W9-ABF-847

WITHDRAWN

American Autobiography 1945–1980

A Bibliography

American
Autobiography
1945–1980

A Bibliography

Mary Louise Briscoe
Editor

Barbara Tobias
and
Lynn Z. Bloom
Associate Editors

The University of Wisconsin Press

Published 1982

The University of Wisconsin Press
114 North Murray Street
Madison, Wisconsin 53715

The University of Wisconsin Press, Ltd.
1 Gower Street
London WC1E 6HA, England

First printing

Printed in the United States of America

ISBN 0-299-09090-6

Publication of this volume has been made possible in part by funds from the
Research Resources Program of the National Endowment for the Humanities.

Library of Congress Cataloging in Publication Data
Main entry under title:
American autobiography, 1945–1980.
Includes index.
1. United States—Biography—Bibliography.
2. Autobiography—Bibliography.
I. Briscoe, Mary Louise.
II. Tobias, Barbara. III. Bloom, Lynn Z., 1934–
Z5305.U5A47   1982   [CT220]   016.92′0073   82-70547
ISBN 0-299-09090-6

For Brenna

CONTENTS

INTRODUCTION

Over five thousand autobiographies have been published since 1945. More appear in print each week, and during the last decade reader interest has increased considerably. Some readers have been drawn to autobiography because they perceive individual life stories as authentic and compelling. Others seek escape through fantasies of unique or unusual experience. Faced by the confusion of modern life, both general and scholarly readers have turned to the voice of personal experience in order to better understand contemporary culture. Scholars in many humanistic fields (e.g., American Studies, Literature, Women's Studies, Black Studies, and Social History) have begun to recognize autobiography as a significant historical resource as well as an important art form. As Albert E. Stone wrote in 1972, the exploration of autobiography has become "one of the striking and promising developments in recent American studies" because of the "wealth of cultural information quite literally unparalleled in other sources."[1]

This bibliography provides access to over 5,000 American autobiographies published in book form by private and commercial presses from 1945 through 1980. It serves as a companion volume to the only other major reference work in this area, *A Bibliography of American Autobiographies* (The University of Wisconsin Press, 1962), by Louis Kaplan, which includes about 6,000 autobiographies published before 1945.

Autobiography is defined broadly in this volume to include the following:
- memoirs, diaries, journals, and collections of letters;
- nonfiction works containing a substantial portion of autobiographical writing;
- alleged autobiographical works employing a ghost writer or amanuensis;
- works by American authors who have lived in a foreign country;
- works by foreign authors who have lived in the United States for a considerable time.

In order to provide continuity with Kaplan's work, autobiographies published before 1945 which have since been reprinted and those published before 1945 (excluding diaries, private journals, and collections of letters) which were not cited in Kaplan's work have been included.

The bibliography does not include autobiographies published in books of genealogy, manuscripts, newspapers, or periodicals, nor does it include works known to be spurious. Works published after 1980, as well as those published previously but identified after the compilation phase of the project, are being noted and recorded for future supplements.

---

[1] "Autobiography and American Culture," *American Studies: An International Newsletter,* 11 (Winter 1972), p. 22.

Methodology and Procedures

Because autobiography has historically had limited cataloging controls, the first task was to determine the most efficient means of identifying autobiographies cited in existing resources tools. Two major problems emerged. First, many resources tools do not distinguish between autobiography and biography. For example, *The Library of Congress Subject Headings* and *The Cumulative Book Index* list autobiography and biography together and rarely list autobiographical works under the class of Autobiography in a specific subject heading. Secondly, autobiography is often catalogued according to the author's occupation or central interest. In short, the subject headings under which autobiographies may be listed are as diversified as their authors.

Some autobiographies could be identified in specialized bibliographies such as H.V. Ribalow, *Autobiographies of American Jews* (1965), which contains selections from autobiographies by twenty-five Jews active in public life, 1880-1920; Russell Brigano, *Black Americans in Autobiography* (1974), containing 300 entries with annotations; and Carolyn Rhodes, Editor, Mary Louise Briscoe and Ernest Rhodes, Associate Editors, *First Person Female,* a supplement to *American Notes and Queries* (1980), containing about 300 reviews of autobiographies by American women living after 1950.

After reviewing the available resources, it was determined that for the purposes of this project, the most inclusive reference for autobiographies was *Biography Index,* which has been consecutively published since January 1946, and lists a variety of biographic materials. The initial author-title list was compiled after a thorough review of each volume of *Biography Index,* 1946-1980. This list was then refined and expanded by comparing it with other specialized bibliographies; with new, rare, and used book catalogs over a five-year period; with current reviews, including those in *Book Review Digest* and *Library Journal;* and with the *Library of Congress MARC (Machine Readable Catalog)* for autobiographies published since 1968.

The resulting author-title list was used only to determine which works were actually autobiographical. Each volume was then reviewed to insure the accuracy of the citations and to derive information for the annotations and the analytic subject index.

The citation elements, subject entries, and annotations for each autobiography were recorded on a work sheet in a standardized form. The data was then encoded in machine-sensible form and computer-processed to create the main entry section and the Subject Index. Following the editing of the computer-generated text, the machine-sensible files were coded for computerized typesetting to produce camera-ready copy of the entire *Bibliography.*

Entry Format

Each main entry may include the following:
- Main entry number
- Woman author indication (*)
- Author entry
- Author's birth-death dates

- Publication title and subtitle
- Joint authors, collaborative authors, and/or editors
- Edition indication
- Imprint data
    Place of publication
    Publisher
    Date of publication or copyright
- Collation
    Pagination
    Index
- Annotation

Main Entry Number. The main entries have been numbered sequentially. These numbers appear to the left of the first line of the entry and are presented in bold face type. They also serve as reference points in the Subject Index.

Women Author Indication. For ease of reference, women authors have been designated with an asterisk (*) preceding the author entry.

Author Entry. Generally, the author's name has been displayed in the traditional format of surname, forename, and middle name or initial. In those instances when an author's pseudonym has been employed on the title page of the work, it has been utilized as the author entry, but usually pseudonyms appear in parenthesis following the author's name. All pseudonyms have been cross-referenced with the original name of the author in the main entry list.

Birth-Death Dates. The birth and death dates for an author have been provided when possible. When only the death date was available, it has been noted with a lower case "d", e.g., *d. 1955.* A birth date followed only by a hyphen indicates that the author is known to be or may be assumed to be living, e.g., *1922-.* Authors born before 1890 have been presumed to be dead even if no death date was available and their birth date has been noted with a lower case "b", e.g., *b. 1826.*

Publication Title and Subtitle. The complete title and subtitle of the work as it appears on the title page has been provided.

Joint Authors, Collaborative Authors, and/or Editors. Joint authors noted on the title page of the work have been cross-referenced alphabetically in the main entry list (e.g., *A Philosophical Correspondence* by John Dewey and Arthur F. Bentley is listed by the first author, Dewey; Bentley is listed by name only, with a cross-reference to Dewey). Collaborative authors, ghost writers, and editors are not cross-referenced.

Edition Indication. Special editions of series have been noted when appropriate (e.g., Private Edition, Revised Edition, 5th Edition, or Eyewitness Accounts of the Revolution).

Imprint Data. Full names of publishers have been listed for ease of reference. Every attempt was made to locate and analyze the most recent edition. In the case of reprints and revised editions, the earliest edition has been given subsequently in parentheses. If both editions were by the same publisher, only the date of the earliest edition has been given in parenthesis.

Collation. Only Arabic pagination of a work has been noted. If the work contains an index, it has been indicated. In most cases, multi-volume works have been cited in one entry, following the Library of Congress format. However, when multi-volume works have different unnumbered titles and different publication dates, they have been listed as separate entries. Because computer searches on systems such as OCLC have made location more convenient for individual users, library locations have not been listed.

Annotation. Each annotation includes the occupation of the author, the major focus of the autobiography, primary geographic locations, and important personal or historic events in the author's life. In general, the annotative style employed has been objective. However, some judgments have been made as to the quality and tone of the individual work.

Subject Index

A major component of the book, the extensive analytic Subject Index includes over 50,000 entries which will enable readers to locate autobiographies related to their diverse interests. It will be stored on computer tape and has the capability for specific subject searches.

The Subject Index includes references to important personal experience and lifestyle (e.g., family life, country life, immigration, illness, death); historic events (e.g., Depression—1929, World War II); historic periods (e.g., Colonial Period, McCarthy Era, The Sixties); significant friends and colleagues; occupation (e.g., artist, wife, executive); time of life described (e.g., childhood, old age); ethnic background; religious background; geographic locations (e.g., by country, state, city or region).

The Subject Index does not repeat the author-title entries listed in the Bibliography. It does not replicate the indexes of individual volumes; it does include whatever is most prominent in each volume. If, for instance, a prominent event is mentioned in an autobiography, it will not appear in the Subject Index unless it has an important function in the author's narrative. The Subject Index does not attempt to be encyclopedic, but to reflect those topics central to the lives of its authors. Its design evolved as the work on the project progressed. Its shape and content reflect the major concerns of American readers during the last thirty years.

ACKNOWLEDGMENTS

The idea for this bibliography evolved from my attempts to locate contemporary American autobiographies for several research projects that interested me in 1973. I soon realized how inadequate existing resources were for locating autobiographies. Except for Louis Kaplan's *Bibliography of American Autobiographies* (1962) which included works published before 1945, there was no central reference. My first debt, then, is to Kaplan, whose work became something of a model for mine.

Over the years, many have assisted me in various ways. Peggy Batten, then Bibliographer for the English Department at the University of Pittsburgh, encouraged me in the early years of the project, especially in generating ideas for the scope and function of the *Subject Index*. Beverly Florey worked with me through the painstaking process of extracting probable items from *Biography Index* for the initial author-title list. H. David Brumble III shared his notes and enthusiasm as his own project, *An Annotated Bibliography of American Indian and Eskimo Autobiographies* (University of Nebraska Press, 1981), developed.

Marilyn DeMario, Kathryn Flannery, Mary Robertson, and Leslie Tobias provided research assistance. Janice Oliver's help went far beyond the call of secretarial duty, with typing assistance from Debra Faggioli and Pat Renkiewicz. Robert Gale generously assisted in the copy-editing of the entire text.

About sixty percent of the books were located in the University of Pittsburgh's Hillman Library and Carnegie Public Library of Pittsburgh. Ingrid T. Glasco and Suzanne B. Crosby were especially helpful in obtaining hundreds of books through Hillman Library's Interlibrary Loan Service. Many more were analyzed at the Library of Congress.

Barbara Tobias, University of Pittsburgh, who joined the project in 1979, helped with many aspects of the book—with innumerable research questions, with book location and analysis, with the design of the *Subject Index,* and with final text editing. Her help and support have been invaluable.

Lynn Z. Bloom, College of William and Mary, joined the project in late 1979 to assist in analyzing books; she was also responsible for initiating the author-title list for 1975-1980. Her student research assistants included Gerald Berdan, Sheila Core, Michael d'Orso, Nancy Fitch, Wendy Gilmer, Donna Hulsey, Maureen Orton, Elsa Travisano, Lana Whited, Midge Stocker and Lisa Seidman. Berna Heyman and Carol Linton of Swem Library, College of William and Mary, were helpful in locating books in Virginia libraries, including Virginia Commonwealth University, Old Dominion University, University of Virginia, and the Richmond Public Library. The College of William and Mary gave Lynn Z. Bloom a Minor Research Grant in 1981.

The computer programs were designed and supervised by Eleanor Dym, Associate Director of the Knowledge Availability Systems Center, University of Pittsburgh. Mary H. Paul was responsible for the computer text-editing, assisted by Mary E. Koller and Nadine M. Green.

The Provost's Research Development Fund, University of Pittsburgh, awarded me three grants (1974-76) which were essential for the development of this project, especially for the identification and location of the initial author-title list.

The Research Resources Program of the National Endowment for the Humanities provided the major financial support for completing the book (1979-1982).

Bibliography

BIBLIOGRAPHY

0001 Aaron, Henry   **1934-**
Aaron, r-f. As told to Furman Bisher. Illustrated. Revised edition. New York: Thomas Y. Crowell Co., 1974. (Cleveland: World, 1968) 236 p. Index.

In a low-key, conversational style, the author tells how he went from shortstop in one of the great Black barnstorming baseball teams to a major league hitter pushing Babe Ruth's career home run record. An afterword written by Bisher is added to the 1968 edition describing Aaron's life up to 1973.

0002 Aaronson, Sammy   **1905-**
As high as my heart: the Sammy Aaronson story. With Al Hirshberg. New York: Coward-McCann, Inc., 1957. 188 p.

The story of his fight against juvenile delinquency in New York's East Side and Brooklyn, where he set up gymnasiums and sports activities for boys.

0003 Abbey, Edward   **1927-**
The journey home: some words in defense of the American West. Illustrated by Jim Stiles. New York: E.P. Dutton, 1977. 242 p.

Author and conservationist Abbey describes his discovery of the West, his passion for the land, and his efforts to preserve it from destruction by machines, land developers, and excessive population.

0004 Abbot, Charles Greeley   **1872-1973**
Adventures in the world of science. Washington, D.C.: Public Affairs Press, 1958. 150 p.

An interesting record of his sixty years among international research scientists by a physicist who pioneered in solar energy and became affiliated with the Smithsonian in 1898, serving as its secretary from 1928 to 1944.

0005 Abbot, Willis J.   **1863-1934**
Watching the world go by. New York: Beekman Publishers, Inc., 1974. (Boston: Little, Brown, 1933) 358 p. Index.

Abbot tells of his lifelong career in newspaper journalism, from his early days in New Orleans, through Kansas City, Chicago, New York, and Boston. Politics fascinated him and most of his recollections concern the political conventions, elections, and maneuverings he observed and took part in.

0006 Abbott, George   **1887-**
Mister Abbott. New York: Random House, 1963. 279 p.

A successful showman writes about Broadway, his memories of friends and enemies among the celebrities of the entertainment world, including an honest appraisal of himself.

0007 Abeel, David   **1804-1846**
Memoir of the Rev. David Abeel, D.D.: late missionary to China. Compiled by G.R. Williamson. Wilmington, Delaware: Scholarly Resources, Inc., 1972. (New York: Robert Carter, 1848) 315 p.

The life of a Dutch Reformed missionary is told through extracts from his simple but formal journals and letters, which reveal his concern with the love of God and the salvation of the "heathen souls." Although plagued with ill health, Abeel nevertheless managed to travel to Greece, England, Europe, the Far East, and China, spreading the gospel.

0008 Abel, Alan   **1924-**
The confessions of a hoaxer. New York: The Macmillan Co., 1970. 252 p.

A professional prankster describes many of his best hoaxes (e.g., a fictitious Mrs. Yetta Bronstein who ran for President of the United States, a fake recording by a phony count that won Billboard's Pick of the Week), his unusual comic theory, and his motivation for living it.

0009 Abington, E.H.   **b.1873**
Back roads and bicarbonate: the autobiography of an Arkansas country doctor. New York: Vantage Press, 1955. 166 p.

Anecdotal recollections largely of the first half of his life. Beginning with post-Civil War rearing on a cotton plantation, he describes his education as a pharmacist and physician and his experience as part-time banker and farmer while he practiced medicine in rural Arkansas and Oklahoma.

0010 Abraham, Abie   **1913-**
Ghost of Bataan speaks. New York: Vantage Press, 1971. 244 p.

An American soldier describes the fall of Bataan, the Death March, the events at Camp O'Donnell and Cabanatuan, and the sufferings of Filipino and American troops after they had made their hopeless stand in defense of Bataan and Corregidor.

0011 *Abrecht, Mary Ellen
The making of a woman cop. With Barbara Lang Stern. New York: William Morrow and Co., 1976. 275 p.

Policewoman describes her development on the Washington, D.C. police force from a naive rookie to an experienced sergeant supervising male officers. She fights crime and sexism with intelligence, level-headedness, and good humor.

0012 Abudadika, Mwlina Imiri (Sonny Carson)   **1935-**
The education of Sonny Carson. New York: W.W. Norton & Co., 1972. 203 p.

Growing up in Brooklyn, being sent to reformatory, serving in the Army, and going to college all contributed to Carson's education. Later he became involved with the activities of CORE but differed with some of their policies. He believes that Black people must control their own police system and educational system in order to control their own destinies in their own communities.

0013 *Abzug, Bella (Savitsky)   **1920-**
Bella! Ms. Abzug goes to Washington. Edited by Mel Ziegler. New York: Saturday Review Press, 1972. 314 p. Index.

The cantankerous and feisty Abzug chronicles her first year in Congress as the representative from New York during the Nixon Administration. A champion of Blacks, women, the poor, and the young, she provides lively, if self-serving, anecdotal accounts of her struggles with the "smug, incestuous, stagnant institution."

0014 Acheson, Dean Gooderham   **1893-1971**
Grapes from thorns. New York: W.W. Norton & Co., 1972. 253 p.

This collection of articles, speeches, and letters assembled from 1950 until his death provide an engaging portrait of a compassionate, humane and witty statesman.

0015 Acheson, Dean Gooderham   **1893-1971**
Morning and noon. Boston: Houghton Mifflin Co., 1965. 288 p. Index.

After a quiet New England boyhood followed by an interlude working on railroad construction in Ontario, Acheson went to Washington as law clerk to Supreme Court Justice Brandeis. There and in private practice he learned to profit from his association and to respect his fellow men. Later under FDR he became involved in great affairs of state.

0016 Acheson, Dean Gooderham   **1893-1971**
Present at the creation: my years in the State Department. New York: W.W. Norton & Co., 1969. 798 p. Index.

Assistant Secretary of State, 1941-45, Under Secretary of State, 1945-47, and Secretary of State, 1949-53, he focuses on the aims, strategies, and development of foreign policy during World War II and in the chaotic, tense postwar period of the Cold War and the Korean War. This highly detailed volume is a repository of names, dates, and information neatly categorized for historians and other political analysts.

0017 Acheson, Dean Gooderham   **1893-1971**
Sketches from life: of men I have known. New York: Harper and Brothers, 1961. 206 p. Index.

An analysis of his long career in the State Department, with personal views of some of the remarkable men he worked with.

0018 Acheson, Edward Goodrich   **1856-1931**
A pathfinder: inventor, scientist, industrialist. Port Huron, Michigan: Acheson Industries, 1965. (New York: The Press Scrapbook, 1910) 63 p.

In spite of early hardship and discouragement the author kept trying again. He was ultimately able to produce revolutionary products including carborundum, graphite, colloidal graphited lubricants, and other products valuable in industry.

0019 *Ackerman, Diane   1948-
Twilight of the tenderfoot: a western memoir. New York: William Morrow and Co., Inc., 1980. 222 p.

A contemporary narrative of frontier life by an Eastern poet who experienced and evaluated life on a large cattle ranch in New Mexico, learning to herd and brand cattle, mend fences, aid heifers in giving birth, and participate in the serious and often comic rituals of cowboy life.

0020 *Acosta, Mercedes de   1893-1967
Here lies the heart. New York: Reynal and Co., 1960. 372 p. Index.

A thoughtful and exuberant account of her quest for a meaningful life, in the context of her experience as a writer of poetry, fiction, plays, and film scripts.

0021 *Adair, Cornelia Wadsworth   1838-1921
My diary: August 30th to November 5th, 1874. Introduction by Montagu K. Brown. Illustrated by Malcolm Thurgood. Austin: University of Texas Press, 1965. 125 p.

Mrs. Adair kept this diary record of the two-month cross-country trip in 1874 she and her family took to New York, Massachusetts, the Great Lakes, the Mississippi River, the Midwest, and Colorado. Because she traveled by train and boat, the diary offers a detailed though not particularly colorful account of largely outmoded means of transportation and attendant social life.

0022 Adamic, Louis   1899-1951
Dinner at the White House. New York: Harper & Brothers, 1946. 276 p.

Starting with an account of a January 1942 dinner at the White House with Roosevelt, Churchill, and the author present, Adamic continues with an examination of the relationship between the President and the English Prime Minister.

0023 Adamic, Louis   1899-1951
My America: 1928-1938. New York: Da Capo Press, 1976. (New York: Harper & Bros., 1938) 669 p. Index.

Adamic's narrative combines his personal history with a social and political history of the United States, 1929-1939. He writes from his perspective as Croatian immigrant, partly insider, partly outsider. He provides a humanistic interpretation of the communist and socialist movements, of labor leaders John L. Lewis and Harry Bridges, of Roosevelt's New Deal, and of a multitude of other people, great and small, who contributed to the social fabric.

0024 Adamic, Louis   1889-1951
The native's return; an American immigrant visits Yugoslavia and discovers his old country. New York: Harper & Brothers, 1934. 370 p. Index.

After emigrating nineteen years earlier to America and establishing himself as a writer, Adamic returned to his native region of Yugoslavia. Struck first by the beauty and richness of the land and people, he was soon confronted by the deteriorating economic/political situation—the rise of fascism, persecution of Slovenes and other groups. He left fearful for his family and convinced that the Russian Revolution would be the salvation of the Yugoslav people.

0025 *Adams, Abigail (Smith)   1744-1818
Familiar letters of John Adams and his wife Abigail Adams, during the Revolution; with a memoir of Mrs. Adams. Edited by Charles Francis Adams. Freeport, New York: Books for Libraries Press, 1970. (New York: Hurd and Houghton, 1876) 424 p. Index.

This well-known collection of letters reveals the depth, the variety, the tenderness of feelings between a famous couple during the period of Revolutionary struggle.

0026 *Adams, Abigail (Smith)   1744-1818
New letters of Abigail Adams, 1788-1801. Edited with introduction by Stewart Mitchell. Westport, Connecticut: Greenwood Press, Inc., 1973. (Boston: Houghton Mifflin Co., 1947) 281 p. Index.

With 141 previously unpublished letters selected from the Cranch-Dawes-Turner Collection, this volume describes Abigail Adams' life between 1789 and 1801, with primary focus on the years John was Vice-President and President.

0027 *Adams, Abigail (Smith)   1744-1818
see also **Adams, John**

0028 Adams, Charles Francis   1807-1886
Diary of Charles Francis Adams. Edited by Marc Friedlaender and L.H. Butterfield. Cambridge: Belknap Press of Harvard University Press, 1964-1974. 6v. Index.

Grandson and son of presidents, Charles Francis Adams continued the family practice of diary-keeping. His diary, never before published in full, is considered by the editor as "unquestionably the most important surviving unpublished journal kept by any American in the 19th century."

0029 *Adams, Cindy (Heller)
see **Adams, Joey**

0030 Adams, Henry   1838-1918
The education of Henry Adams. Edited with introduction by Ernest Samuels. Boston: Houghton Mifflin, 1973. (Boston: Massachusetts Historical Society, 1918) 705 p.

Adams, of the quintessential New England "first family," analyzes the lifelong process of his education, formal and informal, psychological, moral, and intellectual. Burdened with familial precedent to become a statesman, Adams followed his own bent as the interpreter rather than the maker of American history. This work is among the classics of American autobiography, its most widely acclaimed chapter being "The Dynamo and the Virgin."

0031 Adams, Henry   1838-1918
Henry Adams and his friends; a collection of his unpublished letters. Compiled with introduction by Harold D. Cater. New York: Octagon Books, 1970. (Boston: Houghton Mifflin Co., 1947) 797 p. Index.

Over 750 previously unpublished letters written to 100 different people, from 1858 to 1918, giving a rich and varied view of Adams' intellect and an unusual image of his warmth and compassion. Includes series of letters to Mabel Hooper La Farge, John Hay, and Mrs. Henry Cabot Lodge, among others.

0032 Adams, Henry   1838-1918
The selected letters of Henry Adams. Edited with an introduction by Newton Arvin. Great letters series. New York: Farrar, Straus, and Young, Inc., 1951. 279 p. Index.

These letters have all been previously published and cover a period of 60 years, from his student letters from Germany in 1858 to the last year of his life, 1918. The range shows the development of the mind of an interesting and powerful intellectual.

0033 Adams, Joey   1911-
From gags to riches. New York: Frederick Fell, Inc., 1946. 336 p.

Making it as a comic in New York, a narrative filled with quips, show business gossip, and name-dropping.

0034 Adams, Joey   1911-
The God bit. New York: Mason & Lipscomb Publishers, 1974. 252 p.

A comedian, author, and all-around show business personality tells anecdotes—some humorous, others serious—but all emphasizing the faith and belief in God which show people have.

0035 Adams, Joey and *Cindy Adams   1911-
Cindy and I: the real life adventures of Mr. and Mrs. Joey Adams. New York: Crown Publishers, 1957. 320 p.

A wise-cracking, anecdotal account of the first five years of the marriage of comedian Joey Adams and his wife, Cindy (nee Heller). They demonstrate that "Life in the Adams' menage is all laughs. We do hits and play games 24 hours a day."

0036 Adams, John   1735-1826
Adams-Jefferson letters: the complete correspondence between Thomas Jefferson and Abigail and John Adams. Edited by Lester J. Cappon. Chapel Hill: University of North Carolina Press, 1959. 2v. Index.

An early project of the Institute of Early American History and Culture, this edition includes their complete correspondence.

0037 Adams, John   1735-1826
Correspondence between John Adams and Mercy Warren. Edited by Charles F. Adams, including an appendix of specimen pages from the History of the American Revolution. American Women: Images and Realities. New York: Arno Press, 1972. (Boston: Collections of the Massachusetts Historical Society, 1878) 436 p.

A lively and sometimes bitter exchange between John Adams and poetess, playwright, and staunch anti-Federalist, Mercy Warren, over the publication of her history of the American Revolution, showing a remarkable contrast between the caustic Adams and the cool, brilliant Warren.

0038 Adams, John   1735-1826
Diary and autobiography. Edited by L.H. Butterfield. Cambridge, Massachusetts: Harvard University Press, 1961. 4v. Index.

Adams' diaries include Vol. I: Diary 1755-1770; Vol. II: Diary 1771-1781; Vol. III: Diary 1782-1804, fragmentary diaries of Abigail Adams 1784, 1787, 1788, Autobiography Part I to October 1776 ("John Adams"); and Vol. IV: Autobiography Part II, 1777-1778 ("Travels and Negotiations"), Autobiography Part II, 1779-1780 ("Peace").

0039 Adams, John   1735-1826
The earliest diary of John Adams: June 1753-April 1754; September 1758-January 1759. Edited by L.H. Butterfield. Associate editors, Wendell D. Garrett and Marc Friedlaender. Cambridge: Belknap Press of Harvard University Press, 1966. 120 p. Index.

Discovered four years after the 1961 Belknap edition of his diary was published, these fragments help to illuminate the mind and personality of the young John Adams and show his early concern about matters which occupied him greatly in later life.

0040 Adams, John   **1735-1826**
The John Adams papers. Edited by Frank Donovan. New York: Dodd, Mead and Co., 1965. 335 p. Index.
    Selected letters, papers, and other documents are arranged to show John Adams as a lawyer, congressman, diplomat, peacemaker, political philosopher, Vice-President, President, and old man. The sources and dates of the documents are not identified.

0041 Adams, John   **1735-1826**
The papers of John Adams. Edited with introduction by Robert J. Taylor, Mary-Jo Kline, Gregg L. Lint. Illustrated. Cambridge, Massachusetts: Belknap Press of Harvard University Press, 1979. 4v. Index.
    This judicious selection of Adams' papers includes letters to and from friends and acquaintances; committee reports; polemical writings, published and unpublished; and state papers which he contributed, such as instructions to representatives and messages to the royal governor. They reveal Adams' commitment to public service and his increasingly revolutionary spirit, in the eighteenth-century sense of "restoring ancient liberties" (eds.). Thus Adams wrote on the relations between the colonies and the crown, the powers of Parliament, and attempted an extensive legal justification of a commonwealth of American states under the King.

0042 Adams, John Quincy   **1767-1848**
Diary of John Quincy Adams, 1794-1845: American diplomacy and political, social, and intellectual life from Washington to Polk. Edited by Allan Nevins. New York: Frederick Ungar, 1969. (New York: Longmans, Green and Co., 1928) 586 p. Index.
    A selection from a twelve-volume *Memoirs* published between 1874 and 1877 traces a lifetime of public service in domestic and foreign affairs.

0043 Adams, John Quincy   **1767-1848**
John Quincy Adams and American continental empire: letters, papers and speeches. Edited by Walter LaFeber. Chicago: Quadrangle Books, 1965. 157 p. Index.
    A selection of writings by the sixth U.S. president intended to reveal his mind, his passions, his views of the world's political, economical, and ideological systems and his belief in an American continental empire.

0044 Adams, John Quincy   **1767-1848**
John Quincy Adams in Russia: comprising portions of the diary of John Quincy Adams from 1809-1814. Edited by Charles Francis Adams. New York: Praeger Publishers, 1970. (Philadelphia: J.B. Lippincott and Co., 1874) 662 p.
    A reprint of Volume II of his memoirs, comprising the record of his experiences during his successful mission to the court of Czar Alexander I, beautifully written, eloquent in detail.

0045 *Adams, Julia Davis
see **Davis, Julia**

0046 *Addie, Pauline (Betz)   **1919-**
Wings on my tennis shoes. London: Sampson Low, Marston and Co., Ltd., 1949. 198 p. Index.
    The development of her career in tennis and her achievements as a professional player.

0047 Ade, George   **1866-1944**
Letters of George Ade. Edited by Terence Tobin. Illustrated. West Lafayette, Indiana: Purdue University Studies, 1973. 251 p. Index.
    With keen observation tempered by humor, Ade wrote stories and fables populated with characters typical of his small-town Indiana background. His correspondence follows his progress from Chicago journalist to popular author and playwright and back to his Indiana homeland and the life of a gentleman farmer.

0048 Adler, Cyrus   **1863-1940**
I have considered the days. Foreword by A.S.W. Rosenbach. Illustrated. New York: Burning Bush Press, 1969. (Jewish Publication Society of America, 1941) 447 p. Index.
    Adler writes with thoughtful eloquence of his distinguished career as a Middle Eastern scholar, president of the Jewish Theological Seminary of America, and participation in many international educational, cultural, and religious symposia. A benevolent Jewishness pervades his orientation to the world.

0049 Adler, Mortimer Jerome   **1902-**
Philosopher at large: an intellectual autobiography. Illustrated. New York: Macmillan Publishing Co., 1977. 349 p. Index.
    Adler discusses his career as a popularizer of philosophy, particularly under the aegis of Robert Hutchins at the University of Chicago. Adler has been instrumental in the *Great Books* series, and in planning and producing the fifteenth edition of the *Encyclopedia Britannica*.

0050 *Adler, Polly   **1900-1962**
A house is not a home. New York: Rinehart and Co., 1953. 374 p.
    A madam explains her life as a prostitute and madam in New York City. The Roaring Twenties, the era's gangsters, problems with the law, and social stigma are all part of the narrative.

0051 Adlum, John   **1759-1836**
Memoirs of the life of John Adlum in the Revolutionary War. Edited and introduction by Howard H. Peckham. Chicago: Caxton Club, for the William L. Clements Library Associates, 1968. 143 p.
    An engaging account of a young patriot's participation in the Revolutionary War. Adlum, a private, fought in the War when he was fifteen to seventeen years old. He witnessed the British capture of New York City in 1776 and was himself taken prisoner-of-war in 1776. On parole, he became a servant to a group of American officers, lived in a private home, and enjoyed good food and considerable freedom.

0052 Agee, James   **1909-1955**
The last letter of James Agee to Father Flye. Boston: Godine, 1969. 4 p.
    Dated May 11, 1955, this last of a long series of his letters to Father Flye was found unmailed on the mantel of Agee's living room when Agee died.

0053 Agee, James   **1909-1955**
Letters of James Agee to Father Flye. Boston: Houghton Mifflin Co., 1971. (New York: George Braziller, Inc., 1962) 267 p.
    Letters (1925-1955) from the writer to his friend and former teacher reveal the bond of understanding and the shared feelings between them.

0054 *Agle, Nan (Hayden)   **1905-**
My animals and me: an autobiographical story. Photos by Emily Hayden. New York: The Seabury Press, 1970. 119 p.
    Pleasant memories of her childhood in rural Maryland, her first pets, her parents and sisters, and a warm happy life.

0055 Agnew, Spiro Theodore   **1918-**
Where he stands: the life and convictions of Spiro T. Agnew. Introduction by Richard M. Nixon. Biography by Ann Pinchot. Preface by Clement W. Stone. Illustrated. New York: Hawthorn Books, 1968. 116 p.
    A collection of statements articulating Agnew's conservative stand on civil rights, health and welfare, education, the Vietnam War, civil disobedience, and crime, compiled from speeches, press releases, and interviews, mostly in 1967 and 1968. Prefaced by a thirty-page biography, this work, with its subtitle ironic in light of Agnew's demonstrated criminal activity, was intended as an autobiographical adjunct to Agnew's vice-presidential campaign in 1968.

0056 Aherne, Brian   **1902-**
A proper job. Boston: Houghton Mifflin Co., 1969. 355 p.
    Born in England, Aherne acted in movies and on the stage there before coming to the United States and making his debut on Broadway (1931) and in American films (1933).

0057 Aiken, Conrad Potter   **1889-1973**
Ushant: an essay. New York: Oxford University Press, 1971. (Boston: Little, Brown and Co., 1952) 365 p.
    This book by a poet and author is an experimental autobiography. Written in third person, it is "an interior monologue autobiography of a literary man." It does not relate a sequence of physical events, but stresses the emotional and psychological life of the author in England.

0058 Albee, Fred Houdlett   **1876-1945**
A surgeon's fight to rebuild men: an autobiography. London: R. Hale, 1950. (New York: E.P. Dutton and Co., Inc., 1943) 270 p.
    Recollections of a long active life in surgery including descriptions of innovative techniques and world-wide recognition of his work.

0059 Albert, David E.   **b.1878**
Dear Grandson. Philadelphia: Olivier, Maney and Co., 1950. 215 p.
    A letter to the author's 13-year-old grandson, in which the elder tells of his adventures in escaping from Russia to America; his self-education; his employment as singer, bellboy, salesman, cigar-maker, and partner in a chain of drug stores; and his admiration of the free enterprise system.

0060 Albert, Herman W.   **b.1882**
Odyssey of a desert prospector. Norman: University of Oklahoma Press, 1967. 260 p.
    A wonderfully appealing story of prospecting, a lonely but richly rewarding life. As a neophyte, Albert learned by doing and by observing the old timers he met. He found a treasure trove, not of ore, but of memories, experience, animal lore, and human contemporaries.

0061 Alcott, Amos Bronson   **1799-1888**
Letters of A. Bronson Alcott. Edited by Richard L. Herrnstadt. Ames, Iowa: Iowa State University Press, 1969. 846 p. Index.
    The first collection of all extant Alcott letters printed in full, this volume provides a valuable glimpse of nineteenth-century intellectual life as well as insight into the personal character of this man of letters, whose

interests include education, women's rights, communal living, and philosophy.

0062 *Alcott, Louisa May 1832-1888
Louisa May Alcott: her life, letters, and journals. Edited by Ednah D. Cheney. Boston: Roberts Brothers, 1889. 404 p.
Letters and journal entries are arranged with commentary by the editor, following chronologically from a genealogy through the writing of *Little Women* to the last years. Includes entries from family acquaintances such as Emerson. In addition to accounts of her own writing process, some entries include mention of her extensive reading.

0063 *Aldrich, Mildred 1853-1928
A hilltop on the Marne, being letters written June 3-September 8, 1914. Boston: Houghton Mifflin Co., 1915. 187 p.
A polished, often witty and intelligent series of letters written by a New Englander living above the Marne in France at the beginning of World War I. Having retired to this out-of-way spot to spend her remaining days in peace, she was instead confronted by war. Hers is an account of the quiet charm of the area, then the growing tension and the experience of being on the edge of a battlefield.

0064 *Aldrich, Mildred 1853-1928
On the edge of the war zone, from the battle of the Marne to the entrance of the Stars and Stripes. Boston: Small, Maynard and Company, 1917. 311 p.
A continuation of the author's *A Hilltop on the Marne,* this volume contains the human details, the domestic concerns of a small village situated along the Marne and near the battlefront up to the U.S. entry in the war. The author conveys both a sense of the disruption and the surprising normality of daily life as her cottage serves as a hostel of sorts for officers and enlisted men.

0065 Aldrin, Edwin E. "Buzz" 1930-
Return to earth. With Wayne Warga. Illustrated. New York: Random House, 1973. 338 p.
Astronaut Aldrin writes of the training, the trip to the moon and the historic first walk on the moon with Neil Armstrong, the instant fame requiring difficult adjustment, the demanding worldwide public relations tour for NASA, and his resulting mental depression, treatment, and recovery.

0066 *Alexander, Eveline Martin 1843-1922
Cavalry wife: diary of Eveline M. Alexander, 1866-1867, being a record of her journey from New York to Fort Smith to join her cavalry-officer husband, Andrew J. Alexander, and her experiences with him on active duty among the Indian nations and in Texas, New Mexico, and Colorado. Edited with introduction by Sandra L. Myres. College Station: Texas A & M University Press, 1977. 175 p. Index.
This diary contains a good-natured account of the author's journey to join her husband at Ft. Smith, Arkansas, and of their travels with the cavalry throughout the territories of Texas, New Mexico, and Colorado. She is particularly attracted by Indian cultures and settlements, notably Navajo and Taos.

0067 Alexander, Guy B. 1918-
Chromatography: an adventure in graduate school. Washington, D.C.: American Chemical Society, 1977. 165 p. Index.
Alexander tells what it was like to be a graduate student at the University of Wisconsin in the late 1940's, doing doctoral research on chromatography to earn his Ph.D. in chemistry. He focuses on research in ways that he claims are simple, but which are too complex for lay readers to comprehend.

0068 Alexander, Holmes 1906-
Pen and politics: the autobiography of a working writer. Morgantown: West Virginia University Library, 1970. 212 p.
Possessed by a compulsion to write, Alexander gave up teaching, steeplechasing, and a life of security in his father's insurance firm to try to make his way by writing magazine articles, novels, biographies, and eventually syndicated newspaper columns.

0069 Alexander, Lloyd 1924-
My love affair with music. Decorations by Vasiliu. New York: Thomas Y. Crowell Co., 1960. 274 p.
An author of books for children and adults writes of his passion for music, not as a professional but as an ordinary man addicted to the arts.

0070 Alexander, Morris 1909-
Israel and me: a behind-the-scenes look by a longtime U.S. Zionist leader and returned Israeli immigrant. Illustrated. Cambridge, Massachusetts: Schenkman Publishing Co., Two Continents Publishing Group, 1976. 278 p.
Alexander, a lawyer and active Zionist, focuses on the establishment of Israel as a nation and on his role in abetting the emerging country through his activities in B'nai B'rith and other American Zionistic organizations, 1945-1968. He and his family emigrated to Israel for four years

(1968-1972), providing him the opportunity to describe the country's people, politics, education, and social organization from firsthand experience before returning to Ann Arbor, Michigan.

0071 Alger, Philip Langdon 1894
Tales of my life and family. New York: The Author, 1974. 261 p. Index.
Alger, an engineer with General Electric Company for forty years, was instrumental in the adoption of the city manager government for Schenectady in the 1930's and charter government for Schenectady County in the 60's. The appendix includes speeches and papers by him and a list of patents, honors, books and articles.

0072 Allen, Arthur James 1875-1944
A whaler & trader in the Arctic: 1895-1944: my life with the Bowhead. Foreword by Rusty Heurlin. Illustrated. Anchorage: Alaska Northwest Publishing Co., 1978. 213 p.
Allen recounts his adventures throughout fifty years as a whaler and trader of whale ivory and sealskin in Barrow and other places in Alaska. He married Ellnou, an Eskimo, and they had two children, one of whom was killed at sixteen in a storm while on a whaling expedition. Nevertheless, Allen loves his vocation, adopted territory, and people.

0073 Allen, Asa Alonso 1911-1970
Born to lose, bound to win: an autobiography. With Walter Wagner. New York: Doubleday and Co., Inc., 1970. 202 p.
A poor Missouri farmer born again in the middle of the Depression, he became a successful preacher and evangelist for the Pentecostal Church.

0074 *Allen, Charlotte Vale 1941-
Daddy's girl: a memoir. New York: Wyndham Books, 1980. 255 p.
Convinced that no one loved her except her father, Allen began an incestuous relationship with him at age eight, which she describes in graphic detail. Her personal life became more complicated until she found some release in her father's death.

0075 *Allen, Florence Ellinwood 1884-1966
To do justly. Cleveland: The Press of Western Reserve University, 1965. 201 p.
She served as a common pleas judge, a justice of the Ohio Supreme Court, and a judge of the Federal Court of Appeals for the Sixth Circuit. Her book describes growing up in Ohio and Utah, going to law school at Chicago University and New York University where she became involved in the woman's suffrage movement, returning to Ohio to set up her law practice, and becoming a judge.

0076 Allen, Fred (John Florence Sullivan) 1894-1956
Fred Allen's letters. Edited by Joe McCarthy. Garden City, New York: Doubleday & Co., Inc., 1965. 359 p.
Known for his wit both offstage and on, comedian Allen reveals his sharp and zany humor in this selection from the thousands of letters he wrote to fans and friends in and out of show business.

0077 Allen, Fred (John Florence Sullivan) 1894-1956
Much ado about me. Boston: Little, Brown and Co., 1956. 380 p. Index.
He died before completing the book, which is a narrative of his boyhood in the Boston suburbs, his apprenticeship as a comedian, and his gradual success as a vaudeville performer, up to 1929.

0078 Allen, Fred (John Florence Sullivan) 1894-1956
Treadmill to oblivion. Boston: Little, Brown and Co., 1954. 240 p.
A comedian describes the development and early days of radio comedy in New York and his part in the industry. The book contains excerpts from a number of the actual scripts used by Allen on the air.

0079 Allen, George Edward 1896-1973
Presidents who have known me. New York: Simon and Schuster, 1950. 246 p.
Allen, under Franklin Roosevelt a commissioner of Washington, D.C., and a Truman appointee to the Reconstruction Finance Committee, offers an hilarious account of his years in business and politics, focusing on Eisenhower, Henry Wallace, Alben Barkley, Adlai Stevenson, as well as Roosevelt and his favorite, Harry Truman.

0080 Allen, Richard 1760-1831
Life experience and gospel labors of the Rt. Rev. Richard Allen: to which is annexed the rise and progress of the African Methodist Episcopal Church in the U.S.A.; containing a narrative of the yellow fever in the year of our Lord 1793; with an address to the people of color in the U.S. written by himself and pub. by his request. Introduction by George A. Singleton. New York: Abington Press, 1960. 93 p. Index.
Born a slave to a prominent Quaker lawyer in Philadelphia, he became a Methodist minister. In 1787 he and other Negro Methodists withdrew from the Philadelphia Methodist Episcopal Church because of prevailing practices of racial discrimination. In 1816 the A.M.E. Church was formally organized, with Allen consecrated as its first bishop.

0081 Allen, Steve 1921-
Mark it and strike it: an autobiography. New York: Holt, Rinehart and Winston, 1960. 432 p.
A critical review of his career as an entertainer on radio and television, with an interesting analysis on the subject of comedy.

0082 Allin, Benjamin Casey, III 1886-1960
Reaching for the sea. Illustrated. Boston: Meador Publishing Co., 1956. 294 p. Index.
Allin, a civil engineer and expert on port construction, tells about his extensive work at the ports of Houston, Stockton, San Francisco, The Dalles (Oregon), Miami, and Port Bhavnagar, India. He also describes his world travels, 1906-10, illustrated with many photographs.

0083 Allison, John Moore 1905-
Ambassador from the prairie; or, Allison wonderland. Illustrated. Boston: Houghton Mifflin Co., 1973. 400 p. Index.
The author, who started without private means or public influence, writes of his thirty-year career in the Foreign Service, beginning as a clerk and ending as ambassador. He was especially concerned with aspects of American foreign policy with respect to Asia.

0084 Allyn, Joseph Pratt 1833-1869
The Arizona of Joseph Pratt Allyn: letters from a pioneer judge: observations and travels, 1863-1866. Edited by John Nicolson. Tucson: University of Arizona Press, 1974. 284 p. Index.
Allyn, appointed to the first supreme court of the Arizona Territory, wrote these letters to his newspaper editor friend Charles Warner, recording his travels, information about settlements and outposts, mining operations, Indians, Arizona pioneers, and Mexicans. The letters reflect his faith and enthusiasm in Arizona's future as a great mining and ranching state.

0085 Almirall, Leon Vincent b.1884
From college to cow country. Caldwell, Idaho: The Caxton Printers, Ltd., 1956. 471 p.
A college graduate raised in Brooklyn, in 1906 he went to Colorado to become a rancher. A tenderfoot, then a cowboy, he started his own ranch in the high Rockies.

0086 *Alsop, Guliema Fell 1881-1978
Deer Creek; the story of a golden childhood. New York: Vanguard Press, 1947. 310 p.
Describes the author's middle-class childhood in the 1880's, the strong influence of her Grandma May in rural Deer Creek, Pennsylvania, and of her father in his Brooklyn ministry at St. Ann's Episcopal Church. Ambivalence about being a lady, nostalgia for innocence, and respect for learned obedience to the rules of survival.

0087 Alsop, Stewart Johonnot Oliver 1914-1974
Stay of execution; a sort of memoir. Illustrated. Philadelphia: J.B. Lippincott Co., 1973. 312 p. Index.
In 1971 he discovered he had a rare form of leukemia. His book describes his fear and understanding of the disease, his efforts to prepare for his death and yet to survive. He lived as a journalist, with a regular column in *Newsweek*.

0088 *Alsop, Susan Mary (Jay) Patten 1919?-
To Marietta from Paris, 1945-1960. Illustrated. Garden City, New York: Doubleday & Co., Inc., 1975. 370 p. Index.
These letters were written during the fifteen-year period the author spent in Paris as the wife of Bill Patten, a Foreign Service reserve officer. She describes to her friend Marietta Tree her social life, her observations of people and politics, and her own well-considered opinions with style, wit, and intelligence.

0089 Alston, Walter Emmons 1911-
A year at a time. With Jack Tobin. Waco, Texas: Word Books, 1976. 212 p.
Emphasizing landmark ballgames, Walter "Smokey" Alston describes his career as a baseball manager, moving up from the minor leagues, at 44, to a 23-year job with the Dodgers in Brooklyn and Los Angeles.

0090 *Alta 1942-
Momma: a start on all the untold stories. New York: Times Change Press, 1974. 76 p.
A poet closely identified with the Women's Liberation Movement writes of love, motherhood, independence, freedom, and of the importance of learning to live with the paradox of love and independence.

0091 Altman, Irvin Larry 1928-
Call of the cricket. Millbrae, California: Celestial Arts, 1978. 164 p.
Harsh memoirs of a "gentleman thief" con man, from unhappy childhood (including sexual initiation by an aunt on the day of his bar mitzvah) to criminal adulthood. He was encouraged to write it all down by a former school-teacher cellmate at Folsom Prison.

0092 Alvarez, Walter Clement 1884-1978
Alvarez on Alvarez. Illustrated. San Francisco: Strawberry Hill Press, 1977. 152 p.
Alvarez looks back on 93 years as physician and son of a physician, researcher, and medical writer. His research on stomach and intestinal disorders at the Mayo Clinic frequently pointed up emotional causes as well as physiological ones, leading him to write books for lay persons on nervous disorders.

0093 Alvarez, Walter Clement 1884-1978
Incurable physician: an autobiography. Englewood Cliffs, New Jersey: Prentice-Hall, Inc., 1963. 274 p.
Because of his popular newspaper column he became known as "America's family doctor," a kindly man who cares about his patients. His book, like his column, also depicts him as an outspoken critic on many subjects, including Freud, psychoanalysis, conformity, and religion.

0094 Alvin, Joe (Joseph A. Czyzewski) 1908-
Light of Notre Dame. Philadelphia: Dorrance & Co., 1978. 235 p.
Alvin uses "The Lady of the Golden Dome of the University of Notre Dame" as the inspiration of his life and the motif of this book. He focuses on his career as a journalist in Chicago and a public relations man in Hollywood. He particularly enjoyed his stint as head of the News and Special Events of the NBC Pacific Division during World War II.

0095 Alzado, Lyle Martin 1949-
Mile high: the story of Lyle Alzado and the amazing Denver Broncos. With Paul Zimmerman. Illustrated. New York: Atheneum, 1978. 230 p.
This account of a Denver Broncos football player emphasizes his rags-to-riches rise from a Brooklyn slum to Yankton College (South Dakota) to the 1978 Super Bowl (the Broncos lost to Dallas). It juxtaposes Alzado's enormous size (6'3", 260 pounds) and fierce behavior on the football field with his gentle treatment of his wife and his philanthropic endeavors for handicapped children.

0096 Ameringer, Oscar 1870-1943
If you don't weaken: the autobiography of Oscar Ameringer. Illustrated. Foreword by Carl Sandburg. New York: Greenwood Press, 1969. (New York: Henry Holt, 1940) 476 p. Index.
Ameringer narrates his activities as a lifelong socialist committed to devoting his full efforts to unionizing laborers, organizing strikes and political protests, publishing antiwar and various other Socialist statements. After studying art in Munich, Ameringer lived in Milwaukee, Louisiana, Texas, and Illinois, ever fighting the good fight.

0097 Ames, Edward Scribner 1870-1958
Beyond theology: the autobiography of Edward Scribner Ames. Edited and foreword by Van Meter Ames. Chicago: University of Chicago Press, 1959. 223 p.
Ames, a professor of philosophy at Butler College (Indianapolis) and at the University of Chicago, interweaves a narrative of his childhood, education, and career with a spiritual autobiography and statement of his philosophical and theological views as a minister in the Disciples of Christ church. He favors "practical" rather than doctrinaire faith and writes with thoughtful, articulate candor.

0098 Ames, Oakes 1874-1950
Oakes Ames: jottings of a Harvard botanist 1874-1950. edited with introduction by Pauline Ames Plimpton. Foreword by George Plimpton. Illustrated. Cambridge, Massachusetts: Harvard University Press, 1979. 401 p.
This collection of writings, diaries and letters portrays Ames as a botanist, a world authority on orchids, a teacher and administrator, a sportsman, a traveler, and a family man. His letters reveal his ardent devotion to his career and to his wife.

0099 Amram, David 1930-
Vibrations: The adventures and musical times of David Amram. New York: The Macmillan Co., 1968. 469 p.
The story of Amram's lifelong love of music, his education and experience with music from his first instrument—a Boy Scout bugle—to his tenure as composer in residence with the New York Philharmonic and the performance of his own compositions by major orchestras.

0100 Anderson, Clinton Presba 1895-
Outsider in the senate: Senator Clinton Anderson's memoirs. With Milton Viorst. New York: World Publishers, 1970. 328 p. Index.
Major events of the 1950's and 60's, enlivened with anecdotal material by the chairman of the Joint Committee on Atomic Energy, the Senate Aeronautical and Space Sciences Committee, and the Senate Interior Committee.

0101 *Anderson, Edna M. 1907-
From sunflowers to bluebonnets. San Antonio, Texas: The Naylor Co., 1974. 110 p.
Anderson recalls her years as a school teacher, particularly the first

years at a one-room country school in eastern Kansas and her last years in a larger school in a southern Texas town.

0102 *Anderson, Elizabeth Prall   **b.1884**
Miss Elizabeth: a memoir. With Gerald R. Kelly. Illustrated. Boston: Little, Brown and Co., 1969. 315 p.

A fascinating memoir by Sherwood Anderson's wife (1922-27) written after he summarily dismissed her. During her marriage to Anderson she ran a bookstore in New York and knew many authors, whose personalities and idiosyncrasies she describes anecdotally. When the Andersons separated, Elizabeth moved to Taxco, Mexico, and teamed up with silversmith Bill Spratling to sell silver and hand-embroidered clothing.

0103 Anderson, Enoch   **1753?-1824**
Personal recollections of Captain Enoch Anderson, an officer of the Delaware regiments in the Revolutionary War. With notes by Henry Hobart Bellas, LLB. Eyewitness Accounts of the American Revolution, Series III. New York: New York Times, 1971. (Wilmington: The Historical Society of Delaware, 1969) 61 p.

Written to his nephew, these letters constitute a brief and sketchy record of military life in the Delaware regiment.

0104 Anderson, George ("Sparky") Lee   **1934-**
Main spark: Sparky Anderson and the Cincinnati Reds. And Si Burick. Garden City, New York: Doubleday & Co., 1978. 239 p.

Anderson, since 1969 manager of the Cincinnati Reds baseball team, explains his philosophy as a three-time pennant winner: firmness, fairness, and kindness. With down-to-earth good humor he recounts his experiences with notable players, particularly Pete Rose and Johnny Bench, memorable games, and an occasional misjudgment as well.

0105 Anderson, Heartley William   **1898-**
Notre Dame, Chicago Bears, and Hunk: football memoirs in highlight. With Emil Klosinski. Introduction by George Halas. Postscript by Wayne Millner. A Sports Immortals Book. Oviedo, Florida: Florida Sun-Gator Pub., 1976. 191 p. Index.

Anderson recounts his days as a football player for Notre Dame, 1918-1921, when he also played baseball, basketball, and ice hockey. After graduation he coached football at St. Louis University, North Carolina State University, and Notre Dame and played and coached the line for the Chicago Bears. He provides detailed accounts of the games.

0106 Anderson, Jack Northman   **1922-**
The Anderson papers. With George Clifford. New York: Random House, 1973. 275 p.

The power of the press as an adversary to the power of politicians is Anderson's central idea. In this book he writes of ITT, Watergate, the brief vice-presidential candidacy of Eagleton, the FBI, and Bangladesh, each illustrating the ways in which public information and opinion can be used for the abuse of power.

0107 Anderson, John Murray   **1886-1954**
Out without my rubbers: the memoirs of John Murray Anderson. As told to and written by Hugh Abercrombie Anderson. New York: Library Publishers, 1954. 242 p.

A theatrical director and producer describes his productions in New York, England, and Hollywood, including the revues he designed for the circus, and the many famous people he worked with and met.

0108 *Anderson, Leila W.
Pilgrim circuit rider. In collaboration with Harriet Harmon Dexter. New York: Harper & Brothers Publishers, 1960. 200 p.

A Congregational missionary traveling in rural America writes of her early life on an Illinois farm, her education, training and ordination. Her book provides an interesting record of rural society in conflict with urbanization, attempting to preserve the best of the past.

0109 *Anderson, Margaret C.   **1890-1973**
The fiery fountains. Foreword by Gorham Munson. New York: Horizon, 1969. (New York: Hermitage House, 1951) 242 p.

Prominent member of art circles during the Twenties and editor of *The Little Review* (Chicago) describes her life and friendship with Georgette Leblanc. Includes an emotional description of her friend's long and painful death by cancer. Continuation of first volume, *My Thirty Years War* (1930).

0110 *Anderson, Marian   **1902-**
My Lord, what a morning: an autobiography. New York: The Viking Press, 1956. 312 p.

The inspiring story of the author's warm and reverent approach to music and living—the arduous climb to the top of the concert world aided by her own will to work, years of study, her determination to surmount the barriers of racial prejudice, and her outstanding contralto voice.

0111 *Anderson, Mary   **1872-1964**
Woman at work: the autobiography of Mary Anderson. Foreword by Mary N. Winslow. Westport, Connecticut: Greenwood Press, 1973. (Minneapolis: The University of Minnesota Press, 1951) 266 p. Index.

The life story of a working woman, her activities as a union organizer, and her work as director of the Women's Bureau, U.S. Department of Labor for twenty-five years. From the transcription of her interviews and conversations, she emerges as a simple, strong woman who has contributed to the advancement of women.

0112 Anderson, Maxwell   **1888-1959**
Dramatist in America: letters of Maxwell Anderson, 1912-1958. Edited by Laurence G. Avery. Appendices. Chapel Hill: University of North Carolina Press, 1977. 366 p. Index.

In letters to his many correspondents, Anderson describes his careers as journalist, poet, playwright, and screenwriter, often urging that poetry be given its rightful place in the theater. Near the end of his life Anderson was discouraged about both American theater and American life in general.

0113 Anderson, Richard Clough, Jr.   **1750-1826**
The diary and journal of Richard Clough Anderson, Jr.: 1814-1826. Edited by Alfred Tischendorf and E. Taylor Parks. Durham, North Carolina: Duke University Press, 1964. 342 p. Index.

Having first served in the Kentucky legislature and the U.S. House of Representatives, Anderson became in 1823 minister to La Gran Colombia, a union of Ecuador, Venezuela, and New Granada (Colombia). His diary discusses political, social, and economic issues of Kentucky, the United States, and Colombia as well as personal and family concerns.

0114 Anderson, Sherwood   **1876-1941**
Letters. Selected and edited with an introduction and notes by Howard Mumford Jones, with Walter B. Rideout. Boston: Little, Brown and Co., 1953. 467 p. Index.

The letters of this author span the years 1916-1944 and are addressed to friends, relatives, other writers, and publishers. Most of the letters originate from either Illinois or Virginia; a discussion of art, particularly writing, runs throughout.

0115 Anderson, Sherwood   **1876-1941**
Return to Winesburg: selections from four years of writing for a country newspaper. Edited with introduction by Ray Lewis White. Chapel Hill: The University of North Carolina Press, 1967. 223 p.

Having achieved literary and social success after the publication of *Winesburg, Ohio,* Anderson sought to relive his youth in rural late-nineteenth-century America and overcome his sense of creative exhaustion by returning to a small town as a newspaperman.

0116 Anderson, Sherwood   **1876-1941**
Sherwood Anderson/Gertrude Stein: correspondence and personal essays. Edited by Ray Lewis White. Chapel Hill: University of North Carolina Press, 1972. 130 p.

A record of the unlikely literary friendship between Midwestern ex-businessman Anderson and sophisticated esthete Stein—affectionate, if apparently superficial.

0117 Anderson, Sherwood   **1876-1941**
A story teller's story: a critical text. Edited with introduction by Ray Lewis White. Cleveland: The Press of Case Western Reserve University, 1968. (New York: B.W. Huebsch, 1924) 360 p. Index.

Written at the height of his popularity (1923), this work gives authenticity to Anderson's "legends"—his impoverished childhood, his parents, his revolt from business life, and his entrance into avant-garde literary circles.

0118 Anderson, Sherwood   **1876-1941**
Tar: a midwest childhood: a critical text. Edited with introduction by Ray Lewis White. Cleveland: The Press of Case Western Reserve University, 1969. (New York: Boni & Liveright, 1926) 257 p. Index.

A semi-fictional memoir, this book is the story of his pastoral, gently sad boyhood, although he calls himself George Willard and his town, Winesburg, rather than Clyde, Ohio. The book is about his growing up, his grief at his mother's death, and finally his acceptance of that loss as he enters adolescence. This edition includes critical appendixes.

0119 *Andrews, Eliza Frances   **1840-1939**
War-time journal of a Georgia girl, 1864-1865. Edited by Spencer Bidwell King, Jr. Atlanta: Cherokee Publishing Co., 1976. (New York: D. Appleton, 1908) 396 p.

The diary of a young Southern woman who was sent to rural Georgia for protection from Sherman's army, only to find that Sherman brought the war to her area. Her travels and adventures, always from a proper Southern lady's perspective, reflect the rebel philosophy after the war ended as well as during its last few months.

0120 *Andrews, Fannie Fern (Phillips)   **1867-1950**
Memory pages of my life. Boston: Talisman Press, 1948. 205 p.

Author, scholar, educator, worker for international peace; her autobiography includes brief recollections of childhood, with major focus on her career. Includes list of public offices held; partial list of publications.

0121 *Andrews, Marietta (Minnigerode)   **b.1869**
Memoirs of a poor relation; being the story of a post-war Southern girl and her battle with destiny. New York: E.P. Dutton & Co., 1927. 455 p. Index.

A descendant of a prominent Virginia family describes her post-Civil War childhood, the remnants of Virginia society, and her years as an art student in Washington in the 1890's.

0122 Andrews, Robert Hardy   **1903-**
Corner of Chicago. Boston: Little, Brown and Co., 1963. 365 p.

In the late Twenties he was hired by the Chicago *Daily News* where he shared an office with Carl Sandburg and established his reputation writing about Chicago. Later he became a prolific writer of the new American art form, radio soap opera, creating such shows as *Ma Perkins, Just Plain Bill,* and *Jack Armstrong, the All American Boy.*

0123 Andrews, Roy Chapman   **1884-1960**
An explorer comes home: further adventures of Roy Chapman Andrews. With drawings by Thomas W. Voter. Garden City, New York: Doubleday & Co., 1947. 276 p.

A naturalist's look at the people and animals of his rural Connecticut home, Pondwood Farm.

0124 Andrews, Roy Chapman   **1884-1960**
Under a lucky star: a lifetime of adventure. New York: The Viking Press, 1943. 300 p.

Based on journals of his expeditions between 1907 and 1930, plus recollection of personal experiences, the book describes the development of his career, his eighteen years in China, and his directorship of the American Museum of Natural History.

0125 Andrews, William Albert   **1843-1901?**
Dangerous voyages of Captain William Andrews. Illustrated. Compiled by Richard Henderson. New York: Abercrombie and Fitch, 1966. 39 p.

The first of two diaries by Andrews, a fanatical sailor, describes in detail the 1878 transatlantic voyage of the 19-foot *Nautilus* with his brother. The second, *Columbus Outdone,* narrates the record-setting solo transatlantic crossing of the 14 1/2-foot *Sapolio,* capsizable, leaky, without an auxiliary engine, radio, lights, or arrangements for self-steering.

0126 Andrus, Burton C.   **1892-1977**
I was the Nuremberg jailer. New York: Coward-McCann, 1969. 210 p. Index.

For eighteen months during 1945-46, Andrus' job was to guard the 21 top Nazis and maintain the security of the Tribunal that was trying them for war crimes. He writes of the daily events in the prison, of the trials, of the people he guarded.

0127 Angell, Israel   **1740-1832**
Diary of Colonel Israel Angell: commanding the Second Rhode Island Continental Regiment during the American Revolution, 1778-1781. Edited by Edward Field. Eyewitness Accounts of the American Revolution. New York: Arno Press, Inc., 1971. (Providence, Rhode Island: Preston and Rounds Co., 1899) 149 p. Index.

Including notes on his experience at the Battle of Brandywine and during the winter of Valley Forge, the diary is a slim but interesting account.

0128 Angell, James Burrill   **1829-1916**
Reminiscences of James Burrill Angell. Freeport, New York: Books for Libraries Press, 1971. (New York: Longmans, 1911) 258 p.

The story of a prominent educator and diplomat who served as president of the University of Vermont and the University of Michigan and was sent on diplomatic missions to China and the Ottoman Empire.

0129 *Angelou, Maya   **1928-**
Gather together in my name. New York: Random House, 1974. 214 p.

The author has studied and taught dance, helped produce and star in plays, written for newspapers in Cairo and Ghana and for TV, and the theater. In this book she recalls experiences of her youth before she became a successful writer.

0130 *Angelou, Maya   **1928-**
I know why the caged bird sings. New York: Random House, 1970. 281 p.

The life of a young Black girl who later studied dance, starred on the stage, and wrote for newspapers and television. Her story is a sensitive narrative of her gradual awareness of the realities of life, of prejudice, of cruelty, of ignorance, but also of love.

0131 *Angelou, Maya   **1928-**
Singin' and swingin' and gettin' merry like Christmas. New York: Bantam Books, 1977. (New York: Random House, 1976) 269 p.

In this third autobiographical volume, Angelou masterfully recreates her lean years as record shop clerk and B-girl, followed by her rapid ascent to cabaret singer and dancer and her subsequent role with the touring company of *Porgy and Bess.* Along the way she describes her forays into organized religion, a brief marriage, the problems of raising

her beloved son alone, and European travels with the opera company. Her experiences are infused with her evolving sense of Black womanhood and her growth from cautiousness to confidence and self-assurance.

0132 Angoff, Charles   **1902-1979**
When I was a boy in Boston. Freeport, New York: Books for Libraries Press, 1970. (New York: Beechhurst Press, 1947) 182 p.

A collection of stories, several of which were published earlier in little magazines, of the author's boyhood. Most focus on a particular character who had a strong influence on him.

0133 Anonymous (Attributed to a Mr. Matthews or Mathews)
A summer month; or, recollections of a visit to the falls of Niagara, and the lakes . . . Philadelphia: H.C. Carey and I. Lea, 1823. 250 p.

The account of a tour of upper New York and Canada and observations of scenery and people, the joys and the difficulties of travel in the early nineteenth century.

0134 Antel, Francis P.
Ransom & gems: the DeLong Ruby story. Illustrated. Palm Beach, Florida: Literary Investment Guild, Ltd., 1969. 193 p. Index.

The author, a writer, was doing research in south Florida in 1965 on gem thefts when he discovered a clue that led him to the DeLong Ruby, stolen from the American Museum of Natural History by a gang masterminded by socially prominent yacht broker, Dick Pearson. Antel tells how he negotiated for its return and, despite threats to his life, testified at Pearson's trial, which resulted in conviction.

0135 Antheil, George   **1900-1959**
Bad boy of music. Garden City, New York: Doubleday, Doran and Co., Inc., 1945. 295 p.

A glib and brassy narrative by the composer of "Ballet Mecanique" describing his life as a concert pianist and composer among American expatriates in Europe during the 1920's, then among entertainers and musicians in New York and Hollywood.

0136 Anthony, Edward   **1895-1971**
This is where I came in: the impromptu confessions of Edward Anthony. Garden City, New York: Doubleday and Co., Inc. 1960. 381 p. Index.

An anecdotal narrative of the varied career of a writer—his Manhattan boyhood, his days as a cub reporter, his long association with the Crowell-Collier Publishing Company, and his work as a Hollywood script writer.

0137 Anthony, Norman   **1889-1968**
How to grow old disgracefully. New York: Duell, Sloan and Pearce, 1946. 247 p.

Traces author's career as artist-journalist; he became editor of *Ballyhoo,* published by George T. Delacorte, Jr., a men's magazine whose style was later pre-empted by *Esquire.*

0138 *Anthony, Susan B.   **1916-**
The ghost in my life. New York: Chosen Books, 1971. 221 p.

The namesake and grandniece of the famous suffragist writes of a life made difficult by that heritage, of various jobs as a reporter and broadcaster, of being a feminist and an alcoholic.

0139 Arceneaux, George   **1895-**
Youth in Acadie: reflections on Acadian life and culture in Southwest Louisiana. Baton Rouge, Louisiana: Claitor's Publishing Division, 1974. 100 p. Index.

Arceneaux provides a brief history of the 1604 French settlement of Acadie, in what is now Nova Scotia, and explains how the Acadians migrated to Louisiana in 1763. Having grown up in a traditional Acadian home, Arceneaux relates the ancient French customs that prevail in family life, farming, education, and religion.

0140 Ardery, Philip   **1914-**
Bomber pilot: a memoir of World War II. Illustrated. Lexington: The University Press of Kentucky, 1978. 233 p. Index.

After a brief eulogy to the victims of World War II, this book glorifies patriotism, fighting for one's country, war, and being a man among men. Ardery writes of his many bomber missions and colleagues in the U.S. Army Air Corps.

0141 Arlen, Michael J.   **1930?-**
Exiles. Illustrated. New York: Farrar, Straus & Giroux, 1970. 226 p.

Arlen writes of his father, a celebrated novelist in the Twenties, his mother, and himself in a haunting quest of discovery in the movement and meaning of their lives.

0142 Arlen, Michael J.   **1930?-**
Passage to Ararat. New York: Farrar, Straus & Giroux, 1975. 293 p.

Arlen set out on a journey to discover the heritage of his Armenian forebears. He found sadness and horror as well as humor and hope in a land and people that conquerors have been trying to suppress for centuries. He also tried to come to terms with a father and a father's fears.

0143 *Armaghanian, Arsha Louise   1902-
Arsha's world and yours. New York: Vantage, 1977. 96 p.
  Arsha was an Armenian teenager living near Istanbul when World War I broke out and all Armenians were deported to the interior of Turkey. Arsha stowed paper, pencils and her Bible in a sack and kept a diary of her family's forced travels and struggles to survive. As Christians they were considered outcasts in the primitive Turkish village where they were finally allowed to settle. After World War I, Arsha came to America where she went to college, raised a family, and managed a nursery school.

0144 Armes, Jay J.   1940?-
Jay J. Armes, investigator. With Frederick Nolan. New York: Macmillan and Co., 1976. 234 p.
  Armes is to private investigation what Melvin Belli is to trial law. He describes his hyperactive, flamboyant life, and unorthodox, not always legal, methods of solving crimes. Armes analyzes several dozen breathtaking "capers," all of which he solved, and writes partly to demonstrate what can be done without hands; his were destroyed in an accident at age 12.

0145 Armour, Richard   1906-
My life with women: confessions of a domesticated male. New York: McGraw-Hill Book Co., 1968. 180 p.
  A prolific writer of spoofs and humorous books, articles, and poems, Armour here writes about himself, particularly about married life.

0146 *Armstrong, April Oursler   1926-
Cry Babel: the nightmare of aphasia and a courageous woman's struggle to rebuild her life. Garden City, New York: Doubleday and Co., 1979. 252 p.
  At 46, Armstrong was afflicted with aphasia that reduced her from a prolific author and theology professor to the physical and linguistic level of an eighteen-month-old baby. This highly religious, mystical account narrates her seven-year struggle toward psychological, personal, and professional rehabilitation.

0147 *Armstrong, April Oursler   1926-
House with a hundred gates. New York: McGraw-Hill Book Co., 1965. 286 p.
  Armstrong tells of life with her author parents, Fulton and Grace Oursler, including estrangement when her mother's alcoholism became rampant and union when her father and then Armstrong converted to Catholicism. She successfully combined marriage to lawyer Martin Armstrong with motherhood (seven children), a brisk literary career, and increasing involvement with institutional Catholicism.

0148 Armstrong, Henry   1912-
Gloves, glory and God: an autobiography. Westwood, New Jersey: Fleming H. Revell, 1956. 256 p.
  In novelistic form, this third-person autobiography describes a Black athlete's rise to become the world's lightweight champion boxer, followed by a slow decline and many injuries. Later an alcoholic, ultimately he became a Baptist preacher and "fought for God."

0149 Armstrong, Louis   1900-1971
Louis Armstrong—a self-portrait: the interview by Richard Meryman. New York: The Eakins Press, 1971. 59 p.
  The major portion of this interview was published in *Life*, April 15, 1966. In it the famous trumpeter tells anecdotes of his youth in New Orleans and his later success in Chicago and elsewhere.

0150 Armstrong, Louis   1900-1971
Satchmo: my life in New Orleans. New York: Prentice-Hall, Inc., 1954. 240 p.
  A wizard with his horn, Armstrong here tells of his childhood, his start in music, the bumptious life in New Orleans, great bands, great musicians, and his break into the big time in Chicago.

0151 Armstrong, William Howard   1914-
Through troubled waters. New York: Harper & Row, 1973. 86 p.
  The story of a man and his three young children coping with the sudden death of their wife and mother.

0152 Arnold, Eddy   1918-
It's a long way from Chester County. Illustrated. Old Tappan, New Jersey: Hewitt House, 1969. 154 p. Index.
  His career as a country singer was solidly established by his recording of "That's How Much I Love You" in 1946. It peaked, declined, and grew again by the mid-sixties. His book describes the struggle and success of a young man from Tennessee.

0153 Arnold, Henry Harley   1886-1950
Global mission. New York: Harper and Brothers, 1949. 626 p. Index.

Author describes his childhood in Pennsylvania, education at West Point, early years of flying, and detailed account of World War II, ending with his retirement after 42 years of service developing air power.

0154 Arnold, Oren   1900-
A boundless privilege. Introduction by Alan D. LeBaron. Illustrated. Austin, Texas: Madrona Press, Inc., 1974. 159 p.
  Harking back to the first twenty years of the twentieth century, the author examines the accelerated rate of change and its effects on the old simple life in the rural region of Rusk County, Texas. Folk speech and customs, family life, typical characters, and simple pleasures typify the life in a passing era.

0155 Arnold, Thurman Wesley   1891-1969
Fair fights and foul: a dissenting lawyer's life. New York: Harcourt, Brace & World, Inc., 1965. 292 p. Index.
  Arnold's book reviews the cases and causes he has known and describes the legal, economic, and religious ideas which he accepted in his youth and which have since changed through the decades causing conflict and adjustment.

0156 Arnold, Thurman Wesley   1891-1969
Voltaire and the cowboy: the letters of Thurman Arnold. Edited by Gene M. Gressley. Preface. Introduction. Illustrated. Boulder, Colorado: Colorado Associated University Press, 1977. 552 p. Index.
  The detailed, precise, and witty biographical introduction is a fitting prelude to the extensive selection from 17,000 of Thurman Arnold's letters, written from 1910-1969. They cover his college years and the beginning of his career as a lawyer in Laramie, Wyoming (1910-1918); his academic appointments at the University of West Virginia and Yale Law schools (1927-1936); his years in Washington as assistant attorney general; his partnership in Arnold, Fortas, and Porter (1937-1969); and his impassioned and witty defense of victims of the McCarthy anti-communist investigations.

0157 *Arnow, Harriette Louisa Simpson   1908-
Old Burnside. Illustrated. Lexington: University Press of Kentucky, 1977. 129 p.
  With precise details and a homey nostalgia reminiscent of Wilder's *Little House on the Prairie* series, Arnow recreates her turn-of-the-century family life in Burnside, Kentucky, and supplies a history of this small rural town on the Cumberland River.

0158 Arny, William Frederick Milton   1813-1881
Indian agent in New Mexico: the journal of Special Agent W.F.M. Arny, 1870. Introduction and notes by Lawrence R. Murphy. Santa Fe: Stagecoach Press, 1967. 62 p. Index.
  Arny's journal records his visits (May-October, 1870) to various New Mexican Indian tribes—including Abiquiu, Apache, Navajo, and Ute. He knows and loves the Indians, provides much census data and many sensible recommendations.

0159 Aronson, Charles N.   1913-
Free enterprise. Foreword by J.F. Jim Straw. Illustrated. Arcade, New York: C.N. Aronson, 1979. 1655 p.
  This is an extensively detailed history of Aronson's founding and development of the Aronson Machine Company in Arcade, New York. Aronson regards his life as a Horatio Alger story and is proud of his mechanical ingenuity, honesty, and acumen as his business expanded, 1946-1969, to a multi-million-dollar enterprise.

0160 Aronson, John Hugo   1891-
The galloping Swede. And L.D. Brockmann. Missoula, Montana: Mountain Press Publishing Co., 1970. 180 p. Index.
  At fourteen, he had saved enough money to immigrate to America, and he kept traveling west until he reached Montana. There he worked as a rancher, established his own construction company, and eventually served as a two-term governor.

0161 Arthur, Joseph   b.1875
Broken hills: the story of Joe Arthur, cowpuncher and prospector, who struck it rich in Nevada. As told to Zua Arthur. Illustrated. New York: Vantage Press, 1958. 220 p.
  Arthur told his wife this story of rough living in the turn-of-the-century American West, working on cattle ranches and prospecting for precious ores; she recorded it in the first person. Arthur "struck it rich" at the Broken Hills (Nevada) lode. He also tells of deer hunting and other woodland activities.

0162 Ashe, Arthur, Jr.   1943-
Advantage Ashe. As told to Clifford George Gewecke, Jr. Illustrated. New York: Coward-McCann, Inc., 1967. 192 p.
  Ashe was the first Black man to play in the white-dominated amateur tennis circuit. Trained by a Black coach, he played tournaments in the United States and Australia. At 22 he became the ranking amateur in the United States.

0163 Asher, Jeremiah   **b.1812**
Incidents in the life of the Rev. J. Asher: pastor of Shiloh (coloured) Baptist Church, Philadelphia, U.S., and a concluding chapter of facts illustrating the unrighteous prejudice existing in the minds of American citizens toward their coloured brethren. Introduction by Wilson Armistead. The Black Heritage Library Collection. Freeport, New York: Books for Libraries Press, 1971. (London: Charles Gilpin, 1850) 80 p.
   Written and published to raise funds for his ministerial services, Asher's memoir is an account of personal indignities suffered in Northern states prior to the Civil War.

0164 *Ashley, Elizabeth   **1939-**
Actress: postcards from the road. And Ross Firestone. Illustrated. New York: M. Evans & Co., 1978. 252 p.
   A harsh and sometimes vulgar account of Ashley's struggle with success, professional blacklisting, insecurity, and mental instability. A Tony Award-winning Broadway star at 23, she gained the reputation of a rude, high-strung "bad girl," and had to struggle to find work after her stormy marriage to George Peppard broke up.

0165 Ashley, William Henry   **1778-1838**
The West of William H. Ashley: the international struggle for the fur trade of the Missouri, the Rocky Mountains, and the Columbia, with explorations beyond the Continental Divide, recorded in the diaries and letters of William H. Ashley and his contemporaries; 1822-1838. Edited by Dale Lowell Morgan. Denver: The Old West Publishing Co., 1964. 341 p. Index.
   A dominant figure in Western history who was also a Missouri politician and U.S. Congressman, Ashley left a diary that sheds light on fur trading and Western exploration during the early 1800's, here augmented with related papers, letters, and newspaper accounts.

0166 Ashurst, Henry Fountain   **1874-1962**
Many-colored toga: the diary of Henry Fountain Ashurst. Edited by George F. Sparks. Drawings by H. Beaumont Williams. Tucson: University of Arizona Press, 1962. 416 p. Index.
   The diary (1910-1937) of one of Arizona's two first senators who served thirty years in the U.S. Senate and played a leading role in maintaining the independence of the judiciary through his chairmanship of the Committee on the Judiciary.

0167 Ashworth, William   **1942-**
The Wallowas: coming of age in the wilderness. New York: Hawthorn Books, 1978. 165 p.
   Ashworth wrote this evocative account of his decade of mountaineering in the Wallowa Mountains of Oregon as a plea for ecological conservation and to show the progressive stages of his relationship to the wilderness. Initially, the adventure stage pits man against nature. The second and third stages involve man's progressively deepening understanding of the universe and eventual oneness with it. The culminating fourth stage is peace.

0168 Asimov, Isaac   **1920-**
In joy still felt: the autobiography of Isaac Asimov, 1954-1978. Garden City, New York: Doubleday & Co., 1980. 828 p. Index.
   This book is a continuation of Asimov's first autobiographical work, In Memory Yet Green. It describes simultaneous developments of the successful science fiction writer (with 215 books to his credit) and a frustrated academic career. He was promoted to full professor only in 1979, after 31 years on the faculty of the Boston University School of Medicine.

0169 Astaire, Fred   **1899-**
Steps in time. Illustrated. New York: Da Capo Press, 1979. (New York: Harper & Row, 1959) 327 p. Index.
   Astaire describes his years as a touring Vaudeville performer with his sister Adele in revues, musicals, and nightclubs. When Adele retired to marry, his famous partnership with Ginger Rogers was born, as was his movie career. Along with his many roles and dancing partners (including Leslie Caron and Cyd Charisse), Astaire relates his experience as a USO entertainer during World War II; the narrative is infused with his love for his wife and children.

0170 *Astor, Brooke (Russell)
Patchwork child. New York: Harper & Row Publishers, 1962. 224 p.
   Because her father was a high-ranking Marine officer, she spent her childhood in several foreign countries from which she derived what she calls a patchwork of experience. Her book reflects the life of a socialite growing up in military and international settings, including China just before the revolution.

0171 *Astor, Mary   **1906-**
A life on film. New York: Delacorte Press, 1971. 245 p.
   Her second autobiographical work focuses less on her personal problems and more on her life as an actress, stressing the tension, difficulties, and tedium of that world.

0172 *Astor, Mary   **1906-**
My story: an autobiography. Garden City, New York: Doubleday and Co., Inc., 1959. 332 p.
   In the context of her film career, the book focuses on her struggle with and recovery from alcoholism.

0173 Atkins, James A.   **1890-**
The age of Jim Crow. New York: Vantage Press, 1964. 300 p. Index.
   A Black leader writes of his life disciplined by hard work, by illness, by deprivation, but successful in gaining education, knowledge, and the satisfaction of helping in the struggle for racial equality and equal opportunities.

0174 *Atkins, Susan Denise   **1948?-**
Child of Satan, child of God. With Bob Slosser. Plainfield, New Jersey: Logos International, 1977. 290 p.
   A member of Charles Manson's sex-and-drug oriented "family" writes of the sordid events of her alienated life that culminated in the wanton murder of actress Sharon Tate. Beginning her criminal activities early as a shoplifter with interludes as a go-go dancer, she became a fugitive from society and the law in her teens. She was always high on progressively more potent drugs until imprisoned for the Tate murder, when she found Christ. As a born-again Christian she functions as a lay minister in her prison environment.

0175 Atkinson, Carroll   **1896-**
Intellectual tramp: the autobiography of a schoolteacher. New York: Exposition Press, 1955. 390 p.
   An anecdotal illustration of the author's definition of "intellectual tramp"—"a human being . . . with considerable native intelligence, who . . . shifts from place to place as either necessity or opportunity may dictate." Always on the defensive, Atkinson recounts his peripatetic existence as a public schoolteacher, college administrator, and public relations man during innumerable moves, particularly in the West.

0176 Atkinson, Donald T.   **1874-1959**
Texas surgeon: an autobiography. New York: Ives Washburn, Inc., 1958. 180 p.
   An ophthalmologist, internationally recognized for his work on glaucoma, devotes half the book to his early life and hard-earned medical education. He continues with his first years of medical practice in rural Texas and the Oklahoma Territory.

0177 Atkinson, Wilmer   **1840-1920**
Wilmer Atkinson, an autobiography. New York: Beekman Publishers, 1974. (Philadelphia: Wilmer Atkinson Co., 1920) 375 p.
   Atkinson was a journalist in Delaware who founded the Farm Journal, helped found bird clubs, worked to beautify the landscape, improve roads, and supported the Woman's Rights Movement and Women's Suffrage.

0178 Atwood, George   **1892?-**
Along the Alcan. Illustrated by George Atwood. New York: Pageant Press, 1960. 212 p.
   Atwood, a carpenter from Minnesota, was a member of a construction crew that helped to build airports, hangers, line camps, and pumping stations along the Alcan Highway from Edmonton, Alberta, to Fairbanks, Alaska, throughout 1943.

0179 Auchincloss, Louis (Andrew Lee, pseud.)   **1917-**
A writer's capital. Illustrated. Boston: Houghton Mifflin, 1979. (Minneapolis: University of Minnesota Press, 1974) 160 p. Index.
   A privileged life of private schools, travel, homes on Long Island and Bar Harbor furnished much of the background material for Auchincloss's novels. To the story of what led him to become a writer he appends chapters on Ruth Draper, Amelie Rives, and Aileen Tone.

0180 Auden, Wystan Hugh   **1907-1973**
Letters from Iceland. And Louis MacNiece. New York: Random House, 1969. (1937)
   A unique travel book written in the form of verse letters with interspersed prose commentaries. The letters are addressed to the living and the dead—Byron, Isherwood, Betjeman, and others.

0181 Audett, James "Blackie" Henry   **1903-**
Rap sheet: my life story. Foreword by Gene Lowall. New York: William Sloane Associates, Inc., 1954. 284 p.
   An exciting cops-and-robbers tale from the robber's point of view. Audett ran away from home in Canada at thirteen, was impressed into military service in World War I, and returned to a lifetime of robbing trains, bootlegging liquor from Canada to the United States during Prohibition, and smuggling Chinese workers into the United States. In the 1920's and 1930's, he became a big-time bank robber in the Midwest, working with Dillinger and Al Capone, and ultimately spent five years in Alcatraz, after stretches in other prisons.

0182 Audubon, John James   **1785-1851**
Audubon and his journals. Edited by Maria R. Audubon. Notes by Elliott

Coves. New York: Dover Publications, Inc., 1960. (New York: Charles Scribner's Sons, 1897) 2v. Index.

An unabridged edition of the journals of his travels and observations in Europe (1826-1828), Labrador (1833), and along the Missouri River (1843), by a famous naturalist.

0183 Audubon, John Woodhouse   1812-1862
Audubon's western journal: 1849-1850; being the ms. record of a trip from New York to Texas, and an overland journey through Mexico and Arizona to the gold-fields of California. Introduction, notes and index by Frank Heywood Hodder. Biographical memoir by Maria R. Audubon. Glorieta, New Mexico: Rio Grande Press, 1969. (Cleveland: The A.H. Clark Co., 1906) 249 p. Index.

After the war with Mexico had ended, he, like many Americans, went to explore the relatively unknown Southwest. His daily journal is a sensitive depiction of the times, influenced by the painter's trained eye.

0184 Auerbach, Arnold ("Red")   1917-
Red Auerbach: winning the hard way. With Paul Sann. Boston: Little, Brown and Co., 1966. 372 p.

In twenty years as a professional basketball coach, aggressive, colorful Auerbach won more championships (nine with the Boston Celtics), coached more games (1585), and paid more fines ($17,000) than any other coach in professional sports. Here he discusses his players, his strategy, his feuds, and his philosophy of the game.

0185 Auerbach, Arnold Malcolm   1912-
Funny men don't laugh. Garden City, New York: Doubleday and Co., 1965. 176 p.

Auerbach recalls five sober, tense years during the Depression when he worked as a gag writer for Lou Jacobs (pseud.), learning the craft superbly, as did his colleague, Herman Wouk. Their best known client was Fred Allen, "a champion [whose] combination of style, viewpoint and wit" has never been duplicated. This is not a funny book.

0186 August, John, pseud.
see **DeVoto, Bernard Augustine**

0187 *Austin, Barbara Leslie   1946-
Sad nun at Synanon. New York: Holt, Rinehart and Winston, Inc., 1970. 186 p.

She entered a convent at nineteen, taught elementary school, and then at 22 volunteered to work at Synanon, a rehabilitation center for drug addicts. Her book describes the shock and difficulty of that experience, coming to terms with social issues, adjustments in her personal life, and finally leaving the convent.

0188 *Austin, Mary Hunter   1868-1934
Literary America, 1903-1934: the Mary Austin letters. Edited by T.M. Pearce. Illustrated. Westport, Connecticut: Greenwood Press, 1979. 296 p. Index.

Out of the 115 letters in this collection, only eight were written by Mary Austin. Editor Pearce supplies generous commentary and biographical background as well as a section of brief sketches of many of the literary figures who produced the letters contained. He makes frequent reference to Austin's autobiography, *Earth Horizon.*

0189 Autry, Gene   1907-
Back in the saddle again. With Mickey Herskowitz. Illustrated. Garden City, New York: Doubleday & Co., 1978. 282 p. Index.

Autry describes his discovery by Will Rogers as the "singing cowboy," his career in Western movies and television (particularly in the series *Annie Oakley*), and his experience in corporate management and politics.

0190 Averell, William Woods   1832-1900
Ten years in the saddle: his memoirs. Edited with epilogue by Edward K. Eckert & Nicholas J. Amato. Illustrated. San Rafael, California: Presidio Press, 1978. 443 p. Index.

This highly detailed memoir discusses Averell's education at West Point (1851-55), from which he emerged as a cavalry officer sent to subdue the Indians in Arizona and New Mexico. He regarded these territories and Old Mexico as curiosities and presents a thorough description of their culture. At the outbreak of the Civil War Averell was designated commander of the Third Pennsylvania Cavalry, Union Army. The memoir breaks off after a description of the Battle of Bull Run and the Peninsula campaign in 1862, and is concluded with an editorial epilogue.

0191 Averill, Gerald   1896-1949?
Ridge runner: the story of a Maine woodsman. Philadelphia: J.B. Lippincott Co., 1948. 217 p.

Colorful, well-written description of life in the Maine woods, warm relation to grandfather in early youth, later experience in logging camp and as a game warden from 1933-1946.

0192 Avery, Samuel Putnam   1822-1904
Diaries 1871-1882 of Samuel P. Avery, art dealer. Edited with introduction by Madeleine Fidell Beaufort (and others). Foreword by A. Hyatt Mayor. Illustrated. New York: Arno Press, 1979. 936 p. Index.

One of the founding fathers of the Metropolitan Museum of Art, Avery is best remembered for having started the Metropolitan's art library. His diaries, five volumes of which are included here, record his purchases, itineraries, and observations from eleven years of collecting.

0193 *Ayscough, Florence Wheelock   1878-1942
Florence Ayscough and Amy Lowell: correspondence of a friendship. Edited by Harley Farnsworth MacNair. Chicago: University of Chicago Press, 1945. 288 p.

Letters 8 December 1917 to 1 May 1926. Their friendship included an exchange of information about Chinese art and China, where Florence Ayscough lived for years.

0194 Babson, Roger Ward   1875-1967
Actions and reactions: an autobiography of Roger W. Babson. New York: Harper & Brothers Publishers, 1949. (1935) 354 p. Index.

A forthright, moralistic narrative based on a philosophy of common sense, ingenuity, and independence, describing his New England boyhood, his education, and his success as a statistician and founder of three colleges.

0195 *Bacall, Lauren   1926-
By myself. New York: Ballantine Books, 1980. (New York: Alfred A. Knopf, 1978) 506 p.

With candor, integrity, and humor, Bacall describes her upbringing by a strong Jewish mother, her sudden film stardom, and romance with Humphrey Bogart, married and 25 years her senior. Despite improbable odds, their sixteen-year marriage which lasted until Bogie's death in 1957 was dominated by immense love and personal and professional integrity.

0196 Bacigalupa, Drew (Andrea)   1923-
Journal of an itinerant artist. Illustrated by Andrea Bacigalupa. Huntington, Indiana: Our Sunday Visitor, Inc., 1977. 176 p.

Bacigalupa's journal is divided into twelve months, beginning in December ("the format of the liturgical calendar"), and is illustrated with striking woodcuts. He intersperses vignettes of his travels in Europe and Mexico with brief portraits of memorable people. His love for humanity and his own family is paramount.

0197 Backus, Henny
see **Backus, Jim**

0198 Backus, Isaac   1724-1806
Diary of Isaac Backus. Edited by William G. McLoughlin. Providence, Rhode Island: Brown University Press, 1979. 3v. Index.

McLoughlin states of this enormous diary: it "makes clear [Backus's] importance as a [Baptist] leader ... The diary, covering the sixty-year span from the First to the Second Great Awakening, describes [Backus's] ... campaigns for religious liberty ... It reveals his early struggles to fulfill his mission as pastor, ... describes his work in consolidating the growing Baptist denomination, and discusses the situations that led him into theological controversies." The diary also shows Backus as a family man, farmer, bookseller, ironmonger, and citizen of an emerging republic.

0199 Backus, Jim   1913-
Rocks on the roof. With Henny Backus. New York: G.P. Putnam's Sons, 1958. 190 p.

Television and film actor best known as the voice of Mr. Magoo and his wife, Henny, a sculptor, collaborate to tell amusing anecdotes about their sociable years in Hollywood, where their friends included Victor Mature and James Dean.

0200 Badollet, John Louis   1758-1837
Correspondence of John Badollet and Albert Gallatin, 1804-1836. Edited by Gayle Thornbrough. Indianapolis: Indiana Historical Society, 1963. 372 p. Index.

The letters exchanged between two friends, both Jefferson Republicans, who in different ways participated in the development of their adopted country, the one as a frontier official in the Indiana Territory, the other as a U.S. Congressman, Secretary of the Treasury, and minister to France and Great Britain.

0201 *Baez, Joan   1941-
Daybreak. New York: The Dial Press, Inc., 1968. 159 p.

Reminiscences of her childhood and youth as well as incidents during her career and her work for non-violence and resistance, by a famous folk-singer.

0202 Bagby, James Thomas   b.1879
From the tablets of my heart. Introduction by A.L. Dickerson. New York: Vantage Press, 1957. 103 p.

Crippled by polio at fourteen months of age, Bagby nevertheless became a highly successful and inspiring minister to his Tennessee congregations. He was particularly influenced by his parents and teachers.

0203 *Bagley, Merle Lucile (Zane)   1890-
Sidestepping the barbarians: glimpses of a real experience. Illustrated.
Redlands, California: Citrograph Printing Co., 1948. 45 p.
   Reminiscences (May, 1944-February, 1945) of life in the Japanese-oc-
cupied Philippine Islands. The author, a public school teacher, and her
husband evaded the Japanese with the help of their Filipino foster son and
his family, finding temporary shelter in a guerrilla camp. The memoir
ends with their separation from their foster son and return to San
Francisco. Fragmentary, written in the second person.

0204 *Bailey, Alice Anne (La Trobe-Bateman)   1880-1949
Unfinished autobiography of Alice A. Bailey. Foreword by Foster Bailey.
New York: Lucis Publishing Co., 1951. 305 p.
   Occult teacher relates her transition from British socialite and biblical
scholar to believer in the Disciples of Christ, describing her international
work in this field.

0205 *Bailey, Emma
Sold to the lady in the green hat. New York: Dodd, Mead & Co., Inc.,
1962. 213 p.
   In 1944, her husband's health made a family move from urban New
Jersey to rural Vermont imperative. To help their income she opened an
auction house, becoming the first woman auctioneer. Her book describes
their gradual adaption to New England, the development of a successful
business and a new life.

0206 *Bailey, Florence Augusta (Merriam)   b.1863
My summer in a Mormon village. Boston: Houghton, Mifflin and Co.,
1894. 171 p.
   Well-established as a popular writer, she traveled by train and wagon to
a remote Mormon village where she spent the summer recording her
impressions of the Mormon lifestyle.

0207 Bailey, Francis Lee   1933-
The defense never rests. With Harvey Aronson. New York: Stein and
Day, 1971. 262 p.
   The most controversial and talked-about American lawyer since Clar-
ence Darrow, Bailey is an outspoken critic of the system of justice. In this
volume he describes some of the behind-the-scenes events and his part in
some famous cases—the Sam Sheppard case, the Great Plymouth Mail
Robbery, and the Boston Strangler case.

0208 *Bailey, Pearl   1918-
The raw Pearl. New York: Harcourt, Brace & World, Inc., 1968. 206 p.
   The exuberant Pearl tells the story of her life and career and some of
the things she learned along the way. Her book transmits her energy,
warmth, and concern for people as her singing has always done.

0209 *Bailey, Pearl   1918-
Talking to myself. New York: Harcourt Brace Jovanovich, Inc., 1971.
233 p.
   The fantastic success of *Hello, Dolly!* with its accompanying exhilara-
tion, exhaustion, and magical interreaction between the audience and
herself prompted the author to write a second book of reminiscences
about people, attitudes, emotions, and faith.

0210 Baillie, Hugh   1890-1966
High tension: the recollections of Hugh Baillie. Freeport, New York:
Books for Libraries Press, 1970. (New York: Harper and Brothers, 1959)
300 p. Index.
   The story of his forty years in journalism—as a cub reporter in Los
Angeles, as head of the United Press Washington Bureau at 29, and later
as president of United Press.

0211 Baily, Waldron   1871-1953
**The autobiography of Waldron Baily: the life of the novelist and politi-
cian from North Carolina.** Foreword by Frances Baily Morris. New York:
Exposition Press, 1958. 117 p.
   Baily recounts his life history in North Carolina as a buyer of timber
for telephone poles. He was the author of *Heart of the Blue Ridge,* which
was made into a movie, *The Savage Instinct.* For a time he was a somewhat corrupt literary agent. He adorns the book with his poetry and a
puzzling mixture of literary styles: "Here endeth a real good true one! It
never happened again at good old Camp Bryan!"

0212 Bakanowski, Dolf   1840-1919
Polish circuit rider: the Texas memoirs of Adolf Bakanowski, 1866-70.
Translated and annotated by Marion Moore Coleman. Cheshire, Connecticut: Cherry Hill Books, 1971. 49 p.
   After four years serving as a missionary for the Polish Catholic
churches in Texas, where he was responsible for their organization, he
returned to Europe and then was reassigned to Chicago.

0213 Baker, Albie   1917-
Stolen sweets. New York: Saturday Review Press/E.P. Dutton & Co.,
1973. 247 p.
   Baker stole his first bicycle when he was thirteen. Thereafter he took

part in many "capers" and became a notorious jewel thief. Eventually he
went straight and worked in the movies as a script writer and technical
director, although he seems to miss the excitement of his old life.

0214 *Baker, Gladys   1900-1957
I had to know. New York: Appleton-Century-Crofts, Inc., 1951. 309 p.
   Accounts of her experiences with mysticism, serious illness, and her
career as a successful journalist culminate in her conversion to Catholicism under Bishop Fulton J. Sheen's guidance.

0215 *Baker, Josephine   1906-1975
Josephine. And Jo Bouillon. Translated from the French by Mariana
Fitzpatrick. New York: Harper & Row, 1977. 302 p. Index.
   Josephine Baker's memoirs were almost finished at the time of her
death; narrative ellipses have been filled in by friends' recollections of her
remarkable life—poverty as a mulatto child further hindered by her ille-
gitimacy in St. Louis, a glamorous career in Paris as a fabulously clad
dancer in the Folies Bergere, espionage work in World War II for the
French Resistance, and her adoption of twelve children of various races,
her Rainbow Tribe.

0216 *Baker, Louise (Maxwell)   1909-
Out on a limb. New York: Whittlesey House, 1946. 213 p.
   A humorous account of coping with life with only one leg, even roller
skating and horseback riding.

0217 Baker, Ray Stannard (Grayson, David, pseud.)   1870-1946
**More adventures with David Grayson: adventures in understanding, ad-
ventures in solitude, and great possessions.** Garden City, New York:
Doubleday and Co., Inc., 1946. 341 p.
   Previously published as separate volumes, this edition is a sequel to *The
Adventures of David Grayson* which combined three earlier works. Enter-
taining narrative with perceptive analysis of life experience by Baker, who
was a well-known biographer of Woodrow Wilson.

0218 Baker, Robert Gene (Bobby)   1928-
Wheeling and dealing: confessions of a Capitol Hill operator. With Larry
L. King. New York: W.W. Norton, 1978. 296 p. Index.
   Baker tells tales of corruption in Congress and of his close association
with Senators Lyndon Johnson and Robert Kerr. His rise to power behind
the scenes during the 50's and early 60's ended when he was investigated
by a Congressional committee for influence peddling and jailed for tax
evasion. He details his own shady dealings at the behest of Congressmen,
names womanizers and bribers among politicians, and depicts himself as
a scapegoat.

0219 *Baker, Sarah Josephine   1873-1945
Fighting for life. New York: Arno Press, 1974. (New York: The
Macmillan Co., 1939) 264 p.
   Dr. Baker spent her lifetime promoting hygiene, especially for children.
She established the New York Bureau of Child Hygiene in 1908, the first
department of its kind in the world.

0220 Bakker, Jim
Move that mountain! With Robert Paul Lamb. Foreword by Williard
Cantelon. Plainfield, New Jersey: Logos International, 1976. 183 p.
   Evangelist Bakker tells of his estrangement from God during his teen-
age years, his newfound faith after thinking he had killed a child in an
automobile accident when he was eighteen, his two years at North Central
Bible College (Minneapolis), which he left when he married Tammy
LaValley in 1961. Together they spent three years on the road as
evangelists and then became highly successful with two evangelical television shows in Portsmouth, Virginia, "Club 700" and "The Jim and
Tammy Show." Bakker's narrative fluctuates between acts of faith and
cost-accounting.

0221 *Balch, Emily Tapscott Clark   1893-1953
**Ingenue among the lions: the letters of Emily Clark to Joseph
Hergesheimer.** Edited with introduction by Gerald Langford. Austin:
University of Texas Press, 1965. 221 p. Index.
   Emily Clark, editor and moving spirit of *The Reviewer,* a harbinger of
the Southern literary renaissance, wrote these letters giving a daily ac-
count of the journal and the literary world of the Twenties.

0222 Balchen, Bernt   1899-1973
Come North with me: an autobiography. New York: E.P. Dutton and Co.,
Inc., 1958. 318 p. Index.
   An aviator explorer who became a U.S. Air Force Colonel describes his
experience on famous expeditions with Richard E. Byrd, in U.S. operations aiding Norwegian resistance fighters in World War II, and of other
unusual events in modern exploration.

0223 Baldridge, Cyrus LeRoy   b.1889
Time and chance. New York: John Day, 1947. 431 p.
   Newspaper sketch artist, illustrator, and author of books for children
and adults records early training in Chicago, travels to France in World

War I, and to Africa, India, and the Middle East, on which many of his books are based.

0224 *Baldridge, Letitia Katherine   **1926?-**
Of diamonds and diplomats. Boston: Houghton Mifflin Co., 1968. 337 p.
The happy, exciting life of Baldridge, who was social secretary for ambassadors in Paris, Rome, and at the White House, and worked also for Tiffany's and as a consultant at Chicago's Merchandise Mart.

0225 *Baldridge, Letitia Katherine   **1926?-**
Roman candle. Boston: Houghton Mifflin Co., 1956. 308 p.
The story of a six-foot blond from Omaha whose dream was fulfilled when she became social secretary to Ambassador to Italy Clare Boothe Luce. She recalls that life as full, active, and glamorous.

0226 Baldwin, William   **1903-**
Billy Baldwin remembers. New York: Harcourt Brace Jovanovich, 1974. 232 p. Index.
For over forty years he was interior decorator for many of America's well-known celebrities. This volume contains over 100 color photographs of his best achievements along with a narrative account of the logistical, aesthetic, and personality problems he had to deal with during the course of his career.

0227 Baldwin, William   **1779-1819**
Reliquiae Baldwinianae; selections from the correspondence of the late William Baldwin, M.D. New introduction by Joseph Ewan. Compiled by William Darlington. Classica Botanica Americana, Sup. 2. New York: Hafner Publishing Co., 1969. (Philadelphia: Kimber and Sharpless, 1843) 346 p. Index.
Although his career as a botanist was relatively short, Baldwin collected over 3000 species from the coastal plain and the Piedmont, a significant contribution to early natural history. Most of his letters are to Henry Muhlenberg and William Darlington, fellow botanists.

0228 Ball, Thomas   **1819-1911**
My threescore years and ten: an autobiography. Edited with introduction by H. Barbara Weinberg. Illustrated. Series: The Art Experience in Late Nineteenth-Century America. New York: Garland Publishing, 1977. (Boston: Roberts Brothers, 1892) 379 p.
A sculptor best known for his equestrian statue of George Washington in Boston's Public Garden and other heroic-sized statues "documents his major commissions and describes his struggles to bring them to technical and expressive perfection, . . . records methods of study and work, . . . and offers advice to young artists based on the evolution of American art" (ed.).

0229 Ballard, Melvin J.   **1873-1939**
Melvin J. Ballard: crusader for righteousness. Illustrated. Salt Lake City, Utah: Bookcraft, 1966. 293 p.
Born to early Mormon-convert parents, Ballard became a Mormon missionary in South America and was elected to the First Presidency and Council of the Twelve of the Mormon Church. Two hundred pages of this book are devoted to his Mormon-oriented discourses on immortality, church leadership, tithing, motherhood, the resurrection, Temple work, and other matters of concern to Mormon Church members.

0230 Ballou, Adin   **1803-1890**
Autobiography of Adin Ballou, 1803-1890, containing an elaborate record and narrative of his life from infancy to old age with appendixes. Completed and edited by William S. Heywood. Philadelphia: Porcupine Press, Inc., 1975. (Lowell, Massachusetts: Vox Populi Press, 1896) 586 p.
Called to the Christian ministry at age nineteen, Ballou spent his life preaching, teaching, and helping found the Hopedale Community in Massachusetts, a new social experiment, among other good works.

0231 *Balsan, Consuelo (Vanderbilt)   **1877-1964**
Glitter and the gold. London: George Mann, Ltd., 1973. (New York: Harper and Brothers, 1952) 336 p. Index.
Her life as an American heiress, an English duchess, and the fond wife of a French colonel.

0232 Balshofer, Fred J.
One reel a week. And Arthur C. Miller. With Bebe Bergsten. Foreword by Kemp R. Niver. Berkeley: University of California Press, 1967. 218 p.
A motion-picture pioneer who started with the Lubin Company in 1905, Balshofer became a producer; Miller, who writes alternate chapters, was a cameraman. Together they trace much early movie history and chronicle the development of movie-making machinery as well.

0233 Bandelier, Adolph Francis Alphonse   **1840-1914**
Scientist on the trail: travel letters, 1880-1881. Edited by George P. Hammond and Edgar F. Good. Berkeley: Quivera Society, 1949. 142 p. Index.
These travel letters were originally published in a Highland, Illinois, newspaper and describe the explorer-historian's experiences studying Indian pueblos in documents and by observation.

0234 Bandelier, Adolph Francis Alphonse   **1840-1914**
The Southwestern journals of Adolph F. Bandelier. Edited and annotated by Charles H. Lange and Carroll L. Riley. Albuquerque: The University of New Mexico Press, 1966-1975. 3v. Index.
Concerned with Bandelier's initial trip to the Southwest, the first volume, 1880-1882, of his journals shows his early interest in using a common archaeological-historical approach by interpreting archaeological data through an intimate knowledge of ethnological data of the Pueblo Indians. The second volume, 1883-1884, follows his field work among the Pueblo Indians of the Rio Grande Valley and in the Silver City-Gila Cliff Dwellings area. Volume three, 1885-1888, continues his record of the anthropology, botany, folklore, geography, history, and culture of the Indians of the Southwest.

0235 *Bankhead, Tallulah (Brockman)   **1903-1968**
Tallulah: my autobiography. New York: Harper and Brothers, 1952. 326 p. Index.
An actress from Alabama describes her life and career as she traveled and lived in such places as London, New York, Hollywood, and Washington, D.C. She reminisces about famous people she has known and discusses many rumors concerning her life.

0236 Banks, James   **b.1883**
Wing of scarlet. As told to Irving Wallace. Washington, D.C.: Pioneer Publishing Co., 1946. 144 p.
Describes boyhood in Red Wing, Minnesota, homesteading in Lonesome Prairie, Montana (1911-1919), and later life in Cannon Falls, Minnesota; includes accounts of spiritual dreams and visions.

0237 Banta, Albert Franklin   **1843-1924**
Albert Franklin Banta: Arizona pioneer. Edited by Frank D. Reeve. Albuquerque: Historical Society of New Mexico Publications in History, 1953. 143 p. Index.
A colorful, adventure-laden account of one man's participation in the settling and taming of the Wild West. With only twelve months' formal education, he held jobs ranging from bullwhacker, typesetter, and scout for the U.S. Army, to deputy sheriff, district attorney, probate judge, and newspaper publisher.

0238 Baragwanath, John Gordon   **1888-1965**
A good time was had. New York: Appleton-Century-Crofts, Inc., 1962. 245 p.
As an explorer and mining engineer he spent much of his time in Ecuador and other parts of South America. Married to Neysa McMein, a leading illustrator and member of the Algonquin Round Table, he was also close to many of the artists and intellectuals of the New York scene.

0239 Barav, Shmuel
see **Burnstein, Samuel M.**

0240 Barber, Marshall Albert   **1868-1953**
The schoolhouse at Prairie View. Lawrence: University of Kansas Press, 1953. 81 p. Index.
Recollections of his boyhood experience in a one-room schoolhouse in Kansas during the 1870's by a man who became an internationally known biologist specializing in malaria.

0241 Barber, Walter Lanier (Red)   **1908-**
Show me the way to go home. Philadelphia: The Westminster Press, 1971. 192 p.
Red Barber, a seasoned sportscaster and a lay reader in the Episcopal Church, writes of his family and career, but concentrates on his Christian faith, his activities as a lay reader, sermons he has given, services he initiated for the New York Yankees team in 1966, and his experiences in Vietnam on a USO tour.

0242 Barbour, Thomas   **1884-1946**
A naturalist's scrapbook. Cambridge: Harvard University Press, 1946. 218 p. Index.
For many years Director of Harvard's Museum of Comparative Zoology, he writes with care and affection of his life, the museum, his friends, and colleagues.

0243 *Bard, Mary   **1904-1970**
The doctor wears three faces. Philadelphia: J.B. Lippincott Co., 1949. 254 p.
A blunt, earthy, humorous description of her life as a doctor's wife, with a poignant recognition of the life-death center in his work played against her desire to have more of his time for family life.

0244 *Bard, Mary   **1904-1970**
Forty odd. Philadelphia: J.B. Lippincott Co., 1952. 253 p.
Occasionally glib and flippant, the book describes a Nebraska woman's fear of passing forty, of losing her sexual attractiveness and sense of identity, and the way in which she comes to terms with the sense of loss and mortality.

0245 *Bard, Mary   **1904-1970**
Just be yourself. Philadelphia: J.B. Lippincott, 1956. 255 p.
    A lively, pleasantly humorous account of a young mother's initiation
and development as a Brownie troop leader in the Puget Sound region.
Initially lukewarm, she invested her energy, creativity, and love into the
troop of 25 little girls and grew in understanding, practical skills, and
leadership ability.

0246 *Barjansky, Catherine   **1890-1965**
Portraits with backgrounds. In collaboration with Elinore Denniston.
Illustrated. New York: The Macmillan Co., 1947. 223 p.
    Before becoming an American citizen in the 1940's, Madam Barjansky
wandered many European countries, creating portraits of the famous and
unfamous. Here she creates those portraits in words, reflecting her own
life and creative spirit.

0247 Barker, Elliott Speer   **b.1886**
Ramblings in the field of conservation. Foreword by Thomas L. Kimball.
Introduction by Jesse Williams. Santa Fe, New Mexico: Sunstone Press,
1976. 181 p.
    Barker discusses his long career as director of the New Mexico De-
partment of Game and Fish. His particular concerns were wildlife management, overgrazing, forest fires, and soil conservation. A founder of the
National Wildlife Federation, Barker was also three-term president of the
Western Association of State Game and Fish Commissioners. He promoted Smokey the Bear and lobbied for legislation designating wilderness
areas. At 89 he still directed wilderness trail rides.

0248 Barker, John Tull   **1877-1958**
Missouri lawyer. Philadelphia: Dorrance and Co., 1949. 391 p.
    His life in the law from 1898, with anecdotes of prominent characters
and legal matters, including Frank and Jesse James, the Swope Murder
Case, and Thomas J. Prendergast.

0249 *Barkins, Evelyn (Werner)   **1918-**
The doctor has a family. New York: Pellegrini and Cudahy, 1950. 211 p.
    Anecdotes of family life (pregnancy, housebuilding, returning to work)
containing humorous criticism of suburban mores and of the pieties of
modern child-rearing.

0250 *Barkins, Evelyn (Werner)   **1918-**
I love my doctor. New York: Thomas Y. Crowell Co., 1948. 238 p.
    Describes with humor the difficulties of early marriage and establishing
her husband's medical practice.

0251 Barkley, Alben William   **1877-1956**
That reminds me. Garden City, New York: Doubleday and Co., Inc.,
1954. 279 p. Index.
    The politician from Kentucky who became President Truman's
vice-president recalls his political career and his association with various
presidents. The book includes letters and speeches.

0252 *Barkley, Jane (Rucker)   **1911-1964**
I married the Veep. As told to Frances Spatz Leighton. New York: The
Vanguard Press, 1958. 316 p.
    The story of her courtship and marriage to Vice-President Alben
Barkley.

0253 Barnett, Eugene E.   **1888-1970**
**Recollections of growing up in America's Southland and of 26 yrs. in
Pre-Communist China: 1888-1936.** Eugene E. Barnett (available from
University Microfilms International, Ann Arbor, Michigan), 1964. 346 p.
    A well-written account of the author's development as a Christian
missionary and of his 26 years in China (1910-1936), in various leadership
positions with the Young Men's Christian Association. The book provides
a detailed account of the relationship between the YMCA and its Chinese
hosts and a detailed interpretation of its administration.

0254 Barnitz, Albert   **1835-1912**
Life in Custer's cavalry: diaries and letters 1867-1868. And Jennie (Platt)
Barnitz. Edited by Robert M. Utley. New Haven, Connecticut: Yale
University Press, 1977. 302 p. Index.
    This superbly edited collection of letters between Captain Albert
Barnitz and his wife, Jennie, 1867-1868, brings alive frontier fighting
between the Plains Indians and the U.S. Cavalry in unusually vivid and
specific detail. Barnitz's letters are thorough eyewitness accounts of life on
military posts (Fort Hayes and Fort Leavenworth, Kansas), maneuvers on
the Plains, and hostile encounters with the Indians.

0255 *Barnitz, Jennie (Platt)   **1841?-1927**
    see **Barnitz, Albert**

0256 Barnum, Phineas Taylor   **1810-1891**
**Barnum's own story: the autobiography combined and condensed from the
various editions published during his lifetime.** Combined and compiled by
Waldo R. Browne. New York: Dover Publications, Inc., 1961. (New
York: The Viking Press, Inc., 1927) 452 p.

    A reprint of the 1927 edition which condenses two volumes, *The Life
of P.T. Barnum* (Redfield, 1855) and various editions of *Struggles and
Triumphs* (see below).

0257 Barnum, Phineas Taylor   **1810-1891**
Struggles and triumphs of P.T. Barnum: told by himself. Edited by John
G. O'Leary. Rev. ed. London: MacGibbon and Kee, 1967. (Hartford: J.B.
Burr & Co., 1870) 188 p.
    The great impresario recalls the highlights of his career as owner of
"The Greatest Show on Earth." He was particularly pleased with the
popularity and financial success of Jenny Lind, Tom Thumb, and Jumbo
the elephant. Despite catastrophic financial losses in fires, Barnum reveled
in making enormous sums of money.

0258 Baroux, Louis   **1817-1897**
**Correspondence of Rev. Louis Baroux, Missionary Apostolic to Michi-
gan, to Rev. M.J. DeNeve, Superior of the American College at Louvain.**
Translated from French by E.D. Kelly. Introduction by E.D. Kelly. Reprint of 1913 edition. Berrien Springs, Michigan: Hardscrabble Books,
1976. (n.p.: E.D. Kelly, 1913) 95 p.
    Clergyman and missionary Baroux wrote this letter in 1862 to his
superior in France to tell him how his efforts to Christianize the Pokagon
and Potawatomi Indians in Michigan were going and how successful he
was in persuading the savage to "throw away his gun for the ax and the
plow."

0259 Barrett, E. Boyd   **b.1883**
A shepherd without sheep. Milwaukee, Wisconsin: Bruce Publishing Co.,
1956. 143 p.
    An anecdotal account of how a "strayed shepherd," an ordained priest
forbidden to take communion or exercise his priestly powers because of
his earlier rebellion against the Church, can still remain in the fold,
devoutly maintaining his faith and informally ministering to others.

0260 *Barringer, Emily Dunning   **1876-1961**
**Bowery to Bellevue: the story of New York's first woman ambulance
surgeon.** New York: W.W. Norton and Co., 1950. 262 p.
    From the perspective of retirement, the author recalls her internship at
Gouverneur Hospital from 1902 to 1904, especially on ambulance duty,
and combating antagonism from her colleagues because of her sex.

0261 Barringer, Paul Brandon   **1857-1941**
The natural bent: the memoirs of Dr. Paul B. Barringer. Edited by Anna
Barringer. Chapel Hill: University of North Carolina Press, 1949. 280 p.
    Part I contains memories of childhood in Civil War and Reconstruc-
tion periods, with descriptions of hardships and shortages faced by Southern families; Part II contains an account of Barringer's education, from
military school and university through Grand Tour and medical training.

0262 Barrow, Joseph Louis
    see **Louis, Joe**

0263 *Barry, Anne   **1940-**
Bellevue is a state of mind. New York: Harcourt, Brace & Co., 1971.
178 p.
    An investigative report of a week spent in the violent ward of Bellevue;
a grim account of the tragedy, despair, and hope of mental illness.

0264 Barry, David Sheldon   **1859-1936**
Forty years in Washington. New York: Beekman Publishers, 1974. 349 p.
Index.
    Starting as a page in the Senate in 1875, Barry studied in night school
and became Washington correspondent and representative for the Detroit
Post, Chicago *Tribune,* Providence *Journal* and numerous other papers.
He served as secretary to several senators and other public figures. He
records first-hand impressions of people and national and international
events during his long tenure in Washington.

0265 Barry, Henry M.
I'll be seeing you. New York: Alfred A. Knopf, 1952. 239 p.
    Blinded by a shell in World War II, a veteran describes his recupera-
tion and training for a new civilian life.

0266 Barry, Rick   **1944-**
Confessions of a basketball gypsy. With Bill Libby. Englewood Cliffs,
New Jersey: Prentice Hall, 1972. 256 p.
    This story of his rise, fall, and re-entry into the world of sports
superstars offers a view of basketball as big business and athletes as big
businessmen.

0267 *Barrymore, Diana   **1921-1960**
Too much, too soon. And Gerold Frank. New York: Henry Holt and Co.,
1957. 380 p.
    Written after her attempted suicide, the book tries to account for her
turbulent life, beginning with her unhappy, chaotic childhood and adolescence, and the continued difficulty she had in being a Barrymore.

0268 *Barrymore, Elaine (Jacobs)
All my sins remembered. And Sandford Dody. New York: Appleton-Century, 1964. 274 p.
Life with John Barrymore was never dull but punctuated with his violent passion, mercurial temper, romantic interludes, bouts of alcoholism, jealousy and desire for domination. Through it all she remained fascinated and in love.

0269 *Barrymore, Ethel   1879-1959
Memories: an autobiography by Ethel Barrymore. New York: Harper and Brothers, 1955. 310 p. Index.
The story of her long and successful career as a prominent actress on stage and film, with details of her early life and theatrical family.

0270 Barrymore, John   1882-1942
Confessions of an actor. New York: Benjamin Blom, Inc., 1971. (Indianapolis: The Bobbs-Merrill Co., 1926) 138 p.
Dominated by the aura of theatrical egotism, the book is sparse in detail and includes nothing that resembles a confession. It is a superficial stroll through selected memories of his childhood and dramatic career, with references to his famous family.

0271 Barrymore, Lionel   1878-1954
We Barrymores. As told to Cameron Shipp. Westport, Connecticut: Greenwood Press, 1974. (New York: Appleton-Century-Crofts, Inc., 1951) 311 p. Index.
Member of an extensive family of actors and actresses reminisces about his personal and professional life in theater and film.

0272 Bart, Jan   1919-1971
I lost a thousand pounds. With Barney Ruben. Carlton Fredericks, Commentator. New York: Oceana Publications, 1957. 240 p. Index.
A theater and night club entertainer writes to explain the childhood origins of his obesity and to illustrate the thesis that "I've lost a thousand pounds in my time. But I've kept on growing inside while gradually shrinking outside." At intervals, Fredericks psychoanalytically interprets Bart's obesity.

0273 Bartlett, Josiah   1729-1795
The papers of Josiah Bartlett. Edited by Frank C. Mevers. Illustrated. Bibliography. Calendar of unpublished letters. Hanover, New Hampshire: University Press of New England, 1979. 447 p. Index.
This volume consists primarily of letters to and from Bartlett, 1775-1795, culled from a collection of 3,600. They reveal the political activities of Bartlett, second signer of the Declaration of Independence, delegate to the Continental Congress in 1776 and 1778, New Hampshire Superior Court judge, 1784-1794, founder of the New Hampshire Medical Society. His frugality, concern for public health, love of family, and religious faith are also apparent in the letters.

0274 Barton, George A.   1885-1969
My lifetime in sports. Minneapolis, Minnesota: Olympic Press, 1957. 340 p.
A sports reporter and sports editor of the Minneapolis *Tribune* for fifty years reminisces about notable sports events and players, mostly in boxing, football, and baseball, and identifies some of his notable sports scoops.

0275 Bartram, William   1739-1823
Travels of William Bartram. Edited by Mark Van Doren. New York: Dover Publications, 1955. (Philadelphia: James & Johnson, 1791) 414 p. Index.
In 1773 Bartram set out for a trip in the South "for the discovery of rare and useful productions of nature, chiefly in the vegetable kingdom." His record is a major source of information on early American geography, anthropology, and natural history noting the characteristics of rivers, plants, fish, reptiles, birds, and Indian civilization and customs in the Carolinas, Georgia, and Florida.

0276 Baruch, Bernard Mannes   1870-1965
Baruch. New York: Henry, Holt and Co., 1957-1960. 2v. Index.
A distinguished statesman and economist discusses his personal philosophy, his early years, and his success on Wall Street. The second volume emphasizes his active role in public life for fifty years.

0277 Barziza, Decimus et Ultimus   1838-1882
Adventures of a prisoner of war, 1863-1864. Edited by R. Henderson Shuffler. Austin: University of Texas Press, 1964. (Houston: Richardson and Owen, 1865) 140 p. Index.
A Confederate officer, Barziza was wounded and captured at Gettysburg and imprisoned at Johnson's Island, Ohio. A year later he escaped while being transferred to another prison, made his way to Canada and finally back to North Carolina via a Canadian underground system established to assist Rebel soldiers.

0278 Basloe, Frank J.   1887-1966
I grew up with basketball: twenty years of barnstorming with cage greats of yesterday. In collaboration with D. Gordon Rohman. New York: Greenberg, 1952. 210 p.
A retired commissioner of the New York State Basketball League recalls the early years of basketball when he was coach-manager of the Globe Trotters-Oswego Indians (1903-1923).

0279 *Bass, Altha Leah   1892-
see Sweezy, Carl

0280 *Bates, Daisy Gatson   1920-
The long shadow of Little Rock. New York: David McKay Co., 1962. 234 p.
As head of the Arkansas NAACP and a resident of Little Rock, she led the two-year struggle of the Black community to integrate schools. During those violent years she lived under armed guard and carried a gun after her life and those of her sons were threatened repeatedly. As co-publisher of the *State Press* with her husband, she fought against police brutality, for CIO organizers, and for other social causes.

0281 Bates, Edward   1793-1869
The diary of Edward Bates: 1859-1866. Edited by Howard K. Beale. New York: Da Capo Press, 1971. (Washington: U.S. Govt. Printing Office, 1933) 685 p. Index.
A remarkably detailed record of public and private life during these years, including those he served as U.S. Attorney General, with accounts of political and military strategy, of national and local politics in St. Louis, of books he read, of the weather, his garden, the cost of a watch.

0282 *Bauer, Evelyn (Showalter)
Through sunlight and shadow. Illustrated. Scottdale, Pennsylvania: Herald Press, 1959. 221 p.
The story of an American missionary couple in Landour, North India, and Kodiakanal, South India, who learned to enter the exotic world of the Hindi. Their work was interrupted by Evelyn's illness, polio, which occurred when their son was eight months old and which left her paralyzed, but not demoralized. She learned to type with her left hand and wrote religious pieces and this autobiography during her convalescence.

0283 Bauer, Harold   1873-1951
Harold Bauer: his book. Illustrated. New York: Greenwood Press, 1969. (New York: W.W. Norton, 1948) 306 p. Index.
A lively account of Bauer's London upbringing and musical training, twenty years as a concert pianist in Europe based in Paris, followed by forty years' residence and musical activities in America, particularly in New York and Hartford. Full of pleasant anecdotes about his musical contemporaries.

0284 Baughman, Urbanus Edmund   1905-1978
Secret service chief. With Leonard Wallace Robinson. New York: Harper & Row Publishers, Inc., 1961. 266 p.
In 1934 he became a Secret Service agent; in 1948 he became chief. His book describes his work for three presidents and their families and the criminal world he protected them from.

0285 *Baum, Vicki   1888-1960
It was all quite different: the memoirs of Vicki Baum. New York: Funk & Wagnalls Co., Inc., 1964. 372 p. Index.
By the time she immigrated to the U.S. in 1931 she had established herself as a novelist (*Grand Hotel);* soon after that she became a well-known screenwriter in Hollywood. Her book describes her life among writers and intellectuals in Vienna, Berlin, and the U.S.

0286 Bausum, Robert Lord   1893-
Pass it on: four generations of missionary service. Illustrated. New York: Vantage Press, 1977. 283 p.
Bausum tells the story of his career as a third-generation Baptist missionary with his wife in China, mostly in Kweilin. The account of religious zeal and hard work is intertwined with a history of Sino-Japanese politics in the 1920's and 30's, culminating in war which ultimately became part of World War II. For Bausum the war reflected the opposition of Communism (atheism) and Christianity. The Bausum family traveled hundreds of thousands of miles in evangelical activities on furlough in the United States.

0287 *Baxter, Anne   1923-
Intermission: a true story. New York: Ballantine, 1978. (New York: G.P. Putnam's Sons, 1976) 384 p.
Movie actress tells the story of her marriage to rancher and businessman Ron Galt, 1959-63, with whom she learned to love the Australian outback at Giro, Galt's ranch near Worcester. It was an exhilarating struggle to cope with marriage, maternity, and movie-making.

0288 Baxter, Gordon
Bax seat: log of a pasture pilot. Edited by Stephan Wilkinson. Foreword. Illustrated. New York: Ziff-Davis Flying Books, 1978. 212 p.
This collection of the best of Baxter's humorous "Bax Seat" columns and feature articles is a log of his love affair with airplanes and "airplane

people." A pilot in World War I and avid small-plane enthusiast, he also tells the story of how a "good ole boy from southern Texas" found himself working for a New York-based aviation magazine.

0289 Baxter, Gordon   **1923-**
Village creek: the first and only eyewitness account of the second life of Gordon Baxter. New York: Summit Books, 1979. 318 p.
A disc jockey discusses his 27-year marriage to "the perfect mother" of his eight children, whom he left at 51. He married an airline stewardess with whom he had an affair ten years earlier and lived with his bride in a house he had built in the woods. Fired from his job at 53, restricted in activities by a slight stroke, he overcame his ambivalence about midlife fatherhood.

0290 *Bayh, Marvella   **1933-1979**
Marvella: a personal journey. With Mary Lynn Kotz. Introduction by Lady Bird Johnson. Epilogue by Birch Bayh. New York: Harcourt Brace Jovanovich, 1979. 310 p. Index.
Marvella Bayh's forthright, compelling, intensely moving life story begins on an Oklahoma farm, moves to the presidency of Girls' Nation, and marriage at nineteen to Birch Bayh. A loving and energetic wife, she loyally campaigned for her husband's successful Senate victories in 1962 and 1968 and willingly performed all the activities demanded of a Senator's wife, despite her mother's death, her father's alcoholism, and plane and car accidents. Cancer changed her life; she became an inspirational speaker for the American Cancer Society before her untimely death at 46.

0291 *Beach, Barbara   **1933-**
MS and us: an autobiography. Hicksville, New York: Exposition Press, 1976. 167 p.
Beach, a victim of multiple sclerosis, describes the gradual onset of the symptoms, their acceleration, her alternation between hope and despair, and the slow and frustrating pace of daily living. Although the book is meant to be reassuring to other MS victims, the psychological and physical toll of the disease is unbearably grim.

0292 *Beach, Sylvia   **1887-1962**
Shakespeare and company. New York: Harcourt, Brace and Co., 1959. 230 p. Index.
In 1919 she opened a bookshop on the Left Bank. Her book describes her life as book seller, lending librarian, publisher, and patron to many who became prominent in the literary circle of Paris in the Twenties.

0293 Bean, George H.   **b.1886**
Yankee auctioneer: wherein are to be found the reminiscences and philosophy of a country auctioneer, well seasoned with yarns about profits and people. Boston: Little, Brown and Co., 1948. 247 p.
His experience on the back roads of the Connecticut Valley depicts a vanishing life style.

0294 Bean, L.L.   **1872-1967**
My story: the autobiography of a down-East merchant. Introduction by John Gould. Illustrated. Freeport, Maine: L.L. Bean, 1960. 163 p.
L.L. Bean, founder and owner of the Maine sporting goods business renowned for high-quality products, has assembled a miscellany of family photographs, copies of newspaper articles, business letters, in somewhat random order. They emphasize the quality of Bean's merchandise, the volume of business and its centrality to the Freeport, Maine, economy, family life, and numerous hunting and fishing expeditions.

0295 Beard, Frank   **1939-**
Pro: Frank Beard on the golf tour. Edited by Dick Schaap. Cleveland: The World Publishing Co., 1970. 323 p.
A year in the life of a golf pro on tour based on his diary for 1969 when he won more money than any other player.

0296 Beattie, Edward William, Jr.   **1909-**
Diary of a Kriegie. New York: Thomas Crowell Co., 1946. 312 p.
Between September 1944 and May 1945 he was a German prisoner of war. A journalist who spoke fluent German, he completed his diary after the war, expanding his notes and including facts and opinions he could not safely have recorded in prison, even in a secret diary.

0297 Beatty, Charles   **1715-1772**
Journals of Charles Beatty, 1762-1769. Edited with introduction by Guy Soulliard Klett. University Park: Pennsylvania State University Press, 1962. 144 p. Index.
Journals of three trips by Reverend Beatty, two to England (1762 and 1769), preaching and soliciting funds, and one through the Pennsylvania and Ohio wilderness (1766), gathering information and preaching. Letters and other documents are appended.

0298 Beatty, John   **1828-1914**
Memoirs of a volunteer, 1861-1863. Edited by Harvey S. Ford. New York: W.W. Norton and Co., Inc., 1946. 317 p.
First published in 1879 as *The Citizen Soldier*, Beatty's diary records the war with candor, common sense, and humor. He is sympathetic with

the common soldiers and highly critical of the political maneuvers among officers and state officials. In the war he rose from private to brigadier general in the Third Ohio Volunteer Infantry. Afterwards, he resumed presidency of his bank, wrote three novels and many popular tracts on political economy.

0299 Beaulac, Willard Leon   **1899-**
Career ambassador. New York: The Macmillan Co., 1951. 262 p.
Highlights of a 27-year career as Foreign Service officer and ambassador primarily in Central and South America include observations about American diplomacy, world relations, and the author's commitment to democracy and the policy of non-intervention.

0300 Beaumont, William   **1785-1853**
Wm. Beaumont's formative years: two early notebooks, 1811-1821. With annotations and an introductory essay by Genevieve Miller. New York: Henry Schuman, 1946. 87 p. Index.
Self-educated in medicine and physiology, he is well known in early American medical history. These notebooks include notes on his medical observations and travel, principally during the War of 1812.

0301 *Beauvoir, Simone de   **1908-**
America day by day. Translated by Patrick Dudley. New York: Grove Press, 1953. (London: Duckworth, 1952) 337 p.
After traveling the United States for four months in the early 1950's, a French author yields her impressions of America's cities, slums, hotels, bars, gardens, trains, and music. She is delighted by New York, Los Angeles, Santa Fe, and Savannah; appalled by Washington, Niagara, Houston, and Williamsburg. Exploring college campuses, concepts of liberty, hospitality, regional cuisines, and burlesque shows, de Beauvoir finds America "one of the world's pivotal points."

0302 Bechet, Sidney   **1897-1959**
Treat it gentle. New York: Da Capo Press, 1975. (New York: Hill and Wang, 1960) 245 p. Index.
Transcribed from tapes he dictated before his death, the story of his life as a jazz musician in New Orleans and Paris.

0303 *Beck, Daisy (Woodward)   **b.1876**
All the years were grand. Chicago: Erle Press, 1951. 257 p.
An Indiana Methodist minister's wife recalls her earlier, livelier days of work and travel.

0304 Beck, Frederick K.   **1904?-**
Second carrot from the end. Foreword by H. Allen Smith. New York: William Morrow and Co., 1946. 160 p.
Experience with Roger Dahljelm as partner in development of the Farmers Market in Los Angeles.

0305 Beck, Levitt Clinton   **1920-1944**
Fighter pilot. Huntington Park, California: Mr. and Mrs. L.C. Beck, 5965 Pacific Boulevard, 1946. 200 p.
Written near Paris in July 1944, while Beck awaited escape through the French Underground, this narrative reveals the spirit and idealism characteristic of many in World War II.

0306 Becker, Carl Lotus   **1873-1945**
"What is the good of history?": selected letters of Carl L. Becker, 1900-1945. Edited with introduction by Michael Kammen. Ithaca: Cornell University Press, 1973. 374 p. Index.
Historian Becker's letters deal extensively with historical writing, university and higher education, war, peace, domestic politics, family, and friendships. This selection is arranged chronologically to present a self-portrait of the man and his changing opinions on liberalism.

0307 Beckwourth, James Pierson   **1798-1866**
The life and adventures of James P. Beckwourth: mountaineer, scout, and pioneer, and chief of the Crow Nation of Indians; written from his own dictation by T.D. Bonner. Introduction by Delmont R. Oswald. Illustrated. Lincoln: University of Nebraska Press, 1972. (New York: Harper and Brothers, Publishers, 1856) 547 p. Index.
Beckwourth was one of the living legends of the West, a man respected among white men and Indians, who could run faster, trap better, kill more hostile Indians, endure more hardships, marry more wives, outwit more cunning savages, and, apparently, tell more tall tales than any other man before or since. A fascinating book despite its debatable authenticity.

0308 Bedichek, Roy   **1878-1959**
Adventures with a Texas naturalist. Illustrated by Ward Lockwood. Foreword by H. Mewhinney. New rev. ed. Austin: University of Texas Press, 1961. (Garden City, New York: Doubleday, 1947) 330 p.
A naturalist, professor of speech, and friend of J. Frank Dobie describes his experience in the Texas outdoors.

0309 Beebe, Lewis   **1892-1951**
Journal of Dr. Lewis Beebe. Eyewitness Accounts of the American Revo-

lution. New York: Arno Press, Inc., 1971. (Philadelphia: Historical Society of Pennsylvania, 1935) 40 p.

An interesting account of his experience on an expedition against Canada in 1776.

0310 Beecher, George Allen   1868-1951
A bishop of the Great Plains. Epilogue by Walter Herbert Stowe. Philadelphia: Church Historical Society, 1950. 218 p.

Recollections of the romance, obligations, and responsibilities of his life's work by the Episcopal bishop of western Nebraska from 1910 to 1943.

0311 Beecher, Lyman   1775-1863
Autobiography. Edited by Barbara M. Cross. Cambridge: Belknap Press of Harvard University Press, 1961. 2v. Index.

The notes, recollections, and correspondence of a prominent New England minister reflect his staunch devotion to Calvinism and the strength of his character and influence in continual struggles for Christianity.

0312 Beers, Clifford Whittingham   1876-1943
A mind that found itself: an autobiography. Robert Coles, Preface. Pittsburgh: University of Pittsburgh Press, 1981. (New York: Longmans, Green and Co., 1908) 205 p.

During his mid-twenties he had a nervous breakdown followed by a two-year illness. His book records in precise detail his illness, the inadequate and often destructive treatment, and his later years as a philanthropist and moving force in the organization of mental hygiene foundations.

0313 *Begley, Kathleen A.   1948-
Deadline. New York: G.P. Putnam's Sons, 1977. 148 p.

Begley focuses on her career as a reporter, primarily for the Philadelphia *Inquirer.* She covered murders, accidents, local and national political news, the Miss America Pageant (irritating to her feminist views), and writes with gusto of the newspaperwoman's life.

0314 *Behanna, Gertrude Ingram
see *Burns, Elizabeth

0315 Behrman, Martin   1864-1926
Martin Behrman of New Orleans: memoirs of a city boss. Edited with introduction by John R. Kemp. Illustrated. Baton, Rouge: Louisiana State University Press, 1977. 356 p.

Kemp's introduction supplies a balanced correction to Behrman's understandably partisan defense of his years as mayor and political boss of New Orleans, 1904-1920, when he was defeated by a reform movement before regaining office in 1925. Behrman's keen knowledge of party politics and ability to use the system to his party's advantage is apparent throughout.

0316 Behrman, Samuel Nathaniel   1893-1973
People in a diary; a memoir. Boston: Little, Brown & Co., 1972. 338 p. Index.

Author of some two dozen plays of manners as well as essays and filmscripts, Behrman offers a finely crafted account of his life among and fascination with the wealthy, sophisticated and amusing denizens of Hollywood and New York.

0317 Behrman, Samuel Nathaniel   1893-1973
The suspended drawing room. New York: Stein and Day, 1965. 253 p.

A collection of playwright Behrman's shorter prose pieces. Most were previously published in *The New Yorker.*

0318 Behrman, Samuel Nathaniel   1893-1973
Tribulations and laughter: a memoir. London: Hamish Hamilton, 1972. 338 p. Index.

A loosely structured account of a prominent playwright's career in the theatrical worlds of Broadway and Hollywood, his long friendship with Siegfried Sassoon, and many prominent characters of the theater.

0319 Behrman, Samuel Nathaniel   1893-1973
Worcester account. New York: Random House, 1954. 239 p.

A playwright recalls his youth in Worcester, Massachusetts, and his Jewish upbringing.

0320 Beidelman, George Washington   1839-1864
Civil War letters of George Washington Beidelman. Edited by Catherine H. Vanderslice. Illustrated. New York: Vantage Press, 1978. 212 p.

Beidelman was an enlisted man in the Union Army from 1861 until he died, probably of pneumonia, in March, 1864, just before his 25th birthday. In heavily religious letters to family and friends, he describes in detail a number of the major Civil War battles in which he participated, including the Second Battle of Manassas and the Battle of Gettysburg.

0321 Bel Geddes, Norman   1893-1958
Miracle in the evening: an autobiography. Edited by William Kelley. Garden City, New York: Doubleday and Co., Inc., 1960. 352 p.

The extraordinary life of a designer-engineer whose work spanned art, dance, theater, and industry, a modern renaissance architect.

0322 Belden, Josiah   1815-1892
Josiah Belden, 1841 California overland pioneer: his memoir and early letters. Edited with introduction by Doyce B. Nunis, Jr. Georgetown, California: The Talisman Press, 1962. 150 p. Index.

The dictated memoir of Belden's journey with the 1841 Bartleson overland expedition and his description of early days in California. Letters to his sister, extensive notes, commentary, and bibliography are included.

0323 *Bell, Margaret Van Horn (Dwight)   1790-1834
A journey to Ohio in 1810 as recorded in the journal of Margaret Van Horn Dwight. Edited by Max Farrand. New Haven: Yale University, 1912. 64 p.

The witty, lively account of a twenty-year-old woman's wagon trip from New Haven, Connecticut, to Warren, Ohio, recording the accents and actions of the people she meets, the discomfort of poor inns, poor roads, November weather in the mountains, rowdy Pennsylvania Dutch wagoners, and Methodists who fail to observe the sabbath as she would have them.

0324 *Bell, Marguerite N.   b.1888
The lives and times of just Molly: an autobiography. Illustrated. Minneapolis: Golden Valley Press, 1980. 208 p.

At 91, Bell wrote this book as "a celebration of freedom in personal relationships." And a glorious, unsentimental celebration it is. She vividly describes her childhood in Minneapolis, her pleasure in music and love of kindergarten teaching, both traded for marriage with Dwight Bell in 1911. She describes the pleasures of rearing six children before the Depression and the difficulties of getting them all through college in the 1930's. She invented and marketed the Nap-Jac, a baby sleeper, and led a life of the quintessential wife, mother, and grandmother.

0325 Bellah, James Warner   1899-1976
Irregular gentleman. Garden City, New York: Doubleday, 1948. 248 p.

A breezy narrative of travel, sex, and adventure in various exotic ports, by a writer attempting to convey the significance of "real" experience in a meaningful life.

0326 Belli, Melvin Mouron   1907-
Melvin Belli: my life on trial: an autobiography. With Robert Blair Kaiser. New York: William Morrow and Co., 1976. 351 p. Index.

This flamboyant California trial lawyer recounts his childhood, his college days, and notable trials in which he often won large settlements for injured clients such as Maureen Connolly, Jack Ruby, Errol Flynn, Lenny Bruce, and the Rolling Stones.

0327 Bellow, Saul   1915-
To Jerusalem and back: a personal account. New York: The Viking Press, 1976. 182 p.

Jewish novelist Bellow describes a trip he and his wife took to Israel in 1976 and concentrates on describing the country's past, present, and future by characterizing its population. His informants range from leaders in politics (Teddy Kolleck), the arts (Dennis Silk), religion, education, and military strategy, to its general population, which ranges from super-religious Hasidic Jews and Jews of Arabic origin to non-religious but patriotic Zionists.

0328 *Belmont, Eleanor (Robson)   1879-1979
Fabric of memory. New York: Farrar, Straus and Cudahy, 1957. 311 p. Index.

The story of her remarkable career as a prominent actress, her retirement, and her second career as a patron of the arts and welfare leader. Includes letters from G.B. Shaw and Israel Zangwill published for the first time.

0329 Belton, Howard C.   1893-
Under eleven governors. Introduction by Myra Weston. Illustrated. Portland, Oregon: Binford & Mort, 1977. 90 p.

Between 1933 and 1970 Belton, an Oregon farmer in Clackomas County, was a state legislator, twenty years a senator, five years a state treasurer, and a member of several state boards. His brief account of his public service under eleven governors identifies the major accomplishments of each administration, the issues met and public works undertaken, and some major points of political dissension.

0330 Bemelmans, Ludwig   1898-1962
My life in art. New York: Harper and Brothers, 1958. 64 p.

An artist-writer discusses his early interest in painting and the years in Paris when he learned to use oils.

0331 Bench, Johnny (Lee)   1947-
Catch you later: the autobiography of Johnny Bench. And William Brashler. Illustrated. New York: Harper & Row, Publishers, 1979. 245 p. Index.

A catcher recounts his journey from Binger, Oklahoma, through the minor leagues to the Cincinnati Reds, the World Series, and the record books.

0332 Bender, Horace, pseud.
see Greenough, Horatio

0333 Bendiner, Alfred   **1899-1964**
Translated from the Hungarian; notes toward an autobiography. Illustrated. South Brunswick, New Jersey: A.S. Barnes & Co., 1967. 317 p.
After serving in World War I, he became an architect in Philadelphia, where he was well respected for his designs as well as his drawings, paintings, and cartoons. His book reflects the wit of his satire and the enormous pleasure of his life.

0334 Benét, Stephen Vincent   **1898-1943**
Selected letters. Edited by Charles A. Fenton. New Haven: Yale University Press, 1960. 436 p. Index.
A cross-section of letters selected from his extensive correspondence to illustrate the development of his personal and professional life over the years.

0335 Benjamin, Harold Raymond W.   **1893-1969**
Sage of Petaluma: autobiography of a teacher by J. Abner Peddiwell. With a foreword by Harold R.W. Benjamin. New York: McGraw-Hill Book Co., 1965. 233 p.
Purports to be a "mythical autobiography" and claims that the events never happened to anyone in particular and yet "they happened to everyone of my generation and background."

0336 Bennett, Abram Elting   **1898-**
Fifty years in neurology and psychiatry. New York: Intercontinental Medical Book Corporation, 1972. 166 p.
The author describes his own work and achievements, his teacher-scholar contacts in younger days, unusual cases demonstrating the growth of knowledge through research, and hospital activities.

0337 Bennett, James Augustus   **1831-1909**
Forts and forays: the diary of a dragoon in New Mexico, 1850-1856. Edited by Clinton E. Brooks and Frank D. Reeve. Albuquerque: University of New Mexico Press, 1948. 85 p.
A volunteer at 18, Bennett moved with the army from Rochester, New York, to Santa Fe, New Mexico. His diary vividly describes the primitive conditions of army life, the brutal treatment within the army as well as in Indian wars, and the conflict of cultures among Whites, Spanish, and Indians.

0338 *Bennett, Joan   **1910-**
Bennett playbill. With Lois Kibbee. New York: Holt, Rinehart & Co., 1970. 332 p.
Bennett's recollections of her volatile and controversial theatrical family. "The Bennetts," she says, "were like a forest fire; the minute the flames were put out in one spot, they'd pop up in another."

0339 *Bennett, Kay   **1921?-**
Kaibah: recollection of a Navajo girlhood. Los Angeles: Westernlore Press, 1964. 253 p.
A third person narrative about Kaibah (Kay Bennett) describing her life in an "average Navajo family" on a reservation in New Mexico (1928-1935), including good detail of daily life and rituals, the struggle to maintain Navajo ways in a changing culture, and a chapter on the Depression.

0340 Bentley, Arthur F.
see Dewey, John

0341 *Bentley, Elizabeth   **1908-1963**
Out of bondage: the story of Elizabeth Bentley. New York: Devin-Adair, 1951. 311 p.
Agent who worked with the American Communist Party and Russian Secret Police describes what she did, the people with whom she was involved, and her subsequent decision to report all to the FBI.

0342 Bentley, William   **1795-1819**
Diary of William Bentley, D.D., pastor of the East Church, Salem, Mass. Gloucester, Massachusetts: Peter Smith, 1962. 4v. Index.
Volume I: 1784-1792; Volume II: 1793-1802; Volume III: 1803-1810; Volume IV: 1811-1819. A popular pastor noted for his Catholic and liberal views of Christianity and distingushed for his social virtues as well, who helped prepare the way for Unitarianism.

0343 Benton, Joseph
Oklahoma tenor; musical memories of Giuseppe Bentonelli. Foreword by Eva Turner. Introduction by B.A. Nugent. Illustrated. Norman: University of Oklahoma Press, 1973. 150 p.
As Giuseppe Bentonelli, he was the first major American operatic artist to become highly popular in Europe. He made his American debut in Chicago, sang several roles at the Metropolitan, and then toured extensively before he returned to his home state and served as a professor of music at the University of Oklahoma.

0344 Benton, Thomas Hart   **1889-1975**
An American in art: a professional and technical autobiography. Lawrence: University Press of Kansas, 1969. 197 p. Index.
An account of his technical development as an artist, as distinct from his personal autobiography, An Artist in America. This volume includes 68 reproductions of his paintings and "American Regionalism: A Personal History of the Movement."

0345 Benton, Thomas Hart   **1889-1975**
An artist in America. Third edition with seventy-six illustrations. Columbia: University of Missouri Press, 1968. (New York: Halcyon House, 1939) 369 p.
The amplified version of Benton's well-written autobiography includes comments on the artist from the perspective of his role in the regionalist movement in American art. This edition also includes his activity since the 1951 edition when he was contemplating retirement.

0346 Berenson, Bernard   **1865-1959**
Bernard Berenson treasury: a selection from the works, unpublished writings, letters, diaries, and journals of the most celebrated humanist of our times, 1887-1958. Edited by Hanna Kiel. New York: Simon & Schuster, Inc., 1962. 414 p. Index.
An anthology of the art critic's writings, half previously unpublished, affords a record of his thoughts about and reactions to ideas, people, and events through his books, essays, letters, and diaries from 1887 to 1958.

0347 Berenson, Bernard   **1865-1959**
Conversations with Berenson. By Umberto Morra. Translated from the Italian by Florence Hammond. Boston: Houghton Mifflin Co., 1965. 305 p. Index.
A compilation of notes of many conversations, 1931-1940, which Morra had with art critic Berenson at his villa in Italy. Berenson speaks on a variety of subjects: worldly and artistic experience, knowledge of the past and present, of men and of nations, and of art, history, music, literature.

0348 Berenson, Bernard   **1865-1959**
Passionate sightseer: from the diaries, 1947-1956. Preface by Raymond Mortimer. New York: Simon and Schuster, 1960. 200 p. Index.
A distinguished art historian records his passion for the visual world of art and nature in journals of his travels in North Africa and Italy after World War II.

0349 Berenson, Bernard   **1865-1959**
Rumor and reflection. New York: Simon and Schuster, 1952. 458 p. Index.
Written primarily from his villa outside Florence, Italy, from January, 1941, to November, 1944, this wartime diary contains the author's day-to-day impressions of what was happening in Italy and the world beyond.

0350 Berenson, Bernard   **1865-1959**
Sketch for a self-portrait. New York: Pantheon Books, Inc., 1949. 185 p.
Written somewhere in hiding during World War II, this book reflects the warmth and dignity, the wisdom and curiosity of the man who was a major influence in the establishment of American art collections during the early part of the century. His book, The Italian Painters of the Renaissance, is an established classic.

0351 Berenson, Bernard   **1865-1959**
Sunset and twilight: from the diaries of 1947-1958. Edited with epilogue by Micky Mariano. Introduction by Iris Origo. New York: Harcourt, Brace and World, Inc., 1963. 547 p. Index.
Selections from his diaries intended to depict his personal life and thoughts more fully than previous publications from the diaries.

0352 *Berg, Gertrude   **1900-1966**
Molly and me. With Cherney Berg. New York: McGraw-Hill Book Co., Inc., 1961. 278 p.
In 1929 she sold NBC on a script called "The Rise of the Goldbergs." She played the part of Molly; the show grew out of her deeply Jewish family life and entertained radio audiences for years. Her book tells of her real family life and the development of her career.

0353 Berger, Elmer   **1908-**
Memoirs of an anti-Zionist Jew. Washington, D.C.: Institute for Palestine Studies, 1978. 159 p.
The memoirs of an anti-Zionist, pro-Arab Jew whose rabbinical connections led high-level Jewish organizations to oppose the view that Israel should be a real homeland for Jews and to promote the rights of Arab Palestinians. His many experiences with Jews, Arabs, and Christians (especially politicans) are described. The successful existence of the state of Israel does not change Berger's views.

0354 *Bergman, Ingrid 1915-
Ingrid Bergman: my story. And Alan Burgess. New York: Delacorte Press, 1980. 504 p. Index.

Actress Bergman candidly discusses her rise from Stockholm's Royal Dramatic School to international film stardom and the Hollywood Academy Awards. She is both defensive and insightful about the scandal caused by her desertion of husband Peter Lindstrom and daughter Pia for a liaison with Italian director Roberto Rossellini.

0355 Berle, Adolf Augustus 1895-1971
Navigating the rapids, 1918-1971. Edited by Beatrice Bishop Berle and Travis Beal Jacobs. Introduction by Max Ascoli. New York: Harcourt, 1973. 859 p. Index.

A graduate of Harvard and man of broad interests, Berle records in his papers his never-finished study of the interaction between corporate and political power.

0356 Berle, Milton 1908-
Milton Berle, an autobiography. With Haskel Frankel. New York: Delacorte Press, 1974. 337 p. Index.

Using the brusque aggressive tone of his comic image, Berle talks about his sixty years in show business, always emphasizing the importance of his family, especially his mother and his latest wife, Ruth.

0357 Berman, Leonid 1896-1976
The three worlds of Leonid. Translated from French by Olivier Bernier. Preface by Virgil Thomson. New York: Basic Books, Inc., 1978. 275 p. Index.

With a painter's eye for detail, Leonid recounts his privileged life in pre-revolutionary Russia and Germany and his perilous flight from the revolution. Making his way to Paris, Leonid studied painting and found love, Parisian-style. Caught by the war, he served in the French army and was captured by the Germans. After the war, he emigrated to America and continued his painting. The book ends in 1946, although he died thirty years later.

0358 *Bernard, Jessie Shirley 1903-
Self-portrait of a family: letters by Jessie, Dorothy Lee, Claude and David Bernard, with commentary by Jessie Bernard. Boston: Beacon Press, 1978. 344 p.

Sociologist Bernard edits and interprets the letters to and from her children during the 1950's and 60's to illustrate what it is like to rear a family of three children as a single parent (her husband died shortly after David was born in 1951) and working mother whose activities took the family all over the United States, Europe, and North Africa.

0359 Bernardi, Jack
My father, the actor. Foreword by Herschel Bernardi. New York: W.W. Norton & Co., 1971. 233 p.

A sentimental account of an Austro-Hungarian immigrant and his life as an actor in the Yiddish Theater in the United States.

0360 Bernays, Edward L. 1891-
Biography of an idea: memoirs of a public relations counsel. New York: Simon & Schuster, 1965. 849 p. Index.

An account of public relations as a new discipline and profession in this century—the problems, the creativity, and the power it involves. He describes the work he has done in the arts, business, industry, and government.

0361 Bernheim, Bertram Moses 1880-1958
A surgeon's domain. New York: W.W. Norton and Co., Inc., 1947. 253 p.

Written while Bernheim was Associate Professor of Surgery at The Johns Hopkins Medical School, this book is a self-study, as well as an analysis of surgery and surgeons seen through his experienced and somewhat unorthodox eyes. He establishes an interesting and sympathetic context for a key issue: "It was a little odd, men actually liking to operate on people."

0362 *Bernheim, Mary Lilias (Christian) 1902-
A sky of my own. New York: The Macmillan Co., 1974. (New York: Rinehart & Co., Inc., 1959) 244 p.

At age 45 she was a biochemist teaching and doing research. Then after World War II she and her husband decided to learn to fly. Her book describes what she learned and felt, the freedom and fear of flight.

0363 Berra, Lawrence Peter (Yogi) 1925-
Yogi: the autobiography of a professional baseball player. With Ed Fitzgerald. Garden City, New York: Doubleday & Co., Inc., 1961. 234 p.

Rated as one of the best fielding catchers in baseball history, he grew up in St. Louis, played for the New York Yankees, and was widely popular among sports fans. His book is written in the brusque, jocular tone he was famous for.

0364 Berrigan, Daniel 1921-
America is hard to find. Garden City, New York: Doubleday & Co. Inc., 1972. 191 p.

A collection of essays, poems, and letters written during his four months in the underground and eighteen months in prison reveals Berrigan's commitment to the radical reshaping of America during the late 1960's.

0365 Berrigan, Daniel 1921-
Lights on in the house of the dead; a prison diary. Garden City, New York: Doubleday & Co., Inc., 1974. 309 p.

The journal of Berrigan's eighteen months in the Federal Prison in Danbury, Connecticut, August 1970-February 1972, for burning draft files in Catonsville, Maryland, which made him known as one of the Catonsville Nine.

0366 Berrigan, Philip 1923-
Prison journals of a priest revolutionary. Compiled and edited by Vincent McGee. Introduction by Daniel Berrigan. New York: Holt, Rinehart and Winston, 1970. 198 p.

In 1968 he was imprisoned in the Federal penitentiaries at Lewisburg and Allenwood, Pennsylvania, for participating in the napalming of draft files in Catonsville, Maryland. This defense of his action was written during his incarceration.

0367 Berrigan, Philip 1923-
Widen the prison gates; writing from jails, April 1970-Dec. 1972. New York: Simon & Schuster, 1973. 261 p.

Berrigan was ordained a priest in 1955; in 1973 he left the priesthood and married Elizabeth McAlister. He served forty months in the U.S. Army during World War II. He served 39 months in federal and local prisons for resisting the war in Indochina. This volume is a collection of his journals and letters written while imprisoned. It is a compact image of the terrible contradictions suffered by many during the Sixties.

0368 Berry, Jason 1949?-
Amazing grace; with Charles Evers in Mississippi. New York: Saturday Review Press, 1973. 370 p.

Berry records his experiences during the 1971 Mississippi gubernatorial campaign when he worked as press secretary for Charles Evers.

0369 Bertram, John 1796-1882
John Bertram of Salem, Massachusetts: his own account of incidents in his life. Foreword by Rosamond de Laittre. Facsimile of entire handwritten manuscript. Santa Barbara, California: Rosamond de Laittre, 1964. 65 p.

Bertram's account chronicles a long lifetime of maritime activities. As a youthful sailor, he was imprisoned on a ship during the War of 1812; for the next twenty years he sailed the seven seas as a seaman and captain—to South America, Africa, and the East Indies, in particular. When illness forced him landward, he ran a successful business trading by sea, married three times, and traveled abroad by ocean liner.

0370 Best, Tharratt Gilbert 1892-1969
Early memoirs of a country gentleman, Tharratt Gilbert Best, 1892-1969. Compiled and edited by Virginia Best Clarendon. Illustrated. Boonville, New York: North County Books, 1976. 225 p.

Best kept a diary 1902-1925, which records his coming-of-age in fits and starts. Fond of Utica and Boonville in upstate New York, he eventually settled in the latter as a surveyor and city engineer. He enjoyed Princeton after he realized his grades would not be outstanding and flirted continuously until he settled into marriage in 1923. He drove an ambulance in France in World War I, an experience and a country which provoked the most abundant and romantic descriptions in his book.

0371 Beston, Henry 1888-1968
Northern farm: a chronicle of Maine. New York: Rinehart and Co., Inc., 1948. 246 p.

Farm life in the woods of Maine, with an argument against modern man's alienation from nature.

0372 Beston, Henry 1888-1968
The outermost house: a year of life on the great beach of Cape Cod . Baltimore, Maryland: Penguin Books, 1976. (Garden City, New York: Doubleday, Doran and Co., Inc., 1928) 222 p.

Written in solitude, a meditative description of nature and the human spirit.

0373 *Betz, Pauline
see *Addie, Pauline (Betz)

0374 *Bevington, Helen (Smith) 1906-
Charley Smith's girl: a memoir. New York: Simon & Schuster, 1965. 255 p.

The story of a poet's childhood and her gradual estrangement from both of her divorced parents: one strong, stern, and unloving, the other erratic, emotional, and despairing.

0375 Bhikkhu Anuruddha
see Pulley, Sande

0376 Bickford, Charles **1891-1967**
Bulls, balls, bicycles and actors. New York: Paul S. Eriksson, Inc., 1965. 336 p.
After working at a great variety of jobs in his youth, Bickford tried burlesque, vaudeville, road shows, and stock companies, acquiring there the training which led him to his first roles on Broadway and in the movies. His subsequent fifty-year career was marked with a defiance of conformity and a taste for rebelliousness.

0377 Biddle, Francis Beverley **1886-1968**
A casual past. Garden City, New York: Doubleday & Co., Inc., 1961. 408 p. Index.
A record up to 1939 of his illustrious forbears, education, and early career as a Philadelphia lawyer by a man who later became U.S. Attorney General (1941-1945).

0378 Biddle, Francis Beverley **1886-1968**
In brief authority. Garden City, New York: Doubleday & Co., Inc., 1962. 494 p. Index.
A continuation of the author's autobiographical *A Casual Past*, this volume is divided into four sections: 1. The Labor Board, TVA investigation and Circuit Court of Appeals; 2. Solicitor General; 3. Attorney General; and 4. The Nurnberg Trial.

0379 Biddle, George **1885-1973**
Tahitian journal. Minneapolis: University of Minnesota Press, 1968. 207 p.
Prefaced by some memories of his World War I experiences, Biddle's book is mainly the journal he kept during his stay in Tahiti (1920-22) where he went to isolate himself to paint without interruption. He lived in a remote village with the natives, learned their language and customs, and came to understand their ways.

0380 Bierce, Ambrose **1842-1914?**
The letters of Ambrose Bierce. Edited by Bertha Clark Pope. With a memoir by George Sterling. New York: Gordian Press, 1967. (1922) 204 p.
A consummate satirist, Bierce wrote articles for newspapers and creative stories exploring, as he said, "the ways of hate as a form of creative energy." He is a coiner of words, creator of clear description, and master of verbal restraint.

0381 Bierce, Ambrose **1842-1914?**
Twenty-one letters of Ambrose Bierce. Edited by Samuel Loveman. Reprint of 1922 edition. Norwood, Pennsylvania: Norwood Editions, 1976. (Cleveland: G. Kirk, 1922) 33 p.
Samuel Loveman, an aspiring amateur poet, evidently sent several of his poems to author Ambrose Bierce, who functioned as a critic and agent in trying to get them published. These 21 brief letters, 1908-1913, concern this attempt; they contain some criticism of the poems as well as pleasantries.

0382 Biever, John **1951?-**
Young sports photographer with the Green Bay Packers. With George Vecsey. Illustrated. New York: W.W. Norton & Co., 1969. 189 p.
His father was official photographer for the Packers. By the time he was thirteen he was skillful enough with a camera that his father allowed him to help photograph a game. He continued through his high school years, after which he wrote this book.

0383 Bihaly, Andrew **1934-1968**
The journal of Andrew Bihaly. Edited by Anthony Tuttle. New York: Thomas Y. Crowell Co., 1973. 228 p.
A victim of the horrors of World War II, Bihaly reflects on the cataclysmic changes during the sixties in his adopted America. Alone but trying to communicate his feelings, he sought help from a psychiatrist, worked in the Free Store on Cooper Square, but ultimately was overcome by despair and killed himself.

0384 Bingay, Malcolm Wallace **1884-1953**
Of me I sing. Indianapolis: The Bobbs-Merrill Co., Inc., 1949. 300 p.
A plainspoken, humorous narrative about a Michigan high school dropout who worked his way up in journalism to become editor of the Detroit *Free Press*. His book includes much of the social and political history of Michigan in his time.

0385 *Birdwell, Cleo
Amazons: an intimate memoir by the first woman ever to play in the National Hockey League. New York: Holt, Rinehart & Co., 1980. 390 p.
A flip and often funny account of the unconventional characters she encounters in an athletic career as a rookie with the New York Rangers.

0386 Birenbaum, William M. **1923-**
Something for everybody is not enough: an educator's search for his education. New York: Random House, 1971. 293 p.
The President of Staten Island Community College, who describes his career as "checkered" and "rather difficult," writes of those parts of his education that have turned out to be useful.

0387 Birkbeck, Morris **1764-1825**
Notes on a journey in America: from the Coast of Virginia to the Territory of Illinois. Ann Arbor: University Microfilms, Inc., 1966. (London: James Ridgway, 1818) 156 p.
Emigrating to America in 1817, Birkbeck, a knowledgeable English agriculturalist, traveled through eastern America and settled in Illinois. He records his impressions of the country he passed through and evaluates different areas as possible farm sites for his colonization project with an eye toward fertility, salubrious climate, and the character of the present inhabitants.

0388 Birmingham, Frederic Alexander **1911-**
It was fun while it lasted. Philadelphia: J.B. Lippincott Co., 1960. 224 p.
Recollections of his boyhood and family life in Harlem (1915-20) include stories of Sunday outings, apartment life in the then respectable suburb, the first family car, the coming of World War I, the growing pains of maturity, told with a poignant, critical affection for his parents and a deep love for his sister.

0389 Birney, James Gillespie **1792-1857**
Letters of James Gillespie Birney, 1831-1857. Edited by Dwight L. Dumond. New York: D. Appleton-Century Company, 1938. 2v. Index.
Volume I contains letters August 30, 1831-June 1, 1840; Volume II, July 23, 1840-October 29, 1857. Letters written and received by Birney give a contemporary picture of the antislavery movement from the perspective of a Southern abolitionist, advocate of freedom of the press, and Liberty Party candidate for President of the United States.

0390 *Bishop, Isabella Lucy (Bird) **1831-1904**
A lady's life in the Rocky Mountains. Introduction by Daniel J. Boorstin. Norman: Oklahoma Press, 1960. (New York: G.P. Putnam's Sons, 1879-1880) 252 p.
An English lady who traveled alone for her own recreation and interest, the author exercised her geographical knowledge, feeling for beauty, and capacity for description in her letters to her sister. She traveled and lived in Colorado, particularly in the Longs Peak-Estes Park region, enduring hardships cheerfully and appreciating the beauty of the mountains.

0391 Bisno, Abraham **1866-1929**
Abraham Bisno: union pioneer. Foreward by Joel Seidman. Madison: University of Wisconsin Press, 1967. 244 p.
A well-known leader among Jewish garment workers in Chicago and New York gives an account of his early life and the beginning of unions in the women's garment industry.

0392 Bissell, Richard Pike **1913-1977**
My life on the Mississippi, or why I am not Mark Twain. Illustrated. Boston: Little, Brown and Co., 1973. 240 p.
Bissell, who has been called "a modern Mark Twain" because he writes books about the Mississippi and has been a riverboat pilot, protests with tongue in cheek about the comparison. His book contains amusing stories about his steamboating days on the rivers.

0393 Bissonette, A.A. Georges **1921-**
Moscow was my parish. Westport, Connecticut: Greenwood Press, 1978. (New York: McGraw-Hill, 1956) 272 p.
A well-written account of the urbane Father Bissonette's experience as a chaplain in Moscow focuses more on his travels around Russia than on his clerical duties. In 1955 he was suddenly expelled without apparent cause.

0394 *Bjorn, Thyra (Ferre) **1905-1975**
This is my life. New York: Holt, Rinehart and Winston, 1966. 181 p.
Mrs. Bjorn writes warm, humorous anecdotes of her life after the publication of her first book, *Papa's Wife*. No longer content to remain only a housewife and mother, she added lecturing, traveling, and more writing to her full life.

0395 Black, Hugo LaFayette **1886-1971**
Sincerely your friend: letters of Mr. Justice Hugo L. Black to Jerome A. Cooper. University: University of Alabama Press, 1973. 17 p.
A brief collection of letters from the U.S. Supreme Court Justice to one of his law clerks.

0396 Black Elk **1863-1950**
Black Elk speaks Vine Deloria, Jr., Introduction. Lincoln: University of Nebraska Press, 1979. (New York: William Morrow and Co., 1932) 238 p.
A powerful narrative of Indian life, of the changes brought by white

settlers, of Custer's Last Stand, of the Battle of Wounded Knee, but primarily of the old ways and their deep spiritual value.

0397 Black Hawk 1767-1838
Life of MA-KA-TAI-ME-SHE-KIA-KIAK, or Black Hawk, dictated by himself. Fairfield, Washington, Ye Galleon Press, 1974. (Cincinnati: n.p., 1833) 206 p.
The story of the famous Sauk chief, based on the 1833 edition which he is said to have dictated to an army translator.

0398 Blackford, Charles Minor 1901-
Torpedoboat sailor. Illustrated by Paul Simon. Annapolis, Maryland: United States Naval Institute, 1968. 156 p.
Blackford writes of his naval service in World War I aboard the destroyers *Paulding* and *McDougal.* He skillfully evokes the group camaraderie among the enlisted men and re-creates military strategy in his accounts of naval raids on other ships.

0399 *Blackford, Susan Leigh (Colston) b.1835
Letters from Lee's army: memoirs of life in and out of the army in Virginia during the war between the states. Annotated by Charles Minor Blackford. Edited and abridged for publication by Charles Minor Blackford III. New York: Charles Scribner's Sons, 1947. 312 p. Index.
The letters of Susan Leigh Colston Blackford and Charles Minor Blackford record their observations of war-time life in the South, 1861-1865. This is an abridged version of a small edition privately printed in 1894.

0400 *Blackwell, Elizabeth 1821-1910
Pioneer work in opening the medical profession to women: autobiographical sketches. New introduction by Mary Roth Walsh. New York: Schocken Books, 1977. (London: Longmans, Green, 1895) 264 p.
Blackwell fought to study and practice medicine in the mid-nineteenth century, learning first from medical books, then studying at Geneva University. Acceptance was hard won on all fronts, but she emerged as the first woman in America to receive a complete medical education. Dedicated to her profession and to furthering women's opportunities in medicine, Dr. Blackwell never married but adopted a daughter. She also founded a hospital.

0401 Blagden, David 1944-
Very Willing Griffin: the story of the smallest boat ever to compete in the Single-handed Transatlantic Race. Illustrated. New York: W.W. Norton & Co., Inc., 1973. 237 p. Index.
After describing the extensive preparation for his race, the book is primarily his daily log kept for the 52 days of the race. Blagden writes of the technical matter crucial to such a voyage, but also of the mental stress common to this kind of rigorous but lonely adventure.

0402 Blaik, Earl Henry 1897-
The Red Blaik story. New Rochelle, New York: Arlington House, Publishers, 1974. 582 p. Index.
Part I, "You have to pay the price," published separately in 1960, describes Blaik's life as Army head football coach until his resignation in 1959. Part II, "As I knew them," carries the story into the 60's and adds his recollections of other coaches, of presidents, and of generals as well as a re-examination of the West Point Honor Scandal of 1951.

0403 Blaik, Earl Henry 1897-
You have to pay the price. With Tim Cohane. Foreword by General Douglas MacArthur. New York: Holt, Rinehart and Winston, 1960. 430 p. Index.
A football coach for 25 years at Dartmouth and West Point, his book is about the game, the Army, and the values inherent in both.

0404 *Blake, Alma Carwile 1909-
Of life and love and things. Parsons, West Virginia: McClain Printing Co., 1971. 119 p.
The ordinary life of a pleasant, ordinary woman living among friends and family in a small town in West Virginia, emphasizing her work as wife, mother, and Girl Scout Leader.

0405 Blake, Morgan 1889-1953
A sports editor finds Christ. Foreword by Billy Graham. Hopeville, Georgia: Hale Publishing Co., 1952. 192 p.
Blake intermingles the account of his career as a newspaper sports reporter (mostly for the Atlanta *Journal*) with his activities, 1910-1940, as a Christian "saved" from alcoholism by evangelical religion.

0406 Blalock, Alfred 1899-1964
The papers of Alfred Blalock. Edited with preface by Mark M. Ravitch. Illustrated. Bibliography. Baltimore: Johns Hopkins Press, 1966. 2v. Index.
An enormous compendium of the professional papers of Alfred Blalock, M.D., cardiovascular specialist at the Johns Hopkins University Medical School. These range from investigations of biliary tract disease, to mastoid disease, to the regulation of blood circulation, to a great many

papers on shock and various aspects of heart disease. Though highly technical, the papers are lucid, articulate, and to the point.

0407 *Blalock, Jane B. 1945-
The guts to win. And Dwayne Netland. Introduction by Billie Jean King. Illustrated. New York: Golf Digest, Inc., New York Times, 1977. 158 p.
Feminist golfer Blalock describes her career on the Ladies Professional Golf Association circuit, 1969-1976. She devotes two chapters to vindicating herself against LPGA charges that she cheated in tournaments in 1972 by moving the putt marker; she fought ostracism, harassment, and was threatened with suspension from the LPGA. She offers advice on how to play golf and assesses women's future in professional sports.

0408 Blanchard, Paul 1892-1980
Personal and controversial: an autobiography. Boston: Beacon Press, 1973. 308 p. Index.
A graduate of Harvard Divinity School and Brooklyn Law School, Blanchard traces his career "from Christian fundamentalist to humanist atheist, from stodgy Puritan to sexual rebel, from doctrinaire socialist to socialistic pragmatist."

0409 *Blatch, Harriot Stanton 1856-1940
Challenging years: the memoirs of Harriot Stanton Blatch. With Alma Lutz. Westport, Connecticut: Hyperion Press, 1976. (New York: Putnam & Sons, 1940) 347 p. Index.
A brisk narrative of the author's childhood growing up in the "cradle of the feminist movement," her education and marriage, followed by a sometimes intense account of the suffrage movement in New York, the campaign for the Nineteenth Amendment, and finally a tough look at the world's work left yet for women to do—child-labor laws, activities to preserve peace, economic advancement for women, etc.

0410 Blatchford, John 1762-1794
Narrative of John Blatchford: detailing his sufferings in the Revolutionary War, while a prisoner with the British, as related by himself. Introduction and notes by Charles I. Bushnell. Eyewitness Accounts of the American Revolution. New York: Arno Press, Inc., 1971. (New York: Privately Printed, 1865) 127 p.
In 1777 he enlisted as a cabin boy on a continental ship which was soon captured by the British. For the next six years he was on several prison ships, was sent to do forced labor in the East Indies, and finally was returned home.

0411 Blatty, William Peter 1928-
I'll tell them I remember you. New York: W.W. Norton & Co., Inc., 1973. 172 p.
The author of *The Exorcist* writes fondly of the difficult years of urban poverty in New York, his Lebanese immigrant parents, but especially of his mother with whom he believes he has made contact after death.

0412 Bleier, Robert (Rocky) Patrick, Jr. 1946-
Fighting back. With Terry O'Neil. Illustrated. New York: Warner Books, 1976. (New York: Stein and Day, 1975) 268 p. Index.
Pittsburgh Steeler linebacker Bleier offers an unusually candid and critical self-appraisal. After playing football for Notre Dame and for the Pittsburgh Steelers in 1967 and 1968, Bleier was drafted and sent to Vietnam in 1969. His foot was badly damaged by a grenade. Through perseverance and extensive physical therapy and weight lifting, he not only recovered but returned to the Steelers to play much better than before his injury.

0413 *Bloodgood, Lida Louise Fleitmann b.1885
Hoofs in the distance. Foreword by A. Henry Higginson. Lida Lacey Bloodgood, decorations. New York: D. Van Nostrand Co., 1953. 131 p. Index.
"The Gibson Girl of Madison Square Garden" horse shows nostalgically describes the shows she entered, mounts she rode, travels she took to Maine and Europe, and hunts she rode in as Mistress of the Fox Hounds.

0414 *Bloodgood, Mrs. J. Van S.
see *Fleitmann, Lida Louise

0415 Bloom, Sol 1870-1949
Autobiography of Sol Bloom. New York: G.P. Putnam's Sons, 1948. 345 p.
In 1945, Bloom, aged 75, was one of seven American delegates sent to draft the charter of the United Nations. The son of Polish immigrants, he sold newspapers at age six, rose in the entertainment world to become the biggest publisher of popular music in the United States by 29, became a congressman at 54, serving under four presidents for over 25 years.

0416 Bobst, Elmer Holmes 1884-1978
Bobst: the autobiography of a pharmaceutical pioneer. New York: McKay, 1973. 360 p.
A magnate in the modern pharmaceutical industry writes a sentimental account of his rise to wealth and subsequent philanthropic activities.

0417 Bock, August J.   **b.1886**
Knight of the napkin: memoirs of fifty years' experience in many lands.
Foreword by Edward Bryce Bell. New York: Exposition Press, 1951.
61 p.
   A waiter, proud of his work, summarizes his apprenticeship in Europe
before immigrating to the United States, his many years of service in
restaurants here since 1907, with brief opinions about various aspects of
his work life.

0418 Bodenheim, Maxwell   **1893-1954**
My life and loves in Greenwich Village. Afterword by Samuel Roth.
Illustrated. New York: Belmont Books, 1961. (New York: Seven Sirens
Press/Bridgehead Books, 1954) 141 p.
   Poet Max Bodenheim recalls his encounter with a variety of often
seamy, sordid aspects of Bohemian life in Greenwich Village in the 1920's
and 1930's. Through the volume parade mostly impecunious artists,
writers, sexual deviants, lovers at peace and at war, and benevolent land-
lord Albert Strunsky, who donated living quarters to starving artists.

0419 Boettinger, John R., Jr.   **1939-**
Love in Shadow. Illustrated. New York: W.W. Norton & Co., 1978.
279 p.
   Boettinger provides biographies of his parents Anna Eleanor Roosevelt
(the only daughter of F.D.R. and Eleanor) and newspaperman John R.
Boettinger whom Anna met on an F.D.R. campaign tour in 1932. Mar-
ried in 1935, they were divorced in 1949, after successfully editing the
Seattle *Post-Intelligence* for six years. Boettinger's military service in
World War II contributed to his depression and ultimate suicide in 1950.
His son's reminiscences are autobiographical in the last three chapters.

0420 *Bogan, Louise   **1897-1970**
What the woman lived; selected letters of Louise Bogan, 1920-1970. Edited with introduction by Ruth Limmer. New York: Harcourt Brace
Jovanovich, Inc., 1973. 401 p. Index.
   Bogan earned her living by writing literary criticism, but poetry was
her life interest. Her letters are often to major figures on the literary scene,
providing insight into the writer, the receiver, the creative process, and
the struggle and growth of a personality.

0421 Bogardus, Emory Stephen   **1882-1973**
Much have I learned. Los Angeles: University of Southern California
Press, 1962. 115 p. Index.
   A thoughtful analysis of ordinary experience that became significant
for what it taught him, written by a prominent urban sociologist at the
University of Southern California after his retirement.

0422 *Boggs, Marion Alexander   **1877-1970**
Alexander letters, 1787-1900. Edited by Marion Alexander Boggs. Fore-
word by Richard Barksdael Harwell. Reprint of 1910 edition. Savannah:
University of Georgia Press, 1980. (Savannah, Georgia: privately printed
for G.J. Baldwin, 1910) 387 p.
   These letters of the Alexander family begin with their settlement in
Washington County, Georgia, in 1787 and end in 1900. The most numerous represent exchanges among the ten children of Adam Leopold Alexander and his wife, Sarah Hillhouse Gilbert, in the 1850's and 1860's.
They are educated families of plantation owners and bankers and consider
their culture, manners, and breeding vastly superior to the Yankee
invaders during the Civil War.

0423 Bohlen, Charles Eustis   **1904-1974**
Witness to history, 1929-1969. New York: W.W. Norton & Co., Inc.,
1973. 562 p. Index.
   Memoir of a diplomat involved in American-Soviet relations from 1929
to 1969. Bohlen writes his impressions of the men who led the United
States during this period.

0424 Bohn, Dave
Backcountry journal: reminiscences of a wilderness photographer. Illustrated. Santa Barbara: Capra Press, 1974. 62 p.
   Illustrated with thirteen examples of his work, his book reflects the
somewhat mystical quality of his landscape photographs. He aims to
remove the presence of the photographer and if possible that of the
viewer, allowing the landscape to become anthropomorphic.

0425 *Bolster, Alice (Landon)
True adventures of a little country girl: an autobiographical narrative.
New York: Vantage Press, Inc., 1950. 96 p.
   Recalls cheerful childhood on a farm in Rutland, Vermont, with a
loving family and lots of pets.

0426 *Bolton, Isabel, pseud. (Miller, Mary Britton)   **1884-1975**
Under Gemini: a memoir. New York: Harcourt, Brace & World, 1966.
128 p.
   Mary Miller writes about a decade in her childhood after her parents
died when she and her twin sister, Grace, and their three older siblings
were reared in Goshen, New York, first by a loving grandmother and
after her death by an incompetent but well-meaning governess. Neverthe-

less, their childhood was relatively pleasant; its charm and the closeness
of being a twin ended with the maturity imposed by their fourteenth
birthday and boarding school.

0427 *Bolyan, Helen
   see ***Martin, Martha, pseud.***

0428 Bontemps, Arna   **1902-1973**
Letters: 1925-1967. And Langston Hughes. Selected and edited by
Charles H. Nichols. New York: Dodd, Mead, 1980. 576 p. Index.
   Five hundred of the 2300 lively, perceptive letters exchanged between
writers Bontemps and Hughes, 1925-1967, are included here. Section I,
1925-1941, says editor Nichols, "gives us insights into the identity of each
writer, his effort to learn his craft, to experiment, to gain an audience." In
Section II, 1941-1959, the authors are involved "in the social and racial
conflict of a turbulent world." Between 1959-1967 they are reacting to the
Civil Rights revolution and to the revival of interest in African-American
culture.

0429 Boone, Pat   **1934-**
The honeymoon is over. And Shirley Boone. Nashville: T. Nelson, 1980.
(Carol Stream, Ill.: Creation House, 1977) 185 p.
   Traveling as entertainers with four teenage daughters presented many
problems, which were met with Christian resolve and human impulsive-
ness in uneven proportions, but with general success. The authors alternate presenting sections of the book, as in conversation.

0430 *Boone, Shirley
   see **Boone, Pat**

0431 Booth, Edwin Thomas   **1833-1893**
**Between actor and critic: selected letters of Edwin Booth and William
Winter.** Introduction and commentary by Daniel J. Watermeier. Princeton, New Jersey: Princeton University Press, 1971. 329 p. Index.
   These annotated letters which span the twenty-year period of their
friendship (1869-1890) chronicle the professional activities as well as the
straightforward and unpretentious personality of the famed American
Shakespearian actor. Unfortunately only six of Winter's letters have been
preserved.

0432 Booth, Edwin Thomas   **1833-1893**
**Edwin Booth: recollections by his daughter, Edwina Booth Groosmann,
and letters to her and to his friends.** Freeport, New York: Books for
Libraries Press, 1970. (New York: Century, 1894) 292 p. Index.
   The collected letters (pp. 31-284) of a famous nineteenth-century actor
reveal his great affection for his daughter and interesting details of his
personal life while traveling with his theatrical company.

0433 Booth, John Nicholls   **1912-**
Fabulous destinations. New York: The Macmillan Co., 1950. 239 p.
   An author-clergyman travels alone in the Orient during a sabbatical
leave right after World War II.

0434 Borland, Hal Glen   **1900-1978**
Country editor's boy. Philadelphia: J.B. Lippincott Co., 1970. 313 p.
   The transition years of a boy, a town, and an area, the high plains of
eastern Colorado when the days of the Old West were disappearing and
the New West was emerging.

0435 Borland, Hal Glen   **1900-1978**
High, wide and lonesome. Philadelphia: J.B. Lippincott Co., 1956. 251 p.
   A journalist describes his boyhood in eastern Colorado, where frontier
life of the Old West still existed.

0436 Born, Max
   see **Einstein, Albert**

0437 Bossard, Marcus   **b.1864**
Eighty-one years of living. Minneapolis: Midwest Printing Co., 1946.
77 p.
   Boyhood in Wisconsin, medical practice in Spring Green, Wisconsin,
1887-1945.

0438 Bosworth, Allan R.   **1901-**
My love affair with the Navy. Foreword by Ernest M. Eller. Illustrated.
New York: W.W. Norton, 1969. 288 p. Index.
   Bosworth, a career Navy public relations officer eventually promoted
to Captain, mingles accounts of his military service during the Depression, World War II, Korean War, and the Vietnam War with pungent
anecdotes about Navy life in port and at sea; his views on submarines,
battleships, and Sealab; and his opinions on the importance of cooperation
and friendly rivalry between the Marines, the Seabees, and the Navy.

0439 Botein, Bernard   **1900-1974**
Trial judge, the candid, behind-the-bench story of Justice Bernard Botein.
New York: Da Capo Press, 1974. (New York: Simon and Schuster, 1952)
337 p.

In 1941 he was appointed a Justice of the New York Supreme Court. He was at that time a senior member of a prominent law firm with a distinguished public service record. His book describes what it felt like to be a judge, including problems he had not been trained to deal with, the roles of judge and lawyer in a trial, the drama and routine business of the job.

0440 *Botta, Anne Charlotte (Lynch)   **1815-1891**
Memoirs of Anne C.L. Botta, written by her friends. With selections from her correspondence and from her writings in prose and poetry. Compiled by V. Botta. New York: J. Selwin Tait & Sons, 1894. 459 p.

The first half of this collection consists of the recollections by friends from Julia Ward Howe to Andrew Carnegie. The latter half is a selection from Anne Botta's correspondence with friends and acquaintances, particularly those in her literary circle, as well as her own prose and poetry. Included among the prose work are "Leaves from the Diary of a Recluse," part of Mrs. Botta's account of her days as governess to the Gardiner children on Shelter Island, N.Y.

0441 Boudreau, Lou   **1917-**
Player-manager. With Ed Fitzgerald. Illustrated. Rev. ed. Boston: Little, Brown & Co., 1952. (1949) 256 p.

Boudreau, shortstop and manager for the Cleveland Indians, recounts his career in sports. As a student at the University of Illinois he played baseball, football, and basketball, but soon turned pro. His autobiography highlights notable games and players.

0442 *Boulding, Elise (Biorn-Hansen)   **1920-**
Born remembering. Wallingford, Pennsylvania: Pendle Hill, 1975. 30 p.

One of the founders of the Women's International League for Peace and Freedom describes her early education in New Jersey, her career as a social worker in New York, her conversion to Quakerism, her marriage and five children.

0443 *Boulton, Agnes
Part of a long story. Garden City, New York: Doubleday and Co., Inc., 1958. 331 p.

A well-written narrative of her struggling days as a writer in Greenwich Village and of her love and early years of marriage to Eugene O'Neill.

0444 *Boulton, Laura Theresa (Craytor)
Music hunter; the autobiography of a career. Illustrated. Garden City, New York: Doubleday & Co., Inc., 1969. 513 p. Index.

For 35 years Mrs. Boulton traveled in remote parts of the world to discover and record the traditional and liturgical music of people whose cultures were scarcely known. As her book reveals, her work was her life.

0445 Bourke, John Gregory   **1843-1896**
On the border with Crook. New York: Scribner's, 1891. 491 p.

Written by a member of General George Crook's military staff, this is a minutely detailed account of the subjugation and management of the Indian tribes from Mexico to the Dakotas and west to Idaho, including careful descriptions of the flora, fauna, terrain and a sometimes sympathetic account of a number of tribes, particularly the Apaches. A very rich picture of military life in the 1870's and 80's.

0446 *Bourke-White, Margaret   **1905-1971**
Portrait of myself. New York: Simon & Schuster, Inc., 1963. 383 p.

The famed photographer writes a compelling narrative of her world-wide adventures, many on assignments from *Life* magazine. Illustrated with her own expressive photographs.

0447 *Bourne, Eulalia
Ranch schoolteacher. Tucson: University of Arizona Press, 1974. 312 p.

She describes her development as a teacher, primarily of non-English-speaking pupils, in several one-room school houses during the pioneer days of Arizona's statehood. The volume includes some photographs of the teacher and her students.

0448 *Bourne, Eulalia
Woman in Levi's. Illustrated by Vic Donahue. Tucson: The University of Arizona Press, 1967. 208 p.

Teaching school during the week and running a homestead ranch on the weekends made for a very exhausting and busy life, but the author, a keen observer and lover of the out-of-doors, stuck to both jobs and enjoyed them.

0449 Bourne, Randolph   **1886-1918**
The world of Randolph Bourne. Edited with introduction by Lillian Schlissel. New York: E.P. Dutton & Co., Inc., 1965. 333 p.

Mainly an anthology of his writings, this volume includes some letters (1912-1918) by this promising young critic who died just after World War I.

0450 Bouton, James Alan (Jim)   **1939-**
Ball four: my life and hard times throwing the knuckleball in the big leagues. Edited by Leonard Shecter. New York: World Publishers, 1970. 400 p.

A diary of a baseball season (1968) spent on an expansion team by a former New York Yankee who lost his fastball. The intention is to reveal the game as it is viewed by the men who play it.

0451 Bouton, James Alan (Jim)   **1939-**
I'm glad you didn't take it personally. Edited by Leonard Shecter. New York: Morrow, 1971. 220 p.

A humorous account of what happened to the author after the publication of his first autobiography, *Ball Four,* and his subsequent career in the television industry.

0452 *Bouvier, Lee
see *Onassis, Jacqueline (Bouvier) Kennedy

0453 Bove, Mike
Flight 13: thirteen years with Castro. New York: Vantage, 1973. 232 p.

He writes of his work as an independent pilot, supplying arms to Cuban revolutionary forces until his disillusionment with Fidel Castro.

0454 Bowen, Ashley   **1728-1813**
The journals of Ashley Bowen (1728-1813) of Marblehead. Edited by Philip Chadwick Foster Smith. Illustrated. Boston: The Colonial Society of Massachusetts, 1973. 325 p.

Bowen's journals cover the years he spent as a seaman and merchant captain (1740's to 1772). He describes his daily activities and specifics of navigation (longitude, latitude, weather). Also an amateur painter, Bowen designed sails and sketched ships; his drawings are interspersed among his journal entries.

0455 *Bowen, Catherine (Drinker)   **1897-1973**
Adventures of a biographer. Boston: Little, Brown and Co., 1959. 235 p. Index.

Recollections of her experience during research travels for material on the lives of famous people she wrote about.

0456 *Bowen, Catherine (Drinker)   **1897-1973**
Family portrait. Boston: Little, Brown and Co., 1970. 301 p.

A gentle, loving portrait of her mother, father, four older brothers, and sister along with sundry other relatives forms a celebration of and mourning for bygone youth. Her brothers especially were her heroes, older, wiser, and inhabiting a mysterious male world in which she could not participate.

0457 *Bowen, Catherine (Drinker)   **1897-1973**
Friends and fiddlers. Boston: Little, Brown and Company, 1942. (1935) 261 p.

The book concerns her joy in music, not of concert-going but of amateur performance for fun. An amateur violinist herself, she recognizes her music not as an accomplishment, but as a daily comfort and an intimate family activity.

0458 Bowen, Harold G.   **1883-1965**
Ships, machinery and mossbacks: the autobiography of a naval engineer. Foreword by William D. Leahy. Illustrated. Princeton: Princeton University Press, 1954. 397 p. Index.

Vice-Admiral Bowen, a career engineer in the U.S. Navy, 1901-1946, describes the naval engineering activities while he was Chief of the Navy's Bureau of Engineering, and later in charge of the Naval Research Laboratory and overseer of the Naval Office of Research and Inventions. During this time the Navy attained supremacy in steam engineering, pioneered in electronics, and supported extensive basic and applied research.

0459 Bower, William Clayton   **b.1878**
Through the years: personal memoirs. Lexington, Kentucky: Translyvania College Press, 1957. 111 p.

A thoughtful, intellectually and spiritually sophisticated analysis of the author's life as a religious educator, primarily at the College of the Bible in Lexington, Kentucky, and at the University of Chicago Divinity School.

0460 Bowers, Claude Gernade   **1878-1958**
My life: the memoirs of Claude Bowers. New York: Simon & Schuster, Inc., 1962. 346 p. Index.

A historian, politician, newspaperman, and diplomat describes his progress from happy boyhood in Indianapolis through a varied career in and out of politics ending with his ambassadorship in Chile (1939-1953) and the years afterward.

0461 Bowie, Walter Russell   **1882-1969**
Learning to live. Nashville, Tennessee: Abingdon Press, 1969. 288 p. Index.

An eloquent, appealing memoir by an Episcopalian clergyman who served as a chaplain in World War I and at St. Paul's and Grace Churches in Richmond, Virginia, throughout the 1920's and 1930's. In the 1940's and 1950's he was a faculty member at Union Theological Seminary and always an articulate spokesman for civil rights, ecumenism, and enlightened church reform.

0462 Bowles, Chester 1901-
Promises to keep: my years in public life, 1941-1969. New York: Harper & Row, 1971. 657 p.
   A record of his public life which began when he was forty and lasted for 29 years, this volume reflects, in Bowles' words, "one man's futile effort to buck the so-called 'Establishment'."

0463 Bowles, Samuel b.1826
Across the continent: a summer's journey to the Rocky Mountains, the Mormons, and the Pacific States with Speaker Colfax. New York: Hurd & Houghton, 1865. 438 p.
   Although dominated by mannered descriptions of the wealth of Midwestern cities and the unlimited opportunities of Western lands, this account occasionally sparkles with the newspaper editor's surprise and delight in the physical beauty he finds on his journey. He comments on the Indian Question, polygamy, exploitation of natural resources, spicing the lot with what he frankly acknowledges to be gossip.

0464 Bowman, John Gabbert 1877-1962
The world that was. New Brunswick: Rutgers University Press, 1947. (New York: The Macmillan Co., 1926) 83 p.
   A nostalgic recollection of his boyhood, emphasizing the strong influence of his father's wisdom and values by a man who became Chancellor of the University of Pittsburgh.

0465 *Boyd, Belle 1843-1900
Belle Boyd in camp and prison: written by herself; a new edition prepared from new materials by Curtis Carroll Davis. South Brunswick, New Jersey: Thomas Yoseloff, 1968. (New York: Blelock & Co., 1865) 448 p. Index.
   Perhaps the most notorious among women who spied during the Civil War, Belle Boyd worked for the Confederacy, then took her name and fame to the stage and lecture platform where the legends of her days in espionage developed even further.

0466 Boyd, Malcolm 1923-
As I live and breathe: stages of an autobiography. New York: Random House, 1970. (1969) 276 p.
   In 1951 Boyd left Hollywood, where he had been a radio-television partner of Mary Pickford and Buddy Rogers, to study for the Episcopal priesthood. Thereafter he was a college chaplain, civil rights demonstrator, and fighter against poverty, discrimination and the Vietnam War. Here he writes of his angers, his fears, his motivations and beliefs.

0467 Boyington, Gregory (Pappy) 1912-
Baa, baa, black sheep. New York: G.P. Putnam's Sons, 1958. 384 p.
   He gave up his commission in the U.S. Marines to join Claire Chennault's elite mercenaries, The Flying Tigers, which, along with a reputation as a hard-drinking, hard-living adventurer, led him to become a military outcast. By 1943 he was out of work and desperate for an active military assignment. He was assigned to command a group of misfits known as his Black Sheep, who brought him and themselves a certain renown for their courage and heroism. The book was the basis of the TV series by the same name.

0468 *Boyle, Kay 1903-
The long walk at San Francisco State. New York: Grove Press, 1970. 150 p.
   A member of the creative writing faculty at San Francisco State University during the 1968-69 student strikes, she describes the violent clash between youth and the authority represented by S.I. Hayakawa, then university president.

0469 Braden, Spruille 1894-1978
Diplomats and demagogues: the memoirs of Spruille Braden. New Rochelle, New York: Arlington House, 1971. 496 p.
   A graduate of Yale, fervent anti-communist, and longstanding member of the John Birch Society, Braden was Ambassador to Colombia, Cuba, and Argentina, before being appointed Assistant Secretary of State by Harry S. Truman in 1945.

0470 Bradford, Gamaliel 1863-1932
The letters of Gamaliel Bradford: 1918-1931. Edited by Van Wyck Brooks. Boston: Houghton Mifflin Co., 1934. 377 p. Index.
   The letters reveal the breadth of Bradford's interests as critic and scholar, from Shakespeare and other Elizabethans to Darwin, Confederate generals, theater, politics, and sports. His wit, humor and gentleness are expressed in correspondence to a wide and multifarious circle of friends from Cambridge scholars to the young authors such as Robert Frost and H.L. Mencken. Companion volume to his journals.

0471 Bradford, Gamaliel 1863-1932
Life and I: an autobiography of humanity. New York: Greenwood Press, 1968. (Boston: Houghton-Mifflin, 1928) 307 p.
   Bradford presents a psychological and philosophical study of the "I," with chapters on "Love and I," "Power and I," "Thought and I," "Christ and I," and even "Christ and Not-I," concentrating on the many desires which threaten to pull the "I" apart.

0472 Bradford, Perry 1895-
Born with the blues; Perry Bradford's own story; the true story of the pioneering blues singers and musicians in the early days of jazz. New York: Oak Publications, 1965. 175 p. Index.
   The story of his campaign to get commercial recording companies to make records of Negro girl singer, Mamie Smith, and other blues and jazz singers and combination bands, leading to million-dollar profits for Okeh Company and others. He awakened the industry to the tremendous market for the rhythmic beat of the blues.

0473 Bradley, Omar Nelson 1893-1981
A soldier's story. New York: Henry Holt and Co., 1951. 618 p. Index.
   American General of the Army recounts his experience during World War II from the perspective of the field command post. He includes personal relationships with his colleagues, especially Patton, Eisenhower, and Montgomery, in addition to detailed accounts of actions ending with the surrender of Germany in 1945. He writes honestly about his involvement with the Korean War, six years after the events described in his book.

0474 Bradley, Preston b.1888
Along the way: an autobiography. With Harry Barnard. New York: David McKay Co., Inc., 1962. 280 p.
   A minister of the Peoples Church of Chicago for over fifty years writes of his youth, education, and his prominent ministry which became international.

0475 Bradley, William H. 1868-1962
Will Bradley, his chap book: an account in the words of the dean of American typographers, of his graphic arts adventures: as a boy printer in Ishpeming, art student in Chicago, designer, printer, and publisher at the Wayside Press, the years as art director in periodical publishing and the interludes of stage, cinema, and authorship. New York: The Typophiles, 1955. 104 p.
   An American contemporary of William Morris and The Kelmscott Press, his approach to graphic arts was as adventuresome, but more democratic, targeting magazines, newspapers, and advertising houses. In 1954 he was awarded the gold medal of the American Institute of Graphic Arts "for a half-century of typographic achievement."

0476 Bradley, William Warren 1943-
Life on the run. New York: Quadrangle/New York Times, 1976. 299 p.
   New York Knicks basketball star's intriguing analysis of the professional touring athlete's life on the road. Bradley offers an exceptionally sensitive interpretation of the way a professional team functions humanly, on and off the court, at home and away, in its relations with coaches, trainers, rival players, fans, friends.

0477 Bradna, Fred 1871-1955
Big top: my forty years with the greatest show on earth. As told to Hartzell Spence. New York: Simon and Schuster, 1952. 323 p.
   The author, an equestrian director and stage manager, describes his own and his wife's life with the Barnum and Bailey, Ringling, and North circuses. The book traces the development of the circus in the United States and contains a glossary of circus terminology in addition to descriptions of the greatest acts.

0478 Bradshaw, Terry Paxton 1948-
Terry Bradshaw: man of steel. With David Diles. Preface by Pete Rozelle. Foreword by Roger Staubach. Illustrated. Grand Rapids, Michigan: Zondervan Publishing House, 1979. 195 p.
   A candid and articulate account of Bradshaw's career as quarterback for the Pittsburgh Steelers, 1971-1979, interlaced with comments about life in Shreveport, Louisiana, with his parents and brothers, college football at Louisiana Tech., and unsatisfying marriage to skater Jo-Jo Starbuck. Bradshaw's Christian commitment is pervasive.

0479 Brady, James 1928-
Superchic. Boston: Little, Brown and Co., 1974. 266 p.
   The former publisher of *Women's Wear Daily* and *Harper's Bazaar* gives an irreverent and opinionated account of the designers, models, editors, columnists, and advertisers who people the elegant world of haute couture.

0480 Brainard, Joe 1942-
I remember. New York: Full Court Press, 1975. (New York: Angel Hair, 1970) 138 p.
   Painter Brainard's book consists entirely of one-sentence paragraphs, each of which begins, "I remember . . ." These focus mostly on childhood

and adolescent memories of family life, holidays, American culture, and sex: "I remember knowing what 'c-a-n-d-y' meant long before I knew how to spell."

0481 Brainerd, David   **1718-1747**
Journey with David Brainerd: forty days or forty nights with David Brainerd. Downers Grove, Illinois: Inter-Varsity Press, 1975. 120 p.
    A devotional guide compiled of selections from the diary, journal, and letters of Brainerd, a missionary among the Indians during the early Colonial era. The guide is intended to assist people seeking "a dynamic spiritual experience within the evangelical Christian tradition." Each of the forty short selections closes with a prayer.

0482 Brainerd, David   **1718-1747**
Life and diary. Edited by Jonathan Edwards. Newly edited and with a biographical sketch of President Edwards, by Philip E. Howard, Jr. Chicago: Moody Press, 1949. 384 p.
    This account of Brainerd's life and work among the American Indians was originally published in Vol. III of *The Works of President Edwards in Eight Volumes* (London: James Black & Son, 1817). It provides an interesting record of his spiritual growth, the conditions of the Indians, and his perception of the effect of mission work upon them.

0483 Braly, Malcolm   **1925-**
False starts. Boston: Little, Brown and Co., 1976. 375 p.
    An up-beat, witty, and philosophical book about the author's first forty years. By 14, abandoned by mother, father, and stepmother, Braly became a ward of the state and began a career as a thief, which lasted until he was forty. He published his first novel while in prison and went on to become the respected author of *In the Yard,* a novel about San Quentin.

0484 Brandeis, Donald Asa   **1928-**
Fling wide the gates. As told to Byron McKissack. Foreword by Harold G. Sanders. New York: Vantage Press, 1958. 105 p.
    Brandeis, an evangelical Baptist minister, writes "so others may know how Jesus Christ became real to me." High school valedictorian, he joined the Navy at sixteen to fight Hitler. There he traded his Jewish faith for atheism when his best friend was killed in the Battle of Luzon. He became an alcoholic and chronic gambler; car theft resulted in a sentence at Florida State Prison where he was converted to Christianity.

0485 Brandeis, Louis Dembitz   **1856-1941**
Letters of Louis D. Brandeis. Melvin I. Urofsky and David W. Levy, editors. Vol. 1: 1870-1907: urban reformer; Vol. 2: 1907-1912: people's attorney; Vol. 3: 1913-1915: progressive and zionist; Vol. 4: 1916-1921: Mr. Justice Brandeis; Vol. 5: 1921-1941: elder statesman. Albany: State University of New York Press, 1971-1978. 5v. Index.
    A towering figure in his own time and in the broader sweep of American history, Brandeis was a leading reformer in the progressive era, the synthesizer of American Zionism, and a great jurist of the Supreme Court. His letters demonstrate his outstanding character and accomplishments in helping to make the world and his country a better place.

0486 Braun, Bob   **1929?-**
Here's Bob. Introduction by Ruth Lyons. Afterword by Dick Clark. Illustrated. Garden City, New York: Doubleday & Co., 1969. 191 p.
    In the 1960's Braun was a big fish in the Cincinnati TV pond, with the "Fifty-Fifty Club" noontime TV show and others of the "audience participation, guest-star, live music" format. His autobiography, illustrated with many publicity stills, enhances his image as a good-natured entertainer, surrounded by celebrities and housewives.

0487 Brawley, William Hiram   **1841-1916**
Journal of William H. Brawley, 1864-1865. Edited with introduction by Francis Poe Brawley. Charlottesville, Virginia: Privately printed, 1970. 263 p.
    Edited by his grandson, the journal records his experience in England and France where he was apparently sent as a Confederate envoy and law student after losing an arm while fighting for the South Carolina Volunteers.

0488 Breakenridge, William M.   **1846-1931**
Helldorado: bringing the law to the Mesquite. Glorieta, New Mexico: Rio Grande, 1970. (Boston: Houghton Mifflin Co., 1928) 256 p.
    He served as a deputy sheriff in Tombstone, Arizona, and spent many years as a lawman in Tucson, both during the late nineteenth century when the notorious gamblers and guns were in their prime. A vivid recollection of life on the Western frontier.

0489 Brecht, Arnold   **b.1884**
The political education of Arnold Brecht: an autobiography, 1884-1970. Abridged Version. Princeton, New Jersey: Princeton University Press, 1970. (Stuttgart: Deutsche Verlags-Anstalt, 1966-67) 544 p. Index.
    A blend of personal reminiscence and political contemplation form an extraordinary account of German history from the start of World War I through the period of Weimar democracy to the ascent of Hitler.

0490 Bredesen, E. Harald   **1918-**
Yes, Lord. With Pat King. Introduction by Pat Boone. Coverdale House, 1974. (Plainfield, New Jersey: Logos International, 1972) 206 p.
    Minister and man of a thousand schemes, Bredesen recounts his Lutheran seminary days and promotion of various Christian endeavors from fund-raising for the World Counsel on Christian Education to the Gospel Association, followed by marriage and ministry in an upstate New York Church. Meanwhile, his wife fed and looked after all the hard-luck cases he brought home.

0491 Breen, George
An immigrant's shenanigans: thirty-three jobs in twenty years. New York: Exposition Press, 1951. 230 p.
    Proud of his success in America, Breen recalls his childhood and youth in Ireland, his assortment of jobs after immigration, and, later, an extended trip to Europe to visit relatives.

0492 Breig, Joseph Anthony   **1905-**
Life with my Mary. Milwaukee, Wisconsin: Bruce Publishing Co., 1955. 202 p.
    A newspaper reporter and editor (Vandergrift *News,* Pittsburgh *Sun-Telegraph, Universe-Bulletin*) celebrates the joys of marriage and fatherhood, always within the context of Roman Catholicism.

0493 Breitmann, Hans
    see Leland, Charles Godfrey, pseud.

0494 Bremer, Arthur Herman   **1950-**
An assassin's diary. Introduction by Harding Lemay. New York: Harper's Magazine Press, 1973. 142 p.
    The would-be assassin of George Wallace left thirteen handwritten diary entries later found in his car. They represent an interesting though incoherent articulation of his original plans to kill the president and then Wallace.

0495 Brennan, James McClellan   **b.1871**
From mine pit to pulpit. Boston: The Christopher Publishing House, 1954. 226 p.
    A contented reminiscence by a retired Methodist clergyman who, when aged eight to eleven, worked in the Pennsylvania anthracite mines, first picking slate from coal, later as a door-tender and mule-driver's assistant. His interim occupation as a barber and his long-term career as a Methodist clergyman seem easy by comparison and thoroughly pleasurable. Brennan worked his way through Dickinson College and Drew Seminary, later serving congregations in upstate New York and the YMCA during World War I.

0496 *Brent, Linda, pseud.
    see *Jacobs, Harriet (Brent)

0497 Brent, Stuart
The seven stairs. Boston: Houghton Mifflin Co., 1962. 205 p.
    By 1960 he had a prosperous bookshop on Chicago's Michigan Avenue and a daily TV program, "Books and Brent," that *Variety* called the best daytime TV show. He writes about getting started in the book business with little more than a love of good books and a great deal of determination and naiveté.

0498 Brereton, Lewis Hyde   **1890-1967**
Brereton diaries: the war in the air in the Pacific, Middle East and Europe, 3 October 1941-8 May 1945. New York: William Morrow and Co., 1946. 450 p. Index.
    A personal account of World War II by the Commander of the Far East Air Forces, who was later assigned to the Middle East, then to Europe.

0499 *Breshko-Breshkovskaia, Ekaterina Konstantinovna (Verigo) 1844?-1934
The little grandmother of the Russian Revolution; reminiscences and letters of Catherine Breshkovsky. Edited by Alice Stone Blackwell. Boston: Little, Brown and Co., 1917. 348 p. Index.
    Although primarily concerned with Breshkovsky's involvement in the Russian Revolution, this mixture of letters, speeches and secondary material includes an account of Breshkovsky's fund-raising visit to New York, Boston, Philadelphia and Chicago, and her reception by the settlement movement workers. Important because it casts light on American support for the Russian Revolution in its early stages.

0500 Breslau, Alan Jeffry   **1926?-**
Time of my death. New York: E.P. Dutton, 1977. 301 p.
    A chemical engineer analyzes the plane crash in July 1963 in which he was severely maimed and burned and describes in detail the rehabilitation process that required 46 operations and much loving support from his wife and medical personnel.

0501 Breslin, Jimmy   **1930-**
The world of Jimmy Breslin. Annotated by James G. Bellows and Richard C. Wald. New York: The Viking Press, 1967. 282 p.

Breslin became a sportswriter for the New York *Herald Tribune* in 1963. By the time this book, a collection of his columns, was published, his reputation as a serious journalist was well established. He is admired for his Irish humor and sensibility, his compassion, and the strength of his critical insight.

0502 Brewer, Grover Cleveland   **1884-1956**
A story of toil and tears/of love and laughter. Murfreesboro, Tennessee: Deehoff Publishers, 1957. 155 p.
   Brewer emphasizes his lifelong career as a gospel preacher and devotes chapters to confession, salvation, rebaptism, anthropomorphisms—describing God in human terms.

0503 Brewer, Samuel J.G.
My dear wife from your devoted husband: letters from a rebel soldier to his wife. Editor's note and introduction by H. Candler Thaxton. Preface by William F. Thaxton. Warrington, Florida: H. Candler Thaxton, 1968. 155 p.
   This plainspoken narrative of an infantryman's activities during the Civil War is typical and ultimately moving in its accounts of good and poor commanders, tattered clothing and barefoot marches, sickness and health, ample and insufficient food, missing pay, and a dearth of letters from home. Despite these discontents, Brewer decides to stay in the service so his son will not think he is a deserter.

0504 Brewer, William H.   **1828-1910**
Up and down in California, 1860-1864: the journal of William H. Brewer, Professor of Agriculture in the Sheffield Scientific School from 1864 to 1903. Edited by Francis P. Farquhar. Preface by Russell H. Chittenden. Illustrated. Los Angeles: University of California Press, 1966. (New Haven: Yale University Press, 1930) 583 p. Index.
   Brewer wrote three picturesque letters while serving as a horticulturalist for the California State Geological Survey under the direction of Josiah Dwight Whitney. He notes geographical, geological, and botanical facts, and provides abundant detail about the behavior of animals and humans, Indians and white settlers.

0505 Bridge, Horatio   **1806-1893**
Journal of an African cruiser: comprising sketches of the Canaries, the Cape de Verde, Liberia, Madeira, Sierra Leone, and other places of interest on the West Coast of Africa. Edited by Nathaniel Hawthorne. Detroit: Negro History Press, 1968. (New York: George P. Putnam, 1853) 179 p.
   A fascinating account of the author's voyage as a naval officer to the West Coast of Africa, 1843-44, when he visited Liberia, Madeira, Sierra Leone and other West African countries noting customs, trade, religion, and other aspects of their cultures. Of particular interest are his observations on the progress of Liberia, settled by colonies of freed slaves.

0506 Briggs, Ellis Ormsbee   **1899-1976**
Farewell to Foggy Bottom: the recollections of a career diplomat. New York: David McKay Co., Inc., 1964. 306 p.
   A career diplomat for nearly forty years, having been ambassador to seven countries, Briggs reminisces about his experiences in amusing or serious circumstances. He has suggestions for improving the effectiveness of the Foreign Service and decided opinions regarding bureaucrats, government policies, and the operation of the State Department.

0507 *Brinton, Mary (Williams)
My cap and my cape: an autobiography. Philadelphia: Dorrance and Co., 1950. 262 p.
   Socialite Philadelphian recalls her nursing experiences during World War I and II.

0508 Briscoe, Edward Gans   **1937-**
Diary of a short-timer in Vietnam. New York: Vantage Press, 1970. 117 p.
   The diary of a Black surgeon in the Vietnam War, written during the second half of his tour of duty (called "short-time") before he returned to the United States in May, 1968.

0509 Britt, Albert   **1874-1969**
An America that was: what life was like on an Illinois farm seventy years ago. Barre, Massachusetts: Barre Publications, 1964. 196 p.
   A recreation of the author's youth on an Illinois farm makes vivid the self-sufficient and simpler ways of rural living before the turn of the century.

0510 Brock, Jim
The Devils' coach. And Joe Gilmartin. Illustrated. Elgin, Illinois: David C. Cook Publishing Co., 1977. 168 p.
   A baseball coach recalls his experience with the Arizona State University Sun Devils. Before he became a born-again Christian his coaching philosophy was simple: "If we won, it was because I was a great coach; if we lost, it was because the players were a bunch of turkeys." After his conversion he became more compassionate. The Sun Devils won the Col-

lege World Series championships in 1975, 1976, and 1977 and other collegiate championships in 1972 and 1973.

0511 Brockway, Zebulon Reed   **1827-1920**
Fifty years of prison service: an autobiography. Montclair, New Jersey: Patterson Smith, 1969. (New York: Charities Publication Committee, 1912) 437 p. Index.
   Working in prisons in Albany, Rochester, and Detroit before becoming Superintendent of the Elmira Reformatory from the time of its opening in 1876 to 1900, Brockway devoted his long life to the work of reformation and rehabilitation of prisoners and the protection of society.

0512 Brokenshire, Norman   **1898-1965**
This is Norman Brokenshire: an unvarnished self-portrait. New York: David McKay Co., Inc., 1954. 307 p.
   A prominent disc jockey and radio commentator describes his life and his long struggle with alcoholism.

0513 Bromfield, Louis   **1896-1956**
From my experience: the pleasures and miseries of life on a farm. New York: Harper and Brothers, 1955. 355 p. Index.
   A realistic but pleasant account of his years as a farmer, after assessing the experience of World War II and his fame as a writer moved him to return to the land of his boyhood.

0514 Brooke, Francis Taliaferro   **1763-1851**
A family narrative: being the reminiscences of a Revolutionary officer. Eyewitness Accounts of the American Revolution. New York: New York Times and Arno Press, 1971. (Richmond, Virginia: MacFarlane & Fergusson, 1849) 43 p.
   Originally a family memoir issued as a private publication, this is a brief account of a career which he began as a private in Washington's army and ended with forty years as judge of Virginia's Court of Appeals. This is a reprint of the 1921 edition rather than the original 1849 edition entitled *A Narrative of My Life.*

0515 *Brooks, Alice M.   **1887-1957** .
Clenched fist. And Willietta E. Kuppler. Philadelphia: Dorrance and Co., 1948. 206 p.
   The record of their experience as teachers in the federal schools of Alaskan territory during the early 1900's ends with a patriotic plea to preserve Alaska from the U.S.S.R.

0516 Brooks, Audrey Lee   **b.1871**
A Southern lawyer: fifty years at the bar. Chapel Hill: The University of North Carolina Press, 1950. 214 p. Index.
   A pleasant reminiscence by a lawyer and Southern gentleman, describing his boyhood on a North Carolina plantation during Reconstruction, his early days as a lawyer and prosecuting attorney, and his 57-year legal career.

0517 *Brooks, Gladys Rice (Billings)
Gramercy Park: memories of a New York girlhood. New York: E.P. Dutton & Co., Inc., 1958. 220 p.
   Recollections of her girlhood in the 1890's and early 1900's include anecdotes of many celebrities attended by her father, a doctor, and others who came to the Sunday salons held by her mother, a lover of the arts (Mark Twain, Lillian Russell, Enrico Caruso, et al.).

0518 *Brooks, Gwendolyn   **1917-**
Report from part one. Illustrated. Detroit: Broadside Press, 1972. 215 p.
   This autobiographical statement by an outstanding Black poet contains "Report from Part One," previously published in *McCall's* magazine as well as sections on her African experience, photographs, and three interviews in 1967, 1969, and 1971.

0519 Brooks, Van Wyck   **1886-1963**
Days of the phoenix: the nineteen-twenties I remember. New York: E.P. Dutton and Co., Inc., 1967. (1957) 193 p.
   Because he lived at the center of the literary world, his personal reminiscences are also literary history, including his experience with such writers as Lewis Mumford, Sinclair Lewis, Sherwood Anderson, and Theodore Dreiser.

0520 Brooks, Van Wyck   **1886-1963**
From the shadow of the mountain: my post-meridian years. New York: E.P. Dutton & Co., Inc., 1961. 202 p.
   The third volume of the essayist's autobiography concerns his life from 1931, when he returned to normal life after four years in mental hospitals, until 1961.

0521 Brooks, Van Wyck   **1886-1963**
Scenes and portraits: memories of childhood and youth. New York: E.P. Dutton and Co., Inc., 1954. 243 p.
   Recollections of his boyhood and early years to 1914, including his

years at Harvard, his close friendship with Maxwell Perkins, and many prominent artists and intellectuals.

0522 Brooks, Van Wyck   **1886-1963**
Van Wyck Brooks: an autobiography. Foreward by John Hall Wheelock. Introduction by Malcolm Cowley. New York: E.P. Dutton & Co., Inc., 1965. 667 p. Index.
Brooks' autobiographical trilogy describing his life and literary America from the early 1900's to the 1960's— *Scenes and Portraits, Days of the Phoenix,* and *From the Shadow of the Mountains.*

0523 Brooks, Van Wyck   **1886-1963**
Van Wyck Brooks-Lewis Mumford letters: the record of a literary friendship, 1921-1963. Edited by Robert E. Spiller. New York: Dutton, 1970. 461 p. Index.
This collection is unique, according to its editor, "in that it is so unliterary in the usual sense of gossip, incidental literary criticism, and the thrill of entree to the mysterious but nondescript world of literary and artistic personalities." The letters document a deep and moving friendship.

0524 *Brookter, Marie   **1934-**
Here I am take my hand. With Jean Curtis. New York: Harper & Row Publishers, 1974. 248 p. Index.
Although she had previously worked in several election campaigns, her book concerns primarily her work for the George McGovern campaign when she became the first Black advance woman. She describes her duties as publicist for the Women's Rights Division and the frustrations and triumphs of the campaigns.

0525 Broonzy, William   **1893-1958**
Big Bill blues: William Broonzy's story as told to Yannick Bruynoghe.- Foreword by Charles Edward Smith. Introduction by Yannick Bruynoghe. Revised discography by A.J. McCarthy and Ken Harrison. Rev. ed. New York: Oak Publications, 1964. (London: Cassell, 1955) 176 p.
Big Bill Broonzy tells fascinating tales about his development as a country blues singer and guitar player, showing how many of his over three-hundred songs lamented painful incidents in his life or the lives of his friends and lovers. Among the musician friends he describes are Washboard Sam, Tampa Red, and Memphis Minnie.

0526 *Brophy, Eliza (St. John)   **1862-1949**
Twice a pioneer. Introduction by Margaret E. Venne. New York: Exposition, 1972. 125 p.
Stories of homestead life in Minnesota and South Dakota, originally published serially in *The Dakota Farmer* (1945-46).

0527 Brophy, John   **1883-1963**
A miner's life, an autobiography. Edited and supplemented by John O.P. Hall. Madison: University of Wisconsin Press, 1964. 320 p. Index.
Brophy, the CIO's full-time director until 1939, was in the forefront of every organizing campaign 1933-1939. He fought for the eight-hour day, campaigned to become president of the UMW, and was part of the early organization of the CIO. He continued his work on various special assigments until his death.

0528 Brosnan, James Patrick   **1929-**
The long season. New York: Harper and Brothers, 1960. 273 p. Index.
A personal account of the 1959 baseball season, written by a pitcher for the Cincinnati Reds.

0529 Broun, Heywood Hale   **1918-**
A studied madness. Sagaponack, New York: Second Chance Press, 1979. (Garden City, New York: Doubleday, 1965) 298 p.
Broun describes his experiences as an actor of stage, screen, and television; his views on the theater (both from the actor's and the writer's perspectives); and, from his background as a sports writer, makes comparisons between acting, horseracing, and baseball.

0530 Broun, Heywood Hale   **1918-**
Tumultuous merriment. New York: Richard Marek Publishers, 1979. 278 p.
A popular news and sportscaster writes of his working life, with special attention to the ways in which sports has become a business.

0531 Brousch, John J.   **1913-**
John J. Brousch, conqueror of adversity; an autobiography. Minneapolis: T.S. Denison & Co., 1966. 307 p.
Written to show that "with a little common sense, everyone can change his level of thinking and rise to a higher plane of living through a program of personal growth," Brousch's book offers advice illustrated by his own experience on how to conquer oneself, how to profit from illiterate qualities of others, how and what to read, the value of a liberal education and of realizing one's best potential.

0532 Browder, Earl Russell   **1891-1973**
Contempt of Congress: the trial of Earl Browder. Introduction by Louis B. Bouden. Yonkers, New York: Earl Russell Browder, 1951. 192 p.
In the record of his trial and acquittal for contempt of Congress charges, the author cites his belief in Marxist principles, his objections to the paths taken by American communists, and his belief in challenging the Senate Committee rather than invoking the Fifth Amendment.

0533 Brower, Charles Hendrickson (Charlie)   **1901-**
Me, and other advertising geniuses. Garden City, New York: Doubleday & Co., Inc., 1974. 230 p.
A brisk, exuberant narrative of his forty-year career in advertising. He includes stories of his work in newspapers, radio, and television.

0534 Brown, Addison   **1830-1913**
Judge Addison Brown; autobiographical notes for his children. Boyce, Virginia: Carr Publishing Co, 1972. 193 p.
He describes growing up in nineteenth-century Massachusetts, establishing his law practice in New York in 1854, his long years of practice as a lawyer and judge, with sections on the Civil War, notable buildings and events in early New York, and comments on world affairs.

0535 Brown, Arthur Judson   **1856-1963**
Memoirs of a centenarian. Edited by William N. Wysham. New York: World Horizons, 1957. 174 p.
Dr. Brown writes eloquently of his extraordinarily active and distinguished career as a clergyman for twelve years in Wisconsin, Illinois, and Portland, Oregon. Until retirement, he was Secretary to the Board of Foreign Missions of the Presbyterian Church.

0536 Brown, Clinton Giddings   **b.1882**
You may take the witness. Illustrated by Doug Anderson. Austin: University of Texas Press, 1955 223 p.
A vivid, fast-moving account of the author's courtroom experiences as a trial lawyer in San Antonio, written to entertain the general reader rather than a legal audience, though Brown articulately discusses courtroom strategy. His most notable case was Morris Fishbein, M.D. vs. Dr. John R. Brinkley, a proven fraud who implanted goat glands allegedly to restore male potency. Brown won.

0537 Brown, Edmund Gerald   **1905-**
Reagan and reality: the two Californias. New York: Praeger, 1970. 235 p. Index.
Published just prior to the 1970 California gubernatorial election, this book offers Brown's admittedly "unobjective" appraisal of Reagan's first term in office by comparing it to his own performance as Governor and his own perception of California history.

0538 *Brown, Estelle Aubrey   **1876-1958**
Stubborn fool: a narrative. Caldwell, Idaho: The Caxton Printers, Ltd., 1952. 309 p.
A narrative of her sixteen years with the Indian Service working administratively on reservations in South Dakota and Arizona, and her subsequent indictment of its exploitation of the rights of American Indians.

0539 Brown, H. Rap   **1943-**
Die, Nigger, die! New York: Dial Press, 1969. 145 p.
Distinguishing between whites, Blacks, and Negroes, i.e., institutionalized Blacks who are allied with whites, Brown advocates violence, militancy, and whatever means are necessary to secure freedom and destroy the system that oppresses Black people.

0540 Brown, Jack   **1911-**
Monkey off my back: an ex-convict and addict relates his discovery of personal freedom. As told to Allen Groff. Grand Rapids, Michigan: Zondervan Publishing House, 1971. 150 p.
The grim details of his life as a criminal and dope addict, with graphic descriptions of his experience in various prisons, including one in which he shared a cell with Clyde Barrow. Written by a born-again Christian devoting his life to exposing the horrors of drugs and crime.

0541 Brown, James   **1698-1739**
Letter book of James Brown, of Providence, merchant, 1735-1738: from the original manuscript in the library of the Rhode Island Historical Society. Introduction by George Philip Krapp. Freeport, New York: Books for Libraries Press, 1971. (Providence: Printed for the Rhode Island Historical Society, 1929) 66 p.
Details of his merchandise business reveal very little of his personal life.

0542 Brown, Joe Evan   **1892-1973**
Laughter is a wonderful thing. As told to Ralph Hancock. New York: A.S. Barnes and Co., 1956. 312 p. Index.
The story of his development as a comedian and actor, through circus days and vaudeville, stage and screen.

0543 Brown, John Mason   **1900-1969**
Morning faces: a book of children and parents. New York: Whittlesey House, 1949. 187 p.
   Narrative chapters, most previously printed in *The Saturday Review of Literature,* describe the interactions of father and two sons growing up together.

0544 *Brown, Julia Clarise
I testify; my years as an undercover agent for the F.B.I. Boston: Western Islands, 1966. 293 p.
   From 1951 to 1960 Mrs. Brown, as an FBI confidential agent, was inside the communist network. She worked in various subversive organizations, met many top Party functionaries, and reported her activities and contacts to the FBI. This book tells of those activities and of her testimony in 1962 before the House Committee on Un-American Activities.

0545 Brown, Karl   **1897?-**
Adventures with D.W. Griffith. New York: Farrar, Straus and Giroux, 1973. 251 p. Index.
   During his fifty years in the motion-picture business Brown was an important part of cinema history. He was assistant cameraman on all of the D.W. Griffith pictures from 1913 until World War I and later photographed *The Covered Wagon* and directed *Stark Love,* a documentary filmed in the mountains of North Carolina. His book contains vivid reminiscences about the people and the history of film-making.

0546 *Brown, Lilian (MacLaughlin)   **b.1880**
I married a dinosaur. Introduction by Roy Chapman Andrews. New York: Dodd, Mead and Co., 1950. 268 p.
   Humorous account of her first four years of marriage, spent fossil hunting in India and Burma, by a young woman called Pixie by her husband, whom she met and married in India.

0547 Brown, Paul   **1908-**
P.B.: the Paul Brown story. With Jack Clary. Illustrated. New York: Athcneum, 1979. 338 p.
   This forthright, good-natured account of Brown's career as a football coach exemplifies his philosophy that "everything we do must be in terms of our team and doing our best." He moved from high school coaching in the 1930's (Severn-Maryland-Preparatory) to college coaching in the 1940's (Ohio State), to leading the Cleveland Browns to eleven championships in the 1950's and 60's. After being fired by owner Art Modell in a power struggle, he concluded his career as coach and manager of the Cincinnati Bengals.

0548 Brown, Rollo Walter   **1880-1956**
The hills are strong. Boston: Beacon Press, 1952. 238 p.
   A writer and teacher recalls growing up in southeastern Ohio, the events which contributed to his maturity, and his development as an author.

0549 Brown, Silas   **fl.1805-1815**
Aaron Burr expedition: letters to Ephraim Brown from Silas Brown, 1805-1815. Mansfield, Ohio: Mrs. Michael D. Harter, 19??. 46 p.
   Silas Brown left upstate New York as a member of Aaron Burr's expedition to Mississippi in 1908. Brown is aware of Burr's indictment for treason and acquittal; but he is evasive about his connections with Burr and the nature of their enterprise, despite occasional diatribes against slavery.

0550 Brown, William Wells   **1815-1884**
Narrative of William W. Brown: a fugitive slave, and a lecture delivered before the Female Anti-Slave Society of Salem, 1847. Introduction by Larry Gara. Reading, Massachusetts: Addison-Wesley Publishing Co., 1969. (Boston: The Anti-Slavery Office, 1847) 98 p.
   This book by a Kentucky-born slave became a best seller in 1847; two years later he published *Clotel, or the President's Daughter,* the first novel published by an American Negro. His writing is detailed and effective.

0551 Browne, John Ross   **1821-1875**
A dangerous journey: California 1849. Palo Alto: Arthur Lites Press, 1950. 93 p.
   The natural beauty and violence among men and animals recorded during his mule trip between San Francisco and San Luis Obispo in the summer of 1849 as a revenue agent.

0552 Browne, John Ross   **1821-1875**
J. Ross Browne: his letters, journals and writings. Edited with introduction and commentary by Lina Fergusson Browne. Albuquerque: University of New Mexico Press, 1969. 419 p. Index.
   Assessing his limitations and capabilities early in life, Browne set out to accomplish two ambitions: to see the world and to become a writer. He succeeded in both by traveling over most of the then-known world and by writing humorous and shrewd accounts of what he saw.

0553 Browne, John Ross   **1821-1875**
Yusef: or, the journey of the Frangi: a crusade in the East. Series: Amer-

ica and the Holy Land. New York: Arno Press, 1977. (New York: Harper & Bros., 1853) 421 p.
   Browne, an inveterate traveler and sometime statistician, writes with zest and American chauvinism about his trip, c. 1851, to Sicily, Greece, Turkey, Syria, Lebanon, and the Holy Land. He describes in detail the local manners and mores—some curious, many pleasant, some horrifying.

0554 *Browne, Martha (Griffith)   **d.1906**
Autobiography of a female slave. Detroit: Negro Historical Press, 1971? (New York: Redfield, 1857) 401 p.
   Although somewhat melodramatic in style, this is an excellent narrative of slave life, its pain and degradation, written by a woman finally freed by the death of her mistress, who left her a legacy enabling her to move to Massachusetts where she became a teacher of Black children.

0555 Browning, Meshach   **1781-1859**
Forty-four years of the life of a hunter: being reminiscences of Meshach Browning, a Maryland hunter, roughly written down by himself. Middle Atlantic States Historical Publications. Revised and illustrated by E. Stabler. Port Washington, New York: Kennikat Press, 1972. (Philadelphia: J.B. Lippincott Co., 1859) 400 p.
   A remarkable record of early nineteenth-century life in the Maryland mountains, written in an interesting and readable style by a hunter who survived the severe conditions of wilderness life and isolation and who left a legacy of eleven children.

0556 Brownlow, Louis   **1879-1963**
Autobiography of Louis Brownlow. Chicago: University of Chicago Press, 1955-1958. 2v. Index.
   Volume I is a detailed account of the author's childhood in Missouri, his informal education, and his career as a journalist in Tennessee and Washington, D.C. to 1915. Volume II (1915-1945) details his experience in several city governments, including his close contact with Woodrow Wilson and Franklin D. Roosevelt.

0557 Brownson, Orestes Augustus   **1803-1876**
Brownson-Hecker correspondence. Edited with introduction by Joseph F. Gower and Richard M. Leliaert. Illustrated. Notre Dame, Indiana: University of Notre Dame Press, 1979. 345 p. Index.
   The editors have provided extensive notes, biographical sketches, a history of the correspondence, and an appendix to this collection of letters dating from 1841-1872. Brownson, a Boston editor, and Hecker, a Manhattan banker, converted to Roman Catholicism and became devoted to spreading the Catholic faith in the United States.

0558 Broyles, Frank   **1924-**
Hog wild: the autobiography of Frank Broyles. With Jim Bailey. Illustrated. Memphis, Tennessee: Memphis State University Press, 1979. 200 p.
   The athletic director for the Arkansas Razorbacks gives a play-by-play account of his career, both as Georgia Tech football player and in assistant and head coach positions. He recalls many college football games in detail and provides an account of the lifestyle of a coach's family.

0559 *Bruce, Honey Harriet
Honey: the life and loves of Lenny's shady lady. With Dana Benenson. Edited with Bob McKendrick. Chicago: Playboy Press, 1976. 309 p.
   The extraordinarily sordid life of Lenny Bruce's wife for six years. Her adulthood began with a year's sentence in Raiford (Florida) State Penitentiary. Later she worked as a carnival dancer, strip-tease artist, and prostitute. She and Bruce were both addicted to heroin which she quit after his premature death.

0560 Bruce, Lenny   **1925-1966**
How to talk dirty and influence people; an autobiography. Chicago: Playboy Press, 1965. 188 p.
   Some people found Bruce's comedy offensive, some, self-indulgent; some thought him creative and some, obscene and subversive. Most, however, agreed that he was free-speaking and uninhibited, unafraid of shocking audiences and breaking taboos.

0561 *Brucker, Clara H.   **1897-**
To have your cake and eat it. Illustrated. New York: Vantage Press, 1968. 378 p.
   The wife of Wilber M. Brucker describes the social activities and trips (to Europe, the Far East, the Middle East, and around the United States) she participated in while her husband was Secretary of the Army, 1955-61.

0562 Bruff, Joseph Goldsborough   **1804-1889**
Gold Rush: the journals, drawings, and other papers of J. Goldsborough Bruff, Captain, Washington City and California Mining Association, April 2, 1849-July 20, 1851. Edited by Georgia Willis Read and Ruth Gaines. New York: Columbia University Press, 1944. 2v. Index.
   A life-long resident of Washington, D.C., in 1849 he was intrigued by the discovery of gold and formed a mining company. Based on diaries of his overland journey, his extensive journals were revised for publication

when he returned, penniless, to his job as a draftsman for the Bureau of Topographical Engineers. Includes elaborate historical and critical notes.

0563 Brunn, Fritz   **b.1888**
Memoirs of a doctor of the old and new worlds. New York: Crambruck Press, 1969. 135 p.
    After describing his boyhood, medical education, practice, and family life in Vienna, he writes of his immigration to New York in 1938 and the Austrian-American synthesis in his private and professional life.

0564 Brunner, Edmund de Schweintz   **1889-1973**
As now remembered: the interesting life of an average man. N.P.: the author, 1968. 302 p.
    The book describes his personal and professional life, focusing on his contributions to social research.

0565 Brunson, Howard   **b.1884**
The oilman who didn't want to become a millionaire: his own story. New York: Exposition Press, 1955. 84 p.
    Brunson was reared on a Mississippi cotton farm during the Reconstruction and for thirty years worked for others on oil fields in California, Oklahoma, and Texas. At 50 he formed his own company and nearly went broke before making a million dollars. Brunson takes pride in his honesty, family, and coaching baseball.

0566 *Bryan, Mary Baird
    see Bryan, William Jennings

0567 Bryan, William Jennings   **1869-1925**
Memoirs of William Jennings Bryan: by himself and his wife. And Mary Baird Bryan. New York: Port Washington, Kennikat Press, 1971. (Philadelphia: The John C. Winston Co., 1925) 2v. Index.
    Bryan left only a first draft of his life story through his college years. His wife Mary completed their memoirs, using his correspondence, documents, and her diary, leaving an interesting record of their personal and political lives.

0568 *Bryant, Anita   **1940-**
Amazing grace. Old Tappan, New Jersey: Fleming H. Revell Co., 1971. 127 p.
    A spiritual testimony of her Christian faith is based on incidents demonstrating how her faith works.

0569 *Bryant, Anita   **1940-**
Mine eyes have seen the glory. Old Tappan, New Jersey: Fleming H. Revell Co., 1970. 159 p.
    Her childhood in Oklahoma, the Miss America title, her singing career, and marriage are described in the context of Christian witness.

0570 Bryant, Traphes
Dog days at the White House; the outrageous memoirs of the presidential kennel keeper. With Frances Spatz Leighton. New York: Macmillan Publishing Co., 1975. 343 p. Index.
    The White House kennel keeper and electrician tells anecdotes about the presidents, their families, their pets, and their idiosyncracies.

0571 Bryant, William Cullen   **1794-1878**
The letters of William Cullen Bryant. Edited by William Cullen Bryant II and Thomas G. Voss. New York: Fordham University Press, 1975-. v. Index.
    The poet-journalist's letters are written to his wife, Frances, his literary confidante, Richard Henry Dana, and other friends; they comment extensively on literature, politics, and travel.

0572 Bryant, William Cullen   **1794-1878**
William Cullen Bryant and Isaac Henderson: new evidence of a strange partnership; twenty-one letters hitherto unprinted. Edited with introduction and notes by Theodore Hornberger. Austin: University of Texas Library, 1950. 44 p.
    Written between 1852 and 1873, the collection includes letters from Bryant to Henderson, to the New York *Evening Post*, to his caretaker, and many from Bryant and his daughter Julia to the Hendersons during their European tour (1866-67) after Mrs. Bryant's death.

0573 Buaken, Manuel
I have lived with the American people. Caldwell, Idaho: The Caxton Printers, Ltd., 1948. 358 p.
    He writes of his experience as a well-educated Filipino immigrant confronted by American prejudice against Orientals, chiefly in California. In describing his own life he expands his story to include many of other Filipinos, with a plea for better understanding and acceptance in the U.S.

0574 Bubis, J.L.   **1885-1957**
Women are my problem: the autobiography of an obstetrician and gynecologist. Illustrated. New York: Comet Press Books, 1953. 223 p.
    After discussing his childhood and medical training in Cleveland, an obstetrician-gynecologist devotes considerable space to defending and justifying the then radical medical philosophy and techniques of gyneplastic repairs and puerperal gynecology.

0575 Buchanan, James   **1791-1868**
Mr. Buchanan's administration on the eve of the rebellion. Freeport, New York: Books for Libraries Press, 1970. (New York: Appleton and Co., 1866) 296 p.
    Buchanan's formal interpretation of events leading up to the Civil War, filled with excerpts from government documents, is intended to prove that the Northern abolitionists caused not only the Civil War, but most of the country's problems thereafter. He claims that on all occasions he tried to warn his countrymen of this hazard and to tell them to accept compromise rather than to go to war, but "Congress disregarded all the recommendations."

0576 Buchanan, Jerreal B.   **1927-**
Who's calling my name? Nashville, Tennessee: Broadman Press, 1977. 154 p.
    In a series of good-natured parable-like chapters, Buchanan analyzes his "Type A" personality, hard-working, competitive, hyperactive and hyper-reactive to the emotional stress of being a Baptist clergyman.

0577 Buchanan, Joseph Ray   **1851-1924**
The story of a labor agitator. New York: Freeport, Books for Libraries Press, 1971. (New York: the Outlook Co., 1903) 460 p.
    Born in Hannibal, Missouri, he worked on a newspaper there, then in Denver and Leadville, Colorado, where he joined a trade union and soon became prominent as a union organizer. A detailed, readable document for labor history.

0578 Buchanan, Wiley Thomas, Jr.   **1914-**
Red carpet at the White House: four years as Chief of Protocol in the Eisenhower administration. With Arthur Gordon. New York: E.P. Dutton & Co., Inc., 1964. 256 p. Index.
    A behind-the-scenes look at state visits to the White House by foreign dignitaries, written by the Protocol Chief during the second Eisenhower term, 1959-1961.

0579 Bucher, Lloyd Mark   **1927-**
Bucher: my story. With Mark Rascovich. Garden City, New York: Doubleday & Co., 1970. 447 p.
    Bucher was commander of the U.S.S. *Pueblo* which in January 1968 was seized by the North Koreans. Here he writes of that international incident, his eleven-month captivity with his crew, their release, and the Court of Inquiry which followed. Appendixes give crew personnel lists, "confessions," statements, and reports.

0580 *Buck, Pearl (Sydenstricker)   **1892-1973**
American argument. With Eslanda Goode Robeson. New York: The John Day Co., 1949. 206 p.
    An autobiographical dialogue by Buck, a white author raised in China, and Robeson, a Black author raised in the United States, in which they explore the values which formed their characters and the differing ways in which they confront difficult contemporary issues.

0581 *Buck, Pearl (Sydenstricker)   **1892-1973**
A bridge for passing. New York: The John Day Co., 1961. 256 p.
    The story of her return to Japan to work on the filming of her book, *The Big Wave*. A sensitive understanding of the people and an appreciation of Japanese ways.

0582 *Buck, Pearl (Sydenstricker)   **1892-1973**
The child who never grew. New York: The John Day Co., 1950. 62 p.
    Published first as an article in *Ladies Home Journal*, the book is an account of awareness and accommodation to her child's lack of mental development.

0583 *Buck, Pearl (Sydenstricker)   **1892-1973**
My several worlds: a personal record. New York: John Day, 1954. 407 p.
    A Nobel Prize-winning novelist looks back upon her childhood in China and the various visits she made to that country. She describes the experience of being an American physically but Chinese mentally, and the process of finally becoming completely American. Her account spans the time from the Boxer Rebellion to 1953, includes her reactions to American foreign policy concerning China, and indicates how China influenced her life in the United States.

0584 Buckingham, Joseph Tinker   **1779-1861**
Personal memoirs and recollections of editorial life. New York: Arno Press, 1970. (Boston: Ticknor, Reed, and Fields, 1852) 2v.
    These memoirs of his life in printing, publishing, and editing speak of hardships, failures, discouragements, but ultimate satisfactions of a stern, upright man. Includes excerpts from his editorials and articles.

0585 Buckley, William Frank, Jr.   1925-
Airborne: a sentimental journey. New York: Macmillan and Co., 1976. 252 p.
In new journalistic style, laced with pithy observations, and with wit more gentle than acerbic, Buckley narrates the transatlantic voyage of his sailboat *Cyrano* with its crew of six. In the process, he gives his history as a sailor since age 13 and analyzes his close relationships with his wife and son, Christopher.

0586 Buckley, William Frank, Jr.   1925-
United Nations journal; a delegate's odyssey. Garden City, New York: Anchor, 1977. (New York: G.P. Putnam's Sons, 1974) 280 p. Index.
As a member of the U.S. Delegation to the UN General Assembly for three months during 1973, the author saw diplomacy at work. Here he writes a readable and informative analysis of his experiences, including discussions about Cuba, the Mideast War, human rights, African art, and freedom of information.

0587 Buckley, William Frank, Jr.   1925-
The unmaking of a mayor. New York: The Viking Press, 1966. 341 p. Index.
In the 1965 New York mayoralty elections, the voters chose among Lindsay, Beame, and Buckley. Here is Buckley's account of his campaign and the events that led to that election day.

0588 Buckskin Joe
see Hoyt, Edward Jonathan

0589 Budenz, Louis Francis   1891-1972
This is my story. New York: Whittlesey House, 1947. 371 p.
Budenz describes the rationale of his conversion to the Catholic Church. After eleven years in the Communist Party, he resigned as party member and managing editor of the *Daily Worker* to write and teach at Notre Dame and Fordham Universities. The book includes detailed narrative of the conflict between the Catholic worker and the Communist Party; it describes issues and leadership of the C.P. chiefly between 1934 and 1945.

0590 Budge, Donald   1915-
Don Budge: a tennis memoir. With Frank DeFord. Illustrated. New York: The Viking Press, 1969. 184 p. Index.
Budge describes various key tennis matches he played at Forest Hills and Wimbledon, including "the greatest match"—a decisive Davis Cup match in 1937 against Baron Gottfried von Cramm. Interspersed with an account of his professional career is advice on how to play good tennis—singles, doubles, on grass and clay courts—and an explanation of Budge's "grand slam."

0591 Buel, Clarence Clough   1850-1933
The memoirs of Clarence Clough Buel, 1850-1933: condensed from the original manuscript entitled "Sixty Years with the Press." Edited and illustrated by Richard Van Wyck Buel. Tucson, Arizona: Richard Van Wyck Buel, 1967. 165 p.
Unfortunately, only twenty-four copies were printed of this engaging narrative of Buel's life as an English immigrant to Wisconsin, at college in Berlin, as a reporter on the Minneapolis *Tribune*, where "every day [was] a holiday to a reporter." In 1875, he began work on the New York *Herald*, where he interviewed, among others, Mark Twain and politicians such as Congressman Abram S. Hewitt and Senator James G. Blaine. He wrote copiously for periodicals, was associate editor of the *Century Magazine*, knew all the Boston and New York literati, and had a wonderful time.

0592 Buffalo Bill, pseud.
see Cody, William Frederick

0593 *Buford, Harry T., Lieut., pseud.
see *Velazqez, Loreta Janeta

0594 Bulfinch, Charles   1763-1884
The life and letters of Charles Bulfinch, architect, with other family papers. Edited by his granddaughter, Ellen Susan Bulfinch. Introduction by Charles A. Cummings. New York: Burt Franklin, 1973. (Boston: Houghton, 1896) 323 p. Index.
A leading architect in Boston, he designed Boston's first theater, the State House on Beacon Hill, and was appointed to complete the work which Benjamin Latrobe had begun on the National Capitol in Washington. This volume combines diary entries and letters to depict his life chronologically. He was at the time the only architect in New England.

0595 Bullitt, William C
see Roosevelt, Franklin Delano

0596 Bulosan, Carlos   1914-1956
America is in the heart: a personal history. Seattle: University of Washington Press, 1973. (New York: Harcourt, Brace and Co., Inc., 1946) 326 p.
Describes growing up in a poor Filipino village, immigrating to America in the 1920's where he was sold to an Alaskan cannery contractor for $5, working his way down to California where life was never made easier by the difficulties of racial bias, poverty, and labor union conflicts. Seriously ill most of his life, he read widely in American and European literature and finally published his own poetry and fiction.

0597 Bunning, James Paul David   1931-
The story of Jim Bunning. As told to Ralph Bernstein. Philadelphia: J.B. Lippincott Co., 1965. 180 p.
The sixth pitcher in modern major league baseball to pitch a perfect game, i.e., no runner reached base, Bunning tells the story of his rise in baseball in chapters separated by inning-by-inning accounts of that perfect game.

0598 Burgess, Fred E.   1892-
Memoirs of eighty years of farming. Philadelphia: Dorrance & Co., 1974. 131 p.
A story of farm and country living in Oregon and Washington during the first half of the twentieth century.

0599 Burgess, Thornton Waldo   1874-1965
Now I remember: autobiography of an amateur naturalist. Boston: Little, Brown & Co., 1960. 338 p.
Famous as the author of Mother West Wind books for children, he writes here of his childhood days on Cape Cod, his clerking days in Boston, and the gradual development of his career as a writer of over seventy books and more than 15,000 newspaper "Bedtime Stories."

0600 Burk, Wayne
The thief: the autobiography of Wayne Burk. As told to Ted Thackrey, Jr. Los Angeles: Nash Publishing, 1971. 441 p.
Written from interviews and police documents, the book portrays the life of a professional thief and gunman who considers himself happy and successful. At time of publication, he was a fugitive.

0601 *Burke, Billie   1885-1970
With a feather on my nose. With Cameron Shipp. New York: Appleton-Century-Crofts, Inc., 1949. 272 p.
Describes her career on stage, 1903-1944, her marriage to Florenz Ziegfeld, Jr., with details of theater life and people in this period. Includes a brief description of current work in radio and film, showing a sharp if nostalgic contrast between the older, more refined life and the newer, more artificial Hollywood mode. She views her caricature of the "bird-witted lady" as incidental in her long career.

0602 *Burke, Billie   1886-1970
With powder on my nose. New York: Coward McCann, 1959. 249 p.
Her second book explains her mode of being a feminine woman, the techniques of maintaining that appearance, and the values that appearance represents.

0603 *Burke, DeAnn
see Burke, Todd

0604 Burke, Todd
Anointed for burial. And DeAnn Burke. Preface by Charles Farah, Jr. Foreword by John Garlock. Plainfield, New Jersey: Logos International, 1977. 259 p.
Burke and his wife describe their missionary activities for twenty months (1973-1975) in the Khmer Church (Cambodia) where they taught the Bible, oversaw faith healings, found homes for orphans, and performed other benevolent acts until forced to evacuate Phnom Penh in the communist takeover. This book abounds in parables and other forms of religious instruction.

0605 *Burks, Lorna Doone   1900-1945
I die daily: the story of a woman whose love will live forever. Edited by Arthur J. Burks. New York: Rockport Press, Inc., 1946. 208 p.
Moving account of the year before her death by cancer of the uterus.

0606 Burlingame, Roger   1889-1967
I have known many worlds. Garden City, New York: Doubleday and Co., Inc., 1959. 283 p.
Burlingame thoughtfully explains how his career as a writer evolved from his family background (his father edited *Scribner's Magazine*), tastes, talents, and experience. He wrote fiction in Italy and Paris during the late 1920's and early 1930's, then married, settled in Connecticut, and shifted to writing about technology.

0607 Burnett, Peter Hardeman   1807-1895
Recollections and opinions of an old pioneer. New York: Da Capo Press, 1969. (New York: D. Appleton and Co., 1880) 448 p.
Boyhood in Missouri; pioneer in Oregon; jurist and politician in Oregon and California; first Governor of California.

0608 *Burns, Elizabeth 1894?-
The late Liz: the autobiography of an ex-pagan. 2nd ed. New York: Meredith Press, 1968. (New York: Appleton-Century Crofts, 1957) 342 p.
A slangy, semi-tough account of the author's three affluent marriages, three divorces, and two children, one highly religious, one estranged. The narrative culminates in her suicide attempt, cancer operations, addiction to alcohol and pills, sobriety, and discovery of lifesaving evangelical religion.

0609 Burns, George 1896-
I love her, that's why!: an autobiography. With Cynthia Hobart Lindsay. Prologue by Jack Benny. New York: Simon and Schuster, 1955. 267 p. Index.
After a brief description of his early life, he writes mostly of his career as an actor and comedian on stage, radio, and film, with his wife and partner, Gracie Allen.

0610 Burns, George 1896-
Living it up: or, they still love me in Altoona! With Elon Packard and Jack Langdon. New York: G.P. Putnam's Sons, 1976. 251 p.
An account, laden with anecdotes and comedy routines, of comedian George Burns' 72-year career, from the vaudeville circuit to the Palace Theater, to the Burns and Allen and George Burns radio shows, to the movie, *The Sunshine Boys*.

0611 Burr, Aaron 1756-1836
Memoirs of Aaron Burr: with miscellaneous selections from his correspondence. By Matthew L. Davis. New York: Da Capo Press, 1971. (New York: Harper & Brothers, 1836-37) 2v.
Burr turned all of his papers and correspondence over to Davis, who then wrote the "memoirs" and controlled what should not be included, e.g., notes revealing Burr's strong dislike of George Washington.

0612 Burr, Aaron 1756-1836
Private journal of Aaron Burr: during his residence of four years in Europe; with selections from his correspondence. Edited by Matthew L. Davis. Upper Saddle River, New Jersey: Literature House, 1970. (New York: Harper & Brothers, 1838) 2v.
Burr was living in Europe after being found not guilty of treason or a misdemeanor in his fatal duel with Alexander Hamilton. Originally written for his daughter, this is an excellent record of early nineteenth-century life and travel.

0613 Burroughs, John 1837-1921
John Burroughs' America: selections from the writings of the Hudson River naturalist. Edited with an introduction by Farida A. Wiley. Foreword by Julian Burroughs. New York: Devin-Adair Co., 1951. 304 p. Index.
In a selection of essays from his many published books, the author talks about what he sees and thinks about in the natural world around him.

0614 *Burrow, Brunettie
I lay down my cap. San Antonio: The Naylor Co., 1961. 96 p.
The story of her 25 years as a registered nurse, her courage, drive, and common sense.

0615 Burrow, Trigant 1875-1950
A search for man's sanity: selected letters; with biographical notes. Prepared by the Editorial Committee of the Lifwynn Foundation: William E. Galt, Chairman. Foreword by Sir Herbert Read. New York: Oxford University Press, 1958. 615 p. Index.
A collection of letters by a prominent psychiatrist, selected to reveal the thought and feeling of a man engaged in the stress of daily analysis of group and individual behavior, a man genuinely interested in the arts as well as science and highly respected by his colleagues.

0616 Burrows, Abram S. 1910-
Honest, Abe: is there really no business like show business? Boston: Little, Brown, 1980. 369 p. Index.
Author, producer, director Burrows tells the story of his life, from salesman, gag writer, and Wall Street runner during the Great Depression to success in radio and television. Also an articulate drama critic, Burrows enjoys a host of Hollywood celebrity friends.

0617 Burstein, Samuel M. 1921-
Rabbi with wings. Illustrated. New York: Herzl Press, 1965. 134 p.
"The Flying Rabbi" describes four exciting years, 1948-51, when he worked in the fledgling state of Israel, helping to establish an air force and train pilots, as well as to teach aerodynamics, mathematics, physics, and English. With a patriotic Zionistic spirit, Burstein discusses the economic and military development and Sabra spirit of the new country.

0618 *Burton, Katherine (Kurz) 1890-1969
Next thing: autobiography and reminiscences. New York: Longmans, Green and Co., 1949. 246 p.
An author of several books related to Catholic heritage writes of her conversion to Catholicism, her childhood, her marriage to Harry Burton

(editor of *McCalls*), her devotion to the medical theories of Dr. John Henry Tilden.

0619 *Burton, Ruth Guthrie (Thomson) Harding b.1882
Three parts Scotch: an informal biography. Indianapolis, Indiana: The Bobbs-Merrill Co., 1946. 288 p.
A rambling, sentimental narrative by a New England woman describing her life, friends, and her poetry.

0620 Burtsell, Richard Lalor 1840-1912
Diary of Richard L. Burtsell, priest of New York: the early years, 1865-1868. Edited by Nelson J. Callahan. New York: Arno Press, 1978. 422 p.
Recording the day-to-day activities of a busy Catholic priest, the Burtsell diary reveals his concern for difficulties of church law, the parochial school system, celibacy among the clergy, and anti-Catholic bigotry.

0621 Bush, Vannevar 1890-
Pieces of the action. New York: Cassell, 1972. (New York: Morrow, 1970) 366 p. Index.
During a period of evolution, change, and the advancement of science and technology, Bush was a chief actor in his roles as inventor, educator, president of the Carnegie Institution of Washington, director of the Office of Scientific Research and Development, advisor to presidents, and chairman of Merck and Co.

0622 Butcher, Harry Cecil 1901-
My three years with Eisenhower: the personal diary of Captain Harry C. Butcher, USNR, naval aide to General Eisenhower, 1942-1945. New York: Simon & Schuster, 1946. 911 p. Index.
An inside story of the war against Germany and Italy by Eisenhower's naval aide.

0623 Butler, Pierce 1873-1955
Laurel Hill and later: the record of a teacher. New Orleans: Robert L. Crager and Co., 1954. 144 p.
Describes his education at Johns Hopkins and Oxford; professor of literature, and later Dean at Sophie Newcomb College, Tulane University.

0624 Butler, Pierce 1873-1955
Unhurried years: memories of the old Natchez region. Baton Rouge: Louisiana State University Press, 1948. 198 p.
Youth on family plantation near Natchez, Mississippi, 1873-93.

0625 Buttita, Tony
After the good gay times, Asheville—summer of '35: a season with F. Scott Fitzgerald. New York: The Viking Press, 1974. 173 p.
Reconstructed from his own notes of visits, events, encounters, phone calls, and letters, these recollections describe the author's life during the summer of 1935 when he became well acquainted with Fitzgerald.

0626 *Buxbaum, Katherine b.1885
Iowa outpost. Philadelphia: Dorrance and Co., 1948. 253 p.
A mixture of fact and fiction describing life in rural Iowa, specifically of a settlers' community in Lapham, their values, their religion, their recreation and routine life.

0627 Byrd, David Harold 1900-
I'm an endangered species: the autobiography of a free enterpriser. Houston: Pacesetter Press, 1978. 108 p.
Byrd has enjoyed life as a multimillionaire, partly through wildcat drilling of oil wells, for which he obtained leases through ruthless and flamboyant tactics. He married a millionaire's daughter, expanded his various businesses, and became active in the Civil Air Patrol and in philanthropic activities.

0628 Byrd, Harold Eugene
The Black experience in big business. Illustrated. Hicksville, New York: Exposition Press, 1977. 143 p.
Byrd, a Black electronics engineer with a Los Angeles firm, recounts various experiences of racial discrimination, promotion, and the reactions to his race by those he supervised. He describes his marriage and fatherhood and concludes with a survey justifying Affirmative Action programs.

0629 Byrd, Richard Evelyn 1888-1957
Discovery: the story of the second Byrd Antarctic expedition. Introduction by Claude A. Swanson. Freeport, New York: Books for Libraries Press, 1972. (New York: G.P. Putnam's Sons, 1935) 397 p. Index.
An eloquent memoir of the 1934 return voyage to Little America, Antarctica, with striking descriptions of the exploration, geological experiments, and the perils of survival.

0630 Byrd, William 1674-1744
London diary (1717-1721) and other writings. Edited by Louis B. Wright and Marion Tinling. New York: Oxford University Press, 1958. 647 p. Index.

Born in London, he studied law and in 1704 inherited his father's vast estates in Virginia, where he became a prominent leader in colonial America. His diary is meticulous in detail.

0631 Byrd, William   **1674-1744**
The secret diary of William Byrd of Westover, 1709-1712. Edited by Louis B. Wright and Marion Tinling. New York: Arno Press, 1972. (Richmond, Virginia: The Dietz Press, 1941) 622 p. Index.
One of the earliest extensive diaries by a Southern colonist, this work was written in shorthand by Byrd, a prominent planter. It presents a detailed narrative of colonial life in Tidewater Virginia at the beginning of the eighteenth century.

0632 Byrnes, James Francis   **1879-1972**
All in one lifetime. New York: Harper and Brothers, 1958. 432 p. Index.
The life of a distinguished statesman who served as Congressman, Senator, Supreme Court Justice, Secretary of State, and Governor of South Carolina.

0633 Byron, Ralph L.
Surgeon of hope. Preface by Jeanette Lockerbie. Foreword by Raymond C. Ortlund. Old Tappan, New Jersey: Fleming H. Revell Co., 1977. 159 p.
Byron's career as a surgeon at the City of Hope Hospital, Los Angeles, is permeated by his evangelical Christian faith, so strong that he risked court-martial for proselytizing when he was a doctor in the U.S. Marine Corps. The book also contains loving assessments by his wife and son of Bryon's surgical skill and faith.

0634 Cabell, James Branch   **1879-1958**
As I remember it: some epilogues in recollection. New York: The McBride Co., 1955. 243 p.
A narrative about his career as a writer, with extensive descriptions of his interactions with some of the people who most influenced him.

0635 Cabell, James Branch   **1879-1958**
Between friends: letters of James Branch Cabell and others. Edited by Padraic Colum & Margaret Freeman Cabell. Introduction by Carl Van Vechten. New York: Harcourt Brace & World, Inc., 1962. 304 p. Index.
Letters of authors during the post-World War I years reveal their varied opinions on numerous subjects, including Cabell's controversial novel, *Jurgen.*

0636 Cabell, James Branch   **1879-1959**
The letters of James Branch Cabell. Edited by Edward Wagenknecht. Norman: University of Oklahoma Press, 1975. 277 p. Index.
Most of the letters by a Southern novelist are to other literary figures, including Ellen Glasgow, Sinclair Lewis, Carl Van Doren, H.L. Mencken.

0637 Cabell, James Branch   **1879-1958**
Preface to the past. New York: R.M. McBride & Co., 1936. 309 p.
A collection of commentaries and notes, most originally accompanied the several volumes of Cabell's *Biography of the Life of Manuel.* Autobiographical material is strictly confined to the circumstances in which the volumes of the *Biography* were written. Occasional acerbic comments refer to contemporaries such as Howard Pyle, William Faulkner, and H.L. Mencken.

0638 Cabell, James Branch   **1879-1958**
Quiet, please. Gainesville: University of Florida Press, 1952. 105 p.
During short reflections about his feelings and thoughts on his past, the author's present old age is clearly described.

0639 Cabot, Thomas D.   **1898-**
Beggar on horseback: the autobiography of Thomas D. Cabot. Foreword by Robert S. McNamara. Illustrated. Boston: David R. Godine, 1979. 191 p.
Cabot carried on the tradition of his renowned Boston family by succeeding in business as chairman of the multinational Cabot Corporation, a firm producing carbon black by innovative methods. A prominent philanthropist, he was elected as Overseer of Harvard University for two terms. The author, his wife, children and friends enjoy worldwide travel, particularly if it involves sports—mountain climbing, backpacking, skiing, sailing, riding, whitewater canoeing—all in accord with Cabot's conservationist philosophy.

0640 Cacopardo, J. Jerry   **1910-**
Show me a miracle: the true story of a man who went from prison to pulpit. And Don Weldon. New York: E.P. Dutton and Co., Inc., 1961. 220 p.
In 1937 he was framed on a murder charge by his uncle. In 1952 he was finally cleared of the charge, began to study for the Presbyterian ministry, and was ordained in 1957.

0641 Cahan, Abraham   **1860-1951**
The education of Abraham Cahan. Translated from Yiddish by Leon Stein, Abraham P. Conan, Lynn Davison. Introduction by Leon Stein. Philadelphia: Jewish Publication Society of America, 1969. (New York: Forward Ass'n., 1926) 450 p. Index.
After immigrating from Lithuania, he became a teacher, lawyer, socialist agitator, trade unionist—precursors to his editorship of the *Jewish Daily Forward.* Cahan's concern with language and communication almost matches his concern for social justice. Yiddish title: *Bleter/fun mein leben.*

0642 *Cahill, Susan Girlinghausen
Earth angels: portraits from childhood and youth. New York: Harper and Row, 1976. 213 p.
In slangy prose, Cahill describes a succession of losses of faith throughout her Catholic childhood and adolescence, beginning with her discovery that Santa Claus was human. Cynical about her parochial education, Cahill nevertheless enters a nunnery, but leaves after a year, inspired by the secular activities of the Civil Rights Movement.

0643 *Caine, Lynn   **1927?-**
Widow. New York: William Morrow & Co., Inc., 1974. 222 p.
The author shares her experiences and feelings as a widow—"the emotions of bereavement that leave even the strongest psyche tattered." She writes of the onset of her husband's cancer, the months of illness, his death, the progression of her grief.

0644 *Calamity Jane
see ***Canary, Martha***

0645 Calder, Alexander   **1898-1976**
Calder; an autobiography with pictures. New York: Random House (Pantheon Books), 1977. (1966) 285 p.
Famous for his mobile and stabile sculptures, this artist first trained as an engineer. In his twenties he turned to art, creating intricately balanced and shaped structures which changed the direction of twentieth-century art.

0646 Caldwell, Charles   **1772-1853**
Autobiography of Charles Caldwell, M.D. Introduction by Lloyd G. Stevenson. Preface, notes and appendix by Harriot W. Warner. New York: Da Capo Press, 1968. (Philadelphia: Lippincott, Grambo, & Co., 1885) 454 p.
This is the hyperbolic, self-defensive autobiography of "the Horatio Alger of medicine, the enfant terrible of Philadelphia and the West, the fiercest and fightingest of pioneers, the non-stop medical orator." Caldwell was a physician in the War of 1812, professor at the Philadelphia Academy of Medicine and the medical schools of Louisville and Lexington, and a prolific author.

0647 Caldwell, Erskine   **1903-**
Call it experience: the years of learning how to write. New York: Duell, Sloan and Pearce, 1951. 239 p.
Beginning with his early days as a stringer for local Georgia newspapers, Caldwell describes the hard work getting started as a writer, publishing his first fiction, his collaborations with Margaret Bourke-White, and the difficult business of developing his career.

0648 *Caldwell, Janet Taylor (Max Reiner, pseud.)   **1900-**
Growing up tough. Old Greenwich, Connecticut: The Devin-Adair Company, 1971. 159 p.
One of the world's most widely read writers looks at her early years in England and America. Her story becomes a strange polemic for her anti-feminist stance.

0649 Calhoun, Jack   **1923-1945**
Somewhere the sun is shining. Edited by Beryl Calhoun. Foreword by E.R. Quesada. Afterthought by Fenton E. Calhoun. San Diego, California: Grossmont Press, 1976. 70 p.
Calhoun, a journalism major at the University of California, Berkeley, enlisted in the Army Air Force shortly after the bombing of Pearl Harbor and received flight training in Texas before being stationed in England and Belgium as a fighter pilot. His mother, editor of the collection, reports her son's death in battle on February 22, 1945.

0650 Calhoun, John Caldwell   **1782-1850**
The papers of John C. Calhoun. Edited, with preface and introduction by W. Edwin Hemphill. Columbia: University of South Carolina Press, 1959-. v. Index.
This thorough, scholarly collection of Calhoun's papers, mostly letters he wrote as Secretary of War under President Monroe, focuses on his presidential prospects and their gradual disappearance; relations between the U.S. government and various Indian tribes; monitoring the educational quality of the U.S. Military Academy at West Point; discussions of whether to establish military outposts in the Northwest; the Monroe Doctrine; and some minor aspects of his personal life—brief illnesses and trips. Twelve volumes covering the years through 1835 have been published through 1979.

0651 Calkins, Earnest Elmo   **b.1868**
"And hearing not—": annals of an adman. New York: Charles Scribner's Sons, 1946. 387 p.

Deaf from early childhood, the author writes of his difficult adjustment to the world with this handicap. He emphasizes that over six million people of the U.S. are seriously hard of hearing, causing considerable disadvantage in a society which carries on the business of living largely by speech.

0652 Calkins, Frank   **1932-**
Rocky Mountain warden. New York: Alfred A. Knopf, 1971. 265 p.

Primarily a description of life in southern rural Utah where he worked five years as a game warden, the book gives an earthy portrait of Western country life.

0653 Callahan, Kenneth   **1905-**
Kenneth Callahan: universal voyage. Edited by Michael R. Johnson. Introduction by James Harithas. Seattle: University of Washington Press, 1973. 79 p.

Primarily a collection of his paintings printed with a text edited from the recent tape recordings, lectures, and writings of a major artist in the Pacific Northwest, whose work is seen as primordial, metaphysical, mystical.

0654 Calley, William Laws   **1943-**
Lieutenant Calley: his own story. As told to John Sack. New York: Viking, 1971. 181 p.

He gives his own account of what happened before, during, and after the controversial incident in the village of Mylai, Vietnam, which resulted in a military jury finding him guilty of premeditated murder. (Also published as *Body Count: Lieutenant Calley's Story*, New York, Hutchinson, 1971).

0655 Calloway, Cab   **1907-**
Of Minnie the Moocher and me. With Bryant Rollins. New York: Thomas Y. Crowell and Co., 1976. 282 p.

Calloway tells of his exhilarating career as band leader and singer, which included fame, fortune, and bevies of females. He loved his work, which included a full roster of celebrities during the Jazz Age and the Big Band Era. Extended engagements at Harlem's Cotton Club marked his preeminence.

0656 *Calverley, Eleanor Jane (Taylor)   **1886-1968**
My Arabian days and nights. New York: Thomas Y. Crowell Co., 1958. 182 p.

Medical missionary describes her family and professional experience in Kuwait, where she was the first woman doctor (1912-1930).

0657 Cameron, James   **1911-**
Point of departure. Boston: Oriel Press, 1978. (New York: McGraw Hill, 1967) 318 p. Index.

English journalist Cameron writes a compelling philosophical account of his globetrotting career as a reporter of diverse and significant international events since World War II. He intermittently lived with American troops during the Korean and Vietnam wars and often visited America. Journalists, he says, walk "the agonizing narrow line between sincerity and technique, between the imperative and the glib."

0658 Campanella, Roy   **1921-**
It's good to be alive. Boston: Little, Brown and Co., 1959. 306 p.

Paralyzed by an accident in the prime of his career, a popular baseball player describes his early life, his years with the Brooklyn Dodgers, and the difficult recovery from total paralysis.

0659 *Campbell, Litta Belle (Hibben)   **b.1886**
Here I raise mine Ebenezer. New York: Simon and Schuster, 1963. 256 p.

Her life, character, and opinions are reflected in anecdotal sketches of her childhood, married family life, children, legal issues, and incidents related to her career as a lawyer.

0660 *Campbell, Litta Belle (Hibben)   **b.1886**
Marching without banners: and other devices. New York: Simon and Schuster, 1969. 192 p.

A loosely structured narrative which reads like a journal, with entries responding to particular events in her life after retiring from a legal career.

0661 Campbell, Tom W.   **b.1874**
Arkansas lawyer: reminiscences of a lifetime. Illustrated. Little Rock, Arkansas: Pioneer Publishing Co., 1952. 522 p.

Arkansas lawyer Tom Campbell recounts in abundant detail the highlights of his childhood in Randolph County and notable cases of his fifty-year law practice throughout Arkansas. Capsule biographies of friends and associates abound, as do pictures of county courthouses. Campbell concludes with an extensive account of his travels and an elaborate narrative of his abdominal surgery at the Mayo Clinic.

0662 Camuti, Louis J.   **1893-**
All my patients are under the bed: memoirs of a cat doctor. With Marilyn and Haskel Frankel. New York: Simon and Schuster, 1980. 222 p.

Veterinarian Camuti has spent sixty years treating cats—all house calls, which he believes reduces feline anxiety. He recounts his early years as a farm vet and an army vet, his decision to limit his practice to cats, and his frequent dealings with celebrities' pets. Camuti also discusses "cat people" as a social phenomenon.

0663 Canada, J.W.   **b.1871**
Life at eighty: memories and comments by a tarheel in Texas. LaPorte, Texas: J.W. Canada, 1952. 198 p.

Canada describes his childhood, youth, and college education in North Carolina, but focuses on his fifty years of farm work in Texas encouraging farm cooperatives, innovations in milk production and distribution, improved cattle breeding, and other reforms.

0664 *Canary, Martha (Calamity Jane)   **1850-1903**
Copies of Calamity Jane's diary and letters: taken from the originals now on display in the Treasures of the West Exhibit at the Wonderland Museum, Billings, Montana. Preface by Jean Hickok McCormick. Billings, Montana: Foote Pub. Co., 1951. (Billings: Western Trails, 1951) n.p.

In plain, straightforward language, Calamity Jane writes an annual letter to her daughter, Janey, fathered by Jane's first husband, Wild Bill Hickok. She assures Janey of her legitimacy: "You were not a woods colt, Janey, don't let any of these pusgutted blatherskites get by with that lie."

0665 Canby, Henry Seidel   **1878-1961**
American memoir. Boston: Houghton Mifflin Co., 1947. 433 p.

A perceptive, well-written analysis of his childhood in Wilmington, Delaware, in the 1880's, college life and influence around 1900, the experience of World War I, and his work in literary journalism in New York, where he established *The Literary Review*, which later became *The Saturday Review of Literature*.

0666 *Candlin, Enid Saunders
The breach in the wall; a memoir of the Old China. New York: Macmillan Publishing Co., Inc., 1973. 340 p. Index.

Candlin, who lived in China until 1940, describes the country and some of its cities—Shanghai, Peking, and Nanking—as she knew and loved them, as well as the history and politics leading up to the Sino-Japanese War.

0667 Cane, Melville   **b.1879**
All and sundry; an oblique autobiography. New York: Harcourt, Brace & World, Inc., 1968. 253 p.

A miscellany of prose and poetry, some previously published, reveals the stages of Cane's long and apparently pleasant life as a practicing poet and lawyer in New York.

0668 Canfield, Cass   **1897-**
Up and down and around: a publisher recollects the time of his life. New York: Harper & Row, 1971. 272 p. Index.

His long association with Harper's publishers has brought Canfield into contact with many well-known authors, has taken him on trips to various places in America and abroad, and kept him in the forefront of events—prohibition, war, politics.

0669 Cannon, James, Jr.   **1864-1944**
Bishop Cannon's own story: life as I have seen it. Edited with introduction by Richard L. Watson, Jr. Durham, North Carolina: Duke University Press, 1955. 465 p. Index.

The published version of Bishop Cannon's incomplete manuscript autobiography omits 150 of the 900 original pages, mostly about growing up in a border state (Maryland) during the Reconstruction. Cannon discusses in detail his college days at Randolph-Macon and Princeton, his clerical work in Virginia and Texas, and his episcopal activities in Mexico, the Belgian Congo, Brazil, Cuba, and elsewhere. He emphasizes his political efforts as a church lobbyist for the Eighteenth Amendment and international Prohibition, and presents a view of various politically motivated trials (1928-34), in which he was accused of "gambling, flour hoarding, lying, adultery" and corrupt campaign practices. He was ultimately acquitted on all counts.

0670 Cannon, James P.   **1891-**
Letters from prison. Edited by George Lavan. Introduction by Jack Barnes. New York: Merit Publishers, 1968. 354 p.

Cannon, National Secretary of the Socialist Workers Party in the 1930's and early 40's, wrote these 182 letters to his wife, Rose Karsner, while imprisoned at Sandstone, Minnesota, throughout 1944. He opposed World War II, which he interpreted as a capitalistic venture that would ultimately devastate the working class. In sum, the letters offer a coherent system for establishing an organized, structured, effective political party.

0671 Cannon, Joseph Gurney   **1836-1926**
Uncle Joe Cannon: the story of a pioneer American. As told to L. White Bushey. St. Clair Shores, Michigan: Scholarly Press, 1970. (New York: Henry Holt and Co., 1927) 362 p. Index.

A staunch Republican from Illinois who was in national politics from the Civil War through World War I, he was a powerful Speaker of the House under Theodore Roosevelt, McKinley, and Wilson, and was known always as "Uncle Joe."

0672 Cannon, Walter Bradford   **1871-1945**
The way of an investigator: a scientist's experiences in medical research. New York: Hafner Press, 1965. (New York: W.W. Norton & Co., 1945) 223 p. Index.
He writes of his experience as a teacher and researcher during a forty-year career at Harvard Medical School—his problems, his mistakes, and his satisfactions.

0673 Canton, Frank M.   **1849-1927**
Frontier trails: the autobiography of Frank M. Canton. Edited by Edward Everett Dale. New Edition. Norman: University of Oklahoma Press, 1966. (New York: Houghton Mifflin, 1930) 236 p.
Although he was an outlaw in Texas in his youth, he later changed his name, moved north, and became a peace officer, serving as sheriff and deputy U.S. Marshal in various places, then as adjutant general of the Oklahoma National Guard. He showed great courage, risking his life to enforce the law and protect the lives and property of others.

0674 Cantor, Eddie   **1892-1964**
As I remember them. New York: Duell, Sloan and Pearce, 1963. 144 p.
A performer recalls with warmth and affection the events and friends of his show business career.

0675 Cantor, Eddie   **1892-1964**
Take my life. With Jane Kesner Ardmore. New York: Doubleday and Co., Inc., 1957. 288 p.
A Broadway comedian describes his early life on New York's Lower East Side and his long and happy career in entertainment.

0676 Cantor, Eddie   **1892-1964**
The way I see it. Edited by Phyllis Rosenteur. Englewood Cliffs, New Jersey: Prentice-Hall, Inc., 1959. 204 p.
The homespun life and philosophy of a prominent entertainer is full of anecdotes about family, friends, and the famous, written in the tone of the stand-up comedian.

0677 Canutt, Yakima   **1895-**
The autobiography of Yakima Canutt. With Oliver Drake. Foreword by Charlton Heston. Afterword by John Wayne. New York: Walker and Co., 1979. 252 p. Index.
A narration of Canutt's exciting life, ranging from being a championship rodeo rider in his teens, to twenty years as a stunt man for Charlton Heston, John Wayne, Clark Gable and others, to directing others in film stunts and enhancing their safety. Unlike most stunt men who specialize, Canutt was a general practitioner of dangerous escapades with fire, explosives, wild animals, stagecoaches, chariots, horses, parachutes, and railroads.

0678 Canzoneri, Robert   **1925-**
A highly ramified tree. New York: The Viking Press, 1976. 189 p.
Canzoneri writes lyrically of the interplay of generations in his extended Italian family and of the effects—positive and negative—of time and change on them all. The author, a Southern writer and English professor, takes his aging father to Sicily to reaffirm family ties. In exploring his own relationship with his first wife, children, and parents, Canzoneri gains self-knowledge and humility.

0679 Capa, Robert   **1913-1954**
Slightly out of focus. New York: Henry Holt and Co., 1947. 243 p.
A photographer and war correspondent writes of his experience in love and war during World War II. A well-written narrative, with photographs, somewhat in the Hemingway mode.

0680 Capote, Truman   **1924-**
Dogs bark; public people and private places. New York: Random House, 1973. 419 p.
The author's collection of his short pieces—essays, profiles, travel pieces and observations—previously printed in magazines and books. They depict his personal landscape and characters he has found memorable.

0681 Capote, Truman   **1924-**
The Thanksgiving visitor. New York: Random House, 1967. 63 p.
An autobiographical story about Capote's childhood years when he lived with distant, elderly cousins in rural Alabama focuses on his relationship to one of the cousins, Miss Sook Faulk.

0682 Capra, Frank   **1897-**
Frank Capra: the name above the title: an autobiography. New York: The Macmillan Co., 1971. 513 p. Index.
An immensely successful movie director, Capra rose from humble be-

ginnings to eminence in the arts, served his country in military and civilian life, and through a series of widely imitated screen classics made Columbia Pictures a major studio.

0683 *Caraway, Hattie Wyatt   **1878-1950**
Silent Hattie speaks: the personal journal of Senator Hattie Caraway. Edited by Diane D. Kincaid. Westport, Connecticut: Greenwood Press, 1979. 151 p. Index.
Caraway, the first woman elected to the U.S. Senate, served 1931-1945. A late assessment of her career refers to her as "the quiet little grandmother who never won anything, said anything, or did anything . . . thrust by the whim of the electorate into a job far beyond her capacities." The diary, written intermittently between December 1931, and March 1934, verifies this harsh judgment, for Caraway seldom focuses on Senate business.

0684 Carew, Rodney Cline   **1945-**
Carew. With Ira Berkow. Illustrated. New York: Simon & Schuster, 1979. 251 p. Index.
Carew, voted Most Valuable Player in the American League in 1977, describes his rise from an impoverished childhood in the Canal Zone to a comfortable life as a superb batter for the Minnesota Twins. He is particularly concerned with racial discrimination, for as a Black he has intermittently felt victimized. However, he married Marilynn Levvy, a white Jew, and has gradually—not without difficulty—become a devoted husband and father.

0685 *Carey, Ernestine Gilbreth   **1908-**
see Gilbreth, Frank Bunker, Jr.

0686 Carey, Mathew   **1760-1839**
Autobiographical sketches. New York: Arno Press, 1970. (Philadelphia: John Clarke, 1829) 156 p.
Between 1819 and 1828 the author wrote and circulated a series of letters addressed to "a friend" which contain his views on "the rise and progress of the American system, and the efforts made to secure its establishment." He attempted to arouse his fellow citizens from their apathy and indifference to the public welfare, particularly the protection of American manufactures.

0687 *Carlisle, Olga Andreyen   **1930-**
Island in time: a memoir of childhood. Illustrated. New York: Holt, Rinehart & Winston, 1980. 227 p.
Carlisle, a Russian emigrée painter and writer, analyzes her wartime exile on the Île d'Oléron, France, from the dual perspectives of her teenage years during World War II and her current viewpoint. Her father, ever susceptible to betrayal, aided the French Resistance, while she and the rest of her family maintained some semblance of civilized life in territory occupied by Nazis.

0688 Carlisle, William L.   **1890-1964**
Bill Carlisle, lone bandit: an autobiography. Introduction by J.R. Williams. Illustrated by Charles M. Russell. Pasadena: Trail's End Publishing Co., Inc., 1946. 220 p.
Cowboy turned bandit, imprisoned twenty years and rehabilitated.

0689 Carlson, Gerald F.   **1925-**
Two on the rocks. New York: David McKay Co., Inc., 1966. 193 p.
His fascinating adventures among the Eskimos on Little Diomede Island in the Bering Strait, 150 miles from Nome, Alaska. Carlson and his wife served as teacher, do-it-yourself doctor, radio operator, friend, and observer of the struggle to survive on this remote Arctic archipelago.

0690 Carlyle, Thomas   **1795-1881**
see Emerson, Ralph Waldo

0691 Carmichael, Hoagy   **1899-**
Sometimes I wonder. With Stephen Longstreet. New York: Farrar, Straus and Giroux, 1965. 313 p.
A fuller narrative of his life in the center of the jazz world, his boyhood in Indiana, his college bands, his success on radio and in Hollywood, his close friendship with Bix Beiderbecke.

0692 Carmichael, Hoagy   **1899-**
Stardust road. New York: Greenwood Press, 1969. (New York: Rinehart and Co., Inc., 1946) 156 p.
The early days of jazz and Tin-Pan Alley, his close friendships with Bix Beiderbecke and William Moenkhaus, in a rhythmic narrative that carries the droll humor of one of the great jazz pianists and songwriters.

0693 Carothers, Merlin R.
Prison to praise. Edited by Jorunn Oftedal. Watchung, New Jersey: Charisma Books, 1972. (Plainfield, New Jersey: Logos International, 1970) 107 p.
Colonel Carothers writes of his criminal youth, his life as a soldier-paratrooper-demolitions expert during World War II, his conversion to

Christ and service as a U.S. Army chaplain guided by his concept of praising God "in all things."

0694 Carothers, Merlin R.
Victory on Praise Mountain. Plainfield, New Jersey: Logos International, 1979. 177 p.
Carothers describes incidents that occurred during his ministry of Praise Center in Escondido. California, 1975-1977. He focuses on overcoming trials of hostile associates, overwork, marital strain, and illness; dynamic faith solves all problems, physical and spiritual.

0695 Carpenter, Malcolm Scott   **1925-**
We seven: by the astronauts themselves. And others. New York: Simon & Schuster, Inc., 1962. 352 p. Index.
A collective autobiography and description of their training and missions by the seven Project Mercury astronauts.

0696 Carpenter, Will Tom   **1854-1933**
Lucky 7: a cowman's autobiography. Edited with introduction by Elton Miler. Illustrated by Lee Hart. Austin: University of Texas Press, 1957. 119 p.
"Lucky 7" chronicles the odyssey of his adventuresome, peripatetic, hardworking life as a cattle driver and trail boss. Written with homespun language and acute perception, Carpenter's life is a "true Western romance of dusty and freezing work and a man's love of the freedom of the cattle trail."

0697 Carr, Camillo Casatti Cadmus   **1842-1914**
A Cavalryman in Indian country. Ashland, Oregon: Lewis Osborne, 1974. 55 p.
After serving with distinction during some of the fiercest fighting of the Civil War, Carr was assigned to be part of the Arizona garrisons which protected the growing settlements and conducted "police offensives" against the aggressive Apaches. His narrative concerns his three years in the blistering Arizona frontier at Fort McDowell where survival was the soldiers' main duty.

0698 Carr, William George   **1901-**
The continuing education of William George Carr: an autobiography. Washington, D.C.: National Education Association, 1978. 442 p.
Carr, from 1952-1967 Executive Secretary of the National Education Association, focuses on national and international aspects of education as he describes the NEA's involvement in the United Nations, World Conference(s) of the Teaching Profession (1953-1972), school integration, bi-lingual education, the Teacher Corps, civil rights, unionization, publications, and other professional matters.

0699 Carrel, Alexis   **1873-1944**
Voyage to Lourdes. Translated by Virginia Peterson. Preface by Charles A. Lindbergh. New York: Harper and Brothers, 1950. 52 p.
This book is written in the third person but relates a French-American surgeon's personal reconciliation at Lourdes, France, between the Catholic faith and science.

0700 Carrieri, Joe   **1937-**
Yankee batboy. As told to Zander Hollander. New York: Prentice-Hall, 1955. 202 p.
The author, a batboy, discusses his association with the New York Yankees during the time of Mickey Mantle, Casey Stengel, and Yogi Berra.

0701 *Carrighar, Sally
Home to the wilderness. Boston: Houghton Mifflin, 1973. 330 p.
A writer and naturalist describes her childhood and early years, focusing on the tense, confusing, and often bitter relationship she had with her mother.

0702 Carroll, Charles   **1737-1832**
Journal of Charles Carroll, 1776: during his visit to Canada, in 1776, as one of the commissioners from Congress. Introductory memoir by Brantz Mayer. Eyewitness Accounts of the American Revolution. New York: New York Times/Arno Press, 1969. 110 p.
Carroll's journal records his trip from New York to Montreal and his return in the spring of 1776. He describes the still-frozen rivers and lakes, the forts situated on Lakes George and Champlain, and the conditions of the soldiers there.

0703 *Carroll, Gladys (Hasty)   **1904-**
To remember forever: the journal of a college girl 1922-1923. Boston: Little, Brown and Co., 1963. 306 p.
An account of her first year at Bates College portrays life at a women's school, emphasizing the conflicts between expectations of marriage, public service, and the desire to become an independent woman and successful writer.

0704 *Carroll, Gladys (Hasty)   **1904-**
Years away from home. Boston: Little, Brown and Co., 1972. 373 p.
Recalling some experience from her first book, this one shows the influence of her home life on her development as a writer, up to the success of her first novel, *As the Earth Turns.*

0705 Carroll, John   **1735-1815**
The John Carroll papers: Vol. I, 1755-1791; Vol. II, 1792-1806; Vol. III, 1807-1815. Edited by Thomas O'Brien Hanley, S.J. South Bend, Indiana: University of Notre Dame Press, 1976. 3v. Index.
This beautifully printed, carefully edited collection contains about ninety percent letters, but also includes ecclesiastical reports and a journal of Carroll's European tour, 1771-72. Together, these letters illustrate Carroll's concerns, human, theological, and political, pertinent to establishing the Catholic Church in America, and significant communication with Catholic clergy and laity throughout America and Europe.

0706 Carson, Christopher (Kit)   **1809-1868**
Kit Carson's autobiography. Edited by Milo Milton Quailfe. Lincoln: University of Nebraska Press, 1966. (Taos: New Mexico Publishing Corp., 1926) 192 p. Index.
A dictated unsentimental account of his career as a Western scout and Indian fighter by one of America's most romanticized figures. Carson was brave, resourceful, an indefatigible traveler with extraordinary common sense concerning military strategy and peaceful relations with Indian tribes.

0707 Carson, Sonny
see **Abubadika, Mwlina Imiri**

0708 Carter, Forrest Bedford Gunyi Usdi (Little Tree)   **1926?-**
Education of Little Tree: a true story. New York: Delacorte Press, 1976. 216 p.
Carter (named "Little Tree" in Cherokee) was orphaned at five and in 1930 went to live with his grandparents in the Tennessee mountains. Taught the lore of nature by his grandmother and his Cherokee heritage by his grandfather, he had little contact with the world of white prejudice until placed in a Christian orphanage where he was beaten and ostracized. He finally left the orphanage and returned to the mountain cabin to share his grandparents' last years.

0709 Carter, Hugh Alton   **1920-**
Cousin Beedie and Cousin Hot: my life with the Carter family of Plains, Georgia. As told to Frances Spatz Leighton. Illustrated. Englewood Cliffs, New Jersey: Prentice Hall, Inc., 1978. 366 p. Index.
Among various people capitalizing on their relationship to Jimmy Carter is "Cousin Beedie," a Plains, Georgia, worm and cricket farmer, antique dealer, and state legislator. He affably gossips about all the members of the Carter family, their children, wives, cousins, and other relatives, rehashing familiar stories and telling some new ones.

0710 Carter, Jimmy   **1924-**
The spiritual journey of Jimmy Carter: in his own words. Compiled with introduction by Wesley G. Pippert. New York: The Macmillan Co., 1978. 270 p. Index.
The collection of excerpts from speeches, interviews, and writings of Jimmy Carter before and during his presidency is arranged to provide the commentary of a devout, fundamentalist, evangelical Christian on his religion. It covers "The Life of Faith"; "Temptation, Sin, Forgiveness, and Grace"; "Religion and Politics"; and "Teaching and Preaching."

0711 Carter, Landon   **1710-1778**
The diary of Colonel Landon Carter of Sabine Hall: 1752-1778. Edited with introduction by Jack P. Greene. Charlottesville: University Press of Virginia, 1965. 2v. Index.
A rich account of the day-to-day life of a member of the colonial Virginia gentry, this diary includes much information on agriculture, crops, slavery, medical practice, scientific activity, social life, and politics, and a look at his personal traits and values, his problems, his motivation, and the world as he saw it.

0712 *Carter, Lillian   **1898-**
Ms. Lillian and friends: the Plains, Georgia, family philosophy and recipe book. As told to Beth Tartan and Rudy Hayes. Foreword by Jimmy Carter. Illustrated. New York: A & W Publisher, 1977. 254 p.
This peculiar book contains autobiographical interviews with Lillian Carter, mother of President Jimmy Carter, who wrote the foreword. It also contains a history of the Carter hometown, Plains, Georgia; sketches of Southern stereotypes (Good Ole Boy, Poor White Trash, Southern Belle), and recipes of Southern food, including grits 'n greens, catfish stew, and sweet potato pie.

0713 Carter, Robert   **1663-1732**
Letters of Robert Carter: 1720-1727, the commercial interests of a Virginia gentleman. Edited by Louis B. Wright. Westport, Connecticut: Greenwood Press, 1970. (San Marino, California: The Huntington Library, 1940) 153 p. Index.

The letters of a great planter and colonial leader provide important historical information on business relations with English and European merchants and the preoccupation of early Virginians with trade.

0714 Carter, Sidney   **1832-1863**
Dear Bet: the Carter letters 1861-1863: the letters of Lieutenant Sidney Carter, Company A, 14th regiment, South Carolina, Volunteers Gregg's-McGowan's Brigade, CSA, to Ellen Timmons Carter. Edited, with introduction and notes by Bessie Mell Lane. Foreword by Horace Fraser Rudisill. Clemson, South Carolina: Bessie Mell Lane, 1978. 165 p. Index.
Carter's straightforward and unassuming letters to his wife cover the period from his enlistment in the Confederate Army in August 1861, to January 21, 1863. He was killed at Gettysburg a week later. The letters comment on Carter's food supply, supplemented from home when the viands survived the journey, on his intermittently bad health, and on the war in his immediate vicinity.

0715 Carter, Vincent O.   **1924-**
The Bern book: a record of a voyage of the mind. New York: The John Day Co., 1973. 297 p.
Though not strictly either an autobiography or a travel book, this book states the author's faith in himself and describes his experience of being an unpublished writer and the only Black man in Bern, Switzerland, where he gives English lessons and writes.

0716 Carter, William Hodding, Jr.   **1907-1972**
First person rural. Garden City, New York: Doubleday & Co., Inc., 1963. 249 p.
The editor of the *Delta Democrat-Times* in Greenville, Mississippi, recounts stories of Southern life, travels, hunting expeditions, and people he knew.

0717 Carter, William Hodding, Jr.   **1907-1972**
Where Main Street meets the river. New York: Rinehart and Co., Inc., 1953. 339 p.
A journalist describes the first newspaper he started in a small Southern town, the development of his career, his years as a war correspondent, and his return to the South after the war.

0718 Cartwright, Peter   **1785-1872**
Autobiography of Peter Cartwright: the backwoods preacher. Edited by W.P. Strickland. Portraits. Freeport, New York: Books for Libraries Press, 1972. (Carlton, 1856) 525 p.
Cartwright spent much of his very long life as a circuit-riding Methodist preacher in the Western territories of Ohio and Illinois, though he also preached in Kentucky, Tennessee, and New England. His autobiography elucidates church doctrine, describes camp meetings and church conferences, and recounts cultural particulars in travelogue fashion.

0719 Carver, Jonathan   **1710-1780**
The journals of Jonathan Carver: and related documents, 1766-1770. Edited, with preface and introduction by John Parker. Auxiliary editors, Carolyn Gilman and Raymond J. DeMallie. Bicentennial Edition. N.P.: Minnesota Historical Society Press, 1976. 344 p. Index.
A scholarly edition of Carver's journals of his travels throughout Michigan, Wisconsin, and the Great Lakes Region of Canada. It is supplemented by a daily list of places visited and miles traveled; by James Stanley Goddard's "Journal of a Voyage, 1766-1767," and letters, commissions, and travel authorizations to and from Carver, 1766-1770. Carver provides considerable information about the French; the Chippewa, Dakota, and Winnebago Indians; the terrain; fur trade; and buffalo. Appended is his "Dakota Dictionary."

0720 Carver, William F.   **1840-1927**
Life of Dr. William F. Carver of California: champion rifle-shot of the world; being an interesting and truthful story of his capture by the Indians when a child, and romantic life among the savages for a period of sixteen years. The Garland Library of Narratives of North American Indian Captives, v. 92. Wilcomb E. Washburn, series editor. Preface by Wm. F. Carver. New York: Garland Publishing Co., 1977. (Boston: William F. Carver, printed by Rockwell & Churchill, 1878) 177 p.
This oral history focuses on the events identified in the subtitle. It is supplemented by extensive records of Carver's performances in the rifle-shooting matches that comprised his later career.

0721 Carver, William Owen   **1868-1954**
Out of his treasure: unfinished memoirs. Biographical chapter by J.B. Weatherspoon. Nashville, Tennessee: Broadman Press, 1956. 158 p.
Dr. Carver, for fifty years a professor of theology at Southern Baptist Theological Seminary (Louisville), tells of his rural Tennessee upbringing as one of eleven children during the Reconstruction era; his education, secular and sacred; and his experiences as a pastor. He devotes two of five chapters to his theological "heresies" and controversies.

0722 Case, Brayton Clarke   **1887-1944**
Lazy-man-rest-not: the Burma letters of Brayton C. Case. Edited by Randolph L. Howard. Philadelphia: The Judson Press, 1946. 128 p.
Thirty years in Burma as a Baptist missionary.

0723 *Cash, June (Carter)   **1929-**
Among my klediments. Illustrated. Grand Rapids: Zondervan Publishing House, 1979. 152 p.
June Cash, in narrative and song lyrics, focuses on her "klediments," an Appalachian term for "favorite things and people." The daughter of country musician Maybelle Carter, Cash entered the country music circuit at nine, touring throughout the South. In 1961 she began working with Johnny Cash, eventually helped him cure his addiction to drugs, and married him in 1968. They love music, marriage, family, and Christianity.

0724 *Caspary, Vera   **1899-**
The secrets of grownups. New York: McGraw-Hill, 1979. 287 p. Index.
A sparkling account of Caspary's development as a celebrated novelist (*Laura*) and screenwriter (*A Letter to Three Wives*). Even as a child, she wrote stories; at seventeen she wrote advertising copy, and eventually wrote most of the copy for Bernarr MacFadden's *Dance Magazine* before she turned to fiction. At forty, she found her true love, film producer Igee Goldsmith, and enjoyed a stimulating life of travel and writing, despite being blacklisted for communist sympathies.

0725 *Cassady, Carolyn
Heart beat: my life with Jack and Neal. Illustrated. New York: Pocket Books, 1978. (Berkeley, California: Creative Arts Book Co., 1976) 93 p.
Letters, domestic details, and accounts of "tea" parties outline this *ménage à trois* in San Francisco in the 1950's. Cassady writes of the tension caused by her "puritan instinct" for monogamy and her delight in having essentially two husbands in Neal Cassady and Jack Kerouac. Her narrative supplies glimpses of the Beat Generation, its music, art, and drug culture.

0726 Casserly, John J.   **1927-**
Ford White House: the diary of a speechwriter. Boulder: Colorado Associated University Press, 1977. 374 p. Index.
Casserly's diary details the challenge of writing speeches during Gerald Ford's presidency when the country was beset with a "national sense of betrayal." He enjoyed the insider's perspective, but found the work very demanding.

0727 *Cassini, Marguerite   **1882-1961**
Never a dull moment: the memoirs of Countess Marguerite Cassini. New York: Harper and Brothers, 1956. 366 p. Index.
The daughter of an important Czarist diplomat describes her long and colorful career among royalty, diplomats, society leaders, and her unusual success as a couturière.

0728 *Castellani, Aldo   **1875-1971**
Doctor in many lands: the autobiography of Aldo Castellani. Garden City, New York: Doubleday and Co., Inc., 1960. 359 p.
Distinguished in medical research and surgery, he describes his international experience in the field, including prominent figures he has treated, and his research on human reactions to the stress of war.

0729 *Castle, Irene   **1893-1969**
Castles in the air. As told to Bob and Wanda Duncan. Garden City, New York: Doubleday & Co., Inc., 1958. 264 p.
Until her husband Vernon's death in a training accident during World War I, they danced and entertained for the cafe society of New York and Paris, their lives and performances characteristic of the glamour of the pre-war era. Thereafter she continued her life as an entertainer and pace-setter for women's fashions.

0730 *Cather, Willa Sibert   **1873-1947**
Willa Cather in Europe: her own story of the first journey. Introduction and incidental notes by George N. Kates. New York: Alfred A. Knopf, 1956. 178 p.
The journal of her first European travels in 1902 reveals much about the mind of a young writer and the kinds of people and ideas she would later write into her fiction.

0731 Catledge, Turner   **1901-**
My life and the *Times*. New York: Harper & Row, 1971. 319 p. Index.
For many years chief news executive of the New York *Times*, Catledge recounts his rise from poverty-stricken Mississippi boyhood, through his early jobs as a reporter in the South and later in Washington, to his long, eventful service with the *Times*. The book is full of anecdotes and inside views of rivalries, personalities, and crises.

0732 Catling, Patrick Skene   **1925-**
Better than working. New York: The Macmillan Co., 1960. 212 p.
Just out of college, he applied to the Baltimore *Sun* for a reporter's job. His book describes the successful development of his career as a journalist during the next ten years.

0733 Catton, Bruce   **1899-**
Waiting for the morning train: an American boyhood. Garden City, New York: Doubleday & Co., Inc., 1972. 260 p.
   A nostalgic look at his childhood in a small Michigan town by a well-known author of popular histories of the Civil War era and other books.

0734 *Caulfield, Genevieve   **1888-1972**
Kingdom within. Edited by Ed Fitzgerald. New York: Harper and Brothers, 1960. 278 p.
   Blinded as an infant, she studied to be a teacher, became fascinated by Japan, and in 1923 after years of teaching to accumulate savings, went to Japan where she taught the blind. When World War II began, she established a school for the blind in Bangkok and later in Vietnam.

0735 Cebuhar, Steve   **1916-**
Four years behind the iron curtain. New York: Vantage Press, 1971. 208 p.
   In 1942 he joined the U.S. diplomatic service and was immediately sent to Lebanon, then Russia and Yugoslavia. His book is staunchly patriotic, harshly anti-communist.

0736 Celler, Emanuel   **1888-1981**
You never leave Brooklyn: the autobiography of Emanuel Celler. New York: John Day, 1953. 276 p.
   A congressman from Brooklyn, New York, recalls his childhood and the realization of his political ambitions. The book is mainly concerned with the congressman's opinions about U.S. immigration laws.

0737 Cerf, Bennett Alfred   **1898-1971**
At random: the reminiscences of Bennett Cerf. New York: Random House, 1977. 306 p. Index.
   A fascinating account of Cerf's profound influence on American book publishing. Beginning as an assistant to Horace Liveright, he bought the Modern Library, then founded Random House, building it into a multi-million dollar corporation. He fought to have Joyce's *Ulysses* published in the U.S. and helped bring many writers to prominence. His anecdotes illuminate the personalities of many of the century's greatest writers.

0738 Cervantes, Alfonso Juan   **1920-**
Mr. Mayor. With Lawrence G. Blochman. Foreword by Hubert H. Humphrey. Los Angeles: Nash Publishing, 1974. 193 p.
   A two-term mayor of St. Louis, the epitome of mid-America geographically, ethnically, and economically, tells of his struggle to rebuild a faltering city by fostering low-cost housing, by persuading businessmen to combat prejudice and unemployment, by wooing tourists, by tightening anti-crime measures, by fighting social decay.

0739 Cerwin, Herbert   **1908-**
In search of something: the memoirs of a public relations man. Introduction by Frank H. Bartholomew. Los Angeles: Sherbourne Press, Inc., 1966. 318 p.
   Cerwin describes his varied career as a United Press correspondent, as head of the Rockefeller office in Mexico, as a diplomat in Brazil, and as a public relations specialist.

0740 *Chace, Marian   **1896-1970**
Marian Chace: her papers. Edited by Harris Chaiklin. Kensington, Maryland: American Dance Therapy Association, 1975. 261 p.
   Dance therapist Chace briefly discusses her development as a dancer and her increasing understanding of the therapeutic potential of dance throughout the 1930's, as a preface to her papers, published and unpublished, on dance therapy schools and hospitals (notably, St. Elizabeth's, Washington, D.C.), from 1940 to 1970.

0741 *Chadwick, Margaret Lee   **1893-**
Looking at the sunset upside down: the autobiography of Margaret Lee Chadwick. Illustrated. Corte Madera, California: Omega Books, 1976. 173 p.
   Educated in rural Utah, Salt Lake City, later at Western College (Oxford, Ohio) and Stanford, she then taught for six years in Nevada, had a number of offers of marriage that did not work out, and on a round-the-world trip met and married career naval officer, Joseph Chadwick. She bore three children and started a day nursery. For thirty years they directed the Chadwick (boarding) School on the Palos Verdes Peninsula in California.

0742 Chaffee, Burns   **b.1880**
My first eighty years . . . ; the life story of a California surgeon. Foreword by Merton E. Hill. Los Angeles: Westernlore Press, 1960. 264 p.
   Dr. Chaffee describes his childhood in California, his college days at Stanford, his medical education at Johns Hopkins and residency in Maryland, and his military duty during World War I in Georgia and France. The book is particularly useful for its information on American medical education, 1900-1920.

0743 Chaikin, Joseph   **1935-**
Presence of the actor. New York: Atheneum, 1972. 161 p.
   The author, who has received several off-Broadway acting awards, founded the open theater in 1963, which became a celebrated influence in the theater during the sixties. Here he writes notes on productions he has taken part in, on acting experiences and training, and on other influences on his professional work.

0744 *Chamberlain, Henriqueta
Where the Sabia sings: a partial autobiography. Illustrated by Ken Chamberlain. New York: The Macmillan Co., 1955. (1947) 246 p.
   A well-written, empathetic recollection of her childhood in Brazil by a daughter of Baptist missionaries.

0745 Chamberlain, Samuel   **1895-1975**
Etched in sunlight; fifty years in the graphic arts. Illustrated. Boston: Boston Public Library, 1968. 227 p. Index.
   His work in graphic arts is both respected and popular. This book combines reproductions of his etchings, drawings, lithographs and photographs with a well-written account of his life in the arts, conveying the humane perception and intellect for which he is recognized.

0746 Chamberlain, Samuel Emery   **1829-1908**
My confession: the recollections of a rogue. Illustrated by the author. Introduction and postscript by Roger Butterfield. New York: Harper and Brothers, 1956. 302 p.
   The story of his adventures as a cavalryman in the Mexican War (1846-1848), often in the style of flagrant melodrama, but interesting as a comment on the times.

0747 Chamberlain, Wilton   **1936-**
Wilt; just like any other 7-foot black millionaire who lives next door. And David Shaw. New York: Macmillan Publishing Co., 1973. 310 p.
   Chamberlain, who holds innumerable basketball records, knows and writes about his own career, other players, his million-dollar house built to his scale, and his views on racial questions and politics.

0748 Chamberlin, William Henry   **1897-1969**
The evolution of a conservative. Chicago: Henry Regnery Co., 1959. 295 p. Index.
   A journalist and foreign correspondent for many years, including twelve in the Soviet Union, describes his political philosophy in the context of an analysis of world politics since 1940, when he published his life story, *The Confessions of an Individualist.*

0749 Chambers, Whittaker   **1901-1961**
Cold Friday. Edited with an introduction by Duncan Norton-Taylor. New York: Random House, 1964. 327 p.
   A controversial figure in the Alger Hiss case, Chambers here reflects on his formative years at Columbia, his career as a journalist, his family life, and his concern for his children.

0750 Chambers, Whittaker   **1901-1961**
Odyssey of a friend: Whittaker Chambers' letters to William F. Buckley, Jr., 1954-1961. Edited with notes by William F. Buckley, Jr. Foreword by Ralph de Toledano. New York: G.P. Putnam's Sons, 1970. (1969) 303 p. Index.
   Buckley describes the letters as "spontaneous personal and philosophical reflections which will help the reader to judge the plausibility of the attacks on Whittaker Chambers' character," since the case for Alger Hiss "relies increasingly on efforts to discredit Chambers personally."

0751 Chambers, Whittaker   **1901-1961**
Witness. New York: Random House, 1952. 808 p. Index.
   The author's and his family's involvement with the Communist Party from the mid-20's to the celebrated spy case of Alger Hiss in 1948. He interprets his feelings and actions as a confession.

0752 Champion, George   **1810-1841**
Journal of the Rev. George Champion: American missionary in Zululand, 1835-9. Edited and annotated by Alan R. Booth. Cape Town: C. Struik (PTY.) LTD., 1967. 149 p. Index.
   After a period of adjustment in Cape Town and Bethelsdorp, a band of American missionaries journeyed to Dingane to set up a school and missions for the Zulus. Although they were welcomed at first, later the natives turned against them and forced them to leave. Champion's journal records his observations about the people, the country, and the work of the missionaries.

0753 Chandler, Raymond   **1888-1959**
Raymond Chandler speaking. Edited by Dorothy Gardiner and Katherine Sorley Walker. Freeport, New York: Books for Libraries Press, 1971. (New York: Houghton Mifflin Co., 1962) 271 p. Index.
   The extant letters of a prominent mystery writer, edited according to themes, e.g., "Chandler on Chandler," "Chandler on the Mystery Novel," "Chandler on Cats."

0754 *Chaney, Earlyne
Remembering; the autobiography of a mystic. Los Angeles, California: Astara's Library of Mystical Classics, 1974. 382 p.

From humble beginnings to a movie career and eminence as a mystic and founder of Astara, a mystical, religious organization of international scope, Chaney writes of psychic experiences, cosmic illumination, communication with those on the other side, astral flights, and the pilgrimage of the soul upward into light.

0755 *Chanler, Julie (Olin)   1882-1961
From gaslight to dawn: an autobiography by Julie Chanler. New York: Pacific Printing Co., Inc., 1956. 413 p.

Raised in New York high society, she became devoted to the B'hai religion as a young woman. Her book conveys an image of her wealth and privilege, her international travel, her charitable work for B'hai, and her pet terriers.

0756 *Chanler, Margaret (Terry)   1862-1934
Memory makes music. New York: Stephen-Paul Publishers, 1948. 171 p.

Recollections of the changes in musical taste and fashion since the late nineteenth century and the autobiography of her musical interests, by a writer and music critic.

0757 Chanute, Octave   1832-1910
see **Wright, Wilbur**

0758 *Chapelle, Dickey   1919?-
What's a woman doing here? New York: William Morrow and Co., 1962. 285 p.

As a photojournalist and war correspondent, she wrote front-line reports of the battles of Iwo Jima and Okinawa in World War II. Afterwards she and her husband covered the movements of refugees, the Hungarian Revolution, and Castro's overthrow of the Batista regime in Cuba.

0759 Chapin, Charles E.   1858-1930
Charles E. Chapin's story. New York: Beekman Publishers, Inc., 1974. (New York: Putnam, 1920) 334 p.

Chapin was a newspaperman and city editor for forty years before he took the steps that led to his life imprisonment in Sing Sing. Having speculated on stocks and lost everything, he determined to end his life and his wife's to save her from a friendless, helpless future. Instead, after shooting his wife, he gave himself up at a police station.

0760 Chapin, Earl V.
Long Wednesdays. New York: Abelard-Schuman, 1953. 268 p.

The editor of a small country weekly in Minnesota reminisces about his job in the 1930's.

0761 Chapin, Henry   1895-
A countdown at eighty. Illustrated. Dublin, New Hampshire: Bauhan, 1977. 188 p.

An articulate account of Chapin's attempt to lead the simple life he believed conducive to becoming a great writer, first in his native state of Massachusetts, then as a married expatriate in Paris. Fatherhood and the Depression forced him into farming in New Hope, Pennsylvania, where he became attuned to nature and to relieving the plight of the poor.

0762 Chapin, Schuyler Garrison   1923-
Musical chairs: a life in the arts. New York: G.P. Putnam's Sons, 1977. 448 p.

A monied childhood in Mt. Kisco, New York, helped to instill in Chapin a love of music which he pursued at NBC (with time out as an Army pilot in World War II), then at Columbia Records, and finally at Lincoln Center, where he became General Manager of the Metropolitan Opera. From his vantage point as a musical entrepreneur, he relates anecdotes about the many renowned musicians with whom he has worked.

0763 Chaplin, Ralph   1887-1961
Wobbly: the rough-and-tumble story of an American radical. Chicago: University of Chicago Press, 1948. 435 p. Index.

For fifty years he worked in the American labor movement as rebel editor, writer of battle songs, agitator, and organizer. Like others with a similar commitment, he sees his life as the story of a movement; for him, it was the radical labor movement.

0764 Chapman, Frank Michler   1864-1947
Frank M. Chapman in Florida: his journals and letters. Compiled and edited by Elizabeth S. Austin. Gainesville: University of Florida Press, 1967. 228 p. Index.

One of America's great naturalists, Chapman recorded in these letters and journals his own work in Florida in the 1880's and 1890's as well as a later visit from 1932 to 1934. Here are described his explorations of the Indian, Sebastian, and Suwanee River areas; the birds, wildlife, and flora of Florida; and the concerns of the naturalists of his day.

0765 Chapman, John Wight   1858-1939
A camp on the Yukon. Cornwall-on-Hudson, New York: The Idlewild Press, 1948. 214 p.

Episcopal missionary in Anvik, Alaska, 1887-1930.

0766 *Charisse, Cyd, pseud.
see **Martin, Tony**

0767 Charles, Ray   1930-
Brother Ray: Ray Charles' own story. And David Ritz. New York: Dial Press, 1978. 340 p.

The story of a famous Black musician, from his extremely impoverished rural Southern beginnings, his going blind, to those who helped him develop his great talent for playing instruments, singing, and composing. His music, his many sexual experiences, his problems with drugs, and his faith in his creativity make this story a statement of personal philosophy.

0768 *Chase, Edna Woolman (Alloway)   1877-1957
Always in vogue. With Ilka Chase. Garden City, New York: Doubleday and Co., Inc., 1954. 381 p.

The editor of *Vogue* Magazine recalls her years in New York working on that magazine and the people connected with it.

0769 Chase, Harold Beverly   b.1889
Auto-biography: recollections of a pioneer motorist 1896-1911. New York: Pageant Press, Inc., 1955. 174 p.

An entertaining story of Chase's life-long love affair with turn-of-the-century automobiles, experiencing and reporting the difficulties and pleasures of driving early gas-, electric- or steam-driven cars, including an Orient Buckboard, a racing Chadwick ("the Speediest Stock Car in the World"), and a 1907 Model N Ford.

0770 *Chase, Ilka   1905-1978
Carthaginian rose. Drawings by Mircea Vasiliu. Garden City, New York: Doubleday & Co., Inc., 1961. 429 p.

With candor and relish the author-actress recreates her memorable journeys to Europe and the exotic East.

0771 *Chase, Ilka   1905-1978
Free admission. Garden City, New York: Doubleday & Company, Inc., 1948. 319 p.

A shapeless, chatty Hollywood memoir which dwells on gossip and the small details of the author's life.

0772 Chase, Joseph Cummings   1878-1965
Face value: autobiography of the portrait painter. New York: Rolten House, Inc., 1962. 216 p.

Portrait painter, designer, and teacher, Chase tells charming stories about painting presidents, soldiers, statesmen, actors, authors, and explorers.

0773 Chase, Joseph Cummings   1878-1965
My friends look better than ever. New York: Longmans, Green, and Co., 1950. 301 p.

Painter-illustrator reminisces about his life through anecdotes about his friends and people he has painted over the years—actors, writers, artists, generals, and soldiers.

0774 *Chase, Mary Ellen   1887-1973
A goodly fellowship. New York: The Macmillan Co., 1939. 305 p.

A sequel to *A Goodly Heritage,* this volume is a tribute to the author's teachers, from her mother to her professors at the University of Minnesota. It is also an account of the author's own varied teaching career, her wariness of "educators" who are not teachers and "experimentalists" who do not, as she does, come to teaching "as to a sport."

0775 *Chase, Mary Ellen   1887-1973
A goodly heritage. Illustrated by Maitland de Gogorza. New York: Henry Holt & Co., 1936. 298 p.

In tribute to New England at the turn of the century, the author traces the influence of a tempered Puritanism, the simplicity of coastal life, and the value of a classical education in preparing her for the New Age.

0776 *Chase, Mary Ellen   1887-1973
White gate: adventures in the imagination of a child. New York: W.W. Norton, 1954. 185 p.

The book describes the memories of an author's childhood in Maine in the 1890's.

0777 Chase, Salmon Portland   1808-1873
Diary and correspondence of Salmon P. Chase. Annual Report of the American Historical Association, 1902. New York: Da Capo Press, 1971. (Washington: Government Printing Office, 1903) 527 p. Index.

A U.S. Supreme Court Justice during the Civil War, he corresponded with antislavery journalist Edward S. Hamlin, with Charles Sumner, and with George S. Denison, his personal representative in New Orleans

(1802-65), and other contemporaries. He argued strenuously in letters and in the court against slavery.

0778 Chase, Salmon Portland   **1808-1873**
Inside Lincoln's cabinet: the Civil War diaries of Salmon Portland Chase. Edited by David Donald. New York: Longmans, Green, and Co., 1954. 227 p. Index.

The diaries of the author detail his political career during the years Lincoln was president. He relates experiences in Washington, D.C., as Secretary of the Treasury, a Republican candidate for the presidency, and the beginning of his career as a Supreme Court Justice.

0779 Chase, Warren   **1813-1891**
The life-line of the lone one: or autobiography of the world's child. Illustrated. New York: AMS Press, 1975. (Boston: Bela Marsh, 1865) 310 p.

It is difficult to tell whether the subject, identified only as "The Lone One," is autobiographical or not. Chase identifies this book as a "true and literal history" of the struggles of an ambitious mind to "rise from a dishonorable birth"; he published it as a moralistic guide for the humble.

0780 Cheney, Russell   **1881-1945**
Russell Cheney, 1881-1945: a record of his work. Notes by F.O. Matthiessen. New York: Oxford University Press, 1947. 124 p.

This record of a painter's work includes excerpts from his diary and his letters as well as plates of his paintings.

0781 *Chennault, Anna (Chan)   **1925-**
The education of Anna. New York: New York Times Books, 1980. 242 p.

Chennault writes of her luxurious childhood in Peking, reared by her grandparents. Her youth was shattered by the Sino-Japanese War and devastated by World War II, which broke up her family. As a reporter, she fell in love with General Claire Chennault, 35 years her senior. They married in 1947, founded an airline, and were fighting communism when he died in 1958. She moved to Washington, D.C., became prominent in Republican politics and in defending official policy during the Vietnam War.

0782 *Chennault, Anna (Chan)   **1925-**
A thousand springs: the biography of a marriage. Introduction by Lin Yutang. New York: Paul S. Eriksson, Inc., 1962. 318 p.

A description by his wife of General Claire Chennault and their life together, against the background of war and peace, China, and The Flying Tigers.

0783 Chennault, Claire Lee   **1890-1958**
Way of a fighter: the memoirs of Claire Lee Chennault. Edited by Robert Hotz. New York: G.P. Putnam's Sons, 1949. 375 p. Index.

After a few pages about his early life, he describes his army experience in China (1939-49), where he organized the crack bomber squadron The Flying Tigers, converted after the war to transport food, supplies and trade goods throughout China. American air adviser to Chiang Kai-shek.

0784 *Cheshire, Maxine   **1930-**
Maxine Cheshire, reporter. With John Greenya. Illustrated. Boston: Houghton Mifflin Co., 1978. 307 p. Index.

She describes the violence that permeated her hometown, Harlan, Kentucky, and the many scandals she uncovered in later years as a reporter for the Washington *Post.* Cheshire deals specifically with the Tongson Park scandal (Koreagate), the Nixons' keeping of gifts from foreign dignitaries while in office, and John Kennedy's extra-marital affairs as Senator and as President.

0785 *Chesnut, Mary Boykin (Miller)   **1823-1886**
A diary from Dixie. Edited by Ben Ames Williams. Boston: Houghton Mifflin Co., 1949. 572 p. Index.

The diary is edited from a manuscript of 50 notebooks, covering the period of the Civil War, from 1861 to 1865. The author emerges as an intelligent, articulate, well-informed member of Confederate society.

0786 Chessman, Caryl Whittier   **1921-1960**
Cell 2455: Death Row. Englewood Cliffs, New Jersey: Prentice-Hall, Inc., 1960. 271 p.

An expanded version of the 1954 edition, including material from personal letters, interviews, his other books, and his last long letter of appeal to Governor Pat Brown of California, written by a convicted murderer.

0787 Chessman, Caryl Whittier   **1921-1960**
Trial by ordeal. Englewood Cliffs, New Jersey: Prentice-Hall, 1955. 294 p.

A criminal in San Quentin's Death Row describes what it is like living there. The book is essentially an appeal for a reprieve from the death sentence. As a part of his argument, the author discusses capital punishment, sex crimes, and the criminal mentality.

0788 Chester, Henry L.   **1896-**
Memoirs. Hollywood, California: Vantage Press, 1978. 106 p.

Chester is an energetic social activist who served briefly in the army in France in 1918 before World War I ended, worked as a teacher in North Carolina in the 1920's, and as a social worker in Los Angeles until 1935. Determined to be granted his civil rights, he secured a job with the Railway Mail Service, at which he worked nearly twenty years. He was active in gaining social services for the Watts area after violence erupted there in the 1960's, but devotes half the book to detailed accounts of his travels throughout the United States, Canada, the Caribbean, and Europe.

0789 Chevalier, Haakon Maurice   **1902-**
Oppenheimer: the story of a friendship. New York: George Braziller, 1965. 219 p. Index.

Chevalier, for some twenty years a French professor at the University of California, Berkeley, presents in agonizing detail the story of his friendship with J. Robert Oppenheimer in the late 1930's and early 40's, the subsequent betrayal, and its aftermath. In August 1943, Oppenheimer, director of the Los Alamos, N.M., project to develop the atomic bomb, told a military intelligence officer that Chevalier had conspired to obtain information about the atomic bomb for the Soviets. This lie, which led to "the Chevalier Incident," destroyed Chevalier's career; he wrote the book to vindicate himself.

0790 Chevigny, Hector   **1904-1965**
My eyes have a cold nose. New York: Yale University Press, 1946. 273 p.

A radio script writer writes of becoming blind in middle age and learning to adapt to it. An intense, articulate book.

0791 *Chicago, Judy (Judith Gerowitz)   **1939-**
Through the flower: my struggle as a woman artist. Introduction by Anaïs Nin. Garden City, New York: Doubleday and Co., 1977. 226 p. Index.

Reared in Chicago, Illinois, by communist sympathizer parents, feminist painter and sculptor Judy Chicago was devastated as a teenager by her father's death and similarly distressed by widowhood at 23. Psychotherapy and her graduate studies in art at U.C.L.A. were mutually enhancing, as is her supportive marriage to artist Lloyd Hamrol. Chicago analyzes the development of women's art historically and in contemporary California.

0792 Child, Charles   **1902-**
Roots in the rock. Illustrated by the author. Boston, Massachusetts: Little, Brown & Co., Inc., 1964. 346 p.

An artist describes his experiences homesteading on a remote coastal region in Maine.

0793 Child, Francis James   **1825-1896**
see **Lowell, James Russell**

0794 *Child, Lydia Maria (Francis)   **1802-1880**
Letters of Lydia Maria Child. Biographical introduction by John G. Whittier. Appendix by Wendell Phillips. New York: AMS Press, 1971. (Boston: Houghton Mifflin, 1883) 280 p. Index.

The most popular literary woman of her day, she published historical novels, was editor of *Juvenile Miscellany,* a children's periodical, and became an outspoken supporter of abolition, temperance, prison reform, and equality of civil rights, irrespective of sex.

0795 Childs, J. Rives
see **Miller, Henry**

0796 Chillyblast, Wm. Chauncy, pseud.
see **Daugherty, Robert Dodds**

0797 Chippendale, Harry Allen   **1879-1953**
Sails and whales. Introduction by Henry Beetle Hough. Boston: Houghton Mifflin Co., 1951. 232 p.

Whaler captain describes his experiences on several boats fishing for sperm whale in the South Atlantic during the early years of the twentieth century. During World War I and II, he served on cargo ships.

0798 *Chisholm, Shirley (St. Hill)   **1924-**
The good fight. New York: Harper & Row, 1973. 206 p. Index.

Her impressions of events and personalities as she perceived them during the 1972 Presidential primary campaign when she ran for the presidency, despite hopeless odds, in order to open up the political system and "to demonstrate sheer will and refusal to accept the status quo."

0799 *Chisholm, Shirley (St. Hill)   **1924-**
Unbought and unbossed. Boston: Houghton Mifflin Co., 1970. 177 p.

The first Black woman to be elected to the U.S. Congress describes her childhood in Barbados, her education and early political experience, her opposition to the Vietnam War, and many current social issues.

0800 Chodorov, Frank   **1887-1966**
Out of step: the autobiography of an individualist. Introduction by E. Victor Milione. New York: The Devin-Adair Co., 1962. 261 p.

A lively analysis of self and society by a journalist who was a professional individualist. Author of *One is a Crowd* and *The Income Tax: Root of all Evil.*

0801 *Chrisman, Berna Hunter   1877-1963
When you and I were young, Nebraska! Edited by Henry E. Chrisman. Broken Bow, Nebraska: Purcell's Incorporated, 1971. 255 p. Index.
    Written at age 82, her book describes her arrival in Nebraska at age two, the difficult life of pioneering in the late nineteenth century, the loneliness, boredom, physical suffering, as well as the happier moments of daily life and survival.

0802 *Christensen, Inga Hoegsbro   b.1872
"Inga-play!": the memoirs of Inga Hoegsbro Christensen. With Molly Winston Pearson, Alice Randall, and Peggy London. Foreword by James Francis Cooke. Illustrated. New York: Exposition Press, 1952. 202 p.
    Mrs. Christensen's narrative describes her Danish childhood, her musical training in Copenhagen, her immigration to New York, where she specialized in teaching the works of Scandinavian composers to children of the wealthy. She continued her career as a pianist until she was eighty, with satisfaction and acclaim.

0803 *Christian, Linda   1924-
Linda: my own story. New York: Crown Publishers, Inc., 1962. 280 p.
    Her life and loves in Hollywood, including her early romance with Errol Flynn, her marriage to Tyrone Power, and later to Edmund Purdom.

0804 Christie, Joseph William   1904-
Medical missionary to Africa. Illustrated. New York: Vantage Press, 1966. 140 p.
    Christie spent his first fifty years in a fairly conventional American way: he worked his way through medical school, married, raised a family, practiced general medicine in Pontiac, Michigan, and during World War II served in Australia and the South Pacific as a physician with the U.S. Army. In 1964 he went to Zambia as a medical missionary, particularly to treat people with Hansen's disease.

0805 Christman, Enos   1828-1912
One man's gold: the letters and journals of a Forty-Niner. Edited by Florence Morrow Christman. New York: Whittlesey House, McGraw-Hill Book Co., 1930. 278 p.
    The editor acknowledges that the original documents have been "quite freely condensed and edited," augmented by newspaper clippings, and that names have been changed. The letters and journal entries follow Christman's passage from Philadelphia around Cape Horn to California and wealth, and back to Philadelphia. A plainspoken, simple account of one man's three years spent prospecting in the California Gold Rush.

0806 Christowe, Stoyan   1898-
My American pilgrimage. Boston: Little, Brown and Co., 1947. 264 p.
    Describes the experience of a Macedonian immigrant in and around St. Louis, 1915-1920, his first five years in America, working first in a factory, then with his father laying railroad tracks in the Northern Plains.

0807 Christy, Thomas   b.1829?
Road across the Plains 1850: a guide to the route from Mormon Crossing, now Omaha, Nebraska, to the city of Sacramento, California . . . together with his diary of the same journey. Edited by Robert H. Becker. Denver: Fred A. Rosenstock, Old West Publishing Co., 1969. 208 p.
    Especially valuable because it includes route maps and diary, this is an unusual record of the mass overland immigration to the California gold fields in 1849-50.

0808 Chrysler, Walter Percy   1875-1940
Life of an American workman. With Boyden Sparkes. New York: Dodd, Mead and Co., 1950. (New York: Curtis Publishing Co., 1937) 219 p.
    Automobile manufacturer describes his rise from childhood in Kansas in a railroad family to corporate responsibility in the auto industry.

0809 Churchill, Samuel   1911-
Big Sam. Garden City, New York: Doubleday & Co., Inc., 1965. 184 p.
    With warm nostalgia, Churchill writes of his father, his family, and life in the logging camps of Oregon during the early days of the twentieth century. It was magnificent country with what seemed like enough timber to last a thousand years. Life was rough and conditions were crude but the people had vigor, humor, courage, and great hearts.

0810 Churchill, Winston Leonard Spencer
    see Roosevelt, Franklin Delano

0811 Chynoweth, Bradford Grethen   1890-
Bellamy Park: memoirs. Hicksville, New York: Exposition, 1975. 301 p.
    Born into an army family, Chynoweth spent his life at various army posts and duties from Cheyenne, Wyoming, and London to the South Pacific. He concentrates especially on describing his experiences during

World War II when he commanded the Visayan Force with headquarters in Cebu Island.

0812 Ciliberti, Charles   1906-
Backstairs mission in Moscow: the diary of an American worker compiled during three journeys in the forbidden land of the Soviets. New York: Booktab Press, 1946. 127 p.
    Chauffeur to Ambassador and Mrs. Joseph E. Davies, 1936-1938.

0813 *Cirile, Marie
Detective Marie Cirile; memoirs of a police officer. Illustrated. Garden City, New York: Doubleday & Co., Inc., 1975. 222 p.
    As a detective on the New York police force for over ten years, she achieved some notoriety for cases she broke wearing various disguises. Her book reveals the tough, squalid side of urban life, especially crimes affecting women.

0814 Cisler, Walker Lee   1897-
A measurable difference: the reminiscences of Walker Lee Cisler. The Entrepreneurial Autobiographical Series. Introduction by Floyd A. Bond. In collaboration with James P. McCormick. Ann Arbor, Michigan: University of Michigan, Graduate School of Business Administration, 1976. 161 p. Index.
    This volume focuses on the world's energy resources (including atomic energy) and technological developments that contribute to the efficient production of inexpensive power. Cisler, president of the Detroit Edison Company, 1959-1973, has an unusual public-spirited, international perspective on energy production.

0815 Claessens, August   1885-1954
Didn't we have fun!: stories out of a long, fruitful and merry life. New York: The Rand School Press, 1953. 200 p.
    Claessens, a Socialist Party leader elected to the New York State Assembly in 1917, thoroughly enjoyed his career as assemblyman, his speechmaking tours of the United States, and the people he met. Among the most notable were Eugene Debs and Edison's electrical wizard, Alfred Steinmetz. Claessens cleverly delivered Socialist speeches to groups assembled for other purposes—such as to watch beauty contests or attend Ku Klux Klan meetings.

0816 Clancy, Foghorn, pseud.   b.1882
My fifty years in rodeo: living with cowboys, horses and danger. Illustrated by Olaf Wieghorst. Foreword by Gene Autry. San Antonio: The Naylor Co., 1952. 285 p.
    A rambling account of rodeo announcer and promoter Clancy's fifty years on the rodeo circuit, from various Southwestern locations, especially Texas and Wyoming, to Madison Square Garden, in which he has seen "tragedy, thrills, romance, love, comedy and great sportsmanship." The book is useful for information about places, dates, and performers in particular rodeos, 1897-1947.

0817 Clancy, Frank Jeffrey   1892-
Doctor come quickly. Seattle: Superior Publishing Co., 1950. 248 p.
    Chronicle of a urologist-surgeon's experiences with patients during thirty years of practice in Seattle, begun after World War I service as Navy doctor.

0818 Clap, Roger   1609-1691
Memoirs of Roger Clap: 1630. Freeport, New York: Books for Libraries Press, 1971. (Boston: B. Green, 1731) 62 p.
    A brief description of his good fortune in immigrating to New England seeking religious freedom and settling happily there, with directions to his children to serve the Lord.

0819 Clapp, Theodore   1792-1866
Autobiographical sketches and recollections: during thirty-five years' residence in New Orleans. New York: Books for Libraries Press, 1972. (Boston: Phillips, Sampson & Co., 1857) 419 p.
    Raised in Massachusetts, he graduated from Yale Divinity School and took his ministry to New Orleans. His book describes the life of the city, including tragic epidemics of cholera and yellow fever.

0820 Clapp, Theodore   1792-1866
Parson Clapp and the Strangers' Church of New Orleans. Edited by John Duffy. Louisiana State University Studies, Social Science Series, no. 7. Baton Rouge: Louisiana State University Press, 1957. 191 p. Index.
    The autobiographical sketches (pp. 49-174) of a minister in New Orleans, providing a concise view of his life, his ministry, and the city.

0821 *Clappe, Louise Amelia Knapp (Smith)   1819-1906
The Shirley letters from the California mines, 1851-1852. Introduction and notes by Carol I. Wheat. Western Americana. New York: A.A. Knopf, 1949. (San Francisco: T.C. Russell, 1922) 216 p.
    In 23 letters to her sister in New England, the author precisely describes the activities, people, and locale of a California mining camp in Feather River Gorge in the short period of time she lived there with her physician husband enduring the hardships of pioneer existence.

0822 *Clapper, Olive (Ewing)   **1896-1968**
One lucky woman. Garden City, New York: Doubleday & Co., Inc., 1961. 503 p.
　　With her husband, journalist Raymond Clapper, she lived and worked as a writer-lecturer in the midst of the Washington international set from the Harding to the Eisenhower administration.

0823 Clark, Amasa Gleason   **1825-1927**
Reminiscences of a centenarian: as told by Amasa Gleason Clark, Veteran of the Mexican War to Cora Tope Clark. San Antonio: The Naylor Company, 1972. (Bandera, Texas: Privately Printed, 1930) 84 p.
　　Still active at 101, he dictated his recollections of boyhood, friends, and his extensive family. He fathered nineteen children, most of whom remained in Bandera County, Texas, with their own families.

0824 *Clark, Anne
Australian adventure: letters from an ambassador's wife. Foreword by Dame Zara Holt. Austin: University of Texas Press, 1969. 232 p. Index.
　　Out of the need to share her new interests and experiences in Australia as a U.S. ambassador's wife, Anne Clark wrote these engaging letters to her friends and family in the United States describing her travels, her social life, and her observations of the world "down under."

0825 *Clark, Ava Milam   **b.1884**
Adventures of a home economist. With J. Kenneth Munford. Introduction by Betty E. Hawthorne. Illustrated. Corvallis: Oregon State University Press, 1969. 432 p. Index.
　　An articulate, comprehensive account of Clark's career as a professor and Dean of the School of Home Economics at Oregon State College, 1911-1950, intertwined with a history of the Home Economics movement in the United States, the Middle East, and the Orient, where she spent considerable time. She also supplies biographical sketches of some of her notable graduates.

0826 *Clark, Eugenie   **1922-**
Lady and the sharks. New York: Harper & Row, 1969. 269 p.
　　The sequel to *Lady With a Spear* adds twelve years to her memoir as a marine biologist. She developed and managed the Cape Haze Marine Laboratory near Sarasota, Florida, while raising four small children.

0827 *Clark, Eugenie   **1922-**
Lady with a spear. New York: Harper and Brothers, 1951. 243 p.
　　An ichthyologist from New York describes her life-long love affair with fish. She recounts how she made her hobby her work, how being a woman in her field has affected her professional attitudes, and describes her field work in the South Pacific and Egypt.

0828 Clark, Glenn   **1882-1956**
Man's reach: the autobiography of Glenn Clark. New York: Harper and Brothers, 1949. 314 p.
　　After describing his family and educational background, Clark tells how the power of prayer was revealed to him and his subsequent experiences exercising that power.

0829 Clark, Harold W.   **1891-**
Skylines and detours. Washington, D.C.: Review and Herald, 1959. 320 p.
　　An account of the author's life, focusing on his 45 years teaching biology at Pacific Union College, on his strong ties to wife, children and parents, and on his firm Seventh-Day Adventist faith.

0830 Clark, John Kenneth
Telling it like it was; a country preacher tells his story. Halifax, Virginia: J. Kenneth Clark, 1974. 200 p.
　　Clark, who served as minister in twenty different Baptist churches during his career, sometimes had three or more congregations in his charge at one time. He writes with humor and compassion of his busy life which included duties as widely different as babysitting with a drunk and keeping watch with five condemned prisoners on death row.

0831 Clark, Joseph James   **1893-**
Carrier admiral. With Clark G. Reynolds. New York: David McKay Co., Inc., 1967. 333 p. Index.
　　In 1925 he became a naval aviator. After that he was involved with many of the men and events which made naval aviation history, especially those related to the development of the aircraft carrier. He served in World War II, Korea, and Vietnam. When he retired he was Commander of the Seventh Fleet.

0832 Clark, Mark Wayne   **1896-**
Calculated risk: the story of the war in the Mediterranean. New York: Harper and Brothers, 1950. 500 p. Index.
　　Commander of Fifth Army recounts his campaign in Italy (what Churchill called "the soft underbelly of the Axis") as a calculated risk to divert the German army from the French and Russian fronts.

0833 *Clark, Maurine (Doran)   **1892?-1966**
Captain's bride, general's lady: memoirs. New York: McGraw-Hill Book Co., Inc., 1956. 278 p.
　　A warm personal narrative of army life by a general's wife.

0834 *Clark, Septima (Poinsette)   **1898-**
Echo in my soul. With LeGette Blythe. Foreword by Harry Golden. New York: E.P. Dutton & Co., Inc., 1962. 243 p.
　　As Director of Workshops and Director of Education of the Highlander Folk School in Tennessee she continued a lifetime's work educating the poor and ignorant and combatting segregation and prejudice.

0835 Clark, Tom
see Fidrych, Mark

0836 Clark, Walter   **1846-1924**
The papers of Walter Clark. Edited by Audrey Lee Brooks and Hugh Talmage Lefler. Chapel Hill: University of North Carolina Press, 1948-1950. 2v. Index.
　　The letters, speeches, and articles of a prolific writer who became Chief Justice of the Supreme Court of North Carolina; includes descriptions of his boarding school and university experience, life in the Confederate Army, and his career as a country lawyer and Chief Justice. Good description of his work as a social and economic reformer in the context of Southern aristocracy.

0837 Clark, William
see Lewis, Meriwether

0838 *Clarke, Caroline Cowles (Richards)   **1842-1913**
Village life in America 1852-1872, including the period of the American Civil War, as told in the diary of a schoolgirl. New York: Henry Holt and Co., 1912. 202 p.
　　A record of childhood in ideal conditions amid the village life in New York State and of the effects of the Civil War in the Northern states told in an artless and attractive manner by a quick-witted schoolgirl.

0839 Clarke, Donald Henderson   **1887-1958**
Man of the world: recollections of an irreverent reporter. New York: The Vanguard Press, Inc., 1950. 304 p.
　　Recollections of his work and acquaintances while he was a reporter for *The World* precede the author's account of his psychoanalytic treatment for alcoholism at Bloomingdale's in White Plains, New York.

0840 *Clarke, Elizabeth Dodge Huntington   **1884-1976**
Joy of service: memoirs. With Elspeth McClure Clarke and Court Carol Walters. Illustrated. New York: Nat'l. Board of the Young Women's Christian Association, 1979. 316 p. Index.
　　For most of her 91 years, Elizabeth Dodge led an active, joyous life of Christian service, much of it devoted to YWCA work in New York City and in Turkey, where her first husband, George Huntington, was Vice-President of Robert College in Istanbul After Huntington died, Elizabeth married clergyman Dumont Clarke in 1956 and continued her Christian service and world travels until her death.

0841 Clarke, Herman   **1837-1914**
Back home in Oneida: Herman Clarke and his letters. Compiled and edited by Harry F. Jackson and Thomas F. O'Donnell. Foreword. Epilogue. Illustrated. Syracuse: Syracuse University Press, 1965. 212 p.
　　Clarke, a young farmer in Oneida, New York, at the outset of the Civil War, fought with the 117th New York Volunteer Infantry (August 1862—June 1865) up and down the coastal areas of Virginia and South Carolina, concluding his service with a battle at Fort Fisher, North Carolina. He believed that "a soldier's life is serious business; but it has its attractions and recompenses . . . the true soldier will derive from his campaign an education and discipline worth more than money." His letters to relatives and to the editor of the Utica newspaper are forthright, articulate, specific, and patriotic.

0842 Clarke, James Freeman   **1810-1888**
The letters of James Freeman Clarke to Margaret Fuller. Edited by John Wesley Thomas. Hamburg, Germany: Cram, de Gruyter and Co., 1957. 147 p.
　　A fascinating collection of letters (1829-1848) from James Clarke to Transcendentalist intellectual Margaret Fuller, his "first and best friend." These cover a wide range of topics, focusing on theology, literature, religion, and the personal lives of a host of mutual friends.

0843 Clarke, William F.   **1896-**
Over there with O'Ryan's Roughnecks: reminiscences of a Private 1st Class who served in the 27th U.S. Division with the British Forces in Belgium and France. Illustrated. Seattle: Superior Publishing Co., 1968. 176 p.
　　From diaries, memory, and published accounts, Clarke describes the activities of the 27th Division of the U.S. Army, with which he served as a private first class, in World War I. They fought in Belgium, near Ypres, and in France, notably around St. Souplet.

0844 *Clawson, Bertha Fidelia   **1868-1957**
Bertha Fidelia: her story. With Jessie M. Trout. Illustrated by Louis LeVier. St. Louis, Missouri: Bethany Press, 1957. 128 p.
Clawson emphasizes her fifty years of missionary work in Japan, devoted primarily to founding and directing Joshi Sei Gakuin, a Christian girls' school that eventually included an elementary school, high school, and Bible college.

0845 Clay, Cassius Marcellus   **1810-1903**
The life of Cassius Marcellus Clay: memoirs, writings, and speeches showing his conduct in the overthrow of American slavery, the salvation of the Union, and the restoration of the autonomy of the states. New York: Negro Universities Press, 1969. (Cincinnati: J. Fletcher Brennan & Co., 1886) 535 p.
A loosely organized account of his personal and public life, including his early conversion to the anti-slavery movement by William Lloyd Garrison, his political career in Kentucky, his diplomatic appointment in Russia, the context of the Civil War, his divorce, and Reconstruction.

0846 Clay, Henry   **1777-1852**
The papers of Henry Clay. Edited by James F. Hopkins. Associate editor, Mary W.M. Hargreaves. Lexington: University of Kentucky Press, 1961-v. Index.
The letters and personal papers from his developing career as a lawyer and statesman, his growing influence and presidential candidacy, his tenure as Secretary of State, and his position as a political leader. Also included are official documents and consular reports from the newly emerging Latin American countries.

0847 Clay, Henry   **1777-1852**
The private correspondence of Henry Clay. Edited by Calvin Colton. Freeport, New York: Books for Libraries Press, 1971. (New York: A.S. Barnes & Co., 1855) 642 p. Index.
Unlike other collections of Clay's papers, this volume includes only his personal correspondence. The editor has chosen to present those letters to and from Clay which shed light on the history of the period without the cautiousness characteristic of more formal public documents.

0848 *Clayton, Mariam Lawton   **b.1885**
A pioneer grandmother's story of her life. New York: Exposition, 1971. 109 p.
Recollection of a frontier life in the West including her youth, school teaching experiences, wedding trip in Wyoming, and farming in Montana.

0849 Clayton, William Lockhart   **1880-1966**
Selected papers of Will Clayton. Edited by Frederick J. Dobney. Baltimore: The Johns Hopkins Press, 1971. 298 p. Index.
A successful business man and "Southern gentleman," Clayton served in Washington as Deputy Federal Loan Administrator, Assistant Secretary of Commerce, 1940-1944; Assistant Secretary of State, 1944-1946; Undersecretary of State, 1946-1947; was a prime mover in the Marshall Plan; and was an important delegate to the International Trade and Employment Conference in Geneva in 1947, the International Trade Organization, and the Atlantic Union.

0850 Cleaver, Joseph, Jr.   **1833-1909**
The diary of a student at Delaware College: August, 1853, to November, 1854. Edited by William Ditto Lewis. Baltimore: J.H. Furst Co., 1951. 87 p.
From a manuscript of the lost original, entries in the diary record Cleaver's daily activities and feelings and include descriptions of the old college building. The editor has provided extensive notes with information from faculty meeting minutes, Athenean Society minutes, and entries from the manuscript diary of his friend David Lewis Mustard.

0851 Cleaves, Emery N.   **1902-**
Sea fever: the making of a sailor. Boston: Houghton Mifflin Co., 1972. 283 p.
After finishing his undergraduate education at Harvard, he shipped out on cargo vessels for eight months, filled with romantic notions of life at sea. The voyage taught him much—that his love for the sea was real and that life at sea in modern times was impractical. That era had passed.

0852 Cleere, William W.   **b.1884**
Hello, hello, hello, Doc. New York: Exposition Press, 1958. 165 p.
A collection of humorous, occasionally sentimental anecdotes concerning the author's practice of medicine in rural Virginia for 44 years. The autobiographer finds jokes concerning drunkenness and obstetrics particularly amusing and, though white, often writes in Black dialect.

0853 Clemens, Orion   **1825-1897**
    see **Clemens, Samuel Langhorne**

0854 Clemens, Samuel Langhorne (Mark Twain, pseud.)   **1835-1910**
Letters from the Earth. Edited by Bernard De Voto. Preface by Henry Nash Smith. New York: Harper & Row Publishers, Inc., 1962. 303 p.
Consists of two main parts: (1) "Letters from the Earth," "Papers of

the Adam Family," and "Letter to the Earth," all on Biblical themes, and (2) DeVoto's selections from unpublished Twain manuscripts, some autobiographical in nature.

0855 Clemens, Samuel Langhorne (Mark Twain, pseud.)   **1835-1910**
Letters from the Sandwich Islands: written for the Sacramento Union by Mark Twain. Introduction and conclusion by G. Ezra Dane. New York: Haskell House Publishers, Ltd., 1972. (Stanford: Stanford University Press, 1938) 224 p.
In 1866, he convinced the Sacramento *Union* to pay him for journalistic accounts of his travels to Hawaii, still called the Sandwich Islands. Much of the material in these letters was used in *Roughing It* and *Innocents Abroad.*

0856 Clemens, Samuel Langhorne (Mark Twain, pseud.)   **1835-1910**
Letters of Quintus Curtius Snodgrass. Edited by Ernest F. Leisy. Dallas: University Press in Dallas/Southern Methodist University, 1946. 76 p.
A series of letters printed in the New Orleans *Daily Crescent* in 1861 satirizing military life, previously thought to be written by Mark Twain.

0857 Clemens, Samuel Langhorne (Mark Twain, pseud.)   **1835-1910**
The love letters of Mark Twain. Edited with an introduction by Dixon Wecter. Westport, Connecticut: Greenwood Press, 1976. (New York: Harper and Brothers, 1949) 374 p.
Letters to Olivia Langdon from courtship through 34 years of marriage. This edition has a check list of the letters (places, dates, brief note of contents) and a list of persons mentioned in the letters.

0858 Clemens, Samuel Langhorne (Mark Twain, pseud.)   **1835-1910**
Mark Twain, business man. Edited by Samuel Charles Webster. Boston: Little, Brown and Co., 1946. 409 p. Index.
Family and business letters, largely concerned with Twain's publishing venture with the editor's father, Charles L. Webster, in a contextual narrative intended to show Twain was responsible for his business losses.

0859 Clemens, Samuel Langhorne (Mark Twain, pseud.)   **1835-1910**
Mark Twain and the three R's: race, religion, revolution and related matters. Edited with introduction by Maxwell Geismar. Indianapolis: Bobbs-Merrill Co., Inc., 1973. 260 p. Index.
An anthology of Twain's radical social commentary and other matters selected from autobiographical and other writings.

0860 Clemens, Samuel Langhorne (Mark Twain, pseud.)   **1835-1910**
Mark Twain to Mrs. Fairbanks. Edited by Dixon Wecter. San Marino, California: Huntington Library, 1949. 286 p. Index.
Author's development during the years between 1867 and settling with his wife and family in Hartford in 1871 shown in annotated letters to Mary Mason Fairbanks from their meeting on a *Quaker City* cruise to her death in 1899.

0861 Clemens, Samuel Langhorne (Mark Twain, pseud.)   **1835-1910**
Mark Twain to Uncle Remus, 1881-1885. Edited by Thomas H. English. Emory Sources and Reprints, Series 7, no. 3. Atlanta: Emory University Library, 1953. 22 p.
The book contains letters from the writer Samuel Clemens (Mark Twain), in Connecticut, to the writer Joel Chandler Harris (Uncle Remus), in Georgia. The letters are mostly concerned with publishing.

0862 Clemens, Samuel Langhorne (Mark Twain, pseud.)   **1835-1910**
Mark Twain's autobiography. Edited by Charles Neider. New York: Harper's, 1959. (1924) 2v.
Since he at first intended that his autobiography would not be published until after his death, he felt he could speak his "whole frank mind" as freely as in a love letter. In fact, he relented and published selected chapters in the *North American Review.* This work concerns his experiences in the West as a miner and journalist and his later career as a humorist.

0863 Clemens, Samuel Langhorne (Mark Twain, pseud.)   **1835-1910**
Mark Twain's correspondence with Henry Huttleston Rogers, 1893-1909. Edited with introduction by Lewis Leary. Berkeley: University of California Press, 1969. 768 p. Index.
Their letters reveal a business relationship that brought Twain from financial disaster to renewed prosperity, as well as a friendship Twain valued highly, and a notable change in his life style, which now depended on male camaraderie.

0864 Clemens, Samuel Langhorne (Mark Twain, pseud.)   **1835-1910**
Mark Twain's letter to William Bowen: Buffalo, February sixth, 1870. Prefatory note by Clara Clemens Gabrilowitsch. Foreword by Albert W. Gunnison. New York: Haskell House Publishers, Ltd., 1975. (San Francisco: The Book Club of California, 1938) 11 p.
Written to his boyhood friend from Hannibal, Missouri, a warm, lively comment on their past friendship and his recent marriage.

0865 Clemens, Samuel Langhorne (Mark Twain, pseud.)   1835-1910
Mark Twain's letters. Arranged with comment by Albert Bigelow Paine. New York: AMS Press, 1975. (New York: Harper and Brothers, 1917) 2v. Index.
   A collection of his letters (1853-1883) depicts the rich and varied character of the artist and philosopher.

0866 Clemens, Samuel Langhorne (Mark Twain, pseud.)   1835-1910
Mark Twain's letters from Hawaii. Edited with introduction by A. Grove Day. Honolulu: University Press of Hawaii, 1975. (New York: Appleton-Century, 1966) 298 p.
   A collection of travel letters based on his daily log, paid for by American newspapers, still remarkably descriptive of life in the Islands.

0867 Clemens, Samuel Langhorne (Mark Twain, pseud.)   1835-1910
Mark Twain's letters in the Muscatine Journal. Edited with introduction by Edgar M. Branch. Folcroft, Pennsylvania: Folcroft Library Editions, 1973. (Chicago: The Mark Twain Association of America, 1942) 28 p.
   Letters written 1853-1855 for the newspaper owned by his brother Orion in Muscatine, Iowa; his first professional writing for public consumption.

0868 Clemens, Samuel Langhorne (Mark Twain, pseud.)   1835-1910
Mark Twain's letters to his publisher, 1867-1894. Edited with introduction by Hamlin Hill. Berkeley: University of California Press, 1967. 388 p. Index.
   Includes the complete texts of 290 letters Twain wrote to his publishers, revealing his ambivalence toward his business affairs and an interesting view of his complex personality.

0869 Clemens, Samuel Langhorne (Mark Twain, pseud.)   1835-1910
Mark Twain's letters to Mary. Edited with commentary by Lewis Leary. New York: Columbia University Press, 1961. 138 p. Index.
   Written to Mary Benjamin Rogers, 1900-1910, these letters from Mark Twain were for him a way of keeping in touch with the vivacity of youth. One of his own daughters was away, the other ill, so Twain made Mary an honorary niece, a companion to whom he could express his many moods and who would give him quick and sympathetic response.

0870 Clemens, Samuel Langhorne (Mark Twain, pseud.)   1835-1910
Mark Twain's notebook: prepared for publication with comments by Albert Bigelow Paine. St. Clair Shores, Michigan: Scholarly Press, Inc., 1971. (New York: Harper Brothers Publishers, 1935) 413 p. Index
   This is a set of journals or commonplace books in which Twain recorded whatever struck his fancy, 1865-1904.

0871 Clemens, Samuel Langhorne (Mark Twain, pseud.)   1835-1910
Mark Twain's notebooks and journals. Edited by Frederick Anderson, Michael B. Frank, Kenneth M. Sanderson. Berkeley: University of California Press, 1975-. v. Index.
   A wealth of information about Twain's multifarious literary projects, business ventures, and personal life.

0872 Clemens, Samuel Langhorne (Mark Twain, pseud.)   1835-1910
Mark Twain's travels with Mr. Brown, being heretofore uncollected sketches . . . describing the adventures of the author and his irrepressible companion in Nicaragua, Hannibal, New York, and other spots on their way to Europe. Collected and with an introduction by Franklin Walker and G. Ezra Dane. New York: Russell and Russell, 1971. (New York: Alfred A. Knopf, 1940) 296 p.
   Weekly letters for the *Alta California* newspaper covering six months of the author's travels between the time he left San Francisco until he sailed from New York in 1867 on the journey described in *Innocents Abroad.*

0873 Clemens, Samuel Langhorne (Mark Twain, pseud.)   1835-1910
The pattern for Mark Twain's, *Roughing It;* **letters from Nevada by Samuel and Orion Clemens, 1861-1862.** Collected and edited with introduction by Franklin R. Rogers. Berkeley: University of California Press, 1961. 72 p. Index.
   Written by Twain before he had any notion of a literary career to *Gate City*, a newspaper in Keokuk, Iowa, describing what he observed in the frontier mining country around Carson City.

0874 Clemens, Samuel Langhorne (Mark Twain, pseud.)   1835-1910
Selected Mark Twain-Howells letters, 1872-1910. Edited by Frederick Anderson, William M. Gibson, and Henry Nash Smith. Cambridge: Harvard University Press, 1967. (1960) 453 p. Index.
   A selection of their letters from the previous two-volume edition (Harvard Univ. Press, 1960), with the addition of two letters discovered since 1960, revealing the rich, enduring friendship of two outstanding literary figures.

0875 Cleveland, Grover   1837-1908
Letters of Grover Cleveland: 1850-1908. Edited by Allan Nevins. Boston: Da Capo Press, 1970. (Boston: Houghton Mifflin Company, 1933) 640 p. Index.
   Selected from the mass of his correspondence, this edition portrays

more of the political than the private man, essentially, Nevins says, because Cleveland chose to reveal so little of his personal life and feelings.

0876 Clifford, Richard L.
A human touch. Edited by Carol Mulvehill. Illustrated by Robert Handville. Maryknoll, New York: Maryknoll Fathers, 1979. 93 p.
   A collection of parable-essays about his parishioners, primarily in Peru, where he was a Maryknoll missionary. His gently pious prose focuses particularly on the very old and very young.

0877 *Clifton, Lucille   1936-
Generations: a memoir. New York: Random House, 1976. 79 p.
   A Black poet describes ways in which her identity grew within the facts and legends of her parents and ancestors, all storytellers who passed on the pain of slavery and the self-respect to survive it.

0878 Cline, Joseph Leander   1870-1955
When the heavens frowned: an autobiography. Dallas: Mathis, Van Nort and Co., 1946. 221 p.
   Youth and teaching experience in Tennessee; then life as a meteorologist in Galveston, Texas.

0879 Clodfelter, Michael
Pawns of dishonor. Boston: Branden Press, 1976. 467 p.
   Clodfelter devotes all but one chapter of this long book to his experiences as an infantryman in the 101st U.S. Army Airborne Division in the Vietnam War, 1964-1967. It is an anti-war book which paradoxically acknowledges his desire for the thrill and glory of battle.

0880 *Clooney, Rosemary   1928-
This for remembrance. With Raymond Strait. Foreword by Bing Crosby. Chicago: Playboy Press, 1978. 270 p.
   Clooney writes with candor about her mental breakdown and institutionalization, partially brought on by her presence at the assassination of her friend Bobby Kennedy. She describes her Irish Catholic upbringing, marriage to José Ferrer, her rise to fame as a singer and actress, and finally her struggle back to sanity and happiness.

0881 Clower, Jerry   1926-
Let the hammer down! And Gerry Wood. Illustrated. Waco, Texas: Word Books, 1978. 189 p.
   The title means "do the best you can, with maximum effort," and Clower's anecdotes, told in down-home folksy Southern humor and dialect, are intended to make this point. He is a Christian moralist in a comic vein and from that perspective describes his tours, TV appearances, lectures, and people he has met.

0882 Clubb, Oliver Edmund   1901-
The witness and I. New York: Columbia Univ. Press, 1974. 314 p. Index.
   A career diplomat, he was appointed director of the State Department's Office of Chinese Affairs in 1950. In 1951 he was accused of being a communist sympathizer by Whittaker Chambers. His book describes the impact of McCarthyism and the Cold War on the State Department, the Foreign Service, and his life.

0883 Clune, Henry W.   1892-
Main Street beat. New York: W.W. Norton and Co., 1947. 269 p.
   Experience as a journalist in Rochester, New York, 1910-1947.

0884 Clurman, Harold Edgar   1901-
All people are famous (instead of an autobiography). New York: Harcourt Brace Jovanovich, 1974. 327 p. Index.
   A stage director, critic, and founder of the Group Theatre recalls his encounters with many of the great creative people of the twentieth century and his own part in shaping the cultural history of America.

0885 Clytus, John   1929-
Black man in red Cuba. With Jane Rieker. Coral Gables, Florida: University of Miami Press, 1970. 158 p.
   In 1964 Clytus arrived in Cuba determined to leave the capitalist United States behind forever. After three years of attempting to be accepted, he returned disillusioned to America "convinced that a 'Negro' Communist is an absurdity and a black Communist is an impossibility," and that communism exploits all, "rich and poor, who do not dance to the dictatorial tune of its ruling hierarchy."

0886 Coates, Robert Myron   1897-1973
The view from here. New York: Harcourt, Brace and Co., 1960. 215 p.
   Reflections on his childhood, his warm relation to his parents, the coming of the automobile, of World War I, and a personal view of his experience in Paris during the Twenties, which he saw as an era of hope.

0887 *Coatsworth, Elizabeth Jane   1893-
Maine memories. Brattleboro, Vermont: The Stephen Greene Press, 1968. 165 p.

A nostalgic look at the years of early middle age, the work and pleasure, the children growing up, the neighbors, and the simpler life in Maine.

0888 *Coatsworth, Elizabeth Jane   1893-
Maine ways. Illustrated by Mildred Coughlin. New York: The Macmillan Co., 1947. 213 p.
   Contented with her life, Coatsworth writes pleasant, low-keyed stories about daily events, eccentric characters, and the ways of nature down East in her beloved Maine.

0889 *Coatsworth, Elizabeth Jane   1893-
Personal geography: almost an autobiography. Brattleboro, Vermont: A Janet Greene Book/Stephen Greene Press, 1976. 192 p. Index.
   Coatsworth, poet and author of a Newbery award-winning children's book, has assembled a collection of excerpts from her notebooks and accounts of travel to Europe and the Far East, bridged by poetry. The book reveals a perceptive writer who at 36 married another author, Henry Beston, reared two daughters on a beloved Maine farm, and found beauty, inspiration, and joy in the minutiae of nature and family life.

0890 *Cobb, Geraldyn M. (Jerrie)   1931-
Woman into space: the Jerrie Cobb story. With Jane Rieker. Englewood Cliffs, New Jersey: Prentice-Hall, Inc., 1963. 223 p.
   After a brief description of her childhood in Oklahoma and her early interest in flying, she describes the rigorous training and testing program she passed in order to be considered for the position of first female astronaut and the conservative public and congressional reaction to the idea of a woman in space.

0891 Cobe, Albert
Great spirit. With George Elrick and R.E. Simon, Jr. Chicago: Children's Press, 1970. 64 p.
   A golf pro recalls his difficult childhood years in various Indian schools, his happier years at Haskell Institute, his career in professional sports, and the conflict he experienced between his love for Chippewa traditions and his need for success in the white man's world.

0892 Coblentz, Stanton Arthur   1896-
My life in poetry. New York: Bookman Associates, 1959. 182 p.
   A thoughtful account of his development as a poet and, incidentally, as a man of letters, and an articulate defense of traditional verse, metrical and rhymed, against modern verse, which is neither.

0893 Coblentz, William Weber   1873-1962
From the life of a researcher. New York: Philosophical Library, 1951. 238 p. Index.
   In his narrative autobiography, required of academicians in the National Academy of Sciences, Coblentz provides family background, descriptions of four decades of research in physics, and details of his interest in nature, including intense research activity in astronomy and medicine.

0894 Coburn, Alvin Langdon   1882-1966
Alvin Langdon Coburn, photographer; an autobiography with over 70 reproductions of his works. Edited by Helmut and Alison Gernsheim. Illustrated. Introduction by Helmut Gernsheim. New York: Dover, 1978. (New York: Praeger, 1966) 145 p. Index.
   This fascinating book combines Coburn's story of his career as a photographer (mostly in England, the United States, Spain, and France) with many of his photographs. He includes anecdotes about and correspondence with some of his most famous subjects, including George Bernard Shaw and Henry James. Coburn was born in Boston, reared in Los Angeles, but lived most of his life in England and traveled widely, camera in hand.

0895 Coburn, Walt   1889-1971
Walt Coburn: Western word wrangler; an autobiography. Illustrated. Flagstaff, Arizona: Northland Press, 1973. 255 p.
   Coburn, a prolific writer for fifty years, published over one thousand short stories in popular Western pulp magazines as well as nearly one hundred books. His cowboy background lent authenticity to his stories and merited him the appellation King of the Western Pulps.

0896 Cochise, Ciye Nino   b.1874
The first hundred years of Nino Cochise; the untold story of an Apache Indian chief. As told to A. Kinney Griffith London: Abelard-Schuman, 1971. 346 p. Index.
   The grandson of Chief Cochise tells the story of the 38 Chiricahui Apache Indians led by his mother who escaped to Mexico to avoid relocation to the San Carlos Reservation. He writes from his own memories and from tales told him by his mother and his shaman. In later life he tried acting in Hollywood, flying airplanes, and taking part in several unsuccessful business ventures.

0897 *Cochran, Jacqueline (Mrs. Floyd B. Odlum)
Stars at noon. With Floyd Odlum. Boston: Little, Brown and Co., 1954. 274 p.
   The author describes her poverty-stricken youth in Florida, her career as

a cosmetologist, and the beginnings of her career as an aviator. She includes memories of record-breaking flights and her work with other women as aviators in the World War II war effort.

0898 Cochran, Louis   1899-
FBI man: a personal history. New York: Duell, Sloan and Pearce, 1966. 207 p.
   An account of Cochran's pre-World War II years as an FBI Special Agent, written with an eye for the hardboiled, Sam Spade image and an ear for the sanctimonious. Cochran writes from the conviction that the FBI under J. Edgar Hoover rightfully attained an "almost legendary image" and claims that "Criminals, traitors, and bigots, the enemies of the Federal Bureau of Investigation, lawbreakers and extremists of any sort would find no comfort in my book," dedicated to the preservation of law and order in the Cold War era.

0899 Cochran, Mickey   1924-
The Cochran family book of ski racing. And Bill Bruns. New York: Hawthorn Books, Inc., 1977. 167 p. Index.
   Cochran, coach of the 1973-1974 U.S. Ski Team which starred his four children, devotes the first third of the book to an autobiographical account of his family's passion for skiing; they own and operate a mountain ski area in Vermont. The remainder of the book explains Cochran's techniques of ski racing—body position, curved turns, racing turns, speed, mental attitudes, conditioning, and training.

0900 Cockerell, Theodore Dru Alison   1866-1948
Theodore D.A. Cockerell: letters from West Cliff, Colorado, 1887-1889. Edited by William A. Weber. Illustrated by author. Boulder: Colorado Associated University Press, 1976. 222 p.
   These attractive letters, enhanced by the naturalist's drawings of settings, animals, and insects, discuss Cockerell's life and scientific investigations in West Cliff, Colorado, where he was sent from England to recuperate from tuberculosis. He provides a fascinating view of the frontier—animals, vegetation, terrain, and social customs of pioneers, miners, prospectors, and gamblers.

0901 Codrescu, Andrei   1946-
The life and times of an involuntary genius. New York: George Braziller, 1975. 192 p.
   A poet born and brought up under the repression of a communist regime, Codrescu fled from Transylvania after being expelled from the university and sent a notice of military conscription. He wandered through Europe and the U.S., finally settling in California.

0902 Cody, William Frederick (Buffalo Bill)   1846-1917
Letters from Buffalo Bill: taken from the originals now on exhibit at the Wonderland Museum, Billings, Montana. Edited by Stella Adelyne Foote. Illustrated. Billings, Montana: Foote Pub. Co., 1954. 80 p.
   Buffalo Bill Cody's letters (1876-1916) to his "mother-sister," Julia Cody Goodman, discuss business matters pertinent to his Wild West Shows and investments, good and bad, and his relations with women, also good and bad.

0903 Cody, William Frederick (Buffalo Bill)   1846-1917
Life and adventures of Buffalo Bill: Colonel William F. Cody. Freeport, New York: Books for Libraries Press, 1971. (Chicago: Homewood Press, 1917) 352 p.
   A myth in his own time, he includes stories of his childhood in Kansas, his service on the Pony Express, his career as a hunter and Indian scout, and his touring Wild West Show.

0904 Cody, William Frederick (Buffalo Bill)   1846-1917
Life of Hon. William F. Cody: Known as Buffalo Bill, the famous hunter, scout, and guide: an autobiography. Foreword by Don Russell. Illustrated. Lincoln, Nebraska: University of Nebraska Press, 1978. (Hartford, Connecticut: Frank E. Bliss, 1879) 365 p.
   This Bison Book edition claims to be the first complete reprinting of Cody's original 1879 autobiography—a partly plagiarized book that was frequently modified by many ghost writers. The book contains fascinating accounts of Cody's life on the plains as pony express rider, coach driver, scout extraordinaire for the Union Army, buffalo hunter, Indian fighter, guide, and late in life, actor and creator of Buffalo Bill's Wild West Show.

0905 Coe, Charles
Young man in Vietnam. New York: Four Winds Press, 1968. 109 p.
   A striking account of his experience as a Marine lieutenant in Vietnam reveals the horror and confusion of a strange war in a strange time.

0906 Coe, George Washington   1856-1941
Frontier fighter: the autobiography of George W. Coe, who fought and rode with Billy the Kid. As related to Nan Hillary Harrison. Albuquerque: University of New Mexico Press, 2nd ed., 1951. (Boston: Houghton Mifflin Co., 1934) 220 p.
   Recollections by Billy the Kid's best friend of the excitement and hardships of frontier life during the settlement of the Western territory, as outlaw then as homesteader.

0907 Coffin, Levi   **1798-1877**
Reminiscences of Levi Coffin. New York: Arno Press and the New York Times, 1968. (Cincinnati: R. Clarke, 1876) 732 p.
An abolitionist who assisted nearly three thousand runaway slaves to escape was called the President of the Underground Railway. His book tells of many dramatic escapes, of mobs and riots, of risks incurred by the friends of slaves, of the free produce movement, and of his journeys to the North, the South, Canada, and England for the cause.

0908 Coffin, Robert Peter Tristram   **1892-1955**
Lost paradise: a boyhood on a Maine coast farm. St. Clair Shores, Michigan: Scholarly Press, Inc., 1971. (New York: The Macmillan Company, 1934) 284 p.
A poet's third person narrative describes his Maine boyhood with affection for its simplicity, the warmth of his close family life, the strength of their New England values.

0909 Coffin, William Sloane   **1924-**
Once to every man: a memoir. New York: Atheneum, 1977. 344 p.
Coffin aspired to be a concert pianist before World War II made him a Russian Liaison Officer, followed by Yale, Union Theological Seminary, and a stint training Russian agents for the CIA. His aggressiveness as a young officer (remarked on by General Eisenhower) has informed his career as a chaplain, civil rights advocate, and noted practitioner of civil disobedience.

0910 Coffman, William Milo   **b.1883**
America in the rough: the autobiography of W.M. (Bill) Coffman. New York: Simon and Schuster, 1955. 309 p.
The youthful, often rowdy adventures on land and sea of the man who became a promoter for the Shriners, raising millions to establish homes for crippled children.

0911 *Coghlan, Margaret (Moncrieffe)   **b.1762**
Memoirs of Mrs. Coghlan. Eyewitness Accounts of the American Revolution. New York: The New York Times and Arno Press, 1971. (London: J. Lane, 1794) 158 p.
The daughter of Major Moncrieffe includes in her memoirs descriptions of America during the Revolutionary War.

0912 Cogley, John   **1916-1976**
A Canterbury Tale: experiences and reflections: 1916-1976. New York: Seabury Press, 1976. 126 p.
Cogley's editorial career began on *The Catholic Worker*, then *Commonweal*. He became religious news editor of the New York *Times* and editor of the *Center Magazine* at the Center for the Study of Democratic Institutions. Cogley reflects on his spiritual and theological discomfort in a church unresponsive to changing times, which gradually determined his conversion to Episcopalianism in 1973.

0913 Cohan, George Michael   **1878-1942**
Twenty years on Broadway, and the years it took to get there: the true story of a trouper's life from the cradle to the closed shop. Westport, Connecticut: Greenwood Press, Publishers, 1971. (New York: Harper & Brothers, 1925) 264 p.
In his day, his book might have been called scrappy, sometimes fresh. It conveys a sense of what Broadway and New York were like during the early twentieth century, focusing on the theatrical life and family of an actor, composer, and playwright.

0914 Cohen, Julius Henry   **1873-1950**
They builded better than they knew. Freeport, New York: Books for Libraries Press, 1971. (New York: Julian Messner, Inc., 1946) 376 p. Index.
General Counsel for the New York Port Authority for over twenty years, an important contributor to labor law, author of *Commercial Arbitration and the Law*, describes the times, people, and events during his fifty years as a public servant.

0915 Cohen, Morris Raphael   **1880-1947**
Dreamer's journey: autobiography. New York: Arno Press, 1955. (Boston, Massachusetts: The Beacon Press, 1949) 318 p. Index.
Following a description of childhood in Russia and adolescence in New York's East Side, the book primarily describes Cohen's development as a philosopher and teacher at New York City College and Harvard and his important contributions to social, legal and scientific philosophy.

0916 Cohen, Morris Raphael   **1880-1947**
Portrait of a philosopher: Morris R. Cohen in life and letters. Edited by Leonora Cohen Rosenfield. New York: Harcourt, Brace and World, Inc., 1962. 461 p. Index.
The letters, diaries, and other papers of a prominent philosopher at Harvard, edited by his daughter to depict his rich and varied character in his words and those of his friends, including Albert Einstein, Felix Frankfurter, and Oliver Wendell Holmes, Jr.

0917 Colby, William Egan   **1920-**
Honorable men: my life with the CIA. And Peter Forbath. Illustrated. New York: Simon & Schuster, 1978. 493 p. Index.
Colby's account of his directorship of the CIA reads like the penultimate spy novel, as he details the complex, violence-ridden undercover operations.

0918 Colcord, Charles Francis   **1859-1934**
Autobiography of Charles Francis Colcord: 1859-1934. Tulsa, Oklahoma: C.C. Helmerich, 1970. 245 p. Index.
Recognized for many years as "First Citizen of Oklahoma City" and then as "First Citizen of Oklahoma," Colcord's history as cowboy, rancher, sheriff, real estate and oil executive parallels the fortunes of the state in its progress from wild, unsettled early days through the development of its wealth and resources and the evolving of stability.

0919 *Cole, Catherine
see *O'Connor, Patti

0920 *Coleman, Ann Thomas Raney   **1810-1897**
Victorian lady on the Texas frontier: the journal of Ann Raney Coleman. Edited by C. Richard King. Illustrated. Norman: University of Oklahoma Press, 1971. 206 p. Index.
Coleman recalls nineteenth-century Texas—the rough terrain, the Indians, the abundance of men and scarcity of women, the Negro slaves, the rugged transportation, and personal poverty.

0921 Coleman, James Weatherby   **1894-**
Experiences of an Arkansas backwoodsman. Illustrated by Lynn Ellen Coleman. New York: Vantage Press, 1976. 158 p.
Coleman tells of his childhood in rural Arkansas, focusing on daily activities such as farming, hunting, and going to school, punctuated by the circus, pranks, and accidents. He then describes his career as a professor of physical education and coach at Georgetown (Kentucky) College, the University of Akron, State College at Minot, North Dakota, and the University of Nevada at Reno.

0922 Coleman, John Royston   **1921-**
Blue-collar journal: a college president's sabbatical. Philadelphia: J.B. Lippincott Co., 1974. 252 p.
The journal kept for eight weeks during spring of 1973 when Coleman, on sabbatical from his presidency of Haverford College, worked at blue collar jobs in order "to break the lockstep for a while." He started as a ditch digger laying sewer pipe, then was a porter-dishwasher and salad man in a restaurant, and finally a trash collector. His experiences were both amusing and instructive.

0923 Coleman, Thomas W.   **1849-1921**
I buried Custer: the diary of Pvt. Thomas W. Coleman, 7th U.S. Cavalry. Edited by Bruce R. Liddic. Introduction by John M. Carroll. Illustrated by James H. Earle. College Station, Texas: Creative Publishing Co., 1979. 210 p.
This twelve-page diary provides a terse account of Private Coleman's participation in the Battle of the Little Big Horn, June 25-26, 1876. The rest of the book provides a biography of Coleman and amplifies the historical information about the battle and General Custer.

0924 *Colley, Ophelia
see *Pearl, Minnie

0925 Collier, John   **1884-1968**
From every zenith a memoir, and some essays on life and thought. Denver, Colorado: Sage Books, 1963. 477 p.
A committed humanist writes of his life as a social scientist devoted to the struggles of American Indians, with considerable analysis of government policy on Indian affairs.

0926 *Collier, Sophia   **1956-**
Soul rush: the odyssey of a young woman of the '70s. New York: William Morrow & Co., 1978. 240 p.
A wealthy flower child of the late Sixties and Seventies writes to demonstrate how much she has done, and how well. She dropped out of several schools, was raped while hitching, had a number of casual love affairs, and had been a disciple of Guru Marahj Ji and a organizer of Divine Light Mission, from which she resigned in order to write this book.

0927 Collins, Lee   **1901-1960**
Oh, didn't he ramble: the life story of Lee Collins. As told to Mary Collins. Edited by Frank J. Gillis and John W. Miner. Urbana: University of Illinois Press, 1974. 159 p. Index.
One of the great jazz cornet players, first in New Orleans and later in Chicago, started to dictate and write his story in 1943. Later the material was updated and edited to form this chronological account. Included are a discography and a record made by Collins of several performances, 1948-1953.

0928 **Collins, Michael** 1930-
Carrying the fire: an astronaut's journeys. Foreword by Charles A. Lindbergh. New York: Farrar, Straus and Giroux, 1974. 478 p.

Astronaut Collins, who orbited the moon while the first moon-landers Armstrong and Aldrin walked on it, traces his participation in the selection process, the training, the Gemini 10 flight, and the moon orbit. He explains how the machines operated and what it was like living in the artificial, high-pressure environment. An appendix includes information about U.S. manned space flights up to 1974.

0929 **Collins, William J.**
Out of the depths; the story of a priest-patient in a mental hospital. Garden City, New York: Doubleday & Co., Inc., 1971. 287 p.

A description of the ordeal of a young priest who worked his way through emotional illness. He writes with careful detail of his learning experience acquired through therapy.

0930 **Colman, Moses Rich** 1807-1872
Captain Moses Rich Colman: master mariner, Scituate, Massachusetts, 1807-1872; letters of a Yankee clipper ship captain. Compiled and edited by Addie Cushing Colman. Dorchester, Massachusetts: printed for the editor, 1949. 119 p.

Excerpts from his letters depict the life of a typical seaman in nineteenth-century New England.

0931 **Colonel Yay**
see Panlilia, Yay

0932 **Colson, Charles W.** 1931-
Born again. New York: Bantam Books, 1977. (New Jersey: Fleming H. Revell, 1976) 406 p. Index.

Colson, a talented, ambitious lawyer, joined President Nixon's inner circle as one who ruthlessly cut through legal red tape to solve political problems. His illegal actions led to a jail term, but a religious conversion enabled him not only to survive but to prevail. "Nixon's hatchet man found spiritual rebirth," which he emphasizes here.

0933 **Colton, Walter** 1797-1851
Three years in California: together with excerpts from the author's Deck and Port, covering his arrival in California and a selection of his letters from Monterey. Introduction and notes by Marguerite Eyer Wilbur. Stanford: Stanford University Press, 1949. (New York: D.W. Evans, 1860) 376 p.

Responsible for the jurisdiction of a large territory of California around Monterey from 1846 to 1849, a naval officer and chaplain describes military operations and the daily life of a diverse population living there at the time.

0934 *****Colum, Mary Gunning (Maguire)** 1887-1957
Life and the dream. Revised with additional material. Chester Springs, Pa.: Dufour Editions, 1966. (Garden City, New York: Doubleday and Co., Inc., 1947) 378 p. Index.

Before moving to America in 1914, Colum was active in the literary circles of the Abbey Theatre in Dublin, in Paris, and in London. Her book includes rich descriptions of her intellectual growth in the world of letters.

0935 **Colvin, Fred Herbert** 1867-1965
Sixty years with men and machines: an autobiography. With D.J. Duffin. New York: Whittlesey House, 1947. 297 p. Index.

Describes his experience in the world of invention, machinery, and production from 1884-1944, including his participation in the development of the bicycle, the automobile, the airplane, and the railroad locomotive, as well as hundreds of machines and machine tools. Colvin was an editor for *American Machinist* for over thirty years and wrote more than forty technical books that sold over a million copies.

0936 **Commons, John Rogers** 1862-1945
Myself: the autobiography of John R. Commons. Madison: University of Wisconsin Press, 1963. 201 p.

The informal story of a labor historian and economist who held positions on numerous state and federal boards and commissions and whose economic ideas expressed in his writing and teaching have had considerable influence in shaping modern economic theory.

0937 **Compton, Arthur Holly** 1892-1962
Atomic quest: a personal narrative. New York: Oxford University Press, 1956. 370 p. Index.

"A personal story of the release of the atom's energy," by a physicist who was at the center of atomic research through World War II and after.

0938 **Compton, Charles Herrick** 1880-1966
Memories of a librarian. St. Louis: St. Louis Public Library, 1954. 197 p.

A librarian in Seattle and Nebraska discusses libraries, other librarians, and recounts parts of speeches given at various library conferences.

0939 *****Conant, Charlotte Howard** 1862-1925
A girl of the Eighties at college and at home, from the family letters of Charlotte Howard Conant and from other records, by Martha Pike Conant and others. Boston: Houghton Mifflin Co., 1931. 261 p.

As much a family portrait as autobiography, this collage of reminiscences and letters describes the New England girlhood and college life of a woman who was to teach, work in a law office, serve as charity supervisor, and finally became headmistress of the Walnut Hill School for Girls in Natick, Massachusetts.

0940 **Conant, James Bryant** 1893-1978
My several lives: memoirs of a social inventor. New York: Harper & Row, 1970. 701 p. Index.

Conant's lives include several positions of importance including the presidency of Harvard University. He "invented" scholarships, professorships, MAT degrees for future teachers, the Nieman Defense Research Committee, the Committee on Present Danger, and the Education Commission of the States. Here he writes about his busy life of service to his university and his country.

0941 **Condon, Eddie** 1905-1973
The Eddie Condon scrapbook of jazz. And Hank O'Neal. Illustrated. New York: St. Martin's/Galahad Books, 1973. 284 p.

A scrapbook of photos and clippings with explanations and narrative becomes an autobiographical account of a half century of the jazz age by one of its outstanding participants.

0942 **Condon, Eddie** 1905-1973
We called it music; a generation of jazz. Narration by Thomas Sugrue. Westport, Connecticut: Greenwood Press, 1970. (London: Peter Davis, 1948) 341 p. Index.

First-class jazz musicians are few; Condon is one of the best. Here are his memories and assessments of his fellow musicians. Appended is information about ten Chicago bands and an informal Condon discography.

0943 **Condon, Richard** 1915-
And then we moved to Rossenarra; or, the art of emigrating. New York: Dial Press, 1973. 302 p.

The travels of a peripatetic American family which has moved about 29 times—to Ireland, Spain, France, Switzerland, Mexico and back to Ireland several times. Condon writes humorously of people and customs, of food and bathtubs, and of hotels and houses he has known.

0944 **Conlan, John (Jocko) Bertrand** 1899-
Jocko. With Robert Creamer. Illustrated. Philadelphia: J.B. Lippincott, 1967. 240 p.

Conlan describes his career in baseball, first as a player in the AA League and for the Chicago White Sox, 1919-1936, followed by 25 years as an umpire in the major leagues. With candor and down-to-earth language, he discusses the nice and not-so-nice players he has met, the spitball and the beanball, and the umpires' strike.

0945 **Connally, Thomas Terry** 1877-1963
My name is Tom Connally. As told to Alfred Steinberg. New York: Thomas Y. Crowell, 1954. 369 p. Index.

A former senator from Texas discusses his political career from 1915 to 1952, describing politics and government as an integral part of his life.

0946 **Connell, Robert** 1846-1932
Arkansas. New York: The Paebar Company, 1947. 128 p.

Dictated to his daughter when he was 82, the book describes his experience on the Arkansas River and in Arizona Territory, where he worked hard for statehood.

0947 **Connelly, Marc** 1890-1981
Voices offstage: a book of memoirs. New York: Holt, Rinehart & Winston, Inc., 1968. 258 p.

The memoir of an era of outstanding American theater and literary life reflected in the life of an outstanding playwright. Connelly collaborated often with George S. Kaufman and knew most of the celebrities of his time. He is best remembered for his play *The Green Pastures*, which was awarded the Pulitzer Prize.

0948 **Connelly, William Lawrence** 1873-1964
Oil business as I saw it: half a century with Sinclair. Foreword by P.C. Lauinger. Norman: University of Oklahoma Press, 1954. 163 p. Index.

A petroleum executive describes his beginnings in the oil industry, his association with the Sinclair Oil Company in Oklahoma, and his subsequent global adventures in the service of that company.

0949 **Conner, Dennis** 1942-
No excuse to lose: winning yacht races. As told to John Rousmaniere. Illustrated. New York: W.W. Norton & Co., 1978. 192 p. Index.

Conner remains a determined amateur in boat racing and has sailed and won in America's Cup, Congressional Cup, and Southern Ocean Racing Conference races since 1974. He gives advice on how to select boats, crew, and how to prepare and sail a winning boat. He discusses the winning styles of today's outstanding yachtsmen: Ted Hood, Lowell North, Ted Turner, and Buddy Melges, among others.

0950 *Conner, Virginia (Brandreth)   **b.1877?**
What Father forbad. Philadelphia: Dorrance and Co., 1951. 219 p.
     In a sprightly account, the socialite wife of an Army general describes an active life including entertainment, coping with servants, raising children, dealing with numerous illnesses, and enjoying grandchildren.

0951 Conrad, Barnaby   **1922-**
Fun while it lasted. New York: Random House, 1969. 392 p.
     At nineteen he jumped into a Mexican bullring on a dare, full of youthful romanticism he had absorbed while reading Hemingway's *Death in the Afternoon.* Thereafter his life, which had begun in privilege, was a series of adventures and varied careers as a bullfighter, painter, novelist, and restaurateur. His novel *Matador* sold over two and a half million copies and has been translated into eighteen languages.

0952 Conroy, Frank   **1936-**
Stop-time. New York: Penguin Books, 1977. (New York: The Viking Press, 1967) 283 p.
     A re-creation of Conroy's childhood and youth, ranging from rural Chula Vista, Florida, where he enjoyed the privacy of a tree house and expertise on the yo-yo, to New York City, where he was a marginal student at Stuyvesant High School and held a series of odd jobs. He spent a transitional year at an International Folk (High) School in Denmark. Interwoven are painful interludes with his Danish mother and shiftless stepfather.

0953 Conway, Ainslie
The enchanted islands. And Frances Conway. New York: G.P. Putnam's Sons, 1947. 287 p.
     Pioneering for five years in the Galapagos Islands (1937-1942).

0954 Conway, Frances
see Conway, Ainslie

0955 Cook, Frederick Albert   **1865-1940**
Return from the Pole. Edited with introduction by Frederick J. Pohl. New York: Pellegrini and Cudahy, 1951. 335 p.
     Written between 1930 and 1935, Dr. Cook's narrative describes his party's dangerous journey back from the North Pole in 1908-09. The editor discusses the Cook-Peary controversy and Cook's later life.

0956 Cook, Harold Oatman   **b.1885?**
Fifty years a forester. In cooperation with Lewis A. Carter. Boston: Massachusetts Forest and Park Association, 1961. 62 p.
     Cook began his forestry career in 1907 when Theodore Roosevelt and Gifford Pinchot were leading the forest conservation movement. He finds that his career parallels national crises—"State Forests Go to War," "The Civilian Conservation Corps," etc.—as he reminisces a half-century later on the growth of Massachusetts's forests.

0957 Cook, James H. (Captain Jim)   **1857-1942**
Fifty years on the old frontier: as cowboy, hunter, guide, scout, and ranchman. Foreword by J. Frank Dobie. Introduction by Charles King. Illustrated. Norman: University of Oklahoma Press, 1980. (New Haven, Connecticut: Yale Univ. Press, 1923) 253 p. Index.
     Cook went west, learned to be an expert cowboy, hunter, and guide. His description of life on the old frontier is a straightforward statement of both the difficulties and the excitement of those times. He served as an army scout during the Apache War and formed close friendships with many Indians, some of whom petitioned Washington to make Cook their government agent. Late in life he became a rancher but continued to have contacts with his old friends, including a number of Indians.

0958 Cook, John L.   **1945-**
The advisor. Philadelphia: Dorrance & Co., 1973. 287 p.
     For 25 months he was stationed in Vietnam. His book describes in realistic human terms the struggle of one community to rid itself of Viet Cong control.

0959 Cook, Joseph   **1838-1901**
see Cook, William Henry

0960 Cook, William Henry   **1812-1885**
Letters of a Ticonderoga farmer: selections from the correspondence of William H. Cook and his wife with their son, Joseph Cook, 1851-1885. Edited by Frederick G. Bascom. Ithaca, New York: Cornell University Press, 1946. 134 p.
     Farm life in Ticonderoga; son's experience at Andover, Yale, Harvard; and his career as a lecturer for YMCA.

0961 *Cooke, Anne (Strother) Kirk Rogers
The other Mrs. Simpson: postscript to the love story of the century. And Elizabeth Lightfoot. New York: Vantage Press, 1977. 203 p.

A former alcoholic socialite in the 1930's and 1940's writes of her unfulfilled relationship with her sister, Mary, who married Ernest A. Simpson, former husband of the Duchess of Windsor.

0962 Cooley, Mortimer Elwyn   **1855-1944**
Scientific blacksmith: autobiography. Prepared with the assistance of Vivien B. Keatley. New York: Arno Press, 1972. (Ann Arbor: University of Michigan Press, 1947) 290 p.
     Boyhood in western New York; training at the U.S. Naval Academy, Annapolis; professor, then Dean of the College of Engineering, University of Michigan, 1881-1928.

0963 *Coolidge, Elizabeth Sprague   **1864-1953**
Da Capo: a paper read before the Mothers' Club, Cambridge, Mass., March 13, 1951. Washington, D.C.: Library of Congress, Elizabeth Sprague Coolidge Foundation, 1952. 14 p.
     Coolidge describes her activities as a patron of music, 1916-1950, particularly of the Berkshire Quartet and Berkshire Festival, and of concerts in the Library of Congress.

0964 *Coon, Helen L.
Trial and triumph, or, I never gave up, never! Illustrated. Clearwater, Florida: The Eldnar Press, 1973. 95 p.
     Published in the early era of Women's Liberation, this book tells the story of a woman widowed during World War I who kept working, established an independent business, remarried, and developed a life of contentment, all "on her own."

0965 Coons, William R.
Attica diary. New York: Stein and Day, 1972. 238 p.
     A day-by-day account of Coons's fifteen-month's term in Attica prison, his thoughts, conflicts, and rage at the inhuman debasement of prison life. Convicted for possession of LSD, he condemns the prison, its warden, and society for the cruel punishment and terrible conditions existing at the prison. He was released just before the bloody uprising in September 1971.

0966 Cooper, James Fenimore   **1789-1851**
Correspondence of James Fenimore Cooper. Edited by his grandson, James Fenimore Cooper. Freeport, New York: Books for Libraries Press, 1971. (New Haven: Yale University Press, 1922) 2v. Index.
     Despite the fact that much Cooper material was destroyed, his character is revealed in his extant letters. Some of these here presented were written to his wife and family giving account of his activities and news of friends; other letters from his friends reveal indirectly his views on current questions.

0967 Cooper, James Fenimore   **1789-1851**
The letters and journals of James Fenimore Cooper. Edited by James Franklin Beard. Cambridge: The Belknap Press of Harvard University Press, 1960-1968. 6v. Index.
     Cooper's central position in the early development of American literature gives his observations and opinions special cogency. These six volumes of his letters and journals, 1800-1851, have as their central theme his relationship to his country and record almost every phase of American life which caught his wide-ranging curiosity and interest.

0968 Cooper, Kent   **1880-1965**
Kent Cooper and the Associated Press: an autobiography. New York: Random House, 1959. 334 p. Index.
     The title is apt, for much of his sixty-year career in journalism was devoted to organizing the Associated Press. He initiated reporting by telephone, wirephoto, and the role of AP as an international news distributing service.

0969 *Cooper, Miriam   **1891-**
Dark lady of the silents; my life in early Hollywood. Illustrated by Bonnie Herndon. Indianapolis: The Bobbs-Merrill Co., Inc., 1973. 256 p. Index.
     She starred in *Birth of a Nation* and *Intolerance,* directed by D.W. Griffith, and many other silent movies, 1911-23. For many years she was married to Raoul Walsh, who produced and directed several of her movies. Her book describes her life in early Hollywood as a star and later as a friend and participant in the film world.

0970 Copley, John Singleton   **1738-1815**
Letters and papers of John Singleton Copley and Henry Pelham, 1739-1776. New York: AMS Press, 1972. (Boston: Massachusetts Historical Society, 1914) 384 p.
     Somehow these papers became a part of the British State Papers during the American Revolution. Many of the letters are about Massachusetts before the Revolution and provide interesting information on the painter's early work.

0971 Copper, Arnold
Psychic summer. And Coralee Leon. New York: Dial Press, 1976. 184 p.
     Interior decorator Copper describes fourteen Ouija board séances at Fire Island in the summer of 1976 that conjured up tormented spirits

from a nineteenth-century shipwreck. The spirits appeared in a photograph of his friends, left a starfish as a memento, and nearly drowned Copper as he swam offshore.

0972 Coppini, Pompeo   **1870-1957**
From dawn to sunset. San Antonio, Texas: Press of the Naylor Co., 1949. 404 p. Index.
    A sculptor and professor of fine arts, Coppini discusses his life and work, primarily in San Antonio; his interest and involvement with commemorating and preserving historical events and places; his disappointments and awards of recognition in his field.

0973 Corey, Stephen Jared   **b.1874**
As I look back. Lexington, Kentucky: College of the Bible, 1958. 88 p.
    Corey, reared in the Missouri Ozarks, became an ordained Disciple of Christ minister and a member of the Foreign Christian Missionary Society, traveled to Africa, the Orient, Latin America, India, and Palestine. Although the book focuses on his world travels, Corey was also President of the College of the Bible (Lexington, Kentucky), 1939-48.

0974 Corlett, Charles H.   **1884-1971**
Cowboy Pete: the autobiography of Major General Charles H. Corlett. Edited by Wm. Farrington. Santa Fe, New Mexico: Sleeping Fox Enterprises, 1974. 127 p. Index.
    Raised in the cattle country of Colorado, Corlett attended West Point, served in World War I, worked with the CCC in the Thirties, and during World War II was in Alaska, Kwajalein, and Europe. After his retirement from the army, he filled several state government posts in New Mexico under Governor Mechem.

0975 Cornelius, Temple H.   **1891-1964**
Sheepherder's gold. Illustrated. Denver: Sage Books, 1964. 186 p.
    Writing in language surprisingly formal in comparison with the rough-and-ready prospector's life he describes, Cornelius tells of the searches he and others made for gold in New Mexico and Colorado during the early part of the twentieth century. Forgotten or misplaced caches; friendly and hostile Ute Indians, Mexicans, and rural prospectors; and rugged terrain and weather complicate the quest.

0976 Corner, George Washington   **b.1889**
Anatomist at large: an autobiography and selected essays. Essay Index Reprint. Freeport, New York: Books for Libraries Press, 1969. (New York: Basic Books, Inc., 1958) 215 p.
    Corner's details of his student years at Johns Hopkins and his career in biology as a professor and physician. Citing many distinguished members of the profession, he gives a short history of medical advancements in the first half of this century.

0977 *Cornish, Nellie Centennial   **1876-1956**
Miss Aunt Nellie: the autobiography of Nellie C. Cornish. Edited by Ellen Browne and Edward Beck. Foreword by Nancy Wilson Ross. Tribute from Martha Graham. Illustrated. Seattle: University of Washington Press, 1964. 283 p. Index.
    Cornish traces the development of the Cornish School in Seattle, from its birth as a school for music lessons to an academy offering dance, puppetry, and drama as well as instrumental instruction. She recalls many of the 20,000 students she knew in her 25 years with the school, emphasizing their successes all over the world.

0978 *Cornwell, Barbara
Bush rebels: a personal account of Black revolt in Africa. New York: Holt, Rinehart and Winston, 1972. 252 p.
    A white journalist has recorded her experiences and observations while living with Black guerrilla revolutionaries fighting for their independence from Portugal in Mozambique, East Africa, and Portuguese Guinea, West Africa.

0979 Corrothers, James David   **1869-1917**
In spite of the handicap: an autobiography. Introduction by Ray Stannard Baker. Freeport, New York: Books for Libraries Press, 1971. (New York: George H. Doran Co., 1916) 238 p.
    Born in Michigan and educated at Northwestern University, he became a journalist, a poet, and a Baptist minister. His book describes the difficulties faced by Northern Blacks and by intelligent Blacks whose early success made their brothers uneasy.

0980 Corum, Bill (Martene Windsor Corum)   **1894-1958**
Off and running. Edited by Arthur Mann. Illustrated. New York: Henry Holt, 1959. 303 p. Index.
    This is the tape-recorded transcription of Corum's life, focusing on his 35 years as a sports columnist for the New York *Journal*. His specialty was baseball, though he also covered several Kentucky Derby races and some boxing matches. He fought in France in World War I and served as a war correspondent in World War II.

0981 Cosell, Howard   **1920-**
Cosell. Illustrated. Editorial assistance by Mickey Herskowitz. Chicago: Playboy Press, 1973. 390 p.

An interesting account of his life in sports, especially as a sportscaster on radio and television. The book begins with the 1972 Olympics in Munich, where he recorded the scene as Palestinian guerrillas held Israeli athletes hostage. His book frequently focuses on the heroism of athletes.

0982 Cosell, Howard   **1920-**
Like it is. Chicago, Illinois: Playboy Press, 1974. 304 p.
    Cosell thrives on being a controversial and abrasive sportsbroadcaster. In this sequel to his *Cosell,* he continues to follow his self-proclaimed goals of the pursuit of truth and the correction of wrong-doing. He writes of people he respects, answers questions he finds stimulating, and discusses his reactions to issues in sports.

0983 *Coske, Lon
    see *McCloskey, Eunice

0984 Coslow, Sam   **1902-**
Cocktails for two: the many lives of giant songwriter. Illustrated. New Rochelle, New York: Arlington House, 1977. 309 p. Index.
    A composer of over 500 tunes for films and Broadway musicals (including "Just One More Chance" and "My Old Flame") describes his fifty-year career in show business which also involved stints as a vaudevillian, singer, piano player, band leader, and film producer. In the mid-1950's, when music moved from big bands to rock, Coslow became a successful investment service advisor as publisher of *Indicator Digest.*

0985 Coss, Richard David   **1944-**
Wanted. With Jo Ann Summers. Foreword by Charles L. Pippin. Introduction by Chaplain Ray. San Diego, California: Beta Books, 1977. 132 p.
    Coss ecstatically recounts his experience as a born-again Christian, which began in 1969 when he was converted in prison. A twelve-year record of 33 arrests for car theft, assault and battery, and other crimes had landed him in various detention homes and prisons, but Christianity and marriage to another born-again Christian completely reformed him; he now runs a full-time ministry for prisoners.

0986 *Cotton, Ella (Earls)
Spark for my people: the sociological autobiography of a Negro teacher. New York: Exposition, 1954. 288 p.
    A Black teacher who lived in Virginia, Kentucky, and Alabama describes her growing racial and humanitarian awareness and how her teaching developed from such growth.

0987 Cotton, Norris   **1900-**
In the Senate: amidst the conflict and turmoil. New York: Dodd, Mead & Company, 1978. 239 p. Index.
    Cotton covers the years he was a U.S. Senator and Congressman, from Truman to Ford. He discusses presidential policy, the problems in the land of politics. But basically, Cotton uses this book as a soapbox to propound his conservative views: he especially rants against government spending and Democratic presidents.

0988 Cousy, Robert   **1928-**
Basketball is my life. As told to Al Hirschberg. Englewood Cliffs, New Jersey: Prentice-Hall, Inc., 1958. 217 p.
    Basketball player for the Boston Celtics describes his career in the game.

0989 Covello, Leonard   **b.1887**
Heart is the teacher. With Guido D'Agostino. New York: McGraw-Hill Book Co., Inc., 1958. 275 p.
    A teacher and principal in the New York City public schools for 45 years describes his childhood in Italy, his adolescence as an immigrant in East Harlem, and his devotion to education in immigrant neighborhoods.

0990 *Cowles, Fleur Fenton   **1910-**
Friends and memories. Illustrated. New York: Reynal and Co., William Morrow and Co., 1978. 311 p. Index.
    Cowles, an energetic journalist and jet-setter, describes her passion for travel and flying and her interest in art (including publishing the arty *Flair* for one year) and painting. Among famous people she has met, particular favorites are Queen Elizabeth II (whose coronation Cowles attended), Bernard Baruch, Eva Peron, and Harry Truman.

0991 Cowles, Russell   **b.1887**
Russell Cowles: forty-eight reproductions of paintings and twenty letters by the artist. Introduction by Donald Bear. Los Angeles: Dalzell Hatfield, 1946. 53 p.
    This volume consists of a 27-page biographical and critical introduction, 47 reproductions of Cowles' paintings, followed by 24 pages of letters to his representatives explaining the way he painted some of the pictures.

0992 Cowley, Malcolm   **1898-**
The dream of the golden mountains: remembering the 1930's. Illustrated. New York: The Viking Press, 1980. 328 p. Index.
    This sequel to *Exile's Return* focuses on New York in the 1930's as the

focal point of left-wing politics. From his comfortable position as editor of *The New Republic,* Cowley viewed the proletarian and socialist political and social activities of the era, notably the Bonus Marches, the Hunger Marches, the May Day parades, and the Harlan County (Kentucky) coal strikes. Among his friends were Clifford Odets, Allen Tate, and Hart Crane.

0993 Cowley, Malcolm   1898-
Letters and memories: 1944-1962. New York: The Viking Press, 1966. 184 p. Index.
    The letters that passed between novelist William Faulkner and the literary critic over a period of eighteen years, with connecting narrative supplied by Cowley, who was among the first serious critics to recognize the merit of Faulkner's writing.

0994 Cowley, Malcolm   1898-
The view from 80. New York: The Viking Press, 1980. 74 p.
    After he had written an article for *Life* Magazine (December 1978) on growing old, the author received many letters from octagenarians agreeing with or disputing his reflections. Instead of answering each letter, he expanded his article into this book, adding examples, anecdotes and observations, to serve as a "personal message to each of my comrades in age."

0995 Cox, James Middleton   1870-1957
Journey through my years. New York: Simon and Schuster, 1946. 463 p. Index.
    Describes fifty years as journalist and public servant, including experience as Governor of Ohio (elected 1913, 1917, 1919) and Democratic nominee for President (1920).

0996 *Cox, Marian Metcalf   b.1882
The sphinx wore an orchid: memoirs of Marian Cox. Introduction by Maxwell Geismar. Illustrated. New York: Vantage Press, 1967. 244 p.
    Cox writes with venom and velvet about her life as a "feminine parasite," married as a Southern belle of sixteen to Dr. John Watson Cox, who got rich quick from the invention of Anti-Kamnia, a patent medicine similar to aspirin. Living in her gilded Murray Hill cage in New York, Cox was forced to renounce Ray, her socialite lover, and to accept in exchange European travel and material opulence. Her ironic wit and outraged feminism permeate this book and her novel, *The Crowds and the Veiled Woman.*

0997 Craig, Gordon
    see *Duncan, Isadora

0998 Craig, Howard Arnold   1897-
Sunward I've climbed: a personal narrative of peace and war. El Paso: Texas Western Press, 1975. 171 p.
    From the day in 1909 when he saw Walter Brookins, a pupil of the Wright brothers, fly an aeroplane, Craig devoted himself to airplanes and the U.S. Air Service/Air Corps. Eventually he became commandant of the National War College and chairman of the Inter-American Defense Board.

0999 Craig, Robert W.
Storm and sorrow in the High Pamirs. New York: Simon & Schuster, 1980. (Seattle: The Mountaineers, 1977) 223 p.
    A story of adventure and tragedy climbing mountains in the Pamirs Range on the Chinese-Soviet border during a 1974 expedition.

1000 *Crain, Clara (Moore)   1905-
We shall rise. Illustrated. New York: Pageant Press, 1955. 68 p.
    Mrs. Crain tells of the problems that plagued her family: her mother's death when Crain was young; her stepmother's chronic invalidism and eventual mental illness; her stepsister's twenty years of convulsions; her first husband's alcoholism and wife-beating; her second husband's premature death. Her strong religious faith and her nursing career pulled her through. At the book's end, she was an evangelical medical missionary in Hawaii.

1001 Cranch, Christopher Pearse   1813-1892
Life and letters of Christopher Pearse Cranch, by his daughter Leonora Cranch Scott. Illustrated. New York: AMS Press, 1969. (Boston: Houghton Mifflin, 1917) 395 p. Index.
    After an early career as a minister, Cranch became a poet and painter, spending years in Paris, Rome, and Florence, as well as in Cambridge, Massachusetts. His friends included the Brownings, Emerson, James Russell Lowell, and George William Curtis. His daughter has combined passages from his autobiography and letters with her own biographical narrative.

1002 Crane, Clinton Hoadley   1873-1958
Clinton Crane's yachting memories. Illustrated. New York: D. Van Nostrand Co., 1952. 216 p. Index.
    A naval architect describes his sixty-year career which he combined with racing the boats he designed in major competitions. His account,

written with gusto and love, provides a history of twentieth-century yacht design and racing interwoven with autobiography.

1003 Crane, Harold Hart   1899-1932
Letters of Hart Crane, 1916-1932. Edited by Brom Weber. Berkeley: University of California Press, 1965. (New York: Hermitage House, 1952) 412 p. Index.
    The poet's letters are arranged by date and geographic location. The letters originate from New York, the West Indies, Mexico, Europe, and Ohio; the topics primarily discussed are daily events and literature. Many of the letters are to his mother.

1004 Crane, Jasper
    see *Lane, Rose (Wilder)

1005 Crane, Stephen   1871-1900
Letters. Edited by R.W. Stallman and Lillian Gilkes. New York: New York University Press, 1960. 366 p. Index.
    This scholarly edition of Crane's lifetime correspondence includes letters to and from Crane and his relatives, publishers, and other authors, including Joseph Conrad and H.G. Wells. These cover his career as a war correspondent (Greco-Turkish War) and author. Although Crane's longer letters are articulate and present an intimate portrait of the man and artist, the editors also include trivial missives.

1006 Crane, Stephen   1871-1900
Reports of war: war dispatches; great battles of the world. Edited by Fredson Bowers. Introduction by James B. Colvert. Charlottesville: University Press of Virginia, 1971. (New York: New York University Press, 1964) 677 p.
    This volume includes Crane's known newspaper war dispatches from Greece, Florida, Cuba, Puerto Rico, and England as well as his "Great Battles of the World." The book is Volume IX of the University of Virginia edition of *The Works of Stephen Crane.*

1007 Crane, Stephen   1871-1900
Stephen Crane in the West and Mexico. Edited by Joseph Katz. Kent, Ohio: Kent State University Press, 1970. 109 p.
    Seventeen newspaper articles written by Stephen Crane during a trip in 1895 from what the editor calls a sequel to *The Red Badge of Courage.* Crane reports on drought-stricken farmers in Nebraska, the New Orleans Mardi Gras, Texas and Mexico. Important as a record of Crane's playing a role much like the one he created in the protagonist of *The Red Badge of Courage,* and as background in later short stories such as "The Blue Hotel."

1008 Crane, Stephen   1871-1900
Stephen Crane's love letters to Nellie Crouse: with six other letters, new materials on Crane at Syracuse University and a number of unusual photographs. Introduction and notes by Edwin H. Cady and Lester G. Wells. Syracuse: Syracuse University Press, 1954. 54 p.
    The letters were written primarily from New York to Nellie Crouse and his other correspondents. Crane mentions his trip to Mexico in a letter to Crouse.

1009 Crashing Thunder (Sam Blowsnake)   b.1875?
The autobiography of a Winnebago Indian. Edited by Paul Radin. New York: Dover Publications, 1963. 91 p.
    Written around 1917, the book is a series of confessions about his life as a drunkard and womanizer who finally wandered back to his true religion, the Peyote Cult. Considered a major work among Indian autobiographies.

1010 *Craven, Margaret   1901-
Again calls the owl. Illustrated by Joan Miller. New York: G.P. Putnam's Sons, 1980. 120 p.
    From her college days at Stanford during World War I, Craven worked to be a writer and moved from newspaper editorials to short story writing for the *Saturday Evening Post.* Cataracts, the result of an accident, curtailed her ambition to write a novel until corrective surgery and an assignment in British Columbia compelled her to live in a tiny Canadian Indian settlement and write *I Heard the Owl Call My Name* at the age of 69. She was hailed as a literary Grandma Moses.

1011 *Crawford, Cheryl
One naked individual: my fifty years in the theatre. Illustrated. Indianapolis: Bobbs-Merrill Co., 1977. 275 p.
    Crawford's unsentimental account of her fifty-year career as a play producer and director illuminates the process by which plays are financed, cast, directed, and somewhat mysteriously fail or succeed. Crawford was associated with experimental theater at the Provincetown Wharf; as an independent producer she directed a number of hits such as *Brigadoon, Paint Your Wagon,* and *The Rose Tattoo.*

1012 *Crawford, Dorothy Painter   1892-
Stay with it, Van: from the diary of Mississippi's first lady mayor. New York: Exposition Press, 1958. 312 p.

From 1951 to 1953, Dorothy Crawford, who with her husband managed a 650-acre farm in Madison, Mississippi (pop. 541), was the first woman mayor in the town and in the state. Although the book covers her childhood in Oklahoma Territory and her college days at Oklahoma A & M, it focuses on the day-by-day activities of the mayoralty, including clean-up and anti-rabies campaigns, reorganization of the municipal airport, and plans for a municipal water filtration system.

1013 *Crawford, Joan (Lucille LeSueur)   **1908-1977**
A portrait of Joan: the autobiography of Joan Crawford. Garden City, New York: Doubleday & Co., Inc., 1962. 239 p.
  A popular movie actress writes of her poor and difficult childhood and her life in Hollywood, including four marriages, four adopted children, film friends and celebrities.

1014 Crawford, Thomas Edgar   **1867-1941**
The West of the Texas Kid, 1881-1910: recollections of Thomas Edgar Crawford, cowboy, gun fighter, rancher, hunter, miner. Edited with introduction by Jeff C. Dykes. Norman: University of Oklahoma Press, 1962. 202 p.
  The love of the West preserved, and perhaps extended, by entertaining yarns of outlaws, cattlemen and cowboys as told by "The Texas Kid," whose nephew said, "My uncle wrote the truth as closely as he could recall it."

1015 Creel, George   **1875-1953**
Rebel at large: recollections of fifty crowded years. New York: G.P. Putnam's Sons, 1947. 384 p. Index.
  Hard life as journalist in Kansas City and New York, gradually moving toward success as a writer and politician fighting social abuse.

1016 Crews, Harry   **1935-**
Blood and grits. New York: Harper & Row, 1979. 213 p.
  Crews's essays on foxhunting in Florida, hiking the Appalachian Trail in Tennessee, visiting a carnival with a resident gambler, and examining L.L. Bean's sporting goods emporium in Freeport, Maine, are evocative of the author, earthy, Southern, on-the-road, enjoying drugs, booze, and most of all, casual friendships.

1017 Crews, Harry   **1935-**
Childhood: the biography of a place. New York: Harper & Row, 1978. 171 p.
  Crews's re-creation of his childhood on a tenant farm in the backwoods of Macon County, Georgia, mingles the brutality of a drunken father with his gentleness when sober, the poverty of everyday life with the richness of neighboring friendships and oral storytelling. Crews survived polio and scalding with a feisty spirit and a lyrical realist's vision intact.

1018 Crile, George Washington   **1864-1943**
George Crile; an autobiography. Edited with sidelights by Grace Crile. Philadelphia: J.B. Lippincott Co., 1947. 2v. Index.
  The remarkable career of an outstanding surgeon and medical researcher who was one of four founders of the Cleveland Clinic.

1019 Crockett, David   **1786-1836**
Adventures of Davy Crockett: told mostly by himself. New York: Charles Scribner, 1955. 246 p.
  This book concerns Davy Crockett as a frontiersman in Tennessee and Texas. The first section deals with growing up, marriage, travel, and Indian Wars. The part of doubtful authorship, usually ascribed to Richard Penn Smith, describes the Battle of the Alamo.

1020 Crockett, David   **1786-1836**
A narrative of the life of David Crockett . . . Knoxville: University of Tennessee Press, 1973. (Philadelphia: E.L. Carey, 1835) 373 p.
  "Narrative of his life published in 1834; account of his tour to the north and down east, also 1834; and his exploits and adventures in Texas—a pseudo-autobiography generally ascribed to Richard Penn Smith, 1799-1854, published posthumously in 1836." Many differing editions of this work have been published.

1021 Crofut, William
Troubadour; a different battlefield. Foreword by Robert F. Kennedy. Illustrated. New York: E.P. Dutton, 1968. 283 p.
  A modestly told and heartwarming account of the author's tour of 29 countries in eight years as a "troubadour of goodwill." Beginning on his own without official sanction, the author as a PFC in Korea began playing his guitar and banjo for Korean schoolchildren. Eventually with U.S. government backing, Crofut toured with Steve Addiss, sharing in a cultural exchange through music, even in the midst of war.

1022 Crompton, George   **1872-1953**
Mariemont. Worcester, Massachusetts: George Crompton, 1952. 88 p.
  The American dream, embodied in a house, is related in George Crompton's account of the family estate, Mariemont, in Worcester, Massachusetts. It was completed in 1895 after Crompton's father, an English immigrant who followed his father's profession as an inventor of

looms and weaving machinery, established a highly lucrative business in Worcester and became a leading social and civic figure. The author lovingly recalls a happy childhood of stereotypical American opulence in a large, overstuffed house.

1023 Crook, George   **1828-1890**
General George Crook: his autobiography. Norman: University of Oklahoma Press, 1960. 326 p.
  Covers the period from 1852 (graduation from West Point) to June 18, 1876 (day after the battle of Rosebud, preceding Custer's Battle of the Little Big Horn). After the Civil War, Crook led campaigns against the Indians all over the Western territories.

1024 Crosby, Bing (Harry Lillis)   **1904-1978**
Call me lucky. As told to Pete Martin. New York: Simon and Schuster, 1953. 333 p.
  A Hollywood actor recalls his Catholic upbringing, his career in radio, on stage and screen, and his family life until 1952.

1025 *Crosby, Caresse   **1892-1970**
Passionate years. New York: Dial Press, 1953. 342 p.
  A poet and editor explains what it was like being a member of the Lost Generation in New York, Boston, and France, and her association with people such as D.H. Lawrence, Gertrude Stein, Salvador Dali, and Aldous Huxley.

1026 Crosthwait, William Lafayette   **b.1873**
The last stitch. With Ernest G. Fisher. Philadelphia: J.B. Lippincott, 1956. 250 p.
  Crosthwait describes his Mississippi boyhood, his hard work to get a medical education, and his long career as a surgeon in Texas.

1027 Crouch, Cleo
My life on the road: the autobiography of Cleo Crouch. As told to Bill Clark. Introduction by Clifford Clowing. Hicksville, New York: Exposition, 1975. 293 p.
  A trucker from St. Joseph, Missouri, he built a truck line, made his fortune, and then retired in Florida at the age of 57.

1028 *Crouter, Natalie Corona (Stark)   **1898-**
Forbidden diary: a record of wartime internment, 1941-1945. American Women's Diary Series, V. 2. Edited, with introduction and afterword by Lynn Z. Bloom. Illustrated. Drawings by Daphne Bird. New York: Burt Franklin & Co., 1980. 546 p.
  Crouter, a Boston businessman's wife living with her husband and two children in Baguio, summer capital of the Philippines, was captured by the Japanese at the outbreak of World War II and interned with 500 families of American engineers and missionaries in the Philippine mountains (December 1941—February 1945). Her diary, kept secretly throughout the war, focuses on the internees' social organization, family life, resourcefulness, and generally tolerable relations with their Japanese captors.

1029 Crumbine, Samuel Jay   **1862-1954**
Frontier doctor: the autobiography of a pioneer on the frontier of public health. Philadelphia: Dorrance and Co., 1948. 284 p.
  A doctor in Dodge City, Kansas (1880's and 1890's), Crumbine became the State Health Officer of Kansas, and an eminent "sanitary scientist" who helped eliminate the public drinking cup and roller towel. Lively description of the Western frontier.

1030 *Crying Wind   **1950?-**
Crying Wind. Chicago: Moody Press, 1977. 189 p.
  A halfbreed deserted by both parents, she describes her life on a Kickapoo reservation and her solitary adjustment to city life at age 15. An alien in both cultures, she finally found solace in converting to Christianity.

1031 Csonka, Larry   **1946-**
Always on the run. With Dave Anderson and Jim Kiick. New York: Random House, 1973. 223 p.
  Two running backs of the Miami Dolphins exchange thoughts about football, their lives, Coach Shula, and other players. Career statistics are appended.

1032 *Cuero, Delfina   **1900?-**
The autobiography of Delfina Cuero. Edited by Florence Shipek. Morongo Indian Reservation, California: Malki Museum Press, 1970. (1968) 67 p.
  Cuero lived as a hunter-gatherer in the Diegueno Indian traditions for most of her life. Her book reflects the love and wisdom of her people.

1033 Cugat, Xavier   **1900-**
Rumba is my life. Illustrated by the author. New York: Didier Publishers, 1949. 210 p.
  In the Forties he became part of the Hollywood myth, famous as a band leader, composer, entertainer. His book is witty and intelligent.

1034 *Culbertson, Manie
May I speak? Diary of a crossover teacher. Edited with introduction by Sue Eakin. Gretna, Louisiana: Pelican Publishing Co., 1972. 156 p.
The author, an experienced white teacher, kept a diary after she was transferred during the middle of the year from a school with an all-white faculty that had a predominantly white student body to an all-Black school where she was among the first whites ever to teach. This is a stringently honest account by one teacher who is admittedly prejudiced, afraid, and resentful of the court order forcing integration with no consideration for the teachers' preferences.

1035 Culligan, James F. **1917-1970**
Father Culligan; selfless shepherd. Edited by Kenneth C. Bogart. Quezan City, Alteneo de Manila: Culligan Memorial Foundation, 1972. 167 p.
He was educated and ordained a Jesuit priest in Connecticut. In 1950 he was sent to the Philippines where after a few years of parish work he was assigned to the Ateneo de Manila as student counselor and professor of theology and psychology. This is a collection of his letters, homilies, talks, and tributes by several close friends, one of whom edited this volume.

1036 Culligan, Matthew Joseph **1918-**
The Curtis-Culligan story: from Cyrus to Horace to Joe. New York: Crown Publishers, Inc., 1970. 224 p. Index.
The controversial former president of Curtis Publishing Company, who battled to save the company from bankruptcy and himself from character assassination and charges of mismanagement, tells what happened to Curtis between 1945 and 1962 and his part in the events.

1037 *Cullman, Marguerite (Wagner) **1908-**
Occupation: angel. New York: W.W. Norton & Co., Inc., 1963. 256 p.
Along with entertaining stories about the Broadway theatrical world, the author explains something of the workings of stage production and the backing of plays.

1038 Culver, Joseph Franklin **1834-1899**
Your affectionate husband J.F. Culver: letters written during the Civil War. Edited by Leslie W. Dunlap. Notes by Edwin C. Bears. Illustrated. Iowa City: Friends of the University of Iowa Libraries, 1978. 466 p. Index.
This book contains 233 intimate and loving letters from a newly married soldier to his young wife, dealing with his reactions to war and information about the many friends and relatives from his hometown, Pontiac, Illinois.

1039 *Cumming, Elizabeth Wells Randall **1811-1867**
The genteel gentile: letters of Elizabeth Cumming, 1857-1858. Edited with introduction and notes by Ray R. Canning and Beverly Beeton. Salt Lake City: University of Utah Library, 1977. 111 p. Index.
Eighteen letters written by the loyal wife of the first non-Mormon governor of Utah reveal the fundamental opposition between the Mormon and gentile worlds. U.S. troops were brought to Salt Lake City to help "persuade" disaffected Mormons to leave, and the Mormons were prepared to destroy the city rather than let it pass out of their hands. The troops prevailed and the city was spared.

1040 Cummings, Edward Estlin **1894-1962**
Eimi. New York: William Sloane Associates, 1949. (New York: Covici, 1933) 432 p.
Ostensibly a travel diary, this book, like others of his works, shows the author's experimentation with compressed language, dislocated syntax, and typographical variations.

1041 Cummings, Edward Estlin **1894-1962**
Selected letters of E.E. Cummings. Edited by F.W. Dupee and George Stade. New York: Harcourt, Brace & World, Inc., 1969. 296 p. Index.
A selection of some 260 letters written over a sixty-year span to family and friends. The letters are witty and idiosyncratic, showing a range of the emotions and thoughts of this complex, gifted writer.

1042 Cummins, Clessie Lyle **1888-1968**
My days with the diesel: the memoirs of Clessie L. Cummins, father of the highway diesel. Philadelphia: Chilton Books, 1967. 190 p.
With an ample supply of invention, showmanship, and faith in his idea, Cummins set out to reduce the pound-per-horsepower ratio of diesel engines and to perfect a high-speed, light-weight automotive diesel suitable for trucks and other vehicles. After many years of failure and setbacks he achieved his goal, won acceptance of his engine by long-distance truckers, and transformed the industry.

1043 Cunningham, Alfred Austell
Marine flyer in France: the diary of Captain Alfred A. Cunningham, November 1917-January 1918. Washington, D.C.: History and Museums Division Headquarters, U.S. Marine Corps., 1974. 43 p.
In 1917 he became the Marine Corp's first director of aviation. He kept this diary of his tour of the battlefronts and flying fields of France, after which he organized the Marine Corps Aeronautic Company.

1044 Cunningham, James F. **1901-**
American pastor in Rome. Illustrated. Garden City, New York: Doubleday, 1966. 285 p.
A charming account of Father Cunningham's boyhood and early career as a pharmacist in Danbury, Connecticut, followed by 25 years as a pastor, missionary in the United States, and Navy chaplain in World War II. Most of the emphasis, however, is on Cunningham's twelve-year pastorate at Santa Susanna, the American Catholic Church in Rome, which he, his parishioners, and the Romans thoroughly enjoyed.

1045 Curley, James Michael **1874-1958**
I'd do it again: a record of all my uproarious years. Englewood Cliffs. New Jersey: Prentice-Hall, Inc., 1957. 372 p. Index.
The story of his political career in Massachusetts, where he served as mayor of Boston and governor, by a colorful and unpredictable statesman.

1046 Curry, George **1861-1947**
George Curry, 1861-1947: an autobiography. Edited by H.B. Hening. Albuquerque: University of New Mexico Press, 1958. 336 p. Index.
A frontier storekeeper in his teens, he sought work and adventure in New Mexico, joined Teddy Roosevelt's Rough Riders which took him to the Philippines, and returned to devote his energy to the development of New Mexico, where he served as governor and elder statesman.

1047 Curtis, George William **1824-1892**
Early letters to John S. Dwight: Brook Farm and Concord. Edited by George Willis Cooke. Port Washington, New York: Kennikat Press, 1971. (New York: Harper & Brothers, 1898) 293 p.
Interesting because of his early years with Ralph Waldo Emerson and Brook Farm, his letters to his close friend also reflect his philosophy, his views on major issues of the day, and everyday details.

1048 Curtis, Harvey Lincoln **1876-1956**
Recollections of a scientist: an autobiography by Harvey Lincoln Curtis. Foreword by A.V. Astin. Bonn, Germany: Ludwig Leopold Press (private), 1958. 128 p.
Curtis focuses on his work for the National Bureau of Standards, where he was employed as a physicist for 47 years concentrating on ballistics and insulation. He describes his trip to Europe on ballistics matters during World War I. A ballistics table and Curtis family genealogy are appended.

1049 Curtis, James Michael (Curtis, Mike) **1943?-**
Keep off my turf. With Bill Gilbert. Philadelphia: J.B. Lippincott Co., 1972. 179 p.
Written because "there's too much anti-football sentiment in the air these days," the book is a celebration of the game and his life in it.

1050 *Curtiss, Mina Stein Kirstein **1896-**
Other people's letters: a memoir. Illustrated. Boston: Houghton Mifflin, 1978. 243 p. Index.
Had Proust lived longer, Curtiss would have been his Boswell. Drawing heavily upon her own journal and her letters to others, Curtiss writes of the years in which she collected Proust's letters for publication, drifting among the elite of Paris searching out manuscripts and letters.

1051 Curwen, Samuel **1715-1802**
Journal and letters: of the late Samuel Curwen, an American refugee in England from 1775 to 1784. Edited by George Atkinson Ward. New York: AMS Press, 1973. (Boston: C.S. Francis and Co., 1842) 578 p.
An American loyalist, he left for England in 1775. His detailed journals describe the London political circles, travel conditions, and everyday routines in England during the American Revolution.

1052 Cushing, Frank H. **1857-1900**
My adventures in Zuni. Introduction by Okah L. Jones, Jr. Illustrated by Farny. New ed., originally a three-part series in *Century Magazine,* XXV-VI, 1882-1883. Palo Alto, California: American West Publishing Co., 1970. (Santa Fe: Peripatetic Press, 1941) 125 p.
Cushing, a young ethnologist with the Bureau of Ethnology at the Smithsonian Institution, lived with the Zunis, 1879-1884, studying and recording their culture, myths, and folktales in this thoroughly fascinating volume, even though he violated Zuni trust in publishing their secret legends.

1053 Cushman, Dan **1909-**
Plenty of room and air. Great Falls, Montana: Stay Away Joe Publishers, 1975. 260 p.
Cushman tells a series of extended anecdotes, mostly good-natured, about his childhood in Box Elder and Zurich, Montana. Through accounts of wheat farming, chicken raising, and escapades with horses, cows, and rattlesnakes, he conveys some of the rough-and-ready atmosphere of the homesteader's life in the West that was gradually being tamed. Cushman describes his parents as hardy, pragmatic, fearless, happy-go-lucky.

1054 *Cutler, Frances Wentworth
see ***Knickerbocker, Frances Wentworth**

1055 Cutler, G. Ripley   fl.1914-1918
Of battles long ago: memoirs of an American ambulance driver in World War I. Edited with introduction by Charles H. Knickerbocker. Illustrated. Hicksville, New York: Exposition Press, 1979. 280 p.
An American volunteer ambulance driver for the French army in World War I describes hospitals and rescue missions at the front lines, major offensives (Verdun, Marne), and being wounded during combat, with personal observations and photographs of life in wartime France.

1056 Cutler, Robert   1895-1974
No time for rest. Boston: Little, Brown and Co., 1966. 421 p. Index.
In a lifetime marked by enthusiasm and devotion to hard work, Cutler describes his experience as a student, a lawyer, a military officer, and as a government official in several capacities, including Special Assistant to Eisenhower for National Security Affairs, and National Security Council.

1057 Czatt, John Hamill   1896-
Mighty timber. San Antonio: The Naylor Co., 1961. 327 p.
Half of his book is a nostalgic recollection of his early rural life in southern Ohio; the rest depicts his education at Ohio State University, setting up his medical practice in Columbus, then moving to Modesto, California, where he became an active contributing member of the community.

1058 Czyzewski, Joseph A.
see Alvin, Joe

1059 Dabney, Virginius   1901-
Across the years: memories of a Virginian. Illustrated. Garden City, New York: Doubleday & Co., Inc., 1978. 420 p. Index.
A Pulitzer Prize for Journalism winner and lifetime advocate of Virginia reminisces about his childhood in turn-of-the-century Charlottesville, college years at the University of Virginia, and his long career as editor of the Richmond *Times-Dispatch*. He based many editorials on first-hand knowledge from his travels, saw the rise of Nazism and spoke out against Hitler, and chronicled the changing South.

1060 Dahl, Arndt Elstad   1897-
Banker Dahl of South Dakota: an autobiography. Rapid City, South Dakota: Fenske Book Co., 1965. 269 p.
A banker who has "led a full, interesting, and rewarding life" relates his experiences during 48 years of banking, his thinking on various banking matters, and his assessments of his associates.

1061 Dahlberg, Edward   1900-1977
Because I was flesh: the autobiography of Edward Dahlberg. New York: New Directions Publishing Corp., 1964. 234 p.
Colored by background reality of urban life, this is a son's portrait of his relationship with his remarkable mother, who fails repeatedly in her objective to achieve security for them both by acquiring a new husband.

1062 Dahlberg, Edward   1900-1977
The confessions of Edward Dahlberg. New York: George Braziller, 1971. 312 p. Index.
As writer and critic he came into contact with many others among the intelligentsia of the Twenties and Thirties. In remarkable aphoristic prose, he describes Edmund Wilson, Gertrude Stein, Charles Olson, and others.

1063 Dahlberg, Edward   1900-1977
Epitaphs of our times: the letters of Edward Dahlberg. New York: George Braziller, 1967. 308 p. Index.
A sampling from the many letters he wrote to literary and intellectual friends including Theodore Dreiser, Robert M. Hutchins, Herbert Read, William Carlos Williams, and Allen Tate, among others. The letters are grouped according to their recipients rather than by chronology.

1064 Dale, Alan, pseud. (Aldo Sigismondi)   1926?-
The spider and the marionettes: an autobiography. New York: Lyle Stuart, 1965. 315 p.
An unusually egocentric, disturbing autobiography in which the author, a night club, radio, and television singer, discusses the vicissitudes of his career and unsatisfying relationships with women and men—mostly the result of his volatile temper and unstable personality. In abusing others, he abused himself and finally escaped the "spider web" by becoming an independent entertainer in nightclubs.

1065 Dale, Fred Hiner   1881-1969
Oklahoma lawyer. Guymon, Oklahoma: Guymon Publishing Co., 1961. 233 p.
Charming story of his life and career as an attorney in rural Oklahoma, by a man who became a district judge and spent most of his life in Guymon.

1066 Daley, Eliot A.   1936-
Father feelings. New York: William Morrow & Co., 1978. 192 p.
Clergyman and family counselor Daley has written a series of vignettes

of life with his family—wife Patti, adolescent daughters Alison and Shannon, and young son Jad—which become parables about parenthood. He focuses on holiday celebrations, family traditions, changing values between generations (such as a conflict over pierced ears), interpersonal communication, love, respect, and sharing.

1067 Dallas, George Mifflin   1792-1864
Diary of George Mifflin Dallas: United States Minister to Russia, 1837-1839. Edited by Susan Dallas. New York: Arno Press, 1970. (Philadelphia: J.B. Lippincott Co., 1892) 214 p.
An interesting record of diplomatic life in the early nineteenth century and the court of the Czar.

1068 *Dalrymple, Jean   1910-
September child: the story of Jean Dalrymple, by herself. New York: Dodd, Mead & Co., Inc., 1963. 318 p. Index.
Widely respected as a theatrical director and producer, she has directed the Light Opera and Drama Companies for the New York City Center, the performing arts programs for the Brussels World's Fair (1958) and the New York World's Fair (1964-65). Her book is packed with activity and celebrity.

1069 Dalton, John Edward
Forged in strong fires: the early life and experiences of John Edward Dalton. As told to M.P. Wentworth. Edited by M.P. Wentworth. Caldwell, Idaho: The Caxton Printers, Ltd., 1948. 373 p.
World-wide travels of a cowboy, boxer, and adventurer, around the turn of the century.

1070 Damrosch, Walter Johannes   1862-1950
My musical life. Westport, Connecticut: Greenwood Press, 1972. (New York: Charles Scribner's Sons, 1923) 376 p.
His life in music began in Silesia, where his family was visited by Liszt and Saint-Saens, and he lived among the greatest musicians of his time for the rest of his life. His book is rich with stories about them and his career as a prominent orchestra leader.

1071 Dana, Richard Henry, Jr.   1815-1882
An autobiographical sketch (1815-1842). Edited by Robert F. Metzdorf. Introduction by Norman Holmes Pearson. Hamden, Connecticut: Shoe String Press, 1953. 119 p.
A cryptic but eloquent account of Dana's education at Cambridge-Port grammar school, William Wells' boarding school, and Harvard College, where he won the Boylston Prize for oratory; authorship (*Harper's* paid $250 for the copyright of *Two Years Before the Mast)*; and first four months of marriage.

1072 Dana, Richard Henry, Jr.   1815-1882
The journal of Richard Henry Dana, Jr. Edited by Robert F. Lucid. Cambridge: The Belknap Press of Harvard University Press, 1968. 3v. Index.
Prefaced by his "Autobiographical Sketch," this edition follows Dana's text as he wrote it, providing a wide assortment of historical data as well as the opportunity to confront an attractive and remarkable personality. Volumes I and II contain his journal up to 1859, Volume III records his voyage around the world 1859-1860.

1073 Daniele, Francescantonio Michele   1879-1957
Signor Dottore: the autobiography of F. Michele Daniele, Italian immigrant doctor, 1879-1957. Edited by Victor Rosen. New York: Exposition Press, 1959. 237 p.
He settled in Youngstown, Ohio, to practice medicine in the Italian community, returned to Italy from 1911 to 1918, and came again to Youngstown where he became an outspoken leader of the birth control movement.

1074 *Daniell, Rosemary
Fatal flowers: on sin, sex, and suicide in the deep South. New York: Holt, Rinehart and Winston, 1980. 293 p.
A bitter, yet ambivalent analysis of Southern sexual mores in terms of her own life.

1075 *Daniels, Bebe (Virginia)   1901-1971
Life with the Lyons. With Ben Lyon. Illustrated. Long Acre, London: Odhams Press Limited, 1953. 256 p. Index.
With good humor, actress Daniels and actor-producer Lyons, married since 1930, recount their careers in films and film production, separately and together. Their love for each other and for their two children is reflected in their mutual enjoyment of their family; their love for their work is manifested in their long and varied careers; and their love for their country is demonstrated not only in the entertainment of G.I.'s during World War II, but also in a moving series of interviews Bebe conducted with soldiers on the front line, for which she won an American Medal of Freedom.

1076 Daniels, Jonathan   1902-
White House witness, 1942-1945. Garden City, New York: Doubleday & Co., Inc., 1975. 299 p. Index.

During World War II, wartime secrecy shrouded the White House, the key power center of the world. Daniels' diary tells what it was like to work in the hidden corridors of the President's office and captures the hopes, labors and intrigues of the Capital.

1077 Daniels, Josephus 1862-1948
The Cabinet diaries of Josephus Daniels, 1913-1921. Edited by E. David Cronon. Lincoln: University of Nebraska Press, 1963. 648 p. Index.
Woodrow Wilson's Secretary of the Navy kept these diaries during his tenure of office from 1913 to 1921 (1914 and 1916 are missing). Through them can be seen Daniels' relations with the President, other government officials, and subordinates, including Franklin D. Roosevelt, chosen by Daniels as his assistant. Daniels was the subject of much controversy despite the success of the Navy during World War I.

1078 Daniels, Josephus 1862-1948
Editor in politics. Westport, Connecticut: Greenwood Press, 1974. (Chapel Hill: University of North Carolina Press, 1941) 644 p. Index.
Volume two of his memoirs describes his life from 1893 to 1912, when he was an editor and journalist becoming more involved with politics.

1079 Daniels, Josephus 1862-1948
Shirt-sleeve diplomat. Westport, Connecticut: Greenwood Press, 1973. (Chapel Hill: University of North Carolina Press, 1947) 547 p. Index.
The fifth volume of his autobiography, describing his years as U.S. Ambassador to the Republic of Mexico (1933-1942). Previously he had served as Secretary of the Navy (1913-1921). Shirt-sleeve diplomats contrast with stuffed shirt and spats diplomats.

1080 Daniels, Josephus 1862-1948
Tar Heel editor. Westport, Connecticut: Greenwood Press, 1974. (Chapel Hill: University of North Carolina Press, 1939) 544 p.
The first volume of his memoirs, describing his life from 1885-1893, written by a journalist and statesman who was then editing a paper in North Carolina.

1081 Daniels, Josephus 1862-1948
The Wilson era, years of peace—1910-1917. Westport, Connecticut: Greenwood Press, Publishers, 1974. (Chapel Hill: University of North Carolina Press, 1944) 615 p.
A personal memoir of the times, written by Wilson's Secretary of the Navy, with more detailed accounts of the era than of himself, although he calls it the third volume of his autobiography.

1082 Daniels, Josephus 1862-1948
The Wilson era, years of war and after—1917-1923. Westport, Connecticut: Greenwood Press, Publishers, 1974. (Chapel Hill: University of North Carolina Press, 1946) 654 p.
Called the fourth volume of his autobiography, this work is, like the previous one, more a memoir of the times than of the man. This volume is based extensively on Daniels' World War I diary. Both are long and detailed, as well as readable.

1083 Daniels, Josephus 1862-1948
see also **Roosevelt, Franklin Delano**

1084 Dannay, Frederic
see **Nathan, Daniel, pseud.**

1085 Darby, William 1775-1854
A tour from the city of New York, to Detroit in the Michigan territory, made between the 2nd of May and the 22nd of Sept. 1818. New York: Published for the author by Kirk & Mercein, 1819. 228 p. index.
A tour the author took observing the natural history and geography of the region around the southern shores of Lake Ontario and Lake Erie, including the Thousand Islands and Niagara Falls.

1086 Darian, Ralph G.
My safaris via inferno: life and thoughts of an Armenian-American lawyer. Foreword by John V. Brennan. New York: Exposition Press, 1959. 112 p.
A collection of sporadic memories and opinions written by a Detroit lawyer who immigrated to the U.S. from Turkey in 1912 as a young man.

1087 Dark, Alvin 1923-
When in doubt, fire the manager: my life and times in baseball. And John Underwood. Illustrated. New York: E.P. Dutton, 1980. 242 p.
After his career as a baseball player, Dark became a baseball manager, often hired and fired by such teams as the Kansas City Athletics and the Cleveland Indians. His zealous Christianity was compromised by family difficulties and an extramarital relationship of five years that eventually led to a second marriage. This stability led to the reemergence of his strong religion and to professional success.

1088 Daugherty, Edgar Fay 1874-1957
A Hoosier parson: his boosts and bumps (an apologia pro mea vita**).** Boston: Meador Publishing Co., 1951. 224 p.

Individualist, sportsman, and Christian, Daugherty affirms his faith in an autobiography which is candid and friendly.

1089 Daugherty, Hugh Duffy
Duffy: an autobiography. With Dave Diles. Garden City, New York: Doubleday & Co., Inc., 1974. 168 p.
The well-loved coach of the Michigan State Spartans for nineteen years, who later became part of the ABC College Game of the Week team, recalls his successful career and tells tall tales of collegiate sports.

1090 Daugherty, Robert Dodds b.1874
Chillyblast: a narrative. Santa Ana, California: Sewell and Duke, 1948. 85 p.
Youth in rural Iowa; college professor of math at Iowa State Teachers College and Kansas State College; narrated in eighteenth-century comic style.

1091 *Davenport, Marcia (Gluck) 1903-
Too strong for fantasy. New York: Charles Scribner's Sons, 1967. 483 p. Index.
Devoted to the world of music (her mother was opera star Alma Gluck) and of fiction writing, Davenport writes also of her support for Willkie's presidential campaign, her attachment to Czechoslovakia, and her admiration of the Masaryk Republic.

1092 David, Ebenezer 1752?-1778
A Rhode Island chaplain in the Revolution: letters of Ebenezer David to Nicholas Brown, 1775-1778. Edited by Jeannette D. Black and William Greene Roelker. Port Washington, New York: Kennikat, 1972. (Providence, Rhode Island: Society of the Cincinnati, 1949) 82 p. Index.
The author joined the Continental Army soon after his ordination and wrote these letters to Brown, a merchant in Providence. They describe the life and activities of an army chaplain of the time and contain valuable accounts of actions in which Rhode Island troops took part.

1093 David, Solomon D. 1888-1977
Transfigured: the autobiography of Solomon D. David. As told to J. Robert Moffet. Edited, designed and illustrated by Larry Bouchard. Chicago: Disciples Divinity House of the University of Chicago, 1979. 82 p.
In 1908 he immigrated to America from Syria to begin his education. He went first to Macalester College in Minneapolis, then on to medical school at the University of Minnesota. He established a practice as an orthopedic surgeon in Houston where he was also active in the Lebanese community. He published four books of Arabic poetry.

1094 Davidson, Bruce Landon 1933-
Bruce Davidson photographs: (including autobiographical sketch). Preface by Henry Geldzahler. Introduction by Bruce Davidson. Illustrated. New York: Agrinde/Summit Books, 1978. 167 p.
Davidson's eloquent autobiographical introduction to this handsome collection of photographs representative of his life's work reveals the intimate interweaving of life and art. Although he has attempted moviemaking, this collection of still photographs displays his commitment to the Civil Rights movement and his interest in the poor and forgotten people of the world.

1095 Davidson, Donald 1893-1968
The literary correspondence of Donald Davidson and Allen Tate. Edited by John Tyree Fain and Thomas Daniel Young. Athens: University of Georgia Press, 1974. 442 p. Index.
This literary correspondence began when the two were apprentices to poetry and in 1922 agreed to exchange poems and criticism. Although they were different in temperament, personality, and experience, they continued to correspond until 1966, resulting in a remarkable dialogue about the nature of the literary vocation in the past two centuries.

1096 Davidson, John Wynn 1823-1881
The expedition of Capt. J.W. Davidson from Fort Tejon to the Owens Valley in 1859. Edited by Philip J. Wilke and Harry W. Lawton. Illustrated. Socorro, New Mexico: Ballena Press, 1976. 55 p.
Army Captain Davidson was sent to the Santa Clara Valley in California to apprehend the Paiute Indians who were allegedly stealing the white settlers' horses. In precise ethnographic and geographic notations, he describes the territory and the tribes. Although he expected that the Owens Valley would be set aside for an Indian reservation, his lush descriptions aroused the whites' greed and they kept the land for themselves.

1097 Davies, Samuel 1724-1761
Reverend Samuel Davies abroad: the diary of a journey to England and Scotland, 1753-55. Edited with introduction by George William Pilcher. Urbana: University of Illinois Press, 1967. 176 p. Index.
Davies' journal chronicles a trip to England on behalf of American Presbyterians to solicit funds and support for the College of New Jersey and Presbyterians in Virginia. His observations are colorful and, to this age, quaint.

1098 *Davis, Angela   1944-
With my mind on freedom: an autobiography. New York: Bantam Books, 1975. 399 p.

In the late Sixties, Davis emerged as a central figure in revolutionary politics. One of the first Black women to popularize the Afro hair style, she focused most of her energies for several years on political activism and was imprisoned for allegedly supplying guns to members of the Black Panther party. Her story is a significant social document of the times.

1099 Davis, Charles   1922-
On my own. With R.E. Simon, Jr. Chicago: Childrens Press, 1970. 63 p.

Recounting the story of his youth, army experience, and the founding of his own public relations firm, Davis writes in simple language suitable for the guidance of children interested in careers in public relations work.

1100 Davis, Clive   1932-
Clive—inside the record business. With James Willwerth. New York: William Morrow & Co., Inc., 1975. 300 p. Index.

An important figure in the revolution in the record industry, which in the 1960's saw the emergence of rock music as a cultural medium. He focuses on his years with Columbia Records, 1960-1973, when he signed and promoted pioneering rock artists, many of whom he discusses here.

1101 Davis, Clyde Brion   1894-1962
The age of indiscretion. Philadelphia: J.B. Lippincott Co., 1950. 284 p.

Reflections on his childhood and youth in Missouri in the early twentieth century together with observations on how conditions have improved during the intervening fifty years.

1102 Davis, Elmer Holmes   1890-1958
By Elmer Davis. Edited by Robert Lloyd Davis. Indianapolis: The Bobbs-Merrill Co., 1964. 370 p.

This is a collection of fiction and essays, some autobiographical in nature, by a news commentator who dared speak for individual freedom during the McCarthy era.

1103 Davis, Garry   1922-
The world is my country. New York: G.P. Putnam's Sons, 1961. 254 p. Index.

Determined to become a "citizen of the world," Davis renounced his U.S. citizenship in Paris in 1948 and for a decade traveled worldwide, voluntarily and by deportation. He wanted to "prove" that an individual can obtain "world legality grounded in reasoned freedom and justice," but he was most often jailed and ridiculed for his efforts. A self-defense.

1104 *Davis, Harriet Ide (Eager)   1892?-1974
World on my doorstep: a venture in international living. New York: Simon and Schuster, 1947. 274 p.

Life in Geneva 1931-1941, while raising a family; revealing a deep concern for international peace.

1105 Davis, Hassoldt   1907-1959
World without a roof: an autobiography. New York: Duell, Sloan and Pearce, 1957. 436 p.

The international adventures of an explorer, writer, and combat soldier.

1106 Davis, Jefferson   1808-1889
The messages and papers of Jefferson Davis and the Confederacy: including diplomatic correspondence, 1861-1865. Edited and compiled by James D. Richardson. Illustrated. Introduction by Allan Nevins. New York: Chelsea House—Robert Hector, 1966. (Washington, D.C.: Govt. Printing Office, 1905) 2v. Index.

"Without any sectional or political bias," Richardson has "compiled and edited all the messages, proclamations, and inaugural addresses of Jefferson Davis, President of the Confederate States" (Vol. I), as well as the "important and interesting diplomatic correspondence of the Confederacy" (Vol. II). Includes biographical sketches of Davis, Vice-President Stephens, General Robert E. Lee, and three Confederate secretaries of state.

1107 Davis, Jefferson   1808-1889
The papers of Jefferson Davis. Edited by Haskell M. Monroe, Jr. and James T. McIntosh. Baton Rouge: Louisiana State University Press, 1971. 567 p.

Davis, the leader of the Confederacy, was blamed by both sides—by the South, because he failed, and by the North, because he tried to succeed. Later more objective assessments recognized his unquestioned integrity, courage, dedication to duty, and strong leadership qualities. Volume I includes his autobiographical sketches, letters and other papers from 1808 to 1840; other volumes are forthcoming.

1108 Davis, Jefferson   1808-1889
Private letters, 1823-1889. Selected and edited by Hudson Strode. New York: Harcourt, Brace & World, Inc., 1966. 580 p. Index.

This selection of private letters by the President of the Confederacy includes some previously printed, but a large proportion, including those

to and from his wife Varina while he was in prison after the Civil War, have not been printed before in their entirety.

1109 Davis, Jehiel Shotwell   1892-
A teacher's story: an autobiography. Boston: The Christopher Publishing House, 1961. 292 p.

A strict conservative moralist depicts the spiritual and professional achievements of his life as a teacher in Chicago.

1110 Davis, Jerome   1891-1979
A life adventure for peace: an autobiography. Foreword by James A. Pike. Illustrated. New York: Citadel Press, 1967. 208 p.

Davis, a prolific author of books with a social mission and a professor of sociology at Dartmouth and at Yale, describes his life of social activism to promote peace, which took him to Russia and to the German death camps before World War II, and which led him to establish and subsidize Promoting Enduring Peace, Inc.

1111 Davis, Jesse Buttrick   1871-1955
The saga of a schoolmaster; an autobiography. Boston: Boston University Press, 1956. 311 p.

Davis, whose final position was Dean of the Boston University School of Education, achieved eminence as an educator through talent, kindness, and extraordinary energy. His life and career, encompassing jobs as high school teacher, principal, city director of guidance, junior college president, state supervisor of education, provide a micro-history of American secondary education in the "Modern Era" (1890-1950).

1112 *Davis, Julia (Julia Davis Adams)   1900-
Legacy of love. New York: Harcourt Brace and World, Inc., 1961. 237 p.

Memories of life in an extended family surrounded by loving individualists including her grandparents and father, John W. Davis, an attorney, ambassador to London, and presidential candidate.

1113 Davis, Loyal Edward   1896-
A surgeon's odyssey. Garden City, New York: Doubleday & Co., Inc., 1973. 336 p.

A wise, humane review of his medical practice and related experience by a man who became a neurological surgeon and Chairman of Surgery at Northwestern University School of Medicine.

1114 *Davis, Mary Elizabeth (Moragne)   1817-1903
The neglected thread: a journal from the Calhoun Community, 1836-1842. Edited with preface by Delle Mullen. Columbia: University of South Carolina Press, 1951. 256 p. Index.

Diary of the early years of an educated writer gives an account of people and customs of the rural South and her feelings about them; ends with her religious conversion and decision to marry.

1115 Davis, Noah   b.1803
A narrative of the life of Rev. Noah Davis, a colored man: written by himself, at the age of fifty-four. Edited by Maxwell Whiteman. Illustrated. Afro-American History Series. Philadelphia: Rhistoric Publications, 1969. 86 p.

This narrative, "printed solely for the author's benefit," was written to raise money so that Davis could buy his last two children out of slavery, having already purchased his wife and five of his children. His story is simple and to the point—he recounts his early slave life, buying his freedom, religious conversion, marriage, preaching, and multiple efforts to raise money for his family's freedom.

1116 Davis, Owen   1874-1956
My first fifty years in the theatre: the plays, the players, the theatrical managers and the theatre itself as one man saw them in the fifty years between 1897 and 1947. Boston: Walter H. Baker Co., 1950. 157 p.

In recounting many happy memories of his working life, the writer briefly lists his plays, producers, and casts over the years spent in New York and Hollywood. He won a Pulitzer Prize for "Icebound" and served with theatrical organizations.

1117 Davis, Reuben   1813-1890
Recollections of Mississippi and Mississippians. Introduction by William D. McCain. Preface and expanded index by Laura D.S. Harrell. Revised edition. Hattiesburg: University and College Press of Mississippi, 1972. (Boston: Houghton, Mifflin & Co., 1889) 456 p. Index.

Davis served as a U.S. Congressman, was a leading lawyer, and a Brigadier General for the Confederacy. His book describes his prominent role in the development of the state of Mississippi before the Civil War.

1118 Davis, Richard Harding   1864-1916
The adventures and letters of Richard Harding Davis. Edited by Charles Belmont Davis. New York: Beekman Publishers, 1974. (New York: Charles Scribner's Sons, 1917) 417 p.

Davis reported for Philadelphia and New York newspapers and was particularly noteworthy for his accounts of six wars, including the Greco-Turkish War (1897), the Spanish-American, and the first part of

World War I. He wrote novels, short stories, plays, and travel articles featuring his personal adventures in picturesque places.

1119 Davis, Richard Harding 1864-1916
Year from a reporter's notebook. New York: Arno Press, 1970. (New York: Harper & Brothers, 1898) 305 p.
A journalist's notes on major international events from May 1896 to June 1897, including Czar Nicholas II's coronation, President McKinley's inauguration, and wartime letters from Turkey, Greece and Cuba.

1120 Davis, S. Chester b.1883
What? had I shot him? Philadelphia: Dorrance & Co., 1975. 171 p.
Written when he was over ninety, this book describes the long, successful career of a businessman who began his career in Marion, Ohio, and finally settled in Tulsa. He worked in a variety of businesses, the last of which was petroleum.

1121 Davis, Sammy, Jr. 1925-
Yes I can: the story of Sammy Davis, Jr. And Jane and Burt Boyar. New York: Farrar, Straus & Giroux, 1965. 612 p.
After struggling many years to reach star status in show business, he was set back by a serious automobile accident and the loss of an eye, but still made top billing, overcoming racial prejudice along the way.

1122 Davis, Stephen Chapin 1833-1856
California Gold Rush merchant: the journal of Stephen Chapin Davis. Edited by Benjamin B. Richards. San Marino: The Huntington Library, 1956. 124 p. Index.
An interesting view of the Gold Rush by a seventeen-year-old merchant from New England (1850-1854).

1123 Davis, William Heath 1822-1909
Seventy-five years in California: recollections and remarks by one who visited these shores in 1831, and again in 1833, and except when absent on business was a resident from 1838 until the end of a long life in 1909. Edited with preface by Harold A. Small. Publisher's preface by W.R.H. Illustrated. San Francisco: John Howell Books, 1967. (San Francisco: Andrew J. Leary, 1889) 345 p. Index.
A human and mercantile history of San Francisco (1833-1906) from the lively and humanistic viewpoint of a civic-minded merchant. An invaluable account of social, business, and civic customs and manners, published here in a handsome format with tinted plates of early San Francisco geography and portraits of attractive early settlers.

1124 Davison, Peter Hubert 1928-
Half remembered; a personal history. New York: Harper & Row, 1973. 245 p.
A poet examines his life and his parents' gifts to him, remembering and unraveling the past. He concludes that his poetry comes from the midst of life—between childhood and old age, between the conscious and the unconscious, between home and work.

1125 Dawson, Leonard Ray 1935-
Len Dawson: pressure quarterback. With Lou Sahadi. New York: Cowles Book Co., 1970. 245 p.
Star quarterback for the Kansas City Chiefs (1963-69), he wrote his life story after he was accused of gambling connections. The book focuses on his performance in the Super Bowl 1969, the climax of his career.

1126 *Dawson, Sarah (Morgan) 1842-1909
Confederate girl's diary. Foreword and notes by James I. Robertson, Jr. Introduction by Warrington Dawson. Westport, Connecticut: The Greenwood Press, 1972. (Boston: Houghton Mifflin, 1913) 473 p.
Written during her twenties, the diary is a lively and detailed record of her life in Louisiana during the Civil War. One of the best records of activity off the battlefield in the lower Mississippi Valley.

1127 Day, Clarence Burton b.1889
Career in Cathay. San Francisco: Chinese Materials Center, Inc., 1975. 185 p. Index.
After being educated at Hamilton College and San Francisco Theological Seminary, Day followed the family tradition of teaching religion by becoming a teacher at Hangchow Christian College between World Wars I and II. For six months during World War I, Day and his wife were interned without hardship in Shanghai, then repatriated. After the war, the Days went to teach in Lahore, India, before retiring in the United States in 1955. The book gives a lively and pleasant account of a missionary's extensive travels and relations with the host countries.

1128 *Day, Doris 1924-
Doris Day: her own story. With A.E. Hotchner. Illustrated. New York: Bantam, 1976. (New York: William Morrow, 1975) 362 p.
Eighty percent of this volume is Doris Day's as-told-to account of her life, which focuses on her "girl-next-door" career as a movie actress and her prolonged unhappy marriage to Marty Melcher. Lawyer Jerome Rosenthal systematically bilked the Melchers of considerable money; after

Melcher's death, Day collected nearly 23 million dollars from Rosenthal for fraud and damages.

1129 *Day, Dorothy 1897-
The long loneliness. New York: Curtis Books, 1972. 318 p.
Raised an Episcopalian, she converted to Catholicism, became co-founder of the *Catholic Worker,* a newspaper based on a philosophy of anarchism and pacifism.

1130 *Day, Helen Caldwell 1926-
Not without tears. New York: Sheed and Ward, 1954. 270 p.
A Black Catholic convert describes her work as a nurse in Memphis at the Blessed Martin House of Hospitality.

1131 *Day, Ingeborg 1940-
Ghost waltz: a memoir. New York: The Viking Press, 1980. 244 p.
An Austrian immigrant to New York in the late 1950's tells of her quest to learn whether her father, a member of the S.S. in Austria during World War II, had ever been involved in the Holocaust. He forbade discussion of this subject, though she learned more about it when she was an exchange high school student to the United States in the mid-1950's. As an editor and writer in New York in the 1970's, she explores her own ambivalent attitude toward Jews, as well as toward her parents and her native culture, finally coming to terms with both during a New York Bar Mitzvah.

1132 *Day, Laraine 1920-
Day with the Giants. Edited by Kyle Crichton. Garden City, New York: Doubleday and Co., Inc., 1952. 219 p.
An account of family life with Leo Durocher, a famous baseball personality, including many stories about wives and children of baseball figures and her growing involvement with her husband's career.

1133 Day, Wilbur V. 1901-
Through Hell to Heaven. Illustrated. Introduction by Charles L. Allen. New York: Vantage Press, 1978. 49 p.
Day, a Methodist minister in Wabash, Indiana, was seriously injured in an automobile accident in November 1960. Just as he was beginning to recover, an x-ray machine fell on his mending ankle and smashed his foot. Attendant complications sent him into a two-year period of depression; his suicide attempt by sticking his fingers into a light socket failed but the shock helped to cure his depression.

1134 Deady, Matthew Paul 1824-1893
Pharisee among Philistines: the diary of Judge Matthew P. Deady, 1871-1892. Edited with introduction by Malcolm Clark. Illustrated. Portland, Oregon: Oregon Historical Society, 1975. 2v. Index.
A robust account of a vigorous man intimately involved as a judge and state legislator in the development of Portland in particular and Oregon in general. The abundant appendixes following each chapter interpret the significant events and the judge's legal decisions, thereby providing a history of Portland as a supplement to the diary.

1135 Dean, John Wesley, III 1938-
Blind ambition: the White House years. New York: Simon and Schuster, 1976. 415 p. Index.
With compelling and chilling detail, the counsel to President Nixon (1970-73) describes his role and the roles of other principals, including Haldeman, Ehrlichman, Colson, Magruder, Kleindienst, Mitchell, and Richard Nixon, in covering up the break-in at Democratic headquarters in Watergate during the 1972 campaign to reelect Nixon. Dean pleaded guilty and served four months in prison, along with others also convicted in the Watergate cover-up that led to Nixon's resignation.

1136 *Dean, Maureen
"Mo": a woman's view of Watergate. With Hays Gorey. New York: Bantam Books, 1976. (New York: Simon and Schuster, 1975) 270 p. Index.
"Mo" Dean's marriage to John Dean, counsel to President Nixon, began concurrently with the national trauma. Ignorant of any specific Watergate details until they were revealed in John's sworn testimony, she reflects on the stresses in their lives before, during, and after the break with the President over the illegal actions of many top members of Nixon's political team.

1137 Dean, William Frishe 1897-1956
General Dean's story. As told to William L. Orden. New York: The Viking Press, 1954. 296 p. Index.
A major general in the United States Army recounts his days as a prisoner-of-war during the Korean War.

1138 *DeAngeli, Marguerite (Lofft) b.1889
Butter at the old price: the autobiography of Marguerite DeAngeli. Garden City, New York: Doubleday & Co., Inc., 1971. 258 p. Index.
DeAngeli, illustrator and author of many children's books, won the Newbery Prize for the book *The Door in the Wall* in 1950. Her story is full of warm memories of her family and friends.

1139 *DeBidoli, Emi
Reminiscences of a vocal teacher. Cleveland: Emi De Bidoli, 1946. 97 p.
   Voice teacher in Cleveland for 24 years, she was well-known and re-spected in music and literary circles in the United States and Europe.

1140 *Deer, Ada
Speaking out. With R.E. Simon, Jr. Open Door Books. Chicago: Childrens Press, 1970. 63 p.
   The daughter of a Menominee Indian father and a white mother tells of her youth, education, and career in social work. Juvenile career guidance.

1141 *DeForest, Elsie Davis
Out of my cabin. Boston: Christopher Publishing House, 1956. 180 p.
   The author, a schoolteacher, describes how she, her ailing mother, and intermittently invalid husband lived through the Depression in "Owl Center," a home they built on ten wooded acres in the Ozarks, near Neosho, Missouri. Strong religious faith, mutual support, hard work on the property, and DeForest's modest teaching income contributed to their survival.

1142 DeForest, John William   1826-1906
Union officer in the Reconstruction. Edited with an introduction and notes by James H. Croushore and David Morris Potter. Hamden, Con-necticut: Shoe String Archon, 1968. (New Haven: Yale University Press, 1948) 211 p. Index.
   An agent of the Freedman's Bureau in Greenville, South Carolina (1866-67), a young Union officer writes with compassion a first-hand account of whites and Blacks, Northerners and Southerners, the high-minded and the low-down in a country beggared by war.

1143 DeForest, John William   1826-1906
Volunteer's adventures: a Union captain's record of the Civil War. Edited with notes by James H. Croushore. Introduction by Stanley T. Williams. Hamden, Connecticut: Shoe String Archon, 1970. (New Haven: Yale University Press, 1946) 237 p. Index.
   DeForest's outstanding record of camp life in letters mostly to his wife (1862-1864); the author of *Miss Ravenel's Conversion* (1865).

1144 DeForest, Lee   1873-1961
Father of radio: the autobiography of Lee DeForest. Chicago: Wilcox Follett, Co., 1950. 502 p. Index.
   Recollections of his personal life and long years of work in developing radio by electronic engineer and inventor.

1145 DeKruif, Paul Henry   1890-1971
Life among the doctors. In collaboration with Rhea DeKruif. New York: Harcourt, Brace and Co., 1949. 470 p. Index.
   Scientist-writer chronicles ten years (1938-1948) of medical practice advances.

1146 *Demarest, Victoria Booth-Clibborn
God, woman and ministry. Introduction by Cynthia C. Wedel. St. Peters-burg, Florida: Sacred Arts International, 1978. 182 p.
   Demarest, granddaughter of Salvation Army founder William Booth, followed in her parents' and grandparents' evangelical footsteps and spent a vigorous lifetime preaching around the world. She devotes half the book to justifying the case for women clergy and the other half to describing her marriage, motherhood, and career as an internationally known clergywoman.

1147 *DeMille, Agnes   1908-
And promenade home. Boston: Little, Brown and Co., 1958. 301 p. Index.
   The story of her developing success as a dancer and choreographer and of her marriage to Walter Prude during the war years, 1942-1945.

1148 *DeMille, Agnes   1908-
Dance to the piper. Boston: Little, Brown and Co., 1951. 342 p. Index.
   The story of an American dancer and choreographer from her youth and early career to the success of *Oklahoma* and her marriage.

1149 *DeMille, Agnes   1908-
Speak to me, dance with me. Boston: Little, Brown and Co., 1973. 404 p. Index.
   Based on her diaries and correspondence, the book conveys the essence of her driving need to dance and the hardship involved in her struggle to become a successful artist.

1150 *DeMille, Agnes   1908-
Where the wings grow. Garden City, New York: Doubleday & Co., Inc., 1978. 286 p.
   A warm, somewhat nostalgic recollection of her lost youth, innocence, and rapport with the country woods of New England. She conveys a sense of her independence, lively spirit, and temperament which later made her a great dancer and choreographer.

1151 DeMille, Cecil Blount   1881-1959
The autobiography of Cecil B. DeMille. Edited by Donald Hayne. Englewood Cliffs, New Jersey: Prentice-Hall, Inc., 1959. 465 p. Index.
   During his career in Hollywood (1913-1956), he directed seventy films, many of which were spectacular pictures like his last one, *The Ten Commandments*. His book, like his films, has a crowded set, filled with the history of Hollywood.

1152 Dempsey, Jack   1895-
Dempsey. With Barbara Piattelli Dempsey. Introduction by Joseph Durso. Illustrated. New York: Harper & Row, 1977. (New York: Simon and Schuster, 1960) 320 p. Index.
   Dempsey recounts his career as a boxer, culminating in his defeat of Gene Tunney in Chicago in 1927. He was also a Hollywood film star, specializing in "Big Hero" roles in which he beat up an assortment of rivals and villains. For 37 years he ran a popular Broadway restaurant.

1153 Dennis, Eugene   1905-1961
Letters from prison. Edited by Peggy Dennis. New York: International Publishers, 1956. 157 p.
   Eugene Dennis, general secretary of the American Communist Party, wrote letters to his wife and son throughout his imprisonment in the Atlanta Federal Penitentiary (1950-55). Jailed under the Smith Act for his communist activities, Dennis keeps a resolutely optimistic spirit, expresses interest in his young son's activities, and comments extensively on current events during the Cold War Era.

1154 *Dennis, Peggy (Carson/Karasick)   1909-
The autobiography of an American Communist: a personal view of a political life, 1925-1975. Westport, Connecticut: Lawrence Hill & Co., Creative Arts Book Co., 1977. 302 p. Index.
   The common-law wife of American Communist Party leader Eugene Dennis presents their personal lives and the efforts of communists at home and abroad to promote social change, economic equity, and civil rights. They organized California farm laborers in the 1920's, worked for the Comintern in Moscow in the 30's, and left a son to be reared by the communists. Dennis was jailed, 1950-55, in a wave of anti-Communist sentiment, a particularly difficult time for Peggy.

1155 Denny, Ebenezer   1761-1822
Military journal of Major Ebenezer Denny: an officer in the Revolution-ary and Indian Wars, with an introductory memoir. Eyewitness Accounts of the American Revolution. New York: Arno & Press, 1971. (Philadel-phia: Historical Society of Pa., 1859) 288 p.
   Most of the events he describes (1781-1795) occurred in various battles in Pennsylvania among famous contemporary military leaders, providing an interesting record of the men and their war. Appended are letters of the same period by his friend and commander Josiah Harmer. Denny later settled in Pittsburgh where he became a prominent banker.

1156 Dent, Harry Shuler   1930-
The prodigal South returns to power. New York: John Wiley & Sons, 1978. 308 p. Index.
   Special Counsel to the President, Richard Nixon (1969-72), Dent ex-plains the "Southern strategy" which he masterminded and which he claims restored the two-party system to the post-bellum Democratic South and brought Southern politics again into the national mainstream as a force to be reckoned with.

1157 Depew, Chauncey Mitchell   1834-1928
My memories of eighty years. New York: Charles Scribner's Sons, 1924. 417 p. Index.
   A detailed insider's look at New York state and national politics during and following the Civil War. The author's rapid rise to national promi-nence is chronicled with portraits of the important people he knew from Lincoln and Horace Greeley to James Russell Lowell and Commodore Vanderbilt. A who's who of politics, literature, and industry (particularly railroading) during the author's eighty years as a public figure.

1158 DeQuattrociocchi, Niccolo   1899-
Love and dishes. Indianapolis: The Bobbs-Merrill Co., Inc., 1950. 416 p. Index.
   Humorous accounts of his interest in young women and good food by the owner of El Borracho Restaurant in New York; includes large section of recipes from his own and other famous restaurants with accompanying remarks.

1159 Derleth, August William   1909-1971
Walden West. New York: Duell, Sloan and Pearce, 1961. 262 p.
   Sac Prairie, Wisconsin, became his Walden—a microcosm of life in any world. With some nostalgia for passing times and values, he describes his childhood, his grandparents and others whose wisdom marked his experi-ence, his interest in writing, his long correspondence with H.P. Lovecraft.

1160 deRopp, Robert S.   1913-
Warrior's way: the challenging life games. New York: Delacorte Press, 1979. 405 p. Index.

De Ropp discusses his upbringing in England, his education in biochemistry at the Royal College of Science in London, and his subsequent emigration to New York as a cancer researcher at the Rockefeller Institute. The dominant motif of de Ropp's life is his absorption with mysticism as manifested in the Warrior's Way, a philosophy of life that led him to be a disciple of Gurdjieff and Ouspensky.

1161 Derstine, Gerald   **1928-**
Following the fire. As told to Joanne Layman. Illustrated. Foreword by David J. du Plessis. Introduction by Nelson Litwiller. Plainfield. New Jersey: Logos International, 1980. 277 p.
Derstine's story is essentially a string of unusual manifestations of the Holy Spirit as experienced by him, his family, and his church brethren. The events that became commonplace to him included wrestling with Satan, speaking in tongues, being directed in every action by spoken works or mailed letters dictated by God, and on one occasion, his own metamorphosis into a worm. Abandoned and feared by his church and his family, Derstine became a widely known speaker/minister before being readmitted to the Mennonite Church in 1970.

1162 Dessauer, John Hans   **1905-**
My years with Xerox; the billions nobody wanted. Garden City, New York: Doubleday & Co., Inc., 1971. 239 p. Index.
The story of the remarkable development of Xerox from its origin as an invention by Chester Carlson developed by the Haloid Company to the evolution of one of America's largest and most dynamic corporations. The author was a prime maker of this history, having served as executive vice-president of Xerox, vice-chairman of its Board of Directors, and head of Research and Development. He recognized the potential of the invention and aided in its development from the beginning.

1163 Deter, Arthur B.   **1868-1945**
Forty years in the land of tomorrow, 1901-1940. Nashville, Tennessee: The Broadman Press, 1946. 207 p.
A Baptist minister describes his life as a missionary in rural Brazil.

1164 *de Trevino, Elizabeth Borton   **1904-**
The hearthstone of my heart. Introduction by Margaret Cousins. Garden City, New York: Doubleday and Company, 1977. 225 p.
De Trevino writes nostalgically about her family and childhood in Bakersfield, California, in the early 1900's. She talks about her start as a reporter in Boston, her eventual move back to California as a Hollywood reporter, and ends her story in Mexico when she meets her future husband.

1165 *de Trevino, Elizabeth Borton   **1904-**
My heart lies South: the story of my Mexican marriage with epilogue. New York: Thomas Y. Crowell Co., 1972. (1953) 252 p.
While working as a reporter for a Boston newspaper in Mexico during the 1930's, she married Luis Trevino. Her book describes her life and marriage in Mexico. The 1972 edition adds an epilogue emphasizing the economic and social changes that occurred and the continuing centrality of the family in Mexican life.

1166 *Detzer, Dorothy   **1900-**
Appointment on the hill. New York: Henry Holt and Co., 1948. 262 p.
Lobbyist for the Women's International League for Peace and Freedom (1925-1946) describes her activities as a pacifist through the war years.

1167 de Vasconcelos, Mariano Antonio
see **Narvais, Cosme Lozano, pseud.**

1168 Devereux, James Patrick Sinnott   **1903-**
Wake Island. Revised and enlarged edition. Illustrated. Canoga Park, California: Major Books, 1978. (1977) 279 p.
An account of the defense of Wake Island based upon the author's own recollection, some few available records, and the recollections of other Wake Island veterans. Text includes photographs taken before and after the sixteen-day battle.

1169 Devol, George H.   **1829-1903**
Forty years a gambler on the Mississippi: a cabin boy in 1839; could steal cards & cheat the boys at eleven; stack a deck at fourteen; bested soldiers on the Rio Grande during the Mexican War; won hundreds of thousands from paymasters, cotton buyers, defaulters, & thieves; fought more rough-and-tumble fights than any man in America; & was the most daring gambler in the world. Introduction by John O. West. Illustrated. Austin, Texas: Steck-Vaughn Company, 1967. (Cincinnati: Devol & Haines, 1887) 300 p.
In the language of melodrama Devol narrates some 150 anecdotes of life aboard Mississippi River steamboats, 1850-1887. Among them are "It Made a Man of Him," "Lost His Wife's Diamonds," "Don't Dye Your Whiskers," "A Woman With a Gun," and "Ten Thousand in Counterfeit Money."

1170 DeVoto, Bernard Augustine (John August, pseud.)   **1897-1955**
The letters of Bernard DeVoto. Edited by Wallace Stegner. Garden City, New York: Doubleday & Co., 1975. 393 p.

One hundred forty-eight letters selected from the thousands he wrote and arranged in nine topical groups reflect DeVoto's opinions; controversies with Van Wyck Brooks, literary Marxists, art critics and others; and his private life. He was a professor at Northwestern and Harvard, an editor, and wrote the Easy Chair column in *Harper's* for over twenty years.

1171 Dewey, Albert Peter   **1916-1945**
As they were. Epilogue by Geoffrey T. Hellman. New York: The Beechhurst Press, 1946. 233 p.
Describes his life in France, 1939-40, while serving in the Polish Military Ambulance Corps.

1172 Dewey, George   **1837-1917**
Autobiography of George Dewey: Admiral of the Navy. St. Clair Shores, Michigan: Scholarly Press, 1971. (New York: C. Scribner's, Sons, 1913) 337 p. Index.
A narrative of ships, of sailing, of naval battles and strategy, written by one of the first great names in American naval history.

1173 Dewey, John   **1859-1952**
A philosophical correspondence,: 1932-1951. With Arthur F. Bentley. Edited by Sidney Ratner and Jules Altman. Introduction by Sidney Ratner. Associate Editor, James E. Wheeler. New Brunswick, New Jersey: Rutgers University Press, 1964. 737 p. Index.
These wide-ranging, articulate letters form a series of philosophical dialogues between America's renowned philosopher and a foremost theorist in political science, sociology, and psychology. They discuss their respective work, the work of others (from Aristotle to Bertrand Russell), and such philosophical issues as the nature of perception, language, knowing, meaning, fact, experience, cognition, definition, space-time, transaction, and a host of other matters.

1174 *Dewey, Maybelle (Jones)   **b.1888**
Push the button: the chronicle of a professor's wife. Atlanta: Tupper and Love, Inc., 1951. 180 p.
Cheerful account of her love for the South and Professor Malcolm H. Dewey of Emory University.

1175 Dewey, Thomas Edmund   **1902-1971**
Twenty against the underworld. Edited by Rodney Campbell. Garden City, New York: Doubleday & Co., Inc., 1974. 504 p. Index.
Dewey's unfinished memoirs together with public papers, trial transcripts, interviews, and other documents have been arranged and edited into this volume, which deals with his youth, his early career as Special Prosecutor fighting crime and racketeers, and his tenure as New York District Attorney when he became known as the racket-buster.

1176 Diamond, Sigmund   **1920-**
In quest: journal of an unquiet pilgrimage. New York: Columbia University Press, 1980. 227 p. Index.
Diamond is an American Jew who traveled to Jerusalem by way of Eastern Europe and the Soviet Union in search of his family and religious roots. His journal describes numerous synogogues, museums, and art galleries in major cities as well as his reflections upon Jewish history and current Jewish life around the world.

1177 Dick, John Henry   **1919-**
Other Edens: the sketchbook of an artist naturalist. Foreword by S. Dillon Ripley. Illustrated. Old Greenwich, Connecticut: Devin-Adair, 1979. 272 p.
Dick, a naturalist who specializes in bird paintings, describes his world travels in pursuit of elusive species. He has become a conservationist in the course of many trips over the last 25 years to East Africa, India, Greenland, the Antarctic, the Galapagos, Central America, and the King Ranch in Texas.

1178 *Dickerson, Nancy Hanschman
Among those present: a reporter's view of twenty-five years in Washington. Illustrated. New York: Random House, 1976. 238 p.
Personal and professional life mingle as Dickerson describes Washington according to the presidents: the Kennedys she found totally charming, the Johnsons congenial, President Nixon tasteless, and the Fords friendly and reassuring. Recounting dinners, personal friendships, and speculating on the sex lives of the presidents, she paints an attractive picture of Washington journalism.

1179 Dickey, James   **1923-**
Self-interviews. Recorded and edited by Barbara and James Reiss. New York: Dell, 1972. (Garden City, New York: Doubleday, 1970) 190 p. Index.
This is a "talked" book. The poet, roughly following an outline devised by the editors, tape-recorded his thoughts: the first two chapters tell about the young poet's slow self-discovery and his rise to success after his first book of poetry in 1960; Chapter 3 covers a variety of literary problems from the creative process to politics; the remaining chapters are concerned with the poet's thoughts on his "most important" poems.

1180 *Dickinson, Emily   1830-1886
Letters of Emily Dickinson. Edited by Thomas H. Johnson and Theodora Ward. Cambridge: Harvard University Press, 1958. 3v. Index.
  The letters, written 1842-1886, show the poet's sensitive development from girlhood to late middle life. Comprehensive listing of 1049 letters, 124 prose fragments, biographical sketches of recipients and persons mentioned, plus manuscript background of each letter provided.

1181 *Dickinson, Emily   1830-1886
Letters to Dr. and Mrs. Josiah Gilbert Holland. Edited by their granddaughter, Theodora Van Wagenen Ward. Cambridge: Harvard University Press, 1951. 252 p. Index.
  The letters to her close friends, written from her early twenties to the end of her life, sometimes including her poems, have been provided with background by the editor.

1182 *Dickinson, Emily   1830-1886
Selected letters. Edited by Thomas H. Johnson. Cambridge: The Belknap Press of Harvard University Press, 1971. 364 p. Index.
  A selection from the complete edition of "the most meaningful and most important letters plus a representative sampling of others—without losing the spirit of Emily Dickinson."

1183 Dickson, Albert Jerome
Covered wagon days; a journey across the plains in the Sixties, and pioneer days in the Northwest; from the private journals of Albert Jerome Dickson. Edited by Arthur Jerome Dickson. Cleveland: The Arthur H. Clark Co., 1929. 287 p. Index.
  The editor has polished the memoranda, notes, journals, and private papers written by his father recording the life of a plainsman, a journey by covered wagon, mining camps, and a boat trip down the Missouri. It is the story of Indian raids, border treaties, the formation of territorial government, road agents and vigilantes. With photographs, drawings, and map.

1184 *Dickson, Lillian   1901-
Chuckles behind the door: Lillian Dickson's personal letters. Edited by Marilyn Dickson Tank. Illustrated. Taiwan: Lillian Dickson, 1977. 350 p.
  Missionary Dickson, also the wife of a missionary, worked with various groups in the Orient before founding the Mustard Seed, Inc., an independent Christian organization that supported hospitals, clinics, handicraft centers, vocational schools, kindergartens, boys' and girls' schools, and prison work. She approached this work with enthusiasm and faith and tells about it largely through letters to her daughter.

1185 *Dienstag, Eleanor   1938-
Whither thou goest: the story of an uprooted wife. New York: E.P. Dutton, 1976. 187 p.
  Dienstag recounts two painful years in her life when she and her family moved to upstate New York to accommodate her husband's new job. This forced an agonizing readjustment of her own burgeoning career, but she eventually succeeded in juggling the demands of marriage, family, and work. She raises painful questions for a dual-career family: whose career is paramount, who adjusts to moves, and how?

1186 Dietz, Howard   1896-
Dancing in the dark; words by Howard Dietz. Foreword by Alan Jay Lerner. Illustrated. New York: The New York Times Book Co., 1974. 370 p. Index.
  He wrote the lyrics for such shows as *Band Wagon, Sadie Thompson, Inside U.S.A.*, and English versions of *La Boheme* and *Die Fledermaus* for the Metropolitan Opera. His book has the charm and wit of the gentleman his friends in show business claim him to be.

1187 *Dillard, Annie   1945-
Pilgrim at Tinker Creek. New York: Harper's Magazine Press, 1974. 271 p.
  A spiritual autobiography in modern times. Her journal is a meditation in her voice only, as she describes incidents she has observed on her solitary walks near Roanoke, Virginia.

1188 DiMaggio, Joseph Paul   1914-
Lucky to be a Yankee. Foreword by Grantland Rice. New York: Grosset & Dunlap, 1951. (New York: R. Field, 1946) 221 p.
  The story of his outstanding career in baseball during the late Thirties and Forties includes anecdotes about many famous Yankees who were his contemporaries.

1189 Dixon, George   1900-1965
Leaning on a column. Philadelphia: J.P. Lippincott Co., 1961. 215 p.
  A round of embassy parties and White House dinners provides amusing anecdotes for this Washington columnist's account of his life.

1190 Dixon, Paul   1921-1974
Paul Baby: confessions of the mayor of Kneesville. Introduction by Bob Hope. Illustrated. Cleveland: World Publishing Co., 1968. 250 p.
  "Kneesville" is the imaginary locus of Paul Dixon's women-oriented

daily television show on WLW Cincinnati. This book is intended to give his fans a look backstage at Dixon, his band, and backup stars.

1191 Dmytryk, Edward   1908-
It's a hell of a life, but not a bad living. Illustrated. New York: New York Times Books, 1978. 310 p. Index.
  In a fast-paced, rough-cut style, Dmytryk describes Hollywood life, recalling the films he has made and the entertainers with whom he has worked, such as Marlon Brando and Humphrey Bogart. He describes the difficulties of his married life and his affiliation with the Communist Party.

1192 Dobzhansky, Theodosius Grigorievich   1900-1975
Roving naturalist: travel letters of Theodosius Dobzhansky. Edited with introduction by Bentley Glass. Philadelphia: American Philosophical Society, 1980. 327 p.
  A collection of letters written by an expatriated Russian scientist widely recognized for his study of evolutionary processes in the twentieth century. This volume consists of travel letters from exotic lands to his close friends.

1193 *Dodd, Bella (Maria Assunta Isabella Visono)   1904-1969
School of darkness. New York: P.J. Keney and Sons, 1954. 250 p. Index.
  A teacher-lawyer explains how, in order to get union representation for teachers in New York, she became involved with the Communist Party. She discusses her membership, communist and union officials of the 1930's and 40's, her political disillusionment, and her subsequent return to the Catholic faith.

1194 Dodds, Warren   1894-1959
The Baby Dodds story. As told to Larry Gara. Los Angeles: Contemporary Press, 1959. 109 p.
  One of the great New Orleans jazz drummers relates a fascinating history of New Orleans-style jazz in the process of describing his career as a drummer. He played with the best in the business, including Louis Armstrong, Fate Marable, and Sidney Bechet, in New Orleans, St. Louis, Chicago, and New York.

1195 Dodge, David Witherspoon   1890?-1959
Southern rebel in reverse: the autobiography of an idol-shaker. In cooperation with Clair M. Cook. New York: The American Press, 1961. 178 p.
  An impetuous Southern clergyman, teacher, and broadcaster, Dodge fought for human rights and liberalism and against prejudice and narrow-mindedness of many kinds.

1196 Doherty, Bill   1910-
Crime reporter: the autobiography of Bill Doherty. Illustrated. New York: Exposition Press/An Exposition-Banner Book, 1964. 274 p.
  Crime reporter of the Chicago *Sun-Times* and Chicago *Tribune,* Doherty describes the highlights of his 28-year career as one of six brothers, all of whom were reporters. The climax came when he was persecuted by an irate racketeer, Tony Cosmo, and needed a police guard.

1197 Dolgun, Alexander   1926-
Alexander Dolgun's story: an American in the Gulag. With Patrick Watson. New York: Alfred A. Knopf, 1975. 370 p.
  Picked up by a KGB operative in Moscow in 1948, Dolgun, though he had done nothing, was held prisoner for eighteen months of interrogation, isolation, enforced sleeplessness, brutality, and near-starvation. He was sentenced to 25 years of hard labor and managed to survive five years before being released in 1956, but was kept under surveillance until 1971 when he was allowed to leave Russia.

1198 *Dolson, Hildegarde   1909-
We shook the family tree. New York: Random House, 1946. 199 p.
  Growing up in Franklin, Pennsylvania, then making it in New York as a young writer.

1199 Donahue, Phil   1935-
Donahue: my own story. Illustrated. New York: Simon & Schuster, 1979. 183 p.
  Donahue describes how he survived a hectic boyhood in Cleveland and college at Notre Dame to become the most popular syndicated talk-show host in America. He focuses on journalism's "moral contradictions," competition in the media, his experiences as a working husband and divorced parent, and his struggle with Catholicism.

1200 Donato, Joe
Tell it to the Mafia. Plainfield, New Jersey: Logos International, 1975. 154 p.
  After years with the Mafia, he was "touched" by Jesus, quit the underworld, and became an evangelist-healer. This is the story of his conversion.

1201 Doncourt, Kenneth
  see Murray, Ken

1202 *Donlan, Yolande 1920-
Third time lucky. New York: Dial Press/James Wade, 1976. 245 p.
The book's title evidently refers to the author's three-stage career as a chorus girl, a Hollywood starlet, and finally, theatrical success as understudy to Vivien Leigh in *Born Yesterday*, where she had a chance to star with Laurence Olivier. The book abounds in liquor and sex, much of it indulged in by her alcoholic father, Hollywood actor James Donlan, and some by Yolande herself, despite her prim facade.

1203 Dooley, Martin, pseud.
see **Dunne, Finley Peter**

1204 Dooley, Thomas Anthony 1927-1961
Deliver us from evil: the short story of Viet Nam's flight to freedom. New York: Farrar, Straus and Cudahy, 1956. 214 p.
His first book tells of his experience as a Navy doctor in Indo-China, helping to build refugee camps for Vietnamese, learning of the needs and problems which led him to devote the rest of his brief life to that country.

1205 Dooley, Thomas Anthony 1927-1961
Dr. Tom Dooley's three great books: *Deliver us from evil. The edge of tomorrow, The night they burned the mountain.* New York: Farrar, Straus and Co., 1960. 383 p.
A combined edition of the three books describing his humanitarian involvement with the people of Southeast Asia.

1206 Dooley, Thomas Anthony 1927-1961
The edge of tomorrow. New York: Farrar, Straus and Cudahy, 1958. 208 p.
Here he describes his return to Asia where he established a hospital in the primitive Laotian village of Nam Tha, five miles from the border of Red China.

1207 Dooley, Thomas Anthony 1927-1961
The night they burned the mountain. New York: Farrar, Straus and Co., 1960. 192 p.
In his third book he writes of establishing a second hospital in Laos aided by two other American doctors. He was sent back to the United States for cancer surgery, made a rapid fund-raising tour, and returned to Laos once more.

1208 Doran, George Henry 1869-1956
Chronicles of Barabbas, 1884-1934: further chronicles and comment, 1952. Sinclair Lewis, W. Somerset Maugham, H.L. Mencken, Christopher Morley—portrait reviews. Rev. ed. New York: Rinehart & Co., 1952. (1935) 446 p.
A fifty-page autobiographical overview of Doran's life, focusing primarily on his career as a publisher, prefaces Doran's fascinating observations on publishers' concerns—agents, subscriptionists, plagiarism—and portraits of many authors Doran published, including Mary Roberts Rinehart, Michael Arlen, Rebecca West, and Max Beerbohm.

1209 *Dorfman, Elsa
Elsa's housebook; a woman's photojournal. Boston: David R. Godine, 1974. 78 p.
Dorfman arranged poetry readings and set up a poetry circuit. This volume contains photographs she took of some of the poets, her impressions and experiences with them.

1210 Dorn, Frank 1901-
Walkout: with Stilwell in Burma. New York: Thomas Y. Crowell Co., 1971. 258 p. Index.
As Stilwell's senior aide-de-camp, Dorn observed and recorded the men and events of the first Burma Campaign and the retreat march in May 1942 of 115 people after the defeat of the British and Chinese armies by the Japanese.

1211 Dorsey, John Morris 1900-
University Professor John M. Dorsey. Detroit: Wayne State University Press, 1980. 282 p.
Appointed to the honored position of University Professor at Wayne State University, Dorsey reports his experiences and his philosophy of education. His story begins with his years in medical school and deals with his religion, his health, and his individualistic philosophy.

1212 Dos Passos, John 1896-1970
The best times: an informal memoir. New York: The New American Library, 1966. 229 p.
The remembrances of a respected writer illuminate the life and development of the literary circle in the Twenties and Thirties which included Hemingway, Fitzgerald, and others.

1213 Dos Passos, John 1896-1970
The fourteenth chronicle: letters and diaries of John Dos Passos. Edited by Townsend Ludington. Boston: Gambit, 1973. 662 p. Index.
Covering a period from 1910 to two months before his death, these letters and diary entries reveal the author's stand on various social issues. He also talks about his writing, emphasizing how hard he worked to create a distinctive literary style. Text includes a biographical narrative by the editor.

1214 Doten, Alfred R. 1829-1903
The journals of Aldred Doten, 1849-1903. Edited by Walter Van Tilberg Clark. Reno: University of Nevada Press, 1970. 3v. Index.
An extraordinarily complete diary of nearly 54 years by a newspaper man who was part of the Gold Rush days on the mining frontier and the Nevada silver boom. He noted the events of the day, both public and personal, fires, flood, political campaigns, theater programs, weather, vigilante actions, scenery, and business ventures.

1215 Doty, Silas 1800-1876
Life of Silas Doty, 1800-1876: a forgotten autobiography; the most noted thief and daring burglar of his time. Foreword by Randolph G. Adams. Compiled by J.G.W. Colburn. New ed. Detroit, Michigan: Alved of Detroit, 1948. (Toledo, Ohio: Blade Printing & Paper Co., 1880) 288 p.
The adventures of a life-long thief and sometime murderer who stole everything from his teacher's penknife to horses, cattle, and money, and sometimes gave his loot to the poor.

1216 *Doubleday, Rhoda Van Bibber (Tanner)
Atlantic between. New York: Doubleday, Inc., 1947. 682 p.
Gossipy account of society life in New York, California and Europe.

1217 Dougal, William H. 1822-1895
Off for California: the letters, log and sketches of William H. Dougal, Gold Rush artist. Edited by Frank M. Stranger. Foreword by Joseph A. Sullivan. Oakland, California: Biobooks, 1949. 62 p.
In letters to his fiancée and family, Dougal describes his impressions of San Francisco while engaged in business affairs and travel. His sketches are photographic in their detail.

1218 Douglas, Henry Keyd 1840-1903
The Douglas diary; student days at Franklin and Marshall College, 1856-1858. Edited by Frederic Shriner Klein and John Howard Carrill. Illustrated. Lancaster, Pennsylvania: Franklin and Marshall College, 1973. 192 p.
Douglas was one of the first students at the newly formed school joining Marshall College and Franklin College. He comments on college life and mischief, the presidential campaign of James Buchanan, and other contemporary issues before the Civil War.

1219 Douglas, Jack 1908-
A funny thing happened to me on my way to the grave: an autobiography. New York: E.P. Dutton and Co., Inc., 1962. 181 p.
A humorist, author, and script writer for radio and television describes his experiences as an entertainer, a stand-up comedian, and a writer for many prominent comedians, including Bob Hope and Jack Paar.

1220 Douglas, Jack 1908-
Shut up and eat your snowshoes! New York: G.P. Putnam's Sons, 1970. 251 p.
Well-established as a writer for many outstanding radio, movie, and TV comedians, Douglas moved his wife and six-year-old son from Connecticut to Lost Lake in northern Ontario. His book about their life in the wilderness is comic but passionate, with searing criticism of the artificiality of urban living.

1221 Douglas, Lloyd Cassel 1877-1951
Time to remember. Boston: Houghton Mifflin Co., 1951. 238 p.
The author of many novels, including *Magnificent Obsession* and *The Big Fisherman,* claims to have written this volume of reminiscences as a kind of occupational therapy suggested by his doctor during his last illnesses. Although he admits that his life lacked drama, his recollections provide a charming view of late-nineteenth-century mid-America.

1222 Douglas, Mike, pseud. (Dowd, Michael Delaney, Jr.) 1925-
Mike Douglas: my story. Illustrated. New York: G.P. Putnam's Sons, 1978. 320 p. Index.
Douglas got his start on radio singing with "Kay Kyser's Kollege of Musical Knowledge," then worked on local stations during television's early years before his stint as a daytime talk-show host. He recalls numerous "glittering celebrities and super stars" he has had on the show, silly stunts and routines with wild animals, his fan letters, and his loving family.

1223 Douglas, Paul Howard 1892-1976
In the fullness of time; the memoirs of Paul H. Douglas. New York: Harcourt Brace Jovanovich, 1972. 642 p. Index.
Douglas served as U.S. Senator from Illinois from 1948 to 1966. He describes some of his efforts on Capitol Hill—for civil liberties, labor legislation, housing, education, tax reform, truth in lending. He worked hard for what he believed in and championed causes of the poor.

1224 Douglas, Stephen Arnold   **1813-1861**
The letters of Stephen A. Douglas. Edited by Robert W. Johannsen. Urbana: University of Illinois Press, 1961. 558 p. Index.
Letters written by Douglas, the "Little Giant," from 1833 to 1861. He espoused the cause of popular sovereignty and called himself "a radical and progressive democrat."

1225 Douglas, William Orville   **1898-1980**
Court years, 1939-1975: the autobiography of William O. Douglas. New York: Random House, 1980. 434 p. Index.
The second volume of his memoirs, this volume recounts his 35 years on the U.S. Supreme Court, the cases that came before it, the five Chief Justices under whom he served during the administrations of six U.S. presidents. Text includes a list of his law clerks as well as an index of U.S. Supreme Court Cases discussed in the book.

1226 Douglas, William Orville   **1898-1980**
Go East, young man; the early years: the autobiography of William O. Douglas. Illustrated. New York: Random House, 1974. 493 p. Index.
Covering his life from boyhood to his appointment to the Supreme Court in 1939, this book is filled with anecdotes, warm recollections, and personal experiences. It describes his love of the land, his friendship with FDR, his initiation into the world of Washington politics, and the development of his unique political and judicial philosophy.

1227 Douglas, William Orville   **1898-1980**
Of men and mountains. New York: Harper and Brothers, 1950. 328 p.
Recollections of his teen-age experiences in the Cascade Mountains near his home, their spiritual and physical importance, including his recovery from infantile paralysis, by U.S. Supreme Court Justice.

1228 Douglass, David Bates   **1790-1849**
American voyageur: the journal of David Bates Douglas. Edited by Sydney W. Jackman and John F. Freeman. Assisted by Donald J. Richard and James L. Cartes. Marquette: Northern Michigan Univ. Press, 1969. 128 p.
Appointed by Lewis Cass, Governor of Michigan Territory, to explore the Southern coasts and shores of Lake Superior in 1820, Douglass kept a detailed journal of the five-month expedition. He served as surveyor and engineer, returning afterward to his post as a professor of natural science at West Point.

1229 Douglass, Frederick   **1817-1895**
Life and times of Frederick Douglass. Introduction by Rayford W. Logan. New York: Collier Books, 1962. (Boston: DeWolfe, Fiske and Co., 1892) 640 p.
In his third autobiographical volume there is less about his life as a slave and extensive descriptions of his Civil War and postwar activities. Written with evidence of the restraint of old age.

1230 Douglass, Frederick   **1817-1895**
The life and writings of Frederick Douglass New York: International Publishers, 1950-1975. 5v. Index.
This five-volume edition includes all of his known writings, except for his three autobiographical volumes. Volume I: Early years, 1817-1849. Volume II: Pre-Civil War decade, 1850-1860. Volume III: The Civil War, 1861-1865. Volume IV: Reconstruction and after. Volume V: Supplementary volume, 1844-1860.

1231 Douglass, Frederick   **1817-1895**
My bondage and my freedom. Introduction by Dr. James McCune Smith. New York: Arno Press, 1968. (New York: Miller, Orton and Mulligan, 1855) 464 p.
His second autobiographical volume retells his life as a slave and gives a vivid picture of his early years in the abolitionist movement. Includes extracts from his speeches.

1232 Douglass, Frederick   **1817-1895**
Narrative of the life of Frederick Douglass: an American slave. Edited by Benjamin Quarles. Cambridge: Harvard University Press, 1960. (Boston: Published at the Anti-Slavery Office, 1845) 163 p.
The first of his three autobiographies, which describes his life on the Eastern Shore of Maryland through his escape to Massachusetts in 1838.

1233 Dowd, Michael Delaney, Jr.
see Douglas, Mike, pseud.

1234 Downing, John Peter   **1913?-**
At war with the British. Illustrated. Daytona Beach, Florida: John P. Downing, 1980. 204 p.
Downing writes of his service with the American Army during its early involvement in World War II when the British were the dominant allied combat force in Europe, Africa, and the Middle East.

1235 Doyle, Douglas J.   **1906-**
Doctor for the poor: experiences, observations, and opinions of a retired general practitioner after 35 years' practice in Chicago. New York: Vantage Press, 1978. 231 p.
A rambling, sordid account of a general practitioner's medical career in Chicago, beginning during the Depression. Doyle examined W.P.A. applicants in the 1930's and catalogs medical anomalies he encountered. He rabidly opposes abortion, but perversely describes how to self-abort.

1236 Drachman, Bernard   **1861-1945**
The unfailing light: memoirs of an American rabbi. New York: Rabbinical Council of America, 1948. 456 p.
Life in service of promoting modern American Orthodox Judaism; Dean, then faculty member at the Jewish Theological Seminary.

1237 *Dragonette, Jessica   **d.1980**
Faith is a song: the odyssey of an American artist. New York: David McKay Co., Inc., 1951. 288 p.
Recalls her career in radio entertainment and life-long joy in singing for others, with brief glimpses of many people she has worked with.

1238 Drake, Daniel   **1785-1852**
Pioneer life in Kentucky, 1785-1800. Edited from the original manuscript with introductory comments and a biographical sketch by Emmet Field Horine. New York: Henry Schuman, 1948. (Cincinnati: Robert Clarke & Co., 1870. Vol. 6 of the Ohio Valley Historical Series) 257 p.
A detailed portrayal by an eminent physician of farm and family life in late eighteenth-century America, written in letters to his family, who had requested he make a family record.

1239 Dramesi, John A.   **1933-**
Code of honor. New York: W.W. Norton & Co., Inc., 1975. 271 p.
In 1967, the fighter bomber he piloted was shot down over North Vietnam. He spent the next six years as a prisoner of war. His book reveals an extraordinary story of resistance and survival, describing the tricks and games he invented to keep mind and body together, his two escapes, and conflicts between the Code of Conduct for U.S. POW's and the direct orders given by some of his superior officers.

1240 *Draper, Ruth   **1884-1956**
Letters, 1920-1956: a self-portrait of a great actress. Foreword by John Gielgud. Edited with narrative notes by Neilla Warren. Bibliography. Illustrated. New York: Charles Scribner's Sons, 1979. 362 p. Index.
The letters of actress Draper describe her dramatic monologues and her career travels with vitality and humor. She was never in one place for more than three consecutive days. In addition, this volume includes a list of her monologues, with a brief annotation for each, a bibliography, and a discography.

1241 *Dreiser, Helen (Patges) Richardson   **1894-1955**
My life with Dreiser. Cleveland: The World Publishing Co., 1951. 328 p.
A personal record of her love for author Theodore Dreiser and her life with him, adjusting to differences in age and temperament during his last 26 years.

1242 Dreiser, Theodore   **1871-1945**
A Hoosier holiday. London: Constable, 1932. (New York: John Lane Company, 1916) 513 p.
Reminiscences of a journey through New York, Pennsylvania, Ohio, and especially Indiana with attention paid to the scenery, the people, the villages and towns of this American heartland, along with recollections of childhood scenes as well.

1243 Dreiser, Theodore   **1871-1945**
Letters of Theodore Dreiser: a selection. Edited with preface and notes by Robert H. Elias. Philadelphia: University of Pennsylvania Press, 1959. 3v.
Nearly 600 letters written between 1897 and 1945 show a writer of eloquence, power, and feeling. He delights in lyric poetry, pseudo-science, philosophizing. He was intensely interested in political activity and social reform but was essentially isolated from other people, particularly writers, and participated in no organized literary movements.

1244 Dreiser, Theodore   **1871-1945**
Letters to Louise: Theodore Dreiser's letters to Louise Campbell. Edited by Louise Campbell. Philadelphia: University of Pennsylvania Press, 1959. 123 p.
The letters are set in a narrative depicting their long friendship (1917-1945), during which she served as his confidential literary editor.

1245 *Dreisewerd, Edna
The catcher was a lady: the Clem Dreisewerd story. Illustrated. New York: Exposition Press, 1978. 159 p.
Edna Dreisewerd, an aspiring baseball player herself, played the game vicariously through her husband Clem, catcher for various minor league farm clubs (1936-1943) and later with the St. Louis Browns and the Boston Red Sox. She describes their living conditions, road tours, and the pleasures and pains of working with different teams.

1246 *Drew, Louisa Lane   1820-1897
Autobiographical sketch of Mrs. John Drew. Introduction by her son,
John Drew. Illustrated. New York: Benjamin Blom, Inc., 1971. (New
York: Scribner, 1899) 200 p.
 Brief description of her stage life by a well-known nineteenth-century
actress, with notes on many other actors and actresses of her day.

1247 Drewelow, John F.
**In denim and broadcloth: this half century of ours ... with a bit of humor
now and then ...** Illustrated by Eve Drewelow. New York: Vantage Press,
1953. 298 p.
 Country preacher Drewelow writes with sanctimonious good humor
about his preaching and traveling throughout North and South Dakota,
Illinois, Iowa, Ohio, and Wisconsin.

1248 Driscoll, Charles Benedict   1885-1951
Country Jake. New York: The Macmillan Co., 1946. 256 p.
 A rich narrative of his early years on a Kansas farm during his recovery
from rheumatic fever, with interesting description of farm life at the turn
of the century.

1249 Driscoll, Charles Benedict   1885-1951
Kansas Irish. New York: The Macmillan Co., 1943. 320 p.
 The first of two autobiographical books, this one describes his life on a
Kansas farm during the late nineteenth century, emphasizing the impor-
tance of his father's influence and power over the family.

1250 *Drooz, Irma (Gross)   1914-1964
Doctor of medicine. New York: Dodd, Mead & Co., 1949. 308 p.
 A detailed account of her medical education, including many biases
against female doctors, her internships, and specialization in neurosurgery
and psychiatry.

1251 Drucker, Peter Ferdinand   1909-
Adventures of a bystander. New York: Harper & Row, 1979. 344 p.
Index.
 Drucker grew up in the fading world of pre-war Vienna, went to London to escape Nazism in the 1930's, and then came to America, where he
wrote noted works on economics. His own life emerges through lively,
literate portraits of the people who influenced his youth and young
adulthood in Austria, Germany, England, and the United States, including Sigmund Freud and Buckminster Fuller.

1252 Drury, Richard S.
My secret war. Illustrated. Fallbrook, California: Aero Publishers, 1979.
224 p.
 This volume recounts personal experiences and candid reactions of a
young aviator in the Laotian War, a phase of the combat in Southeast
Asia that was not openly acknowledged by the American government
during the Vietnam War years. Flying a heavily loaded World War
II-type plane (the Skyraider A-1) that was used in rescue operations
required great skill. The author's love of flying and his proud militarism
in the face of vacillating political opinions are captured in these chapters
written soon after each combat mission.

1253 Drury, Wells   1851-1932
An editor on the Comstock Lode. Foreword by Ella Bishop Drury. Palo
Alto: Pacific Books, 1948. (New York: Farrar and Rinehart, 1936) 307 p.
Index.
 Well-written descriptive account of the rich and racy era of the
gold-mining days in Nevada by an editor who was later a well-known
journalist in California.

1254 Dubinsky, David   1892-
David Dubinsky: a life with labor. And A.H. Raskin. New York: Simon
& Schuster, 1977. 351 p. Index.
 Labor leader Dubinsky describes his affiliation with the working
classes: his boyhood in Poland, the socialist activities which sent him to
prison in Siberia, escape to America, employment in New York
sweatshops, and rise to the Presidency of the International Ladies Garment Workers Union, a position he held for 34 years.

1255 DuBois, John VanDeusen   1833-1879
**Campaigns in the West, 1856-1861: journal and letters of Colonel John
VanDeusen DuBois.** Edited by George P. Hammond. Illustrated by Jo-
seph Heger. Tucson: Arizona Pioneers Historical Society, 1949. 120 p.
Index.
 A remarkably detailed account of daily life with the U.S. Cavalry in the
Southwest, written by a young lieutenant from New York, commissioned
at West Point.

1256 DuBois, William Edward Burghardt   1868-1963
**The autobiography of W.E.B. DuBois: a soliloquy on viewing life from
the last decade of its first century.** New York: International Publishers,
1968. 448 p. Index.
 A leader since the turn of the century in the Black liberation movement, DuBois surveys his personal involvement in that struggle; his role

in the NAACP, the Pan-African movement and the opposition to coloni-
alism; and his fight for peace during the Cold War. Written in his nineti-
eth year, his third autobiography offers a panoramic view of a great social
revolution.

1257 DuBois, William Edward Burghardt   1868-1963
The correspondence of W.E.B. DuBois. Edited by Herbert Aptheker.
Amherst: University of Massachusetts Press, 1973-78. 3v. Index.
 DuBois discusses racism and pacifism but his main concern is with the
social improvement of Blacks. In letters to Paul Robeson, Lorraine
Hansberry, and scores of others he writes about post-war plans for and
current problems of Black nations.

1258 DuBois, William Edward Burghardt   1868-1963
In battle for peace: the story of my 83rd birthday. New introduction by
Herbert Aptheker. Millwood, New York: Kraus-Thomson Organization,
Ltd., 1976. (New York: Masses and Mainstream, 1952) 192 p.
 Founder of the NAACP and a prominent Black sociologist for over
fifty years describes his experience in the McCarthy era when he was
accused and acquitted of treason.

1259 DuBois, William Edward Burghardt   1868-1963
Seventh son: the thought and writings of W.E.B. DuBois. Edited with
introduction by Julius Lester. New York: Random House, 1971. 2v.
 In Volume I a lengthy biographical sketch liberally weighted with
quotations from DuBois' writings precedes selections of his early work
from the New York *Freeman* and essays from 1896 to 1934 having primarily to do with the Black experience ("The Suppression of the African
Slave Trade," "The Philadelphia Negro," "The Negro in Literature &
Art"). Volume II continues with extensive selections from *The Crisis* and
his later work which concerns Africa as well as the U.S.

1260 Duffus, Robert Luther   1888-1972
Tower of jewels: memories of San Francisco. New York: W.W. Norton &
Co., Inc., 1960. 250 p.
 Duffus worked as a reporter for the San Francisco *Bulletin* from 1911
and later was an editorial writer. He intended his memoir as a tribute to
the great editor, Fremont Older, to the newspaper staff, and to a departed
generation. It was a time of sensational stories meant to increase circulation, of hopes and dreams of a generation, of a dynamic and exciting city
just before the grim reality of the First World War.

1261 Duffus, Robert Luther   1888-1972
Waterbury record: more Vermont memories. New York, New York:
W.W. Norton & Co., Inc., 1959. 272 p.
 His second volume of Vermont recollections is set in 1906, the year
between high school graduation and college days at Stanford when he
worked for the Waterbury *Record* and Stowe *Journal.* He uses that setting
to convey the values and sensibility of small-town life and his adolescent
years.

1262 Duffus, Robert Luther   1888-1972
Williamstown Branch: impersonal memories of a Vermont boyhood. New
York, New York: W.W. Norton & Co., Inc., 1958. 252 p.
 Sketches of his childhood in Vermont when he was a boy of ten convey
the warmth of nostalgic recollection, the wonder of a child's lively imagi-
nation and curiosity.

1263 Dufour, Lou   1895-
Fabulous years: carnival life, world's fairs, and Broadway. With Irwin
Kirby. New York: Vantage Press, 1977. 209 p.
 A well-known entrepreneur in the world of carnivals, amusement
parks, and fairs, he writes of his seventy-year career as a Coney Island
hustler, traveling carnival owner, international showman, and Broadway
and movie producer.

1264 Dufresne, Frank   1898-1966
My way was north: an Alaskan autobiography. Introduction by Corey
Ford. Drawings by Rachel S. Horne. New York: Holt, Rinehart and
Winston, 1966. 274 p.
 This description of his life and love affair during the 1920's and 30's
with the rough, beautiful, and exciting northern wilderness includes un-
derstanding tales of the primitive Eskimos, of dog sledding, of the wild
birds, fish, and animals, of the stark and breathtaking countryside, of life
in a fascinating world far removed from the experiences of ordinary
Americans.

1265 Duke, Florimond   1895-1969
Name, rank, and serial number. With Charles M. Swaart. Illustrated.
New York: Meredith, 1969. 162 p. Index.
 A colonel in the American Air Force during World War II, the author
parachuted into Hungary as part of a secret mission. This military memoir is the account of that mission, the author's subsequent capture and
imprisonment by the Nazis, the life in prison and eventual liberation. The
story is told in the third person with dramatic dialogue.

1266 Duke, Harry
Neutral territory. Philadelphia: Dorrance & Co., 1977. 99 p.
Former racketeer Duke tells of his twenty-year career as a "gangster, hoodlum, cop-beater, stick-up artist, extortionist, shakedown artist, bootlegger, burglar, safecracker, and thief, involved with alcohol, drugs, numbers rackets, and in constant danger of being murdered by Mafia rivals." A persona non grata on both coasts, Duke got married, went straight, and became a businessman, selling damaged cut-up chickens.

1267 Duke, Vernon, pseud. (Dukelsky, Vladimir Alexandrovitch) 1903-1969
Passport to Paris. Illustrated. Boston: Little, Brown, 1955. 502 p. Index.
In fascinating detail, this versatile composer describes his peripatetic existence after being misled by the Bolshevik Revolution (he finally settled in the United States) and his career writing classical music as Vladimir Dukelsky. As Vernon Duke he wrote popular music, mostly scores for films and plays. He knew everyone in popular and classical music, liked most of them, and recreates their fast-moving milieu with charm and wit.

1268 Dukelsky, Vladimir Alexandrovitch
see Duke, Vernon, pseud.

1269 *Dulles, Eleanor Lansing   1895-
Eleanor Lansing Dulles, chances of a lifetime: a memoir. Englewood Cliffs, New Jersey: Prentice-Hall, 1980. 390 p.
Minister in the U.S. State Department for over two decades, she participated in the post-war reconstruction of Austria, ran the Berlin Desk after World War II, and was one of the original team who put the Social Security system into operation. She writes of her professional career and her personal triumphs among an overpowering family of achievers.

1270 *Duncan, Isadora   1878-1927
My life. Illustrated. New York: Victor Gollancz, 1968. (New York: Boni & Liveright, 1927.) 376 p.
Duncan's flamboyant life, of which she was the best press agent, is recounted here with considerable drama. She contributed to the method and style of modern dance until her untimely death. Declaring the inseparability of love and art, she proclaimed that "the artist is the only lover" and enjoyed numerous well-publicized love affairs.

1271 *Duncan, Isadora   1878-1927
Your Isadora: the love story of Isadora Duncan and Gordon Craig. Edited by Francis Steigmuller. New York: Random House, 1974. 399 p.
In 1904 Duncan, the American-born creator of modern dance, met and fell in love with Gordon Craig, an actor and theatrical designer. Their letters spanning sixteen years have been linked with narrative by the editor to reveal two extraordinary personalities, geniuses in their respective worlds of theater and dance, during their years of love and conflict.

1272 Dunglison, Robley   1798-1869
The autobiographical ana of Robley Dunglison, M.D. Edited with notes and introduction by Samuel X. Radbell. Philadelphia: American Philosophical Society, 1963. 212 p. Index
The first full-time professor of medicine in this country, hired by Thomas Jefferson to teach at Jefferson Medical College; he became well-known and respected as one of the great national medical figures of his day. Includes recollections of many famous contemporaries.

1273 Dunglison, Robley   1798-1869
see also Jefferson, Thomas

1274 Dunham, John   1939-
Someday I'm going to be somebody. With Gene Klinger. Chicago: Children's Press, 1970. 63 p.
Growing up in a Chicago ghetto, he decided to use education to get himself out. This is a brief narrative of his upward mobility which resulted in a job as director of computer operations in a large corporation.

1275 *Dunham, Katherine   1910-
Island possessed. Garden City, New York: Doubleday & Co., Inc., 1969. 280 p.
Captivated by the spirit of Haiti, Dunham, who studied its anthropology and dance, returned to the country several times. She learned about its history and politics, met its leaders, came to know its people. She was initiated into voodoo and tells of her reactions to that ceremony.

1276 *Dunham, Katherine   1910-
Katherine Dunham's journey to Accompong. New York: Henry Holt and Co., 1946. 162 p.
While studying anthropology at the University of Chicago, she went to a remote village in Jamaica to observe its culture and dance rituals. Based on her daily notes, her book offers a remarkable picture of her experience in a dwindling culture, which later helped her to develop a prominent career in dance.

1277 *Dunham, Katherine   1910-
Touch of innocence. New York: Harcourt, Brace and Co., 1959. 312 p.

A haunting third person narrative describing the pain, deprivation, loneliness, and confusion of her childhood and adolescence in and around Chicago. Written in Haiti after she had achieved success as a dancer and choreographer.

1278 Dunlap, William   1766-1839
Diary of William Dunlap, 1766-1839: the memoirs of a dramatist, theatrical manager, painter, critic, novelist, and historian. Illustrated. Reissue of 1930 edition. New York: Benjamin Blom, 1969. (New York: New York Historical Society, 1930) 964 p. Index.
Dunlap, in diaries ranging from cryptic to loquacious, comments on events in the American theatrical, political, and artistic milieus in which he was a central figure, a renaissance man in a Revolutionary and post-Revolutionary era. Includes varied, though fragmentary, commentaries on an enormous number of phenomena and people.

1279 Dunn, Arthur Wallace   1859-1926
From Harrison to Harding: a personal narrative, covering a third of a century, 1888-1921. Series on American History and Culture in the Nineteenth Century. Port Washington, New York: Kennikat Press Scholarly Reprints, 1971. (New York: G.P. Putnam's Sons, 1922) 2v.
A political journalist in Washington describes the events of federal government in action for over thirty years, using details from his interactions with major figures as the central focus of the book.

1280 Dunn, Lloyd
On the flip side. New York: Billboard Publishers, 1975. 188 p.
He traveled all over the world in pursuit of songs, artists, and music markets. He writes of his unusual and occasionally bizarre experiences with a humorous yet philosophical attitude.

1281 Dunn, Robert   1877-1955
World alive: a personal story. New York: Crown Publishers, Inc., 1956. 480 p.
Trained as a reporter under Lincoln Steffens, he was a correspondent in five wars, spent considerable time in Alaska during the Gold Rush, and for twenty years was on active duty for Naval Intelligence.

1282 Dunne, Finley Peter (Martin Dooley, pseud.)   1867-1936
Mr. Dooley remembers: the informal memoirs of Finley Peter Dunne. Edited with an introduction and commentary by Philip Dunne. Boston: Little, Brown & Co., Inc., 1963. 307 p.
In this volume of his essays edited with background commentaries by his son, the creator of the Mr. Dooley sketches discusses biography, Warren G. Harding, Theodore Roosevelt, Mark Twain, and the Irish. In the guise of Mr. Dooley he offers observations on current national and world events.

1283 Dunne, Philip   1908-
Take two: a life in movies and politics. Foreword by Anthony Lewis. Illustrated. New York: McGraw-Hill, 1980. 355 p. Index.
Dunne reviews his career in Hollywood as a screen-writer, producer, and director. He analyzes his involvement with such celebrities as Gregory Peck and Susan Hayward and his political activities in the 1940's and 50's defending of constitutional rights, combating rumors of his communist affiliation and fighting blacklisting.

1284 DuPont, Samuel Francis   1803-1865
Samuel Francis DuPont, a selection from his Civil War letters. Vol. I: The Mission: 1860-1862; Vol. II: The Blockade: 1862-1863; Vol. III: The Repulse: 1863-1865. Edited by John D. Hayes. Illustrated. Foreword by Charles W. David. Ithaca, New York: Cornell University Press, 1969. 3v. Index.
Samuel Francis DuPont, Rear Admiral of the U.S. Navy during the Civil War, "played a major part in planning the blockades of the Confederacy and later commanded the squadron which explored tnat operation on the South Atlantic coast." Although he was notably victorious at Port Royal, the ironclads under his command at Charleston were defeated and he was blamed for the failure, relieved of command, and died in shame soon afterward. This enormous collection of his letters is intended, in part, to show that "he acted against his better judgment" at Charleston and to rehabilitate his reputation.

1285 Durand, William Frederick   1859-1958
Adventures in the Navy, in education, science, engineering, and in war: a life story. Foreword by Hugh L. Dryden. New York: American Society of Mechanical Engineers and McGraw Hill Book Co., 1953. 212 p. Index.
Durand, at 93, writes lucidly and humanistically of a vigorous 65-year career as a professor of mechanical engineering at Cornell and Stanford, his research on ship propellers and jet engines, his consultancy on such projects as the Hoover Dam, his government work during World Wars I and II, and his public services that continued into his ninth decade.

1286 Durang, John   1768-1822
The memoir of John Durang, American actor: 1785-1816. Edited by Alan S. Downer. Pittsburgh: University of Pittsburgh Press, 1966. 176 p. Index.
A pioneer actor and Jack-of-all-theatrical-trades, Durang painted scen-

ery, played Shakespeare, danced, did acrobatic feats with a circus troupe, devised stage effects, and organized a company for the Pennsylvania Dutch circuit. His memoir reflects his enthusiastic personality.

1287 *Durant, Ariel   1898-1981
   see Durant, William James

1288 Durant, William James   1885-1981
A dual autobiography. And Ariel Durant. New York: Simon & Schuster, 1977. 420 p. Index.
   The authors of *The Story of Civilization* discuss their lives, their travels, the famous people they have met, and a lifetime of intellectual activity.

1289 Duren, Ryne (Rinold) George, Jr.   1929-
Comeback. With Robert Drury. Dayton, Ohio: Lorenz Press, 1978. 169 p.
   Minor and major league pitcher Duren focuses on his addiction to alcohol which began at thirteen and ended some thirty years later, after his career and marriage had deteriorated because of his drunkenness. Duren now directs an alcoholic rehabilitation program.

1290 Durham, Robert Lee   1870-1949
Since I was born. Edited with foreword by Marshall W. Fishwick. Preface by Margaret Durham Robey. Illustrated. Richmond, Virginia: Whittet & Shepperson, 1953. 217 p.
   Although Durham was President of Southern Seminary and Junior College, 1919-1942, he focuses most of his down-home commentary on notable family and friends, race relations, the Reconstruction era, and local and state politics in North Carolina before 1915.

1291 Durocher, Leo Ernest   1906-
The Dodgers and me: the inside story. Chicago: Ziff-Davis Publishing Co., 1948. 284 p.
   Player-manager recalls his stormy career in baseball, his long association with Branch Rickey, his fierce devotion to the Brooklyn Dodgers, and his wife, Laraine Day. Includes anecdotes about many outstanding players.

1292 Durocher, Leo Ernest   1906-
Nice guys finish last. New York: Simon & Schuster, 1975. 448 p. Index.
   A baseball man through and through, Leo the Lip is famous for his almost daily fights with umpires, suspensions, and legal battles in his long years as player on the Gashouse Gang team of the St. Louis Cardinals, as playing manager of the Brooklyn Dodgers, and then as manager of the rival New York Giants.

1293 Durst, Paul
Roomful of shadows. London: Dobson, 1975. 176 p.
   Durst looks back on his boyhood in the Missouri of the Twenties, when the outlaws of the old West were a fresh memory and model T's drove on dusty, unpaved roads. Raised by a widowed mother and beloved, irascible Irish uncle, Durst poignantly relates family anecdotes and sometimes hair-raising adventures of his own.

1294 *Dusky, Lorraine   1943-
Birthmark. New York: M. Evans and Co., 1979. 191 p.
   Dusky's story is familiar, but movingly told. Working as a reporter fresh out of college, she fell in love with a married man and eventually bore his child in secret. She gave the baby up for adoption immediately, continued her career as a writer, but has regretted the loss of her child to the extent that she has become a prime spokeswoman for the public release of adoptees' birth records.

1295 Duus, Olaus Fredrik   1824-1893
Frontier parsonage: the letters of Olaus Fredrik Duus, Norwegian pastor in Wisconsin, 1855-58. Translated by the Verdandi Study Club of Minneapolis and edited by Theodore C. Blegen. Travel and Descriptive Series, Volume 4. Northfield, Minnesota: Norwegian-American Historical Association, 1947. 120 p.
   A record of family life in pioneer times, these letters reflect the intellectual loneliness of an immigrant clergyman as well as the details and simple pleasures of everyday living.

1296 Dwight, Timothy   1752-1817
Travels in New England and New York. Edited by Barbara Miller Solomon with the assistance of Patricia M. King. Cambridge, Massachusetts: Belknap Press of Harvard University Press, 1969. 4v. Index.
   Dwight's letters concern his travels through New York, Connecticut, and Massachusetts. In them he describes the land, the culture, and the folkways of the inhabitants, particularly before and during the Revolutionary War.

1297 Dye, Jacob   1875-1961
Lumber camp life in Michigan: an autobiographical account by Jacob Dye—1880-1893, and his son Rex J. Dye—1904-1909. Illustrated. Hicksville, New York: Exposition Press, 1975. 48 p.
   Jacob Dye wrote the first half of this wonderfully illustrated book, his

son, Rex, the second half, each recalling the routines of northern lumber camps, the tools, food, pay, men, wildlife, and the amazing advent of the train. Photographs and drawings are from Jacob Dye's personal collection.

1298 Dye, Rex J.
   see Dye, Jacob

1299 *Dykeman, Wilma   1920-
Look to this day. New York: Holt, Rinehart & Winston, 1968. 342 p.
   A novelist and historian writes of her family life and travel in Southern Appalachia, emphasizing the textures of the commonplace, the importance of family life and values.

1300 Dyson, Freeman   1924-
Disturbing the universe. New York: Harper & Row, 1979. 283 p. Index.
   As a physicist Freeman Dyson has worked at the forefront of scientific inquiry. His research has encompassed rockets, nuclear reactors, nuclear weapons, energy sources, and space exploration; his humanitarian concerns extend to the moral and societal consequences of science. He considers the implications of genetic engineering and colonizing space, and writes with admiration about his canoe-building son who explores alternatives of his own. Dyson's work is lively, scientifically enlightening, immensely literate, and great of spirit.

1301 Eager, Samuel Watkins   1900-
Reminiscences of an Orange County lawyer and judge. Illustrated. Middletown, New York: Service Press, 1978. 134 p.
   This privately printed volume combines Eager's account of his career as a lawyer and judge in Orange County, New York, with essays of his views on the court system, trials by jury, wills and estates, and lawyers' fees.

1302 Eagleson, Hodge Macilvain   1895-
Laughing into glory. New York: George W. Stewart, Publisher, Inc., 1947. 192 p.
   The story of his first ministry in a small, rural Methodist church in Hookerstown, Pennsylvania, written with charm and humor.

1303 Eardley, George C.   1926-
A letter for Josephine. Boston: Branden Press, 1975. 232 p.
   A confusing book about the author's confused life. He devotes considerable space to proving that his medical discharge from the U.S. Navy in 1949 for mental instability (schizophrenia) was unjustified, though his later discussion of a "spiritual wedding" with a woman several hundred miles away casts doubt on his mental stability. A sometime mechanic, he led a marginal existence in Arizona and New Mexico. He includes observations on psychiatry, the military, and the nature of religion.

1304 *Earhart, Amelia   1898-1937
The fun of it: random records of my own flying and of women in aviation. Chicago: Academy Press Limited, 1977. (New York: Harcourt Brace, 1923) 218 p.
   Aviator Earhart describes her relatively calm early days as a teacher, social worker, and aviation editor for *Cosmopolitan,* her landmark solo flight across the Atlantic, and her female contemporaries in aviation. Earhart's plane was lost in the South Pacific in 1937.

1305 *Earhart, Amelia   1898-1937
Last Flight. Arranged with foreword by George Palmer Putnam. Illustrated. New York: Harcourt, Brace and Co., 1937. 226 p.
   This book, compiled and arranged by Earhart's husband after her death over the Pacific, was to have been titled *World Flight.* Earhart relates her plans for a round-the-world flight, beginning in 1935 with the acquisition of a twin-engine Lockheed Electra, details stops in Africa and Asia, and carries the narrative as far as New Guinea. Supplemented by facsimiles from her log books and biographical fragments by people who knew her.

1306 Earle, Stephen Carpenter   1839-1913
Journals of Stephen C. Earle, 1853-1858. Edited by Albert B. Southwick. Worcester, Massachusetts: Worcester-Bicentennial Commission, 1976. 72 p.
   Earle's journals cover his adolescence in Worcester, Massachusetts, before the Civil War. After a couple of years of simply noting the daily weather, Earle's observations broaden to include the cultural and social life in Worcester along with some partisan attacks against incumbent President Franklin Pierce.

1307 *Earp, Josephine Sarah Marcus   1869-1944
I married Wyatt Earp: the recollection of Josephine Sarah Marcus Earp. Collated, edited, illustrated, with epilogue by Glenn G. Boyer. University of Arizona Press, 1976. 277 p. Index.
   Josie, third wife of Wyatt Earp, apotheosized in legend as the hero of the gunfight at O.K. Corral, "tells of Wyatt's real-estate flyer in San Diego, his horse racing days, his involvement with the sporting game, his undercover work for Wells Fargo, their Alaskan adventure, and . . . golden years of seasonal prospecting in the vast deserts of California, Arizona, and Nevada." (ed.)

1308 Eastman, Charles Alexander (Ohiyesa)   **1858-1939**
From the deep woods to civilization: chapters in the autobiography of an Indian. Introduction by Raymond Wilson. Illustrated. Lincoln: University of Nebraska Press, 1977. (Boston: Little, Brown, 1916) 206 p. Index.
Eastman, 3/4 Sioux, 1/4 white, was educated at Beloit and Dartmouth and trained as a physician at Boston University. He worked for many years as a physician at Pine Ridge Agency, South Dakota Territory, and treated the injured at the Wounded Knee Massacre, which he describes in detail. He was an articulate spokesman for the Sioux in their fight to remain free, but saw himself foremost as an American.

1309 Eastman, Charles Alexander (Ohiyesa)   **1858-1939**
Indian boyhood. Illustrated by E.K. Blumenschein. Boston, Massachusetts: Corner House Publications, 1975. (New York: McClure, Phillips & Company, 1902) 247 p.
A reverie of his boyhood in Minnesota and Canada written by a Sioux Indian who later assimilated white culture, became formally educated, and achieved success as a physician and writer. The book is dedicated to his son and namesake, Ohiyesa, to whom he hopes to pass on the spirit of the old Indian ways.

1310 Eastman, Max   **1883-1969**
Enjoyment of living. New York: Harper and Brothers, 1948. 603 p. Index.
The first thirty-three years in Eastman's life, describing his development as a writer and socialist; well-written personal and cultural history.

1311 Eastman, Max   **1883-1969**
Great companions: critical memoirs of some famous friends. New York: Farrar, Straus and Cudahy, 1959. 312 p.
A self-portrait is created by means of his interactions with some of the outstanding individuals he has known, such as Albert Einstein, Pablo Casals, Charles Chaplin, and John Dewey.

1312 *Eaton, Evelyn Sybil Mary   **1902-**
I send a voice. Illustrated by Narca Schor. Wheaton, Illinois: Theosophical Publishing House, 1978. 178 p.
Evelyn Eaton is a white woman who became a Pipe Woman through the rites of an Amerindian Sweat Lodge among California Indians. She writes of sweats, feasts, dances, and the ever-important Pipe sacred to the Sweat Lodge. She also discusses the protective grandfathers of various regions, medicine men, and fasting rituals.

1313 *Eaton, Evelyn Sybil Mary   **1902-**
Trees and fields went the other way. Illustrated. New York: Harcourt Brace Jovanovich, Inc., 1974. 342 p.
Eaton, a journalist-novelist-poet and wanderer, includes an account of a 1945 flight with eleven other war correspondents to twenty countries around the world, her teaching experience at several colleges, and her later experiences with the Indians on Big Pine Reservation.

1314 Eaton, Frank (Pistol Pete)   **1860-1958**
Pistol Pete: veteran of the Old West. Dictated to Eva Gillhouse. Boston: Little, Brown and Co., 1952. 278 p.
Old cowboy and former U.S. Deputy Marshal recalls his early years in a series of tales about people and events, his preparation for and final success in finding and shooting his father's killer.

1315 Eby, Kermit   **1903-1962**
For brethren only. Elgin, Illinois: Brethren Press, 1958. 234 p.
A collection of reflections on the proper duty of mankind vis-à-vis fellow humans and God, emphasizing other-worldliness, absence of materialism, and loving fellowship, interspersed with recollections of his farm boyhood in Baugo, Indiana, which centered around the Brethren and Mennonite religions.

1316 Eccles, Marriner Stoddard   **1890-1977**
Beckoning frontiers: public and personal recollections. Edited by Sidney Hyman. New York: Alfred A. Knopf, 1950. 499 p. Index.
A strong supporter of democratic capitalism documents his role in the Federal Reserve during the Roosevelt years and explains his economic philosophy.

1317 *Eddy, Mary Baker   **1821-1910**
Memorabilia: letters by Mary Baker Eddy and excerpts therefrom. Boston: The Trustees under the Will of Mary Baker Eddy, 1952. 16 p.
These letters, excerpted from Eddy's collected letters and miscellany, are not always dated and, although intended to represent significant policy statements and procedures of the Christian Science Church, are full of allusions to factions and to plots for the destruction of the church and Eddy, its founder, that are incomprehensible without a larger context.

1318 Eddy, Sherwood   **1871-1963**
Eighty adventurous years: an autobiography. Introduction by Reinhold Niebuhr. New York: Harper, 1955. 255 p.
A missionary and evangelist for the Young Men's Christian Association describes his faith and work. Since his work involved extensive travel in the East, the author recounts his visits, particularly to India and China.

A chapter entitled "Men I Have Known" surveys the notable people, such as Gandhi, whom Eddy met during his lifetime.

1319 Edelman, John Walter   **1892-1971**
Labor lobbyist: the autobiography of John W. Edelman. Edited by Joseph Carter. Indianapolis: The Bobbs-Merrill Co., 1974. 231 p. Index.
His lifelong service to the cause of labor included posts with several unions—the Hosiery Workers, CIO, Textile Workers—and lobbying for labor-supported bills—St. Lawrence Seaway, Medicare, and housing acts such as the Area Re-Development Act (1961).

1320 *Edey, Marion (Armstrong)   **1879-1957**
Early in the morning. Introduction by John Mason Brown. New York: Harper and Brothers, 1954. 236 p.
A poet recalls her childhood in the Hudson River country in the 1890's.

1321 Edge, Walter   **1873-1956**
A Jerseyman's journal; fifty years of American business and politics. New York: Johnson Reprints, 1972. (Princeton: Princeton University Press, 1948) 349 p. Index.
In fifty years of public life Edge was New Jersey assemblyman, journal clerk of the Senate, secretary of the Senate, Governor of New Jersey, U.S. Senator, and American Ambassador to France. He reiterates his faith in the American system, the flexibility of that system to adjust to the needs of an industrialized society, and the wealth of opportunities for youth to achieve the fullest expression of their lives.

1322 *Edgerton, Mary Wright   **1827-1884**
Governor's wife on the mining frontier: the letters of Mary Edgerton from Montana, 1863-1865. Edited with introduction by James L. Thane, Jr. Salt Lake City: University of Utah Library, 1976. 148 p. Index.
The wife of Montana territorial governor Sidney Edgerton wrote letters to her Ohio relatives, 1863-65, describing the exigencies of daily life in a mining boom town, Bannack, which suffered from inflation, severe weather, and outlaws. The amply detailed introduction puts the letters into their larger political and social context.

1323 Edison, Thomas Alva   **1847-1931**
Diary and sundry observations of Thomas Alva Edison. New York: Greenwood Press Publishers, 1968. (New York: Philosophical Library, 1948) 181 p.
The diary is a record of July 1885; the observations are Edison's comments collected by the editor from various sources. Plainspoken reflections of a lively mind.

1324 Edison, Thomas Alva   **1847-1931**
The diary of Thomas A. Edison. Introduction by Kathleen L. McGuirk. Old Greenwich, Connecticut: The Chatham Press, Inc., 1971. 72 p.
A facsimile edition of his only diary, written in July 1885, during an important personal transition when he was recovering a sense of order after his wife's death and was beginning to seek a new wife. Remarkable details of quest and fancy.

1325 Edmonds, Henry Morris   **1878-1960**
A parson's notebook. Birmingham, Alabama: Elizabeth Agee's Bookshelf, 1961. 310 p.
A well-educated Presbyterian minister from Alabama discusses his travels, his friends, and his philosophy.

1326 Edwards, Frank   **1908-1967**
My first 10,000,000 sponsors. New York: Ballantine Books, 1956. 185 p.
Edwards narrates his adventures as a radio broadcaster in Pittsburgh, Louisville, Indianapolis, and Washington, D.C., in a career lasting from 1924 until he became a TV newscaster in 1955. In his work he found continual pleasure, excitement, and some danger when threatened by gangsters his newscasts exposed.

1327 Edwards, George Clifton   **1914-1961**
Pioneer-at-law. New York: W.W. Norton & Co., 1974. 247 p.
A son's story of his father's career as a Texas lawyer who believed that women should vote and that Blacks have civil rights. His own youth and later life as a lawyer and judge have been shaped by his father's example of selfless devotion to the cause of justice.

1328 *Edwards, India   **1895?-**
Pulling no punches: memoirs of a woman in politics. New York: G.P. Putnam's Sons, 1977. 275 p.
Edwards was for years the main women's page reporter for the Chicago Tribune; her political activity led her to become vice-chairman of the Democratic National Committee and chairman of the Women's Division. She was instrumental in Truman's 1948 election victory and continually lobbied for the appointment of women to prominent political positions.

1329 Eggleston, George Teeple   **1906-**
Roosevelt, Churchill, and the World War II opposition: a revisionist

autobiography. Preface by Devin A. Garrity. Illustrated. Old Greenwich, Connecticut: Devin-Adair Co., 1979. 255 p.

Eggleston, editor of Scribner's *Commentator* and part of the ultra-conservative America First committee, was a vigorous isolationist before World War II in the forefront criticizing the policies of President Roosevelt. When the war came, he volunteered and was commissioned to serve in the navy, but was frequently called before grand juries investigating his alleged pro-Nazi leanings.

1330 Ehrlich, Jacob W. 1900-
A life in my hands: an autobiography. New York: G.P. Putnam's Sons, 1965. 379 p. Index.

"Jake" Ehrlich, a celebrated, successful trial lawyer, tells the story of over forty years of active legal practice, relating some of the courtroom drama and other public battles he has been involved in.

1331 Ehrmann, Max 1872-1945
Journal of Max Ehrmann. Edited by Bertha K. Ehrmann. Boston: Bruce Humphries, 1952. 344 p.

The journal spans the years 1919-1936 and was primarily written in Indiana. The lawyer-poet examines various aspects and incidents of his life in an attempt to develop a philosophy of life and extract the worth of human experience.

1332 Einstein, Albert 1879-1955
Albert Einstein, the human side: new glimpses from his archives. Edited by Helen Dukas and Banesh Hoffmann. Princeton, New Jersey: Princeton University Press, 1979. 167 p.

This collection of Albert Einstein's letters to ordinary people and rhymes composed for special occasions reveals the great scientist's modesty, humor, sensitivity, and compassion. Einstein felt that there is often "too great a disproportion between what one is and what others *think* one is."

1333 Einstein, Albert 1879-1955
Autobiographical notes. Translated and edited by Paul Arthur Schilpp. A Centennial Edition. LaSalle, Illinois: Open Court, 1979. 89 p.

Constituting the only major attempt Einstein made to write autobiography, the text records how, when, and why he thought as he did, and where his conclusions led him at specific times. Original German manuscript is placed beside English translation.

1334 Einstein, Albert 1879-1955
The Born-Einstein letters; correspondence between Albert Einstein and Max and Hedwig Born from 1916-1955, with commentaries by Max Born. Translated by Irene Born. Foreword by Bertrand Russell. New York: Walker and Co., 1971. 240 p. Index.

The letters of two eminent scientists include references to many of their famous contemporaries, major questions of scientific interest, and an uncommon awareness of the social responsibility of the scientist.

1335 Einstein, Lewis David 1877-1967
A diplomat looks back. Edited by Lawrence E. Gelfand. Foreword by George F. Kennan. New Haven: Yale University Press, 1968. 269 p. Index.

In these memoirs written during the 1940's and early 1950's, Einstein reviews his life as a diplomat, events he witnessed, and incidents he was concerned with from the discussions at Algeciras and the life around the Turkish Sultans through a mission to Peking, the "epic" of the Dardanelles, the massacre of the Armenians, and an assignment in Bulgaria.

1336 Eiseley, Loren Corey 1907-1977
The night country. Illustrated by Leonard Everett Fisher. New York: Charles Scribner's Sons, 1971. 240 p.

In a meditative exploration, the author moves from scattered images of his impoverished childhood through his experiences as a young developing scientist to his musings as an established anthropologist. He sees himself as having developed in two separate worlds, one dark, hidden, and self-examining and the other external and boisterous. It is this first world that predominates in this book.

1337 Eisen, Theophilus
The old leather satchel. Illustrated by George Malick. Philadelphia: Christian Education Press, 1954. 88 p.

Clergyman Eisen intersperses the account of his ministry in Oklahoma, Ohio, and Indiana with short sermons and philosophical musings—mostly on ethics and human relationships. After retirement, he contracted diabetes, controlled it, and became a successful door-to-door salesman.

1338 Eisenhower, Dwight David 1890-1969
At ease: stories I tell to friends. Garden City, New York: Doubleday, 1967. 400 p.

The author tells simple anecdotes about his life, his celebrated and little-known acquaintances, and history he has been a part of. Less formal than his other autobiographical writings, this volume emphasizes the genial, relaxed, and amusing facets of his life.

1339 Eisenhower, Dwight David 1890-1969
Crusade in Europe. Garden City, New York: Doubleday and Co., Inc., 1948. 559 p. Index.

Describes the European campaign (1939-1945), drawing on his own significant experience as Allied Commander. Rich in historical fact and the General's point of view.

1340 Eisenhower, Dwight David 1890-1969
Dear general: Eisenhower's wartime letters to Marshall. Edited by Joseph Patrick Hobbs. Baltimore: Johns Hopkins Press, 1971. 255 p. Index.

The editor has selected and annotated these letters sent by Eisenhower to Marshall, 1942-1945, to show that an analysis of Eisenhower's wartime career can be made on a single set of most significant documents. The letters are grouped in four divisions: Planning for Invasion, Commanding in the Mediterranean, Preparing Overlord, and Commanding in Europe.

1341 Eisenhower, Dwight David 1890-1969
In review: pictures I've kept; a concise pictorial "autobiography." Selected and condensed by E. Corbin. Garden City, New York: Doubleday & Co., Inc., 1969. 237 p.

With word pictures drawn from four books by Eisenhower and photographs from his family albums, this book sketches the significant people and events in his life.

1342 Eisenhower, Dwight David 1890-1969
Letters to Mamie. Edited with commentary by John S.D. Eisenhower. Garden City, New York: Doubleday and Company, Inc., 1978. 282 p.

John S.D. Eisenhower's edition of his father's personal letters to Mamie is intended to trace General Eisenhower's slow realization of his stature and to discourage Kay Summersby Morgan's allegation of an affair with Eisenhower. The younger Eisenhower accomplishes both, and the General, "thinking on paper," emerges from his World War II letters homesick and surprisingly romantic.

1343 Eisenhower, Dwight David 1890-1969
Mandate for change, 1953-1956: the White House years. Garden City, New York: Doubleday & Co., Inc., 1963. 650 p. Index.

A president's story from campaign through his first term in the White House.

1344 Eisenhower, Dwight David 1890-1969
The papers of Dwight David Eisenhower: the war years. Baltimore: Johns Hopkins Press, 1970. 5v. Index.

Correspondence and other documents, 1939-1945.

1345 Eisenhower, Dwight David 1890-1969
Waging peace. Garden City, New York: Doubleday & Co., Inc., 1965. 741 p.

This continuation of Eisenhower's account of his presidency details major developments from the elections of 1956 until after the Inauguration of 1961.

1346 Eisenhower, Edgar Newton 1889-1971
Six roads from Abilene: some personal recollections of Edgar Eisenhower. John McCallum, oral historian. Seattle: Wood & Reber, Inc., 1960. 132 p.

In this oral history, Tacoma attorney Edgar Eisenhower reminisces about growing up in Abilene, Kansas, at the turn of the century as one of six brothers, two of whom later became highly successful, Dwight as a World War II General and U.S. President, Milton as president of Johns Hopkins University. Edgar credits his parents with their sons' success and extols their happy, hard-working home life.

1347 Eisenhower, John Sheldon David 1922-
Strictly personal. Garden City, New York: Doubleday & Co., Inc., 1974. 412 p. Index.

The son of President Eisenhower writes of his experiences as a career army officer, as an observer of the Allied high command in World War II, as White House staff officer 1958-1961, and as U.S. Ambassador to Belgium 1969-1971.

1348 Eisenhower, Milton Stover 1899-
The President is calling. Garden City, New York: Doubleday & Co., Inc., 1974. 598 p. Index.

The author, a brother of Dwight D. Eisenhower, carried out policy and program assignments under eight presidents as well as serving in important posts in higher education.

1349 Eisenschiml, Otto 1880-1963
O.E.: historian without an armchair. Indianapolis, Indiana: The Bobbs-Merrill Co., 1963. 224 p.

A recognized historian of the Civil War, he includes stories from his father, a Union officer, and other living veterans he talked with, his impressions of historical sites, and the unusual methods he used in a lifetime of research.

1350 Eisenstaedt, Alfred   **1898-**
The eye of Eisenstaedt. As told to Arthur Goldsmith. New York: The Viking Press, 1969. 199 p.

An informal discussion of photography, his career as a professional photographer, and some of his most famous pictures, including his first cover for *Life,* portraits, landscapes, human interest, animals, and children.

1351 Eisler, Charles   **b.1884**
Million-dollar bend; the autobiography of the benefactor of the radio tube and lamp industry. New York: William-Frederick Press, 1960. 306 p.

An immigrant from Budapest, he founded the Eisler Engineering Company of Newark, New Jersey, in 1920. A saga of an independent spirit and champion of free enterprise in the United States. Text contains many photographs, diagrams, and illustrations of his inventions.

1352 *Elder, Lauren   **1946-**
And I alone survived. With Shirley Streshinsky. New York: Thomas Congdon Books, E.P. Dutton, 1978. 175 p.

This is a compelling account of how Elder and two friends survived a plane crash in the Sierra Nevadas only to have the two friends die overnight, leaving Elder to climb down a steep mountain wall seeking civilization and medical help.

1353 Eldredge, Lawrence H.   **1902-**
Trials of a Philadelphia lawyer. Philadelphia: J.B. Lippincott Company, 1968. 257 p.

Eldredge writes briefly about his childhood but concentrates mainly on some of his most interesting court cases, among them, a little girl horribly burned and disfigured after falling into cement dust and "the phantom killer," a man who robbed and murdered truck drivers as they slept in their cabs.

1354 Eleazer, J.M.   **1895-**
A Dutch Fork farm boy. Illustrated by Corrie McCallum. Columbia: University of South Carolina Press, 1952. 154 p.

An articulate, pleasantly low-key narrative of Eleazer's turn-of-the-century childhood in rural South Carolina, categorized by the seasons of the year. Nostalgic accounts of a country school, farm chores, sports, nature, and friends and family predominate.

1355 Eliade, Mircea   **1907-**
No souvenirs: journal, 1957-1969. Translated by Fred H. Johnson, Jr. New York: Harper & Row, 1977. (Paris: Edition Gallimard, *Fragments d'un Journal,* pp. 229-571, 1973) 343 p. Index.

Eliade, a Rumanian-born, internationally known author and historian of religions, reflects on myths, literature, psychoanalysis, religions, philosophy, culture, the nature of man, the nature of divinity, his travels (Italy, Mexico), his teaching (University of Chicago), his process of writing. He attempts to recover the past in his journal, "a journey which takes place across different landscapes, forms, and colors, arouses a series of associations . . . precious for the secret history of the soul."

1356 Elkins, Frank Callihan   **1939-1966**
The heart of a man. Edited by Marilyn Roberson Elkins. New York: W.W. Norton & Co., Inc., 1973. 139 p.

The diary of a Navy pilot in Vietnam, May-October, 1966, reveals the personal agony, loneliness and fear of a man seen by his friends as brave and heroic. It was edited by his wife for publication six years after his death in action.

1357 Ellicott, Andrew   **1754-1820**
Journal of Andrew Ellicott: late commissioner on behalf of the U.S. for determining the boundary between the U.S. and the possessions of his Catholic majesty. Americana Classics. Chicago: Quadrangle Books, 1962. (Philadelphia: Budd and Bartram, 1803) 300 p.

A journal of his travels (1796-1800) while surveying the boundary of Spanish Florida, including his overland journey to Pittsburgh, then down the Ohio and Mississippi rivers, overland east to the Florida Peninsula, and back to Philadelphia.

1358 Elliot, James   **1927-1956**
The journals of Jim Elliot. Edited by Elisabeth Elliot. Old Tappan, New Jersey: Fleming H. Revell Co., 1978. 477 p.

Elliot began keeping a journal during his junior year at Wheaton College as an exercise in piety and wrote intermittently until his untimely death at 29, murdered in Ecuador by the Auca Indians he was trying to convert to Christianity. Elliott is torn, at times, between his desires of the flesh (for Betty, whom he finally married in 1953) and of the spirit. His religious and missionary zeal are paramount throughout.

1359 *Ellis, Anne   **1875-1938**
The life of an ordinary woman. Introduction by Lucy Fitch Perkins. New York: Arno Press, 1974. (Boston: Houghton Mifflin, 1929) 301 p.

A plainspoken narrative of Ellis's extraordinary adventures in mining towns of Colorado and other Western territories where she was a cook, politician, wife, and friend to miners and pioneer settlers.

1360 Ellis, James Benton   **1870-1946**
Blazing the gospel trail. Foreword and afterword by Vep Ellis. Plainfield, New Jersey: Logos International, 1976. 127 p.

Originally a Methodist who later became a Church of God Pentecostal Holiness gospel preacher in Alabama, Ellis recounts the highlights and bizarre experiences of his career. These include speaking in tongues, snake handlers, arsonists, faith healers, and accounts of divine portents and miracles. During World War I Ellis was imprisoned on false charges of being pro-German. His narrative is full of violent and mystifying events which he interprets according to his faith.

1361 Ellis, James Hervey   **1893-1978**
Jumping frog from Jaspar County: Hoosier boy lands on Madison Avenue. London: Abelard-Schuman, 1970. 240 p.

Ellis rose to a powerful position in advertising, eventually becoming President of the Kudner Agency, Inc., which handled such accounts as Buick and Firestone for many years. He writes of his career, the cutthroat politics in the advertising world, the ulcers and thrombosis, including his own, and the final sense of satisfaction in success.

1362 Ellis, James Hervey   **1893-1978**
Run for your life. With Don Arthur Torgerson and R.E. Simon. Chicago: Childrens Press, 1970. 64 p.

Written to give career guidance for youth, this book tells of Ellis's childhood, his success as a football player, and his career with the Chicago Committee on Urban Opportunity.

1363 Ellison, Jerome   **1907-**
Report to the Creator. New York: Harper and Brothers, 1955. 246 p.

An impressionistic, not fully coherent account of the author's life and his intermittent but ultimately powerful and overwhelming religious faith, enhanced by his ten-year freedom from alcoholism. A humorist despite this humorless book, Ellison had written regular columns for *Life* and other magazines in the 30's, but alcohol and womanizing ruined his marriage, irredeemable even with eight years of psychotherapy.

1364 Ellsworth, Ralph Eugene   **1907-**
Ellsworth on Ellsworth: an unchronological, mostly true account of some moments of contact between "library science" and me, since our confluence in 1931, with appropriate sidelights. Metuchen, New Jersey: Scarecrow Press, 1980. 163 p. Index.

He writes with humor and goodwill about his accomplishments and trials as a serious professional dedicated to the scientific spirit introduced by the University of Chicago Graduate Library School in the early 1930's.

1365 Ely, Richard Theodore   **1854-1943**
Ground under our feet: an autobiography. Illustrated. Series: The Academic Profession. New York: Arno Press, 1977. (New York: Macmillan, 1938) 330 p. Index.

With justifiable pride, Ely tells of his life as a successful economist and author. A "Connecticut Yankee" reared in upstate New York, Ely was educated at Columbia and became enamored of economics on a trip to Germany. He taught and wrote extensively on political economy and related subjects at Johns Hopkins and the University of Wisconsin.

1366 *Emerson, Ellen Louisa (Tucker)   **1809-1831**
One first love: the letters of Ellen Louisa Tucker to Ralph Waldo Emerson. Edited by Edith W. Gregg. Cambridge; Belknap Press/Harvard University Press, 1962. 208 p. Index.

Letters written from 1828 to 1831 by Emerson's first wife, along with some of her verses.

1367 Emerson, Ralph Waldo   **1803-1882**
Correspondence between Ralph Waldo Emerson and Herman Grimm. Edited by Frederick William Holls. Port Washington, New York: Kennikat, 1971. (Boston: Houghton, Mifflin and Co., 1903) 90 p.

Grimm, the son of Wilhelm Grimm of the Grimm's fairy-tale brothers, played an important part in the introduction and interpretation of Emerson to the German people. Although they met only once (in 1873), they corresponded for fifteen years. Grimm's letters are in German accompanied by English translations. Also included are two letters to Gisela von Arnim, afterwards Grimm's wife.

1368 Emerson, Ralph Waldo   **1803-1882**
The correspondence of Emerson and Carlyle. Edited by Joseph Slater. New York: Columbia University Press, 1964. 622 p. Index.

This new edition of their correspondence includes letters cut from earlier editions and some previously unpublished, providing more extensive information about two great literary artists.

1369 Emerson, Ralph Waldo   **1803-1882**
The journals and miscellaneous notebooks of Ralph Waldo Emerson. Edited by William H. Gilman and others. Cambridge: The Belknap Press of Harvard University Press, 1960-. v. Index.

Emerson kept his notebooks and journals as preparation for essays and lectures. They record his observations on many subjects, drafts of poems, and notes for works in process. This carefully annotated edition reveals the process of an active, deeply thoughtful mind at work.

1370 Emerson, Ralph Waldo   **1803-1882**
Letters from Ralph Waldo Emerson to a friend, 1838-1853. Edited by Charles Eliot Norton. Port Washington, New York: Kennikat, 1971. (Boston: Houghton, Mifflin and Co., 1899) 81 p.

Emerson's ideal of friendship, though never perfectly attained, is mirrored in these letters to a younger friend which span fifteen years. The friend offered appreciation, knowledge, practical qualities, and acquaintance with affairs which Emerson lacked. Emerson offered his essential individualism and idealism to their relationship.

1371 Emerson, Ralph Waldo   **1803-1882**
Ralph Waldo Emerson: essays and journals. Selected and with an introduction by Lewis Mumford. Garden City, New York: Doubleday & Co., Inc., 1968. 671 p.

Pages 627-71 contain brief entries from Emerson's journals from 1820 through 1871. The rest of the volume reprints selected essays.

1372 Emerson, William   **1743-1776**
Diaries and letters of William Emerson, 1743-1776, minister of the church in Concord, chaplain in the Revolutionary army. Arranged by Amelia Forbes Emerson. N.P.: privately printed, 1972. 150 p. Index.

The grandfather of Ralph Waldo Emerson, Rev. Emerson recorded his travel in New England exchanging pulpits with fellow ministers, his experiences at the outbreak of the Revolution and in the army camp near Bunker Hill, and the coming of Harvard College to Concord to avoid the smallpox epidemic of 1763.

1373 Emmerson, John Kenneth   **1908-**
Japanese thread: a life in the U.S. Foreign Service. New York: Holt, Rinehart and Winston, 1978. 465 p. Index.

His diplomatic "office" was Japan, where he spent over a third of the twentieth century. Emmerson describes the militaristic Thirties and Forties (including Pearl Harbor), the post-war Occupation, his mission to Communist Chinese Headquarters in 1944 where he met Mao Tse-tung, the Cold War era, the McCarthy period (when Emmerson himself was investigated), and the mid-Sixties, when he was U.S. Minister to Japan.

1374 Endrey, Eugene   **1891-1967**
Beg, borrow, and squeal. New York: Pageant Press. Inc., 1963. 293 p.

A critical review of life in the world of theater and entertainment by a man who immigrated from Hungary and became a journalist, actor, director, and producer, struggling to succeed with the Chicago Hungarian Theatre and his newspaper, the *Hungarian Radio News.*

1375 Engel, Lehman   **1910-**
This bright day: an autobiography. Illustrated. New York: Macmillan Publishing Co., 1974. 366 p. Index.

Well-known as a composer and Hollywood conductor, he writes of his life in theatrical music, recalling many of his famous friends and acquaintances, but emphasizing the fragility of fame and happiness, the effects of time passing in one's life.

1376 Engleman, Finis Ewing   **1895-1978**
The pleasure was mine: 14 years in American Overseas Education, Part II. Foreword by Paul B. Salmon. Danville, Illinois: Interstate Printers & Publishers, 1980. 176 p.

After retiring as an education executive at 68, Engleman launched vigorously into a fourteen-year second career as an educational consultant, mostly for the U.S. State Department. He and his wife traveled extensively throughout the Middle East and Africa as he examined and reported on the American system of overseas schools for the children of American employees abroad. Engleman describes the trips and his findings and concludes with an essay on the major problems of "stateside education" in 1977, including a divided profession and bilingualism.

1377 Engleman, Finis Ewing   **1895-1978**
The pleasure was mine: 70 years in education, Part I. Danville, Illinois: Interstate Printers and Publishers, 1980. (1971) 176 p.

Throughout his life Engleman loved and supported education and educators. His own education began in a rural one-room school where he was switched for misbehavior. After one year of high school he went to college, became superintendent of schools for the state of Connecticut, and finally executive secretary of the American Association of School Administrators. He discusses various aspects of educational philosophy, politics, and practices.

1378 Enos, Edward
    see Canutt, Yakima

1379 *Enters, Angna   **1907-**
Artist's life. New York: Coward-McCann, Inc., 1958. 447 p.

Based on her daily journals and partially on her earlier book, *First Person Plural,* this book analyzes her life in three arts—mime, painting, and writing.

1380 *Enters, Angna   **1907-**
First person plural. Illustrated. New York: Da Capo Press, 1978. (New York: Stackpole, 1937) 386 p.

Enters recounts her performing tours in the United States and Europe from 1927 to 1936, detailing mime acts she performed and the costume designed for each. She comments on the people, customs, and art museums in the countries visited.

1381 Ephron, Henry   **1911-**
We thought we could do anything: the life of screenwriters Phoebe and Henry Ephron. New York: W.W. Norton & Co., 1977. 211 p.

In terse prose resembling a film scenario, Ephron relates the story of his 38-year marriage to Phoebe, mother of their four daughters including novelist Nora, and his 31-year collaboration with her as a writer and adapter of plays for the screen, including *Carousel* and *What Price Glory?* They "thought they could do everything" right as film writers and as partners, lovers, and parents. By 1971 Phoebe became depressed over a pre-cancerous skin condition and died; this book is a eulogy.

1382 *Epstein, Perle   **1938-**
Pilgrimage: adventures of a wandering Jew. Boston: Houghton Mifflin Co., 1979. 364 p.

Epstein recounts the intricacies of her search for the Kabbalah, Jewish mysticism and direct knowledge of God, which had traditionally been vouchsafed only to men. She searched in New York, India, and finally accomplished the goal of her spiritual autobiography after a series of near-misses and frustrations. Throughout, Epstein discusses her dreams and other religiously significant encounters.

1383 Erickson, T.A.   **b.1871**
My sixty years with rural youth. With Anna North Coit. Foreword by Skuli Rutford. Minneapolis: University of Minnesota Press, 1956. 162 p. Index.

Erickson relates his lifelong involvement with agriculture as a farmer's son and ultimately as the Minnesota state leader of 4-H clubs through his position with the University of Minnesota Agricultural Extension Service. His autobiography provides a history of 4-H youth education in twentieth-century Minnesota.

1384 Ericsson, Henry   **1861-1947**
Sixty years a builder: the autobiography of Henry Ericsson. New York: Arno Press, 1972. (Chicago: A. Kroch and Son, 1942) 388 p. Index.

In 1882 he immigrated to Chicago from Sweden and began a career in construction which eventually made him one of the central powers in the development of Chicago. His book is eloquent in details of city life from the turn of the century, providing a document of social, economic, and political history.

1385 Ernst, Morris Leopold   **1888-1976**
So far so good. New York: Harper & Brothers, 1948. 271 p.

His zest for living and passionate defense of human freedom and individual rights are evident in his adventures with family and friends on an individual, national or international level.

1386 Ernst, Morris Leopold   **1888-1976**
Touch wood: a year's diary. New York: Atheneum Publishers, 1960. 370 p.

A prominent New York attorney and proponent of civil liberties, he wrote this diary in his seventieth year as a test and illustration that his life was by no means over, and scarcely diminished. He comments on major political issues, television, the hula hoop, his deep concern for world literacy, sailing in Nantucket, and on time spent with many interesting and famous friends.

1387 Erskine, John   **1879-1951**
Memory of certain persons. Philadelphia: J.B. Lippincott Co., 1947. 439 p. Index.

His education and professional life as a college teacher and writer (Amherst, Columbia, Juilliard School of Music).

1388 Erskine, John   **1879-1951**
My life as a teacher. Philadelphia: J.B. Lippincott Co., 1948. 249 p. Index.

One of three autobiographical volumes by a man who had careers in music, in writing, and in teaching. This one focuses on his experiences as a teacher at Amherst, at Columbia, and Beaune.

1389 Erskine, John   **1879-1951**
My life in music. New York: William Morrow and Co., 1950. 283 p. Index.

The author recounts his work with Columbia University's English Department, as President and Trustee of the Juilliard School of Music, and with the Metropolitan Opera, as well as insights into his personal development with family and friends.

1390 Ervin, Samuel James, Jr.   **1896-**
The whole truth: the Watergate conspiracy. New York: Random House, 1980. 320 p. Index.

Ervin, chairman of the Senate Select Committee to investigate the Watergate break-in and cover-up during 1973 and 1974, was moved to write this book as a corrective to Nixon's *Memoirs,* which he sees as self-serving and inaccurate. Ervin presents incontrovertible evidence that Nixon and his staff (Haldeman, Ehrlichman, Dean, et al.—all of whom were convicted and imprisoned) were guilty of violating the Constitution and that Nixon would have been impeached and convicted if he hadn't resigned. Ervin amply contradicts Nixon's claim that he was hounded from office by a hostile press. The author's candor, respect for the Constitution, and patriotism are evident on every page.

1391 Erwin, John Robert   1930-
The man who keeps going to jail. Foreword by Richard B. Oglivie. Elgin, Illinois: David C. Cook Publishing Co., 1978. 182 p.
Erwin, for thirteen years director of Programmed Activities for Correctional Education (PACE) at Chicago's Cook County Jail, tells of his miserable childhood in seven foster homes, two orphanages, and prison for a variety of delinquencies. At 22 he had a religious conversion to evangelical Christianity, attended Emmaus Bible College, married, and began a jail ministry that is increasingly effective.

1392 Espey, John Jenkins   1913-
Minor heresies. New York: Alfred A. Knopf, 1949. 202 p.
The second volume of his recollections from childhood in Shanghai, where his parents were Presbyterian missionaries, is skillfully written with a dramatic sense of East-West cultural differences.

1393 Espey, John Jenkins   1913-
The other city. New York: Alfred A. Knopf, 1950. 211 p.
The third volume of recollections of his early life in China; this one focuses on his years at the Shanghai American School. All three volumes are skillfully written, with a good sense of drama, humor, and perception of Chinese culture.

1394 Espey, John Jenkins   1913-
Tales out of school. New York: Alfred A. Knopf, 1947. 204 p.
The son of Presbyterian missionaries in China writes of his early life and education there, with interesting details of Chinese culture from a Westerner's point of view.

1395 *Espy, Harriett Newell
see **Vance, Zebulon Baird**

1396 Esses, Michael
Michael, Michael, why do you hate me? Introduction by Pat Boone. Plainfield, New Jersey: Logos International, 1973. 167 p.
A spiritual narrative describing a rabbi's conversion to Christianity, emphasizing his near-fatal illness and recovery.

1397 *Ethridge, Willie (Snow)   1900-
It's Greek to me. New York: The Vanguard Press, Inc., 1947. 297 p.
An account of her impressions of Greece, while traveling there with her husband, Mark Ethridge, Chairman of the American Delegation on the U.N. Balkan Commission. Personalized description of postwar relief and turmoil.

1398 Evans, Charles   1890-1979
The Reverend goes to Hollywood. New York: The Crowell-Collier Press, 1962. 222 p.
A middle-aged minister in rural California, he followed his whim to become a movie star and achieved a moderate success.

1399 *Evans, Dale
see ***Rogers, Dale Evans**

1400 *Evans, Dale
see **Rogers, Roy**

1401 Evans, Norm   1942-
On God's squad: the story of Norm Evans. As told to Ray Didinger and Sonny Schwartz. Carol Stream, Illinois: Creation House, 1971. 192 p.
An offensive tackle for the Miami Dolphins describes his faith in God, his success in professional football, and his belief that the former is responsible for the latter.

1402 Evans, Norm   1942-
On the line. With Edwin Pope. Foreword by Bob Griese. Illustrated. Old Tappan, New Jersey: Fleming H. Revell, 1976. 157 p.
Evans focuses on his twelve years as a professional football offensive lineman, essentially with the Miami Dolphins. He considers the six months per year that he plays football "the most bone-grinding, mind-grinding six months of any business I can think of, . . . [but] my life belongs to Jesus Christ, not to pro football." Nevertheless, he loves football, the fans, and his Christian family.

1403 Everest, Frank Kendall   1920-
Fastest man alive. As told to John Guenther. Foreword by Albert Boyd. New York: E.P. Dutton and Co., Inc., 1958. 252 p.
The experience of an Air Force test pilot who flew more than 1,900 miles per hour.

1404 Evergood, Philip (Philip Blashki)   1901-1973
Philip Evergood. Text by John I.H. Bauer. New York: Harry N. Abrams, Inc., 1975. 215 p. Index.
This collection of Evergood's paintings, many reproduced in color, is prefaced by a biographical sketch and accompanied with interpretive commentary by Evergood and Bauer that relates the paintings to the artist's life and attitudes.

1405 *Evers, Mrs. Medgar
For us, the living. New York: Doubleday & Co., Inc., 1967. 378 p.
Writing after her husband, civil rights leader Medgar Evers, was assassinated, she describes life as a middle-class Black in Mississippi.

1406 Ewald, Johann   1744-1813
Diary of the American War: a Hessian journal. Translated by Joseph P. Tustin. New Haven, Connecticut: Yale University Press, 1979. 467 p. Index.
An erudite, articulate, and detailed diary of six campaigns in the Revolutionary War in which the author, a Captain in an elite corps of Hessian Mercenaries, describes the movements and battles with sharp observations about leaders on both sides. He and his troops were imaginative and skilled at guerrilla warfare, waging battle from Trenton to New York to Charlestown to Yorktown. Sketches of battle plans are included.

1407 *Ewing, Ruth Grimes
Our life with the Garos of Assam, India. Philadelphia: Dorrance & Co., 1971. 197 p.
Mrs. Ewing and her husband set out for India in 1921 with another couple to the mission station at Garo Hills, India. Her book describes their work, their pattern of living, the Garo natives, the mission churches and schools, trips taken, the advances in Garo leadership, and the expansion of Christian influence among the people.

1408 *Exner, Judith Katherine Campbell   1934-
My story. As told to Ovid Demaris. Prologue by Demaris. Illustrated. New York: Grove Press, 1977. 299 p.
Exner, long-time playgirl and mistress to many, writes a sordid account of her life in and out of bed. She focuses on her sexual liaison with John F. Kennedy during his presidential campaign and in the White House. She was investigated by the CIA because she was concurrently involved with Sam Giancana, the King of American racketeers, and the question arose as to whether Exner was in any way a link between the two men.

1409 Eytinge, Bruce Swomley   1893-
Bruce Eytinge: actor, inventor, aviator (an autobiography). San Antonio, Texas: The Naylor Co., 1975. 191 p.
Dedicated to the Boy Scouts of America, this volume describes how the American virtues of self-reliance, discipline, and creative character-building have been incorporated into his personal and professional lives.

1410 Fagan, James Octavius   b.1859
Confessions of a railroad signalman. Boston: Houghton Mifflin, 1980. 181 p.
Less a personal confession than the strongly stated opinions of a telegraph operator, towerman, and time chief clerk for the railroad superintendent concerning railroad safety. Eyewitness to several accidents, the author describes the weaknesses in the system and suggests solutions.

1411 *Fahrner, Mary   1904-
Way of the cross—where it led me: the story of a Franciscan nun. Illustrated. Mountain View, California: Pacific Press Publishing Ass'n., 1977. 56 p.
Fahrner describes the piety of her more than fifty years as a Franciscan nun who taught in a Catholic school. She lovingly fulfilled the rules governing her conduct—"poverty, chastity, and obedience," but approves the loosening of the severe restrictions under which she had lived as a young nun (chaperoned half-day visits to parents every three to five years). Her contented narrative does not prepare readers for her sudden conversion to Seventh Day Adventism at age seventy.

1412 Fairbank, Calvin   1816-1898
Rev. Calvin Fairbank during slavery times: how he "fought the good fight" to prepare "the way." Edited from his manuscript. New York: Negro Universities Press, 1969. (Chicago: Patriotic Publ. Co., 1890) 207 p.
This volume, a reprint of the 1890 edition, tells the story of an active abolitionist clergyman who labored for anti-slavery causes and for the good of the "Africo-American" people.

1413 Fairchild, David Grandison   1869-1954
The world grows round my door: the story of the Kampong, a home on the

edge of the tropics. New York: Charles Scribner's Sons, 1947. 359 p. Index.

A remarkable and readable narrative of his life and work as a botanist, principally his years on Java in the Kampong.

1414 Falk, Louis Austin   **1895-1979**
High windows: an autobiography. Foreword By Samuel Margoshes. New York: Whittier Books, Inc., 1959. 145 p.

Polish immigrant Falk served in the American Army in World War I, fought in Germany, arrived in the United States penniless, and married the daughter of New York's richest Jewish merchant. He studied law and founded a large meat company in Jersey City, New Jersey. Once his business was well-established, he labored effectively for Zionism and many other Jewish causes.

1415 Fall, Albert Bacon   **1861-1944**
The memoirs of Albert B. Fall. Introduction by David H. Stratton. El Paso: Texas Western College Press, 1966. 63 p.

Fall spent his early life as a cowboy, miner, and prospector. This memoir deals with that period, rather than his later years when he became a U.S. Senator, Secretary of the Interior, was convicted of taking a bribe in the Teapot Dome Scandal and went to prison.

1416 Farley, James Aloysius   **1888-1976**
Jim Farley's story: the Roosevelt years. New York: Whittlesey House, 1948. 388 p. Index.

Tells of his political experience during the administration of Franklin D. Roosevelt; in some ways a justification of his fall from Franklin D. Roosevelt's grace.

1417 *Farmer, Frances   **1914-1970**
Will there really be a morning?: an autobiography. New York: G.P. Putnam's Sons, 1972. 318 p.

After a fast and bitter career as a movie star (19 movies, 1935-43), she suffered a total breakdown and was institutionalized for eight years by an unloving mother. She later settled in Indiana where she had a modest career in television, but suffered the rest of her life from bouts with depression and alcoholism, finally dying of throat cancer.

1418 Farnham, Thomas Jefferson   **1804-1848**
Travels in the great Western prairies, the Anahuac and Rocky Mountains, and in the Oregon Territory: an 1839 wagon train journal. Monroe, Oregon: R.R. McCallum, 1977. (London: Richard Bentley, 1843) 108 p.

Farnham travelled widely in the West, including Mexico and California. This journal describes his explorations in the Oregon Territory with descriptions of geography, Indian tribes and customs, and the excitement and danger of travel. He later wrote a history of the Oregon Territory.

1419 *Farrow, Tiera   **b.1881?**
Lawyer in petticoats. Foreword by Edward D. Ellison. New York: Vantage Press, 1953. 214 p.

An inspiring, articulate account by a bright and determined woman who accomplished a number of "firsts" in legal practice in Kansas—the first woman general practitioner of law, the first woman divorce proctor, the first woman judge. She was a feminist from her law school days, conscious of sexism in law, and fought persistently for its eradication.

1420 Farson, Negley   **1890-1960**
A mirror for Narcissus. Garden City, New York: Doubleday & Co., Inc., 1957. 330 p.

After a decade as a foreign correspondent and an autobiography (*The Way of a Transgressor*) that was a best seller, he wrote ten books, did free-lance journalism in Europe and Africa, was a roving adventurer, and struggled to cope with recurring mental strain and alcoholism, all described in vibrant narrative.

1421 Farson, Negley   **1890-1960**
Transgressor in the tropics. Garden City, New York: Doubleday & Co., Inc., 1957. (New York: Harcourt, Brace & Co., 1938) 320 p.

A writer on assignment in South America describes his experience traveling around the continent.

1422 Farson, Negley   **1890-1960**
Way of a transgressor. London: Howard Baker, Ltd., 1970. (London: Gollancz and Co., 1935) 639 p.

Farson led an exciting, adventurous life traveling extensively and trying almost everything with irrepressible *joie de vivre* —from selling American machinery in Tsarist Russia to beachcombing in Vancouver Island to sailing 3600 miles across Europe from the North Sea to the Black Sea—topping it all with ten years as a foreign correspondent.

1423 Faubus, Orval Eugene   **1910-**
In this faraway land. Conway, Arkansas: River Road Press, 1971. 736 p.

A remarkable combat diary which Faubus kept during his service as an infantryman in the 35th Division of the Third Army, with appended letters he wrote about the war to his hometown newspaper, the Madison

County *Record*. His is a striking, personal record of combat life on the front in the major campaigns of France and Germany.

1424 Faulkner, Barry   **1881-1966**
Barry Faulkner: sketches from an artist's life. Dublin, New Hampshire: William L. Bauhan, 1973. 208 p. Index.

A celebrated muralist during his lifetime, he wrote these sketches during his later years, putting them in chronological form when he was quite old. His murals decorate the National Archives, the Eastman School of Music, and many public and private buildings. During World War I he helped design camouflage for the Camouflage Corps.

1425 Faulkner, William   **1897-1962**
Faulkner at Nagano. Edited by Robert A. Jelliffe. Folcroft, Pennsylvania: The Folcroft Press, 1973. (Tokyo: Kenkyusha, 1956) 206 p.

In August 1955 Faulkner went to Japan to take part in the Nagano Seminar. This volume presents the talks, discussions, remarks, interviews, and addresses in which he discussed his work, his opinions, and his impressions of Japan.

1426 Faulkner, William   **1887-1962**
Faulkner on love: a letter to Marjorie Lyons. Edited by Richard Lyons. Fargo: The Merrykit Press, 1974. 11 p.

The introductory note explains how the editor's wife Marjorie on impulse sent a hastily sketched note to Faulkner concerning a character in *Pylon*. Faulkner responded, appropriately, with a note on yellow lined paper torn across the bottom. The note, reproduced in this limited edition, a handset and printed pamphlet, expresses Faulkner's belief that every young man, no matter his condition, "has once in him the capacity for one great love and sacrifice for love."

1427 Faulkner, William   **1897-1962**
Selected letters of William Faulkner. Edited with introduction by Joseph Blotner. New York: Random House, 1977. 488 p. Index.

A representative selection of author William Faulkner's letters, 1918-1962, "to reveal as much as possible . . . about his art—its sources, intentions and process of creation—and beyond that to reveal attitudes basic to that art: aesthetic, philosophical, social, and political," as well as relationships with family, friends, "fellow writers, publishers, editors, agents, directors, producers and readers."

1428 Faulkner, William   **1897-1962**
see also Cowley, Malcolm

1429 Fax, Elton Clay   **1909-**
Through Black eyes; journeys of a Black artist to East Africa and Russia. Illustrated. New York: Dodd, Mead & Co., 1974. 203 p.

Fax records his observations during journeys through Uganda, Sudan, Ethiopia, Tanzania in Africa, and Uzbekistan in Soviet Central Asia. As a Black American he was especially sensitive to human exploitation and found injustice, inequality, and oppression in both Africa and the Soviet Union.

1430 Fay, Paul Burgess, Jr.   **1918-**
The pleasure of his company. New York: Harper & Row, 1966. 262 p.

A friend of J.F. Kennedy from PT boat days during World War II, Fay shared experiences with him through 21 years. His book concentrates on the informal, unguarded moments of the relationship, the fun they had together.

1431 Feather, William   **b.1889**
The business of life. New York: Simon and Schuster, 1949. 424 p.

In a collection of items, some previously printed in magazines and newspaper columns, the writer makes common-sense observations about himself, his family, his business associates, and life around him.

1432 Feelings, Tom   **1933-**
Black pilgrimage. New York: Lothrop, Lee & Shepard Co., 1972. 72 p.

A gentle narrative of his retreat from the American culture and his adoption of Ghana as his new home. He describes without bitterness his feelings of displacement as a Black artist in a culture that knew Black art as merely primitive and his desire to paint the beauty and grace of his people, who suffered poverty in his hometown Brooklyn and the Southern United States.

1433 Feeney, Leonard   **1897-1978**
Survival till seventeen. Introduction by S.M. Clare. Illustrated. Memorial Edition. Still River, Massachusetts: St. Bede's Publications, 1980. (New York: Sheed & Ward, 1948) 88 p.

This elegant, eloquent narrative of a turn-of-the-century Catholic childhood in Lynn, Massachusetts, focuses philosophically on significant people and moments in time before Feeney left home for the Jesuit priesthood at seventeen.

1434 Feibelman, Julian B.   **1897-**
The making of a rabbi. New York: Vantage Press, 1980. 508 p.

Feibelman recalls his childhood, family, education, teachers, Army experience, and rabbinate, taking up many of the social issues of the mid-twentieth century.

1435 Feibleman, James Kern   **1904-**
Philosophers lead sheltered lives: a first volume of memoirs. London: George Allen and Unwin, Ltd., 1952. 321 p. Index.
The author reflects upon his life and development as a philosopher.

1436 Fell, Jesse W.   **1808-1887**
see Lincoln, Abraham

1437 Fell, John   **1721-1798**
Delegate from New Jersey; the journal of John Fell. Illustrated. Edited with introduction by Donald W. Whisenhunt. Port Washington, New York: Kennikat, 1973. 212 p. Index.
Although not an aggressive or spectacular personality, Fell fulfilled his duty as a citizen deeply committed to the goal of independence. He was firm in his convictions, totally dependable, and a staunch, hardworking member of the Continental Congress who represented New Jersey with competence and integrity. Brief biographies of people mentioned in his journal are appended.

1438 Feller, Robert William Andrew   **1918-**
Bob Feller's strikeout story. New York: Grosset and Dunlap, 1947. 242 p.
Pitcher for the Cleveland Indians who broke the record for season strikeouts in 1946 when he returned from four years of service in the Navy. He writes a remarkable tribute to his father who encouraged his success.

1439 Fellig, Arthur   **1899-1968**
Weegee: an autobiography. New York: Ziff-Davis Publishing Co., 1961. 159 p.
At ten he immigrated from Austria, attended school for four years amid New York slums, and started a career as a freelance photographer that made him internationally famous. His *Naked City*, a collection of New York photos, was the basis for a Hollywood movie.

1440 *Ferber, Edna   **1887-1968**
A kind of magic. Garden City, New York: Doubleday & Co., Inc., 1963. 335 p.
Her second autobiographical work begins in 1939, the year she began building a country house in Connecticut—for her the fulfillment of an American dream—and writing *Peculiar Treasure*. She describes both as creative, personal acts, emphasizing the ways in which she converts living material into fiction that is deeply American and that reflects her enthusiastic quest for life.

1441 *Ferber, Edna   **1887-1968**
Peculiar treasure: autobiography. Revised edition. Garden City, New York: Doubleday and Co., Inc., 1960. (1938) 383 p.
Prominent as a novelist and playwright (*Showboat, Giant,* etc.), she writes of her childhood in a Midwestern, middle-class Jewish family, her early years as a reporter in Appleton and Milwaukee, Wisconsin, and as a novelist in Chicago. She writes about writing with spirited enthusiasm (but without personal intimacy), suggesting the relationship between fact and fiction.

1442 *Ferderber-Salz, Bertha
And the sun kept shining . . . Foreword by Meacham Z. Rosensaft. Illustrated; maps. New York: Holocaust Publications, 1980. 233 p.
An eloquent, wrenching account of a Jewish woman's survival and struggle to save her children in the midst of the Nazi Holocaust. She also details post-war atrocities against Jews in Poland and immigration with her daughters to the United States.

1443 Ferguson, Clarence Joseph   **1895-**
Mink, Mary and me: the story of a wilderness trapline. New York: M.S. Mill Co., Inc., Publisher, 1946. 248 p.
Shortly after their marriage, they moved to MacKenzie Territory in northern Canada where he became a fur trapper. After nine years, they returned to the United States where their son was born, but were soon drawn to the wilderness life once more, this time for five years. Their wilderness life was always a success; in civilization they seemed to flounder.

1444 *Ferland, Carol   **1936-**
The long journey home. New York: Alfred A. Knopf, 1980. 294 p.
A diary of the author's thirty-second year spent in a New England mental hospital undergoing psychotherapy, in which she explored her relationship with her husband (loving, bewildered, disapproving of her dependency on alcohol and pills), her five children (all were shy and caring), and her psychiatrist.

1445 Fernald, Charles   **1830-1892**
County judge in Arcady: selected private papers of Charles Fernald; pioneer California jurist. Introduction and notes by Cameron Rogers. Glendale, California: Arthur H. Clark, 1954. 207 p. Index.
The bulk of this book contains commentary about the letters and documents which are, in large part, addressed to the California judge. Approximately 25% of the book's material is by Judge Fernald. Most of the items written by the Judge are to his wife and concern their separation and his political activities.

1446 Ferrier, Denis   **1921-**
Country vet. New York: Taplinger Publishing Co., 1973. (London: Hart-Davis, 1972) 196 p.
A narrative filled with medical detail and antic humor describes the life of a country veterinarian, his patients, their owners, and the satisfying life he established for himself.

1447 *Ferry, Eudora Bundy
Yukon gold: pioneering days in the Canadian North. New York: Exposition Press, 1971. 249 p.
In 1911 the author traveled to Dawson, Yukon Territory, to marry Doug Ferry, a mining engineer for the Yukon Gold Company. Her descriptions of the rugged life, the minus-sixty-degree cold, the breathtaking aurora borealis, her homes, and her neighbors provide a vivid picture of the pioneering days of the Canadian North.

1448 Fichter, Joseph Henry   **1908-**
One-man research: reminiscences of a Catholic sociologist. New York: John Wiley & Sons, 1973. 258 p. Index.
Father Fichter chronicles his research experiences in five sociological studies in order to assist other social scientists by describing the actual processes of research methodology. He studied a New Orleans Catholic parish, school desegregation, police arrests, clergy, and high school students and carefully describes his methods, adding notes after each chapter.

1449 Fidrych, Mark   **1954-**
No big deal. And Tom Clark. Philadelphia: J.B. Lippincott Company, 1977. 251 p.
In the same uninhibited style that characterizes him on the mound, colorful pitcher "Bird" Fidrych tells of his school days in Massachusetts, his two years in the minor leagues, and his overnight success with the Detroit Tigers.

1450 Field, Henry   **1902-**
The track of man: adventures of an anthropologist. New York: Dell, 1967. (1955) 351 p.
This exciting, articulate book records Field's forty-year career as an anthropologist as he studied both old and new cultures in Iraq, Iran, and Saudi Arabia. Many of his early findings are housed in the Chicago (originally Field) Museum of Nature and History and reflected in Malvina Hoffman's sculptures of various tribes; others, sent to Berlin, were destroyed during World War II. Field was employed by President Roosevelt on the "M" Project, which produced 665 studies assessing the world's resources in order to resettle war refugees.

1451 Fields, William Claude   **1880-1946**
W.C. Fields by himself; his intended autobiography. Commentary by Ronald J. Fields. Englewood Cliffs, New Jersey: Prentice-Hall, 1973. 510 p.
W.C. Field's grandson has edited and assembled Field's vast assortment of notes, outlines, scrapbooks, letters, scripts, scenarios, and photographs. Included are glimpses into Field's outrageous comic genius, his hilarious vaudeville and movie routines, his quarrels, opinions, and reminiscences—"the autobiography he would have written."

1452 Filley, Horace Clyde   **1878-1973**
Every day was new: the story of the growth of Nebraska. New York: Exposition Press, 1950. 179 p.
An account of his early farm life, later career and family life in Lincoln, Nebraska, by a college professor who appreciates rural life despite its problems.

1453 Fillmore, Clyde   **1908-**
Prisoner of war. Quanah, Wichita Falls, Texas: Nortex, 1974. 152 p.
The story of the Lost Battalion, a group of mostly Texans who were captured on Java early in World War II and remained prisoners of the Japanese for four years. Of the 456 Americans in the third group, 132 died. Appendixes list the survivors and casualties.

1454 Finck, Henry Theophilus   **1854-1926**
My adventures in the golden age of music. Music Reprint Series. New York: Da Capo Press, 1971. (New York: Funk & Wagnalls Co., 1926) 462 p. Index.
A prominent music critic reviews his childhood in Missouri and Oregon, but writes primarily of his musical career, with stories of famous musical contemporaries he met, performances he attended.

1455 Finn, William Joseph   **1881-1961**
Sharps and flats in five decades: an autobiography. New York: Harper &
Brothers Publishers, 1947. 342 p.
  His belief in music as the spiritual center of his life is demonstrated in
his experience as a choir director and manager for fifty years.

1456 Finney, Charles Grandison   **1792-1875**
The autobiography of Charles G. Finney. Edited and condensed by Helen
Wessel. Minneapolis: Bethany Fellowship, 1977. (Oberlin, Ohio: Oberlin
College, 1876) 230 p.
  Finney provides an impassioned account of his religious conversion and
subsequent career as a fiery and thoroughly compelling evangelical
preacher, first in upstate New York, eventually in major American cities
and in England. He converted over half a million people and spearheaded
an American religious revival in the nineteenth century. (The 1876 edition
was reprinted by AMS Press in 1973.)

1457 Finney, Humphrey S.   **1902-**
Fair exchange: recollections of a life with horses. New York: Charles
Scribner's Sons, 1974. 175 p. Index.
  The colorful life of horse racing is recalled by Finney, who was presi-
dent and then chairman of Fasig-Tipton Company, Thoroughbred Auc-
tioneers. He describes people, horses, and spectacular auctions like the
Louis B. Mayer sales, the sealed-bid sale of the Woodward Estate (with
Nashua alone bringing $1,250,000), and Aly Khan's auction of French
paintings in the sale ring at Saratoga.

1458 Fischer, Anton Otto   **1882-1962**
Focs'le days: a story of my youth. With paintings by the author. New
York: C. Scribner's Sons, 1947. 82 p.
  An illustrator of several seafaring books writes of his own adventures at
sea, including voyages to the Pacific coast.

1459 Fischer, Louis   **1896-1970**
**Men and politics: an autobiography; with an appendix of letters from
Mrs. Eleanor Roosevelt added to the reprint edition.** Westport, Connecticut: Greenwood Press, 1970. (New York: Duell, Sloan and Pearce, 1941)
672 p. Index.
  A remarkable record of life and political developments between World
Wars I and II, given here with a detailed account of Fischer's travel and
observations as a writer-journalist during those years. He utilizes impressions and opinions of common and prominent figures in each European country, providing a dramatic depiction of the between-war years.

1460 Fish, Job   **1828-1923**
Job Fish, pioneer teacher (1828-1923): autobiography. Partly narrated to
his sons, Williston Fish and John Charles Lounsbury Fish. Batavia, New
York: Gertrude Fish Rumsey & Josephine Fish Peabody, 1963. 251 p.
  Fish tells of his early life in Ohio where he did farm work and later
taught at several schools before founding the Berlin (Ohio) Academy.
This folksy account of his long and productive life (he had eleven children) includes information about his ancestors and descendents, lists of
former students, photographs, and newspaper clippings.

1461 Fish, Joseph   **1840-1926**
Life and times of Joseph Fish, Mormon pioneer. Edited by John H.
Krenkel. Danville, Illinois: Interstate Printers and Publishers, 1970.
543 p. Index.
  Kept over a period of seventy years, Fish's diary records many events
in Mormon history, including life in Nauvoo, the trek to Great Salt
Valley, Indian wars, anti-Mormon conflicts in Utah, colonizing attempts
in Arizona and Mexico, and life in several Mormon communities. He was
a versatile worker, holding many different skilled jobs and several public
offices, and he devoted a portion of his time to active membership in his
church.

1462 Fishbein, Morris   **b.1889**
Morris Fishbein, M.D.; an autobiography. Illustrated. Garden City, New
York: Doubleday & Co., Inc., 1969. 505 p. Index.
  He became an important leader in the American Medical Association
and for years edited its journal. His book describes over eighty years as a
medical crusader, encouraging innovation and research, while populariz-
ing an awareness of medical problems in the home through his book,
Modern Home Medical Advisor.

1463 *Fisher, Anna Marie   **1896-**
Omits for obits. Hanover, Indiana: self, 1976. 181 p.
  A personal, disjointed account of the author's Indiana childhood and
her European and Middle Eastern travels after she had become a teacher
and sometime Dean of Women at Hanover College, Indiana. The book is
full of private jokes and allusions.

1464 *Fisher, Mary Francis Kennedy   **1908-**
Among friends. New York: Alfred A. Knopf, 1971. 306 p.
  Best known as a gastronome, Fisher writes here of her childhood in
Whittier, California, a largely Quaker community. The book is full of
loving, nostalgic memories, especially for the odd and unusual character.

1465 *Fisher, Welthy (Honsinger)   **b.1879**
To light a candle. New York: McGraw-Hill Book Co., Inc., 1962. 279 p.
  With humor and conviction she relates her life's work heading a Chinese school, working for the YWCA in France during World War I,
fulfilling missionary duties around the world as a bishop's wife, and establishing Literacy Village for training teachers in India.

1466 Fitch, Jabez   **1737-1812**
**New York diary of Lieutenant Jabez Fitch: of the 17th (Connecticut)
Regiment from August 22, 1776 to December 15, 1777.** Eyewitness Accounts of the American Revolution. Edited by W.H.W. Sabine. New
York: Arno Press, 1971. (New York: Colburn & Tegg, 1954) 288 p. Index.
  An unusually detailed Revolutionary War diary written in camp, on
the battlefield, on prison ships, and in various billets while he was a
prisoner on parole, giving a critical view of the harsh conditions of prison
life in particular.

1467 Fitch, John   **1917-**
Adventures on wheels: the autobiography of a road racing champion.
With William W. Nolan. New York: G.P. Putnam's Sons, 1959. 284 p.
  He writes of his experience as an international road racer since 1948
when this sport was reborn in the United States. Describing the psychology of a man with a compulsive need to compete in a sport entailing
constant exposure to physical danger, he says, "To race is to engage one's
physical and mental powers of endurance, restraint, judgment and discipline with an intensity that renders other enterprises pale in comparison."

1468 Fitzgerald, Francis Scott Key   **1896-1940**
**As ever, Scott Fitz; letters between F. Scott Fitzgerald and his literary
agent Harold Ober, 1919-1940.** Edited by Matthew J. Bruccoli, with the
assistance of Jennifer McCabe Atkinson. Foreword by Scottie Fitzgerald
Smith. Philadelphia: J.B. Lippincott, 1972. 441 p. Index.
  Ober marketed Fitzgerald's stories, cared for his daughter Scottie,
loaned him money, and was both banker and accountant. Their relationship was a mixture of business and the personal because Fitzgerald, unable to handle money, was constantly requesting advances and Ober, out
of concern and friendship, somehow kept the family going.

1469 Fitzgerald, Francis Scott Key   **1896-1940**
Correspondence of F. Scott Fitzgerald. Edited by Matthew J. Bruccoli
and Margaret M. Duggan. Assistant editor, Susan Walker. Illustrated.
New York: Random House, 1980. 640 p. Index.
  This compilation of letters to and from Fitzgerald does not include
those previously published. Most important are the 85 letters exchanged
between the novelist and his wife, including Zelda's 42-page analysis of
their mutual decline from success to madness, alcoholism, and loss of
creativity. Letters, book inscriptions, and an occasional telegram also shed
light on Fitzgerald's writing and literary friendships.

1470 Fitzgerald, Francis Scott Key   **1896-1940**
Dear Scott/Dear Max: the Fitzgerald-Perkins correspondence. Edited by
John Kuehl and Jackson R. Bryer. London: Cassell & Co. Ltd., 1973.
282 p. Index.
  A remarkable record of the complex interaction between two outstanding figures in a major literary epoch. This edition presents selected letters
in a continuous narrative frame, 1919-1940.

1471 Fitzgerald, Francis Scott Key   **1896-1940**
The letters of F. Scott Fitzgerald. Edited by Andrew Turnbull. New
York: Charles Scribner's Sons, 1963. 615 p. Index.
  Candid, warm letters reveal the drama of Fitzgerald's private life, his
dreams and his personal concern for his daughter, wife, and friends, in
addition to his deep interest in his career and the literary scene.

1472 Fitzgerald, Francis Scott Key   **1896-1940**
The notebooks of F. Scott Fitzgerald. Edited by Matthew J. Bruccoli.
New York: Harcourt Brace Jovanovich/Bruccoli Clark, 1978. 359 p.
  A fascinating compilation of Fitzgerald's writer's notebooks,
1932-1940. They are arranged by mode: "Conversation and Things Over-
heard," "Epigrams, Wise Cracks and Voices," "Feelings of Emotions
(without girls)," "Descriptions of Girls," "Jingles and Songs."

1473 Fitzgerald, Francis Scott Key   **1896-1940**
Scott Fitzgerald: letters to his daughter. Edited by Andrew Turnbull.
Introduction by Francis Fitzgerald Lanahan. New York:. Charles
Scribner's Sons, 1965. 172 p. Index.
  These letters, written during the last seven years of his life (1933-1940),
contain fanciful advice to Fitzgerald's daughter Scottie. He describes his
life in Hollywood vividly and tries to direct her life by imposing his
romantic ideas with wit and vitality. Although he was ill and felt neglected by the world, his love for her shines through.

1474 Fitzpatrick, John   **1739-1791**
**The merchant of Manchac: the letterbooks of John Fitzpatrick,
1768-1790.** Edited with introduction by Margaret Fisher Dalrymple. Baton Rouge: Louisiana State University Press, 1978. 451 p. Index.

Fitzpatrick, who worked in Tennessee and the Midwest, was a merchant during the American Revolution. His letters describe his business transactions with suppliers and clients.

1475 *Flach, Vera
A Yankee in German-American Texas hill country. San Antonio, Texas: The Naylor Co., 1973. 175 p.
   When she married a German-American rancher in the hill country, she had to learn what living on a ranch meant. Not only did she have to cope with household chores, but with German customs, taboos, and disapproval. She relates some of the history of the settlement and the pioneer families as well.

1476 Flagg, James Montgomery   1877-1960
Roses and buckshot. New York: G.P. Putnam's Sons, 1946. 224 p.
   His famous "I Want You" Uncle Sam poster during World War II will be remembered, if not his name. His book is a witty, readable narrative of his career as a painter and illustrator, especially popular among Hollywood stars.

1477 Fleischer, Nathaniel S.   1887-1972
Fifty years at ringside. Foreword by Dan Daniel. New York: Greenwood Press, 1969. (New York: Fleet Publishing Co., 1958) 296 p. Index.
   For 35 years a boxing reporter and editor of *The Ring*, an international boxing magazine, Fleischer writes of the "pulse-stirring excitement, humor, pathos, and glamour" of the rise of American and international boxing 1907-1957, and of his role in reporting this. Fleischer writes affectionately of many boxers, promoters, and fellow journalists.

1478 *Fleitmann, Lida Louise (Mrs. J. Van S. Bloodgood)   1894-
Hoofs in the distance. Limited Edition. New York: Van Nostrand Co., Inc., 1953. 131 p. Index.
   Former Master of Hounds reminisces about the glamour of her years of fame hunting and showing horses in the 1920's.

1479 Fletcher, Calvin   1789-1866
Diary of Calvin Fletcher; including letters of Calvin Fletcher, and diaries and letters of his wife Sarah Hill Fletcher. Edited by Gayle Thornbrough. Indianapolis: Indiana Historical Society, 1972. 2v. Index.
   The daily record of a successful lawyer, farmer, landowner, and banker who became deeply religious and was especially concerned with the educational and civic development of the community in which he lived. Volume I includes his diaries and letters from 1817 to 1838, the 1821-1824 diary and other brief journals of Sarah Hill Fletcher, his wife. Volume II, 1838-1843, includes letters to and from Fletcher.

1480 Fletcher, Ebenezer   1761-1831
Narrative of Ebenezer Fletcher, a soldier of the Revolution. Introduction and notes by Charles I. Bushnell. Freeport, New York: Books for Libraries Press, 1970. (New Ipswich, New Hampshire: S. Wilder, 1827) 86 p.
   In 1777, he was wounded and captured by the British. This brief record describes his recovery, treatment and eventual escape; notes appended provide a full historical context of the war.

1481 Fletcher, Elijah   1797-1858
The letters of Elijah Fletcher. Edited by Martha von Briesen. Charlottesville: University Press of Virginia, 1965. 306 p. Index.
   Born and educated in Vermont, Fletcher made his way to Alexandria and later Lynchburg, Virginia, where he taught school, took part in civic affairs, and was publisher of the newspaper, "The Virginian." His 1000-acre plantation, Sweetbriar, was willed by his daughter, Indiana Fletcher Williams, for the establishment of Sweet Briar College "as a living expression of the family's convictions regarding the values of education."

1482 Fletcher, Ernest More   1867-1941
The wayward horseman. Edited by Forbes Parkhill. Denver: Sage Books, Alan Swallow Press, 1958. 217 p. Index.
   A good-humored narrative of his adventures as a cowboy on the Chisholm Trail, between Texas and Kansas, and in Arizona, Colorado, and New Mexico as well. Fletcher served a five-year jail sentence for cattle rustling, then went straight and at 35 married Lillian, who tormented him continually. The book ends with his second marriage and the birth of two children.

1483 *Fletcher, Grace Nies   1900-
Merry widow. New York: William Morrow & Co., Inc., 1970. 255 p.
   "This is a lighthearted story of how I changed from a 'Preacher's Kid' who could not dance, play cards, go to the theater, or even chew gum, to (at sixty) a gay, insouciant widow who, as I jetted from Occident to Orient, could (and did) pick up any man I wanted to and call him 'friend,' and put him down again if I found him uninteresting."

1484 *Fletcher, Inglis (Clark)   1888-1969
Pay, pack, and follow: the story of my life. New York: Henry Holt and Co., 1959. 308 p.
   A popular historical novelist describes the experiences which led to her

development as a writer, including western travels with her husband, a mining engineer, and later life on a restored North Carolina plantation.

1485 *Fletcher, Mrs. John Gould
see *Simon, Charlie May

1486 Fletcher, Tom   1873-1954
One hundred years of the Negro in show business: the Tom Fletcher story. Illustrated. New York: Burdge & Co., Ltd., 1954. 337 p.
   An articulate account of Blacks in show business, 1850-1950, interwoven with the autobiography of Fletcher, an entertainer who, like many Blacks, began his career (and a move away from the plantation) by performing in a minstrel show. Fletcher discusses notable performers and forms of entertainment in which Blacks were popular, such as minstrel shows, Pickaninny Band, the blues, and ragtime music.

1487 Fletcher, Walter R.
My times with dogs. Illustrated. New York: Howell Book House, 1980. 319 p.
   For fifty years he wrote a column on dogs which appeared regularly on the sports pages of the New York *Times*. This is a collection of anecdotes about the people as well as the canines involved in the world of dog breeding, exhibiting, handling, and judging.

1488 Flexner, Abraham   1866-1959
Abraham Flexner: an autobiography; a revision, brought up to date, of the author's *I Remember*, published in 1940. Introduction by Allan Nevins. New York: Simon and Schuster, 1960. 302 p. Index.
   The remarkable story of a distinguished educator who obtained millions from foundations to revolutionize U.S. medical education in the Twenties and later established the Institute For Advanced Study at Princeton, which he directed until his retirement.

1489 Flood, Curtis Charles   1938-
The way it is. With Richard Carter. New York: Trident Press, 1971. 236 p.
   Convinced that baseball does not operate in a social or political vacuum, this baseball player and painter places himself and the national pastime against the backdrop of a ghetto upbringing, and the stupidities and cruelties of racism rampant within and without the sport. Often witty and always highly articulate, the author tells more about people and ideas than batting averages.

1490 Flournoy, Theodore
see James, William

1491 *Flynn, Bethine
The flying Flynns: the remarkable adventures of an animal doctor in the wilderness. New York: Seaview Books, 1979. 359 p.
   Flynn's book is divided into two parts. One focuses on "A Place of Adventure," the British Columbia and Alaskan wilderness where her husband, Wallace Flynn, practiced veterinary medicine with her assistance and provided aid to the Indians and other local residents. After his death, Flynn lived by herself in their "Place of Refuge," a remote cabin and hundred acres on Nootka Island.

1492 Flynn, Edward Joseph   1892-
You're the boss. New York: The Viking Press, 1947. 244 p. Index.
   New York and U.S. political life from the 1920's through World War II described by a practical politician personally involved with machines, bosses, and party politics.

1493 *Flynn, Elizabeth Gurley   1890-1964
The Alderson story: my life as a political prisoner. New York: International Publishers, 1972. (1963) 223 p.
   A socialist labor leader convicted of treason under the Smith Act, she served two years (1955-57) in the Federal Reformatory for Women in Alderson, West Virginia. Her book is a detailed and critical account of the psychological and physical conditions in which she lived.

1494 *Flynn, Elizabeth Gurley   1890-1964
The rebel girl: an autobiography, my first life (1906-1926). New York: International Publishers, 1973. (New York: Masses and Mainstream, 1955) 351 p. Index.
   The early career of a prominent socialist labor leader who spent her life struggling for labor's rights and defending civil liberties.

1495 Flynn, Errol Leslie   1909-1959
My wicked, wicked ways. Illustrated. New York: G.P. Putnam's Sons, 1959. 438 p.
   Actor Errol Flynn recounts his adventuresome youth in Tasmania, his explorations in New Guinea (1927-32), and offers a chaotic account of his turbulent life as a film star in Hollywood and on location around the world. "I have had my fun, my kicks, my vodka, my affairs" (he estimates 12,000-14,000), "my fights and my pictures." Flynn, a heavy drinker, was also accused of statutory rape and named in a number of paternity suits.

1496 Flynn, Thomas   1944-
Tales for my brothers' keepers. Foreword by Tom Wicker. New York: W.W. Norton, 1976. 112 p.
  Flynn's writing is rambling yet graphic as he describes prison life, but gives no clue to his crime. Calling his cell mates by first name only, he stresses that there are "all different ways to do time."

1497 Fokker, Anthony Herman Gerald   1890-1939
Flying Dutchman: the life of Anthony Fokker. And Bruce Gould. Literature and History of Aviation. Introduction by Col. Edward V. Rickenbacker. New York: Arno Press, 1972. (New York: Holt, Rinehart & Winston, 1931) 282 p.
  Fokker was raised in Holland and like the Wright brothers, he grew up with the aviation industry. His fighter planes were crucial to the Germans in World War I, but when he returned to Holland after the war with enormous profits and aircraft designs, he was attracted to the United States, which had been unable to gain his services before the war. An important record of modern invention and aviation.

1498 *Fontaine, Joan   1917-
No bed of roses. Illustrated. New York: William Morrow and Co., 1978. 319 p.
  Fontaine writes of her life in Hollywood, including her long-time feud with her sister, Olivia De Haviland. Of her career, she says: "There is much in my life that might make me the envy of many . . . fame, fortune, romance, self-expression, independence . . . My career is the result of opportunity and luck as much as anything else . . . I am proud that I have carved my path on earth almost entirely by my own efforts."

1499 Fontaine, Robert   1913-
Hello to springtime. New York: Thomas Y. Crowell Co., 1955. 246 p.
  A Canadian-American author describes his boyhood travel and adventures with his parents who were vaudeville musicians.

1500 Fools Crow, Frank   1890?-
Fools Crow. Assisted by Dallas Chief Eagle. Recorded by Thomas E. Mails. Illustrated by the author. Garden City, New York: Doubleday & Co., Inc., 1979. 278 p. Index.
  In this oral history Fools Crow, Oglala Sioux chief and medicine man, recounts the history of his tribe. Their nomadic ways changed to farming and sheep raising when the Indians were herded to the Pine Ridge Reservation in the Black Hills of South Dakota. Fools Crow describes in detail many tribal secrets, including his role as a religious medicine man and the significance of the Sioux dances.

1501 Foote, Arthur William   1853-1937
Arthur Foote. 1853-1937: an autobiography. Norwood, Massachusetts: privately printed at the Plimpton Press, 1946. 135 p.
  Prominent composer and organist describes his life in music, mostly in the Boston area.

1502 Foote, Henry Stuart   1804-1880
Casket of reminiscences. New York: Negro Universities Press, 1968. (Washington: Chronicle Publ. Co., 1874) 498 p.
  In sketches that first appeared in the Washington Chronicle, Foote describes events from his early life and some of his famous contemporaries during his years in the U.S. Senate.

1503 *Foote, Mary (Hallock)   1847-1938
Victorian gentlewoman in the Far West; the reminiscences of Mary Hallock Foote. Edited with introduction by Rodman W. Paul. San Marino, California: The Huntington Library, 1972. 416 p. Index.
  Married to an engineer whose jobs took him to the West during the Victorian era, Mary Foote, an illustrator and author, experienced the boisterous life in the West, greatly at odds with her value system from the genteel tradition of the Eastern upper class. Her husband and his formally educated engineer friends were isolated from the self-made men of the mining communities.

1504 Ford, Arthur A.   1896-1971
Nothing so strange: the autobiography of Arthur Ford. In collaboration with Margueritte Harmon Bro. New York: Harper & Row Publishers, 1958. 250 p. Index.
  Respected as a psychic by the eminent and the ordinary, Ford believes that everyone is potentially a medium. His book is eerie in its straightforward, simple faith in psychic power and the expanding consciousness.

1505 Ford, Corey   1902-1969
Time of laughter. Foreword by Frank Sullivan. Boston: Little, Brown and Co., 1967. 232 p. Index.
  Ford has written what he calls a sentimental journey to the golden age of American humor, the Roaring Twenties. He wrote humor for Life and The New Yorker, he knew many of those now remembered for their wit and/or acidity, he participated in the life style of that decade which danced between world wars.

1506 *Ford, Elizabeth Bloomer   1918-
Times of my life. With Chris Chase. Illustrated. New York: Harper and Row, 1978. 305 p. Index.
  The popular former First Lady recalls her "sunny girlhood," a brief stint dancing with Martha Graham in New York, her unhappy first marriage, and her marriage to young lawyer Gerald Ford. As Ford went from congressman to President, Betty raised four children, underwent psychiatric treatment, had a mastectomy, and weathered life as a public figure.

1507 Ford, George Barry   b.1885
A degree of difference. New York: Farrar, Straus & Giroux, 1969. 271 p.
  For over fifty years he was a parish priest in New York, with long service at Corpus Christi on Morningside Heights. He became well known, respected and loved by many New Yorkers for his early concern with educational and social issues.

1508 Ford, Gerald R.   1913-
A time to heal. New York: Harper and Row, and Reader's Digest Association, 1979. 454 p. Index.
  A pleasant, low-key, straightforward account of Ford's life, largely focusing on the period 1974-76 when he was United States Vice-President and when he became President, succeeding Nixon. He loved being President: "I never felt better physically. I never had a clearer mind. I never enjoyed an experience more." This zest permeates his accounts of American policy in Cambodia, the Mayaguez affair, and other events during Ford's "time to heal" the nation, reeling from the Watergate scandal.

1509 Ford, Henry   1863-1947
My life and work. In collaboration with Samuel Crowther. Series: Big Business: Economic Power in a Free Society. New York: Arno Press, 1973. (New York: Doubleday, Page & Co., 1922) 289 p. Index.
  Ford discusses his experience with the horseless carriage, elaborating on his principles of business management, labor, service, pricing, and ethics. Looking at the technology of his age and speculating on the advancements of the future, Ford preaches against veneration of the past and fear of the future, or fear of failure.

1510 Ford, John Anson   b.1883?
Honest politics my theme: the story of a veteran public official's troubles and triumphs; an autobiography. Foreword by Will Durant. Preface by Thomas Clements. New York: Vantage Press, 1978. 221 p. Index.
  Ford reminisces about his six terms as a member of the Los Angeles County Board of Supervisors. He was associated with a wide range of citizens, including publisher Dorothy Chandler, Governor Earl Warren, and movie magnate Louis B. Mayer. Ford appreciates the terrain, the city, the intricacies of Democratic Party politics, and Lois, his wife for 64 enjoyable years.

1511 Forrest, Nathan Bedford   1821-1877
Gunboats and cavalry: the story of Forrest's 1864 Johnsonville Campaign as told to J.P. Pryor and Thomas Jordan. Edited and reported by E.F. Williams & H.K. Humphreys. Illustrated. Memphis, Tennessee: Nathan Bedford Forrest Trail Committee, 1965. (Memphis, Tennessee, 1867) 24 p.
  Confederate General Forrest recounts the Johnsonville, Tennessee, campaign of 1864, in which his troops destroyed "three gunboats, eleven transports, eighteen barges" and federal supplies valued at eight million dollars, with a loss of only "two men killed and four wounded."

1512 *Forster, Minnie Jane (Wyatt)   b.1875
He led me through the wilderness. Wichita, Kansas: Preston Printing Co., 1947. 207 p.
  A simple narrative of her married life on an Oklahoma homestead.

1513 *Forster, Minnie Jane (Wyatt)   b.1875
Was the hill barren?: the story of an American family. New York: Exposition Press, 1953. 173 p.
  An American Dream inadvertently fulfilled, simply told by a down-to-earth housewife, mother, and grandmother who would have preferred to stay in her beloved Missouri Ozarks but instead followed her wandering husband Tom to a homestead in Oklahoma, and thereafter to New Mexico and Kansas. Tom invented and sold farm machinery and after fifty years of marriage their patents made them rich, to their surprise and pleasure.

1514 *Forten, Charlotte L.   1838-1914
A free Negro in the slave era: the journal of Charlotte L. Forten. Introduction and notes by Ray Allen Billington. The Dryden Press, Inc., 1953. 248 p.
  Born in Philadelphia to a family that had never been slaves, she later moved to Massachusetts, became an abolitionist, and married Francis Grimké, whose mother was a slave.

1515 Fosdick, Harry Emerson   1878-1969
Living of these days: an autobiography. New York: Harper and Brothers, 1956. 324 p. Index.

The life story of a prominent New York minister, author of numerous books on popular religion.

1516 Fosdick, Raymond Blaine   1883-1972
Chronicle of a generation: an autobiography. New York: Harper and Brothers, 1958. 306 p. Index.
A lawyer describes his childhood in western New York, college years at Princeton, experience as a New York public official, appointment as Under-Secretary General of the League of Nations, and later as director of the Rockefeller Foundation.

1517 Foster, George Murphy   1892-1969
Pops Foster: the autobiography of a New Orleans jazzman. As told to Tom Stoddard. Introduction by Bertram Juretzky. Interchapters by Ross Russell. Berkeley: University of California Press, 1971. 208 p. Index.
Recollections from the early jazz era through seventy years by the first famous double bass player in jazz. He knew and worked with many of the great jazzmen, Louis Armstrong, Earl Hines, Duke Ellington. A chronology of musical groups, 1899-1969, and discography are included.

1518 Foster, Tom   1902-
Forty-five years on the Rock Island line: being a true story of my life as I lived and remembered it. Malvern, Arkansas: Foster, 1974. 188 p.
Foster fulfilled his childhood dream to become a railroad man when he went to work on the Rock Island in 1920. As an engine watchman he worked 29 years at night, seven days a week with no vacation; during his other 16 years with the line he worked part daytime. The passing of steam engines brought the end of his job and of an era.

1519 Foster, William Zebulon   1881-1961
More pages from a worker's life. Edited with introduction by Arthur Zipser. Illustrated. New York: American Institute for Marxist Studies, 1979. 48 p.
This is a collection of observations on two dozen people, places, and political incidents that were omitted from Foster's autobiographical *Pages from a Worker's Life* (1939). Foster, communist candidate for U.S. president in 1924, '28, and '32, speaks briefly about people he admired (from Mother Jones and Emma Goldman to Woodrow Wilson); places he visited (Berlin, Budapest, Constantinople, the American South); and incidents of social and political significance, such as strikes and party politics.

1520 Foulois, Benjamin Delahauf   1879-1967
From the Wright brothers to the astronauts: the memoirs of Major General Benjamin D. Foulois. With Colonel C.V. Glines, USAF. Illustrated. New York: McGraw-Hill Book Co., 1968. 306 p. Index.
In 1898 he enlisted in the Army; in 1935 he retired as a Major General and Chief of the Air Corps. His book reveals the exciting, often controversial life of a rather heroic individualist as well as the history of aviation in the United States.

1521 Fountain, Clayton W.   1909-
Union guy. New York: The Viking Press, 1949. 242 p. Index.
The unionization of an American worker and the inside workings of a powerful labor union, the UAW-CIO.

1522 Fountain, Peter Dewey   1930-
A closer walk; the Peter Fountain story. With Bill Neely. Chicago: Henry Regnery Co., 1972. 202 p.
Fountain is a worthy legatee of the continuing New Orleans jazz tradition. A true American art form, jazz began in spiritual and gospel songs of the South and offers the opportunity for a musician to express himself through his own interpretation of traditions.

1523 Fowle, George   1837-1917
Letters to Eliza: from a Union soldier, 1862-1865. Illustrated by Louis Cary. Edited by Margery Greenleaf. Chicago: Follett Pub. Co., 1970. 176 p. Bibliography.
A plainspoken account, through letters to his fiancée, Eliza Caldwell, of Fowle's service in the 39th Massachusetts Volunteers Regiment with the Army of the Potomac. Fowle fought mostly in Virginia against Robert E. Lee's troops at Harper's Ferry, Spotsylvania, Leesburg, Richmond, and Petersburg. Wounded in February 1865, he observes philosophically, "after roughing it for nearly three years a fellow gets used to anything that comes along." Discharged a month after Lincoln's assassination, Fowle married Eliza in July 1865.

1524 Fowler, Gene   1890-1960
Skyline: a reporter's reminiscence of the 1920's. New York: The Viking Press, Inc., 1961. 314 p.
His third autobiographical book tells of his experience as a reporter during the 1920's, the decade which he describes as "a Carnival Spin of mass make-believe—the world's last brief holiday from fear." Included are stories of the famous and the unknown who characterized the era, with extensive memoirs of his close friend, Damon Runyon.

1525 Fowler, Gene   1890-1960
A solo in tom-toms. New York: The Viking Press, 1946. 390 p.
A quest narrative which analyzes the experience and values of the American West through the author's life in Colorado.

1526 Fowler, Jacob   1765-1850
The journal of Jacob Fowler. Edited with notes by Elliott Coues. Lincoln: University of Nebraska Press, 1970. (New York: F.P. Harper, 1898) 152 p. Index.
Fowler's journal, kept while he was on a trading expedition in the Southwest in 1821-22, is the first complete narrative of an expedition to that area after Pike's of 1806-07. Although poorly educated, he was a rugged, intrepid frontiersman who had a good eye for observation and a keen sense of adventure.

1527 Fowlie, Wallace   1908-
Journals of rehearsals: a memoir. Durham, North Carolina: Duke University Press, 1977. 219 p. Index.
Using a backdrop of scenes from a personal notebook, Fowlie discusses his development from student in the 1920's to professor and literary historian. He focuses particularly on his "scandalous and passionate" lifelong love affair with French literature and highlights his contacts with scholars and writers at Harvard and in Paris, and with his students at Bennington.

1528 Fowlie, Wallace
see also **Miller, Henry**

1529 *Fox, Debbie Diane   1955-
A face for me. With Jean Libman Block. New York: Wyden Books, 1978. 197 p.
Fox has written of her extensive birth defects and the 57 operations to correct them as an inspiration for others with severe problems to have faith in God and in modern medicine. Fox amplifies her narrative with optimistic religious poetry.

1530 Fox, Gustavus Vasa   1821-1883
The confidential correspondence of Gustavus Vasa Fox, Assistant Secretary of the Navy, 1861-1865. Edited by Robert Means Thompson and Richard Wainwright. Freeport, New York: Books for Libraries Press, 1972. (New York: Naval History Society, 1920) 2v.
Letters written to and from Fox during the Civil War. The correspondents are prominent leaders, shipmates, and personal friends; most letters have the intimacy of friendship and therefore include interesting, unofficial reflections of the war.

1531 Fox, John   1863-1919
John Fox and Tom Page as they were: letters, an address, and an essay. Edited with introduction by Harriet R. Holman. Coconut Grove, Miami, Florida: Field Research Projects, 1970. 89 p. Index.
The lively correspondence between two contemporary regional writers (1891-1919) of Virginia and Kentucky.

1532 Fox, Monroe L.
Blind adventure. Philadelphia: J.B. Lippincott Co., 1946. 205 p.
Blinded when his ship was shelled during the Battle of Iwo Jima, he describes his recovery and rehabilitation during the first year, after which he became a rancher in northern New Mexico. His experience is striking for the positive approach he took, accepting blindness as a challenge instead of a defeat.

1533 Frackelton, William   1870-1943
Sage brush dentist. 1st rev. ed. As told to Herman Gastrell Seely. Pasadena: Trail's End Publishing Co., Inc., 1947. (Chicago: A.C. McClurg and Co., 1941) 258 p.
Colorful recollections of his life as a frontier dentist in Wyoming, with anecdotes about Calamity Jane, Buffalo Bill Cody, Butch Cassidy, and many others.

1534 France, Royal Wilbur   1883-1962
My native grounds. New York: Cameron Associates, Inc., 1957. 255 p.
After building a successful career as a New York lawyer, he became a college professor. Then in 1951 he became a defense attorney for accused communists who were being tried by the McCarthy Senate Committee.

1535 *Francis, Arlene (Arlene Francis Kazanjian)   1908-
Arlene Francis: a memoir. With Florence Rome. Illustrated. New York: Simon & Schuster, 1978. 204 p. Index.
Francis recounts her career as an entertainer, beginning with the singing of a Lydia Pinkham's commercial when she was seventeen; becoming a personality on *What's My Line?* in the 1950's and hostess on the *Home* show. She concludes with a discussion of her stage and summer stock acting in the 60's and 70's.

1536 Francis, Robert   1901-
Frost; a time to talk, conversation and indiscretions recorded. Amherst: University of Massachusetts Press, 1972. 100 p.

Descriptions of conversations with some verbatim quotations the author had with poet Robert Frost during two periods—April 1932 to July 1935, and May 1950 to April 1959. During the first period Francis was a young poet looking for guidance, which Frost provided. The later conversations were more wide-ranging and versatile.

1537 Francis, Robert **1901-**
Trouble with Francis; an autobiography. Amherst: University of Massachusetts Press, 1971. 246 p.
Although he finds himself to have been growing healthier and happier through the years, Francis considers himself a pessimist impressed with the ills, injustices, and frustrations of life.

1538 Frank, Maurice B. **1904-**
Success is a crime: an autobiography. Francis P. Antel. Rochester, New York: Herman Schwartz, 1973. 235 p.
A high-school dropout, he founded a Chicago newspaper, *The Comet*, made it successful, sold it, lost his profits in the Depression, but has been making money ever since. One of his favorite efforts is raising 86 million to found the John F. Kennedy Hospital in Palm Beach, Florida.

1539 Frank, Waldo David **1889-1967**
Memoirs of Waldo Frank. Edited by Alan Trachtenberg. Introduction by Lewis Mumford. Illustrated. Amherst: The University of Massachusetts Press, 1973. 268 p. Index.
Frank's reflections on his public career constitute a chronicle of a neglected American writer whose activities were associated with nearly all the significant artistic, intellectual, and political movements from 1910 to 1950. He felt himself to be an outsider always struggling to get into life, always failing.

1540 *Franken, Rose D. (Lewin) **1895-**
When all is said and done: an autobiography. Garden City, New York: Doubleday & Co., Inc., 1963. 397 p.
Dividing her life neatly into B.C. and A.C. (before *Claudia,* her best-selling novel, and after), Franken tells amusing tales of her life, family and friends.

1541 *Frankfort, Ellen
The *Voice: life at the *Village Voice. New York: William Morrow, 1976. 272 p.
A reporter for the radical *Village Voice* in the late 60's and early 70's critically analyzes the paper's policies and politics—national, office, and sexual—through portraits of the staff, including a self-portrait. She demonstrates considerable inequity, as when the editor was paid $72,000 a year and the reporters earned $100 a week.

1542 Frankfurter, Felix **1882-1965**
Felix Frankfurter reminisces: recorded in talks with Dr. Harlan B. Phillips. New York: Reynal and Co., 1960. 310 p. Index.
Originally intended for the archives of Columbia University's Oral History Research Office, the book records the development of his career in law and politics and his experience as a Justice of the U.S. Supreme Court.

1543 Frankfurter, Felix **1884-1965**
see also **Roosevelt, Franklin Delano**

1544 Franklin, Benjamin **1706-1790**
The autobiography of Benjamin Franklin. Franklin Center, Pennsylvania: Franklin Library, 1979. (London: J. Parsons, 1793) 228 p.
Perhaps the most famous of American autobiographies, influential as a model of early American experience as well as autobiographical form. Numerous editions have appeared, some including other writings, with various introductions and notes.

1545 Franklin, Benjamin **1706-1790**
Benjamin Franklin and Catherine Ray Greene: their correspondence, 1755-1790. Memoirs of the American Philosophical Society, Vol. 26. Edited and annotated by William Greene Roelker. Philadelphia: American Philosophical Society, 1949. 147 p. Index.
Although they met only five times, their friendship in correspondence lasted 34 years, aided by her friendship with his favorite sister, Jane Mecom. Greene's husband, William, became Governor of Rhode Island.

1546 Franklin, Benjamin **1706-1790**
Letters and papers of Benjamin Franklin and Richard Jackson 1753-1785. And Richard Jackson. Edited with introduction by Carl Van Doren. Memoirs of the American Philosophical Society, Vol. 24. Philadelphia: American Philosophical Society, 1947. 222 p. Index.
Contains sixty items, most printed here for the first time. During 1763-1770, Jackson, of the Inner Temple, served as "Agent for the Province of Pennsylvania, to solicit and transact the Affairs thereof at the Court of Great Britain," an appointment Franklin recommended. That the men were friends and philosophers, as well as officials, is reflected in their letters.

1547 Franklin, Benjamin **1706-1790**
The letters of Benjamin Franklin and Jane Mecom. Memoirs of the American Philosophical Society, Vol. 27. Edited with introduction by Carl Van Doren. Princeton: Princeton University Press, 1950. 380 p. Index.
A collection of 98 letters, many never printed before, between Franklin and his favorite sister, written 1727-1790. A vivid picture of daily life in Revolutionary times.

1548 Franklin, Benjamin **1706-1790**
Memoirs: parallel text edition comprising the text of Franklin's original manuscript, the French tr. by Louis Guillaume le Veillard, the French tr. pub. by Buisson, and the version ed. by William Temple Franklin, his grandson. Edited with an introduction and explanatory notes by Max Farrand. Published in cooperation with The Huntington Library. Berkeley: University of California Press, 1949. 422 p.
The four texts of Franklin's memoirs printed together as source material for study and comparison.

1549 Franklin, Benjamin **1706-1790**
Mr. Franklin: a selection from his personal letters. Edited by Leonard W. Labaree and Whitfield J. Bell, Jr. New Haven: Yale University Press, 1956. 61 p.
A selection of 27 letters intended to provide a glimpse of his genius as a correspondent and to pay tribute to the 250th anniversary of his birth.

1550 Franklin, Benjamin **1706-1790**
My dear girl. Illustrated. New York: Printing Week Library of Benjamin Franklin Keepsakes, 1977. 71 p.
A collection of twenty letters written by Franklin, 1758-64, to Polly Stevenson, daughter of his London landlady. Franklin instructed Polly in science and encouraged her to perform experiments with water pressure, tides, and dyes. Their affection was lifelong, though only one letter of Polly's is included here.

1551 Franklin, Benjamin **1706-1790**
The papers of Benjamin Franklin. Edited by Leonard W. Labaree, William B. Willcox, and others. New Haven, Connecticut: Yale University Press, 1959-. 21v. Index.
This monumental collection of Franklin's papers, intended to be as comprehensive as possible, includes letters he received, drafts and copies of letters sent, business ledgers, invoices, receipts, and household accounts, official and personal papers from his ministry in France, as well as his published works.

1552 Franklin, Charles A.
see **Banta, Albert Franklin**

1553 Franklin, Joe **1930?-**
A gift for people. New York: M. Evans & Co., 1978. 246 p.
Television talk-show host Franklin reminisces about various celebrities he has interviewed over his 25-year career, including Bing Crosby and Barbra Streisand. He offers advice on how to get along with people, including how to say "I love you," how to add zest to human encounters, and other good-natured homilies.

1554 Franklin, Sidney **1903-1976**
Bullfighter from Brooklyn: an autobiography. With an evaluation of Sidney Franklin from *Death in the Afternoon,* by Ernest Hemingway. New York: Prentice-Hall, Inc., 1952. 245 p.
At nineteen he left home to wander in Mexico, where he saw his first bullfight and began his training, accepting the challenge that an American could not succeed in the profession. His career was remarkable; he was praised by Hemingway as one among seven of the best matadors of his day.

1555 Frederic, Harold **1856-1898**
The correspondence of Harold Frederic. Edited by George E. Fortenberry and others. Text established by Charlyne Dodge. Fort Worth: Texas Christian University Press, 1977. 615 p. Index.
The abundant letters of Frederic, a journalist and author, prefigure Hemingway in subject and style as a man of diverse experiences whose personal life remains controversial and who seldom wrote "literary" letters. As a robust, adventuresome American, he was a spokesman of his era.

1556 Freeman, Allen Weir **1881-1954**
Five million patients: the professional life of a health officer. New York: Charles Scribner's Sons, 1946. 299 p. Index.
Written in third person, the book speaks through the student, the apprentice, the journeyman, and the professor, giving the chronology of his medical life and training, as well as a history of public health issues in the United States.

1557 Freeman, Benjamin H. **b.1842**
The Confederate letters of Benjamin H. Freeman. Compiled and edited by Stuart T. Wright. Hicksville, New York: Exposition Press, 1974. 65 p.

He was a patriot soldier of the South who fought ungrudgingly for his state and country during the Civil War. His letters contain evidence of his increasing concern about the war, his nostalgia, his weariness. Copious notes are appended.

1558 Freeman, John Davis   **1884-1974**
Death loses the game. Chicago: Moody Press, 1954. 188 p.
A combination of Freeman's spiritual autobiography, religious philosophy of life, sermons, and parables to illustrate his view that if one is in harmony with God and the universe, "Time" will be "the referee between Life and Death."

1559 Freeman, Lawrence   **1906-**
You don't look like a musician. Detroit: Balamp, 1974. 125 p. Index.
Observations and bon mots on the world of jazz from a 45-year veteran. Freeman played with the greats, both famous and lesser known, in New Orleans, Detroit, San Francisco, England, Lisbon. He also explores the phenomenon of a white man playing "black men's music" and the changing significance and audience of modern jazz.

1560 Freiwirth, Paul K.   **1927-**
Why I left the Seventh-Day Adventists. New York: Vantage Press, 1970. 120 p.
Freiwirth, who holds a doctorate in history from Vanderbilt University, explains the elaborate process by which he and his wife, Nellie, formerly Seventh Day Adventist proselytizers and solicitors of money for the church, discovered the errors in Seventh Day Adventist doctrine and became astrologers instead.

1561 Frémont, John Charles   **1813-1890**
The expeditions of John Charles Frémont. Edited by Donald Jackson and Mary Lee Spence. Urbana: University of Illinois Press, 1970-1973. 4v. Index.
Frémont led bands of courageous men in exploratory expeditions across the Plains and Rockies five times before he was forty years old. These volumes present the story of those years by means of letters, journal entries, and other documents. Volume I: Travels from 1838 to 1844; Volume II: The Bear Flag Revolt and the Court-Martial; Volume II Supplement: Proceedings of the Court-Martial; and Volume IV: Map Portfolio.

1562 Freud, Sigmund
see Putnam, James Jackson

1563 *Friday, Nancy   **1937-**
My mother/my self: the daughter's search for identity. New York: Dell, 1978. (New York: Delacorte, 1977) 475 p.
A psychological examination of crucial aspects of mother-daughter relationships, from childhood through middle and old age, focusing on love/hate, dependency/independence, reality/illusion. Interspersed among evidence from specialists and mothers and daughters is Friday's autobiographical account of her relationship with her own mother, about whom she is highly ambivalent.

1564 *Friedan, Betty   **1921-**
It changed my life: writings on the women's movement. New York: Random House, 1976. 388 p.
Friedan, founder of National Organization for Women and the National Women's Political Caucus, has collected her writings which chronicle her personal experiences and the evolution of her views on women's place in the world since the publication of *The Feminine Mystique* in 1963. Also included are dialogues with Pope Paul and Simone de Beauvoir, accounts of her travels with Indira Gandhi, and of the International Women's Year Conference in Mexico City in 1975.

1565 Friede, Donald   **1901-1965**
Mechanical angel: his adventures and enterprises in the glittering 1920's. New York: Alfred A. Knopf, 1948. 246 p. Index.
Describes his work in the publishing world (Knopf and Liveright), and the fast, shallow world of the avant-garde, with many references to the world of books and literature.

1566 Friedheim, Arthur   **1859-1932**
Life and Liszt: the recollections of a concert pianist. Edited by Theodore L. Bullock. New York: Taplinger Publishing Co., Inc., 1961. 335 p. Index.
A concert pianist, pupil and secretary of Franz Liszt, acquaintance or friend of kings, czars, and musical giants, Friedheim here portrays the musical circles of the Victorian and Edwardian eras in European capitals and in North America.

1567 Friedman, Bob
What's a nice Jewish boy like you doing in the First Baptist Church? Glendale, California: Regal Books, 1972. 102 p.
A Los Angeles hippy writes of his conversion from Judaism to Christianity during the late Sixties. He uses Biblical stories and fast talk to describe his experience.

1568 *Friemantle, Anne   **1910-**
Three-cornered heart. New York: The Viking Press, 1971. 316 p.
A third person narrative by a novelist-historian who immigrated from England in 1947. She reminisces about celebrities and intellectuals she has known (Einstein, Lady Gregory) and describes England during and after World War I.

1569 *Friermood, Elisabeth Hamilton   **1903-**
Frier and Elisabeth: sportsman and storyteller. Consultant, Harold Thomas Friermood. New York: Vantage Press, 1979. 386 p.
A joint autobiography by Elisabeth and Harold Friermood. She is the author of well-received children's books; his career with the national YMCA brought him high acclaim, especially in connection with sports programs, including American Olympic teams.

1570 *Frisbie, Florence   **1933-**
Miss Ulysses from Puka-Puka: the autobiography of a South Sea trader's daughter. Edited and translated by her father, Robert Dean Frisbie. New York: The Macmillan Co., 1948. 241 p.
Written at age 12 by the daughter of a Polynesian mother and an American trader-author, describing life on one of the northern Cook Islands; perhaps the first book written by a South Sea Islander.

1571 Frisch, Frank   **1898-1973**
Frank Frisch: the Fordham Flash. As told to J. Roy Stockton. Garden City, New York: Doubleday and Co., Inc., 1962. 287 p. Index.
His long career as a professional baseball player and manager with the New York Giants, the St. Louis Cardinals, the Pittsburgh Pirates, and many of baseball's great names.

1572 Fromm, Herbert   **1905-**
The key of see: travel journals of a composer. Boston: Plowshare Press, Inc., 1967. 191 p.
Fromm, who immigrated to America when exiled from his German homeland by the Nazi pogroms in 1936, kept diaries of his travels to California in 1952, Israel and Germany in 1960, and Germany in 1962. A synagogue organist and composer, Fromm writes music in transit and pays particular attention to the local musical offerings in this often privately focused account.

1573 *Frooks, Dorothy   **1899-**
Lady lawyer. New York: Robert Speller & Sons, 1975. 201 p. Index.
Her busy life included speaking for women's right to vote, becoming legal counsel to the Salvation Army, working to establish Small Claims Court in New York, admission to the bar in several regions, publishing the *Murray Hill News,* earning a doctorate in psychology, serving in two world wars, and traveling extensively to serve humanity.

1574 *Frost, Elinor   **1875?-1938**
see **Frost, Robert**

1575 *Frost, Lesley   **1899-**
New Hampshire's child: the diary journals of Lesley Frost. With notes and index by Lawrance Thompson and Arnold Grade. Albany: State University of New York Press, 1969. Index.
The childhood journals of poet Robert Frost's daughter (1905-09) written during their years on a Derry, New Hampshire, farm. Subject index is organized according to her interests: fears, berries, birds by name, Christmas, games, landmarks.

1576 Frost, Robert   **1874-1963**
Family letters of Robert and Elinor Frost. Edited by Arnold Grade. Foreward by Lesley Frost. Albany: State University of New York Press, 1972. 293 p. Index.
A narrative of the Frost family life recorded in letters, primarily from parents to children, depicts their affection, concern, and an exchange of ideas as well as of routine details.

1577 Frost, Robert   **1874-1963**
Interviews with Robert Frost. Edited by Edward Connery Lathem. New York: Holt, Rinehart and Winston, 1966. 295 p.
Interviews drawn from a wide range of printed sources (1915-1962) reveal the life and thought of a major American poet.

1578 Frost, Robert   **1874-1963**
Letters of Robert Frost to Louis Untermeyer. New York: Holt, Rinehart & Winston, Inc., 1963. 388 p.
These letters (1915-1962) record a friendship as well as portray Frost the man and Frost the poet, his growth and thought.

1579 Frost, Robert   **1874-1963**
Selected letters of Robert Frost. Edited by Lawrance Thompson. New York: Holt, Rinehart and Winston, 1964. 645 p. Index.
The collection includes 123 letters by Frost and others written to him by a variety of friends and antagonists. Also included are a detailed chronology, genealogy, analytical index, and annotations by the editor.

1580 Fry, Varian   **1907-1967**
Assignment: rescue. Revised. New York: Four Winds Press, 1968. (New York: Random House, *Surrender on Dermond* [earlier title], 1947) 187 p.

In 1940-41 Fry worked as a secret agent in Vichy, France, to smuggle out French and German refugees on Hitler's blacklist. Before he was arrested and deported by the Gestapo, Fry had helped over a thousand people to escape, including Wanda Landowska, Marc Chagall, and Max Ernst.

1581 Fuerbringer, Ludwig Ernest   **1864-1947**
Persons and events: reminiscences of Ludwig Ernest Fuerbringer, continuation of 80 eventful years. St. Louis: Concordia Publishing House, 1947. 274 p.

A professor of theology at Concordia Seminary for fifty years and its president for twelve, he was a major force in the Evangelical Lutheran Church. His recollections focus on the history of the church and its leaders, ending with a backward glance at St. Louis at the turn of the century.

1582 Fuertes, Louis Agassiz   **1874-1927**
To a young bird artist: [his] letters to George Miksch Sutton. Commentary by George Miksch Sutton. Illustrated. Norman: University of Oklahoma Press, 1979. 147 p.

This charming book reveals the development of a mentor-pupil relationship. In 1915 Sutton, an aspiring painter of birds, wrote to Fuertes, a noted bird painter, for advice and received thoughtful comments on his early drawings. Their correspondence deepened into friendship, as Sutton continued to send Fuertes his drawings for criticism.

1583 Fuess, Claude Moore   **1885-1963**
Independent schoolmaster. Boston: Little, Brown and Co., 1952. 371 p. Index.

A teacher and headmaster at Phillips Academy and Andover for over forty years, he played a prominent role in the development of secondary education in America.

1584 *Fuldheim, Dorothy   **1894-**
I laughed, I cried, I loved: a news analyst's love affair with the world. Illustrated. Cleveland: World Publishing Co., 1966. 204 p. Index.

Television commentator Fuldheim describes her travels from 1930 to 1965 to Europe, Africa, India, Hong Kong, Formosa, and Egypt. She devotes one chapter to various celebrities she has interviewed on television, one to a favorite aunt, Molly, and another to her best childhood friend, Roseka.

1585 Fullam, George Townley   **1841-1879**
The journal of George Townley Fullam: boarding officer of the Confederate sea raider Alabama. Edited by Charles G. Summersell. Illustrated. University: The University of Alabama Press, 1973. 229 p. Index.

This is the journal and log of a Britsh naval officer who fought during the Civil War as second officer on the CSS *Alabama*. He provides a detailed account of his fellow officers, his views of the North, and his delight in Southern victories.

1586 Fuller, Alfred Carol   **1885-1974**
Foot in the door: in life appraisal of the original Fuller Brush man. As told to Hartzell Spence. Hightstown, New Jersey: McGraw-Hill Book Co., 1960. 250 p. Index.

The founder of the Fuller Brush Company and its legendary salesmen tells of his childhood in a conservative religious family of fourteen, his first small shop in Hartford, and the gradual growth of a financial empire.

1587 *Fuller, Margaret (Sarah Margaret Fuller Ossoli)   **1810-1850**
Love-letters of Margaret Fuller, 1845-1846: to which are added the reminiscences of Ralph Waldo Emerson, Horace Greeley and Charles T. Congdon. Introduction by Julia Ward Howe. Illustrated. Prefatory note by James Nathan Gotendorf. New York: AMS Press, 1970. (London: Fisher Unwin, 1903) 228 p.

In 1845-1846 social reformer Margaret Fuller was in New York with Horace Greeley's family, writing copiously for the *Tribune* and visiting the shore, including the tranquil beaches of Coney Island and Rockaway for inspiration and solace. She describes these activities and comments at length on other people, known and unknown, in her highminded but emotional love letters to James Nathan, a German immigrant broker.

1588 *Fuller, Margaret (Sarah Margaret Fuller Ossoli)   **1810-1850**
Margaret Fuller, American romantic: a selection from her writings and correspondence. Edited by Perry Miller. Gloucester, Massachusetts: Peter Smith, 1969. (New York: Anchor Books, 1963) 319 p.

Selections from the dynamic Trancendentalist social reformer's correspondence and essays are arranged to provide a fascinating intellectual autobiography of an unconventional, freethinking feminist. Miller's antagonistic interpretations precede each selection.

1589 *Fulton, Eileen
How my world turns. As told to Brett Bolton. New York: Taplinger, 1970. 208 p.

In addition to acting in the theater and movies, the author played the part of the lovable but conniving Lisa in the long-running soap opera, *As the World Turns.*

1590 *Furman, Bess   **1894-1969**
Washington by-line: the personal history of a newspaper woman. New York: Alfred A. Knopf, 1949. 348 p. Index.

After learning journalism in Iowa, in 1928 she went to work in Washington, where she developed a successful career, marriage, and family. Her book includes interesting details of the administrations she covered and the political celebrities she knew.

1591 Furman, James Clement   **1897-**
From movies to ministry: (and victory over alcohol). Introduction by D.P. McFarland. Illustrated. Raleigh, North Carolina: Christian Action League of North Carolina, 1977. 121 p.

From the time he took his first drink at seventeen until his mid-thirties, Furman was an alcoholic. Nevertheless, he became a successful public relations man for Paramount Pictures. His rehabilitation was begun through the influence of Moral Rearmament, for which he and his supportive wife became proselytizers. At 46 Furman entered Southern Baptist Theological Seminary, was ordained at 49, and for the next sixteen years was Executive Secretary of the United Tennessee League, a temperance educational organization.

1592 *Furness, Thelma (Morgan), Viscountess
   see ***Vanderbilt, Gloria (Morgan)**

1593 Fyodrov, Michael   **1910-**
Death my generation: an autobiography. New York: Roy Publisher, 1946. 301 p.

Son of Russian nobleman and American mother describes growing up in America as an immigrant, eventually becoming a journalist in Europe during World War II.

1594 Gaige, Crosby   **1882-1949**
Footlights and highlights. New York: E.P. Dutton and Co., 1948. 320 p. Index.

Highlights of the life of a Broadway producer who also engaged in various food enterprises.

1595 Gaine, Hugh   **1726-1807**
The journals of Hugh Gaine, printer. Edited by Paul Leicester Ford. New York: Arno Press and the New York Times, 1970. (New York: Dodd, Mead & Co., 1902) 235 p. Index.

Born and apprenticed in Ireland, Gaine emigrated to New York in 1745. He published newspapers, especially *The Mercury*, pamphlets, and other materials, and was outspoken on political issues such as the Stamp Act. This volume includes a biographical statement, a bibliography of the issues of his press, real estate transactions, his journals through 1798, and his letters.

1596 *Gallagher, Mary (Barelli)
My life with Jacqueline Kennedy. Illustrated. Edited by Frances Spatz Leighton. New York: David McKay Co., Inc., 1969. 396 p.

In 1953 she became secretary to John F. Kennedy. She became Jacqueline Kennedy's personal secretary shortly after the Kennedy marriage and remained with her through the White House years and after. She writes a personal account of the Camelot era.

1597 Gallahue, Edward   **1902-1971**
Edward's odyssey; an autobiography. Garden City, New York: Doubleday & Co., Inc., 1970. 216 p.

Although his story contains some elements of the success-in-business stereotype, it also examines his conflicts, problems, emotional difficulties, and anxieties. His interests include the study of psychology, theology, and philosophy; he took part in promoting the Mental Health Association and World Religious Conferences.

1598 Gallatin, Albert   **1761-1849**
   see **Badollet, John Louis**

1599 Gallery, Daniel Vincent   **1901-**
Eight bells, and all's well. New York: W.W. Norton & Co., Inc., 1965. 308 p. Index.

Memories of a naval career by Admiral Gallery including the capture of the German submarine V-505, now on display at Chicago's Museum of Science and Industry. It was the first enemy ship captured in action by the United States since the War of 1812 and the only U-boat captured intact during World War II.

1600 Gallico, Paul   **1897-1976**
Confessions of a story writer. London: Michael Joseph Ltd., 1961. (New York: Alfred Knopf, 1946) 434 p.

Twenty stories previously published, but here printed with additional articles describing the background of each story, the evolution of these ideas, the effect of his personal life and problems on his fiction, and an autobiographical essay.

1601 Gallier, James 1798-1868
Autobiography of James Gallier, architect. With a new introduction by Samuel Wilson, Jr. Illustrated. New York: Da Capo Press, 1973. (Paris: E. Briere, 1864) 150 p.

Gallier immigrated from Ireland in 1827 and established himself as an architect in New Orleans. He became famous as the chief architect of mid-nineteenth-century New Orleans, especially for Greek revival buildings. His book is interesting for its details on architectural practice as well as of a significant life in an interesting time.

1602 Gallo, Fortune T. 1878-1970
Lucky Rooster: the autobiography of an impresario. New York: Exposition Press, 1967. 304 p.

The rags-to-riches story of an Italian immigrant boy who became a successful impresario bringing musical events—operas, ballets, symphonies, military bands—to the public and setting the pace in America's musical taste with such spectacles as the San Carlo Opera Company and performances under the stars in amphitheaters across the country.

1603 *Galloway, Grace (Growden) d.1789
Diary. Edited by Raymond C. Werner. Eyewitness Accounts of the American Revolution. New York: New York Times, 1971. 189 p.

This reprint of her diary, first published in the *Pennsylvania Magazine of History and Biography* in 1931 and 1934, furnishes an account of her life during 1778-1779. She and her husband had been prominent in the social life of Philadelphia. His loyalty to Britain made it necessary for him to seek refuge behind the British lines and eventually to sail for England. She remained behind in the vain hope of saving their property for her daughter.

1604 Gambino, Thomas 1942-
Nyet: an American rock musician encounters the Soviet Union. Englewood Cliffs, New Jersey: Prentice-Hall, 1976. 183 p.

Rock musician Gambino writes about his band's tour of Russia (Moscow and Leningrad), Latvia (Riga), and Lithuania (Vilnus) in November-December, 1974. Although this book purports to offer insight into the lives of typical citizens living under the Communist regime, it is written from a tourist's perspective combined with the "cool" viewpoint of a suave musician.

1605 Gamow, George 1904-1968
My world line: an informal autobiography. Foreword by Stanislaw M. Ulam. New York: The Viking Press, 1970. 178 p. Index.

Gamow's unfinished autobiography covers mainly his life until he arrived in the United States in 1934. His ideas played important parts in the foundation of physics, in cosmology, and in recent discoveries in biology. His books are classics on the history of physics, new ideas in physical science, and especially the popularization of physics, astronomy, and other natural sciences.

1606 Gann, Ernest Kellogg 1910-
A hostage to fortune. New York: Alfred A. Knopf, 1978. 504 p.

Gann describes his many encounters with fortune, good and bad: expulsion from military academy, minimal success in the theatre at Yale, a rowdy trip around the world, the great passion of his life—flying—his entry into the airline industry, the death of his son, the disaster of his first marriage and success of his second.

1607 Gannett, Lewis Stiles 1891-1966
Cream Hill: discoveries of a week-end countryman. With lithographs by Ruth Gannett. New York: The Viking Press, 1949. 191 p.

In the early 1920's he and his wife bought a farmhouse in Connecticut. His book describes the pleasures of their irregular country life while maintaining their New York jobs, especially their delight in gardening.

1608 Garai, Bert 1892-
The man from Keystone. Illustrated. New York: Living Books, Inc., 1966. 248 p. Index.

Garai immigrated from Hungary to New York before World War I and soon obtained a job as a news photographer for the Keystone View Company, which he later managed. Although he obtained American citizenship, he and his family lived abroad for many years, often in London, which was the base for his quest of photographs of the famous and newsworthy that took him all over Europe, America, and into Africa. He writes as he photographs, with brash self-confidence.

1609 Garbus, Martin 1934-
Ready for the defense. New York: Farrar, Straus and Giroux, 1971. 306 p.

An attorney involved in civil rights during the Sixties writes of some cases he was associated with, including those of Lenny Bruce and Timothy Leary. He was "seeking radical change by representing the people whose conflict with the system might result in the creation of new rights and the clarification of old ones."

1610 Garcia, Andrew 1853?-1943
Tough trip through paradise, 1878-1879. Edited by Bennett H. Stein. Boston: Houghton Mifflin Co., 1967. 446 p.

Garcia was a colorful character who lived nine years with Indian wives and became known as the Squaw Kid. Here he tells of adventures in the Musselshell country of Montana and Idaho among the Nez Perce and Flathead Indians during the end of the era of the Plains Indians.

1611 Gardner, Erle Stanley 1889-1970
Host with the big hat. Illustrated. New York: William Morrow and Co., 1969. 247 p.

Gardner describes his railroad trip to Mexico City via special train as a guest of the Mexican government and his visit to the controversial Julsrud Collection of 33,000 primitive figurines which may establish an earlier date and ethos of Mexican civilization, if their authenticity can be established.

1612 Gardner, Hy 1908-
Champagne before breakfast. Foreword by Fred Allen. New York: Henry Holt and Co., 1954. 304 p.

Brief narratives about himself and his writing are interspersed in a collection of stories and incidents about the people and parties he writes about for his Broadway column.

1613 *Gardner, Jeanne 1930-
A grain of mustard. With Beatrice Moore. Foreword by Mahalia Jackson. Introduction by Harold E. Hughes. New York: Trident Press, 1969. 189 p.

Clairvoyant Gardner describes her impoverished childhood in West Virginia, her youthful marriage, motherhood, and the gradual emergence of her psychic, prophetic, and interpretive powers, represented by "The Voice," which supernaturally dictates a variety of spiritual and political messages that determine Gardner's actions and beliefs.

1614 Garfield, James Abram 1831-1881
The diary of James A. Garfield. Edited with introduction by Harry James Brown and Frederick D. Williams. East Lansing: Michigan State University Press, 1967- v. Index.

Born in a log cabin east of Cleveland, Ohio, Garfield spent his early years there and later at what became Hiram College and at Williams College. He returned to Ohio as a teacher, then entered politics as a state senator and later served in the House of Representatives for seventeen years. Unfortunately the diary has gaps during the Civil War years as well as other periods of his life, but on the whole it is rich in candid remarks and presents a vivid self-portrait.

1615 Gargan, William 1905-1979
Why me? an autobiography. Illustrated. Garden City, New York: Doubleday & Co., Inc., 1969. 311 p.

Gargan began acting in films during the Twenties; in the Fifties he starred in *Martin Kane, Private Eye,* the first television detective series. In 1960 he had surgery for cancer of the larynx. When he recovered, he made a new life and career as a popular fund-raiser for the American Cancer Society.

1616 Garis, Roger 1901-1967
My father was Uncle Wiggily. New York: McGraw-Hill Book Co., 1966. 217 p.

The son of a father and mother who both wrote popular juvenile fiction—Uncle Wiggily, Motor Boys, Bobbsey Twins, and Tom Swift. His autobiography tells about living in small-town America with an enthusiastic and imaginative family which among them wrote more than a thousand books.

1617 Garland, Hamlin 1860-1940
Back-trailers from the middle border. St.Clair Shores, Michigan: Scholarly Press, 1974. (New York: The Macmillan Co., 1928) 379 p.

This reprint covers the years 1914 to 1928 in the lives of the author and his family, during which they moved east to New York and spent several summers in England visiting writers and the other men of note.

1618 Garland, Hamlin 1860-1940
Hamlin Garland's diaries. Edited by Donald Pizer. San Marino, California: The Huntington Library, 1968. 281 p. Index.

The entries from author Garland's 43 diaries, 1898-1940, do not duplicate material in any of his other autobiographical volumes. Organized thematically by the editor, the entries discuss his social and literary experiences, his gloomy thoughts on the decline of his career in old age, literary personalities, political events, and social problems.

1619 Garlits, Don 1932-
King of the dragsters: the story of Big Daddy Don Garlits. And Brock Yates. Enlarged and updated edition. Philadelphia: Chilton Book Co., 1970. (1967) 246 p.

The story of his career in drag-racing is centered in the development of this sport during the 1950's and 1960's.

1620 Garner, William Robert   **1803-1849**
Letters from California 1846-1847. Edited with a sketch by Donald Munro Craig. Berkeley: University of California Press, 1970. 262 p. Index.

Prefaced by a 75-page biographical sketch, this volume presents a series of letters first printed in the Philadelphia *North American* and *United States Gazette* and intended to draw farmers, craftsmen, and merchants to develop the California Territory. Garner describes the customs, resources, and economic prospects based on his 22 years of personal experiences in California.

1621 *Garrett, Eileen Jeanette (Lyttle)   **1893-**
Adventures in the Supernormal; a personal memoir. New York: Creative Age Press, Inc., 1949. 252 p.

Like *My Life As a Search . . .* this book explores in detail her childhood, youth and marriage, and coming to terms with the discovery that she has psychic powers. She includes discussions of different kinds of psychic power, as well as the research done by J.B. Rhine of Duke University and Gardner Murphy of the College of the City of New York.

1622 *Garrett, Eileen Jeanette (Lyttle)   **1893-**
Many voices; the autobiography of a medium. Introduction by Allan Angoff. New York: G.P. Putnam's Sons, 1968. 254 p. Index.

She is a trance medium through whom disembodied voices speak. In 74 years she has become something of an international figure, participating in psychic research, reporting facts and events that she has no evident way of knowing, and making no claims to supernatural powers.

1623 *Garrett, Eileen Jeanette (Lyttle)   **1893-**
My life as a search for the meaning of mediumship. New York: Oquaga Press, 1939. 224 p.

A psychic medium writes of her childhood and adolescence, marriage, and the gradual awareness she had of her special powers. The major focus of the book is her attempt to understand and cope with being a medium, which includes participating in psychic research at Duke University.

1624 Garrison, James Holley   **1801-1842**
Behold me once more: the confessions of James Holley Garrison, brother of William Lloyd Garrison. Edited by Walter McIntosh Merrill. Illustrated. Boston: Houghton Mifflin Co., 1954. 146 p. Index.

Garrison, brother of abolitionist William Lloyd Garrison, wrote these memoirs of his life as a youth and seaman, 1810-1840, as a form of penance for his lifelong alcoholism, allegedly conquered in 1840. His candid narrative conveys a moving account of a difficult, sordid life often spent in stupor and in irons.

1625 Garrison, William Lloyd   **1805-1879**
Letters. Edited by Walter M. Merrill and Louis Ruchames. Illustrated. Cambridge: Belknap Press of Harvard University Press, 1971. 3v. Index.

Projected to include letters up to his death in 1879, the present three volumes follow the journalist and abolitionist from his apprenticeship, founding of his newspaper and New England and American anti-slavery societies, his trip to England, courtship and marriage (Vol. I); his objections to orthodox observance of the Sabbath, 1838 Peace Convention, his efforts in support of women (Vol. II); to his urging disunion, his lecture circuit with Frederick Douglass, the Anti-Sabbath Convention, and his work for woman's suffrage (Vol. III).

1626 Garry, Charles R.
Streetfighter in the courtroom: the people's advocate. And Art Goldberg. Foreword by Jessica Mitford. New York: E.P. Dutton Co., 1977. 268 p.

This volume traces Garry's development from a poverty-stricken childhood to his position as folk hero of the New Left. As a lawyer, he used the courtroom to expose the system and attack the establishment.

1627 Garvey, Michael Joseph
Confessions of a Catholic worker. Chicago: Thomas More Press, 1978. 132 p.

Garvey is a young man who has been keeping the Catholic faith by living and working at the Catholic Worker House in Davenport, Iowa, 1976-1977. He expresses his faith and the spirit of the Catholic Worker Movement in anecdotes about the poor people who receive the House's services.

1628 Gaston, Arthur George   **1892-**
Green power; the successful way of A.G. Gaston. Illustrated. Birmingham, Alabama: Southern University Press, 1968. 175 p.

The grandson of slaves, Gaston grew up in rural Alabama, served in France during World War I, and returned to Birmingham where he began a series of hardworking business ventures that eventually made him a millionaire. He argues that green power must precede black power.

1629 Gates, Frederick Taylor   **1853-1929**
Chapters in my life: with the Frederick Taylor Gates lectures by Robert Swain Morison, M.D. Foreword by John Romano. Illustrated. New York: The Free Press/Macmillan, 1977. 305 p. Index.

A Baptist minister raised puritanically, Gates describes the liberal ed-

ucation he provided for his children, based on his belief that with maturity comes a natural personal religion. He also discusses his work with John D. Rockefeller, Sr. and his role in establishing the American Baptist Educational Society, the University of Georgia, the Rockefeller Foundation, and the General Education Board.

1630 Gauss, Christian Frederick   **1878-1951**
The papers of Christian Gauss. Edited by Katherine Gauss Jackson and Hiram Haydn. New York: Random House, 1957. 373 p.

A collection from the autobiographical notebooks, journals, and diaries of a prominent educator, who joined the Princeton faculty in 1905 and later became Dean (1925-1945).

1631 Gayle, Addison, Jr.   **1932-**
Wayward child: a personal odyssey. Garden City, New York: Anchor Press/Doubleday, 1977. 182 p.

Gayle analyzes his life as a Black "bookworm" and writer from the South, a child and man prone to fantasies of violence and fond of passionate women. His lifetime inspirations have been Dostoevski and Richard Wright.

1632 *Gebhard, Anna Laura (Munro)   **1914-**
Rural parish: a year from the journal of Anna Laura Gebhard. New York: Abingdon-Cokesbury Press, 1947. 121 p.

An affectionate record of a year in the daily life of a young couple working with three small churches in neighboring towns that form their parish in rural Minnesota.

1633 Geddes, Norman Bel   **1893-1958**
see Bel Geddes, Norman

1634 Geiser, Peter   **1826-1901**
Autobiography of Peter Geiser: inventor, the Geiser separator, patented 1852-1855. Waynesboro, Pennsylvania: Caolon Press, 1968. 45 p.

Although the story is centered on the separator, it reveals the curiosity and inquisitive mind of the plainspoken inventor of the thresher.

1635 *Gellhorn, Martha   **1908-**
Travels with myself and another. Illustrated. New York: Dodd, Mead & Co., 1978. 283 p.

This is an entertaining, sometimes acid-etched description of Gellhorn's lifetime travels to China, the Caribbean, Russia, and particularly East Africa, which she loved.

1636 *Geoffrey, Theodate, pseud.
see *Wayman, Dorothy

1637 George, Otto
Eskimo medicine man. Illustrated. Portland: Oregon Historical Society, 1978. 278 p. Index.

As the last "traveling physician" for the Department of Interior's Indian Service, Dr. George worked among Eskimos and traders in Alaska's remote north and northwest during the 1930's, accompanied by his wife and two small children. He describes the culture, medical practices, and superstitions of his Eskimo patients and conveys an unromaticized affection for Alaska.

1638 George, Willis DeVere   **1897-**
Surreptitious entry. New York: Appleton-Century Co., Inc., 1946. 214 p.

An operative for Naval Intelligence describes his experience in counterespionage during World War II.

1639 Geraway, William R.   **1936?-**
There's $50,000 on my head. Hicksville, New York: Exposition Press, 1976. 280 p.

Geraway's straightforward account of his life of crime, his "quarter century of human and social failure," including counterfeiting, check forgery, and being an accessory to murder, is told without the defensiveness that characterizes many such tales. His cooperation with the law while in prison caused the Mafia to put out a $50,000 contract for his murder. He lived to evade their grasp, to be freed from prison, and to find God and a good wife.

1640 Gerdy, Robert S.   **1919-1965**
From the letters of Robert S. Gerdy, 1942-1945: a personal record of World War II. Introduction by William Knapp. Edited by Donald Harrison. Philadelphia: Dorrance & Co., 1969. 355 p.

Gerdy, later a *New Yorker* editor, wrote over five hundred letters to relatives throughout World War II, which he spent in the U.S. Army as an enlisted man who eventually rose to captain, "because I can write a bit, because I know the news when I see it, and because I can take news in and get it out fast and accurately." The letters from Florida, France, and England reflect a sensitive newsman's eye for personalities, places, and events, thoughtfully interpreted.

1641 Gero, Eugene
see Sakall, S.Z.

1642 *Gerowitz, Judith
see *Chicago, Judy

1643 Gerry, Elbridge   **1744-1814**
Letterbook, Paris, 1797-1798. Edited by Russell W. Knight. Salem, Massachusetts: Essex Institute, 1966. 92 p.
One of the three ministers to France during the XYZ Affair which ruptured Franco-American relations, Gerry suffered the most censure, condemnation, and abuse from his countrymen. The editor hopes "that the publicaton of his Paris letterbook will invalidate much of the obloquy that has been heaped upon Gerry's head."

1644 Gertz, Elmer   **1906-**
To life: the story of a Chicago lawyer for more than forty years a defender of personal rights and civil liberties, a Don Quixote of the legal world. New York: McGraw, 1974. 252 p.
A renowned libel and civil liberties lawyer from Chicago, he is known for his celebrated defense of Henry Miller's *Tropic of Cancer* and for overturning Jack Ruby's death sentence for the murder of Lee Harvey Oswald. He is also the author of several books, articles, and radio plays. In this volume he celebrates a rich, full life.

1645 Getty, Gerald W.
Public defender. And James Presley. New York: Grosset & Dunlap, Publishers, 1974. 376 p.
For a number of years he worked in and then was head of the public defender's office in Cook County, Illinois. His book is in some ways a defense of the public defender; he includes discussions of the crimes and trial practice typical in the Chicago area, with a lengthy section on the Richard Speck murder trial.

1646 Getty, Jean Paul   **1892-1976**
How to be rich. Chicago: Playboy Press, 1965. 264 p.
A billionaire who made his first million at age 24 tells his methods of doing business and gives advice about building and using a fortune, about characteristics of the true executive, and about dealing fairly with labor. He cites events from his own career in support of his candidly expressed views.

1647 *Geva, Tamara   **1908-**
Split seconds: a remembrance. New York: Harper & Row, 1972. 358 p.
Mostly about her youth in Russia, this book tells of her education and great desire to become a ballerina, finally being accepted at the Theatre School in Petrograd. After dancing throughout Europe, she traveled to the United States, where she danced in musical comedies including *On Your Toes* with its famous Richard Rodgers masterpiece "Slaughter on Tenth Avenue."

1648 Gibbons, Euell   **1911-1975**
Stalking the faraway places, and some thoughts on the best way to live. Illustrated by Freda Gibbons. New York: David McKay Co., Inc., 1973. 279 p. Index.
His first book, *Stalking the Wild Asparagus,* has made him famous as an expert on wild and natural foods. In this volume he describes several journeys in North America looking for foods used by ancient Indians and comments extensively on his philosophy of living.

1649 Gibbs, Mifflin Wistar   **b.1823**
Shadow and light: an autobiography. With an introduction by Booker T. Washington. New York: Arno Press, 1968. (Washington, D.C.: n.p., 1902) 372 p.
A judge writes of interesting people he met and his impressions of widely scattered parts of the world he visited, especially Madagascar where he was U.S. Consul. He intersperses his recollections with moral commentary.

1650 *Gibson, Althea   **1927-**
I always wanted to be somebody. Edited by Ed Fitzgerald. New York: Harper and Brothers, 1958. 176 p.
The first Black woman to play in white tennis tournaments, she was voted Woman Athlete of the Year in 1957 and was the Wimbleton championship winner in 1958.

1651 *Gibson, Althea   **1927-**
So much to live for. With Richard Curtis. New York: G.P. Putnam's Sons, 1968. 160 p. Index.
By 1958 she had become the women's world champion in tennis, winning the titles at Wimbleton and Forest Hills. In need of money, she quit amateur tennis and became a professional golfer. She writes of her personal need for competititon and the rewards of her success.

1652 Gibson, Hugh   **1883-1954**
Hugh Gibson, 1883-1954: extracts from his letters and anecdotes from his

friends. Introduction by Herbert Hoover. Edited by Perrin C. Galpin. Illustrated. New York: Belgian American Educational Foundation, Inc., 1956. 163 p.
Selected personal letters of diplomat and humanitarian Hugh Gibson are arranged in reverse chronological order in this edition of one thousand copies printed for his friends. Although he was stationed in Geneva, Brazil, Belgium, Poland, Paris, and Cuba, and worked extensively with Herbert Hoover on war relief after World War I, his official correspondence was unavailable and the focus here is on witty intimacy.

1653 Gibson, Jerry   **1952-**
Big league batboy. With Ed Wilks. Photographed by Rich Clarkson. New York, Random House/Random House Sports Library, 1970. 129 p. Index.
In this book for youths, Gibson describes his job as a batboy for the St. Louis Cardinals, 1966 and 1967. Highlights were his association with some of the players, including Lou Boudreau, Roger Maris, and Orlando Cepeda, and the 1966 All-Star game.

1654 Gibson, Robert ("Hoot")   **1935-**
From ghetto to glory: the story of Bob Gibson. With Phil Pepe. Illustrated. Library ed. Englewood Cliffs, New Jersey: Responsive Environments Corp./Prentice Hall, 1970. (New York: Prentice Hall, 1968) 200 p.
An articulate, forthright account of Gibson's career as a pitcher for the St. Louis Cardinals (including World Championships in 1964 and 1967) and of his firm views on racial equality. Raised in the Omaha ghetto by a widowed laundress, Gibson has made it on his own terms and talent into a white world which he is determined to integrate.

1655 Gibson, Walter Murray   **1823-1888**
The diaries of Walter Murray Gibson 1886, 1887. Edited with introduction and notes by Jacob Adler and Gwynn Barrett. Honolulu: The University Press of Hawaii, 1973. 199 p. Index.
As Hawaii's prime minister, Gibson was a controversial figure who served under King Kalakaua, tried to advance Hawaii's position in the Pacific, was overthrown in the revolution of 1887, and was exiled to San Francisco. His diaries here shed light on his complex character, his devotion to his daughter and grandchildren, and his unrequited love for Mother Marianne, who ministered to the lepers at Kakaalo and Molokai.

1656 Gibson, William Charles   **1914-1961**
Mass for the dead. New York: Atheneum, 1968. 431 p.
Written in the form of a mass for the dead with sections matching those of the mass—Introit, Kyrie, Paternoster, etc., this volume is not so much about Gibson's life as it is a requiem for his mother, her living and her dying.

1657 Giesler, Harold Lee
see Giesler, Jerry, pseud.

1658 Giesler, Jerry, pseud. (Giesler, Harold Lee)   **1886-1962**
The Jerry Giesler story. With Pete Martin. New York: Simon and Schuster, 1960. 341 p. Index.
Giesler, a noted California attorney, tells the dramatic stories of some of his most famous cases, including those of Errol Flynn, Charles Chaplin, Robert Mitchum, Lili St. Cyr, "Bugsy" Siegel, and Murder, Inc. He also offers observations on legal strategies and his courtroom tactics and a chapter each on his early and current personal life. The narrative is fast-paced except for some lengthy courtroom transcripts.

1659 Gilbert, Alfred Carlton   **1884-1961**
Man who lives in paradise: the autobiography of A.C. Gilbert. With Marshall McClintock. New York: Rinehart and Co., Inc., 1954. 374 p.
An Olympic gold medal winner, later a famous toy manufacturer (erector sets, American flyer trains), discusses the two main interests of his life: business and sports. His major geographic ties are with Connecticut, Idaho, and Oregon.

1660 Gilbert, Gustave Mark   **1911-1977**
Nuremberg diary. New York: Farrar, Straus and Co., 1947. 471 p. Index.
The journal notes of the prison psychologist at the Nuremberg trial of Nazi war criminals include his observations of and responses to the accused throughout the trial and execution.

1661 Gilbert, Louis Wolfe   **1886-1970**
Without rhyme or reason. Introduction by Jimmy Durante. New York: Vantage Press, 1956. 240 p. Index.
Gilbert focuses on his fifty-year career as a writer of song lyrics, mostly for New York vaudeville and legitimate theater, and in Hollywood for movies. Full of names and anecdotes about hundreds of entertainment personalities, 1900-1950. "The Robert E. Lee" and "Ramona" are among Gilbert's best-known songs.

1662 Gilbert, Stirling Price   **1862-1951**
Georgia lawyer: his observations and public service. Athens: University of Georgia Press, 1946. 257 p.
Colorful descriptions of his life in Georgia during the late-nineteenth

and early-twentieth century, by a man who served as a state judicial officer (1893-1936) and a State Supreme Court Justice (1916-1936). Includes legal and social history.

1663 Gilbreth, Frank Bunker, Jr.   **1911-**
Bells on their toes. And Ernestine Gilbreth Carey. New York: Thomas Y. Crowell Co., 1950. 237 p.
  The second volume of their collective autobiography of life in a large family, organized according to the time and motion studies made famous by their parents.

1664 Gilbreth, Frank Bunker, Jr.   **1911-**
Cheaper by the dozen. And Ernestine Gilbreth Carey. New York: Thomas Y. Crowell Co., 1963. 245 p.
  Delightful story of life in the large family of two industrial engineers who used theories of motion study to help raise their twelve children.

1665 Gilder, Richard Watson   **1844-1909**
Letters of Richard Watson Gilder. Edited by Rosamond Gilder. Boston: Houghton Mifflin Co., 1916. 515 p. Index.
  Poet, *Scribner's* and *Century Magazine* editor, publicist, man of affairs, Gilder's letters reveal his ideals, ambitions, and impulses to literary or civic achievement. Here the letters are connected by a narrative written by his daughter.

1666 *Gildersleeve, Virginia Crocheron   **1877-1965**
Many a good crusade: memoirs of Virginia Crocheron Gildersleeve. New York: The Macmillan Co., 1954. 434 p. Index.
  Her life as an educator and administrator is recalled by a scholar active in the International Federation of University Women, in organizing the Women's Reserve in the Navy (WAVES), in drafting the Charter of the United Nations, and numerous other "crusades," although she says "quiet efforts" would be a more appropriate name.

1667 *Giles, Nell   **1920?-**
Punch in, Susie! New York: Harper and Brothers, 1943. 143 p.
  A series of articles written for the Boston *Globe* describing her life as a factory worker at General Electric during World War II.

1668 Gill, Brendan   **1917-**
Here at the *New Yorker* New York: Random House, 1975. 406 p. Index.
  This affectionate account of the *New Yorker* and the eccentrics who made it was published on its fiftieth anniversary. Since Gill was part of that institution for nearly forty of those years, the book is something of an autobiography of its author and a memoir of those merry days.

1669 Gill, William Hanson   **b.1886**
Always a commander: the reminiscences of Major General William H. Gill. As told to Edward Jaquelin Smith. Colorado Springs: The Colorado College, 1974. 124 p.
  This career army man served through two wars, but reminisces here especially about action in the South Pacific Theater on the Villa Verde Trail on Luzon during World War II. In 1946 he became President of Colorado College.

1670 *Gillespie, Janet
With a merry heart. New York: Harper & Row, Publishers, 1976. 231 p.
  Author Gillespie recounts her family's adventures through the New England seasons, characterizing her father, a minister, her mother, a homemaker, her brothers and sisters, and many other close relatives.

1671 Gillette, James B.   **1856-1937**
Six years with the Texas Rangers, 1875 to 1881. Edited by Milo Milton Quaife. Lincoln: University of Nebraska Press, 1976. (Texas: Privately Printed, 1921) 259 p.
  A short history of the Texas Rangers during the years he was a member describes the dangers, the rugged life, the scouting expeditions, the Indian raids, the remarkable individuals who made up this famous frontier force.

1672 Gillham, Charles Edward   **1898-1970**
Raw north. New York: A.S. Barnes and Co., 1947. 275 p.
  A tale of seven years in the far northern regions of Canada and Alaska told with realism and admiration for the varied people the author lived and worked with.

1673 *Gilman, Caroline (Howard)   **1794-1888**
Recollections of a Southern matron. Philadelphia: Keystone, 1899. (New York: Harper & Brothers, 1838) 272 p.
  This story of her personal observations and experience is intended to depict local habits and manners in South Carolina.

1674 *Gilman, Charlotte Perkins Stetson   **1860-1935**
The living of Charlotte Perkins Gilman: an autobiography. Foreword by Zona Gale. New York: Arno Press, 1972. (New York: D. Appleton-Century Co., 1935) 341 p. Index.
  After a failed marriage and mental collapse, she led a busy life writing

and lecturing on labor, suffrage, and socialism. She achieved international fame by attacking the conventional concepts of the dependence and subservience of women.

1675 *Gilman, Dorothy   **1923-**
A new kind of country. Garden City, New York: Doubleday & Company, 1978. 125 p.
  Tired of inflation and crime and of being a single woman raising two sons in the suburbs, Gilman sent her sons to college and bought a 125-year-old house in a fishing village in Nova Scotia. She writes with pleasure about meeting new people with different ways of life while examining the changes in her suburban values.

1676 Gilmer, Francis Walker   **1790-1826**
  see **Jefferson, Thomas**

1677 Gilmore, Eddy   **1907-1967**
Me and my Russian wife. Garden City, New York: Doubleday and Co., Inc., 1954. 313 p.
  Personal narrative of the author's work, friends, and family during his twelve years' assignment in Russia as head of the Moscow Bureau of the Associated Press (1941-1952).

1678 Ginsberg, Allen   **1926-**
Indian journals, March 1962-May 1963, notebooks, diary, blank page, writings. San Francisco: City Lights books (Dave Haselwood books), 1970. 210 p.
  Musings, observations and miscellaneous poetic jottings in diary form written during the poet's visit to India.

1679 Ginsberg, Allen   **1926-**
Journals: early fifties, early sixties. Edited by Gordon Ball. Illustrated. New York: Grove Press, 1977. 313 p. Index.
  Ginsberg's journal is a random collection of dreams, fantasies, observations, wishes, drawings, and poetry that reflects his shyness, his desire to "do something," and his preoccupation with sex and drugs.

1680 Ginsberg, Allen   **1926-**
To Eberhart from Ginsberg: a letter about *Howl*, 1956; an explanation by Allen Ginsberg of his publication *Howl* and Richard Eberhart's New York *Times* article "West Coast Rhythms," together with comments by both poets. Relief etchings by Jerome Kaplan. Preface by Richard Eberhart and Allen Ginsberg. Lincoln, Massachusetts: Penmaen Press, 1976. 45 p.
  Ginsberg explains to critic and poet Eberhart the genesis, meaning, and poetic techniques of the best-known poem of the Beat Generation, *Howl*, "an 'affirmation' of individual experience of God, sex, drugs, absurdity, etc."

1681 Ginzburg, Ralph   **1929-**
Castrated: my eight months in prison. New York: Avant-Garde Books, 1973. 35 p.
  A terse record describing his prison term, the difficulty of obtaining parole, and the absurdity of his conviction for obscenity charges, by the man who was editor of *Eros* magazine.

1682 *Giovanni, Nikki   **1944-**
Gemini: an extended autobiographical statement on my first twenty-five years. New York: Viking Compass Edition, 1973. 149 p.
  A Black poet writes of the major influences in her life, intellectual and emotional. Her book emphasizes the warmth and stability of her family, especially her grandmother, mother, sister, and son.

1683 *Giovanni, Nikki   **1943-**
Poetic equation: conversations between Nikki Giovanni and Margaret Walker. And Margaret Walker. Washington, D.C.: Howard University Press, 1974. 135 p.
  Both women are Black writers with the temperament of the poet. In these taped conversations the two exchange ideas on their careers, personal lives, the issues of the time, on literature, on being Black.

1684 Girandola, Anthony J.   **1924-**
The most defiant priest; the story of the priest who married. New York: Crown Publishers, Inc., 1968. 277 p.
  Still a devout Catholic, he was excommunicated after his marriage, then opened a church in St. Petersburg, Florida, for excommunicated Catholics. He continues to argue for changes in the Church policies on celibacy, confession, divorce, birth control, and the privileges of the clergy.

1685 Girard, James W.   **b.1877**
The man who knew trees: the autobiography of James W. Girard. St. Paul: Minnesota Historical Society, 1949. 35 p.
  A third person description of his long career in the U.S. Forest Service.

1686 *Gish, Lillian   1896-
Dorothy and Lillian Gish. Edited by James E. Frasher. Illustrated. New York: Charles Scribner's Sons, 1973. 311 p.

Hundreds of photographs from their vaudeville, stage, and movie careers connected by Lillian's narrative tell the story of the Gish sisters, who established their reputations in the classic silent films of the legendary D.W. Griffith. Included are the "filmography" and "stageography" of both sisters.

1687 *Gish, Lillian   1896-
Lillian Gish: the movies, Mr. Griffith, and me. With Ann Pinchot. Illustrated. Englewood Cliffs, New Jersey: Prentice-Hall, Inc., 1969. 388 p. Index.

A real trouper and an actress from the age of five, Lillian Gish grew up with the movies as they grew with her. Her book also describes her sister Dorothy and the life and career of D.W. Griffith, the great film pioneer who taught them the art of the film. An impeccable professional, Gish has remained a highly respected actress known for her discipline, enthusiasm, good humor, and dedication to her craft.

1688 *Glasgow, Ellen Anderson Gholson   1873-1945
Letters. Compiled and edited with introduction and commentary by Blair Rouse. New York: Harcourt, Brace and Co., 1957. 384 p. Index.

A selection of her letters (1897-1945) revealing her development as an outstanding novelist, her character interacting with friends, and her role in the literary and artistic life of her time.

1689 *Glasgow, Ellen Anderson Gholson   1873-1945
Woman within. New York: Harcourt, Brace and Co., 1954. 307 p. Index.

A writer recalls her childhood in Virginia, her development as a writer, and the experience of being part of a literary circle in New York. Includes geneology and bibliography of her works.

1690 *Glass, Willie Elmore   b.1887
Miss Willie: happenings of a happy family (1816-1926). Illustrated. Essington, Pennsylvania: Huntingdon Press, 1976. 419 p.

Anecdotes of the Elmore family when Willie was growing up in Alabama, including a collection of turn-of-the-century photographs of various family members. Glass focuses on the good times and sustenance from her enormous extended family and many friends, which helped during her stormy marriage, divorce, and remarriage to an alcoholic proprietor of many failed businesses.

1691 Glasser, Arthur Frederick   1914-
And some believed: a chaplain's experiences with the Marines in the South Pacific. Chicago: Moody Press, 1946. 208 p.

Narrative includes very little description of the war or combat, focusing mainly on his functions as a chaplain.

1692 Glick, Carl   1890-1971
I'm a busybody. New York: Thomas Y. Crowell Co., 1949. 238 p.

After interesting recollections of his childhood and adolescence in Iowa and Montana and his early attempts at writing, the book becomes a glib portrayal of a writer hustling on the periphery of significance.

1693 Glickman, Harry
Promoter ain't a dirty word. Illustrated. Foreword by Don McLeod. Forest Grove, Oregon: Timber Press, 1978. 186 p.

Glickman focuses on his efforts to promote various boxing, football, basketball, and hockey teams, particularly in Portland, Oregon. His happiest moments occurred when the Portland Trail Blazers won the National Basketball Association world championship in 1977.

1694 Glover, John   1732-1797
General John Glover's letterbook, 1776-1777. Edited with introduction by Russell W. Knight. Foreword by Walter Muir Whitehill. Salem, Massachusetts: Essex Institute, 1976. 64 p. Index.

A collection of letters sent in 1776-77 which focus on military strategy, day-to-day procedures in running an army (including food, clothing, supplies), Glover's problems with money, family matters, and the uncertain postwar period.

1695 *Gluck, Gemma (La Guardia)   b.1881
My story. Edited with a preface by S.L. Shneiderman. New York: David McKay Co., Inc., 1961. 116 p.

Born in the U.S., a sister of Fiorello LaGuardia, she lived in Budapest with her husband, a Hungarian Jew. In 1944 she was arrested by the Gestapo and imprisoned in Ravensbruck. Her book recalls early family life in New York, her life and imprisonment in Europe, and her return to the U.S. in 1947.

1696 Glueck, Sheldon   1896-
Lives of labor, lives of love: fragments of friendly autobiographies. Hicksville, New York: Exposition Press, 1977. 222 p.

This autobiography includes incidents in the personal lives of Sheldon and Eleanor Glueck and their daughter, Joyce, but concentrates on their fifty years of joint research in criminology at Harvard Law School,

conferences attended, awards given. It also includes Eleanor's diary and a bibliography of their voluminous writings.

1697 Goddard, George William   b.1889
Overview; a lifelong adventure in aerial photography. With DeWitt S. Copp. Garden City, New York: Doubleday & Co., Inc., 1969. 415 p. Index.

In 1917 he entered the Air Service and trained to be an aerial photographer and pilot. During the next fifty years he played a major role in the development of aerial photography as an inventor and practitioner.

1698 Goddard, Robert Hutchings   1882-1945
Papers: including the reports of the Smithsonian Institution and the Daniel and Florence Guggenheim Foundation; Vol. I: 1898-1924; Vol. II: 1925-1937; Vol. III: 1938-1945. Edited by Esther C. Goddard (and others). Illustrated. New York: McGraw-Hill Book Co., 1970. 3v. Index.

These letters, diary entries, reports, and other papers tell the story of a pioneer in rocket research whose farsighted ideas, inventions, and accomplishments have made possible the space age. It has been said that it would be impossible "to design a rocket, construct a rocket, launch a rocket, guide a rocket, or fly in space without infringing a Goddard patent" (they number over 200).

1699 Godkin, Edwin Lawrence   1831-1902
The gilded age letters of E.L. Godkin. Edited by William M. Armstrong. Albany: State University of New York Press, 1974. 583 p. Index.

A selection of letters by Godkin, who was first editor of the *Nation,* a national weekly founded after the Civil War to perpetuate the hard-won goals of freedom, to heal the divisions that had split the American Anti-Slavery Society, and to work for the well-being of the freed men.

1700 *Godowsky, Dagmar   1897-1975
First person plural: the lives of Dagmar Godowsky. New York: The Viking Press, 1958. 249 p.

With verve and great comic spirit, Dagmar Godowsky, daughter of pianist-composer Leopold Godowsky, tells of her flamboyant career as a film star in Hollywood in the 1920's and in Paris and Berlin in the 30's. She spent freely of her money and herself in days of champagne and roses with actors, musicians (including Rubenstein, Heifitz, Stravinsky), and no regrets.

1701 Gogolak, Peter   1942-
Nothing to kick about: the autobiography of a modern immigrant. With Joseph Carter. Illustrated. New York: Dodd, Mead, 1973. 274 p.

Gogolak's family escaped from Hungary during the uprising and came to America where young Peter learned about a new culture. He eventually became a New York Giants football player famed for his kicking ability. He has never forgotten his Hungarian culture that made him special among American athletes.

1702 Gold, Herbert   1924-
My last two thousand years. New York: Random House, 1972. 246 p.

A second generation American, novelist Gold tells of the journey back to his European roots in search of answers to "Who am I?" and "Is America enough?" His travels took him to Paris, Rome, Haiti, and Israel where he found some answers and other people on similar journeys.

1703 *Gold, Mary Jayne
Crossroads Marseilles, 1940. New York: Doubleday & Co., Inc., 1980. 412 p. Index.

A wealthy debutante from Evanston, Illinois, she was in France at the outbreak of World War II. Instead of returning home, she stayed there to become a valuable member of Varian Fry's Emergency Rescue Committee, spiriting hundreds of refugees out of France.

1704 Gold, Victor (Vic Gold)   1928?-
I don't need you when I'm right; the confessions of a Washington P.R. man. New York: William Morrow & Co., 1975. 218 p.

A humorous look behind the scenes in the world of public relations. He worked for presidents and vice-presidents, senators and other Washington luminaries, experiencing the PR dream world of politics and power.

1705 Goldberg, Reuben Lucius   1883-1970
Rube Goldberg vs. the machine age: a retrospective exhibition of his work with memoirs and annotations. Illustrated. Edited by Clairk Kinnaird. New York: Hastings House, Publishers, 1968. 214 p.

The title, the book, and its narrative reflect Goldberg's main interest as a humorist: he saw himself as a rebel against the gadgetry of the machine age that enslaves rather than frees him.

1706 Golden, Harry Lewis   1902-
The right time: an autobiography. Illustrated. New York: G.P. Putnam's Sons, 1969. 450 p. Index.

The crusty editor of the *Carolina Israelite* for 26 years has written a very readable account full of wit and wry humor but with a serious purpose. He was successful in his pursuit of the American Dream, fighting for the rights of others, particularly for racial and religious minorities.

1707 Golden, Jeffrey 1950-
Watermelon summer; a journal. Philadelphia: J.B. Lippincott Co., 1971. 152 p.

A revolutionary temporarily without a cause, Golden spent the summer of 1970 working on a farm in Georgia, "a way of life completely alien to his affluent, middle-class background." It was a frustrating, enlightening and sometimes funny experience far removed from his previous world.

1708 *Goldfrank, Esther Schiff 1896-
Notes on an undirected life: as one anthropologist tells it. Illustrated. Bibliography. Flushing, New York: Queens College Press, 1978. 244 p. Index.

Anthropologist Goldfrank draws from her journal and from letters to document her years as secretary to Franz Boaz at Columbia University and working with Pueblo Indians in New Mexico and Blackfoot Indians in Alberta, Canada. Her detailed chapters provide both a history of anthropology in the 1920's and 1930's and a glimpse at how a field anthropologist approaches a "new" culture.

1709 Goldhaft, Arthur D. 1885-1960
The golden eggs. Edited with introduction by Meyer Levin. New York: Horizon Press, 1957. 314 p.

Veterinarian and proprietor of Vineland (N.J.) Poultry Laboratories, Dr. Goldhaft pioneered in making vaccines for fowl pox and fowl cholera. His life story is also the story of a Jewish agricultural colony in America, of a haven for refugees from pogroms, and of a multiple generation family closely knit by Judaism and veterinary medicine.

1710 *Goldman, Emma 1869-1940
Living my life. New York: Da Capo, 1970. (New York: A.A. Knopf, 1931) 2v. Index.

The turbulent life of anarchist Goldman, who believed in "perfect, unrestrained freedom for everyone." She was a labor agitator, published *Mother Earth,* was accused of complicity in the assassination of President McKinley, traveled, lectured, went to Russia but became disillusioned with the Bolshevik regime in 1921, aided Spanish anarchists against France in 1936.

1711 *Goldman, Emma 1869-1940
My disillusionment in Russia. Introduction by Rebecca West. Biographical sketch by Frank Harris. New York: Crowell, 1970. (New York: Doubleday, 1925) 263 p.

A biographical sketch of the author's childhood in Russia, immigration to the U.S., and growing involvement in the Anarchist movement includes material from Goldman's notes. The remainder of the volume contains Goldman's account of her deportation from the U.S. and her initial hope and excitement in traveling to Russia after the Revolution. What she finds on arrival is a Russia "grotesque, totally unlike the great ideal that had borne me upon the crest of high hope." A meticulous and scathing denunciation of Leninist Russia is colored always by her disillusion with the U.S.

1712 *Goldman, Emma 1869-1940
Nowhere at home; letters from exile of Emma Goldman and Alexander Berkman. Edited by Richard and Anna Maria Drinnon. New York: Schocken Books, Inc., 1975. 282 p. Index.

Because she was an exile, letters became anarchist Goldman's favored medium of expression; in them the gap between the spoken and written word was narrow and she could express her ideas with feeling and intensity.

1713 Goldman, Eric Federick 1915-
The tragedy of Lyndon Johnson. New York: Alfred A. Knopf, 1969. 531 p. Index.

From his position as Special Consultant to the President, 1963-1966, Goldman observed and analyzed the triumphs and failures of the Johnson Administration and the strengths and weaknesses of Lyndon Johnson himself.

1714 Goldman, Raymond Leslie 1895-
Even the night. New York: The Macmillan Co., 1947. 196 p.

A moving account of his struggle to overcome the effects of infantile paralysis and diabetes, by a man who achieved moderate success as a writer.

1715 Goldmann, Nachum 1895-
Memories: the autobiography of Nachum Goldmann; the story of a life-long battle by world Jewry's ambassador at large. Translated by Helen Sebba. London: Weidenfeld & Nicholson, 1970. (New York: Holt Rinehart & Winston, 1969) 358 p. Index.

In 1923 he began working on the *Encyclopaedia Judaica* in Berlin and within two years began to engage in Zionist political and organizational work. His book reflects his own history as well as impressions of Jewish life in his time.

1716 Goldmark, Peter Carl 1906-1977
Maverick inventor: my turbulent years at CBS. With Lee Edson. New York: E.P. Dutton, 1973. 278 p. Index.

CBS engineer and inventor Goldman recounts his career of "crazy ideas"—ideas which helped produce television, sophisticated military communications equipment, LP records, cassettes, and electronic devices for the NASA space program. He writes of his ideas and their usually skeptical reception, concentrating particularly on his lengthy fight for color television.

1717 Goldovsky, Boris 1908-
My road to opera: the recollections of Boris Goldovsky. As told to Curtis Cate. Illustrated. Boston: Houghton Mifflin Company, 1979. 401 p. Index.

Singer, pianist, conductor, producer, director Goldovsky was a child prodigy in Moscow and studied in Berlin, where he experienced the excitement of one of the great European music centers. After immigrating to the United States, through his performances and productions and his role as commentator for Texaco's broadcasts for the Metropolitan Opera, he has contributed much to America's understanding of opera.

1718 Goldschmidt, Richard Benedict 1878-1958
In and out of the ivory tower: the autobiography of Richard B. Goldschmidt. Seattle: The University of Washington Press, 1960. 352 p. Index.

A distinguished zoologist describes his early years in Frankfurt, his world travels as a research scientist, his internment as an alien in the United States during World War I, the rise of Hitler, and his immigration to the United States in 1936, when he joined the faculty of the University of California.

1719 Goldschmidt, Richard Benedict 1878-1958
Portraits from memory: recollections of a zoologist. Seattle: University of Washington Press, 1956. 181 p.

Describes his years in Germany among many celebrated zoologists whom he knew as a student or colleague in the 1890's and after.

1720 Goldstein, Ruby 1905-
Third man in the ring. As told to Frank Graham. New York: Funk & Wagnalls, 1959. 216 p.

As a kid on New York's Lower East Side, he started boxing at age ten; by seventeen he had become professional. He won considerable success as a lightweight boxer, but after World War II began to referee. He writes of the fights, the tough social world boxers and referees operate in, and many of the fighters and managers he has worked with.

1721 Goldwater, Barry Morris 1909-
With no apologies: the personal and political memoirs of United States Senator Barry M. Goldwater. New York: William Morrow and Company, Inc., 1979. 320 p. Index.

Conservative Senator Goldwater offers opinions on political and economic problems, comments on the chaos of the Sixties, and appraises presidents and other important government officials. His autobiography supports his reputation as a straightforward, uncompromising public figure.

1722 Gomez, Al V. 1905-
The foundation stock. Preface by Monte LeNoir. New York: Vantage Press, 1976. 173 p.

Gomez articulately explains how to breed and train thoroughbred race horses. His general recommendations are buttressed by numerous anecdotes of his own experiences with his favorite winning horses.

1723 Gompers, Samuel 1850-1924
Seventy years of life and labor: an autobiography. New York: Augustus M. Kelley, Publishers, 1967. (New York: E.P. Dutton and Co., Inc., 1925) 2v. Index.

A narrative remarkable for its detail and precision describing his life as a prominent labor organizer and founder of the American Federation of Labor.

1724 Gonzales, Richard Alonzo (Pancho) 1928-
Man with a racket: autobiography. As told to Cy Rice. New York: A.S. Barnes and Co., 1959. 254 p. Index.

One of the best tennis players of his time, he recalls here his early dedication to the game while growing up in the slums of Los Angeles, his first tournaments during adolescence, and his championship years in tennis.

1725 *Goodman, Ellen 1940?-
Close to home. New York: Simon and Schuster, 1979. 251 p.

This collection of Goodman's columns written in the 1970's for the Boston *Globe* conveys her personal, feminist reactions to the decade and some of its major figures (Pat Nixon, Bella Abzug) and contemporary phenomena, such as the Equal Rights Amendment. Over half of the book focuses on Goodman's personal relationships, determined by her roles as a writer and as a divorced single parent.

1726 Goodman, Julien M. 1913-
M.D. P.O.W. New York: Exposition Press, 1972. 218 p.

Captured by the Japanese on Bataan, he was held in several prison camps, April 3, 1942-September 14, 1945. His book, written thirty years later, reveals his bitter resentment of the degradation of imprisonment.

1727 Goodrich, Samuel Griswold (Peter Parley, pseud.)   1793-1860
Recollections of a lifetime: or, men and things I have seen; in a series of familiar letters to a friend, historical, biographical, anecdotical, and descriptive. Detroit: Gale Research Co., 1967. (New York: Miller, Orton and Mulligan, 1857) 2v. Index.
   The author, under his pen name Peter Parley, wrote for children over 100 educational books set in fictional framework. He also wrote textbooks, histories and dictionaries, was a state legislator, a consul in Paris, a poet, and editor.

1728 Goodspeed, Edgar Johnson   1871-1962
As I remember. New York: Harper and Brothers, 1953. 303 p. Index.
   A biblical scholar recalls the beginning of the University of Chicago and his own work on a new translation of the Bible.

1729 Goodwin, Grenville   1907-1940
Grenville Goodwin; among the Western Apache, letters from the field. Edited by Morris E. Opler. Illustrated. Tucson: The University of Arizona Press, 1973. 103 p. Index.
   During the 1930's Goodwin and Morris Opler were both studying different Apachean cultures. With a common sense of exploration and discovery and a similar set of empirical problems, they exchanged information and ideas in order to compare systematically the Western Apache beliefs and customs and contribute ethnographic details to American anthropology.

1730 *Goodwin, Ruby Berkley   1903-
It's good to be black. Preface by Carmen Kenya Wadley. Reprint of 1954 edition with new preface. Carbondale: Southern Illinois University Press, 1976. (Garden City, New York: Doubleday, 1953) 256 p.
   Goodwin's penetrating, beautifully written analysis of what it meant to grow up Black and proud as a coal miner's daughter in DuQuoin, Illinois, takes the form of memorable vignettes about quintessential experiences: the home birth of her sister; family cooperation to care for a blind aunt; the accidental destruction of her church by fire; the miner's trade. As a child, Berkley discovered that a Black pride is Black power and universal brotherhood.

1731 Goodwyn, Frank   1911-
Life on the King Ranch. New York: Thomas Y. Crowell Co., 1951. 293 p.
   The son of the ranch boss of the Norias section of King Ranch in Texas describes his childhood and youth with cowboys, riding and roping horses, and folklore of the Mexican hands.

1732 *Gordon, Barbara   1935-
I'm dancing as fast as I can. New York: Harper and Row, 1979. 313 p.
   Award-winning television producer Gordon discovered at 41 that she was addicted to valium; within a few weeks, she lost her lover, her career, her identity, and nearly her life. She writes movingly of her courageous battle to regain sanity.

1733 Gordon, Benjamin Lee   1871-1965
Between two worlds: the memoirs of a physician. New York: Bookman Associates, Inc., 1952. 354 p. Index.
   Memoirs of a scholar (both Jewish and secular) and physician who records his joys and sorrows, his zest for living, and his wish to leave a spiritual legacy.

1734 Gordon, Max   1892-1978
Max Gordon presents. With Louis Funke. New York: Bernard Geis Associates, 1963. 314 p. Index.
   From New York's Lower East Side Gordon worked up through burlesque and vaudeville, coped with success and failure, and became a major Broadway producer.

1735 *Gordon, Ruth   1896-
My side: the autobiography of Ruth Gordon. New York: Harper and Row, 1976. 502 p. Index.
   Actress Ruth Gordon tells the story of her career in the theater and, in later life, in the movies, in dramas ranging from *A Doll's House* to *Harold and Maude*. Gregory Kelly, her first husband, taught her to act; Jed Harris fathered her son; Garson Kanin is her second, supportive husband.

1736 *Gordon, Ruth   1896-
Myself among others. New York: Atheneum, 1971. 389 p.
   This autobiographical work is devoted almost entirely to her life in the theater, with anecdotes of dramatic celebrities described in a rather disjointed narrative.

1737 *Gordon, Ruth   1896-
Ruth Gordon: an open book. New York: Doubleday & Co., Inc., 1980. 395 p. Index.

Anecdotes, advice, and remembrances of her seventy-odd years in the theater comprise Gordon's lively, humane memoirs. Of colonial ancestry, she was reared in Quincy, Massachusetts. She discusses her tours with innumerable plays and friendships with many of the great actors and actresses of her time. Among her lessons for living is such advice as "Do not face the facts."

1738 *Gordon, Ruth   1896-
Years ago: a play. New York: The Viking Press, 1947. 173 p.
   An autobiographical play describing her family and their reactions to her preparations to go to New York to become an actress.

1739 Gordon, William A.   1921-
Writer and critic: a correspondence with Henry Miller. Baton Rouge: Louisiana State University Press, 1968. 88 p.
   The confrontation between writer and critic is illustrated by this exchange of fifteen letters between Gordon and Henry Miller concerning the manuscript of Gordon's *The Mind and Art of Henry Miller*. Miller comments minutely on specific points, while Gordon answers. Some of the arguments are not resolved, but they constitute an interesting dialogue between the critic, who in this case is the author, and the author, who is acting as critic.

1740 Gordy, Berry, Sr.   1888-1978
Movin' up: Pop Gordy tells his story. Illustrated. New York: Harper & Row, Publishers, 1979. 144 p.
   Gordy writes about his boyhood in Georgia and his early married years in Detroit. His story, a fulfillment of the American Dream, reveals that a hard-working man from a hard-working family can successfully run his own business in spite of being Black and struggling during the Depression. He became an executive at Motown Records.

1741 Gore, Albert   1907-
Let the glory out; my South and its politics. New York: The Viking Press, 1972. 307 p.
   Drawing on his experience in county, state, and national politics, Gore interprets events and conditions of the South as they relate to American politics of the 1960's and 1970's. He hopes to inspire able youth to worthy public service and conscientious leadership.

1742 Gorgas, Josiah   1818-1883
Civil War diary. Edited by Frank E. Vandiver. University: University of Alabama Press, 1947. 208 p.
   The 1861-1865 section of Gorgas' private journal is interesting as a description of his personal sensibility more than a record of battles and events. After twenty years in the Union Army, he became Chief of Ordnance for the Confederacy (April 8, 1861).

1743 Gorman, Tom   1919-
Three and two! As told to Jerome Holtzman. Illustrated. New York: Charles Scribner's Sons, 1979. 216 p. Index.
   Gorman focuses on his short-lived career as a player for a Mexican baseball team and his subsequent decision to become an umpire. He provides amusing tales about baseball players and managers, including Leo Durocher and Casey Stengel.

1744 Gottehrer, Barry H.   1935-
The mayor's man. Garden City, New York: Doubleday & Co., 1975. 326 p. Index.
   New York Mayor Lindsay's right-hand man during the tumultuous late sixties, Gottehrer played a part in the changes made in the city by the administration to meet the challenge of the times.

1745 Gottschalk, Louis Moreau   1829-1869
Notes of a pianist. Edited with a prelude, a postlude, and explanatory notes by Jeanne Behrend. New York: Da Capo Press, 1979. (Philadelphia: J.B. Lippincott & Co., 1881) 420 p. Index.
   An American concert pianist and musician conscious of his role as cultural ambassador, Gottschalk traveled widely in the United States, Latin America, and Europe. His journal teems with observations of people of many different cultures and social levels and with comments on politics, industrial progress, and problems of his era.

1746 Gough, John Bartholomew   1817-1886
Sunlight and shadow; or gleanings from life work. Comprising personal experiences and opinions, anecdotes, incidents, and reminiscences, gathered from 37 years experience on the platform and among the people. Hartford, Connecticut: A.D. Worthington and Co., 1882. 542 p.
   These reminiscences of a temperance lecturer lean heavily on little moral sermons illustrated by anecdotes and personal experiences. Chapters include discussions of "War with vice," "Society's curse," and "Footprints of rum—stories of ruined homes and broken hearts."

1747 *Gould, Beatrice Blackmar
   see **Gould, Bruce**

1748 Gould, Bruce   **1898-**
American story; memories and reflections of Bruce Gould and Beatrice Blackmar Gould. And Beatrice Blackmar Gould. New York: Harper & Row, Publishers, 1968. 330 p.

The remarkable story of a Midwestern couple who became joint editors of the *Ladies' Home Journal* during the Twenties, sharing a rich and cheerful life amid their interesting contemporaries.

1749 Gould, Charles Newton   **1868-1949**
Covered wagon geologist. Edited by B.W. Beebe. Norman: University of Oklahoma Press, 1959. 282 p.

A lively, vivid account of Gould's career as a geologist in Oklahoma, a professor at the University of Oklahoma, consultant to oil companies, director of the Oklahoma Geological Survey, and state geologist. Gould, who was reared in a log cabin and sod house, explored rocky sites by mule and covered wagon, met Indians and colorful prospectors as well as eminent geologists, and wrote widely.

1750 Gould, Franklin Farrar   **1885-1966**
A Maine man in the making. New York: Harper and Brothers Publishers, 1949. 212 p.

A tale of growing up on a farm in Maine with his father, a strong, wise man. After a brief time working outside the state, the author returns to Maine to stay.

1751 Gould, John   **1908-**
And one to grow on: recollections of a Maine boyhood. With drawings by F. Wenderoth Saunders. New York: William Morrow & Co., Publishers, 1949. 253 p.

An easy-going narrative about his childhood in rural Maine which captures the character of time and place with droll humor.

1752 Gould, John   **1908-**
This trifling distinction: reminiscences from Down East. Boston: Little, Brown, 1978. 211 p.

Asserting that all citizens of Maine are either authors or characters, Gould portrays a rainbow of local color in personal vignettes. Each chapter centers on the individuality and essential goodness of one person. As he says, people from out of state just love to hear how rugged Maine life is, especially "in January, about seed-catalogue time."

1753 Gould, Milton Samuel   **1909-**
The witness who spoke with God: and other tales from the courthouse. New York: The Viking Press, 1979. 309 p. Index.

Gould, one of America's leading criminal lawyers, focuses his forensic skills on the New York State Court System, in which he practices. He concentrates both praise and satire on judges and lawyers he has known.

1754 Gould, Ralph Ernest   **1870-1954**
Yankee boyhood: my adventures on a Maine farm seventy years ago. New York: W.W. Norton and Co., Inc., 1950. 251 p.

Recollections of the harshness poverty imposed in his boyhood on a farm in Maine during the late nineteenth century, by the oldest child in a large family. With Yankee integrity he includes many redeeming features of his youth.

1755 Gould, Ralph Ernest   **1870-1954**
Yankee drummer. New York: McGraw-Hill Book Co., Inc., 1947. 236 p.

A drummer (traveling salesman) tells marvelous tales of his experiences traveling through New England selling plows, manure spreaders, and other farm machinery.

1756 Gould, Ralph Ernest   **1870-1954**
Yankee storekeeper. New York: Whittlesey House, 1946. 195 p.

Life of a country storekeeper in Somerset County, Maine, for four decades.

1757 Goulet, Emil Oliver   **1900-**
Rugged years on the Alaska frontier. Philadelphia: Dorrance and Co., 1949. 304 p.

Description of his sixteen years in Alaska, beginning in the early Depression and ending after World War II, by a man who kept careful records of the events and people he encountered while working and prospecting throughout the territory.

1758 Gowdy, Curt   **1919-**
Cowboy at the mike. With Al Hirshberg. Garden City, New York: Doubleday & Co., Inc., 1966. 213 p.

When a back ailment precluded a career as an athlete, Gowdy began broadcasting sporting events and became one of the most versatile of sports commentators. He covered baseball, "The Game of the Week," All-Star Games, the World Series, the Olympic Games, and is known to millions of fans.

1759 Grace, Richard (Dick) Virgil   **1898-**
Visibility unlimited. New York: Longmans, Green and Co., 1950. 276 p.

Recollections of thirty years of adventure as an aviator and stuntman by a pilot who served on active duty in both World Wars.

1760 Grady, Billy   **1890-**
Irish peacock; the confessions of a legendary talent agent. New Rochelle, New York: Arlington House, 1972. 288 p. Index.

Grady was an agent for many famous stars of stage and screen in the heydays of the business. His book is well-written, interesting in its straightforward descriptions of his clients and the times, and void of the usual slick, snappy language of similar writers.

1761 Graham, Andrew J.   **b.1854**
Autobiographical notes, verses and other writings. Second edition. Charles River, Massachusetts: The Runnymede Co., 1938. (1936) 265 p. Index.

The life and work of an Episcopal minister who became a Christian Scientist during the late-nineteenth and early-twentieth centuries in Ohio, Massachusetts, Nebraska, Minnesota, and Rochester, New York.

1762 *Graham, Elinor (Mish)   **1906-**
Maine charm string. New York: The Macmillan Company, 1946. 231 p.

A curious view of her life in rural Maine described through a series of stories and events relating to her hobby, collecting antique buttons.

1763 *Graham, Elinor (Mish)   **1906-**
My window looks Down East. New York: The Macmillan Co., 1951. 218 p.

Thoughtful reminiscences about her experiences living fifteen years on a rural coast of Maine with her husband and young daughter, including her appreciation of natural life and neighbors.

1764 *Graham, Elinor (Mish)   **1906-**
Our way Down East. New York: The Macmillan Co., 1943. 173 p.

In 1934 they bought a farm in Maine, where they lived for many years. This book, the first of several she wrote about country life, tells of their first eight years on the farm, getting acquainted with the land, the people, and country ways.

1765 *Graham, Martha   **1893-**
The notebooks of Martha Graham. Introduction by Nancy Wilson Ross. Illustrated. New York: Harcourt Brace Jovanovich, 1973. 464 p.

Dancer, choreographer, and teacher, Graham is regarded as the greatest single influence on modern dance. These notebooks contain brief memos ranging from symbolism and classic mythology to legends from many lands and times. Notes for creative interpretations in dance form show some of the evolution of her ideas.

1766 *Graham, Morrow   **1892-**
They call me Mother Graham. Illustrated. Old Tappan, New Jersey: Fleming H. Revell Co., 1977. 64 p.

The mother of evangelist Billy Graham tells of her up-bringing near Charlotte, North Carolina, her forty-year marriage to Frank Graham, and her mothering of four children, focusing on Billy's religious experience at fourteen, his education at Florida Bible College and Wheaton, and his evangelistic career. The book, intended to be inspirational, is filled with Bible passages, homilies, and pious reflections.

1767 Graham, Robin Lee   **1949?-**
The boy who sailed around the world alone. With Derek L.G. Gill. Illustrated. New York: Golden Press, 1973. 140 p.

In 1965 he started sailing around the world; he completed his journey in five years. Here he tells the story of learning to sail at age ten, sailing the South Seas with his family for a year, and the fascinating, courageous experience of his solo trip. He stopped at length in various ports to rest, to repair his boat, to marry, and to honeymoon, before returning to his home and starting point in Los Angeles.

1768 Graham, Robin Lee   **1949?-**
Dove. With Derek L.T. Gill. New York: Harper & Row, 1972. 199 p.

In 1965 at age sixteen, Graham set sail on his 24-foot sloop *Dove*. Five years and 33,000 miles later he had circumnavigated the globe, weathered tropical storms, lost his mast, battled loneliness, but met and married a girl who was also looking for a different kind of life and adventure. Numerous color photographs.

1769 *Graham, Sheilah   **1908?-**
Beloved infidel: the education of a woman. And Gerold Frank. New York: Henry Holt and Co., 1958. 338 p.

The story of her difficult childhood in London, her early success as a chorus girl, her move to New York and Hollywood as a celebrity columnist, and her three-year romance with F. Scott Fitzgerald.

1770 *Graham, Sheilah   **1908?-**
College of one. New York: The Viking Press, 1967. 245 p.

In the years just before he died, F. Scott Fitzgerald devised and supervised a unique two-year liberal arts course for Sheilah Graham. Here she tells the interesting story of this educational experiment and includes reproductions of the original curriculum typescript sheets.

1771 *Graham, Sheilah   **1908?-**
The rest of the story. New York: Coward-McCann, 1964. 304 p.
From 1941 to 1963 she recovered from Fitzgerald's death, became a war correspondent in London, married twice, raised two children, and had her own radio and television shows.

1772 *Graham, Sheilah   **1908?-**
Scratch an actor: confessions of a Hollywood columnist. London: Mayflower Books Ltd., 1970. 268 p.
Primarily a book of Hollywood gossip, her book represents, she says, the *danse macabre* of the film world, the illusion of fame and glitter which, when it vanishes, leaves nothing.

1773 *Graham, Sheilah   **1908?-**
State of heat. New York: W.H. Allen, 1973. (London: Grosset & Dunlap, 1972) 223 p.
Written in the tone suggested by the title, her book is an argument for the power of sex in a successful life, which she demonstrates by descriptions of her own sexual tastes and exploits.

1774 *Graham, Sheilah, pseud. (Shiel, Lily)   **1908?-**
The late Lily Shiel. Illustrated. New York: Grosset & Dunlap, 1978. 223 p.
At six, cockney Lily Shiel was placed in a Jewish orphanage by her ailing mother; there she stayed until she was fourteen. Although she was the brightest and most energetic of the orphans, a male relative prevented her from applying for a scholarship and insisted that she go to work as a housemaid. Through her personal attractiveness, grit, and enterprise, Lily obtained progressively more attractive jobs. She fell in love with her employer and married him at nineteen, over the objections of Monty Collins, her millionaire fiancé whom she did not love.

1775 Grange, Harold (Red) Edward   **1903-**
Red Grange story: the autobiography of Red Grange. As told to Ira Morton. Foreword by Robert C. Zuppke. New York: G.P. Putnam's sons, 1953. 178 p.
A football player writes about his athletic career, emphasizing his experience at the University of Illinois, in professional football, and in film.

1776 Granlund, Nils Thor   **1894-1957**
Blondes, brunettes, and bullets. With Sid Feder and Ralph Hancock. New York: David McKay, 1957. 300 p.
"Granny" relates anecdotes about his career as a publicist and producer of vaudeville and night club shows before, during, and after Prohibition. The Silver Slipper was his best known club. He chats about a variety of entertainers, especially beautiful women such as Hilda Ferguson, Jean Harlow, and Lucille Ball.

1777 Grant, Daniel T.   **1914-**
When the melon is ripe: the autobiography of a Georgia Negro high school principal and minister. New York: Exposition Press, 1955. 174 p.
A bitter, defensive narrative by a Black principal of several high schools in Georgia. He was often at odds with the local white citizens because he encouraged social and academic racial intermingling in a highly segregationist region. Unjustly accused of sex crimes, his job and life were often threatened.

1778 *Grant, Dorothy (Fremont)   **1900-**
Born again. Milwaukee: The Bruce Publishing Co., 1950. 254 p.
Written in response to public reaction to her first autobiographical account of her conversion to Catholicism, here she argues the importance of faith as a power to change life.

1779 *Grant, Julia (Dent)   **1826-1902**
The personal memoirs of Julia Dent Grant (Mrs. Ulysses S. Grant). New York: G.P. Putnam's Sons, 1975. 346 p.
Mrs. Grant's story spans her life from childhood through the Civil War, the White House years, and up to the death of her husband.

1780 Grant, Ulysses Simpson   **1822-1885**
General Grant's letters to a friend 1861-1880. Introduction and notes by James Grant Wilson. New York: AMS Press, 1973. (New York: Crowell, 1897) 132 p. Index.
These letters to his friend Elihu Washburne, Illinois congressman and later American representative in France, were written from famous battlefields, from the White House, and from around the world during Grant's extended tour. They contain Grant's views on men and affairs in America and foreign lands, particularly on British rule in India and on the Japanese.

1781 Grant, Ulysses Simpson   **1822-1885**
Mr. Lincoln's general: U.S. Grant, an illustrated autobiography. Edited by Roy Meredith. New York: E.P. Dutton And Co., Inc., 1959. 252 p. Index.

Over 300 illustrations selected by the editor to match major extracts from Grant's outstanding autobiography, originally published in its entirety in 1885-86.

1782 Grant, Ulysses Simpson   **1822-1885**
The papers of Ulysses S. Grant. Edited by John Y. Simon. Illustrated. Carbondale: Southern Illinois University Press, 1967-. v. Index.
After 1843 when he graduated from West Point, Grant served in the U.S. Army until he was elected President in 1868. Named General of Union Armies in the West in 1863, he was put in command of all Union armies five months later and accepted Lee's surrender April 9, 1865. After two terms as President, he retired, traveled extensively, ran unsuccessfully for a third nomination as Republican candidate in 1880, and wrote his Memoirs, the royalties from which saved his family from poverty after his death.

1783 Grant, Ulysses Simpson   **1822-1885**
Personal memoirs of U.S. Grant. Edited with notes and introduction by E.B. Long. New York: AMS Press, 1972. (New York: C.L. Webster, 1885-86) 666 p. Index.
In a careful account of his life up to the end of the Civil War, the general, writing the year before his death, tells his story as an ordinary man.

1784 Grant, Ulysses Simpson   **1822-1885**
Personal memoirs of U.S. Grant: a modern abridgment. Introduction by Philip Van Doren Stern. Gloucester, Massachusetts: Peter Smith, 1969. (Greenwich, Connecticut: Fawcett Pubs., 1962) 464 p. Index.
This is an abridgment of the factual, moving account of Grant's life. Although he eventually became U.S. president, this book focuses on the Civil War and provides detailed accounts of the battles, campaigns, and personalities involved, including most of the prominent Civil War generals, Northern and Southern. Mark Twain suggested that Grant write this book to help pay his enormous debts; indeed, the book did become a posthumous bestseller.

1785 Gray, Charles Glass   **b.1820**
Off at sunrise: the overland journal of Charles Gray. Edited with introduction by Thomas D. Clark. San Marino, California: Huntington Library, 1976. 182 p. Index.
Gray, a young Forty-Niner, records in his journal the 2,498 mile trek from Independence, Missouri, to San Francisco, May 1—November 19, 1849, as a member of the Newark Overland Company. He describes the scenery, the weather, difficulties with the wagons, sickness, wild animals, and appears continually to be drawn by the spirit of adventure, rather than by a lust for the precious metal.

1786 *Gray, Edna
One woman's life, the steppings of faith: Edna Gray's story. Atlanta, Georgia: The Franklin Printing and Publishing Co., 1900. (1898) 352 p.
A novelistic narrative of her marriage to a tyrannical husband and the difficulty she had surviving his cruelty. When she left him, she was ostracized by church and community, but finally recovered her four children and began a new life with them.

1787 Gray, Frank S.   **b.1861**
Pioneer adventures. Cherokee, Texas: J.T. Gray, 1948. 384 p.
Frontier and pioneer life in area of Cherokee, Texas.

1788 Gray, George H.   **1917-**
Sole survivor: the battle of Midway and its effect on his life. Naples, Florida: Naples Ad/Graphics Service, 1979. 230 p.
An ensign in the U.S. Navy aboard an aircraft carrier during the Battle of Midway, he was the only one in his squadron to survive the shots from enemy aircraft, the crash of his own aircraft, and the treacherous ocean which supported him until his miraculous rescue. Text includes photographs.

1789 Gray, Jerry (pseud.)   **1902-**
Third strike. Edited by Glenn Clark, with a foreword by Starr Daily. New York: Abington-Cokesbury Press, 1949. 59 p.
The unfinished diary of a sailor suffering from alcoholism gives a striking impression of his mental anguish prior to suicide.

1790 Gray, Martin   **1925-**
For those I loved. With Max Gallo. Foreword by David Douglas Duncan. Translated from the French by Anthony White. Boston: Little, Brown and Co., 1972. 351 p.
The story of Gray's survival through the Holocaust and annihilation of his people in the ghetto of Warsaw and the "lower camp" at Treblinka. He was later a member of the Resistance, a Soviet Army officer and an importer in New York. After he had established an idyllic life in southern France, fate struck again in the form of a flash forest fire which destroyed his wife and four children. Despite the repeated blows, he struggles to keep going and to fight for the environment through the Dina Gray Foundation.

1791 *Gray, Millie 1800-1851
The diary of Millie Gray, 1832-1840: recording her family life before, during and after Col. Wm. F. Gray's journey to Texas in 1835; and the small journal, giving particulars of all that occurred during the family's voyage to Texas in 1838. Edited by William R. Graham. Illustrated. Houston, Printed in the name of Rosenberg Library Press, Galveston: F. Young Pub. Co., 1967. 158 p.
The diaries kept by the wife of Colonel William Fairfax Gray in Fredericksburg, Virginia, and later in Texas contain glimpses of her nineteenth-century character and everyday personal life. Her description of the ship voyage to Houston is of particular interest.

1792 Grayson, David, pseud.
see Baker, Ray Stannard

1793 Graziano, Rocky 1921-
Somebody up there likes me. With Rowland Barber. New York: Simon and Schuster, 1955. 375 p.
Former middle-weight champion writes of the street life of his New York boyhood, his years in prison, and his hard work for the championship title.

1794 Greco, Jose 1918-
The gypsy in my soul: the autobiography of Jose Greco. With Harvey Ardman. Garden City, New York: Doubleday & Co., Inc., 1977. 279 p. Index.
Dancer and choreographer Greco intermingles accounts of the financial and artistic successes of his flamenco dance company with tales of his multiple marriages and love affairs, often concurrent. His tastes in dancing and beautiful women reinforce the Spanish dancer stereotype he cultivates in this book.

1795 Greeley, Horace 1811-1872
An overland journey: from New York to San Francisco in the summer of 1859. Edited with notes and introduction by Charles T. Duncan. New York: Alfred A. Knopf, 1964. (New York: C.M. Saxton, Barker & Co., 1860) 326 p. Index.
The major purpose of his journey was to explore for himself the Western territories in order better to promote a transcontinental railroad and the development of the West. A magnificent frontier travel book.

1796 Greeley, Horace 1811-1872
Recollections of a busy life. Port Washington, New York: Kennikat Press, 1971. (New York: J.B. Ford and Co., 1868) 624 p.
Originally published in the New York Ledger, these essays describe the life and times of a prominent journalist, with sections on Margaret Fuller, Henry Clay, Abraham Lincoln, Jefferson Davis, the Civil War, socialism, literature, politics.

1797 *Green, Anne 1899-
With much love. New York: Harper and Brothers, 1948. 276 p.
After early childhood in Savannah, Green describes her family life in Paris through 1920, where her father was business agent for an American cottonseed oil company.

1798 Green, Benny 1927-
Drums in my ears; jazz in our time. New York: Horizon Press, 1973. 188 p.
A musician and celebrated jazz critic, the author presents a potpourri of jazz pieces full of the history of the era. He writes from personal experience as well as with critical acumen, for he lived and worked in the jazz clubs himself and knew personally the musicians he describes.

1799 Green, Gerald 1922-
The stones of Zion; a novelist's journal in Israel. New York: Hawthorn Books, Inc., 1971. 386 p. Index.
Every stop on his itinerary in modern Israel reminded Green of biblical events. Friends and guides presented historical and archaeological evidence which enforced or redefined his understanding of the scriptures and brought to life the ancient religious stories.

1800 Green, Paul (Aknik) 1901-
I am Eskimo—Aknik my name. Edited by Abbe Abbott. Juneau: Alaska Northwest Publishing Co., 1959. 86 p.
Written in the style of oral tradition, his book mingles folk tales and hunting lore with his life story among the Alaska Eskimos.

1801 Greenbaum, Everett
The Goldenberg who couldn't dance. New York: Harcourt Brace Jovanovich, 1980. 160 p.
Greenbaum writes about his childhood in Buffalo and his brief career in the Navy, but he focuses mainly on his career as a television writer for shows like Mr. Peepers, Gomer Pyle, and Mash. He discusses Hollywood friends like Wally Cox and Marlon Brando, but the book is also a paean to his friend and co-writer, Jim Fritzell.

1802 Greenberg, David 1943-
Play it to a bust: The Super Cops. New York: Hawthorn Books, Inc., 1975. 247 p.
A controversial policeman in the New York Police Department, the "Batman" of the "Batman and Robin" detective team writes of their work in Bedford-Stuyvesant, the tough Brooklyn ghetto.

1803 Greene, Catherine Ray 1731-1794
see Franklin, Benjamin

1804 Greene, Clarence Wilson b.1873
Life at Greene's Corners. Boston: Meador Publishing Co., 1956. 148 p. Index.
Greene's account of his childhood years at Greene's Corners, Michigan, focuses on children's common experiences such as blackberrying, the village blacksmith, washing and shearing sheep, school, and holidays.

1805 Greene, Edgar C. (Doc Greene) 1920?-1970
Memory collector. Introduction by Bob Considine. Garden City, New York: Doubleday & Co., Inc., 1970. 275 p.
A collection of memories, topical and trivial, from his long experience as a columnist for the Detroit News.

1806 *Greene, Gael 1936-
Don't come back without it. New York: Simon and Schuster, 1960. 214 p.
Greene humorously narrates her first two and a half years as a reporter on the New York Post, including an evening with Elvis Presley, an attempt to lose weight at Slenderella, an exposé of Arthur Murray Dance Studios, and a variety of amorous escapades.

1807 Greene, Nathanael 1742-1786
Papers of General Nathanael Greene. Edited by Richard K. Showman and others. Illustrated. Chapel Hill: University of North Carolina Press, 1980. 2v. Index.
Volume I details the significant part he played in the triumph at Trenton as general in Washington's army. Volume II follows his career from the battles of Brandywine and Germantown in 1777 through his joining Washington at Fredericksburg. N.Y. in Oct. 1778. His letters lend insight into the economic and political history of the time.

1808 Greene, Robert W. 1911-
Calvary in China. New York: G.P. Putnam's Sons, 1953. 244 p.
A Catholic missionary priest tells of his treatment, imprisonment, and deportation while in China between the years 1949-52 when the communists took over the country.

1809 *Greene, Ruth Altman 1896-
Hsiang-Ya journal. Foreword by James C. Thomson. Hamden, Connecticut: Archon Books for The Yale China Association, 1977. 171 p. Index.
A missionary analyzes the "war-to-the-death conflict of ideas between the forces of Chiang Kai-shek and the forces of Communism" which she and her medical missionary husband, Phil, experienced during the 1920's-40's as representatives of the Yale-in-China Missionary Program in various mid-Chinese provinces. Much of her moving account is derived from letters.

1810 Greene, Warwick 1879-1929
Letters of Warwick Greene: 1915-1928. Edited by Richard W. Hale. Freeport, New York: Books for Libraries Press, 1971. (Boston: Houghton Mifflin Co., 1931) 309 p. Index.
From 1910 to 1915 he was director of the Bureau of Public Works in Manila. He was with the American Red Cross in France, and after serving in several significant positions during World War I, he was discharged in 1919 as a lieutenant colonel. He later became president of the New England Oil Refining Company. His letters focus primarily on political events during and after the war.

1811 Greenfeld, Josh
A child called Noah; a family journey. New York: Holt, Rinehart and Winston, 1972. 193 p.
The painful diary of a family through the first five years in the life of their autistic child Noah. Although at first Noah seemed completely normal, by the time he was two and a half, he could not perform simple tasks or communicate. His parents and his brother had to find ways to cope with their despair and his autistic condition.

1812 *Greenman, Frances Cranmer 1890-
Higher than the sky. Illustrated by Frances Cranmer Greenman. New York: Harper & Bros., 1954. 305 p.
In an evocative, perceptive, entertaining autobiography, Greenman narrates her upbringing in rural South Dakota as a daughter of a dynamic suffragist mother and understanding father. She received art training at Washington, D.C.'s Corcoran Gallery, traveled throughout Europe painting, married and lived the good life in New York City until her husband went broke in the Depression. Thereafter, she traveled over the United States, painting portraits of the famous, the infamous, the rich and the vain, and had a wonderful time on her own forthright terms.

1813 Greenough, Horatio (Horace Bender, pseud.)   1805-1852
Letters of Horatio Greenough: American sculptor. Madison: The University of Wisconsin Press, 1972. 456 p. Index.

In addition to family letters, this collection includes many to artists and architects known by Greenough, America's first sculptor. Among other projects, he was commissioned to do two sculptural groups for the National Capitol. Robert Gilmor, Jr., who designed the Washington Monument, was his patron.

1814 Greenough, Horatio (Horace Bender, pseud.)   1805-1852
Letters of Horatio Greenough to his brother, Henry Greenough. Edited by Frances B. Greenough. New York: AMS Press, 1973. (Boston: Ticknor and Co., 1887) 250 p.

A reprint of the edition originally published by the sister-in-law of America's first sculptor.

1815 Greenspun, Herman Milton   1909-
Where I stand: the record of a reckless man. With Alex Pelle. New York: David McKay Co., Inc., 1966. 304 p.

An editor often at the center of controversy, the author has fought against corruption and the abridgement of freedom taking on such adversaries as Senator Pat McCarran, columnist Westbrook Pegler, and Senator Joe McCarthy. His activities in behalf of Israel ran him afoul of the U.S. Neutrality Act and his feuds involved him in libel suits which he always won.

1816 *Greenwood, Grace, pseud.
see *Lippincott, Sara Jane (Clarke)

1817 Greer, Howard   1896-1974
Designing male. New York: G.P. Putnam's Sons, 1949. 310 p.

An account of his younger life, primarily in Paris and New York after World War I, and Hollywood during the Twenties, by a custom dress designer who started out as a Nebraska farm boy wanting to be a writer. Numerous anecdotes about royalty, socialites, theater, and movie personalities reflect his attraction to the "right" people and places.

1818 *Gregg, Elinor D.
The Indians and the nurse. Norman: University of Oklahoma Press, 1965. 173 p.

From 1922 to 1924 Miss Gregg was nurse on the Rosebud and Pine Ridge Sioux Indian reservations, after which she became supervisor of nursing for the Indian Service in Washington, D.C. During the next dozen years she recruited public health nurses and made field trips to the Southwest, North, and other areas organizing and improving health service for the Indians.

1819 Gregg, Josiah   1806-1850?
Diary and letters of Josiah Gregg. Edited by Maurice Garland Fulton. Norman: University of Oklahoma, 1941-44. 2v. Index.

Gregg, a Santa Fe trader, knew the central plains, the Plains Indians, and the Mexicans during the 1830's, and wrote the classic *Commerce of the Prairies*. These letters and diary entries concern his experiences after 1840 when he traveled more and took part in the Mexican War. Volume I: Southwestern enterprises, 1820-1847; Volume II: Excursions in Mexico & California, 1847-1850.

1820 Gregory, Dick   1932-
Nigger: an autobiography. With Robert Lipsyte. New York: E.P. Dutton & Co., Inc., 1964. 224 p.

The compelling story of Gregory's youth and continuing fight against racial prejudice and poverty. He writes of his successes in high school and college bands and athletics, his recognition as an entertainer, and his deep involvement in the cause of civil rights in Chicago, Birmingham, Jackson, and Selma.

1821 Gregory, Horace   1898-
The house on Jefferson Street; a cycle of memoirs. New York: Holt, Rinehart and Winston, 1971. 276 p. Index.

Gregory recaptures a vanishing era in a spiritual journey from his grandfather's house in Milwaukee through the literary worlds of Chicago, New York, and London to his ancestral Irish heritage. He met other poets and writers on his quest for identity and describes here those meetings and the literary atmosphere of the times, particularly the Thirties.

1822 Gresens, Harold
Just call me Doc! Fifty years as a pharmacist. New York: Vantage Press, 1977. 95 p.

The author recalls everyday events he observed while working behind the counter as a pharmacist.

1823 Grew, Joseph Clark   1880-1965
Ten years in Japan: a contemporary record drawn from the diaries and private and official papers of Joseph C. Grew. New York: Arno Press, 1972. (New York: Simon & Schuster, 1944) 554 p. Index.

An ambassador to Japan from 1932 until the attack on Pearl Harbor, Grew witnessed a series of crises in the internal and external affairs of Japan. His diary follows the progress of Japan's drive for world power from his unique vantage point.

1824 Grew, Joseph Clark   1880-1965
Turbulent era: a diplomatic record of forty years, 1904-1945. Edited by Walter Johnson. Assisted by Nancy Harvison Hooker. Freeport, New York: Books for Libraries Press, 1970. (Boston: Houghton Mifflin, 1952) 2v. Index.

The books contain the recollections, letters, and diaries of an American diplomat's forty years in the foreign service. Because he served in Berlin at the outbreak of World War I and was Ambassador to Japan just before World War II, these books contain close personal accounts of both wars.

1825 Grierson, Francis (Benjamin Henry Jesse Francis Shepard) 1848-1927
Valley of shadows. Boston: Houghton Mifflin Co., 1948. 278 p.

An outstanding account of his early life in Illinois and Missouri (1858-1863) that perceptively anticipates the effects of the inevitable war.

1826 Griffen, John Howard   1920-
Black like me: with a new epilogue by the author. Boston: Houghton Mifflin & Co., 1977. (1961) 208 p.

Through the use of skin dyes, Griffen masqueraded as a Black man in the Deep South, where he encountered the fear, prejudice, and hatred whites have for Blacks. He writes compassionately of the Southern Black experience in the latter part of 1959.

1827 Griffin, Archie   1954-
Archie: the Archie Griffin story. With Dave Diles. Garden City, New York: Doubleday & Co., Inc., 1977. 192 p.

This as-told-to narrative is a mixture of biography and autobiography, for the ghostwriter interjects considerable adulation of Griffin. The book emphasizes Griffin's athletic career at Eastmoor High School (Columbus, Ohio), his football career at Ohio State University where he won the Heisman Trophy in 1974 and 1975, and his family whose motto is "work hard, play whenever you can, love without ceasing, and respect everyone."

1828 Griffis, Stanton   1887-1974
Lying in state. Garden City, New York: Doubleday, 1952. 315 p.

A businessman and diplomat relates his career in business, his World War II experiences in Finland and the Pacific, and finally his postwar diplomatic missions to such countries as Poland, Egypt, Argentina, and Spain.

1829 *Griffith, Corinne   1906-1979
Papa's delicate condition. Boston: Houghton Mifflin Co., 1952. 178 p.

Describes her early affection for her father during his fight with alcoholism, which eventually made family reconciliation possible. Interesting description of small-circus people and customs.

1830 *Griffith, Corinne   1906-1979
This you won't believe. New York: Frederick Fell, Inc., 1972. 115 p.

Light, chatty stories of her earlier years of fame and glamour as a Hollywood star.

1831 Griffith, David Wark   1875-1948
The man who invented Hollywood; the autobiography. Edited with annotations by James Hart. Louisville, Kentucky: Touchstone Publishing Co., 1972. 170 p.

The unfinished autobiography of movie pioneer Griffith is presented as originally dictated. Also included are biographical notes and many photographs of movies, movie-making, and movie actors from the Golden Age of Hollywood.

1832 Griffith, George P.   1902-
Life and adventures of Revenooer No. 1. Illustrated. Birmingham, Alabama: Gander Publishers, 1975. 288 p.

Griffith, a lawyer by training and an Internal Revenue Service agent, Alcohol and Tax Division, for 35 years, has written an account of his experiences trying to capture moonshiners, primarily in the South. Proud of the large numbers of successful raids and prosecutions he conducted, Griffith was indignant over other "revenooers" who let their quarry go free on technicalities so they could keep their jobs.

1833 Griffith, Thomas   1915-
Waist-high culture. New York: Harper and Brothers, 1959. 275 p.

A philosophical analysis of his childhood, his college years, his early days as a journalist in Seattle, then at Time-Life, gradually moves into a discussion of the ideals of political systems and a criticism of American culture.

1834 Grigsby, Hugh Blair   1806-1881
see Randall, Henry Stephens

1835 Grimes, Martin   1918-
Turnip greens and sergeant stripes. New Rochelle, New York: Arlington House, 1972. 272 p.

Written in Southern dialect, with a glossary included, his book is a down-home memoir of rural life in Alabama and his service on the Japanese front during World War II.

1836 *Grimke, Sarah Moore   **1792-1873**
Letters on equality of the sexes, and the condition of woman, addressed to Mary S. Parker. New York: Burt Franklin, 1970. (Boston: I. Knapp, 1838) 128 p.

Fifteen letters written in 1837 by a now famous feminist discuss the conditions of women in America, Europe, Asia, and Africa. Some argue the right of women to be ministers; one notes that Adam was as responsible as Eve for the fall of man.

1837 Grimm, Charles John   **1898-**
Jolly Cholly's story: baseball, I love you! With Ed Prell. Introduction by Bill Veeck. Chicago: Henry Regnery Co., 1968. 242 p.

One of the great characters of baseball history writes of his experience as a player or manager of the Philadelphia Athletics, the St. Louis Cardinals, the Pittsburgh Pirates, the Chicago Cubs, the Milwaukee Brewers and Braves.

1838 Grimm, Herman   **1828-1921**
see **Emerson, Ralph Waldo**

1839 Griscom, George L.   **1837-1901**
Fighting with Ross' Texas Cavalry Brigade, C.S.A.; the diary of George L. Griscom, adjutant, 9th Texas Cavalry Regiment. Edited by Homer L. Kerr. Illustrated. Introduction by Harold B. Simpson. Hillsboro, Texas: Hill Jr. College Press, 1976. 255 p.

Griscom became Adjutant of a Confederate Texas regiment, Company D; he reports on its efforts from 1862 to 1865 in cryptic diary entries.

1840 Grisham, Noel   **1916-**
Beyond the schoolhouse. San Antonio, Texas: The Naylor Co. 1974. 118 p.

A school superintendent's background offers perspectives on his efforts and philosophy of education. He compares his own development with the current conditions and attitudes, concluding that many youths today lack the kind of experiences which generate a better outlook.

1841 Griswold, Thomas   **1870-1967**
Time of my life. Introduction by Arthur E. Turner. Midland, Michigan: Northwood Institute, 1973. 201 p.

Griswold, a chemical engineer, married the daughter of J.H. Dow and spent his entire career at the Dow Chemical Company in Midland, Michigan. He discusses a number of chemical processes he developed and devotes half the book to advice for successful living: hard work and wisdom equal health and wealth.

1842 Groosman, Edwina Booth
see **Booth, Edwin Thomas**

1843 Gross, Benjamin Samuel   **1891-1979**
I looked and listened: informal recollections of radio and television. New Rochelle, New York: Arlington House, 1970. (New York: Random House, 1954) 334 p. Index.

A newspaper columnist in New York City describes the early days of radio and television broadcasting as he saw it.

1844 Gross, Fred William   **1896-**
The pastor: the life of an immigrant. Philadelphia: Dorrance & Co., 1973. 182 p.

An immigrant from Russia started his new life in North Dakota and eventually became a clergyman. His parishes, his missionary work, and counseling occupied his life in the United States and abroad, where he experienced Nazi attacks during the early Hitler era.

1845 Grosz, George   **1893-1959**
His life and work. Edited by Uwe M. Schneede with contributions by Georg Bussman and Maria Schneede-Szcesny. Translated by Susanne Flatauer. Illustrated. New York: Universe Books, 1979. 182 p. Index.

This comprehensive volume presents a chronological view of Grosz's drawings and paintings, accompanied by interpretive biographical and autobiographical commentary. In 1933, disgusted with German Fascism and captivated by America, Grosz immigrated to New York, where he lived until he died in 1959. In contrast to the Dadaistic and satiric styles of his earlier works, his American art became more realistic and serene.

1846 Grosz, George   **1893-1959**
A little yes and a big no: the autobiography of George Grosz. Illustrated by the author. Translated by Lola Sachs Dorin. New York: The Dial Press, 1946. 343 p.

A famous painter and cartoonist writes of his early life and career in Germany, his early awareness of the Holocaust, his immigration to the United States. A beautiful, sensitive, and frightening narrative.

1847 *Gruber, Ruth   **1911-**
I went to the Soviet Arctic. New York: The Viking Press, 1944. (New York: Simon and Schuster, 1939) 333 p.

The author set out to find out for the Herald-Tribune syndicate about the status of women in the Soviet Union. She discovered much about the people of the Soviet Arctic and the newly developed areas of that country through her interviews and meetings, especially with women pioneers.

1848 Gruen, John   **1926-**
The party's over now; reminiscences of the Fifties—New York's artists, writers, musicians, and their friends. New York: The Viking Press, 1972. 282 p. Index.

An active participant in New York art circles during the 1950's, Gruen reconstructs the activities of avant-garde painters, poets, writers, composers, critics, and gallery chiefs who made the New York cultural "scene" so dazzling and outrageous.

1849 Gruening, Ernest   **1887-1974**
Many battles; the autobiography of Ernest Gruening. New York: Liveright, 1973. 564 p. Index.

The battles were fought during his sixty-year career as a journalist, editor, public official, governor and senator of Alaska. A strong opponent of the Vietnam War and the draft, he and Wayne Morse were the only senators to vote against the Tonkin Gulf Resolution. His is the story of an energetic, productive life.

1850 Gue, Benjamin F.   **1828-1904**
Diary of Benjamin F. Gue in rural New York and pioneer Iowa, 1847-1856. Edited by Earl D. Ross. Ames: Iowa State University Press, 1962. 137 p.

As a young man, he and his brother bought farm land in Iowa and successfully established themselves as respected citizens. Later, he was a state senator, influential in the founding of the State Agricultural College, and then a journalist, owner and editor of the *Iowa North West* of Fort Dodge.

1851 Guerard, Albert Joseph   **1914-**
Touch of time: myth, memory, and the self. Illustrated. Stanford, California: Stanford Alumni Associations, 1980. 195 p.

Novelist, literary critic, and literature professor Guerard reflects on his much traveled youth, wartime experiences in France, the world of literary thought, and his French-American heritage in a series of connected essays. Student and teacher of many notable writers and scholars at Harvard and Stanford, Guerard describes his memoirs as "meditations on remembered experience and the creation of personal fictions and myths."

1852 Guerard, Albert Leon   **1880-1959**
Personal equation. New York: W.W. Norton & Co., 1948. 317 p.

Educated in France and England, he taught at American colleges and universities across the country and became unshakably Americanized.

1853 *Guerin, Elsa Jane
Mountain Charley: or, The adventures of Mrs. E.J. Guerin, who was thirteen years in male attire; an autobiography. Introduction by Fred W. Mazzulla and William Kostka. Western Frontier Library, New ed. Norman: University of Oklahoma Press, 1968. (Dubuque, Iowa: The Author, 1861) 112 p.

An intriguing story of a woman who, dressed as a male, went on a wagon trek to California in 1855, prospected for gold at Pikes Peak in 1859, ran a saloon in Denver, and enjoyed her freedom from the repressions most women endured. Other stories appeared in periodicals of the day about characters called "Mountain Charley" who may or may not have been the same person. This volume includes the story by General George West, publisher of the Golden, Colorado, *Colorado Transcript,* of Mountain Charley as he knew her.

1854 *Guffy, Ossie   **1931-**
Ossie: the autobiography of a Black woman. As told to Caryl Ledner. New York: W.W. Norton & Co., 1971. 224 p.

Because she feels herself to be more representative of Blacks in America than the bright, militant, or talented Blacks who make the news, Ossie Guffy writes about her life and work fighting against discrimination, poverty, and ignorance. She recognizes that most whites are not like Richard Nixon or George Wallace, just as most Blacks are not like Ralph Bunche or Rap Brown—most are ordinary people who need to get to know and understand each other better.

1855 *Guggenheim, Marguerite   **1898-1979**
Confessions of an art addict. New York: The Macmillan Co., 1960. 175 p. Index.

A woman of great wealth and influence in the world of modern art describes her "gilded" childhood, early unhappy marriages, and her evolution as a gallery owner, patron and promoter of many modern artists since the 1920's.

1856 *Guggenheim, Marguerite   **1898-1979**
Out of this century: the informal memoirs of Peggy Guggenheim. New York: Universe Books, 1979. (New York: The Dial Press, 1946) 396 p.

Very personal, informal description of a wealthy woman whose patronage of the arts helped balance her rather shapeless, eccentric life.

1857 *Guidry, Sister Mary Gabriella   1914-
The Southern Negro nun: an autobiography. New York: Exposition Press, 1974. 156 p.
The writer is a member of a religious congregation of Black nuns in the South who work in education and human relations. The Congregation of the Sisters of the Holy Family sent her to several assignments in Texas, to British Honduras, and to New Orleans, where she worked in schools as a teacher and principal.

1858 *Guild, Caroline
Rainbow in Tahiti. Foreword by James Norman Hal. Garden City, New York: Doubleday and Co., Inc., 1948. 253 p.
Describes new life she established with her husband on ten acres in Tahiti, 1923-1940, a kind of paradise regained by a pair of Bostonians, with a sense of humor about cultural conflicts.

1859 *Guiney, Louise Imogen   1861-1920
Letters of Louise Imogen Guiney. Edited by Grace Guiney. New York: Harper Brothers, 1926. 2v.
The author took much pleasure from writing letters, a form of literary composition through which she could express her free spirit, comment on public figures and events, give critical verdicts, and communicate with sympathetic friends about her life, her experiences, her poetry.

1860 Gunther, John   1901-1970
Death be not proud. New York: Harper and Brothers, 1971. (1949) 264 p.
A moving account of his son's illness and death from a malignant brain tumor, including the son's letters and diary, a comment by the wife and mother, and a connecting narrative by the author.

1861 Gurnee, Russell   1923?-
Discovery at the Rio Camuy. And Jeanne F. Gurnee. Illustrated. New York: Crown Publishers, Inc. 1974. 183 p. Index,.
A caving enthusiast, Gurnee writes of his exploration of the Rio Camuy cave in Puerto Rico, supported by the National Speleological Society and the National Geographic Society.

1862 Gurtov, Melvin   1942-
Making changes: the politics of self liberation. Oakland, California: Harvest Moon Books, 1979. 203 p.
Gurtov describes his metamorphosis from a stereotypic Brooklyn Jew oriented to success (which he found for a time at the Rand Corporation think-tank) and from a conventional marriage to a subservient wife, to a communal humanist and free-thinking political science professor at the University of California. Although he praises group living, egalitarian friendships with both men and women, vegetarianism, and interpersonal understanding, his self-absorbed focus makes him seem less of an individual than a stereotypic southern Californian of the 1970's.

1863 Gustafson, Walter   1915-
My time in the army: the diary of a World War II soldier. Illustrated. Chicago: Adams Press, 1968. 182 p.
Private First Class Gustafson, a mailman who performed the same functions in the U.S. Army from September 1942, to February 1945, uses a diary and letters he wrote during this time to provide an account of the minutiae of army life. He served in the United States until April 1945, when he was transferred to Germany. He was a draftee who was not an enthusiastic soldier but was "resigned to army life and tried to make the best of it."

1864 *Gustaitis, Rasa   1934-
Turning on. New York: The Macmillan Co., 1969. (1968) 326 p.
Seeking to learn more about being "turned on" without drugs, the author explored various consciousness-expanding experiments: Esalen Institute, Zen, Sadhana, Rolfing, and others. She defines being turned on as "to be fully present at whatever one is in at a particular moment and ready to accept the next moment, whatever it might bring."

1865 Gustorf, Frederick Julius   1800-1845
The uncorrupted heart: journal and letters of Frederick Julius Gustorf, 1800-1845. Edited with introduction and notes by Fred Gustorf. Translated from German by Fred Gustorf and Gisela Gustorf. Columbia: University of Missouri Press, 1969. 182 p. Index.
Naturalized a U.S. citizen in September 1834, during the following spring and summer German-born Gustorf undertook a journey from Philadelphia to St. Louis to inspect the German immigrant colonies in Illinois and Missouri. His travel journal provides a rich and varied record of the people and places he visited.

1866 Guthrie, Alfred Bertram, Jr.   1901-
Blue hen's chick: a life in context. New York: McGraw-Hill Book Co., 1965. 164 p.
A nostalgic story of his youth in Montana, followed by college days, newspaper work in Kentucky, his Nieman Fellowship days at Harvard,

and eventual return to Montana. His love for the land, particularly for Montana and the West, and his closeness to nature are evident here as in his novels.

1867 Guthrie, Woody (Woodrow Wilson Guthrie)   1912-1967
Bound for glory. Illustrated with sketches by the author. Introduction by Studs Terkel. Reprint of 1943 edition. New York: E.P. Dutton, 1976. (1943) 426 p.
Born in Oklahoma, Guthrie went west much like the characters in The Grapes of Wrath, riding the rails and singing songs in saloons to earn money. The book is a tribute to the grit and goodness of America's plain people, including migrant workers and manual laborers. Of his music Guthrie says, "a song, you sing it out, and it soaks in people's ears and they all jump up and down and sing it with you, and then when you quit singing it, it's gone, and you get a job singing it again."

1868 Guthrie, Woody (Woodrow Wilson Guthrie)   1912-1967
Seeds of man: an experience lived and dreamed. New York: E.P. Dutton and Co., 1976. 401 p.
In dialect and song, with a mixture of fact and fiction, folk singer Woody Guthrie narrates a rambling tale of the adventures that he, his father, his Uncle Jeff, and his older brother, Ray, had in 1931 en route from Pampas, Texas, to romantic Big Bend country, searching for his prospector grandfather's lost silver mine. Guthrie appreciates freedom, sex, and the land's beauty, and sympathizes with exploited workers.

1869 Guthrie, Woody (Woodrow Wilson Guthrie)   1912-1967
Woody sez. Preface by Studs Terkel. New York: Grosset & Dunlap, 1975. 172 p.
Folk poet, folk singer, author, ballad maker—Guthrie was an individualist with a worldly vision. His was a major influence in the folk revival of the 1950's. These articles first appeared in his column in People's World in 1939-1940.

1870 Hackett, Francis   1883-1962
American rainbow: early reminiscences. New York: Liveright Publishing Corp., 1971. 292 p.
The story of his immigration to the United States from Ireland, his boisterous youth, his early struggles and adventures as a writer up to 1910, when he and others founded The New Republic.

1871 Hadley, James   1821-1872
Diary (1843-1852) of James Hadley: tutor and professor of Greek in Yale College, 1845-1872. Edited with foreword by Laura Hadley Moseley. New Haven: Yale University Press, 1951. 334 p. Index.
An eminent Yale professor's diary describes campus life, his colleagues, and his experience in the university community.

1872 *Hadley, Martha E.   1852-1915
Alaskan diary of a pioneer Quaker missionary. Mt. Dora, Florida: Loren S. Hadley, 1969. 210 p.
Her diary is a daily record of her life in a remote Alaskan mission, 1899-1903; it includes details of temperature, climate, living conditions, and converts.

1873 Hagan, John W.   1836-1918
Confederate letters of John W. Hagan. Edited by Bell Irvin Wiley. Athens: University of Georgia Press, 1954. 55 p.
A collection of letters written 1861-64 by a Confederate soldier to his wife. His sense of duty remained constant in adversity, even when he was underfed, unpaid, or captured. This edition reproduces the original misspellings and punctuation.

1874 Hagedorn, Herman   1882-1964
The hyphenated family: an American saga. New York: The Macmillan Co., 1960. 264 p.
Although he was born in Brooklyn, his parents had emigrated from Germany, but sent their eldest sons back to their paternal grandmother to be educated. Thereafter, the family lived in two countries. The book describes the painful conflict in loyalty and patriotism that continued through World War I, recorded by the son, who became a poet and author.

1875 Hagen, Walter   1892-1969
The Walter Hagen story: by the Haig himself. As told to Margaret Seaton Heck. New York: Simon and Schuster, 1956. 342 p. Index.
The story of an internationally famous professional golfer.

1876 Hagerty, Cornelius J.   1885-1977
Diary of my European trip. Huntington, Indiana: Our Sunday Visitor, Inc., 1976. 496 p.
This diary records Father Hagerty's sabbatical tour of Europe and the Holy Land, August 1959—September 1960. He consistently records his daily religious devotions and the duties of the churches in which he worshipped, his meals, and major points of interest.

1877 Haggerty, James Edward   **1903-1963**
Guerrilla padre in Mindanao. Manila: Bookmark, 1964. (New York: Longmans, 1946) 257 p. Index.
 The story of a Jesuit priest who had been a college rector on Mindanao, Philippines, until the island was captured by the Japanese. He lived and worked with the guerrilla forces for the next three years, an experience he describes with eloquence and precision.

1878 *Hahn, Emily   **1905-**
England to me. Garden City, New York: Doubleday and Co., Inc., 1947. 271 p.
 After recovering from their life in a Japanese concentration camp, Emily Hahn and her husband, Major Charles Boxer, returned to her husband's estate in Dorset, England, for several years. Good description of postwar England.

1879 Halaby, Najeeb Elias   **1915-**
Crosswinds: an airman's memoirs. Garden City, New York: Doubleday and Company, Inc., 1978. 371 p. Index.
 Halaby, former head of the Federal Aviation Agency and Chairman of the Board of Pan American Airways, candidly recounts his rise and fall in corporate aviation. A World War II test pilot and Charles Lindbergh devoté, Halaby describes the drama of being an airline executive during the SST controversy and the days of burgeoning civil aviation.

1880 Halas, George Stanley   **1895-**
Halas by Halas: the autobiography of George Halas. With Gwen Morgen and Arthur Veysey. Illustrated. New York: McGraw-Hill, 1979. 351 p. Index.
 The only man qualified to be elected to the Football Hall of Fame in three categories—player, coach, and owner, Halas recounts his life and the history of his sport, revealing why he is often called "the greatest man in football."

1881 Haldeman-Julius, Emanuel   **1889-1951**
My second 25 years: instead of a footnote, an autobiography. Girard, Kansas: Haldeman-Julius Publications, 1949. 117 p.
 A potpourri of autobiographical essays from Haldeman-Julius's Socialist monthly, *The American Freeman*, 1914-1939, including accounts of his publishing the Little Blue Books, appreciations of Eugene Debs and "a mechanical man in a store window," and bizarre street characters.

1882 Haldeman-Julius, Emanuel   **1889-1951**
The world of Haldeman-Julius. Foreword by Harry Golden. Compiled by Albert Mordell. New York: Twayne Publishers, 1960. 288 p.
 This is a collection of personal essays from his Socialist monthly, *The American Freeman*, which he edited and published along with three hundred million copies of the classics in the "Little Blue Books" series. The essays include reminiscences of childhood in Philadelphia, an appreciation of his Kansas farm, and his love of good food.

1883 Hale, Edward Everett   **1822-1909**
A New England boyhood. New York: Grosset and Dunlap, 1970. (New York: Cassell Publishing Co., 1893) 208 p.
 Hale became a leading Congregationalist preacher in Boston, a well-respected author (*A Man without a Country*), and spent most of his 87 years in the city where he was raised. His boyhood book, contemporary with Twain's *Tom Sawyer*, Alcott's *Little Men*, and Howells' *A Boy's Town*, is unusual in its depiction of urban childhood.

1884 *Hale, Nancy   **1908-**
Life in the studio. Boston: Little, Brown and Co., 1969. 209 p.
 The daughter of two artists—her father a teacher of painting and drawing and her mother a portrait painter—the author writes a sensitive reminiscence of her exceptional parents and an examination of the nature of art and the artist.

1885 *Hale, Nancy   **1908-**
New England girlhood. Boston: Little, Brown and Co., 1958. 232 p.
 Recollections of a warm and happy childhood with her artist parents, described with the recognition that memory evokes fantasy.

1886 *Hale, Susan   **1833-1910**
Letters of Susan Hale. Edited by Caroline P. Atkinson. Boston: Marshall Jones Co., 1919. 472 p.
 In the nineteenth century letters were an easy and natural means of self-expression. Susan Hale's letters are conversational in style, expressing her thoughts while revealing a life comprised of teaching school, studying art, traveling in Europe and elsewhere, and keeping house in Rhode Island.

1887 *Haley, Alex   **1921-**
Roots. Garden City, New York: Doubleday & Co., 1976. 688 p.
 In novelistic form, author and journalist Haley has written a bestselling account of his family history, tracing his ancestors back to their "roots" in Gambia, West Africa, birthplace of Kunta Kinte. He follows with Kinte's importation to the United States as a slave; proceeds to his relatives' survival as house and field slaves until the Civil War; through the Reconstruction Era in Tennessee; to emergence in the twentieth century as middle-class citizens. Haley's last chapter describes his own life, focusing on his gradual emergence as a writer and his research on *Roots*.

1888 Haley, Nelson Cole   **1832-1900**
Whale hunt: the narrative of a voyage by Nelson Cole Haley, harpooner in the ship Charles W. Morgan, 1849-1853. New York: Ives Washburn. Inc., 1948. 304 p.
 Written after Haley's retirement (1864), the book is based on his journal kept during the voyage; a vivid description of the early whaling industry.

1889 Hall, Carl Mitchel   **1899-**
Personal memoir: an unforgettable autobiography. Illustrated. Baltimore: Gateway Press, 1976. 639 p.
 Engineer Hall's account of his life as an engineer, husband, and father includes his observations on a multitude of topics, from nuclear energy to birth control, minutely detailed and sincere. He focuses on his work with the Kentucky and Missouri Highway Departments and on his service during World War II with the U.S. Army Corps of Engineers.

1890 Hall, Charles Francis   **1821-1871**
Life with the Esquimaux: a narrative of Arctic experience in search of survivors of Sir John Franklin's expedition. Introduction to new edition by George Swinton. Rutland, Vermont: Charles E. Tuttle Co., Publishers, 1970. (London: S. Low, Son and Marston, 1864) 547 p.
 A remarkably detailed account of his Arctic exploration and search party (1860-62); includes descriptions of daily routine and survival, of Esquimaux life and culture, of the treachery of snow and icebergs, and an amazing sense of adventure.

1891 Hall, Daniel Weston   **b.1841**
Arctic rovings and the adventures of a New Bedford boy on sea and land. Edited by Jerome Beatty. Designed and illustrated by William Hogarth. New York: William R. Scott, Inc., 1968. (Boston: A. Tompkins, 1861) 144 p.
 He left school at fifteen and with his father's reluctant approval joined the crew of a whaling ship. Because of the captain's cruelty, he jumped ship off the coast of Siberia and finally returned to New Bedford in another whaler four years later.

1892 Hall, Donald Andrew   **1928-**
String too short to be saved. New York: The Viking Press, 1961. 143 p.
 A beautifully written, if somewhat nostalgic, recollection of his boyhood in rural New Hampshire and his special relation with his grandfather.

1893 Hall, Edwin Presley   **1902-**
Doctor reminisces. Huntsville, Alabama: Strode Publishers, 1978. 332 p.
 Hall recounts his years as a doctor from medical school to the present, primarily by presenting case histories during his long career. He worked as an intern, a coal mine doctor, a ship's surgeon, an army surgeon in World War II in North Africa and in the United States in Veterans' hospitals. His career allowed him to travel extensively in the Southern United States and in Europe; he describes his travels and colleagues with precise detail.

1894 Hall, Granville Stanley   **1844-1924**
Letters to Jonas Gilman Clark. Edited by N. Orwin Rush. Worcester, Massachusetts: Clark University Library, 1948. 38 p.
 Correspondence from his European "pedagogic tour" (1888-89) when he was interviewing leading scientists and studying the forms of higher education prior to the establishment of Clark University, where he became president.

1895 Hall, James Norman   **1887-1951**
Forgotten one and other true tales of the South Seas. Boston: Little, Brown and Co., 1950. 246 p.
 Author sketches his experiences with people living in Tahiti during the 1920's.

1896 Hall, James Norman   **1887-1951**
My island home: an autobiography. Epilogue by Edward Weeks. Westport, Connecticut: Greenwood Press, 1970. (Boston: Little, Brown and Co., 1952) 345 p. Index.
 A writer tells of his early days in Iowa, the years he spent as a social worker in Boston, travel to England, Iceland, and the South Pacific. The book's main focus is on the author's interest in literature as both reader and writer.

1897 Hall, Melvin Adams   **1889-1962**
Bird of time. New York: Charles Scribner's Sons, 1949. 307 p. Index.
 The second of his memoirs, written with a sense of sadness for time and values lost to technological society, a sense of romance for people living close to the land, and a questing spirit for further adventures.

1898 Hall, Melvin Adams   **1889-1962**
Journey to the end of an era: an informal autobiography. New York: Charles Scribner's Sons, 1947. 438 p. Index.
   The worldwide travels of an adventurer with a romantic sensibility and a restless spirit always in search of the new and unusual.

1899 *Hall, Minta   **b.1878**
Do you remember?: memories of a schoolteacher. New York: Exposition Press, 1956. 44 p.
   Elementary schoolteacher writes an elementary account of her forty years in the classroom, lacing it with children's remarks and misspellings collected over the years.

1900 Hall, Ralph J.   **1891?-**
The main trail. Edited by Vic Jameson. San Antonio, Texas: The Naylor Co., 1971. 193 p.
   Unable to finish school because of eye trouble, Hall began his career riding circuit in New Mexico as a lay missionary. He later preached from coast to coast at churches, conferences, colleges, and seminaries sharing his spiritual power and the Gospel of Christ.

1901 Hall, Robert Anderson   **1911-**
Stormy petrel in linguistics. Ithaca, New York: Spoken Language Services, 1975. 230 p. Index.
   A professor at Cornell for many years, Hall studied under or worked with many of the principal contributors to the profession, including Leonard Bloomfield, Edward Sapir, and Hans Kurath. Hall's autobiography verifies his reputation as a scholar and an ill-tempered polemicist.

1902 *Hall, Sharlot Mabridth   **1870-1943**
Sharlot Hall on the Arizona Strip: a diary of a journey through northern Arizona in 1911. Edited by C. Gregory Crampton. Flagstaff, Arizona: Northland Press, 1975. 97 p.
   Serving as territorial historian of Arizona, the author traveled by wagon through the Arizona Strip, a region north of the Colorado River, in order to survey its people, resources, and history. In terse prose, she describes the territory and by the way gives some sense of the experience of camping and traveling in this rugged land. Includes bibliography.

1903 Hall, William Preston, Jr.   **1918-**
Admired and condemned. Honea Path, South Carolina: William Preston Hall, Jr., 1974. 300 p.
   A Baptist minister has written the history of his life and struggles to overcome evil in order to carry out God's will and to help others. He finds life rewarding when lived according to the rules of God and organized society.

1904 Hallinan, Vincent   **1896-**
A lion in court. New York: G.P. Putnam's Sons, 1963. 319 p.
   A flamboyant and controversial lawyer in San Francisco describes his career in litigation, with bold criticism of the judiciary system, penal codes, and American society.

1905 Halper, Albert   **1904-**
Good-bye, Union Square; a writer's memoir of the thirties. Chicago: Quadrangle Books, 1970. 275 p.
   Halper recalls his life during the thirties when he went to New York to find his way as a writer. He nostalgically remembers literary and political conversations, sales of his stories, people he met, a productive summer at Yaddo, his acquaintance with Whittaker Chambers and others.

1906 Halpern, Samuel Eliott   **1936-**
West Pac '64. Boston: Brandon Press, 1975. 236 p.
   He writes of his experience as a Navy doctor serving in the West Pacific in 1964. His story ends with an account of the Battle of Tonkin Gulf.

1907 *Halsell, Grace   **1948?-**
Bessie Yellowhair. New York: William Morrow & Co., 1973. 213 p.
   Halsell changed clothes, names, and identities with an Indian woman to live among the Navajos and then "pass" as a Navajo among whites. As when she previously "passed" for Black (described in *Soul Sister*), she found the transition shocking, necessitating considerable psychological adjustment.

1908 *Halsell, Grace   **1948?-**
Soul sister. New York: The World Publishing Co., 1969. 221 p.
   Influenced by John H. Griffin's **Black Like Me**, the author determined to pass herself as Black and live in Harlem and Mississippi as part of the Black community. Her experiences—terrifying, shameful, and nightmarish—reveal much that she learned about the struggle between the races for survival, identity, and dignity.

1909 *Halsey, Margaret   **1910-**
No laughing matter: the autobiography of a WASP. Philadelphia: J.B. Lippincott, 1977. 250 p.
   Halsey describes her WASP upbringing in a Germanic,

achievement-oriented, Yonkers, New York, family. After college, she got a job with Simon and Schuster, married publisher Simon's brother, Henry, a peaceful professor, and began to write in earnest. During World War II, she fell in love with Joseph Bloch, who patiently tolerated her increasing agoraphobia, alcoholism, and irascible temperament until he divorced her when she was 58. She copes with grit and wry humor.

1910 Halsey, William Frederick   **1882-1959**
Admiral Halsey's story. With Joseph Bryan. New York: Whittlesey House, 1947. 310 p. Index.
   Retired as a fleet admiral in 1947, Halsey served the Navy over 45 years. Describes his life, primarily military, primarily in the Pacific, with few traces of his personal life.

1911 Hamilton, Alexander   **1712-1756**
Gentleman's progress: the itinerarium of Dr. Alexander Hamilton, 1744. Edited with introduction by Carl Bridenbaugh. Westport, Connecticut: Greenwood Press, 1973. (Chapel Hill: University of North Carolina Press, 1948) 267 p.
   The diary of his journey from Maryland to Maine is lively, witty, and informative, with incisive descriptions of people, lodgings, taverns, countryside, and manners, an interesting view of eighteenth-century life.

1912 Hamilton, Alexander   **1757-1804**
The papers of Alexander Hamilton. Edited by Harold C. Syrett. New York: Columbia University Press, 1979. (1961) 26v. Index.
   This edition of Hamilton's papers contains letters to and from him and documents written by or concerning him. All are in chronological order. Hamilton occupied a central position in the government of the United States, serving as Washington's aide-de-camp, as Major General in the Army, Secretary of War, Secretary of the Treasury, author of *The Federalist Papers,* and a major contributor to economic and fiscal policy.

1913 *Hamilton, Esther (Yerger)
Ambassador in bonds. East Stroudsburg. Pennsylvania: Pinebrook Book Club, 1946. 246 p.
   A Christian missionary describes life in a Japanese concentration camp in the Philippines, 1941-1945. She draws an analogy between "bonds" of prison camp and "bonds" of marriage.

1914 Hamilton, Peter Joseph   **1859-1927**
Little boy in Confederate Mobile. Arranged for publication by Rachel-Duke Hamilton Cannon. Illustrated by William Bush. Mobile, Alabama: Colonial Mobile Book Shop, 1947. 31 p.
   Brief recollection of his boyhood in Alabama during and shortly after the Civil War.

1915 Hamilton, William Thomas   **1822-1908**
My sixty years on the Plains: trapping, trading, and Indian fighting. From the original edition by E.T. Sieber (1905), with an introduction by Donald J. Berthrong. Illustrated by Charles M. Russell. The Western Frontier Library. Norman: University of Oklahoma Press, 1960. (New York: Forest and Stream Publishing Co., 1905) 184 p.
   Most of the book describes trapping, trading, or fighting with different Plains Indians, 1842-1845. Begun when he was on a hunting expedition at twenty, the book concludes with a summary of his later years as trader, agent, scout.

1916 *Hamlin, Anna M.
Father was a tenor. Illustrated. Hicksville, New York: Exposition Press, 1978. 96 p.
   Hamlin focuses on the career of her father, George Hamlin, as a tenor in oratorios and recitals around the United States and in Europe, 1890-1920. She made her own musical debut as a singer in Lake Placid in 1920, but her account of her own career is fragmentary and ends in 1925.

1917 Hamlin, James D.   **1871-1950**
Flamboyant judge: James D. Hamlin, a biography. As told to J. Evetts Haley and Wm. Curry Holden. Canyon, Texas: Palo Duro Press, 1972. 312 p.
   The editors have integrated two manuscripts which they persuaded Hamlin to dictate—one on a wire recorder, one to a typist—in the mid-1940's. The result is an interesting account of a lively character deeply involved in the economic and social development of the Southwest, especially western Texas and Santa Fe-Taos, New Mexico.

1918 Hammerberg, Kuno   **1901-**
Kuno: one of the last of the general practitioners. Hicksville, New York: Exposition Press, 1979. 124 p.
   The son of Swedish immigrants, he became a general practitioner in the town of Clare, Michigan. The book recounts his four decades of service delivering babies under adverse circumstances, performing many kinds of surgery, and making life and death decisions.

1919 Hammond, John   **1910-**
John Hammond on record: an autobiography. With Irving Townsend. Illustrated. Discography. New York: Ridge Press/Summit Books, 1977. 416 p. Index.

Hammond, a Vanderbilt heir, was the family maverick because he dropped out of Yale and hung around Harlem musicians in the Twenties. He turned this fascination into a useful and engaging autobiography which discusses all the musicians (mostly jazz) he has known and their performances he recorded for 45 years with Columbia Records and other producers. His career is related to his other equally engrossing commitment to civil rights, as his long service on the NAACP board testifies.

1920 Hammond, John Hays   **1855-1936**
The autobiography of John Hays Hammond. Illustrated. New York: Arno Press, 1974. (New York: Farrar & Rinehart, 1935) 813 p.

After his youth on the Western frontier, the author went to Africa where he became a business associate of Cecil Rhodes, worked with the Reform Movement there, was charged with high treason, condemned to death, then released, and went on to other adventures. Later he was a political figure in the Republican Party before and after World War I.

1921 Hammond, William Gardner   **1829-1894**
Remembrance of Amherst: an undergraduate's diary, 1846-1848. Edited by George F. Whicher. New York: Columbia University Press, 1946. 307 p. Index.

Vivid, precise description of his individual development as a student and of the contemporary educational process.

1922 *Hancock, Cornelia   **1840-1926**
South after Gettysburg: letters of Cornelia Hancock, 1863-1868. Edited by Henrietta Stratton. Foreword by Bruce Catton. Illustrated by Edward Shenton. New York: Thomas Crowell Co., 1956. (Philadelphia: University of Pennsylvania Press, 1937) 288 p.

Raised a Quaker in New Jersey, she was a prominent nurse in the Civil War, setting up aid stations and hospitals at Gettysburg, the Battle of the Wilderness, the White House, and Richmond after its capture. Later she established a Quaker School for Blacks in South Carolina, described in the second half of this volume in letters not included in the earlier edition. A later selected edition has been published in 1971 by Books for Libraries Press.

1923 *Hancock, Joy (Bright) Little   **1898-**
Lady in the Navy: a personal reminiscence. Annapolis: The Naval Institute Press, 1972. 289 p. Index.

She served as Yeoman (F) First Class, USNR, during World War I; later she learned to fly and as a civilian worked for the Bureau of Aeronautics. She was one of the first officers commissioned in the WAVES when it was mobilized in 1942 and was Director of the WAVES, 1946-53, when she retired. Her book documents the history of women in the U.S. Navy.

1924 Handerson, Henry Ebenezer   **1837-1918**
Yankee in gray: the Civil War memoirs of Henry E. Handerson with a selection of his wartime letters. Cleveland: The Press of Western Reserve University, 1962. 132 p.

He was raised in northeastern Ohio, but his family moved to Tennessee in 1852. His memoir, written in the 1890's, describes his life in Civil War times (1859-65), when he served as a Confederate officer. He later became a highly respected medical historian in Cleveland.

1925 Handy, William Christopher   **1873-1958**
Father of the blues: an autobiography. Edited by Arna Bontemps. Illustrated. Foreword by Abbe Niles. London: Sidgwick and Jackson, 1957. (New York: Macmillan, 1941) 317 p. Index.

Saved from a career as a clergyman by an early desire to play the trumpet and to sing with minstrel groups, Handy provides an engaging story of his lifelong career as a jazz musician, blues composer, and music publisher, interwoven with a history of blues music. This includes the reception (and plagiarism) of his most notable works, such as "St. Louis Blues," "Memphis Blues," and "A Good Man is Hard to Find." Handy's prose is as rhythmic and vigorous as his music.

1926 *Hangen, Patricia Dana
Tell him that I heard. New York: Harper & Row, 1977. 217 p.

A moving tribute to an international correspondent's dangerous, peripatetic way of life, and to the man himself, NBC newsman Welles Hangen. Married in Cairo in 1958, for the next fourteen years they lived in Lebanon, Egypt, Kuwait, Jordan, India, Germany, and Hong Kong as Welles covered revolutions, wars, invasions, and other highly charged events. Pat loved her husband and their adventuresome life. Her description of his capture and disappearance in Cambodia (1972) is especially poignant.

1927 *Hansberry, Lorraine   **1930-1965**
To be young, gifted and Black. New York: Prentice-Hall, 1969. 266 p.

A pastiche of her own words from letters, speeches, diaries, and plays, compiled by her husband, Robert Nemiroff, after she died of cancer. Her first play, A Raisin in the Sun (1959), won the New York Drama Critics Award; she was widely respected for her involvement in the Civil Rights movement as well.

1928 *Hansen, Karen, pseud.
see *Millberg, Karen Schwencke

1929 Hapgood, Hutchins   **1869-1944**
A Victorian in the modern world. Introduction by Robert Allen Skotheim. Seattle: University of Washington Press, 1972. (New York: Harcourt, 1939) 604 p. Index.

Because he was born and brought up during the Victorian Era, Hapgood pictures the modern world "strained through the Victorian temperament." He views the revolutionary significance of the labor movement, political and social conditions, and standards of life and ethics as changes rooted in our democratic history.

1930 Haraszthy de Mokesa, Agoston   **1812-1869**
Father of California wine, Agoston Haraszthy: including grape culture, wines, & wine making. Edited by Theodore Schoenmann. Foreword by Robert L. Balzar. Illustrated. Santa Barbara, California: Capra Press, 1979. 126 p.

A diary of travels to European wine-growing areas that describes quality and character of grapes for use in selecting cuttings to take back to California, with some attention to the culture of other fruits and nuts. The author was in large part responsible for the development of California vineyards. A biographical introduction sketches his fascinating life—a Hungarian nobleman immigrant who made and lost fortunes in various ventures.

1931 Harbison, Massy (White)   **b.1770**
A narrative of the sufferings of Massy: from Indian barbarity, giving an account of her captivity, the murder of her two children, her escape, with an infant at her breast. Rpt. 1825 & 1836 eds. Narratives of North American Indian Captives, v. 42. Edited by John Winter. Illustrated. New York: Garland Publishing Co., 1977. (Pittsburgh: S. Engles, 1825) 192 p.

In 1791 Harbison was captured by the Indians. She had a horrifying escape and recounts the events in lurid detail.

1932 Hardin, John Wesley   **1853-1895**
The life of John Wesley Hardin: as written by himself. Edited by Robert G. McCubbin. Norman: University of Oklahoma Press, 1961. 152 p.

Notorious as a Texas gunfighter, he finally received a pardon, studied law, and briefly led a reputable life before he became involved in the saloon life of El Paso, where he was shot.

1933 *Hardy, Irene   **1841-1922**
An Ohio school mistress: the memoirs of Irene Hardy. Edited by Louis Filler. Kent, Ohio: The Kent State University Press, 1980. 310 p. Index.

Hardy writes about her childhood in Ohio, her desire to be educated and later to become a teacher. She fought for women's rights, better education, and an eradication of racial prejudice.

1934 *Hardy, Martha
Skyo. Seattle: Superior Publishing Co., 1949. 256 p.

Describing herself as "an old maid school Ma'am," a math professor retired from the University of Washington writes of her adventures in the woods of Washington where she had a cabin and many friends among the mountain folk and forest animals.

1935 *Hardy, Mary (McDowell) Duffus, Lady   **1825?-1891**
Through cities and prairie lands. Sketches of an American tour by Lady Duffus Hardy. New York: Arno Press, 1974. (London: Chapman & Hall, 1881) 338 p.

A light and airy account of this British noblewoman's tour of North America from Quebec to New York, westward to California and back to Boston. The author passes judgment on everything she sees without reserve, from behavior of the Chinese in California to the reading of the "Act of Independence," as she calls it, in Boston.

1936 Hardy, William Harris   **1837-1917**
No compromise with principle: autobiography and biography of William Hardy Harris. Arranged and compiled by Toney A. Hardy. New York: American Book-Stratford Press, Inc., 1946. 344 p.

The long and active life of a prominent attorney in Mississippi, including his service in the Civil War, his work during Reconstruction, and his major contribution to the development of the railroad in the state.

1937 Hare, James M.   **1910-**
With malice towards none: the musings of a retired politician. Foreword by Russel B. Nye. East Lansing: Michigan State University Press, 1972. 196 p.

An official in Michigan state government for over 25 years, Hare evaluates his experience, analyzes what he believes to be the failure of big government, and recommends several measures for reform which he urges are imperative for adjusting to the complex needs of modern society.

1938 Hargis, Billy James   **1925-**
Why I fight for a Christian America. Nashville, Tennessee: Thomas Nelson Inc., 1974. 179 p.

Christian crusade leader Hargis writes about experiences influencing his life, his beliefs, the founding of American Christian College, conspiracies he sees undermining the United States, and "continual government harassment" against him, particularly by the IRS.

1939 *Harkness, Georgia   1891-1974
Grace abounding. Nashville, Tennessee: Abingdon Press, 1969. 192 p.
  Through scripture, poetry, prayer, and autobiographical meditation, theologian Harkness praises her parents, comments with pleasure on her rural upbringing and the natural settings in which she has lived and taught theology, and voices opinions on social action, particularly the benefits of pacifism, racial integration, and the Civil Rights movement.

1940 Harlow, LeRoy F.
Without fear or favor: odyssey of a city manager. Provo, Utah: Brigham Young University Press, 1977. 350 p. Index.
  Harlow describes the ups-and-downs of managing various cities in Minnesota, Oregon, Florida, and elsewhere. He dealt with politicians, antagonistic citizens, and local crime syndicates, sometimes failing but often succeeding.

1941 *Harman, Jeanne (Perkins)   1919-
Such is life. New York: Thomas Y. Crowell Co., 1956. 210 p.
  The story of her seven-year experience as a writer-researcher for *Life* magazine; a vivid description of the spirited and competitive world of Time-Inc.

1942 Harned, Thomas Biggs   b.1851
Memoirs of Thomas B. Harned, Walt Whitman's friend and literary executor. Edited with detailed index by Peter Van Egmond. Hartford: Transcendental Books, 1972. 58 p. Index.
  Harned's life touched on those of many political and social leaders of his time including clergymen, scholars, and writers, particularly Walt Whitman, who said that Harned's "integrity was beyond any corrupting influence."

1943 Harrelson, Kenneth Smith (Hawk Harrelson)   1941-
Hawk. With Al Hirshberg. Illustrated. New York: The Viking Press, 1969. 244 p.
  A flashy, popular baseball personality, he played with the Kansas City Athletics before going to the Boston Red Sox. In 1968 he was American League Player of the Year, and then was traded to the Cleveland Indians. His book conveys his pride in sensationalism, image clothes, and baseball.

1944 *Harriman, Margaret (Case) Morgan   1904?-1966
Blessed are the debonair. New York: Rinehart and Co., Inc., 1956. 254 p.
  Growing up in New York's Algonquin Hotel, owned by her father, Frank Case, she was surrounded by those who brought fame and glamour to the 1920's and 30's. She became a well-known writer and journalist.

1945 Harrington, Bob   1927-
Chaplain of Bourbon Street: an autobiography. With Walter Wagner. Garden City, New York: Doubleday & Co., Inc., 1969. 214 p.
  The story of a Baptist minister who opened a church in the middle of New Orleans' French Quarter. Flamboyant and outspoken, he also travels extensively as an evangelist, describing himself as "a man on fire for God."

1946 *Harris, Bernice Kelly   1894-
Southern savory. Chapel Hill: University of North Carolina Press, 1964. 256 p.
  Harris shapes her memories into a collection of local-color vignettes filled with family and friends, but she rarely provides last names. Sensitive to people and language, Harris began early to imitate those around her and to write stories, games that later worked into her career as author and playwright.

1947 Harris, Charles
One man's medicine/Charles Harris. New York: Harper, 1975. 294 p.
  Described by the author as a "fictionalized memoir about medicine," this book describes a thirty-year career in cancer research and clinical medicine.

1948 Harris, Charles William   1916-
Your father's business: letters to a young man about what it means to be a priest. Illustrated. Notre Dame, Indiana: Ave Maria Press, 1978. 110 p.
  Harris, a chaplain at Oregon State University, wrote a series of autobiographical sermon-letters to Bill, a college senior, to help him decide whether to enter the priesthood or to get married after graduation. The letters are clear, honest, simple, and exploratory; they point unequivocally to the priestly vocation—but Bill got married anyway.

1949 Harris, David   1946-
I shoulda been home yesterday. New York: Delacorte Press/Seymour Lawrence, 1976. 234 p.
  Harris was sentenced to three years in Federal prison for refusing to be inducted into the Army. His story is about his time in prison, the brutality

of the guards and prisoners, the friendships one makes, and what one does to survive.

1950 Harris, Frank   1855-1931
Frank Harris: his life and adventures, an autobiography. Introduction by Grant Richards. London: The Richards Press, 1947. 552 p. Index.
  Revised and abridged version of four volumes previously published. The lively story of a man who was both author and powerful editor of several literary journals. As a boy he ran away to America where he worked, studied, and had a variety of adventures before returning to Europe and to England where he spent most of his adult life.

1951 Harris, Frank   1855-1931
Frank Harris to Arnold Bennett; fifty-eight letters, 1908-1910. Folcroft, Pennsylvania: Folcroft Library Editions, 1973. (n.p.: privately printed, 1936) 40 p.
  Bennett, who signed his book reviews Jacob Tonson, and Harris began to correspond after Harris had sent him early proof copies of some of his work. The letters included in this volume contain both professional and personal matters as their friendship grew.

1952 Harris, Frank   1855-1931
My life and loves. Edited with introduction by John F. Gallagher. New York: Grove Press, 1963. (Paris: Obelisk Press, 1952-54) 983 p.
  The first unexpurgated U.S. edition of his autobiographical writing, including five volumes in one.

1953 Harris, Frank   1855-1931
My secret life. Introduction by G. Legman. New York: Grove Press, 1966. 11v. in 2.
  Further autobiographical writing by the controversial Irish writer and editor.

1954 Harris, Fred R.   1930-
Potomac fever. New York: W.W. Norton, 1977. 214 p. Index.
  An anecdotal account of his career as an Oklahoma state senator, a U.S. senator, and a presidential candidate in 1972. Harris writes with warm humor of the friendships that developed during his legislative career; he provides a political history of Washington from 1964 to 1976.

1955 Harris, Jed   1900-1979
A dance on the high wire: recollections of a time and a temperament. New York: Crown Publishers, 1979. 188 p.
  A disjunctive, anecdotal account of Harris's days at Yale before he was expelled, months of being a tramp, and years as a producer of *Coquette*, *The Front Page*, *Our Town*, *Uncle Vanya*, and other hits. He reminisces about personalities, on and off stage, and money, earned and lost, though, he says, "I have traveled light, a voyageur sans baggage, all my life."

1956 Harris, Jed   1900-1979
Watchman, what of the night? Garden City, New York: Doubleday & Co., Inc., 1963. 154 p.
  Although his book centers on his 1947 Broadway production of *The Heiress*, it conveys a sense of the theatrical world beyond the play, including Harris's role as a major producer and director.

1957 Harris, John   b.1870
Tears and triumphs: the life story of a pastor-evangelist. Louisville: Pentecostal Publishing Co., 1948. 445 p.
  A rich, colorful narrative of his life on preaching circuits in West Virginia and surrounding states; very readable social history by a skilled storyteller.

1958 Harris, Mark   1922-
Twenty-one twice: a journal. Boston: Little, Brown and Co., 1966. 288 p.
  Asked to write a special report about the Peace Corps, Harris waited five months for security clearance and then went overseas, spending sixteen days traveling, meeting volunteers and evaluating risks. Written as a journal, this book reflects on the events of those days.

1959 Harris, Paul Percy   1868-1947
My road to Rotary: the story of a boy, a Vermont community and Rotary. Chicago: A. Kroch and Son, 1948. 318 p.
  In most of his book, the founder of Rotary International recalls the friends and values of his New England boyhood which remained significant throughout his life. The last fourth describes the founding of Rotary, its subsequent growth and influence.

1960 Harris, T.H.   1869-1942
The memoirs of T.H. Harris: State Superintendent of Public Education in Louisiana, 1908-1940. Foreword by John A. Hunter. Edited by Donald A. Shipp. Epilogue by Sadie Harris Baskin. Baton Rouge: Bureau of Educational Materials & Research, College of Education, Louisiana State University, 1963. 194 p.
  Harris, Louisiana State Superintendent of Education in the 1920's and 1930's, discusses his rural upbringing and his career in education, which

he began as a public schoolteacher, continued as a part-time student, part-time teacher at Louisiana State University, and proceeded upward. Harris's administration promoted music, vocational instruction, better education (including Blacks) based on reforms in school financing.

1961 Harris, Townsend   **1804-1878**
The complete journal of Townsend Harris: first American Consul and Minister to Japan. Introduction and notes by Mario Emilio Cosenza. Preface by Douglas MacArthur II. Rev. ed. Rutland, Vermont and Tokyo, Japan: Charles E. Tuttle Co., 1959. (New York: Doubleday, Doran and Co., Inc., 1930) 616 p. Index.
    The daily journals (1855-1858) include detailed descriptions of household routines, climate, customs, economics, politics, and diplomacy.

1962 Harrison, Benjamin   **1833-1901**
Benjamin Harrison, 1833-1901: chronology-documents-bibliographical aids. Edited by Harry J. Sievers. Bibliography. Dobbs Ferry, New York: Oceana Publications, 1969. 89 p. Index.
    Harrison's writings include letters to his wife and political speeches given as Governor of Indiana and President of the United States. The editor has provided a detailed chronology and an annotated bibliography.

1963 Harrison, Charles Yale   **1898-1954**
Thank God for my heart attack. New York: Henry Holt and Co., 1949. 144 p.
    This detailed, well-written account of his heart attack and subsequent recovery is both moving and informative, with specific descriptions of his physical and psychological reactions at every stage.

1964 Harrison, Eddie   **1942-**
No time for dying. And Alfred V.J. Prather. Englewood Cliffs, New Jersey: Prentice-Hall, 1973. 259 p.
    The story of Harrison's unremitting attempts to win his case and be released from prison in spite of the many obstacles and injustices of the criminal justice system. He and his lawyer, both of whom possessed exceptional faith and conviction, combined their efforts through four separate trials, finally winning an unprecedented presidential commutation.

1965 *Harrison, Edith (Ogden)   **1861-1955**
Strange to say: recollections of persons and events in New Orleans and Chicago. Chicago: Kroch and Son, 1949. 188 p. Index.
    Southern lady recalls her long life in political society with detailed stories about friends, parties, and travels.

1966 Harrower, John   **1733-1777**
Journal of John Harrower: an indentured servant in the colony in Virginia, 1733-1766. Edited with introduction by Edward Miles Riley. Williamsburg, Virginia: Colonial Williamsburg, 1963. 202 p. Index.
    Said to be the only diary of an indentured servant, it is a vivid record of ordinary life in eighteenth-century Tidewater Virginia by a Scot who was assigned to tutor his master's children.

1967 *Hart, Marion (Rice)   **1891-**
I fly as I please. New York: Vanguard, 1953. 247 p.
    A woman from New York describes her experience becoming an aviator in her later years.

1968 *Hart, Marion (Rice)   **1891-**
Who called that lady a skipper? The strange voyage of a woman navigator. New York: The Vanguard Press, 1938. 313 p.
    Working in London as a sculptor, she bought a used yacht, persuaded friends to help her repair it, and set out on a world cruise. Their adventures are recorded in her letters.

1969 Hart, Moss   **1904-1961**
Act one: an autobiography. New York: Random House, 1959. 444 p.
    After a brief description of boyhood poverty in New York, he writes of his first theatrical job as an office boy, the disaster of his first play, and then the development of his career as a successful Broadway playwright.

1970 *Hart, Sara Liebenstein   **b.1869**
The pleasure is mine: an autobiography. Chicago: Valentine-Newman, Publishers, 1947. 288 p. Index.
    An interesting record of her active life as a social worker at Chicago's Hull House, supporting the Juvenile Court, and helping to organize many activities that aided women and children in the Chicago area. Well-written social history.

1971 Harte, Bret   **1836-1902**
The letters of Bret Harte. Assembled and edited by Geoffrey Bret Harte. New York: AMS Press, 1973. (Boston: Houghton Mifflin, 1926) 515 p.
    Letters written 1866-1902, mostly to his wife, when he held consular posts in Scotland and lived in London.

1972 *Hartman, May Weisser   **1900-**
I gave my heart. New York: Citadel Press, 1960. 350 p.

Mae Weisser Hartman focuses on the seventeen years (age 17-34) she worked with Judge Gustave Hartman (d.1936) directing the Judge's charity, the Israel Orphan Asylum of New York. She relates the Home's history, dwelling on the annual fund-raising extravaganza she arranged at Madison Square Garden.

1973 Hartney, Harold Evans   **1888-1945**
Up and at 'em. Edited by Stanley M. Ulanoff. Garden City, New York: Doubleday, 1971. (Harrisburg, PA.: Stackpole Sons, 1940) 359 p.
    Colonel Hartley presents his own story which is inextricably joined with the early history of military aviation, especially during World War I. He was shot down four times, once by Baron Richthofen, and was in the thick of the fighting while commanding the outstanding aviation unit, the First Pursuit Group.

1974 Hartney, Harold Evans   **1888-1945**
Wings over France. Edited by Stanley M. Ulanoff. Folkstone: Bailey Brothers & Swinfen, 1971. (1940) 360 p.
    A Canadian commissioned a major in the U.S. Air Service during World War I, Hartney writes of his experience in air combat over France, providing a history of America's participation in this aspect of aviation history.

1975 Harvey, Eli   **1860-1957**
The autobiography of Eli Harvey: Quaker sculptor from Ohio. Edited by Dorothy Z. Bricker, Jane Z. Vail, and Vernon G. Wills. Foreword by Norman Rockwell. Epilogue by Edith James Harvey. Illustrated. Wilmington, Ohio: Clinton County Historical Society, 1966. 100 p.
    Harvey, a noted sculptor of animals, including a trumpeting elephant at the Smithsonian and many sculptures at the Bronx Zoo, writes about his career, marriages, and residences in Ohio, New York, and California.

1976 *Hathaway, Katharine (Butler)   **1890-1942**
Journals and letters of the little locksmith. Illustrated by the author. New York: Coward-McCann, inc., 1946. 395 p.
    As a child she suffered from a tubercular infection of the spine which kept her bedridden for ten years. A delicate, fanciful sensibility developed in those years, eventually expressing itself in sketches and an informal autobiography, *The Little Locksmith* (1942).

1977 *Hathaway, Katharine (Butler)   **1890-1942**
The little locksmith. New York: Coward-McCann, 1943. 237 p.
    Even though her life was dominated by physical frailty and deformity, her imagination and penetrating mind sustained an inner world of excitement and an outreaching understanding and love.

1978 Haupt, Herman   **1817-1905**
Reminiscences of General Herman Haupt. Milwaukee: Wright & Joys Co., 1901. 331 p.
    General Haupt held many engineering and executive positions with railroad, pipeline, and other companies, was Chief of the Bureau of U.S. Military Railroads in the Civil War, and took part in important Military operations. Included with his narrative are interviews and correspondence with President Lincoln, Secretary Stanton and several generals, as well as his impressions of them.

1979 *Hautzig, Esther Rudomin   **1931-**
The endless steppe: growing up in Siberia. New York: Thomas Y. Crowell, 1968. 215 p.
    This unsentimental book describes 1941-45, when Jewish Esther Rudomin, her mother, father, and grandmother were deported by the Russians from their home in Vilna, Poland, to Siberia. Conditions were predictably harsh, but even in the land of climatic extremes and with severe deprivation of food and space, Esther went to school, worked in the potato fields, and survived psychologically, thanks to her closely knit family.

1980 Havlicek, John   **1940-**
Hondo: Celtic man in motion. And Bob Ryan. Illustrated. Englewood Cliffs, New Jersey: Prentice-Hall, 1977. 192 p.
    Basketball player Havlicek settled on basketball after making the all-state teams in football, basketball and baseball; nevertheless, his first pro contract was in football with the Cleveland Browns. Strategies, injuries and descriptions of championship games make up the bulk of Havlicek's story of fourteen seasons with the Boston Celtics.

1981 Havner, Vance Houston   **1901-**
That I may know him: a personal testimony. New York: Fleming H. Revell Co., 1948. 94 p.
    A spiritual autobiography describing his Christian upbringing, his call to the Baptist ministry, and his career as an evangelist of simple faith in the Bible.

1982 *Havoc, June   **1916-**
Early Havoc. New York: Simon and Schuster, 1959. 313 p.
    A harrowing account of Havoc's 3000+ hour stint as a marathon dancer in the 1930's in a four-month ordeal in which she came in second

and earned only $50 from the exploiting manager. Interspersed are flash-back accounts of Havoc's childhood career on the vaudeville circuit, managed by a callous mother from whom she escaped through marriage.

1983 Hawes, Hampton   1928-1977
Raise up off me. And Don Asher. New York: Coward, McCann & Geoghegan, Inc., 1974. 179 p.
   The life of a dedicated and pioneering jazz pianist who with others of his race made a rebellion through music, overcoming the dark world of drugs, despair, and prison and finding new expression through his art.

1984 Hawthorne, Nathaniel   1804-1864
The English notebooks: based on the original manuscripts in the Pierpoint Morgan Library. New York: Russell & Russell, Inc., 1962. 667 p. Index.
   Composed between 1853 and 1857, the notebooks, here freed from Mrs. Hawthorne's expurgations and revisions, present Hawthorne's reactions to England, his irritations, resentments, and affections for that country.

1985 Hawthorne, Nathaniel   1804-1864
Letters of Hawthorne to William D. Ticknor, 1851-1864. Foreword by C.E. Frazer Clark, Jr. Washington: N.C.R. Microcard Editions, 1972. (Newark, NJ: Carteret Book Club, 1910) 2v. in 1. Index.
   One hundred letters chronicling the friendship and business relation-ship between Hawthorne and his publisher Ticknor are a record of the later years of Hawthorne's career. Most were written from Liverpool where Hawthorne was American consul. Remarkable for its intimacy and detail, Hawthorne's correspondence provides insights into the mind and heart, as well as the activities of the mature Hawthorne.

1986 Hawthorne, Nathaniel   1804-1864
Love letters of Nathaniel Hawthorne, 1839-1863. Foreword by C.E. Frazer Clark, Jr. Washington: NCR Microcard Editions, 1972. (Chicago: privately printed, 1907) 2v. in 1.
   The love letters Hawthorne wrote to his future wife, Sophia Amelia Peabody. This edition of the Dofobs publication of 1907 includes 102 letters from the 1839-1842 period together with 62 additional letters after 1842 and restores many of the passages Mrs. Hawthorne had expurgated.

1987 Hay, John   1838-1905
Letters of John Hay and extracts from his diary. New York: Gordian Press, 1969. (Washington: printed but not published, 1908) 3v.
   A quick wit and warm humor shine through Hay's writings, portraying him as a man always more aware of his blessings than of his hardships. He has made his diplomacy appear as effortless as his poetry and prose, always correct but never tedious.

1988 *Hayden, Melissa   1923-
Melissa Hayden, off stage and on. Photographs by Fred Fehl. Garden City, New York: Doubleday & Co., Inc., 1963. 127 p.
   A great ballerina tells her own story as well as those of some ballets, what she thinks and feels as she dances them, how she brings them to life.

1989 Hayden, Thomas Emmett   1940-
Trial. New York: Holt, Rinehart & Winston, 1970. 168 p.
   A restrained anger marks this minutely detailed account of the conspir-acy trial following the Chicago Riots of 1968. Hayden contends: "Our crime was that we were beginning to live a new and contagious life style without official authorization. We were tried for being out of control." In chronicling this often absurd trial that the author sees as the first main sign of a swing to the repressive right, Hayden also captures the cultural forces operating at the time.

1990 Hayden, William   b.1785
Narrative of William Hayden, containing a faithful account of his travels for a number of years, whilst a slave, in the South. Afro-American Histor-ical Series. Philadelphia: Rhistoric Publishers, 1969. (Cincinnati: The author, 1846) 156 p.
   Hayden was an atypical slave determined to be free without running away. While traveling with his master, a domestic slave trader, he ignored several opportunities to escape; finally in 1824 he bought his freedom and settled legally in Cincinnati.

1991 Haydn, Hiram Collins   1907-1973
Words and faces. New York: Harcourt Brace Jovanovich, 1974. 346 p. Index.
   The author relates his experiences in book and journal publishing for thirty years and recalls the stimulating people he has known and worked with. He was an editor of the Phi Beta Kappa publication, *The American Scholar*, a teacher, and an editor and publisher for Crown, Harcourt, Atheneum, and Random House.

1992 *Hayes, Helen   1900-
Gift of joy. With Lewis Funke. New York: M. Evans and Co., Inc., 1965. 254 p.
   In chapters on various subjects—Shakespeare, gardening, age, work—the actress recalls incidents from her life along with favorite

poems, excerpts from plays, essays, and novels relating to the chapter topics.

1993 *Hayes, Helen   1900-
On reflection: an autobiography. With Sanford Doty. New York: M. Evans (distributed by Lippincott), 1968. 253 p.
   A shy child who became the first lady of the American stage, Helen Hays writes of her family, their famous friends, their pets, and the lessons life has taught her. With gentle and affectionate humor she sets down anecdotes from her private and public life in this legacy for her grandchil-dren.

1994 Hayes, Rutherford Birchard   1822-1893
Hayes: the diary of a President, 1875-1881, covering the disputed elec-tion, the end of Reconstruction, and the beginning of Civil Service. Edited by T. Harry Williams. New York: David McKay Co., Inc., 1964. 329 p. Index.
   A President's record of the period of his life covering nomination, campaign, his disputed election, and his term of office.

1995 *Hayhurst, Emma Luethy
I will: an autobiography. Hicksville, New York: Exposition Press, 1978. 245 p.
   Confined to a wheelchair after she was stricken with crippling polio as a child, she went on to become an artist, an inspiring teacher, and a poet.

1996 Hayne, Donald   1908-
Batter my heart. New York: Alfred A. Knopf, 1963. 303 p.
   A priest's thoughtful, well-written, philosophical search for meaning in his life in relation to the church and modern times.

1997 Hayne, Paul Hamilton   1830-1886
A collection of Hayne letters. Edited by Daniel Morley McKeithan. Westport, Connecticut: Greenwood Press, 1970. (Austin: The University of Texas Press, 1944) 499 p.
   Raised in an aristocratic Charleston family, Hayne was a prominent Southern writer after the Civil War, publishing poems, reviews and critiques widely. His letters are written to literary contemporaries such as William Dean Howells, James Russell Lowell, and William Gilmore Simms.

1998 *Hays, Brooks   1898-
A hotbed of tranquility; my life in five worlds. With an appreciation by Donald G. Herzberg. New York: The Macmillan Co., 1968. 238 p. Index.
   Hays, who lost his congressional seat because of his moral stand on Civil Rights, writes about his life emphasizing the uses and abuses of humor in campaigning, in Congress, in the courtroom, and in academia.

1999 *Hayward, Brooke   1937-
Haywire. Illustrated. New York: Alfred A. Knopf, 1977. 325 p.
   The daughter of actress Margaret Sullavan and theatrical producer Leland Hayward has written an unsentimental, compelling memoir about her family's life, centering on the themes of "carelessness and guilt, and the wreckage they can make of lives." Despite the best of intentions and the bestowal of "grace, joy, beauty, privilege, and power" on their chil-dren, the Haywards divorced and the children suffered mental breakdowns, an undiagnosed death at 21, and enormous conflicts with their mother.

2000 *Hayward, Helen (Harry)   1898?-
The other foot. New York: Vantage Press, 1951. 122 p.
   Lively account of growing up in a stern, father-dominated family in impoverished Methodist parsonages in the South.

2001 Haywood, Harry   1898-
Black Bolshevik: autobiography of an Afro-American communist. Illus-trated. Chicago: Liberator Press, 1978. 700 p. Index.
   Haywood's consciousness of discrimination against workers and Blacks was heightened when he served as a member of the all-Black Eighth Regiment of the U.S. Army in World War I. Upon discharge, he became involved with the Communist Party in America and internationally, and devotes much of this voluminous book to analyzing the Party's activities in the 1920's, '30's and '40's. In the process, he also explores a number of Civil-Rights issues of particular significance to Blacks, such as the case of the Scottsboro boys, and provides a history of Black involvement in com-munism.

2002 Hazard, Leland   1893-
Attorney for the situation. Illustrated. Pittsburgh, Pennsylvania: Carnegie-Mellon University Press, 1975. 314 p. Index.
   After his early legal career in Kansas City, Hazard moved to Pitts-burgh, serving as an officer of Pittsburgh Plate Glass and becoming active in planning the "Renaissance," helping to initiate the first educational TV station, WQED, and working to improve the quality of urban life by means of modern mass transit, cultural events, international exchange, and community development programs.

2003 *Hazlitt, Margaret   **1770-1841**
Journal; recollections of England, Ireland, and America. Edited and annotated by Ernest J. Moyne. Lawrence: The University of Kansas Press, 1967. 195 p. Index.
She was the daughter of Reverend William Hazlitt, the first Apostle of Unitarianism in Boston, and the sister of William Hazlitt, the distinguished essayist and critic. Half of her journal describes her impressions of America, with notes on Boston, Philadelphia, and Pittsburgh, among other places.

2004 *Head, Edith   **1907-**
Dress doctor. With Jean Kesner Ardmore. Boston: Little, Brown and Co., 1959. 249 p.
A prominent costume designer in Hollywood writes of her work, of the Oscars she earned, and of the glamorous clients she has served.

2005 Healy, George Peter Alexander   **1813-1893**
Reminiscences of a portrait painter. New York: Kennedy Graphics, Inc., 1970. (Chicago: A.C. McClurg and Co., 1894) 221 p.
Healy's story recalls his youth, his determination to become an artist, and his meetings with and paintings of famous people of his era: nobility and crowned heads of state, American and French statesmen, and men of letters.

2006 Healy, George William, Jr.   **1905-**
A lifetime on deadline: self-portrait of a Southern journalist. Foreword by Turner Catledge. Illustrated. Gretna, Louisiana: Pelican Publishing Co., 1976. 294 p. Index.
Healy focuses on his fifty-year career as a journalist, primarily with the New Orleans *Times-Picayune,* which he eventually edited; during World War II he worked in Washington, D.C. as director of censorship with the Office of War Information. Portions of the book are accounts of Healy's childhood in Nachez and his college days at Ole Miss, where he played cards and golf with "shiftless" William Faulkner.

2007 *Hearst, Patricia Campbell   **1954-**
The trial of Patty Hearst. Edited by Kenneth J. Reeves. Illustrated by Jack Lucey. Introduction and epilogue by Carolyn Andpacher. San Francisco: Great Fidelity Press, 1976. 738 p. Index.
This is the transcript of the trial of Patty Hearst for bank robbery in April, 1974. She was captured by the terrorist Symbionese Liberation Army, eventually identified with her captors, was a fugitive for fifteen months, and was convicted despite her claim of brainwashing.

2008 Hearst, William Randolph   **1863-1951**
William Randolph Hearst: a portrait in his own words. Edited by Edmond D. Coblentz. New York: Simon and Schuster, 1952. 309 p.
Using the publisher's letters and writings, the editor, who was an associate of Hearst's for fifty years, has composed a story of the long career of a controversial and influential journalist.

2009 Heath, William   **1737-1814**
Heath's memoirs of the American War: reprinted from the original edition of 1798. Introduction and notes by Rufus Rockwell Wilson. Freeport, New York: Books for Libraries Press, 1970. (Boston: I. Thomas & E.T. Andrews, 1798) 435 p. Index.
A collection of diary entries and letters, 1775-1783, providing "one of the most valuable of the contemporary narratives of the Revolution" from the point of view of a general, who, though "worthy and patriotic, [was] better fitted for muster service and barrack duty than active command in the field." Heath, not a strategist, failed despite considerable advantage to defeat the Hessians at Fort Independence, New York, in 1777; thereafter Washington never assigned any important field missions to him.

2010 Heatter, Gabriel   **1890-1972**
There's good news tonight. Edited by Edwin Palmer Hoyt, Jr. Garden City, New York: Doubleday and Co., Inc., 1960. 216 p.
Heatter, originator of "We the People," a 1930's network radio show, regards his inspirational motto, "Ah there's good news tonight," and the upbeat broadcast itself as a means of encouraging listeners to conquer their fears. Obsessed with and sometimes incapacitated by fears, he credits his broadcasting and his loyal wife with helping him to control his own life.

2011 Hebert, Feux Edward   **1901-**
Last of the Titans: the life and times of the Congressman of Louisiana. With John McMillan. Preface by Bascom N. Timmons. Edited by Glenn R. Conrad. Lafayette, Louisiana: Center for Louisiana Studies, University of Southwestern Louisiana, 1976. 478 p. Index.
Hebert regards himself as "the prototype of a vanishing breed," a Southern conservative Democrat and powerful congressman for over 35 years. He was a militant foe of communism, particularly harsh on Whittaker Chambers and, as chairman of the House Armed Services Committee since 1971, a staunch advocate of military preparedness.

2012 Hecht, Ben   **1894-1964**
A child of the century. New York: Simon and Schuster, 1954. 654 p. Index.

Hecht started his career as a newspaper reporter in Chicago, writing short stories, novels, non-fiction books, and plays in his spare time. He became one of the Chicago literary group that included Sherwood Anderson, Theodore Dreiser, and Carl Sandburg. Later he wrote for Broadway and Hollywood as well.

2013 Hecht, Ben   **1894-1964**
Letters from Bohemia. Garden City, New York: Doubleday & Co., Inc., 1964. 203 p.
Hecht remembers seven of his artist-friends through amusing and affectionate anecdotes and informal letters from them. They were all talented, artistic, and unconventional; their letters reflect Hecht's personality as well as their own.

2014 Heckewelder, John   **1743-1823**
Thirty thousand miles with John Heckewelder. Edited by Paul A.W. Wallace. Pittsburgh: University of Pittsburgh Press, 1958. 474 p. Index.
A remarkable record of an eighteenth-century Moravian missionary's sixty years among Indians of the Ohio Valley, edited from twelve manuscript journals and two histories.

2015 Heckman, William L. ("Steamboat Bill")   **b.1869**
Steamboating: sixty-five years on Missouri's rivers; the historical story of developing the waterway traffic on the rivers of the Middlewest. Introduction by Dan Saults. Kansas City: Burton Publishing Co., 1950. 284 p.
Reminiscences of a long life on a long river by a captain who left school at twelve to learn river piloting and knows the Missouri from its mountain beginning in Montana to St. Louis and the Mississippi River. Includes descriptions of steamboats and river lore from the mid-nineteenth century.

2016 Heckscher, August   **1913-**
Alive in the city: memoir of an ex-commissioner. Illustrated. New York: Scribner, 1974. 294 p.
As New York City Parks Commissioner for six years, Heckscher was responsible for making the city more livable and enjoyable. He pictures city government clearly and considers the complex, contradictory recreational needs of a great metropolis which he tried to fulfill.

2017 Hedrick, Ulysses Prentiss   **1870-1951**
Land of the crooked tree. New York: Oxford University Press, 1948. 350 p.
Frontier life in the woods of northern Michigan during the 1870's and 80's, the author's boyhood. Interesting details of daily life in a well-written narrative.

2018 *Hedwig, Eva Kiesler
see *Lamarr, Hedy

2019 Heidenreich, Steve   **1954-**
Running back. And Dave Dorr. New York: Hawthorn Books, 1979. 219 p.
Heidenreich, an Indiana University runner whose under-four-minute miles made his racing of Olympic Games caliber, was badly injured by a hit-and-run driver in 1976. This book chronicles his gradual recovery, his overcoming of aphasia, his successful return to racing, and his hopes of qualifying for the 1980 Olympics.

2020 *Heiner, Marie Hays   **1907-**
Hearing is believing. Introduction by Rupert Hughes. Cleveland: The World Publishing Co., 1949. 126 p.
Describes deafness in her youth and her adaption to it, leading her to become a dominant force in the Cleveland Hearing and Speech Center for thirteen years.

2021 Heinsheimer, Hans Walter   **1900-**
Best regards to Aida; the defeats and victories of a music man on two continents. New York: Alfred A. Knopf, 1968. 267 p. Index.
The author was at the center of music publishing in Europe and the United States during most of the twentieth century. Here he tells about his career and the composers and performers of serious modern music he has known.

2022 *Hellman, Lillian   **1905-**
Pentimento, a book of portraits. Boston: Little, Brown and Co., 1973. 297 p.
Reminiscences from different stages of her life from childhood to the present reveal facets of the playwright's life—Hollywood days, New York in the 30's, her long love affair with Dashiell Hammett, her career in the theater.

2023 *Hellman, Lillian   **1905-**
Scoundrel time. Introduction by Garry Wills. Boston: Little, Brown and Co., 1976. 155 p.
Twenty-four years after being investigated by the House Un-American Activities Committee and subsequently blacklisted for alleged (but

unproven) communist sympathies, playwright Hellman, with a fine mixture of anger and scorn, analyzes the experience and its devastating short- and long-term effects on American life and on her career.

2024 *Hellman, Lillian   1905-
Three. Introduction by Richard Poirier. Illustrated. Boston: Little, Brown and Co., 1979. 726 p.
This volume contains three of Hellman's autobiographical works previously published as separate volumes— *An Unfinished Woman, Pentimento, Scoundrel Time.*

2025 *Hellman, Lillian   1905-
Unfinished woman—a memoir. Boston: Little, Brown and Co., 1969. 280 p.
Although she was close to many well-known figures, Hellman chose to focus this book on mostly obscure people who have meant much to her. "The daily stuff," she says, is "the real truth," not the gossip or celebrities.

2026 *Helm, Edith (Benham)
Captains and the kings. Foreword by Mrs. Franklin D. Roosevelt. New York: G.P. Putnam, 1954. 300 p. Index.
The book tells about the author's childhood and youth and how she became social secretary at the White House. She served in that capacity for 25 years, though not continuous ones, under Wilson, Roosevelt, and Truman.

2027 *Helmericks, Constance   1918-
Our Alaskan winter. And Harmon Helmericks. Boston: Little, Brown and Co., 1949. 271 p.
The authors learned to survive in the wintertime while exploring the Arctic, living Eskimo-style in a tent-snowhouse, eating caribou and boiled fish, and getting to know the Eskimos.

2028 *Helmericks, Constance   1918-
Our summer with the Eskimos. And Harmon Helmericks. Boston: Little, Brown and Co., 1948. 239 p.
An exciting summer spent on the Colville River and the shores of the Arctic Ocean living as the Eskimos do and learning their ways.

2029 *Helmericks, Constance   1918-
We live in the Arctic. And Harmon Helmericks. Boston: Little, Brown and Co., 1947. 329 p.
Another of their exciting books about living in the Far North, hunting, living simply as the Eskimos do, being self sufficient and battling for survival in the face of formidable odds, but reveling in the freedom.

2030 Helmericks, Harmon
see *Helmericks, Constance

2031 Helpern, Milton   1902-1977
Autopsy: the memoirs of Milton Helpern, the world's greatest medical detective. With Bernard Knight, M.D. New York: St. Martin's Press, 1977. 273 p. Index.
After a brief account of his New York childhood and education (C.C.N.Y. and Cornell Medical College), Helpern focuses on the various deaths with which he had to deal as Chief Medical Examiner of New York City, in performing many autopsies and testifying at many court trials. Among the most notorious murder trials were the cases of Alice Crimmins, Dr. Carl Coppolino, and Dr. Hermann Sander. *Autopsy* is also a history of forensic medicine, which Helpern's engaging narrative style does much to make palatable.

2032 *Hemenway, Ruth V., M.D.   1894-1974
A memoir of revolutionary China, 1924-1941. Edited with introduction by Fred W. Drake. Illustrated. Amherst: The University of Massachusetts Press, 1977. 220 p.
Hemenway writes about her life as a missionary doctor in China before the Communist revolution (1924-1941). Not a strong believer in organized religion, she fought with religious missionaries, communists, and Japanese to bring medicine and schooling to Chinese orphans.

2033 Hemingway, Ernest   1899-1961
Moveable feast. New York: Charles Scribner's Sons, 1964. 211 p.
People, places, impressions—an inside view of the literary scene in Paris in the Twenties.

2034 *Hemingway, Mary Welsh   1908-
How it was. Illustrated. New York: Alfred A. Knopf, Inc., 1976. 537 p. Index.
The fourth wife of novelist Ernest Hemingway tells the poignant, often humorous story of her life, from her "Huck Finn" childhood through early newspaper days, her first marriage, her life with Hemingway during his most turbulent years, and her struggle to adjust after his suicide. Her memoir defines her as a successful journalist and sportswoman in her own right.

2035 *Hemphill, La Breeska Rogers   1940-
La Breeska: an autobiography. Nashville, Tennessee: Hemphill Music Co., 1976. 220 p.
Singer La Breeska Hemphill nostalgically recalls her childhood and the beginnings of her gospel singing career with a family ensemble, the Happy Goodmans. Following marriage to a Pentacostal preacher, La Breeska and her husband embarked on their own traveling ministry, culminating in a performance at the Grand Ole Opry.

2036 Hemphill, Paul   1936-
The good old boys. New York: Simon & Schuster, 1974. 255 p.
Most of the chapters appeared previously in essay form. Considered by the author to be an epitaph to the good old boys of the South, this collection is a sympathetic description of his father, a trucker, the importance of baseball and sports in general, the world of evangelists and Lester Maddox, Nashville, and Roller Derby—an attempt to convey the sense of place the author has as a Southerner.

2037 Henderson, Brantley   b.1884
Only the happy memories: reminiscences of a Virginia boyhood. New York: Exposition Press, 1954. 197 p.
Henderson reminisces about his boyhood in South Boston, Halifax County, Virginia, where he was nurtured by a loving family and superstitious Blacks on a tobacco plantation. He describes his rural schooling, his first cigar, and his first love.

2038 Henderson, Ernest   1897-1967
World of Mr. Sheraton. New York: David McKay Co., Inc., 1960. 277 p.
President of the Sheraton Hotel Corporation, he writes of his first business ventures in merchandising and the development of the chain. He presents the factors that led to a successful business and the image of a disciplined ambition, arguing that his book and his business career are a tribute to the merits of the free enterprise system.

2039 Hendricks, Joseph Edward   1903-
Little Joe: my memories. Kissimmee, Florida: Cody Publications, Inc., 1966. 417 p.
Hendricks, reared in Florida and educated at Stetson University, was elected in 1936 as Democratic Congressman from Florida's Fifth District (including Orlando, St. Augustine, and Daytona Beach), partly because of his support of the Townsend Plan. He served in Congress for twelve years and tells trivial, unconnected anecdotes about Senators William Bankhead, Lyndon Johnson, and others. Hendricks ends with a personalized account of his later business career building sub-divisions in his former Congressional district.

2040 Hennacy, Ammon   1893-1970
The book of Ammon. Introduction by Steve Allen and Dorothy Day. Illustrated. Salt Lake City: Ammon Hennacy, 1964. 490 p.
An overly detailed, discursive account of the radical, pacifist activities of a social worker and sometime migrant laborer. Persecuted during World War I for his pacifism, Hennacy continued to communicate with and support the anarchistic activities of people such as Alexander Berkman and Emma Goldman and the socialism of Eugene Debs. Strongly influenced by Thoreau, Tolstoy, and Gandhi, he temporarily converted to Roman Catholicism in the 1950's and between 1953-1961 was an associate editor of *The Catholic Worker.*

2041 *Henrichsen, Margaret (Kimball)   1900-
Seven steeples. Cambridge: Houghton Mifflin, 1953. 238 p.
A Methodist woman minister in Maine discusses how she got into her profession and the reactions she encountered because she was a woman. As a part of her story she reviews her own spiritual growth.

2042 Henry, Joseph   1797-1878
The papers of Joseph Henry. Edited by Nathan Reingold. Washington, D.C.: Smithsonian Institution Press, 1972- . v. Index.
A founder of the Library of Congress and of the American scientific community, Henry was concerned with the proper application of science to technology. Volume I: December 1797-October 1832, The Albany Years; Volume 2: November 1832-December 1835, The Princeton Years.

2043 Henry, William Mellors (Bill Henry)   1890-1970
Behind the headlines with Bill Henry, 1903-1970. Edited by Patricia Henry Yeomans. Los Angeles: The Ward Ritchie Press, 1972. 304 p.
A prominent journalist in print, radio, and television, he was a columnist for the Los Angeles *Times* for thirty years, an enthusiastic promoter of the Olympic Games, and chief commentator on NBC television's "Window on Washington."

2044 Henson, Josiah   1789-1883
Father Henson's story of his own life. Introduction by Mrs. H.B. Stowe. Williamstown, Massachusetts: Corner House Pub., 1973. (Boston: A.D. Phelps, 1849) 212 p.
Although Harriet Beecher Stowe used him as an inspiration for Uncle Tom, the real Henson narrative reveals a different person, courageous and determined, who, having escaped to Canada, later with skill and resource-

fulness led other slaves to freedom and had subsequent careers as a preacher, community leader, and agent of the Underground Railway. This is a reprint of the 1858 edition. The numerous editions have varying titles, including *Uncle Tom's story of his life, Truth stranger than fiction,* and *An Autobiography of the Rev. Josiah Henson.*

2045 Henson, Matthew Alexander 1866-1955
A Black explorer at the North Pole; an autobiographical report by the Negro who conquered the top of the world with Admiral Robert E. Peary. Foreword by Robert E. Peary. Introduction by Booker T. Washington. New York: Walker and Co., 1969. (New York: Frederick A. Stokes Co., 1912) 190 p.
The exciting and arduous expedition to the North Pole described by Henson, a Black explorer who accompanied Admiral Peary on all of his trips since 1891 and proved his stamina, courage, and fitness by long and thorough apprenticeship. Originally published under the title, *A Negro Explorer at the North Pole.*

2046 Herff, Ferdinand Peter 1883-1965
The doctors Herff: a three-generation memoir. Edited by Laura L. Barker. San Antonio: Trinity University Press, 1973. 2v. Index.
A remarkable record of his family medical heritage. His father and grandfather were physicians; from them he derived an unusual sense of responsibility to his profession and commitment to society. All practiced in San Antonio after Ferdinand Ludwig Herff's immigration from Germany.

2047 Hergert, Jacob J. 1892-
"I was born among the Russian subversives": A saga of why it was possible for the Bolsheviks to effect the transition from one absolutism to another/What are we facing? Illustrated by James Hadlow. "Warning" by Arthur Park Tracy. Santa Barbara, California: J.J. and A.J. Hergert, 1967. 673 p.
Hergert attempts to rewrite, from an insider's vantage point, the history of the Russian people and their leaders with an eclectic religious bent. He includes the details of his Russian childhood (up to 1913, when he immigrated to the United States) and his opinions of events concerning the United States and Russia.

2048 Herman, Leon
A surgeon thinks it over. Philadelphia: University of Pennsylvania Press, 1962. 159 p.
A Pennsylvania Dutch boy's journey from the farm to, as he says in the Introduction, "an honorable, if not exalted, estate in the ultra conservative atmosphere of Philadelphia surgery."

2049 Herman, Victor 1915-
Coming out of the ice: an unexpected life. Illustrated. New York: Harcourt Brace Jovanovich, 1979. 369 p.
Herman became Russianized as a consequence of living in Russia with his auto-worker father. Befriended by a famous Russian general, he entered an aviation school and won a world parachuting contest but had problems because of his American citizenship. Arrested as an enemy of the state, Herman experienced years of imprisonment and torture in Siberia, but received a surprise exoneration after eight years and left Russia for the U.S.A.

2050 Hermanns, William
Holocaust, from a survivor of Verdun. Drawings by Paul Bacon. New York: Harper & Row, 1972. 141 p.
Urged by his students at San Jose State College who felt that what had happened at Verdun was happening in Vietnam, Hermanns published his experiences during World War I as a German soldier. He had been in the trenches of the Argonne Forest and a prisoner of the French, but the horror of his four days in the Battle of Verdun had the most profound effect on the rest of his life.

2051 Herndon, Angelo 1913-
Let me live. New York: Arno Press, 1969. (New York: Random House, 1937) 409 p.
The son of a poor Black miner, he went to work in the Kentucky coal mines at thirteen. In the late 1920's he moved to Birmingham, continuing to suffer from poverty and racial discrimination. During the Depression he joined the Communist Party as a labor organizer. He was indicted in Georgia under an anti-slave insurrection law of 1861 and was eventually exonerated by the U.S. Supreme Court in 1937.

2052 Herrgesell, Oscar 1926-1972
Dear Margaret, today I died... letter from Vietnam. Compiled by Margaret Rawton Herrgesell. San Antonio: The Naylor Co., 1974. 93 p.
He arrived in Vietnam February 19, 1972; he was killed in a helicopter hit by artillery on July 29, 1972. These letters written to his wife during that time convey the anxiety, fear, and hope of a dedicated lieutenant colonel in a frustrating war.

2053 Herrick, James Bryan 1861-1954
Memories of eighty years. Introduction by the author. Chicago: University of Chicago Press, 1949. 270 p. Index.

Recollections of conditions in medical education and practice for eight decades by physician in general practice and diagnostic consultation; includes reflections on old age and descriptions of his colleagues' work.

2054 Herron, Jim 1866-1949
Fifty years on the Owl Hoot Trail: Jim Herron, the first sheriff of No Man's Land, Oklahoma Territory. Edited by Harry E. Chrisman from an original manuscript. Introduction by Edward Everett Dale. Chicago: Sage Books, 1969. 355 p.
Herron dictated his story to his teenage granddaughter in the 1940's when he was old and blind. Chrisman used the original typescript, supplemented by letters from pioneers and cattlemen who knew Herron and with information from county records. Herron's life story as a cowboy, sheriff, and outlaw is a remarkable document of ranch life in the Southwest.

2055 Herst, Herman 1909-
Nassau Street: a quarter century of stamp dealing. New York: Duell, Sloan and Pearce, 1960. 305 p.
He started collecting stamps when he was a boy in Portland, Oregon, and later decided to become a dealer and collector. His career as a philatelist on Nassau Street in New York, the center of the nation's stamp dealers, is the major theme of his book.

2056 Hertzler, Arthur Emanuel 1870-1946
The horse and buggy doctor. Foreword by Milburn Stone. Lincoln: University of Nebraska Press, 1970. (New York: Harper & Brothers, 1938) 322 p.
A well-written narrative of a prominent Kansas doctor, his rural boyhood, his early medical interest and training, the development of his country practice, the building of his outstanding clinic.

2057 *Herz, Alice d.1974
Phoenix: letters and documents of Alice Herz: the thought and practice of a modern day martyr. Edited by Shingo Shibata. Amsterdam, B.R. Gruner B.V., 1976. 216 p.
A refugee from Nazi Germany, in 1974 she chose "the flaming death of the Buddhists" as an act of protest against U.S. intervention in Vietnam. Her letters document her growing moral outrage with the unrestrained power of the U.S. Executive.

2058 Herz, Jacob
Fair ball in foul territory; the confessions of a little league manager on the field and in the clubhouse. Jericho, New York: Exposition Press, 1974. 122 p.
A bitter and inflated account of five years as manager of a Little League program. He describes how the actual practice of running a Little League program falls far short of instilling American ideals and values in boys as exemplified by Jack Armstrong.

2059 Heston, Charlton 1916-
The actor's life: journals 1956-1976. With Carol Lanning. Edited by Hollis Alpert. Illustrated. New York: A Henry Robbins Book /E.P. Dutton, 1978. 482 p.
Heston identifies these daily jottings as impressionistic notations about his acting career, world travels, wife Lydia, son Fraser, and daughter Holly, which "have taught me a lot, mainly about myself, but also about makeup, and scripts, and shooting schedules, and leading ladies, and studio heads." He deleted, before publication, much personal miscellany. Heston emerges as a consummate craftsman, a lover of his family and of travel, and highly principled in work and friendships.

2060 Heth, Edward Harris 1909-1963
My life on earth. Illustrated by Edwin Schmidt. New York: Simon & Schuster, 1953. 247 p.
An evocative, moving, often humorous account of Heth's friends and neighbors in rural Wisconsin, where the living is relaxed and where people dwell harmoniously with each other and with nature. This is contrasted with New York City, where such values do not exist; Heth makes intermittent forays there to transact business pertinent to his career in advertising (short-lived) and as a writer (for a lifetime) and is always delighted to return to the country. Good-natured line drawings enhance this pleasant text.

2061 Heth, Henry 1825-1899
The memoirs of Henry Heth. Edited by James L. Morrison, Jr. Westport, Connecticut: Greenwood Press, 1974. 303 p. Index.
Heth was a professional soldier schooled at West Point and seasoned on the Western frontier, who served as a Confederate general during the Civil War. He was less effective than his immediate contemporaries; he acted impulsively and without being able to foresee the enemy's reactions, but he was brave, tenacious, and loyal.

2062 Heusken, Henry 1832-1861
Japan journal, 1855-1861. Translated and edited by Jeannette C. van der Corput and Robert A. Wilson. New Brunswick, New Jersey: Rutgers University Press, 1964. 247 p. Index.

Because he knew Dutch, which was the language of diplomacy and medium of communication with Japanese scholars interested in Western science and technology, Heusken became secretary and interpreter for the first American Consul-General to Japan, Townsend Harris. Arriving just after the Perry expedition, Harris acted to improve upon the previous agreements and procure a full commercial treaty.

2063 *Hewins, Caroline Maria   1846-1926
Caroline M. Hewins: her book: containing *A Mid-century Child and her Books* (by Caroline M. Hewins) and *Caroline M. Hewins and Books for Children* (by Jennie D. Lindquist). Preface by Bertha Mahony Miller. Introduction by Anne Carroll Moore. Illustrated. Boston: Horn Book, Inc., 1954. (New York: Macmillan, 1926) 107 p.
   Hewins, an outstanding and pioneering children's librarian, shows a love of her profession and what it symbolizes through this eloquent account of her childhood and adolescence as manifested through her reading of the best and the brightest of children's literature.

2064 Hewitt, Arthur Wentworth
Old brick manse. New York: Harper and Row, 1966. 246 p.
   The colorful recollections of a small Vermont town pastorate written in a friendly, homespun, direct style. The book speaks of many phases of his life including his election to the state legislature and battles in the senate over local option, education, women's suffrage.

2065 Hewitt, Edward Ringwood   1866-1957
Days from seventy-five to ninety. New York: Duell, Sloan and Pearce, 1957. 128 p.
   A chronicle of his zest for life and activity in old age (he typed the manuscript at ninety) by the author of *Those Were the Days.*

2066 Hewitt, Edward Ringwood   1866-1957
A trout and salmon fisherman for seventy-five years. New York: C. Scribner's Sons, 1948. (1922) 338 p.
   A revised edition of two of his earlier published books with much new material added, this book contains fishing lore about tackle, baits, life cycle and habits of fish, their foods and habitats, all in considerable and careful detail.

2067 Hewitt, Joe   1931-
I was raised a Jehovah's Witness. Denver: Accent Books, 1979. 191 p.
   A third-generation Jehovah's Witness who turned Baptist minister, Hewitt writes about his mother's conversion to the Witnesses and of his childhood ministry for the Watchtower Society, eventual disillusionment, and conversion to Christianity. He provides a primer on, and argument of, Jehovah's Witnesses doctrines, organization, and tactics, emphasizing how the Witnesses have employed scripture out of context and continually updated their doctrines and dates for Armageddon.

2068 Hewitt, John Michael   b.1867
The Alaska vagabond, Doctor Skookum: memories of an adventurous life. New York: Exposition Press, 1950. 284 p.
   Hewitt focuses on the most exciting time of his life, 1898-1902, when as camp physician he joined a party of prospectors in the Alaska Gold Rush of 1898. He loved the rustic, frontier environment and mores, the outdoors, the colorful people, and recalls anecdotes of miscellaneous medical cases he attended in the wilds.

2069 *Heymanns, Betty   1932-
Bittersweet triumph. Garden City, New York: Doubleday & Co., Inc., 1977. 191 p.
   Heymanns writes of her battle against cerebral palsy, fighting not only to walk and speak but to become recognized as a professional photographer.

2070 *Heyward, Carter
A priest forever. New York: Harper & Row, 1976. 146 p.
   She was one of eleven women "irregularly" ordained to the priesthood of the Episcopal Church in 1974. Her book describes her childhood, her call to the priesthood, and documents the heated controversy caused by her ordination.

2071 *Heywood, Martha Spence   b.1873
Not by bread alone: the journal of Martha Spence Heywood, 1850-1856. Edited by Juanita Brooks. Illustrated. Salt Lake City: Utah State Historical Society, 1978. 141 p. Index.
   Martha Spence traveled from Iowa to Utah Territory by covered wagon to become the third wife of Mormon Joseph Heywood. Her journal recounts the hardships of the trip. She was chronically ill and did not get along well with Heywood's other wives or their traveling companions. She also discusses activities of the Mormon church at Nephi and Zion, Utah.

2072 Hicks, Elias   1789-1849
Journal of the life and religious labours of Elias Hicks, late of Newtown, Bucks County, Pennsylvania. New York: Arno Press, 1969. (Philadelphia: Merrihew & Thompson, printers, 1851) 451 p.

A narrative, including diary entries, of his spiritual reveries, written by a prominent Quaker leader during the last six years of his life.

2073 Hicks, Granville   1901-
Part of the truth. New York: Harcourt, Brace & World, Inc., 1965. 314 p. Index.
   Desiring to produce a book that was "objective, selective, honest as far as it went, as straightforward" as possible, Hicks examines his life, his writing, his friends, and the causes he espoused, particularly communism, with which he eventually became disillusioned.

2074 Hicks, Granville   1901-
Small town. New York: The Macmillan Co., 1946. 276 p.
   Hicks writes about his fellow townsmen (although their names are changed), himself, and the small busy fragment of life that is a New England town, its schools and other institutions, the minds and human nature of its citizens, and his own part in the life of the town.

2075 Hicks, John Donald   1890-1972
My life with history; an autobiography. Illustrated. Lincoln: University of Nebraska Press, 1968. 366 p. Index.
   Although his book started out to be primarily an academic autobiography, Professor Hicks included personal experiences which help to illustrate the changing customs of the times. He has found himself typical of the small-town, middle-class, Midwestern American who left the country for the city and who brought some of the old agricultural influences into the dominant urban society.

2076 Hicks, John Edward
Adventures of a tramp printer, 1880-1890. Kansas City: MidAmericana Press, 1950. 285 p.
   After working ten years as an apprentice in many different American cities, a young printer decides to become a journalist. Good detail about the history of early newspapers, other printers and editors, and the social conditions of the time.

2077 *Higgins, Marguerite   1920-1966
News is a singular thing. Garden City, New York: Doubleday, 1955. 256 p.
   A Pulitzer Prize-winning journalist for the New York *Herald Tribune* writes of her years as a foreign correspondent during World War II, the Korean War, and in the Eastern European countries. She also relates the difficulties she encountered in her profession because she was a woman.

2078 Higginson, Henry Lee   1834-1919
Life and letters of Henry Lee Higginson: By Bliss Perry. Freeport, New York: Books for Libraries Press, 1972. (Boston: The Atlantic Monthly Press, 1921) 557 p. Index.
   The letters are set in a biographical frame by the editor, providing a continuous narrative of a prominent Bostonian—a major in the Civil War, a partner in the wealthy brokerage firm of Lee, Higginson and Company, a founder and patron of the Boston Symphony Orchestra, and a generous contributor to the development of Harvard University and other educational institutions.

2079 Higginson, Thomas Wentworth   1823-1911
Army life in a Black regiment. Introduction by Howard Mumford Jones. Williamstown, Massachusetts: Corner House, 1971. (East Lansing: Michigan State Univ. Press, 1870) 296 p.
   Higginson, a prominent Bostonian, was commander of the First South Carolina Volunteers, the first slave regiment organized for the United States during the Civil War. His book records regimental life in camp and on the battlefield; it also conveys the yearning of the North for a simpler, healthier way of life than was experienced in industrialized cities.

2080 Higginson, Thomas Wentworth   1823-1911
Cheerful yesterdays. New York: Arno Press, 1968. (Boston: Houghton Mifflin, 1898) 374 p.
   Born into one of the established families in Salem, Massachusetts, he became a Unitarian minister, a militant abolitionist, and a crusader for women's rights. He spent his life moving back and forth between political theory and its demonstration, achieving a remarkable balance.

2081 Higginson, Thomas Wentworth   1823-1911
Letters and journals of Thomas Wentworth Higginson, 1846-1906. Edited by Mary Thacher Higginson. New York: Negro Universities Press, 1969. (Boston: Houghton Mifflin Co., 1921) 358 p.
   The record of this prominent Boston clergyman and man of letters includes his early life in Cambridge and Worcester, a remarkable document of his Civil War experience, and interactions with many of his famous contemporaries.

2082 *Hildegarde, pseud.
   see *Sell, Hildegarde Loretta

2083 *Hilf, Mary Asia b.1874
No time for tears. As told to Barbara Bourns. New York: Thomas Yoseloff, 1964. 271 p.
An articulate, engaging account of Hilf's formative years in Teofipol, Russia, immigration to Wisconsin, and marriage to Jake Rosenberg, a successful merchant. An optimistic activist, she was devoted to her husband, daughter, extended family, and various Jewish philanthropic causes.

2084 Hill, George Handel (Yankee) 1809-1849
Scenes from the life of an actor. Illustrated. Completed by anon. New York: Garrett & Co., Publishers, 1969. (1853) 246 p.
Above all, "Yankee" Hill was impulsive. This comic actor who visited prisons, asylums, almshouses, and similar establishments in his character researches, entered Harvard and later practiced medicine solely because of a pleasant encounter with his own physician.

2085 Hill, George Henry 1900-
Yankee photographer. New York: Coward-McCann, 1953. 184 p.
A former newspaper photographer for the New York *Times-Wide World Photos* relates the memorable stories he covered in New England, 1919-1944.

2086 Hill, Jasper Smith 1832-1858
The letters of a young miner: covering the adventures of Jasper S. Hill during the California Gold Rush, 1849-1852. Edited with introduction and notes by Doyce B. Nunis. Illustrated. San Francisco: John Howell-Books, 1964. 111 p.
In 1849 17-year-old Jasper Hill journeyed from his home in Mt. Pleasant, Iowa, to California with a group of fellow townspeople, The Mt. Pleasant Mining Company, in hopes of striking it rich. His letters home throughout the next two years, from Placerville, Nevada City, and Hang Town, California, reflect perseverance and hard work with little reward.

2087 Hill, Shandy
Dear Sir: you cur. Illustrated. Philadelphia: Whitmore Publishing Co., 1969. 190 p.
Shandy Hill was editor and publisher of the Pottstown (Pa.) *Mercury* (1930-1960), which reflected his "personality, character, toughness, pugnacity, kindness, humor, compassion." This third person account focuses on notable newspaper stories and crusades.

2088 Hilleary, William M. 1840?-1917
A webfoot volunteer: the diary of William M. Hilleary, 1864-1866. Oregon State Monographs, Studies in History No. 5. Edited by Herbert B. Nelson and Preston E. Onstad. Corvallis: Oregon State University Press, 1965. 240 p. Index.
As prospectors, traders, and others sought to advance into the interior of Oregon in the 1860's, two volunteer regiments were called upon to put an end to the guerrilla warfare with which the Indians harassed the immigrants. The citizen-soldiers kept the trails open and defended settlements east of the Cascade Mountains, thereby protecting their homes and families in the Willamette Valley.

2089 Hilton, Conrad Nicholson 1887-1979
Be my guest. Englewood Cliffs, New Jersey: Prentice-Hall, Inc., 1957. 372 p. Index.
Although some of his book describes his successful years as head of an international hotel corporation, much of it describes his early experience in boyhood and business, revealing the amazing drive and pioneer spirit which helped him develop his empire.

2090 Himes, Chester Bomar 1909-
My life of absurdity: autobiography II. Illustrated. Garden City, New York: Doubleday & Co., Inc., 1976. 398 p.
Himes, a Black writer of mystery stories (*Pink-Toes, Blind Man With a Pistol, Cotton Comes to Harlem*) reviews the events of his literary and sexual adventures in Europe (primarily Paris) 1955-1970. Himes intermittently laments his rejections by European and American publishers.

2091 Himes, Chester Bomar 1909-
The quality of hurt: the autobiography of Chester Himes. Illustrated. Garden City, New York: Doubleday and Co., Inc., 1972-1976. 2v.
Intense, densely packed volumes that trace the author's growing up in the South, his unorthodox education, his seven-and-a-half-year stint in the Ohio State Penitentiary, his growth as a writer, his desire to leave the United States, and the eventual fulfillment of that desire. Often painful, sometimes funny, an intimate and intelligent portrait of the Black artist.

2092 Hinckle, Warren James 1938-
If you have a lemon, make lemonade. New York: G.P. Putnam's Sons, 1974. 370 p. Index.
Hinckle, from 1964 to 1969 editor of *Ramparts* which became the leading magazine against the Vietnam War, describes his view of the Sixties and the political, religious, and cultural transformations which occurred—changes within the Catholic Church, the hippie movement, the Kennedy assassination controversy and other headline-making events.

2093 Hinckley, Robert Henry 1891-
I'd rather be born lucky than rich: the autobiography of Robert Hinckley. Provo, Utah: Brigham Young University Press, 1977. 160 p. Index.
Raised a Mormon, Hinckley began government administrative work during the Depression, first with the Federal Emergency Relief Act, then with the Water Development and Conservation Program and the WPA. He attempted to reconcile Mormon opposition to federal assistance projects. In later years he worked for Sperry and the Civil Aeronautics Authority, fulfilling a lifelong commitment to political participation.

2094 Hindus, Maurice Gershon 1891-1969
A traveler in two worlds. Introduction by Milton Hindus. Garden City, New York: Doubleday & Co., Inc., 1971. 326 p.
A peasant boy from Eastern Europe, Hindus appreciates the opportunities he found in America, especially the opportunity of obtaining a first-class education at Colgate and Harvard despite his poverty and lack of influential connections. In this book covering the years up to 1923 when he revisited his native Russia for a writing assignment, he remembers his youth and marvels at the freedom he found in America: "I had been subject to no social or class discrimination, to no political oppression."

2095 Hines, Jerome 1921-
This is my story, this is my song. Westwood, New Jersey: Fleming H. Revell Co., 1968. 160 p.
Trained in chemistry and math as well as voice, Hines became a basso at the Metropolitan Opera in his early twenties. Shortly after his marriage, he had a religious experience which transformed his life, giving him inner strength during the strain of performance and leading him to do volunteer work on various skid rows while his reputation as a basso continued.

2096 Hines, John Chesterfield b.1877
Minstrel of the Yukon: an Alaskan adventure. Foreword by Lucius Beebe. New York: Greenberg Publisher, 1948. 231 p.
Colorful description of frontier life in Nome, Alaska (1900-1906), before the Gold Rush, by a man who worked as a prospector, entertainer, newspaper apprentice, and mining company executive.

2097 Hinkle, John 1851-1941
I saw my Savior: a true story. New York: Pageant Press, 1953. 63 p.
Elder Hinkle tells of his conversion and of his preaching experiences as a Primitive Baptist in Kentucky. This spiritual autobiography, full of morals and parables, is written in simple language with the fervor and conviction of righteousness. Hinkle often rewrites portions of the Bible as his personal narrative.

2098 *Hinkley, Anita W. b.1884
Wickford memories. Boston: Branden Press, 1972. 118 p.
Nostalgic memories of life in an old village on Narragansett Bay in Rhode Island where her family has lived for generations. She describes in loving detail the people, houses, activities, and her serene contentment with her surroundings.

2099 Hinricks, Everard
see Sloan, Eric

2100 Hirsch, William 1892-
Treat them human. As told to Victor Ullman. Foreword by Joe E. Brown. Introduction by Danny Thomas. Illustrated. New York: Crown Publishers, 1964. 253 p.
For sixty years Hirsch provided humanitarian law enforcement, treatment, and rehabilitation of prisoners as superintendent of the Toledo, Ohio, workhouse and as sheriff of Lucas County, Ohio. He and his wife, Rose, have personally helped thousands of prisoners, Boys' Club members, and newsboys to lead useful, moral lives and have earned Toledo's respect and love. An appealing book that does much to dispel the media images of insensitive sheriffs and brutal lawbreakers.

2101 Hirschmann, Ira Arthur 1906-
Caution to the winds. New York: David McKay Co., Inc., 1962. 312 p.
In 1921 he was a copy boy in a Newark department store; in the early thirties he became vice-president of Saks Fifth Avenue. During World War II he secretly negotiated for the release of Jewish children and adults in several European countries. His book is rich with anecdotes of celebrities in the arts and politics.

2102 Hiss, Alger 1904-
In the court of public opinion. New York: Alfred A. Knopf, 1957. 424 p. Index.
In 1948 Whittaker Chambers testified before the House Un-American Activities Committee that Hiss, a State Department official, was a communist. Hiss describes the hearings, his evidence of fraud and forgery used against him, and the climate of opinion of the time.

2103 Hitchcock, Ethan Allen 1798-1870
Fifty years in camp and field; diary of Mayor-General Ethan Allen

Hitchcock. Edited by W.A. Croffut. New York: G.P. Putnam's Sons, 1909. 514 p. Index.

Diary entries connected by the editor to form a narrative of an eminent American soldier, the grandson of Ethan Allen. Hitchcock recorded a vivid account of the Mexican War. During the Civil War he declined the command of the Union Army and became military advisor to Lincoln and Stanton.

2104 Hoard, Edison   1933-
Curse not the darkness. With Michael Reuben. Chicago: Children's Press, 1970. 64 p.

Orphaned at eleven, he became determined to do well in school. He lived with various relatives, worked after school and on weekends, and ultimately became a successful lawyer in Chicago.

2105 *Hobart, Alice Tisdale   1882-1967
Gristy's child. New York: Longmans, Green and Co., 1959. 343 p.

A novelist writes of her mother's early death and her own subsequent quest for life, which took her to China during its revolution and again before World War II, experiences which formed the basis of several novels.

2106 Hobbs, Thomas Hubbard   1826-1862
The journals of Thomas Hubbard Hobbs: a contemporary record of an aristocrat from Athens, Alabama; written between 1840, when the diarist was fourteen years old, and 1862, when he died serving the Confederate States of America. Edited by Faye Acton Axford. University: University of Alabama Press, 1976. 272 p. Index.

Hobbs's diary covers his active years as a member of Alabama's privileged plantation class, his years as a state legislator, and his brief service as a captain in the Confederate Army, before he died of a severe leg wound in 1862.

2107 Hobbs, William Herbert.   1864-1953
An explorer-scientist's pilgrimage: the autobiography of William Herbert Hobbs. Illustrated. Ann Arbor, Michigan: J.W. Edwards, Inc., 1952. 222 p. Index.

Hobbs, a professor of geology at the University of Wisconsin and at the University of Michigan, describes his career as a geologist. He traveled over the world in geological explorations, including Germany, Spain, Italy, Africa, Australia, New Zealand, and Greenland. He was a prolific author of scientific papers, a noted contributor to international geological congresses, and a distinguished teacher.

2108 Hodges, Luther Hartwell   1898-1974
Businessman in the statehouse: six years as Governor of North Carolina. Chapel Hill: University of North Carolina Press, 1962. 324 p. Index.

The story of his six years as Governor of North Carolina during which he dealt with state government in a businesslike fashion in order to handle problems efficiently, cut red tape, and get things done.

2109 Hodgin, Edwin Stanton   b.1868
Confessions of an agnostic clergyman: a lifelong search for a satisfying faith. Boston: The Beacon Press, 1948. 235 p.

Quaker boyhood in Iowa farm country, Unitarian ministry in California and Massachusetts (1906-1946).

2110 Hoffa, James Riddle   1913-1975?
The trials of Jimmy Hoffa; an autobiography. As told to Donald I. Rogers. Chicago: Henry Regnery Co., 1970. 308 p.

Hoffa's life story covers his poverty-stricken childhood, his various jobs, his association with the Teamster's Union, and his rise to the presidency of the Union. He discusses at length his prosecution by Robert Kennedy and what he calls the "frame-up." Some of the trial testimony is included with Hoffa's accusations that the basic guarantees of American justice were violated and he was deprived of a fair hearing.

2111 Hoffman, Abbie   1936-
Soon to be a major motion picture. Introduction by Norman Mailer. Illustrated. New York: Perigree Book (G.P. Putnam's Sons), 1980. 304 p.

A mordantly witty saga of Hoffman's activities as a free spirit and social revolutionary. The book covers Hoffman's Jewish childhood in Worcester, Massachusetts, college at Brandeis, and first marriage, but it focuses on his radical activities in the Civil Rights movement in the South during the early 1960's and as protester during the 1968 Democratic Convention, for which he stood trial as a member of the "Chicago Seven." To escape imprisonment for a "coke bust," Hoffman went underground for seven years, then wrote this upon his reemergence.

2112 Hoffman, Charles Anthony   1904-
God, man and medicine. Edited by Elizabeth A. Nichols. Illustrated. Parsons, West Virginia: McClain Printing Co., 1978. 205 p.

Urologist and past president of the American Medical Association, Hoffman details his commitment both to the individual patient and to political medicine. As AMA president he traveled throughout the world, encountering the problems and practices of socialist- and communist-administered medicine and exploring common moral and scientific concerns with fellow physicians. Problems of birth control and sex education were particularly prominent during his administration; Hoffman's conservatism led him to oppose legalized abortions and physicians' attempts to unionize.

2113 *Hoffman, Helen   1900-
    see ***Hoffman, Ruth**

2114 *Hoffman, Malvina   1887-1966
Yesterday is tomorrow: a personal history. New York: Crown Publishers, Inc., 1965. 378 p.

Born into a musical family, she grew up appreciating the arts and turned to sculpture as her medium. She studied in Paris, worked with Rodin, and portrayed many different segments of society. Her work brought her world-wide acclaim and recognition as America's foremost woman sculptor, especially as an interpreter of dance and of the races of mankind. Generously illustrated.

2115 Hoffman, Richard   1831-1909
Some musical recollections of fifty years. Biographical sketch by his wife. Introduction by Frank E. Kirby and John G. Doyle. Detroit Reprints in Music. Illustrated. Detroit: Information Coordinators, Inc., 1976. (New York: Charles Scribner's Sons, 1910) 168 p.

Hoffman recalls exposure in his early youth to performances of Mendelssohn and Liszt in England and the development of his own fifty-year career as a pianist, mostly in the United States. His belief in the importance of individual interpretation in music is emphasized by his article "How to Stimulate Thought and Imagination in a Pupil," reprinted here.

2116 *Hoffman, Ruth and *Helen Hoffman   1900-
We lead a double life. Philadelphia: J.B. Lippincott Co., 1947. 264 p.

A lively and unusual story of identical twins who lived nearly identical lives, became commercial artists, studied and traveled extensively in Europe and North Africa. Interesting analysis of the psychology of twins, their anxiety about being "different," and their pleasure in leading inseparable lives.

2117 Hoffman, William S.   1937?-
The loser. New York: Funk, 1968. 213 p.

He describes his compulsive fascination for gambling which caused him to abandon a wife, four children, and middle-class comfort to embark on a life on the run.

2118 Hogan, John Joseph   1829-1913
On the mission in Missouri, 1857-1868. Ltd. edition. Westminster, Maryland: Christian Classics, 1972. (Kansas City, Missouri: J.A. Heilmann, 1892) 211 p.

The story of a missionary traveling on horseback and railroad to small Missouri towns, with details of his expenses, the dangers of travel, the tension before, during, and after the Civil War.

2119 Hohn, Caesar   1887?-1962?
Dutchman on the Brazos: reminiscences. Foreword by Agnes Meyer. Austin: University of Texas Press, 1963. 194 p. Index.

The story of a frontier Texan, his boyhood, college years at Texas A. and M., and his long career in agricultural services and development.

2120 Holden, William Curry   1903-
Alton Hutson: reminiscences of a South Plains youth. Edited by William Curry Holden. Oral historian, William Curry Holden. Illustrated. San Antonio, Texas: Trinity University Press, 1975. 151 p. Index.

Hutson's first thirty years in Lubbock, Texas, compiled from his written account, brief diaries, and oral history told to Holden. Hutson's parents were typical rancher-homesteaders who eventually went broke. He worked his way through high school and college with a variety of menial jobs, eventually earned a law degree, but lived on the profits from a cactus wax-rendering business on the Mexican border.

2121 *Holiday, Billie   1915-1959
Lady sings the blues. With William Dufty. New York: Lancer, 1969. (Garden City, New York: Doubleday and Co., Inc., 1956) 250 p.

Jazz singer writes of the poverty and prejudice in her early life and career, her seduction by men and drugs, with a tentative optimism about her future. Discography included.

2122 Holley, Joseph Winthrop   1874-1958
You can't build a chimney from the top: the South through the life of a Negro educator. New York: The William-Frederick Press, 1949. 226 p.

After graduating from Phillips Academy and Lincoln University, Holley returned to the South, where in 1903 he founded and became president of Albany State College (Albany, Georgia).

2123 *Holley, Mary (Austin)   1784-1846
Texas diary, 1835-1838. Edited with an introduction by J.P. Bryan. Illustrated. Austin: University of Texas, 1965. 120 p. Index.

Her diary covering two trips to Texas in 1835 and 1837-8 gives glimpses of prominent Texans as well as descriptions of transportation, living conditions, political and social activities during the infancy of Texas. Includes pencil sketches she made of the Houston area.

2124 *Holley, Sallie   1818-1893
A life for liberty: anti-slavery and other letters of Sallie Holley. Edited with introductory chapters by John White Chadwick. Illustrated. New York: Negro Universities Press, 1969. (New York: G.P. Putnam's Sons, 1899) 292 p. Index.

Sallie Holley devoted her quiet life to the betterment of Blacks, as her abundant letters, assembled here with biographical connections, make clear. Educated at Oberlin College, she worked first for the abolition of slavery and, that accomplished, taught Black children in Virginia for the last twenty years of her life. She was in communication with many contemporary notables, intellectual and liberal.

2125 Holmes, Burton   1870-1958
The world is mine. Illustrated by Burton Holmes. Culver City, California: Murray & Gee, Inc., 1953. 267 p.

Holmes, bon vivant and world traveler who earned a handsome living giving illustrated lectures about his travels, focuses on travels before and during World War I in Morocco, Japan, Spain, and Mexico. He accompanies the narrative with numerous photographs of the interiors of his ornate house, of erupting volcanoes, of colorful natives, and of himself in elaborate costumes.

2126 Holmes, Edison Parker   1896-
The disadvantage of being a preacher's son. Winston-Salem, North Carolina: Clay Printing Co., 1950. 167 p.

A journalist writes of his boyhood in North Carolina, where he was raised in a rural Methodist parsonage.

2127 Holmes, Frank Lincoln Duane   b.1881
Covered wagon memories. New York: Vantage Press, 1971. 142 p.

The story of a boy's fifth year when he and his family lived in a covered wagon in Minnesota with the vain hope that the open-air living would cure his mother's consumption. After her death the boy and his father used the wagon for living and business quarters when Mr. Holmes became a peddlar.

2128 Holmes, James   1804-1883
Dr. Bullie's notes: reminiscences of early Georgia and of Philadelphia and New Haven in the 1800's. Edited, compiled, with introduction by Delma Eugene Presley. Atlanta: Cherokee Publishing Co., 1976. 247 p. Index.

A physician and Georgia state legislator followed the pattern of his second cousin, Oliver Wendell Holmes, by writing autobiographical and regional essays in the manner of *The Autocrat of the Breakfast Table.* He discusses his education at Yale and Penn, the Georgia coastal culture, Georgia political figures, the sea islands of Georgia, the Civil War, and his medical practice.

2129 Holmes, John Clellon   1926-
Nothing more to declare. New York: Deutsch, 1968. (New York: E.P. Dutton, 1967) 253 p.

Holmes's book, focusing on the 1950's, is divided into three sections. I, Recollections of his friendships with four significant visitors, Jay Landesman, Gershon Legman, Jack Kerouac, and Allen Ginsberg. II, Essays of literary criticism. III, His autobiography, emphasizing two marriages (to wives unnamed), many love affairs, literary successes, the writing process—and his own protracted bouts with writer's block.

2130 Holmes, John Haynes   1879-1964
I speak for myself: the autobiography of John Haynes Holmes. New York: Harper and Brothers, 1959. 308 p. Index.

The life of a liberal who was minister of the Community Church of New York City for over fifty years, who helped found both the American Civil Liberties Union and the NAACP.

2131 *Holmes, Marjorie   1910-
You and I and yesterday. Illustrated. New York: William Morrow & Co., 1973. 191 p.

A prolific author of popular and religious books reflects on her childhood in Storm Lake, Iowa, during the 1920's. Acknowledging that everything was not good in the good old days, she nevertheless recalls those times with a certain nostalgia for a simpler life.

2132 Holmes, Oliver Wendell   1809-1894
Our hundred days in Europe: the writings of Oliver Wendell Holmes. Vol. X. Riverside Edition. Boston: Houghton Mifflin and Co., 1896. 301 p. Index.

Holmes tells of his 1886 voyage to Europe, comparing his experiences and observations to those of this 1833-35 visit—marveling in the changes made in the fifty intervening years.

2133 Holmes, Oliver Wendell   1841-1935
Holmes-Laski letters: the correspondence of Mr. Justice Holmes and

Harold J. Laski, 1916-1935. Edited by Mark DeWolfe Howe. Foreword by Felix Frankfurter. Cambridge: Harvard University Press, 1953. 2v. Index.

An unusual friendship and correspondence developed between them when Holmes was 75 and Laski 23, a young professor of government at Harvard. Their letters document an adventuresome intellectual exchange.

2134 Holmes, Oliver Wendell   1841-1935
Holmes-Pollock letters: the correspondence of Mr. Justice Holmes and Sir Frederick Pollock, 1874-1932. Edited by Mark DeWolfe Howe. 2nd ed. Cambridge: Harvard University Press, 1961. (1941) 2v. Index.

A remarkable record of a friendship and an era. Both were intelligent, cultured members of the legal profession and began their American-English correspondence on legal and social matters soon after they met.

2135 Holmes, Oliver Wendell   1841-1935
Holmes-Sheehan correspondence: the letters of Justice Oliver Wendell Holmes and Canon Patrick Augustine Sheehan. Edited with preface and introduction by David H. Burton. Port Washington, New York: National University Publications/Kennikat Press, 1976. 70 p.

These 43 letters and the excerpts from letters exchanged in 1903-1913 between Irish Canon Sheehan and the "essentially religious" legal scholar, . . . free-swinging intellectual, dissenting Justice" Holmes reveal the affection and common human sympathies that united these two men, although they were almost diametrically opposed on matters of doubt and belief, science and religion.

2136 Holmes, Oliver Wendell   1841-1935
Justice Holmes to Doctor Wu: an intimate correspondence, 1921-1932. New York: Central Book Co., Inc., 1947. 58 p.

Originally published in the October 1935 issue of the *T'ien Hsia Monthly,* these letters were written to Dr. John C.H. Wu when he was an unknown law student of 22. Subsequently, he became a prominent attorney, politician, and Dean of the Comparative Law School of China. The letters were prompted by Wu's great admiration for Holmes, as indicated in a series of articles he published in the *Michigan Law Review* (1921-23).

2137 Holmes, Oliver Wendell   1841-1935
Touched with fire: Civil War letters and diary of Oliver Wendell Holmes, Jr., 1861-1864. Edited by Mark DeWolfe Howe. Cambridge: Harvard University Press, 1946. 158 p. Index.

Letters primarily to his mother and fragments of his diary, both written when he was a young officer in the Civil War, depict life in the field, daily hardships and supply shortages, and the perils of being wounded with only primitive medical aid available.

2138 Holmes, Robert Masten   1844-1864
Kemper County rebel: the Civil War diary of Robert Masten Holmes, C.S.A. Edited by Frank Allen Dennis. Foreword by Thomas L. Connelly. Jackson: University and College Press of Mississippi, 1973. 115 p. Index.

Holmes, a private in the 24th Mississippi Regiment (the "Kemper Rebels") of the Confederate Army, kept a diary from May 1862, through May 1863. He was cheerful and stoic in the campaigns in Kentucky and East and Middle Tennessee, bearing no malice to the North.

2139 *Holmes, Sarah Katherine (Stone)   1841-1907
Brokenburn: the journal of Kate Stone, 1861-1868. Edited by John Q. Anderson. Baton Rouge: Louisiana State University Press, 1972. (1955) 400 p. Index.

The Civil War experiences of a well-educated, sensitive, patriotic girl in her twenties, living on a large cotton plantation in northeast Louisiana; a remarkably intense and wide-ranging view of the times.

2140 Holmes, Wilfred Jay   1900-
Double-edged secrets: U.S. naval intelligence operations in the Pacific during World War I. Foreword by Daniel K. Inouye. Illustrated. Annapolis, Maryland: Naval Institute Press, 1979. 231 p. Index.

Captain Holmes recounts his service in intelligence from June 1941 to the end of World War II.

2141 Holt, John Caldwell   1923-
Never too late: my musical life story. New York: Delacorte Press, 1978. 245 p.

Holt was well along in a career as a writer and speaker when he took up the cello in his forties. Here he tells of his musical family, childhood trips to Carnegie Hall, listening to jazz after "lights out" at Exeter, and his self-instructed discovery of classical music. Like Holt's other books, this one is about learning and making a commitment to an art—at any age.

2142 Holtz, Paul R.   1895-
Sixty years in medicine. New York: Vantage Press, 1977. 108 p.

A good-natured reminiscence about Holtz's farm boyhood in rural Maryland, his early medical practice in Wyoming, and notable cases he has encountered. He itemizes important medical discoveries during his lifetime and concludes with a brief discussion of immunology.

2143 *Homans, Abigail (Adams)   **1881-1974**
Education by uncles. Illustrated with decorations by Pauline Baynes.
Boston: Houghton Mifflin Co., 1966. 148 p.
  A spirited account by the great-great-grandaughter of President John
Adams describes her youth, much of which she spent with her uncles
Henry and Brooks after the death of her father. With Henry in Washing-
ton and London she was in the midst of a circle of the famous people of
the day; with Brooks she lived in Paris until the Spanish-American War
broke out and he sent her to live in a convent.

2144 Honnell, William Rosecrans   **1860-1946**
**Willie Whitewater: the story of W.R. Honnell's life and adventures
among the Indians as he grew up with the state of Kansas.** As told to
Caroline Cain Durkee. Introduction by Kirke Mechem. Kansas City:
Burton Publishing Company, 1950. 309 p.
  Recollections of three generations of homesteading in Kansas with
some descriptions of American Indian customs.

2145 *Hooper, Alice Forbes Perkins
  see Turner, Frederick Jackson

2146 Hooper, Ben W.   **1870-1957**
Unwanted boy: the autobiography of Governor Ben W. Hooper. Edited by
Everett Robert Boyce. Knoxville: University of Tennessee Press, 1963.
258 p. Index.
  After two terms as Governor of Tennessee, he became a key figure in
arbitration on the U.S. Railroad Labor Board.

2147 Hooten, William J.   **1900-**
Fifty-two years a newsman. El Paso: The University of Texas at El Paso,
1974. 193 p. Index.
  For 52 years (1918-1970) Hooten had a ringside seat watching local,
national, and international news unfold. He started to work for the Associated Press in Arizona and retired as editor of the El Paso *Times* after
thirty years, longer than any other person had held the job. He tells of
many famous people he met and memorable events he reported.

2148 Hoover, Calvin Bryce   **1897-1974**
Memoirs of capitalism, communism, and nazism. Durham, North Carolina: Duke University Press, 1965. 302 p. Index.
  Although Hoover was at one time hostile toward old-style capitalism,
his experiences and observations of various economic, political, and social
systems have facilitated his change in attitude to support for the current
form of "modified capitalism." His government service in Intelligence
together with his knowledge and research as an economist have helped
him understand concepts of "balance between the power of the state and
personal liberty."

2149 *Hoover, Helen   **1910-**
A place in the world. New York: Alfred A. Knopf, 1969. 292 p.
  She and her husband gave up their jobs in Chicago to live in the
Minnesota woods. She was a research metallurgist, he an art director for
a publishing house. In their simpler life they established new careers as a
nature writer and illustrator.

2150 *Hoover, Helen   **1910-**
The years of the forest. New York: Alfred A. Knopf, 1973. 318 p.
  This work is a continuation of her life with her husband in Minnesota
until "progress" forced them to leave their life in the woods.

2151 Hoover, Herbert Clark   **1874-1964**
**The Hoover-Wilson wartime correspondence, Sept. 24, 1914 to Nov. 11,
1918.** Edited by Francis William O'Brien. Ames: The Iowa State University Press, 1974. 297 p. Index.
  During World War I Hoover was Food Administrator for the U.S.
under President Wilson, overseeing the acquisition of food for America,
the Allies, and the neutral nations. Though the two were personally very
different in background and personality, they had to cooperate closely in
their service to the country and the world.

2152 Hoover, Herbert Clark   **1874-1964**
The memoirs of Herbert Hoover. New York: The Macmillan Company,
1952. (1951) 3v. Index.
  The memoirs give a detailed account of domestic and world affairs,
reflecting Hoover's personal and professional point of view. Volume I.,
Years of Adventure 1874-1920; Volume II., The Cabinet and the Presidency 1920-1933; Volume III., The Great Depression 1929-1941.

2153 Hope, Bob   **1903-**
Five women I love: Bob Hope's Vietnam story. Garden City, New York:
Doubleday & Co., Inc., 1966. 255 p.
  The story of his famous Christmastime USO trips to do shows for
American soldiers in Vietnam and Southeast Asia. He always included
five beautiful girls along with the other entertainers in the shows which
played at military camps, bases, and often areas close to the front lines.

2154 Hope, Bob   **1903-**
Have tux, will travel: Bob Hope's own story. As told to Pete Martin.
Illustrated by Ted Sally. New York: Simon and Schuster, 1954. 308 p.
Index.
  Comedian Hope humorously describes his childhood in Cleveland,
Ohio, where as a teenager he broke into show business as a dancer and
singer. He soon became a comedian, made Hollywood movies, traveled
worldwide entertaining U.S. troops during World War II, and amassed a
fortune. Unlike many of his peers who have been married and divorced
many times, he remains devoted to his wife, Dolores, and four children.

2155 Hope, Bob   **1903-**
I owe Russia $1200. Garden City, New York: Doubleday & Co., Inc.,
1963. 272 p.
  A breezy, humorous book describing many of his international tours to
armed force bases during the Cold War years.

2156 Hope, Bob   **1903-**
Road to Hollywood: my 40-year love affair with the movies. And Bob
Thomas. Illustrated. Garden City, New York: Doubleday and Company,
1977. 271 p.
  Comedian Hope describes the "road" from his birthplace in Cleveland,
Ohio, to Hollywood. Through a mixture of humor and backstage anecdotes, he pays tribute to his leading ladies and his fellow actors, especially
his good friend Bing Crosby. Editor Thomas adds a critical appreciation
of Hope's films.

2157 Hopkins, Albert L.   **1893-**
Autobiography of a lawyer. Chicago: Albert L. Hopkins, 1966. 236 p.
  A Chicago attorney describes his Mississippi upbringing and his education at Ole Miss, University of Chicago, and Harvard. Founder of the
esteemed legal firm of Hopkins, Sutter, Owen, Mulray, Wentz & Davis,
he emphasizes some of the significant legal issues involved in notable law
cases he has argued concerning interstate commerce and revenue matters.
His concluding chapter expresses his political conservatism and isolation-
ism.

2158 Hopkins, Claude C.   **b.1866**
My life in advertising: scientific advertising. Foreword by S.R. Bernstein.
Chicago: Advertising Publications, Inc., 1966. (New York: Harper &
Brothers, 1927) 318 p.
  Hopkins describes over fifty years' experience in advertising for such
companies as Swift, Van Camp, Quaker Oats, and Pepsodent. He writes
not a life story but a "business story" full of common sense and insight
into uncommon salesmanship.

2159 *Hopkins, Sarah Winnemucca
Life among the Piutes: their wrongs and claims. Bishop, California: Sierra
Media, Inc., 1969. (1883) 268 p.
  She sees her life in the context of her tribe, their first contact with
whites, their early trust and good faith and the dishonesty and violence
they got in return. Her book emphasizes the wrongs her people endured.

2160 Hopkins, William Foster   **1899-1977**
Murder is my business. Dayton, Ohio: Landfall Press, 1970. (Cleveland:
World Pub. Co., 1970) 344 p.
  "Foss" Hopkins has been a Cincinnati lawyer specializing in murder
trials for over fifty years. His hard-hitting, hard-boiled style provides
dramatic accounts of courtroom trials of the famous, such as Harry Gold,
for his association with the Klaus Fuchs international nuclear secrets spy
case, the infamous, and the unknown. "The afternoon you call my office
in need of help and I do not respond, I will not be retired. I will be dead."

2161 Hoppe, Willie   **1887-1959**
Thirty years of billiards. Edited by Thomas Emmett Crozier. New York:
Dover, 1975. (New York: G.P. Putnam's Sons, 1925) 254 p. Index.
  The book chronicles his years as a child prodigy and his rise to the
Balkline billiards championship. Text includes thirty-eight illustrated
lessons in billiards.

2162 *Hopper, Hedda   **1890-1966**
Whole truth and nothing but. With James Brough. Garden City, New
York: Doubleday & Co., Inc., 1963. 331 p.
  Her second Hollywood memoir is filled with anecdotes of famous celeb-
rities she interacted with during her career as a gossip columnist.

2163 Hopping, Richard Coke   **b.1875**
A sheriff-ranger in chuckwagon days. Illustrated by J. Smith. New York:
Pageant Press, 1952. 246 p.
  In novelistic form, with vivid, natural dialogue, Coke narrates an adventuresome tale of the life he and his wife, Leila, led as pioneers and
ranchers in West Texas and New Mexico, "the last of the frontier
outposts" at the turn of the twentieth century. Coke eventually became a
sheriff and describes some of his more dangerous conquests.

2164 Horgan, Paul   **1903-**
Encounters with Stravinsky: a personal record. New York: Farrar, Straus
and Giroux, 1972. 224 p. Index.

A sketchbook of recollections and anecdotes about the author's relationship with Igor Stravinsky before and after their friendship began. He calls it a "personal record . . . a modest act of homage to a transcent artist" who brought him aesthetic fulfillment for almost forty years.

2165 Horn, Tom 1860-1903
Life of Tom Horn, Government Scout and interpreter: written by himself: together with his letters and statements by his friends. A vindication. John C. Coble, Preface, Afterword. Glorieta, New Mexico: Rio Grande Press, 1976. (Denver: John C. Coble, 1904) 328 p.
A stock detective schooled by the Pinkertons, Horn had been a government scout fighting the Apaches and had served in Cuba in the Spanish-American War. Horn's autobiography offers interesting letters, testimony, and transcripts appended to the life story but does not quite "vindicate" or explain the murder of a teenaged boy for which Horn was hanged.

2166 *Horne, Lena 1917?-
In person, Lena Horne. As told to Helen Arstein and Carlton Moss. New York: Greenberg, 1950. 249 p.
Description of her struggle to develop a career as a singer, with her mother's help, by an entertainer who encountered racial discrimination in her working and family life.

2167 *Horne, Lena 1917?-
Lena. As told to Richard Schickel. New York: Doubleday & Co., Inc., 1965. 288 p.
An extraordinary entertainer tells of beginning her career at sixteen in Harlem's Cotton Club to support her parents, through recognition and achievement in nightclubs, films, theater, and television.

2168 *Horney, Karen 1885-1952
The adolescent diaries of Karen Horney. New York: Basic Books, 1980. 271 p.
These five diaries, 1899-1911, span Horney's school days, medical education, marriage to Oskar Horney, psychoanalysis, and first pregnancy. She was always in love, sometimes with love itself. Her letters to "Homvieh," whom she married in 1909, convey an intellectual friendship before the correspondents eventually fell in love.

2169 Hornsby, Rogers 1896-1963
My kind of baseball. Edited with foreword by J. Ray Stockton. New York: David McKay Co., 1953. 185 p.
Hornsby, who led the National League in batting for seven years in the 1920's with a 400+ batting average, tells about his baseball career as an outfielder with the St. Louis Cardinals, New York Giants, and Chicago Cubs, and as manager of the Cincinnati Reds.

2170 Hornung, Paul Vernon 1935-
Football and the single man. As told to Al Silverman. Garden City, New York: Doubleday & Co., Inc., 1965. 252 p.
An All-American quarterback at Notre Dame and later a fine all-around halfback for the Green Bay Packers, Hornung describes his life as pro-football's Golden Boy, his scrapes with his coaches, his "fiancées," his supercharged life.

2171 Hosmer, Horace R. 1830-1894
Remembrances of Concord and the Thoreaus: letters of Horace Hosmer to Dr. S.A. Jones. Edited by George Hendrick. Urbana: University of Illinois Press, 1977. 157 p.
Journeyman Hosmer's plainspoken letters to Jones reveal "the desperation, not always quiet" that surrounds Thoreau's *Walden*, as he focuses on the "materialism, drunkenness, brutal treatment of mentally retarded children, and suicides "(ed.) in Concord, Massachusetts. Hosmer comments on Thoreau's love of nature and absence of sexuality.

2172 *Hotchner, A.E.
see *Day, Doris

2173 Hough, Henry Beetle 1896-
Once more the thunderer. New York: Ives Washburn, Inc., 1950. 316 p.
Newspaper editor in Martha's Vineyard, Massachusetts, describes his thirty years on the *Vineyard Gazette* with stories about people and events, and reflections on his legacy from the past.

2174 Hough, Henry Beetle 1896-
To the harbor light. Drawings by Donald Carrick. Boston: Houghton Mifflin Co., 1976 210 p.
Charming reminiscences of a gentle, easy-going way of life on Martha's Vineyard.

2175 Hough, John T., Jr. 1946?-
A peck of salt; a year in the ghetto. Boston: Little, Brown and Co., 1970. 245 p.
A Vista volunteer's story of his year working in the Black ghettos of Chicago and Detroit. Despite his determination to understand and help,

his efforts failed, though it was an "honorable failure" caused by the magnitude of the task, not by any lack of integrity or industry.

2176 *Houghton, Adelaide (Louise) Wellington b.1867
The London years: the diary of Adelaide Wellington Houghton, 1925-1929. Washington, D.C.: privately printed at the Spiral Press, New York, 1963. 274 p.
The 1925-1929 diary of the wife of the U.S. Ambassador to Great Britain, Allen B. Houghton, is replete with details of teas, luncheons, motor tours, court appearances, and ambassadorial protocol. Menus, guest lists, and daily schedules of Mrs. Houghton and her five children comprise most of the entries, with an occasional reference to weightier diplomatic matters.

2177 House, Edward Mandell 1858-1938
The intimate papers of Colonel House: arranged as a narrative by Charles Seymour. St. Clair Shores, Michigan: Scholarly Press, 1976. (Boston: Houghton Mifflin Co., 1926-28) 4v.
A close advisor and confidant of President Wilson, House first became involved in politics in Texas where he was identified with the reform faction of the Democratic Party. Later he advised Wilson on cabinet appointments, acted as liaison and intermediary between Wilson and government, financial and business leaders, and during World War I acted as the President's right-hand man in dealings with the Allies. Because he compromised instead of standing on principle during the Paris Peace Conference, he lost the trust of Wilson thereafter.

2178 House, Edward Mandell 1858-1938
Letters from the Colonel: Edward M. House to Frank Andrews, 1899-1902. Edited by James A. Tinsley. Vol. IV, no. 1. Houston: Texas Gulf Coast Historical Association, 1960. 20 p.
Eighteen letters of Colonel House's private correspondence with prominent Houston lawyer Frank Andrews show the extreme control that House and his friends exercised over Texas politics through supporting a gubernatorial candidate sympathetic to their business interests. They also reveal House's enterprise in promoting the economic development of the Southwest Texas Gulf area.

2179 Houseman, John 1902-
Front and center. Illustrated. New York: Simon and Schuster, 1979. 512 p. Index.
Houseman writes about the years 1942-1955, including his contributions to Voice of America during World War II and anecdotes of actors, directors, writers, and producers involved in many of his plays and motion pictures, especially *Galileo*, *The Bad and the Beautiful*, and *Lust for Life*.

2180 Houseman, John 1902-
Run through; a memoir. New York: Simon & Schuster, 1972. 507 p. Index.
During the 1930's and early 40's, Houseman was director or producer of many plays, including *Four Saints in Three Acts*, *The Shoemaker's Holiday*, *Heartbreak House*. He worked with the WPA Negro Theatre, the Mercury Theatre, The Mercury Theatre of the Air, and many movies, including *Citizen Kane*.

2181 Houston, David Franklin 1866-1940
Eight years with Wilson's cabinet, 1913 to 1920: with a personal estimate of the President. St. Clair Shores, Michigan: Scholarly Press, 1970. (Garden City, New York: Doubleday, Page & Co., 1926) 2v.
He served as Wilson's Secretary of Agriculture, then of Treasury. His book is a closely detailed record of the people and politics of Wilson's administration.

2182 Houston, Fred F. 1912-
Sam Houston's navy. New York: Grossmont Press, 1976. 135 p.
A series of personal recollections of a high school dropout's twenty years in the navy and fifteen years in navy-related maintenance work.

2183 Houston, Robert J. 1917-
D-Day to Bastogne: a paratrooper recalls World War II. Illustrated with maps. Hicksville, New York: Exposition Press, 1980. 172 p.
Houston provides detailed and energetic accounts of his months with the 501st Parachute Infantry Regiment, Company H, in Normandy, Holland, and Germany in 1944-1945. On a return visit to the region in 1976 he notes the changes made in thirty years, paying particular attention to the thousands of military graves in European cemeteries. He contends that World War II was necessary but closes with a plea that the world learn from history.

2184 Houston, Sam 1793-1863
The autobiography of Sam Houston. Edited by Donald Day and Harry Herbert Ullom. Norman: University of Oklahoma Press, 1954. 298 p. Index.
Selected from his massive written records, including speeches, letters, and an 1855 published memoir, this book describes his childhood, his

political career in Tennessee, and his leadership in the army and in politics on behalf of Texas.

2185 *Howar, Barbara   1935?-
Laughing all the way. New York: Stein and Day, 1973. 298 p.
  Centering her book on Washington in the bizarre period of the 1960's, Howar reports on her life among the politicians. Qualified by right of her eye for nonsense and hypocrisy as well as physical stamina, she feels entitled to judge the local character both on and off TV.

2186 *Howard, Dorothy Gray Mills   1902-
Dorothy's world: childhood in Sabine Bottom, 1902-1910. Englewood Cliffs, New Jersey: Prentice-Hall, 1977. 298 p.
  Folklorist Howard anatomizes her preschool learning in turn-of-the-century Texas to show what she learned, how, where, when, and why. She focuses on farm activities, clothing, home life, games, music, schooling and religious education.

2187 Howard, Henry   1868-1951
Charting my life. Boston: The Merrymount Press, 1948. 398 p. Index.
  The story of his life as a chemical engineer, steamship promoter, and expert yachtsman, by a man who kept his hobby and career in remarkable balance.

2188 *Howard, Katherine Graham   1898-
With my shoes off. New York: Vantage, 1977. 347 p.
  Howard, a disinherited Southerner who followed her husband to Massachusetts where he was actively engaged in elective and appointive offices, found herself gradually drawn into politics. As secretary of the Republican National Committee in 1952, she campaigned vigorously for Eisenhower. She served sixteen months as deputy administrator of the Federal Civil Defense Administration and was also a delegate to the NATO Civil Defense Committee in Paris. She presents an interesting perspective on the emergence of women in politics.

2189 *Howard, Mattie   1895-
The pathway of Mattie Howard: to and from prison; autobiography; true story of the regeneration of an ex-convict and gangster woman. Illustrated. Revised. New York: Pageant Press, Inc., 1963. (1937) 317 p.
  This story of spiritual salvation is told by an unidentified writer who had the "privilege to spend many happy hours in the company of Mattie Howard since [her] conversion." From an innocent childhood, Howard fell into the company of a murderer, spent years in prison, and returned to a religious life, directing her evangelism toward prison wardens and inmates. Although identified on the title page as an autobiography, the book is an as-told-to volume in the third person.

2190 *Howard, Maureen   1930-
Facts of life. Boston: Little, Brown and Company, 1978. 182 p.
  In anecdotal form Howard writes nostalgically about love, growing up Catholic, death, and her parents' relationship.

2191 Howard, Oliver Otis   1830-1909
Autobiography of Oliver Otis Howard, Major General, United States Army. Black Heritage Library Collection. Freeport, New York: Books for Libraries Press, 1971. (New York: Baker & Taylor Co., 1907) 2v.
  Howard's book details his youth, education, service during the Civil War, and work during the Reconstruction Era as commissioner of the Freedmen's Bureau and as a founder and then president of Howard University. Among his later activities were travels in the United States, Europe, and Egypt to attend conferences, lecture, and carry out official duties.

2192 Howard, Oliver Otis   1830-1909
My life and experiences among our hostile Indians; a record of personal observations, adventures, and campaigns among the Indians of the Great West with some account of their life, habits, traits, religion, ceremonies, dress, savage instincts and customs in peace and war. New Introduction by Robert M. Utley. New York: Da Capo Press, 1972. (Hartford, Connecticut: A.D. Worthington & Co., 1907) 570 p.
  A detailed record of his early life, his Civil War service, and primarily of his long career as a frontier general and diplomat among the Indians. A man of strong Christian faith, he is viewed as one of the frontier's humanitarian generals.

2193 Howard, Oscar C.
Oscar C. Howard—master of challenges: an autobiography. Introduction by Dr. Frederick D. Patterson. Minneapolis: T.S. Denison & Co., Inc., 1974. 211 p.
  He grew up in rural Georgia, was educated at Tuskeegee Institute, and moved to Minneapolis where he began working in the restaurant business. His book tells of his success as a Black man in white society, of starting his own industrial catering company, of establishing a four-year course in lodging and food at the University of Minnesota.

2194 Howbert, Irving   1846-1934
Memories of a lifetime in the Pike's Peak region. Glorieta, New Mexico:

The Rio Grande Press, Inc., 1970. (New York: G.P. Putnam's Sons, 1925) 298 p. Index.
  Howbert was a cattleman in his early years, but his life follows the pattern of development of his city, Colorado Springs, where his career was identified with its financial, educational, and social growth.

2195 Howe, Edgar Watson   1853-1937
Plain people. St. Clair Shores, Michigan: Scholarly Press, 1974. (New York: Dodd, Mead & Co., 1929) 317 p.
  Plainspoken and direct, the author gives an intimate portrait of his family under the guardianship of a harsh, unloving father who was a Methodist minister and abolitionist. The author chronicles his own apprenticeship in the newspaper business, the mishaps of his courtship, marriage and eventual divorce, and his success as a journalist. The final chapter contains bits and pieces of this seventy-year-old man's plain wisdom.

2196 Howe, Frederic C.   1867-1940
The confessions of a reformer. Introduction by John Braeman. Chicago: Quadrangle Books, 1967. 352 p. Index.
  The shaping of a reformer and polemicist, his involvement in municipal government (Cleveland), state and national politics, and his continuing confidence in and fight for the eventual triumph of justice over privilege.

2197 *Howe, Julia Ward   1819-1910
Reminiscences, 1819-1899. Illustrated. New York: Negro Universities Press, 1969. (Boston: Houghton Mifflin, 1899) 465 p. Index.
  Howe's reminiscences constitute her effort "to do justice" to individuals she knew and to the events she experienced. Considered by her friend Oliver Wendell Holmes "eminently clubable," this writer and feminist traveled widely, championing many causes, particularly women's rights. Howe later became the first woman member of the National Institute of Arts and Letters.

2198 Howe, Samuel Gridley   1801-1876
Letters and journals of Samuel Gridley Howe: the Greek revolution. Edited by Laura E. Richards. Notes by F.B. Sanborn. New York: AMS Press, 1973. (Boston: Dana Estes, 1909) 2v.
  Howe's daughter has written his biography incorporating entries from his journal and letters into her narrative. Howe was a leading American philanthropist and humanitarian, particularly devoted to the struggle for Greek independence from Turkey and the relief of refugees from that war.

2199 Howells, William Dean   1837-1920
Life in letters of William Dean Howells. Edited by Milldred Howells. New York: Russell & Russell, 1968. (Garden City, New York: Doubleday, Doran & Co., 1928) 2v. Index.
  After a short introduction touching on his ancestry and early life, Volume I contains the letters to and from Howells during the years 1857-1889. He spent several years abroad, lived and worked in Boston, wrote articles, books, and plays, and edited the *Atlantic*. Volume II (1890-1920) covers his later years and work including his interest in other writers, his own work, and further travels.

2200 Howells, William Dean   1837-1920
Literary friends and acquaintance; a personal retrospect of American authorship. Edited by David F. Hiatt and Edwin H. Cady. Illustrated. A selected edition of W.D. Howells, Vol. 32. Bloomington: Indiana University Press, 1968. (New York: Harper & Brothers, 1900) 397 p. Index.
  Throughout his career Howells was fascinated by literary memoirs. He knew most American authors of all regions from 1860 to 1920; he published, edited, reviewed, and corresponded with scores of them. Most of these pieces were originally published separately in various periodicals.

2201 Howells, William Dean   1837-1920
Years of my youth: and three essays. Introduction and notes by David J. Nordlot. Illustrated. Bloomington: Indiana University Press, 1975. 420 p.
  In writing of his childhood, youth, and young manhood, Howells concentrates on his passion for poetry writing, printing, and journalism. This volume, one of several of Howells' autobiographical writings, includes information on his early family life and family relationships. The three concluding essays concern Venice.

2202 Howells, William Dean   1837-1920
  see also Clemens, Samuel Langhorne

2203 Howland, Larry O.
Going straight. Irvine, California: Harvest House, 1979. 142 p.
  Howland recounts his violent childhood, abused by an alcoholic father, as a prelude to his criminal activities in and out of the U.S. Army. He was dishonorably discharged from the army and eventually sent to San Quentin for burglary, auto theft, kidnapping, and murder. In prison he was baptized a Jehovah's Witness; and on release, he married a good woman and attended John Wesley College. His narrative ends with graduation and an evangelizing visit to prisoners.

2204 Hoyt, Charles Sherman   **b.1879**
Memoirs. Edited and designed by Eugene Virginius Connett. New York: Van Nostrand Co., Inc., 1950. 348 p. Index.
   Recollections of sixty years in yacht racing under sail, with many detailed stories about sea cruising and racing yachts.

2205 Hoyt, Edward Jonathan (Buckskin Joe)   **1840-1918**
Buckskin Joe, being the unique and vivid memoirs of Edward Jonathan Hoyt, hunter-trapper, scout, soldier, showman, frontiersman, and friend of the Indians, 1840-1918. Edited by Glenn Shirley. Lincoln: University of Nebraska Press, 1966. 194 p. Index.
   Hoyt describes his enjoyment of a varied life including hunting and trapping, organizing and directing bands, touring with circuses, serving in the Civil War, mining for silver, leading immigrants to the West, working in Pawnee Bill's Wild West Show, and mining in Honduras.

2206 Hoyt, Henry Franklin   **1854-1930**
Frontier doctor. Edited by Doyce B. Nunis, Jr. Illustrated. Chicago: (Lakeside Press) R.R. Donnelly and Sons Co., 1979. 518 p. Index.
   A fifty-page "Historical Introduction" precedes this generously illustrated Wild West tale of outlaws, Indians on the warpath, and beautiful women. Hoyt recalls surveying in the Northwest, doctoring in the Southwest, and serving as Chief Surgeon during the Spanish-American War and in Manila.

2207 *Hoyt, Jo Wasson
For the love of Mike. With Frank Graham, Jr. New York: Random House, 1966. 210 p.
   As wife of a U.S. diplomat stationed in the Congo, Jo Hoyt was endangered by the 1964 rebellion and violence. She tells of the diplomatic posts where her husband served in Pakistan, Morocco, and the Congo, and of amusing as well as dramatic events occurring as she set up house and raised four children in a succession of unfamiliar situations.

2208 *Hubbard, Barbara Marx   **1929-**
Hunger of Eve. Harrisburg, Pennsylvania: Stackpole Books, 1976. 224 p.
   The author describes "the hunger that drove me out of my own Eden of comfort to search for universal action and consciousness" by founding SYNCON (a synergistic convergence) in 1970 and the Utopian Committee for the Future. She is the daughter of toy czar Louis Marx, ex-wife of painter Earl Hubbard, and mother of five children.

2209 Hubbard, Harlan   **1846-1903**
Shantyboat. New York: Dodd, Mead and Co., 1953. 352 p.
   A painter describes the experience of traveling from Cincinnati to New Orleans on a houseboat.

2210 Hubbard, Louis Herman   **b.1882**
Recollections of a Texas educator. Illustrated. Salado, Texas: Louis Herman Hubbard, 1954. 288 p.
   Hubbard, from 1926 to 1950 President of Texas State Women's University, describes his upbringing in Puerto Rico and Texas and his long career as an administrator at TSWU, intimately intertwined with the history of that institution.

2211 *Hubbard, Mina (Benson)
A woman's way through unknown Labrador; an account of the exploration of the Nascaupee and George Rivers. London: John Murray, Albemarle Street W, 1908. 338 p. Index.
   A record of two pioneering journeys to a land whose climatic conditions are similar to those of the Arctic Circle. This account of Hubbard's expeditions constituted the only geographical data recognized by European and American geographical authorities.

2212 Hubbell, Ralph   **1909-**
Come walk with me. Englewood Cliffs, New Jersey: Prentice-Hall, Inc., 1975. 150 p.
   For forty years the best-known sportscaster of Buffalo and western New York state, Hubbell relates anecdotes and fond memories of the development of big-time sports in that area. Included is his own "one man's Hall of Fame" with recollections of great athletes and great sports characters.

2213 *Hufford, Georgia (Hastings)   **1882-**
Then came May. Philadelphia: Dorrance and Co., 1950. 273 p.
   Recollections of her pioneer girlhood in northern Michigan, with vivid details of the humor and hardships of everyday life.

2214 *Hughes, Adella (Prentiss)   **1869-1950**
Music is my life. Photographs. Cleveland: The World Publishing Co., 1947. 319 p. Index.
   Prominent as an impresario, manager, and patron of music in Cleveland, her book describes her life in music, the establishment of the Cleveland Symphony Orchestra, its home in Severance Hall, and many famous musicians and friends.

2215 Hughes, Charles Evans   **1862-1948**
The autobiographical notes of Charles Evans Hughes. Illustrated. Edited by David J. Danelski & Joseph S. Tulchin. Cambridge: Harvard University Press, 1973. 363 p. Index.
   Hughes was a judge, statesman, lawyer, and investigator. He served as Governor of New York, Justice of the Supreme Court, presidential candidate in 1916, Secretary of State, 1921-1925, Judge of the World Court, and Chief Justice of the U.S. Supreme Court. During his distinguished career, he was noted for opinions strongly upholding human liberties.

2216 *Hughes, Emmy   **1863-1934**
Dissipations at Uffington House: the letters of Emmy Hughes, Rugby, Tennessee, 1881-1887. Introduction by John R. Debruyn. Memphis, Tennessee: Memphis State University Press, 1976. 80 p. Index.
   Emmy Hughes, niece of Thomas Hughes (author of *Tom Brown's Schooldays*), settled in Rugby, Tennessee, with her grandmother in 1881, as a member of a colony Hughes helped found to aid unemployed workers from New England. Through this series of letters to her English friend, Lucy Taylor (daughter of the editor of *Punch*), Emmy reveals a fascinating juxtaposition of English upper-class home life transplanted to America, the practical realities of managing servants and a household, and participating in the activities of a small town.

2217 Hughes, Harold Everett   **1922-**
The man from Ida Grove: a senator's personal story. With Dick Schneider. Illustrated. Waco, Texas: Word Books, 1979. 346 p.
   Hughes describes his personal battles: against poverty as an Iowa farmboy; against his fellow man as a World War II foot soldier; against alcoholism and suicidal tendencies; and against political opponents who considered him profane, reckless, weak, violent, and simple. Against these overwhelming odds, Hughes was elected governor of Iowa and U.S. senator.

2218 Hughes, Howard Robard   **1905-1978**
My life and opinions. Edited by Robert P. Eaton. Chicago: Best Books Press, 1972. 244 p.
   The editor claims the book is from an authentic collaborative manuscript he worked on with Hughes. However, he frames the text in a science-fiction setting (2025 A.D.) in which Hughes is revived from a frozen state. Authentic or not, the book reflects the sensational mythology surrounding the powerful, eccentric, and private industrialist.

2219 Hughes, Langston   **1902-1967**
I wonder as I wander: an autobiographical journey. New York: Rinehart and Co., Inc., 1956. 405 p.
   At thirty he decided he wanted to make a living as a writer and then began his travels in the United States and abroad to discover if a Black writer could succeed without compromise.

2220 Hughes, Langston   **1902-1967**
see also **Bontemps, Arna**

2221 *Hughes, Lora Wood   **b.1870?**
No time for tears. Life-in-America Series. Boston: Houghton Mifflin Co., 1946. 305 p.
   Describes a full and rugged life, from childhood on a Kansas homestead in the 1870's to later years in the Northwest states; primitive frontier to wartime nursing after Pearl Harbor at age 70.

2222 *Hughes, Russell Meriwether (La Meri)   **1898-**
Dance out the answer: an autobiography. Foreword by John Martin. Illustrated. New York: Marcel Dekker Inc., 1977. 194 p. Index.
   "La Meri"'s energetic autobiography chronicles her transition from Kentucky schoolgirl to world-famous ethnic dancer. She describes her trek across the globe, learning native dances of many countries. In later years she taught at her Cape Cod home and directed a touring repertory company.

2223 Huizenga, Lee Sjoerds   **1881-1945**
Pressing on: an autobiographical sketch. Grand Rapids, Michigan: William B. Eerdmans Publishing Co., 1946. 83 p.
   Brief spiritual autobiography by a Catholic medical missionary who later died in a Japanese concentration camp.

2224 Hull, Cordell   **1871-1955**
Memoirs of Cordell Hull. Prepared with the assistance of Andrew Berding. New York: The Macmillan Co., 1948. 2v. Index.
   Primarily a narrative of his role as Franklin D. Roosevelt's Secretary of State (1933-1945), the book begins with Hull's origins in the hills of Tennessee, his early days as an attorney and Spanish Civil War soldier.

2225 *Hulme, Kathryn Cavarly   **1900-**
Undiscovered country; a spiritual adventure. Boston: Little, Brown and Co., 1966. 306 p.
   As a young girl she became determined to be a writer. Along the way she went to college, worked a few years in factories, traveled with a

wealthy milliner in Europe. In Paris she met the Russian mystic Gurdjieff and became his disciple, changing the course of her life.

2226 Humbard, Rex   **1919-**
Miracles in my life. Old Tappan, New Jersey: New American Library, 1971. 128 p.

Gospel preacher Humbard started out traveling and preaching with an old patched tent and a guitar, but his success grew until his Cathedral of Tomorrow in Cuyahoga Falls, Ohio, and his extensive TV appearances have made him a familiar purveyor of old-time religion to thousands. Day-care centers, senior citizens' housing, a college, and other social services are all part of his crusade.

2227 Hume, Edward Hicks   **1876-1957**
Doctors East, doctors West: an American physician's life in China. New York: W.W. Norton and Co., Inc., 1946. 278 p.

Brought to China in 1905 to organize what became the Hsiangya Medical College for Yale University, Hume describes many years of service in circumstances that offered an awesome combination of primitive superstition and sophisticated competence.

2228 Hume, Robert Deniston   **1845-1908**
Pygmy monopolist: the life and doings of R.D. Hume written by himself and dedicated to his neighbors. Edited with introduction by Gordon B. Dodds. Madison: The State Historical Society of Wisconsin, 1961. 87 p.

Written as a defense against charges of business monopoly, the book describes the ventures of a prominent businessman and entrepreneur in the Oregon salmon industry.

2229 *Humphrey, Doris   **1895-1958**
Doris Humphrey, an artist first; an autobiography. Edited and completed by Selma Jeanne Cohen. Foreword by Charles Humphrey Woodford. Introduction by John Martin. Middletown, Connecticut: Wesleyan University Press, 1972. 305 p. Index.

In a lifetime of fighting for the creation, development, and acceptance of American modern dance, Humphrey first performed, then when physical disability curtailed her activities, composed and choreographed dances. Her brief unfinished autobiography is contained in the first 65 pages of this book. An appendix, pp. 233-269, includes her writings about dance, advice to choreographers, and other related subjects.

2230 *Humphrey, Doris   **1895-1958**
New dance: an unfinished autobiography. Introduction by John Martin. Edited by Selma Jeanne Cohen. New York: Dance Perspectives Foundation, 1966. 81 p.

Humphrey recalls her training and early professional experiences as a dancer, first in Chicago and later in Los Angeles with the Denishawn Company. She provides an interesting background of her development into "one of the half-dozen women of great vision and total dedication" who made possible the growth of American dance.

2231 Humphrey, Hubert Horatio   **1911-1978**
Hubert Humphrey: the man and his dream. Compiled with foreword by Heldon D. Engelmeyer and Robert J. Wagman. Introduction by Muriel Humphrey. New York: Methuen, 1978. 358 p. Index.

This collection of Humphrey's speeches, letters, and articles is arranged to reflect his career as freshman senator, a member of "the loyal opposition," a presidential candidate, and his return to the Senate. They express his concerns with civil rights, international interdependence, defense of Israel as a nation, desegregation, party politics, and full employment, revealing Humphrey to be a man of principle and integrity.

2232 *Humphrey, Inez Faith
From the prairies to the mountains: memories/ especially of Illinois and Eastern Kentucky. New York: Exposition Press, 1968. 146 p.

A chatty reminiscence about the author's long career as an English teacher, primarily at Morehead State College (Ky.), full of details about people, places, and events. Humphrey was deeply committed to the Christian Church, particularly its missionary activities, and in retirement enjoyed European travel.

2233 Humphrey, William   **1924-**
Farther off from heaven. New York: Alfred A. Knopf, 1977. 242 p.

A writer's memories of his boyhood cluster around the death of his father in an automobile accident and the end of his childhood years which that event brought about.

2234 Huncke, Herbert E.   **1915-**
Evening sun turned crimson. Introduction by Allen Ginsberg. Cherry Valley, New York: Cherry Valley Ed., 1980. 224 p.

Allen Ginsberg states in the introduction that just after World War II, "the first information and ritual of the emergent hip subculture passed through Huncke's person." A fictional character in several novels of the period (Clellon Holmes, Jack Kerouac, William Lee, William Burroughs, Allen Ginsberg), Huncke tells his own stories of friendship, drugs, jails, hospitals, and "hanging out."

2235 *Hungry Wolf, Beverly   **1950-**
The ways of my grandmothers. New York: William Morrow and Co., 1980. 256 p.

A young, white-educated Blood Indian describes her self-conscious attempt to re-discover the old ways of her people. Her book also includes tribal history and practical advice on daily life (sewing, beadwork, cooking).

2236 Hunt, Everette Howard   **1918-**
Give us this day. Illustrated. New Rochelle, New York: Arlington House, 1973. 235 p.

Hunt spent nineteen months on the Cuba Project (which became known as the Bay of Pigs Invasion) as an officer of the Central Intelligence Agency and here writes his account of the way the project was organized and why it failed. His later notoriety in connection with the Watergate affair led him to publish this account in an effort to clarify and correct details of his CIA connection.

2237 Hunt, Everette Howard   **1918-**
Undercover: memoir of an American secret agent. Berkeley, California: Berkeley Publishing Corp., 1974. 338 p. Index.

A key operative in the Watergate episode, Hunt recalls his role in the wartime OSS, in the CIA during the Cold War, Bay of Pigs, and Gemstone operations. He writes also of his own conviction and imprisonment and the downfall of Nixon and his administration.

2238 Hunt, Rockwell Dennis   **1868-1966**
Boyhood days of "Mr. California": Rockwell Hunt and four brothers in the 1870's. Introduction by Stuart C. Gibbons. Stockton, California: Rockwell D. Hunt, 1965. 176 p.

Hunt reminisces about growing up on the family ranch in the Sacramento River Valley, Freeport, California. He describes his parents, four brothers, friends, and their activities: attending a one-room country school and small church; gardening, haymaking, and threshing; hunting with bows and arrows; and surviving floods of the Sacramento River.

2239 Hunt, Rockwell Dennis   **1868-1966**
"Mr. California": autobiography of Rockwell D. Hunt. Introduction by Emory S. Bogardus. San Francisco: Fearon Publishers, 1956. 380 p. Index.

A sprightly account of Hunt's long career as an economics professor and Dean of the Graduate School at U.C.L.A. When he retired at 77, he assumed duties at the College of the Pacific for another six years. This volume emphasizes two of Hunt's major loves, education and the state of California.

2240 Hunter, George   **1755-1824**
The Western journals of Dr. George Hunter: 1796-1805. Edited by John Frances McDermott. Transactions of the American Philosophical Society. n.s., vol. 53, pt. 4. Philadelphia: The American Philosophical Society, 1963. 133 p. Index.

Commissioned by Thomas Jefferson to accompany William Dunbar in exploring the Louisiana Territory, he traveled in parts of Kentucky, Louisiana, and Mississippi, recording his observations of the land, climate, Indians, and the daily life.

2241 Hunter, John Dunn   **1798?-1827**
Memoirs of a captivity among the Indians of North America. Edited by Richard Drennon. New York: Schocken Books, 1973. (London: Longmans, 1823) 252 p.

Orphaned and raised by Kansas and Osage tribes, he was nearly twenty when he learned to read and write. His book was published in early 1823, resulting in immediate fame as well as suspicions about the verity of his story. Finally rejected by white society, he went to the Southwest to help organize Indians against white exploitation. There he was murdered.

2242 *Hunter, Rodello
Daughter of Zion. New York: Alfred A. Knopf, 1972. 285 p.

Daughter of a prominent Mormon family, she writes critically but lovingly of her life as a Mormon in contemporary society.

2243 *Hunter, Rodello
Wyoming wife. New York: Alfred A. Knopf, 1969. 330 p.

Raised in Utah, she and her husband settled in Freedom, Wyoming, when they were married. Here she writes about country life in modern times, the pleasures of living close to nature while living within the borders of society and technology.

2244 Huntington, James
On the edge of nowhere. As told to Lawrence Elliott. Introduction by Lowell Thomas. New York: Crown Publishers, Inc., 1966. 183 p.

His father was a white trapper, his mother an Indian. Huntington grew up in the rugged, primitive Alaskan countryside. Because his life spanned two worlds, the white and the Indian, the new and the old, he had to learn many kinds of survival. His book depicts the stark drama of a contemporary frontier.

2245 Huntley, Chester Robert (Chet)				**1911-1974**
The generous years; remembrances of a frontier boyhood. New York: Random House, 1968. 215 p.
    The well-known TV commentator tells of his early years growing up on one of America's last frontiers, the prairies and towns of Montana from before World War I into the mid-1920's.

2246 *Hurlbut, Gladys
Next week—East Lynne! Introduction by Howard Lindsay and Russell Crouse. Postscript by Dorothy Stickney. New York: E.P. Dutton and Co., Inc., 1950. 254 p.
    The actress recalls with humor her stock company experience as a leading lady during the Twenties and early Thirties and ends with her return to the stage, after fifteen years spent writing plays and movies, in *Life with Mother.*

2247 Hurok, Solomon					**1888-1974**
Impresario: a memoir. With Ruth Goode. New York: Random House, 1946. 291 p.
    Filled with backstage anecdotes about artists in ballet, opera, and on the concert stage, the book describes the life of one of the great American impresarios. A significant part of his life and work is integral to the growth of American ballet.

2248 Hurok, Solomon					**1888-1974**
S. Hurok presents: a memoir of the dance world. New York: Hemitage House, 1953. 336 p. Index.
    A narrative of dance in America and his role in organizing and promoting it in this country.

2249 *Hurst, Fannie					**1889-1968**
Anatomy of me: a wanderer in search of herself. Garden City, New York: Doubleday and Co., Inc., 1958. 367 p.
    A popular fiction writer traces her development as a writer, growing up in St. Louis, living in Greenwich Village during the Twenties, moving around New York's literary circle.

2250 Hurst, Lawrence					**b.1883**
Sixty-one years in the school room. Boston: Meador Publishing Co., 1952. 255 p.
    Rambling reminiscences of his school years, from age six to retirement in 1950, by a farm boy who became a college professor with some years of high school teaching and athletic coaching in between.

2251 Huse, Raymond Howard				**1880-1954**
Autobiography of a plain preacher. Boston: Meador Publishing Co., 1949. 121 p.
    A Methodist minister whose pastorates were in Vermont, New Hampshire, and Ithaca, New York, writes of the early influence of the church on his life, his call to the ministry, and his service as minister and superintendent.

2252 Husing, Edward Britt				**1901-1962**
My eyes are in my heart. With Cy Rice. Introduction by Ralph Edwards. New York: Bernard Geis Associates, Inc., 1959. 287 p.
    A pioneer in the development of radio broadcasting, his voice was familiar in American households for over thirty years. At 55, surgery for a brain tumor left him blind and partially paralyzed. His book tells of his career, his illness, his limited recovery, and his spiritual growth during the last years of his life.

2253 Hussey, Harry					**b.1881**
My pleasures and palaces; an informal memoir of forty years in modern China. Introduction by V.K. Wellington Koo. Garden City, New York: Doubleday & Co., Inc., 1968. 384 p. Index.
    Born in Canada, Hussey was a successful architect in Chicago when, in 1911, he was sent to China to design buildings for the International Y.M.C.A. He set up a residence and office in Peking and soon became popular in many Oriental countries as a designer-builder. He remained in China most of his life, observing major changes in Chinese government and culture and often acting as an informal diplomat for the United States.

2254 Hutchinson, Thomas					**1711-1780**
Diary and letters of His Excellency Thomas Hutchinson: captain-general and governor-in-chief of his late Majesty's province of Massachusetts Bay in North America; complied by Peter Orlando Hutchinson. New York: Burt Franklin, 1971. (London: S. Low, Marston, Searle & Rivington, 1883-86) 2v.
    Hutchinson, as the King's representative and governor of Massachusetts during the outbreak of the American Revolution, was later the subject of much abuse and misrepresentation. This volume of his writings attempts to vindicate him by presenting materials showing him to be carrying out his duty in supporting the constitutional principles of Parliament and the Mother Country against the aspirations of the Colonies, as he was bound to do.

2255 Hutson, Alton
   see **Holden, William Curry**

2256 Hyams, Joe						**1923-**
Mislaid in Hollywood. New York: Peter H. Wyden, Inc., 1973. 244 p.
    Hyams writes intimately about some of Hollywood's greatest actors—Cary Grant, James Dean, Humphrey Bogart, to name a few—describing personal encounters with them in interviews or casual friendships. He combines stories about their private lives with tales about his own life in Hollywood in the Fifties and Sixties.

2257 Hyatt, Henry (Jimmy Valentine)			**1871-1945**
Alias Jimmy Valentine himself, by himself. Introduction by Mary Flowers Hyatt. Philadelphia: Dorrance and Co., 1949. 362 p.
    Account of thirty years of criminal life, after escaping from an orphanage and living in various prisons, by a well-groomed burglar specializing in jewelry robberies.

2258 Hyde, William J.					**1864-1953**
Dig or die, Brother Hyde. As told to Harriet Harmon Dexter. Epilogue by Harriet Harmon Dexter. Illustrated by Susanna Suba. New York: Harper & Brothers, 1954. 253 p.
    An engaging account of Hyde's career as a Methodist clergyman, which began in 1886 in the Dakota Territory, where he built countless churches ("dig or die"), married, and served his parishioners well, including the town bootlegger, who attended the "dry" church. His later congregations were in Berea, Ohio, and Evanston, Illinois.

2259 Hyman, Mac						**1923-1963**
Love, boy: the letters of Mac Hyman. Southern Literary Studies. Illustrated. Selected and edited by William Blackburn. Introduction by Max Steele. Baton Rouge: Louisiana State University Press, 1969. 227 p.
    The letters of the author of *No Time for Sergeants* reveal him to be at ease in his small-town world, but isolated from it while observing it.

2260 Ickes, Harold LeClaire				**1874-1952**
The autobiography of a curmudgeon. Introduction by Bernard Sternsher. Chicago: Quadrangle Books, 1969. (New York: Reynal & Hitchcock, 1943) 350 p. Index.
    A story of a fiercely honest, highly principled newspaperman who after years of being active in Republican politics was offered the post of Secretary of the Interior by President Roosevelt. Most of the book involves his life and views before his appointment, but it also gives some insight into his approach to the Public Works Administration that included major projects like the Grand Coulee Dam.

2261 Ickes, Harold LeClaire				**1874-1952**
The secret diary of Harold L. Ickes. Edited by Jane D. Ickes. New York: Simon and Schuster, 1953-1954. 3v. Index.
    Appointed by Franklin D. Roosevelt as Secretary of the Interior and a catalytic agent of the New Deal, Ickes kept a precise record of his personal and official life in Washington. Few knew he kept it; fewer still ever saw parts of it. Every weekend he transcribed his daily notes into a full text. The complete manuscript is in the Library of Congress; this edition has some omissions, at the editor's discretion. Volume I encompasses The first thousand days, 1933-1936; Volume II, The inside struggle, 1936-1939; Volume III, The lowering clouds, 1939-1941.

2262 Ignatow, David					**1914-**
Notebooks. Edited with introduction by Ralph J. Mills. Chicago: The Swallow Press, 1973. 375 p.
    Not a chronological autobiography, this work incorporates some of the poet's experiences, largely of inward, emotional significance, as well as his uninhibited thinking on many public and private subjects through a number of years.

2263 Ilfrey, Jack
Happy Jack's go-buggy: a WW II fighter pilot's personal document. With Max Reynolds. Foreword by Eddie Rickenbacker. Illustrated. Hicksville, New York: Exposition Press, 1979. 167 p.
    A generally cheerful account of Ilfrey's experiences as a P-38 fighter pilot during World War II, as a member of the 94th Hat in the Ring Fighter Squadron, First Fighter Group. He flew 142 combat missions before being shot down in France six days after D-Day. He was hidden by a French family and eventually escaped to British lines. An ace in 1942, he was much decorated.

2264 Imperato, Pascal James				**1937-**
Medical detective. New York: Richard Marek Publishers, 1979. 272 p. Index.
    Imperato writes about his work in Africa fighting various epidemics from smallpox to cholera, his years in medical school, as well as his decision to become an epidemiologist. Afterwards he returned to New York and battled with bureaucrats and red tape while working as director for the Bureau of Infectious Diseases in New York City.

2265 Infeld, Leopold d.1968
Quest: an autobiography. New York: Chelsea Publishing Co., 1980. (New York: Doubleday, Doran & Co., 1941) 361 p.

This is the story of a physicist from a Polish ghetto who became a colleague of Albert Einstein at Princeton. His journey is marked by recurrent barriers of anti-Semitism as well as lucky breaks that provided opportunities to leave Poland just before Hitler invaded. The epilogue briefly relates his decade in Canada and his eventual return to Poland, clouded by the suspicion he would give away "atomic secrets" which he did not possess.

2266 Ingersoll, Ralph McAllister 1900-
Point of departure: an adventure in autobiography. New York: Harcourt Brace & World, Inc., 1961. 247 p.

The beginnings of a colorful, successful career are described with relish up through his stint as first managing editor of the fledgling *New Yorker*.

2267 Ingersoll, Ralph McAllister 1900-
Top secret. New York: Harcourt, Brace and Co., 1946. 373 p. Index.

An officer in the planning group of the Chief of Staff to the Supreme Allied Commander (COSSAC) during the final two years of World War II writes of the large-scale planning, direction, and execution of the Allied victory and the lessons learned and applied.

2268 Ingersoll, Robert Green 1833-1899
The letters of Robert G. Ingersoll. Edited with a biographical introduction by Eva Ingersoll Wakefield. Preface by Dr. David Saville Muzzey. New York: Philosophical Library, 1951. 747 p. Index.

These letters, arranged by subject matter and preceded by interpretive essays, show Ingersoll as a family man, humanist, orator, and lover of the arts as well as articulate agnostic. Letters about his career as a lawyer have been left for another volume.

2269 Ingersoll, Robert Green 1833-1899
The life and letters of Robert G. Ingersoll. Edited with biographical introduction by Eva Ingersoll Wakefield. Edited and preface by Royston Pike. Edition for the English Reader. London: C.A. Watts & Co., Ltd., 1952. 309 p. Index.

Distinguished lawyer Robert Ingersoll's witty, principled, forthright letters to a multitude of correspondents, known (Walt Whitman, Annie Besant) and unknown, are arranged topically: patriotism, religion, literary criticism, epicureanism, birth control, capital punishment, freedom of thought, sex equality, etc. His heroes are Voltaire and Thomas Paine; his messages, humanitarianism and agnosticism: "I thank God every day that he does not exist."

2270 Inouye, Daniel Ken 1924-
Journey to Washington. With Lawrence Elliott. Englewood Cliffs, New Jersey: Prentice-Hall, Inc., 1967. 297 p.

Born of Japanese parents in the Territory of Hawaii, he served in Europe during World War II, receiving the Congressional Medal of Honor. Later he worked for Hawaiian statehood, served as U.S. Representative and then as U.S. Senator.

2271 Ireman, Allan H. 1899-1977
As I remember: recollections. Edited by Joyce H. Finch. Illustrated. Ithaca, New York: Cornell University Libraries (Department of Manuscripts and University Archives), 1979. 131 p.

Ireman recounts a joyous life in and around Ithaca and Cornell University where he lived and worked. His illustrious family had helped to settle this area. A Cornell graduate, he practiced law in Ithaca until his retirement. His love of life and music, of the natural splendors around Ithaca, and his philanthropic services are all well reported in this book.

2272 Irigaray, Louis 1930?-
A shepherd watches, a shepherd sings. And Theodore Taylor. New York: Doubleday & Company, Inc., 1977. 300 p.

He grew up in a Basque family in California, was apprenticed as a shepherd at age six. His book recalls life in a little-known ethnic group in a vanishing way of life.

2273 Irving, Clifford Michael 1930-
Clifford Irving: what really happened; his untold story of the Hughes affair. With Richard Suskind New York: Grove Press, Inc., 1972. 378 p.

Irving's bizarre story of the Hughes hoax, a fake autobiography of Howard Hughes supposedly based on tape-recorded interviews. Eventually the whole scheme was discovered and Irving was sentenced to two-and-a-half years imprisonment.

2274 Irving, Washington 1783-1859
Crayon miscellany. Edited by Diane Terrell. Illustrated. New Haven, Connecticut: Twayne Publishers, 1979. 502 p. Index.

This volume contains a textual study of *A Tour on the Prairies* and *Abbotsford and Newstead Abbey*, both of which record personal experiences and have a basis in Irving's journals. The former deals with a brief expedition he made of his native land after a seventeen-year absence; the

latter records his respective visits to the homes of Sir Walter Scott and Lord Byron.

2275 Irving, Washington 1783-1859
Journals and notebooks: complete works of Washington Irving. Illustrated. Edited by Nathalia Wright. Madison: University of Wisconsin Press, 1969- . v.

Most of Irving's journals were written while he was traveling abroad and contain accounts of daily activities, miscellaneous notes, expense accounts, anecdotes, observations, and reminiscences. Although he was the first American writer after the Revolution to come into extended contact (over 22 years) with European culture, he makes no comparisons or penetrating analysis of the American and European character.

2276 Irving, Washington 1793-1859
Letters. Edited by Ralph M. Aderman and others. Boston: Twayne Publishers, 1978- . v.

Irving was a typical representative of middle-class, nineteenth-century America whose work reflected prevalent attitudes and satisfied popular taste. His letters to friends and relatives, however, express his own ideas more forcefully and directly though with warmth and geniality. In his diplomatic role he corresponded with other officials about delicate political, social, and economic issues.

2277 Irving, Washington 1783-1859
Letters from Sunnyside and Spain. Edited by Stanley T. Williams. Norwood, Pennsylvania: Norwood Editions, 1976. (New Haven: Yale University Press, 1928) 80 p.

This book consists of nine letters Irving wrote to his sister and nieces while living at Sunnyside, his Tarrytown, New York, home, 1840-1841, and nine written 1842-1845 from Spain, where he was the American minister. They deal primarily with his observations of social events he attended—receptions, parties, a coronation, parades—and sketches of some of the participants.

2278 Isaac, Godfrey 1913-1980
"I'll see you in court". And Richard Kleiner. Chicago: Contemporary Books, 1979. 262 p.

Isaac recounts a number of his most memorable cases as a trial lawyer, including an investigation and defense of Sirhan Sirhan for client Teddy Charach, who wanted to prove that a "second gun" had killed Bobby Kennedy. Isaac's legal acumen was often supported by the intuitive hunches of his tempestuous second wife, Roena.

2279 Isham, Asa Brainerd 1844-1912
Autobiography of Asa Brainerd Isham, M.D. Edited with preface by A. Chapman Isham, M.D. Ann Arbor, Michigan: His Kin, 1957. 107 p.

Isham grew up in Ohio and worked briefly as a printer's devil and as a reporter before enlisting in the Seventh Michigan Cavalry of the Union Army. Much of the book deals with his Civil War experiences, including being wounded at Haymarket, Virginia, and taken prisoner at Richmond. After the war he became a physician, taught at the Cincinnati College of Medicine and Surgery, and aided in the development of a unified medical education program for Cincinnati.

2280 Isherwood, Christopher 1904-
Christopher and his kind: 1929-1939. New York: Farrar, Straus, and Giroux, 1976. 339 p.

Writing of himself in the third person, Isherwood blithely describes a decade of his life and the "boys" he loved in that time.

2281 Isherwood, Christopher 1904-
Lions and shadows: an education in the twenties. New York: New Directions Pub. Co., 1977. (1947) 249 p.

Playwright Isherwood writes of his experiences in and loathing of British boarding schools and universities, raging "against the dictatorship of [his] elders." He expresses enthusiasms he is "shy of confessing to, because they are so passionate" and writes of his anxieties and the roles he plays.

2282 Isherwood, Christopher 1904-
My guru and his disciple. New York: Farrar, Straus, Giroux, 1980. 338 p.

Isherwood describes how his friendship with a Hindu monk from 1939 to 1976 influenced his life in terms of religion, friendship, and self-awareness. Diary entries are interspersed; Isherwood's reminiscences are more factual than spiritual.

2283 Israelsen, Orson Winso 1887-1968
Forty years of sound and forty years of silence: an autobiography. Illustrated. Logan, Utah: Orson Israelsen, 1968. 130 p.

Israelsen, a devout Mormon, is proud of his 59-year marriage, four children, and various homes in Logan, Utah, where he taught irrigation engineering at Utah State University. Although the book exhibits considerable stylistic naiveté, Israelsen tells movingly of his deafness at forty from an illness and of his "soundless" but highly successful career—including testifying at many court trials.

2284 Ives, Burl   **1909-**
Wayfaring stranger. New York: Whittlesey House, 1948. 253 p.
Written at about age 30, a warm personal narrative of Ives' boyhood in Illinois, the hard work and travels which led to his career as a writer and singer of modern ballads.

2285 Ives, Charles Edward   **1874-1954**
Memos. Edited by John Kirkpatrick. New York: W.W. Norton & Co., 1972. 355 p. Index.
These memos by a distinguished composer were dictated to a secretary or jotted down to form an autobiographical scrapbook of reminiscences demonstrating to derogatory critics that they did not know what they were talking about and supplying information to Ives enthusiasts. Numerous appendixes include letters and other information.

2286 Ives, Joseph Christmas   **1828-1868**
Steamboat up the Colorado: from the journal of Lieutenant Joseph Christmas Ives, United States Topographical Engineers, 1857-1858. Edited by Alexander L. Crosby. Illustrated by Lorence Bjorklund. Boston: Little, Brown and Company, 1965. 112 p. Index.
In 1857 Ives, a U.S. Army engineer, was sent by the War Department to explore the Colorado River to find out how far north it could be navigated and to learn whether, near Needles, California, it could be linked with a Mormon road to Los Angeles. His return route, 320 miles to Ft. Defiance, was successfully made by mule train, though threatened by Indians and drought.

2287 Ivy, Robert Henry   **1881-1974**
Link with the past. Baltimore: The Williams and Wilkins Co., 1962. 148 p.
The achievements of a prominent oral and plastic surgeon at the University of Pennsylvania.

2288 Jackson, Andrew   **1767-1845**
The papers of Andrew Jackson. Edited by Sam B. Smith and Harriet Chapell Owsley. Knoxville: University of Tennessee Press, 1980-. v. Index.
This is a well-edited collection of business papers and letters to and from Jackson during the years when he was successively a schoolteacher, lawyer, United States representative, senator from Tennessee, and superior court judge. They reveal his role in helping his country to gain political independence from Great Britain, to become a republic and to expand westward. The letters reveal his developing leadership, loyalty, honesty, and sometimes irascible pride.

2289 *Jackson, Anne Jane   **1926-**
Early stages. Boston: Little, Brown & Co., 1979. 212 p.
Anne Jackson describes her childhood in rural areas outside of Pittsburgh, where her freethinking Croatian immigrant father and Irish Catholic mother led an unconventional, sometimes hand-to-mouth existence. After their move to Brooklyn, Anne metamorphosed into a "show-off and a hellion," stealing, flirting, and even threatening suicide to pursue her favorite pastime, watching movies. Her native talent led her to acting classes; her mother's mental illness ended her childhood.

2290 Jackson, Frederick E.   **b.1883**
Memories and reveries: a physician's philosophical review of eight decades. New York: Exposition Press, 1958. 153 p.
Jackson's chapters follow his train of thought rather than chronology, as informal prose intermingles anecdotes of rural boyhood activities such as hunting and fishing with his views on "time," "fate and destiny," "egocentricity," and religious faith. He barely alludes to his career as a physician.

2291 Jackson, George   **1941-1971**
Blood in my eye. New York: Random House, 1972. 197 p.
Finished just a week before he was shot and killed inside San Quentin Prison in 1971, this book expresses Jackson's rebellion against imprisonment and the conditions that lead to it. In prison he became committed to the ideas of Marx, Lenin, and Mao and to the idea of Black revolution, which he discusses here.

2292 Jackson, George   **1941-1971**
Soledad brother; the prison letters of George Jackson. Introduction by Jean Genet. New York: Coward McCann, Inc., 1970. 330 p.
In the first letter of this collection, the author unashamedly sketches his double life—one part of him at home in a loving family, the other part in the streets. It is the second life, the life in the streets that leads to Soledad prison and a charge of murder. In the letters that follow expressing his anger and frustration and chronicling prison abuse, Jackson does not look for excuses, but the finger he points is directed at what he sees as a racist society in which Black men and women must rebel or be destroyed.

2293 *Jackson, Harrisene   **1941-**
There's nothing I own that I want. Englewood Cliffs, New Jersey: Prentice Hall, 1974. 168 p.
A Black woman's story of her struggle to escape the ghetto: her love for

her mother whom she saw murdered when she was six, her pregnancy and marriage at sixteen, the mental illness of her oldest daughter, and her dogged sense of survival.

2294 Jackson, James   **1810-1834**
Memoir of James Jackson, Jr., M.D., with extracts from his letters to his father, and medical cases, collected by him. New York: Arno Press, 1972. (Boston: I.R. Butts, 1835) 444 p.
This book includes a memoir written by his father, followed by James Jackson's letters (pp. 81-194) and his observations on various medical cases. The letters were written from Paris (1831-33) where he was studying medicine.

2295 *Jackson, Madeline Manning   **1948-**
Running for Jesus. As told to Jerry B. Jenkins, author of preface. Waco, Texas: Word Books, 1977. 192 p.
Jackson straightforwardly recounts how her major concerns, Christianity and running, have been inextricably intertwined from early childhood. She won a gold medal at the Mexico City Olympic Games in 1968, but ran the worst race of her life in an attempted comeback at the Montreal Olympic Games in 1976. For a number of years after graduation from Tennessee State University, Jackson worked for the Salvation Army in Cleveland, her hometown, but always spent considerable time promoting the gospel.

2296 *Jackson, Mahalia   **1911-1972**
Movin' on up. With Evan McLeod Wylie. New York: Hawthorn Books, Inc., 1966. 212 p.
The warm story of a simple, loving woman who spreads the joy of her faith through her gospel singing. Through hard times, poverty, and prejudice she has faced the world with good humor, determination, and religious dedication.

2297 Jackson, Richard   **1721?-1787**
see Franklin, Benjamin

2298 *Jackson, Shirley   **1919-1965**
Life among the savages. New York: Farrar, Straus and Young, 1953. 241 p.
The book describes the move a writer and her husband make to Vermont, the birth of her third child, and her experiences as a housewife and mother to three young children.

2299 *Jackson, Shirley   **1919-1965**
Raising demons. New York: Farrar, Straus and Young, 1956. 310 p.
A novelist known for her fiction on themes of horror and paranoia writes of her more cheerful side—pets, kids, Little League baseball, and being a housewife.

2300 Jackson, Ulys   **1905-**
Autobiography of Ulys Jackson, M.D., Harrison, Arkansas, 1905-19. Compiled by Mrs. Ulys Jackson (Mary Ruth). Illustrated. Genealogy. Harrison, Arkansas: Mrs. Ulys Jackson, 1977, c. 1978. 178 p. Index.
After much effort Jackson graduated from the University of Arkansas School of Medicine and became a surgeon in Arkansas. In World War II he served in North Africa and India and was among the 500 survivors of the sinking of the H.M.T. *Rohna*, in which over 1000 troops were drowned. After the war he returned to Arkansas as a physician and coroner.

2301 Jackson, William Henry   **1843-1942**
The diaries of William Henry Jackson: frontier photographer; to California and return, 1866-67; and with Hayden Surveys to the Central Rockies, 1873, and to the Utes and Cliff Dwellings, 1874. Edited with introduction and notes by LeRoy R. Hafen and Ann W. Hafen. The Far West and the Rockies Historical Series, 1820-1875, Vol. X. Glendale, California: The Arthur H. Clark Co., 1959. 345 p. Index.
During his long and productive life, he was well-known for his photographs and murals of Western frontier life. Three of his numerous diaries of Western exploration are included here. In addition to paintings, photographs, and diaries left to libraries in New York and Colorado, forty thousand glass negatives were left to the State Historical Society of Colorado.

2302 Jacobi, John E.
Professor's odyssey: a portrait of a profession. Hicksville, New York: Exposition Press, 1976. 80 p.
A retired professor of sociology reflects on his fifty-year career working in nine colleges and universities. He compares large and small colleges, pre- and post-war teaching, and administrative and academic tasks.

2303 *Jacobs, Harriet (Brent) (Linda Brent, pseud.) **1818-1896**
Incidents in the life of a slave girl. Edited by L. Maria Child. New York: Harcourt, Brace, 1973. (Boston: The author, 1861) 210 p.
Born a slave, she remained in the South until she was 27 before escaping to the North. This story of the hardships, indignities, and abuses she suffered was written "to arouse the women of the North [and] . . . to

convince the people of the Free States what Slavery really is . . . how deep, and dark, and foul is that pit of abominations."

2304 Jacobs, Michel   **1877-1958**
Epigramus of an ignoramus: the life of Michel Jacobs. Illustrated by Michel Jacobs. Rumson, New Jersey: Primatic Art Co., 1953. 241 p.

Jacobs, who was a lieutenant colonel in World War I, may have found his true vocation in military service, but he regards painting (mostly stereotyped portraits) as his true love.

2305 Jacobs, Paul   **1918-1978**
Is Curly Jewish?: A political self-portrait illuminating three turbulent decades of social revolt, 1935-1965. New York: Atheneum, 1965. 339 p.

Jacobs attempts to describe the period 1935 to 1965 from the point of view of a radical and "to discover whether that view is related to how I feel about being a Jew." He was a union organizer, an international union representative, a labor consultant, and an active participant in the struggles between anti-Stalinist radicals and the communists.

2306 *Jacobs, Victoria   **1838-1861**
Diary of a San Diego girl, 1856. Edited by Sylvia Arden. Santa Monica: Norton B. Stern, 1974. 75 p. Index.

Written during the year before her marriage, the diary depicts a young woman's courtship in the context of middle-class life in the then small, rustic town of San Diego.

2307 *James, Alice   **1848-1892**
Alice James, her brothers—her journal. Boston: Milford House, 1972. (New York: Dodd, 1934) 252 p.

The journal describes her life in England, 1884-92, where she had moved for reasons of health. Her entries are caustic and tender, but always acute. She speaks with appreciation and love of her brother Henry, but she sometimes shocked him. She exhibits a lively interest in life around her.

2308 *James, Alice   **1848-1892**
The diary of Alice James. Edited with introduction by Leon Edel. New York: Dodd, Mead & Co., 1964. (Cambridge: John Wilson and Son, 1894) 241 p. Index.

Long unpublished at her brother Henry's insistence, the diary of Alice James records her sickroom world during the final months of her life and adds a page in the annals of an intellectual family. Four copies were originally printed for her brothers in 1894.

2309 James, Allen   **1904-**
Chief of the Pomos: life story of Allen James. Edited by Ann M. Connor. Santa Rosa, California: Ann M. Connor, 1972. 144 p.

An account of his life up to 1933 which describes the traditions of his tribe in order to preserve them (the design and construction of wigwams, ways to cook buckeyes, making poisons and medicines).

2310 James, Frank Lowber   **1841-1907**
Years of discontent: Doctor Frank L. James in Arkansas, 1877-1878. With David Baird. Edited with introduction by David Baird. Memphis, Tennessee: Memphis State University Press, 1977. 84 p. Index.

A candid account of medical practice in backwater Osceola, Arkansas, by a witty, urbane young physician who was bored in the small town and escaped to Memphis for the theater, balls, and other forms of culture. James' observations on folk medicine and current medical practices are informative.

2311 James, Henry   **1843-1916**
Autobiography. Edited with an introduction by Frederick W. Dupee. New York: Criterion Books, 1956. 622 p. Index.

A Small Boy and Others (1913), *Notes of a Son and Brother* (1914), and *The Middle Years* (1917), edited here in one volume on the fortieth anniversary of the death of one of America's finest writers.

2312 James, Henry   **1843-1916**
Henry James and H.G. Wells: a record of their friendship, their debate on the art of fiction, and their quarrel. And Herbert George Wells. Edited with introduction by Leon Edel & Gordon N. Ray. Urbana: University of Illinois Press, 1958. 272 p. Index.

Their letters (1895-1915) contain a debate about art as individual expression and art as social welfare.

2313 James, Henry   **1843-1916**
Henry James and Robert Louis Stevenson: a record of friendship and criticism. Introduction by Janet Adam Smith. London: Rupert Hart-Davis, 1948. 284 p. Index.

All surviving correspondence between James and Stevenson (1884-1894). Includes James' review of an 1899 edition of Stevenson's letters. A remarkable record of two outstanding literary artists.

2314 James, Henry   **1843-1916**
Letters. Edited by Leon Edel. New York: Macmillan, 1978. (Cambridge: Harvard University Press, 1974-) 2v. Index.

A selection of letters intended to be "representative" and "useful," showing the evolution in a personal literary form by one of the masters of the art.

2315 James, Henry   **1843-1916**
Letters to A.C. Benson and Auguste Monod: now first published, and edited with an introduction by E.F. Benson. Folcroft, Pennsylvania: Haskell House, 1969. (London: Elkin Mathews & Morrot; New York: Charles Scribner's, 1930) 118 p.

James's correspondence with poet Arthur Christopher Benson (1892-1915) explains why he hasn't written to or seen Benson for long intervals: "I was brutally preoccupied and distracted"; "My long silence . . . has not been baseness of any species: it has been high consideration and exquisite delicacy." James's letters to Auguste Monod (1905-1915) focus on translating James's stories into French accurately.

2316 James, Henry   **1843-1916**
Notebooks of Henry James. Edited by F.O. Matthiessen and Kenneth B. Murdock. New York; Oxford University Press, 1947. 425 p. Index.

Notebooks beginning in 1878 and recording his work in progress during thirty years reveal the mind and spirit of the writer, the germination of his ideas, his approach to technical problems, and the shape of the finished work.

2317 James, Henry   **1843-1916**
The selected letters of Henry James. Edited with an introduction by Leon Edel. Great Letters Series. New York: Farrar, Straus and Cudahy, 1955. 235 p. Index.

A selection of 120 letters intended to provide a guide to the varied types of letters written by an outstanding American author.

2318 James, Jasper E.   **d.1864**
Letters from a Civil War soldier. Edited by Vera Dockery Elkins. New York: Vantage Press, 1969. 61 p.

Jasper James, a Confederate soldier in the Civil War, wrote letters to his parents and siblings (1861-1864) at random intervals. These focus mostly on the food and living conditions (not bad at the war's beginning, but they deteriorated steadily). He was captured in 1863; a letter a year later indicates that he was again fighting for the Confederate Army. He was killed by Sherman's troops in Jonesboro, Georgia, in 1864.

2319 James, John Garland   **1844-1930**
Selected letters of John Garland James to Paul Hamilton Hayne and Mary Middleton Michel Hayne. Edited by Daniel Morley McKeithan. Austin: The University of Texas Press, 1946. 96 p.

James was raised in Virginia but settled in Texas where he became a prominent educator and banker. These letters to a famous contemporary poet and his wife relate primarily to some books of poetry and oratory he was developing, but reveal a growing friendship with the Haynes.

2320 James, Thomas   **1782-1847**
Three years among the Indians and Mexicans. Edited with introduction by Milo Milton Quaife. Garland Library of Narratives of North American Indian Captives, vol. 61. New York: Garland Publishing, 1978. (Waterloo, Illinois: War Eagle Office, printers, 1846) 130 p.

The perils of life on the frontier amid grizzly bears by a daring fur trapper. James recalls Indian raids, bitter winter encampments, the business endeavors of the Missouri Fur Company, Spanish "treachery," thefts, and debts.

2321 James, W.E.   **1894-**
Hanging and rattling: an autobiography of W.E. "Ed" James. As told to Dulcimer Nielsen. Illustrated. Caldwell, Idaho: Caxton Printers, 1979. 186 p.

James has lived most of his life in the back country of Idaho (now known as the Primitive Area) as a rancher, guide, packer, trapper, and horse raiser. He is a hard-bitten, hard-working veteran of the American West.

2322 James, William   **1842-1910**
Letters of William James and Theodore Flournoy. And Theodore Flournoy. Edited by Robert C. LeClair. Madison: University of Wisconsin Press, 1966. 252 p. Index.

For twenty years the American and the Swiss psychologist corresponded, sharing professional interests, news of publications, meetings, and colleagues. They were kindred spirits, two students of human nature in an intellectually vital world at the end of an optimistic era before World War I.

2323 James, William   **1842-1910**
Selected letters. Edited with introduction by Elizabeth Hardwick. New York: Farrar, Straus and Cudahy, 1961. 271 p. Index.

Most of these letters have been previously published. Hardwick selected an interesting range to reflect the pleasure James was fond of giving in his correspondence, a view of his charm and brilliance, and that of many of his famous contemporaries, including Henry Adams, Henry James, Oliver

Wendell Holmes, and John Jay Chapman, as well as the fascinating era they lived in.

2324 Jameson, John Franklin 1859-1937
An historian's world: selections from the correspondence of John Franklin Jameson. Edited by Elizabeth Donnan and Leo F. Stock. Memoirs of the American Philosophical Society, vol. 42. Philadelphia: American Philosophical Society, 1956. 382 p. Index.

A selection from the correspondence of a prominent historian, founder of the American Historical Association, and promoter of the National Archives Building.

2325 *Jannopoulo, Helen (Phiambolis) b.1875
And across big seas. Caldwell, Idaho: The Caxton Printers, Ltd., 1949. 353 p.

Grandmother's tale for her grandchildren about childhood in Braila, Rumania, and immigration to America with her family.

2326 Janssens, Victor Eugene August 1817-1894
Life and adventures in California of Don Augustin Janssens 1834-1856. Edited by William H. Ellison and Francis Price. Translated by Francis Price. San Marino: The Huntington Library, 1953. 165 p. Index.

Born in Belgium, when he was eight his family moved to Mexico, and at seventeen he migrated to what is now southern California, where he became a prominent rancher and businessman.

2327 Jarratt, Devereux 1733-1801
The life of the Reverend Devereux Jarratt in his letters to Rev. John Coleman. New York: Arno Press & The New York Times, 1969. (Baltimore: Warner & Hanna, 1806) 223 p.

Written as a series of letters to Coleman, Jarratt's autobiography describes his youth, his beliefs, his work for the church, and religious questions.

2328 Jarvis, Howard Arnold 1902-
I'm mad as hell: the exclusive story of the tax revolt and its leader. With Robert Pack. New York: Times Books, 1979. 310 p. Index.

This spirited autobiography chronicles Jarvis's struggle to convince the people of California to adopt his tax-cut proposal—Proposition 13. Jarvis's book follows the campaign from inception through election and reverberations. Toward the end, the author describes portions of his childhood in Utah—how he came to be "mad as hell"—and encourages his countrymen to follow his example as reformer.

2329 *Jastrow, Marie
A time to remember: growing up in New York before the Great War. Illustrated. New York: W.W. Norton & Co., 1979. 174 p.

Jastrow nostalgically recalls immigrant life in New York City, 1905-1917. Despite her family's initial poverty, their hard work and a support system of neighbors, shopkeepers, school teachers, and policemen made her childhood and acculturation pleasant and secure.

2330 Jaworski, Leon 1905-
Confession and avoidance: a memoir. With Mickey Herskowitz. Garden City, New York: Anchor Press/Doubleday, 1979. 325 p. Index.

Jaworski discusses various significant criminal cases in which he has participated as prosecutor, defense attorney, or judge, and in the process communicates his personal philosophy. Among these cases are prosecutions of Nazi war criminals (at Nuremberg), Mississippi Governor Ross Barnett over Civil Rights, and U.S. congressmen in the Tong Sun Park scandal.

2331 Jaworski, Leon 1905-
The right and the power: the prosecution of Watergate. New York, Houston: Readers Digest Press/Gulf Publishing Co., 1976. 305 p. Index.

In an exciting narrative, Watergate Special Prosecutor Jaworski describes the investigation of the break-in at Democratic campaign headquarters conducted by the Senate Watergate Committee and the federal courts. This culminated in the prosecution at which Jaworski officiated, which ultimately led to the convictions of various officials in the Nixon administration and to Nixon's resignation to avoid impeachment.

2332 Jay, John 1745-1829
Correspondence and public papers. Edited by Henry P. Johnston. New York: Da Capo, 1971. (New York: G.P. Putnam's Sons, 1890-1893) 4v. in 1.

Jay was the first Chief Justice of the United States, a member and president of the Continental Congress, minister to Spain, envoy to Great Britain, and twice Governor of New York. This edition reprints in one volume the earlier four-volume selection of his important personal and semi-official letters to and from him, along with public correspondence and documents.

2333 Jeffers, Robinson 1887-1962
The selected letters of Robinson Jeffers: 1897-1962. Edited by Ann N. Ridgeway. Foreword by Mark Van Doren. Photos by Leigh Wiener. Baltimore: The Johns Hopkins Press, 1968. 407 p. Index.

Jeffers' gentle humor and genuine concern for people are evident in these letters, which reflect on his own work and the work of others, on the art of poetry, on events, and on friendship and love.

2334 Jefferson, Isaac b.1775
Memoirs of a Monticello slave, as dictated to Charles Campbell in the 1840's by Isaac, one of Thomas Jefferson's slaves: life of Isaac Jefferson of Petersburg, Virginia, blacksmith, containing a full and faithful account of Monticello and the family there, with notices of many of the distinguished characters that visited there, with his revolutionary experience and travels, adventures, observations and opinions, the whole taken down from his own words. Edited with introduction by Rayford W. Logan. Charlottesville: University of Virginia Press for the Tracy W. McGregor Library, 1951. 45 p. Index.

Recollections by Isaac, a slave at Monticello, recorded during an interview in 1847 with Campbell, a scholar and editor.

2335 Jefferson, Joseph 1829-1905
The autobiography of Joseph Jefferson. Edited with introduction by Alan S. Downer. Illustrated. Cambridge, Massachusetts: Harvard University Press, 1964. (New York: Century Co., 1890) 363 p. Index.

Jefferson was the epitome of the Yankee peddler turned actor. He toured the American South, West, and Mexico, helping to introduce the drama of Europe and the English Reformation to the Western Hemisphere. He is best remembered for his portrayal of Rip Van Winkle.

2336 Jefferson, Thomas 1743-1826
The autobiography of Thomas Jefferson. Introduction by Dumas Malone. New York: G.P. Putnam's Sons, 1959. 119 p.

Written at 77, the book recalls the events of 1776 and others significant in the prime of his political career.

2337 Jefferson, Thomas 1743-1826
The complete Jefferson: containing his major writings, published and unpublished, except his letters. Edited by Saul K. Padover. Illustrated. Select Bibliographies Reprint Series. Freeport, New York: Books for Libraries Press, 1969. (New York: Duell, Sloan & Pearce, 1943) 1322 p. Index.

Jefferson's Autobiography, written January 6-July 28, 1821 (pp. 1119-1194), focuses on the drafting of the Declaration of Independence, his governorship of Virginia, the Peace Pact of 1783, the establishment of the federal government and Constitution, observations on the French Estates General, Declaration of the Rights of Man, and the French Revolution. The rest of this compendium consists of Jefferson's speeches, essays, notes, memos, poems, travel memoranda, diary excerpts, and some letters, arranged topically: religion, science, education, Indians, foreign policy, etc.

2338 Jefferson, Thomas 1743-1826
Correspondence between Thomas Jefferson and Pierre Samuel du Pont de Nemours, 1798-1817. Edited by Dumas Malone. Translated by Linwood Lehman. Supplemented by Gilbert Chinard. New York: Arno Press, 1979. (Boston: Houghton Mifflin, 1930) 210 p. Index.

Sixty letters between two modern-minded practical idealists, both of whom wished to contribute to the establishment of a just and happy state. The 100-page supplement contains Gilbert Chinard's essay "Jefferson and the Physiocrats."

2339 Jefferson, Thomas 1743-1826
Correspondence of Thomas Jefferson and Francis Walker Gilmer, 1814-1826. Edited with introduction by Richard Beale Davis. Columbia: University of South Carolina Press, 1946. 163 p. Index.

"An exchange between two alert minds of broad interest"; Jefferson appointed Gilmer to the Chair of Law at Central College (University of Virginia) and sent him to England to find additional outstanding faculty.

2340 Jefferson, Thomas 1743-1826
The family letters of Thomas Jefferson. Edited by Edwin Morris Betts and James Adam Bear, Jr. Columbia: University of Missouri Press, 1966. 506 p. Index.

The correspondence of Jefferson and his family (1783-1826) concerns family matters, local affairs, farm problems, the construction of Monticello, the fine arts, and a multitude of other subjects. The letters reiterate Jefferson's enjoyment of family society and his dislike of the occupation of politics.

2341 Jefferson, Thomas 1743-1826
Jefferson himself; the personal narrative of a many-sided American. Edited by Bernard Mayo. Charlottesville: The University Press of Virginia, 1970. (Boston: Houghton Mifflin, 1942) 384 p. Index.

An intimate portrait of Jefferson constructed from his own words, using materials from his voluminous writings, especially his letters, woven into "a narrative account of the man, of his private and public life, his varied interests and achievements."

2342 Jefferson, Thomas 1743-1826
A Jefferson profile, as revealed in his letters. Selected and arranged with

an introduction by Saul K. Padover. New York: The John Day Co., 1956. 359 p. Index.

A selection of 180 letters intended to portray his character and extensive range of interests.

2343 Jefferson, Thomas   **1743-1826**
The Jefferson-Dunglison letters. Edited by John M. Dorsey. Charlottesville: University of Virginia Press, 1960. 120 p. Index.

Letters between Jefferson and his physician (May 27, 1825-April 7, 1826) concern Jefferson's health, but primarily deal with matters related to the Medical School of the University of Virginia.

2344 Jefferson, Thomas   **1743-1826**
Letters of Thomas Jefferson. Introduction by Frank Irwin. Tilton, New Hampshire: The Sanbornton Bridge Press, 1975. 249 p.

Arranged by subject rather than chronology, this selection covers such topics as The Rights of Man, Alien and Sedition Laws, Foreign Wars and Treaties, Slavery and the Missouri Question.

2345 Jefferson, Thomas   **1743-1826**
The papers of Thomas Jefferson. Edited by Julian P. Boyd and others. Princeton: Princeton University Press, 1950-. v.

This edition of Thomas Jefferson's papers aims to present his writings and actions as completely as possible. The records of his life and career constitute a record of the origin, formation, and early growth of the Republic. His letters, notes, observations, reports, and many other writings testify to his insatiable thirst for knowledge and the versatility of his mind in exploring every avenue of science, culture, political, social and technical endeavor.

2346 Jefferson, Thomas   **1743-1826**
To the boys and girls: being the delightful, little-known letters of Thomas Jefferson to and from his children and grandchildren. Selected with historical notes by Edward Boykin. New York: Funk & Wagnalls Co., Inc., 1964. 210 p. Index.

A concerned and devoted father and grandfather, Jefferson filled his letters to his daughters and his grandchildren with playful, scolding, or anxious advice. Linked here with the editor's comments and biographical material, the letters give a picture of Jefferson's life from 1783 to its end.

2347 Jefferson, Thomas   **1743-1826**
see also **Adams, John**

2348 Jelke, Ferdinand Frazier   **1884-1953**
An American at large. New York: Duell, Sloan and Pearce, 1947. 337 p.

Raised in a hardworking Midwestern family of some wealth, he attained considerable wealth and social status on his own with the Newport and and international set. His travels led him to conclude that races and cultures are different and America should not attempt to Americanize the world.

2349 Jenkins, Herbert T.   **1907?-**
Forty years on the force, 1932-1972; Herbert Jenkins reminisces on his career with the Atlanta police department. Atlanta: Center for Research in Social Change, Emory University, 1973. 159 p.

Chief of the Atlanta Police Department 1947-1972, Jenkins also served as president of the International Association of Chiefs of Police, and on President Johnson's National Advisory Commission on Civil Disorders. After he retired from the force in 1972 he became senior consultant to the Center for Research in Social Change. His book reflects on the history of Atlanta's police department, with interesting comments on race relations, integration, and the social crises of the late Sixties.

2350 Jenkins, Ray Howard   **1897-**
Terror of Tellico Plains: the memoirs of Ray H. Jenkins. Foreword by Howard H. Baker, Jr. Illustrated. Knoxville, Tennessee: East Tennessee Historical Society, 1978. 199 p.

With humor and confidence Jenkins, aged 81, recounts his life, primarily dealing with legal cases in his career as an East Tennessee trial lawyer and judge. His family life centers on his two wives named Eva and his daughter Eva; his political life on the Army-McCarthy hearings; and major concerns of East Tennessee, including the Tellico Dam and the Clinch River Breeder Reactor.

2351 Jenkins, William Marshall, Sr.   **1892?-**
And . . . I'll throw in the socks; the memoirs of a Kentucky storekeeper. Written and illustrated by William M. Jenkins, Jr. Based on conversations and tape-recorded interviews with his father. Nashville, Tennessee: Parthenon Press, 1972. 196 p.

In an era of rugged individualism now fading into history, Jenkins left the farm to become a country storekeeper who brought fashion, learning, and a bit of elegance from the outside world into the rural Kentucky community of Guthrie.

2352 *Jenner, Chrystie   **1950-**
I am Chrystie. With Patricia Wood. Millbrae, California: Les Femmes Publishing, 1977. 187 p.

Chrystie Jenner, wife of 1976 Olympic decathalon winner Bruce Jenner and sometime stewardess, has written an autobiography to prove that she is a person in her own right. She vacillates between her desire to be a helpmate and mother and her wish to be independent.

2353 Jervis, John Bloomfield   **1795-1885**
The reminiscences of John B. Jervis, engineer of the Old Croton. Edited with introduction by Neal Fitzsimons. Syracuse: Syracuse University Press, 1971. 196 p. Index.

The leading consulting engineer of the antebellum era, Jervis was chief engineer for the Delaware and Hudson Canal project, a member of the Erie Canal engineering staff, an inventor and designer of railroad equipment and lines, director of the building of the Croton water-supply aquaduct system for New York City, and builder of dams, bridges, and railroad systems.

2354 Jessel, George   **1898-**
This way, miss. Foreword by William Saroyan. New York: Henry Holt, 1955. 229 p.

An entertainer from California discusses the entertainment profession in Hollywood, various personalities he has known, his renown as a toastmaster, and the Jewish faith, from 1941 to 1954. The book is in the form of thoughts to his daughter and includes speeches by and to him.

2355 Jewell, Bradbury   **1752-1828**
The fishbasket papers: the diaries, 1768-1823, of Bradbury Jewell, Esquire, of Tamworth, Durham and Sandwich, N.H. Edited by Marjory Gane Harkness. Peterborough, New Hampshire: Richard R. Smith, 1963. 236 p.

Originally given to the editor in a fishbasket, the diaries are the record of an ordinary man prominent in his day; historical context is supplied between entries by the editor.

2356 Jewett, Albert C.   **1870?-1926**
An American engineer in Afghanistan: from the letters and notes of A.C. Jewett. Edited by Marjorie Jewett Bell. Minneapolis: The University of Minnesota Press, 1948. 335 p.

Entering Afghanistan in 1911 to supervise the installation of a hydro-electric plant, Jewett notes experiences during eight years in an informative and entertaining portrait of a little-known part of the world.

2357 *Jewett, Sarah Orne   **1849-1909**
Letters. Introduction and notes by Richard Cary. Enlarged and revised edition. Waterville, Maine: Colby College Press, 1967. (Boston: Houghton Mifflin, 1911) 186 p. Index.

Contains 142 letters, 125 of which are in the Colby College Library. Inclusive dates, 1869-1908.

2358 *Jewett, Sarah Orne   **1849-1909**
Letters of Sarah Orne Jewett now in the Colby College Library. Notes by Carl J. Weber. Waterville, Maine: Colby College Press, 1947. 75 p. Index.

A small collection of 33 letters, many published for the first time, showing the Maine author's development as a writer. Inclusive dates, 1879-1904.

2359 Jewitt, John Rodgers   **1783-1821**
Narrative of the adventures of John R. Jewitt: only survivor of the crew of the ship Boston, during a captivity of nearly three years among the savages of Nootka Sound. Edited by Richard Alsop. New York: Garland Publishing, Inc., 1925. 203 p.

Jewitt, a young armorer on the ship *Boston,* was held captive for nearly three years by an Eskimo tribe in Nootka Sound, Alaska. He describes their clothing, houses, customs, hunting, fishing, waging war, and division of labor. Befriended by the chief, Maquina, Jewitt was eventually obliged to marry an Eskimo. When another ship came along, he tricked Maquina, who was captured and briefly held for ransom until Jewitt was released.

2360 Jimmy the Greek (James Snyder)   **1919-**
Jimmy the Greek. With the editing assistance of Mickey Herskowitz and Steve Perkins. Chicago: Playboy Press, 1975. 247 p.

Gambler and odds-maker Jimmy the Greek tells about his rise to big-time gambling on anything from horse racing to prizefighting to political contests. He has tips to offer on casino gambling but has a strong belief in luck as well as common sense and skill.

2361 *John, Sally
see **John, Thomas**

2362 John, Thomas Edward   **1943-**
Tommy John story. And Sally John with Joe Musser. Illustrated. Foreword by Tom Lasorda. Old Tappan, New Jersey: Fleming A. Revell, 1978. 175 p.

This is a baseball player's story of a rising career with the Los Angeles Dodgers which was apparently ended by an injury to his pitching arm. By great effort and religious faith, John recovered and continued his career. The book also emphasizes the closeness of marriage and the joys of parenthood.

2363 Johnson, Alvin Saunders   1874-1971
Pioneer's progress: an autobiography. New York: The Viking Press, 1952. 404 p. Index.
    An economist and educator recalls his childhood, youth, and college career in Nebraska during the late-nineteenth century. The author also writes about various colleges for which he worked and the political side of his economic career. The book primarily covers the time from the author's birth to World War II.

2364 Johnson, Andrew   1808-1875
The papers of Andrew Johnson. Leroy P. Graf and others. Knoxville: The University of Tennessee Press, 1967-. v.
    Andrew Johnson rose from abject poverty to become President of the United States at the death of Abraham Lincoln. He held virtually every elective office available from local Tennessee alderman through state and national positions and, although born into the lowest stratum of Southern society, came to associate with the great men of the nation. A Southern Democrat who supported the Union, a provincial among sophisticates, he faced enormous handicaps in his presidency because of his disagreements with Congress about the process of Reconstruction.

2365 Johnson, Axel P.   b.1886
Smuggled into paradise: saga of an immigrant youth. Philadelphia: Dorrance & Co., 1958. 156 p.
    Johnson came to America from Sweden as a child and from his early teens supported himself as a telegraph operator and newspaperman. In spite of never having completed high school, he eventually graduated from law school and was elected to the Colorado legislature for one term. He practiced criminal law and served on the faculty of Westminster Law School. After anecdotes of his courtroom experiences, the memoir ends with an account of a journey to Sweden. The large type and abundant dialogue make this book suitable for children, though its content is of equal interest to adults.

2366 Johnson, Benjamin C.   1840-1889
A soldier's life: the Civil War experiences of Ben C. Johnson. Foreword by George G. Mallinson. Edited with introduction by Alan S. Brown. Kalamazoo: School of Graduate Studies/Western Michigan University Press, 1962. 121 p.
    Johnson writes simply and clearly of his participation in the Civil War as an enlisted man in the Sixth Regiment, Michigan Infantry, 1861-1865. From March 1862 to August 1865 this regiment served under General Benjamin F. Butler in and around New Orleans, where enemies included reptiles and innumerable diseases in addition to Confederate soldiers. Over twenty-five percent of his compeers did not survive. Originally published serially in *The Veteran* (1883-84).

2367 *Johnson, Claudia Alta (Taylor) "Lady Bird"   1912-
White House diary. New York: Holt, Rinehart and Winston, 1970. 806 p. Index.
    The diary of her days in the White House presents a thorough, honest picture of those five years in a candid and warm style. In addition to being wife, mother, and manager of the busiest household in the world, Mrs. Johnson campaigned for and advised her husband and worked for her own beautification and arts programs.

2368 *Johnson, Edith Eugenie   b.1872
Leaves from a doctor's diary. Foreword by Alvin Johnson. Palo Alto, California: Pacific Books, 1954. 279 p.
    Dr. Johnson kept a diary from 1932 to 1953 and here publishes excerpts concerning her practice of obstetrics and gynecology in Palo Alto, California, particularly among Orientals.

2369 Johnson, Frank Thomas   b.1860
Autobiography of a centenarian. Denver: Big Mountain Press, 1961. 296 p. Index.
    The boyhood, family life, education, and long career in law of a prominent U.S. District Judge in Denver, Colorado.

2370 Johnson, Frederick   1932-
The Tumbleweeds: somersaulting up and out of the city streets. New York: Harper and Row, 1977. 246 p.
    Johnson, a social worker in a Puerto Rican area of New York in the 1950's, rehabilitated five youths and gave them strong identity as members of a performing acrobatic group, the Tumbleweeds. The book's implicit message is that through pride in a skill comes the responsibility, maturity, and self-reliance necessary to propel oneself out of the ghetto and into the middle class.

2371 Johnson, Hallett   1888-1968
Diplomatic memoirs: serious and frivolous. New York: Vantage, 1963. 207 p.
    Recollections of 35 years in the U.S. Diplomatic Service.

2372 Johnson, Jack (John Arthur)   1878-1945
Jack Johnson is a dandy: an autobiography. Preface, The Lampman. Introduction by Dick Schaap. Epilogue by Irene Johnson (Mrs. Jack Johnson). New York: Chelsea House Publishers, 1969. 262 p.

Johnson examines his career as a boxer (1908-1915, the first Black heavyweight world champion) and in detail narrates his key fight against Jim Jeffries, "the great white hope" to defeat Johnson and thereby to demean Blacks. But Johnson won. He was married four times, twice to white women. For a time Johnson went into exile and was eventually sentenced to Leavenworth Prison for violating the Mann Act. He remained a bon vivant and Black activist to the end, when he died in a car crash.

2373 Johnson, James Welden   1871-1938
Along this way: the autobiography of James Weldon Johnson. New York: Da Capo Press, 1973. (New York: The Viking Press, 1933) 418 p.
    Johnson, a man of varied talents, was a teacher, editor, journalist, lawyer, songwriter, school principal, author, poet, and U.S. Consul in Venezuela and Nicaragua. Throughout his life he worked on behalf of minority groups and the maintenance of free speech.

2374 Johnson, John Arthur
    see Johnson, Jack

2375 Johnson, Joseph Mitchell
The story of a county pastor. New York: Vantage Press, 1967. 260 p.
    Father Johnson was pastor at St. John's Church in Hollywood, Maryland, for 31 years (1922-53). During that time he directed the renovation of the buildings, the improvement of the church grounds, and the establishment of parochial schools. The story is told primarily in the third person, especially when the author is describing the everyday duties of a pastor: "The pastor put his best efforts behind his work. He did the best he could and the best he knew, and he would gladly have given more to the cause if he had more to give."

2376 *Johnson, Josephine Winslow   1910-
Seven houses; a memoir of time and places. New York: Simon & Schuster, 1973. 157 p.
    Stories from her life are organized around the seven houses her family lived in. She evokes vivid memories of the houses as places and describes with sensitivity the natural world surrounding them.

2377 Johnson, Lyndon Baines   1908-1973
Vantage point; perspectives of the presidency 1963-1969. Illustrated. New York: Holt, Rinehart & Winston, 1971. 636 p. Index.
    Beginning with his experience of the assassination of John F. Kennedy, the former president moves selectively through what he considers to be the most important problems, goals and accomplishments of his career including Viet Nam, the War on Poverty, Civil Rights, and Cold War politics. His intent is, as he puts it, to give a president's point of view documented as much as possible with letters, addresses, etc.

2378 Johnson, Sam Houston   1913?-
My brother Lyndon. Edited by Enrique Hank Lopez. New York: Cowles Book Co., Inc., 1969. 278 p. Index.
    Focusing on the development of his brother's political career, Johnson describes public and personal events in their life, often with a dour, critical perspective on power politics and the personalities involved.

2379 Johnson, Samuel   1696-1772
Samuel Johnson, president of King's College, his career and writing. Edited by Herbert and Carol Schneider. Foreword by Nicholas Murray Butler. New York: AMS Press, 1972. (New York: Columbia University Press, 1929) 4v.
    Volume I of this work contains biographical and historical documents including the autobiography (p. 1-49) and most of the letters of Samuel Johnson, a distinguished, eighteenth-century leader in American thought and education. The other three volumes contain historical documents and papers valuable to an understanding of the intellectual life during this period.

2380 Johnson, Samuel Wallace   b.1872
Autobiography. Illustrated. Denver: Big Mountain Press, 1960. 232 p. Index.
    Johnson's crusty autobiography emphasizes his impoverished childhood in rural Nebraska and his career as a lawyer and politician in Denver, where he was district attorney for six years and district court judge for twenty-four. In formal, sometimes stilted language Johnson offers critical vignettes of Colorado politicians and some turn-of-the-century Denver history.

2381 Johnson, Sherman Ellsworth   1896-
From the St. Croix to the Potomac: reflections of a bureaucrat. Foreword by Wayne D. Rasmussen. Illustrated. Bozeman: Big Sky Books, Montana State University, 1974. 289 p. Index.
    Hutchinson, a career bureaucrat with the U.S. Department of Agriculture 1936-1960, defends both the bureaucracy and the Department in a detailed account of his activities as Deputy Administrator, Economic Research Service, and of the activities of the bureau itself. The book provides an understanding of governmental policies to enhance agriculture from the Depression through the 1960's.

2382 Johnson, Tom Loftin   **1854-1911**
My story. Edited by Elizabeth J. Hauser. Introduction by Melvin G. Holli. Seattle: University of Washington Press, 1970. (New York: B.W. Huebsch, 1911) 326 p. Index.

Elected mayor of Cleveland in 1901, Johnson brought his resourcefulness and his training in big business to bear on city government. He applied the merit system to city departments, instituted a model building code, built public bathhouses, laid out parks, and increased the city's assets.

2383 Johnson, Wallace Edwards   **1901-**
Work is my play. With Eldon Roark. New York: Hawthorn Books, Inc., 1973. 198 p.

He was born in a Mississippi sharecropper's cottage. In 1953 he and Kemmons Wilson started the first national motel chain, Holiday Inn. In 1968 he received the Horatio Alger Award. His book is a version of that great American myth.

2384 Johnson, William   **1809-1851**
William Johnson's Natchez: the ante-bellum diary of a free Negro. Edited by William Ransom Hogan and Edwin Adams Davis. Preface by Edwin Adams Davis. Critical introduction by Frank A. Burdick. Illustrated. Series in Negro Culture and History. Port Washington, New York: Kennikat Press, 1968. (Baton Rouge: Louisiana State University Press, 1951) 2v. Index.

Johnson's diary spans 1835-51, when he was murdered in a dispute over land ownership. This narrative provides an extensive account of his barbering business and farming in Nachez (population then around 4700) and dispels the myth of the totally polarized Mississippi society of rich planters and poor slaves. Johnson comments on relations between whites and free Blacks, some of whom were themselves slaveholders, from the vantage point of a socially and economically successful freed slave.

2385 Johnston, William Graham   **1828-1913**
Overland to California: by a member of the wagon train first to enter California in the memorable year of 1849. Foreword by Joseph A. Sullivan. First California Edition. Oakland, California: Biobooks, 1948. (Pittsburgh, 1892) 272 p.

His party originated in Pittsburgh, traveled by steamer to Independence, Missouri, and after six weeks preparing for the journey, started on the Overland Trail to Sacramento. Based on his diary of the trip, the narrative was written over forty years later and includes a description of his return trip through the Isthmus of Panama in 1850.

2386 *Johnstone, Margaret (Blair)   **1913-**
When God says "no": faith's starting point. New York: Simon and Schuster, 1953. 311 p.

A woman Congregational minister in Illinois discusses her spiritual struggles as well as her struggle against sexual prejudice in her profession.

2387 Jones, Charles and Eugene Simmons Jones   **1925-**
Double trouble: the autobiography of the Jones Twins. With Dale Kramer. Boston: Little, Brown and Co., 1952. 317 p.

A first person plural narrative by twin photographers, their training in the Marines, and their experience in the Korean War.

2388 Jones, Cleon Joseph   **1942-**
Cleon. With Ed Hershey. New York: Coward-McCann, Inc., 1970. 191 p.

After a brief description of his boyhood in a small Alabama town, Jones writes of his career in baseball, focusing on the 1969 World Series win by the New York Mets.

2389 Jones, E. Stanley   **1885-1973**
A song of ascents: a spiritual autobiography. Foreword by James K. Mathews. Nashville, Tennessee: Abingdon Press, 1968. 400 p. Index.

Jones, a Methodist evangelist who has carried gospel messages to India, China, Japan, Korea, and throughout the United States, writes an eloquent though extremely detailed spiritual autobiography to explain why and how "God is the heart of everything." This book abounds in abstractions and biblical references but has very little personal information, despite Jones's international significance.

2390 Jones, Eugene Simmons   **1925-**
   see Jones, Charles

2391 Jones, Henry Boswell   **1792-1882**
Diary of Henry Boswell Jones of Brownsburg (1842-1871). Edited by Charles W. Turner. Illustrated. Verona, Virginia: McClure Press, 1979. 126 p. Index.

Evidently a very busy and conscientious man, Jones recorded many details of thirty years' farm life: sales and purchases, plantings and harvests, droughts and floods, children born to the servants, tallies of town votes, and who preached each Sunday's sermon.

2392 Jones, Howard Mumford   **1892-**
Howard Mumford Jones: an autobiography. Madison: University of Wisconsin Press, 1979. 292 p. Index.

Believing that "each human being is more than the totality of his own history," Mumford draws an engaging picture of the various academic settings in which he taught and wrote, including the University of Texas, the University of North Carolina, the University of Michigan, and Harvard. Among his numerous awards was a Guggenheim Fellowship to write the biography of Thomas More.

2393 Jones, James   **1921-1977**
Viet journal. New York: Delacorte Press, 1974. 257 p.

In 1973, he was contracted by the New York Times Magazine to do a book on Vietnam. He arrived shortly before the cease-fire, his assignment to describe the war as a novelist, not a politician. The result was this journal which captures the chaos and confusion, the human elements of that strange war.

2394 Jones, John Paul   **1747-1792**
John Paul Jones' memoir of the American Revolution: presented to King Louis XVI of France. Translated and edited by Gerard W. Gewalt. Introduction by John R. Sellers. Illustrated. Washington, D.C.: American Revolution Bicentennial Office/Library of Congress, 1979. 116 p.

A patriot and naval officer writes of his service during the American Revolution aboard the *Alfred,* and as commander of the sloops *Providence, Ranger, Ariel,* and *Bonhomme Richard.* After the war he tried in vain to obtain service in Louis XVI's royal navy, as letters appended to the memoir attest.

2395 Jones, John Paul   **1747-1792**
Life of Rear-Admiral John Paul Jones, Chevalier of the Military Order of Merit . . . Compiled from his original journals and correspondence. Illustrated by James Hamilton. Philadelphia: Walker & Gillis, 1845. 399 p.

The editor has compiled this book from the original journals and correspondence of Admiral Jones, including an account of his services in the American Revolution and in the Russo-Turkish War in the Black Sea.

2396 Jones, Joseph   **1727-1805**
Letters of Joseph Jones of Virginia, 1777-1787. Edited by Worthington Chauncey Ford. Eyewitness Accounts of the American Revolution. New York: Arno Press, 1971. (Washington, D.C.: Department of State, 1889) 157 p.

Judge Jones' letters, chiefly to James Madison, depict the condition of Virginia politics subsequent to the treaty of peace with Great Britain. The struggle of internal factions in his state is typical of what happened in other states, but in Virginia questions of constitutional development were deliberated with especially intense bitterness and a wide array of very talented opponents.

2397 Jones, Marvin   **1886-1976**
Memoirs: 1917-1973, fifty-six years of continuing service in all three branches of the federal government. Edited and annotated by Joseph M. Ray. El Paso: Texas Western Press, 1973. 183 p. Index.

Jones, who first took up his duties as congressman from Texas in 1917, writes of some of the significant legislation he supported. Later he served as war-price administrator and federal judge, still holding the post of senior judge at the time this book was published.

2398 *Jones, Mary (Harris)   **1830-1930**
Autobiography of Mother Jones. Edited by Mary Field Parton. Introduction by Clarence Darrow. Illustrated. Chicago: Charles H. Kerr Publishing Co., 1974. (1925) 242 p.

With gusto and panache, the grandmotherly-looking Mother Jones tells the story of her life as a labor organizer, particularly among the coal miners in Virginia and West Virginia, the steelworkers in Pittsburgh, and child laborers everywhere. Fearless and forthright, Mother Jones endured arrests and jail but fought staunchly for her cause.

2399 Jones, Robert Tyre (Bobby)   **1902-1971**
Golf is my game. Garden City, New York: Doubleday & Co., Inc., 1960. 255 p.

He began playing golf at age six. For the next forty years it was the central passion in his life, until he suffered a disabling disease. He writes of his active life as an amateur, a professional player, and an avid supporter with devoted enthusiasm.

2400 Jones, Thomas Elsa   **1888-1973**
Light on the horizon: the Quaker pilgrimage of Tom Jones. Richmond, Indiana: Friends United Press, 1973. 225 p. Index.

For many years he was the president of Earlham College. His book describes his early education, his Quaker philosophy, and his international work with the American Friends Service Committee.

2401 Jones, Tristan   **1924-**
The incredible voyage: a personal odyssey. Foreword by John Hemming. Kansas City: Sheed Andrews and McMeel, 1977. 390 p.

Jones has sailed over 345,000 miles in boats under forty feet long. This volume is his first account of his voyages.

2402 Jones, Tristan 1924-
Saga of a wayward sailor. Kansas City, Missouri: Andrews and McMeel, 1979. 264 p.

Jones describes his voyage from Norway through the Baltic Sea, the English Channel, the Bay of Biscay, the Atlantic Ocean, and the inland waterways of western Europe. He was accompanied by his best friend, a one-eyed, three-legged Labrador retriever.

2403 Jones, Weimar
My affairs with a weekly. Winston-Salem, North Carolina: John F. Blair, 1960. 116 p.

Jones has compiled a pleasant collection of brief, personal essays describing his experiences as the editor of *The Franklin Press*, the Macon County, North Carolina, weekly newspaper. This includes commentary on country editor-subscriber relationships and chatty anecdotes about his good-natured wife.

2404 *Jordan, Barbara Charline 1936-
Barbara Jordan: a self-portrait. And Shelby Hearon. Preface. Illustrated. Garden City, New York: Doubleday & Co., Inc., 1979. 269 p.

Jordan discusses the sources of the drive, energy, business acumen, and oratorical gifts that took her from Girl of the Year at Phyllis Wheatley High School (Houston, 1952) through Boston University Law School to the Texas State Senate, to two terms as U.S. Representative (1972-1976). She is noted for her forthright willingness to vote to impeach Nixon during the Watergate investigations, her active work for Civil Rights, and an honorary degree from Harvard.

2405 Jordan, Pat 1941-
A false spring. New York: Dodd, Mead & Co., 1975. 277 p.

Jordan relives his three-year minor-league baseball career playing for such teams as McCook, Eau Claire, and Palatka before he realized the hopelessness of ever being a successful player and quit the game.

2406 Jordan-Smith, Paul 1885-1971
The road I came: some recollections and reflections concerning changes in American life and manners since 1890. Caldwell, Idaho: The Caxton Printers, Ltd., 1960. 474 p.

Literary editor for the Los Angeles *Times*, he writes here about his boyhood in the Upper Valley of Virginia, extolling the benefits of country ham, country values, and his 25 years as a literary critic, commenting on the changes in values and taste over the years.

2407 *Jordon, Nell (Sutton)
The doctor's daughters. San Antonio, Texas: The Naylor Co., 1972. 113 p.

The author writes of her girlhood as one of five daughters of a small-town doctor in the rough hill country of northwestern Arkansas and in Oklahoma. Her life in the early part of the century included chores, school, box socials, spelling bees, hard work, and simple pleasures.

2408 Josephson, Matthew 1899-1978
Infidel in the temple; a memoir of the nineteen-thirties. New York: Alfred A. Knopf, 1967. 513 p. Index.

Focusing on the period between the two World Wars, the author writes of his own life and ideas but also records his observations of a critical decade, the Thirties. He writes of the Depression, leftists, communism, the banking crisis, situations in France and Spain, the New Deal, the labor movement, and in general, the state of the country and the world.

2409 Josephson, Matthew 1899-1978
Life among the surrealists; a memoir. New York: Holt, Rinehart and Winston, 1962. 403 p.

A group portrait of his friends who were active in the literary and art movements of the 1920's is developed around his own life experience.

2410 Josselyn, Amos Piatt 1820-1885
The overland journal of Amos Piatt Josselyn: Zanesville, Ohio to the Sacramento Valley, April 2, 1849 to Sept. 11, 1849. Edited by J. William Barrett. Illustrated. Baltimore: Gateway Press, 1978. 129 p. Index.

This heavily footnoted journal chronicles the American West—its land, beasts, people, and hardships—during the South Zanesville Company's journey toward California gold. Supplementing the journal are Josselyn's letters to his wife, the company's financial accounts, and an "Emigrants Guide" describing the territory along the California-Oregon Trail. Originally published in a series of articles in the Zanesville *Sunday Times Signal* in 1953 from the original manuscripts in the California State Library.

2411 Journeyman, pseud.
see Nock, Albert Jay

2412 Judd, Lawrence McCully 1887?-1968
Lawrence M. Judd & Hawaii; an autobiography. As told to Hugh W. Lytle. Rutland, Vermont: Charles E. Tuttle Co., 1971. 296 p.

Grandson of Laura Fish Judd, an early nineteenth-century missionary, Lawrence Judd became a territorial Governor of Hawaii. After he retired, he worked among the leprosy patients at Molokai helping the sick and aged. His kindness, humor, and compassion are evident in these stories of his experiences in the Islands.

2413 Judd, Neil Merton 1887-1976
Men met along the trail; adventures in archaeology. Illustrated. Norman: University of Oklahoma Press, 1968. 162 p. Index.

The reminiscences of fifty years as an archaeologist largely spent exploring Indian ruins in Arizona, Utah, New Mexico, and Guatemala. He has seen his profession "evolve from curio-collecting to radiocarbon dating and pollen analysis." He was curator of archaeology at the Smithsonian Institution.

2414 Judge, William Quan 1851-1896
Practical occultism: from the private letters of William Q. Judge. Edited with preface by Arthur L. Conger. Pasadena: Theosophical University Press, 1951. 307 p.

Selections from correspondence (1882-1891) written to colleagues and others in United States, England, and India concerning theosophical ideas and activities.

2415 Juelich, Walter 1895-
My human zoo: the story of a refugee doctor. New York: Exposition Press, 1959. 110 p.

A well-written account of the author's experiences in New York City (1940-59) as a physician to patients of diverse races and nationalities. Emphasizes his pride in being Jewish and an American immigrant and his horror of German genocide and concentration camps, in which he was imprisoned for a month. Juelich also discusses alcoholism, obesity, smoking, and other medical problems.

2416 Julian, Hubert Fauntleroy 1897-
Black eagle. As told to John Bulloch. Illustrated. London: Jarrold's Publishers, 1964. 200 p. Index.

Julian describes his exciting life as a pilot and international arms dealer (supplying Tshombe of Katanga), although his firm did not sell arms for revolutionary purposes or to enable one state to invade another. Julian's race (Black) motivates and dominates all his actions and beliefs, including his perspectives on international politics, his love of travel, and his elegant life style.

2417 Kabotie, Fred 1900-
Hopi Indian artist: an autobiography. As told to Bill Belknap. Foreword by Barton Wright. Flagstaff, Arizona: Museum of Northern Arizona with Northland Press, 1977. 149 p. Index.

With a strong sense of the customs and culture of the Hopi Indians, Kabotie demonstrates how his own life both fits the pattern and expands it. He attained success (including a Guggenheim Fellowship) as a painter of Hopi dance scenes and murals. He taught painting and silversmithing to other Hopis and was instrumental in founding the Hopi Cultural Center of Shungopavi, Arizona, the heart of the Hopi reservation.

2418 Kaeo, Peter Young 1836-1880
News from Molokai: letters between Peter Kaeo & Queen Emma, 1873-1876. Edited with introduction and notes by Alfons L. Korn. Illustrated. Honolulu: University Press of Hawaii, 1976. 345 p.

Peter Kaeo, cousin of Queen Emma of Hawaii, was obliged to go to the island of Molokai because of his leprosy. This book is a collection of letters between him and the Queen, in which he reports on his illness and the tragic events in the lives and deaths of other lepers. The Queen sympathizes, sends provisions, reports on political intrigues, and awaits his return home.

2419 Kahn, David E. 1893-1968
My life with Edgar Cayce. As told to Will Oursler. Garden City, New York: Doubleday & Co., Inc., 1970. 214 p.

Kahn writes of his lifelong friendship and association in psychic discovery with Cayce, a well-known prophet and psychic. His book is a spiritual autobiography as well as a personal reading of Cayce.

2420 Kahn, Edgar Adolph 1900-
Journal of a neurosurgeon. Foreword by Bronson S. Ray. Springfield, Illinois: Charles C. Thomas, publisher, 1972. 172 p.

Dr. Kahn recalls his part in the development of neurosurgery, his experiences in training during World War II and afterwards.

2421 Kahn, Ely Jacques 1916-
About the New Yorker and me: a sentimental journal. New York: G.P. Putnam's Sons, 1979. 453 p. Index.

A fascinating diary of the author's sixtieth year, his fortieth as a writer, for many years on the *New Yorker* staff. During the year, he travels to Greece, Africa, Georgia, and elsewhere on magazine assignments; relishes life with his second wife, writer Eleanor Munro, and their son; converses with innumerable writers, politicians, and others of international interest of whom he provides vignettes and colorful background information.

2422 Kahn, Roger
Boys of summer. Illustrated. New York: Harper & Row, 1972. 442 p.

With a strong sense of his participation in a profession marked by the likes of Ring Lardner, the author recounts his early love affair with the Brooklyn Dodgers and his serving as the New York *Herald Tribune's* sportswriter covering the Dodgers in the 1950's. Rich in newspaper, baseball, and Brooklyn lore, this is also the personal story of a newspaperman.

2423 Kaltenborn, Hans Von 1878-1965
Fifty fabulous years: 1900-1950: a personal review. New York: G.P. Putnam's Sons, 1950. 312 p. Index.
Radio news analyst describes world travel, interviews with national leaders, and opinions on current affairs in recorded interviews with his son, which Kaltenborn edited and revised.

2424 *Kaminska, Ida 1899-1980
My life, my theatre. Illustrated. Edited and translated by Curt Leviant. New York: Macmillan Publishing Co., Inc., 1973. 310 p. Index.
Her mother was known as the Mother of Yiddish Theater; she herself soon followed in the theatrical footsteps traveling and acting throughout Europe. She and her husband directed the nationalized Yiddish State Theater in Poland after World War II and she continued acting on the stage and in films, emigrating from Poland when anti-Zionist hatred became unbearable after the Six-Day War.

2425 Kanin, Garson 1912-
Hollywood: stars and starlets, tycoons and fleshpeddlers, movie makers and moneymakers, frauds and geniuses, hopefuls and has-beens, great lovers and sex symbols. New York: The Viking Press, 1974. 393 p.
In 1937 he was hired by Samuel Goldwyn to learn the movie business. His book recalls almost forty years among the personalities of film and theater. In addition to many of the famous, there are stories of figures lesser known or past their prime, such as Mrs. Patrick Campbell.

2426 Kantor, MacKinlay 1904-1977
But look, the morn: the story of a childhood. New York: Coward-McCann, Inc., 1947. 308 p.
An excellent recollection of a writer's boyhood in Webster City, Iowa, written without nostalgia but depicting the character and values of middle America in the early twentieth century.

2427 *Kappu, Myrtle King 1898-
I married a prince: a Cinderella story from Hawaii. Hicksville, New York: Exposition Press, 1977. 271 p.
After fifteen years of worldwide traveling and hiking with a friend (in Hawaii, Japan, China, and Iraq), she settled in Hawaii to teach school until her retirement in 1962. In 1935 she married a Hawaiian prince, David Kaapuawao Kamehameha, and lived in a grass house for most of their marriage until his death in 1971.

2428 Karcher, Joseph T. 1903-
Main Street lawyer. Illustrated by Bill Canfield. Foreword by Emma E. Dillon. Boston: Meador Publishing Co., 1959. 189 p.
A pleasant reminiscence that focuses on Karcher's life-long relationship with his hometown, Sayreville, New Jersey. There he grew up, studied law, became a practicing lawyer and, for twenty years, magistrate judge. His love for the law, the town, his family, and "The American Heritage" is pervasive.

2429 Karpis, Alvin 1908?-
The Alvin Karpis story. With Bill Trent. Illustrated. New York: Coward, McCann & Geoghegan, 1971. 256 p.
A boastful, colorful look at the underworld figures of the 1930's when Karpis and the Ma Barker gang made headlines with payroll heists, bank robberies, and kidnapping. After many daring escapades, the author finally lost the battle of nerve and wits with J. Edgar Hoover and the FBI and spent 33 years in jail for kidnapping.

2430 Karras, Alexander 1935-
Even big guys cry. With Herb Gluck. New York: Holt, Rinehart and Winston, 1977. 246 p.
Karras tells of his childhood in Gary, Indiana, as the son of a Greek immigrant doctor. His father's premature death forced the entire family to work; the three sons (Louie, Teddy, and Alex) went through college on football scholarships. Karras was an All-American tackle at the University of Iowa and played defensive lineman for the Detroit Lions for thirteen years until he was fired in 1971. He includes a serious attack on the pro-football system.

2431 Katz, Israel
My brother's keeper: a lifetime of reminiscences, poetry, speeches, and articles. New York: Vantage Press, 1978. 75 p.
This collection of a chemical researcher's poetry, speeches, articles, and essays focuses on his love for his family. His life as a Jewish Lithuanian immigrant embodies fulfillment of the American Dream: becoming a worthy citizen, earning a college degree, and working hard.

2432 Katz, Josef 1918-
One who came back; the diary of a Jewish survivor. Translated by Hilda

Reach. New York: Herzl Press and Bergen-Belsen Memorial Press, 1973. 277 p.
The experience during the 1933-1945 Nazi period of a German Jew who endured the horrors of the Holocaust—human suffering, starvation, torture—but managed to survive the death camps. Although written in 1946 when all the anguish was fresh in his mind, these memoirs remained unpublished for 25 years.

2433 Katz, Meyer Myron 1909-
Papa, play for me: the hilarious, heartwarming autobiography of comedian and bandleader Mickey Katz. As told to Hannibal Coons. Introduction by Joel Grey. New York: Simon & Schuster, 1977. 223 p.
Katz describes his lifelong career (from age 14) as an entertainer. He began by playing in dance bands in Cleveland, his home town; eventually he switched to Yiddish comedy songs ("The Barber of Shlemiel," "The Herring Boats are Coming") and being a Yiddish disc jockey. His biggest success was *Borscht Capades,* with son Joel Grey.

2434 Katzman, Jacob 1911-
Commitment: the Labor Zionist life-style in America: a personal memoir. Foreword by Marie Syrkin. New York: Labor Zionist Letters, 1975. 211 p.
Katzman, an ardent Zionist, lectured and devoted a lifetime to the establishment of a Jewish socialist state in Palestine. He describes the activities of and his family's involvement with the Boston *Chavershaft,* a social and cultural brotherhood of Jews who worshiped and promoted Zionist causes together.

2435 Kaufmann, Arthur b.1888
Excerpts from Arthur Kaufmann's memoirs: old canvas, new varnish. The Hague: Albani, 1963. 50 p.
A painter reviews his life, studies, his flight from Germany to Holland and then America. He discusses influences on his development and his beliefs about art and democracy. Reproductions of some of his portraits and paintings are included.

2436 *Kazanjian, Arlene Francis
see ***Francis, Arlene***

2437 Kazin, Alfred 1915-
New York Jew. New York: Alfred A. Knopf, 1978. 307 p. Index.
Kazin's third autobiographical volume covers the 1940's, 50's, and 60's, and focuses on the New York literary and intellectual milieu in which he was a central figure. He first worked for *The New Republic* and *Fortune,* then contributed distinguished literary criticism and social analysis to a myriad of publications. Ever conscious of his Jewishness, he regards this background as central to his world view.

2438 Kazin, Alfred 1915-
Starting out in the Thirties. Boston: Little, Brown and Co., 1965. 160 p.
The years from 1934 to 1940 were formative ones for this critic. He speaks here of the beginnings of his career, the writers, editors, and others who influenced his writing, and the events that shaped his thinking.

2439 Kazin, Alfred 1915-
Walker in the city. New York: Harcourt, Brace and Co., 1951. 176 p.
In a narrative tour through Brooklyn, Kazin remembers growing up in a tenement and developing an awareness of himself in the world.

2440 Kean, Robert Winthrop 1893-
Dear Marraine (1917-1919). Illustrated. Livingston, New Jersey: The author, 1969. 289 p. Index.
The story of America's part in the fighting in France during World War I told by an American artillery officer who took part in some of the fiercest battles—Chateau-Thierry, Vaux, and Soissons. Many photographs and maps are included.

2441 Kean, Robert Winthrop 1893-
Fourscore years, my first twenty-four. N.P.: privately printed., 1974. 264 p.
Kean, who later served in Congress for twenty years, writes of his privileged childhood and youth—winters in the family brownstones on Park Avenue and Murray Hill, summers at the ocean at Elberon and Deal, prep school, Harvard, travel in the West, a big-game hunting trip to Alaska, and National Guard duty on the Mexican Border.

2442 Keane, Walter 1921-
Walter Keane. Foreword by Eric Schneider. Redwood City, California: Johnson Myers Publishing Co., 1964. n.p.
Keane, whose painting trademark is a large-eyed, melancholic child, here comments on 48 paintings and drawings he made between 1945 and 1963, explaining what he was trying to achieve in each instance.

2443 *Kearney, Belle 1863-1939
A slaveholder's daughter. New York: Negro Universities Press, 1969. (New York: Abbey Press, 1900) 269 p.

A post-Civil War story of a Southern woman from a proud Mississippi family who breaks traditions by teaching public school, by helping Blacks get an education, by becoming a suffragist, and by working as a Temperance leader. Kearney is a "new Southern" woman.

2444 Kearns, Jack ("Doc") 1882-1963
Million dollar gate. With Oscar Fraley. New York: The Macmillan Co., 1966. 335 p.
Both a saint and scoundrel, a soft touch and a financial wizard, a glib hard-sell expert and a polished persuader, Kearns was a brash man who "manipulated" Jack Dempsey to the heavyweight championship of the world and originated the million-dollar gate.

2445 Keating, Edward 1875-1965
Gentleman from Colorado: a memoir. Foreword by Eleanor Connolly Keating, Illustrated. Denver: Sage Books/Alan Swallows, 1964. 522 p. Index.
Keating calls his book a collection of "stories"—about life as a newspaperman, the Western frontier, state and national politics, labor organization, and, as he titled one chapter, "interesting people." A politically active Irish Democrat who battled Denver's political machine in his early years, Keating geared most of his actions to the benefit of the blue-collar worker.

2446 Keating, Michael
White man/black man. And Jimmy Watson. New York: Praeger Publishers, 1974. 227 p.
Two men, one Black and one white, tell the story of their friendship which began when Keating as Editorial Director of WCBS-TV recruited Watson for an apprenticeship program to train young Blacks to become journalists.

2447 *Keckley, Elizabeth (Hobbs) 1824-1907
Behind the scenes; thirty years a slave and four years in the White House. American Negro: his history and literature. New York: Arno Press, 1968. (New York: G.W. Carleton & Co. Pub., 1868) 371 p.
A restrained but moving account of the author's childhood and young adulthood as a slave, the sadism of a schoolmaster who beat her, her rape by a white man, her eventual freedom after she earned the money to buy her son's and her own freedom, serves as preface to the story of her life in Washington and New York with Mrs. Lincoln during and after Lincoln's presidency.

2448 Keemer, Edgar Bass 1913-
Confessions of a pro-life abortionist. Illustrated. Vinco Press, 1980. 240 p. Index.
A Black gynecologist and abortionist, Keemer performed hundreds of abortions both privately and openly, lost his medical license, and served time in prison. He remains firmly supportive of a woman's right to abortion. The seemingly paradoxical "pro-life" segment of his title refers to the woman, not to the unborn child.

2449 Keene, Donald 1922-
Meeting with Japan. Tokyo: Gakuseisha Publishing Co., 1979. 168 p.
Keene has written a profound account of the growth and development of his love for Japan—the country, people, and literature, of which he is a world-famous interpreter, historian, and translator. He first learned Japanese as a naval officer in World War II, then studied and taught at Cambridge before living in Japan. He explains why he feels at home and at peace there, particularly in Kyoto, and describes his friendships with various writers and scholars, including Yukio Mishima and Abe Kotso.

2450 Keiner, Samuel S. 1910-
Doctor, don't let me die! And Dan Gorden. Boston: Meador Publishing Co., 1947. 486 p.
The education, internship, and practice of a physician; his experience with life and death; his thoughts about the cavalcade of humanity that has touched his life; and his devotion to the social responsibilities of his profession.

2451 Keiser, Albert 1887-1959
The way up; an autobiography. Peterborough, New Hampshire: Richard R. Smith, 1961. 223 p.
After immigrating from Holland at fourteen, he was raised on a Nebraska farm, went to college, served as a Lutheran missionary and minister, and later became a professor of literature at a small Lutheran college in North Carolina.

2452 *Keith, Agnes Newton 1901-
Three came home. Sketches by the author and Don Johnston. Boston: Little, Brown and Co., 1947. 316 p.
Main focus is survival in a Japanese concentration camp with her small son and husband; stark, descriptive, well-written. The intimate horror of war.

2453 *Keith, Agnes Newton 1901-
White man returns. Line drawings by the author. Boston: Little, Brown and Co., 1951. 310 p.

The author writes about her personal experiences with people and customs in Borneo when returning there with her family to help with reconstruction after World War II.

2454 Keith, Charles Alexander b.1883
Fast balls and college halls: an autobiography of Charles A. Keith. Foreword by Nell Stuart Donovan. New York: Vantage Press, 1959. 146 p.
Keith emphasizes his rural Arkansas upbringing, his college years, his playing of amateur and professional baseball (St. Louis Browns), and his forty-years' service at Eastern Kentucky State University as head of the history department, coach of various teams, and Dean of Men.

2455 Keith, Elmer 1899-
"Hell, I was there!" Los Angeles: Peterson Publishing Co., 1979. (New York: Winchester Press, 1974) 308 p.
An expert on guns, hunting, and the outdoors, he learned to shoot as a young boy. Here he describes his lifelong enthusiasm for hunting and the natural world. His wife of fifty years has shared this passion, frequently hunting and traveling with him. His book captures the spirit of the American West.

2456 Keith, Herbert F.
Man of the woods. Introduction and notes by Paul F. Jamieson. Syracuse, New York: Syracuse University Press, 1972. 164 p.
Keith writes about his life in the community of Wanakena, New York, a lumber camp which became a village surrounded by forest preserve, about the guides of the Oswegatchie River, and of the forest that has survived logging, fire, blowdown, and sportsmen.

2457 Keller, George Jacob 1896-1960
Here, Keller, train this. New York: Random House, 1961. 246 p.
While teaching art at Bloomsburg State College (Pa.), a friend sent him a full-grown mountain lion and challenged him to train it. He did. Subsequently he entered animal acts in several small circuses during the summers before finally giving up teaching. The last two years of his life he spent with the Ringling Brothers Barnum and Bailey Circus.

2458 *Keller, Helen Adams 1880-1968
Helen Keller, her socialist years; writings and speeches. Edited with introduction by Philip S. Foner. New York: International Publishers, 1967. 128 p.
This collection of Helen Keller's political and social writings and speeches include her arguments for women's suffrage, her defense of the Industrial Workers of the World (Wobblies), her opposition to World War I, her views on birth control, her support of Eugene V. Debs, her pleas on behalf of the unemployed and the labor movement, her defense of the Soviet Union, and her eulogy of Lenin. For a dozen years socialism provided a viable response to the social ills about which Keller was particularly concerned.

2459 *Keller, Helen Adams 1880-1968
Helen Keller's journal. Bath: Cedric Chivers, 1973. (London: Michael Joseph, Ltd., 1938) 296 p.
A record of her thoughts and feelings during her trip to England in 1936-1937, after the death of Anne Sullivan, her teacher and companion for almost fifty years.

2460 *Keller, Helen Adams 1880-1968
Midstream: my later life. New York: Greenwood Press, 1968. (New York: The Crowell Publishing Co., 1929) 362 p. Index.
Her second autobiographical volume continues the story of her life after her sophomore year at Radcliffe, including chapters about her friendships with Mark Twain and Alexander Graham Bell.

2461 *Keller, Helen Adams 1880-1968
The story of my life: with her letters (1887-1901) and a supplementary account of her education, including passages from the reports and letters of her teacher, Anne Mansfield Sullivan, by John Albert Macy. Introduction by Ralph Barton Perry. New York: Lancer Books, 1968. (New York: Doubleday Page, 1903) 525 p.
Written during her sophomore year at Radcliffe, the book depicts the remarkable story of her learning and intellectual growth after her blindness, emphasizing her unusual relationship with her teacher, Anne Sullivan.

2462 Keller, James Gregory 1900-1977
To light a candle: the autobiography of James Keller, founder of the Christophers. New York: Doubleday & Co., Inc., 1963. 260 p.
Ordained at 25, he was deeply affected by a brief visit to the Far East which convinced him of the power of individuals to take responsibility for their fellow men and thereby change the human condition. Here he tells how the Christophers grew into a wide-ranging movement.

2463 *Kelley, Shirley Dyckes 1933-
Love is not for cowards. As told to Elizabeth Cullander. Englewood Cliffs, New Jersey: Prentice-Hall, Inc., 1978. 281 p.
Kelley grew up in Miami, was educated at St. Mary's College (South

Bend, Indiana), where she decided to become a nun. Her extensive account of her religious training is a reflection of her decisive, resilient, effervescent personality, which contributed to her success as a history teacher. After she left the order in 1971, she enjoyed an active social life and married FBI Director Clarence Kelley in 1976.

2464 *Kellogg, Clara Louise   1842-1916
Memoirs of an American prima donna. Illustrated. New York: Da Capo Press, 1978. (New York: G.P. Putnam's Sons, 1913) 382 p. Index.
   A confident, spirited account of Kellogg's youth and operatic career, 1860-1880. She writes of many wealthy and famous figures she met and describes operatic tours to Europe and Russia singing for the crowned heads of Europe.

2465 Kellogg, David S.   1847-1909
Doctor at all hours; the private journal of a small-town doctor's varied life 1886-1909. Edited by Allan S. Everest. Brattleboro, Vermont: Stephen Greene, 1970. 229 p.
   A turn-of-the-century family G.P. with a large rural practice in upstate New York writes of his patients, family, and his avocational interests, including local history, nature observations, mountain climbing, collecting china and Indian relics, and archaeology.

2466 Kellogg, Miner Kilbourne   1814-1889
M.K. Kellogg's Texas journal, 1872. Illustrated. Edited with introduction by Lerena Friend. Austin: University of Texas Press, 1967. 183 p. Index.
   A journal kept by a non-Texan who was employed as an artist on the Texas Land and Copper Association Expedition of 1872. Although his sketches have not been found, the journal describes vividly the progress of a mineral expedition, largely unsuccessful, across northern Texas.

2467 Kelly, Emmett   1898-1979
Clown. With F. Beverly Kelley. New York: Prentice-Hall, Inc., 1954. 271 p.
   After his boyhood on a Missouri farm, he joined a circus and later became one of the most famous clowns in circus history. Here, his story of Willie the Tramp.

2468 Kelly, Luther Sage (Yellowstone Kelly)   1849-1928
"Yellowstone Kelly": the memoirs of Luther S. Kelly. Edited by M.M. Quaife. Foreword by Nelson A. Miles. Lincoln: University of Nebraska Press, 1973. (New Haven: Yale University Press, 1926) 268 p. Index.
   The life story of a prominent Indian Scout on the western frontier.

2469 Kelly, Walter C.   1873-1934
Of me I sing: an informal autobiography. Foreword by George Ade. Illustrated. Epilogue by Grantland Rice. New York: Dial Press, 1953. 246 p.
   Kelly, a comic actor and monologist, describes his travels, triumphs, and tribulations on the vaudeville circuit in the Midwest and East. As "The Virginia Judge," Kelly presided over comic mock trials on and off stage, including some involving retired prizefighter Jim Jeffries.

2470 Kelty, Matthew
Flute solo: reflections of a Trappist hermit. Kansas City: Andres & McMeel, Inc., 1979. 128 p.
   Kelty writes introspectively of his life as a priest and his decision to become a Trappist hermit in New Guinea. He dwells at length on his love for solitude and on his constant quest for a complete spiritual union with God.

2471 *Kemeny, Jean Alexander   1930-
It's different at Dartmouth: a memoir. Illustrated. Preface. Brattleboro, Vermont: The Stephen Greene Press, 1979. 199 p.
   The wife of Dartmouth College's thirteenth president writes of the frustration and satisfaction of her "profession." Warm, funny, and sometimes irreverent, Mrs. Kemeny describes an ill-defined, thankless job as she portrays an institution, its personable president, and her life with both.

2472 Kendall, Amos   1789-1869
Autobiography of Amos Kendall. Edited by William Stickney Smith, his son-in-law. New York: Peter Smith, 1949. (Boston: Lee and Shepard, 1872) 700 p.
   The author gives an extensive account of his family life and career affairs in public life as selected by his editor from the mass of written material Kendall produced.

2473 Kendall, Messmore   1872-1959
Never let weather interfere. New York: Farrar, Straus and Co., Inc., 1946. 423 p. Index.
   Steeped in the traditions of the American dream, the book describes the life of a lawyer in a family of lawyers, confident of achievement, independence, and success.

2474 *Kenmore, Carolyn
Mannequin; my life as a model. New York: Bartholomew House, Ltd., 1969. 313 p.
   The ups and downs of a modeling career make it plain that a model's life is not all glitter and glamour, but involves hard work and determination. Despite the fact that photographs are basic to her career, the book does not contain pictures.

2475 Kennan, George Frost   1904-
Memoirs: 1925-1950. Boston: Little, Brown and Co., 1967. 583 p. Index.
   After a brief summary of his youth, Kennan devotes his memoirs to his training in Foreign Service School for service in Russia and his subsequent service abroad in Moscow, Prague, Germany, and Portugal. After World War II he worked at the National War College, on the State Department Planning Staff and with various policy-making functions in Washington until his retirement from government service in 1950.

2476 Kennan, George Frost   1904-
Memoirs: 1950-1963. Boston: Little, Brown and Co., 1972. 368 p. Index.
   Based on his later years of government service as Ambassador to Moscow and to Yugoslavia, this volume continues Kennan's description of the evolution of his philosophy of public affairs and, particularly, foreign affairs.

2477 *Kennedy, Florynce   1916-
Color me Flo: my hard life and good times. Englewood Cliffs, New Jersey: Prentice-Hall, 1976. 177 p.
   A Black lawyer and political activist describes her family, education, and social philosophy. Often outrageously blunt, she was a founding member of NOW, but left it in 1971 to form the Feminist Party which backed Shirley Chisholm for President.

2478 *Kennedy, Rose (Fitzgerald)   1890-
Times to remember. Illustrated. Garden City, New York: Doubleday & Co., Inc., 1974. 501 p.
   A remarkable history of three generations, written to reveal them "in their settings, their humanity, their natures, and destinies," by the woman who has often appeared to be the power behind the throne of this modern American "royal" family.

2479 Kennerly, David Hume   1947-
Shotter. Illustrated. New York: Newsweek Books, 1979. 269 p. Index.
   A Pulitzer Prize-winning photographer assesses the risks and rewards of photojournalism. He discusses his successful career as apprentice in Oregon, bureau reporter covering Spiro Agnew's downfall and Robert Kennedy's final days, UPI's Saigon Bureau chief photographer at 24, and President Ford's personal photographer at 27.

2480 Kent, Henry Watson   1866-1948
What I am pleased to call my education. Edited by Lois Leighton Comings. New York: The Grolier Club, 1949. 208 p. Index.
   Kent's purpose in writing is to record the events of his life and how they fitted him for his career working in museums and libraries—Norwich Free Academy, Slater Memorial Museum, The Grolier Club, and the Metropolitan Museum of Art, New York. A bibliography of his writing and editing is appended.

2481 *Kent, Louise (Andrews)   1886-1969
Mrs. Appleyard and I. Illustrated. Boston: Houghton Mifflin Co., 1968. 414 p.
   Mrs. Kent wrote about a dozen children's books and several for adults featuring a Mrs. Appleyard, a thinly disguised projection of her own character and life in small-town New England. She writes fondly of the simpler life and values of her earlier years.

2482 Kent, Rockwell   1882-1971
It's me, O Lord: the autobiography of Rockwell Kent. New York: Dodd, Mead and Co., 1955. 617 p.
   A multi-faceted artist whose talents led him to careers as a painter, writer, explorer, illustrator, farmer, sailor, book designer, architect, orator, lithographer, wood engraver, and political figure tells the story of his life from birth to marriages and his travels and trials (literal and figurative). He describes the places he has been (New York, Newfoundland, Virginia, etc.) and his political work which included Spanish Civil War activities.

2483 Kent, Rockwell   1882-1971
Of men and mountains: being an account of the European travels of the author and his wife, Sally, following their release from continental imprisonment. Ausable Forks, New York: Asgaard Press, 1959. 46 p.
   From 1950 to 1958, Kent was confined to the United States by refusal of the State Department to issue a passport because of his Communist sympathies. Vindicated by the Supreme Court in 1958, Kent and his wife traveled to Ireland, Switzerland, and spent several weeks in Russia, where he extolled the joys of the Communist political state and the beauties of the countryside.

2484 Kentfield, Calvin   1924-
Great green; a loose memoir of merchant marine life in the middle of the
twentieth century with examples of true experience being turned into
fiction. New York: The Dial Press, 1974. 256 p.
   Kentfield reminisces about his adventures as a sailor on merchant ships
and tankers. He transformed some of his experiences into fiction; after
automation took over many shipboard jobs, he went ashore permanently.
The appendix includes samples of his fiction, first published in *The New
Yorker* and *Harper's Bazaar*.

2485 Kenworthy, Leonard Stout   1912-
Worldview: the autobiography of a social studies teacher and Quaker.
Richmond, Indiana: Friends United Press, 1977. 262 p.
   He reflects on a lifetime of learning and teaching which was dominated
by three main concerns: a desire to improve social studies instruction, an
interest in international education, and the revitalization of the Religious
Society of Friends.

2486 Kenyon, Melvin   1933-
Burned to life. As told to Bruce A. Darnall and Mike Christopulos.
Foreword by A.J. Foyt. Harrison, Arkansas: New Leaf Press, 1976. 128 p.
   Kenyon, a born-again Christian after being badly burned in the 1965
Langhorne 100 USAC championship race, exhibits his resilience, religious
faith, and devotion to auto-racing in this book filled with frightening
details of wrecks. He was once run over in the Indy 500 while trying to get
out of his wrecked car. Midget-car racing, of which he is the four-time
U.S. champion, is of particular interest to him.

2487 Kephart, George S.
Campfires rekindled: a forester recalls life in the Maine woods of the
Twenties. Illustrated. Marion, Massachusetts: Channing Books, 1977.
146 p.
   Kephart, a forester for lumber companies in Maine in the 1920's, before
logging became mechanized, describes his expeditions along northern
Maine's Allegash and Penobscot rivers, canoeing, camping, hunting, fish-
ing, and scouting the woods for suitable stands of timber for logging.

2488 Kepner, William Allison   b.1875
William Allison Kepner: teacher, scientist, philosopher. Edited by Bruce
D. Reynolds. Charlottesville, Virginia: Jarman's Inc., Printers, 1946. 49 p.
   A revered professor of biology at the University of Virginia for over
forty years, he wrote his life story at his students' request, emphasizing his
developing curiosity and scientific education.

2489 Kerkhoff, Jack   1901?-1958?
How thin the veil: a newspaperman's story of his own mental crack-up
and recovery. New York: Greenberg Publishers, 1952. 311 p.
   The story of 45 days in a mental institution after his attempted suicide.

2490 Kerouac, Jack (Jean-Louis Lebris de Kerouac)   1922-1969
Lonesome traveller. New York: McGraw Hill, 1960. 183 p.
   A guru of literature and lifestyle in the 1950's, he describes his book as
"a mishmosh of life as lived by an independent educated penniless rake
going anywhere."

2491 Kerouac, Jack (Jean-Louis Lebris de Kerouac)   1922-1969
Satori in Paris. New York: Grove Press, Inc., 1966. 118 p.
   Kerouac, searching for his ancestral roots in Paris, experiences satori,
"sudden illumination," in retrospective contemplation of his ten-day trip
(c. 1965). The book, written in Kerouac's typically impressionistic, disjunctive mixture of slang and literary allusions, validates Kerouac's
self-description as: "this rage and rake and rack of lacks, this 'trunk of
humours' as Shakespeare said of Falstaff, this false staff . . . this
fear-of-death tumor, with tumescences in the bathroom . . . this farceur
jokester at art galleries in New York and whimperer at police stations and
over longdistance telephones . . ."

2492 Kerouac, Jean-Louis Lebris de
see Kerouac, Jack

2493 Kertzer, Morris Norman   1910-
Tell me, Rabbi. New York: Bloch Publishing Co., 1976. 196 p.
   Rabbi Kertzer, a descendant of Sholom Aleichem, writes humorous
anecdotes with pungent messages. Kertzer tells of his boyhood in frozen
Cochrane, Ontario, but focuses on various aspects of Jewish life, including
weddings, Bar Mitzvahs, circumcisions, keeping kosher, Israel, education,
and family life.

2494 Kesselring, Joseph Otto   1902-1967
My life, love, and limericks; an autobiography in verse. New York: Exposition Press, 1973. 189 p.
   Known principally as the author of *Arsenic and Old Lace* and other
Broadway plays, Kesselring also wrote short stories and sketches, directed
and acted in amateur theatricals, and was a singer. His poems trace the
progress of his life.

2495 Kessler, Henry Howard   1896-1978
Knife is not enough. Illustrated. New York: W.W. Norton & Co., Inc.,
1968. 295 p. Index.
   As a young surgeon, Kessler began to be concerned with the major
issues of post-operative rehabilitation. Ultimately he spent fifty years on
this enterprise, attaining international recognition for his work and special
gratification from the founding of the Kessler Institute for Rehabilitation
in West Orange, New Jersey.

2496 Ketchum, Carlton G.   1892-
Recollections of Colonel Retread, USAAF 1942-1945, Pittsburgh, Pennsylvania: Hart Books (printers), 1976. 296 p.
   Ketchum, a colonel in the U.S. Army Air Force, 1942-1945, has collected and privately printed the letters he wrote to his wife about his
experiences. They contain detailed interpretations of personnel and military strategy he observed during his duty in New Jersey, the Middle East,
and Europe, and are punctuated by accounts of occasional meetings with
his son David, also in the service.

2497 *Keyes, Evelyn   1917-
Scarlett O'Hara's younger sister: my lively life in and out of Hollywood.
Illustrated. Secaucus, New Jersey: Lyle Stuart Inc., 1977. 318 p. Index.
   Pampered by Cecil B. DeMille and cast as Scarlett O'Hara's younger
sister Suellen, Keyes achieved movie stardom in the 1930's. She recounts
a dramatic life of marriages, divorces, and Hollywood life.

2498 *Keyes, Frances Parkinson (Wheeler)   1885-1970
All flags flying: reminiscences of Frances Parkinson Keyes. New York:
McGraw-Hill Book Co., 1972. 655 p.
   This volume covers 1904-1931, the early years of her marriage and
career as a novelist and journalist. Because her husband was a U.S. Senator from New Hampshire, her time was filled with social obligations; she
also published "Letters from a Senator's Wife" in *Good Housekeeping* for
fourteen years, which started her writing career.

2499 *Keyes, Frances Parkinson (Wheeler)   1885-1970
The cost of a best seller. New York: Julian Messner, Inc., 1950. 126 p.
   Description of the difficulty of writing, particularly in acquiring authentic backgrounds for her fiction by an author who perseveres despite
frequent physical illnesses, achieves fame, and is sustained by her faith in
prayer and her dedication to the global human family.

2500 *Keyes, Frances Parkinson (Wheeler)   1885-1970
Roses in December. New York: Liveright Publishing Co., 1966. (Garden
City, New York: Doubleday & Co., New York) 1960) 352 p. Index.
   Reflections of her New England childhood in a prominent, aristocratic
family, of nineteenth-century elegance and charm, of her poignant struggle to become a writer in spite of her family's wishes, of her brilliant
father's untimely death when she was two, and her early devotion to and
engagement to Harry Keyes, a family friend more than twice her age.

2501 Kieran, John   1892-
Not under oath: recollections and reflections. Boston: Houghton Mifflin
Co., 1964. 282 p. Index.
   Raconteur, naturalist, newspaper man, sportswriter, and scholar,
Kieran is also well known as one of the regular panel members on radio's
"Information Please," a high-speed genial war of wits. His autobiography
reveals his own vivacity and warmth, his love of nature, and his regard for
humanity.

2502 Kiesler, Frederick John   1892-1965
Inside the endless house: art, people and architecture: a journal. New
York: Simon & Schuster, 1966. 573 p.
   This personal journal covering 1956 to 1964 touches on the whole
range of the author's artistic and intellectual activity, his accounts of
travel in Italy and Brazil, descriptions of people and events, and his
creation of the Shrine of the Book, the sanctuary for the Dead Sea scrolls.

2503 Kiick, Jim
see Csonka, Larry

2504 Kikuchi, Charles   1915?-
The Kikuchi diary: chronicle from an American concentration camp: the
Tanforan journals of Charles Kikuchi. Edited with introduction by John
Modell. Illustrated. Urbana: University of Illinois Press, 1973. 258 p.
   A Nisei relocated during World War II, Kikuchi recorded events in the
camp, his psychological adjustments, and the ambivalence typical of his
ethnic group.

2505 Killian, James Rhymeir, Jr.   1904-
Sputnik, scientists, and Eisenhower: a memoir of the First Special Assistant to the President for Science and Technology. Illustrated. Cambridge, Massachusetts: MIT Press, 1977. 315 p. Index.
   Eisenhower's Special Assistant for Science and Technology articulately
discusses America's scientific efforts to surpass Russia in the space race
that began in 1957 when the Soviets orbited Sputnik I and continued into
the Kennedy administration. Killian also provides a history of the Presi-

dent's Science Advisory Committee during the Eisenhower administration and a fond personal recollection of Eisenhower.

2506 Kimball, Dexter Simpson   **1865-1952**
I remember. Foreword by Senator Ralph K. Flanders. New York: McGraw-Hill, 1953. 226 p. Index.
    The author, an engineer and educator, looks back at his 87 years and particularly recalls the various jobs he held as well as his close association with Cornell University.

2507 *Kimbrough, Emily   **1899-**
Forty plus and fancy free. New York: Harper and Brothers, 1954. 240 p.
    In some ways this seems strictly a travel book, but it reflects Kimbrough's style of life and writing, her humor, and her sense of adventure as she describes a European tour with three other grandmothers.

2508 *Kimbrough, Emily   **1899-**
The innocents from Indiana. New York: Harper and Brothers, 1950. 229 p.
    Humorous account of Emily (11 yrs.) and her brother (4 yrs.) moving from Muncie, Indiana, to Chicago. Good description of family and school experience.

2509 *Kimbrough, Emily   **1899-**
It gives me great pleasure. Illustrated by Helen Hokinson. New York: Dodd, Mead & Co., 1948. 227 p.
    Three years of lecture tours throughout the country provide many humorous episodes of mishaps, pitfalls, and amusing confusion.

2510 *Kimbrough, Emily
    see also *Skinner, Cornelia Otis

2511 King, Alexander   **1900-1965**
May this house be safe from tigers. Illustrated by the author. New York: Simon and Schuster, 1960. 374 p.
    His second autobiographical work depends again on humorous anecdotes but focuses more on affectionate recollections of individuals, prominent and unknown, who were significant to his work as a journalist-illustrator.

2512 King, Alexander   **1900-1965**
Mine enemy grows older. New York: Simon and Schuster, 1958. 374 p.
    A humorous, almost impersonal narrative with moments of emotional depth in which a prominent journalist-illustrator describes his career with Henry Luce, Eugene O'Neill, and others, and, in a subordinate way, his recovery from drug addiction.

2513 *King, Billie Jean   **1943-**
Billie Jean. With Kim Chapin. New York: Harper and Row, 1974. 208 p.
    With few references to her personal life, she describes her development as a tennis star and her fight for equality for women athletes.

2514 *King, Caroline Blanche (Campion)   **1871-1947**
This was ever in my dream. Caldwell, Idaho: The Caxton Printers, Ltd., 1947. 297 p.
    After her husband's death, she acquired an acre of rural Pennsylvania and gradually converted it to a beautiful garden and cultivated woods surrounding the house she built there. This and other gardening experiences formed the basis of many articles she wrote for *The Flower Grower* and *Country Gentleman*.

2515 *King, Coretta (Scott)   **1927-**
My life with Martin Luther King, Jr. Illustrated. New York: Holt, Rinehart and Winston, 1969. 372 p. Index.
    The story of the remarkable King family, who with faith and courage were heroic in their devotion to justice. Mrs. King writes of the dream they had, their work together for the cause of racial equality, her husband's assassination, and her determination to continue to support the Civil Rights Movement.

2516 *King, Eleanor   **1906-**
Transformations: the Humphrey-Weidman era: a memoir. Illustrated. Brooklyn: Dance Horizons, 1978. 324 p. Index.
    Interwoven with this well-written story of four figures of modern dance in America, Doris Humphrey, Charles Weidman, Pauline Lawrence, and José Limón, is the story of King's development as a dancer, 1928-1941, at Denishawn, Bennington, and with dance groups in New York. King provides vivid portraits of the major dancers of the 1930's and interprets the dynamics of the dance climate during this artistically exciting time.

2517 King, Ernest J.   **1878-1956**
Fleet Admiral King: naval record. And Walter Muir Whitehill. Illustrated. New York: W.W. Norton & Co., 1952. 674 p. Index.
    This third person autobiography deals mainly with King's part in World Wars I and II and his tours of command in between.

2518 King, Ernest LaMarr   **1875-1954**
Main line: fifty years of railroading with the Southern Pacific. As told to Robert E. Mahaffay. Garden City, New York: Doubleday and Co., Inc., 1948. 271 p. Index.
    A good narrative of railroad history, from the rough and primitive days in the 1890's through World War II, by a man who began as a telegraph operator and later became a railroad executive.

2519 King, Frank Marion   **1863-1953**
Wranglin' the past: reminiscences of Frank M. King. Illustrated by Charles M. Russell. 1st Rev. ed. Pasadena, California: Trail's End Publishing Co., Inc., 1946. (Pasadena, California: Frank M. King, 1935) 284 p.
    The colorful story of a cowboy's life in the Southwest during the last quarter of the nineteenth century includes anecdotes about Billy the Kid and other famous gunfighters but deals primarily with the difficulties of common everyday life.

2520 King, George S.   **1878-1966**
Doctor on a bicycle. New York: Rinehart and Co., 1958. 275 p.
    King went straight from high school to medical school, became a general practitioner at 21 and soon established a large practice on Long Island by being the first to arrive at crisis cases (by bicycle, no less). He writes of colorful cases throughout his sixty-year practice and lovingly of the sea, on which he often cruised as ship's doctor on luxury yachts.

2521 *King, Grace Elizabeth   **1851-1932**
Memories of a Southern woman of letters. Freeport, New York: Books for Libraries Press, 1971. (New York: Macmillan, 1932) 398 p.
    Born into a prominent New Orleans family, King writes about her experiences before and after the Civil War. As in her novels and stories, her major focus is on the development of women in Louisiana and their attempts to preserve social amenities in a climate of disruption.

2522 King, Harry
Box man; a professional thief's journey. As told to and with commentary by Bill Chambliss. New York: Harper and Row, 1972. 179 p.
    For the better part of fifty years, King was a professional thief specializing in safe-cracking. He tells the story of how he became a thief, his time spent in Folsom and San Quentin prisons, and his ultimate decision to "go straight."

2523 King, Hiram Burris   **1890-**
Memoir of an Oklahoma jurist. San Antonio, Texas: The Naylor Co., 1973. 123 p.
    He recalls his experience as a soldier in World War I, travel to tourist sites in the U.S. such as Mt. Rushmore, but very little about life in early Oklahoma.

2524 King, Larry L.   **1929-**
... And other dirty stories. Foreword by Willie Morris. New York: The World Publishing Co., 1968. 236 p.
    A contributor of articles and essays to various periodicals has collected some of them for this book which captures the flavor of his life. He sees the deeply serious yet extravagantly hilarious aspects of American life.

2525 King, Larry L.   **1929-**
Confessions of a white racist. New York: The Viking Press, 1971. 173 p.
    The author, a writer and journalist, traces his steps from boyhood to manhood in order to understand for himself the insanities of racial prejudice and his own involvement in racism as a white growing up among whites. He is not writing about Blacks or other "minorities" but about whites, about being white in a white-dominated society.

2526 King, Martin Luther, Sr.   **1899-**
Daddy King: an autobiography. With Clayton Riley. Foreword by Benjamin E. Mays. Introduction by Andrew J. Young. New York: William Morrow and Co., 1980. 215 p.
    Born of a poor Southern farming family, King, who witnessed lynchings and beatings as a youth, became a country preacher and laborer. With great effort he obtained a divinity degree from Morehouse College and became the minister of Ebenezer Baptist Church in Atlanta. He led voter registration drives and other civil liberties endeavors long before the Civil Rights Movement began—excellent preparation for the upbringing of his son, Martin Luther King, Jr. Despite the assassination of King, Jr., and the murder of his wife, Rev. King continues to maintain his belief in non-violence and racial integration.

2527 *King-Salomon, Frances W.   **1894-**
House of a thousand babies: experiences of an American woman physician in China (1922-1940). Illustrated. New York: Exposition Press, 1968. 168 p.
    A lucid, alternately amusing and suspenseful account of King's experiences as a physician-obstetrician at the Margaret Williamson Hospital in Shanghai. King comments on Chinese obstetrical custom, Chinese family life, cooking and culture. She eventually met a British professor of chemistry at St. John's University (Shanghai); they married, had two daugh-

ters, and she taught physiology until evacuated when World War II began.

2528 *Kingsley, Myra   1897-
Outrageous fortune: how I practice astrology. Introduction by Jay Franklin. New York: Duell, Sloan, and Pearce, 1951. 240 p.

A personal narrative which focuses on her interest and work in astrology.

2529 *Kingston, Maxine Hong
The woman warrior: memoirs of a girlhood among ghosts. New York: Alfred A. Knopf, 1976. 209 p.

She sees her life in the ghosts of female figures from her Chinese family history, in the clash of two cultures growing up in San Francisco's Chinatown. Her fantasy-memoir won the National Book Critics Circle Award and became an unexpected best-seller.

2530 Kinley, David   1861-1944
The autobiography of David Kinley. Introduction by Robert Murray Haig. Urbana: University of Illinois Press, 1949. 167 p. Index.

Memoirs of a college professor of economics who relinquished teaching and research for administrative work and led the growth of the University of Illinois for forty years until his retirement in 1930.

2531 Kinney, Curtis
I flew a camel. With Dale M. Titler. Drawing by Don Wootton. Philadelphia: Dorrance & Co., 1972. 122 p.

A nostalgic look at the dramatic days of World War I and the adventuresome fliers who manned single-seater planes for the RAF in air battles with the Red Baron and his countrymen. Kinney piloted a Sopwith Camel and came to love this "bucking bronco of the air."

2532 Kinney, Henry   1816-1854
Kinney journals: Boston to the Sandwich Islands, 1847-1848. Edited by Charlotte Morris Thompson. Illustrated. Introduction by Maria Kinney. Geneology. Lafayette, California: Charlotte Morris Thompson, 1978. 149 p.

Henry Kinney and his bride Louisa sailed from Boston, November 3, 1847, and arrived in Hawaii, February 26, 1848, to become missionaries. Each kept a journal of the voyage and each focused on the weather, unusual fauna (albatrosses, flying fish), and their continual seasickness.

2533 *Kinney, Maria Louisa Walsworth
see Kinney, Henry

2534 Kirby, Gustavus Town   1874-1956
I wonder why? Edited by Mrs. Thomas Mercer Waller. New York: Coward-McCann, Inc., 1954. 180 p.

With urbane wit Kirby relates the highlights of a long, vigorous life as a lawyer devoted to public service and to fun. He was educated at Columbia University, where he played football, fenced, and was a member of the 1908 U.S. Olympic fencing team. He toured the world in 1905, enjoying sightseeing and beautiful women. Married to his wealthy employer's daughter, he settled in Bedford, Connecticut, practiced law, and eventually became an art patron and President of the United States Olympic Association.

2535 Kirby, Louis Paul   b.1870
Fourscore breathless years. Boston: Meador Publishing Co., 1951. 429 p.

Journalist who has worked on many city newspapers across the country reflects upon the issues of his times.

2536 Kirkham, George   1942?-
Signal zero: the true story of a professor who became a street cop. Philadelphia: Lippincott, 1976. 208 p.

A professor of criminology attempts to reconcile his theoretical training with the professional experience of a particular student who is a full-time police officer. To do this, he spent several months working behind a badge and uniform in a large American city.

2537 Kirkland, Wallace   1892-1979
Recollections of a *Life* photographer. Photographs by the author. Boston: Houghton Mifflin Co., 1954. 272 p.

Chapters are not continuous, but show him in the context of a variety of assignments during his career with *Life* magazine.

2538 Kirkwood, Joe   1897-1970
Links of life. As told to Barbara Fey. Foreword by Barbara Fey. Introduction by Lowell Thomas. Oklahoma City: privately printed, 1973. 141 p.

Born in Sydney, Australia, Kirkwood established an international reputation as golf's premier trick-shot artist. Winner of many of the world's most coveted golfing championships, he was best known for promoting the game of golf throughout the world.

2539 Kirstein, Lincoln   1907-
For John Martin: entries from an early diary. Edited by Selma Jean Cohen. Illustrated. New York: Dance Perspectives Foundation, 1973. 55 p.

Kirstein's fragmentary diary entries cover the summer of 1933, spent largely in Paris learning his craft. He was Director of the American Ballet, which later became the New York City Ballet.

2540 Kirstein, Lincoln   1907-
Thirty years: Lincoln Kirstein's The New York City Ballet (Expanded to include the years 1973-1978, in celebration of the company's thirtieth anniversary). New York: Alfred A. Knopf, 1978. (1973) 398 p. Index.

In discussing the thirty-year history of the New York City Ballet, of which he was manager, Kirsten demonstrates a history of modern ballet and demonstrates the powerful artistic influence and innovations of Balanchine and Stravinsky, among others. Kirsten invents a "diary" entry as a preview of each segment of his discussion offering considerable insight into costuming, scenery, fund raising, and arts management.

2541 Kiser, Bill   1927-
New light of hope. New Canaan, Connecticut: Keats Publishing Co., 1974. 223 p.

In an inspiring but unsentimental account, Kiser, handicapped by cerebral palsy, writes of home schooling, surgery and physical therapy, nursing homes, emotional instability, and frustrated sexuality. Spurred by a period of prayer and faith-healing, he has sought to become as independent as his handicap will allow and has successfully earned a living as a writer.

2542 Kissinger, Henry Alfred   1923-
White House years. Cartography by Dick Sanderson. Illustrated. Boston: Little, Brown and Company, 1979. 1521 p. Index.

The highlights of Kissinger's memoir of his first four years as Assistant to the President for National Security Affairs (1969-1973) are the discussion of his relationship with Richard Nixon, portraits of major foreign leaders, and his views on the art of diplomacy.

2543 Kistiakowsky, George Bogdan   1900-
Scientist at the White House: the private diary of President Eisenhower's special assistant for science and technology. Introduction by Charles S. Maier. Illustrated. Cambridge, Massachusetts: Harvard University Press, 1976. 448 p. Index.

This diary reveals the U.S. transition from conventional warfare to the missile age, and its increasing Cold War rivalry with Russia over atomic delivery systems and satellite intelligence. It discloses the ambiguous policies of the Eisenhower administration, which promoted advanced missile development to compete with Sputnik I while the President himself was trying to check the nuclear-arms race.

2544 *Kitt, Eartha   1928-
Alone with me: a new autobiography. Illustrated. Chicago: Henry Regnery Co., 1976. 276 p. Index.

Kitt, a sensuous singer, dancer, and actress, recounts her impoverished childhood in South Carolina and, after her mother abandoned her, in Harlem with a stern aunt. As a teenager Kitt won a scholarship for dance training with Katherine Dunham. She toured Mexico and the United States and became wildly popular in *New Faces of 1952*. Since then she has had a demanding career on the stage and in cabarets. In this forthright account Kitt considers herself "Thursday's Child," a loner who has "far to go."

2545 *Kitt, Eartha   1928-
Thursday's child. New York: Duell, Sloan and Pearce, 1956. 250 p.

Her first autobiographical book describes the poverty and hardship of her girlhood in New York, her years with the Katherine Dunham Dancers, and her first success as an entertainer.

2546 *Klaben, Helen   1941?-
Hey, I'm alive! With Beth Day. New York: McGraw-Hill Book Co., 1964. 206 p.

In 1963 she and the pilot of a small plane crashed in the Yukon wilderness. For 49 days they lived on melted snow, a few cans of food, some toothpaste, and an amazing will to live in spite of the conditions which daily suggested almost certain death.

2547 *Klasner, Lily   1862-1946
My girlhood among outlaws. Illustrated. Edited by Eve Ball. Tucson: The University of Arizona Press, 1972. 336 p. Index.

As a child on the New Mexico frontier, Mrs. Klasner encountered the hardships of migration and settlement in a raw, sparsely populated land. Harassed by outlaws and Indian raids, her family lost most of its possessions. From her letters, clippings, diary, and other documents she wrote this account of her life which several people have attempted to edit, but it had not been published until this edition. Also included are excerpts from J.S. Chisum's personal diary, Jan. 1878 (pp. 261-287).

2548 Klavan, Gene (Eugene)
We die at dawn: the true to life story of America's No. 1 radio team, or No. 2, or No. 3, Klavan and Finch. Illustrated. Garden City, New York: Doubleday & Co., Inc., 1964. 172 p.
With in-group humor designed for his listeners, Klavan describes typical radio broadcasts, 6-10 a.m. on New York's WNEW, that he and his partner, Dee Finch, conducted daily during the 1950's and early 1960's. He analyzes their comic style (parody, situation humor, nonsense) and identifies their total absorption in their work, including rising daily at 4:30 a.m. to make the 6 a.m. show.

2549 Klein, Woody   1929-
Lindsay's promise; the dream that failed; a personal account. New York: The Macmillan Co., 1970. 349 p. Index.
Klein was New York City Mayor Lindsay's press secretary in 1966 and later served as an assistant administrator in the Housing and Development Administration. This is his view of the first year of Lindsay's administration and the nature of the pressures, trials, and crises confronting the man who was trying to create order out of the previous corruption and chaos in New York.

2550 Kleinholz, Frank   1901-
A self portrait. Introduction by Philip Evergood. Illustrated by Frank Kleinholz. New York: Shorewood Publishers, Inc., 1964. 95 p.
Kleinholz writes a pleasant eighteen-page autobiographical introduction to a volume of reproductions of his paintings, explaining how he became a lawyer somewhat inadvertently, floundering in search of a more satisfying profession. When his first wife died in 1945, he decided to become a full-time painter and embarked on this new and satisfying career, aided by his second wife, Lidia.

2551 *Kligman, Ruth   1933?-
Love affair; a memoir of Jackson Pollock. New York: William Morrow & Co., Inc., 1974. 220 p.
Kligman, an aspiring artist, met painter Jackson Pollock in 1956, resulting in a passionate, mercurial affair which lasted five months until his fatal automobile accident. Her memoir makes vivid the happiness, the despair, the exultation, and the suffering of their relationship.

2552 *Kluball, Carolyn   1948-
Will everyone please stand still for the picture. Philadelphia: Dorrance & Co., 1973. 86 p.
A junior high school teacher recalls some of the typical experiences she had teaching in a small school in the South. Her main point is that teachers are inadequately and unrealistically prepared for their jobs.

2553 *Knauff, Ellen (Raphael) Boxhornova   1915-
The Ellen Knauff story. Preface by the author. Introduction by Arthur Garfield Hays. New York: W.W. Norton and Co., Inc., 1952. 242 p. Index.
War bride's account of her three-year fight to be admitted to the United States despite unjust charges that detained her on Ellis Island.

2554 Knauth, Percy   1914-
Season in hell. New York: Harper, 1975. 111 p.
A successful writer, journalist, and editor for over 28 years describes his battle with suicidal depression.

2555 *Knepper, Verna Weiser   b.1886?
My papa's daughter. San Antonio, Texas: The Naylor Co., 1971. 140 p.
Interspersed with brief anecdotes of her life in the early days after the opening of the Oklahoma Territory are facts about the history of the area, the "Run" of 1889, and territorial schools.

2556 *Knickerbocker, Frances Wentworth Cutler   1887-1973
Minister's daughter; a time exposure photograph of the years 1903-04. Philadelphia: Dorrance & Co., 1974. 148 p.
During her fifteenth and sixteenth years the author kept this diary of her observations of family and acquaintances, her favorite authors, and her own activities. She provides a picture of happy American family life at the turn of the century.

2557 Knight, John   1915?-
The story of my psychoanalysis. New York: McGraw-Hill Book Co., Inc., 1950. 225 p.
One of the first accounts by a patient who undertook psychoanalysis, describing his inquiry, dreams, and associations during the process of his search for self-knowledge.

2558 *Knight, Sarah (Kemble)   1666-1727
Journal of Madam Knight. Introductory note by Malcolm Freiberg. Wood engravings by Michael McCurdy. Boston: David R. Godine, 1972. (New York: Theodore Dwight, 1825) 72 p.
A sprightly picture of provincial New England in colonial times, Madam Knight's journal describes her journey on horseback from Boston to New York. She enjoys the bustle of New York, thinks New Haveners too rigid and puritanical, and displays her own intelligence and energy in

the candor and humor of her comments on events and people along the way.

2559 Knowles, John   1926-
Double vision: American thoughts abroad. New York: The Macmillan Co., 1964. 210 p.
Both a personal travelogue and a review of American attitudes, this book includes acute observations of foreign lands and people Knowles visited in addition to his feelings about his own country. The sharply contrasting ways of life he encountered gave him constant reminders of America and taught him much about himself as well.

2560 Knox, George L.   1841-1927
Slave and freeman: the autobiography of George L. Knox. Edited with introduction by Willard B. Gatewood, Jr. Lexington: University Press of Kentucky, 1979. 247 p. Index.
Knox's account of his life, originally published in installments in his newspaper, *The Indianapolis Freeman* (1894-1895), is divided into three parts. I: his childhood as a slave in Tennessee, which culminated in his freedom as a soldier with the Union Army. II: His years as a barber in Greencastle, Indiana, 1864-1884, and his increasing involvement in Republican politics. III: A decade as the "Foremost Black Citizen of Indiana," the owner of several prosperous hotel barber shops and publisher of a Black newspaper.

2561 Koch, Howard
As time goes by: memoirs of a writer. Introduction by John Houseman. Illustrated. New York: Harcourt Brace Jovanovich, 1979. 220 p.
Koch, a lawyer-turned-writer at an early age, had the good fortune for his first radio script to be the cataclysmic *War of the Worlds*. This led to a Hollywood screenwriting career and scripts for *Sea Wolf, Casablanca, Sergeant York,* and many others. Gray-listed and eventually black-listed during the 1950's for alleged left-wing politics, Koch and his family lived in Rome, Paris, and London for several years before he resumed his writing career from Woodstock, New York.

2562 Koch, Oscar W.   1897-1970
G-2; intelligence for Patton. With Robert G. Hays. Philadelphia: Army Times Pub. Co., 1971. 167 p.
Koch, who was chief of intelligence for General George S. Patton, traces the role of military intelligence in some of the most important battles during World War II, revealing the practical problems and the routine excitement of life as an army spy.

2563 Kofoed, John Christian (Jack)   1894-1979
Fifty-fifty: or, you can't hide a man who is riding on a camel. Introduction by John S. Knight. Coral Gables, Florida: Wake-Brook House, 1963. 289 p.
Kofoed discusses his life in terms of the topics his fifty years of newspaper columns covered: men and women (the entertainers and the entertained), restaurants (mostly in Miami), sports (baseball, cycling, boxing, bullfighting), and trips (Egypt, Denmark, Jamaica) he has taken.

2564 Kofoed, John Christian (Jack)   1894-1979
Leg man in seven-league boots. Introduction by Eustace L. Adams. Coral Gables, Florida: Glade House, 1946. 167 p.
A prominent New York reporter and columnist describes his life in journalism with many anecdotes about celebrities and journalists.

2565 Kohl, Herbert R.
Half the house. New York: E.P. Dutton & Co., Inc., 1974. 269 p.
An elementary teacher who taught and directed Other Ways, an open school in Berkeley, and has assisted in the struggle for community control of schools in Harlem and East Harlem, Kohl describes his search for better ways of educating young people.

2566 Komroff, Manuel   1890-1974
Big city, little boy. Growing Up in America Series. New York: A.A. Wyn, 1953. 182 p.
The book describes a writer's childhood in New York City at the turn of the century and the realization that he wanted to be a writer.

2567 Kopay, David
The David Kopay story: an extraordinary self-revelation. And Perry Deane Young. Illustrated. New York: Arbor House, 1977. 247 p.
Kopay gives a simplistic account of his life as a homosexual football player, explaining repeatedly why he thinks it is all right. He includes numerous football pictures, descriptions of his athletic stardom, and examples of his persecution since declaring his homosexuality.

2568 Kopperl, Bert   1917-
With two wheels and a camera. Illustrated. Foreword by Helen Hayes. Hicksville, New York: Exposition Press, 1979. 242 p.
"Wheelchair photographer" Kopperl, crippled by polio during World War II, provides humorous accounts of numerous celebrities and places he has photographed, often juxtaposing the misery of his condition with the joy of a busy life. His mother always at his side, Kopperl has produced

thousands of excellent photographs, about one hundred of which are included in this work.

2569 *Koren, Else Elizabeth Hysing   1832-1918
The diary of Elizabeth Koren, 1853-1855. Edited, translated with introduction by David T. Nelson. Preface by Theodore C. Blegen. Northfield, Minnesota: Norwegian-American Historical Association, 1955. 381 p. Index.
   A beautifully written account, similar to Wilder's *Little House on the Prairie*, of the immigration from Norway to Decorah, Iowa, by the author and her newlywed pastor husband. The sea and overland journeys are described with loving attention to domestic detail, as is pioneer life in the new settlement—from the making of log cabins and furniture to the cooking and incessant floor scrubbing.

2570 Korfmacher, Ronald C.   1936-1973
Journey to a far country: the parish papers. Edited with preface by J. Elmo Agrimson. Bismarck, North Dakota: Tumbleweed Press, 1977. 360 p.
   This collection of essays (1962), *The Badlands Bugle* (1962-1968), and letters from Vietnam (1968-1972), provides an autobiographical account of the adult life of the author, a Lutheran clergyman who was the pastor of two remote parishes in western North Dakota. He ministered to the American troops in Vietnam for two years and then returned to the land he loved, where he died of a heart attack at 37.

2571 Kovic, Ron   1946-
Born on the Fourth of July. New York: McGraw-Hill Book Co., 1976. 208 p.
   Kovic's story, told in a mixture of first and third person chapters, includes his grim experiences in the Vietnam War and his agonizing re-entry into society handicapped by being paralyzed from the chest down.

2572 Kraft, Hy   1899-1975
On my way to the theatre. Illustrated. New York: The Macmillan Co., 1971. 216 p.
   Kraft's journey into the world of Broadway theater includes stopovers in the lower East Side, Hollywood, Washington, D.C., and London. He played a part in the House Hearings on Un-American Activities and has bitter comments about those show-business luminaries who cooperated with the Committee rather than standing up for their rights.

2573 Kramer, Gerald Louis   1936?-
Jerry Kramer's farewell to football. Illustrated. Edited by Dick Schaap. Foreword by Rod McKuen. New York: The World Publishing Co., 1969. 202 p.
   A popular player with the Green Bay Packers, Kramer had a series of medical problems that led him to retire from football at 32. His book recalls the life and values he grew up with in Idaho, the challenge, hard work, and pleasure of professional football, and a philosophy of life that is surprising in its depth and maturity.

2574 Kramer, Jack (John Albert)   1921-
The game: my 40 years in tennis. With Frank Deford. Illustrated. New York: G.P. Putnam's Sons, 1979. 318 p. Index.
   Kramer, a lifelong professional tennis player, discusses the strategy of winning by playing "percentage tennis," which includes pacing one's energy and attacking on a second serve. In discussing the various matches he has played in (especially at Wimbledon and Forest Hills), Kramer assesses the playing styles of the major twentieth-century pros and provides a history of modern tennis.

2575 Kramer, Jerry   1936-
Instant replay; The Green Bay diary of Jerry Kramer. Edited by Dick Schaap. Photographs by John and Vernon J. Biever. New York: The World Publishing Co., 1968. 286 p.
   During the football season of 1967, Kramer kept a diary several times a week, using a tape recorder and occasional written notes. His motive: to show what it is like for a professional player to struggle through a season.

2576 Kraus, Hans Peter   1907-
Rare book saga: the autobiography of Hans Peter Kraus. New York: G.P. Putnam's Sons, 1978. 386 p. Index.
   The memoirs of a well-known book collector who has secured and purveyed many of the greatest books and manuscripts in the world from the first edition of *King Lear* to the first printing of the Declaration of Independence.

2577 Kraus, John Daniel   1910-
Big ear. Powell, Ohio: Cygnus-Quasar Books, 1976. 228 p.
   A graduate of the University of Michigan, he writes a fairly technical account of his career as astronomer and professor at Ohio State University. Big Ear was the huge radio telescope built in Ohio in the late 1950's.

2578 Krause, Walter C.
So I was a sergeant: memoirs of an occupation soldier. Hicksville, New York: Exposition Press, 1978. 206 p.

Krause sympathetically recounts anecdotes of his experiences in Germany after World War II as an occupation soldier. He was an American army sergeant in charge of a hospital for German prisoners-of-war awaiting "denazification"—determination of their guilt or innocence of war crimes.

2579 Krenek, Ernst   1900-
Horizons circled: reflections on my music. With preface, biographical sketch, and music criticism by Will Ogdon and John L. Stewart. Berkeley: University of California Press, 1974. 167 p.
   Krenek describes his philosophical approach to his musical compositions and to life. He discusses electronic music and the twelve-tone system, the development of which he influenced significantly. His sense of history and his interest in politics, both reflected in his compositions, stem from his having survived both world wars.

2580 Krenov, James
Cabinetmaker's notebook. New York: Van Nostrand Reinhold Co., 1976. 132 p. Index.
   Siberian-born Krenov writes of the skill, discipline, and dedication required of a craftsman, and of the trade and tools of cabinet making. His work has been exhibited and praised world-wide.

2581 Krents, Harold
To race the wind; an autobiography. Illustrated. New York: G.P. Putnam's Sons, 1972. 282 p.
   A bright, upbeat memoir of his youth by a blind boy who set energetic goals for himself and pursued them despite handicaps and discouragement. He graduated from Harvard College and Law School and passed the bar exams. Krents was the inspiration for the main character of the play, *Butterflies Are Free*.

2582 Kresge, Sebastian Spering   1867-1966
S.S. Kresge story. As told to Steve Spilos. Illustrated. Racine, Wisconsin: Western Publishers, 1979. 373 p.
   Very little autobiographical information appears in this book, which is primarily a biography of the author's father and a history of the Kresge Company from its first five-and-dime store in 1900 to the K-Mart Corporation. Photos are of Kresge buildings, executives, and employees.

2583 Kreye, Eric
Under the blood banner: the story of a Hitler Youth. As told to Norma R. Youngberg. Illustrated by John Steel. Mountain View, California: Pacific Press Publishing Assn., 1968. 120 p.
   A novelistic tale about Kreye's childhood in Germany as a fairly young and innocent member of the Hitler Youth, living with his loving parents but terrorized by media presentations of "Der Führer." Born in Michigan, he returned to the United States after the war, where relatives introduced him to Seventh Day Adventism, the faith the book promotes.

2584 Kriegel, Leonard   1933-
Long walk home. New York: Appleton-Century, 1964. 213 p.
   At eleven he contracted polio during summer camp. His book is a moving account of his partial recovery, his gradual adaptation to life without the use of his legs. It is a dramatic record of the physical and psychological agony of his illness. He later became an English professor.

2585 Krielewitch, Melvin L.   1895-
Now that you mention it. New York: Quadrangle, 1973. 257 p. Index.
   He served in both world wars and Korea, retiring as a Marine Corps General. Later he had an active life in New York State politics; his last position was as Chairman of the New York State Athletic Commission.

2586 Krist, Gary Steven   1945-
Life, the man who kidnapped Barbara Mackle. New York: Olympia Press, 1972. 370 p.
   With the qualities of suspense fiction, Krist recounts his life from an impoverished childhood in Alaska through his bizarre abduction of heiress Barbara Mackle.

2587 Kriyananda, Swami (Donald Walters)   1926-
Path: autobiography of a Western Yogi. Preface by John W. White. Illustrated. Nevada City, California: Ananda Publications, 1977. 640 p. Index.
   Swami Kriyananda relates his search for God through the path of yoga, under the instruction of his guru Paramahansa Yogananda. The author portrays himself as a Westerner preserved from the destructive life of most Westerners, having followed the path of honesty and intensity to find the truth of the East.

2588 Krock, Arthur   1886-1974
Memoirs; sixty years on the firing line. New York: Funk & Wagnalls, 1968. 508 p. Index.
   Washington correspondent for the New York *Times* for over thirty years, Krock was a friend of the powerful and an eyewitness to history. His purpose in writing "is to portray the men of government as I have known them in the context of great events." The book concentrates on his

view of the transformation of the American governmental system in his time and the men who reshaped it.

2589 Kroll, Stanley
Professional commodity trader (look over my shoulder). New York: Harper, 1974. 178 p.
An over-the-shoulder look at the dealings of a professional commodities trader as he attends meetings and conferences, engages in private maneuvers, lets profits run and cuts losses.

2590 Kronenberger, Louis   **1904-1980**
No whippings, no gold watches; the saga of a writer and his jobs. Boston: Little, Brown and Co., 1970. 309 p. Index.
Reminiscences of work, the people he worked with, and a variety of jobs he has had—as a reader, reviewer, editor, writer, teacher, and critic at publishing houses, national magazines, universities, and newspapers during his extensive literary career.

2591 Krutch, Joseph Wood   **1893-1970**
More lives than one. New York: William Sloane Associates, 1962. 378 p. Index.
Drama critic for *The Nation* (1924-1952), professor of literature at Columbia (1937-1950), naturalist, and author—Krutch led an interesting and gratifying life, qualities beautifully revealed in his book.

2592 Kuhler, Otto   **1894-**
My iron journey: an autobiography of a life with steam and steel. Illustrated by Otto Kuhler. Foreword by Palmer Hoyt. Denver, Colorado: Intermountain Chapter, National Railway Historical Society, Inc., 1967. 244 p.
An exciting tale intertwining the design and development of twentieth-century steam and diesel locomotives and trains with the life of their designer. Kuhler was born in Germany, served briefly in the German army during World War I, and afterward with his Belgian wife emigrated to the United States, where he had a thriving career as a train designer. Kuhler's evocative writing is supplemented with many of his nostalgic drawings and paintings of trains.

2593 *Kuhn, Isobel
In the arena. London: China Inland Mission/Overseas Missionary Fellowships, 1959. 192 p.
After receiving missionary training at Chicago's Moody Bible Institute, the author went to China in 1928 as a member of the China Inland Mission to work among the Chinese peasants. There she married a fellow missionary, John Kuhn, and together they spent nearly twenty years in Yunnan among the Lisu people, until driven out by the Communists after World War II. A compelling, exciting tale, written while Kuhn was dying of cancer.

2594 *Kuppler, Willietta
see *Brooke, Alice M.*

2595 Kushin, Nathan   **b.1884**
Memoirs of a new American. Foreword by Solomon Grayzel. New York: Bloch Publishing Co., 1949. 157 p.
Real-estate businessman recalls his childhood and adult experiences in Russia and the United States, emphasizing his family responsibilities and his appreciation of freedom.

2596 *LaBastille, Anne
Assignment: wildlife. Foreword by Gerald Durrell. Illustrated. New York: E.P. Dutton, 1980. 243 p.
Whether saving an endangered species in Guatemala, staking out a national wildlife reserve in the Caribbean, or analyzing the Amazonian ecosystem, LaBastille is an award-winning conservationist and a very good writer.

2597 Lacy, Leslie Alexander
Native daughter. New York: Macmillan Publishing Co., Inc., 1974. 205 p.
His book is both a confession and a love story. A middle-class urban Black, he was well educated, traveled to Africa to understand his heritage, and returned to Chicago to teach in a program for unmarried Black girls. For the first time he learned to love a woman; the conflicts between her Black tenement poverty background and his forced a dramatic situation in which both had to challenge their prejudice and move beyond racial stereotypes.

2598 Lacy, Leslie Alexander
The rise and fall of a proper Negro; an autobiography. New York: The Macmillan Co., 1970. 244 p.
Lacy grew up in the United States, became bitter and angry with discrimination and with the draft, and went to Africa searching for a new definition of emotional freedom and a way to be absorbed by the culture. He discovered the Africa of his thoughts was an illusion; anger and corruption existed there too.

2599 LaFarge, John, S.J.   **1880-1963**
The manner is ordinary. New York: Harcourt, Brace and Co., 1954. 408 p. Index.
His father a famous artist and friend of Henry Adams, the son became the first priest in the family, attained success in his calling, and became Editor-in-Chief of *America,* a national Catholic weekly.

2600 LaFollette, Philip Fox   **1897-1965**
Adventure in politics: the memoirs of Philip LaFollette. Illustrated. Edited by Donald Young. New York: Holt, Rinehart and Winston, 1970. 299 p. Index.
A member of the Progressive LaFollette family of Wisconsin, the author recounts the part he and his family played in the struggle for creative and vigorous state government and the difficulties they had because of their stand against war.

2601 LaFollette, Robert Marion   **1855-1925**
La Follette's autobiography: a personal narrative of political experiences. Foreword by Allan Nevins. Madison: The University of Wisconsin Press, 1960. (Madison: Robert M. La Follette Co., 1913) 349 p. Index.
The political life of a prominent statesman in Wisconsin and national government, who is best remembered as a pioneer in the Progressive movement for more representative government.

2602 LaGuardia, Fiorello Henry   **1882-1947**
Making of an insurgent: an autobiography, 1882-1919. Philadelphia: J.B. Lippincott Co., 1948. 222 p. Index.
Written during the last six months of his life, the book describes LaGuardia's formative years as a statesman, including work for the consular service in Hungary, as a translator on Ellis Island, as Deputy Attorney General for New York State—all preceding his years as congressman and Mayor of New York City.

2603 *Laird, Carobeth Tucker Harrington   **1895-**
Encounter with an angry god: recollections of my life with John Peabody Harrington. Foreword by Harry Lawton. Decorations by Don Perceval. New York: Ballantine Books, 1977. (Banning, California: Malki Museum Press, 1975) 220 p.
Laird writes an unsparing account of the seven years she spent as the wife of John Peabody Harrington, an eccentric ethnologist who devoted his life to learning as much as possible about the Southwest Indian culture and dialects, particularly Shoshonean, Chumashan, and Yumen. Laird served as interpreter, transcriber, secretary, and housekeeper in their rudimentary and meager dwellings. Eventually the author divorced Harrington, married George Laird, a Chemehuevi blacksmith, and settled on an unproductive ranch near San Diego. The book is particularly valuable for its analysis of linguistic methodology.

2604 *Laird, Carobeth Tucker Harrington   **1895-**
Limbo. Epilogue by Anne Buffington-Jennings. Novato, California: Chandler and Sharp, 1979. 178 p.
Laird's personal narrative describes a typical life in the "Golden Mesa Nursing Home," which she, as an unwilling patient, detested because of "the dreadful food, the mingling of the mentally incompetent with the mentally competent, the dehumanizing effect of treating everyone as senile, the underpaid, frequently incompetent and occasionally callous aides and the absence of any sort of medical care except for a patient obviously in extremis."

2605 Laite, William E., Jr.   **1932-**
The United States vs. William Laite. Washington, D.C.: Acropolis Books, Ltd., 1972. 250 p.
Convicted of perjury and making false statements in relation to overtime pay for employees of his firm which was working on a government contract, Laite was sentenced to a year and a day in prison. Here he relates his prison experiences and sets forth his indictment of the system.

2606 *Lake, Veronica, pseud. (Constance Ockleman)   **1919-1973**
Veronica. With Donald Bain. Illustrated. New York: Citadel Press, 1971. (1969) 281 p. Index.
An account of Lake's career as a Hollywood actress in the 1940's and early 1950's, when she made *The Blue Dahlia, I Married a Witch, So Proudly We Hail, Ramrod,* and twenty-two other films. With three disastrous marriages, three children (one disastrous), a protracted bout with alcoholism, she sank professionally but made a comeback in television and in summer stock.

2607 *Lamar, Eugenia Dorothy (Blount)   **1867-1955**
When all is said and done. Athens: University of Georgia Press, 1952. 286 p. Index.
Memoirs of a long, busy life disciplined by "Old South" ideals, by a woman proud of her Southern heritage.

2608 *Lamarr, Hedy, pseud. (Eva Kiesler Hedwig)   **1915-**
Ecstasy and me: my life as a woman. Introduction by J. Lewis Bruce. Preface by Philip Lambert. Illustrated. New York: Bartholomew House, 1966. 318 p.

Lamarr offers a superficial account of her career as a film actress in Austria and Hollywood, her six marriages, innumerable sexual affairs, and her spending of thirty million dollars—mostly on herself. The nude scenes in *Ecstasy*, an early film, established her as the sex-goddess whose image she perpetuates here: "My sex drive is uncontrollable."

2609 Lamb, Edward   **1902-**
No lamb for slaughter: an autobiography by Edward Lamb. Foreword by Estes Kefauver. New York: Harcourt, Brace & World, Inc., 1963. 248 p. Index.
    A practicing lawyer in Toledo, he was a labor lawyer for the C.I.O. during the 1930's. Exonerated on a charge of being a communist in the McCarthy Era, he found time to be a writer, business executive, and newspaper publisher. His book reflects the incredible drive and enthusiasm that led to an interesting life.

2610 Lambert, Gerard Barnes   **1886-1967**
All out of step: a personal chronicle. New York: Doubleday and Co., Inc., 1956. 316 p.
    The unusual, remarkably successful life of an advertising pioneer, yachtsman, and unorthodox businessman (Listerine, Gillette).

2611 Lambie, Thomas A.   **1885-1954**
A doctor's great commission. Foreword by V.R. Edman. Illustrated. Wheaton, Illinois: Van Kampen Press, 1954. 288 p.
    An account of Lambie's sixty years as a Presbyterian medical missionary in Ethiopia, Egypt, and, after World War II, Palestine. Though he encountered illnesses, insects, snakes, and inhospitable climate, he was nevertheless successful in establishing hospitals and clinics for treatment of local people, particularly the Shilluk. Lambie describes the geography in exotic detail.

2612 Lame Deer, John (Fire)   **1900?-**
Lame Deer: seeker of visions. Edited by Richard Erdoes. New York: Simon and Schuster, 1972. 288 p.
    In addition to being a Sioux shaman, he was at various times a soldier, tribal policeman, sign painter, farmhand, drunkard, and jail inmate.

2613 Lamneck, John Howard   **1891-**
From lamplight to satellite: an autobiography. Boston: The Christopher Publishing House, 1961. 390 p.
    A detailed account of his early life and education, his career as a lawyer, and later as Justice of the Ohio Supreme Court, by a man famous for his contributions to juvenile law.

2614 *Lamont, Florence (Corliss)   **d.1952**
Far Eastern diary, 1920. Edited by Corliss Lamont. New York: Horizon Press, Inc., 1951. 95 p.
    The private diary of her travels to Japan and China by a member of a wealthy, prominent New England family.

2615 Lamont, Thomas Stilwell   **1899-1967**
Thomas Stilwell Lamont. Edited by Edward M. Lamont. Illustrated. New York: Horizon Press, 1969. 221 p.
    A memorial collection of eulogies and reminiscences about international banker Lamont, a partner in Morgan Guaranty Trust, including commentaries by a brother, a son, and by the presidents of Harvard University and Exeter Academy, at both of which he was an alumnus and loyal trustee. His reports to Harvard, letters to his family, and speeches reveal a man of principle, intense family love, loyalty, and wit.

2616 Lamont, Thomas William   **1870-1948**
Across world frontiers. New York: Harcourt, Brace and Co., 1951. 278 p. Index.
    A banker recalls his career and involvement in world affairs through post-World War I.

2617 Lamont, Thomas William   **1870-1948**
My boyhood in a parsonage: some brief sketches of American life toward the close of the last century. New York: Harper and Brothers, 1946. 203 p.
    Pleasant, nostalgic recollections of his boyhood in the Hudson River Valley and his education at Phillips Exeter and Harvard College.

2618 *Lamour, Dorothy   **1914-**
Dorothy Lamour: my side of the road. As told to Dick McInnes. Illustrated. Englewood Cliffs, New Jersey: Prentice-Hall, Inc., 1980. 244 p. Index.
    Lamour describes her childhood in Louisiana, her struggles as a beginning actress, and her first success, starring in the motion picture *The Jungle Princess*. She offers a candid view of life in Hollywood as well as of her struggles to balance her career with motherhood, especially during the *Road* movie days with Bob Hope and Bing Crosby.

2619 *Lance, La Belle   **1931-**
This, too, shall pass. With Gary Sledge. Illustrated. Chappaqua, New York: Christian Herald Books, 1978. 150 p.

An articulate testament of faith in God, man, and her husband, Bert Lance. The Lances were childhood friends, college sweethearts, and rose to prosperity through Bert's freewheeling banking activities. With fortitude drawn from her Christianity and her roots in Calhoun, Georgia, LaBelle proclaims his innocence of the charges of fiscal manipulation and mismanagement while a member of Jimmy Carter's administration.

2620 Land, Emory Scott   **1879-1971**
Winning the war with ships: land, sea, and air—mostly land. Introduction by Charles A. Lindbergh. New York: Robert McBride Co., Inc., 1958. 310 p. Index.
    President Roosevelt assigned him to develop a vast program of ship construction for the Navy and Merchant Marine in World War II. The result was 5,600 ships. His book describes his long working relationship with Roosevelt (1913-1945) and the Navy, and his amazing success in the Maritime Commission.

2621 *Landis, Jessie Oryce   **1904-1972**
You won't be so pretty (but you'll know more). London: W.H. Allen, 1954. 256 p.
    An actress reminisces about her life, loves, and acting, particularly on stage in London and New York.

2622 Landress, M.M.
I made it myself. With Bruce Dobler. New York: Grosset & Dunlap, 1973. 276 p.
    A printer in New York, he was kidnapped by the mob and forced to counterfeit twenty-dollar bills. Soon he began to like it, but when the Secret Service arrested him, he was relieved and cooperative. His book emphasizes the ease and temptations of his crime.

2623 Landreth, Earl   **1893-1969**
Washington diaries, 1933-35. New York: Vantage Press, 1964. 335 p.
    Landreth was in Washington from 1933 to 1935 to serve on the Puerto Rican Hurricane Relief Committee. This diary, covering approximately one and a half years, comments both on political and social activities.

2624 Lane, Franklin Knight   **1864-1921**
The letters of Franklin K. Lane, personal and political. Edited by Anne Wintermute Lane & Louise Herrick Wall. Boston: Houghton Mifflin Co., 1922. 473 p. Index.
    Working first as a newspaperman, Lane went on to practice law, become city and county attorney, Interstate Commerce Commissioner, and U.S. Secretary of the Interior. The letters selected for this volume tell chiefly of his services to his country.

2625 *Lane, Rose (Wilder)   **1887-1968**
The lady and the tycoon; letters of Rose Wilder Lane and Jasper Crane. Edited by Roger Lea MacBride. Caldwell, Idaho: The Caxton Printers, Ltd., 1973. 401 p. Index.
    Mrs. Lane, the daughter of Laura Ingalls Wilder of *Little House* fame, wrote short stories, novels, and articles. Her correspondence with Crane, a DuPont executive, scholar, and businessman, covers twenty years of their friendship and mutual admiration.

2626 *Lang, Lucy (Fox) Robins
Tomorrow is beautiful. New York: The Macmillan Co., 1948. 303 p. Index.
    Through four decades of labor struggles Mrs. Lang fought to promote the economic, social, and industrial welfare of workers. She lived an unconventional life filled with drama, excitement, and devotion to a cause.

2627 Langer, William Leonard   **1896-1977**
In and out of the ivory tower: autobiography of William L. Langer. Illustrated. New York: Neale Watson Academic Publications, 1977. 268 p. Index.
    A scholar and historian recounts his years in schools as student and as professor. These were interspersed with periods of military duty, government research work in Europe, and the assistant directorship of the CIA, work in which he traveled all over the world.

2628 Langford, J. Oscar
Big Bend: a homesteader's story. With Fred Gipson. Austin: University of Texas Press, 1973. (1952) 159 p. Index.
    Langford brought his wife and child to the Big Bend country of Texas in 1909 to prove out a homestead. Although the way of life was hard, the country was beautiful, his health, which had been precarious, improved greatly, and the four years there were among the best of their lives.

2629 Langford, Nathaniel Pitt   **1832-1911**
The discovery of Yellowstone Park, journal of the Washburn Expedition to the Yellowstone and Firehole rivers in·the year 1870. Foreword by Aubrey L. Haines. Lincoln: University of Nebraska Press, 1972. (St. Paul, Minnesota: The Hayes Foundation, 1905) 125 p. Index.
    The expedition led by Henry D. Washburn, surveyor general of the Montana Territory, explored the Yellowstone wilderness region. Two

important outcomes of that journey were the naming of main features of the region and the beginning of the national park concept, particularly for the Yellowstone area. Langford was the expedition's effective scribe and an enthusiastic organizer within the group.

2630 Langner, Lawrence   **1890-1962**
G.B.S. and the lunatic; reminiscences of the long, lively, and affectionate friendship between George Bernard Shaw and the author. New York: Atheneum, 1963. 313 p.
Langner worked at the Theatre Guild on productions of several Shaw plays in the U.S. This led to a series of letters between Shaw and the author—a record of Shaw's views on his plays and other subjects from sex to socialism.

2631 Langner, Lawrence   **1890-1962**
The magic curtain: the story of a life in two fields, theatre and invention, by the founder of the Theatre Guild. New York: E.P. Dutton and Co., Inc., 1951. 498 p. Index.
Story of his activities in art and invention with descriptions of notable plays and figures in theater as well as notable inventions of the era (1915-1950).

2632 Lanier, Sidney   **1842-1881**
Poems and letters. Introduction and notes by Charles R. Anderson. Baltimore: The Johns Hopkins Press, 1969. (1945) 227 p.
Selections from the Centennial Edition (1945) include 25 poems and a series of letters relating to his professional life in music and literature.

2633 Lano, David   **b.1874**
Wandering showman, I. East Lansing: Michigan State University Press, 1957. 290 p.
At age five, he became a puppeteer, joining a family tradition that derived from sixteenth-century Italy. His book describes his 78 years as a puppet-master, with an unusual view of small-town, rural America.

2634 Lappin, Samuel Strahl   **b.1870**
Run Sammy run: sixty-five years a preacher man. St. Louis: Bethany Press, 1958. 224 p.
An evangelical preacher characterizes himself as perpetually running—moving fast and working hard to support his blind, widowed mother, to gain an education, to preach wisely and well. Half the book focuses on his formative years in backwoods Dry Fork and Geff, Missouri.

2635 Larkin, Thomas Oliver   **1802-1858**
First and last consul: Thomas Oliver Larkin and the Americanization of California; selection of letters. Edited by John A. Hawgood. Palo Alto, California: Pacific Books, Publishers, 1970. (San Marino, California: Huntington Library, 1962) 147 p. Index.
Letters written to Abel Stearns and William A. Leidesdorff when Larkin was U.S. consul in Monterey (1834-46) concentrate on his significant role in the movement to secure California for the United States.

2636 Larkin, Thomas Oliver   **1802-1858**
Larkin papers: personal, business, and official correspondence of Thomas Oliver Larkin, merchant and U.S. Consul in California. Edited by George P. Hammond. Index by Anna Marie Hager and Everett G. Hager. Berkeley: University of California Press for the Bancroft Library, 1951-68. 10v. Index.
A massive collection of the records of one of California's most prominent early citizens. Appointed U.S. Consul in 1843, his letters record many significant incidents of his personal and professional life and the history of Western development.

2637 *LaRoe, Else Kienle   **1900-**
Woman surgeon: the autobiography of Else K. LaRoe, M.D. New York: The Dial Press, 1957. 373 p.
Born and educated in Germany, she developed an outstanding career as a restorative surgeon.

2638 Laski, Harold Joseph   **1893-1950**
see Holmes, Oliver Wendell

2639 *Lasky, Bessie Mona Gainess   **1890-**
Candle in the sun. Los Angeles: De Vorss and Co., 1957. 316 p.
The high points of her life as wife of Hollywood and New York film producer Jesse Lasky, and as mother to Jesse, Jr., Betty, and Bill. In early years, she entertained and traveled a great deal. Later, she concentrated more on her painting and spiritualistic religion.

2640 Lasky, Jesse Louis   **1880-1958**
I blow my own horn. With Don Weldon. Garden City, New York: Doubleday and Co., Inc., 1957. 284 p. Index.
A film producer who became prominent in Hollywood, including a partnership with Mary Pickford, describes his difficult but rewarding career.

2641 Lasky, William Raymond   **1921-**
Tell it on the mountain. With James F. Scheer. Garden City, New York: Doubleday & Co., Inc., 1976. 271 p.
Lasky, son of moviemaker Jesse Lasky, tells of his Jewish ancestors and upbringing in a Hollywood seaside mansion. His passion for animals domestic and exotic led to his career as an animal trainer in films. After divorce, electroshock therapy, and alcoholic bouts he was on the verge of suicide, but several escapes from death led him to conversion from Judaism to born-again Christianity.

2642 Latham, Harold Strong   **1887-**
My life in publishing. Introduction by Sterling North. New York: E.P. Dutton & Co., 1965. 256 p.
An entertaining memoir of the publishing profession by the editor-in-chief of the Macmillan Company, who before retirement spent 42 active years in the book world. He reminisces about his own life and about noted authors and others he has known.

2643 Latrobe, Benjamin Henry   **1764-1820**
Impressions respecting New Orleans: diary and sketches, 1818-1820. Edited by Samuel Wilson, Jr. New York: Columbia University Press, 1951. 196 p. Index.
Acknowledged as the founder of professional architecture in the United States, Latrobe gives vivid details of the turbulent, growing city, its clashes of culture, and comments on philosophical and moral questions that stimulated him during his working visit.

2644 Latrobe, Benjamin Henry   **1764-1820**
The Virginia journals of Benjamin Henry Latrobe: 1795-1798. Edited by Edward C. Carter, II, and others. New Haven, Connecticut: Yale University Press, 1977. 2v. Index.
Latrobe's journals are divided into two parts: half the entries are anecdotal stories of daily life, opinions, and amusing accounts of colonial life in Virginia. The other half consists of his watercolor sketches, snatches of songs, and blueprints for buildings.

2645 Lattimore, Owen   **1900-**
Ordeal by slander. Boston: Little, Brown and Co., 1950. 236 p.
A consecutive account of the author's defense before the Senate subcommittee following the accusation of espionage by Senator Joseph McCarthy.

2646 *Laune, Seigniora (Russell)   **b.1875**
Sand in my eyes. Flagstaff, Arizona: Northland Press, 1974. (Philadelphia: J.B. Lippincott Co., 1956) 256 p.
As a young bride in 1896, she began life in the Oklahoma Territory with her husband. Her book describes their life together in the developing frontier town, reflecting her simplicity, charm, and devotion to Woodward, Oklahoma.

2647 *Laurence, Jeanne   **b.1887**
My life with Sydney Laurence. Seattle, Washington: Salisbury Press Book, 1974. 159 p.
Mrs. Laurence, herself a painter, married Sydney Lawrence and together they spent happy years living and painting in Alaska, enjoying the wild beauty of the vigorous, challenging country they both loved. Included are 106 color reproductions of her husband's paintings.

2648 Laurens, Henry   **1724-1792**
The papers of Henry Laurens. Edited by Philip M. Hamer. Columbia: Published for the South Carolina Historical Society by the University of South Carolina Press, 1968- . v. Index.
An almost forgotten patriot of the American Revolution, Laurens of South Carolina was a merchant, planter, defender of American liberty, diplomat, and President of the Continental Congress during a critical period of the Revolution, 1777-1778. During his term the French Alliance and the Articles of Confederation were approved by the Congress. Later he was captured at sea by the British, imprisoned in the Tower of London for fifteen months, and exchanged in 1781 for General Cornwallis.

2649 Lauro, Joseph   **1912-**
Action priest; the story of Father Joe Lauro. And Arthur Orrmont. Foreword by Richard Cardinal Cushing. New York: William Morrow and Co., 1971. 357 p.
A bomber pilot in World War II, Lauro finally achieved his ambition of becoming a priest in 1949. Thereafter he served in the Arkansas Ozarks and later, as a member of Cardinal Cushing's Society of St. James, ministered to the poor and disadvantaged people of Ecuador.

2650 Laussat, Pierre Clément de   **1756-1835**
Memoirs of my life: to my son during the years 1803 and after. Translated with introduction by Agnes-Josephine Pastwa. Edited by Robert D. Bush. Historic New Orleans Collected Monograph Series. Baton Rouge: Louisiana State University Press, 1978. 137 p. Index.
Laussat's journal chronicles the years 1803 and 1804 when he was Prefect of Louisiana for France. He describes his daily activities, among them being his role in the Louisiana Purchase. This journal provides

insight into the attitudes, mostly unfriendly, of an aristocratic Frenchman living in the American wilderness.

2651 Lavender, David Sievert   1910-
One man's West. Line drawings by William Arthur Smith. Lincoln: University of Nebraska Press, 1977. (New York: Doubleday, 1943) 316 p.
     The author uses first person narrative to describe the life of a modern cowboy, a lifestyle which he saw would change quickly.

2652 *Lawrence, Andrea Mead   1932-
Practice of mountains. And Sara Burnaby. New York: Seaview Books, 1980. 213 p.
     An Olympic skiing champion describes how her commitment to the sport has influenced her life. Text includes photographs.

2653 *Lawrence, Frieda (von Richthofen)   1879-1956
Memoirs and correspondence. Edited by E.W. Tedlock. New York: Alfred A. Knopf, 1964. 481 p. Index.
     The narrative of her life, edited from unfinished manuscripts plus letters, portrays her understanding of her nature and affections, her relationship with D.H. Lawrence, and the years after his death.

2654 *Lawrence, Mary Chipman   1827-1906
The captain's best mate: the journal of Mary Chipman Lawrence on the whaler _Addison_, 1856-1860. Edited by Stanton Garner. Providence, Rhode Island: Brown University Press, 1966. 311 p. Index.
     A remarkable journal written by the wife of a whaling captain, who with her five-year-old daughter accompanied her husband on his dangerous voyage. Warm, courageous, and pious, she presents an overview of the whaling armada and recreates the people and places of the Pacific and the hopes, despair, and common purpose of the whalemen themselves.

2655 Lawrence, Robert   1912-
A rage for opera; its anatomy as drawn from life. New York: Dodd, Mead & Co., 1971. 176 p. Index.
     Conductor Lawrence writes his views on opera as a performing medium, discussing the audience, the repertoire, the singers, conductors, producers, and the impresarios from his large experience with them all. He laments the limited repertoire and shrunken outlook of today's opera world and wishes for fresh composers and new trends to be explored.

2656 *Lawrenson, Helen   1907-
Stranger at the party: a memoir. New York: Random House, 1975. 244 p.
     She has published over sixty articles in _Esquire_, and many in _Harper's_, _Vogue_, _McCall's_, and others; for a time she was managing editor of _Vanity Fair_. This book begins with her husband's death in 1957; it becomes a quest to rediscover a sense of self and independence in spite of her grief.

2657 *Lawrenson, Helen   1907-
Whistling girl: candid confessions of a chameleon. Garden City, New York: Doubleday and Co., 1978. 182 p.
     A journalist tells of her interviews with Hollywood celebrities, her introduction to oral sex in a Havana brothel, drinking "viper brandy" with an artist in Paris, experiences as a newspaper reporter and magazine editor, and her best-known article, "Latins are Lousy Lovers."

2658 Lawson, Robert   1892-1957
At that time: with decorations by the author. New York: The Viking Press, 1947. 126 p.
     His New England boyhood in another time and place, recalled with eloquence, charm, and nostalgia.

2659 Lax, David   1910-
One man show: a personal adventure in American art. Illustrated. New York: Washington Irving Gallery, 1976. 353 p. Index.
     Painter Lax reflects on his life and career as an artist, prolific but impoverished, living in New York during the Depression on $50-$75/month, serving in the U.S. Army Transportation Corps in France in World War II, having difficulty re-entering the art world and earning a living afterward until he attained some financial stability and recognition (beginning in 1958) as a faculty member of Dutchess Community College. Lax paints in an interesting variety of styles and writes with equal interest on art, society, and politics.

2660 Lax, Robert
     see Merton, Thomas

2661 Layden, Elmer   1902?-
It was a different game; the Elmer Layden story. With Ed Snyder. Illustrated. Englewood Cliffs, New Jersey: Prentice-Hall, Inc., 1969. 175 p.
     One of the Four Horsemen of Notre Dame coached by Knute Rockne in the Twenties, Layden writes with nostalgia about playing football when it was "a sport more than a business."

2662 Leach, Frank Aleamon   b.1846
Recollections of a newspaperman (a record of life and events in Califor-

nia). New York: Beekman Publishers, Inc., 1974. (San Francisco: S. Levinson, 1917) 146 p. Index.
     Memories of more than sixty years spent mostly on the central California frontier—Sacramento, Napa, Vallejo, Oakland. Leach was a newspaperman, establishing and running several papers. Later he became Superintendent of the U.S. Mint in San Francisco and eventually Director of the U.S. Mint in Washington.

2663 Leach, Henry Goddard   1880-1970
My last seventy years. New York: Bookman Associates, 1956. 232 p.
     Leach, an educator and aficionado of Scandinavia, has written his life story in an unusual format, with most chapters focused on his association, intimate or remote, continuing or momentary, with a notable person. These include his professors at Princeton and Harvard (Kittredge), people he met or interviewed while teaching in Scandinavia and Europe (Selma Lagerlof), or in writing for _The Forum_ (Shaw, V. Woolf), which he edited.

2664 Leachman, Harden Bryant   b.1881
The early advertising scene. Wood Dale, Illinois: H.B. Leachman, 1950. 253 p.
     Recollections of his first twenty years in the advertising field (1900-1920) by a successful practitioner, including anecdotes about businessmen, products, and customers.

2665 *Leak, Zenolia   1936?-
Mission possible. With George Elrick and Emmett Smith. Chicago: Children's Press, 1970. 62 p.
     In this book intended to offer high school students career guidance in the airlines industry, Leak writes also of an impoverished childhood, illegitimate pregnancy, beatings from her husband, and finally her acquittal of charges of homicide.

2666 Leary, Timothy Francis   1920-
Confessions of a hope fiend. New York: Bantam Books, 1973. 296 p.
     This is a personal account of Leary's imprisonment on drug charges, culminating in a much-publicized escape after two hundred days in various jails. He obtained passage to the Middle East with a forged passport and made contact with Black Panther leader Eldridge Cleaver. Drug and sexual experiences prominently figured in his life. Eventually political pressure forced him to move to Switzerland.

2667 Leavell, William Hayne   1850-1930
William Hayne Leavell, 1850-1930: an autobiography. Seattle: Alec Bayless and Larry Noble, 1979. 171 p.
     Leavell presents a minutely detailed account of his South Carolina upbringing during the Civil War and Reconstruction; for a time he was a Ku Klux Klan member determined to restore Blacks to their antebellum subservience. After marriage he turned his energies and considerable business acumen to building various Presbyterian congregations and churches in New York, New Hampshire, Boston, Mississippi, and Houston. He concluded a vigorous life with appointment as Minister to Guatemala.

2668 Lebrun, George Petit   b.1862
It's time to tell. As told to Edward D. Radin. New York: William Morrow and Co., 1962. 255 p. Index
     The credits of his professional life as an active public servant in New York include 36 years as the mainstay of the New York Board of Coroners, the initiation of the Sullivan Law requiring gun registration, his ten-year fight for licensing automobile drivers, and agitation for public safety in city buildings. He describes many of the rich, famous, and infamous people he worked around.

2669 Lederer, John   d.1670
The discoveries of John Lederer: with unpublished letters by and about Lederer to Governor John Winthrop, Jr. and an essay on the Indians of Lederer's _Discoveries_ by Douglas L. Rights and William P. Cumming. Edited by William P. Cumming. Charlottesville: University of Virginia Press, 1958. 148 p. Index.
     A record of his three journeys exploring the tidewater settlements of Virginia, the Piedmont, and the Blue Ridge Mountains in 1670, including interesting commentary on Indian tribes encountered. (_Discoveries_ was first published in 1672, by J.C. for S. Heyrick).

2670 Lederer, William Julius   1916-
All the ships at sea. New York: William Sloane Associates, Inc., 1950. 292 p.
     Humorous account of his eighteen years of shipboard and shore experiences by a naval officer who became a public relations specialist.

2671 Ledyard, John   1759-1789
John Ledyard's journal of Captain Cook's last voyage. Edited by James Kenneth Munford. Introduction by Sinclair H. Hitchings. With notes on plants by Helen M. Gilkey and notes on animals by Robert M. Storm. Corvallis: Oregon State University Press, 1963. 264 p. Index.
     A native of Connecticut, he joined Cook's expedition (1776-1780) to explore the Northwest Passage. His journal, compiled in 1783, conveys

the spirit of a romantic adventurer while recording precise details of their travels in the South Seas, the Sandwich Islands, and the Northwest coast.

2672 Lee, Andrew, pseud.
see **Auchincloss, Louis**

2673 *Lee, Gypsy Rose   1914-1970
Gypsy: a memoir. New York: Harper and Brothers, 1957. 337 p.
    Stripteaser Lee, "the greatest no-talent star" in show business, narrates the story of her life on the vaudeville and burlesque circuits. Her ruthless mother promoted her career from the time Lee was four until she struck it rich with a long Ziegfeld Follies run. June Havoc, Lee's sister, also figures prominently.

2674 Lee, J.D.   1929-
Testament of intent. Foreword by Edward Uhlar. Hicksville, New York: Exposition Press, 1977. 233 p.
    This book discusses the disbarment proceedings instituted against the author, a nationally prominent attorney who was active in reform of the bar association and in setting up a "Citizens' Legal Clinic" for the poor. The plaintiff was the Tennessee Bar Association. After a long trial the charges were dismissed. The plaintiff has appealed and the case is still pending. The author suggests the charges are a harassment because he won important cases against clients served by some plaintiff lawyers.

2675 Lee, Jesse   1758-1816
Memoir of the Rev. Jesse Lee; with extracts from his journals. Compiled by Milton Thrift. New York: Arno Press and The New York Times, 1969. (New York: N. Bangs and T. Mason, 1823) 360 p.
    A minister in the Church of Christ, Lee traveled between New York and Virginia to strengthen the organizational ties of the church.

2676 Lee, John Doyle   1812-1877
Morman chronicle: the diaries of John D. Lee, 1848-1876. Edited and annotated by Robert Glass Cleland and Juanita Brooks. San Marino: The Huntington Library, 1955. 2v. Index.
    Five diaries of a prominent Morman leader describe the Morman settlement of Utah, his devout, uncompromising practice of Morman beliefs, and the details of everyday life on the wilderness frontier.

2677 *Lee, Mabel Barbee   b.1886
Memories beyond bloomers: 1924-1954. Foreword by George Anderson. Illustrated. Washington, D.C.: American Alliance for Health, Physical Education, and Recreation, 1978. 458 p. Index.
    Lee discusses her thirty-year career as chairman of Women's Physical Education at the University of Nebraska and her involvement in the Academy of Physical Education; the American Alliance for Health, Physical Education and Recreation; and other organizations in which she dynamically labored and lobbied for women's physical education to be on par with men's. Lee provides a history of the development of women's physical education in the United States, 1920-1960.

2678 *Lee, Mabel Barbee   b.1886
Memories of a bloomer girl: 1894-1924. Foreword by Celeste Ulrich. Washington, D.C.: American Alliance for Health, Physical Education, and Recreation, 1977. 384 p.
    Lee, a pioneer professor of physical education, uses a lifetime of detailed diaries and considerable dialogue to narrate her upbringing in Centerville, Iowa, her education at Coe and at Wellesley, and her early teaching career. Interwoven is a history of women's physical education and women's liberation in the early 1920's.

2679 Lee, Raymond Eliot   1886-1958
The London journal of General Raymond E. Lee, 1940-1941. Edited by James Leutze. Foreword by Dean Acheson. Boston: Little, Brown and Co., 1971. 489 p. Index.
    As military attaché to the American Embassy in London during 1940 and 1941, he had a first-hand experience with British morale and the heroic efforts of plain citizens and the military. His urbanity, sense of history, and appreciation of life color his evaluations of the wartime British scene.

2680 Lee, Robert Edward   1807-1870
Lee's dispatches: unpublished letters to Jefferson Davis and the War Department of the Confederate States of America, 1862-65; from the private collection of Wyberley Jones De Renne, of Wormsloe, Georgia. Edited with introduction and notes by Douglas Southall Freeman. Additional dispatches and foreword by Grady McWhiney. New York: G.P. Putnam's Sons, 1957. (1915) 416 p. Index.
    An interesting contribution to our understanding of the man, the general, and Civil War history.

2681 Lee, Robert Edward   1807-1870
The story of Robert E. Lee: as told in his own words and those of his contemporaries. Edited by Ralston B. Lattimore. Illustrated. Source Book Series, No. 1, 1964. Philadelphia: Eastern National Park and Monument Association, 1964. 96 p.

Writings by Lee, to Lee, and by others about him fill this beautifully illustrated volume. The portrait that emerges is of a modest man of high moral standards, a military genius with a great sensitivity for the hardships of others and a particular fondness for his large family. The book also outlines the movements of the Civil War.

2682 Lee, Robert Greene   b.1886
Payday everyday. Nashville: Broadman Press, 1974. 146 p.
    A southern Baptist preacher's story of his life in the church, with comments on selected issues such as smoking and evolution, and notes on some famous people he has known.

2683 Lee, Robert M.
Man and me, M.D. Hicksville, New York: Exposition Press, 1977. 173 p.
    Upon retiring from a thirty-year medical practice, he traveled all over the world with an anthropologist's interest in observing how certain peoples have developed. Text includes photographs, charts, and illustrations.

2684 Lee, Roger Irving   1881-1965
The happy life of a doctor. Boston: Little, Brown and Co., 1956. 278 p.
    A physician for fifty years, president of the American Medical Association, and founder of the Harvard School of Public Health describes his life in medicine.

2685 Lee, William   1739-1795
Letters of William Lee, 1766-1783. Edited by Worthington Chauncey Ford. Eyewitness Accounts of the American Revolution. New York: New York Times & Arno Press, 1971. (Brooklyn: Historical Printing Club, 1891) 987 p. Index.
    Lee, brother of Richard Henry Lee, was the only American who served as Alderman of London. His letters reveal his chequered career; he promoted the Revolutionary cause, but he "made his own (diplomatic) negotiations an instrument to discredit the American Commissioners" during the Revolutionary War; he erroneously submitted to his brother Arthur's political plots, which subverted his diplomatic missions to the Courts of Vienna and Berlin; and he was unduly suspicious and critical of other American diplomats, such as Benjamin Franklin.

2686 Lee, William   1772-1840
A Yankee Jeffersonian: selections from the diary and letters of William Lee of Massachusetts written from 1796-1840. Edited by Mary Lee Mann. Cambridge: Harvard University Press, 1958. 312 p. Index.
    A candid, perceptive record of his life as a businessman and diplomat, based on his experience in Napoleon's court, the Washington of Presidents Monroe and John Quincy Adams, and the ordinary life of a moderately successful career in early America.

2687 Leeth, John   1755-1832
A short biography of John Leeth: with an account of his life among the Indians. And Ewel Jeffries. Narratives of North American Indian Captives, v. 47. New York: Garland Publishers, 1977. (Lancaster, Ohio: Gazette Office, 1831) 90 p. Index.
    The record of the author's captivity and life among the Indians for over eighteen years, written by Ewel Jeffries from Leeth's recollections. Originally published in 1831, this volume reprints the 1883 edition (R. Clarke, Cincinnati) with Consul Willshire Butterfield's introduction and notes.

2688 LeFlore, Ron   1952?-
Breakout: from prison to the big leagues. With Jim Hawkins. Illustrated. New York: Harper & Row, Publishers, 1978. 180 p. Index.
    LeFlore's autobiography is an honest, earthy account of his youth spent stealing and drug-taking, his 38-month stay in the State Prison of Southern Michigan, where he discovered baseball, and his rise to the major leagues as one of the Detroit Tigers' best centerfielders.

2689 Left Handed   b.1868
Left Handed: a Navajo autobiography. Edited by Walter and Ruth Dyk. Introduction by Ruth Dyk. Foreword by Fred Eggan. Illustrated. New York: Columbia University Press, 1980. 578 p. Index.
    This book is a sequel to *Son of Old Man Hat* (Harcourt Brace, 1938) and covers three years in the life of a Navajo herdsman in the Black Mesa area of Arizona in the late 1880's. Translated from the Navajo, his book focuses on the trials of Left Handed's early marriage, family life, and tribal practice.

2690 *LeGallienne, Eva   1899-
With a quiet heart. Westport, Connecticut: Greenwood Press, 1974. (New York: The Viking Press, 1953) 311 p. Index.
    Written in her fifties, this book begins with the story of her near-fatal accident by fire, her subsequent recovery in Paris, and her return to continued success as one of America's most outstanding stage actresses.

2691 *Lehmann, Lotte   1885-1976
Midway in my song: the autobiography of Lotte Lehmann. Illustrated. Freeport, New York: Books for Libraries Press, 1970. (Indianapolis: Bobbs-Merrill Co., 1938) 250 p. Index.
    The famous opera diva's story of her life and her career, her disap-

pointments and triumphs throughout Europe and the United States, up to her disillusionment with Nazi Germany and new life at the New York Metropolitan Opera.

2692 *Lehmann, Lotte 1885-1976
My many lives. Westport, Connecticut: Greenwood Press, Publishers, 1974. (New York: Boosey & Hawkes, Inc., 1948) 262 p.

Her experiences and conceptions of operatic roles she has performed, dwelling particularly on her acting and insight into the characters rather than the musical aspects of that art form. Separate chapters concern her individual roles, i.e., Elsa— *Lohengrin,* Elizabeth—*Tannhäuser,* and Sieglinde— *Die Walküre.*

2693 Lehmberg, Paul
In the strong moods: a season alone in the North Country. New York: St. Martin's Press, 1980. 149 p.

With his marriage threatening to die from neglect and enervated by just-completed doctoral orals, graduate student Lehmberg elected to spend a summer by himself in the remote Ontario lakes region. There, in a cabin accessible only by canoe, isolated from human contact, he sagely contemplates his natural surroundings and rejoices in a daily routine stripped of the infringements of civilization. His north-woods cabin is for him "a place to regain your senses and your sense."

2694 *Lehr, Elizabeth Drexel
"King Lehr" and the gilded age. Series: Leisure Class in America. New York: Arno Press, 1975. (Philadelphia: Lippincott, 1935) 332 p. Index.

Lehr writes of the "tragic farce of [her] marriage" to a dictator of society and king of jokes who told her the night of their marriage he had married her for her best asset—her money. Despite his being the darling of society's "top" women, he claimed to hate all women but his mother. The author nonetheless describes the society and women of America's "gilded age" with humor.

2695 *Leigh, Dorian 1920-
The girl who had everything: the story of 'The Fire and Ice Girl.' With Laura Hope. Illustrated. Garden City, New York: A Giniger Book/Doubleday, 1980. 227 p.

Dorian Leigh (sister of model Suzy Parker), a mechanical engineer, became a high-fashion model in the late 1940's and 1950's, wandered in and out of innumerable affairs, four marriages, and irresponsible motherhood. Her negligence hit home with a vengeance when, after becoming a born-again Christian in 1972, she had to cope with poverty and the suicide of her drug-addicted son.

2696 Leistad, Einar 1900-
Man with the white horse: memoirs. Illustrated. Hicksville, New York: Exposition Press, 1979. 96 p.

Leistad describes his childhood in the Strinda district of Norway, where he did heavy farm labor. He emigrated to Iowa, where he also did heavy labor, eventually specializing in the construction of grain elevators. With his two trick horses, Frank and Twinkle, he performed feats of strength and skill at carnivals and circuses.

2697 Leitch, John David
see *Leitch, Mary Sinton (Lewis)

2698 *Leitch, Mary Sinton (Lewis) and John David Leitch 1876-1954
Himself and I: our sea saga; in collaboration with himself. New York: The Fine Editions Press, 1950. 246 p.

In three sections, one for her sea captain husband's early life, one for hers, and finally their sea travels together, a socialite-author reminisces about social customs of the early twentieth century and gives a detailed description of their long trip on the *Ripley* after their marriage.

2699 Le Jau, Francis 1665-1717
The Carolina chronicle of Dr. Francis Le Jau, 1706-1717. Edited with introduction and notes by Frank J. Klingberg. California University Publications in History, Vol. 53. Berkeley: University of California Press, 1956. 220 p. Index.

A collection of correspondence and annual reports written by an Anglican missionary in Charleston, South Carolina.

2700 Leland, Charles Godfrey, pseud. (Hans Breitmann) 1824-1903
Memoirs. Detroit: Gale Research Co., 1968. (New York: D. Appleton, 1893) 439 p.

Leland, a prominent journalist (Philadelphia *Bulletin, Vanity Fair*) and translator, wrote numerous articles for magazines and encyclopedias. He writes of his upbringing in Philadelphia and New England; his education at Princeton, Munich, Heidelberg, and Paris; his journalistic career (he knew all the prominent Boston literati); abolitionist efforts; and post-Civil War travels in Europe and England.

2701 Lema, Anthony David 1933?-
Golfers gold: an inside view of the pro tour. With Gwilym S. Brown. Boston: Little, Brown and Co., 1964. 248 p.

A champion player in the 1960's describes tournament life, money, and celebrities.

2702 Leman, Walter Moore 1810-1888?
Memories of an old actor. St. Clair Shores, Michigan: Scholarly Press, 1969. (San Francisco: A. Roman Co., 1886) 406 p.

Bitten by stage mania in his teens, Leman here recalls actors and actresses, theaters, travel throughout the United States and Europe, playing in theaters during a large part of the nineteenth century.

2703 Lemmon, Ed 1857-1946
Boss cowman: the recollections of Ed Lemmon, 1857-1946. Illustrated. Edited by Nellie Snyder Yost. Pioneer Heritage Serials, v. 6. Lincoln: University of Nebraska Press, 1969. 321 p. Index.

Lemmon was a cowhand, trail rider, wagon boss, range manager, and ranch owner who at one time managed the largest fenced pasture in the world (865,000 acres) and bossed the largest single roundup in history. He witnessed and participated in the development of the Western Plains from the early cattle days onward and was named among the first South Dakota cowmen in the National Cowboy Hall of Fame.

2704 *L'Engle, Madeleine 1918-
A circle of quiet. New York: Farrar, Straus and Giroux, 1972. 245 p.

Her first autobiography describes her life in rural Connecticut as wife, mother, grandmother, and writer until the success of *A Wrinkle in Time* which won the Newbery Medal.

2705 *L'Engle, Madeleine 1918-
The irrational season. New York: The Seabury Press, 1977. 215 p.

L'Engle writes about her family, teaching, and the influence of religious inspiration on her writing. She discusses other religions and her reactions to them, dwelling particularly on the plight of the Jews during World War II. Interspersed throughout the book are inspirational poems.

2706 *L'Engle, Madeleine 1918-
The summer of the great-grandmother. New York: Farrar, Straus and Giroux, 1974. 245 p.

A study of her maternal ancestry written during the last year of her mother's life in an attempt to come to terms with her creativity and mortality.

2707 Leonard, John 1940?-
Private lives in the Imperial City. New York: Alfred A. Knopf, 1979. 209 p.

Leonard's collection of "Private Lives" columns from the New York *Times,* 1976-79, provides insights into the relationships of husbands and wives, parents and children, viewed from the perspective of a fortyish, sensitive writer. Most focus on the events of daily life in Manhattan, but transcend the trivial to reveal the profound significance of the commonplace.

2708 Leonard, Zenas 1809-1857
Adventures of Zenas Leonard, fur trader. American Exploration and Travel Series, Number 28. Edited by John C. Ewers. Norman: University of Oklahoma Press, 1959. 172 p. Index.

Born in Clearfield County, Pennsylvania, he moved down the Ohio River to St. Louis in 1831 and on to the Rocky Mountains to become a trapper. He was associated with Captain B.L.E. Bonneville's party (1833-35), returned to Pennsylvania for six months, and then headed west to establish himself as a fur trader in St. Louis. First published serially in the Clearfield *Republican,* 1839.

2709 Lerner, Alan Jay 1918-
The street where I live. Illustrated. New York: W.W. Norton and Company, 1978. 320 p. Index.

The book is an engaging, "highly personal biography of three great shows": *Camelot, My Fair Lady, Gigi.* Lerner, who won Academy Awards as librettist for all three shows, pays tribute to the actors and actresses who made his lyrics famous, and especially to his colleagues and friends, composer Fritz Loewe and producer Moss Hart.

2710 LeRoy, Mervyn 1900-
Mervyn LeRoy; take one. As told to Dick Kleiner. New York: Hawthorn Books, 1974. 244 p. Index.

LeRoy started out in vaudeville, but in the 1920's went to Hollywood where he directed and produced movies from 1928 on. Some of his greatest hits are *Wizard of Oz, Mister Roberts,* and *Gypsy.*

2711 *Leslie-Melville, Betty
There's a rhino in the rose bed, Mother. And Jock Leslie-Melville. Garden City, New York: Doubleday & Co., Inc., 1973. 253 p.

As the authors point out, this book is half frothy, half serious, an account of their lives in South Africa and in America. While describing many of the practical and political problems in South Africa, they frequently compare those stories with comparable ones of life in the U.S., in effect making the point that life may be strange in a strange land, but it's also strange at home.

2712 Lester, Julius B.   **1939-**
All is well. New York: William Morrow & Co., 1976. 319 p.
Black author Lester reveals consistent malaise through an autobiographical narrative interspersed with poetry, letters, diary entries, and excerpts from his essays and reviews. He focuses on his increased self-knowledge gained through marriage to a white woman, participation in the Civil Rights Movement, and numerous love affairs.

2713 LeTourneau, Robert Gilmour   **1888-1969**
Mover of men and mountains: the autobiography of R.G. LeTourneau. Chicago: Moody Press, 1967. 290 p. Index.
Self-educated, he invented giant earth-moving machinery: power shovels and rooters, scoops, scrapers, rollers, bulldozers, landing-craft retrievers, tree stringers, log stackers, log transporters, bridge builders, missile launchers, and others. He eventually owned four factories worth 50 million that produced these machines. Claiming that "God needs businessmen as partners as well as preachers," LeTourneau and his wife became involved in missionary work in Liberia and Peru, contributing money, time, and enormous dedication.

2714 Levant, Oscar   **1900-1972**
Memoirs of an amnesiac. New York: G.P. Putnam's Sons, 1965. 320 p.
Levant's autobiography recounts episodes of his life with typical frenetic and sardonic wit. He looks at his psyche, his long battle with drugs and doctors, his friendships with musicians, film stars, and bookies, his *Information Please* days, and his concert appearances—all with ruthless irreverence.

2715 Levant, Oscar   **1900-1972**
The unimportance of being Oscar. Illustrated. New York: G.P. Putnam's Sons, 1968. 255 p. Index.
Written after his *Memoirs of an Amnesiac*, this book continues his fast-moving reminiscences about show business and the great and famous people he has known. Although he claims to feel "a kind of creeping mellowness," his remarks are tinged with acid humor as always.

2716 Levenson, Samuel   **1911-1980**
Everything but money. New York: Simon and Schuster, 1966. 285 p.
Amid nostalgic and amusing stories of the good old days of his youth, Levenson mixes humorous criticism of today's society and a plea for old-fashioned values.

2717 Levenson, Samuel   **1911-1980**
In one era and out the other. New York: Simon & Schuster, 1973. 190 p.
His book describes his childhood and youth in New York, the "younger generation" of the late Sixties, and the problems common to both, like adjusting to unsettling change. A down-to-earth humorist, he recalls: his grandmother who preserved her food in her icebox and used her new refrigerator to cool her house; and the confused rebellion of the young who practice transcendental meditation but do not call it prayer, who reject "Amen!" but say "Right On!"

2718 *Levertov, Denise   **1923-**
The poet in the world. New York: New Directions, 1973. 275 p. Index.
A collection of scattered prose pieces which express her thoughts and opinions on poetry, writing, politics, and other writers.

2719 LeVier, Anthony William   **1913-**
Pilot. As told to John Guenther. Foreword by Arthur Godfrey. New York: Harper and Brothers, 1954. 263 p.
At fifteen he quit school and had his first flying lesson, followed by a sketchy career as stunt flyer, teacher, and barnstormer until 1941, when he became a test pilot for Lockheed.

2720 Levin, Meyer   **1905-**
In search: an autobiography by Meyer Levin. New York: Horizon Press, 1950. 524 p.
Examines his own sense of being a Jew, discussing the history of the Jews through World War II and the development of Israel as the Jewish state.

2721 Levin, Meyer   **1905-**
The obsession. New York: Simon & Schuster, 1973. 316 p.
Obsessed with the conviction that his staging of *The Diary of Anne Frank* had been unjustly debarred because he was too political, Levin tried through twenty years and four analysts to overcome his blind conviction that he was the victim of "doctrinaire censorship of the Stalinist variety." Here he describes the progress of his obsession and his efforts to come to terms with it.

2722 Levine, Isaac Don   **1892-**
Eyewitness to history; memoirs and reflections of a foreign correspondent for half a century. Illustrated. New York: Hawthorn Books, Inc., 1973. 305 p. Index.
The dramatic peaks in the uneven career of a rebel whose life was always influenced by the Russian Revolution. Other interests have included the lore and post-World War II awakening of Africa, the Moscow

Art Theater, other theater projects, a paperback book club, the writing of biographies (Josef Stalin and Billy Mitchell among them) and other books on political affairs.

2723 Levy, Julien
Memoir of an art gallery. Illustrated. New York: G.P. Putnam's Sons, 1977. 320 p. Index.
Levy, a Manhattan art dealer, specialized in work by Dadaists and Surrealists, including Dali, de Chirico, Man Ray, and Joseph Cornell. He knew them and their conferees well, and has arranged these memoirs topically by artist. This mélange of personal anecdotes and serious art criticism vividly depicts the avant-garde art world of the 1930's.

2724 Levy, Newman   **b.1888**
My double life: adventures in law and letters. Garden City, New York: Doubleday & Co., Inc., 1958. 316 p. Index.
Levy writes engagingly about his dual careers as a successful trial lawyer (with Greenbaum, Wolff, and Ernst in Manhattan) and an equally successful author of essays, light verse, collaborator on a play with Edna Ferber, and briefly as a Hollywood screenwriter. Levy loves both careers and describes with sympathy some of his most significant trials, including the defense of several maligned communists who were all convicted during the McCarthy era.

2725 *Lewandowski, Michalene Doskotch   **1920-**
Human island: the story of a woman's dedication to the hopeless. Jerico, New York: Exposition Press, 1970. 193 p.
Lewandowski writes of her six years of visiting, ministering to, and comforting the infirm and elderly, her own strength and determination stemming from her Christian faith. Narratives of individual patients and of family members, along with religious poems, shape her episodic story. She concludes with a warning against the common neglect of the aged and a checklist to consult when choosing a nursing home.

2726 *Lewis, Carola Regester
Ramblings. Parsons, West Virginia: McClain Printing Co., 1974. 194 p.
Entries from a travel journal of trips throughout the West, Midwest, and East which the author wrote and sent to local newspapers in West Virginia. When she and her husband settled down, she continued to write about people, places, and things that interested her.

2727 *Lewis, Cecilia   **1892-**
I remember. Illustrated. Waterloo, Iowa: The author, 1979. 104 p.
As a teenager she began missionary work in Seattle with her parents, who were Salvation Army evangelists. Later she married and when her husband became an invalid, she worked for 26 years as a police matron in Waterloo, Iowa. Her book reflects the values of small-town Midwestern America.

2728 *Lewis, Faye Cashatt
Nothing to make a shadow. Ames: Iowa State University Press, 1971. 155 p.
The first woman graduate of the University of South Dakota College of Medicine and Washington University School of Medicine describes her family's homesteading years (1909-17) near Dallas, South Dakota.

2729 *Lewis, Grace (Hagger)
With love from Gracie: Sinclair Lewis: 1912-1925. New York: Harcourt, Brace and Co., 1955. 335 p.
The story of her life with the famous author.

2730 Lewis, Jack   **1912-**
Bay and River Delaware. Illustrated. Bridgeville, Delaware: The author, 1980. 189 p.
Profusely illustrated with his watercolors and ink drawings, Lewis's book is a folk history of the Delaware Bay area. He mixes local legends with notes on his own experience traveling the area and painting, providing vivid descriptions verbally as well as artistically of the area and its residents.

2731 Lewis, Jerry   **1926-**
The total film maker. Illustrated. New York: Random House, 1971. 208 p.
A versatile comedian turned film maker, Lewis provides an inside look at acting, screen writing, directing, and producing and writes with enthusiasm about his experiences during the adventure of putting a film together.

2732 Lewis, John   **b.1878**
The strange story of a minister's life. Boston: Christopher Publishing House, 1956. 171 p.
Beginning with his childhood in Wales and religious training in England, Lewis recounts the high points of his ministry, including being framed for the arson of his own church in Milwaukee because of his opposition to bingo, and serving time in prison. Much of the book relates the questions of his parishioners and his answers to them; he concludes, "The supreme need of the world today is not to adjust the Christian

gospel to modern thought, but to adjust modern thought to the Christian gospel."

2733 Lewis, Lloyd Downs   1891-1949
Letters from Lloyd Lewis: showing steps in the research for his biography of U.S. Grant. Boston: Little, Brown and Co., 1950. 83 p.
  Historian describes the progress of his research, including reflections on reading and conversation while writng his biography of Ulysses S. Grant, in letters to his publisher, 1945-1949.

2734 Lewis, Meriwether   1774-1809
The journals of Lewis and Clark: a new selection with an introduction by John Bakeless. Edited by John Bakeless. New York: Mentor Book/New American Library, 1964. (Dayton, Ohio: B.F. Ellis, 1840) 384 p.
  An exciting account of the expedition of Lewis and Clark, 1804-1806, who, with 28 men, a Shoshone squaw (Sacajawea) and her indestructible infant, explored American territory from the upper Missouri River, across the Rockies, to the Pacific Coast. Written in plain-spoken language, the dual accounts tell of the dangers and wonders of the wilderness, the Indians (friendly and hostile), animals they encountered, and the explorers' mode of living and survival as they opened the Western frontier to expansion and trade. Many editions have been published.

2735 Lewis, Sinclair   1885-1951
From Main Street to Stockholm: letters, 1919-1930. Edited with an introduction by Harrison Smith. New York: Harcourt, Brace and Co., 1952. 307 p. Index.
  Letters between Lewis and Alfred Harcourt, whom he encouraged to start his own publishing company and who became his publisher. An interesting record of their friendship and of Lewis's determination to change America's conception of itself through his fiction. In 1930, he became the first American to receive the Nobel Prize for literature.

2736 Lewis, Sinclair
  see also **London, Jack**

2737 Lewis, Wilmarth Sheldon   1895-1979
One man's education. New York: Alfred A. Knopf, 1967. 488 p. Index.
  An account of his education, both formal and informal, by a book collector whose passion was Walpoliana, not only what Horace Walpole wrote, printed, and owned but things of his period. His collection and house at Farmington were willed to Yale as the Lewis Walpole Library.

2738 Lewisohn, Ludwig   1882-1955
Up stream: an American chronicle. St. Clair Shores, Michigan: Scholarly Press, 1977. (New York: Boni & Liveright, 1923) 248 p.
  Lewisohn provides a progressively more ironic and bitter account of his family's immigration from Prussia in 1899 to South Carolina, where as Jews (though he went faithfully to the Methodist Church) they were cultural and spiritual aliens. He became a writer and professor of English for eight years at the University of Central City. He survived the attempted purge of Germans from the faculty during World War I, but regrets the "aimless business and sapless pleasures" of middle-American life in the early Twenties.

2739 Lewiston, Harry   1900-1965
Freak show man: the autobiography of Harry Lewiston. As told to Jerry Holtman. Los Angeles: Holloway House, 1968. 327 p.
  Lewiston describes his life as a barker and showman with the sleazy side of the circus—exploiting lewd customers at hootchy-kootchy shows, cheating people, gambling and drinking excessively. In his younger and middle years, he was self-centered, callous toward those he loved, and intermittently jailed or threatened by the law. In old age, he suffered blindness and despair.

2740 L'Heureux, John   1934-
Picnic in Babylon; a Jesuit priest's journal, 1963-1967. New York: The Macmillan Co., 1967. 301 p.
  The journal records three years of his life before ordination, commenting on the training of a Jesuit, the gratification and loneliness of his commitment, and the conflict between being a poet and a priest.

2741 Liber, Benzion   1875-1958
A doctor's apprenticeship (autobiographical sketches). New York: Rational Living, 1956. 611 p. Index.
  Liber recounts his childhood in Paris and Rumania, his development as a Socialist, and his medical education in Vienna, where he was also a reporter for Socialist newspapers. After immigrating to America in 1904, he was a general practitioner for fifty years, supporting liberal social and political causes throughout.

2742 Liberace, Wladziv Valentino   1919-
Liberace; an autobiography. Illustrated. New York: G.P. Putnam's Sons, 1973. 316 p.
  One of the most flamboyant show biz figures since early Hollywood, he uses the book to extend his highly cultivated image even further. He writes, as he says, "to be entertaining and to make money."

2743 Liberace, Wladziv Valentino   1919-
The things I love. Edited by Tony Palmer. Illustrated. New York: Grosset & Dunlap, 1976. 222 p.
  Popular pianist Liberace offers a genial account of his career as a flamboyant, sequined entertainer, mostly in Hollywood and Las Vegas. He provides amply illustrated tours of two of his seven opulent houses, a commentary on his wardrobe (including rhinestone-studded red, white, and blue hotpants), and an introduction to his fancy cars, collections of jeweled pianos, miniature and oversized, and exotic dogs.

2744 Lichtenfeld, Julius
A pharmacist's memoirs: fifty years of Ukrainczyk's Brighton pharmacy. New York: Exposition Press, 1952. 108 p.
  Recollections of a neighborhood pharmacist in Brooklyn, the customers and doctors he has known over the years.

2745 *Lichtenstein, Grace
Desperado. New York: The Dial Press, 1977. 213 p.
  The New York-nurtured author encountered the American West as the first female regional bureau chief of the New York *Times*. She writes of her adventures meeting and interviewing cowboys, Indians, mining company executives, ecologists, and movie idols.

2746 Lichtiger, Joshua   1919-
The odyssey of a Jew. New York: Vantage Press, 1979. 174 p.
  Lichtiger describes his odyssey of 1940-41 when he fled his native Kobrin, Poland, after Hitler's invasion and persecution of the Jews. His escape route led to Vilna, Lithuania, then to Kobe, Japan, where he spent seven months before going to Palestine. Eventually he joined relatives in New York.

2747 Liddy, George Gordon Battle   1930-
Will: the autobiography of G. Gordon Liddy. Illustrated. New York: St. Martin's Press, 1980. 374 p. Index.
  Attorney and former Presidential Counsel Liddy describes his pleasant childhood, early career in the FBI, marriage and fatherhood, law school, and his appointments to the Treasury Department and President Nixon's Special Advisory Staff. In the White House he became involved in the Watergate break-in and cover-up and offered to kill or be killed for the cause. His complicity resulted in a prison sentence, shortened for good behavior.

2748 Lieb, Frederick George   b.1888
Baseball as I have known it. Illustrated. New York: Coward, McCann & Geoghegan, 1977. 349 p. Index.
  The history of major-league baseball through the eyes of the sportswriter who covered the game for sixty years, starting in 1909. Lieb reported the games from New York and was official New York scorekeeper for the American League, the grand old man of the baseball writers' fraternity. The author of more than ten books on baseball, Lieb tells of memorable games and players and of electing players to the Baseball Hall of Fame.

2749 Liggett, William Verner   b.1882
My seventy five years along the Mexican border. New York: Exposition Press, 1964. 139 p.
  Recollections of difficult times on the Mexican border in Arizona and Texas, remembered from his boyhood and his adult life as a car-rental executive.

2750 Ligon, Robert Leonard   1867-1959
Just Dad: a pioneer history of the Southwest; collection of letters and writings to his son Ernest which highlight the pioneer days in the Southwest 1867-1959. Schenectady, New York: Character Research Press, 1976. (n.p.: Ernest M. Ligon, 1972) 306 p.
  This retrospective view of the author's pioneer life in Missouri, Kansas, Texas, and Oklahoma is written as an extended, book-length letter from an 84-year-old retired lumber and construction businessman to his Ph.D. son. His good-humored narrative exemplifies many ways to try to fulfill the American Dream—through homesteading, hard work, business investments, luck, a good marriage, successful children, church and community involvement.

2751 Lilienthal, David Eli   1899-1981
The journals of David E. Lilienthal. Including a selection of journal entries from the 1917-1939 period. Introduction by Henry Steele Commager. New York: Harper & Row, 1964-1971. 5v. Index.
  Volume I: The TVA years: 1939-1945 includes his public service under FDR and with the Tennessee Valley Authority. Volume II: The atomic energy years, 1945-1950. Volume III: Venturesome years, 1950-1955 describes his private careers in business and consulting. Volume IV: The road to change, 1955-1959 shows his interests in aiding people of underdeveloped nations. Volume V: The harvest years, 1959-1963 concerns his resumption of interest in public affairs.

2752 Lilienthal, Meta Stern   **1876-1949**
Dear remembered world: childhood memories of an old New Yorker. New York: Richard R. Smith, 1947. 248 p.
Interesting story of middle-class life in Victorian New York.

2753 *Liliuokalani   **1838-1917**
Hawaii's story by Hawaii's queen. Rutland, Vermont: Charles E. Tuttle Co., Inc., 1963. (Boston: Lee & Shepard, 1898) 414 p.
A personal account of the last years of the Hawaiian monarchy that was inevitably and inexorably swept along toward democracy. She believed in the divine right of monarchy but supported efforts to improve health, welfare, and education among her people. She writes of the revolution and annexation by the U.S. and asks for sympathy toward the cause of Hawaiian autonomy.

2754 *Lilly, Antonietta Lena F.
The dyadic cyclone: the autobiography of a couple. And John Lilly. New York: Simon & Schuster, 1976. 285 p.
Psychoanalyst Lilly and his wife, an artist, focus on the question to which they have devoted considerable investigation during their five years together: "Is it possible to merge two centers, cyclones, one male, one female, in such a way that there can be a rising center shared by both?" They discuss their explorations of the question, via meditation, but particularly through hour-long flotations in a dark tank of epsom salts and 93 degrees F. water, to replicate the womb.

2755 Lilly, John   **1915-**
see *Lilly, Antonietta Lena F.

2756 Lincoln, Abraham   **1809-1865**
Abraham Lincoln: an autobiographical narrative. Edited by Ralph Geoffrey Newman. Chicago, Illinois: The Lincoln Mint, 1970. (New Brunswick: Rutgers University Press, 1948) 77 p.
Two sketches, the second originally written in third person, edited here in first person, describing his life through his presidential campaign in 1856.

2757 Lincoln, Abraham   **1809-1865**
Abraham Lincoln: his speeches and writings. Preface by Carl Sandburg. Notes by Roy P. Basler. Cleveland: The World Publishing Co., 1946. 843 p.
A selection of Lincoln's best writings, mostly letters, as Lincoln wrote them, selected on the basis of "literary significance, historical importance, and human interest," with long introduction analyzing his development as a writer.

2758 Lincoln, Abraham   **1809-1865**
Abraham Lincoln's autobiography: with an account of its origin and history and additional biographical material by Robert Dale Richardson. Boston: The Beacon Press, 1947. 45 p.
A copy of the original manuscript (pp. 21-25) is printed in the context of correspondence between Lincoln and Jesse W. Fell, who persuaded him to write it in 1859. Edited by Fell's grandson.

2759 Lincoln, Abraham   **1809-1865**
Lincoln: his words and his world. Edited by Michael P. Dineen. Edited and illustrated by Robert L. Polley. Fort Atkinson, Wisconsin: Home Library, 1976. (Waukesha, Wisconsin: Country Beautiful Foundation/Hawthorn Books, 1965) 96 p.
This handsome volume consists of excerpts from Lincoln's letters and speeches on topics such as the Lincoln-Douglas debates, the Civil War, and his private life. Prints, cartoons, and photographs, many in color, enhance the text.

2760 Lincoln, Abraham   **1809-1865**
Lincoln and the Lincoln country: a Souvenir Guidebook containing a pictorial biography, illustrations, Lincoln's life in his own words, maps, handwritten manuscripts and letters, typical Lincoln humor, frameable Lincoln portrait. Illustrated. Springfield, Illinois: Octavo Press, 1968. 29 p.
Written in the third person in June, 1860, as a campaign autobiography, this tells of Lincoln's self-education, his migration from Indiana to Illinois, life in a log cabin and his storekeeping venture, but without the colorful anecdotes often associated with these tales of a folk hero.

2761 Lincoln, Abraham   **1809-1865**
Literary works of Abraham Lincoln. Introduction by David D. Anderson. Columbus, Ohio: Charles E. Merrill Publishing Co., 1970. 274 p.
While not strictly autobiography, this volume contains orders, directives, stump and courtroom speeches, letters and telegrams which lend insight into Lincoln's mystical vision of human experience. Materials cover the period 1824-1865.

2762 Lincoln, Abraham   **1809-1865**
The living Lincoln: the man, his mind, his times, and the war he fought, reconstructed from his own writings. Edited by Paul M. Angle and Earl Schenck Miers. New Brunswick: Rutgers University Press, 1955. 673 p. Index.

Selections from Lincoln's collected works including letters, speeches, and notes.

2763 *Lincoln, Evelyn (Norton)   **1912?-**
My twelve years with John F. Kennedy. New York: David McKay Co., Inc., 1965. 371 p.
Secretary to John F. Kennedy for twelve years while he was senator and president, Mrs. Lincoln writes of her experiences on the job and relates anecdotes that are both revealing and heartwarming.

2764 Lincoln, Murray Danforth   **1892-1966**
Vice-president in charge of revolution. As told to David Karp. New York: McGraw-Hill Book Co., Inc., 1960. 342 p. Index.
The story of his successful career as a creative and controversial business executive, who at time of writing was head of Nationwide Insurance and had served as first president of CARE, as president of the Cooperative League of the U.S.A., and in several major positions in the United Nations.

2765 *Lindbergh, Anne (Morrow)   **1906-**
Bring me a unicorn: diaries and letters of Anne Morrow Lindbergh, 1922-1928. Illustrated. New York: Harcourt Brace Jovanovich, Inc., 1972. 259 p. Index.
Diary entries and letters shaped into a continuous autobiography record the significant impressions and events of her life through 1928.

2766 *Lindbergh, Anne (Morrow)   **1906-**
The flower and the nettle. New York: Harcourt, Brace, Jovanovich, 1976. 605 p.
The fourth collection from her letters and diaries covers 1936-39, when she lived in England and Brittany, moving in European diplomatic circles with her famous husband and beginning to develop her career as a writer.

2767 *Lindbergh, Anne (Morrow)   **1906-**
Gift from the sea. New York: Random House Inc., 1955. 127 p.
Reflecting on her past during a private retreat on the beach, Lindbergh sees many aspects of her life as representative of American womanhood. She argues the need for cultivating a spiritual center, the need for solitude and privacy, in order to balance the complex demands of social obligation.

2768 *Lindbergh, Anne (Morrow)   **1906-**
Hour of gold, hour of lead: diaries and letters of Anne Morrow Lindbergh, 1929-1932. Illustrated. New York: Harcourt Brace Jovanovich, 1973. 340 p. Index.
This second volume of Anne Morrow Lindbergh's diaries and letters covers her early married life. She learned to fly, to navigate, to live in the glare of publicity. Then came the tragedy of the kidnapping and murder of their young son, which brought the bitterness and despair they overcame by the strength of their love and marriage.

2769 *Lindbergh, Anne (Morrow)   **1906-**
Locked rooms and open doors; diaries and letters of Anne Morrow Lindbergh, 1933-1935. Illustrated. New York: Harcourt Brace Jovanovich, 1974. 352 p. Index.
In this volume the author traces her life after the kidnapping of her son and all the attendant publicity. She and her husband undertook a pioneering flight around the North Atlantic to seek air routes to Europe. Her diary and letters reveal some of the hardships they endured—fear, homesickness, discomforts—but also the beauty, excitement, and adventure of the trip.

2770 *Lindbergh, Anne (Morrow)   **1906-**
War within and without: diaries and letters of Anne Morrow Lindbergh, 1939-1944. Illustrated. Second edition. (A limited first edition was privately printed). New York: Harcourt Brace Jovanovich, 1980. 471 p. Index.
Lindbergh is here an apologist for her husband, whom she says was scorned by the American public and went into a self-imposed two-year exile during World War II because of his alleged pro-Nazi sympathies. In reality, she claims, he was an isolationist; she vehemently denies Lindbergh's anti-Semitism.

2771 Lindbergh, Charles Augustus   **1902-1974**
Autobiography of values. Foreword by William Jovanovich and Judith A. Schiff. New York: Harcourt Brace Jovanovich, 1978. 423 p. Index.
Lindbergh reaches far beyond the notable achievements of his life to discuss many of the values of modern life—advances in science and technology, civilizations of the world, military priorities and weapons, the environment, freedom and responsibility of the individual, life and death, war, and marriage.

2772 Lindbergh, Charles Augustus   **1902-1974**
Spirit of St. Louis. New York: Charles Scribner's Sons, 1953. 562 p.
Primarily the story of his planning and execution of the first intercontinental flight, written over a period of fourteen years.

2773 Lindbergh, Charles Augustus 1902-1974
The wartime journals of Charles A. Lindbergh. Illustrated. New York: Harcourt Brace Jovanovich, Inc., 1970. 1038 p. Index.
During the World War II years, 1938-1945, Lindbergh studied European aviation, sought to alert Western leaders to military imbalance, and to lack of preparation, made a dedicated effort to keep the United States out of a war which threatened to destroy Western civilization. Although his views were controversial and sometimes misunderstood, he maintained his position with sincerity and determination.

2774 Linderman, Frank Bird 1869-1938
Montana adventure; the recollections of Frank B. Linderman. Illustrated. Edited by H.G. Merriam. Lincoln: University of Nebraska Press, 1968. 224 p. Index.
Although he served in the Montana legislature for two terms and was Assistant Secretary of State for Montana as well as a successful insurance agent, Linderman's first love was the great outdoors. He also devoted a large share of his life to the Indians, learning their lore and writing books and articles about them.

2775 Lindsay, John Vliet 1921-
Journey into politics; some informal observations. New York: Dodd, Mead & Co., 1967. 152 p. Index.
With the exception of the final chapter, written after his mayoralty campaign in 1965, Lindsay's book is devoted mainly to his seven years in Congress. The substance appeared first in articles, book reviews, and speeches he wrote between 1958 and 1965.

2776 Lingle, Walter Lee 1868-1956
Memories of Davidson College. Richmond, Virginia: John Knox Press, 1947. 157 p.
Lingle entered Davidson as a freshman in 1888, was president (1929-1941), and was asked by the trustees to write this memoir in retirement; it describes the life of the college and his own years as a part of its history.

2777 Lininger, Clarence 1880-1970?
The best war at the time. New York: Robert Speller and Sons, 1964. 272 p. Index.
In 1898, he volunteered for the infantry to serve in the war with Spain, and afterwards served in the Philippines, in Mexico in pursuit of Pancho Villa, and in World War I, working through the ranks to retire as a general.

2778 Linsley, Kenneth Williams
Advocate for God: a lawyer's experience in personal evangelism. Valley Forge, Pennsylvania: Judson Press, 1977. 80 p.
Linsley, a born-again Christian lawyer with the Judge Advocate General's staff of the U.S. Army, intends each chapter of this book of short, personal religious essays to be used as the basis for a prayer meeting or religious discussion group. They exhibit a belief in the efficacy of faith, prayer, and good works, as manifested in the lives of Linsley, his family, friends, and fellow worshippers.

2779 Lipphard, William Benjamin 1886-1971
Fifty years an editor. Valley Forge, Pennsylvania: The Judson Press, 1963. 256 p.
As editor of *Missions,* a Baptist magazine, he participated extensively in the organizational structure of the church and travelled widely to report on social and political, as well as religious events that concerned the church.

2780 *Lippincott, Sara Jane (Clarke) (Grace Greenwood, pseud.) 1823-1904
Haps and mishaps of a tour in Europe. Boston: Ticknor, Reed & Fields, 1854. 437 p.
A minutely detailed account of the author's tour of Europe, 1852-1853. Although she dines with Charles Dickens, Walter Savage Landor, and becomes close friends with Kossuth and Mazzini, this is less the story of a writer's visits to great people than an American tourist's diary of viewing the Queen, Parliament, and traipsing about the seven hills of Rome.

2781 Lipscomb, David 1831-1918
David Lipscomb: journalist in Texas, 1872. Biographical note by John Louis Robinson. Quanah, Wichita Falls, Texas: Nortex, 1973. 59 p. Index.
Preacher-journalist-educator Lipscomb wrote travel dispatches during his 1872 journey through Texas for the religious journal *Gospel Advocate.* His descriptions remind us of our pioneer heritage, of Indian fights, of railroad robber barons, of wide prairies and open spaces.

2782 Lipsky, Louis 1876-1963
Memoirs in profile. Foreword by Ben Halpern. Philadelphia: Jewish Publication Society of America, 1975. 669 p. Index.
Zionist leader Lipsky prefaces this collection of portraits of notable international Jewish leaders and essays on Zionism with a 57-page autobiography of his childhood in Rochester, N.Y., and his first twenty years as a Zionist newspaper editor and organizer in New York City. His love of the Yiddish theater stimulates him to see life in scenes and vignettes.

2783 Litchfield, Paul Weeks 1875-1959
Industrial voyage: my life as an industrial lieutenant. Illustrated by Richard Bartlett. Garden City, New York: Doubleday and Co., Inc., 1954. 347 p. Index.
In 1900 he moved from Boston to Akron, Ohio, to work as a young supervisor for Goodyear Tire and Rubber Co., then in its second year. Later, as Goodyear's Chairman of the Board, he pioneered in mass production and marketing, labor relations, and export business, his life story becoming emblematic of the rise of modern industry.

2784 Littauer, Vladimir Stanislas 1893-
Russian Hussar. Foreword by Bruce Lockhart. Illustrated. London: J.S. Allen & Co., 1965. 295 p. Index.
A colorful, witty account of Littauer's military career in the pre-revolutionary Russian army. Educated at the Nicholas Cavalry School, Littauer became an officer (cornet) in the Sumsky Hussars, a light cavalry division of the Russian Imperial Army. He describes typical training of the regiment (shooting, swordsmanship, horsemanship), their fighting in World War I, in East Prussia and in the Baltic Provinces, and their ultimate disorganization and dispersal after the Bolshevik Revolution in 1917.

2785 Little, Malcolm (Malcolm X) 1925-1965
The autobiography of Malcolm X. With the assistance of Alex Haley. Introduction by M.S. Handler. Epilogue by Alex Haley. New York: Grove, 1964. 455 p.
The remarkable story of Malcolm X, the outspoken, forceful Black Muslim leader who worked for Black separation and secession as the only acceptable way to liberate his people. In 1964, however, his attitude underwent a change and he broke from Elijah Muhammad, recognizing the advantages of Black integration into the American community.

2786 Littler, Gene Alec 1930-
The real score. With Jack Tobin. Illustrated. Waco, Texas: Word Books, 1976. 199 p.
A golfer writes of 25 years of golfing tournaments; he won the U.S. Open in 1961 and by September 1974, after 487 matches, had won over a million dollars. In 1972 he was operated on for melanoma of the upper arm. Although he feared he would never be able to play golf again, within sixteen months he was playing and winning.

2787 *Liu, Aimee 1953-
Solitaire. New York: Harper & Row, 1979. 215 p.
A bizarre story of Aimee Liu's self-deluding insistence that she was too "fat" and her near-starvation, which brought her weight down to the ninety pounds she maintained throughout high school. A victim of anorexia nervosa, her obsession with not eating was reinforced by a modeling career. As a Yale freshman, she finally decided there was more to life than not eating and snapped out of it.

2788 *Livermore, Mary Ashton Rice 1820-1905
The story of my life. Illustrated. Series: Women in America from Colonial Times to the 20th Century. New York: Arno Press, 1974. (Hartford, Connecticut: A.D. Worthington, 1899) 730 p.
Livermore presents a lively, penetrating account of the major social movements in which she participated during her long life: upbringing in intellectual Boston; living in a log cabin in western New York State; tutoring on a Southern plantation, where she became a firm opponent of slavery; working as one of the Commissioners of the U.S. Sanitary Commission during the Civil War; involvement in temperance, Women's Suffrage, and pacifistic activities thereafter. All this she combined with a fifty-year marriage and motherhood.

2789 Livermore, Robert 1876-1959
Bostonians and bullion; the journal of Robert Livermore, 1892-1915. Illustrated. Edited by Gene M. Gressley. Lincoln: University of Nebraska Press, 1968. 193 p.
Extracting from lengthy diary entries, Livermore, a mining engineer, wrote this journal covering his life to the termination of his Telluride residence in 1910. Later he added a chapter on Canada. Despite labor unrest and natural catastrophes such as avalanches, Livermore found his adventurous life a full and good one.

2790 *Livingston, Anne Home (Shippen) 1763-1841
Nancy Shippen, her journal book: the international romance of a young lady of fashion of colonial Philadelphia. Edited by Ethel Ames. Philadelphia: J.B. Lippincott Co., 1935. 348 p. Index.
A selection of journal entries and letters provides a record of the life, thought, and background of a family before, during, and after the Revolution. The writer was a belle and beauty of Philadelphia, the daughter of the aristocratic Shippen family of Virginia; her mother was a Lee of Stratford Hall, Virginia.

2791 Livingston, Robert R.   **1746-1813**
The original letters of Robert R. Livingston, 1801-1803: written during his negotiations of the purchase of Louisiana to which is prefixed a brief history of the Louisiana Purchase from original documents. Edward Alexander Parsons, author of history and editor of letters. New Orleans: The Louisiana Historical Society, 1953. 126 p.

Livingston, Minister Plenipotentiary to France, arrived in Paris in December 1801, to pursue for the next eighteen months advocacy of "the right of the United States to the free navigation of the Mississippi and the Right of Deposit of merchandise in Louisiana." He also investigated whether "Spain had actually retroceded Louisiana to France," and, if so, whether France would settle United States claims for injuries to American merchantmen. The letters on these subjects were exchanged between Livingston and Rufus King, the American minister in London.

2792 *Livingstone, Belle   **1875-1957**
Belle out of order. Preface by Cleveland Amory. New York: Henry Holt and Co., 1959. 341 p.

The curious story of a woman who left poverty on a Kansas farm for the stage, worked her way into society life in New York, London, Monte Carlo, and was notorious for her unconventional life.

2793 Lochner, Louis Paul   **1887-1975**
Always the unexpected: a book of reminiscences. New York: The Macmillan Co., 1956. 339 p. Index.

Winner of the Pulitzer Prize in 1939 for distinguished service as a foreign correspondent, he describes his career in journalism, including his long association with the Berlin Bureau of the Associated Press (1924-1942).

2794 Locke, Walter   **1875-1957**
This world, my home. Yellow Springs, Ohio: The Antioch Press, 1957. 171 p.

Born in a West Virginia log cabin, he spent his boyhood in Nebraska, where he began his career in journalism, and at 51 became editor of the Dayton (Ohio) *Daily News*. His personal history is also a social and spiritual history of the times.

2795 Lockwood, John C.   **1857-1928**
Custer fell first: the adventures of John C. Lockwood. Edited, compiled, with introduction by J.C. Ryan. Illustrated by S.M. Vena. San Antonio: The Naylor Co., 1966. 119 p.

Lockwood was a soldier at Custer's last stand, then became a stage-coach driver in the Dakota Territory and Idaho. As a consequence of protecting a beautiful woman passenger from her drunken husband, he fled from the ensuing fracas, wanted by federal marshals. A series of coincidences led him to encounter the damsel in San Francisco, save her life, be exonerated by the law, and marry her.

2796 Lodge, Henry Cabot   **1850-1924**
Early memories. Leisure Class in America Series. New York: Arno Press, 1975. (New York: Charles Scribner's Sons, 1913) 362 p. Index.

Lodge discusses the first thirty years of his life, focusing on his illustrious ancestors ("The Olympians"), his Boston upbringing and education at Harvard, two trips to Europe, and his acquaintance with a myriad of New England politicians and literati. Lodge writes with perspicacity and includes many letters from eminent New Englanders.

2797 Lodge, Henry Cabot   **1902-**
The storm has many eyes; a personal narrative. Illustrated. New York: W.W. Norton, 1973. 272 p.

Lodge has served his country in a variety of posts: senator from Massachusetts, Ambassador to Vietnam and to Germany, U.S. Representative to the United Nations, envoy to the Vatican, G.O.P. vice-presidential candidate in 1960. He sees the working of politics and government with the special perspective of his experience.

2798 Lodge, Henry Cabot
see also **Roosevelt, Theodore**

2799 Lodge, John Christian   **1862-1950**
I remember Detroit. Detroit: Wayne University Press, 1949. 208 p.

The former mayor of Detroit recalls his long, active personal and professional life in that city.

2800 Logan, Joshua Lockwood   **1908-**
Movie stars, real people, and me. Illustrated. New York: Delacorte Press, 1978. 368 p. Index.

Logan discusses his career as a film director and theatrical producer from his first movie, *Picnic*, to 1977. He tells anecdotes, some hilarious, some poignant, of hundreds of actors on set and off, focusing on Marilyn Monroe, Kim Novak, Marlon Brando, Bette Davis, and others. He is realistically unsentimental about himself and his work.

2801 Lois, George   **1931-**
George, be careful; a Greek florist's kid in the roughhouse world of advertising. With Bill Pitts. Illustrated. New York: Saturday Review Press, 1972. 245 p.

In rapid-fire prose laced with street language from his Bronx boyhood, a self-made millionaire tells how he made it big in the advertising world, rising from the Greek florist's son among "lace-curtain" Irish to the brain behind Volkswagen and Xerox ad campaigns and political advertiser for Jacob Javits and Robert F. Kennedy.

2802 Lomax, John Avery   **1867-1948**
Adventures of a ballad hunter. New York: The Macmillan Co., 1947. 302 p.

Recalls life as an avid ballad hunter since boyhood in Texas, including his discovery of Leadbelly in 1934 and his collection, with his son Alan, of over 10,000 folk songs now housed in the Library of Congress.

2803 Lombardo, Guy   **1902-1977**
Auld acquaintance. With Jack Altschul. Introduction by Jules Stein. New York: Ballantine Books, 1976. (New York: Doubleday, 1975) 385 p.

A well-written account of Lombardo's successful, joyous career as a bandleader, "playing for people who demanded the melody of their favorite songs and the beat that encouraged them to dance," which provides an overview of "big band" dance music in the 1930's and 40's. A portrait of Lombardo's warm extended family and a chapter on his hobby, speedboat racing.

2804 London, Jack   **1876-1916**
Jack London, American rebel: a collection of his social writings, together with an extensive study of the man and his times. Edited by Philip S. Foner. New York: The Citadel Press, 1947. 533 p.

Included with fiction, articles, and essays are some autobiographical writings—selections from *John Barleycorn, My Life in the Underworld,* and *The People of the Abyss,* as well as "How I Became a Socialist," and "What Life Means to Me."

2805 London, Jack   **1876-1916**
John Barleycorn: or alcoholic memoirs. Introduction by Arthur Calder-Marshall. Cambridge, Massachusetts: Robert Bentley, Inc., 1978. (New York: Century Co., 1913) 210 p.

The major characters in this "alcoholic memoir" are London, laborer, sailor, and writer; his wife, Charmian; and "John Barleycorn," alcoholism personified. Although London first got drunk at five, again at seven, and drank steadily throughout his life, he claims he was not an alcoholic. Nevertheless, London was increasingly dependent on drink and continued to write his self-imposed thousand words a day, often while drunk.

2806 London, Jack   **1876-1916**
Letters from Jack London, containing an unpublished correspondence between London and Sinclair Lewis. Edited by King Hendricks and Irving Shepard. New York: The Odyssey Press, 1965. 502 p. Index.

A prolific writer, who by the time he died at forty had written fifty books plus many newspaper articles, London also wrote thousands of letters. This selection aims to "create a fairly accurate image of London, his intellectual and physical vigor, his impetuousness, his dreams and doubts and frustrations."

2807 London, Jack   **1876-1916**
No mentor but myself: a collection of articles, essays, reviews, and letters on writing and writers. Edited by Dale L. Walker. Foreword by Howard Lachtman. Port Washington, New York: Kennikat Press, 1979. 197 p.

In this collection of articles, essays, letters, prefaces, reviews, and excerpts from his fiction, London comments on "the economics of authorship, the demands of editors, the expectations of readers, and the specifications of critics." He also considers his authorial image, reader psychology, and the conflict between truth and fiction. London derives particular pleasure from shaping a plausible, profitable tale and from the freedom his literary career affords his life.

2808 London, Jack   **1876-1916**
The road. Edited by King Hendricks. Santa Barbara: Peregrin Publishers, Inc., 1970. (New York: Macmillan, 1907) 224 p.

London recounts his experiences as a hobo in 1894, jumping freights and riding the rods—and even the cowcatcher—cross country, evading "bulls" (policemen), hostile moralists who want to make him work, and organized society generally. He was arrested and jailed a month for vagrancy in Niagara Falls without a lawyer, trial, or other legal protection. Hobos, though social outcasts, have their own culture, which London describes in vivid detail.

2809 *Lone Dog, Louise   **1915?-**
Strange journey: the vision life of a psychic Indian woman. Healdsburg, California: Naturegraph Books, 1964. 68 p.

Beginning with a discussion of her Mohawk-Delaware heritage, she writes of the early encounters she had with ghosts and spirits which encouraged her development as a psychic.

2810 Long, Breckinridge   **1881-1958**
The war diary of Breckinridge Long; selections from the years 1939-1944. Selected and edited by Fred L. Israel. Lincoln: University of Nebraska Press, 1966. 410 p. Index.

Having served in various State Department positions and as Ambassador to Italy, Long became Special Assistant Secretary of State to handle emergency war matters in 1939, and in 1940 Assistant Secretary of State, a policy-making post. His diary presents a primary source of diplomatic history in an exciting period of American and world history.

2811 Long, John Davis   1838-1915
The journal of John D. Long. Edited by Margaret Long. Rindge, New Hampshire: Richard R. Smith Publisher, Inc., 1956. 363 p. Index.

Based on his 24-volume journal, this edition gives a rounded portrait of the boyhood and adult life of a popular statesman who was a three-term Governor of Massachusetts and Secretary of the Navy under McKinley.

2812 *Long, Mary Alves   b.1864
High time to tell it. Durham, North Carolina: Duke University Press, 1950. 314 p.

Primarily a recollection of her childhood on a plantation in North Carolina and her extended family, with a brief description of her work for the League of Nations.

2813 *Longfellow, Fanny (Appleton)   1817-1861
Mrs. Longfellow: selected letters and journals of Fanny Appleton Longfellow. Edited by Edward Wagenknecht. New York: Longmans, Green and Co., 1956. 255 p. Index.

The life records of Mrs. Henry Wadsworth Longfellow, providing a remarkable portrait of her experience in the intellectual aristocracy of Boston.

2814 Longfellow, Henry Wadsworth   1807-1882
The letters of Henry Wadsworth Longfellow. Edited by Andrew Hilen. Cambridge: The Belknap Press of Harvard University Press, 1966. 2v. Index.

Although he disliked writing letters, Longfellow wrote, by the time he was 36, an estimated 1200, 805 of which are included in these volumes. The first volume, 1814-1836, covers the years until he assumed the chair as Smith Professor of Modern Languages at Harvard and reveals a young, well-mannered man of keen and expansive mind, but does not foreshadow his later poetic ambition or accomplishment. Volume II, 1837-1843, includes letters from the beginning of his Harvard tenure and a trip to Europe through his marriage to Frances Appleton.

2815 Longfellow, Henry Wadsworth   1807-1882
Life of Henry Wadsworth Longfellow: with extracts from his journals and correspondence. Edited with biography by Samuel Longfellow. Illustrated. New York: Greenwood Press, 1969. (Boston: Houghton Mifflin, 1891) 3v. Index.

Vol. I consists of a biography of poet Longfellow's first 35 years, when he was educated at Bowdoin College, traveled in Spain, Italy, and Germany, and taught at Bowdoin and Harvard, heavily documented with correspondence and journal entries. Volumes II and III, which cover the rest of Longfellow's life, are comprised largely of impressionistic journals and letters, many with humorous or pithy observations: "I think that poems had better be left as they are written; their imperfections are often only imaginary."

2816 Longo, Gabriel Anthony   1926-
Spoiled priest; the autobiography of an ex-priest. New Hyde Park, New York: University Books, Inc., 1966. 252 p.

The moving, frank story of a priest from his boyhood through his seminary days, his ordination, his years in the priesthood, and his difficult decision to leave.

2817 *Longo, Joan Marie   1935-
I married a priest. New York: Grosset & Dunlap, 1969. 242 p.

Longo writes briskly and candidly about her experience as the wife of a former Catholic priest. Both from an Italian Catholic heritage, they have been ostracized by their families and church members, as well as praised and asked for guidance by other priests desiring to leave the church. Her account is a mixture of exposé and loving concern.

2818 Longstreet, Stephen   1907-
Boy in the Model-T: a journey in the just gone past. Illustrated by the author. New York: Simon and Schuster, 1956. 309 p.

At twelve, his mother and grandfather took him on a cross-country trip in a Model-T. His story of their journey is vivid and nostalgic, while portraying a significant stage in his maturity.

2819 Longyear, Edmund Joseph   1864-1954
Mesabi pioneer: reminiscences of Edmund J. Longyear. Edited by Grace Lee Nute. St. Paul, Minnesota: The Minnesota Historical Society, 1951. 116 p. Index.

Recollections of a mining engineer's exploration for iron ore in Minnesota's Mesabi Range and formation of his own company, 1890-1911.

2820 *Loos, Anita   1893-1981
Cast of thousands. Illustrated. New York: Grosset & Dunlap, 1977. 280 p. Index.

With more photographs than copy, this volume celebrates the glitter and glamour of Hollywood from silent films to the fifties. At times Loos gossips about star personalities and the highlights and pitfalls of many Hollywood careers.

2821 *Loos, Anita   1893-1981
A girl like I. New York: Ballantine Books, 1975. (New York: The Viking Press, 1966) 275 p.

An amusing story of her climb up the ladder of success from the early days of silent films onward. Loos became known for the fact that she was one of the first writers to make fun of sex, especially in her character, Lorelei Lee, of *Gentlemen Prefer Blondes.*

2822 *Loos, Anita   1893-1981
Kiss Hollywood good-by. New York: The Viking Press, 1974. 213 p.

The second volume of Loos' autobiography carries the story of her adventures beyond her first stay in Hollywood to the "outside world," where she enjoyed great celebrity in literary and social circles. Back in Hollywood in 1931 she worked with Irving Thalberg and continued her irreverent observations. She wrote novels, plays, and two hundred screenplays.

2823 *Lopez, Nancy   1957-
The education of a woman golfer. With Peter Schwed. Illustrated. New York: Simon and Schuster, 1979. 191 p.

Professional golfer Nancy Lopez describes her education, which since age eight has largely been through golfing. She includes the physical and psychological aspects of the game, the friends and rivals in women's golf, and her earnings, $200,000 in 1978.

2824 Lopez, Vincent   1895-1975
Lopez speaking: an autobiography by Vincent Lopez. New York: Citadel Press, 1960. 351 p.

Lopez describes his career as an entertainer which he began as a jazz and ragtime pianist, but shifted in his twenties to leading dance bands in posh New York hotels and nightclubs. He discusses a variety of love affairs, a failed first marriage, and an unstable life complicated by gambling, until numerology helped him become born again and he achieved a stable marriage and career.

2825 Lord, Daniel Aloysius   1888-1955
Played by ear. Introduction by R. Bakewell Morrison. Chicago: Loyola University Press, 1956. 383 p.

A Jesuit priest who wrote thirty adult books, 48 children's books along with booklets, pamphlets, plays, pageants, and musical compositions, here writes episodes of his own life. Although he does not write solely for adolescents, he has a youthful outlook and some of his chapter headings reflect his purposes, "To a young man considering his vocation," "To a young hospital nun," and "To a young Jesuit about to be ordained."

2826 *Lose, M. Phyllis
No job for a lady: autobiography. As told to Daniel Mannix. New York: Macmillan Publishing, 1979. 217 p.

Lose enthusiastically explains how her early love of horses led her to the job of "exercise boy" at Garden State Race Track at fifteen, and then through grueling veterinarian's training at the University of Pennsylvania. She specializes in horses and has been the veterinarian to the Barnum and Bailey Circus and the Philadelphia police force. She has invented several major techniques for equine surgery and established her own equine clinic and hospital.

2827 *Lothrop, Eleanor (Bachman)   1901?-1963
Throw me a bone: what happens when you marry an archaeologist. New York: McGraw-Hill Book Co., Inc., 1948. 234 p.

The wife of Samuel Lothrop describes her experiences traveling with him to various fieldwork sites in Central and South America, often with strong reactions to primitive conditions, laced with her sharp sense of humor.

2828 *Louchheim, Katie Scofield   1903-
By the political sea. Garden City, New York: Doubleday & Co., Inc., 1970. 293 p. Index.

As vice chairman of the Democratic National Committee and later as a State Department official, the author gives an insider's view of political campaigns and off-year maneuverings from 1948 to the late 60's. Among other concerns, the author expresses her efforts to bring more women into political life.

2829 *Loud, Patricia (Russell)   1926-
Pat Loud; a woman's story. With Nora Johnson. New York: Coward, McCann & Geoghegan, Inc., 1974. 223 p.

Pat Loud, the wife on the nationally televised *An American Family,* tells what went wrong with her dream. Her affluent, successful marriage and happy family failed, leaving her to confront her own self-doubts and to build a new life.

2830 Louis, Joe (Joseph Louis Barrow)   1914-1981
The Joe Louis story. Edited by Chester L. Washington and Haskell Cohen. Illustrated. New York: Grosset & Dunlap, 1953. (New York: Duell, Sloan & Pearce, 1947) 197 p.

Boxer Joe Louis, in sports-page jargon and dialogue that must have been concocted by his ghost writers, narrates his rise from poverty to wealth and fame as a heavyweight boxer, including victories over Max Schmeling (1938), Lou Nova (1941), and Billy Conn (1946). He retired from boxing in 1951, defeated by Rocky Marciano.

2831 Louis, Joe (Joseph Louis Barrow)   1914-1981
My life story. New York: Duell, Sloan and Pearce, 1947. 188 p.

World heavyweight-boxing champion writes of his early life, training for the ring, service in World War II, and the championship.

2832 *Love, Bessie (Juanita Horton)   1898-
From Hollywood with love. Introduction by Kevin Brownlow. Illustrated. Filmography. London: Elm Tree Books, Hamish Hamilton, 1977. 160 p. Index.

This account of the actress's life, emphasizing her career in quality silent films (*Intolerance*) followed by mediocre talkies (*Battle Beneath the Earth*), is epitomized by Love's comment, "Having begun at the top, by the early twenties I was working my way down, taking anything to keep the wolves from whelping on my doorstep." She had a career in vaudeville until *The Broadway Melody* gave her a start in talking films. In 1935 she began an acting career on stage in London.

2833 Love, Nat   b.1854
The life and adventures of Nat Love, better known in the cattle country as Deadwood Dick, by himself. Illustrated. New York: Arno Press, 1968. (Los Angeles, 1907) 162 p.

Born a slave, Love headed West after the Civil War and led a rambunctious, adventurous life as cowpuncher. There, he says, he met no discrimination, but took part in wild escapades, amazing feats, and battles with wild animals, Indians, and other cowmen. When the wide-open West calmed down, he became a Pullman porter, the only kind of position open to Negroes at the time.

2834 Lovecraft, Howard Phillips   1890-1937
Lovecraft at last. Preface by Willis Conover. Foreword by Harold Taylor. Illustrated. Arlington, Virginia: Carrollton, Clark, 1975. 272 p. Index.

In 1936 Conover, as a teenage horror story fan, initiated a correspondence with H.P. Lovecraft, whose stories in *Weird Tales* he admired. Their correspondence, reproduced in facsimile, reveals that Lovecraft treated Conover as an adult and Conover addressed Lovecraft as an equal and an astute critic as well as practitioner of his literary medium.

2835 Lovecraft, Howard Phillips   1890-1937
Selected letters, 1911-1924. Edited by August Derleth and Donald Wandrei. Sauk City, Wisconsin: Arkham House, 1965. 362 p.

A prolific writer of often long, but always direct and spontaneous letters, Lovecraft used them as a kind of conversation with his friends discussing his childhood, his travels, his experiences, his nightmares. He is known chiefly for his poems, articles on astronomy, and his macabre tales of fantasy and terror. This volume prints his letters up to the time of his wife's illness and the impending dissolution of his marriage.

2836 Lovecraft, Howard Phillips   1890-1937
Selected letters, 1925-1929. Edited by August Derleth and Donald Wandrei. Sauk City, Wisconsin: Arkham House, 1968. 359 p.

This volume covers the period of his happy return to Providence from New York and the broadening of his interests in outlook and tolerance. He wrote more tales, did revision work, and expanded his correspondence until it nearly precluded all other activities.

2837 *Lovelace, Linda   1948-
Ordeal. With Mike McGrady. Secaucus, New Jersey: Citadel Press, 1980. 253 p.

A star of pornographic films describes her life as a modern Gothic horror tale—physical beatings, threats of permanent disfigurement, several perversions, and finally her escape through the love of a good man and her faith in God.

2838 Loveridge, Arthur   1891-
Tomorrow's a holiday (Kesho siku kuu). New York: Harper & Brothers Publishers, 1947. 278 p.

A naturalist describes his field work in Africa, the specimens he collected, the explorations he made to find them, and his interactions with Africans who helped or observed him in his travels.

2839 Lovett, Cummings Samuel   1917-
C.S. Lovett, maranatha man: an autobiography. Illustrated. Baldwin Park, California: Personal Christianity, 1978. 232 p.

Lovett began his career in Christianity as a Baptist preacher, moved into evangelism with a series of books and pamphlets aimed at establishing "Jesus' boot camp" among his followers, and finally founded Personal

Christianity, "a worldwide ministry." The child of a broken home, he says he found in God "the joy of having a real father at last."

2840 Lovett, Robert Morss   1870-1956
All our years: autobiography. New York: The Viking Press, 1948. 373 p. Index.

Richly detailed life of an outstanding man of letters, professor of English at the University of Chicago for 45 years, president of the socialist "League for Industrial Democracy" for 20 years, a writer and editor involved with many well-known figures in literary and public life. Accused in 1943 of "Un-American activities" by the House Committee on Appropriations; cleared.

2841 *Lowell, Amy   1874-1925
see ***Ayscough, Florence Wheelock**

2842 Lowell, James Russell   1819-1891
Scholar-friends: letters of Francis James Child and James Russell Lowell. Edited by M.A. DeWolfe Howe and G.W. Cottrell, Jr. Westport, Connecticut: Greenwood Press, 1970. (Cambridge: Harvard University Press, 1952) 84 p.

The letters between the scholar, Francis Child, and the poet, James Russell Lowell, deal with such topics as scholarship, literature, and travel to Europe. Both men had ties to Cambridge, Massachusetts, and their letters frequently originated from there.

2843 Lowenberg, Henry A.   1903-1971
Until proven guilty: forty years as criminal defense counsel. As told to Robin Moore. Boston: Little, Brown and Co., 1971. 236 p.

Lowenberg describes cases he has had a part in, including some unusual or amusing ones. He offers his observations and opinions concerning several types of criminal behavior—drug addiction, gambling, prostitution—and social questions, such as capital punishment and organized crime.

2844 Lowie, Robert Harry   1883-1957
Robert H. Lowie: ethnologist. Berkeley: University of California Press, 1959. 198 p.

A prominent professor of anthropology at the University of California writes about field work, its methods and applications, using his experience as illustrative material.

2845 *Lowry, Ira Marie
Second landing. Philadelphia: Dorrance & Co., 1974. 53 p.

The author tells of her nursing experiences helping TB patients and of her own illness from tuberculosis which she eventually overcame.

2846 Lubbock, Francis Richard   1815-1905
Six decades in Texas; or memoirs of Francis Richard Lubbock, Confederate governor of Texas. Edited by C.W. Raines. Austin, Texas: Pemberton Press, 1969. (Austin, Texas: B.C. Jones & Co., 1900) 685 p. Index.

In addition to autobiographical material, Lubbock recollects much of Texas history, descriptions of war, public events, and adventure with a strong thread of politics. Appendixes include poetic tributes on the death of his brother, his own 1891 speech to the legislature on Jefferson Davis, and a report on the Texas penitentiary.

2847 Lucas, George Aloysius   1824-1909
The diary of George A. Lucas: an American art agent in Paris, 1857-1909. Transcribed with introduction and foreword by Lilian M.C. Randall. Illustrated. Princeton, New Jersey: Princeton University Press, 1979. 2v. Index.

Lucas's diaries begin loquaciously in 1852, but most of those dealing with his 52-year career in Paris as an agent for American art dealers and collectors are terse and abbreviated. They provide valuable information on the Paris art market of that time (1857-1909), when he bought vast collections for Samuel Avery, William T. Waters, John T. Johnston, and William H. Vanderbilt.

2848 Lucas, Lawrence   1933-
Black priest/White church; catholics and racism. New York: Random House, 1970. 270 p.

A Black Catholic priest, Lucas writes about his life in order to prove his contention that the Catholic Church is a white racist institution and to offer suggestions for righting the wrongs and incorporating equality into the principals and practices of the Church, which he loves despite its failings.

2849 Luce, Henry Robinson   1898-1967
Ideas of Henry Luce. Edited with an introduction by John K. Jessup. New York: Atheneum, 1969. 405 p. Index.

Taken from speeches, letters, and published articles and arranged to define the range of Luce's serious interests and the messages he wanted to communicate, this book attempts to present Luce's thoughts on journalism, politics, law, business, art, religion, and people.

2850 Luckey, Henry Carl   **1868-1956**
Eighty-five American years: memoirs of a Nebraska Congressman. New York: Exposition Press, 1955. 230 p.

The son of German immigrants, Luckey grew up on a Nebraska farm; he farmed and taught school before completing degrees in law and political science at the University of Nebraska. He describes with considerable detail his years as a businessman, his travels, the role of Congress during his terms, 1934-1938, his views of the European political situation as he observed it on a trip in 1937, and his opinions of America in 1953.

2851 Luckman, Sidney   **1916-**
Luckman at quarterback: football as a sport and a career. Chicago: Ziff-Davis Publishing Co., 1949. 233 p.

Recollections of his life in football by a quarterback who achieved renown at Columbia and went on to play professionally with the Bears. He discusses the development of strategies such as the T-formation and the interaction between college and professional team personnel.

2852 Luisi, Gerard   **1884-1962**
How to catch 5000 thieves. And Charles Samuels. New York: The Macmillan Co., 1962. 285 p.

The "happily violent life" of an insurance detective, who describes his successful interest in the business as well as some of its fraudulent practice.

2853 *Lumpkin, Katharine DuPre   **1897-**
Making of a southerner. New York: Alfred A. Knopf, 1947. 247 p.

Detailed account of her Southern family history from the early 1800's, through her own childhood at the turn of the century, college education in Georgia and New York, where she began to understand segregation and her Southern heritage very differently.

2854 Lundborg, Louis Billings   **1901?-**
Up to now. Illustrated. New York: W.W. Norton, 1978. 241 p.

The chairman of the board of the Bank of America uses this narrative as an implicit illustration that hard work and belief in the American ideals of honesty, fair play, and perseverance can enable even the most humble people to attain success. He focuses on his homesteading childhood in Billings, Montana, his college years (three at Stanford), and his career as a fund raiser, director of the California Chamber of Commerce, and banker. His book vividly captures the spirit of the American frontier and the more benign aspects of American capitalism.

2855 Lundy, Benjamin   **1789-1839**
The life, travels and opinions of Benjamin Lundy. Compiled by Thomas Earle. New York: Negro Universities Press, 1969. (Philadelphia: William D. Parrish, 1847) 316 p.

Lundy was known principally through his devotion to the cause of emancipation, one of the most energetic, indefatigable, and self-sacrificing pioneers in anti-slavery agitation, traveling widely for the cause. This book was compiled from his letters and publications adapted into narrative form "under the direction and on behalf of his children."

2856 *Lutes, Della Thompson   **d.1942**
The country kitchen. Boston: Little, Brown and Co., 1938. (1936) 264 p.

Culinary memories of her rural southern Michigan childhood. Chapters deal with Sunday-school picnics, the county fair, old-style breakfast, and Christmas dinner; an index to the recipes is included.

2857 *Lyde, Elsie (Leslie)   **1881-1966**
Trustable and preshus friends. Edited with prologue by Jane Douglass. Foreword by Julie Harris. Illustrated. New York: Harcourt Brace Jovanovich, 1977. 95 p.

Elsie Leslie, America's foremost child actress of the 1890's, starred in *Little Lord Fauntleroy* and the *The Prince and the Pauper*, playing both major roles. She kept a precocious diary so well-written one suspects adult alteration and corresponded with notables about her work, including Mark Twain and Helen Keller. Her only comeuppance was from Oliver Wendell Holmes, who at her request criticized her poetry and said "if you MUST write I strongly advise you to keep to prose."

2858 Lyle, John H.   **1882-1964**
Dry and lawless years. Englewood Cliffs, New Jersey: Prentice-Hall, Inc., 1960. 311 p. Index.

During the Prohibition era in Chicago he was called "Fighting Judge Lyle" because he used the legal system as a forceful weapon against Al Capone and the Mafia syndicate that boasted it "owned" the city. His book describes his ongoing battle during and since the 1920's with dramatic stories of the corruption by major Mafia figures and the public outrage he helped to generate against them.

2859 Lyman, Chester Smith   **1814-1890**
Around the Horn to the Sandwich Islands and California 1845-1850; being a personal record. Illustrated. Edited by Frederick J. Teggart. Freeport, New York: Books for Libraries Press, 1971. (New Haven: Yale University Press, 1924) 328 p.

Lyman's three-fold record includes a seven-months' voyage around

Cape Horn to Hawaii, a year's stay in the Sandwich Islands, and a nearly three-year stay in California. It provides exact and detailed descriptions of life, customs, natural scenery, the discovery of gold, and other events seen through his scientist's eye.

2860 Lyman, Theodore   **1833-1897**
Meade's headquarters, 1863-1865; letters of Colonel Theodore Lyman from the Wilderness to Appomattox. Selected and edited by George R. Agassiz. Freeport, New York: Books for Libraries Press, 1970. (Boston: Atlantic Monthly Press, 1922) 371 p. Index.

A member of General Meade's staff commanding the Army of the Potomac, Colonel Lyman wrote these letters to his wife from the front, giving vivid descriptions of Army life.

2861 Lynch, John Roy   **1847-1939**
Reminiscences of an active life; the autobiography of John Roy Lynch. Edited with introduction by John Hope Franklin. Chicago: University of Chicago Press, 1970. 521 p. Index.

A surprisingly restrained treatment of life in a slave family and the rise to prominance as a Black politician in the Reconstruction period, this autobiography of the first Black to be elected to Congress from Mississippi is intended by the author to alter what he sees as incorrect views of the Reconstruction and the situation of Blacks in the post-Civil War South.

2862 Lynk, Miles Vandahurst   **1871-1957?**
Sixty years of medicine: the life and times of Dr. Miles V. Lynk; an autobiography. Memphis, Tennessee: The Twentieth Century Press, 1951. 125 p. Index.

A Black doctor writes of his life, the history of the University of West Tennessee which he founded, and contemporary medical policy.

2863 *Lynn, Loretta (Webb)   **1935?-**
Loretta Lynn: coal miner's daughter. With George Vecsey. Illustrated. Chicago: Henry Regnery Company, 1976. 204 p. Index.

She "waded out of the mud" in Butcher's Holler, Kentucky, to become the "first lady of country music." She reflects on her career, her unorthodox marriage to Doolittle Lynn, her religion, and the four babies she had while still a teenager.

2864 Lyon, Ben
see ***Daniels, Bebe [Virginia]**

2865 Lyon, Cecil Burton   **1903-**
Lyon's share. New York: Vantage, 1973. 266 p.

Raised in New York City and a graduate of Harvard University, Lyon entered the Foreign Service which took him to Hong Kong, Tokyo, Peking, Chile, and Paris.

2866 Lyon, John   **b.1814**
John Lyon, nurseryman and plant hunter, and his journal, 1799-1814. Edited by Joseph and Nesta Ewan. Transactions of the American Philosophical Society, New series, Vol. 53, Part 2. Philadelphia: American Philosophical Society, 1963. 69 p. Index.

A horticulturist's record of ten trips along the Central and South Atlantic states (pp. 15-54) edited in the context of trade and the times.

2867 Lyons, Lorenzo   **1807-1886**
Makua Laiana: the story of Lorenzo Lyons, lovingly known to Hawaiians as Ka Makua Laiana, Haku Mele o ka Aina Mauna (Father Lyons, lyric poet of the mountain country). Compiled with prologue by Emma Lyons Doyle. Illustrated by F. Gordon Chadwick. Revised and enlarged edition. Honolulu, Hawaii: Emma Lyons Doyle (printed by Advertiser Publishing Co.), 1953. (1945) 278 p. Index.

Lyon's own story, told largely in diary form, is supplemented with accounts by his first wife, Betsey, with letters to and from other family members. Together they form an interesting narrative of the life of one of the early missionaries in Hawaii, where he lived at Waimea, established a church and a post office, and where his second wife taught school (English and Hawaiian).

2868 *Lyons, Ruth   **1907?-**
Remember with me. Illustrated. Introduction by John T. Murphy. Garden City, New York: Doubleday & Co., Inc., 1969. 272 p.

Beginning with a local Cincinnati radio show, she developed her routine into one of the most popular early daytime television programs, *The Fifty-Fifty Club.* Her book recalls many of the celebrities who visited her show. It ends with a moving tribute to her daughter who died of cancer at 21.

2869 *Mabie, Catharine Louise Roe   **b.1872**
Congo cameos. Foreword by Kenneth Scott Latourette. Illustrated. Philadelphia: Judson Press, 1952. 191 p.

Mabie, a Baptist medical missionary with an M.D. from Rush Medical College, served for 43 years at Kimpese, Belgian Congo, dispensing Christianity along with treatment for dysentery, eye infections, malaria, and other diseases and afflictions. She includes considerable information about native customs and particular tribespeople whom she describes with affection.

2870 *Mabie, Janet   **1893-1961**
Heaven on earth. New York: Harper and Brothers, 1951. 242 p.
  Recollections of her childhood summers in Northfield, Massachusetts, as a minister's child with a love of nature.

2871 *Mabuce, Ethel Lincy   **b.1886**
I always wore my topi: the Burma letters of Ethel Mabuce, 1916-1921. Edited with introduction by Lucille Griffith. University: University of Alabama Press, 1974. 336 p. Index.
  Accepted for an overseas assignment by the Women's Foreign Missionary Society of the Methodist Episcopal Church after her graduation in 1916 from Taylor University, she traveled to Burma and served as an evangelical missionary until 1921. Her letters describe her delight in the people, customs, foods, and country of the Burmese, conveying a sense of adventure in an exotic land.

2872 MacArthur, Douglas   **1880-1964**
Duty, honor, country: a pictorial autobiography. New York: McGraw-Hill Book Co., 1965. 218 p.
  The vivid and varied life of MacArthur is told here both in his words and with over 200 photographs.

2873 MacArthur, Douglas   **1880-1964**
Reminiscences. New York: McGraw-Hill Book Co., 1964. 438 p. Index.
  General MacArthur's story of his life and military career dedicated to his country gives insight into the issues which influenced the course of World War II, the occupation of Japan, the Korean War. He gives his side of the disagreements with President Truman which led to MacArthur's removal from command and return to the United States.

2874 MacArthur, Douglas   **1880-1964**
A soldier speaks: public papers and speeches of General of the Army Douglas MacArthur; prepared for the U.S. Military Academy, West Point, N.Y., by the Department of Military Art and Engineering. Edited by Major Vorin E. Whan, Jr. Introduction by General Carlos P. Romulo. New York: Praeger Publishing, 1965. 367 p.
  This collection demonstrates MacArthur's life-long concern for the educational program at West Point, his intense patriotism, his Christian faith, his efforts in the Philippine liberation, his commitment to a strong, well-defended America and "the most vital quality of Americanism—economic freedom." In two world wars, in the Philippines, Korea, Europe, and finally in retirement, MacArthur's speeches tell of a soldier's soldier who acknowledges that "history is the only competent teacher."

2875 Macartney, Clarence Edward Noble   **1879-1957**
The making of a minister: the autobiography of Clarence E. Macartney. Edited with introduction by J. Clyde Henry. Foreword by Frank E. Gaebelin. Great Neck, New York: Channel Press, Inc., 1961. 224 p.
  After a brief recollection of his boyhood in Beaver Falls, Pennsylvania, a Presbyterian minister writes of his pastorates in Philadelphia and Pittsburgh and his major debate with Harry Emerson Fosdick about Fundamentalist principles in the church.

2876 Macaulay, Neill
A rebel in Cuba; an American's memoir. Chicago: Quadrangle Books, 1970. 199 p. Index.
  An American guerrilla fighter in the Cuban Rebel Army under Fidel Castro writes of his experiences, the hopes of the men who fought, the power struggle that ensued following the overthrow of the Batista dictatorship, the differences between the urban revolutionaries and the provincial guerrillas, and his own eventual disillusionment.

2877 MacCampbell, Donald
Don't step on it—it might be a writer; reminiscences of a literary agent. Los Angeles: Sherbourne Press, Inc., 1972. 190 p. Index.
  The personal record of a literary agent offers insights into an often misunderstood occupation, providing an amusing and instructive look at authors and publishers as well.

2878 MacCracken, Henry Noble   **1880-1970**
Family on Gramercy Park. New York: Charles Scribner's Sons, 1949. 213 p.
  Lively story of boyhood in Manhattan by the man who was president of Vassar, 1915-1946. His father was Mitchell Henry McCracken, Chancellor of New York University.

2879 *MacDonald, Betty Bard   **1908-1958**
Anybody can do anything. Philadelphia: J.B. Lippincott Co., 1950. 256 p.
  Humorous family adventures and misadventures of the author of *The Egg and I* egged on particularly by her sister Mary.

2880 *MacDonald, Betty Bard   **1908-1958**
Onions in the stew. Philadelphia: J.B. Lippincott, 1955. 256 p.

Amusing, homey stories of her life on an island with clamming, beachcombing, gardening, pets, and neighbors furnishing the subjects of individual chapters.

2881 *MacDonald, Betty Bard   **1908-1958**
The plague and I. Philadelphia: J.B. Lippincott Co., 1948. 254 p.
  The story of her recovery from tuberculosis after nearly nine months in a sanatorium, by the author of *The Egg and I.*

2882 *MacDonald, Betty Bard   **1908-1958**
Who, me? Philadelphia: J.B. Lippincott Co., 1959. 352 p.
  Selections from previously published autobiographical books are placed here in chronological order: her life on a chicken farm, her conquest of tuberculosis, her career as a writer, and her family life on Vashon Island, helping her daughters through adolescence.

2883 Macdonald, Donald
Diaries of Donald Macdonald 1824-1826. Clifton, New Jersey: Kelley, 1973. 379 p. Index.
  Born in County Carlow, Ireland, Captain Macdonald made two journeys to the U.S. and spent some time in the intellectual community of New Harmony, Indiana. Although he never settled there, he was remembered as a highly romantic figure in the folklore of the community. These are the diaries kept during his two journeys to New Harmony.

2884 *MacDonald, Elizabeth P.
Undercover girl. New York: The Macmillan Company, 1947. 305 p.
  During World War II she worked for the Morale Operations branch of the Office of Strategic Services (OSS) and was one of relatively few women sent overseas. Her assignments in psychological warfare, or forms of subversion to create confusion and division in enemy territories, took her to India and China.

2885 Mack, Connie
see **McGillicuddy, Cornelius**

2886 Mack, John B.   **1935-**
Nobody promised me. With Don Arthur Torgersen and Emmett Smith. Chicago, Illinois: Childrens Press, 1970. 64 p.
  The story of how Mack succeeded in becoming a librarian and teacher in Chicago City College's Black studies program, this book is part of a series meant to provide career guidance for young people.

2887 MacKay, Robert   **1772-1816**
The letters of Robert MacKay to his wife: written from ports in America and England, 1795-1816. Athens: University of Georgia Press, 1949. 325 p.
  In letters written to his wife over a period of 21 years, MacKay describes the life of a Southern merchant during the early nineteenth century, including trade along the Atlantic seaboard and with England as well as social functions in port cities.

2888 MacKay, William   **1943-**
Salesman surgeon: the incredible story of an amateur in the operating room. As told to Maureen Mylander. Introduction by Albert E. Arenen. New York: McGraw-Hill, 1978. 187 p.
  An amazing but frightening account of the experiences of MacKay, a salesman of prosthetic devices. As an amateur orthopedic surgeon, McKay, with a ninth-grade education, often knew more about the prostheses than the surgeons did; he describes in detail how he assisted in and occasionally performed orthopedic operations. His amateur surgical career ended when some of the doctors he helped were prosecuted.

2889 MacKaye, Percy   **1875-1956**
Poog's pasture: the mythology of a child, a vista of autobiography. New York: The Bond Wheelwright Co., 1951. 187 p.
  Poetic revelation of the author's identification with childhood, based on a belief that life is a mythology impersonated by wonderful beings.

2890 MacKey, Joseph
The froth estate. New York: Prentice-Hall, Inc., 1946. 236 p.
  Cynical, frothy reflections of a reporter's ten years on the New York *Sun.*

2891 *MacLaine, Shirley   **1934-**
Don't fall off the mountain. New York: W.W. Norton & Co., Inc., 1970. 270 p.
  The author, known for her dancing and acting on Broadway and in Hollywood, tells of her "discovery," her public success, her personal odyssey, her jaundiced view of fame, and her active political and humanitarian concerns.

2892 *MacLaine, Shirley   **1934-**
You can get there from here. New York: W.W. Norton & Co., Inc., 1975. 249 p.
  During the early 70's the author, an actress and dancer, worked for

presidential candidate McGovern and then led the first American women's delegation to China. This volume covers the details of these two phases of her life, concentrating particularly on the China experience.

2893 *MacLane, Mary   **1881-1929**
I, Mary MacLane: a diary of human days. New York: Frederick A. Stokes Co., 1917. 317 p.
Not a diary per se, the book is a collection of prose images depicting herself and the world of Butte, Montana. H.L. Mencken called her the "Butte Bashkirtseff."

2894 *MacLane, Mary   **1881-1929**
The story of Mary MacLane by herself. New York: Duffield & Co., 1911. (Chicago: Herbert S. Stone and Co., 1902) 322 p.
Written when she was nineteen, this book contains MacLane's thoughts about her unhappy childhood, her desolate life, her assessment of herself—"a philosopher of the peripatetic school . . . a genius . . . filled with anguish and hopeless despair."

2895 Maclay, William   **1737-1804**
The journal of William Maclay: United States Senator from Pennsylvania, 1789-1791. Introduction by Charles A. Beard. New York: Frederick Ungar Publishing Co., 1965. (New York: Appleton and Co., 1890) 429 p. Index.
This journal kept during the inaugural years of the federal government under the Constitution contains Maclay's outspoken views on political issues and customs of the day, on statesmen and their ideas (he voiced sentiments of Democratic-Republicanism before Jefferson did), and on a wide variety of other topics from religion to menus to rheumatism.

2896 MacLeish, Archibald   **1892-1982**
Champion of cause; essays and addresses on librarianship. Compiled and with an introduction by Eva M. Goldschmidt. Chicago: American Library Association, 1971. 248 p.
Poet-turned-librarian MacLeish was confirmed as Librarian of Congress in 1939, a position he held until 1944. Although he lacked training in library science, he proved to be a vigorous leader who introduced modern fiscal and administrative concepts, defined goals and priorities, and initiated progressive personnel policies. This collection features essays and speeches he gave during his tenure in office and later.

2897 *MacMillan, Miriam (Look)
Green seas and white ice. Introduction by Lowell Thomas. New York: Dodd, Mead and Co., 1948. 287 p.
Raised in a family heritage of Maine sea captains, she was fascinated by arctic explorer Donald MacMillan when she was eight years old. She later married him and joined his explorations, recording here their experiences while traveling 40,000 arctic miles.

2898 Macneil, Malcolm F.   **1896?-**
The rewarding path: an autobiography. Illustrated. Boston: Christopher Publishing House, 1961. 177 p.
A self-serving account covering Macneil's rural Nova Scotia childhood; emigration to Boston where he attended a nursing school for 21 months but failed to graduate because he assumed the physician's prerogative as diagnostician; and his career as a businessman (manufacturing light switches) and banker in Worcester, Massachusetts. Orphaned twice, declared 4-F by the Canadian and American armies, not formally educated, Macneil writes to provide a moral example of determination and business success intended to inspire comparable youth.

2899 MacNicol, Roy   **b.1889**
Paintbrush ambassador. Illustrated. New York: Vantage Press, 1957. 255 p. Index.
From an early acting career, MacNicol turned to painting. His second marriage to singer Fay Courtney led to various travels and temporary jobs, from Miami to China, until her untimely death. He took on the honorific role of goodwill ambassador by means of his Mexican painting exhibitions.

2900 Maddry, Charles Edward   **1876-1962**
Charles E. Maddry: an autobiography. Introduction by Hight C. Moore and E.C. Routh. Illustrated. Nashville, Tennessee: Broadman Press, 1955. 141 p.
Maddry, a lifelong Southern Baptist, was educated at the University of North Carolina, near his home, and at the Southern Baptist Theological Seminary. After a career of domestic leadership as a clergyman, in 1933 he became Executive Secretary of the Southern Baptist Foreign Mission Board and traveled over the world to visit every Southern Baptist mission field. He also saved the organization from bankruptcy and established its financial stability.

2901 *Maddux, Rachel   **1913-**
The orchard children. New York: Harper & Row, 1977. 248 p.
Maddux describes how she and her husband moved from southern California to a farm in Tennessee, took in two foster children, lost them

to their biological parents through a court ruling, and eventually adopted a baby girl.

2902 *Madeleva, Mary, C.S.C.   **1887-1964**
My first seventy years. Preface by Leo A. Pursley. New York: Macmillan Co., 1959. 172 p.
A lively, precise account of Sister Madeleva's German-American upbringing in Wisconsin; her extensive education, sacred and secular, at St. Mary's College (Notre Dame, Indiana), University of California-Berkeley, and Oxford; her writing of poetry; and her 25-year presidency of St. Mary's College. Several chapters are devoted to her educational philosophy and her joyous views of religion.

2903 *Madison, Dolley (Payne) Todd   **1768-1849**
Memoirs and letters of Dolley Madison. Edited by her grandniece Lucia B. Cutts. Port Washington, New York: Kennikat, 1971. (Boston: Houghton Mifflin, 1886) 210 p.
The volume contains letters written to and from Dolley Madison during 1796 to 1836 connected with a biographical narrative by her grand-niece. They concern personal and domestic matters in addition to her views on current events and people she met.

2904 Madison, James   **1751-1836**
The papers of James Madison. Edited by William T. Hutchinson and others. Chicago: University of Chicago Press, 1962- . v.
The documents reveal Madison's steadily increasing involvement from 1774 as a county committeeman, then as delegate to the Virginia Convention, member of the council of the state of Virginia, delegate to the Continental Congress, many posts in the federal government, and finally President. He was an outstanding and illustrious figure in public life for almost sixty years.

2905 *Madruga, Lenor   **1942-**
One step at a time: a young woman's inspiring struggle to walk again. Illustrated. New York: McGraw-Hill, 1979. 200 p.
Madruga's account of her hemipelvectomy, the removal of half her pelvis and one leg to halt bone cancer, is optimistic, designed to show other amputees and cancer victims that it is possible to adjust to a prosthesis, to overcome pain, addiction to painkillers, and the loss of a limb, ultimately leading a normal life—including dancing, horseback riding, and waterskiing.

2906 *Maeder, Clara (Fischer)   **1811-1898**
Autobiography of Clara Fisher Maeder. Edited by Douglas Taylor. New York: Burt Franklin, 1970. (New York: Dunlap Society, 1897) 138 p.
Mrs. Maeder, who made her acting debut at the Drury Lane Theater, London, in 1817, continued for sixty years to be a theater personality in England, Ireland, and America. Her account recalls her own experiences and the world of nineteenth-century theater. Appended are several critical and biographical notices of the actress.

2907 Magee, David
Infinite riches; the adventures of a rare book dealer. Introduction by Lawrence Clark Powell. New York: Paul S. Eriksson, 1973. 274 p. Index.
A volume about the adventure of selling rare books, the unusual persons he met, the delight in a business which most people know nothing about. His was a lifelong love affair with books, people, and two cities, San Francisco and London.

2908 *Magidoff, Nila Ivanovna (Shevko)   **1905-**
Nila: her story. As told to Willie Snow Ethridge. New York: Simon and Schuster, 1956. 241 p.
The story of her life in Russia, her marriage to an NBC foreign correspondent in Moscow, her immigration to the United States, her popularity as a speaker on Russia, and her gradual adaptation to life in the United States.

2909 *Magnes, Beatrice L.
Episodes: a memoir. Foreword by James Marshall. Berkeley, California: Judah L. Magnes Memorial Museum, 1977. 124 p.
Magnes narrates her memories in stream-of-consciousness format, recalling hundreds of friends, family members, and servants and writing knowingly of many parts of the globe, describing the local customs of the places she has lived. Judaism is the linking factor for her memories, but her own personal warmth provides the appeal of the book.

2910 Magnuson, Paul Budd   **1884-1968**
Ring the night bell: the autobiography of a surgeon. Edited by Finley Peter Dunne, Jr. Boston: Little, Brown, and Co., 1960. 376 p.
The development of his career as a bone and joint surgeon in Chicago and later as head of the medical section of the Veterans' Association in Washington.

2911 *Magoffin, Susan (Shelby)   **1827-1855**
Down the Santa Fe Trail and into Mexico. The diary of Susan Shelby Magoffin, 1846-1847. Edited by Stella M. Drumm. New Haven: Yale University Press, 1962. (1926) 294 p. Index.

In 1846 the author set out with her husband, a Santa Fe trader, to journey from Missouri to New Mexico and Mexico. She kept an excellent daily journal of her observations along the Santa Fe Trail, which carried a busy trade with the northern Mexico provinces. Her diary contains historical material on Mexican life and customs, Kearny's conquest of New Mexico, and the progress of the Mexican War in the border provinces.

2912 *Magri, M. Lavinia (Lavinia Warren or Mrs. Tom Thumb) 1841-1919
The autobiography of Mrs. Tom Thumb: Some of my life experiences. With the assistance of Sylvester Becker. Edited with introduction by A.H. Saxon. Hamden, Connecticut: Archon Books, 1979. 199 p. Index.
Lavinia Warren Stratton reminisces about her travels as a dwarf circus performer, including extensive tours in the U.S. and Great Britain as well as Japan, China, India, and the Mediterranean. Her arisocratic self-image dominates even in meetings with General Grant and Queen Victoria. In manuscript, she quoted extensively without acknowledgment from P.T. Barnum's autobiography and publicity pamphlets; Becker notes those segments.

2913 Magruder, Jeb Stuart   1934-
An American life: one man's road to Watergate. New York: Atheneum, 1974. 338 p. Index.
The author writes mainly of his job in the Nixon administration focusing on the Watergate affair, the coverup, and its causes.

2914 Magruder, Jeb Stuart   1934-
From power to peace. Foreword by Mark O. Hatfield. Illustrated. Waco, Texas: World Books, 1978. 224 p.
This is a confessional by a convicted Watergate conspirator who served six months in Allenwood and Fort Holabird Federal Prisons in 1974. It describes his participation in the political cover-up, his remorse and acceptance of Christ as his redeemer, and demonstrates the positive impact of that faith on his mental attitude during his trial and imprisonment. After release he worked two years as a fund raiser for the Christian Young Life Organization, preparatory to entering Princeton Theological Seminary.

2915 Mahan, Alfred Thayer   1840-1914
From sail to steam: recollections of naval life. The American Scene Series. New York: Da Capo Press, 1968. (New York: Harper & Brothers, 1907) 458 p.
Mahan provides a detailed account of his naval career that began as a cadet at the U.S. Naval Academy (1860-1864) and ended with his presidency of the War College (1886-1888). He also furnishes an extensive history of pre-Civil War naval vessels, the operation of the Naval Academy, and of the American naval penetration of China and Japan in the 1870's.

2916 Mahan, Asa   1800-1899
Autobiography: intellectual, moral, and spiritual. Philosophy in America Series. New York: AMS Press, 1979. (London: T. Woolmer, 1882) 458 p.
A spiritual autobiography by a Congregational minister includes few particulars of his life except the principles by which he guided his presidencies of Oberlin and Adrian Colleges.

2917 Mahoney, Stanley M.
Stan Mahoney: the adventures of a working man. And Frederick I. Taft. Foreword by Frederick I. Taft. Illustrated. Shaker Heights, Ohio: Corinthian Press, 1978. 230 p.
This is a candid, engaging account of Mahoney's varied occupations as a truckdriver (who raced motorcycles and cars on weekends); ship's fireman, oiler, and mechanic; welder; and commerical fisherman. His analysis of a typical workingman's life is unusually articulate.

2918 Mailer, Norman   1923-
Advertisements for myself. New York: G.P. Putnam's Sons, 1959. 532 p.
This is anything but a conventional autobiography; it is, however, an analysis of his life in writing to date, with running commentary or advertisements providing a continuous structure for his development as a writer.

2919 *Maiullo, Minerva (Tarquinio)
A tapestry of memories. South Brunswick, New Jersey: A.S. Barnes and Co., 1972. 335 p. Index.
Desiring to share with others her unusual experiences, the author has recorded episodes from her travels and singing engagements in Italy and Spain.

2920 Majors, Alexander   1814-1900
Seventy years on the frontier: Alexander Majors' memoirs of a lifetime on the border. Preface by "Buffalo Bill" (General W.F. Cody). Edited by Colonel Prentiss Ingraham. Illustrated. Columbus, Ohio: Long's College Book Co., 1950. (Chicago: Rand McNally, 1893) 325 p.
Drawing upon his broad experiences of hunting, trapping, mining, farming, shipping, and traveling, Majors recalls the Western frontier of the 1800's—its country and crops, its wildlife, Indians, gold rushes,

plagues, floods, rivalries, and the settlement of the Mormons under Joseph Smith. Cherishing his memories, Majors also writes of modern technological and industrial changes and promises for the future.

2921 Malcolm X
see **Little, Malcolm**

2922 Malkin, Maurice L.   1900-
Return to my father's house; a charter member of the American Communist Party tells why he joined—and why he later left to fight communism. Edited by Charles W. Wiley. New Rochelle, New York: Arlington House, 1972. 256 p.
Disillusioned with the Communist Party, he came to believe that modern communism leads inevitably to the totalitarian state in which all but a few party bosses become slaves. Malkin here tells of his experiences before and after communism.

2923 Maloney, Arnold Hamilton   1888-1955
Amber gold: an adventure in autobiography. Boston: Meador Publishing Co., 1946. 448 p. Index.
Born in Trinidad, Maloney was educated in the United States and became professor of pharmacology at Howard University. His book traces the development of his personality and character.

2924 Maltz, Maxwell   1899-1975
Adventures in staying young. New York: Thomas Y. Crowell Co., 1955. 214 p.
Dr. Maltz recounts the fifteen significant cases that taught him the most during his thirty-year career as a plastic surgeon in New York City and points out the moral of each, such as, "If you keep going, your heart will remain forever young."

2925 Maltz, Maxwell   1899-1975
Doctor Pygmalion: the autobiography of a plastic surgeon. New York: Thomas Y. Crowell, 1953. 261 p.
The book recounts the life of a New York plastic surgeon, his patients, and the various operations he performed.

2926 *Mandel, Ursula Greenshaw   1898-
I live my life. Illustrated. New York: Exposition Press, 1965. 647 p.
A sprawling account of the author's California upbringing, education at Vassar and the University of California, practice of general medicine, and three unsuccessful marriages to professional inferiors. Over half of the book is devoted to accounts of her travels in the United States, Canada, Japan, Africa, India, and Europe.

2927 Mandell, Arnold J.   1934-
The nightmare season. New York: Random House, 1976. 216 p.
In 1972 Mandell, a psychiatrist at the University of California-San Diego Medical School, agreed to help Harland Suare, coach of the losing San Francisco Chargers, revitalize the football team. His two-year involvement with the team became a nightmare of hulking players, groupies, and paranoid management. Mandell prescribed pre-game amphetamines for eleven players "to protect them from street drugs," for which he was banished from the National Football League.

2928 *Mander, Anica Vesel   1934-
Blood ties: a woman's history. Sarika Finci Hofbauer, collaborator. Berkeley and New York: Moon Books and Random House, Inc., 1976. 297 p.
A feminist autobiography focusing on the Jewish author's birth and early childhood in Yugoslavia, the family's escape to Italy in 1943, emigration to California in the late 1940's, and her teenage initiations into sexuality, male and female. Interspersed are chapters of her grandmother's reminiscences of World Wars I and II.

2929 Maney, Richard   1892-1968
Fanfare: the confessions of a press agent. New York: Harper and Brothers, 1957. 374 p. Index.
Raised in Montana, in 1919 he traveled to New York to become a press agent. His book describes his life in the theatrical world over several decades.

2930 Manfred, Frederick Feikema   1912-
Conversations with Frederick Manfred. Moderated by John R. Milton. Foreword by Wallace Stegner. Salt Lake City: The University of Utah Press, 1974. 169 p.
Taped interviews with Manfred are the basis for this volume. He talks about the fictional world of his novels, which are regional in character, set in a Western area called Siouxland and peopled with heroes bigger than life.

2931 Mangiolardo, Michael   d.1968
My days in Vietnam. Photographs by author. New York: Vantage Press, 1969. 115 p.
Mangiolardo, a soldier in Vietnam for six months in 1967-68, kept a

diary of his experiences. Although it begins with routine preoccupations (the quality and quantity of the food), as he becomes more involved in the war his observations become more keen (the Vietnamese burn marijuana to heat their food) and more cynical ("They don't want us in their country, so just what are we fighting for?"). Mangiolardo was killed in January, 1968, in a Viet Cong air attack.

2932 Mann, Ambrose Dudley   **1801-1889**
"My dearest friend": the letters of A. Dudley Mann to Jefferson Davis, 1869-1889. Edited with introduction by John Preston Moore. Confederate Centennial Studies, No. 14. Tuscaloosa, Alabama: Confederate Publishing Co., Inc., 1960. 114 p. Index.
     A diplomat of some experience before 1861, he was appointed by Davis as one of three commissioners to obtain European recognition for the Confederacy. Their correspondence records their long friendship in later life.

2933 Mann, William M.   **1886-1960**
Ant hill odyssey. Boston: Little, Brown and Co., 1948. 338 p.
     As a boy he had a strong interest in insects and animals. His book traces the development of that interest through his college years, graduate study, and field work in Brazil, Haiti, the Fiji and Solomon Islands. A Horatio Alger story in the context of natural history.

2934 *Mannes, Marya   **1904-**
Out of my time. London: Gollancz, 1972. (Garden City, New York: Doubleday & Co., Inc., 1971) 251 p.
     The book is written as if she were looking through a carton of diaries and letters from age five; the narrative weaves excerpts from the past with an imaginary dialogue between Mannes and one of her fictional characters. Her main theme: her life was less successful than it should have been because of the rigidity of sex roles, which she struggled against continually.

2935 Mannix, Daniel Pratt   **1911-**
Step right up! New York: Harper and Brothers, 1950. 270 p.
     The story of a traveling American carnival and the people working in various concessions, by an author who spent three years under the canvas learning techniques of the side show.

2936 Manone, Wingy (Joseph Wingston Manone)   **1904-**
Trumpet on the wing. With Paul Vandervoort. Garden City, New York: Doubleday and Co., Inc., 1948. 256 p.
     Growing up in and around the world of jazz, from youth in New Orleans to many major cities in the United States; includes discography.

2937 Mansfield, Edward Deering   **1801-1880**
Personal memories, social, political, and literary, with sketches of many noted people, 1803-1843. New York: Books for Libraries Press, 1970. (Cincinnati: Clarke, 1879) 348 p.
     The reminiscences of a lawyer and writer who spent a large part of his life in Cincinnati. He describes the city and its prominent citizens as well as national events, political figures, and other areas of the country which he lived in or visited during the early nineteenth century.

2938 *Mansfield, Jayne   **1933-1967**
Jayne Mansfield's wild, wild world. And Mickey Hargitay. Los Angeles, California: Holloway House Publishing Co., 1963. 128 p.
     Movie actress Jayne Mansfield, Hollywood's "smartest dumb blonde," exploits her sexuality in this disjointed account of her nude and near-nude escapades and of her on-again off-again marriage in 1955 to Mickey Hargitay, "Mr. Universe."

2939 Mantle, Mickey Charles   **1931-**
The education of a baseball player. New York: Simon and Schuster, 1967. 219 p. Index.
     His second book gives a more detailed picture of his father's influence on his baseball career, the difficulties of his rapid move into the major leagues, his continual medical problems, his ongoing success, and some strategies of the game.

2940 Mantle, Mickey Charles   **1931-**
Mickey Mantle story. As told to Ben Epstein. Foreword by Casey Stengel. New York: Henry Holt & Co., 1953. 108 p.
     Written after his first two years with the New York Yankees, the book tells of his early interest in baseball and the events that made him a young super-star after the Yankees picked him to replace the ailing Joe DiMaggio.

2941 *Marble, Alice   **1913-**
Road to Wimbleton. New York: Charles Scribner's Sons, 1946. 167 p.
     A champion at Wimbleton (1937-1939) describes her childhood in a large, poor family in northern California, the difficult years of training, and the responsibilities of success, including her entertainment tours in World War II.

2942 Marcus, Stanley   **1905-**
Minding the store; a memoir. Boston: Little, Brown and Co., 1974. 383 p. Index.
     A remarkably erudite review of the Nieman-Marcus enterprise emphasizes the strength of the Marcus family in building the business, the social and political events in each era of the business history, and an acute analysis of Texas and national politics, all relating to the amazing success of the store.

2943 Marcy, Randolph Barnes (Colonel)   **1812-1887**
Thirty years of army life on the border. Comprising descriptions of the Indian nomads of the plains, explorations... New York: Harper & Brothers, 1866. 442 p.
     As an army officer for thirty years serving on the frontiers, the prairies, and the Western mountains, Marcy had first-hand experience with the people and customs of a disappearing and changing part of America. He sought to record his observations of Indians, wild territory, animals, and frontiersmen.

2944 Mardikian, George Magar   **1902-**
Song of America. New York: McGraw-Hill Book Co., Inc., 1956. 312 p.
     A leading restaurateur and public figure in San Francisco writes of his boyhood in Armenia and Turkey, his immigration to California, and his adaption to the American way of life, all in a tone of genuine patriotism.

2945 Mares, William
see **Polk, William Roe**

2946 Maresca, James V.
My flag is down: the diary of a New York taxi driver. New York: E.P. Dutton and Co., Publishers, 1948. 188 p.
     Primarily anecdotes of people who got in and out of his cab during seven years, his book describes city life—the sordid and the rich—from a personal viewpoint.

2947 Maretzek, Max   **1821-1897**
Crotchets and quavers: on revelations of an opera manager in America. Preface by Jan Popper. New York: Da Capo Press, 1966. (New York: S. French, 1855) 346 p.
     Written in the form of letters, this autobiography reveals colorful details of the operatic, concert, and popular musical life during the pre-Civil War era in America. A manager and conductor, Maretzek brought the Italian Opera Company to the United States in 1848, then remained here as a leading operatic impresario and influential figure on the musical scene.

2948 Margolin, Arnold Davidovich   **1877-1956**
From a political diary: Russia, the Ukraine, and America, 1905-1945. New York: Columbia University Press, 1946. 250 p. Index.
     Political analysis of his experience in Russia through the Revolution (1900-1919), and America (1922-1945), by a former Justice of the Supreme Court of Appeals of Ukraine and current member of the Massachusetts Bar.

2949 Marin, John   **1872-1953**
The selected writings of John Marin. Edited with introduction by Dorothy Norman. New York: Pellegrini & Cudahy, 1949. (New York: Privately printed for An American Place, 1931) 241 p.
     This volume includes letters and occasional writings from a 1931 edition of painter Marin's letters as well as additional letters written between 1910 and 1949. Most of the correspondence is addressed to Alfred Stieglitz, Marin's greatest lifelong friend, who encouraged him, exhibited his paintings, and fought selflessly and unceasingly to establish his reputation.

2950 Maris, Roger   **1934-**
Roger Maris at bat. And Jim Ogle. New York: Duell, Sloan and Pearce, 1962. 236 p.
     During the 1961 baseball season he broke Babe Ruth's home-run record. This is the story of his success in the game.

2951 Marke, Ernest Charles Melvin Patrick Ekundio
Old man trouble. London: Weidenfeld and Nicholson, 1975. 159 p.
     Born in Sierra Leone, Marke writes of his life as a seaman in and out of trouble, beginning with his stowing away for America, at age fourteen, on a ship that was torpedoed. He shipped from port to port, often jail to jail, a prey to thieves, hustlers, and bigots. He blames most of his troubles on racial prejudice, although, by his accounts, many problems appear to stem also from determined naiveté.

2952 Markham, William Colfax   **1868-1961**
Autobiogaphy of William Colfax Markham. Washington, D.C.: Ransdell, Inc., 1947. 241 p.
     Editor of the Baldwin Ledger in Baldwin, Kansas, he was also the local postmaster, later became Secretary of the National Association of Postmasters, and was increasingly active in state and national politics.

2953 Marks, Richard E.   **1946-1966**
The letters of PFC Richard E. Marks, USMC. Philadelphia: J.P.
Lippincott, 1967. 190 p.
    During fifteen months in the Marine Corps, 1964-1966, Pfc. Marks
wrote almost one hundred letters home, mostly to his mother and sister in
New York. After training in North Carolina, he was sent to Vietnam in
May 1965. His letters reveal his experiences in training and in combat up
until a few days before his death in February 1966, at the age of nineteen.

2954 *Marlowe, Julia   **1865-1950**
Julia Marlowe's story. As told to E.H. Sothern. Edited by Fairfax
Downey. New York: Rinehart and Co., Inc., 1954. 237 p.
    Recorded by her husband and co-star, the narrative depicts her career
as an outstanding stage actress until their retirement in 1924.

2955 Marquart, Frank   **1898-**
An auto worker's journal: the UAW from crusade to one-party union.
Illustrated. University Park: Pennsylvania State University Press, 1975.
161 p.
    In this articulate, incisive volume Marquart discusses his life as an auto
worker, focusing on his radical activities as a labor leader in the 1920's
and 30's. He analyzes the impact of the communists, socialists, and
Trotskyites on the labor unions and provides an intimate view of the
American labor movement and worker education from the Twenties
through the Forties.

2956 Marrs, Elijah P.   **b.1840**
Life and history of the Rev. Elijah P. Marrs. Miami, Florida:
Mnemosyne Publishing Co., 1969. (Louisville, Kentucky: The Bradley &
Gilbert Co., 1885) 146 p.
    His experiences of twenty years as a slave, nineteen months in the
twelfth U.S. Colored Artillery of the Union Army, eighteen years as a
school teacher in Kentucky, and thirteen years in the Baptist ministry.

2957 Marsh, Benjamin Clarke   **1877-1952**
Lobbyist for the people: a record of fifty years. Washington, D.C.: Public
Affairs Press, 1953. 224 p. Index.
    For over thirty years he organized and ran The People's Lobby in
Washington and became well-known as an unconventional but forceful
character in national politics.

2958 Marsh, James   **1794-1842**
**The remains of the Rev. James Marsh, D.D., late president, and professor
of moral and intellectual philosophy, in the University of Vermont; with
a memoir of his life.** Compiled by Joseph Torrey. Port Washington, New
York: Kennikat Press, 1971. (Boston: Crocker and Brewster, 1843) 642 p.
    This volume contains a memoir of Marsh's life by Torrey plus various
letters, discourses, remarks, tracts, and addresses which Marsh wrote
during his career as professor at Hampton Sidney College and president
of the University of Vermont.

2959 Marshall, Edison   **1894-1967**
The heart of the hunter. New York: McGraw-Hill Book Co., Inc., 1956.
328 p.
    The memoir of a big-game hunter and popular novelist describes his
early discovery of hunting and his adventures hunting big game on five
continents. It is a book of passion and honesty, quest and discovery.

2960 Marshall, Edison   **1894-1967**
Shikar and safari: reminiscences of jungle hunting. New York: Farrar,
Straus & Co., 1947. (1946) 263 p.
    Tales of hunting for elephant, tiger, moose, and bear in Alaska, Africa
and Asia, written by a hunter who enjoys the skill, the danger, and the
adventure of the sport.

2961 Marshall, George Catlett   **1880-1959**
Memoirs of my services in the World War, 1917-1918. Foreword and
notes by James L. Colling, Jr. Illustrated. Boston: Houghton Mifflin
Company, 1976. 267 p. Index.
    Marshall, then a captain in the U.S. Army, First Division, and aide,
ultimately to General Pershing, describes his experiences in France with
the U.S. Army in 1917-18. Appended are the texts of Marshall's travels
with Pershing during this time to England, the Western Front, and Italy.

2962 Marshall, J.T.
**Miles expedition of 1874-1875; an eyewitness account of the Red River
war.** Edited by Lonnie J. White. Austin, Texas: Encino Press, 1971. (Ann
Arbor: University of Michigan Press, 1937) 74 p. Index.
    Marshall, a Kansas newspaperman, served throughout the Red River
campaign as a civilian scout with Colonel Miles. His running account of
people, places, and troop activities in Texas, Oklahoma, and Kansas is
factual, compact, and contributes to an understanding of this phase of the
Indian Wars.

2963 Marshall, John   **1755-1835**
**An autobiographical sketch by John Marshall: written at the request of
Joseph Story and now printed for the first time from the original manu-**
script preserved at the William L. Clements Library, together with a
letter from Chief Justice Marshall to Justice Story relating thereto.
Edited by John Stokes Adams. New York: Da Capo Press, 1973. (Ann
Arbor: University of Michigan Press, 1937) 48 p. Index.
    Written in 1827 and unknown to scholars until 1932, it provides most
of the sparse history of Marshall's personal life that is available.

2964 Marshall, John   **1755-1835**
The papers of John Marshall. Edited by Charles T. Cullen. Chapel Hill:
University of North Carolina Press in association with the Institute of
Early American History and Culture, 1974- . v. Index.
    The papers of Supreme Court Chief Justice Marshall include the corre-
spondence, account books, and other documents.

2965 *Marshall, Katherine Tupper   **1882-1978**
Together: annals of an Army wife. New York: Tupper and Love, Inc.,
1946. 292 p.
    Recollections of her marriage to General George C. Marshall, from
1930 through 1945, in effect a personal memoir of their life and the war
years.

2966 Marshall, Oscar Seth   **1870-1953**
Journeyman machinist en route to the stars: Stellafane to Palomar. Edited with preface by Eva Marshall Douglas. Introduction by Ernest V.
Flanders. Illustrated. Taunton, Massachusetts: William S. Sullwold Publishing, 1979. 156 p. Index.
    An inspiring, well-written account of Marshall's lifetime occupation as
a journeyman machinist whose interest in astronomy led him from association with the Springfield (Massachusetts) Telescope Makers to being the
master machinist on the Mt. Palomar telescope. He put himself through
Syracuse University in his late twenties and became an accomplished
amateur painter and writer as well.

2967 Marshall, Otis   **b.1884**
Memories of a G.P. New York: Vantage Press, 1958. 155 p.
    He describes his career as a "horse and buggy" doctor who grew with
the rapid advances in the medical profession. He served as physician in a
coal-mining camp, in industry, for the American Red Cross, and finally as
director of one of the first research centers devoted to geriatric research at
Penney Farms, Florida.

2968 Marshall, Samuel Lyman Atwood   **1900-1977**
Bringing up the rear: a memoir. Edited by Cate Marshall. Illustrated. San
Raphael: Presidio Press, 1979. 310 p. Index.
    During World War II he became chief military historian for the U.S.
Army. His career took him from the days of Pancho Villa to Vietnam, a
life he considers the most exciting of any American.

2969 *Martin, Betty   **1908-**
Miracle of Carville. Edited by Evelyn Wells. Garden City, New York:
Doubleday and Co., Inc., 1950. 302 p.
    Woman who is cured of leprosy after twenty years of treatments at
Carville Hospital in Louisiana describes her experience, including mar-
riage to a patient who is also cured, and their efforts over the years to
dignify conditions and allay unreasonable fears of the disease.

2970 Martin, Frederick Townsend   **1849-1914**
Things I remember. Series: Leisure Class in America. New York: Arno
Press, 1975. (London: E. Nash, 1913) 255 p.
    Martin reminisces about his life among the rich at Newport, in New
York (as a member of the "400"), and in Florida. He dwells with amusing
relish on anecdotes involving British and French titled nobility and is
intrigued by European travel, fancy-dress balls, hunting parties, and financial investments.

2971 Martin, John Bartlow   **1915-**
**Overtaken by events; the Dominican crisis from the fall of Trujillo to the
civil war.** New York: Doubleday & Co., Inc., 1966. 821 p. Index.
    Mainly concerned with the years 1962 to 1965, Martin shows the
day-to-day experience of living abroad representing the United States as
Ambassador to the Dominican Republic, the attempts and failures to
translate policy into reality, the workings of a U.S. embassy in a difficult
country, the pressures building from the time of Trujillo's death through
the presidency and fall of Juan Bosch, and up to the Civil War of 1965.

2972 Martin, Joseph Plumb   **b.1761?**
**Yankee Doodle boy: a young soldier's adventures in the American Revo-
lution told by himself.** Edited by George F. Scheer. Maps and illustrations
by Victor Mays. New York: William R. Scott, Inc., 1964. (Hallowell,
Maine: Glazier, Masters & Co., 1830) 190 p. Index.
    An edition for young readers of Martin's good-humored, detailed de-
scription of his life as a private soldier in the Continental Army during the
Revolution. He saw action in skirmishes and in major campaigns,
marched through heat and cold, played pranks and suffered the dangers
and privations of war for seven years. First published in 1830 under title:
*A narrative of some of the adventures, dangers and sufferings of a Revolu-
tionary soldier.*

2973 *Martin, Martha, pseud. (Helen Bolyan)   d.1959
Home on the bear's domain. New York: The Macmillan Co., 1954. 246 p.
    After surviving against incredible odds, she and her husband found a
new gold claim on a large island in southeastern Alaska. This volume
describes more challenges of wilderness life—shooting bear, clearing land,
logging, and mining.

2974 *Martin, Martha, pseud. (Helen Bolyan)   d.1959
O rugged land of gold. New York: The Macmillan Co., 1953. 223 p.
    Prospecting for gold with her husband in an uninhabited section of
Alaska, she was forced by a series of circumstances to spend a winter
alone. She survived severe injuries from a landslide, she delivered her own
daughter, and she developed the self-confidence demanded to live one day
to the next.

2975 *Martin, Mary   1913-
My heart belongs. New York: William Morrow and Co., 1976. 320 p.
Index.
    Actress Mary Martin describes her exciting life as a star in such
musicals as *South Pacific, Annie Get Your Gun,* and *The Sound of Music.*
Her exhilarating career, managed by her husband, Richard Halliday, was
studded with theatrical success, family happiness (except for Halliday's
alcoholism), good friends, and a Brazilian farm.

2976 Martin, Tony, pseud. (Alvin Morris)   1913-
The two of us. And Cyd Charisse. As told to Dick Kleiner. New York:
Mason/Charter, 1976. 286 p.
    Singer Martin and dancer Charisse collaborate on a duet about their
backgrounds, careers in film, and 28 years of marriage. Their lives have
been glamorous, fun, full of friendships, loving families, world travel, and
adulation.

2977 Martin, William   1895-1950
Bill Martin, American. And Molly Radford Martin. New York: Vantage
Press, 1973. (Caldwell, Idaho: The Caxton Printers, 1959) 263 p.
    He immigrated from Switzerland to Canada in 1911 and then to the
U.S. In 1923 he settled in New Mexico where he became a detective. He
died of injuries he received in the South Pacific during World War II. His
wife recorded the conversations for this book on wire and later edited
them for publication.

2978 Marvin, Dwight   1880-1972
The faith I found. New York: Thomas Y. Crowell, 1954. 149 p.
    Marvin, a journalist, writes his spiritual autobiography for skeptical
laity to present a "provable foundation" for his (and their) subsequent
beliefs. Thus he defines Jesus as a mystic and becomes one himself, "making divine fatherhood real" and believing in a unified universal church
and the "life everlasting."

2979 Marx, Groucho (Julius H. Marx)   1890-1977
Groucho and Me. New York: Random House, Inc., 1959. 344 p.
    Groucho's story of his youth, his family's ventures into show business,
on stage, movies, radio, and TV, told in his familiar comic style.

2980 Marx, Groucho (Julius H. Marx)   1890-1977
Groucho letters: letters to and from Groucho Marx. New York: Simon &
Schuster, 1967. 319 p.
    Witty ripostes and amusing remarks fill these letters exchanged be-
tween Groucho and other comics, corporation presidents, his doctor,
critics, and publishers.

2981 Marx, Groucho (Julius H. Marx)   1890-1977
The Groucho phile: an illustrated life. Introduction by Hector Arce. Illustrated. Indianapolis: Bobbs-Merrill Co., 1976. 384 p. Index.
    A re-creation of Marx's life in pictures, anecdotes, and comedy
routines, with emphasis on his career in theater and film as the sardonic
member of a comedy team that included his brothers Harpo, Zeppo,
Chico, and, less often, Gummo. Marx's three marriages, children, and his
radio program, *You Bet Your Life,* figure somewhat less prominently. The
abundant illustrations will appeal particularly to old movie buffs.

2982 Marx, Groucho (Julius H. Marx)   1890-1977
Marx Bros. scrapbook. And Richard J. Anobile. Illustrated. New York:
Darien House; distrib. by W.W. Norton & Co., 1973. 256 p.
    The narrative of this book is based on interviews taped by Anobile. The
photographs are organized according to each brother's career, with narrative connecting the sections.

2983 Marx, Harpo   1893-1964
Harpo speaks! With Rowland Barber. New York: Bernard Geis Associates, 1961. 475 p.
    The public never heard the voice of Harpo, the silent Marx Brother.
His book makes up for that in a long and lively description of his career
as a comedian on Broadway and in Hollywood and of warm family ties
with his brothers, wife and children.

2984 Marx, Julius H.
    see Marx, Groucho

2985 *Mary Bernard, Sister   1917-
I leap for joy. Plainfield, New Jersey: Logos International, 1974. 241 p.
    A nun, now a member of the Sisters for Christian Community, tells of
her early decision to become a sister and the joyful life of service she lived
as well as the difficulties she encountered living in a community.

2986 Masachele, Opa B.
    see Price, Con

2987 Maslow, Abraham Harold   1908-1970
Journal of A.H. Maslow. Edited by Richard J. Lowry in cooperation with
Bertha G. Maslow. Monterey, California: Brooks/Cole Publishing Company, 1979. 2v.
    These journals of a humanistic psychologist contain brief observations,
comments, and reactions to his reading, his developing ideas, and current
events involving family, friends, students, and many others. Though rich
in revealing the changing ideas and health of a major psychologist, the
journals also contain comments on events and people without benefit of
context.

2988 Mason, Daniel Gregory   1873-1953
Music in my time: and other reminiscences. Illustrated. Freeport, New
York: Books for Libraries Press, 1970. (New York: Macmillan, 1938)
409 p. Index.
    A composer and author of several books on music writes of classical
music and some of its most noted performers and patrons of the 1920's
and '30's, particularly in Boston and in Pittsfield, Massachusetts. Mason
enjoys his work, friends, family, and travel throughout Europe and the
United States; his commentary on his own works candidly acknowledges
the failures as well as the successes.

2989 Mason, Gabriel Richard   b.1884
Gabriel blows his horn; the evolution of a rebel. Philadelphia: Dorrance
& Co., 1972. 200 p.
    Accepting life as a challenge, Mason has been a rebel in education,
politics, religion, and philosophy, advancing humanitarian and compas-
sionate views with earnest idealism. He was one of the founders of the
Teachers' Union in 1912 and has been honored for his contributions to
education and to philosophy with the Townsend Harris Medal and the
Lincoln High School Lincoln Award.

2990 Mason, George   1725-1792
The papers of George Mason. Edited by Robert A. Rutland (and others).
Chapel Hill: University of North Carolina Press, 1970. 3v. Index.
    These volumes contain all available public and private papers written
by Mason or addressed to him; routine business papers and memoranda
have only brief entries. Mason was active in the Virginia Legislature, the
Continental Congress, was a delegate to the Contitutional Convention,
and participated in various governmental commissions.

2991 Mason, William   1829-1908
Memories of a musical life. New York: AMS Press, 1970. (New York:
Century, 1901) 306 p. Index.
    Mason reminisces about friends and pupils of a long professional musi-
cal career. Son of a musician, hymn-writer, choir director, he began his
musical performances at an early age on the piano and organ, studied in
Europe, met Schumann, Moscheles, Moritz Hauptmann, Wagner, and
became a pupil of Franz Liszt. Several letters from Liszt are appended.

2992 Massari, Angelo   b.1885
The wonderful life of Angelo Massari: an autobiography. Translated by
Arthur D. Massolo. New York: Exposition Press, 1965. 311 p.
    Italian immigrant Massari recounts his fifty-year career in Florida,
"advancing from a factory worker to the head of the International Bank
of Tampa, which I organized almost entirely by myself, and of which I
was president from the day of its opening, in 1926, to the day of my
retirement, in 1958." Massari also boasts of his numerous trips to Europe,
Cuba, and Mexico.

2993 Massey, Raymond   1896-
A hundred different lives: an autobiography. Foreword by Christopher
Plummer. Illustrated. Boston: Little, Brown and Company, 1979. 447 p.
Index.
    Massey describes his career as an actor, encompassing over seventy
movies and, most notably, the role of Dr. Gillespie in the popular "Dr.
Kildaire" television series. Massey has received seven honorary
doctorates, retired from acting, and written several other volumes of
memoirs.

2994 Massey, Raymond   1896-
When I was young. Boston: Little, Brown & Co., 1976. 271 p.
    This volume covers Massey's privileged childhood in Toronto, heir to
the Massey-Harris farm-machinery fortune. It focuses not on wealth, but
on the pleasures that wealth could buy and the pains it could produce.

Much of this book is devoted to Massey's service in France and Russia as a Canadian officer in World War I.

2995 Massie, Robert Kinlach 1929-
Journey. And Suzanne Massie. New York: Alfred A. Knopf, 1975. 417 p.
   A moving, sensitive account of their family life which focuses on their son's struggle to survive hemophilia, a condition that causes profuse bleeding. Each wrote separate sections of this book. Robert is the author of *Nicholas and Alexandra,* a novel about the last Czar of Russia and his son, also a victim of hemophilia.

2996 Masters, Edgar Lee 1868-1950
Across Spoon River: an autobiography. Illustrated. New York: Octagon Books, 1969. (New York: Farrar and Rinehart, 1936) 426 p. Index.
   Masters' gloomy cast of mind imposes a pessimistic interpretation on most of the events of his unhappy life, ridden by disease, cursed by a loveless marriage, an unsatisfying career as a lawyer, and by many fruitless love affairs.

2997 Mather, Cotton 1663-1728
Diary of Cotton Mather D.D., FR.S. for the year 1712. Edited with introduction and notes by William R. Manierre II. Illustrated. Charlottesville: The University Press of Virginia, 1964. 143 p. Index.
   This year of Mather's diary, undiscovered by publishers until 1919, was, as all of his diary, written for his children. Mather notes his proposed G.D.'s (good deeds) for each day and relates his achievements and shortcomings in prayer; the education of his children; duties to church, family, and society; ministry to the Indians; and his sermons.

2998 Mather, Cotton 1663-1728
Selected letters of Cotton Mather. Compiled with commentary by Kenneth Silverman. Baton Rouge: Louisiana State University Press, 1971. 446 p. Index.
   Mather's letters touch on virtually every aspect of colonial American life and delineate the life and habits of one of colonial New England's most famous families. He dedicated himself to seeing that God's Word prevailed among mankind and to furthering the worldwide triumph of Reformation through his intellectual and financial support, watchdog activities, efforts to convert the Indians to Puritanism, and publications.

2999 *Mather, Winifred Holt 1870-1945
First Lady of the Lighthouse: a biography of Winifred Holt Mather. Edited by Edith Holt Bloodgood in collaboration with Rufus Graves Mather and Albert Wall. Preface by Edward Ellis Allen. R.G. Mather, "An Interpretation." New York: The Lighthouse/New York Association for the Blind, 1952. 209 p.
   For forty years Winifred Holt worked tirelessly to establish lighthouses for rehabilitation, education, and employment of the blind, including many war veterans in New York City, Rome, and Paris. Married in 1922 to Rufus Mather, she accepted donations for the Lighthouse in lieu of wedding gifts; these totalled $500,000. Her principled, energetic life and letters are exciting and inspirational.

3000 Mathers, James H. b.1877
From gun to gavel: the courtroom recollections of James Mathers of Oklahoma. As told to Marshall Houts. New York: William Morrow and Co., 1954. 246 p.
   After completing his legal education in Tennessee, he went to Oklahoma, then still a territory, to begin the practice of law, specializing in cases involving the death penalty in the rough frontier culture.

3001 Mathews, John Joseph 1895-
Talking to the moon. Chicago: University of Chicago Press, 1945. 244 p.
   An Osage Indian educated at the University of Oklahoma and Oxford describes his years of retreat in the Oklahoma hills. His book recalls Osage myth and history but is also reminiscent of Thoreau's *Walden* in his close affiliation with primitive existence.

3002 Mathewson, Christopher (Christy) 1880-1925
Pitching in a pinch: or, baseball from the inside. Introduction by Red Smith. Foreword by John N. Wheeler. Edited by Vic Ziegel and Neil Offen. New York: Stein and Day, 1977. (New York: G.P. Putnam's Sons, 1912) 306 p.
   A legendary, likeable pitcher for the New York Giants, 1900-1912, offers thoughtful, well-written advice on how to understand and to play baseball—pitching, batting, base running, and coaching. He discusses the significance of spring training and players' jinxes. He also analyzes the highly controversial Giants-Cubs game "that cost the Giants a pennant" in 1908.

3003 Mathieson, Peter John Riber 1871-1954
Master of the moving sea: the life of Captain Peter John Riber Mathieson from his anecdotes, manuscripts, notes, stories and detailed records, by Gladys M.O. Gowland. Edited by J. Ferrell Colton and Antoinette G. Smith. Illustrated by Barton A. Wright. Flagstaff, Arizona: J.F. Colton and Co., 1959. 304 p. Index.
   "The epic of the ship's boy of the Norwegian wooden barque, *Norma,*

in 1885 who, wandering the world in craft of sail and steam through peace and war, rose to command fourteen vessels under the flags of five nations, including the clipper, *Antiope,* the lofty *Carrabin,* the mighty *Moshulu,* and finally in 1944, the U.S. steamer, *Joseph E. Wing.* " (ed.)

3004 Matthews, Herbert Lionel 1900-1977
Education of a correspondent. New York: Harcourt, Brace and Co., 1946. 550 p. Index.
   Educated as a man of letters, an experienced journalist on the New York *Times* works toward a well-conceived philosophy of liberalism through his observations of several totalitarian and fascist states in the 1940's.

3005 Matthews, Herbert Lionel 1900-1977
A world in revolution; a newspaperman's memoir. New York: Charles Scribner's Sons, 1972. 462 p. Index.
   Matthews has been secretary, reporter, cable editor, foreign correspondent, war correspondent, bureau chief, and editorial writer during his more than 45 years with the New York *Times.* He has organized his book by countries and parts of the world where his work has taken him, using passages from his newspaper articles for part of his narrative.

3006 Matthews, Thomas Stanley 1901-
Under the influence: recollections of Robert Graves, Laura Riding, and friends. London: Cassell, 1979. (New York: Harper & Row, 1977) 354 p.
   The poet composes his autobiography by devoting chapters to the description of significant people in his life—his mentor, his friends, his lovers. (American title, *Jacks or Better.*)

3007 Matthews, Vincent
My race be won. With Neil Andur. New York: Charterhouse, 1974. 396 p.
   After winning the Gold Medal in the 400-meter dash at the 1972 Olympics, he refused to stand during "The Star Spangled Banner." His book describes the grueling ordeal of track and field events, his story of 1972, surgery for an ulcer a few months later, and settling into professional sports.

3008 Mattson, Hans 1832-1893
Reminiscences: the story of an emigrant. Illustrated. Scandinavians in America Series. New York: Arno Press, 1979. (Saint Paul, Minnesota: D.D. Merrill Co., 1891) 314 p.
   During Mattson's varied life he emigrated to Minnesota from Sweden, worked as a laborer, studied law, became county auditor, then a colonel in a regiment of Swedish soldiers in the Civil War. After the war, he helped found two Swedish-American newspapers and built up a family farm in Red Wing, Minnesota. He served as Consul-General to India in the 1880's, returned home to become Minnesota Secretary of State. He is justifiably proud of Swedish contributions to American life.

3009 Maudslay, Robert 1855-1939
Texas sheepman: the reminiscences of Robert Maudslay. Edited by Winifred Kupper. Freeport, New York: Books for Libraries Press, 1971. (Austin: University of Texas Press, 1951) 138 p. Index.
   Memoirs of his life as a sheepman on the open range in Texas from 1880 to 1905 by an immigrant (with his mother, sisters, and brother) from Manchester, England. Written in the form of letters to one of his nieces, "My Dear Amy," the manuscript was part of a presentation for a master's degree by the editor, who provides informative notes for each letter.

3010 Mauldin, William Henry (Bill) 1921-
Back home. New York: William Sloane Associates, 1947. 315 p.
   After serving five years in World War II, publishing *Up Front,* a successful account of his war years, winning the Pulitzer Prize by age 25, Mauldin writes a perceptive account of his postwar years.

3011 Mauldin, William Henry (Bill) 1921-
The brass ring. New York: W.W. Norton & Co., Inc., 1971. 275 p.
   Considered the best of all World War II cartoonists, Mauldin worked for the huge overseas army daily, *Stars and Stripes* and won a Pulitzer Prize before he was 25. His characters Willie and Joe came to symbolize the typical G.I. of the war in Europe.

3012 Maxey, Chester C. 1890-
The world I lived in: a personal story. Philadelphia: Dorrance & Co., 1966. 496 p.
   A forthright memoir by Maxey, a professor of political science at Western Reserve University, 1920-25, and thereafter associated with his alma mater, Whitman College, Walla Walla, Washington, as a professor, 1925-1948, and ultimately as its president, 1948-1959. Maxey, a highly successful fund-raiser, was an indefatigable, no-nonsense administrator who insisted on high-quality performance and was not afraid of incurring the wrath of slothful faculty. He combines his life story with a history of the college he served so well.

3013 *Maxwell, Elsa 1883-1963
RSVP: Elsa Maxwell's own story. Illustrated. Boston: Little, Brown and Co., 1954. 326 p. Index.

Two-hundred pound Elsa Maxwell, the uneducated daughter of a failed Iowa insurance salesman, pulls no punches in explaining how she became an "arbiter of international society," giver of lavish parties, and sponsor of social climbers, and loved nearly every minute of it. The book abounds in name-dropping anecdotes, gossip, social chit-chat, and royal titles.

3014 May, George Oliver   **1875-1961**
Memoirs and accounting thought of George O. May. Edited by Paul Grady. New York: The Ronald Press Co., 1962. 313 p. Index.
    A senior executive partner of Price Waterhouse & Co. writes of his first fifty years (pp. 1-52), chiefly in terms of his identity in big business. The remainder of the book is a series of his essays on accounting theory, followed by a chronological list of his published work.

3015 May, Rollo Reese   **1909-**
Paulus; reminiscences of a friendship. New York: Harper & Row, 1973. 113 p.
    A book about the friendship of the author and Paul Tillich, describing the way their lives intermingled from 1934, when Tillich arrived as an exile from Germany, until his death in 1966.

3016 Mayer, Frank H.   **1850-1954**
The buffalo harvest. And Charles B. Roth. Denver, Colorado: Sage Books, 1958. 96 p.
    A tough, moving, and realistic story of his life as a buffalo runner, which conveys a sense of the decline of the Old West as well as the buffalo herd.

3017 Mayer, Tom   **1943-**
Climb for the evening star. Boston: Houghton Mifflin Co., 1974. 115 p.
    A writer and licensed pilot, Mayer depicts the romance, adventure, and excitement of flying. For him "flight . . . is a vehicle for self-discovery."

3018 *Maynard, Joyce   **1953?-**
Looking back; a chronicle of growing up old in the Sixties. Garden City, New York: Doubleday & Co., Inc., 1973. 160 p.
    A member of the generation that grew up in the Sixties records the events, fads, political movements, and experiences of the decade. She admits, however, that "a generation can't be generalized about" and that her recollections are of "too many passing fads, too little that is lasting."

3019 Mayo, Charles William   **1898-1968**
Mayo; the story of my family and my career. Illustrated. Garden City, New York: Doubleday & Co., Inc., 1968. 351 p.
    His father founded Mayo Clinic in Rochester, Minnesota. Living with that legacy, he became an outstanding surgeon and an innovative authority on the art of healing. His book is a personal and professional history.

3020 Mays, Benjamin Elijah   **1895-**
Born to rebel; an autobiography. New York: Charles Scribner's Sons, 1971. 380 p.
    Raised in rural Black poverty in South Carolina, Mays earned a Ph.D. at the University of Chicago and was for 27 years President of Morehouse College. He writes of black-white relations, the role of the church in race relations, and his hopes and efforts toward bringing about equality for all.

3021 Mays, Willie Howard   **1931-**
Born to play ball. As told to Charles Einstein. New York: G.P. Putnam's Sons, 1955. 168 p.
    A Black baseball player from Alabama reminisces about his career with the New York Giants, the 1954 season, and other players.

3022 Mazzuchelli, Samuel   **1806-1864**
The memoirs of Father Samuel Mazzuchelli, O.P.: Memorie Istoriche ed Edificanti d'un Missionario Apostolico dell' Ordine dei Predicatori Fra Varie Tribu di Selvaggi fra i Cattolici e Protestanti negli Stati-Uniti d'America. Foreword by James P. Shannon. Translated by Maria Michele Armato, O.P., and Mary Jeremy Finnegan, O.P. Illustrated. Third edition. Chicago: The Priory Press, 1967. (Chicago: W.F. Hall Pr. Co., 1915, First English transl., Mary Benedicta Kennedy; Milan, 1844.) 329 p.
    Milanese Dominican Samuel Mazzuchelli's memoirs relate his "missions among various Indian tribes, . . . the Canadians in the territories of Wisconsin and Michigan, . . . [and] the Catholics and Protestants in the territories of Iowa and Wisconsin and in the state of Illinois" between 1828 and 1844, as well as his observations on Protestantism and Catholicism in the United States.

3023 McAllister, Robert   **1813-1891**
The Civil War letters. Edited by James I. Robertson, Jr. Preface by Donald Flamm. Illustrated. New Brunswick, New Jersey: Rutgers University Press for New Jersey Civil War Centennial Commission, 1965. 638 p. Index.
    A collection of 637 letters by Colonel McAllister from his Union Army campaigns in New Jersey and Virginia to his family throughout the Civil War. This well-documented selection (culled from 900 extant letters) provides an intimate, humane, sometimes critical view of battles, military strategy, morale, Southerners, the Virginia terrain where he fought, religion, and his own health, severely affected by a war wound.

3024 McAllister, Samuel Ward   **1827-1895**
Society as I have found it. Edited by Leon Stein. New York: Arno Press, 1975. (New York: Cassell, 1890) 469 p.
    McAllister describes his rise to social arbiter of America, as he shuttled between New York, Newport and Savannah and identified the supreme, socially acceptable 400 families. He tells how to enter society, hire cooks, give balls and other parties, and act fashionable. Original title, *The Leisure Class in America.*

3025 McAlmon, Robert   **1896-1956**
Being geniuses together; 1920-1930. Illustrated. Revised and with supplementary chapters By Kay Boyle. Garden City, New York: Doubleday & Co., Inc., 1968. 392 p.
    McAlmon published his autobiography in 1938. Boyle has added alternating chapters in this edition, expanding and correcting descriptions of their life in Paris during the Twenties, when they were close to most of the great artists associated with Sylvia Beach's bookstore, *Shakespeare and Company* —Hemingway, Joyce, Gertrude Stein, Scott and Zelda Fitzgerald, William Carlos Williams.

3026 McAlmon, Robert   **1896-1956**
McAlmon and the lost generation: a self-portrait. Edited with commentary by Robert E. Knoll. Lincoln: University of Nebraska Press, 1962. 396 p. Index.
    Prominent as an author and publisher in the Twenties, his work fell into obscurity when that of many close friends became famous. He published Hemingway's first novel and was regarded with affection by many well-known expatriates for years after he left their company. His book depicts a man involved in and typical of the Lost Generation.

3027 McBey, James   **1883-1959**
Early life of James McBey: an autobiography, 1883-1911. Edited by Nicolas Barker. Illustrated. New York: Oxford University Press, 1977. 131 p.
    In this account of his early life, McBey does not reach the United States. He records his school life and experience in banking and etching in Scotland, including his blind mother's suicide and his first early successes in art exhibitions.

3028 *McBride, Mary Margaret   **1899-1976**
A long way from Missouri. New York: G.P. Putnam's Sons, 1959. 254 p.
    The uneven years of struggle and success in her early career as a journalist.

3029 *McBride, Mary Margaret   **1899-1976**
Out of the air. Garden City, New York: Doubleday & Co., Inc., 1960. 384 p.
    For twenty years she did a radio show in New York which included reviews of books and theater bits and interviews with authors, actors, and other celebrities. Here she recalls her life in the heyday of radio.

3030 *McBride, Michele   **1945-**
The fire that will not die. Palm Springs, California: ETC Publications, 1979. 240 p.
    McBride's anger impelled her to write this account of the fire which swept Our Lady of the Angels School in Chicago, Illinois (December, 1958), killing 92 children and horribly burning and maiming others, including herself. Hospitalized for four and a half months, she still suffers physical debility and psychological damage.

3031 McCaba, Joseph   **d.1973**
Teacher who laughs. Foreword by R.T. Ketcham. Des Plaines, Illinois: Regular Baptist Press, 1973. 148 p.
    McCaba tells of his religious education at Moody Bible Institute, focusing on his life as a Baptist missionary in Niger Colony, Africa. He concentrates on his domestic life rather than on mission work; this includes the difficulties of building a house with unskilled workmen in inclement weather and the problems of day-to-day living (training servants, getting the proper food).

3032 *McCall, Dorothy (Lawson)   **1888-**
The copper king's daughter; from Cape Cod to Crooked River. Introduction by Governor Tom Lawson McCall. Portland, Oregon: Binford & Mort, 1972. 190 p.
    Mrs. McCall, the mother of Oregon governor Tom Lawson McCall, describes her privileged youth as the daughter of Tom Lawson, broker, banker, yachtsman, who showered his fortune on his family. She moved from the storybook wealth of Dreamworld, her father's estate on Cape Cod, to a central Oregon ranch in the Rimrock country east of the Cascades, which she wrote about in *Ranch Under the Rimrock.*

3033 *McCall, Dorothy (Lawson)   **1888-**
Ranch under the Rimrock. Portland, Oregon: Binford & Mort, 1971. 204 p.

In 1911, she moved to central Oregon where she and her husband, Hal McCall, raised five children while building one of the largest dairy farms in Oregon. Her story includes accounts of floods, fires, gunplay, as well as the building of a New England-style colonial manor.

3034 *McCall, Lenore
Between us and the dark. Foreword by C.C. Burlingame. Philadelphia: J.B. Lippincott Co., 1947. 303 p.
A moving account of her mental illness, of the painful discovery that she was not in control of her life, and of nearly five years spent in mental hospitals struggling for her recovery.

3035 McCall, Thomas Lawson   **1913-**
Tom McCall, maverick: an autobiography. With Steve Neal. Illustrated. Portland, Oregon: Binford & Mort, 1977. 296 p.
McCall's engaging life story depicts a dynamic person actively committed to Oregon, the state he governed, 1966-1974. Among his accomplishments were tax reforms, an anti-litter bottle-return drive, cleaning up the Willamette River, an energy-saving edict requiring businesses to dim their advertising signs, and the initiation of the campaign "Visit Oregon, But Don't Stay."

3036 *McCambridge, Mercedes   **1918-**
The two of us. London: Peter Davies, 1960. 182 p.
Actress McCambridge describes her year of travel (1947) with her five-year-old son, John, to recover from a painful divorce. The trip to the Caribbean, England, Ireland, and Italy proved hectic, exhilarating, and therapeutic.

3037 *McCarthy, Abigail (Quigley)
Private faces/public places. Illustrated. Garden City, New York: Doubleday & Co., 1972. 448 p. Index.
Abigail McCarthy relates her experiences with her husband as they began life together teaching and working for Christian renewal and then moved into the political scene. She evaluates the traditional role of political wives and of women in politics, telling also of important people and events including the 1968 campaign with its new constituency and tragic violence.

3038 McCarthy, Eugene Joseph   **1916-**
The year of the people. Garden City, New York: Doubleday and Co., Inc., 1969. 323 p.
The story of one year, 1968—his year as presidential candidate, when McCarthy challenged the traditional system in his attempt to run his campaign on issues rather than personalities, to restore power to the people, and to engender a new vitality in politics.

3039 *McCarthy, Mary Therese   **1912-**
Memories of a Catholic girlhood. New York: Harcourt, Brace and World, Inc., 1972. (1957) 245 p.
The story of a well-known writer's traumatic but often humorous childhood, spent with various relatives and in a Catholic girls' school, after the early death of her parents.

3040 McClain, Dennis Dale Denny   **1940-**
Nobody's perfect. New York: Dial Press, 1975. 208 p.
A story, both funny and sad, of the Detroit Tigers pitcher who was ostensibly a highly successful athlete and businessman, but was also hopelessly in debt and seriously debilitated by gambling, doctors, drugs, and sex.

3041 *McClanahan, Alice M.   **1892-**
Her father's partner: the story of a lady lawyer. Foreword by Joel D. Hunter. New York: Vantage Press, 1958. 122 p.
McClanahan recounts amusing, poignant, and otherwise memorable cases from her law practice in Chicago, 1915-1918, with the Legal Aid Society, and thereafter as her father's partner until he died in 1940. She is proud of women in the legal profession and champions their professionalism.

3042 McClellan, George Brinton, Jr.   **1865-1940**
The gentleman and the tiger: the autobiography of George B. McClellan, Jr. Edited by Harold C. Syrett. From the original manuscript in the possession of the New York Historical Society. Philadelphia: J.B. Lippincott Co., 1956. 375 p. Index.
The boyhood, political career, and professional life of a man who was associated with Tammany Hall as Mayor of New York (1903-09) and a professor of economic history at Princeton for over twenty years.

3043 McClenahan, William U.   **1899-**
G.P. Edited by John L. McClenahan. Philadelphia: Dorrance & Co., 1974. 132 p.
A physician describes his childhood in Egypt with his missionary parents, his education in the U.S., and experiences in medical school, in World War II, and in practice in Chestnut Hill, Pennsylvania.

3044 *McClendon, Sarah   **1910-**
My eight presidents. Illustrated. New York: Wyden Books, 1978. 239 p. Index.
McClendon, a White House press correspondent since Franklin Roosevelt's day, claims she asks some of the toughest questions at press conferences. Here she discusses her relationship with eight presidents but specifically deals with Eisenhower through Carter. Her closing chapters concern her fight against secrecy in the government.

3045 McClintic, Guthrie   **1893-1961**
Me and Kit. Boston: Little, Brown and Co., 1955. 341 p. Index.
The story of his life in the theater, as a drama student, young actor, director, producer, and his long and interesting marriage to Katharine Cornell.

3046 *McCloskey, Eunice (Lon Coske)   **1906-**
Potpourri: an autobiography. Philadelphia: Dorrance and Co., 1966. 157 p.
In her second autobiographical volume, she describes her girlhood in the Allegheny Mountains and her happiness with husband, daughter, and her art.

3047 *McCloskey, Eunice (Lon Coske)   **1906-**
So dear to my heart. Boston: Bruce Humphries, Publishers, 1964. 228 p.
A Pennsylvania artist and poet reminisces about her childhood and early career.

3048 McClure, McKinley M.   **1901-**
Hey! Major, look who's here. Philadelphia: Dorrance, 1972. 92 p.
He joined the U.S. Army at the age of fifteen and did a year and a half of overseas service during World War I. After the armistice, he remained in Germany as part of the Army of Occupation.

3049 McClure, Samuel Sidney   **1857-1949**
My autobiography. Introduction by Louis Filler. New York: Frederick Ungar Publishing Co., 1963. (New York: Frederick A. Stokes, Co., 1914) 266 p.
The founder and editor of *McClure's Magazine* writes of his Irish boyhood, his immigration to New York, the hardships of establishing a career as an editor, and the rewarding years of success. He was a friend and editor of many now famous writers, including Willa Cather, Robert Louis Stevenson, Ida Tarbell, and Stephen Crane.

3050 McCollough, John M.   **1895-**
We flew with one wing. Philadelphia: Dorrance & Co., 1977. 50 p.
McCollough wrote for his great-grandsons this account of his childhood near Oil City, Pennsylvania, and of his service as a machine gunner during World War I with the 168th Squadron, U.S. Air Service. He learned early to work hard, especially to keep the pump on the family's oil well running, even during blizzards. He taught in a one-room country school for two years before entering Gettysburg College at twenty. At the end of his junior year he joined the service and thoroughly enjoyed the excitement and danger of his air battles over France and Germany.

3051 McCollum, Elmer Verner   **1879-1967**
From Kansas farm boy to scientist: the autobiography of Elmer Verner McCollum. Foreword by Edwards A. Park. Illustrated. Lawrence: University of Kansas Press, 1964. 253 p. Index.
A fascinating account of McCollum's childhood on a Kansas farm; his education as a biochemist at the University of Kansas and at Yale; and his biochemical research in nutrition at the University of Wisconsin and at Johns Hopkins. McCollum speaks modestly about his discoveries of Vitamins A and D and international awards in nutrition and biochemistry.

3052 McConnell, Francis John   **1871-1953**
By the way: an autobiography. New York: Abingdon-Cokesbury Press, 1952. 286 p. Index.
The vivid recollections of a crusading Methodist bishop who lived at the center of social and religious reform movements from the 1890's. After the Great Steel Strike of 1919, he led a vigorous campaign for labor reforms.

3053 *McConnell, Lela Grace   **b.1884**
Faith victorious in the Kentucky mountains: the story of twenty-two years of spirit-filled ministry. Winona Lake, Indiana: The author, by Light and Life Press, 1946. 237 p.
Spiritual autobiography describing the education and work of a fundamentalist minister.

3054 McConnell, Robert Earll   **1889-1971**
The autobiography of Robert Earll McConnell. Introduction by Lucius D. Clay. Illustrated. New York: Cross, Hinshaw & Lindberg, Inc., 1966. 133 p. Index.
McConnell's autobiography depicts a successful fulfillment of the American dream. Born in Durango, Colorado, McConnell worked during school vacations in mines and on ranches. He graduated from the Colum-

bia University School of Mines in 1910 and was employed in Mexico, Texas, and California as a mining engineer. In the 1920's as a partner of Foster, McConnell, Inc., a Wall Street brokerage specializing in mining-related businesses, he made a fortune. At 49 he retired and enjoyed living in Virginia and Florida while performing public service, especially on energy-related matters as Chairman of the National Engineers' Committee during World War II.

3055 McCord, James Bennett   1870-1950
My patients were Zulus. With John Scott Douglas. New York: Rinehart and Co., Inc., 1951. 308 p.
   Medical missionary describes forty years of work with the Zulus, including opening a dispensary and hospital and forming a medical school and nurses' training school.

3056 McCord, James Walter, Jr.   1918-
A piece of tape: the Watergate story; fact and fiction. Washington, D.C.: Washington Media Services, 1974. 329 p.
   A key participant in the Watergate affair, McCord writes his account of that historic series of events. The book is divided into "The breakin and its aftermath," "Key testimony before the Senate Watergate Committee," and "Summation and the future."

3057 *McCormick, Patricia   1930-
Lady bullfighter: the autobiography of the North American matador. New York: Henry Holt and Co., 1954. 209 p.
   After seeing her first bullfight at seven, she dreamed of becoming a bullfighter and at 21 made her debut in the bull ring of Juarez. Her story is of the art, its discipline, sacrifice, and rewards.

3058 McCormick, Robert Rutherford   1880-1955
Memoirs: broadcast over WGN, WGNB and the Mutual Broadcasting System. n.p., Robert Rutherford McCormick, 1952. 29 p.
   A brief, superficial sketch of autobiographical incidents from the youth of publisher McCormick, reflecting social and political events from the perspective of a wealthy and politically powerful scion. He briefly mentions the Spanish-American War, President McKinley, Mark Hanna, and other people and phenomena.

3059 McCoy, Tim   1891-1978
Tim McCoy remembers the West: an autobiography. With Ronald McCoy. Garden City, New York: Doubleday & Co., 1977. 274 p. Index.
   An exceptionally well-written account of McCoy's varied life as a cowboy, rancher, movie star, and director of a circus cowboy-and-Indian show. McCoy became intimately acquainted with the last denizens of the open range, the Cheyenne, Blackfeet, and Sioux Indians, and was adopted into the Arapaho tribe. He brought hundreds of Indians from Wyoming, where his ranch was, to Hollywood to act in *The Covered Wagon.*

3060 McCracken, Harold   1894-
Roughnecks and gentlemen: memoirs of a maverick. Illustrated. Garden City, New York: Doubleday & Co., Inc., 1968. 441 p. Index.
   Kicked out of high school, he earned money for a train ticket to British Columbia where he stayed with an aunt and uncle and began to learn the ways of the woods and wilderness. His life became a series of adventures—exploring Alaska; becoming a self-taught archaeologist, naturalist, and movie producer; becoming recognized as an expert on Frederic Remington and Charles Russell.

3061 McCracken, James   1926-
A star in the family; an autobiography in diary form. And Sandra Warfield. Illustrated and edited by Robert Daley. New York: Coward-McCann & Geoghegan, 1971. 388 p.
   Tenor McCracken and his wife, mezzo-soprano Sandra Warfield, both opera singers, together tell the story of their careers, the discouragement, auditions, successes, and amusing incidents. One of their happiest experiences was singing together in the title roles of *Samson and Delilah.*

3062 McCrea, Tully   1839-1918
Dear Belle: letters from a cadet and officer to his sweetheart, 1858-1865. Narrative and editing by Catherine S. Crary. Foreword by Bruce Catton. Drawings by Cecile Johnson. Middletown, Connecticut: Wesleyan University Press, 1965. 256 p. Index.
   A narrative constructed from parts of McCrea's letters to Belle which were connected by Catton to tell the story of McCrea's experience at West Point and with the Army of the Potomac. The Civil War has been called the "West Point War" since so many of the officers on both sides were Academy graduates (over 800 out of 1,000 at the beginning of the war). McCrea represents those well-trained graduates.

3063 *McCullers, Carson Smith   1917-1967
The mortgaged heart. Boston: Houghton Mifflin Co., 1971. 292 p.
   A collection of essays, some previously unpublished, depicts her childhood in Georgia, her later life in New York, and the development of themes in her writing from personal moments to larger social commitments.

3064 McCune, Billy George   1928-
The autobiography of Billy McCune. Introduction by Danny Lyon. San Francisco: Straight Arrow Books, 1973. 154 p.
   In 1950 he was convicted of raping a Fort Worth suburban housewife, which sent him to Death Row. He was misclassified as psychotic, which placed him in a section reserved for lunatics and homosexuals; he spent much of his time in isolation wards and has never been seriously considered for parole. Lyon managed with great difficulty to get his manuscript approved and let out of prison.

3065 McDaniel, Henry Dickerson   1836-1926
With unabated trust: Major Henry McDaniel's love letters from Confederate battlefields as treasured in Hester McDaniel's bonnet box. Edited by Anita P. Sams. Illustrated. Monroe, Georgia: Historical Society of Walton County, 1977. 276 p. Index.
   Major McDaniel's letters to his fiancée Hester Felker reflect life in a Confederate Army unit as it fought and traveled throughout the South, particularly in Virginia. The letters are courtly and provide an understanding of military strategy as well as of events.

3066 McDonald, David John   1902-1979
Union man. Illustrated. New York: E.P. Dutton & Co., 1969. 352 p. Index.
   McDonald, who was president of the United Steelworkers of America for thirteen years, tells the story of the steel strikes of the postwar years, of John L. Lewis and the union movement, of the battle between the AFL and CIO, of industrial and political leaders, and of his own involvement in the union movement.

3067 McDonald, James Grover   1886-1964
My mission in Israel, 1948-1951. New York: Simon and Schuster, 1951. 303 p. Index.
   Experiences and impressions of the first U.S. Ambassador to Israel during its early years by a man active in international affairs, particularly with refugees.

3068 McFarland, Ernest William   1894-
Mac: the autobiography of Ernest W. McFarland. Illustrated. Foreword by J.E. Wallace Sterling. N.P.: MacFarland, 1979. 342 p.
   The book, abundantly illustrated with photographs and anecdotes, reveals the essence of a politician's life and relations with constituents and colleagues. His expertise on water law was helpful in his local political offices. Elected to the U.S. Senate in 1942, he served as majority leader in the 82nd Congress and sponsored the G.I. Bill of Rights before returning to Arizona as governor, and then as Chief Justice of the Arizona Supreme Court.

3069 McFarland, John Horace   1859-1948
Memoirs of a rose man: tales from Breeze Hill. Emmaus, Pennsylvania: Rodale Press, 1949. 144 p.
   Charming story of a well-known Pennsylvanian horticulturist and his garden.

3070 McGarvey, John William   1829-1911
The autobiography of J.W. McGarvey. Edited by DeLoris Stevenson and Dwight E. Stevenson. Lexington, Kentucky: The College of the Bible, 1960. 93 p. Index.
   Written as notes for a biography he intended his son to write, the book has curious switches from first to third person. It is the record of a Baptist minister and college professor who taught for 46 years at College of the Bible in Lexington, Kentucky.

3071 McGillicuddy, Cornelius (Connie Mack)   1862-1956
My 66 years in the big leagues: the great story of America's national game by Connie Mack, with official photographs from the Mack family and from other authentic sources. Philadelphia: The John C. Winston Co., 1950. 246 p. Index.
   Memoirs of both the man and the game to which he gave his life, written in commemoration of seventy-five years of the National League and fifty years of the American League. Connie Mack's recollections of his career as player, manager, and businessman include baseball lore and anecdotes about famous players.

3072 McGinley, Gerard   1906-1955
A Trappist writes home: letters of Abbot Gerard McGinley, O.C.S.O. to his family. Introduction by Father Raymond, O.C.S.O. Preface by McGinley family. Milwaukee: Bruce Publishing Co., 1960. 175 p.
   A collection of letters written 1926-55 by a Trappist-Cistercian monk at Our Lady of Gethseminai, Trappist, Kentucky, and Our Lady of the Genesee, Piffard, New York. The Trappist vows of silence and austerity are congenial to this devout ascetic whose correspondence continually proclaims: "The Trappist life when lived to the core is so sweet; the core of Trappist life is Jesus, He is in me and I in Him, with Mary. Love is sweet and love is joy-giving. That is just what our life is if it be anything at all—love. All for Jesus, all for Jesus."

3073 *McGinley, Phyllis 1905-1978
Sixpence in her shoe. New York: The Macmillan Co., 1964. 281 p.
Written as a rebuttal to Betty Friedan's *Feminine Mystique*, this is a celebration of housewifery by the author of light verse and 17 books for children.

3074 McGinnis, Joe 1943-
Heroes. New York: The Viking Press, 1976. 178 p.
McGinnis laments the loss of American heroes, describing such men as Eugene McCarthy, George McGovern, William Westmoreland, Daniel Berrigan, and expresses his sense of personal failure and depression.

3075 *McGinnis, Vera 1895-
Rodeo road; my life as a pioneer cowgirl. New York: Hastings House, 1974. 225 p.
From age three when she jumped her burro over an irrigation ditch, the author rode horses—racing, jumping, trick riding, and rodeo riding all over the United States, in Europe, and the Orient.

3076 *McGovern, Eleanor (Stegeberg) 1921-
Uphill; a personal story. Boston: Houghton Mifflin Co., 1974. 234 p.
Mrs. McGovern recalls what it was like to be the wife and partner of a politician—the official duties, the family decisions, the campaigning, especially presidential conventions and campaigning, the adversity and the rewards.

3077 McGovern, George Stanley 1922-
Grassroots: the autobiography of George McGovern. New York: Random House, 1977. 307 p. Index.
McGovern analyzes his career as a grassroots politician (trained first as a Methodist minister), serving as a South Dakota Congressman, 1957-62, and as a U.S. Senator for the next decade. As a liberal dove during the hawkish Vietnam War years, McGovern lost a Presidential campaign in 1972; he comments with insightful detail on both the war and the state of American politics.

3078 McGrady, Mike 1933-
The kitchen sink papers: my life as a househusband. New York: Signet/New American Library, 1976. (New York: Doubleday, 1975) 217 p.
With humor and insight, McGrady narrates the highs, the lows, and the humdrum moments of the year (1973-74) he stayed home to care for the house and three school-age children while his wife worked full-time to establish her plastics business. He learned firsthand the meaning of the women's movement as he experienced a life of caring for others, grocery shopping, cooking, running errands, and financial dependence.

3079 *McGrail, Joie Harrison 1922-1977
Fighting back: one woman's struggle against cancer. Creative associate, Phyllis Nevins. New York: Harper & Row, 1978. 196 p.
The author tells the story of the difficult treatment for lung cancer in the United States and in Germany that enabled her to live three years more than expected, but with great physical pain and difficulty. Her valiant spirit to fight cancer, and her husband's help, are pervasive; various therapies (diet, medicine) help intermittently, but McGrail's condition eventually deteriorated.

3080 McGratty, Arthur Raymond 1909-1975
I'd gladly go back. Westminster, Maryland: The Newman Press, 1951. 205 p.
Recollections of childhood escapades in a large, loving family in Brooklyn from the perspective of middle age, by a Catholic priest.

3081 McGregor, Charles Donald 1927-
Up from the walking dead: the Charles McGregor story. With Sharon Sopher. Illustrated. Garden City, New York: Doubleday & Company, Inc., 1978. 490 p.
Most of McGregor's first forty years were spent either as an armed robber or in prison (27 years, mostly in Sing Sing) for robbery or for murder, of which he claims he was wrongfully convicted. Released in 1968 for the third time, McGregor found friendship and a constructive purpose in life through Reality House and the Fortune Society for ex-convicts in New York. He achieved movie stardom in *Blazing Saddles* and *Superfly*.

3082 McGregor, James 1922-
Called for travelling. And Ron Rapoport. New York: Macmillan Publishing Co., Inc., 1978. 243 p. Index.
McGregor writes about coaching basketball all over the world, in countries as diverse as the Soviet Union and Peru. His book concerns his adventures teaching basketball clinics in European countries as well as supervising his American team worldwide.

3083 McIntire, Ross T. 1889-1960
White House physician. In collaboration with George Creel. New York: G.P. Putnam's Sons, 1946. 244 p.
This is the story of FDR's health, his battle against the effects of infantile paralysis, his efforts to overcome the fatigue of his wartime exertions, and the final moments of cerebral hemorrhage brought on by overwork, as told by his friend and official physician, who denies the rumors that Roosevelt ever had cancer, stroke, or various operations.

3084 McKay, Claude 1890-1948
A long way from home: an autobiography. Introduction by St. Clair Drake. New York: Harcourt Brace & World, Inc., 1970. (New York: Lee Furman, 1937) 354 p.
The sensitive story of a Black poet from Jamaica who came to the United States in search of education and expression as a writer. Aided by editors Frank Harris, Max Eastman, and others, McKay published and joined radical literary circles, including the "Harlem Renaissance." He traveled to Russia but returned, repelled by communism. His prose work, including *Home to Harlem* and *Banjo*, won international acclaim.

3085 McKay, Claude 1890-1948
The passion of Claude McKay; selected poetry and prose, 1912-1948. Edited with introduction by Wayne F. Cooper. Illustrated. New York: Schocken Books, 1973. 363 p. Index.
Although primarily a collection of his poetry and prose, this volume includes a selection of his letters. Of special interest are letters written to Max Eastman, which include comments on social problems in Harlem, his struggles to survive as a Black writer, and his later conversion to Catholicism.

3086 McKay, Jim 1921-
My wide world. Illustrated. New York: Macmillan Publishing Co., Inc., 1973. 272 p. Index.
McKay had been featured on ABC's Wide World of Sports for a dozen years before the Munich Olympics in 1972. He uses his experience of that summer season to frame the story of his life as a sportscaster, though half the book is a detailed dramatic account of terrorism, death, and survival at Munich.

3087 McKay, John H. 1923-
McKay: a coach's story. With Jim Perry. New York: Atheneum, 1974. 333 p.
He began coaching the University of Southern California Trojans in 1969. He produced three national championships, seven Rose Bowl teams, and Heisman Trophy winners Mike Garrett and O.J. Simpson. His book tells that story.

3088 *McKenney, Ruth 1911-1972
All about Eileen. New York: Harcourt, Brace, and Co., 1952. 283 p.
A collection of essays, many previously published, about her life with her sister. Eileen and her husband, Nathaniel West, were killed in an automobile accident in 1941; the volume serves as memorial to her.

3089 *McKenney, Ruth 1911-1972
Far, far from home. Illustrated by Susan Knight. New York: Harper and Brothers, 1954. 210 p.
In 1947 the author and her husband, both writers, moved to Belgium for two years, ostensibly to write screenplays on European locations. The book tells the humorous story of their adapting to life with their three small children in a country foreign to them in every way, including the language.

3090 *McKenney, Ruth 1911-1972
Love story. New York: Harcourt, Brace and Co., 1950. 303 p.
The author of *My Sister Eileen* describes her life in Greenwich Village after her secret marriage to Mike Lyman, editor of the left-wing publication, *New Masses*. Both became screenwriters in Hollywood, where they were divorced. The book satirizes many groups, from labor organizers to avant-garde writers.

3091 McKeogh, Michael James 1916-
Sgt. Mickey and General Ike. And Richard Lockridge. New York: G.P. Putnam's Sons, 1946. 185 p.
Assigned as an orderly to Colonel Eisenhower when he was at Fort Sam Houston, he stayed with him through the duration of the war. His book provides an informal, behind-the-scenes picture of Eisenhower and a rather shy, simple self-portrait.

3092 McKuen, Rod 1933-
Finding my father: one man's search for identity. Illustrated. New York: Coward, McCann & Geoghegan, Inc., 1976. 253 p.
This is the story of the poet's exhaustive search for his father who had abandoned his mother before McKuen's birth. He describes his youth, the shock of discovering he was illegitimate, and the reasons for his decision to find his father. Interspersed throughout the book are McKuen's poems.

3093 McLane, Robert Milligan 1815-1898
Reminiscences, 1827-1897. Wilmington, Delaware: Scholarly Resources, Inc., 1972. 165 p.
Since his father was a senator from Delaware and U.S. Minister to London, McLane was from an early age aware of political and diplomatic affairs. Here he writes of his youth and his own career as lawyer, state

legislator, congressman, commissioner to China, and governor of Maryland.

3094 *McLean, Evalyn Walsh   **1886-1947**
Father struck it rich. Ghostwritten by Boyden Sparkes. New York: Arno Press, 1975. (Boston: Little, Brown, 1935) 316 p. Index.
A salty tale of her flamboyant, outrageous progression through Eastern high society. A good-hearted, hard-drinking, high-living free spender, owner of the Hope Diamond, and friend of President Harding, McLean was sobered by her son's death and her husband's permanent hospitalization for alcoholism.

3095 McLoughlin, Emmett   **1907-**
People's Padre: an autobiography. Boston: The Beacon Press, 1954. 288 p. Index.
After 25 years in a Franciscan seminary and priesthood, he left the church to become a hospital administrator. His book includes an account of his persecution and harassment by Catholic priests and lay people.

3096 McLoughlin, John   **1784-1857**
John McLoughlin's business correspondence, 1847-48. Illustrated. Edited by William R. Sampson. Seattle: University of Washington Press, 1973. 179 p.
An important pioneer businessman in Oregon, McLoughlin worked for Hudson's Bay Company and played a major part in the problems and struggles of the frontier community of Oregon City. Appendixes provide shipping data, biographical notes, and a bibliography.

3097 McLoughlin, John   **1784-1857**
Letters of Dr. John McLoughlin: written at Fort Vancouver 1829-1832. Edited by Burt Brown Barker. Portland, Oregon: Binford and Mort for the Oregon Historical Society, 1948. 376 p. Index.
Letters copied in a book by an assistant from the head of the Columbia District of the Hudson's Bay Company in Fort Vancouver, Washington, provide a remarkable view of the work and living conditions in the Northwest. Well-written appendixes give useful information and details.

3098 McMahon, Thomas S.
What, you a priest!: Father Tom, pastor. Foreword by Bill Gleason. Chicago: Franciscan Herald Press, 1976. 287 p.
McMahon, pastor of St. Jude the Apostle Church in South Holland, Illinois, recalls special masses, a visit from Pope Paul VI, athletic contests, banquets, communions, and other activities within his parish.

3099 McNary, James G.   **1877-1962**
This is my life. Foreword by Clarence Budington Kelland. Albuquerque: University of New Mexico Press, 1956. 271 p.
With obvious pride in family, accomplishments, and material wealth, McNary discusses his career as a banker in El Paso, Texas, and lumber company president in Arizona and Louisiana. Active in business (lumber), fraternal and political organizations, McNary was almost rewarded in 1924 when President Harding nominated him for Comptroller of the Currency, but the Senate refused to confirm the appointment.

3100 *McNeal, Violet   **b.1888**
Four white horses and a brass band. Garden City, New York: Doubleday and Co., Inc., 1947. 267 p.
A plainly told but rather grisly story of a young girl from Minnesota, addicted to opium at 18 by a medicine show operator who pretended to marry her, then trained her in the "arts" of his profession.

3101 *McNeil, Marian W.
Lord, give me this mountain. Illustrated. Collingswood, New Jersey: Christian Beacon Press, 1976. 187 p.
With zealous thanksgiving to God, McNeil provides an account of the Mwingi Mission she helped establish in Kenya. Bible verses and testimonies are the backdrop for the building of Christian faith among the natives there and the missionaries' efforts to receive a land grant from the Kenyan government for their mission and hospital.

3102 McNeir, Forest W.   **1875-1957**
Forest McNeir of Texas. San Antonio, Texas: Naylor Co., 1956. 316 p.
A garrulous account of McNeir's life, including several courtships, a fifty-year marriage to Stella, mother of his five adored children, and an occupation as a building contractor. McNeir was a member of the 1920 U.S. Olympic trapshooting team and recounts innumerable trapshooting meets in which he won many championships.

3103 McNulty, John   **1895-1956**
My son Johnny. New York: Simon and Schuster, 1955. 174 p.
A journalist best known for his work in the *New Yorker* describes his delight in being a father and his warm affection for his son.

3104 *McPherson, Aimee Semple   **1890-1944**
The story of my life. Edited by Raymond L. Cox. Waco, Texas: Word Books, 1973. 255 p.

The manuscript on which this book is based was written before her death; in addition, sermon notes, publications, and other documents furnished material which the editor has arranged to make a continuous narrative of her ministry.

3105 McShean, Gordon   **1936-**
Running a message parlor: a librarian's medium-rare memoir about censorship. Illustrated by Terry Down. Palo Alto, California: Ramparts Press, 1977. 237 p.
McShean writes in anecdotal form about his constant battle against censorship of library books and records in Roswell, New Mexico, home of the John Birch Society.

3106 McWilliams, Carey   **1905-**
The education of Carey McWilliams. New York: Simon and Schuster, 1978. 363 p. Index.
A highly analytic, thoroughly detailed account of the author's long liberal political education for 25 years as editor of *The Nation* and as a writer of numerous books, including four on victimized minorities—Jews, Japanese-Americans, Hispanics, and migrant workers. A highly principled man, he used his talents to crusade against the Cold War and the Vietnam War, to which he devotes considerable space here.

3107 McWilliams, LeRoy E.   **1894-1968**
Parish priest. With Jim Bishop. Illustrated. New York: McGraw-Hill Book Co., 1953. 250 p.
Father McWilliams describes his 25-year career as priest of St. Michael's parish in the tough horseshoe district of Jersey City, New Jersey. His parishioners, Irish, Polish, Italian, experienced the joys and traumas of birth and death, sin and salvation, material hardship and sometimes spiritual wealth, all of which McWilliams willingly shared.

3108 *Mead, Margaret   **1901-1978**
Blackberry winter; my earlier years. New York: William Morrow & Co., Inc., 1972. 305 p. Index.
Anthropologist Mead writes of her life up to World War II, including her schooling, the influence of professors on her choice of career, her family, friends, three marriages, pioneering early field trips to Samoa, New Guinea, and Bali, and the opposition she overcame as a young woman studing primitive peoples in the South Seas.

3109 *Mead, Margaret   **1901-1978**
Letters from the field, 1925-1975. Edited by Ruth N. Anshen. Series: World Perspectives, Vol. 52. New York: Harper & Row, 1977. 343 p. Index.
Mead's collected letters discuss her field work in Samoa, Manus, the Admiralty Islands, New Guinea, Bali, and on an Omala Indian Reservation in 1930. She describes the anthropological methodology she was developing and her immersion in the ongoing life of other peoples, other cultures.

3110 *Mead, Margaret   **1901-1978**
Margaret Mead: some personal views. Edited by Rhoda Metraux. New York: Walker & Co., 1979. 286 p. Index.
This collection of Mead's columns from *Redbook Magazine*, 1963-1979, contains her forthright views on cultures around the world. Her topics include the relations among men, women, and children; primitive and more "civilized" societies; government and politics; religion; education; and "personal choices"—places she would like to live, her daydreams, her views on the proper balance between solitude and sociality, and sketches of her female role models.

3111 Means, Alexander   **1801-1883**
Diary for 1861. Emory University Publications: Sources and Reprints, Series 6, no. 1. Edited with introduction by Ross H. McLean. Atlanta: The Library, Emory University, 1949. 46 p.
The diary recalls events in the life and work of a prominent Georgia citizen.

3112 *Mecom, Jane   **1712-1794**
see Franklin, Benjamin

3113 Medema, Ken
Come and see. With Joyce Norman. Waco, Texas: Word Books, 1976. 142 p.
Medema, a Christian composer and pianist, describes his musical ministry and his happy marriage to Joyce, a music therapist and student at Union Theological Seminary. Blind from birth, Medema nevertheless leads an energetic life of concert tours. His book is intended to provide an inspiring example of faith, optimism, and love.

3114 Medill, Robert Bell   **1869-1945**
Klondike diary: true account of the Klondike Rush, 1897-1898. Portland, Oregon: Beattie and Co., 1949. 188 p.
Written in his seventies on the basis of letters, notes, and his diary, the book describes his adventures in the Alaskan Gold Rush.

3115 Meek, Stephen Hall   **1805-1889**
Autobiography of a mountain man, 1805-1889. Introduction by Arthur Woodward. Pasadena: Glen Dawson's Book Shop, 1948. 17 p.
    Brief narrative of the fortunes and failures of a trapper, prospector, and guide in the Western frontier.

3116 Meeker, Arthur   **1902-1971**
Chicago, with love: a polite and personal history. New York: Alfred A. Knopf, 1955. 293 p.
    He grew up in Chicago society of the rich and famous, his father a millionaire, the family moving in the same set with Marshall Field, the Potter Palmers, Edith Rockefeller McCormick, the Jo Ogden Armours, and others. His book recreates the time, place, and characters of an era now vanished.

3117 Meeropol, Robert   **1947-**
We are your sons; the legacy of Julius and Ethel Rosenberg; written by their children. And Michael Meeropol. Boston: Houghton Mifflin Co., 1975. 419 p. Index.
    The sons of the Rosenbergs tell their own story of the trial, appeals, and execution of their parents, the court battles over guardianship, their adoptive parents and their own growth in the politically turbulent 60's. They present arguments and evidence of their parents' innocence as well as letters Ethel and Julius wrote in prison.

3118 Meggyesy, Dave   **1941-**
Out of their league. Berkeley, California: Ramparts, distrib. by Simon & Schuster, 1970. 257 p.
    The author, a former linebacker for the St. Louis Cardinal football team, explains why he quit the sport in the middle of his career. He has come to view the game as vicious and dehumanizing, involving racism and fraud as well as unbelievable brutality that affects the mind as much as the body.

3119 *Megquier, Mary Jane (Cole)
Apron full of gold: the letters of Mary Jane Megquier from San Francisco, 1849-1856. Edited by Robert Glass Cleland. San Marino, California: Huntington Library, 1949. 99 p.
    Vivid description of her journey from Maine through the Panama Canal to California with her husband and of life in San Francisco during the Gold Rush as lived by two ordinary people. She ran boardinghouses while her husband set up a medical practice.

3120 *Mehdevi, Anne Sinclair
From pillar to post. New York: Alfred A. Knopf, 1956. 272 p.
    More cultural conflicts, as her husband's business interests move their family through Mexico, the U.S., and Europe.

3121 *Mehdevi, Anne Sinclair
Persia revisited. New York: Alfred A. Knopf, 1964. 271 p.
    This volume describes their return to and residency in Iran, again emphasizing cultural differences with an attempt to appreciate some universal human characteristics.

3122 *Mehdevi, Anne Sinclair
Persian adventure. New York: Alfred A. Knopf, 1953. 271 p.
    A novelist's record of her marriage to Mohammed Mehdevi and their subsequent journey to Iran reflects dramatic clashes between their two cultures.

3123 *Meir, Golda   **1898-1978**
My life. New York: G.P. Putnam's Sons, 1975. 480 p.
    The remarkable story of the woman who became Prime Minister of Israel. Born in Russia, raised in Milwaukee, she became a Zionist, a socialist, and a significant leader in the struggle for human rights.

3124 Mellnik, Stephen Michael   **1907-**
Philippine diary, 1939-1945. Illustrated. Foreword by Carlos P. Romulo. New York: Van Nostrand Reinhold Co., 1969. 316 p.
    Serving in the Philippines when MacArthur had to surrender, Mellnik was imprisoned by the Japanese; later he escaped and worked with guerrillas until he could be transported back to the U.S. His book, based on his diary, records the agony and humiliation of life in the Japanese penal colony as well as the heroism of survival.

3125 Melrose, Paul C.
On being a missionary. New York: Pageant Press, 1957. 73 p.
    Melrose describes his years between World Wars I and II as a Christian missionary in China, focusing on the training, missionary methods, "sacrificial living," and politics (difficult in China because of communists, guerrillas, friction with Japan and Russia).

3126 Melton, Frederick
    see Clancy, Foghorn, pseud.

3127 Melville, Herman   **1819-1891**
Journal of a visit to Europe and the Levant, October 11, 1856-May 6, 1857. Edited by Howard C. Horsford. Princeton University Studies in English, no. 35. Princeton: Princeton University Press, 1955. 299 p. Index.
    Written in the prime of his literary career, the journal is interesting as a record of his observations and their influence on his later work.

3128 Melville, Herman   **1819-1891**
Journal of a visit to London and the continent, 1849-1850. Edited by Eleanor Melville Metcalf. Cambridge: Harvard University Press, 1948. 189 p. Index.
    A journal, previously unpublished, of Melville's first trip abroad, at age 30, which records his thoughts on the cities he visited while seeking a publisher for *White Jacket* and traveling for several months. His journal, with his granddaughter's notes, creates a sharp image of mid-nineteenth-century life.

3129 Melville, Herman   **1819-1891**
The letters of Herman Melville. Edited by Merrell R. Davis and William H. Gilman. New Haven: Yale University Press, 1960. 398 p. Index.
    A collection of 271 letters, 55 published in full for the first time and 42 previously unpublished, written to family, friends, publishers, and newspaper editors, by a prominent author.

3130 Melville, Marjorie
    see Melville, Thomas

3131 Melville, Samuel Joseph   **1935?-1971**
Letters from Attica. Profiles of the author by Jane Alpert and John Cohen. Foreword by William Kunstler. New York: William Morrow & Co., 1972. 181 p.
    Melville was sentenced to thirteen to eighteen years in prison after pleading guilty to a series of politically motivated bombings. He was shot and killed during the Attica Prison riots of 1971, of which he was one of the leaders. His letters show his despair but later hope and defiance as he led the prisoners' struggle for justice.

3132 Melville, Thomas
Whose heaven, whose earth? And Marjorie Melville. New York: Alfred A. Knopf, 1971. 303 p.
    A young priest, assigned to a mountain parish in Guatemala but sent home after his over-zealous attempts to Christianize the Indians, and a nun, outraged at government and church indifference to the plight of the Indians, joined their efforts to form a guerrilla band to champion the cause of the poor. Betrayed, they fled to Mexico, were married, and continued their activist activities as part of the Catonsville Nine.

3133 Mencken, Henry Louis   **1880-1956**
A choice of days: essays from *Happy Days, Newspaper Days* and *Heathen Days*. Selected with introduction by Edward L. Galligan. New York: Alfred A. Knopf, 1980. 337 p.
    This commemoration of the centenary of Mencken's birth combines twenty chapters from three of his previous works, describing his happy childhood in Baltimore, his early newspaper days, and culminating in his triumph over a five-star newspaper crisis.

3134 Mencken, Henry Louis   **1880-1956**
Days of H.L. Mencken: happy days, newspaper days, heathen days. New York: Alfred A. Knopf, 1947. 958 p.
    "A series of random reminiscences, not always photographically precise, of a life that, on the whole, has been very busy and excessively pleasant," by one of the great journalists of the twentieth century.

3135 Mencken, Henry Louis   **1880-1956**
Letters of H.L. Mencken. Selected and annotated by Guy J. Forgue, with a personal note by Hamilton Owens. New York: Alfred A. Knopf, 1961. 506 p. Index.
    Selected from the thousands of letters he wrote, this volume includes correspondence with many of his important contemporaries. The collection depicts both the tone and the power of his influence in the literary world as well as a fascinating sample of the Mencken philosophy.

3136 Mencken, Henry Louis   **1880-1956**
The new Mencken letters. Edited with introduction by Carl Bode. New York: Dial Press, 1977. 635 p. Index.
    Mencken, flamboyant journalist and editor famed for *Prejudices* and *The American Language*, wrote over 100,000 letters from 1905-1955, from which this representative selection is culled. He wrote often to journalists, authors, and intellectuals letters charged with "malicious animal magnetism" (ed.) expressing the spirit of the Prohibition Era, rowdy political conventions, and a grudging love for Baltimore, his home town.

3137 Mendelson, Ralph Waldo   **1888-1968**
I lost a king. New York: Vantage Press, 1964. 287 p.
    Mendelson has written an articulate account of his lifetime of overseas service as a physician. During World War I, as a member of the American

Red Cross Sanitary Service in the Balkans, he was commissioned to help conquer the typhus epidemic. He then worked in Siam for a decade, as Principal Civil Medical Officer of Health for the Royal Siamese government and surgeon to the king. He was an Air Force surgeon during World War II and Chief of (Medical) Professional Services at Kirtland Air Force Base until his retirement in 1951.

3138 Menjou, Adolphe   **1890-1963**
It took nine tailors. With M.M. Musselman. New York: Whittlesey House, 1948. 238 p.
  Describes boyhood in Cleveland and New York with primary emphasis on his career as a film actor since 1913.

3139 Menninger, Karl Augustus   **1893-**
Sparks. Edited by Lucy Freeman. New York: Thomas Y. Crowell Co., 1973. 290 p. Index.
  Dr. Menninger, a founder of the Menninger Clinic, the Menninger Foundation, and the Menninger School of Psychiatry, changed the thinking of scholars and students with his book, *The Human Mind*, in 1930. This volume is compiled from his reading notes, articles, speeches, and letters to reveal a man of many interests whose mind never seems to rest.

3140 Menuhin, Yehudi   **1916-**
Unfinished journey. Introduction by George Steiner. New York: Alfred A. Knopf, 1977. 393 p. Index.
  Menuhin, a superb violinist, writes with scrupulous literary craftsmanship of his musical career, family and friends, world travels, Zionism, and humanistic concerns. He and his sister, Hepzibah, were both child prodigies; their talent was an entree into the international world of great musicians and concert tours.

3141 Meredith, James Howard   **1933-**
Three years in Mississippi. Bloomington: Indiana University Press, 1966. 328 p.
  Meredith's story of his struggle to attend the University of Mississippi and the events, the trial, and the precedent-shattering success in being the first Black admitted to and graduated from that institution. Still to be attained is his goal of being recognized as a man without regard to race.

3142 Meriwhether, David   **1800-1893**
My life on the mountains and on the plains; the newly discovered autobiography. Edited with introduction by Robert A. Griffen. Norman: University of Oklahoma Press, 1965. 301 p. Index.
  Dictated to his granddaughter when he was 85, this account is based on Meriwhether's remarkable memory plus letters, papers, and clippings. He speaks of his youth, his trip up the Missouri in 1819, his imprisonment by Mexicans, his experiences as an Indian trader, farmer, legislator, and New Mexico territorial governor during a period of incessant war with surrounding Indian tribes.

3143 *Merman, Ethel Agnes (Zimmerman)   **1909-**
Merman: an autobiography. With George Eells. New York: Berkeley Book, 1979. (New York: Simon and Schuster, 1978) 344 p. Index.
  A brassy account of Merman's life, focusing on her theatrical career from preschool to the present, including such hits as *Annie Get Your Gun, Call Me Madam*, and *Mame*. She refers to many actors and composers in show business, comments on her two marriages, and mourns the drug-related death of her daughter.

3144 *Merman, Ethel Agnes (Zimmerman)   **1909-**
Who could ask for anything more. With Pete Martin. Illustrated. Garden City, New York: Doubleday, 1955. 252 p.
  Ethel Merman writes of her theatrical career in such successes as *Call Me Madam* and *Annie Get Your Gun*, and her marriage to publicist Bob Levitt, whom she divorced when their children, Bobby and Ethel, were adolescent. Merman's brash, boastful theatrical style is mirrored in her autobiographical commentary.

3145 Merrick, Elliott   **1905-**
Green Moutain farm. New York: The Macmillan Co., 1948. 209 p.
  Driven out of New York in 1932 by unemployment and the Depression, he took his wife and child to a small farm in Vermont, where they learned to live off the land and find a more peaceful existence.

3146 Merrill, John   **b.1875**
Son of Salem: the autobiography of John Merrill. Illustrated. New York: Vantage Press, Inc., 1953. 202 p.
  Merrill's pleasantly written book emphasizes his formative years in Salem, Massachusetts, his education at Emerson College, his brief career as an actor at the Castle Street Theater, Boston (1897-1898), which he left because of financial insecurity, his 5'7" height which made him too short for some parts, and his moral disapproval of some roles he was obliged to act. Merrill devotes only one chapter to his long career as a teacher of drama at the Francis W. Parker School in Chicago, though he does provide a sample curriculum and rationale.

3147 Merrill, Robert   **1919-**
Between acts: an irreverent look at opera and other madness. With Robert Saffron. Illustrated. New York: McGraw-Hill Publishing Co., 1976. 240 p.
  Opera-singer Merrill has written, as he says, "an irreverent mosaic of tales from the performing arts that I have reveled in for over 40 years . . . vaudeville, radio, film, television, Las Vegas clubs, musical comedy, and for three decades, the Metropolitan Opera."

3148 *Merritt, Onera Amelia (Mary Weston, pseud.)   **b.1887**
An American child: the beginning of an autobiography, by Mary Weston (pseud.). London: Allan Wingate, 1949. 192 p.
  An author recalls her girlhood in New York, her English boarding-school, and the beginning of her quest for womanhood.

3149 Merritt, Wesley   **1834-1910**
Merritt and the Indian wars; three Indian campaigns. Biographical essay by Barry C. Johnson. London: Johnson-Taunton Military Press, 1972. 32 p.
  In his article on the Indian Wars of the post-Civil War period, first published in 1890 in *Harper's New Monthly Magazine*, General Merritt describes his attitudes toward "war-making" against the Indians. He says "finding them, not fighting them, is the difficult problem to solve."

3150 Merrow, Chester Earl   **1906-1974**
My twenty years in Congress: a summary of his major votes, his accomplishments for New Hampshire, his work in international affairs, his philosophy of government both at home and abroad and his predictions of United States policy and courses of action for the future. Illustrated. Concord: The Society for the Publication of New Hampshire Biographies, 1968. 394 p.
  The subtitle aptly summarizes the contents, which express a conservative view on keeping "Red China" out of the United Nations, fears of a communist takeover of the United States, outlawing the Communist Party in the United States, and the need for continuous "military preparedness." Nevertheless, Merrow regards the Peace Corps as "the fulfillment of a vision" and Israel as "the focus of democracy in the Middle East."

3151 Merton, Thomas   **1915-1968**
A catch of anti-letters: Thomas Merton and Robert Lax. Mission, Kansas: Sheed Andrews and McMeel, Inc., 1978. 128 p.
  Their close friendship began in the Thirties at Columbia University when they collaborated on a magazine. Later both converted to Catholicism and in their way retreated from the world, Merton in a Kentucky Trappist monastery, Lax on a Greek island. Their friendship endured.

3152 Merton, Thomas   **1915-1968**
The secular journal of Thomas Merton. New York: Farrar, Straus, and Cudahy, 1959. 270 p.
  Written during 1939-1941 when he was a student at Columbia, then an instructor at St. Bonaventure University, but before he became a Trappist monk, his journal comments on a wide range of topics, often depicting his struggle to resolve the conflict between his desire to write and to serve the Church.

3153 Merton, Thomas   **1915-1968**
The seven storey mountain. Bergenfield, New Jersey: New American Library, 1975. (New York: Harcourt, Brace and Co., 1948) 429 p. Index.
  A philosophical narrative that explores the conflict he experiences between his roles as a Trappist monk and a poet.

3154 Meryman, Richard   **1926-**
Hope: a loss survived. Boston: Little, Brown, 1980. 246 p.
  Writer Meryman traces with wrenching detail the course of his wife's cancer, from the first change in a mole on her back to her painful death at home and his subsequent life as widowed father of two young daughters.

3155 *Mesta, Perle   **1891-1975**
Perle: my story. With Robert Cahn. New York: McGraw-Hill Book Co., Inc., 1960. 251 p. Index.
  Wealthy society leader in Washington, D.C., discusses her life as a party-giver for the elite, her brief career as Ambassador to Luxembourg, and varied political travels and activities.

3156 Metcalf, Keyes DeWitt   **1889-**
Random recollections of an anachronism; or seventy-five years of library work. Illustrated. New York: Readex Books, 1980. 401 p. Index.
  Metcalf, who began library work at thirteen, held key positions in both the largest public library and the largest academic library in the U.S. and was president of the American Library Association. This volume of recollections spans his first 48 years, marked by energy, ambition, curiosity, immense capacity and enthusiasm for library work.

3157 *Meyer, Agnes Elizabeth (Ernst)   **1887-1970**
Out of these roots: the autobiography of an American woman. Boston: Little, Brown and Co., 1953. 385 p. Index.

After beginning a career as an art critic, she married Eugene Meyer, who became owner of the Washington *Post*, and developed a new career as a journalist with an outstanding reputation for social and cultural analysis.

3158 Meyer, Armin Henry 1914-
Assignment Tokyo; an ambassador's journal. Indianapolis: The Bobbs-Merrill Co., Inc., 1974. 396 p. Index.
A career diplomat, Meyer became Ambassador to Japan in 1969, when Japan had become one of the world's three leading industrial powers. His book concentrates on his diplomatic role, emphasizing the significance and gravity of America's relationship with Japan.

3159 *Meyer, Edith (Patterson) 1895-
For goodness sake! Growing up in a New England parsonage. Illustrated. Nashville: Abingdon Press, 1973. 176 p.
One of five children in a Methodist minister's family, she writes of the lively mischievous days of her childhood in a home ruled by codes of physical and spiritual economy.

3160 Meyer, Ernest Louis 1892-1952
Hey! Yellowbacks; the war diary of a conscientious objector. Foreword by William Ellery Leonard. Englewood, New Jersey: J.S. Ozer, 1972. (New York: The John Day Co., 1930) 209 p.
Expelled from the University of Wisconsin for his refusal to serve in World War I, imprisoned, tried three times, and finally released after the armistice, Meyer described his experiences in various military camps. Despite his unpleasant treatment, he feels that "the American government, officially, dealt more humanely and generously with war objectors than did any other nation."

3161 Meyers, Michael 1946-
Goodbye Columbus, hello medicine. New York: William Morrow and Co., 1976. 288 p.
Meyers writes of becoming a family practitioner, beginning with medical school, through internship and residency. He includes anecdotes about typical cases, ranging from obstetrical to alcoholic to pediatric. While in medical school, Meyers played a role in *Goodbye, Columbus* and other films and was on various television talk shows.

3162 Mezvinsky, Edward Maurice 1937-
A term to remember. With Kevin McCormally and John Greenya. Illustrated. New York: Coward, McCann, and Geoghegan, 1977. 256 p. Index.
Mezvinsky was elected to Congress in 1972 as a Democrat from Iowa's first district, just as the taint of the Watergate scandal was about to reach the Oval Office. He joins an account of the Congressional hearings, which he attended as a member of the House Judiciary Committee, with fragments of his disintegrating family life and ultimate divorce, another consequence of the stress of politics.

3163 Mezzrow, Milton 1899-1972
Really the blues. And Bernard Wolfe. New York: Random House, 1946. 388 p. Index.
The world of jazz by one who knew it well, including translations and a glossary of jive talk, discussions of what is jazz, and the ways in which Chicago style differs from that of New Orleans.

3164 *Michel, Trudi 1921-
Inside Tin Pan Alley. Foreword by I. Michel. New York: Frederick Fell, Inc., 1948. 172 p.
Her experience trying to make a career as a songwriter, with one song that did become a hit, "Strange and Sweet," focuses on the difficulty a woman had breaking into the business world.

3165 Mickle, Isaac 1822-1855
Gentleman of much promise: the diary of Isaac Mickle, 1837-1845. Edited with introduction by Philip English Mackey. Illustrated. Philadelphia: University of Pennsylvania Press, 1977. 2v.
A diary reflecting Mickle's growth from a precocious, pious young man of fourteen to a more worthy gentleman of twenty-two. Comments include his political views (Democrat), his literary, musical, scientific, and historical interests—all areas in which he made some local contributions. His enormous energy and enterprise produced remarkable accomplishments in a few years—becoming a lawyer, editing a local newspaper, becoming a political force in Camden, New Jersey, printing a local history.

3166 Middleton, Drew 1913-
Our share of night: a personal narrative of the war years. New York: The Viking Press, 1946. 380 p.
An outstanding, dramatic account of World War II by a journalist who served as an Associated Press correspondent in the British sector. Perceptive analysis of officers and enlisted men in the Allied war zones provides a vivid sense of what the war was like.

3167 Middleton, Drew 1913-
Where has last July gone? Memoirs. New York: New York Times Book Co., 1973. 284 p.

In the spring of 1939 he began working in London for the Associated Press. His book describes his experience there and as a foreign correspondent or bureau chief for the New York *Times* through late 1971. This is the personal history of a journalist who observed and wrote about many of the significant people and events of his time.

3168 Middleton, George 1880-1967
These things are mine: the autobiography of a journeyman playwright. New York: The Macmillan Co., 1947. 448 p. Index.
Well-written narrative of his life in the theater—stage and screen—with interesting details about his literary friends and famous contemporaries.

3169 Middleton, George W. b.1866
Memoirs of a pioneer surgeon. Foreword by Howard A. Kelly. Illustrated by R.P. Middleton. Salt Lake City, Utah: Richard P. Middleton, 1976. 286 p.
This book, written in 1936, is a straightforward account of Middleton's experiences as a Mormon farm youth in Utah, his medical education in Baltimore and London, and his pioneering surgical practice in Cedar City, Utah, 1895-1932. The surgeon loves his work, his Mormon heritage, the hardiness of the Western pioneers, and the rocky terrain of Utah and the Colorado River area.

3170 *Midler, Bette 1945?-
A view from a broad. Photographs by Jean Russell. Illustrated. New York: Simon and Schuster, 1980. 159 p.
A series of one-liners that describe a comic entertainer's tour of Europe, including England, Scandinavia, France, and Australia. She calls it a "monumental schlep."

3171 *Mieir, Audrey
The laughter and the tears. Burbank, California: Manna Books, 1976. 144 p.
In a style highlighted by underlinings, ellipses, and Bible quotations, gospel musician Mieir recounts her musical ministry to the United States and the Orient. She intersperses her story with lyrics and music she has written. Her work has included support of Korean orphans and mixed-blood offspring of American servicemen in Korea and placement with foster parents in America. Two of her own children are adopted.

3172 Miers, Earl Schenck 1910-1972
The trouble bush. Chicago: Rand McNally & Co., 1966. 342 p. Index.
Miers explains his metamorphosis from a scrawny Brooklyn child with cerebral palsy through training as a journalist, first as a high school stringer and later at Rutgers. His editorial positions at Rutgers University Press and Alfred A. Knopf are proof that a handicapped person can lead a useful and enjoyable life.

3173 Miers, Earl Schenck 1910-1972
Why did this have to happen? New York: St. Martin's Press, 1958. 63 p.
An author-editor discusses the challenging difficulty of living with cerebral palsy, an affliction he suffered as a result of injury at birth.

3174 Mikan, George Lawrence 1924-
Mr. Basketball: George Mikan's own story. As told to Bill Carlson. New York: Greenberg Publisher, 1951. 80 p.
A professional basketball player with the Minneapolis Lakers writes of his training and success in the game.

3175 Milam, Carl Hastings 1884-1963
Carl H. Milam and the United Nations Library. Edited with introduction by Doris Cruger Dale. Metuchen, New Jersey: The Scarecrow Press, Inc., 1976. 132 p. Index.
Director of the United Nations Library from 1948 to 1950, Milam kept a diary reflecting his concern for general library policy, budget, personnel, and services, as well as personal events and experiences.

3176 Milland, Ray 1907-
Wide-eyed in Babylon; an autobiography. New York: William Morrow & Co., Inc., 1974. 264 p.
An urbane account of his career in films, beginning with his boyhood in Cardiff, Wales, his early acting career in England, and the long years in Hollywood. He received an Academy Award for his role as an alcoholic in *The Lost Weekend*.

3177 *Millay, Edna St. Vincent 1892-1950
Letters of Edna St. Vincent Millay. Edited by Allan Ross Macdougall. Westport, Connecticut: Greenwood Press, 1972. (New York: Harper and Brothers, 1952) 384 p. Index.
A selection of available letters (1900-1950) reflecting her profound concern for poetry and self-criticism and her deep love of family and friends.

3178 *Millberg, Karen Schwencke (Hansen, Karen, pseud.)
Flight against the wind. New York: The Odyssey Press, 1947. 182 p.
As a young widow in the late Twenties, the author immigrated to New

York from Denmark, describing here her struggle to survive, to bring her son to join her, and finally to establish a small interior decorating business.

3179 Miller, Alexander Quintella, Jr.   **b.1874**
Jayhawk editor: a biography of A.Q. Miller, Sr., compiled and edited by James D. Callahan, from the recollections, writings, and papers of A.Q. Miller, Sr. Compiled and edited by James D. Callahan. Los Angeles: Sterling Press, 1955. 256 p.

A biographical narrative of the life of a newspaper editor for fifty years publisher of the weekly, Belleville (Kansas) *Telescope,* interspersed with his personal reminiscences of early days in Kansas and in his publishing career, notable events in Kansas history (such as Prohibition and the spread of highways), and his editorial views on national defense, right-to-work laws, and politics.

3180 *Miller, Ann   **1923-**
Miller's high life. With Norma Lee Browning. Garden City, New York: Doubleday & Co., Inc., 1972. 283 p.

Ann Miller tap-danced her way to fame in more than forty movies, played in musicals on Broadway, on the road, and on television. Her unremitting hard work and striving for perfection have kept her in top form during her long career.

3181 Miller, Arthur   **1915-**
Theater essays of Arthur Miller. Edited with introduction by Robert A. Martin. New York: The Viking Press, 1978. 401 p.

This collection of 23 erudite, cogent essays and three interviews, 1949-1972, reveals Miller's views on his plays, on the human condition, on the Cold War climate, and contemporary theater. He examines "Tragedy and the Common Man," "The Family in Modern Drama," and defends his Jewish heritage. He claims that he was harassed by the HUAC investigation because of the publicity surrounding his marriage to Marilyn Monroe.

3182 Miller, Arthur C.
see Balshofer, Fred J.

3183 Miller, Francis Pickens   **1895-**
Man from the valley; memoirs of the 20th-century Virginian. Chapel Hill: University of North Carolina Press, 1971. 253 p.

A leader in political, religious, and humanitarian groups, the author worked to bring progressive government to Virginia. His campaign for the governorship and the senatorship (1949, 1952) emphasized equal rights regardless of race, a cause later espoused by Byrd machine candidates.

3184 Miller, Henry   **1891-1980**
Collector's quest: the correspondence of Henry Miller and J. Rives Childs, 1947-1965. Illustrated edition. Introduction by Richard Clement Wood. Charlottesville: Published for Randolph-Macon College by University Press of Virginia, 1968. 216 p. Index.

The correspondence showing the growth of a friendship between the well-known author Miller and Childs, a foreign service officer who was collecting Miller's published works and other Milleriana. The collection, enumerated in an appendix, is now at Randolph-Macon College.

3185 Miller, Henry   **1891-1980**
Henry Miller's book of friends: a tribute to friends of long ago. Illustrated. Santa Barbara, California: Capra Press, 1976. 138 p.

Miller writes warmly of his friends; his references to himself are generally crude and always arrogant. He traces various friendships from childhood through adulthood, though he does not always identify them by last names.

3186 Miller, Henry   **1891-1980**
Letters of Henry Miller and Wallace Fowlie (1943-1972). Introduction by Wallace Fowlie. New York: Grove Press, Inc., 1975. 184 p. Index.

When they first corresponded, Miller was already an established writer, Fowlie an unknown critic. Their letters reveal the interplay and enthusiasm of two extraordinary minds who have greatly influenced contemporary literature.

3187 Miller, Henry   **1891-1980**
Letters to Anaïs Nin. Edited with introduction by Gunther Stuhlmann. New York: G.P. Putnam's Sons, 1965. 356 p. Index.

A selection of letters (1931-46) to his friend and confidante of many years gives an unvarnished portrait of Miller during this fruitful and difficult period of his life.

3188 Miller, Henry   **1891-1980**
My life and times. Illustrated. Edited by Bradley Smith. Chicago: Playboy Press, 1971. 204 p. Index.

An album of photographs, copies of manuscript pages from *Tropic of Cancer,* prints of Miller's own paintings interspersed with text in which Miller rambles through bits and pieces of his life, muses about his career and his philosophy of life. The editor "created and produced" this "visual

autobiography" from taped interviews and materials supplied by Miller and taken from *The Henry Miller Odyssey,* a documentary film.

3189 Miller, Henry   **1891-1980**
This is Henry, Henry Miller from Brooklyn; conversations with the author from *The Henry Miller Odyssey,* by Robert Snyder. Los Angeles: Nash Publishing, 1974. 125 p.

Here in interview form with Robert Snyder, Miller discusses his childhood and family, his marriages, his difficulties in getting published, the influences on his writing, and his life in Europe and California. Includes photos from Snyder's documentary film *The Henry Miller Odyssey.*

3190 Miller, Henry
see also Gordon, William A.

3191 Miller, Loye
Lifelong boyhood: recollections of a naturalist afield. Berkeley: University of California Press, 1950. 226 p.

A naturalist describes the development of his interest in biology and archaeology, reflecting his genuine pleasure in his work.

3192 *Miller, Madelaine Hemingway   **1904-**
Ernie; Hemingway's sister "Sunny" remembers. Preface by Robert Traver. Illustrated. New York: Crown Publishers, Inc., 1975. 146 p.

Her famous brother was both her hero and best friend. In her book she captures memories of their life in Oak Park, Illinois, and summers in upper Michigan, illustrated with many family photographs.

3193 *Miller, Mary Britton
see *Bolton, Isabel, pseud.

3194 Miller, Max Carleton   **1901-1967**
No matter what happens. New York: E.P. Dutton and Co., Inc., 1949. 249 p.

Well-written story of a boy's youthful ideas of adventure and the ways he chose to live them as he grew older and became a professional writer. Miller is the author of *I Cover the Waterfront* and many other books of non-fiction and fiction.

3195 Miller, Max Carleton   **1901-1967**
Shinny on your own side: and other memoirs of growing up. Illustrated by Ray Houlihan. Garden City, New York: Doubleday & Co., 1958. 240 p.

A writer describes his boyhood in Montana and Washington, including stories about the railroad roundhouse, floating on the rivers, horses and buggies, circus life, and learning about girls, adventures which shaped him as a man and author of two dozen novels, including *I Cover the Waterfront.*

3196 Miller, Minor C.   **b.1885**
These things I remember. Foreword by Charles H. Huffman. Philadelphia: Dorrance & Co., 1968. 226 p.

Miller, a lifelong and devoted member of the Church of the Brethren, describes his childhood in rural Virginia, his education at Bridgewater (Va.) College, and longtime teaching of religious education there.

3197 Miller, William ("Fishbait") Moseley
Fishbait: the memoirs of the Congressional Doorkeeper. With Frances Spatz Leighton. New York: Warner Books, 1978. (New York: Prentice-Hall, 1977) 527 p. Index.

Democratic Doorkeeper to the House of Representatives for 24 years fills his disorganized, good-natured reminiscences of twentieth-century politics with anecdotal accounts concerning congressmen, senators, presidents, and their spouses and staffs.

3198 *Millett, Kate   **1934-**
Flying. New York: Alfred A. Knopf, 1974. 545 p.

The author writes of her inner and outer life during one decisive year, revealing her memories, fantasies, fears, doubts, and feelings. She speaks of making a movie, the hard work of sculpture, her love affairs, her political commitment, and her struggle to live out personal ideals denied by convention and tradition.

3199 *Millett, Kate   **1934-**
Sita. New York: Ballantine Books, 1977. (New York: Random House, 1976) 313 p.

Millett sentimentally anatomizes her passion for Sita, her lover in San Francisco and New York in the early 1970's, focusing on the year of rejection and ultimate break-up in detail.

3200 Millette, Ernest Schlee   **b.1884?**
The circus that was; the autobiography of a star performer. With Robert Wyndham. Philadelphia: Dorrance & Co., 1971. 180 p.

Millette started his circus life at age fourteen with the Millette Brothers Acrobatic Troupe and soon was accomplishing feats never equaled since. After ten years he left the circus, completed his education and taught at Robert College, acting as coach and supervising physical education in addition to other duties. In 1968 he was elected by his peers to the Circus Hall of Fame.

3201 Millikan, Robert Andrews   **1868-1953**
The autobiography of Robert A. Millikan. New York: Prentice-Hall, Inc., 1950. 311 p. Index.
Research physicist with international administrative responsibilities reflects upon the events of his life and career, including philosophic observations about the prolific growth of scientific knowledge during the past hundred years.

3202 *Mills, Nettie Elizabeth (West)   **b.1880**
The lady driller: the autobiography of N. Elizabeth Mills. New York: Exposition Press, 1955. 176 p.
Mills chronicles a varied descriptive life from near poverty and warring over homestead claims in Nebraska to eventual success as "The Lady Driller" of oil wells in Oklahoma and Texas. When a novice in business, she successfully operated cafes and hotels, then married a philandering, drug-addicted physician, divorced him, and went into the oil business, where she survived such calamities as dry wells and the machinations of giant companies to become rich.

3203 *Milner, Lucille (Bernheimer)   **1888-1975**
Education of an American liberal. Introduction by Alvin Johnson. New York: Horizon Press, 1954. 312 p. Index.
A social worker from Missouri describes her work as a secretary for the American Civil Liberties Union in New York City from the time the organization began.

3204 Mingus, Charles   **1922-1979**
Beneath the underdog; his world as composed by Mingus. Edited by Nel King. New York: Alfred A. Knopf, 1971. 365 p.
A self-portrait of a musician and jazz composer confronts his experiences in poverty-stricken childhood, outcast adolescence, and an adulthood haunted by guilt and self-hatred. Throughout his search for self and peace of soul he always returned to his music.

3205 Minnelli, Vincent   **1910-**
I remember it well. With Hector Arce. Foreword by Alan Jay Lerner. Illustrated. Garden City, New York: Doubleday & Co., Inc., 1974. 391 p. Index.
A remarkable narrative of Hollywood in the Forties, Fifties, and Sixties, written by an outstanding director of musicals when they were at the center of the movie industry. His book reflects the glamour, self-indulgence, talent and enthusiasm of the era and the stars.

3206 Mirov, Nicholas Tiho   **1893-**
The road I came: the memoirs of a Russian-American forester. Illustrated. Kingston, Ontario: Limestone Press, 1978. 225 p. Index.
A well-written, richly descriptive story of the author's life in pre-revolutionary Russia where he studied forestry, the beginning of his lifelong and worldwide career. He entered the Russian navy just as the revolution broke. Mirov was essentially apolitical and by luck ended up working in Manchuria on a forestry project. After he and his wife immigrated to America, he worked his way up in the California Forest Service and later became lecturer at the University of California.

3207 *Mitchell, Elizabeth Ann (Oldacre)   **b.1876**
Anchored to the rock. Anderson, Indiana: Printed for the author by Gospel Trumpet Co., 1950. 142 p.
A third person narrative of her lifelong devotion to the church, as a minister and minister's wife in the rural South.

3208 Mitchell, Frank   **1881-1967**
Navajo Blessingway singer: the autobiography of Frank Mitchell. Edited by Charlotte J. Frisbie and David P. McAllester. Tucson: University of Arizona Press, 1978. 446 p.
One of the first Navajo children to attend the Fort Defiance boarding school, he later worked as a handyman and interpreter at reservation missions and trading posts. His book is especially interesting, however, for its descriptions of the Blessingway rites he practices.

3209 *Mitchell, Lucy Sprague   **1878-1967**
Two lives: the story of Wesley Clair Mitchell and myself. New York: Simon and Schuster, 1953. 575 p.
The story of a "remarkable marriage and two notable careers." Before marrying a prominent economist, she became Dean of Women and the first woman on the faculty of the University of California. Later she became well-known for her educational work with children and teachers and was for 34 years Chairman of the Bureau of Educational Experiments.

3210 *Mitchell, Margaret   **1900-1949**
Margaret Mitchell's *Gone with the Wind* letters: 1936-1949. Edited by Richard Harwell. New York: Macmillan Publishing Co., 1976. 441 p. Index.
Mitchell's correspondence concerning her only book, *Gone With the*

Wind, focuses on details of publishing, publicity (which she disliked), the movie version, translations (including Russian and Chinese), reviews, and lawsuits over plagiarism and piracy. The book reveals some interesting aspects of Mitchell's composing process—she wrote the book in reverse order, last chapter first. An Atlantan born and bred, Mitchell's loyalty to location is epitomized in her letters, as in her novel.

3211 *Mitchell, Maria   **1818-1889**
Maria Mitchell, life, letters, and journals. Compiled by Phebe Mitchell Kendall. Boston: Lee & Shepard, 1896. 293 p.
Selections from the astronomer's letters and journals from 1847 to her death are bound together by the compiler's commentary. This volume contains Maria Mitchell's observations on her discovery of a comet in 1847, her work as scientist and teacher, her travels in the United States, Europe, and Russia, as well as her views concerning slavery and woman suffrage.

3212 *Mitchell, Suzanne
My own woman: the diary of an analysis. New York: Horizon Press, 1973. 269 p.
Diary entries during the six years in which she consulted an analyst reveal her struggle to overcome depression and develop an independent identity.

3213 Mitchell, Sydney B.   **1878-1951**
Mitchell of California: the memoirs of Sydney B. Mitchell, librarian, teacher and gardener. Preface by Lawrence Clark Powell. Berkeley: California Library Association, 1960. 263 p.
Mitchell describes the places he lived and worked during the first half of his life—Montreal, where he was born and educated; Albany, New York, where he received his education in librarianship; Palo Alto, where he had his first major librarianship at Stanford, married, and began gardening seriously. He died before completing the memoir, which is supplemented by his observations on the library school at Berkeley, Cora Brandt's essay on Mitchell's horticultural work, notably iris breeding, and an annotated bibliography of Mitchell's extensive publications.

3214 *Mitford, Jessica Lucy   **1917-**
A fine old conflict. New York: Alfred A. Knopf, 1977. 333 p.
One of the famous daughters of an eccentric British peer, the author describes her membership in the American Communist Party, her gadfly activities within the party, and her disenchantment and resignation. In addition she writes of her marriages, family, and her battle to expose the funeral industry, which resulted in her book, *The American Way of Death*.

3215 *Mitford, Jessica Lucy   **1917-**
Hons and rebels. London: Quartet Books, 1978. (London: Gollancz, 1960) 222 p.
This first volume of her autobiography (followed by *A Fine Old Conflict*) concerns her childhood and life up to World War II. Her extraordinary family included parents and two sisters who supported Hitler; Nancy, the novelist, and Jessica herself, who ran off to the Spanish Civil War, later came to the United States, and joined the Communist Party.

3216 *Moats, Alice-Leone   **1909-**
Violent innocence. New York: Duell, Sloan and Pearce, 1951. 312 p.
Account of privileged and precious childhood in Mexico (1911-1921), including experiences with tutors and travel to the United States during the Mexican Revolution.

3217 Mockridge, Norton   **1905-**
Mockridge, you're slipping! Drawings by Jerry Schlamp. New York: The John Day Co., 1967. 325 p. Index.
He began his career as a reporter in White Plains, New York, at 21. Four years later he began working for the New York *World-Telegram* as a reporter, then as a feature writer, in various editorial positions, and as a columnist. He writes of his life in journalism with humorous nostalgia.

3218 *Modjeska, Helena (Opido)   **1840-1909**
Memories and impressions; an autobiography. New York: Benjamin Blom, 1969. (1910) 571 p. Index.
A magnificent actress in her time, Modjeska writes of her early life and theatrical experience in Poland, the establishment of her career in San Francisco and New York, with eloquent recollections of many famous people in the theater and high society.

3219 Moffat, Jay Pierrepont   **1896-1943**
Moffat papers: selections from the diplomatic journals of Jay Pierrepont Moffat, 1919-1943. Edited by Nancy Harvison Hoeker. Foreword by Sumner Welles. Cambridge: Harvard University Press, 1956. 408 p. Index.
The diaries of a prominent diplomat provide detailed accounts of his personal, family, and professional interests.

3220 Mollhausen, Baldwin   **1825-1905**
Diary of a journey from the Mississippi to the coasts of the Pacific: with

a United States Government expedition. Introduction by Peter A. Fritzell. Translated by Mrs. Percy Sinnett. Illustrated. Preface by Alexander von Humboldt. New York: Johnson Reprint Corp., 1969. (London: Longman, Brown, Green, Longmans, and Roberts, 1858) 2v.

Mollhausen, a German artist and naturalist, accompanied an American expedition under Lt. W.A. Whipple "to explore the prospects for a railroad along the thirty-fifth parallel" from Little Rock, Arkansas, to Los Angeles. Mollhausen emphasizes the "coherent relationship" of geography, landscape, history, and Indian, Mexican, and white populations, and romanticizes it for a popular readership. His novelistic narrative techniques, embryonic here, led him to a career as a highly popular author of novels with Western American settings.

3221 Molloy, Paul   1920-
And then there were eight. Garden City, New York: Doubleday and Co., Inc., 1961. 189 p.

A journalist writes of his pride and pleasure in his eight children and the importance of family-centered values. His book is the basis for the TV series, *Eight is enough.*

3223 Momaday, Navarre Scott   1934-
Names: a memoir. Illustrated. New York: Harper & Row, Publishers, 1976. 170 p.

Momaday pays homage to his Cherokee and Kiowa ancestors in this warm memoir which he characterizes as "an act of the imagination." He was raised in the shadow of the "Trail of Tears" on reservations in Arizona and New Mexico, where his mother taught and his father worked for the Bureau of Indian Affairs. The account ends with his departure for Virginia, military school, and beyond—a departure forever from a treasured way of life.

3224 Momaday, Navarre Scott   1934-
The way to Rainy Mountain. New York: Ballantine Books, 1973. (1969) 119 p.

At the center of this book is his journey to his birthplace in the heartland of the Kiowa Indians. He sees his journey as analogous to the Kiowa migration from the Rocky Mountains to the Oklahoma plains.

3225 *Monroe, Harriet   1860-1936
A poet's life: seventy years in a changing world. Illustrated. New York: AMS Press, 1969. (New York: Macmillan, 1938) 488 p. Index.

Poet, dramatist, and critic tells of her Chicago childhood, education in a Georgetown convent, and her literary and artistic careers in New York and Chicago (as art critic for the Chicago *Tribune*). Her commission in 1891 to write an ode for the dedication of the World's Columbian Exposition was of paramount importance, as were her travels to Europe and the West (particularly to the annual Snake Dance of the Hopi Indians), and the establishment of *Poetry Magazine.* The narrative is interspersed with fragments of poetry and letters from E.A. Robinson, Ezra Pound, Vachel Lindsay, etc., as well as comments on art, architecture, and dance.

3226 Monroe, James   1758-1831
The autobiography of James Monroe. Edited with introduction by Stuart Gerry Brown. Syracuse: Syracuse University Press, 1959. 236 p. Index.

From an unfinished manuscript previously unpublished, the book focuses on the years 1776-1807, in which his political career prepared him for the Presidency.

3227 Monroe, James   1758-1831
The writings of James Monroe, including a collection of his public and private papers and correspondence, now for the first time printed. Edited by Stanislaus Murray Hamilton. New York: AMS Press, 1969. (New York: Putnam, 1898-1903) 7v.

Distinguished by more than fifty years of public service to the country, he was soldier, legislator in Virginia, member of Congress, Senator, Minister to France, Governor of Virginia, shaper of the Monroe Doctrine, and President.

3228 *Monroe, Marilyn   1926-1962
My story. New York: Stein and Day, 1974. 143 p.

She became a movie queen beset by the fabrications of gossips and press agents but decided to tell her own version of her sad, loveless childhood and the difficulties she had in breaking into Hollywood's charmed circle.

3229 Monroe, William G.   1905-
It was fun while it lasted: the memories and musings of a real American "Old-Timer." New York: Greenwich Book Publishers, 1959. 153 p.

A complacent, disjointed narrative of an army lieutenant's life and philosophy written during a tour of duty in Panama, with comments on the Canal, religion ("The Upper Room"), hillbilly music, animals, Halley's comet, and diverse other subjects.

3230 Montana, Pietro   1895?-
Memories: an autobiography. Illustrated. Hicksville, New York: Exposition Press, 1977. 192 p.

Montana describes his childhood in Italy, his emigration to New York, where he discovered his love of and talent for art, and his six years of

studies at Cooper Union. He became a successful sculptor, making many busts and war memorials, which he discusses articulately.

3231 *Montgomery, Ruth (Shick)   1912-
Hail to the chiefs; my life and times with six presidents. New York: Coward-McCann, Inc., 1970. 320 p. Index.

On the Washington scene for 25 years as a widely syndicated columnist, she writes about White House anecdotes, presidents and their families. In addition, she tells how she became involved with psychic personalities, principally Jeane Dixon.

3232 *Moody, Anne   1940-
Coming of age in Mississippi. New York: The Dial Press, Inc., 1968. 348 p.

Her childhood, education, and involvement in the Civil Rights movement in Mississippi, beginning with the sit-in at Woolworth's lunch counter in Jackson.

3233 Moody, Ralph   1898-
Home ranch. New York: W.W. Norton and Co., Inc., 1956. 280 p.

Recollections of his boyhood in the cattle country of Colorado, by the author of *Little Britches.*

3234 Moody, Ralph   1898-
Little britches: father and I were ranchers. Illustrated by Edward Shenton. New York: W.W. Norton & Co., Inc., 1950. 260 p.

After his father developed lung disease working in a New Hampshire woolen mill, his family moved to a broken-down ranch in Colorado. His book tells of his delight in ranch life, the values of country living, and the close ties that developed between him and his father.

3235 Moody, Ralph   1898-
Man of the family. New York: W.W. Norton, 1951. 272 p.

A restaurateur and author recalls his experience in Colorado after his father's death. He describes all the jobs he held in order to help his family in the early part of the twentieth century.

3236 Moody, Ralph   1898-
Mary Emma & company. Illustrated by Tran Mawicke. New York: W.W. Norton & Co., Inc., 1961. 233 p.

Shortly after his father died, his mother, Mary Emma, moved with her three children to Medford, Massachusetts, to start a new life. This book describes their struggle to make a living in their new home, the children delivering groceries and doing other odd jobs, the mother doing laundry, all with a sense of spirit and love.

3237 Moody, Samuel B.   1920-
Reprieve from hell. Introduction by E.P. King, Jr. and Maury Allen. Illustrated. New York: Pageant Press, 1961. 213 p.

A dramatic account of Moody's participation as a soldier in the American defeat at Corregidor and in the Bataan Death March. As a prisoner-of-war he was sent first to Camp O'Donnell, then to Cabanatuan and Clark Field. Moody approaches the war, his Japanese captors, and the Tokyo War Crimes trials with remarkable understatement, considering his starvation and savage treatment.

3238 Moody, William Vaughn   1869-1910
Some letters of William Vaughn Moody. Edited with an introduction by Daniel Gregory Mason. New York: AMS Press, 1969. (Boston: Houghton Mifflin Co., 1913) 170 p.

Moody's letters are doubly interesting for their literary charm and power to liberate the imagination and for their revelations of the qualities of his mind.

3239 Moore, Allen Hoyt   1890-
Mustard plasters and printer's ink: a kaleidoscope of a country doctor's observations about people, places, and things. Foreword by James A. Michener. Introduction by Lindsay C. Warren. New York: Exposition Press, 1959. 262 p.

A sentimental, folksy account of Moore's boyhood in rural North Carolina (including the obligatory view of Halley's comet), his education at the University of North Carolina (including "testing" the effects of marijuana), his brief service as an army physician in World War I, his European travels, and his friends and neighbors. Moore focuses on his medical practice in Buck's County, Pennsylvania, and in North Carolina.

3240 Moore, Archie   1916-
The Archie Moore story. New York: McGraw-Hill Book Co., Inc., 1960. 240 p.

He started professional boxing in 1936; he still held the World Light Heavyweight title when he returned in 1959. His book describes his life in the ring, emphasizing at times common prejudices about boxing and about Negroes.

3241 Moore, Arthur James   b.1888
Bishop to all peoples. Nashville: Abingdon Press, 1973. 144 p.

He grew up and began his Methodist ministry in Georgia. During his years as a bishop, 1930-1960, he was instrumental in expanding the church's role in evangelism at home and abroad. He was responsible for missions in Southeast Asia and Africa before the church united and later became president of the Board of Missions for twenty years.

3242 Moore, Ben   **1891-**
Heritage of freedom. Introduction by Bolita J. Lewis. Minneapolis, Minnesota: T.S. Denison & Co., 1957. 273 p.
   Moore, for sixteen years (1940-1956) U.S. district judge for the Southern District of West Virginia, emphasizes the backwoods Methodist and Baptist religions of his childhood in Kentucky, his rural schooling, and his judicial career, with his landmark ruling to uphold the Turnpike Act authorizing construction of the West Virginia Turnpike (1953).

3243 *Moore, Colleen   **1902-**
Silent star. Illustrated. Garden City, New York: Doubleday & Co., Inc., 1968. 262 p.
   She started playing in silent movies in 1917. In the early Twenties she bobbed her hair and became the first flapper in the movies. She starred in *Flaming Youth, Lilac Time, So Big,* plus many others, including six talkies. Her memoir is well-stocked with the glitter of Hollywood's golden era.

3244 Moore, Edward Roberts   **1894-1952**
Roman collar. New York: The Macmillan Co., 1950. 251 p.
   Written in response to the frequent question "what does a priest do with his time?" by a priest who ministered at St. Peter's in New York and worked for years at Catholic charities.

3245 *Moore, Ellen C.   **1915-**
Lead me to the exit. Washington, D.C.: Ariadne Press, 1977. 209 p.
   Born in poverty, she writes of her unconventional career as domestic servant, social worker, and college teacher.

3246 Moore, Frank Lincoln   **1866-1935**
Souls and saddlebags: the diaries and correspondence of Frank L. Moore, western missionary, 1888-1896. Edited by Austin L. Moore. Denver: Big Mountain Press, 1962. 207 p. Index.
   Arranged chronologically with editorial explanations of time, place, and history in between, his letters and diary entries provide an interesting view of frontier life in Wyoming and northern Colorado during territorial days.

3247 Moore, Gilbert Stuart   **1935-**
A special rage. New York: Harper & Row, 1971. 276 p. Index.
   As a Black journalist assigned to write about the Black Panther Party for *Life* Magazine, Moore came to know its leaders and followed closely the Huey Newton affair. His work led him to a fuller understanding of the party's problems and goals, but left him with unanswered questions.

3248 *Moore, Martha B.
Unmasked; the story of my life on both sides of the barrier. New York: Exposition Press, 1964. 106 p.
   Speaking out for equality of women of minority groups, she recalls her youth and later life and her struggles against prejudice from Blacks, who mistook her for white, and from whites. She found discrimination in employment, housing, and social acceptance, but overcame many such obstacles to run for the Pennsylvania state legislature and work for the Republican Party.

3249 *Moore, Mary Olga
I'll meet you in the lobby. Philadelphia: J.B. Lippincott Co., 1949. 250 p.
   Lively, energetic story of her work as a lobbyist in Washington, D.C., and as a staff writer for the U.S. Office of War Information in England during World War II.

3250 Moore, Nathaniel Fish   **1782-1872**
Diary: a trip from New York to the Falls of St. Anthony in 1845. Edited by Stanley Pargellis and Ruth Lapham Butler. Chicago: University of Chicago Press, 1946. 102 p.
   A travel diary by the president of Columbia College (N.Y.) depicts the conditions of river and coach travel and an interesting view of the times.

3251 Moore, Paul   **1942-**
Shepherd of Times Square. With Joe Musser. Nashville: Thomas Nelson, 1979. 249 p.
   An account in short episodes of clergyman Moore's dynamic leadership of the Manhattan Church of the Nazarene, where he ministered to the Lamb's Club congregation of prostitutes, derelicts, drug addicts, homosexuals, street people and others. Moore's business enterprises, a restaurant in the old Lamb's Club and the manufacture of religious jewelry, sustained the church but his marriage faltered from the stress.

3252 Moore, William Taylor   **1901-**
Dateline Chicago; a veteran newsman recalls its heyday. Foreword by

Robert Cromie. Illustrated. New York: Taplinger Publishing Co., 1973. 191 p.
   Moore recreates the "Front Page" era of Chicago journalism when gangsters, dance marathons, and spicy divorces were of more interest than Washington or world news.

3253 Moorman, Lewis Jefferson   **1875-1954**
Pioneer doctor. Norman: University of Oklahoma Press, 1951. 252 p. Index.
   Physician reflects upon his medical practice during a fifty-year period of growth and change in scientific knowledge; his experience includes country and city practices, with emphasis on tuberculosis, and teaching and administrative duties in Oklahoma.

3254 Moorman, Madison Berryman   **1824-1915**
Journal of Madison Berryman Moorman, 1850-1851. Biographical sketch of the author by his granddaughter, Louise Parks Barnes. Edited by Irene D. Paden. San Francisco: California Historical Society, 1948. 150 p.
   Well-written narrative of his travels west over part of the Oregon Trail, then through Utah and the California Plains. Picturesque description of the Gold Rush era.

3255 Moran, Benjamin   **1820-1886**
The journal of Benjamin Moran, 1857-1865. Edited by Sarah Agnes Wallace and Frances Elma Gillespie. Introduction by F.E. Gillespie. Preface by S.A. Wallace. Chicago: University of Chicago Press, 1948-1949. 2v. Index.
   An assistant secretary of the U.S. legation in London records the friction between the two countries and describes people and incidents in his daily life.

3256 Moran, Thomas   **1837-1926**
Home-thoughts, from afar: letters of Thomas Moran to Mary Nimmo Moran. Introduction and notes by Fritiof Fryxell. Illustrated by Thomas Moran. Edited by Amy O. Bassford. New York: East Hampton Free Library, 1967. 152 p.
   A collection of 32 letters Moran, a painter and engraver, wrote to his wife during various trips: Lake Superior, 1860; North Rim of the Grand Canyon, 1873, with Major John Wesley Powell; Mount of the Holy Cross (Colorado), 1874, with a Hayden Survey party; Mexico, 1883; Venice, 1886; and the Grand Canyon, Devil's Tower, and the Yellowstone, 1892, with William H. Jackson. Most of the letters are brief, but the expert illustrations are eloquent.

3257 Moreau de Saint Mery, Mederic Louis Ellie   **1750-1819**
Moreau de St. Mery's American journey: 1793-1798. Translated and edited by Kenneth Roberts and Anna M. Roberts. Garden City, New York: Doubleday and Co., Inc., 1947. 394 p. Index.
   A frank and detailed commentary on American life in the late eighteenth century, with descriptions of travel conditions, the habits and manners of American women, food, warehouses and suppliers, prostitution, children, workers, chiefly in New York and Philadelphia.

3258 *Morehead, Willie Carhart
The saving grace. New York: Vantage Press, Inc., 1953. 57 p.
   "The saving grace" of the title is the author's sense of humor, manifested in amusing anecdotes of her many years in nursing. Her work required extensive travel, particularly in the South, and included jobs in a penitentiary, in an asylum, and with the Margaret Sanger Foundation.

3259 Morehouse, Ward   **1898-1966**
Just the other day: from Yellow Pines to Broadway. New York: McGraw-Hill Book Co., Inc., 1953. 240 p.
   The story of his boyhood in rural Georgia, his early years in journalism, and his success as a drama critic for the New York *Sun.*

3260 Morelock, Horale Wilson   **b.1873**
Mountains of the mind. San Antonio, Texas: The Naylor Co., 1956. 246 p.
   Morelock pleasantly describes his upbringing in Appalachian Tennessee, his education at the University of Nashville and the University of Tennessee, and his thirteen years as an English professor at West Texas State Normal College. His major accomplishments are the 23-year presidency of Sul Ross State College and his efforts in establishing Big Bend National Park.

3261 Morey, Lloyd W., Sr.   **d.1976**
Magic city doctor. Boston: Branden Press, 1977. 266 p.
   Morey, an osteopath, focuses on his career in Millinocket, Maine. He describes his invention, the Morey lymphatic pump, that applies pressure to the chest of a patient with breathing difficulties. He narrates accounts of his favorite cases—obstetrical, venereal disease, pneumonia, appendicitis—and feels that over the years osteopathy has become increasingly accepted as a bona fide medical specialty.

3262 Morgan, Charles, Jr.   **1930-**
One man, one voice. New York: Holt, Rinehart, & Winston, 1979. 348 p. Index.

As a lawyer Morgan concerns himself with Civil Rights and the injustices Blacks have suffered in America. He writes of the progress and setbacks Blacks have encountered during integration. The final third of his book is devoted to the events that led to the Watergate scandal and its abuse of the legal system.

3263 Morgan, Charles, Jr.   1930-
Time to speak. New York: Harper & Row, Publishers, 1964. 177 p.
    The day after a bomb killed four little girls in a Black Baptist church in Birmingham, Morgan made an intensely critical speech about segregation at the Birmingham Young Men's Business Association. Thereafter he and his family were threatened regularly, until they finally decided to move out. His book is a moving account of his life in the city, his long commitment to improve conditions there, his sense of despair at Birmingham's decline.

3264 *Morgan, Elizabeth   1948-
The making of a woman surgeon. New York: G.P. Putnam's Sons, 1980. 368 p.
    Morgan relates her odyssey through medical school, from her first anatomy class through residency in surgery, in a field difficult for women to enter or to survive.

3265 Morgan, Lewis Henry   1818-1881
The Indian journals, 1859-1862. Edited with introduction by Leslie A. White. Ann Arbor: The University of Michigan Press, 1959. 229 p. Index.
    Trained as an attorney, he devoted most of his life to the study of kinship roles among various tribes of Plains Indians. His journals record his observations while studying Indians in the Kansas-Nebraska Territory, on the Red River of the North, and on the Missouri River.

3266 *Morgan, Lucy   1889-1981
Gift from the hills; Miss Lucy Morgan's story of her unique Penland School. With LeGette Blythe. Chapel Hill: University of North Carolina Press, 1971. (Indianapolis: The Bobbs Merrill Co., 1958) 331 p.
    Miss Lucy was the director and guiding light for the Penland Craft School in the Blue Ridge Mountains of North Carolina. Here were preserved and taught the old-time craft skills: carding, spinning, dying with natural dyes, weaving, pottery making, metal working, jewelry making. Under her direction for 43 years, the school grew and became a model for others to emulate.

3267 Morgan, Manie (Kendley)   1848-1938
The new stars: life and labor in old Missouri. Arranged by Jennie A. Morgan. Edited by Louis Filler. Yellow Springs, Ohio: The Antioch Press Co., 1949. 301 p.
    Recollections in old age (88) of life during the Civil War in the border state of Missouri.

3268 *Morgan, Robin   1941-
Going too far: the personal chronicle of a feminist. New York: Random House, 1977. 333 p.
    A variety of prose pieces record her evolution from leftist activist to radical feminist, from unmarried woman to wife and mother.

3269 Morgan, William Henry   b.1836
Personal reminiscences of the war of 1861-5; in camp, en bivouac, on the march, on picket, on the skirmish line, on the battlefield and in prison. Freeport, New York: Books for Libraries Press, 1971. (Lynchburg, Virginia: J.P. Bell, 1911) 286 p. Index.
    After a lapse of forty years, Morgan recorded memories of his experiences as a Confederate soldier during the Civil War. The scenes and events of battle, his friends, relations, and comrades in arms, fierce loyalty to Virginia and heroic deeds—all play an important part in his personal recollections.

3270 Morgenstern, Joseph   b.1889
I have considered my days. Illustrated by Esther Morgenstern-Gilman. Foreword by Nachman Meisel. New York: YKUF Publishers (Yiddisher Kultur Farband), 1964. 237 p.
    Morgenstern describes his early life in Lithuania, his voyage to the United States, and his eventual rise to prosperity. His account deals with Jewish life in both countries. His later activities included participation in the Zionist movement and socialist-revolutionary organizations.

3271 Morison, James   1818-1882
By sea to San Francisco, 1849-1850. Edited by Lounie J. White and William R. Gillaspie. Memphis: Memphis State University Press, 1977. 61 p. Index.
    Morison writes of experiences in traveling six months by ship from New England to San Francisco around the tip of South America. A doctor by training, Morison makes many interesting observations about the flora, fauna, and conditions of the trip, and many brief stopovers in Rio de Janeiro, Lima, Panama City, and elsewhere.

3272 Morison, Samuel Eliot   1887-1976
One boy's Boston: 1887-1901. Boston: Houghton Mifflin Co., 1962. 81 p.

A prominent historian writes of his childhood in a prominent Boston family, giving an eloquent, nostalgic description of family life, values, social activities, even menus of dinner parties.

3273 Morley, Felix   1894-
For the record. South Bend, Indiana: Regnery/Gateway, 1979. 472 p. Index.
    Morley reflects philosophically on a long life in and out of journalism and public service. Educated at Haverford and at Oxford as a Rhodes Scholar, he early became a world traveler through ambulance corps service in World War I, work for the League of Nations afterward, and activities as a foreign correspondent for the Baltimore Sun. As editor of the Washington Post, 1933-1940, he greatly improved its quality and international scope. As Haverford president, 1940-45, he restored its financial solvency through the expedient measure of training soldiers at this Quaker institution.

3274 Morrall, Earl   1934?-
Comeback quarterback; the Earl Morrall story. And George Sullivan. New York: Grosset & Dunlap, 1971. 216 p.
    Traded to the Baltimore Colts in 1968 when he was 34, Morrall became starting quarterback for that team which won the NFL championship and was named pro football's Player of the Year. Although they lost in the Super Bowl that year, in January 1971, they beat the Dallas Cowboys to become Super Bowl Champions.

3275 Morrell, Benjamin   1795-1839
A narrative of four voyages. Upper Saddle River, New Jersey: The Gregg Press, 1970. (New York: J & J Harper, 1832) 492 p.
    Between 1822 and 1831, Morrell made four voyages of exploration and discovery during which he observed and surveyed coasts, islands, and inhabitants around the world. First voyage, South Seas and Pacific Ocean; second, Pacific Ocean, South America, Sandwich Islands; third, South and West Coast of Africa; fourth, North and South Pacific, Indian Ocean.

3276 Morris, Alvin
    see Martin, Tony, pseud.

3277 Morris, Ed   1932-
Born to lose. New York: Mason & Lipscomb Publishers, 1974. 216 p.
    The author, who spent 22 out of 40 years in prison, asserts that his purpose in writing is "to awaken the public to the desperate need for the reevaluation of treatment for the neglected child and criminal offender."

3278 *Morris, Edita Toll   1902-
Straitjacket: an autobiography. New York: Crown Publishers, 1978. 147 p.
    In novelistic form, with many short profane dialogues, Morris relates the story of her childhood and adolescence as the daughter of Swedish nobility. She sympathized with the commoner; rebelled against pomp, circumstance, and a domineering mother; and felt isolated from her peers and family. At the book's end she vowed to emigrate and marry Ira Morris, a glamorous, wealthy American and aspiring writer like herself.

3279 Morris, Gouverneur   1752-1816
Diary and letters. Edited by Anne Cary Morris. New York: Da Capo Press, 1970. (New York: C. Scribner's Sons, 1888) 2v. Index.
    Diary notes and letters written during the French Revolution. He was a member of the Continental Congress, the Constitutional Convention, and served as U.S. Minister to France, remaining there during the Reign of Terror. Later he was a member of the U.S. Senate.

3280 Morris, Ira Nelson   1875-1942
Heritage from my father: an autobiography. New York: The author, privately printed, 1947. 263 p.
    A U.S. diplomat in Sweden and Russia describes his early years in Chicago, the importance of his family and education to his growth and development, and his long years in the diplomatic service.

3281 *Morris, Jan   1926-
Destinations: essays from Rolling Stone. New York: Oxford University Press, 1980. 242 p.
    Morris interprets Washington, D.C., Manhattan, Los Angeles, Delhi, Panama, South Africa, Rhodesia, Cairo, Istanbul, Trieste, and London. Her evocative description and deft wit reveal her preferences, prejudices, and love of the diversities and paradoxes of contemporary life.

3282 *Morris, Margaret (Hill)   1737?-1816
Private journal kept during the Revolutionary War. New York: New York Times & Arno Press, 1969. (Philadelphia: privately printed, 1836) 36 p.
    This journal, kept for the amusement of her sister during 1776-1777, relates something of the life of a private family during the Revolution, the effect of the war, the gossip and rumors—a small picture of the times.

3283 Morris, Robert   **1734-1806**
The papers of Robert Morris, 1781-1784. Edited by E. James Ferguson. Associate editor, John Catanzariti. Assistant editor, Mary A. Gallagher. Illustrated. Pittsburgh, Pennsylvania: University of Pittsburgh Press, 1973-78. 4v.
   This edition includes the official diary, correspondence, and other documents of Robert Morris during his administration as Superintendent of Finance, 1781-1784, a position from which he greatly influenced the economic foundation of the emerging United States. Letters to and from every major figure of the Revolutionary period are presented, all related to financial matters, both small and large.

3284 Morris, Willie   **1934-**
North toward home. Boston: Houghton Mifflin Co., 1967. 438 p.
   Raised on the Mississippi Delta, educated at the University of Texas and Oxford, and then transplanted to New York City, the editor of *Harper's* Magazine tells of his growth and maturation in this probing and sometimes funny book.

3285 Morrison, John Arch   **1893-1965**
As the river flows: the autobiography of John A. Morrison. Anderson, Indiana: Anderson College Press, 1962. 214 p.
   Raised in a large, poor family in the Missouri Ozarks, educated only through the eighth grade, he trained himself for the ministry of the Church of God, founded and became president of Anderson College in Indiana.

3286 Morros, Boris M.   **1895-1963**
My ten years as a counterspy. With Charles Samuels. New York: The Viking Press, 1959. 248 p.
   During 1948-58 Russian-born film producer Morros was an F.B.I. counterspy to track down Jack and Myra Soble and others in league with the Russians during the Cold War. His book is filled with the exciting, realistic detail of his profession.

3287 *Morrow, Elizabeth Cutter   **1873-1955**
The Mexican years: leaves from the diary of Elizabeth Cutter Morrow. New York: Elizabeth Cutter Morrow, The Spiral Press, 1953. 272 p.
   Selections from Mrs. Morrow's diary during the time her husband was U.S. Ambassador to Mexico, 1927-30. She mentions political and diplomatic issues in passing, but gives more attention to social and family life, particularly to her daughter Anne's marriage to Charles Lindbergh and to her husband's political campaign, though she never indicates the office he seeks.

3288 Morrow, James   **1820-1865**
Scientist with Perry in Japan: the journal of Dr. James Morrow. Edited by Allan B. Cole. Chapel Hill: University of North Carolina Press, 1947. 307 p. Index.
   A record of his agricultural work and travels with the Perry Expedition in Japan and China (1853-1854), as a representative of the Department of Agriculture. He was to take seeds and agricultural machinery and information to Japan, as well as collect seeds and specimens to bring back.

3289 Morrow, John Howard   **1910-**
First American Ambassador to Guinea. Illustrated. New Brunswick, New Jersey: Rutgers University Press, 1968. 291 p. Index.
   Morrow's tenure as U.S. Ambassador to the newly independent country of Guinea lasted from 1959 to until 1961 when he was appointed to the American delegation at the United Nations.

3290 Morse, Bliss   **1837-1923**
Civil War diaries of Bliss Morse. Compiled and published by Loren J. Morse. Pittsburg, Kansas: Pittcraft, 1964. (1963) 92 p.
   Diaries for the years 1858, 1860, and 1862 through 1866 provide a view of an infantry corporal from Ohio who fought through the South on Sherman's march to the sea and then returned to peacetime occupations.

3291 Mortimer, Wyndham   **1884?-1966**
Organize! my life as a union man. Edited by Leo Fenster. Boston: Beacon Press, 1971. 274 p.
   Mortimer was close to the center of labor union activities in the 1930's. His local union of auto workers was the first in Cleveland's auto industry to achieve recognition and an agreement. He was active in UAW conventions and a strategist in the landmark General Motors strike of 1936-37.

3292 Morton, Charles W.   **1899-1967**
It has its charms . . . . Philadelphia: J.B. Lippincott Co., 1966. 252 p.
   A newspaperman and editor, he worked on the Boston *Evening Transcript*, then for the government Social Security Board, and finally for *The Atlantic Monthly.* Here he tells the story of his life up to 1941 when he started working for the *Atlantic.*

3293 *Morton, Leah, pseud.
   see ***Stern, Elizabeth**

3294 *Morton, Lena Beatrice   **1904?-**
My first sixty years; passion for wisdom. New York: Philosophical Library, 1965. 175 p.
   Her struggles to win her education and to overcome discrimination have shaped her life. She became the first Negro to receive a doctorate in English at Western Reserve and thereafter devoted herself to educating young people. A number of her poems are included in the book.

3295 Moser, William H.   **b.1869**
Seventy years a preacher: the life story of the Rev. William H. Moser, Ph.D., militant Methodist preacher. Oral history and preface by Chester A. Smith. Introduction by Historical Society of the New York Annual Conference of the Methodist Church. Peekskill, New York: The Historical Society of the New York Annual Conference of the Methodist Church, 1959. 110 p. Index.
   Moser, a militant, itinerant Methodist preacher, crusaded for fifty years throughout New York State for God and for temperance. He enjoyed revival meetings, visiting the faithful in their homes, and an occasional court battle over prohibition.

3296 *Moses, Anna Mary (Robertson)   **1860-1961**
The art and life of Grandma Moses. Edited by Otto Kallir. New York: The Gallery of Modern Art, 1969. 168 p.
   This edition contains reproductions of her pictures, essays about her by Louis Bromfield, Jean Cassou, and John Canaday, comments on her art by European papers, a list of documents by and about her in the Bennington Museum, letters, and her own descriptions of her life depicted in her works.

3297 *Moses, Anna Mary (Robertson)   **1860-1961**
Grandma Moses: my life's history. Edited by Otto Kallir. New York: Harper and Brothers, 1952. (New York: Dryden Press, 1946) 140 p.
   Recollections of her childhood in New York state, her young married life in Virginia, her return to New York state, and her development as a painter, told in a simple, direct style that resembles her paintings.

3298 Moss, James E.   **1875-1962**
Jimmy Moss. Salt Lake City: Deseret Book Co., 1963. 243 p. Index.
   The story of a Mormon teacher who devoted his life to education, sports, and the church. The first half of the book describes his childhood, family life and education; the second, his principal role in organizing Utah high school sports events, particularly basketball.

3299 Moss, William Paul   **b.1886**
Rough and tumble: the autobiography of a West Texas judge. New York: Vantage Press, 1954. 77 p.
   Moss describes his fifty years as a lawyer and cattle rancher, mostly in his beloved Odessa, Texas. He writes proudly of his judicial accomplishments and material acquisitions and of his adopted town.

3300 Motley, John Lothrop   **1814-1877**
The correspondence of John Lothrop Motley. New York: AMS Press, 1973. (New York: Harper and Brothers, 1900) 3v.
   An historian and diplomat, Motley studied and wrote about the history of the Dutch Republic and of the United Netherlands and was a leader of the mid-nineteenth-century romantic school of historiography. He served as minister to Austria (1861-1867) and Britain (1869-1870).

3301 Motley, Willard Francis   **1909-1965**
The diaries of Willard Motley. Edited with introduction by Jerome Klinkowitz. Foreword by Clarence Majors. Ames: Iowa State University Press, 1979. 196 p. Index.
   Covering the years 1926 to 1943, a Black writer's diary contains personal notes to himself about high school, football, girl friends, and odd jobs. Siphoning gas to travel across country, he ends up in several town jails, experiences he accepts as colorful material for his diary.

3302 Mott, Frank Luther   **1886-1964**
Time enough: essays in autobiography. Chapel Hill: The University of North Carolina Press, 1962. 248 p.
   In essays about his life in the business and profession of journalism, he emphasizes the need to avoid the tyranny of time and the need to insist for oneself: "I have time enough—enough and to spare for what I really wish most to do."

3303 *Mott, Lucretia (Coffin)   **1783-1880**
Slavery and "The Woman Question": Lucretia Mott's diary of her visit to Great Britain to attend the World's Anti-Slavery Convention of 1840. Edited by Frederick B. Tolles. Supplement no. 23 to the Journal of the Friends' Historical Society. Haverford, Pennsylvania: Friends' Historical Association, 1952. 86 p. Index.
   A revealing picture of the convention to which she was sent as a delegate, but was refused official recognition and participation because she was a woman.

3304 Motta, Dick   **1931-**
Stuff it: the story of Dick Motta, toughest little coach in the NBA. With Jerry Jenkins. Radnor, Pennsylvania: Chilton Book Co., 1975. 187 p.

.A controversial coach in the NBA, Motta was named Coach of the Year in 1971, his third season with Chicago Bulls. At 5'9", he never played varsity basketball in high school or college, making his success in the giant sport somewhat remarkable.

3305 Moultrie, William 1730-1805
Memoir of the American Revolution: so far as it related to the states of North and South Carolina and Georgia. Eyewitness Accounts of the American Revolution. New York: New York Times/Arno Press, 1968. (New York: William Moultrie, 1802) 2v.

Moultrie, a major general in the U.S. Army during the Revolutionary War, has compiled his terse correspondence with other commanders about military matters in North Carolina, South Carolina, and Georgia, including the blockade of Charleston. Some of the letters are imbedded in an interpretive narrative account derived from histories by other people.

3306 *Mountain Wolf Woman 1884-1960
Mountain Wolf Woman, Sister of Crashing Thunder: the autobiography of a Winnebago Indian. Edited by Nancy Oestreich Lurie. Ann Arbor: University of Michigan Press, 1961. 142 p.

Written from taped interviews, the book describes growing up in and between two cultures in Wisconsin with what appears to be an amazing serenity and independence.

3307 *Mowrer, Lilian (Thomson)
Journalist's wife. New York: William Morrow & Co., 1937. 414 p.

She married Edgar Mowrer, the Paris correspondent of the Chicago *Daily News,* in 1916 and spent the next twenty years inside the news in Europe. He fought for freedom of the press and was ousted from two countries rather than submit to censorship. While she was involved with him in large history-making events, she was also a mother and homemaker able to share and record the feelings of ordinary people around her.

3308 Moyle, James Henry 1858-1946
Mormon Democrat: the religious and political memoirs of James Henry Moyle. Edited by Gene A. Sessions. Salt Lake City: Historical Department of the Church of Jesus Christ of Latter-day Saints, 1975. 503 p. Index.

A lawyer and Assistant Secretary of the Treasury under Henry Morgenthau until 1940, Moyle was also a leader in the Mormon church. His memoirs comment on Mormon life in Utah, local and national politics, and his own role in church and political life.

3309 Moynihan, Daniel Patrick 1927-
A dangerous place. With Suzanne Weaver. Boston: Little, Brown & Co., 1978. 297 p. Index.

A journal and commonplace book, this volume describes the author's part "in recent ideas and events that contributed to the emergence of human rights as an issue of American foreign policy."

3310 Moynihan, Donald T.
Skin deep: the making of a plastic surgeon. And Shirley Hartman. Boston: Little, Brown and Co., 1979. 339 p.

A vigorous, engrossing narrative of Dr. Moynihan's two-year residency in plastic surgery at a university hospital in southern California. Moynihan discusses the typical cases: face lifts, rhinoplasty, breast augmentation or reduction; and the dramatic cases to repair victims of accidents or physical abuse. He concludes with a moving account of his two-year-old son's cancer surgery and survival.

3311 Mozier, Aloysius Eugene Francis Patrick 1902-
Bell in the heart: the autobiography of Patty Gardenseed, America's ambassador of goodwill. As told to Trixie-Ann Schubert. Los Angeles: Western Publishers, Ltd., 1963. 285 p.

The adventures of a U.S. Navy boxer who became the Navy welterweight champion during World War I and later received international attention as "Patty Gardenseed," so-named for his program of distributing seeds to alleviate world hunger.

3312 Mueller, Gustav Emil 1898-
Instead of a biography. New York: Philosophical Library, 1970. 237 p.

Several independent but sometimes overlapping parts make up this volume: letters written on a freighter trip across the Atlantic; reminiscences of the years after 1935; and documents including articles and lectures on philosophical subjects. An appendix contains an incomplete bibliography and a chronology of his life.

3313 Muenchhausen, Friedrich Ernest von 1753-1795
At General Howe's side, 1776-1778; the diary of General William Howe's aide de camp. Monmouth Beach, New Jersey: Philip Frenau Press, 1974. 84 p.

Muenchhausen's command of German, French, and English made him a valuable aide to Howe and an intermediary between the General and the German commanders; he was almost constantly at the center of the British-German war effort during the American Revolution. He kept an accurate day-to-day account of his headquarters activities during the eighteen months of his service with General Howe.

3314 Muhlenberg, Henry Melchior 1711-1787
The journals of Henry Melchior Muhlenberg. Translated by Theodore G. Tappert and John W. Doberstein. Philadelphia: Muhlenberg Press, 1942-1958. 3v. Index.

An important religious leader of eighteenth-century America, Muhlenberg acted as a missionary bishop, organizing new congregations, securing pastors, settling disputes, masterminding the preparation of congregational and synodical constitutions. He considered keeping a diary a spiritual exercise as well as a record and source of material for his reports to the authorities in Halle. Volume I concerns his life up to 1763, Volume II describes 1764-1776, Volume III covers 1777-1786.

3315 Muhlenberg, Henry Melchior 1711-1787
The notebook of a colonial clergyman: condensed from the journals of Henry Melchior Muhlenberg. Edited and translated by Theodore G. Tappert and John W. Doberstein. Philadelphia: Muhlenberg Press, 1959. 250 p. Index.

The record of a German Lutheran minister in southeastern Pennsylvania, selected by the editors from their three-volume edition (Muhlenberg Press, 1942-58).

3316 *Muir, Florabel 1890-1970
Headline happy. New York: Henry Holt and Co., 1950. 248 p.

Primarily the work experience of a journalist who was an outstanding reporter for the New York *Daily News* and the Los Angeles *Mirror,* writing extensively about the criminal underworld.

3317 Muir, John 1838-1914
John of the mountains: the unpublished journals of John Muir. Edited by Linnie Marsh Wolfe. Madison, Wisconsin: University of Wisconsin Press, 1979. (Boston: Houghton Mifflin Co., 1938) 459 p. Index.

These journals, starting with 1869, are some of the most noteworthy of the sixty written by Muir covering his career as a naturalist, describing his wanderings, and recording his scientific research as well as his thoughts on the transcendental meaning of nature.

3318 *Muirhead, Sara Alyne Guynes (Angela Sagsam, pseud.) b.1885
I was a country girl. Philadelphia: Dorrance and Co., 1947. 211 p.

Life in rural Texas and Louisiana by a woman who "was brought up according to the teaching of the Good Book" during the late nineteenth century.

3319 Mullan, Fitzhugh 1942?-
White coat, clenched fist: the political education of an American physician. New York: Macmillan Publishing Co., 1976. 222 p.

Mullan dramatically recounts his years of social and political activism as a medical student at the University of Chicago, 1965-1969, and as an intern at Lincoln Hospital, New York City, 1969-1971. As a non-traditional, egalitarian physician Mullan provided medical care for participants in the Southern Civil Rights movement and Puerto Ricans in the Bronx and organized health collectives for medical personnel.

3320 Mullen, James Morfit b.1877
Let justice be done. Philadelphia: Dorrance and Co., 1952. 371 p.

Partially intended as a model for young lawyers, the book focuses on his life in the law.

3321 Muller, Jack 1919?-
I, pig, or how the world's most famous cop, me, is fighting City Hall. With Paul Neimark. New York: William Morrow & Co., Inc., 1971. 159 p.

A tough Chicago cop who has spent his life enforcing the letter of the law and taken much abuse for doing it, Muller has fought corruption among the police and refused to be corrupted himself. He is credited with making more arrests of serious criminals than any other policeman in Cook County history.

3322 *Mullings, Gwendolyn Lydia 1928-
My pilgrim journey: the making of an evangelist. New York: William-Frederick Press, 1976. 91 p.

Housewife evangelist Mullings has written an account of her childhood and Presbyterian schooling in Jamaica, of her marriage and emigration to New York in 1945, and her subsequent life there. Autobiographical passages are interspersed with homilies.

3323 Mulloy, Gardnar 1913-
The will to win: An inside view of the world of tennis. New York: A.S. Barnes & Co., 1960. (1959) 206 p.

At 47 a tennis champ tells the story of his notable athletic achievements, particularly at Wimbledon and as U.S. Davis Cup captain. He grew up in Miami, Florida, served in the U.S. Navy as an L.S.T. captain during World War II, but except for that interlude played tennis steadily for thirty years, beginning in college at the University of Miami.

3324 Mulzac, Hugh Nathaniel 1886-1971
Star to steer by. As told to Louis Brunham and Norval Welch. New York: International Publishers, 1963. 251 p.

The story of a West Indian boy who in 1918 became the first Black in the United States to win his Master's license, but then struggled for 24 years to achieve a position as captain of his own ship, the *Booker T. Washington,* which he commanded through World War II and after.

3325 Mumford, Lewis C.   **1895-**
The letters of Lewis Mumford and Frederic J. Osborn: a transatlantic dialogue 1938-70. And Frederic J. Osborn. Edited by Michael R. Hughes. New York: Praeger Publishers, 1972. (Bath, England: Adams & Dart, 1971) 493 p.
The origin of Mumford and Osborn's friendship lay in their common interest in the ideas of Ebenezer Howard, English originator of the Garden City concept of cities and town planning. Osborn played a central role in the establishment of a government program for building New Towns in Great Britain; Mumford altered world consciousness toward the meaning of city life.

3326 Mumford, Lewis C.   **1895-**
My works and days: a personal chronicle. New York: Harcourt Brace Jovanovich, 1979. 545 p. Index.
A social and literary critic, poet, and historian offers a fascinating series of discussions on 27 topics, including his intellectual history; his "New York adolescence"; his wife of fifty years, Sophy; his mistress of four; travel and study in London and Geneva; his work on Herman Melville. He also offers views on death, nuclear power, and the nature and future of civilization.

3327 Mumford, Lewis C.
see also **Brooks, Van Wyck**

3328 Munson, Charlie   **b.1877**
Mister Charlie: memoir of a Texas lawman, 1902-1910. Edited with introduction by Kenneth E. Munson. Austin: Madrona Press, Inc., 1975. 122 p.
Written in his ninety-eighth year, his book describes life at the turn of the century in Lavaca County, Texas.

3329 Munson, Thurman   **1947-1979**
Thurman Munson: an autobiography. With Martin Appel. Illustrated. New York: Coward, McCann & Geoghegan, 1978. 199 p.
As a baseball player for the New York Yankees he achieved exceptional fame—Rookie of the Year (1970), Most Valuable Player award (1976)—and was the Yankees' captain in 1976. Munson was also successful in real estate investments and devoted to his family, but was killed in 1979 while piloting his new jet plane.

3330 Murdick, Olin John   **1917-**
Journey into truth: The autobiography of a Catholic convert. Foreword by George N. Shuster. New York: Exposition Press, 1958. 177 p.
The Reverend Murdick focuses on his education, secular and sacred, as it occupied 35 years of his life. Reared as a Methodist, Olin became fascinated with Catholicism during his undergraduate years at the University of Michigan, continued his interest during his training at the Chicago Theological Seminary, finally converted at 31, and trained at Catholic University.

3331 Murie, Olaus Johan   **1889-1963**
Journeys to the far North. Illustrated. Palo Alto, California: The Wilderness Society and American West Publishing Co., 1973. 255 p. Index.
For 31 years, he was a field biologist for Carnegie Museum and later for the U.S. Fish and Wildlife Service. He worked primarily in northern Canada and Alaska, collecting specimens and studying the intricate relationship between living things and their environment.

3332 *Muro, Diane P.
Woman on patrol. Valley Forge, Pennsylvania: Judson Press, 1976. 128 p.
Muro first became a police matron to help put her husband through college; then, when the mother of four young children, she became a patrolman in Ocean Grove, California. She describes her rookie year dealing with murder, rape, theft, domestic brawls, alcoholism, and a host of other human ills. She was sustained by her clergyman husband Al and by her strong religious faith.

3333 Murphey, Cecil B.
But God has promised. Carol Stream, Illinois: Creation House, 1976. 169 p.
Murphey tells how he became a missionary, trained in Chicago, and with his wife Shirley went to Kenya in 1960 to convert the natives and direct mission schools.

3334 Murphey, Cecil B.
Somebody knows I'm alive. Atlanta, Georgia: John Knox Press, 1977. 168 p.
Presbyterian clergyman Murphey tells of his religious conversion as a sailor in the Navy. He emphasized the spiritual growth that led to seminary study and six years' missionary work in Kenya. A good-humored workaholic, Murphey provides a picture of the incessant demands on a

clergyman's life (including housing various people with problems) and the need to balance these with commitments to one's family and to God.

3335 Murphy, Frank   **1916-**
The Frank Murphy story: his years in Florida prisons, his rehabilitation, and his conquest of alcoholism. As told to Thomas Helm. New York: Dodd, Mead and Co., 1968. 312 p.
An exciting cops-and-robbers story from the perspective of the robber, Frank Murphy, who served time in Florida's Raiford and Deep Creek penitentiaries. Murphy attributes most of his problems—divorce, extravagance, inability to work, prison escapes, and parole violation, to alcoholism. At the book's end, Murphy is building a new life, thanks to Alcoholics Anonymous, energy, and a good woman.

3336 Murphy, George   **1902-**
Say . . . didn't you used to be George Murphy? With Victor Lasky. New York: Bartholomew House, Ltd., 1970. 437 p. Index.
A man of several successful careers, Murphy danced and sang on the stage and in many movies, turned to public relations for MGM and Desilu Productions, was president of the Screen Actors Guild, and then was elected U.S. Senator for California, defeating Pierre Salinger in 1964 for that position.

3337 *Murphy, Grace E. (Barstow)   **1888-1975**
There's always adventure: the story of a naturalist's wife. New York: Harper and Brothers, 1951. 299 p.
In her recollections of their long life together, the wife of a well-known ornithologist describes their travels, their children, growing up, and her view of the responsibilities wives have in such marriages.

3338 *Murphy, Patricia   **1905-1979**
Glow of candlelight: the story of Patricia Murphy. Englewood Cliffs, New Jersey: Prentice-Hall, Inc., 1961. 260 p. Index.
As a teenager from Newfoundland, she arrived in New York during the Depression and started a restaurant. With good instincts for business and simple, pleasant dining, she built a successful empire and also established herself as a society hostess and horticulturist.

3339 Murphy, Patrick V.   **1925?-**
Commissioner: a view from the top of American law enforcement. And Thomas Plate. New York: Simon and Schuster, 1977. 270 p. Index.
Having served as police commissioner in New York, Detroit, Washington, D.C., and Syracuse, he writes about urban police forces, the failure of the FBI, and small police forces across the U.S. within the context of his own career.

3340 Murphy, Robert Daniel   **1894-1978**
Diplomat among warriors. Garden City, New York: Doubleday & Co., Inc., 1964. 470 p. Index.
He began working for the Department of State in 1917, just after the United States entered World War I. During his subsequent career as a professional diplomat, he was involved in many major world events. As President Roosevelt's personal representative to French Africa he was centrally involved in World War II. Afterward, he served as Ambassador to Japan and played a significant role in the negotiations to end the Korean War.

3341 Murphy, Willie   **1933-**
Black and trying. And C. Dudley. Foreword by Jim Spillman. Afterword by Joy Dawson. Mary Murphy, "Highlights." Harrison, Arkansas: New Leaf Press, 1976. 165 p.
Murphy writes of his life in rural Alabama as a preacher's son. There he developed a hatred for and suspicion of whites that was only gradually erased through his contacts with a generous white employer in Pittsburgh. He became a born-again Christian through the missionary efforts of evangelist Kathryn Kuhlman and joined her troupe as a singer and sometime preacher.

3342 Murray, James   **1713-1781**
Letters of James Murray, Loyalist. Edited by Nina Moore Tiffany. Assisted by Susan I. Lesley. New introduction and preface by George Athan Billias. American Revolution Series, The Loyalist Library. Boston: Gregg Press, 1972. (Boston: Susan I. Lesley, 1901) 324 p. Index.
One of the few Loyalists who lived both in the South and the North prior to the Revolution, Murray was politically prominent in North Carolina, where he was a planter, and later entered the business of sugar-refining in Boston. His sympathy for the British antagonized local Boston patriots who assaulted him in 1769; later his estate in North Carolina was confiscated.

3343 Murray, Ken (Kenneth Doncourt)   **1903-**
Life on a pogo stick: autobiography of a comedian. With John T. Watts. Foreword by Bing Crosby. Note by Chic Young. Introduction by Edgar Bergen. Philadelphia: John C. Winston Co., 1960. 180 p.
Murray's narration of the ups and downs of his career as an entertainer in vaudeville, film, nightclubs, and T.V. is highlighted by the seven-year Hollywood success of *Blackouts* and by *Bill and Coo,* a film with a cast of

300 birds. Murray achieves pathos in describing his search for the mother who abandoned him.

3344 Musial, Stanley Frank   **1920-**
Stan Musial: the Man's own story. As told to Bob Broeg. Garden City, New York: Doubleday & Co., Inc., 1964. 328 p. Index.
Growing up in a Polish neighborhood in Donora, Pennsylvania, Musial decided at age eight he wanted to become a major league baseball player. His interest, talent, and skill in the game developed from this point on. The St. Louis Cardinals signed him for a farm club when he was seventeen; by the time he retired in 1963 he had become one of the best and most popular players of all time.

3345 Muskie, Edward Sixtus   **1914-**
Journeys. Garden City, New York: Doubleday & Co., Inc., 1972. 204 p.
Senator Muskie describes his experiences and ideals, reflecting on the growth of our social and political system. He served as governor of Maine and U.S. Senator and was candidate for the Presidential nomination when this memoir was published.

3346 Musmanno, Michael Angelo   **1897-1968**
Verdict: The adventures of the young lawyer in the brown suit. 384 p.
The working life of a Philadelphia lawyer depicts the drama of the court room, the daily routines of legal practice, and his genuine pleasure in the law.

3347 Musselman, Morris McNeil   **1899-1952**
I married a redhead. New York: Thomas Y. Crowell Co., 1949. 244 p.
Life in New York by the radio script writer who did "Dick Tracy" and other well-known shows; written with Manhattan humor.

3348 Myers, Charles Ellsworth   **b.1866**
Memoirs of a hunter: a story of fifty-eight years of hunting and fishing. Davenport, Washington: The author, 1948. 309 p.
Raised in Ohio, in 1888 he married and shortly thereafter traveled by train to Washington Territory, where he established a homestead and a country store. His book includes marvelous stories of homesteading life, but a special admiration and respect for the hunter's experience because it encourages good citizenship, "begets health, prolongs life, and makes enduring friendships."

3349 *Mytinger, Caroline
New Guinea head hunt. New York: The Macmillan Co., 1946. 441 p.
Traveling with her friend and fellow painter, Margaret Warner, she set out to paint the portrait of the Melanesian race. Her previous book, *Headhunting in the Solomon Islands*, records the present group and subraces. This volume records their experience tracing and painting contemporary representatives of Melanesian ancestors in New Guinea.

3350 Nabokov, Nicolas   **1903-**
Bagázh: memoirs of a Russian cosmopolitan. New York: Atheneum, 1975. 307 p. Index.
Composer Nabokov writes this tribute to "memory's capacity" with evocative eloquence comparable to the *Speak, Memory* of his cousin, Vladimir Nabokov. He discusses his youth in Russia, privileged and protected; his exile and musical studies in Yalta after the Russian Revolution; life in Europe between World Wars where he conducted as well as composed. A particular friend of Stravinsky's, Nabokov moves in international musical and literary circles, where he maintains treasured friendships.

3351 Nabokov, Vladimir Vladimirovich (Vladimir Sirin, pseud.) 1899-1977
Speak, memory; an autobiography revisited. New York: G.P. Putnam's Sons, 1966. (New York: Harper & Bros., 1951) 361 p. Index.
Made up of chapters previously published in various periodicals, this autobiography covers the years 1903 to 1940 of Nabokov's life. He speaks of his family, his education, chess, and especially his passion for studying butterflies. Geographically he ranges from St. Petersburg to Cambridge, to St. Nazaire, to Biarritz.

3352 Namath, Joe Willie   **1943-**
I can't wait until tomorrow ... cause I get better-looking every day! With Dick Schaap. New York: Random House, 1969. 279 p.
A proud, brash narrative of his life in and around professional football by a quarterback for the New York Jets.

3353 Namath, Joe Willie   **1943-**
Matter of style. With Bob Oates, Jr. Illustrated. Boston: Little, Brown and Co., 1973. 196 p.
With a coffee table format and glossy photographs, this book reflects the famous quarterback's style on and off the football field. The narrative includes personal comments on his techniques in the game, with illustrative pictures.

3354 Narvias, Cosme Lozano, pseud. (de Vasconcelos, Mariano Antonio) 1748-1815
Journal of a Texas missionary, 1767-1802 (Diario Historico). Benedict

Leutenegger, Engl. translator. Introduction by Marion A. Habig. San Antonio, Texas: Old Spanish Missions Historical Research Library at San Jose Mission, 1977. 47 p. Index.
These brief excerpts from Father Vasconcelos' diaries, 1770-1815, cover his missionary endeavors in Texas, 1771-1783 and 1785-1787. The diary entries focus on the comings and goings of missionaries, on ordinations, and on Indian attacks.

3355 Nathan, Daniel, pseud. (Dannay, Frederic)   **1905-**
The golden summer. Boston: Little, Brown, 1953. 215 p.
The author of Ellery Queen mysteries tells in novelistic fashion the story of his tenth summer in upstate New York, where, though undersized and bespectacled, he masterminded the building of the JGH clubhouse in his backyard. As leader of a group of boys, he thoroughly enjoyed his many roles in their activities: "theatrical manager, bibliophile, merchant, poet, judge, artist, detective, auctioneer, industrial magnate."

3356 *Nathan, Maud Nathan   **1862-1946**
Once upon a time and today. New York: Arno Press, 1974. (New York: G.P. Putnam's Sons, 1933) 327 p. Index.
A suffragist and worker for the cause of peace, Mrs. Nathan was one of the first Jewish women to preach in a synagogue. She was director of Mt. Sinai Nursing School and the New York Exchange for Women's Work, organized schools for immigrants and the Consumers' League, was a speaker and delegate for the International Council of Women and the International Woman Suffrage Alliance.

3357 Neal, Harry Lee   **1928-**
Wave as you pass. Philadelphia: J.B. Lippincott Co., 1958. 212 p.
He and his wife, Allison, became the duo pianist team, Nelson-Neal. His book describes his early musical training, but focuses mainly on their life on the concert tour, driving their own truck with two grand pianos, a compact household, and two small children.

3358 Nef, John Ulric   **1899-**
Search for meaning; the autobiography of a nonconformist. Washington: Public Affairs Press, 1973. 349 p. Index.
Nef believes that "the most stable foundation for happiness rests with a new humanism for a united humanity." His story makes his devotion to this precept clear as he writes about the friendships and passions he holds dear: artists, musicians, intellectuals, poets, and their works.

3359 Neider, Charles   **1915-**
Edge of the world; Ross Island, Antarctica: a personal and historical narrative. Illustrated. Garden City, New York: Doubleday & Co., Inc., 1974. 461 p. Index.
Neider became a member of the U.S. Antarctic Research Program and traveled to Antarctica in 1970-71 in order to write a book describing the aesthetic experience of living there. This fascinating account of the trip is furnished with numerous maps and spectacular photographs.

3360 Nelson, Ozzie   **1906-1975**
Ozzie. Englewood Cliffs, New Jersey: Prentice-Hall, 1973. 309 p.
The Ozzie and Harriet Show cast the entire family as characters and used cheerful family stories as plots. Nelson's book does the same, emphasizing the importance of his early family life, his wife, children, and grandchildren at the center of his life in and out of show business.

3361 *Nelson, Teresa (Leopando) Lucero   **1917-**
White cap and prayer. New York: Vantage Press, 1955. 226 p.
A devout Catholic tells of her childhood in the Philippines, her marriage at 23 to a man killed on the Bataan Death March in 1942, and her motherhood. Her career as a nurse began in 1939 and continued, with additional postwar training in Winona, Minnesota, throughout her life.

3362 Nemours, Pierre Samuel du Pont de
    see **Jefferson, Thomas**

3363 *Nesbitt, Henrietta (Kugler)   **1874-1963**
White House diary. Garden City, New York: Doubleday and Co., Inc., 1948. 314 p.
Housekeeper for the White House throughout Franklin D. Roosevelt's presidency describes her experience as provisioner in the context of the Depression and World War II.

3364 Nesbitt, Lowell Blair   **1933-**
An autobiography: January 23-February 21, 1976. Introduction by Andrew J. Crispo. Illustrated by Lowell Nesbitt. New York: Andrew Crispo Gallery, 1976. 110 p.
Nesbitt, a New York painter specializing in photorealistic canvases representing his studio interior, chairs, windows, plants, work clothes, robes, shoes, and his dog, comments on the genesis and development of each series in a fleeting autobiographical context.

3365 *Nestor, Agnes   **1880-1948**
Woman's labor leader: an autobiography of Agnes Nestor. Rockford, Illinois: Bellevue Books Publishing Co., 1954. 307 p. Index.

Well-written narrative of an outstanding leader in the Woman's Labor Movement for almost forty years. Originally a child worker in a Chicago glove factory, she was central in achieving the eight-hour work day for women and headed the Chicago Women's Trade Union League.

3366 Netherton, Thomas J.   **1947-**
In the morning of my life. With Marie Chapian. Foreword by Norma Zimmer. Foreword by Lawrence Welk. Illustrated. Wheaton, Illinois: Tyndale House Publishers, 1979. 262 p.
   Netherton's good-natured narrative focuses on his childhood in a peripatetic family, his advancement in the U.S. Army, the experience of being a born-again Christian, and its impact on his career as a popular singer.

3367 Neuhaus, Karl Eugen   **1879-1963**
Drawn from memory: a self portrait. Palo Alto, California: Pacific Books, 1964. 208 p.
   Because German-born Neuhaus was forbidden by a harsh guardian uncle to study art, he became a house painter until he won a scholarship to art school in Berlin at the Royal Museum of Decorative Art. Later Neuhaus emigrated to America and eventually settled on the Monterey Penninsula. His art lectures proved popular, and in 1920 he became a faculty member at the University of California, where he taught and painted until retirement.

3368 Neumann, Emanuel   **1893-**
In the arena: an autobiographical memoir. Foreword by Arthur Hertzberg. Illustrated. New York: Herzl Press, 1976. 375 p. Index.
   Neumann narrates the story of a life devoted to Zionism with its central goal the establishment of the State of Israel, accomplished in 1947. Neumann was an outstanding leader in American and international Zionist organizations. He knew and worked with the world's notable Jewish leaders, including Chaim Weizmann, Louis D. Brandeis, and Rabbi Abba Hillel Silver.

3369 Neutra, Richard Joseph   **1892-**
Life and shape. New York: Appleton-Century-Crofts, 1962. 374 p. Index.
   A respected Austro-American architect, he tells of the forces that shaped him and his awareness of the intricate relationship between physical surroundings and the creative mind and spirit.

3370 *Nevelson, Louise (Berliawsky)   **1900-**
Dawn & dusks: taped conversations with Diana MacKown. Illustrated with introduction by John Canady. New York: Charles Scribner's Sons, 1976. 190 p.
   In a series of candid conversations with her longtime assistant, Nevelson describes the metamorphosis of her life from unconventional wife and mother to one of America's foremost innovative sculptors. Nevelson is articulate and candid in explaining her artistic modes, motifs, and preference for black. The book's text complements the numerous photographs of the sculptor and her creations.

3371 *Newberry, Julia Rosa   **1853-1876**
Julia Newberry's diary. New York: W.W. Norton & Co., 1933. 176 p.
   The journal of two years of the life of a young girl whose travels in Europe are overlaid with nostalgia for her home. The Newberry family was important in Chicago history (Newberry Library) and Julia's roots were deep in Chicago soil; she mourns for it after news of the Great Fire reaches her in Paris.

3372 Newcomb, Charles King   **1820-1894**
Journals of Charles King Newcomb. Edited with introduction by Judith Kennedy Johnson. Studies, vol. 10, Americana Series, no. 1. Providence, Rhode Island: Brown University Press, 1946. 299 p. Index.
   Following a long and informative introduction by the editor, selections from Newcomb's journals are organized thematically (pp. 93-292); transcendentalist poet and diarist whom Emerson thought brilliant.

3373 *Newman, Frances   **1880?-1928**
Frances Newman's letters. Edited by Hansell Baugh. New York: Horace Liveright, 1929. 372 p. Index.
   Letters between Frances Newman and various literary and personal friends give a taste of her personal and professional character. In her book reviews and letters she held high standards based on sound scholarship and dealt ruthlessly, but with a sense of humor, with what she judged to be bad writing.

3374 Newman, Henry   **1670-1743**
Henry Newman's Salzburger letterbooks. Edited and transcribed by George Fenwick Jones. Wormsloe Foundation Publications, no. 8, ltd. ed. Athens: University of Georgia Press, 1966. 626 p. Index.
   A New Englander and colonial subject of Great Britain, Newman, as secretary of the Society for Promotion of Christian Knowledge, worked to bring Protestant Germans afflicted by "Popish Persecution" to the society's lands in Georgia. His letters chronicle the details of providing transport, land, and "Temporal Necessities" for the new settlers.

3375 Newton, Huey P.   **1942-**
Revolutionary suicide. With the assistance of J. Herman Blake. New York: Harcourt Brace Jovanovich, Inc., 1973. 333 p.
   Newton writes of his youth and development, the emergence and strategy of the Black Panther Party, his imprisonment and associates. He distinguishes between revolutionary suicide and reactionary suicide and assesses the future course of the Black Power movement.

3376 Newton, Joseph Fort   **1876-1950**
River of years: an autobiography. Philadelphia: J.B. Lippincott Co., 1946. 390 p. Index.
   Fully detailed narrative of the life and development of an Episcopal minister, famous for his syndicated feature in the *American Press* (1933-1944).

3377 Newton, Louie DeVotie   **1892-**
Why I am a Baptist. New York: Thomas Nelson and Sons, 1957. 306 p.
   Written at the request of the publisher for its "Why I Am" series, the book places his personal history in the context of his Baptist faith, from his first declaration at age ten to his successful career as a minister in Atlanta.

3378 *Ney, Elisabet   **1834-1907**
Sursum!: Elisabet Ney in Texas. Edited by Mr. J.W. (Willie B.) Rutland. Austin: Hart Graphics & Office Centers, 1977. 200 p.
   All but the last twenty pages of this book are letters to or from the German-American artist concerning various commissions for sculptures, mostly in Texas, including a marble bust of Lady Machett. She also worked in Germany and Italy.

3379 Nichols, Frederick George   **1878-1954**
Frederick G. Nichols' memoirs, 1878-1954: the early view of business education. St. Peter, Minnesota: Delta Pi Epsilon, Inc., 1979. 202 p.
   Nichols' memoirs comprise a "written photograph" of one of the great personalities in business education during the first half of the twentieth century. Also a prolific writer, Nichols taught at Harvard for 22 years, where he directed doctoral studies and was secretary to the graduate faculty, despite his lack of minimal educational requirements.

3380 Nichols, George   **1778-1865**
George Nichols, Salem shipmaster and merchant; an autobiography. Edited with introduction and notes by his granddaughter, Martha Nichols. Freeport, New York: Books for Libraries Press, 1970. (Salem, Massachusetts: The Salem Press, 1914) 89 p.
   In an autobiography dictated when he was eighty years old, Nichols tells of his sailing days during the late eighteenth and early nineteenth century.

3381 Nichols, James Wilson   **1820-1891**
Now you hear my horn: the journal of James Wilson Nichols 1820-1887. Edited by Catherine W. McDowell. Illustrated by Eldridge Hardie. Austin: University of Texas Press, 1967. 212 p. Index.
   Nichols's swashbuckling journal of life on the Texas frontier, 1820-1887, tells of continual skirmishes with Indian tribes and various battles of the Mexican-American War, including the Battle of the Hondo in 1842. During the Civil War Nichols, a Union supporter, was persecuted by Confederate sympathizers.

3382 Nichols, John Treadwell   **1941-**
If mountains die: a New Mexico memoir. Introduction by William Davis. Photographs. New York: Alfred A. Knopf, 1979. 144 p.
   With lyricism and humor, a novelist describes his first eight years in Taos, New Mexico (1969-77), a spiritual homeland and refuge from the "frenzied outrage" of New York City and the anti-war movement. Here Nichols "could see all aspects of weather and landscape and wildlife," ally with exploited Chicanos and Indians against encroaching middle-class Anglos, form an intricate network of human ties, and weather his divorce.

3383 *Nichols, Ruth   **1901-1960**
Wings for life. Edited by Dorothy Roe Lewis. Foreword by Richard E. Byrd. Philadelphia: J.B. Lippincott Co., 1957. 317 p.
   A pioneer in aviation, she established many international records in the Twenties and Thirties, then became involved in several organizations for world peace, including UNICEF. Her book depicts the challenge and adventure of the aviation frontier.

3384 Nichols, Thomas Low   **1815-1901**
Forty years of American life: 1812-1861. Westport, Connecticut: Negro Universities Press, 1968. (London, 1864) 2v.
   Nichols, a Black New Hampshire physician, writes engagingly of the years before and after the Civil War. Focusing on "the moral and social condition," he describes his travels to Boston, Buffalo, New York, Cincinnati, New Orleans, and Memphis. He established the Memnonia Institute in Yellow Springs, Ohio, which advocated asceticism, fasting, and spiritual penance.

3385 *Nicholson, Lillie M. 1892-1975
Vagabond schoolmarm. North Newton, Kansas: Mennonite Press, 1977. 173 p.

A collection of personal anecdotes and observations penned just prior to and after her retirement from teaching school; these were originally published by the *Evening Kansas Republican* and *The Newton Journal* under the heading "Zig-Zags." Her up-beat observations are infused with pride in Kansas, the state in which her wanderings as the "vagabond schoolmarm" end.

3386 *Nicholson, Martha Snell 1886-1951
His banner over me. Preface by Louis T. Talbot. Illustrated. Chicago: Moody Press, 1953. 192 p.

Nicholson, who became a religious poet in her adulthood, writes of her childhood in Tacoma, Washington, where her resourceful and beautiful mother was the focal point of a Christian upbringing for herself and her two sisters. On the verge of marriage she developed tuberculosis, the cure of which postponed her wedding for seven years. Her husband, religious faith, and the writing of poetry sustained her subsequent lifetime of chronic illness.

3387 Nicholson, Ralph 1899-1972
A long way from Greens Fork. Illustrated. Tallahassee, Florida: Peninsular Publishing Co., 1968. 224 p.

This self-congratulatory volume focuses on Nicholson's rags-to-riches career as a journalist and newspaper publisher. After graduation from Earlham College he became a foreign correspondent, but soon began the profitable business of buying faltering newspapers throughout the East and South, modernizing their printing plants, and improving their news coverage and design.

3388 Nicklaus, Jack 1940-
Greatest game of all: my life in golf. With Herbert Warren Wind. Foreword by Robert Tyre Jones, Jr. New York: Simon & Schuster, 1969. 416 p. Index.

He began golf at age ten and became the longest driver in the game, winner of many championship tournaments. He writes about his life in golf, including six chapters of instruction.

3389 Niebuhr, Reinhold 1892-1971
Leaves from the notebook of a tamed cynic. Hamden, Connecticut: The Shoe String Press, 1956. (Chicago: Willett, Clark & Colby, 1929) 198 p.

His journal notes (1915-1928) are critical but optimistic about his role as a minister.

3390 Nimoy, Leonard
I am not Spock. New York: Del Rey/Ballantine Books, 1977. (Milbrae, California: Celestial Arts, 1975) 150 p.

Leonard Nimoy, the actor famous for his role as Spock in the *Star Trek* science-fiction TV series, uses this good-natured book to try to demonstrate that he is a versatile, capable actor in television, films and on the stage.

3391 *Nin, Anaïs 1903-1977
The diary of Anaïs Nin. Edited by Gunther Stuhlmann. New York: The Swallow Press and Harcourt, Brace & World, Inc., 1966-76. 7v.

Nin's diary, including a supplementary photographic volume, discusses art, drugs, beauty, and psychology, with comments on plays, books, and films and accounts of visits to Sweden, Belgium, and the south of France. Her psychological exploration of friends, acquaintances, and self is sensitive and illuminating.

3392 *Nin, Anaïs 1903-1977
Unpublished selections from The Diary. Athens, Ohio: Duane Schneider Press, 1968. 43 p.

This selection from unpublished portions of Nin's diary focuses on Henry Miller and Dr. René Allendy, 1932-1938, when she was living in Paris.

3393 Nininger, Harvey Harlow b.1887
Find a falling star. Introduction by Fred L. Whipple. New York: Paul S. Eriksson, Inc., 1972. 254 p. Index.

From 1923 when his interest was first aroused, Nininger, with single-minded persistence, set out to find, collect, study, and educate others about meteorites. His enthusiasm and perseverance have stimulated interest and research by laymen and scientists so that today meteoritical research and analysis have become greatly intensified.

3394 Nitschke, Ray
Mean on Sunday; the autobiography of Ray Nitschke. As told to Robert Wells. Garden City, New York: Doubleday & Co., Inc., 1973. 302 p.

An outstanding middle-line backer for the Green Bay Packers for fifteen years describes his life on that team and the genuine pleasure he derived from his work.

3395 *Nixon, Lily Lee 1890-
Long ago: the story of a public school teacher. Philadelphia: Dorrance & Co., 1977. 125 p.

Nixon integrates the narrative of her long career as a teacher (elementary, junior high, and eventually high school) in Pittsburgh with current events—World Wars I and II and the Depression, in particular. Her life was shaped by her mother, with whom she lived until her mother's death, her education at Slippery Rock and the University of Pittsburgh, and by the Chautauqua movement.

3396 Nixon, Richard Milhous 1913-
R.N.: the memoirs of Richard Nixon. Illustrated. New York: Grossett and Dunlap, 1978. 1120 p. Index.

A controversial President tells the story of his rise from boyhood in California to this nation's highest office. Nixon's memoir candidly recounts six of the American presidency's most turbulent years, focusing on foreign affairs. Nixon offers no apology for the events surrounding the Watergate affair which ultimately forced his resignation.

3397 Nixon, Richard Milhous 1913-
Six crises. Garden City, New York: Doubleday & Co., Inc., 1962. 460 p.

Written after he lost the presidential election to John F. Kennedy, his book analyzes six events crucial in his political life, with comments on the growth which resulted. Events include the Alger Hiss case, President Eisenhower's heart attack, and the 1960 presidential campaign.

3398 Nixon, Richard Milhous 1913-
The White House transcripts; submission of recorded presidential conversations to the Committee on the Judiciary of the House of Representatives. New York: The Viking Press, 1974. 877 p.

The full text of the White House tapes, long withheld by Nixon, printed here with a Watergate Chronology, the White House legal argument that accompanied the transcripts, Nixon's April 29, 1974, address to the nation, and other background material.

3399 Nizer, Louis 1902-
My life in court. Garden City, New York: Doubleday & Co., Inc., 1961. 524 p.

Convinced that stage, movie, and TV trials cannot approximate the drama and excitement of real court contests, Nizer proves his point by re-creating some trials he has participated in: libel (Quentin Reynolds vs. Westbrook Pegler), divorce, plagiarism, malpractice, negligence, proxy fights.

3400 Nizer, Louis 1902-
Reflections without mirrors: an autobiography of the mind. Garden City, New York: Doubleday & Company, Inc., 1978. 469 p. Index.

Nizer, a lawyer who specializes in the motion-picture industry, writes about abuses of the law, his law cases, and his great respect for some of the Supreme Court Justices, especially Benjamin Cardozo. He also deals with censorship in the motion-picture industry and movies used for propaganda (*Up the Down Staircase*) by the Russians.

3401 Noble, Harold Joyce 1903-1953
Embassy at war. Edited with introduction by Frank Baldwin. Illustrated. Seattle: University of Washington Press, 1975. 328 p. Index.

An account of the American Embassy in Korea during the first three months of the Korean War, 1950, and its part in supporting the South Korean government. As the first secretary and third-ranking political officer of the embassy, during that summer Noble was in close contact with Korean politics.

3402 *Noble, Helen (Klaffky)
Life with the Met. New York: G.P. Putnam's Sons, 1954. 246 p. Index.

The technical secretary at the Metropolitan Opera in New York recounts her thirty years on the job. She tells about life backstage and discusses Edward Ziegler along with other operatic personalities.

3403 Nock, Albert Jay (Journeyman, pseud.) 1872-1945
Letters from Albert Jay Nock, 1924-1945: to Edmund C. Evans, Mrs. Edmund C. Evans and Ellen Winsor. Edited with introduction by Frank W. Garrison. Preface by Rebecca Evans and Ellen Winsor. Caldwell, Idaho: The Caxton Printers, Ltd., 1949. 224 p. Index.

In letters to his friends written during the years of his literary activity, the author comments on his life and work.

3404 Nock, Albert Jay (Journeyman, pseud.) 1872-1945
Memoirs of a superfluous man. Chicago: Regnery, 1964. (New York: Harper, 1943) 326 p.

The literary and philosophical autobiography of an active mind, Nock's book has been compared with *The Education of Henry Adams;* however, he teases and outrages the reader while probing into the spirit of early twentieth-century America.

3405 Nock, Albert Jay (Journeyman, pseud.) 1872-1945
Selected letters of Albert Jay Nock. Collected and edited by Francis J. Nock. Caldwell, Idaho: The Caxton Printers, Ltd., 1962. 201 p.

A selection of Nock's letters meant to show his development during the period from 1910 up to the time his *Memoirs* were published. The editor wished to present Nock's human side to counteract the idea conveyed by his published writings that he was a "cantankerous old curmudgeon."

3406 Noguchi, Isamu   **1904-**
A sculptor's world. Illustrated. Foreword by R. Buckminster Fuller. New York: Harper & Row, Publishers, 1968. 259 p.
A sculptor and designer of remarkable intellect and originality, Noguchi writes of his life and work, emphasizing the importance of his Japanese heritage and the conceptual development of his art.

3407 Nolen, William A.   **1928-**
The making of a surgeon. New York: Random House, 1974. 308 p.
A surgeon writes of his five years of training at New York's Bellevue Hospital—his success, mistakes, disasters, and a description of how surgeons work, think and feel.

3408 Nolen, William A.   **1928-**
Surgeon under the knife. New York: Dell Publishing Co., 1977. (New York: Coward, McCann, & Geoghegan, Inc., 1976) 221 p.
At the age of 47 Nolen had an angina attack triggered by strenuous exercise. An angiogram revealed two blocked coronary arteries and in July 1975 he had a double coronary by-pass operation. Nolen offers suggestions for avoiding heart attacks and explains the necessity for operations like his. He also advises that hospital patients be vigilant about their medical care; mistakes can happen.

3409 Nomad, Max   **1881-1973**
Dreamers, dynamiters and demagogues; reminiscences. New York: Waldon Press, 1964. 251 p. Index.
Sketches of many "heroes and non-heroes" he has admired during his lifetime of alternating attraction to and disenchantment with anarchism, various revolutionary causes, and violent acts of protest. Although he gradually shed his illusions about the lofty ideals of the beneficiaries and opponents of the world's injustices, he has never shed his indignation at those injustices and the opportunists who seek to benefit from them.

3410 Norelius, Eric   **1833-1916**
Journals of Eric Norelius, a Swedish missionary on the American frontier. Edited with an introduction by G. Everett Arden. Philadelphia: Fortress Press, 1967. 207 p. Index.
Drawn to America for economic reasons, Norelius left Sweden and became a clergyman, missionary, and educator attempting to establish schools and children's homes, publish a Swedish newspaper, and carry out other humanitarian endeavors. He was an important participant and founding member of the Augusta Lutheran Synod.

3411 *Norman, Frida Elvira   **1900-**
My fifty years with the angels. New York: Vantage Press, 1978. 240 p.
Norman, an elementary school teacher for over fifty years in Minnesota, Iowa, and Washington, D.C., describes each position in minute detail. Norman's energy, cheerful spirit, and love of children remain high despite illnesses, birth defects, the Depression, and problem children in the schools where she taught.

3412 Norris, Clarence (Willie)   **1912-**
Last of the Scottsboro boys: an autobiography. And Sybil D. Washington. New York: G.P. Putnam's Sons, 1979. 281 p.
The state of Alabama granted him an unconditional pardon after reviewing evidence that had convicted him for rape three times. He recalls his five years on death row, ten in the penitentiary, and life as a fugitive after breaking parole in 1946.

3413 Norris, Frank   **1870-1902**
Letters. Edited by Franklin Walker. San Francisco: Book Club of California, 1956. 98 p.
Fewer than a hundred letters have survived the author of *McTeague,* who died at the age of 31. Those that have been preserved almost always have his writing as their subject.

3414 Norris, Jack Clayton   **1899-**
Gleanings from a doctor's eye. Illustrated. Atlanta, Georgia: Jack C. Norris, 1953. 120 p.
These "gleanings" include stories and fragments of a philosophy of life, among them observations on grandfatherhood, television addiction, alcoholism, the maintenance of health after forty, and a religious creed. Norris also comments on Samoa and the Philippines, where he served as a naval doctor in World War II.

3415 *Norris, Kathleen (Thompson)   **1880-1966**
Family gathering. Garden City, New York: Doubleday & Co., Inc., 1959. 327 p.
Author of about eighty popular novels, Norris writes her life story as a family memoir, focusing on family events, members, and activities, mostly in the San Francisco area.

3416 North, Joseph   **1904-1976**
No men are strangers. New York: International Publishers, 1958. 255 p.
A fast-moving account of the development of North's liberal ideals and principles as a Jewish immigrant's child in Pennsylvania, as a University of Pennsylvania student, and in the late 1920's and early 30's as a reporter for *New Masses, The New Republic,* and *The Daily Worker.* A consistently forthright defender of the downtrodden, including Blacks, poor immigrants, Spanish Civil War victims, and Dachau concentration camp victims.

3417 North, Luther Hedden   **1846-1935**
Man of the Plains: recollections of Luther North, 1856-1882. The Pioneer Heritage Series, Vol. IV. Edited by Donald F. Danker. Foreword by George Bird Grinnell. Lincoln: University of Nebraska Press, 1961. 350 p. Index.
In 1864 North and his brother Frank joined the Pawnee Scouts, a unit of the U.S. Army which played a significant role in the long wars for control of the Great Plains, chiefly against the Sioux and Cheyenne tribes.

3418 Northrop, Solomon   **b.1808**
Twelve years a slave. Illustrated. Edited by Sue Eakin and Joseph Logsdon. Baton Rouge: Louisiana State University Press, 1968. (Auburn: Derby and Miller, 1853) 213 p. Index.
Born a free Negro in the North, Northrop was kidnapped at age 33 and enslaved in the South, but finally was rescued twelve years later. His autobiography presents a detailed description of slave life and plantation society from the special perspective of his earlier education and freedom.

3419 Norton, Edwin Clarence   **1856-1943**
The Dean speaks again: giving hitherto unpublished excerpts from personal papers, diaries, and letters; together with portions of previously published speeches. Edited by Edith P. Hinckley and Katharine N. Benner. Art supervision by Alan Benner. Foreword by James A. Blaisdell. Claremont, California: The Creative Press, 1955. 121 p.
With love, faith, and gentle humor, Norton tells about his youth and early education in Minnesota and focuses on his career as the first Dean of Pomona College, 1888-1937. His life, so intertwined with Pomona's, provides a history of that institution's inception and growth.

3420 Noyes, Pierrepont Burt   **1870-1959**
A goodly heritage. New York: Rinehart and Co., Inc., 1958. 275 p.
His first autobiography, *My Father's House* (1937, 1966), describes his early life in the Oneida Community which his father founded. This volume begins in 1879, the year the Community was dissolved, describing his shock in having to contend with the outside world, his return at 24 to direct the new Oneida Community, Ltd., and his long career as a community leader and pacifist who aided Woodrow Wilson's organization of the League of Nations.

3421 Noyes, Pierrepont Burt   **1870-1959**
My father's house: an Oneida boyhood. Gloucester, Massachusetts: Peter Smith, 1966. (New York: Farrar & Rinehart, 1937) 312 p.
Noyes analyzes the first sixteen years of his life, growing up in a Utopian society, a communal religious sect, the Oneida community, founded by his father, John Humphrey Noyes. Raised in relative poverty, Noyes was a happy child, oblivious to the drawbacks of his limited formal and informal education. The major stress of his life was the breakdown and secession of part of the Oneida community.

3422 Nugent, Elliott   **1899-1980**
Events leading up to the comedy; an autobiography. New York: Trident Press, 1965. 304 p.
The story of Nugent's life is full of ancedotes about his careers as an actor and director in theater and movies and as a writer of successful comedies such as *The Seven Year Itch* and, with his friend James Thurber, *The Male Animal.* His bouts with a hypo-manic-depressive cycle periodically interrupted the course of his life but were finally brought under control.

3423 Nugent, William Lewis   **1832-1897**
My dear Nellie: Civil War letters to Eleanor Smith Nugent. Edited by William M. Cash and Lucy Somerville Howorth. Illustrated. Jackson: University Press of Mississippi, 1977. 247 p. Index.
In his effusively romantic letters to his betrothed, Nugent frequently upbraids her for her gaity—as, for example, her dancing, which must mean she intends to abandon the church—only to insist, several letters later, that she must have misunderstood his tone. After their marriage his letters fill with war news and exhortations to be cheerful and not fear the Yankees. He details the progression of the war in Mississippi and Tennessee.

3424 *Nuñez, Bonita Wa Wa Calachaw   **1888-1972**
The spirit woman: the diaries and paintings of Bonita Wa Wa Calachaw Nuñez. New York: Harper and Row, 1980. 243 p.
Taken from her mother at birth by a white woman who had worked for Indian rights in the Southwest, Nuñez became a painter in Greenwich

Village. She spent much of her adult life trying to discover her parents and working for Indian rights.

3425 Nunn, Henry Lightfoot   1878-1972
Whole man goes to work: the life story of a businessman. New York: Harper and Brothers, 1953. 214 p. Index.
   As President of the Nunn-Bush Shoe Company in St. Louis, he encouraged unionization and many forms of labor-management cooperation. His personal philosophy of life and industrial management is the major focus of his book.

3426 Nuttall, Thomas   1786-1859
Nuttall's travels into the Old Northwest: an unpublished 1810 diary. Edited by Jeannette E. Graustein. Chronica Botanica, Vol. 14, No. 1/2. Waltham, Massachusetts: Chronica Botanica Co., 1951. 88 p.
   A botanist's record of his explorations in the Northwest (now Michigan and Minnesota) collecting specimens of flora.

3427 Nye, Bill, pseud.
   see Nye, Edgar Wilson

3428 Nye, Edgar Wilson (Bill Nye, pseud.)   1850-1896
Bill Nye, his own life story. Continuity by Frank Wilson Nye. Freeport, New York: Books for Libraries Press, 1970. (New York: Century, 1926) 412 p.
   This volume is "compiled largely from his letters and articles, with connecting comments written by his son." Nye wrote weekly newspaper stories and magazine articles and fifty or more personal letters a week, chiefly about himself, with gentle, humorous self-ridicule but ringing sincerity.

3429 Nye, Edgar Wilson (Bill Nye, pseud.)   1850-1896
Letters now in the University of Wyoming Library. Edited by Nixon Orwin Rush. Limited edition. Laramie: University of Wyoming Library, 1950. 29 p.
   Thirty-three letters written by a popular frontier humorist and historian.

3430 Oakie, Jack   1903-1978
Jack Oakie's double takes. Preface by Victoria Oakie. Edited by Diane Sipes. Illustrated. San Francisco: Strawberry Hill Press, 1979. 217 p. Index.
   This book is arranged topically to focus on Oakie's particular friends among the hordes of Hollywood stars he worked with (including Chaplin and Garbo) and to accommodate the many diverse categories of movies he acted in for fifty years, ranging from comedies (*The Great Dictator*) to romances (*Song of the Islands*) to westerns (*The Texas Rangers*). Oakie loved all the films, most of the stars, his wife, and his mother.

3431 Ober, Harold
   see Fitzgerald, Francis Scott Key

3432 Oberndorf, Clarence Paul   1882-1954
An autobiographical sketch. Foreword by Norman S. Moore. Ithaca, New York: Cornell University Infirmary and Clinic, 1958. 31 p.
   Oberndorf's narrative tells of his early life, his medical training, and his decision to enter psychiatry. His career was intertwined with the development of analytic psychiatry and his associates included noted psychiatrists such as Freud, under whom he studied. He emphasizes the difficulty in having reputable medical schools accept psychoanalysis as a valid medical specialty.

3433 Obolensky, Serge   1890-1978
The memoirs of Serge Obolensky. New York: McDowell, Obolensky, 1958. 433 p. Index.
   Born a Russian prince, he grew up in the midst of elegant aristocracy and court life, was educated at Oxford University, eventually married Alice Astor, became prominent in the hotel business, and joined the U.S. Paratroopers during World War II, making his first jump at age 53. His book reflects the excitement, variety and wealth of his experience.

3434 O'Brien, Howard Vincent   1888-1947
All things considered: memories, experiences, and observations of a Chicagoan. Indianapolis: The Bobbs-Merrill Co., 1948. 345 p.
   His book bears the name of his daily column, which appeared in the Chicago *Daily News* (1932-1947) and was characterized by "the quiet humor, the gentle irony, the searching honesty, the unaffected good manners that made his personality one of the most winning any newspaper office ever had." (Preface) Many columns are included.

3435 O'Brien, Lawrence Francis   1917-
No final victories; a life in politics—from John F. Kennedy to Watergate. Garden City, New York: Doubleday & Co., Inc., 1974. 394 p. Index.
   The author's life in politics from his early days as an organizer, specializing in registration and get-out-the-vote drives to his important work as Democratic Party strategist, spokesman, and party chairman striving for

united leadership during the 60's and 70's. He was a primary target for the "bugging" operation of Nixon's "plumbers."

3436 *O'Brien, Margaret (Angela Maxine)   1937-
My diary. Drawings by the author. Foreword by Lionel Barrymore. Philadelphia: J.B. Lippincott Co., 1947. 117 p.
   Her diary for 1947, written after she had been a child actress for five years.

3437 O'Brien, Pat Alva
Outwitting the Hun; my escape from a German prison camp. New York: Harper & Brothers Publishers, 1918. 283 p.
   An Irish Canadian, he enlisted in the British Royal Air Corps during World War I, was captured by the Germans, escaped through Belgium, and returned to settle in Illinois.

3438 *Ockleman, Constance
   see *Lake, Veronica, pseud.

3439 *O'Connor, Flannery   1925-1964
The habit of being: letters. Edited with introduction by Sally Fitzgerald. New York: Farrar, Straus, and Giroux, 1979. 617 p. Index.
   O'Connor's warm personal letters to friends and associates reveal her notions about the writing of good fiction, her attitude toward racial problems in the South, her orthodox Catholic convictions, her acceptance of her terminal illness, and many practical, less serious, everyday matters.

3440 *O'Connor, Patti
One summer in Israel. And Catherine Cole. Introduction by Joe D. Seger. Illustrated. Chicago: Academy Press Ltd., 1978. 227 p.
   O'Connor and Cole spent six weeks in Israel in the summer of 1977, partly on a kibbutz, partly touring the country. Cole took thousands of photographs recording her impressions of the people, places, customs, and her own deepening awareness and self-understanding.

3441 O'Connor, Paul   1909-1974
Eskimo parish. Milwaukee: The Bruce Publishing Co., 1947. 134 p.
   A Catholic missionary in Alaska describes his parish, the people, their work and society.

3442 *Odlum, Mrs. Floyd B.
   see *Cochran, Jacqueline

3443 *Offenberg, Bernice
The angel of Hell's Kitchen. New York: Harcourt, 1963. (New York: Bernard Geis Associates, 1962) 277 p.
   At 21 she was working as an investigator for the New York Welfare Department. Her cases involved the poor, the derelict, the hardened mobsters. Her investigative skills and sense of humanity made her work legendary. The film *House on 92nd Street* is about a Nazi espionage ring she helped uncover.

3444 Ogle, George E.   1929-
Liberty to the captives: the struggle against oppression in South Korea. Atlanta: John Knox Press, 1977. 188 p.
   This Methodist missionary in Korea worked along with the urban poor seeking to change the terrible working conditions. These efforts brought the urban industrial mission into conflict with industry, government, and foreign (American) commercial interests. When President Park Chung Wee formed a dictatorship, Ogle was deported for his efforts to aid the people who protested oppression.

3445 O'Grady, John   1925-
O'Grady: the life and times of Hollywood's no. 1 private eye. And Nolan Davis. Los Angeles: J.P. Tarcher, Inc., 1974. 238 p.
   After twenty years as an L.A. policeman, the author opened his own investigative agency catering to despondent wives, blackmailed industrialists, beleaguered celebrities, and others who wanted to keep their affairs out of newspapers and away from official police.

3446 *O'Hara, Constance Marie   1907-
Heaven was not enough. Philadelphia: J.B. Lippincott Co., 1955. 381 p.
   Constance O'Hara details her development as a Catholic playwright and her continual association with the Catholic faith. She worked in Philadelphia and New York and reminisces about the convent school, priests, and nuns.

3447 *O'Hara, Mary, pseud. (Sture-Vasa, Mary Alsop)   1885-1980
Novel in the making, by Mary O'Hara (pseud.) New York: David McKay Co., Inc., 1954. 244 p.
   The "journal of a job," based on her diaries while writing a novel, revealing the progress of her thoughts and craft, by the author of *My Friend Flicka*.

3448 *O'Keeffe, Georgia   1893?-
Georgia O'Keeffe. Illustrated. New York: The Viking Press, 1976. 228 p.

In a verbal style resembling her painting, she writes of her art teachers (William Merritt Chase and Arthur Dow) and education, the genesis of her own work.

3449 Old Mexican   **b.1865?**
Navaho autobiography. Recorded by Walter Dyk. New York: The Viking Fund, 1947. 218 p.
    The themes of acculturation, the difficulties of farming, and the troubles of married life run through this story of a Navaho's life revealing the sufferings and frustrations of his own complex personality and society's imposition on him of expectations, attitudes, ideals and reactions.

3450 *Olds, Sarah Thompson   **1875-1963**
Twenty miles from a match: homesteading in western Nevada. Foreword by Leslie Zurfluh. Illustrated. Reno: University of Nevada Press, 1978. 182 p.
    Olds explains her life as a homesteader and rancher in western Nevada for the first half of the twentieth century. There she reared five children; raised a garden, mules, and lambs; trapped and skinned coyotes; and at times ran a dude ranch and a boardinghouse.

3451 O'Leary, Brian Todd   **1940-**
The making of an ex-astronaut. Boston: Houghton Mifflin Co., 1970. 243 p. Index.
    A scientist-astronaut who left the program a year before the first manned moon landing writes of his desire to become an astronaut, the applications, tests, interviews, training, flight school, and studies involved. He discusses his agonizing decision to quit and offers his views about the future of the space program.

3452 *Olender, Terrys T.
For the prosecution: Miss Deputy D.A. Foreword by Jerry Giesler. Philadelphia: Chilton Co., 1961. 380 p.
    A lively account of her legal education and career as a Deputy District Attorney in California. In spite of continuous opposition from male colleagues, she placed high in her class and began a difficult but successful career as a trial lawyer.

3453 *Oleson, Thurine   **b.1866**
Wisconsin, my home: [her] story. As told to her daughter, Erna Oleson Xan. Illustrated. Madison, Wisconsin: University of Wisconsin Press, 1975. 230 p.
    Oleson recounts the history of her parents, Norwegian immigrants to Wisconsin in 1866, as well as the life stories of herself, her mother-in-law, her husband, and her children. She provides a history of the Norwegian-American community of Winchester, Wisconsin, in which she lived most of her long life. The book presents fond memories of a culture of hard-working, clean, religious farmers, seen from a housewife's point of view.

3454 Oliver, L. Stauffer   **1879-1966**
The bench is a hard seat: an autobiography. Philadelphia: Dorrance & Co., 1965. 177 p.
    Employing the experience gained in 62 years as a lawyer and judge, Oliver gives practical information and advice on successful conduct of a law practice. He also relates his own progress from a young, naive lawyer to a seasoned, competent jurist.

3455 Olmsted, Frederick Law   **1822-1903**
A journey through Texas; or a saddle-trip on the southwestern frontier. New York: Dix, Edwards & Co., 1857. 516 p.
    This narrative, undertaken to describe "the great extent and capacities of Texas, as well as its distinct position and history," was compiled from the author's record of the journey he took in order to improve his health with invigorating outdoor life.

3456 Olmsted, Frederick Law   **1822-1903**
Papers: Vol. 1: The Formative Years, 1822 to 1852. Edited by Charles Capen McLaughlin. Associate editors, Charles E. Beveridge and Victoria Post Ranney. Illustrated. Baltimore: Johns Hopkins Press, 1977. 423 p. Index.
    This splendidly printed, edited, and annotated edition of Olmsted's letters focuses on a voyage to China (1843), "Connecticut Interlude" (1844-1845), "The Search for Love and Certitude" (1846), and Olmsted's years as a "Gentleman Farmer" (1847-49). They are eclectic, vibrant, and witty.

3457 Olsen, Nils Andreas   **1886-1940**
Journal of a famed bureaucrat: Nils A. Olsen and the BAE, 1925-1935. Edited by Richard Lowitt. Ames: The Iowa State University Press, 1980. 245 p. Index.
    Olsen's diaries cover the years 1925 to 1935 and concern his meetings with various Department of Agriculture bureaucrats to discuss farming policy, politics, and programs—among them, taking farmland out of circulation to cut farm surplus.

3458 Olsen, Viggo B.
Daktar/Diplomat in Bangladesh. With Jeanette Lackerbie. Chicago: Moody Press, 1973. 351 p.
    He was a medical missionary in East Pakistan when a bloody civil war led to the establishment of the new state of Bangladesh. Here he writes of his early life, his medical training, becoming a surgeon, and becoming a medical missionary. A major portion of the book is devoted to his family and professional life in Bangladesh.

3459 Olson, Charles   **1910-1970**
Letters for origin, 1950-1956. Edited by Albert Glover. New York: Cape Goliard Press, 1970. 141 p.
    The editor has tried to respect the poet's spelling, spacing, and punctuation while "seeing clearly that bounding outline already present in the mass and of bringing it out, visible, for public view." The letters are written to Cid Corman, editor of *Origin,* a quarterly periodical.

3460 Olson, Sigurd F.   **1899-**
Open horizons. Illustrated by Leslie Kouba. New York: Alfred A. Knopf, 1969. 231 p.
    A deep appreciation and understanding of the spiritual value of the wilderness have been central in the life of Olson, a pre-eminent naturalist, woodsman, writer, and conservation leader.

3461 Olzendam, Roderic Marble   **1892-**
Liberty's grandson: an unconventional autobiography. With Gordon Keith. Hicksville, New York: Exposition Press, 1977. 178 p. Index.
    Olzendam's autobiography is aimed "to help parents and grandparents in their dealings with their own progeny." He attributes his success as industrialist, horticulturist, and public relations person to "love for America, old time patriotism, and a sincere belief in Almighty God."

3462 O'Meara, Walter   **1897-**
We made it through the winter; a memoir of northern Minnesota boyhood. St. Paul: Minnesota Historical Society, 1974. 128 p. Index.
    O'Meara, who later became a journalist, worked for the OSS and OPA during World War II, and was a publicist for Adlai Stevenson in 1956, here writes of his childhood in the raw sawmill town of Cloquet, Minnesota, just after the turn of the century.

3463 *Onassis, Jacqueline (Bouvier) Kennedy   **1929-**
One special summer. Written and illustrated by Jacqueline and Lee Bouvier. New York: Delacorte Press, 1974. 63 p.
    Jackie, aged twenty-two, and her sister Lee, eighteen, spent a summer in Europe and wrote this book together as a thank-you gift to their parents. They shared the printing, drawing, and fun of their adventures in this amusing record.

3464 Oppenheimer, George   **1900-1977**
The view from the Sixties; memories of a spent life. New York: David McKay Co., Inc., 1966. 273 p. Index.
    During his years in publishing, in writing Hollywood screenplays, in the Air Corps' First Motion Picture Unit making training films, and as a playwright, Oppenheimer got to know many famous show business people. Here he describes events, parties, and a glamorous way of life.

3465 Orchard, Hugh Anderson   **b.1871**
Old Orchard farm. Edited by Paul F. Sharp. Ames: The Iowa State College Press, 1952. 235 p.
    The day-to-day adventures of a rural Iowa youth are recalled by one of the post-frontier pioneers who shared in the years of semi-subsistence farming and experimenting to improve the soil culture, the crop strains, the livestock breeds. He recaptures the boy's world of excitement and delight in a difficult but rewarding era.

3466 *Origo, Iris (Cutting), Marchesa   **1902-**
Images and shadows; part of a life. New York: Harcourt Brace Jovanovich, Inc., 1970. 278 p. Index.
    Writing about three distinct periods of civilization—pre-World War I of 1914, the world between the two wars, and the time after World War II—the author attempts to describe her life in various homes she has had in the United States, Ireland, and Italy. Recognizing the barriers imposed by her privileged status, she feels that the price she paid was in being cut off from possible friends and experiences.

3467 Orlando, Guido   **1906-**
Confessions of a scoundrel. As told to Sam Merwin. Philadelphia: John C. Winston, 1954. 275 p.
    An Italian-American press agent narrates the story of his career working for actresses, government officials, and royalty on two continents. Most of his work originated, however, in New York and Hollywood.

3468 Ortman, Elmore Jan   **b.1881**
To rear the tender thought: the autobiography of a modern educator. New York: Exposition Press, 1960. 124 p.
    Ortman's career in education embracing the first half of the twentieth century includes teaching in a wide range of educational institutions:

county, village, and city schools as well as colleges and large universities. Here he also tells about the philosophy that has guided him.

3469 *Osato, Sono   **1919-**
Distant dances. Illustrated. New York: Alfred A. Knopf, 1980. 301 p. Index.

Osato's career as a dancer began at fourteen as a member of the Ballet Russe de Monte Carlo, with which she toured Europe, Australia, and the United States throughout the 1930's. She also danced with the American Ballet Theatre in New York, but after marriage and motherhood in the Forties switched to stage acting because of the difficulty of keeping in top physical shape. Osato's portraits of the luminaries of ballet are lively and insightful.

3470 Osborn, Frederic J.
see **Mumford, Lewis C.**

3471 *O'Shaughnessy, Edith Louise (Coues)   **1870-1939**
Diplomat's wife in Mexico. New York: Arno Press, 1970. (New York: Harper & Brothers, 1916) 355 p.

In letters to her mother, Mrs. O'Shaughnessy writes from the American Embassy in Mexico City describing the beauty of the country, the dramatic events between October 1913, and the breaking off of diplomatic relations in April 1914, and the occupation of Vera Cruz.

3472 Osiek, Paul Henry   **1904-**
Emergency surgeon. And Robert S. Richardson. Philadelphia: Dorrance & Co., 1946. 291 p.

His experience at Emergency Hospital in Pasadena beginning in 1933 conveys a sense of his life and the life of the city, especially its tragic side.

3473 *Ossoli, Sarah Margaret Fuller
see ***Fuller, Margaret**

3474 Oswald, Russell George   **1908-**
Attica—my story. Edited by Rodney Campbell. Garden City, New York: Doubleday & Co., Inc., 1972. 418 p.

Oswald, who was in charge at Attica Prison, was both acclaimed and vilified for terminating that four-and-a-half day riot in September 1971. In an attempt to "set the record straight," he tells of his previous training and work and gives a detailed report of the events before and during the Attica riots. He still believes in prison reform and his "faith in the correctibility of most criminal behavior remains unshaken."

3475 Otash, Fred
Investigation Hollywood! Foreword by Mickey Spillane. Chicago: Henry Regnery Co., 1976. 252 p. Index.

Since 1955, Otash has been a private detective. This book focuses on his famous and intriguing cases which have ranged from tracking down Walter Winchell's daughter, to guarding Judy Garland, to tailing mobster Mickey Cohen during Attorney General Robert Kennedy's investigation of racketeering. Otash writes as he lives, with a terse, hard-boiled style.

3476 Otero, Jesus   **1896-**
Schoolmaster's son: an autobiography. New York: Azteca Press, 1947. 130 p.

Leaving Spain at age 14, he immigrated to Cuba, then to New York, where he began to work at restaurants and gradually learned to be a chef.

3477 Otis, Johnny   **1921-**
Listen to the lambs. New York: Norton, 1968. 256 p.

Born of Greek parents in California, he was drawn into the Black community during his early adolescence by what he calls the "special mysteries of Black 'soul'." He became a jazz musician, working with such outstanding figures as Count Basie; his first hit record with his own combo was "Harlem Nocturne." This book combines an analysis of the American Black-white dilemma with his own unusual story.

3478 *Ovington, Mary White   **1865-1951**
The walls came tumbling down. New York: Harcourt, Brace and Co., 1947. 307 p. Index.

The story of a New England social worker who devoted her life to the Negro question and worked to establish the NAACP.

3479 *Owen, Maggie, pseud.
see ***Wadelton, Maggie Jeanne (Melody)**

3480 Owen, William   **1802-1842**
Diary: from November 10, 1824 to April 20, 1825. Edited by Joel W. Hiatt. Clifton, New Jersey: Augustus M. Kelley, Publishers, 1973. (Indianapolis: Bobbs-Merrill Co., 1906) 134 p. Index.

His father, a wealthy Scottish manufacturer, bought the village of New Harmony, Indiana, in order to develop a benevolent working community there, as he had in New Lanark, Scotland. William was specially educated to become a leader in the utopian society; he devoted himself to publishing a newspaper and later helping to run the family business.

3481 Owens, Jesse   **1913-1980**
Blackthink: my life as black man and white man. With Paul G. Neimark. New York: William Morrow and Co., Inc., 1970. 215 p.

The famous Black athlete tells of discriminatory experiences he has had and suggests solutions to some of the blackthink vs. whitethink problems.

3482 Owens, Jesse   **1913-1980**
Jesse Owens story. With Paul G. Neimark. New York: G.P. Putnam's Sons, 1970. 109 p. Index.

Written for young people, Owen's book describes his outstanding career as a runner. An American Black who won three gold medals in the 1936 Olympic Games, he got even more publicity because Hitler refused to shake his hand.

3483 *Ozawa, Martha Naoko
The foreign student in the United States: with special reference to Martha (Naoko Ozawa). And Helen I. Clarke. Preface by C.A. Engman. Introduction by Martin B. Loeb. Madison: School of Social Work, University of Wisconsin, 1970. 189 p.

After a survey of "the characteristics of over 100,000 foreign students engaged in higher education in the United States" in the late 1960's, the book focuses on Martha Ozawa's account of her experience as a foreign graduate student in social work at the University of Wisconsin. Although from an affluent family, in the United States Martha depended for support on her own earnings, scholarships, gifts, and occasional income from her ex-husband. A picture emerges of a selfless, abstemious young scholar devoted to her profession and her clients.

3484 Paar, Jack   **1918-**
I kid you not. With John Reddy. Boston: Little, Brown & Co., Inc., 1960. 226 p.

With many jokes and one-liners, this book tells anecdotes of the life of a fast-talking comedian from his youth through his big break as summer replacement for *The Jack Benny Show* and his hosting of *The Tonight Show*.

3485 Paar, Jack   **1918-**
My saber is bent. With John Reddy. New York: Simon and Schuster, 1961. 236 p.

The second of his books about his life in television by the originator of the late-night talk show. The monologue is fast, glib, and entertaining.

3486 Pacheco, Ferdie   **1927-**
Fight doctor. Introduction by Muhammad Ali. New York: Simon & Schuster, 1977. 237 p.

Pacheco, a Miami Beach physician, writes of his relationship with boxer Muhammad Ali, whom he attends medically throughout his training and boxing matches. Pacheco, who admires Ali greatly, describes Ali's fights with Sonny Liston, Rocky Marciano, Ken Norton, George Foreman, and Joe Frazier.

3487 *Page, Ruth   **1900-**
Page by Page. Edited with introduction by Andrew Mark Wentink. Brooklyn: Dance Horizons, 1978. 224 p. Index.

Forty-seven essays and a hundred photographs portray the life and career of dancer Ruth Page, an American member of a Russian dance troupe. She writes of the many places in which she has danced, the dancers with whom she has performed, and of the changes in the art of dance during the twentieth century.

3488 Page, Thomas Nelson   **1853-1922**
see **Fox, John**

3489 *Pahk, Induk
The cock still crows. New York: Vantage Press, 1977. 144 p. Index.

Christian missionary and educator Pahk uses the metaphor of a cock, herald of a beginning day, along with numerous other legends, Oriental fables and allegories to punctuate the story of her establishment of schools and colleges for Korean men and women. Faith and energy propelled Pahk through fifty years in America as she worked to create the Induk schools, touring and speaking throughout the country. The legends and bits of poetry reveal her quiet yet exuberant Oriental perspective.

3490 Paige, Leroy (Satchel)   **1906-1982**
Maybe I'll pitch forever. Garden City, New York: Doubleday and Co., Inc., 1962. 285 p.

At 42 Paige was signed to play for the Cleveland Indians, the first Black to pitch in the American League and the fifth ever to play in the major leagues. He was still pitching and playing in his fifties.

3491 Paige, Leroy (Satchel)   **1906-1982**
Pitchin' man. As told to Hal Lebovitz. Cleveland, Ohio: H.P. Lebovitz, 1948. 96 p.

A collection of short comments by one of baseball's great players and characters, originally printed in the Cleveland *News*, as recorded by Hal Lebovitz.

3492 Paine, Philbrook   **1910-**
Squarely behind the beavers. Illustrated by Larry Lurin. New York: W.W. Norton and Co., Inc., 1963. 188 p.

After eighteen years as a public relations man in Boston, he went "back to the land," became a columnist and feature writer in New Hampshire, began renovating the family homestead near Durham, and immersed himself in the curious and independent lifestyle of rural New England.

3493 *Painter, Charlotte   **1926-**
Confession from the Malaga Madhouse: A Christmas diary. New York: Dial Press, 1971. 212 p.

A widowed writer travels to Spain with her six-year-old son, struggling to find some sense of sanity and self in a world gone mad.

3494 Palermo, Louie
'Atsa Louie, I'ma Phil. And Phil Palermo with Bernard Palmer. Foreword by Robert A. Cook. Illustrated. Wheaton, Illinois: Victor Books, 1975. 135 p.

Gospel musicians Phil and Louie Palermo describe their conversion from lukewarm Roman Catholicism to fervent evangelical Christianity as a consequence of their mother's miraculous "cure" from cancer in 1926. They became lifelong crusaders, mixing gospel music, jokes, and ventriloquism with spaghetti suppers; this good-natured mixture has taken them to Brazil for Youth-for-Christ rallies, to Vietnam to entertain troops during the Vietnam War, and throughout the United States on gospel missions.

3495 Palermo, Phil
see **Palermo, Louie**

3496 Paley, William Samuel   **1901-**
As it happened: a memoir. Illustrated. Garden City, New York: Doubleday & Co., Inc., 1979. 418 p. Index.

Founder and chairman of CBS, Paley describes his experience in transforming the small, struggling United Independent Broadcasting into the giant communications empire CBS. As a brilliant and creative businessman he foresaw the cultural and informational potential of radio and TV, discovered and promoted many entertainers, and helped set the trends and tastes of his time.

3497 Palmer, George Herbert   **1842-1933**
Autobiography of a philosopher. New York: Greenwood Press, 1968. (Boston: Houghton Mifflin Co., 1930) 137 p.

His memories of the intellectual growth and struggles in reaching his convictions "about ultimate things on which he now relies." He and his colleagues at Harvard composed the outstanding group of philosophers of their day.

3498 Palmer, Thomas Waverly   **1891-1968**
Gringo lawyer. Gainesville: University of Florida Press, 1956. 176 p. Index.

In 1919, after studying law at Harvard and in Spain, he began to practice law in Chile. His book describes his experience as a lawyer in Latin America during the next thirty years.

3499 Palmquist, Al
Miracle at City Hall. With Kay Nelson. Minneapolis: Bethany Fellowship, Inc., 1974. 173 p.

The author felt a God-given directive to help drug addicts in Minneapolis. He became a policeman and learned first-hand about violence and lawlessness, which he sought to overcome through his distinctive Christian ministry.

3500 Panlilia, Yay (Colonel Yay)
The crucible: an autobiography. New York: The Macmillan Co., 1950. 348 p.

Courageous narrative of experience as a guerrilla fighter in Luzon during the Japanese occupation, 1942-1945, by a journalist.

3501 Panos, Chris   **1935-**
God's spy. Foreword by Pat Boone. Foreword by Brother Andrew. Introduction by Mary W. Stevens. Plainfield, New Jersey: Logos International, 1976. 269 p.

An exuberant account of Panos's life as a teenage hoodlum and hustler, followed by success as a brash businessman selling houses, Western clothing, and boots in Houston. He had been a carousing Greek Orthodox backslider, but when a vision of Christ appeared to him, he became born-again and turned his high-pressure salesmanship to selling Christ and giving Bibles away behind the Iron Curtain at considerable personal cost. Panos also has an evangelical TV show in Houston.

3502 Papanek, Ernst   **d.1973**
Out of the fire. With Edward Linn. New York: William Morrow & Co., Inc., 1975. 299 p.

In 1938 Papanek became director of a group of castles in southern France which served as shelters for refugee Jewish children, many of whose parents had been killed by the Nazis or sent to concentration

camps. He tried to provide a normal life using progressive educational theories. Eventually he brought some of the children to America with him.

3503 Papashvily, George   **1898-**
Anything can happen. And Helen (Waite) Papashvily. New York: Harper & Brothers Publishers, 1945. 202 p.

The story of his immigration to the U.S. from Georgia in Russia includes his first impression of Ellis Island, his early attempts at farming, being cast as a Russian Cossack in Hollywood movies, and working for the war effort in World War II.

3504 Papashvily, George   **1898-**
Home, and home again. And Helen (Waite) Papashvily. New York: Harper & Row, Publishers, 1973. 175 p.

He emigrated to the U.S. in 1922 from Russian Georgia, an experience recorded in *Anything Can Happen.* This volume tells of his return visit forty years later to the village he grew up in, with recollections of childhood at the center of his narrative.

3505 *Paquette, Georgiana S.   **1905-**
My book. New York: Exposition Press, 1949. 32 p.

A whimsical and anecdotal review of her adult life during which she found satisfaction in nursing and journalism.

3506 Paris, Beltran   **b.1888**
Beltran: Basque sheepman of the American West. And William A. Douglass. Illustrated. The Basque Series. Reno: University of Nevada Press, 1979. 186 p.

This unusual book provides an oral history of Basque sheepherders in Wyoming and Nevada as epitomized in the experiences of Paris, who immigrated from French Basque country in 1912. He comments on the difficulties of protecting sheep from predators and disease and on the continual tension between cowmen and sheepmen.

3507 *Park, Etta Wolcott   **1863-1940**
A story for my children. Introduction by Nettie Wolcott Park. Photographs. New York: Vantage Press, 1968. 253 p.

The author intended these recollections of farm life in Michigan and upstate New York, the accompanying geneology, and family photographs for her fourteen children and their families. Its primary interest for outsiders is its detailed record of the daily activities of a closely knit, religiously oriented, resourceful American farm family.

3508 *Park, Maud Wood   **1871-1955**
Front door lobby. Edited by Edna Lamprey Stantial. Boston: Beacon Press, 1960. 278 p.

A settlement worker describes her experience in the suffrage movement, 1916-1919, when she served as vice-chairman and then chairman of the congressional committee of the National American Woman Suffrage Association charged with getting the Suffrage Amendment through Congress.

3509 Parker, George Howard   **1864-1955**
The world expands: recollections of a zoologist. Cambridge: Harvard University Press, 1946. 252 p. Index.

Primarily recollections of his professional life, the book describes some boyhood memories, his Harvard College days, his field work on the Pacific Gold Coast, Japan and China, and his prominent career on the Harvard faculty.

3510 Parker, Morris B.   **1871-1957**
Mules, mines and me in Mexico, 1895-1932. Edited with introduction and notes by James M. Day. Illustrated. Tucson: University of Arizona Press, 1979. 239 p. Index.

At the age of 24 he became manager of an ore-buying agency in Mexico. He was witness to one of Mexico's most turbulent periods of history.

3511 Parker, Theodore   **1810-1860**
The trial of Theodore Parker, with the defence by Theodore Parker. The Black Heritage Library Collection. Freeport, New York: Books for Libraries Press, 1971. (Boston: The author, 1855) 221 p.

In 1854 Parker gave a speech in Boston's Faneuil Hall objecting to the activities of slave hunters under the Fugitive Slave Law, which he called kidnapping. When a disturbance broke out at a fugitive slave trial at the Court House and one of the marshal's guards was killed, Parker and others were charged with inciting the action and resisting the officer. His book records the arguments for his defense.

3512 Parker, Willie J.   **1924-**
Halt! I'm a Federal Game Warden: the amazing career of "the toughest game warden of them all." And Conway Robinson. Foreword by Nathaniel T. Reed. Illustrated. New York: David McKay Co., 1977. 210 p.

A salty, straightforward account of Parker's 25-year career as an agent for the U.S. Fish and Wildlife Service. Integrity personified, Parker is devoted to protecting waterfowl, eagles, alligators, and other endangered or out-of-season species, and is a tough, uncompromising foe of lawbreakers.

3513 Parkman, Francis   **1823-1893**
Journals of Francis Parkman. Edited by Mason Wade. New York: Harper and Brothers, 1947. 2v. Index.
　　Journals of explorer-historian's travels in New York, Maine, Canada, Europe, and on the Oregon Trail.

3514 Parkman, Francis   **1823-1893**
Letters of Francis Parkman. Edited with introduction by Wilbur R. Jacobs. Norman: University of Oklahoma Press, 1960. 2v. Index.
　　The letters (1841-1893) of a famous nineteenth-century explorer and historian record the history of his ambitions, his frustrations, his attainments, and his long struggle against illness, with vivid accounts of his personal life and thought.

3515 Parks, Gordon   **1912-**
Born Black. Philadelphia: J.B. Lippincott, 1971. 192 p.
　　Essays originally commissioned by *Life* Magazine present Park's observations of and interviews with Black people who helped shape the Sixties—Black Muslims, Malcolm X, Muhammad Ali, Stokely Carmichael, Martin Luther King, Jr.

3516 Parks, Gordon   **1912-**
A choice of weapons. New York: Harper & Row, Publishers, 1973. (1965) 274 p.
　　A man of many talents, Parks has been a correspondent, professional basketball player, composer, novelist, and photographer. He made documentaries for Standard Oil Company and received many awards for his photo-journalism in *Life* Magazine.

3517 Parks, Gordon   **1912-**
To smile in autumn: a memoir. New York: W.W. Norton, 1979. 249 p.
　　Parks continues his serial autobiography with an account of his career as a photographer in New York and in the South during the 1940's, 50's and 60's, focusing on segregation, civil rights efforts, life in Harlem, and the Baptist and Muslim religions. He describes his three marriages, each shorter than the previous, to beautiful women; his fatherhood (including mourning a son killed in Africa), his film-making (*The Learning Tree, Shaft*), his composing, his poetry, and his hope for the future.

3518 *Parks, Lillian Rogers   **1896?-**
It was fun working at the White House. And Frances S. Leighton. Introduction by Frances S. Leighton. Illustrated by Isadore Parker. New York: Fleet Press Corp., 1969. 208 p.
　　An engaging book for children and adults about Parks's forty-year career as a maid and seamstress in the White House during the administrations of Hoover, Franklin D. Roosevelt, Truman, and Eisenhower. She particularly liked Eleanor Roosevelt and the open, happy, helpful, magnanimous atmosphere the Roosevelts generated.

3519 *Parks, Lillian Rogers   **1896?-**
My thirty years backstairs at the White House. With Frances Spatz Leighton. New York: Fleet Publishing Corp., 1961. 346 p.
　　Parks, lifelong maid and seamstress at the White House, was the daughter of another White House maid, whose reminiscences she also recounts. Together their service spanned the administrations from Taft to Eisenhower. The Roosevelts, with their largesse, extensive family, and sense of democracy were her favorites.

3520 Parley, Peter, pseud.
　　see **Goodrich, Samuel Griswold**

3521 Parrish, Robert   **1916-**
Growing up in Hollywood. Illustrated. New York: Harcourt Brace Jovanovich, 1976. 220 p. Index.
　　Parrish details his interesting career in films—as a child actor in the 1920's, as a film cutter in the 1930's, and as a director, beginning in the early 1940's. He loved every aspect of film production and learned his craft from such masters as Charlie Chaplin and John Ford.

3522 *Parsons, Geneve Shaffer
Geneve. Foreword by Lenore D. Underwood. New York: Vantage Press, 1969. 103 p.
　　A chaotic, energetic account of Parsons's diverse occupations, some obtained more on bravado and perseverance than on talent. They include stints as a real estate agent, actress, journalist, and political candidate—she finished a strong second in an unsuccessful race for Lieutenant Governor of California. Her jumbled chronology makes it difficult to tell what happened when, or why, but the book continually manifests optimistic egocentrism.

3523 *Parsons, Louella (Oettinger)   **1893-1972**
Tell it to Louella. New York: G.P. Putnam's Sons, 1961. 316 p.
　　In one sense the book is an autobiography of Hollywood in her time.

But it is her work, her life, and that of the famous people she knew well during a long career as a Hollywood columnist.

3524 Parsons, Schuyler Livingston   **1892-1967**
Untold friendships. Boston: Houghton Mifflin Co., 1955. 252 p. Index.
　　As a member of one of New York's oldest families, he inherited traditions of wealth, style and entertainment that prepared him for his own position as a professional host and society leader. The index of his book is studded with celebrities, the rich and the famous.

3525 *Parton, Margaret
Journey through a lighted room. New York: The Viking Press, 1973. 248 p.
　　A journalist for the New York *Herald-Tribune* who spent many years on assignment in Japan and India writes of her personal struggles with love, marriage, divorce, death, and her son's death by leukemia, in a moving affirmation of her will to live and endure.

3526 *Parton, Margaret
The leaf and the flame. New York: Alfred A. Knopf, 1959. 277 p.
　　The book distills her diaries of five years during which she lived in India as a staff correspondent of the New York *Herald Tribune* and the wife of a British correspondent. Entries are colorful and precise in her account as the Western observer of Eastern culture.

3527 *Parton, Sara Payson (Willis)   **1811-1872**
Fern leaves from Fanny's port-folio. Auburn, New York: Derby & Miller, 1853. 400 p.
　　Short pieces, many previously published in newspaper columns, include vignettes of people and places. Some contain moral lessons, some appear to be autobiographical.

3528 Pasternak, Joseph   **1901-**
Easy the hard way. As told to David Chandler. New York: G.P. Putnam's Sons, 1956. 301 p.
　　A Hollywood producer writes of his boyhood in Hungary, his early days as an immigrant in New York, and the development of his career in the movies. He helped establish the success of Deanna Durbin, Marlene Dietrich, and many others.

3529 Patrick, George Thomas White   **1857-1949**
George Thomas White Patrick: an autobiography. Iowa City: University of Iowa Press, 1947. 180 p.
　　Writing at age 90 for the University of Iowa Centennial, Patrick describes his long and productive life as a student, teacher, and philosopher.

3530 Patrick, Marsena Rudolph   **1811-1888**
Inside Lincoln's army: the diary of Marsena Rudolph Patrick, Provost Marshall General, Army of the Potomac. Edited by David S. Sparks. New York: Thomas Yoseloff, 1964. 536 p.
　　A remarkable record of the day-to-day operation of staff departments and personal staffs of the army commanders, the social life in Washington, and many major Washington figures who contributed to the war effort.

3531 Pattee, Fred Lewis   **1863-1950**
Penn State Yankee: the autobiography of Fred Lewis Pattee. State College: Pennsylvania State College, 1953. 384 p. Index.
　　Raised in New Hampshire, he studied at Dartmouth and was a professor of literature at Pennsylvania State College, 1894-1928. He introduced the serious study of American writers into colleges and is acknowledged to be the first professor of American Literature.

3532 Patten, Gilbert (Burt L. Standish, pseud.)   **1866-1945**
Frank Merriwell's "father": an autobiography by Gilbert Patten ("Burt L. Standish"). Edited by Harriet Hinsdale. Assisted by Toni London. Norman: University of Oklahoma Press, 1964. 331 p. Index.
　　Patten, whose Frank and Dick Merriwell books have sold more than 500 million copies since the first was published in 1896, became the real king of the dime novelists. This account of his own life he left unfinished but the last phase has been reconstructed by the editor.

3533 Patterson, Edmund DeWitt   **b.1842**
Yankee rebel: the Civil War journal of Edmund DeWitt Patterson. Edited with introduction by John G. Barrett. Biographical essay by Edmund Brooks Patterson. Chapel Hill: University of North Carolina Press, 1966. 207 p.
　　Patterson's lively and detailed account of Civil War battles is notable for its vivid, elegant language and understated humor.

3534 Patterson, Floyd   **1935-**
Victory over myself. With Milton Gross. New York: Bernard Geis Associates, 1962. 244 p.
　　His book is the story of his personal emancipation—lacking confidence as a child, he could neither read nor write at age ten—and his professional

development as a boxer. In 1960 he regained the world heavyweight championship from Ingemar Johanssen.

3535 Patterson, Grove   **1881-1956**
I like people: the autobiography of Grove Patterson. New York: Random House, 1954. 300 p.

Patterson recounts his childhood upbringing in Carlyle, Ohio, but concentrates on his career as a newspaper editor, primarily of the Toledo *Blade*. During travels abroad, he interviewed Mussolini, Winston Churchill, and Eva Peron, among other notables. Patterson concludes with paeans to his faith in God and faith in people.

3536 Patterson, Harry Norton   **1853-1919**
Afield with plant lovers and collectors: botanical correspondence of the late Harry N. Patterson with the great botanical collectors and distributors of America from 1870 to 1919. Foreword by T.E. Musselman. Edited by Alice L. Kibbe. Quincy, Illinois: Alice M. Kibbe, Carthage College, and Gem City Business College, 1953. 565 p. Index.

Correspondence, 1870-1915, between botanist and printer Harry N. Patterson and a host of other botanical collectors, including Samuel Barnum Mead, H.G. Jessup, and Edwin Hunt, is mostly concerned with the exchange, location, and identification of various plant specimens in the West and Midwest. The collection is now housed at the Field Museum, Chicago.

3537 Patterson, Heywood   **1913-1952**
Scottsboro boy. And Earl Conrad. Garden City, New York: Doubleday and Co., Inc., 1950. 309 p.

One of the central figures in the Scottsboro case tells the story of his arrest, his trial, the harrowing life in Alabama jails and prisons, and his escape.

3538 Pattie, James Ohio   **1804-1850?**
Personal narrative of James O. Pattie. Edited by Timothy Flint. New York: Garland Publishers, 1976. (Cincinnati: John H. Wood, 1831) 300 p.

A fur trapper's formal but classic account of his journeys of trade and exploration to New Mexico and Mexico, with forays along the Platte and Colorado rivers. In addition to describing relations with Pawnee, Comanche, and Apache Indians, he graphically describes encounters with buffaloes and grizzly bears and a revolution in Mexico.

3539 Patton, George Smith   **1885-1945**
War as I knew it. Annotated by Colonel Paul D. Harkins. Boston: Houghton Mifflin Co., 1947. 425 p.

Essentially a study of Patton in the West-European campaign of 1944-45, the book is based heavily on his unpublished war diary and includes letters written to his wife from Africa and Sicily.

3540 Paul, Elliot Harold   **1891-1958**
Desperate scenery. New York: Random House, 1954. 302 p.

The last in his autobiographical series, *Items on the Grand Account*, which describes his youthful experience working on construction crews in Wyoming and Idaho around 1910.

3541 Paul, Elliot Harold   **1891-1958**
Ghost town on the Yellowstone. New York: Random House, 1948. 341 p.

Youthful adventures on a project of the U.S. Reclamation Service in Montana (1907-08), with good details of Western frontier life. One of several in his autobiographical series, *Items on the Grand Account*, by the author of *The Last Time I Saw Paris*.

3542 Paul, Elliot Harold   **1891-1958**
Linden on the Saugus Branch. New York: Random House, 1947. 401 p.

The third volume in his autobiographical series, *Items on the Grand Account*, describing his early years growing up in a suburb of Boston.

3543 Paul, Elliot Harold   **1891-1958**
My old Kentucky home. New York: Random House, 1949. 438 p.

Another in his autobiographical series, *Items on the Grand Account*, describing his life in Louisville around 1910.

3544 Paul, Elliot Harold   **1891-1958**
A narrow street. London: The Cresset Press, 1942. 342 p.

A journalist's well-written account of his experience in Paris during the Twenties and Thirties until the Nazi takeover of the city, with powerful and precise details of personal and political struggles.

3545 Paxton, Elisha Franklin   **1828-1863**
Civil War letters of General Frank "Bull" Paxton, CSA: a lieutenant of Lee & Jackson. Edited by John Gallatin Paxton. Introduction by Harold B. Simpson. Preface by Dick Paxton. Hillsboro, Texas: Hill Junior College Press, 1978. 102 p. Index.

Paxton's letters to his wife and an occasional speech to his troops are embedded in an interpretive matrix that provides a much larger picture of the Civil War as fought primarily in Virginia 1861-63. Paxton was a

Brigadier General of the Stonewall Regiment of the Confederate Army when he was killed in battle on May 2, 1863.

3546 *Peabody, Marian Lawrence   **b.1875**
To be young was very heaven. Boston: Houghton Mifflin Co., 1967. 366 p.

A description of a charming and privileged youth in the 1890's and early twentieth century by a bishop's daughter. Her life was composed of teas, balls, European trips, art school, debutante parties, and charity work which she recorded in eighteen volumes of diary here condensed into one.

3547 *Pearl, Minnie (Ophelia Colley)   **1912-**
Minnie Pearl: an autobiography. With Joan Dew. Illustrated. New York: Simon and Schuster, 1980. 256 p.

This fast and funny narrative moves from early family life to road shows to the Grand Ole Opry. Ophelia Colley traces the development of character Minnie Pearl with humorous anecdotes and witty insight, writing lovingly of the many people, common and celebrated, with whom she has worked during her career.

3548 Pearson, Billy   **1920-**
Never look back: the autobiography of a jockey. With Stephen Longstreet. Introduction by John Huston. New York: Simon and Schuster, 1958. 370 p.

An exciting, fast-moving account of Pearson's career around horses. He began as a stable boy and continued into his thirties as a jockey, racing primarily in California. As a sailor in the Pacific during World War II, he added to his art collection, which grew in quality to the extent that he now runs an art gallery.

3549 Pearson, Drew   **1897-1969**
Diaries, 1949-1959. Edited by Tyler Abell. New York: Holt, Rinehart and Winston, 1974. 592 p. Index.

Pearson lived to communicate. He wrote daily columns for thirty-seven years, weekly broadcasts for twenty years, plus books, articles, lectures, and letters. This volume of his diaries extends his view of the history of his time—a record of the people and events that made history during the decade of the 50's.

3550 Pearson, Hayden Sanborn   **1901-1967**
Country flavor. Foreword by William F. Berghold, editor of The Rural New Yorker. New York: Whittlesey House, division of McGraw-Hill, 1945. 112 p.

In this collection of essays which originally appeared on the editorial pages of the New York *Times*, Pearson writes of the charm of rural life. Text includes photographs of country scenes and farm activities.

3551 Pearson, Hayden Sanborn   **1901-1967**
Countryman's year. Introduction by Dorothy Canfield Fisher. New York: Whittlesey House-McGraw Hill, 1949. 192 p.

Reprinted from the Boston *Herald*, the Providence *Journal*, the New York *Times*, the Richmond *Times-Dispatch*, and the Washington *Evening Star*, these essays express the poetry and wisdom of a man who has retained his country boy's appreciation of the sights, smells, and feelings associated with rural life.

3552 Pearson, Hayden Sanborn   **1901-1967**
New England flavor: memories of a country boyhood. Illustrated by Leonard Vosburgh. New York: W.W. Norton & Co., 1961. 249 p.

A nostalgic recollection of life in a New Hampshire farming community includes stories of Fogg's General Store, covered bridges, fringe-top surreys, the tin peddlar, homemade ice cream, and other happy memories.

3553 Pearson, Hayden Sanborn   **1901-1967**
Sea flavor. Essay Index Reprint Series. Freeport, New York: Books for Libraries Press, 1948. 178 p.

A collection of editorials, articles, and essays reprinted from various newspapers, this volume contains Pearson's impressions and observations of life in a small New England fishing village.

3554 *Pearson, Virginia Edwards (Taylor)   **1899-**
Everything but elephants. New York: Whittlesey House, 1947. 211 p.

Lively, well-written narrative by a doctor's wife during a two-year assignment in the jungle of Colombia.

3555 *Peary, Josephine Diebitsch (Mrs. Joseph)
My Arctic journal, a year among ice-fields and Eskimos: with an account of The Great White Journey across Greenland by Robert E. Peary. Illustrated. New York: Contemp. Pub. Co., 1897. (1893) 240 p.

This is the plain and simple narrative of a white woman's year on the shores of McCormick Bay, midway between the Arctic Circle and the North Pole. It includes observations of a small band of Eskimos as well as a frank account of the hardships of existence.

3556 Pease, Arthur Stanley   **1881-1964**
Sequestered vales of life. Cambridge: Harvard University Press, 1946. 129 p.

Charming sketches of his relatives, friends, neighbors, and surroundings by a keen, thoughtful observer of nature and human nature.

3557 Peck, John Mason   1789-1858
Forty years of pioneer life: memoir of John Mason Peck, D.D. Edited by Rufus Babcock. Introduction by Paul M. Harrison. Foreword by Herman R. Lantz. Series: Perspectives in Sociology. Carbondale: Southern Illinois University Press, 1965. (Philadelphia: American Baptist Publication Society, 1864) 360 p.
Peck's memoir, culled from 53 handwritten volumes by his 1864 editor, Rufus Babcock, reveals an energetic, perceptive Baptist-pioneer clergyman dedicated to observing frontier civilization throughout the Midwest as well as to proselytizing. Peck's typology of frontier social classes provided the basis for Frederick Jackson Turner's analysis; his interpretation of frontier life, social institutions, and communities has a sociological as well as historical base.

3558 Peck, Joseph Howard   1885-
What next, Doctor Peck? Englewood Cliffs, New Jersey: Prentice-Hall, Inc., 1959. 209 p.
In 1916-18 he was a doctor for the Utah Construction Company in a bleak, isolated area in the western part of the state. His book tells of the rough, uncivilized but pleasant life on this twentieth-century frontier.

3559 Pelham, Henry   1749-1806
see Copley, John Singleton

3560 Pellegrini, Angelo   1904-
The unprejudiced palate. New York: The Macmillan Co., 1948. 235 p.
A university professor describes his family's immigration from Italy to the United States, his culinary philosophy, and some practical suggestions about his culinary craft.

3561 Peller, Sigismund   1890-
Not in my time: the story of a doctor. New York: Philosophical Library, 1979. 374 p. Index.
In gruesome detail Peller writes about his life as a doctor. He describes various diseases and symptoms in terms difficult for a layman to understand. Peller also mentions battling against anti-Semitism as well as bureaucrats for better health-care and medical research facilities.

3562 Peltier, Leslie C.   1900-
Starlight nights: the adventures of a star-gazer. Illustrated by Leslie C. Peltier. New York: Harper & Row, 1965. 236 p.
A unique autobiography in which the simple, clear style of an amateur astronomer transports the reader into the starry skies above rural Delphos, Ohio, where the author has lived his entire life, farmed, and raised strawberries and a family. The discoverer of many comets observes, "For the dedicated watcher of the skies each nightfall is a time fraught with suspense. Will the skies tonight be just the same or has something happened since I saw them last?"

3563 Pender, William Dorsey   1834-1863
General to his lady: the Civil War letters of William Dorsey Pender to Fanny Pender. Edited by William W. Hassler. Illustrated. Chapel Hill: University of North Carolina Press, 1965. 271 p. Index.
Pender's letters combine general news of the war's progress (1861-1863) with domestic concerns—inquiries after health, his need for new undershirts, and even accounts of flirtations, which draw swift responses from his young wife. He died of a battle wound before he could return to his family.

3564 Pendleton, Edmund   1721-1803
The letters and papers of Edmund Pendleton, 1734-1803. Collected and edited by David John Mays. Charlottesville: Published for The Virginia Historical Society by The University Press of Virginia, 1967. 2v. Index.
Prominent as a lawyer, judge, and politician in Virginia, he worked with the major figures in colonial history. His letters document his political activity and the times.

3565 Penfield, Wilder Graves   1891-1976
No man alone; a neurosurgeon's life. Foreword by Lord Adrian. New York: Little, Brown & Co., 1977. 398 p. Index.
Dr. Penfield recounts his studies at Princeton and Oxford during World War I, followed by medical practice in New York City and his founding of the Montreal Neurological Institute. A pioneering neurological researcher and surgeon, he details his medical investigations and innovations, including epilepsy research.

3566 Penna, Tony   1908-
My wonderful world of golf. With Oscar Fraley. Foreword by Jimmy Demaret. New York: Centaur House, 1965. 239 p.
Penna, winner of various middle-level golf tournaments in the 1930's, discusses his career as a golfer, comments on changes in tournament golf between 1925-1965, and concludes that the more recent stakes are higher and the players are more gentlemanly. He offers tips on how to play pro

golf, advice to beginners, and identifies his top ten great golfers (Jack Nicklaus is no. 1).

3567 Penney, James Cash   1875-1971
Fifty years with the Golden Rule. New York: Harper and Brothers, 1950. 245 p.
Successful businessman recounts his adherence to Christian principles in his working and family life.

3568 Penney, James Cash   1875-1971
View from the ninth decade: jottings from a merchant's daybook. Foreword by Norman Vincent Peale. New York: Thomas Nelson & Sons, 1960. 222 p.
With self-congratulatory good humor, multimillionaire Penney expounds the religiously-oriented philosophy that governed his business dealings as founder of a department store empire ("The best goods for the least money"). The Golden Rule dominates, girded by faith, hope, charity, optimism, abstinence from smoking and drinking—and by devotion to business and to God.

3569 Pennington, Levi I.   b.1875
Rambling recollections of ninety happy years. Portland, Oregon: Metropolitan Press, 1967. 187 p.
Pennington, a lifelong Quaker clergyman and professor and for over thirty years president of Oregon's Pacific College (now George Fox College), reminisces about significant aspects of the college; his beloved wife, Rebecca; notable Quaker friends (including Herbert Hoover); and his cheerful philosophy of life.

3570 Pepper, Art   1925-
Straight life: the story of Art Pepper. And Laurie Pepper. Discography by Todd Selbert. Illustrated. New York: Schirmer Books, 1979. 516 p. Index.
The story of Art Pepper's life as musician, drug abuser, and prisoner, as reflected by taped interviews with Pepper and others who know him. His experiences at Synanon at the depths of his drug abuse are described, as is his eventual return to music and a straight life.

3571 Percival, James Gates   1795-1856
Uncollected letters of James Gates Percival: poet and geologist, 1795-1856. Edited with introduction and notes by Harry R. Warfel. University of Florida Monographs in Humanities, No. 1. Gainesville: University of Florida Press, 1959. 76 p.
Fifty-two letters previously unpublished confirm the impression held by scholars that Percival was a romantic, melancholic recluse, usually dissatisfed with his place in the world, but nonetheless productive.

3572 Percy, William Alexander   1885-1942
Lanterns on the levee; recollections of a planter's son. Introduction by Walker Percy. Baton Rouge: Louisiana State University Press, 1973. 347 p.
He writes of his noble and tragic view of life, his gloomy assessment of the spiritual health of Western civilization, the collapse of morality, and life in the Southern aristocracy.

3573 *Perenyi, Eleanor Spencer (Stone)   1918-
More was lost. Boston: Little, Brown and Co., 1946. 278 p.
Most of the book describes the war years in Hungary, 1937-1940, when she fell in love, married, and had a child by a young man who joined the underground. A bittersweet recollection of family life and traditions, their country estates and upper-middle-class heritage, before she and her child fled the coming war, seeking refuge in New York.

3574 Perez, Luis   1904-
El coyote: the rebel. New York: Henry Holt and Co., 1947. 233 p.
Orphaned at birth, Perez lived with an uncle until he was eleven, when he joined the Mexican rebel army. In his teens he went to a mission school in New Mexico and later became a U.S. citizen.

3575 Perkins, Elisha Douglass   1823-1852
Gold rush diary; being the journal of Elisha Douglass Perkins on the Overland Trail in the spring and summer of 1849. Illustrated. Edited by Thomas D. Clark. Lexington: University of Kentucky Press, 1967. 206 p. Index.
When the news of 1848 gold discoveries in California reached Perkins in Marietta, Ohio, he assembled a group called the "Marietta Gold Hunters" and set out for the West. His diary records his enthusiastic observations of people, the countryside, the Indians, and animal life on the rugged overland trail.

3576 Perkins, George Hamilton   1836-1899
Letters of Capt. Geo. Hamilton Perkins, U.S.N. , edited and arranged. Also, a sketch of his life by Commodore Geo. E. Belknap, U.S.N. Dedication by Susan G. Perkins. George E. Belknap, biographical sketch. Illustrated. Freeport, New York: Books for Libraries Press, 1970. (Concord, N.H.: I.C. Evans, 1886) 254 p.
Perkins, a naval lieutenant aboard the U.S.S. *Cayuga* and the *Chicka-*

saw during the Civil War, writes colorful letters describing the Louisiana and Alabama terrain and military strategy and events, especially the Battle of Mobile. Thirty years later he wrote an equally fascinating series of letters describing a diplomatic cruise to the Orient, especially to Siam, Indochina, and Canton.

3577 Perkins, Maxwell Evarts   1884-1947
Editor to author: the letters of Maxwell E. Perkins. Selected and edited with commentary and introduction by John Hall Wheelock. New York: Charles Scribner's Sons, 1950. 315 p. Index.
    In these letters to authors written from 1914 to 1947, the editor of *Scribner's* reveals his personality and his interest in the development of American literary talent, especially in fiction.

3578 Perkins, Maxwell Evarts   1884-1947
    see also **Fitzgerald, Francis Scott Key**

3579 Perls, Frederick Salomon   1893?-1970
In and out the garbage pail. Illustrated by Russ Youngreen. New York: Bantam, 1972. (Lafayette, California: Real People Press, 1969) 298 p.
    Psychiatrist and founder of gestalt therapy, Perls uses writing as a means to explore his own struggle with self-esteem, self-love, and self-image.

3580 Perrella, Robert (Father Bob)
They call me the showbiz priest. New York: Trident Press, 1973. 287 p.
    In New York Broadway became his parish. By contacting stars to do church benefits, he became acquainted with many stars and was especially close to Perry Como for a number of years. His book describes his great relish for his work.

3581 Perry, John Edward   1870-1962
Forty cords of wood: memoirs of a medical doctor. Jefferson City, Missouri: Lincoln University, 1947. 459 p.
    Well-written, dramatic story of a Black man who wanted as a young boy to become a doctor and who succeeded in an extraordinary way as a surgeon, medical educator, and founder of hospitals in Missouri.

3582 Perry, Matthew Calbraith   1794-1858
The Japan expedition, 1852-1854: the personal journal of Commodore Matthew C. Perry. Illustrated. Edited by Roger Pineau. Introduction by Samuel Eliot Morison. Washington: Smithsonian Institution Press, 1968. 241 p. Index.
    Enhanced by numerous water colors and pen or pencil sketches, this handsome volume describes Perry's 1852-1854 journey to Japan and includes material omitted from the official narrative such as personal observations, correspondence, and many of the paintings.

3583 Perry, Thomas Sergeant   1845-1928
Selections from the letters of Thomas Sergeant Perry. Introduction by Edwin Arlington Robinson. St. Clair Shores, Michigan: Scholarly Press, 1971. (New York: Macmillan, 1929) 255 p.
    An aristocrat by birth, instinct, and environment, Perry was editor of the *North American Review* and a literary critic. He published several volumes of translations from Russian literature and collections of critical articles. This edition of his letters includes many to the contributors of his journal, notably Henry James.

3584 *Perry-Cowen, Frances
Chautauqua to opera: an autobiography of a voice teacher and daughter of a Chautauqua pioneer. Illustrated. Hicksville, New York: Exposition Press, 1978. 127 p.
    Perry-Cowen focuses on her musical career, including nine years performing with her singer father on road tours with Ye Olde New England Choir and a year's voice lessons in Paris. After marriage she performed "Scenes from the Operas," gave music lessons, and sang in church choirs in New Jersey.

3585 *Pesotta, Rose
Bread upon the waters. Edited by John Nicholas Beffel. New York: Dodd, Mead & Co., 1944. 435 p. Index.
    As a union organizer, the author traveled throughout the U.S. helping to reshape the lot of workers in many industries. With great spirit and energy she pursued her goal of helping workers through World War I, the disturbances after the War, the despairing times during the Depression, and the resurgence when the New Deal sanctioned the right of workers to organize and bargain collectively.

3586 Peters, Arthur Anderson (Fritz Peters)   1913-1979
Boyhood with Gurdjieff. New York: E.P. Dutton Co., Inc., 1964. 176 p.
    An intense and remarkable study of his early education in Paris at the school of Georges Gurdjieff, a well-known educator and theologian, which pays high tribute to the significant influence Gurdjieff had on his life.

3587 Peters, Nathan
The correspondence of Captain Nathan and Lois Peters: April 25, 1775-February 5, 1777. Edited with introduction by William H. Guthman. Hartford: The Connecticut Historical Society, 1980. 54 p.
    The letters exchanged between an officer in the Continental Army serving in Massachusetts and his wife, who was raising their four children and running the family business, a saddle shop in Preston, Connecticut, provide a striking glimpse of the Revolutionary Era.

3588 *Peters, Roberta   1930-
A debut at the Met. With Louis Biancolli. New York: Meredith Press, 1967. 86 p.
    At age ten she went with a friend to her singing lesson. At twenty she made her debut at the Metropolitan Opera as Zerlina in Mozart's *Don Giovanni.* Her book describes the years of study, excitement, and hard work in between that sustained her dream to become a successful musician.

3589 Peterson, Frederick William   b.1869
Desert pioneer doctor: and, experiences in obstetrics. Calexico, California: Calexico Chronicle, 1947. 130 p.
    Two separate volumes published together, the first being autobiographical experiences of medical practice in poor and primitive conditions in Southern California, early twentieth century.

3590 *Peterson, Virgilia   1904-1966
A matter of life and death. New York: Atheneum, 1961. 334 p.
    Written in the form of a letter to her mother, the book is a haunting quest for life's meaning, for reconciliation with her mother and the Catholic faith, for self-justification.

3591 Pettengill, Samuel B.   1886-1974
My story. Edited by Helen M. Pettengill. Illustrated. Grafton, Vermont: H.M. Pettengill, 1979. 388 p.
    In this quiet, charming autobiography, Pettengill tells of his childhood and traces his ancestry, college and law school years, his stint as a lawyer, professor at Middlebury College, and Congressman, ending with the purchase of his home, Robin Lawn.

3592 Pettit, Hermon   1894-
Jubilee!: autobiography of Hermon Pettit. With Helen Wessel. Foreword by Helen Wessel. Preface by John A. Strain. Illustrated. Fresno, California: Bookmates International, 1979. 177 p.
    Pettit, religious all his life, graduated from Occidental College and became an evangelical Presbyterian preacher. His vows of abstinence from worldly pleasures strained his marriage and precipitated both his divorce and his expulsion from the pulpit. Often penniless and for a time hospitalized as a consequence of mental illness and a suicide attempt, Pettit found a new congregation, tranquility, reunion with his children, and peace in nature in old age.

3593 Pettit, Ira S.   fl.1861-1864
Diary of a dead man: letters and diary of Private Ira S. Pettit, Wilson, Niagara County, N.Y. who served ... U.S. Army during the War Between the States. Compiled by Jean P. Ray. Privately printed in Waverly, Iowa (by) Ray, 1976. (Waverly, Iowa: Jean Ray, 1964) 430 p. Index.
    The first half of this book consists of brief diary entries and some letters by Pettit, a private in the Union Army, 11th Regiment, 2nd Brigade, 2nd Division, 5th Army Corps, written June 1862-June 1863, when he was captured by the Confederates. He died in the notorious Andersonville (Georgia) Prison of scurvy and diarrhea, without medical care. The rest of the book consists of fragmentary eulogistic biographies of people who may have known Pettit while he was in the army.

3594 Pettit, Robert E. Lee   1932-
Bob Pettit: the drive with me. With Bob Wolff. Englewood Cliffs, New Jersey: Prentice-Hall, Inc., 1966. 170 p.
    Along with the story of his rise to success as a basketball player, Pettit presents anecdotes of player high jinks, the serious side of competition, and tips on training, playing, and winning.

3595 Petty, Richard   1937-
King of the road. Photographs and drawings by Ellen Griesedieck. New York: Rutledge Books; Macmillan, 1977. 200 p.
    This description of stock car racer Petty's technique, philosophy, and major races is particularly compelling because of the photographs and drawings of life in the machine shop, at the track, and on the road. Petty has won the Daytona 500 five times, surpassing all other winners.

3596 Peyton, Patrick   1908-
All for her: the autobiography of Father Patrick Peyton, C.S.C. Illustrated. Garden City, New York: Doubleday & Co., Inc., 1967. 286 p.
    The progress of his career as a priest—seminary days, his work with the network radio program, "Family Theater of the Air," his crusades world-wide in behalf of the Family Rosary concept, and further efforts to strengthen family ties through prayer.

3597 Peyton, Thomas Roy   **1897-1968**
Quest for dignity: an autobiography of a Negro doctor. Los Angeles: Warren F. Lewis, 1950. 156 p.
     Raised in Long Island, he supported his medical education as a jazz pianist in New York, London, and Paris. In a constant battle with racial prejudice, he moved his practice to several American cities, to Brazil, and finally back to New York, with hopes of racial reconciliation.

3598 Pfau, Ralph   **1904-1967**
Prodigal shepherd. With Al Hirshberg. Foreword by Karl Menninger, M.D. Indianapolis: SMT Guild, 1977. (Philadelphia: J.B. Lippincott, 1958) 252 p.
     Father Pfau tells the interrelated stories of his career in the priesthood, mostly in Indianapolis; his incessant neuroticism, which led to twenty years of alcoholism and intermittent hospitalization for his mental state; and his 25-year maintenance of sobriety through Alcoholics Anonymous.

3599 *Phelps, Orra Almira (Parker)   **b.1867**
When I was a girl in the martin box. New York: Island Press, 1949. 157 p.
     A charming account of her girlhood in nineteenth-century rural Connecticut, with detailed descriptions of games, daily activities, education, and household chores.

3600 Phelps, Richard "Digger"
Coach's world. And Larry Keith. New York: Thomas Y. Crowell Co., 1974. 254 p.
     The author was basketball coach of Notre Dame University in 1974 when his team beat UCLA, breaking its string of 88 straight college basketball wins. Phelps tells of the pressures and rewards he faced as he built up the winning team and how the efforts affected his family, the players, and himself.

3601 Phillips, Claude Anderson   **1871-1960**
Fifty years of public school teaching: from rural school teacher to university professor. Columbia: Missouri State Teachers Association, 1948. 145 p.
     Beginning with his early rural education in Missouri, he describes his life in the context of the development of public education in the state. A good source book for history of education.

3602 Phillips, John Aristotle   **1955?-**
Mushroom: the story of the A-bomb kid. And David Michaelis. New York: William Morrow and Co., 1978. 287 p.
     An average physics student at Princeton, he received national publicity after he designed an atomic bomb for a physics project, drawing entirely on available, unclassified data. His experiences in college, in Hollywood, with the FBI, and with reporters provide entertaining reading while he presents his concerns for nuclear safety.

3603 *Phillips, Kathryn (Sisson)   **b.1879**
My room in the world: a memoir. As told to Keith Jennison. Introduction by Ralph W. Sockman. New York: Abington, 1964. 157 p.
     She grew up in western Kansas where her father was a minister. Educated at Ohio Wesleyan and Columbia Teachers College, she was active in education and church work throughout her life, including her years as a college dean, as first president of the American Association of Women Deans and Counselors, and with her husband, Ellis Phillips, a major supporter of Christ Church in New York.

3604 *Phillips, Marie (Tello)   **1874-1962**
Grow old along with me: the autobiography of Marie Tello Phillips (February 23, 1874-). London: The Mitre Press, 1962. 117 p.
     Author of two novels and six books of poetry and a great promoter of contemporary poetry societies, she writes of her life as a writer and member of polite society, chiefly in Pittsburgh.

3605 Phillips, William   **1878-1968**
Ventures in diplomacy. Boston: The Beacon Press, 1952. 477 p. Index.
     A personal record of his long career as a diplomat, including his assignment to Peking (1905-07), as Undersecretary of State (1922-24), and assignments in Canada, Italy, India, and Palestine. Detailed recollections of major events during almost fifty years of service.

3606 Pickens, Champ   **b.1876**
A rebel in sports: the autobiography of the father of the colorful Blue-Gray football game. Foreword by John McCallum. Introduction by Bob Considine. New York: A.S. Barnes, 1956. 175 p. Index.
     Sports-promoter Pickens reminisces about his rural Alabama childhood, business ventures in New York, his penchant for betting on horses, and particularly his promotion of the Blue-Gray football games, 1939-1955.

3607 *Pickering, Catherine Yates
see **Yates, Richard**

3608 Pickett, Clarence Evan   **1884-1965**
For more than bread: an autobiographical account of twenty-two years' work with the American Friends Service Committee. Boston: Little, Brown and Co., 1953. 420 p. Index.
     A Quaker relief worker details his experience with a Quaker organization, the American Friends Service Committee. He recalls the war relief given to Germany, Spain, and Japan, the aid to conscientious objectors, and the help to poor Americans.

3609 Pickett, George Edward   **1825-1875**
Soldier of the South: General Pickett's war letters to his wife. Edited by Arthur Crew Inman. Freeport, New York: Books for Libraries Press, 1971. (Boston: Houghton Mifflin, 1913) 157 p.
     An unusual collection of letters to LaSalle Corbett Pickett portraying their courtship, marriage, and the birth of their first son during the Civil War. The letters are rich in details of his emotional reactions to love and war.

3610 *Pickford, Mary   **1893-1979**
Sunshine and shadow. Foreword by Cecil B. DeMille. Garden City, New York: Doubleday and Co., 1955. 382 p.
     Her story as a child star of stage and screen, her fame as "America's Sweetheart," her marriages to Douglas Fairbanks, Jr. and Buddy Rogers told in a style that conveys gentle serenity.

3611 *Picon, Molly   **1898-**
So laugh a little. As told to Eth Clifford Rosenberg. New York: Julian Messner, Inc., 1962. 175 p.
     A popular actress in the Yiddish theater describes growing up in Philadelphia and New York's Lower East Side, focusing on the character of her grandmother, a lively, loving, humorous Russian immigrant.

3612 *Piersall, James Anthony   **1929-**
Fear strikes out: the Jim Piersall story. And Al Hirshberg. Boston: Little, Brown and Co., 1955. 217 p.
     During his first season with the Red Sox, he had a mental breakdown which hospitalized him for months. Here he tells of his boyhood, his early career, his breakdown, his amazing recovery, and renewal of an outstanding baseball career.

3613 *Pierson, Louise John (Randall)   **1890-**
. . . Roughly speaking. New York: Simon and Schuster, 1943. 332 p.
     Her well-off family was left with little money when her father died, but she set out to be a self-made woman. During all her ups and downs she met life head-on with humor and resilience.

3614 *Pike, Diane (Kennedy)   **1938-**
Life is victorious!: how to grow through grief; a personal experience. New York: Simon and Schuster, 1976. 209 p.
     Diane Pike analyzes her grief when her new husband, Episcopal Bishop James A. Pike, was lost and died in the Judean wilderness in 1969. She moved from shock to suffering to recovery to building a new life. She and a partner have founded "The Love Project" to intensify union with God. She maintains psychic communion with Pike.

3615 *Pike, Diane (Kennedy)   **1938-**
My journey into self: Phase one. Introduction by R. Scott Kennedy. San Diego, California: L.P. Publications, 1979. 161 p.
     Pike, widow of Bishop James Pike, explains in mystical language her quest for an expansion of her consciousness and self-knowledge.

3616 *Pike, Diane (Kennedy)   **1938-**
Search; the personal story of a wilderness journey. Garden City, New York: Doubleday & Co., Inc., 1970. 198 p.
     The story of her husband, Bishop James A. Pike, his trip into the Judean wilderness, and the tragic missteps that turned it into his last journey.

3617 Pike, James   **1834-1867**
Scout and Ranger; being the personal adventures of James Pike of the Texas Rangers in 1859-60. New York: Da Capo Press, 1972. (Cincinnati: J.R. Hawley and Co., 1865) 164 p. Index.
     A grandnephew of the discoverer of Pike's Peak, the author tells the story of his adventures in the Indian Campaigns with the Texas Rangers. Courageous and forthright, he was curious about the customs and habits of the Indians and describes them, the battles, and other events with unusual attention to detail.

3618 Pike, James Albert   **1913-1969**
The other side; an account of my experiences with psychic phenomena. With Diane Kennedy. Garden City, New York: Doubleday & Co., Inc., 1968. 398 p.
     The controversial bishop writes of events preceding and following his son's death: his attempts to save his son from psychedelic drugs, the son's death, poltergeist occurrences, communications with the son, and other psychic phenomena. Includes a bibliography of works on psychical re-

search, extrasensory perception, and related subjects and a list of research organizations.

3619 Pike, Zebulon Montgomery   **1779-1813**
The journals of Zebulon Montgomery Pike: with letters and related documents. Norman: University of Oklahoma Press, 1966. (Philadelphia: C. & A. Conrad & Co., 1810) 2v.
  Pike's expeditions to the West are second only to those of Lewis and Clark. Volume I includes his journals, reports, and correspondence during the Mississippi River expedition, 1805-1806, and his journals and reports of the later Western expedition. Volume II has his 1806-1807 expedition correspondence as well as his dissertation on Louisiana Territory and his observations on New Spain.

3620 Pike, Zebulon Montgomery   **1779-1813**
Southwestern expedition of Zebulon M. Pike. Edited by Milo Milton Quaife. Freeport, New York: Books for Libraries Press, 1970. (Chicago: Donnelley, 1925) 239 p. Index.
  At the age of 27, Pike was sent by President Jefferson to discover the headwaters of the Red and Arkansas rivers. This journal records the perseverance and suffering experienced as he and his party blazed the trail which later became the main route for the "forty-niners."

3621 *Pilon, Juliana Geran   **1947-**
Notes from the other side of night. Introduction by Mircea Eliade. Illustrated. South Bend, Indiana: Regnery/Gateway, 1979. 146 p.
  This poetic account of the author's return to her native Romania seventeen years after emigrating to the United States to escape communism and anti-Semitism presents vignettes alternating between past and present. Pilon juxtaposes current portraits of family members, etched in philosophical consciousness of the meaning of freedom and persecution, with her only partly understood images from the past.

3622 Pinchot, Gifford   **1865-1946**
Breaking new ground. New York: Harcourt, Brace and Co., 1947. 522 p. Index.
  His "personal story of how Forestry and Conservation came to America" begins with his early training under Louis Brandeis and then describes his political career, especially during his years as U.S. Forester under Teddy Roosevelt, when many of the major policies affecting national forests and reserves were enacted.

3623 *Pinckney, Elizabeth (Lucas)   **1723-1793**
The letterbook of Eliza Lucas Pinckney, 1739-1762. Edited by Eliza Pinckney and others. Chapel Hill: University of North Carolina Press, 1972. 192 p. Index.
  An energetic, intelligent eighteenth-century woman, Eliza Pinckney managed three plantations while her father was away on military duty. She experimented successfully with raising and processing indigo and, after her marriage, with flax, hemp, and silk culture. Her letters reveal part of her remarkable life and have been quoted in numerous other places.

3624 Pincoffs, Maurice C.   **1886-1960**
Maurice C. Pincoffs, M.D.: letters from two world wars and a sketch of his life by his wife. Foreword by Katharine R. Pincoffs. Afterword by Theodore E. Woodward. Illustrated. Baltimore: Garamond/Pridemark, 1967. 287 p.
  Pincoffs, a professor of medicine and preventive medicine at the University of Maryland, served as a U.S. Army physician in France during World War I and as the Chief Consultant in Medicine to the U.S. Army, Far East, during World War II when he was stationed in Hollandia and Manila. The bulk of this volume is comprised of eloquent letters to his wife, Katharine, written while on military duty; they offer valuable insights into military medical problems and practices.

3625 Pinelli, Ralph Arthur (Babe)   **1896-**
Mr. Ump. As told to Joe King. Philadelphia: The Westminster Press, 1953. 184 p.
  The story of his years in professional baseball, as player, then as umpire, with anecdotes of many popular players.

3626 Pink, Arthur Walkington   **1886-1952**
Letters of Arthur W. Pink. Carlisle, Pennsylvania: Banner of Truth Trust, 1978. 135 p.
  A collection of 44 letters by Pink, editor of an obscure magazine of biblical exposition, *Studies in the Scriptures,* 1922-1952, on various religious subjects: God, premillenialism, Satan's devices, books, baptism, worship services, and glorifying the Lord.

3627 *Pinzer, Maimie (pseud.)   **b.1885**
The Maimie papers. Edited with introduction by Ruth Rosen. Textual editor, Sue Davidson. Old Westbury, New York: Feminist Press in cooperation with Schlesinger Library of Radcliffe College, 1977. 439 p. Index.
  A collection of 119 of the 143 letters that Maimie, a reformed prostitute, wrote to her proper Bostonian mentor, Fanny Quincy Howe, 1910-1922. Straightforward and detailed, they reveal a great deal about

the poverty and degradation that accompanied turn-of-the-century prostitution and specify the ways in which reform can be effected. Maimie herself founded a mission to aid such outcast women.

3628 Pistol Pete
  see Eaton, Frank

3629 Pius XII, Pope
  see Roosevelt, Franklin Delano

3630 *Plath, Sylvia   **1932-1963**
Letters home: correspondence 1950-1963. Selected and edited by Aurelia Schober Plath. New York: Harper and Row, Publishers, 1975. 502 p.
  A selection of 396 letters by the poet arranged chronologically, beginning with her freshman year at Smith College, continuing with her marriage to poet Ted Hughes, until her death in London.

3631 Platt, Thomas Collier   **1833-1910**
The autobiography of Thomas Collier Platt. Compiled and edited by Louis J. Lang. New York: Arno Press, 1974. (New York: B.W. Dodge & Co., 1910) 556 p.
  Throughout a 53-year political career Senator Platt became virtually an absolute dictator of the Republican Party in the East and "made" four presidents of the United States (Garfield, Harrison, McKinley, and T. Roosevelt) and four governors of New York.

3632 Pleasants, Henry   **1884-1963**
Doctor in the house. Philadelphia, J.B. Lippincott Co., 1947. 286 p.
  A detailed account of the practical problems occurring in his daily life as a doctor, including a section describing his service as an army doctor in World War I and problems of his patients, their personalities, and diagnoses.

3633 *Plummer, Rachel Parker   **b.1839**
Narrative of the capture and subsequent sufferings of Mrs. Rachel Plummer during a captivity of twenty-one months among the Comanche Indians: written by herself, 1839. Waco, Texas: Texian Press, 1968. 28 p.
  This is the story of the author's capture and captivity by Comanche Indians in 1836, with observations about their culture and the environment. She was eventually reunited with those of her family who survived.

3634 Poe, Clarence Hamilton   **1881-1964**
My first eighty years. Chapel Hill: The University of North Carolina Press, 1963. 267 p.
  At 18 he became editor of *The Progressive Farmer,* which grew from 5,000 to 1,000,000 circulation in 1930. His book conveys his loyalty to the South and rural values and to North Carolina in particular, where he lived most of his life.

3635 Poe, Edgar Allan   **1809-1849**
Letters of Edgar Allan Poe. Edited by John Ward Ostrom. Cambridge: Harvard University Press, 1948. 2v. Index.
  Includes authentic versions of all accessible letters and "offers what seem to be the best texts of lost or unavailable originals, accessible now only in printed form or in typescript."

3636 Pohl, Frederick   **1919-**
The way the future was: a memoir. Illustrated. New York: Ballantine Books, 1978. 312 p.
  Winner of the first Skylark Award for science fiction in 1966 and later the Hugo Award, he writes of his early education, his work as a writer and as editor of *Galaxy* magazine. Text contains several photographs of the author and well-known colleagues.

3637 Poindexter, Hildrus Augustus   **1901-**
My world of reality (an autobiography). Detroit: Balamp Publishing, 1973. 342 p.
  This is the story of a Black farm boy from Tennessee and his determination and success in becoming a physician. He served in public and academic medical positions, traveled extensively, especially in underdeveloped countries for the U.S. Public Health Service, and participated in numerous projects concerning health and tropical disease as officer, and then medical director, of the U.S. Public Health Service.

3638 Poitier, Sidney   **1924-**
This life. Illustrated. New York: Alfred A. Knopf, 1980. 374 p.
  Born to a large, poor family in the Bahamas, Poitier became an actor almost accidentally, and an Academy Award winner almost naturally. Now a director and producer as well, Poitier helps many struggling Black actors.

3639 Polgar, Franz Julius   **1900-1979**
The story of a hypnotist. With Kurt Singer. New York: Hermitage House, 1951. 222 p.
  The discovery of his unusual psychic powers and the career he developed from them.

3640 Poling, Daniel Alfred   **1884-1968**
Mine eyes have seen. New York: McGraw-Hill Book Co., Inc., 1959. 297 p.
    A prominent minister and editor of the *Christian Herald* writes of his boyhood in Oregon, his energetic ministerial career, his service as a chaplain in three wars, and his contact with many important contemporaries.

3641 Polk, Frank   **1908-**
F-F-F-Frank Polk: an uncommonly frank autobiography. Illustrated by Joe Beeler. Foreword by Slim Pickins. Flagstaff, Arizona: Northland Press, 1978. 123 p.
    Writing in Western dialect, Polk describes his wild life as a cowboy and rodeo rider for many years, drinking all the while. He worked as a cowboy gigolo in Reno and Lake Tahoe, and intermittently as a bit player in cowboy movies. Most of his adult years were punctuated by heavy drinking. Polk reformed at seventy, but his narrative is still full of ginger.

3642 Polk, James Knox   **1795-1849**
Correspondence of James K. Polk. Edited by Herbert Weaver and Paul H. Pergeron. Nashville: Vanderbilt University Press, 1969- . 5v. Index.
    The collected letters of James K. Polk, elected President in 1844. Vol. I, 1817-1832; Vol. II, 1833-1834; Vol. III, 1835-1836; Vol. IV, 1837-1838; Vol. V, 1839-1841.

3643 Polk, James Knox   **1795-1849**
Polk: the diary of a presidency, 1845-1849, covering the Mexican War, the acquisition of Oregon, and the conquest of California and the Southwest. Edited by Allan Nevins. London: Longmans, Green and Co., 1952. (1929) 412 p. Index.
    A selection from the four-volume edition (Chicago, A.C. McClurg & Co., 1910) which included only 500 copies, this volume portrays a man serious but uninspiring, competent but not visionary, with remarkable detail in daily entries.

3644 Polk, William Roe   **1929-**
Passing brave. And William J. Mares. New York: Alfred A. Knopf, 1973. 206 p.
    A record of a 1,200-mile camel-back journey across the Arabian desert from Ridyadh to Jordan by two Americans seeking to live unburdened by modern Western trappings, to find the remnants of ancient Bedouin civilization, and to follow the trail of the sixth-century Arab poet, Labid. They found beauty, danger, hospitality, and adventure.

3645 Pollock, Frederick   **1845-1937**
    see Holmes, Oliver Wendell

3646 Pollock, Robert W.
The education of a country doctor. New York: Vantage Press, 1978. 211 p.
    A salacious account of an Oregon country doctor's more bizarre cases, particularly those involving venereal disease, adultery, illegitimate pregnancy, and weird physical phenomena.

3647 *Polykoff, Shirley   **1908?-**
Does she . . . or doesn't she? And how she did it. Garden City, New York: Doubleday and Co., Inc., 1975. 131 p.
    A highly successful advertising executive describes her childhood in a Russian immigrant family and her rise in the competitive business world. Her Clairol account brought her fame, as suggested in the title and other slogans she designed ("Is it true blondes have more fun?" "You can be a rich brunette—the kind men marry").

3648 Pontier, Raymond J.   **1916-**
On the cutting edge: reflections of a minister in suburbia. Foreword by Philip Berrigan. An Exposition-Testament Book. Hicksville, New York: Exposition Press, 1978. 175 p.
    Pontier was for thirty years a clergyman in the Dutch Reformed Church of America and for eighteen years pastor of the Allwood Community Church in Clifton, New Jersey. In 1974 he resigned as pastor under congregational pressure against his support of draft-resistance activities by his son. In 1975 he became a Unitarian and Coordinator of the New Jersey Religious Coalition for Abortion Rights.

3649 Poole, Ernest   **1880-1950**
The bridge: my own story. New York: Johnson Reprint Co., 1971. (New York: Macmillan, 1940) 442 p.
    Poole traveled to Russia, Europe, and parts of the United States observing the "mass life of the common people." He writes about their efforts to rise, the wars that stopped their progress, the failure of the League of Nations, and the rise of dictatorship. He believes that the threats of wars and revolutions will eventually force cooperation among nations and that each land will achieve political and industrial democracy.

3650 Pope, J. Keith   **1919-**
Decade of adventure: archaeology and exploration. Illustrated. Singer, Florida: Singer Island Press, 1979. 295 p.
    An account of the author's adventures looking for lost historical objects such as the burial place of an early nineteenth-century pirate. He served as an enthusiastic, though untrained, volunteer at archeological sites in Mexico and Israel.

3651 *Pope, Lena Holston   **b.1881**
A hand on my shoulder: the story of Lena Pope and the home that evolved from her dreams. Illustrated. Fort Worth, Texas: Branch-Smith, Inc., 1966. 218 p.
    Pope writes with religious fervor about her life, whose principal work was devoted to the founding and support of the Lena Pope Home for children in need of shelter, whether temporary, for victims of floods, fires, or prolonged, as a result of parental desertion, neglect, abuse, or long illness.

3652 *Popkin, Zelda   **1898-**
Open every door. New York: E.P. Dutton & Co., Inc., 1956. 379 p.
    A writer tells of her apprentice years as a reporter in Wilkes-Barre, Pennsylvania, the gratifying years of a successful marriage to Louis Popkin, and her later experience as an international journalist and novelist.

3653 Popov, Dusko   **1912?-**
Spy/counterspy; the autobiography of Dusko Popov. Foreword by Ewen Montagu. Illustrated. New York: Grosset & Dunlap, 1974. 339 p.
    A master spy during World War II, Popov was an espionage agent for the British while ostensibly working for the Germans. He was sent by the Germans to the United States; his advance notice to the FBI of the intended Pearl Harbor attack was mistrusted.

3654 Porter, Cole   **1893-1964**
The Cole Porter story. As told to Richard G. Hubler. Introduction by Arthur Schwartz. Cleveland: The World Publishing Co., 1965. 140 p.
    Only the first 53 pages of this book are Porter's—the "first act" of his life, as he calls it. A prodigious outpouring of melody for Broadway musicals and movies has insured his fame as one of America's composers of popular music for over 35 years. Included is a sixteen-page bibliography of his songs.

3655 Porter, Russell Williams   **1871-1949**
The Arctic diary of Russell Williams Porter. Edited by Herman Frisis. Preface by Caroline Porter Kier. Foreword by R.W. Porter. Charlottesville: University Press of Virginia, 1976. 171 p.
    Porter's vivid text, derived from diaries of his annual Arctic expeditions, 1897-1906, is enhanced by his abundant watercolor illustrations of arctic settings, animals, people, and of ships caught in the ice. Porter expresses a keen appreciation for the joys, hardships, scientific significance, and politics of such explorations—but he did it essentially because he loved it. He later became a maker of precision telescopes and spent years on the Mt. Palomar installation.

3656 Posey, Jake   **b.1863**
Last of the 40-horse drivers: the autobiography of Jake Posey. New York: Vantage Press, 1959. 90 p.
    A pedestrian account of life as a circus hostler that focuses more on detailed accounts of the traveling shows' itineraries (especially the Barnum and Bailey Circus) and lists of performers (including Buffalo Bill) than on circus life and circus personalities or the intricacies of driving a forty-horse team, which Posey did for many years.

3657 Potok, Andrew   **1932?-**
Ordinary daylight: portrait of an artist going blind. New York: Holt, Rinehart, & Winston, 1980. 290 p.
    A gifted painter who lost his eyesight to retinitis pigmentosa, a disease inherited from his father, tells of his rehabilitation, challenging his limitations by learning a new art—writing.

3658 Potter, Charles Francis   **1885-1962**
The preacher and I (an autobiography). New York: Crown Publishers, Inc., 1951. 429 p. Index.
    He began his ministry as a Fundamental Baptist, became a Unitarian-Universalist, and finally a Humanist, participated in the Straton-Potter debates on Fundamentalism versus Modernism, and was a major figure in the Scopes Evolution Trial.

3659 Pound, Ezra Loomis   **1885-1972**
EP to LU: nine letters written to Louis Untermeyer by Ezra Pound. Edited by J.A. Robbins. Bloomington: Indiana University Press, 1963. 48 p.
    Just before his fourth edition of *Modern American Poetry* (1930), Untermeyer and his wife visited Pound in Rapallo. The most interesting letter in this collection Pound wrote at that time, condensing his life and career in five pages, noting his contributions and influence on other writers.

3660 Pound, Ezra Loomis   **1885-1972**
Pound-Joyce: the letters of Ezra Pound to James Joyce; with Pound's essay on Joyce. Edited with commentary by Forrest Read. New York: New Directions, 1967. 314 p. Index.

The friendship of two great writers is revealed in this collection. Pound recognized Joyce's genius early and dedicated himself to Joyce's welfare, assisting him in many ways, from advice and criticism to collecting money from editors.

3661 Pound, Ezra Loomis   1885-1972
The selected letters of Ezra Pound, 1907-1941. Edited by D.D. Paige. New York: New Directions, 1971. 358 p. Index.

The poet's letters include arguments about the art of poetry, his search for perfection, his critical opinions, his interest in problems of language. His correspondents, T.S. Eliot, James Joyce, William Carlos Williams, and others, were among the most outstanding poets, writers, and artists of his time.

3662 *Powdermaker, Hortense   1900-1970
Stranger and friend; the way of an anthropologist. New York: W.W. Norton & Co., Inc., 1967. 315 p. Index.

A trained anthropologist must be immersed in a culture as well as a detached observer. The author tells of four field-work experiences she had: a late Stone-Age Melanesian society in the southwest Pacific—Lesu in New Ireland (1929-30); a rural Mississippi community—half Negro and half white (1933-34); Hollywood, California (1946-47); and an African mining township in northern Rhodesia (1953-54).

3663 Powell, Aaron Macy   1832-1899
Personal reminiscences of the anti-slavery and other reforms and reformers. Westport, Connecticut: Negro Universities Press, 1970. (Plainfield, New Jersey: Caulon Press, 1899) 279 p.

Among the youngest of the radical anti-slavery workers, Powell was a faithful and energetic worker for the cause of abolition just preceding the Civil War. Afterward he continued to support good causes, helping Blacks and Indians, working for peace, temperance, education, and the personal purity movement.

3664 Powell, Adam Clayton   1908-1972
Adam by Adam; the autobiography of Adam Clayton Powell. New York: Dial Press, 1971. 260 p. Index.

A rich, detailed account of the author's middle-class childhood, his education, and his calling to the ministry serves as preface to the story of his rise in politics, his controversial tenure as congressman, and his subsequent expulsion from the U.S. House. This intelligent and sometimes combative autobiography closes with a manifesto of sorts in which Powell presents his outlook on the future of Black Americans.

3665 Powell, Edward Alexander   1879-1957
Adventure road. New York: Doubleday & Co., 1954. 356 p. Index.

Powell, a world traveler and prolific author, has assembled an eclectic series of travel anecdotes from memory and his earlier books; he discusses his travels ranging from British Columbia to Mexico, India to Zanzibar, Egypt to Malaysia. The incidents themselves are high-spirited and well-told, but their sequence is arbitrary and confusing.

3666 Powell, John Benjamin   1886-1947
My twenty-five years in China. China in the 20th Century Series. New York: Da Capo Press, 1976. (New York: Macmillan, 1945) 436 p. Index.

An old China hand describes the political intrigues and alliances in the Orient between World Wars I and II. He went to Shanghai in 1917 as a journalist and to South China, Russia, and Japan as an editor. Captured in Shanghai by the Japanese in December 1941, he suffered from extreme malnutrition, and though eventually hospitalized and repatriated early in 1943, his gangrenous feet had deteriorated to the extent that he had required over two and a half years of surgical restoration at the time he wrote the book.

3667 Powell, John Wesley   1834-1902
Down the Colorado; diary of the first trip through the Grand Canyon, 1869. Illustrated. Foreword & notes by Don D. Fowler. Photos & epilogue by Eliot Porter. New York: E.P. Dutton & Co., Inc., 1969. 168 p. Index.

This journal of a dramatic trip down the wild Colorado River by ten men in four boats recaptures the excitement and wonder of their adventure. Contemporary photographs and drawings in addition to modern color photos beautifully illustrate the vivid descriptions.

3668 Powell, Lawrence Clark   1906-
Fortune & friendship: an autobiography. New York: R.R. Bowker Co., 1968. 227 p. Index.

A bookman from his earliest years, the author has been a reader, seller, librarian, and writer. He writes of his teachers, pupils, colleagues, family, and friends, and of the fortune which led him to travel widely and to achieve his current status.

3669 Powell, Lyle Stephenson   1893-
Surgeon in wartime China. Lawrence: University Press of Kansas, 1946. 233 p. Index.

Although this is essentially a wartime memoir, it includes interesting

comments on the Chinese land and culture as well as the author's personal experience as an army surgeon.

3670 *Powers, Barbara Moore   1934-
Spy wife. With W.W. Diehl. Introduction by W.W. Diehl. New York: Pyramid Books, 1965. 188 p.

The wife of Francis Gary Powers (U-2 spy pilot shot down over Russia in 1960) tells of her cloak-and-dagger life as the wife of a CIA spy, including his letters to her from Russia and his appearance before the Senate Armed Services Committee, as well as their divorce proceedings, which are reproduced in detail. The purpose of the book is to tell the "true story" of their relationship, i.e., to refute Powers' charge of his wife's drunkenness and cruelty and to vindicate her character.

3671 Powers, Francis Gary   1929-
Operation overflight; the U-2 spy pilot tells his story for the first time. With Curt Gentry. Illustrated. New York: Holt, Rinehart and Winston, 1970. 375 p.

Flying over Russia on a reconnaissance mission in a U-2 "spy" plane on May 1, 1960, Powers was shot down and captured by the Soviets, thereby precipitating a serious incident and the official admission that authorized espionage had been occurring. Powers here discloses the details of his recruitment by the CIA, his training, the mission, his trial and imprisonment, his exchange for Soviet spy, Rudolph Abel, and the aftermath when he was made a scapegoat and discouraged from publishing his account of the incident.

3672 Powers, Richie   1931-
Overtime! an uninhibited account of a referee's life in the NBA. With Mark Mulvoy. New York: David McKay Co., Inc., 1975. 212 p.

In his diary of the 1974 basketball season, referee Powers explains how he keeps control of the game and strives to be aware of every aspect of the action. He has open, controversial opinions about pro basketball, players, coaches, and owners and still loves the game after over sixteen years of officiating.

3673 Powers, Robert Merrill   1900-
Prairie preacher: a tale of our yesterdays along the middle border; memoirs. New York: Exposition Press, 1974. 165 p.

Born of second-generation homesteaders, he tells a story of human tragedy and spiritual triumph during the great Depression and drought years. He holds two honorary degrees of Doctor of Divinity and has conducted his pulpit ministry for over 42 years.

3674 Prange, Erwin E.   1917-
The gift is already yours. Minneapolis: Bethany Fellowship, 1980. (Plainfield, New Jersey: Logos International, 1973) 163 p.

After his wartime stint as a pilot, Prange returned to school to become a Lutheran clergyman. His first pastorate was in a tough area of New York City. His calls took him to Montana, Maryland, and other places where he and his parishoners experienced charismatic faith healing.

3675 Pratt, Orson   1811-1881
Orson Pratt journals. Compiled and arranged by Elden J. Watson. Salt Lake City, Utah: E.J. Watson, 1975. 583 p. Index.

The journals, which cover a period prior to 1848, chronicle Pratt's leadership in the early Mormon church. In 1830 he was ordained an elder by Joseph Smith. He went on numerous missions in America and Great Britain, experienced the persecution leveled against the early church, and was finally created an apostle in the Church of the Latter-day Saints. He was in the party that found the site where Salt Lake City was to be built.

3676 Preminger, Otto   1906-
Preminger: an autobiogrpahy. Illustrated. Garden City, New York: Doubleday and Co., Inc., 1977. 208 p. Index.

Preminger's exciting account of his career as a motion-picture director and producer focuses on his years in Hollywood (after immigrating from Austria in 1935), where he made such films as *Carmen Jones* and *Advise and Consent.* Preminger speaks forthrightly about his work, his marriages, his defiance of segregation, anti-Semitism, and other violations of human rights.

3677 Prescott, Orville   1906-
Five-dollar gold piece: the development of a point of view. New York: Random House, 1956. 243 p.

The engaging life story of a man who became a prominent literary critic for the New York *Times,* his unconventional education, prosperous family background, and career in literary journalism.

3678 Prescott, Peter S.
A darkening green; notes from the silent generation. New York: Coward, McCann & Geoghegan, Inc., 1974. 222 p.

In diary entries joined by narrative passages, the author describes the raw, half-understood experience of late adolescence—the rivalry, the searching for purpose, the bull sessions, the anxieties. The record of his freshman year in college captures the emotions, customs, and rites of passage to present a portrait of the Fifties.

3679 Prescott, Philander   b.1801
The recollections of Philander Prescott; frontiersman of the Old North-west, 1819-1862. Edited by Donald Dean Parker. Lincoln: University of Nebraska Press, 1966. 272 p. Index.

His position as sutler's clerk in Detroit, and later Fort Snelling, helping with the supply of goods for military communities in the Northwest Territory was the starting point for his participation in the events that shaped the history of the Northwest frontier from 1819 to 1862. He worked as Indian trader, riverman, interpreter, innkeeper, and supervisor of Indian farmers.

3680 Prescott, William Hickling   1796-1859
The correspondence of William Hickling Prescott, 1833-1847. Transcribed and edited by Roger Wolcott. New York: Da Capo Press, 1970. (Boston: Houghton Mifflin Co., 1925) 691 p. Index.

At a time when documented accuracy was a rare virtue in a historian, Prescott wrote with painstaking care. Despite continued trouble with his eyes, he pursued his research and wrote several monumental works on Spanish history. This volume contains a large portion of his most significant correspondence.

3681 Prescott, William Hickling   1796-1859
The papers of William Hickling Prescott. Selected and edited by C. Harvey Gardiner. Urbana: University of Illinois Press, 1964. 441 p. Index.

This selection, consisting mainly of letters, covers the years 1808 to 1858 of historian Prescott's life. The earlier letters are to family members, then come those concerning his career choice and scholarly interest. Later letters focus on research and publications; others are to friends and family. He had an international reputation as a writer of very readable history, especially his works on the conquests of Mexico and Peru.

3682 *Presley, Dee Elliott Stanley
Elvis: we love you tender. As told to Martin Torgoff. With other authors. Illustrated. New York: Delacorte Press, 1979. 395 p. Index.

Elvis Presley's stepmother tells of her marriage to Vernon Presley, the rise of Elvis' popularity and the "Elvis craze," his close relationship with her three sons, and the events and abuses which led to Elvis' death and her failed marriage to his father.

3683 Preuss, Charles   1803-1854
Exploring with Frémont: the private diaries of Charles Preuss, cartographer for John C. Frémont on his first, second, and fourth expeditions to the Far West. Translated and edited by Erwin G. and Elizabe K. Gudde. American Exploration and Travel Series, no. 26. Norman: University of Oklahoma Press, 1958. 162 p. Index.

Diaries of his overland explorations as Fremont's right-hand man (1842, 1843-44, 1848-49).

3684 *Previn, Dory (Langan)   1925-
Bog-trotter: an autobiography with lyrics. Drawings by Joby Baker. Garden City, New York: Doubleday and Co., Inc., 1980. 383 p.

"I am a freak. Fragmented as this book, a monstrous hydraheaded woman-man dwarf-soul girl-child," an apt description of lyricist Previn, who writes of her career in Hollywood, her several marriages, two abortions, and mental breakdowns. Two-thirds of the book is composed of examples of her lyrics.

3685 *Previn, Dory (Langan)   1925-
Midnight baby: an autobiography. New York: The Macmillan Co., 1976. 246 p.

In poetry and oblique, angry prose composer Dory Previn relates her childhood aspirations of social status and theatrical success, overshadowed by poverty and her crazed father's fear of sterility, which culminated in nightmare when he entombed Dory, her mother, and the newborn baby in a boarded-up room for several months.

3686 Price, Con (Masachele, Opa B.)   b.1869
Memories of old Montana. Introduction by Elting E. Morison. Hollywood: The Highland Press, 1945. 154 p.

Well-written story of a cowboy's life in the Old West; no romance, but interesting and realistic narrative of the times with some references to the author's close friend, Charles M. Russell.

3687 Price, Con (Masachele, Opa B.)   b.1869
Trails I rode. Illustrated by Charles M. Russell. Pasadena: Trail's End Publishing Co., Inc., 1947. 262 p. Index.

A cowboy's memoir of the Old West; well-written, capturing the humor and pathos of hard life in Montana and South Dakota.

3688 Price, Raymond Kissam   1930-
With Nixon. New York: The Viking Press, 1977. 398 p. Index.

A staunch supporter of former President Richard Nixon, presidential speechwriter Price offers a view of his administration and Watergate which focuses on the triumphs as well as the downfalls. Price emphasizes his respect for Nixon the man.

3689 Price, Vincent   1911-
I like what I know: a visual autobiography. Garden City, New York: Doubleday & Co., Inc., 1959. 313 p.

Well-known as an actor, he has since childhood had a major interest in art. Here he describes his first awareness of art around him, his first acquisitions, and many experiences as a student, a collector, and a dealer of art.

3690 Price, Vincent   1911-
Vincent Price: his movies, his plays, his life. Illustrated. Conceived and produced by Whitehall, Hadlyme, & Smith, Inc. Garden City, New York: Doubleday & Co., Inc., 1978. 117 p. Index.

Price provides for children a simple, engaging account of his lifelong career as an actor in theater, films, and on radio and television. Among his most famous films are *Laura, The Masque of the Red Death,* and *The Abominable Dr. Phibes.* Price is a devotee of art and cooking and has written books on both subjects.

3691 Price, Willard DeMille   b.1887
I cannot rest from travel: an autobiography of adventure in seventy lands. New York: The John Day Co., 1951. 313 p.

An inveterate adventurer describes his experience as a roving correspondent and field worker for a museum and a geographic society.

3692 *Priest, Ivy (Baker)   1905-1975
Green grows Ivy. New York: McGraw-Hill Book Co., 1958. 270 p.

The story of her childhood in a small Utah town where her father was a miner and her mother ran a boardinghouse, her marriage and early experience in state politics, and her prominent career as Treasurer of the United States in the Eisenhower administration.

3693 Prince, Harold Smith   1928-
Contradictions; notes on twenty-six years in the theatre. New York: Dodd, Mead & Co., 1974. 242 p. Index.

Prince, who has directed and produced some of the most successful Broadway shows, especially musicals, answers a number of questions about his work and twenty shows he has worked on in a quarter of a century.

3694 Prince, Hezekiah, Jr.   1800-1843
Journals of Hezekiah Prince, Jr.: 1822-1828. Foreword by Robert Greenhalgh Albion. Introduction by Walter Muir Whitehill. Illustrated. New York: Maine Historical Society/Crown Publishers, 1965. 448 p.

These plainspoken journals of a customs official in Thomaston, Maine, offer a day-to-day glimpse of small-town life in Maine in the 1820's from the viewpoint of a young upper-middle-class bachelor. His involvement in the town's social life and his knowledge of the numerous small workaday ships (packets) vital to nineteenth-century transportation provide useful information about both.

3695 *Prouty, Olive (Higgins)   b.1882
Pencil shavings: memoirs. Cambridge, Massachusetts: The Riverside Press, 1961. 234 p.

The author of *Stella Dallas* describes the history of her New England family in Worcester, Massachusetts. Her story includes details of daily life and manners set in the context of her own development and that of her town and family.

3696 Pruden, Edward Hughes   1903-
Window on Washington. New York: Vantage Press, 1976. 136 p.

A minister of the First Baptist Church in Washington, D.C., 1935-1960, recounts his experiences with presidents from Roosevelt to Johnson. Pruden gave the invocation at the inauguration of Harry Truman who was a member of the church. He was an effective fund raiser for an imposing church building.

3697 Pte-san-hunka
see **White Bull, Joseph**

3698 Pugh, Emerson Martindale   1896-
Wyoming scientist, horses to spaceships: memoirs. Illustrated. Hicksville, New York: Exposition Press, 1979. 283 p.

Pugh, for many years a physics professor at Carnegie Institute of Technology, devotes extraordinary detail to an account of his childhood in Evanston, Wyoming, and to his work as a banker (1919-21) in Mountain View, Wyoming. He briefly summarizes his teaching career, work on magnetism and electricity, family illnesses, love of sailing, and travel to Europe.

3699 Pugh, Herbert Lamont   1895-
Navy surgeon. Philadelphia: J.B. Lippincott & Co., 1959. 459 p.

The former Surgeon General of the Navy (1951-55) describes his 33 years in the military, mostly as a Navy surgeon and hospital administrator. He discusses a variety of administrative issues and medical cases with which he dealt and devotes about half the book to colorful descriptions of his worldwide travels.

3700 Puharich, Andrija   **1918?-**
Uri; a journal of the mystery of Uri Geller. Garden City, New York: Doubleday & Co., Inc., 1974. 285 p.

Trained in internal medicine at Northwestern, he later set up his own laboratory in Maine for the study of extrasensory perception. He met Uri Geller, an Israeli psychic, in 1971, brought him to the U.S. to be studied, and established a friendship that led to extensive psychic research. They believe they have made contact with non-earthly beings.

3701 Pulley, Sande (Bhikkhu Anuruddha)
A Yankee in the yellow robe: an American Buddhist monk's role in East-West cultural exchange. Illustrated. New York: Exposition Press, 1967. 130 p.

This is the autobiography of an American whose spiritual journey into Buddhism is reflected in his literal journey from San Francisco to Rangoon, Burma, in 1956. Pulley explains his experiences in Buddhist meditation, ordination, begging, and other religious practices.

3702 Putnam, James Jackson   **1846-1918**
James Jackson Putnam and psychoanalysis; letters between Putnam and Sigmund Freud (and others). Edited with introductory essay by Nathan G. Hale, Jr. Translated by Judith Bernays Heller. Cambridge: Harvard University Press, 1971. 384 p. Index.

Putnam took up the cause of psychoanalysis at age 63, having previously been recognized as a distinguished specialist in nervous diseases. In 1908 and 1909 he met Ernest Jones and Sigmund Freud, thereafter corresponding with them and others. The letters reveal their patients' and their own symptoms, dreams, and feelings with candor.

3703 Putnam, Peter   **1920-**
Cast off the darkness. New York: Harcourt, Brace and Co., 1957. 253 p.

The courageous recovery of a man who was blinded by his attempted suicide, became an author-historian and promoter of various activities for the blind, including "talking books."

3704 Putnam, Samuel   **1892-1950**
Paris was our mistress: memoirs of a lost and found generation. New York: The Viking Press, 1947. 264 p. Index.

Set in the context of a social and intellectual history of American expatriates (1926-1933), the editor of *The New Review* describes his own development before and after World War I. Well-written, nearly a collective autobiography of the times.

3705 Pyle, Ernest Taylor   **1900-1945**
Last chapter. New York: Henry Holt and Co., 1946. 150 p.

In this the final book of Pyle's war reporting, he tells of the war in the Pacific, writing as before with honesty and no pretensions.

3706 Quimby, Paul Elmore
Yankee on the Yangtze: one missionary's saga in Revolutionary China. With Norma Youngsberg. Preface by Denton E. Rebock. Nashville, Tennessee: Southern Publishing Association, 1976. 176 p.

Seventh-Day Adventist missionary Quimby describes his attempts to administer the China Training Institute in Peking and to perform other teaching duties for the church during the military and social upheaval in China between 1927 and 1946.

3707 Quincy, Josiah, Jr.   **1744-1775**
Memoir of the life of Josiah Quincy, Jr. Edited by Josiah Quincy. Era of the American Revolution. New York: Da Capo Press, 1971. (Boston: Cummings, Hilliard & Co., 1825) 498 p.

Josiah Quincy, Jr., was active in politics before the Revolutionary War. He made a deep impression on his contemporaries through his eloquence in political debates at Faneuil Hall and his zeal in upholding freedom and rights of the Colonies. This collection edited by his son includes extracts from his writings, journals, letters to and from distinguished contemporaries, and his pamphlet on the Boston Port Bill.

3708 Quinlan, Joseph
Karen Ann: the Quinlans tell their story. And Julia Quinlan. With Phyllis Battelle. Garden City, New York: Doubleday & Co., Inc., 1977. 343 p.

A sensitive account of the parents' struggle with the court system, their own religious beliefs, and their love for their comatose daughter, who they believed was being kept alive by medical machinery despite apparent brain death.

3709 Quinn, Anthony   **1916-**
Original sin; a self-portrait. Boston: Little, Brown and Co., 1972. 311 p.

Born in Mexico, Quinn worked at a variety of jobs before becoming a movie actor. His career includes over a hundred movie and stage roles. Here he examines his personal triumphs and failures, his self-doubts and his search for self-understanding.

3710 Quinn, Michael A.   **1895-1971**
Love letters to Mike: forty months as a Japanese prisoner of war: April 9, 1942 to September 17, 1945. New York: Vantage Press, 1977. 331 p.

Quinn's diary, written in the form of letters to his wife, covers the

period of his imprisonment by the Japanese in the Philippines, on Formosa, and in Mukden, Manchuria. Quinn's account focuses on the minutiae of daily life; the special days of the Catholic year; and on the activities of his family at home. His morale and health were relatively good throughout the war, as were his relations with his fellow prisoners and the Japanese.

3711 R.S., pseud.
see **Zinsser, Hans**

3712 Rabinow, Paul
Reflections of field work in Morocco. Foreword by Robert Bellah. Berkeley: University of California Press, 1977. 164 p.

A series of reflections about the author's two years of fieldwork in rural Morocco. These contain interesting character sketches of his chief informants in various stages of the work and observations by the author on self and culture. Culture, Rabinow claims, involves interpretation, and to understand one's own culture (and oneself), one must take a detour into another culture.

3713 *Rachewiltz, Mary de
Discretions. Boston: Little, Brown and Co., 1971. 320 p.

Brought up by the Sama family in Gais in the mountains of Italy, the daughter of Ezra Pound gained "pleasure in counterpoint" in "looking back on things at their beginning." She writes of her father's views, her own situation during World War II, and the despair that overcame her then, as well as of happier pre- and postwar times.

3714 Radisson, Pierre Esprit   **1636-1710?**
Voyages of Peter Esprit Radisson, being an account of his travels and experiences among the North American Indians, from 1652 to 1684; transcribed from original mss. in the Bodleian Library and the British Museum. Introduction by Gideon D. Scull. New York: Burt Franklin, 1971. (Boston: The Prince Society, 1885) 385 p.

Radisson's papers, which remained in manuscript for more than two hundred years, were first published in 1885. They tell of his voyages and expeditions in Canada and the United States, including his captivity by the Iroquois.

3715 Rallo, Joseph S.   **1930-**
The Rallo family: the great American saga. And Mary Hulbert. New York: Frederick Fell, Inc., 1966. 248 p.

Rallo, a success in the construction business, happily describes the immigrant's dream become reality. His parents were reared in Sicily, immigrated to St. Louis, married, and reared ten children in an unusually loving, materially prosperous extended family, of which Rallo is proud.

3716 Ramsey, James Gettys McGready   **1797-1884**
Autobiography and letters. Edited by William B. Hesseltine. Nashville: Tennessee Historical Commission, 1954. 367 p. Index.

An aristocrat of the Old South, he was a practicing physician and prominent citizen of Tennessee, as well as a respected historian of his life and times.

3717 Randall, Clarence Belden   **1891-1967**
Over my shoulder: a reminiscence. Boston: Little, Brown and Co., 1956. 248 p.

The story of his boyhood and early career as a lawyer in Michigan, his presidency of Inland Steel Co., and his life in public service where he served as Iron and Steel Consultant for the Marshall Plan under President Eisenhower.

3718 Randall, Clarence Belden   **1891-1967**
Sixty-five plus: the joy and challenge of the years of retirement. Boston: Little, Brown and Co., 1963. 210 p.

A philosophical and practical exploration of his retirement years, his recovery from a heart attack, and his return to a pleasant routine of leisure and activity.

3719 Randall, David Anton   **1905-1975**
Dukedom large enough: reminiscences of a rare-book dealer, 1929-1956. Illustrated. New York: Random House, 1969. 368 p. Index.

A book collector and bookseller for forty years, Randall managed the rare book department at Scribner's, 1935-1956, afterward becoming librarian of the Lilly Library, Indiana University. Here he relates his adventures with books, manuscripts, collections, and authors.

3720 Randall, Henry Stephens   **1811-1879**
Correspondence between Henry Stephens Randall and Hugh Blair Grigsby, 1856-1861. Edited with introduction and notes by Frank J. Klingberg and Frank W. Klingberg. University of California Publications in History, v. 43. New York: Da Capo Press, 1972. (Berkeley: University of California Press, 1952) 196 p. Index.

An edition of the Huntington Library collection of letters between Randall, the New York biographer of Thomas Jefferson, and Grigsby, the leading Virginia historian of his generation. Their letters reveal an intense common interest in Jefferson and depict a wide range of intellectual and cultural interests as well.

3721 *Randall, Margaret (Randall)   1936-
Part of the solution: portrait of a revolutionary. New York: New Directions, 1973. 192 p.
A poet, writer, and social activist, she became dedicated to socialist revolution during the late Sixties when she went to Cuba to work, live, and write. Included here are diary entries, prose pieces, and poetry.

3722 *Randall, Ruth (Painter)   1892-
I Ruth; autobiography of a marriage. Illustrated. Boston: Little, Brown and Co., 1968. 266 p. Index.
The wife of prominent Lincoln scholar, James G. Randall, tells the story of her marriage and the way her interest in her husband's work shaped her own work as an author.

3723 Ransom, Reverdy Cassius   1861-1959
Pilgrimage of Harriet Ransom's son. Nashville, Tennessee: Sunday School Union, 1949. 336 p. Index.
The life and career of a Black minister who became a bishop in the African Methodist Episcopal Church, serving in Ohio and Pennsylvania.

3724 Rascoe, Burton   1892-1957
We were interrupted. Garden City, New York: Doubleday and Co., Inc., 1947. 342 p.
Richly detailed description of his life in the Roaring Twenties by an editor and critic who was at the center of literary and intellectual activity.

3725 *Rasey, Marie J.   1887-1957
It takes time: an autobiography of the teaching profession. Foreword by Karen Horney. New York: Harper and Brothers, 1953. 204 p.
A third person narrative describing the events which motivated her to become a teacher and shaped her life in that career.

3726 *Rasmussen, Anne Marie   1938-
There was once a time; of islands, illusions and Rockefellers. New York: Harcourt Brace Jovanovich, 1975. 236 p. Index.
Born the daughter of a Norwegian fisherman, she was married to Steven Clark Rockefeller for ten years. Her book describes her Cinderella marriage, the pain and happiness of living in the Rockefeller family, and her desire to reshape her life after their divorce.

3727 Rathbone, Basil   1892-1967
In and out of character. Garden City, New York: Doubleday & Co., Inc., 1962. 278 p.
Written in the restrained style and studied perfection that characterized his theatrical roles, his book traces his career, the drama of his life on and off stage or camera, his long and happy marriage, and many of his famous friends.

3728 Rather, Dan   1931-
The camera never blinks: adventures of a TV journalist. With Mickey Herskowitz. New York: William Morrow and Co., 1977. 362 p. Index.
Rather describes the hectic world of a television newsman. Through Watergate, Vietnam, the Kennedy and King assassinations, and his daring coverage of the People's Republic of China's army, Rather's incentive has been a lesson from his obscure Texas college: "Don't let the bastards scare you."

3729 Ravenel, Henry William   1814-1887
The private journal of Henry William Ravenel, 1859-1887. Edited by Arney Robinson Childs. Columbia: University of South Carolina Press, 1947. 428 p. Index.
In selections from the original notebooks on deposit in the South Carolinian Library, this edition provides a remarkable view of Southern life during the Civil War and Reconstruction. An outstanding botanist, Ravenel's eye for detail and his compassionate will to survive result in an unusual record of the man and his times.

3730 Ray, Man   1890-1976
Self-portrait. Boston: Little, Brown & Co., 1963. 402 p.
Pioneer Dadaist and Surrealist Ray has written a word portrait of his career in America and Paris, with anecdotes and vignettes of expatriate artists and writers.

3731 Raymond, Father M., O.C.S.O.   1903-
Forty years behind the wall. Huntington, Indiana: Our Sunday Visitor, 1979. 336 p.
Having lived forty years within the silent Trappist monastery of Gethsemane in Kentucky, Father Raymond provides a detailed account of the life there. His is a lively, witty, intelligent account of daily routines, friends, faith, philosophy, publishing, cancer, and the many ex-GI's who flocked to American monasteries after the World Wars. In the chapter "God's Name Must Be Murphy," he admits that he is flippant, but faithful.

3732 Raymond, Robert S.   1913-
A Yank in bomber command. Edited by Michael Moynihan. Preface by Noble Frankland. New York: Hippocrene Books, 1977. 159 p.
Raymond flew with the Royal Air Force Bomber Command during England's darkest hours, 1940-1943. His accounts of bombing missions to various target sites in Germany and Italy are exciting but understated; only three bombing crews in ten could hope to survive. Soon after transferring to the U.S. Air Force he married Betty, the recipient of his letters.

3733 Reb, Paul   1925?-
Confessions of a future Scotsman. New York: George Braziller, 1973. 127 p.
As a young man he discovered he was Scottish instead of Irish. He uses this discovery to explore his sense of his identity and heritage, to dramatize how we become what we think we are.

3734 Red Fox   1870-1976
The memoirs of Chief Red Fox. Introduction by Cash Asher. New York: McGraw-Hill Book Co., 1971. 208 p.
At age 101 Chief Red Fox assembled this record of the Indian's fight for survival and retention of his rights and identity. His own life spans the early days when he hunted on foot with bow and arrow, traveled with the Buffalo Bill Wild West Show, fought at the battles of Little Big Horn and Wounded Knee, and watched the sad decline of his once-proud race.

3735 Redfield, William Henry   1927-1976
Letters from an actor. New York: The Viking Press, 1967. 243 p.
Written to Robert Mills between January and August 1964, this series of letters describes daily events during the rehearsals, tryouts and opening of the Gielgud-Burton production of *Hamlet*. The writer, who played Guildenstern, conveys lively observations and impressions of the workings of the theater and the performers involved.

3736 Reed, Nathanial (Texas Jack)   1862-1950
The life of Texas Jack; eight years a criminal—41 years trusting in God. Introduction and notes by Glenn Shirley. Quanah, Texas: Nortex Press, 1973. (Tulsa, Oklahoma, 1936) 66 p.
Texas Jack was an outlaw who claimed credit for numerous bank and train robberies. After a prison sentence and parole he turned evangelist, wrote accounts of his exciting life, sold the pamphlets, and preached about moral and respectable living.

3737 Reeder, Russell Peter (Red)   1902-
Army brat: life story of a West Pointer. Condensation of *Born at Reveille*. New York: Meredith Press, 1967. (New York: Duell, Sloan, and Pearce, 1966) 240 p.
Reeder colorfully describes his lifelong Army career. He was an "army brat" and lived all over the United States, first with his army-officer father and Southern mother and later as an officer himself, with his wife, four children, and eleven hunting dogs. He was expelled from West Point twice for academic failure, eventually graduated, and performed various duties at U.S. Army posts before World War II. He wrote the training manual, *Fighting in Guadalcanal*, was wounded in the Battle of Normandy, had his leg amputated, and then taught at West Point.

3738 Reese, Mason   1965?-
Memoirs; in cahoots with Lynn Haney. New York: Dodd, Mead and Company, 1974. 62 p.
Best known for his work in TV commercials, the moppet-haired, gravel-voiced third-grader tells about his life and work through pictures and anecdotes.

3739 Reeves, Donald   1952-
Notes of a processed brother. New York: Random House (Pantheon), 1972. 480 p.
In clipped, reportorial style, the author traces his education from Detroit to the West Indies—sent away from American racism—to the Brownsville section of Brooklyn, where he became one of the leaders in a struggle for a student Bill of Rights. The student struggle is the focus, but what is central to this account is the story of a young Black man coming of age and not yet coming to terms with a racist society.

3740 Regan, John Henninger   1818-1905
Memoirs, with special reference to secession and the Civil War. Edited by Walter Flavins McCaleb. Introduction by George P. Garrison. Brasada Reprint Series. Austin, Texas: The Pemberton Press, 1968. (New York: Neale, 1906) 351 p. Index.
As a top statesman of the Confederacy, Regan served as its Postmaster General and Secretary of the Treasury. Imprisoned after the war with Jefferson Davis and other Confederate Cabinet members, he was in solitary confinement for nearly a year. After release he helped the South in its struggle to overcome the ills of the Reconstruction.

3741 Regnery, Henry   1912-
Memoirs of a dissident publisher. New York: Harcourt Brace Jovanovich, Inc., 1979. 260 p. Index.
After a brief resumé of his life prior to 1948, a political conservative

discusses the founding and 25-year operation of his publishing company. He championed such conservative authors as Russell Kirk, Wyndham Lewis, and William F. Buckley, thoroughly enjoyed his work, and lost money.

3742 Reich, Peter   **1944-**
A book of dreams. New York: Harper & Row, 1973. 172 p.

Reminiscences and dreams contribute to the story of his relationships with his mother and father and his experience with Orgone Energy, the cloudbuster, and the accumulator, all part of the experiments of his father, Wilhelm Reich.

3743 *Reid-Renison, Clara Shepherd
see **Renison, William T.**

3744 Reilly, Michael Francis   **1910?-1973**
Reilly of the White House. As told to William J. Slocum. New York: Simon and Schuster, 1947. 248 p.

Shortly after Pearl Harbor was bombed, Reilly was made Supervising Agent of the White House Secret Service, charged with protecting President Roosevelt. Here he describes that work (1941-1945) from a personal and professional point of view.

3745 Reiner, Max, pseud.
see ***Caldwell, Janet Taylor**

3746 Reinhold, Hans Ansgar   **b.1875**
The autobiography of Father Reinhold. Foreword by W.H. Auden. New York: Herder and Herder, 1968. 150 p.

A simple, compelling narrative of Father Reinhold's lifetime of religious struggles, which began in Nazi Germany after World War I and led to his persecution and ultimate exile in America in 1936. As a parish priest in Yakima, Washington, he suffered from American suspicion of both Communists and Germans throughout World War II and felt intermittently beleaguered. However, by the time of this writing, he had attained a measure of peace, though paralyzed by Parkinson's disease.

3747 *Reis, Claire (Raphael)
Composers, conductors, and critics. New introduction by the author. New preface by Aaron Copland. Foreword by Darius Milhaud. Detroit: Detroit Reprints in Music, 1974. (New York: Oxford University Press, 1955) 264 p. Index.

In the early Twenties she helped organize the League of Composers, serving as executive chairman for the next 25 years. The League worked to bring out unknown composers, to educate the public about contemporary music, and to influence the granting of commissions to composers, rather than awards to a few for finished pieces. In her life's work is reflected a history of modern music and musicians.

3748 Reisman, Marty   **1930-**
The money player; the confessions of American's greatest table tennis champion and hustler. New York: William Morrow & Co., Inc., 1974. 241 p.

Addicted to the sport at age thirteen, he played and hustled table tennis all over the world, winning seventeen singles or doubles championships. His tense, aggressive playing style is reflected in his writing.

3749 Renison, William T.   **b.1876**
Afterglow: memories of a happy ministry. And Clara Shepherd Reid-Renison. New York: Exposition Press, 1953. 121 p.

Renison tells anecdotes about selected moments during his lifelong career as an Episcopal clergyman. With gentle humor he discusses his unsuccessful attempt to find a euphemism for Baalam's "ass" in New Mexico, his ministry at the Seamen's Church Institute in New York, and his enjoyment of his career in Billings, Montana, and semi-retirement in San Francisco. His second wife, whom he married when he was 73, discusses his beloved dogs and his ministry in Billings in a brief volume appended to the autobiography—"Mostly About Dogs."

3750 *Rennert, Maggie
Shelanu: an Israel journal. Englewood Cliffs, New Jersey: Prentice-Hall, Inc., 1979. 446 p.

Rennert, an American widow, decided to live in the Israeli frontier city of Beersheba in the 1970's, to be near her son and his family and to explore the country. She writes with great pleasure of discovering a country, its people, its history, and a niche for herself.

3751 Rentzel, Lance   **1943-**
When all the laughter died in sorrow. New York: Saturday Review Press, 1972. 265 p.

Lance Rentzel, an outstanding student and later a professional football player, was charged with indecent exposure. In this moving account, Rentzel shares his experience of being charged, of the publicity covering the sports pages, of his on and off the field confrontations over his "psychological flaw," and of coming to terms with himself.

3752 *Resnick, Rose
Sun and shadow. New York: Atheneum, 1975. 274 p.

Blinded at the age of two, she was educated in public schools, received undergraduate and graduate degrees in teaching and special education and was trained in several music conservatories. Her life has been devoted to establishing recreation programs and camps for the blind, helping blind children gain admission to San Francisco public schools, and other such projects to increase the human opportunities for blind children.

3753 Revere, Paul   **1735-1818**
Paul Revere's three accounts of his famous ride. Introduction by Edmund S. Morgan. Bibliography. Facsimiles. Boston: Massachusetts Historical Society, 1968. (1961) 36 p.

A map of Boston and facsimiles of Revere's three accounts—actually two drafts of a deposition and a letter to Jeremy Belknap—precede modern type-set versions of the accounts and Longfellow's poem, "Paul Revere's Ride." The second deposition draft eliminates the British officers' profanity so evident in the first, but maintains the repeated threat that they would "blow [Revere's] brains out."

3754 Revson, Peter Jeffrey   **1939-1974**
Speed with style: the autobiography of Peter Revson. And Leon Mandel. Garden City, New York: Doubleday & Co., Inc., 1974. 221 p.

The book is confined to his life on and off the grand prix circuit in 1973, his last year of racing. It is a tense, realistic, and critical description of life in a dangerous game.

3755 Rexroth, Kenneth   **1905-**
An autobiographical novel. Garden City, New York: Doubleday & Co. Inc., 1966. 367 p.

Writing of his formative years, Rexroth describes the picaresque adventures of his youth and intellectual awakening in order to understand himself better and to communicate his story to those he loves.

3756 Reynolds, Bede   **1892-**
A rebel from riches: the autobiography of an unpremeditated monk. Canfield, Ohio: Alba Books, 1975. 150 p.

He began working as a laborer but by 1926 he was a millionaire. He married a Catholic and later was converted to Catholicism. After his wife's death in 1945, he gave away his fortune to spend the rest of his life as a Benedictine monk.

3757 *Reynolds, Bertha Capen   **b.1885**
Uncharted journey: fifty years of growth in social work. New York: The Citadel Press, 1963. 352 p. Index.

Her deep concern for social welfare has shaped her sometimes controversial social philosophy in a lifetime as a dedicated caseworker, group worker, teacher, and guide.

3758 Reynolds, Paul Revere   **1904-**
The middle man; the adventures of a literary agent. New York: William Morrow & Co., Inc., 1972. 223 p. Index.

During 44 years as a literary agent, he has known authors, editors, and the publishing industry. Here he depicts the variety, charm, and excitement of that industry and how writers, editors, motion-picture executives, and publishers operate.

3759 Reynolds, Quentin James   **1902-1965**
By Quentin Reynolds. London: McGraw-Hill Book Co., Inc., 1963. 356 p.

As a foreign correspondent Reynolds was eyewitness to world events before, during, and after World War II in Europe, North Africa, and the South Pacific. He writes of his experiences, his beliefs, and his friends.

3760 *Rhodes, Harrie Vernette   **b.1871**
In the one spirit; autobiography. As told to Margueritte Harmon Bro. New York: Harper and Brothers, 1951. 192 p.

A faith healer writes of her experiences as a clairvoyant and those of her children, as well as many examples of her apparent success as a healer.

3761 Rice, Elmer   **1892-1967**
Minority report: an autobiography. New York: Simon & Schuster, 1963. 473 p.

Recounting a busy lifetime, the author describes his successes and failures, his marriages, his life in the theater, the causes he has fought for, and many famous theater and public figures he has known.

3762 *Rice, Grantland   **1880-1954**
Tumult and the shouting: my life in sport. New York: A.S. Barnes and Co., 1954. 368 p. Index.

A well-respected sportswriter and journalist for over fifty years, he called this book a "summing up . . . the story of my life and of the great men of sport who helped make it an exciting and rich history."

3763 *Rich, Adrienne   **1929-**
Of woman born: motherhood as experience and institution. New York: W.W. Norton and Co., 1976. 318 p.

Contending that her life is representative, a feminist poet writes of her experience of motherhood and the history of that institution. At the center of the book is her experience with her mother and her own child.

3764 *Rich, Louise (Dickinson)   **1903-**
Happy the land. Philadelphia: J.B. Lippincott Co., 1946. 259 p.
She had lived for twelve years in the Rangely Lake region of north-western Maine when her husband died. This book records the lifestyle of the Maine woods they loved, which she continued after his death.

3765 *Rich, Louise (Dickinson)   **1903-**
Innocence under the elms. Philadelphia: J.B. Lippincott, 1955. 283 p.
A writer recalls her early childhood in Bridgewater, Massachusetts, and her relations with her sister, Alice.

3766 *Rich, Louise (Dickinson)   **1903-**
Only parent. Chicago: Peoples Book Club, 1953. 245 p.
A writer explains how she coped with widowhood and the rearing of two children in New England.

3767 *Richards, Eva Alvey
Arctic mood: a narrative of Arctic adventures. Caldwell, Idaho: Caxton Printers, 1949. 281 p.
A schoolteacher's experience in a remote Alaskan village, 1924-26, is described with realistic, practical details of everyday life and a strong sense of what it is like to survive in an Arctic climate.

3768 *Richards, Linda Ann Judson   **1841-1930**
Reminiscences of Linda Richards: America's first trained nurse. Philadelphia: J.B. Lippincott Co., 1949. 121 p.
Brief descriptions of her training in Massachusetts and England, her work at Boston City Hospital, and her medical consulting work in Japan.

3769 Richardson, Bobby (Robert Clinton)   **• 1935-**
The Bobby Richardson story. Westwood, New Jersey: Spire Books/Fleming H. Revell Co., 1965. 156 p.
A second baseman for the New York Yankees since 1963 describes his career as a member of a very good team; his best season was 1962 when he played all but one game and had a .302 batting average in 692 times at bat. A Christian, Bobby is guided on and off the field by his religious principles.

3770 Richardson, Edward H.   **1877-1971**
A doctor remembers. New York: Vantage Press, 1959. 252 p.
Dr. Richardson, for nearly fifty years a gynecological surgeon at Johns Hopkins Medical School, writes in very formal language to demonstrate "conclusively that an average American lad, even when orphaned early in his childhood, who exercises purposeful and discriminating judgment in grasping the opportunities offered by our free enterprise system can achieve through perseverance, determination, and sustained hard work a gratifying measure of success in . . . medicine."

3771 Richardson, George C.
Get up, you're not dead. With Ingrid Frank. New York: W.W. Norton & Co., Inc., 1975. 319 p.
He served in the Army during World War II, returned to his home in Newark where he could not find a job, and joined the newly integrated Air Force. While stationed in Japan he started shooting heroin with friends and was given an undesirable discharge from the service. He rehabilitated himself, eventually returning to Newark, where he later became a Civil Rights worker, state legislator, and organizer of The National Committee to Declare War on Drugs.

3772 Richardson, James Hugh   **1894-1963**
For the life of me: memoirs of a city editor. New York: G.P. Putnam, 1954. 312 p.
A journalist who was at one point in his career city editor of the Los Angeles *Examiner* recalls his start in the profession, his bout with alcoholism, and the famous stories he covered.

3773 Richberg, Donald Randall   **1881-1960**
My hero: the indiscreet memoirs of an eventful but unheroic life. New York: G.P. Putnam's Sons, 1954. 376 p. Index.
The story of a lawyer whose career placed him near the sources of national power, but never quite at their center. In describing his experience with prominent leaders, he discusses "the failure of human leadership to guide mankind away from self-destruction in the greatest era of material growth of human power."

3774 Richman, Harry   **1894-1972**
A hell of a life. With Richard Gehman. Foreword by Richard Gehman. New York: Duell, Sloan and Pearce, 1966. 242 p.
Richman tells of his fast life as a nightclub singer and owner of a New York nightclub, Club Richman. He was befriended by gangster Al Capone and movie magnate Joe Schenck; Richman loved Clara Bow, Jean

Harlow, and a multitude of other flashy beauties, but had no enduring relationships. He earned thirteen million dollars and spent nearly all of it.

3775 Richmond, Alexander   **1913-**
Long view from the left; memoirs of an American revolutionary. Boston: Houghton Mifflin Co., 1973. 447 p. Index.
Three essays (Chapters II, V, and VII) dealing with problems of American radicalism interrupt the course of these personal memoirs. The author considers them to be integral elements of the whole since the interplay between what he did and what he thinks helps to delineate what he is. His object is to convey the communist experience, thought, and actions of those purposefully committed to a revolutionary reconstruction of American society.

3776 *Richmond, Bernice, pseud.
see *Robinson, Bernice (Nelke)*

3777 Rickard, Clinton   **1882-1971**
Fighting Tuscarora; the autobiography of Chief Clinton Rickard. Edited by Barbara Graymond. Illustrated. Syracuse: Syracuse University Press, 1973. 182 p. Index.
Chief Clinton Rickard was the Tuscarora leader of the Indian Rights movement, founder of the Indian Defense League of America, and an expert on Indian-American legal history. Because of his work Indian civil liberties have been better upheld, New York high schools have been opened to Indians, and Indians have taken more pride in their own culture.

3778 Rickenbacker, Edward Vernon   **1890-1973**
From father to son; the letters of Captain Eddie Rickenbacker to his son William, from boyhood to manhood. Edited with notes and introduction by William F. Rickenbacker. New York: Walker and Co., 1970. 204 p.
Written between 1937 and 1965, these letters contain the advice and direction of the World War I flying ace and captain of industry to his son. The collection reveals his forceful and generous character.

3779 Rickenbacker, Edward Vernon   **1890-1973**
Rickenbacker. Illustrated. Englewood Cliffs, New Jersey: Prentice-Hall, Inc., 1967. 458 p. Index.
An American aviation hero in and out of wartime, Rickenbacker tells the story of his lifelong role in automotive and aviation history. Over 32,000 copies of this book were donated to high school and college libraries by contributions through America's Future, Inc. in the hope of making his story available as an inspiration to America's youth.

3780 Rider, Fremont   **b.1885**
And master of none: an autobiography in the third person. Limited edition. Middletown, Connecticut: Godfrey Memorial Library, 1955. 253 p. Index.
During his checkered career, Rider was an editor, poet, publisher, author, printer, real-estate developer, dramatist, inventor, and genealogist. He failed at or gave up some of these occupations, but his principal occupation was that of librarian at Wesleyan University Library.

3781 Ridgway, Matthew Bunker   **1895-**
Soldier: the memoirs of Matthew B. Ridgway. As told to Harold H. Martin. Foreword by George C. Marshall. Westport, Connecticut: Greenwood Press, 1974. (New York: Harper and Brothers, 1956) 371 p. Index.
The wartime memoirs of a general who was Commander of the 82nd Airborne Division in Europe, Commander of the Eighth Army in Korea, Supreme Commander of NATO, and finally, Chief of Staff of the Army.

3782 Riedel, Richard Lanham   **1908-**
Halls of the mighty, my 47 years at the Senate. Illustrated. Foreword by Everett McKinley Dirksen. Washington: Robert B. Luce, Inc., 1969. 313 p. Index.
In spite of the subtitle, Riedel's book reveals more of the Senate and its membership than it does of his own life. He first worked in the Senate as a nine-year-old page; when he retired 47 years later he was its first Press Liaison.

3783 Riegert, Wilbur A.   **d.1974**
Quest for the pipe of the Sioux; as viewed from Wounded Knee. Edited by Paul Manhart. Rapid City, South Dakota: Jean M. Fritze, 1975. 164 p.
Portraying the deep wisdom and traditions of the Sioux, the author, a Chippewa by birth, tells of discovering among the Sioux a real sense of himself as an Indian and his life interest in the religious habit of prayer.

3784 Riegle, Donald Wayne   **1938-**
O Congress. With Trevor Armbrister. Garden City, New York: Doubleday & Co., 1972. 297 p.
A personal account of one year, 1971-1972, in a congressman's life during which he observed his colleagues in moments of tension, tedium and horseplay, behaving courageously, viciously or with respect for each other. He writes of his own activities, official and personal, and his independent and sometimes agonizing decisions voting for crucial bills.

3785 Riggs, Robert (Bobby) Larimore   **1918-**
Court hustler. Philadelphia: J.B. Lippincott Co., 1973. 203 p.
His second autobiographical book, this one spurred by his well-publicized matches in 1973 against Margaret Court and Billie Jean King.

3786 Riggs, Robert (Bobby) Larimore   **1918-**
Tennis is my racket. New York: Simon and Schuster, 1949. 245 p.
In 1946 Riggs won the world championship in tennis. Here he writes of his tennis life from early years of play, sketches several famous players, and gives pointers on the game.

3787 Riley, James Whitcomb   **1849-1916**
Letters of James Whitcomb Riley Edited by William Lyon Phelps. New York: AMS Press, 1973. (Indianapolis: The Bobbs-Merrill Co., 1930) 349 p. Index.
Riley's poems, many in dialect and many about children, won for him the title of "The Hoosier Poet." His simple, affectionate humor, careful technique, and enthusiasm for the works of his contemporaries shine through in these letters to personal friends and literary acquaintances.

3788 *Rinehart, Mary Roberts   **1876-1958**
My story: a new edition and seventeen new years. Illustrated. New York: Rinehart and Co., Inc., 1948. 570 p.
Remembered mainly for her mystery novels, Rinehart engaged in an amazing variety of social and literary activity. Always ambivalent about her successful career, she stresses the importance of her husband and family while describing her life as writer, literary socialite, war correspondent, and adventuresome traveler.

3789 Rinn, Joseph Francis   **b.1868**
Sixty years of psychical research: Houdini and I among the spiritualists. New York: The Truth Seeker Co., 1950. 618 p.
A stockbroker who investigated psychic phenomena as an avocation describes his hope of discovering empirical evidence of a future life and the widespread fraud among most who claimed to have found it.

3790 *Ritchie, Eveline
Taking out my bucketful. And Violet T. Pearson. Illustrated. Denver: Accent Books, 1978. 160 p.
Schoolteacher Ritchie describes her whirlwind retirement years of industry and Christian love. She made thousands of dresses, knitted hundreds of caps, donated considerable money for toys and blankets for children in orphanages in Korea, Taiwan, and Greece, and traveled worldwide "to visit her children." She writes her autobiography to inspire other retirees to comparable undertakings.

3791 *Ritter, Lucy Elizabeth   **1910-**
Lucy's twentieth century. New York: Vantage, 1974. 142 p.
The author recalls her childhood in Hong Kong, followed by high school and college in California. Later she became an insurance executive, a delegate to two Democratic National Conventions, co-chairman of Citizens for Kennedy, collected art objects, and supported cultural activities.

3792 Rivas, Rafael Alberto   **1943-**
Survival: my life in love and war. Hicksville, New York: Exposition Press, 1977. 165 p.
Rivas's autobiography describes his loves and disillusionments, his alternate wealth and poverty. Resiliency and self-confidence enable him to survive skirmishes with the law, antagonists, and physical danger.

3793 *Rivers, Caryl   **1938-**
Aphrodite at mid-century: growing up Catholic and female in post-war America. Garden City, New York: Doubleday & Co., Inc., 1973. 283 p.
Memoirs of an upper-middle-class Catholic girlhood in and around Washington emphasizing the mild and mundane conventionality of the 1950's, "a world of changeless truth, simple moral choices, and nodding assent."

3794 *Rives, Hallie Ermine (Mrs. Post Wheeler)   **1876-1956**
see **Wheeler, Post**

3795 Rives, James Davidson   **1893-1975**
Essays of a Louisiana surgeon. Edited with foreword by S. Sparkman. Memoir by Isidore Cohn, Jr. Illustrated. New Orleans: James D. Rives Surgical Society, 1977. 136 p.
Rives' essays on medical education, doctors, and the practice and frustrations of surgery are wise, witty, and elegantly written. He regards surgeons as "hewers of flesh and drawers of blood." His observations on teaching and on the practice of medicine maintain equal measures of realism and idealism.

3796 Robbin, Edward   **1905-**
Woody Guthrie and me: an intimate reminiscence. Berkeley, California: Lancaster-Miller Publishers, 1979. 160 p.
This is a nostalgic account of the friendship between Robbin and Guthrie from their meeting in 1938 until Guthrie's death in 1967. Robbin always believed in Guthrie and tried to bring his music to the attention of the country. Scattered throughout the book are interviews with Guthrie's close friends and family and some of the folksinger's most moving lyrics.

3797 Roberts, Cecil E.   **1919-**
Soldier from Texas. Foreword by Vernon A. Walters. Illustrated. Fort Worth: Branch-Smith, 1978. 210 p.
Roberts' account of his life focuses with pride on his years as an army captain in World War II, where he successfully commanded American troops in the Battle of the Bulge and the Battle of Remagen. After the war, as a member of the regular army, he served as a military attaché at American embassies in Greece and Bolivia. He retired to a ranch in Texas with the rank of colonel in 1966.

3798 *Roberts, Evelyn (Lutman)   **1917-**
His darling wife, Evelyn: The autobiography of Mrs. Oral Roberts. New York: Dial Press/Damascus House, 1976. 273 p.
Evelyn Roberts emphasizes the Christian joy of their marriage and the many roles she has played as "his inspiration, his helpmate, his comfort, his wife, and the mother of his [four] children." In detail she discusses evangelism, faith, and Oral Roberts University.

3799 Roberts, Isaac Phillips   **1833-1928**
Autobiography of a farm boy. Ithaca: Cornell University Press, 1946. (1916) 207 p.
The author, for thirty years Dean of the College of Agriculture at Cornell University, recalls his boyhood in rural New York, his early manhood in the Middle-West, and his life and work at Cornell. His wide knowledge of and love for farming led him to devote his lifetime to observing and teaching agriculture and encouraging the study of the whole farm rather than specialized aspects.

3800 *Roberts, Joan (Seagrist)   **1918-**
Never alone. New York: McMullen Books, Inc., 1954. 204 p.
Roberts writes pleasantly, with an ingénue's rapturous first love for her theatrical debut, about the factors that contributed to her ultimate success as a Broadway star in *Oklahoma*: her family who subsidized music and dance lessons; her first-rate voice teacher, Estelle Liebling; her excellent direction from Oscar Hammerstein and others; and her strong Catholic faith.

3801 Roberts, Kenneth Lewis   **1885-1957**
I wanted to write. Garden City, New York: Doubleday and Co., Inc., 1949. 471 p. Index.
Roberts analyzes the experience of being a writer—no formulas or routines describing how to write, but details of what it is like to live as a professional writer, including research, hard work, dealing with publishers and agents, frustrations, and the satisfaction of writing well. Journalist and author of historical novels, including *Northwest Passage* and *Lydia Bailey*.

3802 Roberts, Oral   **1917?-**
My story. Tulsa: Summit Book Co., 1961. 213 p.
Oklahoman Roberts describes his evangelistic career, which began shortly after his recovery from tuberculosis through faith healing in his late teens. His evangelical crusades attract thousands to his tent revival meetings in the United States, Africa, and elsewhere; others watch on television. He claims thousands of Christian converts and hundreds of faith healings, at short and long distance.

3803 Roberts, Oral   **1917?-**
Oral Roberts' life story: as told by himself. Illustrated by Eloise Gray. Introduction by Lee Braxton. Tulsa: The author, 1955. 160 p.
Evangelist Roberts focuses on his career as a faith healer and conductor of revival meetings at which ten thousand people are sometimes saved on a single evening. With fervor he describes being healed at twelve of tuberculosis. Subsequently constant prayer, fasting, and a vigilance against the devil became of paramount importance to Roberts and his family.

3804 Roberts, Paul Henley   **1891-**
Them were the days. San Antonio: The Naylor Co., 1965. 134 p.
From the early days of the U.S. Forestry Service, Roberts was a part of the group of rangers who walked or rode into the unmapped Western ranges, climbing fire towers and helping control forest fires, making maps and surveying the remote back country, overseeing grazing and logging operations, and getting to know the people and the country intimately.

3805 Robertson, Alton E.   **1903-**
And they went down into the water: a story about two young hoodlums written by one of them. Waco, Texas: Texian Press, 1975. 80 p.
A witty, tongue-in-cheek account of growing up in Tilmon, Texas, a "town that does not have a Post Office anymore," written by a successful financier and community leader.

3806 Robertson, Frank Chester   **1890-**
A ram in the thicket: an autobiography. New York: Abelard Press, 1950. 357 p.

The story of his difficult life on the Idaho frontier, a boyhood of poverty and hardship, changed in later life only by his developing career as a popular Western writer during the Thirties.

3807 *Robeson, Eslanda Goode (Mrs. Paul Robeson)
see *Buck, Pearl (Sydenstricker)

3808 Robeson, Paul   1898-1976
Paul Robeson speaks: writings, speeches, interviews, 1918-1974. Edited with introduction and notes by Philip S. Foner. Illustrated. New York: Brunner/Mazel, 1978. 623 p. Index.
A compilation of speeches, articles, editorials, and interviews by and about singer Paul Robeson. These cover his days as a Phi Beta Kappa All-American football player at Rutgers (1917-1919), his years in Columbia Law School (1920-23), his career as a singer and actor, tours and residence in England and Russia in the 1930's, 40's and 50's. A communist whose American passport was revoked (1958-63), Robeson lived abroad during those years but never ceased to defend Black rights, the rights of labor unions, and peace and freedom everywhere—the focus of these articulate documents.

3809 Robillard, Fred S.   1890-1971
As Robie remembers. Foreword by Dick King. Wright Investor's Service, 1969. 110 p.
A collection of brief, funny (and a few serious) narratives "that go back to the start of the automobile business and carry [the author] through the city of Chicago," the racing cars [he] drove, . . . [and his] entry into the Marine Corps.

3810 *Robins, Elizabeth (C.E. Raimond, pseud.)   1862-1952
Raymond and I. Foreword by Leonard Woolf. New York: The Macmillan Co., 1956. 343 p.
She was the first and many said the best actress of Ibsen in English, as well as a writer. This book tells of her journey to Alaska in 1900, the first year of the Gold Rush, to find her brother who was seeking his fortune. She discovered him serving as a minister and was determined he should leave instead of "wasting his life." The book depicts their two strong characters in Nome when it was a raw and wild tent city. An absorbing account of the people and the times.

3811 *Robinson, Bernice (Nelke) (Bernice Richmond, pseud.)   1899-
Our island lighthouse. New York: Random House, 1947. 275 p.
In 1938 the author and her husband spent the summer in a lighthouse on a Maine island. Four summers later they began staying all year round. Her book describes their life on the island, their interests in the sea, plant life, gardens, winds, and the sense of peace they enjoyed.

3812 Robinson, Brooks Calbert   1937-
Third base is my home. As told to Jack Tobin. Waco, Texas: Word Books, 1974. 202 p.
Personal glimpses into the life of a Baltimore Orioles' third baseman; he writes of his family, the game, and his abiding personal faith.

3813 *Robinson, Dorothy Redus   1910-
The bell rings at four: a Black teacher's chronicle of change. Foreword by John Hill Westbrook. Illustrated. Austin, Texas: Madrona Press, 1978. 142 p.
Robinson has had a vigorous and effective 46-year career as a classroom teacher, teacher of home economics, special education to physically handicapped and mentally retarded children, and school principal. She emphasizes the racial discrimination prevalent in Texas during much of her career and her satisfaction with the progress Blacks have made in recent years.

3814 Robinson, Duncan W.   1905-
Duncan Robinson, Texas teacher and humanist: collected writings of Duncan Robinson, Professor Emeritus, University of Texas at Arlington. Edited by Thomas Sutherland and Benjamin Capps. Introduction by Ben Capps. "The Heartland," Tom Sutherland. Illustrated. Arlington: English Department, University of Texas at Arlington, 1976. 321 p.
A selection of Robinson's published and unpublished writings covering more than a half century of his life, including high school and college poetry; essays; portions of his biography of Judge Robert McAlpin Williamson; editorials; speeches; and a section of comments by his friends.

3815 Robinson, Edward G.   1893-1973
All my yesterdays; an autobiography. With Leonard Spigelgass. Illustrated. New York: Hawthorn Books, Inc., 1973. 344 p. Index.
Robinson started in stock and went on to road companies, Broadway, and movies, achieving stardom with his portrayal of the title role in *Little Caesar.* He supported liberal political and social causes and was blacklisted as a communist sympathizer. He was a well-known and discriminating art collector as well.

3816 Robinson, Edwin Arlington   1869-1935
Edwin Arlington Robinson's letters to Edith Brower. Edited by Richard Cary. Cambridge: The Belknap Press of Harvard University Press, 1968. 233 p. Index.

Edith Brower, a reader for Dr. Coan's "Bureau of Criticism and Revision" for authors, initiated her correspondence with the poet in 1897 with an impulsive note praising his collection, *The Torrent and the Night Before.* From then until her death in 1931, they wrote regularly, Robinson's letters recording his development as a poet.

3817 Robinson, Edwin Arlington   1869-1935
Untriangulated stars: letters to Harry de Forest Smith, 1890-1905. Edited by Denham Sutcliffe. Cambridge: Harvard University Press, 1947. (Colorado Springs: privately printed, 1945) 348 p. Index.
The first major collection of Robinson's early letters, previously unpublished, which discuss his difficulties as a struggling and as yet unknown poet, written to one of the few friends to whom he confided his personal unhappiness and discussed many of the ideas which later became central to his major work.

3818 Robinson, Frank   1935-
Frank: the first year. With Dave Anderson. New York: Holt, Rinehart, Winston Co., 1976. 259 p.
Robinson recounts his first year (1975) as the first Black manager of a major league baseball team, the Cleveland Indians, telling in diary form how he shaped a losing, demoralized team into a winner, which led to a renewal of his contract for 1976.

3819 Robinson, Frank   1935-
My life is baseball. With Al Silverman. Garden City, New York: Doubleday & Co., Inc., 1975. (1968) 237 p.
Traded by the Cincinnati Reds to the Baltimore Orioles in 1966, he helped the Orioles win the World Series that year, won the triple crown, and became the first player in history to win the Most Valuable Player Award in both leagues.

3820 Robinson, George L.   1864-1958
Autobiography of George L. Robinson: a short story of a long life. Grand Rapids, Michigan: Baker Book House, 1957. 142 p.
At 93 Robinson, a Princeton-educated Presbyterian clergyman, wrote this recollection of his long career as a religious educator and author and researcher in the Holy Land. In 1900 he discovered "the high place of Petra," an ancient Hebrew settlement on a Turkish mountain plateau.

3821 *Robinson, Irene   1910-
A wall to paint on. New York: E.P. Dutton and Co., Inc., 1946. 451 p. Index.
Her letters (1927-1939) to her mother, brother, and small daughter reflect deep love and family ties, details of her wandering career as an artist with descriptions of many artist friends and lovers (e.g., Diego Rivera), and moving accounts of her experience in Spain during the Civil War and in Europe just before World War II.

3822 Robinson, James Herman   1907-1972
Road without turning: the story of Reverend James H. Robinson, an autobiography. New York: Farrar, Straus and Co., 1950. 312 p.
A frank and courageous story of a Black man's struggle to overcome racial discrimination begun in his childhood in Tennessee and continued as his education and conflicts with prejudice progressed.

3823 Robinson, John Roosevelt (Jackie Robinson)   1919-
Breakthrough to the big league: the story of Jackie Robinson. With Alfred Duckett. Breakthrough Books. New York: Harper & Row, 1965. 178 p. Index.
In this book written for young people, Robinson tells the story of his break through the racial barrier to become the first Black major-league baseball player. He was named Rookie of the Year in 1947, a member of the Baseball Hall of Fame in 1962, and took an active role in the struggle for civil rights.

3824 Robinson, John Roosevelt (Jackie Robinson)   1919-
I never had it made. As told to Alfred Duckett. New York: G.P. Putnam's Sons, 1972. 287 p.
His second book is dramatically different from his first, which captures the gratitude of the young Black man who had been given an historic opportunity. This one is more honest, more realistic, more detailed in its description of the hatred and insults he endured, the importance of his family life, the price of fame, his grief at his son Jackie's death, the pain of racial prejudice.

3825 Robinson, John Roosevelt (Jackie Robinson)   1919-
My own story. As told to Wendell Smith. Foreword by Branch Rickey. New York: Greenberg Publisher, 1948. 172 p.
In 1947, he became the first Black to play baseball in the major leagues. His book describes his childhood and family life, his college years at UCLA, and the difficulties he met as a Black in sports. He includes an interesting portrait of Branch Rickey, who engineered his dramatic break through the color bar.

3826 *Robinson, Laura
A life partially relived in vignettes: memoirs. Hicksville, New York: Exposition Press, 1977. 156 p.

A professor of classical studies at Southwestern College with a doctorate from Johns Hopkins describes herself as "a deep South woman, a conservative and an owner of some inherited AT&T stock [who] does not easily make friends in these days and times."

3827 Robinson, Lewis G.   **1929-**
The making of a man; an autobiography. Cleveland: Green & Sons, 1970. 213 p.
Robinson helped form the Freedom Fighters in Cleveland and became vitally involved in demonstrations and actions for racial equality. He describes the summer of 1964, the formation of the Jomo "Freedom" Kenyatta House, the 1966 riots in Hough, and problems connected with race relations.

3828 Robinson, Ray   **1921-**
Sugar Ray. With Dave Anderson. New York: The Viking Press, 1970. 376 p.
He grew up in the ghettos of Detroit and New York to become a world championship boxer, made and spent four million dollars, and retired to enjoy his wife, family, and personal religion.

3829 Rockwell, George Lincoln   **1918-1967**
This time the world. Illustrated. Liverpool, West Virginia: White Power Publications, 1979. 264 p.
Rockwell documents his development from a bright, independent-minded, and puritanical youth into fanatic leader of the American Nazi Party. Experiences at Brown University and as a wartime Navy pilot led him to hate Jews, Communists, and Blacks. His "heroes," Joe McCarthy and Hitler, shaped his political thinking as he struggled to earn a living after the war. Rockwell became an open, aggressive Nazi, advocating mass murders of Jews and others.

3830 Rockwell, Norman   **1894-1978**
Norman Rockwell, my adventures as an illustrator. As told to Thomas Rockwell. New York: Ballantine Books, 1972. (Garden City, New York: Doubleday, 1960) 464 p.
Rockwell is one of America's best-known illustrators, famous for his *Saturday Evening Post* covers portraying down-home America in a warm and entertaining style. Here he relates his frustrations, failures, and triumphs as well as serious reflections on his art and the state of the country.

3831 *Rodgers, Dorothy   **1909-**
A personal book. New York: Harper and Row, 1977. 189 p.
The story of her pampered and privileged upbringing. Married at twenty to composer Richard Rodgers, who at 27 was already a celebrity, she enjoyed a delightful marriage of maternity, travel, notable and loving friends, and wealth augmented by her invention of the "johnny mop" and her authorship of books on decorating and entertaining.

3832 Rodgers, Franklin C. ("Pepper")   **1931-**
Pepper!: the autobiography of an unconventional coach. And Al Thomy. Illustrated. Garden City, New York: Doubleday & Co., 1976. 176 p.
A low-keyed, good-humored account of Rodgers's life, focused primarily on football. He was a quarterback for the Georgia Tech team that won the 1951 Orange Bowl game; he was a pilot and football coach in the Air Force; he coached the U.C.L.A. Bruins and in 1973 returned to his alma mater as head football coach.

3833 Rodney, Thomas   **1744-1811**
Diary of Captain Thomas Rodney, 1776-1777. New York: Da Capo Press, 1974. (Wilmington: The Historical Society of Delaware, 1888) 53 p.
Captain Rodney was in command of a company of Kent County militia, the only Delaware troops engaged in the battles of Trenton and Princeton. His company left Dover on December 14, 1776, and he recorded in his diary the events of the next six weeks.

3834 *Rodzinski, Halina (Lilpop-Wieniawski)   **1904-**
Our two lives. New York: Charles Scribner's Sons, 1976. 403 p.
Her book tells of her early life in Poland, where she met and married Arthur Rodzinski; its main focus is on her life with the famous, somewhat temperamental conductor of the Chicago Symphony, the Cleveland Symphony, and the New York Philharmonic Orchestra.

3835 Roeben, Frederick B.   **b.1878**
Lure of the sea. New York: Vantage Press, Inc., 1950. 64 p.
As a boy of twelve in Germany, he decided to go to America, ran away from home to be a sailor, and after fifteen years finally settled in Covington, Kentucky, working at Procter and Gamble until he retired.

3836 Roethke, Theodore   **1908-1963**
Selected letters. Edited with introduction by Ralph J. Mills, Jr. Illustrated. Seattle: University of Washington Press, 1968. 273 p. Index.
This small selection was chosen to illustrate particularly his career as poet. Included among the letters to such people as Louise Bogan, Kenneth Burke, Rolfe Humphries, and William Carlos Williams are a selection of unpublished poems and early versions of poems, some of which were sent to friends for their criticism. Letters of the Thirties represent his appren-

tice years; the Forties brought critical recognition and was a time of experimentation; the Fifties to early Sixties, the last decade of his life, continue to show a poet wishing for critical attention and experimenting with his art.

3837 Roff, Charles Luther   **1894-**
A boom town lawyer in the Osage, 1919-1927. Quanah, Texas: Nortex Press, 1975. 122 p.
Fresh out of law school, Roff set out to establish a practice in an Oklahoma boom town during the 1920's. In those exciting and rough times he encountered big-time operators, bank robbers, murderers, bootleggers, and all kinds of crooks and petty outlaws.

3838 Roff, Charles Luther   **1894-**
We were young together. New York: Vantage Press, 1973. 204 p.
His boyhood and youth, spent in the Oklahoma and Indian territories, provide background for adventurous and amusing stories of frontier life, especially cattle herding, ranching, rough-and-tumble escapades, and education, both formal and informal.

3839 *Rogers, Dale Evans   **1912-**
My spiritual diary. Westwood, New Jersey: Fleming H. Revell Co., 1955. 144 p.
A Western actress discusses her spiritual joys (the evangelical conversions of others, aid for the mentally retarded, her family of five children, including an adopted Indian) and tribulations (the death of her mongoloid daughter, Robin; her own spiritual backsliding; illness). She, her husband, Roy Rogers, and horse Trigger accompanied Billy Graham on a Christian Crusade in the British Isles.

3840 Rogers, Henry C.   **1914-**
Walking the tightrope: the private confessions of a public relations man. Foreword by Irving Wallace. Illustrated. New York: William Morrow, 1980. 256 p.
Although Rogers, a Hollywood public relations man, uses tightrope walking as a metaphor for the tension of his job, he appears a relaxed but energetic participant in promoting his movie star clients with the press and television. Rita Hayworth was his first well-known client, followed by Claudette Colbert, Joan Crawford, Danny Kaye, and a host of others. His ingenuity, gregariousness, and perseverance have greatly enhanced his career.

3841 Rogers, Henry Huttleston   **1840-1909**
see **Clemens, Samuel Langhorne**

3842 Rogers, John (Chief Snow Cloud)   **1890-**
Red world and white: memories of a Chippewa boyhood. Foreword by Joseph W. Whitecotton. Norman: University of Oklahoma Press, 1974. (1957) 153 p.
The book is chiefly about his boyhood in Indian schools, but stresses the difficulty of living in a world of two cultures.

3843 Rogers, Kenneth Paul
For one sweet grape: the extraordinary memoir of a convicted rapist-murderer. Chicago: Playboy Press, 1974. 224 p.
An explicit book written in his cell at the suggestion of the prison psychiatrist describes the rape he committed and his attempts to understand himself, his childhood, and the chaos of his adult life.

3844 Rogers, Kenny   **1938?-**
Making it with music: Kenny Rogers' guide to the music business. And Len Epand. New York: Harper & Row, 1978. 224 p.
The author's hard-won experience forms a basis for this account of how to succeed in the music business. Anecdotes and vignettes mingle with information about forming a group, finding bookings, agents, publishers and managers, writing songs, understanding contracts, living on the road, and handling success.

3845 Rogers, Peter V.
Tragedy is my parish: working for God in the streets of New Orleans. Illustrated. New York: Macmillan Publishing Co., 1979. 159 p.
Father Rogers discusses the most thrilling and poignant episodes in his career as the Chaplain of the New Orleans Police and Fire Departments. His tales center on the French Quarter, scene of exotic murders and devastating fires.

3846 Rogers, Roy   **1912-**
Happy trails: the story of Roy Rogers and Dale Evans. With Carlton Stowers. Filmography. Waco, Texas: Word Books, 1979.
In the first section of this joint autobiography, Roy Rogers briefly describes his youth and his entry into the motion-picture industry in which he was "King of the Cowboys" from 1943 to 1954. In the second section, Dale Evans similarly talks about her ascent in show business and her dislike of Westerns. The third section presents their life together after their conversion to Christianity.

3847 Rogers, Will 1879-1935
The autobiography of Will Rogers. Selected and edited by Donald Day. New York: Lancer, 1963. (Boston: Houghton Mifflin Co., 1949) 410 p. Index.

With down-home humor, Rogers talks about his life and world affairs during the 1920's and early 30's.

3848 Rogers, Will 1879-1935
Will Rogers scrapbook. Selected and edited by Bryan B. Sterling. New York: Grosset, 1976. 190 p.

A collection of photographs, newspaper columns and interviews with people who knew and worked closely with Rogers. He tells the story of his own life in five brief essays. "Memoirs," he says, "is an old Cherokee word which means that you put down the good things you ought to have done, and leave out the bad ones you did do."

3849 Rolleston, Thomas William 1857-1920
  see Whitman, Walt

3850 *Rollin, Betty 1936?-
First you cry. New York: J.B. Lippincott, 1976. 206 p.

Reporter and television newscaster recounts with anger and anguish the delayed discovery that she had breast cancer at 38. She had a mastectomy, enjoyed all the attention, was grieved and embarrassed over her altered anatomy, but learned: "If I don't have a recurrence of cancer and die soon, all I've lost is a breast, and that's not so bad."

3851 Romanoff, Alexis Lawrence 1892-
Diaries through war and peace: one life in two worlds: Part I. A military officer; Part II. A university scholar. Illustrated. Part I, translated. Ithaca, New York: Ithaca Heritage Books, 1977. 217 p. Index.

In Part I, Romanoff's diaries describe the stress and danger of his life as a young military officer in Soviet Russia and his departure from Russia through Manchuria in 1920, to emigrate to New York. Part II covers Romanoff's "period of professional self-assertion" (1936-48) —his travel in Europe and sabbaticals at Harvard, Yale, the University of Florida, and in Washington, D.C.

3852 *Romig, Emily Craig b.1871
A pioneer woman in Alaska. Caldwell, Idaho: The Caxton Printers, Ltd., 1948. (Colorado Springs: privately printed, 1945) 140 p.

At fourteen, she immigrated to Chicago from Denmark, later married A.C. Craig, and traveled with him to Alaska when gold was discovered in the Klondike. The book is based on her diaries of Alaskan pioneer life, 1897-1944.

3853 Romualdi, Serafino 1900-1967
Presidents and peons: recollections of a labor ambassador in Latin America. Illustrated. New York: Funk & Wagnalls, 1967. 524 p. Index.

Romualdi was AFL representative (later AFL-CIO) for Latin America from 1946 to 1965. His book is intended to describe the U.S. labor movement's combatting of "Communist and other totalitarian forces [attempts] to gain control of labor in Latin America." He believes the efforts of the labor movement have been raising the standard of living for workers through unionization, strengthening representative democracy, and developing labor leadership committed to constructive labor-management relations.

3854 *Ronan, Mary b.1852
Frontier woman: the story of Mary Ronan as told to Margaret Ronan. Edited by H.G. Merriam. Missoula: University of Montana, 1973. 172 p.

The spirited reminiscences of a pioneer lady re-create the covered wagon days in Last Chance Gulch, which became Helena, Montana, in rowdy Virginia City, in southern California in the 1860's, and on the Flathead Indian reservation, where her husband was appointed Government Agent.

3855 Roney, Frank 1841-1925
Frank Roney: Irish rebel and California labor leader: an autobiography. Edited with introduction by Ira B. Cross. Illustrated. New York: AMS Press, 1977. (Berkeley: University of California Press, 1931) 573 p. Index.

After being imprisoned in Ireland in 1866 for political activities, Roney emigrated to America. He worked his way across the country to San Francisco, where he became a noted trade-union organizer, 1876-1886, favoring the open shop because people who joined voluntarily would be more fully committed to their cause. Roney fought anything that lowered worker's wages including non-union men and immigrant Chinese.

3856 Ronne, Finn 1899-1980
Antarctica my destiny: a personal history by the last of the great Polar explorers. Introduction by Lowell Thomas. Illustrated. New York: Hastings House, 1979. 278 p. Index.

With vivid and precise detail Ronne describes his forty years of Antarctic expeditions, twenty as a member of the U.S. Navy. He worked with Admiral Byrd, whose claim to have discovered the North Pole in 1926 Ronne disputes, with U.S. Navy teams, and later on his own. He enjoys

the beauty and the challenges of the sub-zero temperatures and treacherous terrain.

3857 Rooney, Mickey 1920-
I.E.: an autobiography of Mickey Rooney. Illustrated. New York: G.P. Putnam's Sons, 1965. 249 p.

Rooney's "love song to show business, sung at times off-key" testifies to his enjoyment of his profession. Despite five marriages, four divorces, bankruptcy, near-alcoholism, and a "size-psychosis," Rooney professes overwhelming satisfaction with his life.

3858 *Roosevelt, Eleanor 1884-1962
Autobiography. New York: Harper & Row, 1961. 454 p.

An edition combining most of the previous three volumes, *This is My Story, This I Remember,* and *On My Own,* plus additional material.

3859 *Roosevelt, Eleanor 1884-1962
On my own. New York: Harper & Brothers, 1958. 241 p. Index.

After the death of her husband in 1945 Mrs. Roosevelt undertook many useful ventures on her own. She was a member of the U.S. Delegation to the UN General Assembly organization meeting and other UN groups interested in human rights. She traveled throughout the world supporting the work of the UN. She campaigned for Adlai Stevenson and maintained a busy life contributing to causes of world-wide understanding, economic and cultural welfare.

3860 *Roosevelt, Eleanor 1884-1962
This I remember. Westport, Connecticut: Greenwood Press, 1975. (New York: Harper and Brothers, 1949) 387 p. Index.

With dignity and humor, Eleanor Roosevelt discusses her life with FDR during his terms as Governor of New York (1929-1933) and President (1933-1945).

3861 *Roosevelt, Eleanor 1884-1962
Your teens and mine. With Helen Ferris. Garden City, New York: Doubleday & Co., 1961. 189 p.

Addressed to a teenage audience, the book analyzes her own teen years, comparing the problems she faced in growing up with those of modern girls, in a context which implies she succeeded against rather unusual odds.

3862 *Roosevelt, Eleanor 1884-1962
  see also Fischer, Louis

3863 *Roosevelt, Eleanor Butler (Alexander) 1888-1960
Day before yesterday: the reminiscences of Mrs. Theodore Roosevelt, Jr. Garden City, New York: Doubleday & Co., Inc., 1959. 478 p. Index.

An interesting narrative of her life as a Roosevelt, beginning with her New York girlhood at the turn of the century, but focusing on her husband's achievements as Governor of Puerto Rico, Governor General of the Philippines, founder of the American Legion, and Brigadier General during World War II.

3864 Roosevelt, Elliott 1910-
Rendezvous with destiny: the Roosevelts in the White House. With James Brough. New York: G.P. Putnam's Sons, 1975. 446 p. Index.

More a biography embracing the personal life and public concerns during the White House years of his father, FDR, than his own autobiography.

3865 Roosevelt, Franklin Delano 1882-1945
F.D.R.: his personal letters. Edited by Elliott Roosevelt. Foreword by Eleanor Roosevelt. New York: Kraus Reprint Co., 1970. (New York: Duell, Sloan and Pearce, 1947-50) 4v. Index.

Volume I, *The Early Years* (1887-1904), includes letters from childhood and early manhood. Volume II (1905-1928) includes letters from his private and early public life. Volume III-IV (1928-1945) cover the years he was Governor of New York and President of the U.S.

3866 Roosevelt, Franklin Delano 1882-1945
For the President, personal and secret: correspondence between Franklin D. Roosevelt and William C. Bullitt. Edited by Orville H. Bullitt. Introduction by George F. Kennan. Boston: Houghton Mifflin Co., 1972. 655 p. Index.

The correspondence between two men who played important parts in world affairs during the critical years from 1932 to 1945. Bullitt held diplomatic posts in Moscow, Paris, North Africa, and the Middle East.

3867 Roosevelt, Franklin Delano 1882-1945
Franklin D. Roosevelt and foreign affairs. Edited by Edgar B. Nixon. Cambridge: The Belknap Press of Harvard University Press, 1969. 3v. Index.

The three volumes contain the principal documents in the Roosevelt Library at Hyde Park pertaining to foreign relations during his first administration. Volume I—January 1933 to February 1934; Volume II—March 1934 to August 1935; Volume III—September 1935 to January 1937. Includes letters, speeches, memoranda, press conferences, and other documents.

3868 Roosevelt, Franklin Delano   **1882-1945**
Roosevelt and Churchill, their secret wartime correspondence. Edited by Francis L. Lowenheim and others. New York: Saturday Review Press/E.P. Dutton & Co., Inc., 1975. 805 p. Index.
A collection of some of the World War II messages between the two leaders revealing the cooperation, understanding, and growing friendship in their working together toward common goals.

3869 Roosevelt, Franklin Delano   **1882-1945**
Roosevelt and Daniels: a friendship in politics. Chapel Hill: University of North Carolina Press, 1952. 226 p. Index.
Thirty-year correspondence on career and personal matters between Roosevelt and Josephus Daniels, the editor of *The News and Observer* (Raleigh, North Carolina), both politically active in the Democratic Party. The friendship begins with their association in the Navy Department under Wilson and includes Daniels' service as Ambassador to Mexico under Roosevelt.

3870 Roosevelt, Franklin Delano   **1882-1945**
Roosevelt and Frankfurter; their correspondence 1928-1945. Illustrated. Annotated by Max Freedman. Boston: Little, Brown and Co., 1967. 772 p. Index.
Since Frankfurter was outside the administration but in Roosevelt's confidence, the correspondence between them furnishes "a record of friendship, a chronicle of the New Deal, a manual . . . on political leadership, and a testament of citizenship."

3871 Roosevelt, Franklin Delano   **1882-1945**
Wartime correspondence between President Roosevelt and Pope Pius XII. With introductory explanatory notes by Myron C. Taylor. New York: The Macmillan Co., 1947. 127 p.
Messages between the President and the Pope (1939-45) emphasize the endeavors of both to alleviate suffering and establish enduring peace in a better postwar world.

3872 Roosevelt, James   **1907-**
My parents: a differing view. With Bill Libby. Chicago: Playboy Press, 1976. 369 p. Index.
James Roosevelt tells a personal story of his life with his parents, analyzing their marital relationship; their styles of parenting (Franklin warm, Eleanor cool but always to be counted on); their relationships with family, friends, political associates—including possible love affairs. He also analyzes his own life in the public eye.

3873 Roosevelt, Nicholas   **1893-**
Front row seat. Norman: University of Oklahoma Press, 1953. 304 p. Index.
A journalist and diplomat for over forty years, he records his personal observations of major figures and events during that time, with recollections of the Roosevelt family.

3874 Roosevelt, Theodore   **1858-1919**
Autobiography: condensed from the original edition; supplemented by letters, speeches, and other writings. Edited with introduction by Wayne Andrews. Centennial edition. New York: Octagon, 1975. (New York: Charles Scribner's Sons, 1958) 372 p. Index.
A man of violent likes and dislikes, Teddy Roosevelt here discusses important reforms of his administration, diplomatic moves, and his hopes for America. His charm and humor are evident in vigorous accounts of his youth, cowboy days, work on New York's Police Commission, the Rough Riders, and his love of the outdoor life.

3875 Roosevelt, Theodore   **1858-1919**
Cowboys and kings: three great letters by Theodore Roosevelt. Cambridge, Massachusetts: Harvard University Press, 1954. 117 p. Index.
The book contains three letters written by a President of the United States. The first letter is to John Hay and discusses a 1903 trip west. The second letter, written in 1911 to Sir George Otto Trevelyan, describes the 1910 trip to the Middle East and Europe and the many heads of state he met there. The letter to David Gray concerns a 1910 trip to England and includes accounts of British political figures and royalty.

3876 Roosevelt, Theodore   **1858-1919**
Hunting and exploring adventures of Theodore Roosevelt. Edited by Donald Day. Introduction by Elting E. Morison. New York: Dial Press, 1955. 431 p.
The book narrates, in chronological order, President Theodore Roosevelt's hunting and exploring exploits in the western United States, Africa, and Brazil. Donald Day provides a context and commentary on aspects of Roosevelt's life other than hunting.

3877 Roosevelt, Theodore   **1858-1919**
Letters. Selected and edited by Elting E. Morison, et al. Cambridge, Massachusetts: Harvard University Press, 1951-54. 8v. Index.

A record of the interplay of a remarkable personality and politics while he was Governor of New York and U.S. President. Volume I, The Years of Preparation, 1868-1898; Volume II, The Years of Preparation, 1898-1900; Volume III, The Square Deal, 1901-1903; Vol. IV, The Square Deal, 1903-1905; Vol. V, The Big Stick, 1905-1907; Vol. VI, The Big Stick, 1907-1909; Vol. VII, The Days of Armageddon, 1909-1914; Vol. VIII, The Days of Armageddon, 1914-1919.

3878 Roosevelt, Theodore   **1858-1919**
Letters to Kermit from Theodore Roosevelt, 1902-1908. Edited with introduction by Will Irwin. New York: Charles Scribner's Sons, 1946. 296 p. Index.
The first complete collection of over two hundred letters from Roosevelt to his son, Kermit, all written during Roosevelt's presidency, forming "a study almost unique in the relations between an understanding father and a growing son." (Irwin)

3879 Roosevelt, Theodore   **1858-1919**
Selections from the correspondence of Theodore Roosevelt and Henry Cabot Lodge, 1884-1918. Edited by Henry Cabot Lodge and Charles F. Redmond. New York: Da Capo Press, 1971. (New York: Charles Scribner's Sons, 1925) 72 p. Index.
Letters selected from the 34-year correspondence between two men of public affairs showing their wide-ranging interests and activities in common. Their letters cover general topics, their families and friends, literature and life of the times, politics and international affairs.

3880 Roosevelt, Theodore   **1858-1919**
Theodore Roosevelt treasury: a self-portrait from his writings. Compiled with an introduction by Hermann Hagedorn. New York: G.P. Putnam's Sons, 1957. 342 p.
A remarkable selection from many kinds of his writing reveals the private as well as the public man, the historian, the frontiersman, the statesman, in a vigorous, perceptive style.

3881 Roosevelt, Theodore   **1858-1919**
Theodore Roosevelt's letters to his children. Edited by Joseph Bocklin Bishop. Prologue and epilogue by Elting E. Morison. Illustrated. New York: New American Library, 1964. 159 p.
President Roosevelt offers bully exhortations and fatherly advice to his six children, 1898-1911: "I always believe in going hard at everything; whether it is Latin . . . or football, but . . . it is never worthwhile to absolutely exhaust one's self or to take big chances unless for an adequate object." His descriptions of pets, horses, family outings, and holidays show a loving, exuberant parent and an idyllic world of childhood.

3882 *Root, Esther Sayles
Over Periscope Pond; letters from 2 American girls in Paris, Oct. 1916-Jan. 1918. And Marjorie Crocker. Boston; Houghton Mifflin Co., 1918. 295 p.
These two American girls first met in Paris, where they had volunteered to do relief work among the refugees during World War I. Their letters to their families shine with youthful good spirits despite the horrors of wartime.

3883 Root, George Frederick   **1820-1895**
The story of a musical life; an autobiography. New York: Da Capo Press, 1970. (Cincinnati: The John Church Co., 1891) 256 p.
Root's life was indeed dedicated to music: he played many different instruments, including flute, piano, and organ; sang in and directed choirs; taught music classes; wrote books; and composed hymns, war and patriotic songs including "Just before the battle, Mother" and "Tramp, tramp, tramp, the boys are marching." An appendix lists his compositions and includes the words and music for several of his songs.

3884 Roper, Daniel Calhoun   **1867-1943**
Fifty years of public life. In collaboration with Frank H. Lovette. New York: Greenwood Press, 1968. (Durham, North Carolina: Duke University Press, 1941) 422 p. Index.
Roper's fascinating account of his varied career covers his work as a South Carolina state legislator, U.S. Assistant Postmaster General, Commissioner of Internal Revenue, Minister to Canada, and Secretary of Commerce, 1933-1938. Roper's public service, like his book, is characterized by a detailed understanding of significant issues, practical administrative ability, a liking of people, and a sense of humor. This book offers an especially valuable understanding of the Wilson and Franklin Roosevelt administrations.

3885 Rorem, Ned   **1923-**
Critical affairs; a composer's journal. New York: George Braziller, 1970. 216 p. Index.
Rorem's music neither scorns nor adheres to a particular school of experimental music, but seeks to express his ideas, as these essays, written during 1968 and 1969, express his thoughts in words.

3886 Rose, Alexander   **1901-**
Memoirs of a heterosexual. New York: Simon & Schuster, 1968. (1967) 286 p.

Amusing anecdotes of writer-actor Rose who has appeared on TV and in movies, been a court-reporter and an inventor, as well as an author of scripts and humorous books.

3887 Rose, Billy 1899-1966
Wine, women and words. Illustrated by Salvador Dali. New York: Simon and Schuster, 1948. 295 p.
Broadway producer and journalist describes show business experience; includes many of his syndicated columns.

3888 Rose, Donald Frank 1890-1964
Full house. Philadelphia: J.B. Lippincott Co., 1951. 256 p.
A journalist writes of lively family experience with his wife and ten children, with amusing anecdotes of their activities, management, and the inevitable complexities of life in a large family. His family provided material for several thousand columns he wrote for the Philadelphia *Evening Ledger* and *Bulletin*.

3889 *Rose, Helen
Just make them beautiful: the many worlds of a designing woman. Foreword by Sidney Sheldon. Illustrated. Santa Monica, California: Dennis-Landman, 1976. 186 p.
Costume designer to some of the most beautiful women in the world, Helen Rose discusses the trials and tribulations of creating, sewing, and repairing illusions in cloth. She later became an exclusive dress designer to clients such as Princess Grace of Monaco and Nancy Reagan.

3890 Rose, Peter Edward 1941-
Charlie Hustle. With Bob Hertzel. Englewood Cliffs, New Jersey: Prentice-Hall, 1975. 227 p.
A day-by-day account of his 1974 baseball season with the Cincinnati Reds by the controversial Rose. He includes flashbacks of his preceding eleven years in the big leagues and outspoken assessments of other players and the game.

3891 Rose, Peter Edward 1941-
Pete Rose: my life in baseball. Illustrated. Garden City, New York: Doubleday and Co., Inc., 1979. 134 p. Index.
Rose's book provides an insider's view of "America's favorite pastime" for children who aspire to a career in major-league baseball. One of the greatest hitters of all time, he highlights his long career with the Cincinnati Reds.

3892 Rose, Stuart 1899-1975
There's a fox in the spinney; memories of fox-hunting, racing, and publishing. Garden City, New York: Doubleday & Co., Inc., 1967. 328 p.
The two strong attractions of his life, horses and writers, furnish the basis for Rose's book. He began his acquaintance with horses as a cavalry recruit at age sixteen and continues his story through episodes of steeplechase riding, fox hunting, editing, and publishing ventures.

3893 Rosen, Samuel 1897-
The autobiography of Dr. Samuel Rosen. New York: Alfred A. Knopf, 1973. 268 p.
After operating as an otologist for many years, Rosen discovered a new method, stapes surgery, which restored hearing to patients suffering from osteosclerosis. Afterwards, he operated on hundreds of patients at Mount Sinai Hospital and traveled internationally to teach his method to other surgeons. His book includes a great deal of technical information while revealing his genuine commitment to medicine and to humanity.

3894 Rosenbach, Abraham Simon Wolf 1876-1952
The unpublished memoirs. London: John Castle, 1924. (New York: M. Kennerley, 1917) 151 p.
A bibliophile relates in third person many of his experiences as a book collector and dealer in this volume and two others, *Books and Bidders* and *A Book Hunter's Holiday*. He was known as the world's foremost dealer and collector of rare books and manuscripts and spent a lifetime studying, writing about, buying, selling, and loving books.

3895 *Rosenberg, Ethel (Greenglass) 1915-1953
Death house letters of Ethel and Julius Rosenberg. New York: Jero Publishing Co., 1953. 148 p.
A collection of letters to and from Ethel Rosenberg during her imprisonment at Sing Sing, after she and her husband were convicted for treason. The letters record their thoughts, feelings, and protestations of innocence during their final days.

3896 Rosenberg, James Naumberg 1874-1970
Painter's self-portrait. Edited with introduction by Milton S. Fox. Illustrated. New York: Crown Publishers, Inc., 1958. 203 p.
Prominent as an artist, humanitarian, and promoter of American art, he writes of giving up his law practice, of his belief in the ability of art to communicate, of the significance of his landscape painting as a means of escape from an embittered world.

3897 Rosenberg, Julius
see *Rosenberg, Ethel (Greenglass)

3898 Rosenblatt, Samuel 1902-
The days of my years: an autobiography. Illustrated. New York: Ktav Publishing House, 1976. 207 p.
Rosenblatt's autobiography depicts the typical life of a devout German-Jewish immigrant. His values of education, culture, a close family life, Zionism, and philanthropy to Jewish organizations are reflected in his career as an Orthodox Rabbi in Trenton and Baltimore and in his numerous trips to Israel and publications about Judaism.

3899 Rosenfield, Joe, Jr. 1900-
The happiest man in the world. Garden City, New York: Doubleday and Co., 1955. 292 p.
For thirty years Rosenfield, then a salesman of newspaper advertising in Memphis and New Orleans, was an alcoholic, gambler, and womanizer, despite the love of his wife, Dollie. Life on Skid Row drove him to Alcoholics Anonymous and, sober thereafter, he broadcast "Happiness Exchange," a philanthropic New York radio program that relieved the misery of thousands of unfortunates through collecting and distributing donations of money, goods, and services.

3900 *Rosenthal, Jean 1912-1969
Magic of light; the craft and career of Jean Rosenthal, pioneer in lighting for the modern stage. And Lael Wertenbaker. Illustrated by Marion Kinsella. Boston: Little, Brown in assoc. with Theatre Arts Books, 1972. 256 p. Index.
A pioneer in the art and craft of lighting design, she writes of her upbringing in a strong-willed family and her education in the theater. The bulk of the book, however, is devoted to her development of lighting techniques for plays, musicals, operas, and dance. Rosenthal died before the completion of the book; her collaborator carried on using notes from interviews.

3901 Rosenthal, Leonard 1872-1955
Pearl and I. New York: Vantage Press, 1955. 223 p.
Written in his eighties, his book conveys a vigorous enthusiasm for life as he describes his career as a multimillionaire in the pearl business.

3902 Roskolenko, Harry 1907-
Time that was then; the lower East Side, 1900-1914; an intimate chronicle. New York: The Dial Press, 1971. 218 p.
The teeming life of the New York's lower East Side during the early twentieth century furnishes the colorful background for the story of the author's Russian-Jewish immigrant family. It was a time of poverty, of hard work, and mutual support within the family. He writes of the Clockmakers' Strike of 1910, of the Yiddish Press, the Yiddish Theatre, of rabbis and doctors, of revolutionaries and politicians.

3903 Ross, Albion 1906-
Journey of an American. Indianapolis: The Bobbs-Merrill Co., Inc., 1957. 346 p.
An international journalist writes of his travel and his continued quest for life's meaning in troubled times.

3904 Ross, Alexander Milton 1832-1897
Recollections and experience of an abolitionist, from 1855-1865. New foreword by Donald Franklin Joyce. Northbrook, Illinois: Metro Books, 1972. (Toronto: Rowsell and Hutchinson, 1875) 224 p.
An active Canadian abolitionist, Dr. Ross traveled to the South aiding slaves in escaping to freedom in Canada. He arranged secret meetings, drilled groups of determined slaves on routes and methods of travel, equipped them with food, money, and pistols, and during the Civil War watched over and exposed secret Confederate activities in Canada.

3905 Ross, Barney 1909-1967
No man stands alone: the true story of Barney Ross. And Martin Abramson. Foreword by Eddie Cantor. Philadelphia: J.B. Lippincott Co., 1957. 256 p.
Well-known as a prize fighter in the Twenties, he stayed in the headlines because of his Marine service in World War II, his drug addiction, divorce and remarriage. His story moves from the depths of Chicago slum life to fame as a boxer to a painful slump as an addict and then to a resolution of many of his problems.

3906 *Rostenberg, Leona
Old and rare: thirty years in the book business. And Madeleine B. Stern. New York: Abner Schram, 1947. 234 p. Index.
A memoir of years in the rare-book trade enlivened by fascinating searchs and detection, guided by wide knowledge and expertise, and highlighted by devotion to and love of books.

3907 *Roth, Lillian 1910-1980
Beyond my reach. New York: Frederick Fell, Inc., Publishers, 1958. 317 p.

In her second book she tells of the long and difficult years between overcoming alcoholism and her comeback as a singer.

3908 *Roth, Lillian   **1910-1980**
I'll cry tomorrow. New York: Frederick Fell, Inc., Publishers, 1954. 347 p.
An actress who worked primarily in New York and Hollywood describes her experience as a child actor and her later career, but the main focus is her struggle against alcoholism and mental illness.

3909 *Rothstein, Margaret   **1936-**
And other foolish questions I have answered. Ann Arbor, Michigan: Arbor Publications, 1979. 212 p.
With insight, compassion, and humor Rothstein narrates the story of her repeated initiation into teaching for a decade after her graduation from the University of Michigan. She taught high school English, sometimes as a substitute, sometimes part-time, sometimes on a temporary basis to accommodate marriage and motherhood, until she finally attained a permanent position. She is sensitive to the mores, morals, and problems of contemporary teenagers, many of whom are indifferent to school.

3910 Routh, Eugene Coke   **b.1874**
Adventures in Christian journalism. Nashville, Tennessee: Broadman Press, 1951. 92 p.
An editor for the *Baptist Standard* (Texas) and the *Baptist Messenger* (Oklahoma) depicts his work as a missionary in journalism.

3911 Rovere, Richard Halworth   **1915-1979**
Arrivals and departures: a journalist's memoirs. New York: Macmillan, 1976. 274 p.
A journalist has compiled his autobiography from previously published articles about such matters as his innocent flirtation with communism in the 1930's and his subsequent meeting with Senator Joseph McCarthy, whose investigation he found inane. Rovere's portraits of H.W. Ross, *The New Yorker* editor for whom he worked in the 1940's, Walter Lippmann, and John Gunther provide a human focus for the decades of World War II, the Cold War, and the Korean War.

3912 Rowe, Basil Lee   **1896-1973**
Under my wings. Indianapolis: The Bobbs-Merrill Co., Inc., 1956. 256 p.
He started learning how to fly in 1914 and by 1955 had made a Ripley's record by logging 35,000 air hours. The rugged narrative tells of his world-wide adventures in a variety of flying jobs during the early years of aviation.

3913 *Rowlandson, Mary (White)   **1635?-1678**
The narrative of the captivity and restoration of Mrs. Mary Rowlandson: first printed in 1682 at Cambridge, Mass. & London, England, whereunto are annexed a map of her removes & biographical & historical notes. The National Bicentennial ed. (6th ed., 2nd Lancaster ed.). Lancaster, Massachusetts: Lancaster Bicentennial Comm., 1975. (Cambridge, 1682) 96 p.
Captured by the Indians at Lancaster, Massachusetts, in 1675, she was forced to live with them until redeemed for twenty pounds. Her narrative describes vividly the battle, the journeys with her capturers through the wilderness, and her suffering.

3914 *Royall, Anne Newport   **1769-1854**
Letters from Alabama: 1817-1822. Introduction and notes by Lucille Griffith. Southern Historical Publication, No. 14. University: University of Alabama Press, 1969. 292 p. Index.
In eighteenth-century novelistic style replete with scenes, dialogues, and sotto-voce asides, a widow writes of how she traveled in 1817 from Monroe County, Virginia (now West Virginia), to Huntsville, then a frontier town in Alabama territory, where she stayed until July 1923. During this time she wrote fifty letters to "Matt," a young lawyer, commenting perceptively on the geography, manners, and mores of the areas through which she traveled. As a woman in some difficulty herself (her deceased husband's relatives were trying to disinherit her), she is particularly sensitive to the problems of women.

3915 Royce, Josiah   **1855-1916**
The letters of Josiah Royce. Edited with introduction by John Clendenning. Chicago: The University of Chicago Press, 1970. 696 p. Index.
Letters selected "for the light they shed on Royce's life, his character, his intellectual development, and on the period in which he lived." Royce was a philosopher who represented post-Kantian idealism and sought a bond between the individual and the social order.

3916 Royster, Robert Stuart   **1948-1973**
Unquiet pilgrimage: the journal of Robert Stewart Royster. Foreword by Paul S. Rees. Preface by Powell & Helene Royster. Introduction by Helene S. Royster. Afterword. Illustrated. Louisville, Kentucky: Operation Appreciation, 1979. 403 p.
The diary covers Royster's years spent among the Colombian Indians, 1969-1973. He was a profoundly Christian anthropology student who functioned as the Indians' helper as well as analyst of their culture. He

died in 1973 from a snakebite as he was transporting some sick Indian children to obtain medical care; his parents edited (and censored) this detailed diary as a memorial tribute.

3917 Ruark, Robert Chester   **1915-1965**
Old man and the boy. Illustrated by Walter Dower. New York: Henry Holt and Co., 1957. 303 p.
The story of his boyhood in rural North Carolina and his relationship with his grandfather, by an author-journalist.

3918 Ruark, Robert Chester   **1915-1965**
The old man's boy grows older. New York: Holt, Rinehart and Winston, 1961. (1957) 302 p.
More about his unusual grandfather's influence on his life and values during his boyhood and adult years.

3919 *Rubens, Doris
Bread and rice. Foreword by Carlos P. Romulo. New York: Thurston Macauley Associates, 1947. 235 p.
A journalist caught in the Philippines when the Japanese took over describes her capture, her escape to the mountains where she and her husband survived for over a year, and their recapture and internment by the Japanese for another eighteen months. Excellent detail and narrative.

3920 Rubenstein, Arthur   **1886-**
My many years. New York: Alfred A. Knopf, 1980. 626 p. Index.
His second volume, like *My Young Years*, is an astonishing record of the pianist's long and active life. This one begins after World War I and includes tales of his world tours, American citizenship, famous personalities he has known and loved, experience he has enjoyed, all described with wit, style, and vitality.

3921 Rubenstein, Arthur   **1886-**
My young years. Illustrated. New York: Alfred A. Knopf, 1973. 478 p. Index.
Beginning with his childhood in Poland, he writes of "the struggles, the mistakes, the adventures, and of the miraculous beauty and happiness" of his first thirty years. He describes many of the great artists who were his contemporaries through the years of World War I which he spent in England.

3922 Rubin, Jerry   **1938-**
Growing (up) at thirty-seven. New York: M. Evans and Co., Inc., 1976. 208 p.
Rubin, a Sixties radical yippie leader, writes of trying various popular ideas and therapies, from est to vegetarianism to acupuncture, in search of maturity and the New Consciousness.

3923 Rubin, Theodore Isaac   **1923-**
Emergency room diary. New York: Grosset & Dunlap, 1972. 193 p.
The journal of an intern's four-months' duty in the E.R. of a large city hospital. Amid the stream of patients were dramatic, curious, tragic, and even funny events which contributed to his education, his self-esteem, his frustrations, his triumphs.

3924 *Rubinstein, Helena   **1870?-1964**
My life for beauty. Simon and Schuster: New York, 1965. 251 p.
An eventful and successful long life is the subject of the first half of this book. At age 94 Rubenstein wrote this story of her rise in the beauty industry to head a world-wide cosmetic house, her position as a multimillionairess, international hostess, and friend and patroness of artists and writers. The second part of the book comprises a manual of beauty care and secrets.

3925 Ruby, Bob   **1938-**
Ruby in the rough. Illustrated. Gretna, Louisiana: Pelican Publishing Co., 1976. 179 p.
Ruby describes his rough-and-tumble childhood as the son of an ailing mother and traveling-salesman father. In 1959 Ruby tried to crack Broadway as a member of a singing trio, but he was drafted and sent to Germany during the Cold War. Thereafter, he became a talk show radio announcer. He quotes some of his scripts, which range from humorous to inane and include his favorite with Ted Hinton, the Texas lawman who ambushed Bonnie and Clyde.

3926 Runyon, Damon, Jr.   **1918-1968**
Father's footsteps. New York: Random House, 1953. 181 p.
This book is a combination biography-autobiography. Damon Runyon, Jr., a journalist in New York, writes about growing up and his relationship with his famous father, Damon Runyon. The book contains letters Damon Runyon wrote to his son.

3927 Rush, Benjamin   **1745-1813**
Autobiography of Benjamin Rush: his "travels through life" together with his *Commonplace Book* for 1789-1813. Edited with introduction by George W. Corner. Memoirs of the American Philosophical Society, Vol.

25. Westport, Connecticut: Greenwood Press, 1970. (Princeton: Princeton University Press, 1948) 399 p. Index.

Originally written only for his family, his book describes his early life, medical training, career as a practicing physician and teacher of medicine in Philadelphia, and the context of the Declaration of Independence, which he signed.

3928 Rush, Benjamin   **1745-1813**
Letters of Benjamin Rush. Edited by L.H. Butterfield. American Philosophical Society Memoirs, Vol. 30, pts. 1-2. Princeton: Princeton University Press for The American Philosophical Society, 1951. 2v. Index.

In over 650 letters to the first five American presidents, to leaders in science and philosophy both American and European, and to his family, a prominent eighteenth-century physician is observant and honest about his wide-ranging interests.

3929 Rush, Benjamin   **1745-1813**
My dearest Julia: the love-letters of Dr. Benjamin Rush to Julia Stockton. Illustrated. New York: Neale Watson Academic Publications, in association with the Philip H. & A.S.W. Rosenbach Foundation, Philadelphia, 1979. 62 p.

These eighteen charming letters from physician Rush to his sixteen-year-old fiancée, Julia Stockton, were written between October 25, 1975, and January 5, 1776, just before their marriage. Rush commends the "conjugal felicity" of their respective parents and devises a "matrimonial thermometer." Although he is "not insensible" to her physical charms, he is enamored, he says, by her pure mind, gentle disposition, strength of understanding, and sanctity of principles.

3930 Rusk, Claude Ewing   **1871-1931**
Tales of a Western mountaineer: a record of mountain experiences on the Pacific Coast. Portrait of C.E. Rusk by Darryl Lloyd. Illustrated. Seattle: The Mountaineers, 1978. (Cambridge, Massachusetts: Houghton Mifflin, 1924) 309 p.

Rusk, a mountaineer's mountaineer, climbed many mountains in Washington and Oregon from about 1890 until his death from heart disease caused by overexposure during an aborted climb. He describes the majestic terrain and intermingles tales of adventure (including various rescues and close calls) with accounts of the various climbs and trails and observations on flora, fauna, astronomy, and geology.

3931 Rusk, Howard Archibald   **1901-**
A world to care for: the autobiography of Howard A. Rusk, M.D. New York: Random House, 1972. 307 p.

In a half century of medical practice, Dr. Rusk has been especially interested in helping to rehabilitate those patients with paralysis or orthopedic disabilities—paraplegics, stroke victims, polio patients, amputees. The Institute of Rehabilitation Medicine and World Rehabilitation Fund have helped countless patients to overcome their disabilities and get back into life.

3932 *Ruskay, Sophie   **b.1887**
Horse cars and cobblestones. Illustrated by Cecil B. Ruskay. New York: The Beechurst Press, 1948. 240 p.

Her parents came to New York from Russia and started a clothing factory. Her book recalls their life as a middle-class immigrant family at the turn of the century, emphasizing a child's view of school days, family rules and recreation, art and dancing lessons, the advent of the bicycle.

3933 Russ, Witten Booth   **b.1874**
A doctor looks at life. Revised and enlarged edition. San Antonio, Texas: The Naylor Company, 1961. (1952) 235 p.

A curious collection of essays and letters which depict the ultra-conservative medical and political philosophy of a prominent surgeon in San Antonio.

3934 Russell, Elbert   **1871-1951**
Elbert Russell, Quaker: an autobiography. Jackson, Tennessee: Friendly Press, 1956. 376 p.

Based in part on his diaries and correspondence, this book by a professor of religion recalls his boyhood in the Midwest and his long, fulfilling career, including his position as Dean of the Duke University Divinity School (1928-41).

3935 Russell, Fred   **1906-**
Bury me in an old press box: good times and life of a sportswriter. Illustrated. New York: A.S. Barnes, 1957. 235 p. Index.

Russell believes that "happiness is found most readily in sport"; from this perspective he writes joyously about his lifelong career as a sportswriter for the Nashville *Banner*. He recollects notable players and games of football, baseball, golf, and the Kentucky Derby, with engaging anecdotes about other notable sportswriters, including Red Smith and Damon Runyon.

3936 Russell, Harold   **1914-**
Victory in my hands. With Victor Rosen. New York: Creative Age Press, Inc., 1949. 280 p.

In his training as a paratrooper, Russell's hands were blown off in a demolition practice. His book describes the agony of mental and physical adjustment, which for him led to an amazing recovery. In 1946 he received an Academy Award as best supporting actor for his role as a double amputee in *The Best Years of Our Lives*.

3937 *Russell, Rosalind   **1913-1976**
Life is a banquet. With Cris Chase. New York: Ace Books, 1979. (New York: Random House, 1977) 260 p. Index.

A witty, entertaining, forthright account of Russell's effervescent career as an actress on stage and screen, vignettes of many likeable people she has known through her work, and a loving commentary on her marriage (since 1941) to press agent Freddie Brisson. *The Women* and *Auntie Mame* are among her favorite productions.

3938 Russell, William Felton   **1934-**
Go up for glory. As told to William McSweeny. New York: Coward-McCann, Inc., 1966. 224 p.

The basketball success story of Bill Russell, who overcame discrimination to become a star of the National Champion Boston Celtics. His lifetime NBA records are listed as well as the honors he has won, but one of his primary purposes in writing is to plead for human dignity and human rights.

3939 Russell, William Felton   **1934-**
Second wind: the memoirs of an opinionated man. With Taylor Branch. New York: Random House, Inc., 1979. 265 p.

Russell's memoirs are lively, witty, and pull no punches. His personality resembles that of his grandfather, the "Old Man," and his father, "Mister Charlie," whom he loved and admired while growing up in Louisiana and Oakland, California. At the University of San Francisco he was a basketball star distinguished on and off the courts for skill, aggressiveness, and wit. He exhibited these talents for nearly two decades as a player for the Boston Celtics and manager of the Seattle Supersonics, and in his fight for civil rights.

3940 Ruth, George Herman (Babe Ruth)   **1895-1948**
Babe Ruth story as told to Bob Considine. New York: E.P. Dutton & Co., Inc., 1948. 250 p.

Baseball was his life, and his book makes that very clear, beginning with his first move directly into the major leagues, his long career with the New York Yankees, his ups and downs as the great home-run king of the game.

3941 Ruthven, Alexander Grant   **1882-1971**
Naturalist in two worlds: random recollections of a university president. Ann Arbor: University of Michigan Press, 1963. 162 p.

Recollections of experiences which influenced his thinking as President of the University of Michigan emphasize his undergraduate education, his career as a prominent zoologist and curator of the University Museum in Ann Arbor.

3942 Ryan, Cornelius John   **1920-1974**
A private battle. With Kathryn Morgan Ryan. New York: Simon & Schuster, 1979. 448 p.

Ryan's account of his battle against cancer is combined with thoughts and diary entries by his wife. From July, 1970, when Ryan first learned he had cancer, until November 1974, when he died, the author kept a detailed account of the progress of the disease and attempted cures, while fighting against it.

3943 Ryan, Nolan   **1947-**
The other game. And Bill Libby. Illustrated. Waco, Texas: Word Books, 1977. 216 p.

Major-league pitcher Ryan covers the high and low points of his career, frequently comparing the game of baseball to "the game of life." A brief section written by wife Ruth precedes each chapter, providing domestic insights into Ryan's career. Because arm and leg injuries put an end to pitching, Ryan ends the book uncertain of his future.

3944 Sacco, Nicola   **1891-1927**
The letters of Sacco and Vanzetti. Edited by Marion Denman Frankfurter and Gardner Jackson. New York: Octagon Books, 1971. (New York: The Viking Press, 1928) 414 p. Index.

This collection includes a portion of the English letters written during the seven years of their imprisonment in Massachusetts. The letters reflect the depth of their reliance on the doctrine of anarchy and the consistency of their belief that what happened to them occurred only because they were anarchists. Their long struggle for freedom culminated in their execution although they maintained to the end that they were innocent of crime.

3945 Sachs, Ernest   **1879-1958**
Fifty years of neurosurgery: a personal story. New York: Vantage Press, 1958. 186 p. Index.

Dr. Sachs was a pioneer in the field of neurosurgery, largely at the Washington University Medical School in St. Louis where he was chief of neurosurgery until he retired at seventy, whereupon he became a research fellow in physiology at Yale. Sachs was a prolific author of medical papers and a world traveler.

3946 Sackheim, Maxwell B.   **1890-**
My first 65 years in advertising. Blue Ridge Summit, Pennsylvania: Tab Books, 1975. (Englewood Cliffs, New Jersey: Prentice-Hall, 1970) 209 p.

One of the giants of mail-order, direct-response advertising, Sackheim writes of his beginnings and later career as well as demonstrating how to write ads. He was one of the founders of Book-of-the-Month Club (with sales totaling over a billion volumes), worked on Literary Guild, Sears Roebuck, record clubs, American Express Credit Cards, and numerous other advertising campaigns.

3947 Sadler, Barry   **1940?-**
I'm a lucky one. With Tom Mahoney. New York: The Macmillan Co., 1967. 191 p.

The composer of "The Ballad of the Green Berets" and other songs writes of his nine-year career, much of it spent as a member of the Special Forces, known as the Green Berets, in Vietnam. For the children of men who did not come back from Vietnam, he established a foundation to help with their college education.

3948 Sadler, Robert   **1911-**
The emancipation of Robert Sadler. Minneapolis: Bethany Fellowship, Inc., 1975. 254 p.

In 1916 his widowed father sold him and two of his sisters as slaves. When he was fourteen he ran away to Greenville, North Carolina, not knowing how to read, write, or eat with utensils. After working as a laborer, he finally became a minister and evangelist in Minneapolis.

3949 *Sagsam, Angela, pseud.
see *Muirhead, Sara Alyne Guynes

3950 Sahl, Mort   **1927-**
Heartland. New York: Harcourt Brace Jovanovich, 1976. 158 p.

Satiric, intellectual comedian writes a chaotic account of his life as an entertainer, intermingled with his social and political views. He is particularly outraged by the Women's Movement and the official interpretation of John Kennedy's assassination. He sees himself as a "professional nonconformist" deliberately at odds with most people, movements, issues.

3951 *St. Denis, Ruth   **1878-1968**
An unfinished life: an autobiography. Brooklyn: A Dance Horizons Republication, 1969. (New York: Harper, 1939) 391 p.

Her life as dancer and the spiritual philosophies that shaped her dance. Of major significance were her conversion to Christian Science, a psychic identification with the Orient, and her marriage to Ted Shawn, a dancer many years her junior who with her formed the Denishawn dance company.

3952 *St. Johns, Adela (Rogers)   **1894-**
Final verdict. Garden City, New York: Doubleday and Co., Inc., 1962. 512 p.

Recollections of her childhood emphasize her father, a notable trial lawyer who defended Clarence Darrow. As a teenager she followed her father into courtrooms, jails, funeral parlors, and whorehouses, living essentially in a man's world.

3953 *St. Johns, Adela (Rogers)   **1894-**
Honeycomb. Illustrated. Garden City, New York: Doubleday & Co., 1969. 598 p.

A journalist and writer of short stories and novels, many for women's magazines, tells of her life, marriages, children, and friends, including William Randolph Hearst and Huey Long.

3954 *St. Johns, Adela (Rogers)   **1894-**
Love, laughter and tears: my Hollywood story. Illustrated. Garden City, New York: Doubleday & Co., Inc., 1978. 342 p.

Through anecdotes of famous friends and celebrities, she writes of her life in the golden days of Hollywood.

3955 *St. Johns, Adela (Rogers)   **1894-**
Some are born great. Garden City, New York: Doubleday & Co., Inc., 1974. 297 p.

In her book about great American women, she has chosen women who had gallantry—"high-spirited defiance in the face of danger." She has known most of these women personally and relates first-hand impressions and incidents revealing something of her own life as well.

3956 Sakall, S.Z. (Eugene Gero)   **1890-1955**
The story of Cuddles: my life under the Emperor Francis Joseph, Adolf Hitler, and the Warner Brothers. Translated by Paul Tabori. London: Cassell & Co., Ltd., 1954. 231 p.

Sakall writes humorously of his life as a comic actor. The orphaned son of a Budapest tombstone maker, Sakall was reared by his Aunt Emma,

who appreciated his humor and encouraged his burgeoning career as a writer of comic routines and as a comedian. He performed throughout Europe and made a number of movies before emigrating to the United States in 1938 to act in Hollywood films.

3957 Salinger, Pierre Emil   **1925-**
With Kennedy. Garden City, New York: Doubleday & Co., Inc., 1966. 391 p. Index.

After joining Robert Kennedy's staff in 1957 as an investigator for the Rackets Committee, working on the Teamsters' Union affairs, Salinger became John Kennedy's press secretary in 1959 and worked with him during the election campaign and presidency. He served under Johnson during the transition period, filled the Senate seat of California Senator Clair Engle briefly, and then was defeated in the next election. He argues strongly for better communications between the press and the government.

3958 Salisbury, DeWitt Clinton   **1843-1915**
Pages from the diaries of DeWitt Clinton Salisbury, 19th century Wisconsin citizen and Civil War soldier. Selected with comments by Mildred Hansen Osgood. Wauwatosa, Wisconsin: Mildred H. Osgood, 1974. 120 p.

In his diaries describing life in mid-nineteenth-century Wisconsin, Salisbury writes of his education, the Civil War and his part in it, and his postwar return to farming and family life. Continuity between diary excerpts is provided by his granddaughter's commentary.

3959 Salisbury, Harrison Evans   **1908-**
Moscow journal: the end of Stalin. Chicago: The University of Chicago Press, 1961. 450 p. Index.

A reporter's journal and correspondence (1949-1953) record the worst years of the Cold War in Moscow as experienced by a prize-winning New York *Times* correspondent.

3960 Salsbury, Clarence Grant   **b.1886**
Salsbury story; a medical missionary's lifetime of public service. With Paul Hughes. Illustrated. Tucson: University of Tucson, 1969. 277 p.

With his wife and nurse, Cora, he spent ten years as a medical missionary in China; 23 years as superintendent and medical director of Garado Mission in the Navajo country of Arizona; and eleven years as head of the Arizona State Health Department. His is the story of a kindly and devoted humanitarian.

3961 Saltonstall, Leverett   **1892-**
Salty; recollections of a Yankee in politics. As told to Edward Weeks. Boston, Massachusetts: Boston Globe, 1976. 218 p.

From a long line of politicians and "Yankee Democrats," Saltonstall became a lawyer and moved into public office through the famous Boston "machine politics" of the Twenties. In his rise from alderman to state senator, Governor of Massachusetts, and finally U.S. Senator, Saltonstall worked with politicians and presidents and, as chairman of the Senate Armed Services Committee in the Fifties, was involved in controversies over the CIA and the censure of Senator McCarthy.

3962 Samish, Arthur H.   **1897-1974**
The secret boss of California; the life and high times of Art Samish. And Bob Thomas. New York: Crown Publishers, Inc., 1971. 192 p. Index.

Although he never held elective office, Samish controlled a large bloc of votes in the California state legislature, was instrumental in electing the mayor of San Francisco, and had the power to make or break governors. Eventually he was convicted of income-tax evasion, imprisoned, and gave up politics.

3963 Sampey, John Richard   **1863-1946**
Memoirs. Nashville, Tennessee: Broadman Press, 1947. 286 p.

For 67 years a Baptist preacher, professor of theology, and the President of Southern Baptist Theological Seminary: a record of his spiritual life's work.

3964 Samuel, Maurice   **1895-1972**
Little did I know: recollections and reflections. New York: Alfred A. Knopf, 1963. 326 p.

Born in Rumania and educated in England, he spent his adult life traveling and lecturing on Jewish values and relations between Jewish and Christian worlds. He served in the American Army during World War I and on the Morgenthau Pogrom Investigation Commission to Poland in 1919.

3965 Samuel, Maurice   **1895-1972**
Words of Maurice Samuel: selected writings. Edited with introduction by Milton Hindus. Foreword by Cynthia Ozick. Philadelphia: Jewish Publishing Society of America, 1977. 445 p.

This compilation of extracts from Samuel's voluminous writings offers a polemicist's view of what it means to be Jewish in a world oriented to Gentiles, accompanied by an autobiographical account of his Rumanian background, English education, and service in the U.S. Army during World War I.

3966 Samuels, Samuel   **1823-1908**
From the forecastle to the cabin. New York: MacDonald & Janes, 1974.
(New York: Harper & Brothers, 1887) 308 p.
    Captivated by romantic ideas of life at sea, Samuels ran away from
home at eleven years and signed on as cook and cabin boy. The story of
his seafaring life and rise to captaincy is full of adventure, mutinies,
storms, pirates, hair-breath escapes, and excitement of all sorts.

3967 Samuels, Thomas W.   **b.1886**
Lawyer in action. Hicksville, New York: Exposition Press, 1975. 224 p.
    These unconnected episodes and cases reflect the author's views and
philosophy of law and justice gained in over sixty years of active practice.

3968 Sanborn, Franklin Benjamin   **1831-1917**
Recollections of seventy years. Illustrated. Lives and Letters/American
Writers Series. Detroit: Gale Research Co., 1967. (Boston: Richard G.
Badger Gorham Press, 1909) 2v. Index.
    After discussing his rural childhood and adolescence in Hampton Falls,
New Hampshire, Sanborn focuses on his increasing involvement in poli-
tics and the abolitionist movement, particularly as it affected politics in
Kansas Territory. He devotes half of Volume I to the abolitionist activities
of John Brown, which culminated in the raid on Harper's Ferry, Virginia,
in 1858. Sanborn championed the man and his cause in national publications he edited.

3969 *Sanborn, Katherine Abbott   **1839-1917**
A truthful woman in Southern California. New York: D. Appleton and
Co., 1893. 192 p.
    A popular, widely read writer, she wrote this book recording her travel
by train to the West Coast. She gives advice for the traveller and observations on life style and customs at a time when the West was still a
mysterious frontier to the Eastern reader.

3970 Sandburg, Carl   **1878-1967**
Always the young strangers. New York: Harcourt, Brace and Co., 1953.
445 p. Index.
    An account of daily life in the home of his Swedish immigrant parents
in Galesburg, Illinois, which reveals the development of his faith in American tradition.

3971 Sandburg, Carl   **1878-1967**
Letters of Carl Sandburg. Edited by Herbert Mitgang. New York:
Harcourt, Brace & World, Inc., 1968. 577 p. Index.
    Letters from 1898 to 1963 tell the life story of this great poet: his
dreams and achievements, his knowledge of America and Americans, his
literary and other friendships, his political opinions.

3972 Sandburg, Carl   **1878-1967**
Prairie-town boy. New York: Harcourt, Brace and Co., 1952. 179 p.
    A poet reminisces about growing up in a small town in Illinois. The
book is taken from a larger work, *Always the Young Stranger,* and is
directed toward a young audience.

3973 Sanders, George   **1906-1972**
Memoirs of a professional cad. New York: G.P. Putnam's Sons, 1960.
192 p.
    Writing with the droll, sardonic humor that characterized him on the
screen, he recalls twenty-five years in the movies. His conclusion: "In the
face of hostility and opposition that would have staggered lesser men we
have succeeded in creating an art out of movie-making."

3974 Sanders, George Douglas   **1933?-**
Come swing with me: my life on and off the tour. With Larry Sheehan.
Garden City, New York: Doubleday & Co., Inc., 1974. 272 p.
    A colorful figure on the pro-golf circuit, winner of fifteen tournaments
and nearly a million dollars, runner-up in many championships, Sanders
recounts some of the high jinks, friendships, disasters, and successes of his
stormy career and offers amusing advice on a variety of golf-related subjects.

3975 Sanderson, Ivan Terence   **1911-1973**
Green silence: travels through the jungles of the Orient. Edited by Sabina
W. Sanderson. New York: David McKay Co., Inc., 1974. 263 p. Index.
    Starting off around the world at the age of sixteen, a budding naturalist
encountered in the East Indies and Malay States the TEF (tall equatorial
forest). This type of jungle fascinated and haunted him as he studied its
rich and complex world of animals and insects.

3976 *Sanford, Mollie Dorsey   **1838?-1915**
**Mollie: the journal of Mollie Dorsey Sanford in Nebraska and Colorado
Territories, 1857-1866.** Introduction by Donald F. Danker. Pioneer Heritage Series. Lincoln: University of Nebraska Press, 1976. (1959) 199 p.
    Homesteading in the raw new land West of the Missouri was an excit-
ing and difficult life full of adventure, hardship, and isolation. Here Mollie
Sanford tells of that part of her life and of the years following, when she
went with her husband on to the Colorado mining camps and to forts and

army camps. Her journal displays her courage, humor, and common sense
throughout her rugged life.

3977 *Sanger, Margaret Higgins   **1883-1966**
Margaret Sanger; an autobiography. New York: Dover, 1971. (New
York: Norton, 1938) 504 p. Index.
    The personal history of the leader of the birth-control movement, who
has written of her youth, her nursing career, her own determination and
views as well as the history of the movement and the people involved.

3978 Sankey, Ira David   **1840-1908**
My life and the story of the gospel hymns and of sacred songs and solos.
Introduction by Theodore L. Cuyler. New York: AMS Press, 1974. (Philadelphia: P.W. Ziegler Co., 1907) 410 p. Index.
    The first part of this volume contains the events of his own life by
song-evangelist Sankey. The second part is comprised of the history of
gospel hymns and incidents connected with the composition and use of
some well-known ones.

3979 Santayana, George   **1863-1952**
George Santayana's America; essays on literature and culture. Collected
and with a biographical sketch by James Ballowe. Urbana: University of
Illinois Press, 1967. 176 p.
    These collected essays present the author's opinions on American liter-
ature and culture between 1886 and 1922. In addition to autobiographical
matter, he writes about a variety of topics including Emerson, Walt
Whitman, Philistinism, poetry, and young radicalism.

3980 Santayana, George   **1863-1952**
The letters of George Santayana. Edited with introduction by Daniel
Cory. New York: Charles Scribner's Sons, 1955. 451 p. Index.
    The letters of the prominent philosopher span 66 years, beginning in
1866 after he graduated from Harvard, giving a fascinating view of the
development of his personality and central philosophy.

3981 Santayana, George   **1863-1952**
The middle span: Vol. II of *Persons and Places*. New York: Charles
Scribner's Sons, 1945. 187 p. Index.
    The second volume of his autobiography begins in 1866 with his stu-
dent days in Germany, travels to London and Spain, and his career as
professor of Philosophy at Harvard until his resignation in 1912.

3982 Santayana, George   **1863-1952**
My host the world: Vol. III of *Persons and Places*. New York: Charles
Scribner's Sons, 1953. 149 p. Index.
    The last thing ever written by the outstanding modern philosopher,
which describes his experience in England, especially after he resigned his
post at Harvard, and his later years of retirement in Rome.

3983 Santayana, George   **1863-1952**
Persons and places: the background of my life. New York: Charles
Scribner's Sons, 1944. 262 p. Index.
    The first of three volumes, this one describes his boyhood in Spain, his
immigration to Boston at age nine, and his college years at Harvard,
where he began training himself to become a philosopher.

3984 Santee, Ross   **1889-1965**
Lost pony tracks. New York: Charles Scribner's Sons, 1953. 303 p.
    Author-illustrator describes his life as a horse wrangler in Arizona.

3985 Sardi, Vincent   **1885-1969**
Sardi's: the story of a famous restaurant. With Richard Gehman. New
York: Henry Holt and Co., 1953. 227 p.
    The owner of the famous Sardi Restaurant in New York City writes
about his life and his restaurant. The book includes memories of some of
the famous people who ate at Sardi's, and one chapter describes some
famous Sardi menu items.

3986 *Sargent, Wyn   **1930-**
My life with the headhunters. Garden City, New York: Doubleday & Co.,
Inc., 1974. 310 p.
    A photo-journalist's narrative of exciting explorations in the Central
Borneo jungle to locate the Dyak headhunters explains how she came to
understand their rituals, their culture, and the people themselves.

3987 *Sargent, Wyn   **1930-**
People of the valley. New York: Random House, 1974. 302 p.
    Sargent writes the moving story of her stay with the Papuan people, the
Dani, and of the Baliem Valley. She was deported because she photographed and documented evidence against the Indonesian government
when it illegally occupied the territory of West Irian whose people wanted
to be free.

3988 Saroyan, William   **1908-1981**
Bicycle rider in Beverly Hills. New York: Charles Scribner's Sons, 1952.
178 p.

A narrative without chronology in which he reflects on experiences which have been significant to him. "The subject of the book is not so much myself, now and sometime ago, as it is the action of the human soul, to which there is no start or stop."

3989 Saroyan, William   1908-1981
Chance meetings. Boston: G.K. Hall & Co., 1978. 135 p.
Saroyan presents a series of vignettes of colorful people he has met by chance; he finds a surprise element in all relationships, including that with his own son. Among those who particularly impressed him are a Paris street vendor with a pet owl and a sailor in San Francisco, adrift without an anchor.

3990 Saroyan, William   1908-1981
Here comes, there goes, you know who. New York: Simon and Schuster, 1961. 273 p.
Immigrant Armenian family life and the author's experiences, jobs, education, and escapades create a human comedy in a series of short vignettes.

3991 Saroyan, William   1908-1981
Letters from 74 rue Taitbout, or, Don't go, but if you must, say hello to everybody. New York: The World Publishing Co., 1969. 162 p.
Comments and observations about his meetings (real and imagined) with people, some famous and some not.

3992 Saroyan, William   1908-1981
Not dying. With drawings by the author. New York: Harcourt, Brace & World, Inc., 1963. 244 p.
One of several memoirs, this book describes a year in Paris (1958) during which he worked on three books and helped his teenage son and daughter explore the city and themselves.

3993 Saroyan, William   1908-1981
Places where I've done time. Illustrated. New York: Praeger Publishers, 1972. 182 p.
A famous writer and world traveler, Saroyan reminisces about the past by recalling 68 key places in his life. He juxtaposes ordinary places with fabulous ones in his free-wheeling travels through the past and present.

3994 Saroyan, William   1908-1981
Sons come and go, mothers hang in forever. Edited by Frederic W. Hills. New York: McGraw-Hill Book Co., 1976. 211 p.
This is a collection of 67 essays in which Saroyan offers vignettes of his meetings with celebrities (Greta Garbo, Jack Benny), his views on other celebrities (James Joyce, Will Rogers). The essays offer a portrait of the 65-year-old writer, newly divorced, worried about his children, money, and loneliness.

3995 Saroyan, William   1908-1981
The twin adventures: the adventures of William Saroyan, a diary; the adventures of Wesley Jackson, a novel. New York: Harcourt, Brace and Co., 1950. 2v.
In Saroyan's words, this is a "chronicle of a writer at work on the writing of a novel, and the novel itself." Written during the summer of 1944 in London.

3996 Sartain, John   1808-1897
The reminiscences of a very old man, 1808-1897. Illustrated. New York: Benjamin Blom, 1969. (New York: D. Appleton, 1899) 297 p. Index.
A noted engraver applies his pictorial finesse to descriptions of his childhood and youth in England, particularly London, and his adulthood in New York and Philadelphia. He learned engraving from William Young Ottley, a splendid teacher, and discusses the state of the art in the two countries where he lived and worked, notably as an engraver for *Graham's* magazine, where he met Edgar Allan Poe, and on his own magazine, *Sartain's.*

3997 *Sarton, May   1912-
I knew a phoenix: sketches for an autobiography. New York: W.W. Norton & Co., Inc., 1969. (New York: Rinehart and Co., Inc., 1959) 222 p.
A poet and novelist analyzes her search for a world of her own, the influence of her father, George Sarton, a brilliant historian of science, her English mother, her early education, her apprenticeship at Eva LeGallienne's Repertory Theater, and her own experimental theater company.

3998 *Sarton, May   1912-
Journal of a solitude. New York: G.K. Hall, 1979. (New York: W.W. Norton & Co., 1973) 294 p.
In a series of brief journal entries, she comments on her appreciation of rural life in New Hampshire, of friends and pets, but also of the psychic costs of living and writing alone.

3999 *Sarton, May   1912-
Plant dreaming deep. New York: W.W. Norton & Co., 1967. 189 p.
Written in middle age, this book describes her life in Nelson, New Hampshire, where the house she bought and restored becomes a metaphor for establishing an orderly life. Although she maintains a tone of serenity, the anxiety of loneliness and aging hovers near the surface of her narrative.

4000 *Sarton, May   1912-
Recovering: a journal. Illustrated. New York: W.W. Norton, 1980.
Sarton's journal covers December 1978, through November 1979, and recounts "a change in the landscape of my heart." At the year's beginning, she "felt devalued as a woman, as a lover, and as a writer," having been labeled by the New York *Times* as a "lesbian writer." In June she had a radical mastectomy which left her vulnerable and depressed. By the year's end she had triumphed, healthy again in body and spirit, and in control of her creative powers.

4001 *Sarton, May   1912-
A world of light: portraits and celebrations. Portraits. New York: W.W. Norton & Co., 1976. 254 p.
Novelist and poet Sarton's collection of a dozen personal portraits of her father, mother, and special friends (including Louise Bogan and Elizabeth Bowen) and what they meant to her conveys the essence of their personalities, love, and friendship. Every page abounds with observations in memorable language: "something knots a friendship, or raises the emotional content to a new plane, some final door must open between two people if they are to become true friends; a total acceptance of each other."

4002 Savage, Joseph P.   1894-1977
A man named Savage. New York: Vantage Press, 1975. 402 p.
The success story of a lawyer who worked his way up from a poverty-stricken Chicago youth through law school to become an assistant state's attorney, a lawyer in private practice, a member of the Chicago School Board, and a supporter of the Republican Party. Throughout his life he has maintained confidence in the basic virtues and opportunities of America.

4003 Savala, Refugio   1904-
The autobiography of a Yaqui poet. Edited by Kathleen M. Sands. Tucson: University of Arizona Press, 1980. 228 p.
Born in Mexico, he and his family moved to southern Arizona. His book describes his family's flight from persecution by the Mexican government and the growth of the Yaqui culture in a new land.

4004 Savitsch, Eugene de   1903-1959
In search of complications: an autobiography. London: Andre Deutsch, 1958. (New York: Simon and Schuster, 1940) 352 p. Index.
In 1918 he immigrated to San Francisco and later attended the University of Colorado School of Medicine. He pursued his interests in medical research at the University of Chicago School of Medicine and finally had a successful career as a surgeon in Washington. His book includes well-written critical analysis of national and international culture.

4005 Savo, Jimmy   1895-1960
I bow to the stones: memories of a New York childhood. Introduction by George Freedley. Drawings by Victor J. Dowling. New York: Howard Frisch, 1963. 144 p.
Well-known as a comedian on Broadway and in vaudeville, he writes here of his childhood in New York's Italian ghetto with a warm sense of humor and nostalgia.

4006 Sayre, Francis Bowes   1885-1972
Glad adventure. New York: The Macmillan Co., 1957. 356 p. Index.
A devoted diplomat and humanitarian writes of his college adventures, his marriage to Jessie Woodrow Wilson, seventeen years on the Harvard law faculty, and several important assignments during World War II, including the years as Assistant Secretary of State under Cordell Hull.

4007 Scarne, John   1903-
Amazing world of John Scarne: a personal history. New York: Crown Publishers, Inc., 1956. 412 p.
Called the world's number-one expert on games and gambling, he describes the inside of the world of gambling, magic and games, exposing tricks and gimmicks, and establishing his reputation as The Authority on gaming and the occult.

4008 Schaaf, James Edward   1898-
Mamie Doud Eisenhower and her chicken farmer cousin. Whitehouse Station, New Jersey: Wilkie Printing, 1974. 75 p.
There are two parts to this book: the first covering the background of the Doud-Schaaf families from 1859 to 1950; the second telling about Mamie's cousin and his wife Anna from 1950 to 1973 in brief anecdotes and reminiscences.

4009 Schacht, Alexander   **1894-**
My own particular screwball: an informal autobiography. Edited by Ed Keyes. Garden City, New York: Doubleday & Co., 1955. 254 p.

Schacht humorously recounts his childhood of skipping school in New York City to play ball, his twenty-year career as a pitcher for the New York Giants and Washington Senators, and his eventual ownership of two restaurants in New York. While plagued with bone and joint problems and ulcers that affected his pitching, he developed comedy routines to entertain the baseball fans and troops during World War II.

4010 *Schaffer, Dori   **1938-1963**
Dear Deedee: from the diaries of Dori Schaffer. Edited with annotations by Anne Schaffer. Secaucus, New Jersey: Lyle Stuart, 1978. 222 p.

Schaffer kept a diary from the time she was sixteen until she committed suicide from despair at 25. She was bright, pretty, intelligent, thoughtful, deeply committed to Judaism and an academic career as a sociologist, to which her graduate work at U.C.L.A. and Columbia was intended to lead. But she was ambivalent about a profession, which she saw as incompatible with her great loves for her indifferent father, her husband (a homosexual whom she soon divorced), and two lovers, one killed in an auto accident, the other a sexual betrayer.

4011 Schary, Dore   **1905-**
For special occasions. New York: Random House, 1962. 200 p.

A prominent playwright and screenwriter describes his childhood in Newark, where his father ran a catering business near the family home on Mulberry Street.

4012 Schiano, Anthony (Tony Solo)
Solo! self-portrait of an undercover cop. With Anthony Burton. New York: Dodd, Mean & Co., 1973. 247 p.

Nine years of dangerous duty with the New York Police Department as an undercover narcotics detective furnished Schiano with the material for much of this book. He became known as Tony Solo because he worked alone relying on his own courage, strength, bravery, humor, and startlingly unconventional weapons.

4013 Schildkraut, Joseph   **1895-1964**
My father and I. As told to Leo Lani. New York: The Viking Press, 1959. 246 p. Index.

His father, Rudolph, was recognized internationally as a fine actor on stage and in film; Joseph worked with him in theater from childhood on, which led to an unusual father-son bond that influenced his entire life. After they immigrated from Austria, Joseph's career gradually waned, until he regained stature with a fine performance as Otto Frank in *The Diary of Anne Frank.*

4014 Schlesinger, Arthur Meier (Sr.)   **1888-1965**
In retrospect: the history of a historian. New York: Harcourt, Brace and World, 1963. 212 p. Index.

A professor, historian, and supporter of liberal causes records his beginnings, his academic career, his observations of great events, and their effect on his study of history.

4015 *Schlesinger, Marian Cannon
Snatched from oblivion: a Cambridge memoir. Illustrated by the author. Boston: Little, Brown and Co., 1979. 243 p.

A family memoir focusing on her mother, Cornelia James Cannon; her father, Walter B. Cannon, was an eminent physiologist at Harvard. Her childhood memoirs are set in a large Victorian house near Harvard Yard, with visits by students, relatives, and visiting intellectuals.

4016 Schlossberg, Harvey
Psychologist with a gun. And Lucy Freeman. New York: Coward-McCann & Geoghegan, Inc., 1974. 222 p.

He was the first policeman to become a psychologist and help troubled officers as an official of a police department. His book describes his experience on the NYPD before and after he got his Ph.D. in psychology, giving a detailed account of modern police work, its confusion, stress, and rewards.

4017 Schmelzenbach, Elmer   **1910-**
Sons of Africa: stories from the life of Elmer Schmelzenbach. As told to Leslie Parrot. Illustrated. Kansas City, Missouri: Beacon Hill Press of Kansas City, 1979. 217 p.

Schmelzenbach writes of his childhood in Swaziland as the son of missionaries. He was eight before he realized he was white and at about that time began to learn English to supplement his native Zulu. Malaria, poison snakes, witch doctors, and persecutors were among the torments he and his family had to contend with, despite a relatively benign childhood. He was sent to school in Nampa, Idaho, 12,000 lonesome miles from home; after seminary training he and his nurse wife returned to Swaziland and East Transvaal for 36 more years of missionary work.

4018 Schmidt, Sven Erich Heinrich
see **Smith, Whitey, pseud.**

4019 Schmitz, John G.   **1930-**
Stranger in the arena. Santa Ana, California: Rayline Printing Co., 1974. 322 p.

In a political autobiography with selections from his political writings, Schmitz tells about his career as a conservative California legislator and U.S. congressman. In 1972 he was a candidate for president of the United States for the American Party advocating an "essentially apostolic mission of making America Christian."

4020 Schneider, Delano Douglas
Deep the roots of hope. Foreword by Orion Ulrey. Muskegon, Michigan: Creative Design Books, 1976. 264 p.

Schneider, an agricultural missionary for the United Church of Christ, focuses on life in the province of West Orissa, India, where he and his family served, 1962-70. He writes clearly and precisely about village life; agricultural methods for raising crops and poultry; human problems of drunkenness, poverty and illiteracy; and church problems related to obstinacy and short-sightedness. This is, for the most part, an analysis of the country struggling to develop and survive in the 1960's and only secondarily an autobiography.

4021 *Schneiderman, Rose   **1882?-1972**
All for one. New York: Paul S. Eriksson, Inc., 1967. 264 p.

After describing the poverty of her childhood in Poland and New York in the 1890's, she focuses primarily on her work with the New York Women's Trade Union League. She became a dominant figure in the women's labor movement, serving as president of the NYWTUL as well as the national WTUL, and promoting women's political rights in the suffrage movement.

4022 Schnitzer, Ewald W.   **1910-**
Selected adventures of my first fifty years. Idyllwild, California: Strawberry Valley Press, 1974. 149 p.

In diary entries, letters and articles Schnitzer tells of his high adventures around the world: mountain climbing in the Alps, Himalayas, Andes; running rapids in Hell's Canyon; trekking in Bhutan and Sikkim; and collecting art in Hollywood.

4023 Schoenberg, Arnold   **1874-1951**
Letters. Edited by Edwin Stein. Translated from the original German by Eithne Wilkins and Ernst Kaiser. New York: St. Martin's, 1965. (1964) 309 p. Index.

Written between 1910 and 1951, some in German and later in his newly learned English, these letters emphasize the uncompromising creative spirit of the innovative composer Schoenberg, showing a man kind and ready to help friends, but with a stringent code of artistic honor.

4024 Schoenrich, Otto   **1876-1977**
Reminiscences of an itinerant lawyer. Illustrated. Baltimore: J.H. Furst Co., 1967. 664 p.

Written and privately printed for his family and friends, his book is "a rambling account of the rambling life of an American lawyer whose work happened to be connected with incidents of American political and economic expansion since the Spanish-American War." He served as a judge in Puerto Rico and Mayaguez, practiced law in Cuba, Nicaragua, Haiti, Europe and Greece.

4025 Schoenstein, Ralph   **1933-**
Citizen Paul: a story of father and son. Illustrated. New York: Farrar, Straus Giroux, 1978. 156 p.

Bitter-sweet reminiscences by a man whose father is a powerful editor of the New York *Journal-American.* Holding back his son's career development in the newspapers, the father appears like a superman privy to secrets and important people, but not the kind of father the author wants to become to his own children.

4026 Schollander, Donald Arthur   **1946-**
Deep water. And Duke Savage. New York: Crown Publishers, 1971. 276 p.

Winner of four gold medals in the 1964 Tokyo Olympics, Schollander is deeply concerned with the conduct of amateur athletics. He writes of the effort it takes to become a champion, the pressure, the grueling schedule, the intense training, and the single-minded commitment necessary in sports with superb contenders who are nearly equal in performance.

4027 Schoolcraft, Henry Rowe   **1793-1864**
Narrative journals of travels from Detroit northwest through the great chain of American lakes to the sources of the Mississippi River, in the year 1820. New York: Arno, 1970. (Albany: Hostford, 1821) 419 p. Index.

The record of a journey undertaken to learn about the Indian tribes, to survey the topography of the country, to locate a garrison on Lake Superior, to investigate mining possibilities, to purchase tracts from the Indians.

4028 Schooley, William   **1794-1860**
Journal of Dr. William Schooley: pioneer physician, Quaker minister,

abolitionist, philosopher, and scholar, 1794-1860. Illustrated. Zanesville, Ohio: The author, 1977. 261 p. Index.

A collection of speeches, essays, poems, letters, and journal entries by a physician-minister who was active in the abolitionist movement before the Civil War. This volume also contains a list of his patients, prescriptions (herbal medicines), and a genealogy of the Schooley family.

4029 Schorr, Daniel   **1916-**
Cleaning the air. Illustrated. Boston: Houghton Mifflin Co., 1977. 333 p. Index.

After a lifetime of reporting the news, Schorr himself was newsworthy because he caused to be published a House committee report on intelligence against the wishes of the CIA, the White House, the House of Representatives, and CBS. CBS took him off the air; he appeared before the House Ethics Committee; but he refused to reveal his sources, and was finally vindicated.

4030 Schrank, Robert
Ten thousand working days. Cambridge, Massachusetts: M.I.T. Press, 1978. 243 p.

He describes dozens of different jobs held and careers pursued, from plumber, coal miner, and farm hand to union organizer, politician, and sociologist, over a period of 42 years. His intention is to capture the humanity, poetry, and community of workers at their work place which he believes behaviorial scientists often miss.

4031 Schulberg, Budd Wilson   **1914-**
The four seasons of success. Garden City, New York: Doubleday & Co., Inc., 1972. 203 p.

In appraising the effects of success and instant celebrity on American writers, Schulberg assesses six authors as he has known them.

4032 Schultz, James Willard   **1859-1947**
My life as an Indian. Williamstown, Massachusetts: Corner House, 1977. (Forest and Stream Publishing Co., 1907) 204 p.

Schultz, a trader and hunter, writes about his adventures in the romantic Montana Territory, where he gradually became acquainted with the Piegan Blackfeet, married Nat-ah'-ki, a young Blackfoot woman, and enjoyed "the thrill of the open plains, of seeing a shaggy brown sea of buffalo as far as the eye could reach, [and] the sharp evenings when I rode home after a good hunt to my comfortable lodge of skins . . . and the warm kindness of our Piegan friends and kinfolks." The enclosing of Indians on reservations, where he lived out his life raising cattle, sadly ended the romance and adventure.

4033 Schulz, Charles Monroe   **1922-**
Peanuts jubilee: my life and art with Charlie Brown and others. Illustrated. New York: Holt, Rinehart and Winston, 1975. 222 p.

Although the major attraction of his book is a chronological collection of the comic strip, it also includes Schulz's story of his boyhood in St. Paul, his first interest in drawing, and the evolution of his cast of characters—all from friends—into a multimillion dollar enterprise.

4034 Schurmacher, Emile Carlos   **1903-1976**
Knee pants. New York: Thomas Y. Crowell Co., 1950.

Charming story of a journalist's middle-class boyhood in old New York, with nostalgic recollections of button shoes, pianolas, horse-drawn vehicles, and, of course, knee pants as a symbol of youth.

4035 Schurmacher, Emile Carlos   **1903-1976**
Nothing's sacred on Sunday. New York: Thomas Y. Crowell Co., 1951. 243 p.

An interesting, self-critical analysis of his experience as a journalist during the ten years he worked for *The American Weekly,* a Hearst publication, emphasizing the limitations of commercial journalism.

4036 Schurz, Carl   **1829-1906**
The autobiography of Carl Schurz. Introduction by Allan Nevins. An abridgement in one volume by Wayne Andrews. New York: Charles Scribner's Sons, 1961. (New York: McClure, 1907-1908) 331 p. Index.

Born and educated in Germany, he immigrated to Wisconsin in his early twenties, became active in state politics, served in the Civil War, served as a Senator, and as Secretary of the Interior in the Hayes administration. His book reflects his political fervor and strong personality and includes remarkable portraits of many important contemporaries.

4037 Schurz, Carl   **1829-1906**
Intimate letters of Carl Schurz, 1841-1869. Translated and edited by Joseph Schafer. New York: Da Capo Press, 1970. (Madison: State Hist. Soc. of Wisconsin, 1928) 491 p. Index.

His letters constitute a running commentary on the changing political phases during a period of his leadership of liberal German Americans, of political speech-making during the Lincoln campaign, of practical statesmanship leading up to his election as senator from Wisconsin.

4038 Schutz, Anton   **1894-1977**
My share of wine: the memoirs of Anton Schutz. Greenwich, Connecticut: New York Graphic Society, 1972. 224 p. Index.

After fighting for Germany during World War I, Schutz came to America and became a reputable etcher. Later he entered the art publishing world, founding the successful New York Graphic Society, and subsequently created the UNESCO World Art Series, traveling extensively around the world to hunt for little-known art work.

4039 Schuyler, George Samuel   **1895-1977**
Black and conservative: the autobiography of George S. Schuyler. New Rochelle, New York: Arlington House Publishers, 1966. 362 p. Index.

During his years as a journalist, he worked to bring fact and logic to the news media. He believes in a conservative stance for overcoming prejudice, consolidating gains, and advancing by slower-but-surer methods than those advocated by radical Black agitators, who cause resentment and hatred.

4040 *Schwandt, Mary (Mrs. Mary Schwandt-Schmidt)   **b.1848**
The captivity of Mary Schwandt. Fairfield, Washington: Ye Galleon Press, 1975. 31 p.

In 1894, Mary Schwandt recalled her capture by the Sioux Indians in Minnesota in 1862. For a few months she lived with Snana, a Christian tribe member who treated her like a daughter, concealing her with quilts and buffalo robes against marauding tribesmen. Snana's appended account corroborates and reaffirms the loving mother-daughter relationship that existed while they were together.

4041 *Schwartz, Helene E.
Lawyering. New York: Farrar, Straus and Giroux, 1976. 308 p.

Having begun her legal career with the defense of William F. Buckley and *The National Review* against the Linus Pauling libel suit, Schwartz went on to represent the defendants in the Chicago Seven appeal and to counsel demonstrators at the 1972 Miami Beach political convention.

4042 Schwartz, Samuel   **b.1880**
Tell thy children: the autobiography of an American rabbi. Foreword by Leonard J. Mervis. New York: Exposition Press, 1959. 98 p.

Rabbi Schwartz describes his Jewish childhood in Hungary; his college education, still oriented to Judaism, in Budapest; and his immigration to the United States, completing his rabbinical studies in the reform Hebrew Union College in Cincinnati. He ministered to congregations in Cleveland, Florida, Montreal, and ultimately, Chicago, where for 26 years he was the mainstay of temple B'nai Abraham Zion, in Oak Park.

4043 Schwed, Peter   **1911-**
God bless pawnbrokers. New York: Dodd, Mead & Co., 1975. 217 p.

Schwed worked for ten years during the 1930's for the Provident Loan Society of New York and here tells fascinating stories of that institution, a kind of non-profit pawnbroker loaning money on personal collateral at low interest rates, returning profits from auctions to the borrower, and turning over any year-end profits to charity.

4044 *Schwerin, Doris
Diary of a pigeon watcher. New York: William Morrow and Co., Inc., 1976. 288 p.

An introspective portrait exploring her discovery of her talents as a writer, dramatist, and composer, the meaning of her life, the worth of her experience.

4045 Sciaky, Leon   **1893-**
Farewell to Salonica: portrait of an era. New York: Current Books, Inc., A.A. Wyn, Publ., 1946. 241 p.

Well-written narrative of his boyhood in Turkey, the deterioration of that society, the chaos and war which led his family to come to America during World War I.

4046 Scipio, Lynn Adolphus   **1876-1963**
My thirty years in Turkey. Rindge, New Hampshire: Richard R. Smith Publisher, Inc., 1955. 364 p.

Raised in Indiana, he was educated at Purdue, taught engineering at the University of Nebraska, and for thirty years was associated with Robert College Engineering School in Istanbul, chiefly as dean.

4047 *Scott, Audrey
I was a Hollywood stunt girl. Philadelphia: Dorrance & Co., 1969. 119 p.

Scott led an adventurous life as a movie stuntwoman, substituting for such stars as Bette Davis, Judith Anderson, and Rosalind Russell, mostly in scenes involving horse riding and jumping, though occasionally in sequences requiring airplanes or cars. Always close to danger, she was served well by her horses, but received a painful back injury in a stunt fall with a parachute and eventually became a real estate saleswoman.

4048 Scott, Elmer   **1866-1954**
Eighty-eight eventful years: being the intimate story of Elmer Scott in industry and the humanities and of the Civic Federation of Dallas over a third of a century. Illustrated. Dallas: Civic Federation of Dallas, 1954. 164 p. Index.

Scott managed and modernized the first Sears, Roebuck stores in Dallas, 1906-1913, but focuses most of this fragmented book on his multifarious social work and activities for civic improvement from 1910-1954. Among his diverse endeavors the Civic Federation of Dallas was foremost; this book presents the history of this organization, intermingled with personal narrative.

4049 Scott, Fraser
Weigh-in: the selling of a middleweight. New York: Thomas Y. Crowell Co., 1947. 217 p. Index.
    A boxer describes his rise in the prize-fighting world and his disillusionment and decline, when, after being disqualified in a title fight, he began to realize the sham and brutality of his role.

4050 Scott, Jack Denton   **1915-**
Journey into silence. New York: Readers Digest Press, dist. by Crowell, 1976. 200 p. Index.
    An account of an adventurous trip to Spitsbergen to explore a peaceful, silent land behind a towering Chinese Wall Front Glacier only 400 miles from the North Pole. The author writes with enthusiasm of all he saw and experienced: animal life, the sea, the glaciers, the great beauty of the silent North.

4051 Scott, Orange   **1800-1847**
The life of Rev. Orange Scott. Black Heritage Library Collection. Freeport, New York: Books for Libraries Press, 1971. (New York: C. Prindle and L.C. Matlack, 1847-48) 307 p.
    The first forty pages of this volume contain the personal narrative of Scott, whose anti-slavery activities in the Methodist Episcopal Church were opposed by the authorities. Thereafter he withdrew and organized the Wesleyan Methodist Connection, continuing to work against slavery. The remainder of the book includes extracts from letters, other documents, and remarks by Lucius C. Matlack, the editor.

4052 Scott, Winfield   **1786-1866**
Memoirs of Lieut.-General Scott, LL.D. Freeport, New York: Books for Libraries Press, 1970. (New York: Sheldon & Co., 1864) 2v.
    Scott, who ran unsuccessfully for the presidency in 1852, served in the U.S. Army during the War of 1812, the Mexican War, and in the Indian conflicts.

4053 *Scott-Maxwell, Florida (Pier)   **b.1883**
The measure of my days. New York: Alfred A. Knopf, 1972. (1968) 150 p.
    Written in her eighties, this book contains musings and opinions on a variety of subjects such as age, beauty, evolution, and love. The author has written plays, worked for women's suffrage, and studied to become an analytical psychologist in the course of her long life.

4054 Scripps, Edward Wyllis   **1854-1926**
Damned old crank: a self-portrait of E.W. Scripps drawn from his unpublished writings. Edited with introduction by Charles R. McCabe. Westport, Connecticut: Greenwood Press, 1971. (New York: Harper and Brothers, 1951) 259 p.
    From autobiographical papers locked up for 26 years after Scripps' death, the editor has chosen material from the years 1906 to 1925 for a self-portrait. Scripps comments on his varied public and private life and his troubled search for a new way of thinking.

4055 Scripps, Edward Wyllis   **1854-1926**
I protest; selected disquisitions of E.W. Scripps. Edited with biographical introduction by Oliver Knight. Madison: University of Wisconsin Press, 1966. 799 p.
    Many of these disquisitions deal with the thoughts and feelings of this prominent, eccentric journalist, revealing his character, attitudes, habits of mind, and world view.

4056 Scully, Frank (Joseph Xavier)   **1892-1964**
Cross my heart. Illustrated. New York: Greenberg, 1955. 378 p. Index.
    A wisecracking, anecdotal narrative of Scully's first forty years, many in Italy and France, during which his severe medical problems (osteomyelitis, tuberculosis, leg amputation) alternated with journalistic accomplishments (*Fun in Bed,* a collection of sickroom jokes, was a best seller) and encounters, mostly friendly, with famous people—Isadora Duncan, Frank Harris, Jimmy Walker, and others.

4057 Scully, Frank (Joseph Xavier)   **1892-1964**
In armour bright: cavalier adventures of my short life out of bed. With an introduction by Jack Paar. Philadelphia: Chilton Books, 1963. 285 p.
    Because he spent about two-thirds of his life in bed recovering from tuberculosis and over forty operations, he wrote *Fun in Bed,* intended to cheer others who were bedridden. His third autobiographical volume describes more of his adventures as a writer and social reformer of remarkable energy and optimism.

4058 Scully, Frank (Joseph Xavier)   **1892-1964**
This gay knight: an autobiography of a modern chevalier. Introduction by Dale Francis. Philadelphia: Chilton Co., 1962. 232 p. Index.
    The second of three volumes describes his attempts at social and politi-

cal reform in California after he moved there as a screen writer for Fox Studios.

4059 Seagle, Nathan A., D.D.   **1868-1957**
The memoirs of a metropolitan minister: sixty years of service in the diocese of New York. Foreword by Horace W.B. Donegan, D.D. New York: Exposition Press, 1955. 99 p.
    Though a native of North Carolina, the Reverend Seagle spent his entire career as the rector of St. Thomas's and St. Stephen's Episcopalian Churches in New York City, 1894-1945.

4060 Seagrave, Gordon Stifler   **1897-1965**
Burma surgeon returns. New York: W.W. Norton and Co., Inc., 1946. 268 p.
    As a medical missionary, Seagrave started a hospital in Namkham, Burma, was commissioned a major in the U.S. Army Medical Corps in World War II, and joined the retreat on the Burma Road led by General Stilwell. Here he describes his experience during the return to Burma in 1942 and the recovery of his hospital, in a personal narrative of one of the major actions of World War II.

4061 Seagrave, Gordon Stifler   **1897-1965**
The life of a Burma surgeon. Foreword by Chester Bowles. Edited by C.B. Pintchman and B. Wechsler. New York: W.W. Norton & Co., Inc., 1961. 224 p.
    This volume is an abridgement of Dr. Seagrave's *Burma Surgeon,* and *Burma Surgeon Returns,* excerpts from his combat diary. It describes his struggle against disease and death, his building a hospital, and training nurses. During World War II Japanese bombing forced him to retreat to India, but afterward he returned to resume his humanitarian work.

4062 Seagrave, Gordon Stifler   **1897-1965**
My hospital in the hills. New York: W.W. Norton and Co., Inc., 1955. 253 p.
    His third book describes his life and work as a medical missionary in Burma during the decade after World War II.

4063 Seale, Bobby   **1936-**
Seize the time; the story of the Black Panther party and Huey P. Newton. New York: Random House, 1970. 429 p.
    The book derives from tape recordings made by the author in the fall of 1968 and 1969-70, the latter taking place in the San Francisco County Jail. This is a tough-talking history, first briefly sketching Seale's education into radical consciousness, then more extensively the development of the Black Panther Party.

4064 Searcy, Harvey Brown   **b.1884**
We used what we had. Northport, Alabama: Colonial Press, 1962. 102 p.
    Episodes from a doctor's life during the early part of the twentieth century told in amusing and unpretentious vignettes.

4065 Sears, Jesse Brundage   **b.1876**
Jesse Brundage Sears: an autobiography. Palo Alto: Jesse Brundage Sears, 1959. 194 p.
    A narrative of the author's busy career as a professor of education at Stanford and of his 54-year marriage to Stella Sears, followed by reflective essays on parenthood, his career, higher education, and human nature.

4066 Sears, William   **1902-1976**
God loves laughter. London: George Ronald, 1960. 181 p.
    As a child Sears repeatedly dreamed of a "shining man" and experienced a precocious religious faith. He wrote plays professionally for a time, then turned to work in radio and television. In his mid-thirties, he met Marguerite, who later became his second wife; she introduced him to the B'hai faith and he realized that Baha'u'llah was the "shining man" of his dream. Sears proselytized around the world.

4067 *Seaton, Grace Mary (Watson)   **1894?-**
A double life in the Kaiser's capital. Canaan, New Hampshire: Phoenix Publishing, 1973. 121 p.
    Because her father was the court dentist in Berlin before World War I, Grace Watson grew up in Berlin. It was a sheltered youth spent as a part of both the American Colony and the German city in a bygone era of splendor and innocence.

4068 Sedgwick, Ellery   **1872-1960**
The happy profession. Boston: Little, Brown and Co., 1946. 343 p. Index.
    Editor of the *Atlantic Monthly* for thirty years, he writes of his work, his friends, and a literary life style that has since passed.

4069 Seeger, Peter   **1919-**
The incompleat folksinger. Edited by Jo Metcalf Schwartz. Illustrated. New York: Simon and Schuster, 1972. 596 p. Index.
    Folk-singer Pete Seeger offers a low-key, personalized, entertaining history of folk music, instruments, and musicians around the world, interspersed with his views on politics, society, music, human nature, and a

variety of other subjects. A brief autobiographical afterword concludes this volume.

4070 Seel, David John 1925-
Challenge and crisis in missionary medicine. Illustrated. Pasadena, California: William Carey Library, 1979. 149 p.
This articulate, well-organized book presents Dr. Seel's ideas on both the practical and theological aspects of organizing and maintaining appropriate health-care facilities and health education among primitive Korean villagers. His emphasis is on prevention of disease, proper sanitation, and health education compatible with the native culture.

4071 Sego, James 1927-
Sego. Preface by Robert Paul Lamb. Foreword by Jim Bakker. Illustrated. Plainfield, New Jersey: Logos International, 1977. 156 p.
Born of a poor evangelist family in Enigma, Georgia, he grew up amid poor but fervently religious folk. Married young to Naomi Easter, he struggled for years to establish himself, his brothers, and eventually Naomi as a financially solvent gospel-singing group. Ultimately he succeeded, after many years of severe alcoholism and two alcohol-related strokes. The Sego Brothers and Naomi travel throughout the South by bus and often perform on television.

4072 *Seibels, Fanny Marks b.1884
Wishes are horses: Montgomery, Alabama's first lady of the violin. New York: Exposition Press, 1958. 251 p.
Although covering her life from affluent birth to contented old age in Montgomery, Alabama, Seibels focuses on her years between ten and twenty-six, when she became enamored of the violin, studied in Montgomery, New York, and Europe, taught violin at Judson College (Alabama), and had a variety of suitors and many friends. After marriage, she settled into a musically oriented life.

4073 *Sekaquaptewa, Helen 1898-
Me and mine: the life story of Helen Sekaquaptewa. As told to Louise Udall. Illustrated by Phillip Sekaquaptewa. Tucson: University of Arizona Press, 1969. 262 p. Index.
The life of a Hopi Indian woman who tells with beautiful simplicity of the old customs and mores of the tribe. She learned new ways of doing things, such as canning food rather than drying it and having preventative shots for her children, but kept some of the best parts of her Indian culture as well.

4074 Seldes, George 1890-
Tell the truth and run. New York: Greenberg, 1953. 288 p. Index.
A journalist recalls the beginning of his career in Pittsburgh with its corrupt press, his later experiences as a World War II foreign correspondent, and then his work as a peacetime foreign correspondent in places such as England, France, Europe, and Russia.

4075 *Seldes, Marian 1927?-
The bright lights: a theatre life. Illustrated. Boston: Houghton Mifflin Co., 1978. 280 p.
The author examines the serious business of acting as a profession and the joys, the discipline, the technique of her craft.

4076 *Sell, Hildegarde Loretta 1906-
Over 50—so what. With Adele Whitely Fletcher. Garden City, New York: Doubleday and Co., Inc., 1963. 184 p. Index.
A chatty memoir of her life as an entertainer by a singer popular in the Forties.

4077 Sellers, Cleveland 1944?-
The river of no return; the autobiography of a Black militant and the life and death of SNCC. With Robert Terrell. New York: William Morrow & Co., 1973. 279 p.
A Black leader writes of his part in the struggle for equality in the 1960's, the beginnings of SNCC, his work in the Civil Rights Movement in Mississippi, Alabama, and South Carolina. He concludes with an expression of his commitment to building bridges between American and African Blacks because "American Blacks are Africans in exile."

4078 Seltzer, Louis Benson 1897-1980
Years were good. Introduction by Bruce Catton. Cleveland: The World Publishing Co., 1956. 317 p. Index.
At thirteen he left school to become a cub reporter. Editor of the Cleveland *Press* since 1928, he describes his long career as a journalist.

4079 Selvig, Conrad George 1877-1953
A tale of two valleys: an autobiography. Los Angeles: Grover Jones Press, 1951. 144 p.
Born and raised on a Minnesota farm, he became central in the development of the University of Minnesota's Northwest School of Agriculture and served as U.S. congressman for Minnesota (1927-1933).

4080 Selznick, David Oliver 1902-1965
Memo from David O. Selznick. Illustrated. Selected and edited by Ruby Behlmerl. Introduction by S.N. Behrman. New York: The Viking Press, 1972. 518 p. Index.
The legendary producer of such films as *Rebecca* and *Gone with the Wind,* Selznick was an inveterate and prolific writer of telegrams, letters, and especially memos. Here portions are spliced together to form an autobiographical account of his career and the inner workings of Hollywood.

4081 Semmes, Raphael 1809-1877
Rebel raider: being an account of Raphael Semmes's cruise in the C.S.S. Sumter; composed in large part of extracts from Semmes's Memoirs of Service Afloat written in the year 1869. Selected and supplemented by Harpur Allen Gosnell. Chapel Hill: University of North Carolina Press, 1948. 218 p. Index.
Journal entries describing Semmes' command of the *Sumter* (April 18, 1861—April 11, 1862), while assigned to drive enemy commerce from the Southern seas. Includes detailed comments on international law during wartime.

4082 Sennett, Mack 1880-1960
King of comedy. As told to Cameron Shipp. Garden City, New York: Doubleday and Co., Inc., 1954. 284 p.
His life in show business, from New York burlesque to Hollywood film, with a major focus on Mabel Normand, his great love and one of his major comedians.

4083 Sergievsky, Orest 1911-
Memoirs of a dancer: shadows of the past, dreams that came true, memories of yesterdays. Illustrated. New York: Dance Horizons, 1979. 276 p.
The first third of the book concerns the author's upbringing in the luxury of pre-revolutionary Odessa and the poverty of Kiev after the revolution and his parents' divorce. The middle section focuses on Sergievsky's emigration to the United States as the son of a famous test pilot and on his education and career as a dancer with the Metropolitan Opera Company. His love of dancing is mixed with regret in the third portion, where after retirement from the stage at 38 he taught dance and organized "Dance Varieties."

4084 *Seton, Elizabeth Ann 1774-1821
Letters of Mother Seton to Mrs. Julianna Scott. Edited by Rt. Rev. Msgr. Joseph B. Code. New York: Father Salvator M. Burgio Memorial Foundation in Honor of Mother Seton, 1960. 294 p.
Letters written from 1798 until Mother Seton's death in 1821 exhibit a thoughtful, tender spirit, ever devout through childbirth, a happy marriage terminated by her husband's death in 1803, and ostracism by many relatives and friends when she converted to Catholicism in 1805. Although Mother Seton was a powerful organizer and strong leader of the Baltimore Mother House, her letters here focus on more intimate family matters, such as her children's growth and development.

4085 Seton, Ernest Thompson 1860-1946
Trail of an artist-naturalist: the autobiography of Ernest Thompson Seton. Illustrated by author. New York: Arno Press, 1978. (New York: Charles Scribner's Sons, 1940) 412 p.
A naturalist, illustrator, and popular writer about wildlife (*Wild Animals I Have Known*) writes of his youth in northern England, emigration to Canada, and subsequent travels throughout the Canadian Northwest, Alaska, and the American Southwest; he ultimately settled in New Mexico. He tells fascinating anecdotes of birds and wolves in particular.

4086 Seton, Ernest Thompson 1860-1946
The worlds of Ernest Thompson Seton. Edited, with introduction and commentary by John G. Samson. New York: Alfred A. Knopf, 1976. 204 p.
A beautifully illustrated compilation of Seton's commentary on the habits of animals and birds he has encountered in the Canadian and American North, East, and West, prefaced by a brief biography by John Samson.

4087 *Settle, Mary Lee 1918-
All the brave promises: memories of Aircraftwoman 2nd class-2146391. Seymour Lawrence Books. New York: Delacorte Press, 1966. 176 p.
An American, the author volunteered for the WAAF (Women's Auxiliary Air Force) of the British Royal Air Force during World War II. Her moving story of that experience makes vivid the difficulty of adjustment to wartime Britain, to the hierarchy of war, to life without privacy or dignity, to the grim facts of militarized existence.

4088 Sevareid, Eric 1912-
Not so wild a dream. New York: Alfred A. Knopf, 1946. 516 p. Index.
A strong, well-written commentary on his early years in South Dakota and Minnesota, the formation of his liberal philosophy, and a moving account of his experience as a foreign correspondent in World War II.

4089 Sewall, Samuel   **1652-1730**
Diary of Samuel Sewall. Edited with introduction by Harvey Wish. New York: G.P. Putnam's Sons, 1967. 189 p.
This abridgment of Sewall's diary records New England witch trials, Indian massacres, "small pocks" epidemics, and other acts of God with pious musings on the significance of all. Each December 25 he notes with joy how many refrain from idleness on that pagan holiday before he goes on to tell who has been condemned to death for adultery. Upon his wife's death, Sewall actively pursues several widows, keeping strict accounts of his presents to them (and their cost) and of the monetary restrictions of each proposal.

4090 Sewall, Samuel   **1652-1730**
Diary of Samuel Sewall, 1674-1729. Edited by M. Halsey Thomas. Newly edited from the manuscript at the Massachusetts Historical Society. New York: Farrar, Straus and Giroux, 1973. (Boston: Massachusetts Hist. Soc., 1878-82) 2v. Index.
A full diary kept for 56 years by an important and respected man of learning who knew and kept contact with notable people of his place and time. It provides a panorama of life and events in early Boston. Vol. 1, 1674-1708; Vol. 2, 1709-1729.

4091 *Sexton, Anne Harvey   **1924-1974**
Anne Sexton: a self-portrait in letters. Edited by Linda Gray Sexton and Lois Ames. Illustrated. Boston: Houghton Mifflin Co., 1977. 433 p. Index.
In this selection from her private letters, the character of the poet is revealed—her struggle with mental illness, her gift for friendship, craving for love, search for faith, and fascination with death.

4092 Seymour, Whitney North, Jr.   **1923-**
United States attorney: an inside view of "Justice" in America under the Nixon Administration. New York: William Morrow and Co., 1975. 248 p. Index.
In his key role as U.S. Attorney during the early 1970's he observed or participated in important events including Watergate, FBI operations, the Agnew payoffs, and national-security paranoia.

4093 Shadid, Michael Abraham   **1881-1966**
Crusading doctor: my fight for cooperative medicine. Boston: Meador Publishing Co., 1956. 312 p.
Born in Syria, he immigrated to America in 1898, finished his education and became a doctor, spending most of his career in Oklahoma where he worked seriously to organize cooperative medicine.

4094 Shantz, Bobby (Robert Clayton)   **1925-**
The story of Bobby Shantz. As told to Ralph Bernstein. Philadelphia: J.B. Lippincott, 1953. 190 p.
Shantz proudly recounts the story of his career in baseball as a left-handed pitcher, emphasizing his two years pitching for the Philadelphia Athletics, 1951 and 1952. In 1952 he was rated the Most Valuable Player in the American League, an award he especially appreciates because of his small size, 5'4", 140 pounds. He gives advice on how to pitch and regards himself as a role model for other aspiring athletes of small stature.

4095 Shapell, Nathan
Witness to the truth. New York: David McKay Co., Inc., 1974. 386 p.
A moving and dramatic account of the destruction of Polish Jews, written by one who survived and worked to help others who lived through concentration camps in post-war Germany until 1951, when he immigrated to America.

4096 Sharp, John Kean   **1892-1979**
Old priest remembers, 1892-1978. 2nd. Edition, enlarged. Hicksville, New York: Exposition Press, 1978. (1977) 216 p.
Father Sharp writes evocatively and lovingly of his youth in turn-of-the-century New York City, of his seminarian training in Baltimore and Washington, D.C., and of his career as a priest which ranged from being a parish priest to a hospital chaplain to a priest on a cruise ship. He was primarily concerned with teaching in Catholic preparatory schools in New York and on Long Island. Sharp's thoughts on retirement are particularly incisive and poignant; he wants to die as he has lived, with dignity.

4097 Sharpe, William   **1878-1960**
Brain surgeon: autobiography of William Sharpe. Foreword by John Haynes Holmes. New York: The Viking Press, 1952. 271 p.
A brain surgeon who practiced in New York and China recounts his schooling and career while reminiscing about his colleagues and patients.

4098 Shaub, Earl L.   **b.1886**
All in a day's work. New York: G.S. Rand Publications, Inc., 1961. 158 p.
A journalist writes of his early training on the job for small-town papers in the South and Midwest, followed by fifteen years as a feature writer for Universal Service for the Hearst papers and others.

4099 *Shaw, Anna Moore   **1898-**
A Pima past. Tucson: University of Arizona Press, 1974. 262 p.
An Indian family saga unfolding the twentieth-century cultural assimilation of her generation, the inevitable changes in lifestyle, the impact of Anglo culture without loss of proud Pima identity.

4100 Shaw, Artie   **1910-**
The trouble with Cinderella: an outline of identity. New York: Da Capo Press, 1979. (New York: Farrar, Straus and Young, 1952) 394 p.
A narrative of discovery, written after he had achieved success as a band leader and jazz musician but was still searching for a meaningful life.

4101 Shaw, Gary
Meat on the hoof; the hidden world of Texas football. Illustrated. New York: St. Martin's, 1972. 234 p.
A high school and college football player, the author intelligently and often movingly relates his education in what he calls "extremely neurotic male behavior." This is the story of his rite-of-passage, first into the win-at-any-price mentality of Texas football, and then to a more difficult, profound sense of himself as free of football, free of other people's plans for him, and free to express himself as a full human being.

4102 Shaw, Henry B.
In the shadow of Peter. Paterson, New Jersey: St. Anthony Guild Press, 1950. 158 p.
An introspective account of his spiritual growth, from boyhood acquaintance with the Episcopal faith through his college and seminary years when he finally converted to Catholicism and became a priest.

4103 Shaw, Nate   **1885-1973**
All God's dangers: the life of Nate Shaw. Edited and compiled by Theodore Rosengarten. New York: Alfred A. Knopf, 1974. 561 p. Index.
An illiterate Black tenant farmer who in 1932 stood his ground against deputy sheriffs sent to confiscate a neighbor's livestock, spent twelve years in prison, and then returned to try to regain his former status. Here he tells his story to the compiler and editor.

4104 Shaw, Wilbur   **1902-1954**
Gentlemen, start your engines. New York: Coward-McCann, 1955. 313 p.
An automobile racer describes automobile racing and speed records in Indiana, California, Florida, and Utah.

4105 Shawn, Ted   **1891-1972**
One thousand and one night stands. With Gray Poole. New York: Da Capo Press, 1979. (Garden City, New York: Doubleday and Co., Inc., 1960) 288 p.
In 1914 he began his career as a dancer, met and married the already-famous Ruth St. Denis, and was well on his way to the international fame he enjoyed for the next 45 years. This is a narrative of dance and his importance in its development and in establishing the legitimacy of male dancers.

4106 Shea, George Beverly   **1909-**
Songs that lift the heart: a personal story. With Fred Bauer. Old Tappan, New Jersey: Fleming H. Revell Co., 1972. 125 p.
A veteran gospel singer of many years with Billy Graham's Crusades, Shea here writes about his favorite songs and tells personal anecdotes about their meaning for him.

4107 Shea, George Beverly   **1909-**
Then sings my soul. With Fred Bauer. Introduction by Billy Graham. Old Tappan, New Jersey: Fleming H. Revell Co., 1968. 176 p.
A simple narrative of his career as a singer and evangelist, first on radio, then for many years with Billy Graham.

4108 *Shea, Margaret Hammel   **1910-**
Tavern in the town. New York: Ives Washburn, Inc., 1948. 215 p.
Co-owner of a rustic restaurant in Maine right after World War II writes of postwar nostalgia and its effects.

4109 Sheean, Vincent   **1899-1975**
Between the thunder and the sun. New York: Random House, 1943. 428 p. Index.
The time leading up to World War II and the early years of the War (through 1942) as seen by an outspoken civilian correspondent who later entered the armed services.

4110 Sheean, Vincent   **1899-1975**
First and last love. New York: Random House, 1956. 305 p.
Known primarily as a journalist and foreign correspondent, he writes here of his love of great music, his experience with outstanding international performers and composers.

4111 Sheean, Vincent   **1899-1975**
Not peace but a sword. New York: Doubleday, Doran & Co., Inc., 1939. 367 p.

A journalist describes Europe in 1938-39, analyzing the conflicts leading to World War II.

4112 Sheean, Vincent   **1899-1975**
This house against this house. New York: Random House, 1946. 420 p.
His fourth book of personal experience in important historical events with a liberal analysis of international affairs. This volume deals with World War II, its causes, and the making of peace.

4113 Sheehan, Patrick Augustine
see Holmes, Oliver Wendell

4114 *Sheerin, Maria Ward Skelton (Williams)
The parson takes a wife. New York: The Macmillan Company, 1948. 204 p.
Raised in Richmond, Virginia, to be a lady, she had some difficult and humorous experiences learning the conventional behavior of a parson's wife. Her book reflects the mores of a ministry and her own wit and common sense which helped her survive.

4115 Shelby, Carroll Hall   **1923-**
Cobra story. As told to John Bentley. Originally produced by Lyle Kenyon Engel. Minneapolis: Motor Books Int., 1974. (New York: Trident Press, 1965) 272 p. Index.
Racing-driver Shelby's courageous, colorful American individualism won him the admiration and respect of his European counterparts at Le Mans and in the Gran Turismo picture. He came close to snatching the laurels from the long-dominant Ferrari with his American-designed and built Cobras.

4116 *Shelton, Carol
How to succeed in business without being a man! Introduction by Jeri Parker. Salt Lake City, Utah: Quest, 1977. 182 p.
Shelton illustrates her theory that women can be wives and mothers and millionaires, too, with the saga of her divorces, debts, single parenthood, and ventures into the "man's world" of life insurance and real estate. Interspersed (and summarized at the end) are tips on personal and professional motivation.

4117 Shepard, Benjamin Henry Jesse Francis
see Grierson, Francis

4118 *Shepard, Elaine
Forgive us our press passes. Englewood Cliffs, New Jersey: Prentice-Hall, Inc., 1962. 301 p.
As an international correspondent she achieved a spectacular career, covering stories on heads of state, on major political events, on the social scene of Washington.

4119 Shepard, Martin   **1934-**
Memoirs of a defrocked psychoanalyst. Sagaponack, New York: Permanent Press, 1978. (1972) 269 p.
Shepard published this pornographic account of his experiences with group sex, homosexuality, voyeurism, and other orgiastic variations in 1972. Five years later, as a consequence, his medical license was revoked.

4120 Sheppard, Samuel H.   **1923-1970**
Endure and conquer. Cleveland: The World Publishing Co., 1966. 329 p.
On July 4, 1954, Dr. Sheppard's wife was murdered. Everything connected with that and subsequent events was endlessly and sensationally debated: his accusation, trial, conviction, appeals, and then imprisonment. Finally in 1966 the Supreme Court voted to set aside the conviction. This is his own story of the efforts to prove his innocence from the time of the murder and his conviction through the retrial and his vindication.

4121 Sher, Philip   **b.1875**
From the diary of Dr. Philip Sher: a physician who has reflected on life—with a point of view on volunteer social service. Foreword by Joseph B. Wiener. Biographical sketch. New York: Comet Press Books, 1953. 174 p.
Memoirs, human-interest stories, contributions to newspapers, correspondence, and community testimonials comprise this diary of a rabbi-physician whose primary interest was social welfare. As founder of the Jewish Welfare Federation, Sher was instrumental in the promotion of Jewish education and various medical and social services in Omaha, Nebraska, during the first half of the twentieth century.

4122 Sherburne, Andrew   **1765-1831**
Memoirs of Andrew Sherburne: a pensioner of the navy of the Revolution. Freeport, New York: Books for Libraries Press, 1970. (Utica, New York: William Williams, 1828) 262 p.
Sherburne served on the Continental ship-of-war *Ranger* from the age of thirteen and later on other ships, including privateers. He was captured by the British three times during the Revolution. After the war he became a Baptist minister.

4123 Sheridan, Philip Henry   **1831-1888**
Personal memoirs of P.H. Sheridan: General United States Army. Illustrated. St. Clair Shores, Michigan: Scholarly Press, Inc., 1977. (New York: Charles L. Webster & Co., 1888) 2v. Index.
Volume I details Sheridan's military career from West Point to midway through the Civil War. He recounts his experiences with "the savages," Indians in California and Vancouver, and traces the military maneuvers of Generals Granger Nelson, Sill, Grant Wilson, Rosecrans, Bragg, Hunter, and Early. Volume II chronicles his career as general through the Civil War, Reconstruction, and the Franco-German war, with extensive descriptions of battles.

4124 *Sherman, Jane   **1908-**
Soaring: the diary and letters of a Denishawn dancer in the Far East, 1925-1926. Middletown, Connecticut: Wesleyan University Press, 1976. 278 p. Index.
As the youngest member of the famed Denishawn Company during their fifteen-month Far Eastern tour in 1925-26, Sherman wrote these letters and diary entries detailing her adventures, impressions, and thoughts. They reveal not only the conditions of travel and performance in exotic places but also her own maturation and growth.

4125 Sherman, Stuart Pratt, ed.
Letters to a lady in the country, together with her replies. New York: Charles Scribner's Sons, 1925. 232 p.
Letters between "Paul," a Kentuckian living in New York, and "Caroline," a New Yorker living in Kentucky, were published serially in *Books*, 1924-1925. At the beginning of the correspondence each wished to be back home, but gradually their desires changed as did their relationship to each other.

4126 Sherman, William Tecumseh   **1820-1891**
Memoirs. Civil War Centennial Series. Foreword by B.H. Liddell Hart. Westport, Connecticut: Greenwood Press, 1972. (New York: D. Appleton and Co., 1875) 2v. in 1.
Although chiefly a Civil War memoir, his book includes recollections of California (1846-1859), Missouri, Louisiana, Kansas, and New York. The detailed account of his war experience is deftly told, revealing the great military strategist in the vivid context of war.

4127 Sherman, William Tecumseh   **1820-1891**
War is Hell! William T. Sherman's personal narrative of his march through Georgia. Edited by Mills Lane. New York: Arno, 1978. (Savannah: The Beehive Press, 1974) 196 p.
Sherman's account of his famed march through Georgia provides a fascinating look at history, highlighted here by striking photographs and drawings and touching correspondence, much of it with his wife, Ellen. ("Taken principally from the second volume of the *Memoirs* of General William T. Sherman, by himself.")

4128 Shero, Fred Alexander   **1925-**
Shero: the man behind the system. In cooperation with Vijay S. Kothare. Introduction by Bernie Parent. Radnor, Pennsylvania: Chilton Book Co., 1975. 138 p.
A hockey enthusiast from an early age, he was spotted by a New York Rangers scout when he was seventeen. Later, thanks to his special system, he coached the Philadelphia Flyers to their Stanley Cup championship.

4129 Sherrill, Henry Knox   **1890-1980**
Among friends: an autobiography. Boston: Little, Brown and Company, 1962. 340 p. Index.
An Episcopal bishop, well known and loved by many friends and colleagues, writes of his ministry. Rector of Trinity Church, Boston, he served as Bishop of Massachusetts for twelve years.

4130 *Shiel, Lily
see *Graham, Sheilah, pseud.

4131 *Shields, Brooke   **1965-**
Brooke book. Illustrated. New York: Pocket Books, 1978. 150 p.
Twelve-year-old Brooke Shields collects her school essays, press clippings, poems, and six-page autobiography in a slick, lavishly illustrated book. The child of an ex-model and a cosmetics executive, she began her modeling career as Ivory soap baby at eight months and has probably been one of the most photographed pre-teens in America. She touches on her emerging film career, but only mentions briefly "Pretty Baby," a film in which she plays a child prostitute.

4132 Shinnick, Don   **1935-**
Always a winner: on Route 66. As told to James C. Hefley. Introduction by Raymond Berry. Grand Rapids, Michigan: Zondervan Publishing House, 1969. 223 p.
Shinnick intermingles the story of his career as a linebacker for the Baltimore Colts, 1959-1969, with commentary on the importance of the Christian faith and a discussion of his off-season speaking tours for the Fellowship of Christian Athletes. He is devoted to his wife, Marsha, and four children.

4133 Shipp, Nelson McLester   **1892-**
A vagabond newsman. Atlanta: Cherokee Publishing Co., 1974. 230 p.
Index.
    Raised in Georgia during the depression of the 1890's, he left college at
nineteen to edit a weekly newspaper and then traveled about working at
various newspaper and other jobs in the South and Midwest. Later he was
a reporter and editor in Savannah and Macon, became involved in art and
politics, and editorialized against the Ku Klux Klan.

4134 Shippey, Lee   **1884-1969**
**Luckiest man alive: being the author's own story, with certain omissions,
but including hitherto unpublished sidelights on some famous persons and
incidents.** Los Angeles: Westernlore Press, 1959. 203 p. Index.
    Blinded when a teenage aspiring journalist, Shippey nevertheless suc-
ceeded in his chosen career, writing for the Kansas City *Star* and the Los
Angeles *Times*. In between, he covered World War I in France, where he
met and married Madeleine Babin and worked in Tampico, Mexico.

4135 Shirer, William Lawrence   **1904-**
Berlin diary: the journal of a foreign correspondent 1934-1941. London:
Sphere Books Limited, 1970. (New York: Knopf, 1941) 493 p.
    Shirer's journal, written mostly in Berlin during and just before World
War II, is, he says, "a first hand account of a Europe that was already in
agony and that, as the months and years unfolded, slipped inexorably
toward the abyss of war and self-destruction."

4136 Shirer, William Lawrence   **1904-**
End of a Berlin diary. New York: Alfred A. Knopf, 1947. 369 p. Index.
    A continuation of his *Berlin Diary*, this volume records the end of the
war, the beginnings of peace, the inner workings of the Nazi military
machine, the high hopes for the fledgling United Nations, the widening
gulf between Russia and the West.

4137 Shirer, William Lawrence   **1904-**
**Twentieth century journey: a memoir of a life and the times, the start,
1904-1930.** Illustrated. New York: Simon and Schuster, 1976. 510 p. Index.
    Shirer evokes the turn-of-the-century Chicago of his early childhood
and Cedar Rapids, Iowa, where he grew up as a neighbor of Grant Wood
and Carl van Vechten and attended Coe College. After that he went to
Paris, became a foreign correspondent there and in London, and interviewed many notable world figures, whose portraits he presents here,
including Gertrude Stein, Isadora Duncan, Charles Lindbergh, and James
Thurber.

4138 Shores, Cyrus Wells   **1844-1934**
Memoirs of a lawman. Edited by Wilson Rockwell. Denver: Sage Books,
1962. 378 p.
    Liberally edited to insure the accuracy and readability of the original
manuscript, written when Doc Shores was over eighty, the book includes
a section of frontier reminiscences and another describing his eight years
as sheriff of Gunnison, Colorado.

4139 Shotwell, James Thomson   **1874-1965**
Autobiography. Indianapolis: Bobbs-Merrill Co., 1961. 347 p. Index.
    The distinguished historian and humanitarian worked for the cause of
world peace by helping to avert international crises and to negotiate
agreements.

4140 Shula, Don   **1930-**
The winning edge. With Lou Sahadi. Illustrated. New York: E.P. Dutton
& Co., Inc., 1973. 250 p.
    "The Winning Edge" is inscribed on the rings worn by the Miami
Dolphins as mementos of their Super Bowl victory in 1973. In 1971 Shula
was voted AFC Coach of the Year; in 1972 he became the first NFL
coach to win 100 games in his first 10 years. His book describes his
coaching experience and philosophy.

4141 Shuster, George Nauman   **1894-1977**
Ground I walked on: reflections of a college president. South Bend: University of Notre Dame Press, 1969. (New York: Farrar, Straus and
Giroux, 1961) 270 p. Index.
    The history of his 21-year presidency of Hunter College and his service
as U.S. Deputy Commissioner in Bavaria reflect his concerns for education.

4142 Sibley, George
Part of a winter: a memory more like a dream. New York: Harmony
Books, 1978. 245 p.
    Sibley's version of we-took-to-the-woods focuses on the four years of
life in the Colorado wilderness that he shared with his wife, Barbara, and
their two young children, one of whom was born there. Editor of a
newspaper in Crested Butte, Colorado, he searched throughout this time
for the fundamental simplicity and existential unity of life as exemplified
by his hero, Henry David Thoreau.

4143 Sigismondi, Aldo
see **Dale, Alan, pseud.**

4144 Sikorsky, Igor Ivan   **1889-1972**
**Story of the Winged-S: new chapters and illustrations on recent develop-
ments of the helicopter; an autobiography.** New York: Dodd, Mead and
Co., 1967. (1938) 314 p.
    A pioneer in aviation, Sikorsky developed the helicopter, immigrated to
the United States from Russia after the Revolution, and continued to play
an important role in the development of helicopters and planes. Those of
his company carry the Winged-S emblem.

4145 Silbert, Samuel H.   **b.1883**
"Judge Sam." With Sidney A. Eisenberg. Manhasset, New York: Channel
Press, 1963. 192 p.
    Liberally peppered with anecdotes, this account describes a judge's
lifetime on the bench.

4146 Sillman, Leonard   **1908-1976**
Here lies Leonard Sillman: straightened out at last/an autobiography.
New York: The Citadel Press, 1959. 377 p. Index.
    Theatrical producer Leonard Sillman is credited with introducing to
the stage many people who later became stars in theater and films. His
various productions of *New Faces* (1934, 1936 . . .) are his most notable
accomplishments; 1952 introduced Eartha Kitt.

4147 *Sills, Beverly   **1929-**
Bubbles: A Self-Portrait. New York: Warner Books, 1978. (Indianapolis:
Bobbs-Merrill, 1976) 260 p. Index.
    Opera singer Sills provides an exuberant, delightful, abundantly illus-
trated survey of her life, generally pleasant and professionally successful.
She focuses on her career (especially with the New York City and San
Francisco operas) and family—her beloved mother; devoted husband,
Peter Greenough; and children, whose birth defects prompted her
fund-raising efforts for the March of Dimes.

4148 Silvers, Phil   **1911-**
The man who was Bilko: the autobiography of Phil Silvers. With Robert
Saffron. London: W.H. Allen, 1974. 276 p.
    A performer since childhood, Silvers played in all kinds of theatrical
undertakings from burlesque to movies, but many people remember him
best as Sergeant Bilko in the long-running TV comedy series.

4149 Silvers, Phil   **1911-**
This laugh is on me: the Phil Silvers story. With Robert Saffron.
Englewood Cliffs, New Jersey: Prentice-Hall, Inc., 1973. 320 p.
    The private life and the up-and-down show-biz career of Silvers, a
comedian of vaudeville, burlesque, Broadway, Hollywood, nightclub and
television fame.

4150 Simmons, Edward   **1852-1931**
From seven to seventy: memories of a painter and a Yankee. With an
interruption by Oliver Herford. Edited with introduction by H. Barbara
Weinberg. New York: Garland Publishing, 1976. (New York: Harper &
Brothers, 1922) 344 p.
    Simmons, best known for his mural paintings including those in the
Library of Congress, writes with good humor about his Puritan forbears
(he grew up in Concord in Hawthorne's "Old Manse"), his art studies in
Paris, and his exploration of painting sites in England and in Brittany.
Instrumental in founding "Ten American Painters" in 1898, he also ex-
plores the dual allegiance of his peers to tradition and to Impressionism.

4151 Simmons, Lee   **1873-1957**
Assignment Huntsville: memoirs of a Texas prison official. Austin: University of Texas Press, 1957. 233 p. Index.
    Simmons was general manager of the Texas Prison System 1930-1935,
after having been a banker and the manager of the Sherman, Texas,
Chamber of Commerce. A fluent writer and good storyteller, he focuses
on the highlights of his prison management (including the capture of
Clyde Barrow and Bonnie Parker) and his philosophy of treating prisoners—education, hard work, sports, and no-nonsense corporal punishment, if warranted.

4152 Simms, William Gilmore   **1806-1870**
Letters. Collected and edited by Mary C. Simms Oliphant (et al.). Introduction by Donald Davidson. Biographical sketch by Alexander S. Salley.
Columbia: University of South Carolina Press, 1952-56. 5v. Index.
    The extensive correspondence (1830-1870) of a South Carolina writer
who published 82 volumes of poetry and fiction gives a vivid account of
the man, his intellect, and the times.

4153 *Simon, Charlie May (Mrs. John Gould Fletcher)   **1897-**
Johnswood. New York: E.P. Dutton, 1953. 249 p.
    The author of children's books and the widow of John Gould Fletcher
relives the last years of her husband's life in Arkansas in an effort to come
to terms with his death. The book includes some letters and poetry by Mr.
Fletcher.

4154 Simon, Howard 1903-
Cabin on a ridge. Illustrated. Chicago: Follett Publishing Co., 1970. 159 p.

During the Depression when he could no longer earn a living as a painter and book illustrator in New York, the author went to the Ozarks, built a log cabin on a homestead, and settled down to work among the simple mountain people. In the five years he spent there he found a beautiful environment, a simpler, fulfilling life, and friendly, hospitable neighbors.

4155 Simon, Kenneth
see Simon, M. Raphael

4156 Simon, M. Raphael (Kenneth Simon) 1909-
Glory of thy people: the story of a conversion. Preface by Fulton J. Sheen. New York: Macmillan, 1948. 139 p.

Describes conversion of a New York Reformed Jew, a psychiatrist, who became a Trappist monk.

4157 *Simonis, Mother M. Raphaela
Deo Gratias et Mariae: Thanks Be to God and Mary. New York: Vantage, 1973. 122 p.

Born in a small village in Lithuania, she became a teacher and then a Benedictine nun. She writes of her religious education, her study at the Art Academy, her life as a nun during the German occupation, and later her visit to Rome.

4158 Simpson, George Gaylord 1902-
Concession to the improbable: an unconventional autobiography. New Haven, Connecticut: Yale University Press, 1978. 291 p. Index.

Simpson discusses his career as a paleontologist and his world-wide fieldwork (often on expeditions for the American Museum of Natural History). A prolific author (during 1939-41 he wrote 63 articles), much of his work focuses on findings in Venezuela, Brazil, and Argentina, though he also did work in Africa, Australia, and the American West.

4159 Simpson, Louis Aston Marantz 1923-
Air with armed men. London: London Magazine Editions, 1972. 285 p.

A poet writes of his youth, his wartime army experiences, his education, and teaching career. He examines his relationships with the world of contemporary poetry and literature and particularly his friendships with other poets.

4160 Simpson, Louis Aston Marantz 1923-
North of Jamaica. New York: Harper & Row, 1972. 285 p.

In an autobiography that has the character of a novel, the author creates the scenes of his childhood in Jamaica, his emigration to the U.S. to attend Columbia, his experience as a rifleman in World War II, and his writing, giving the sounds and smells, the conversations, and occasional reflections on the life he is recalling. The later chapters include a careful look at the literary movements with which he was involved.

4161 Simpson, Orenthal James 1947-
O.J., the education of a rich rookie. With Pete Axthelm. Illustrated. New York: The Macmillan Co., 1970. 255 p.

Simpson's rookie year in professional football did not measure up to his expectations or the expectations others had of him. He had a lucrative contract and endorsements, but his team, the Buffalo Bills, were disjointed and unbalanced, just managing to salvage private triumph from public defeat that year.

4162 Sims, James Marion 1813-1883
The story of my life. Foreword by C. Lee Buxton, M.D. Introduction by T.J.M. Editor's preface by H. Marion-Sims. New York: Da Capo Press, 1968. (New York: D. Appleton & Co., 1884) 471 p.

Sims' professional peers rate him as the foremost gynecologist of his time because of his innovations with "Sims' speculum," "Sims' position," and the vesicovaginal repair. Sims focuses here on his childhood in South Carolina, his frustratingly long courtship, and debilitating intestinal problems which overshadow the most significant aspects of his work.

4163 Sims, William
West Side cop. With G.C. Skipper. Illustrated. Open Door Books. Chicago: Children's Press, 1970. 64 p.

A career guidance book for young people, this volume examines Sims' youth, education, and the events which led him to become a police officer in Chicago.

4164 *Sinclair, Mary Craig (Kimbrough) 1882-1967
Southern belle. Foreword by Upton Sinclair. New York: Crown Publishers, Inc., 1957. 407 p.

Raised as a Southern lady, she describes her New York education, her successful marriage to Upton Sinclair, and the life they shared among intellectuals, reformers, and politicians.

4165 Siragusa, Charles 1913-
Trial of the poppy; behind the mask of the Mafia. As told to Robert Wiedrich. Englewood Cliffs, New Jersey: Prentice-Hall, Inc., 1966. 235 p.

For 25 years he worked for the Federal Bureau of Narcotics, exposing the network of international drug traffic and the Mafia bosses who ran it. His book focuses particularly on the Mafia, their codes and methods. It includes a glossary of illegal drug terms.

4166 Sirica, John Joseph 1904-
To set the record straight: the break-in, the tapes, the conspirators, the pardon. Illustrated. New York: W.W. Norton & Company, 1979. 394 p. Index.

Sirica records his involvement with the Watergate affair, a five-year struggle from the first indictments through a series of legal altercations to the final judgment against the high-level conspirators and the eventual presidential resignation. Finally, Sirica renders his judgment on Nixon and the Ford pardon.

4167 Sirin, Vladimir, pseud.
see Nabokov, Vladimir Vladimirovich

4168 Siringo, Charles A. 1855-1928
A Texas cowboy: or, fifteen years on the hurricane deck of a Spanish pony, taken from real life. Introduction by J. Frank Dobie. Illustrated. Lincoln: University of Nebraska Press, 1979. (Chicago, Illinois: M. Umbdenstock & Co., 1885) 216 p.

A rocky account of Siringo's escapades as a cowboy in Texas, with occasional excursions to New Mexico and St. Louis. His work of cowpunching and driving stock to market along the Chisholm Trail was punctuated by encounters with Indians, benign and hostile, buffalo, the capture of Billy the Kid, an attack of smallpox, and amorous misadventures.

4169 Siskovsky, Jaroslav b.1888
Fiddler on the roof: the odyssey of concert violinist Jaroslav Siskovsky. Philadelphia: Dorrance & Co., 1975. 307 p.

Having received his first violin lesson at age five, he thereafter fiddled his way through various dance band and orchestra engagements until he became a member of the highly respected New York String Quartet. A large portion of his book is devoted to travels throughout the world.

4170 Sites, David Eston 1888-
My first eighty years. Philadelphia: Dorrance & Co., 1970. 145 p.

Sites happily recollects his West Virginia upbringing as one of a blacksmith's thirteen children, his education at Manchester College in Indiana, his career as a schoolteacher in Indiana, as a Y.M.C.A. secretary for a decade in Milwaukee, and as a traveling salesman thereafter for Rand McNally. Over half the book is devoted to an account of his retirement travels throughout the United States, Canada, and Mexico with his wife.

4171 *Sizemore, Chris Costner
I'm Eve. And Elen Sain Pittillo. Illustrated. Garden City, New York: Doubleday & Co., Inc., 1977. 461 p.

A candid self-portrayal, written as part of her therapy, by the woman whose classic case of multiple personality became the subject of *The Three Faces of Eve.* She writes of the heretofore unknown details of her childhood, two marriages, and continuing struggle with her illness.

4172 Skinner, Burrhus Frederic 1904-
Particulars of my life. New York: Alfred A. Knopf, 1976. 319 p.

From small town boyhood through his early groping toward his lifework, a controversial behaviorist recalls his beginnings with simple clarity.

4173 *Skinner, Cornelia Otis 1902-1979
The ape in me. With drawings by Alajalov. Boston: Houghton Mifflin Co., 1959. 172 p.

The book is intended to describe her life as an actress, but it is full of anecdotes about a variety of things that have interested her for a few minutes here and there.

4174 *Skinner, Cornelia Otis 1902-1979
Bottoms up! New York: Dodd, Mead and Co., 1955. 208 p.

A collection of short reminiscences describing her girlhood, life on the stage, playing the straw-hat belt, traveling, and lecturing.

4175 *Skinner, Cornelia Otis 1902-1979
Happy family. Illustrated with photographs. Boston: Houghton Mifflin Co., 1958. (1948) 310 p.

A family memoir, with good descriptions of the world of American theater evolving from personal details of the Skinner family—Otis, Maud and Cornelia—up to Cornelia's debut as an actress on Broadway. Previously published under title, *Family Circle.*

4176 *Skinner, Cornelia Otis 1902-1979
Nuts in May. New York: Dodd, Mead and Co., 1950. 188 p.

In chapters previously printed in *The New Yorker* magazine, the author humorously describes incidents in her family and stage life.

4177 *Skinner, Cornelia Otis   **1902-1979**
Our hearts were young and gay. And Emily Kimbrough. Illustrated by Alajalov. New York: Dodd, Mead & Co., 1942. 247 p.
  The hilarious adventures of two young ladies off to Europe on an unchaperoned trip with main stops in London and Paris.

4178 Skinner, Otis   **1858-1942**
Footlights and spotlights: recollections of my life on the stage. Illustrated. Westport, Connecticut: Greenwood Press, 1972. (Indianapolis: The Bobbs-Merrill Co., 1924) 366 p. Index.
  An actor from his youth, Skinner tells of his first part, his rise in the theater, the great actors and actresses of his day, the roles he loved best out of the 325 he played, including 38 parts in 14 Shakespeare plays, and of the plays he produced himself.

4179 Skinsnes, Casper C.   **b.1886**
Scalpel and cross. Illustrated. Minneapolis: Augsburg Publishing House, 1952. 254 p.
  A modestly told account of the compassionate endeavors of Dr. Skinsnes, a Lutheran medical missionary, and his wife, a nurse, to build and maintain a hospital in Sinyang, China, during the 1920's and 30's. He was extremely successful in his low-key pursuit of the ideals of good medical care and Christianity, but his endeavors were halted when the Japanese bombed the hospital during the Sino-Japanese War. Evacuated during World War II, he oversaw the successful postwar rebuilding of the hospital.

4180 Skolsky, Sidney   **1905-**
Don't get me wrong—I love Hollywood. New York: G.P. Putnam's Sons, 1975. 258 p. Index.
  A collection of anecdotes and profiles add to this nostalgic look at the star-studded days of Hollywood by a columnist who was part of that scene since 1933.

4181 Skutch, Alexander Frank   **1904-**
A naturalist in Costa Rica. Illustrated. Gainesville: University of Florida Press, 1971. 378 p. Index.
  The author is a naturalist who has spent forty years in wild parts of tropical America, principally in Costa Rica. He records here his experiences and observations of plants, birds, insects, animals as he found and studied them in their natural state.

4182 Slack, Charles W.
Timothy Leary, the madness of the Sixties and me. New York: Peter H. Wyden, 1974. 264 p.
  More a biography of Timothy Leary than an autobiography of Slack, this book tells of Leary's rise and fall, his travels with Slack through the unrest of the Sixties: the campus riots, the Vietnam protests, the use of marijuana and hallucinogenic drugs, and the hedonism.

4183 *Slaughter, Linda (Warfel)   **1843-1911**
Fortress to farm, or twenty-three years on the frontier. Edited with introduction and epilogue by her granddaughter Hazel Eastman. New York: Exposition Press, 1972. 172 p.
  First published serially in the Bismarck *Tribune* in 1893-1894, this account describes the author's eventful and dangerous frontier experiences in the unsettled Dakota Territory as the wife of an Army surgeon.

4184 *Slayden, Ellen (Maury)   **1860-1926**
Washington wife: journal of Ellen Maury Slayden from 1897-1919. New York: Harper & Row, 1963. 385 p. Index.
  During 21 years in Washington as wife of a U.S. congressman, she kept this diary candidly appraising events, experiences, and the people she met, which included almost everyone of note.

4185 *Slenczynska, Ruth   **1925-**
Forbidden childhood. And Louis Biancolli. Garden City, New York: Doubleday and Co., 1957. 263 p.
  A gripping, haunting narrative of a child prodigy's early musical career, rebellion, and discouragement in her mid-teens and early twenties, and re-emergence as a master pianist in her late twenties and early thirties. Her father forced her to practice nine hours a day when she was four, beating her for mistakes. At eighteen she married George Born, who encouraged her comeback.

4186 Slezak, Walter   **1902-**
What time's the next swan? As told to Smith-Corona model 88E. Garden City, New York: Doubleday & Co., Inc., 1962. 227 p.
  The son of a famous opera star writes with affection and humor of his engaging family and his own career as an actor.

4187 Sloan, Alfred Pritchard   **1875-1966**
Adventures of a white-collar man. In collaboration with Boyden Sparkes.

Illustrated. Freeport, New York: Books for Libraries Press, 1970. (New York: Doubleday, Doran, 1941) 208 p.
  In a career which paralleled the growth of America to a powerful industrial economy, Sloan rose from a draftsman's job in a factory to the leadership of the giant General Motors. The mass-production techniques of the automotive industry have been the model of efficient methods throughout the business world and Sloan's recollections of the era of industrial expansion and its pioneers comprise a history of that adventurous period.

4188 Sloan, Alfred Pritchard   **1875-1966**
My years with General Motors. Edited by John McDonald and Catharine Stevens. Garden City, New York: Doubleday & Co., Inc., 1964. (1963) 472 p. Index.
  His own story and that of General Motors, the corporation he served as chief executive officer for 23 years and as board member and committee participant for 45 years.

4189 Sloan, John   **1871-1951**
John Sloan's New York scene; from diaries, notes and correspondence, 1906-1913. Edited by Bruce St. John. Introduction by Helen Farr Sloan. New York: Harper & Row, 1965. 658 p. Index.
  Sloan started his career as an illustrator for books and magazines and by the time he was fifty he had sold only six paintings. His diaries record his daily routine, his life as an artist, and his professional struggles.

4190 Sloan, Stephen C.   **1944-**
Calling life's signals: the Steve Sloan story by Steve Sloan. With James C. Hefley. Introduction by Paul W. (Bear) Bryant. Illustrated. Grand Rapids, Michigan: Zondervan Publishing House, 1967. 143 p.
  With reference to his career in sports, Sloan, a rookie quarterback for the Atlanta Falcons, expounds his Christian philosophy of life: God, the "Master Coach," instructs us to become members of "the best team, Christianity," and to reject alternative teams, such as communism and beatnik social rebellion. He promotes Christianity through marriage.

4191 Sloan, Stephen C.   **1944-**
A whole new ball game. Nashville: Broadman Press, 1975. 168 p.
  Coach Sloan writes of his life and football, which are inextricably interwoven. He went from sandlot to high school, college, and professional football before a shoulder injury cut short his playing career. Thereafter he turned to coaching. His objectives are, first, to "seek the kingdom of God," second, look after his family; and third, perform his job of coaching.

4192 Sloane, Eric (Everard Hinricks)   **1905-**
Legacy. Illustrated by author. New York: Funk & Wagnalls/Thomas Y. Crowell, 1979. 77 p.
  Using "the providence of God is my inheritance" as a motif, Sloane discusses his philosophy of life. He enjoys painting and writing as a dual career; he appreciates awareness of life and environment, solitude, collecting art and artifacts, and being an American.

4193 Sloane, Eric (Everard Hinricks)   **1905-**
Recollections in black and white. New York: Ballantine Books, 1974. 64 p.
  Incidents from his life and the development of his illustrator's art are combined with black-and-white drawings to form a graphic journey through the American landscape. The sketches of covered bridges and rural scenes recall the vanishing American past.

4194 Slonaker, Arthur Gordon   **1919-**
Recollections and reflections of a college dean: including a brief history of the 103rd Barrage Balloon Battery. Parsons, West Virginia: McClain Printing Co., 1975. 218 p. Index.
  Written mainly during summer camp at the U.S. Army Reserve, Slonaker's book tells the story of his career in education from high school teacher to dean of Potomac State College. Also included are sections on the war years in the 103rd Barrage Balloon Battery and on hunting stories.

4195 *Sloop, Mary T.   **1873-1962**
Miracle in the hills. With LeGette Blythe. New York: McGraw-Hill, 1953. 232 p.
  The book narrates Dr. Mary Sloop's experiences as a rural mountain doctor in North Carolina in joint practice with her husband, Dr. Eustase Sloop. Also described are the author's efforts to establish worthwhile education in the area and her receipt of the Mother of the Year Award for 1951.

4196 Smallwood, Franklin   **1927-**
Free and independent. Brattleboro, Vermont: Stephen Greene Press, 1976. 235 p. Index.
  A Dartmouth political science professor explains and interprets the three-year period (1972-74) when he ran for and was elected to the Vermont State Senate. He chronicles "the ongoing dynamics of the political

process," beginning with the campaign, emphasizing the work, intractible governmental bureaucracy, constituents, and legislative housekeeping.

4197 Smart, Charles Allen   **1904-1967**
The long watch. Cleveland: The World Publishing Co., 1968. 237 p.
    Five months after Pearl Harbor, the author, aged 37, enlisted in the Navy; later he became an Executive Officer. His book is a moving recollection of the stress of combat, the battle fatigue coming after days without sleep, the teamwork of military life, the fear of separation, loss, and death.

4198 Smith, Albert E.   **1875-1958**
Two reels and a crank. With Phil A. Koury. Garden City, New York: Doubleday and Co., Inc., 1952. 285 p.
    The story of his life as one of the first film producers, of his company, Vitagraph, and of the outrageous early days of silent film-making.

4199 Smith, Arthur Donaldson   **1864-1939**
Through unknown African countries; the first expedition from Somaliland to Lake Lamu. Illustrated. New York: Greenwood Press, 1969. (London: Edward Arnold, 1897) 471 p.
    Combining his interests in sporting trips and in scientific exploration, Smith joined a friend on a journey to Somaliland in 1893 to acquire the requisite knowledge to mount a future expedition. In June 1894 he set out to explore the country, learn as much as possible about the land, the natives, the animals, insects, fish, fossils, and plants.

4200 Smith, Charles Henry   **1875-1948**
Mennonite country boy: the early years of C. Henry Smith. Mennonite Historical Series. Newton, Kansas: Faith and Life Press, 1962. 261 p. Index.
    The youth, education, and early career of a Mennonite farm boy who later taught and wrote about the beliefs, faith, and principles of the Mennonites and Anabaptists.

4201 Smith, Charles Merrill
Different drums: how father and son bridged generations with love and understanding. Foreword and afterword by Terrence Lore Smith. New York: Saturday Review Press, 1975. 166 p.
    A serious rift between father and son, its effect on their relationship, and the understanding they developed in order to bridge the gap. Written by a clergyman.

4202 Smith, Charles Perrin   **1819-1883**
New Jersey political reminiscences, 1828-1882. Edited by Hermann K. Platt. New Brunswick, New Jersey: Rutgers University Press, 1965. 278 p. Index.
    A condensation of three journals and reminiscences, this book covers Smith's years in Salem, New Jersey, as a newspaper editor, his political career as a leader of the Whig and Republican parties in New Jersey, legislator, and Clerk of the Supreme Court, perhaps the most lucrative sinecure in the state. He records anti-monopoly activities of the 1850's, New Jersey's support for the Union war effort, and the factional rivalry within the Republican Party after the Civil War.

4203 Smith, Chester Allen   **1884-1972**
Chester A. Smith of Peekskill: his memoir. Foreword by The Historical Committee of the New York Annual Conference. Hudson: The Historical Committee of the New York Annual Conference of the Methodist Church, 1966. 37 p. Index.
    Written in response to a resolution of the New York Annual Conference of the Methodist Church, this memoir concentrates on Smith's "participation in the affairs of the General Conferences of The Methodist Church," and includes his civic, educational, and church activities in his home town of Peekskill, New York. Smith toured the Holy Land, built a school in India, and fought liquor traffic during Prohibition. He also advocated racial integration of the church conventions and objected to the huge sums of money (profits on tobacco) that the Duke Foundation contributed to the church, but was overruled.

4204 Smith, Clark Ashton   **1839-1961**
Black book of Clark Ashton Smith. Illustrated by Andrew Smith. Foreword by Marvin R. Hiemstra. George F. Haas, "As I Remember Klarkash-Ton," pp. 109-130; and "Memories of Klarkash-Ton," pp. 131-141. Sauk City, Wisconsin: Arkham House, 1979. 141 p.
    A notebook by Clark Ashton Smith, a writer of science fiction (mostly for *Weird Tales*) and occult poetry, which contains plots for stories, drafts of poems, and observations on life and philosophy: "Communism: the utopia of army ants" and "Do others—the modern perversion of the Golden Rule."

4205 Smith, David   **1906-1965**
David Smith by David Smith. Photographs by David Smith. Edited by Clere Gray. New York: Holt, Rinehart and Winston, 1968. 176 p.
    This stunning collection of photographs of Smith's sculptures and preliminary drawings for them is accompanied by commentaries culled from 10,000 of Smith's Whitmanesque poems, letters, and notes in the Archives

of American Art. They reveal a great deal about Smith's life as well as his artistic techniques and aesthetic philosophy.

4206 Smith, Dennis E.   **1941-**
Report from Engine Co. 82. New York: McCall Books, 1972. 215 p.
    A frightening insider's account of the life and work of a group of firefighters in the South Bronx and a scathing condemnation of the kind of politics that complicates the already dangerous job of firefighting.

4207 Smith, Edgar H.   **1930-1968**
Brief against death. Introduction by William F. Buckley, Jr. Maps by J. Maestro. New York: Alfred A. Knopf, 1968. 365 p.
    In an articulate but unsentimental style, Smith recounts the process by which he claims he was wrongly accused of the brutal murder of teenager Victoria Zielinski in 1957 and how, acting as his own lawyer, he pursued every legal means available to gain a new trial and a stay of execution, battling the state of New Jersey, the appellate courts, and occasionally the Supreme Court. Written from Death Row in prison in Trenton.

4208 Smith, Elihu Hubbard   **1771-1798**
The diary of Elihu Hubbard Smith. Edited by James E. Cronin. Philadelphia: American Philosophical Society, 1973. 481 p.
    After graduating from Yale at fifteen, Smith was sent to Timothy White's Academy at Greenfield Hill for a year before he returned home to study medicine with a doctor. After three years he went to the College of Philadelphia, where he studied with Benjamin Rush. Still too young to become a doctor, he turned to writing poetry and drama, editing, taking part in a literary circle, the Manumission Society, and other groups.

4209 Smith, Frank Ellis   **1918-**
Congressman from Mississippi. New York: Random House (Pantheon Books), 1964. 338 p. Index.
    During his twelve years in Congress Smith tried to maintain a moderate course while working toward the gradual elimination of racial discrimination. His book describes his personal and political life in the events that led him to Washington, his conduct in office, the bitter opposition by racists who accomplished his defeat in 1962, and his views about the future.

4210 Smith, Frank Kingston   **1919-**
Flights of fancy. New York: Random House, 1960. 247 p.
    A successful Philadelphia lawyer, he took up flying as an escape from his busy schedule described in his earlier book, *Week-end Pilot*. Here he tells of more flying adventures, including the fanciful pleasures as well as some highly practical information.

4211 Smith, Frank Kingston   **1919-**
Week-end pilot. Introduction by Gill Robb Wilson. New York: Vintage, 1974. (New York: Random House, 1957) 236 p.
    When his law career made him overwrought and tense, Smith searched for a hobby as a release. After several abortive tries, he fell in love with flying his own plane. He found it exhilarating and liberating, opening a new door to happiness for himself and his family.

4212 Smith, George Edward   **1938-**
P.O.W.: two years with the Vietcong. Introduction and epilogue by Donald Duncan. Berkeley: Ramparts Press, 1971. 304 p.
    Smith, a U.S. Army Special Forces sergeant, was captured by the Vietcong north of Saigon in November 1963. For two years he traveled and lived with the Vietcong in jungle camps. He writes sympathetically of his life in the National Liberation Front's safe areas and of the people we call the VC.

4213 *Smith, Hannah (Merriam)
For heaven's sake. Boston: Little Brown and Co., 1949. 266 p.
    Describes strict upbringing of her younger years as an evangelist's daughter, through her final reconciliation with her father, his acceptance of her on her terms—her marriage and her private life.

4214 Smith, Harry Allen   **1907-1975**
To hell in a handbasket. Garden City, New York: Doubleday & Co., Inc., 1962. 341 p. Index.
    A writer-humorist writes of growing up in Illinois and Ohio and of his work on such newspapers as the Denver *Post*, the Huntingdon *Press*, and the New York *World-Telegram*.

4215 Smith, Harry Allen   **1907-1975**
The world, the flesh, and H. Allen Smith. Edited with introduction by Bergen Evans. Garden City, New York: Hanover House, 1954. 301 p.
    A humorous compilation of anecdotes about Smith's Midwestern upbringing, his family, his career as a newspaperman, and the flamboyant and bizarre people he has known in New York, Hollywood, "The Wild West," and suburbia—mostly writers and actors.

4216 Smith, Howard Worth   **1883-1976**
Our paternal hearth. Illustrated by Juan Flores. The author, 1976. 108 p.

Virginia congressman Smith's writing takes the form of a letter to his grandchildren, signed "Affectionately, Grandaddy." Delightful nostalgia of Virginia country life from the Civil War era on is punctuated by quotations and line drawings as Smith concentrates on the lives of people around him rather than on his own achievements.

4217 Smith, Joseph, III   1832-1914
Joseph Smith III and the restoration. Edited by Mary Audentia Smith Anderson. Condensed with preface by Beth Audentia Anderson Holmes. Independence, Missouri: Herald House, 1952. 639 p.

An articulate account of the life of Mormon founder Joseph Smith's grandson, Joseph Smith III, also a prominent Mormon leader. In the book, which is topically organized and divided into short segments that reflect its initial serial publication, Smith discusses his three successive happy marriages and sixteen children; the history of the Mormon Church and settlements at Nauvoo, Illinois, and Utah; leaders, religious philosophies and tenets, disagreements and persecutions—the latter two dominated by church conflict over polygamy, which the Smiths did not practice. Published serially in *The Saints Herald,* 1932-1937.

4218 *Smith, Kate   1909-
Upon my lips a song. New York: Funk & Wagnalls, 1960. 213 p.

Famous as a singer on radio and television, she writes of her early career experience, the pain of being ridiculed as a "fatgirl," her long and gratifying friendship with her manager/announcer Ted Collins, and many great names in radio and television.

4219 Smith, Leonard Francis   1838-1874
Diaries, 1859-1874, of the Reverend Leonard Smith, circuit rider. Foreword & afterword by Blanche Beal Lowe. Stanton, California: privately printed, 1974. 952 p. Index.

This huge volume is a typed transcription of ten diaries by Reverend Smith, who was a pious clergyman and rode circuit in Ontario and later in Illinois. His diaries are filled with comments on sermon subjects and biblical quotations, observations of nature and the weather, temperance statistics, gossip, current events, and lists of expenses.

4220 *Smith, Lillian Eugenia   1897-1966
The journey. Cleveland: The World Publishing Co., 1954. 256 p.

A personal, spiritual quest for the meaning of self and life in contemporary times by the author of *Killers of the Dream.*

4221 Smith, Malcolm   1938-
Follow me! The apprenticing of disciples. Plainfield, New Jersey: Logos International, 1976. 168 p.

A Pentacostal clergyman explains how he began a divinely inspired discipleship ministry in Brooklyn in 1972, converting disillusioned Vietnam war veterans and hippies to become active disciples who eventually conducted ministries on their own.

4222 *Smith, Margaret (Chase)   1898-
Declaration of conscience. Edited by William C. Lewis, Jr. New York: Doubleday & Co., 1972. 512 p. Index.

Mrs. Smith, the first woman elected to both houses of Congress, often took controversial stands on issues—military affairs, the Nuclear Test Ban Treaty, equality for women in the Armed Forces. She was the first elected official to denounce McCarthyism. In this volume she discusses some of the most important speeches and statements she made during more than three decades of public service.

4223 Smith, Paul Clifford   1908-1976
Personal file. New York: Appleton-Century, 1964. 476 p. Index.

A variety of occupations from rum-running at thirteen, to vice-presidency of a bank at twenty, to editor and general manager of the San Francisco *Chronicle* at twenty-six began his phenomenal career. He went on to be a respected journalist, an officer in the Navy and Marines in the Pacific during World War II, and later head of the Crowell-Collier publishing empire.

4224 Smith, Philip Hillyer
Perennial harvest. Illustrated by William Thomas Woodward. New York: Harper & Brothers Publishers, 1948. 272 p.

In the early 1930's problems with his job and family sent him to a farm in upper New York State to recover a sense of self and work as a free-lance writer. He remained for twelve years, developed self-sufficiency, a sense of inner peace, and a deep appreciation for life.

4225 Smith, Robert S.   1906-
Idaho surgeon: an autobiography. Boise, Idaho: Syms-York, 1974. 151 p.

A description of a full professional life in middle America and then in the West. After medical school and two years in England as a Rhodes Scholar, he became a practicing surgeon and a professional leader in the Northwest. The victim of a stroke that paralyzed his left side in 1971, he had to give up surgery, but has adapted his activities and continues to enjoy life.

4226 Smith, Robert Taylor   b.1875
"Dear Mr. President": the story of fifty years in the White House mail room. With Joe Alex Morris. New York: Julian Messner, Inc., 1949. 238 p.

In 1897 Smith became a mail clerk in the White House, opening mail for nine presidents from McKinley through Truman. Here he describes his work, the events, and people associated with the White House during those years.

4227 Smith, Roy Lemon   1887-1963
Why I am a Methodist. New York: Hermitage House, 1955. 217 p. Index.

A Methodist clergyman in Kansas relates how important his faith has been in his work and life and discusses aspects of the Methodist faith itself.

4228 *Smith, Susy (Ethel Elizabeth Smith)   1911-
Confessions of a psychic. Illustrated. New York: The Macmillan Co., 1971. 315 p.

Smith recounts her search for a philosophy of life leading to her conviction that spirits communicated with her through automatic writing, ghosts, poltergeists, séances, and other supernatural occurrences.

4229 *Smith, Susy (Ethel Elizabeth Smith)   1911-
Conversion of a psychic. Garden City, New York: Doubleday & Co., 1978. 127 p.

A psychic narrates a series of anecdotes and parables that involve a curious mixture of the occult, supernatural, and charismatic Christianity, including speaking in tongues and faith healings. The book combines her history as a Christian with her life as a psychic. She frequently consults both God and her deceased mother for solutions to personal problems, despite advice from the spirit of William James, who told her that attempts to communicate with spirits were more trouble than they were worth.

4230 Smith, Thomas Vernor   1890-1964
Non-existent man: an autobiography. Austin: University of Texas Press, 1962. 280 p. Index.

Throughout a wide-ranging career as professor at several universities, Texas state senator, U.S. congressman, military governor in Sicily and Italy, radio personality, and debater on the *Chicago Round Table,* he maintained strong convictions of truth and conscience.

4231 Smith, Whitey, pseud. (Sven Erich Heinrich Schmidt)
I didn't make a million. With C.L. McDermott. Introduction by Ford Wilkins. Manila: Philippine Education Company, 1956. 219 p.

A slangy account of a nightclub bandleader's exotic life in Shanghai before World War II (full of wine, women, song, and gambling) and of the rock-bottom hardscrabble existence he and his wife led, 1942-45, in Santo Tomas, Philippine Islands, as civilians interned by the Japanese throughout World War II.

4232 Smith, William Ward   1893-1968
A letter from my father: the strange, intimate correspondence of W. Ward Smith to his son Page Smith. Edited by Page Smith. New York: William Morrow and Co., 1976. 472 p.

Written in the form of one long letter to his son, this strange autobiography is about a father who was a failure in business and as a provider, but who writes of overwhelming success in sexual exploits.

4233 Smith, Willie the Lion   1897-1973
Music on my mind: the memoirs of an American pianist. With George Hoefer. Foreword by Duke Ellington. New York: Da Capo Press, 1976. (Garden City, New York: Doubleday, 1964) 318 p. Index.

An exciting account of Willie the Lion's sixty-year career as a jazz pianist, beginning in Newark's Tenderloin district and moving quickly to New York City, downtown, midtown, uptown, and Harlem, where he spent most of his time. He knew and played with all the jazz greats, from George Gershwin to Fats Waller, and the book consequently provides a history of modern jazz.

4234 Smithdas, Robert Joseph   1925-
Life at my fingertips. Garden City, New York: Doubleday & Co., Inc., 1958. 260 p.

At five years he lost sight and hearing when he had spinal meningitis. Inspired by Helen Keller, he became the second deaf-blind person to complete college, earned a Master's Degree from New York University, developed a career as a lecturer and independence in his own apartment.

4235 *Snow, Carmel (White)   1890-1961
The world of Carmel Snow. With Mary Louise Aswell. Design by Alexey Brodovitch. New York: McGraw-Hill Book Company, Inc., 1962. 212 p.

Hired by Condé Nast to work for *Vogue* Magazine, she became a well-known editor and central figure in the world of fashion. Later she was hired to develop *Harper's Bazaar,* which became a potent rival of *Vogue.*

4236 Snow, Edgar   **1905-1972**
Journey to the beginning. New York: Random House, 1958. 434 p. Index.
    At 22 he planned to travel around the world, but became fascinated with China, remained as a journalist, and did not return to the United States for thirteen years. In 1941 he joined the *Saturday Evening Post* and became a well-known specialist on the Far East and Russia, producing articles, books, and photographs as an international journalist.

4237 Snow, Edgar   **1905-1972**
The long revolution. New York: Random House, 1972. 269 p. Index.
    Drawing on his experiences while living and working in China during the 1930's and 40's and his later visits in the 60's and 1970, Snow analyzes aspects of modern China—medical care, population control, the cultural revolution, the Chinese Communist Party, the people, and the communes—and assesses the progress being made.

4238 Snow, Jimmy   **1936-**
I cannot go back. With Jim and Marti Hefley. Introduction by Johnny Cash. Illustrated. Plainfield, New Jersey: Logos International, 1977. 157 p.
    The son of country music singer Hank Snow regretfully delineates his childhood as a thief, troublemaker, school dropout, boozer, and motorcycle maniac. In spite of a burgeoning career in country music in Nashville, Snow was addicted to alcohol and pills, contemplated suicide, then converted to Christianity. He married Carol Cooper soon afterward and they became an evangelical team, eventually establishing the Evangel Temple in Nashville, where many country music stars worshiped.

4239 Snow, Manvel Horn
God-called man: a series of supernatural experiences. New York: The William-Frederick Press, 1950. 76 p.
    Written as a personal testimony to God's truth, this book by a Methodist circuit rider in rural Maine is in fact rather impersonal, though it conveys his experience in the rhetoric of fire and brimstone.

4240 Snow, Thad   **1881-1955**
From Missouri. Boston: Houghton Mifflin Co., 1954. 341 p.
    Snow's compelling autobiography describes small-town life in Greenfield, Indiana (home of James Whitcomb Riley), 1880-1900, and rural life in "Swampeast" Missouri, the Delta region, 1920-1950. Snow, a farmer and spokesman for the rights of farmers and tenant farmers, offers a hard-hitting analysis of the agricultural change (from growing corn and wheat to growing cotton) in the Missouri Delta between 1920 and 1930 and the economic disaster and human hardships this caused, exacerbated by urban financial interests, the U.S. Army Corps of Engineers and Federal Farm policies that favored farm owners' exploitation of sharecroppers.

4241 Snow, Wilbert   **1884-1977**
Codline's child: the autobiography of Wilbert Snow. Middletown, Connecticut: Wesleyan University Press, 1974. 489 p.
    A wandering teacher who worked his way through college and continued through a long life following his two loves, learning and the out-of-doors, describes the serenity of that life, sometimes through his own poems.

4242 Snyder, Eugene F.   **1899-**
From a doctor's heart. Foreword by Paul Dudley White. New York: Philosophical Library, 1951. 251 p. Index.
    A Russian immigrant doctor writes of his serious heart disease in a narrative which explains a great deal about the illness, his physical and psychological reactions to it, and the stress of modern life which induces it.

4243 Sobel, Bernard   **1887-1964**
Broadway heartbeat: memoirs of a press agent. New York: Hermitage House, 1953. 352 p. Index.
    A journalist and press agent for over thirty years on Broadway, he writes of the outstanding producers and stars he publicized and of his life in the theatrical world.

4244 Sobol, Louis   **1896-1948**
The longest street: a memoir. New York: Crown Publishers, Inc., 1968. 448 p.
    A Broadway columnist since 1929, Sobol writes of his life and work in show business.

4245 Sobol, Louis   **1896-1948**
Some days were happy. New York: Random House, 1947. 210 p.
    A few of these pieces were previously published, but most are newly written descriptions of his boyhood in rural Connecticut, capturing something of the nostalgia of life after World War II, by a well-known Broadway columnist.

4246 Solo, Tony
    see Schiano, Anthony

4247 *Solomon, Barbara Probst
Arriving where we started. New York: Harper & Row, 1972. 261 p.
    Growing up as part of the "war generation," the novelist was searching for answers she had not learned from her privileged youth. She went to Franco's Spain and helped two political prisoners to escape, came to know Spanish anarchists in Paris, and learned about postwar politics and their personal consequences for her friends and herself.

4248 Solomon, Franklin Delano Roosevelt   **1934-**
A hell of a life. Edited with foreword by A. Peter Bailey. New York: Vantage Press, 1976. 100 p.
    Solomon paints a bitter picture of his childhood in Allendale County, South Carolina, and describes his attempts as a young activist in the Civil Rights movement to integrate local employment and to register Blacks to vote. Although he feels that middle-class Blacks have benefited from enhanced opportunities, he remains bitter about the limited chances for lower-class Blacks.

4249 *Solomon, Hannah (Greenebaum)   **1858-1943**
Fabric of my life: the autobiography of Hannah G. Solomon. New York: Bloch Publishing Co., 1946. 263 p.
    Raised in one of the pioneer Jewish families in Chicago, she became a prominent citizen and feminist, founded the National Council of Jewish Women, and was, with Susan B. Anthony, an American delegate to the International Council of Women in Berlin, 1904.

4250 Somerville, John Alexander   **b.1882**
Man of color: an autobiography; a factual report on the status of the American Negro today. Publishers Library, No. 5. Los Angeles: L.L. Morrison, 1949. 170 p.
    At nineteen he immigrated to California from Jamaica, learned for the first time of racial prejudice, and worked his way through college. He was the first Negro to graduate from the University of Southern California, ranked the highest in his dental school class, and became a prominent citizen of Los Angeles.

4251 *Sone, Monica (Itoi)   **1919-**
Nisei daughter. Introduction by S. Frank Miyamoto. Seattle: University of Washington Press, 1979. (Boston: Little, Brown and Co., 1953) 238 p.
    The story of her childhood in Seattle, the brutal humiliation of family life in concentration camps for Japanese immigrants, and her gradual adaption and reconciliation to the main stream of American life.

4252 Sonfist, Alan   **1946-**
Autobiography of Alan Sonfist: a self-presentation published in connection with an exhibition of his work at the Herbert F. Johnson Museum of Art, Cornell Univ., March 19-May 4, 1975. Ithaca, New York: Cornell University Press, 1975. 32 p.
    Composed primarily of photographs of his art, Sonfist's book also includes some autobiographical writing, most of it about the creation of artistic arrangements of natural objects such as stones, twigs, and leaves.

4253 Sontag, Alan   **1945?-**
The bridge bum: my life and play. Introduction by Alfred Sheinwold. New York: William Morrow and Co., Inc., 1979. (1977) 240 p.
    A professional bridge player and winner at 31 of more than fifty sectional and regional championships and four national championships describes his most fascinating hands and winning games, set in international contexts (Rome, Monte Carlo). A surprisingly good-humored view of a tense occupation.

4254 Sorensen, Charles E.   **1881-1968**
My forty years with Ford. With Samuel T. Williamson. New York: W.W. Norton and Co., 1956. 345 p. Index.
    A personal account of his long career as an executive of the Ford Motor Co., including the birth of the Model-T and the development of an automobile empire.

4255 Sorokin, Pitirim Aleksandrovich   **b.1889**
Long journey: the autobiography of Pitirim A. Sorokin. New Haven, Connecticut: College & University Press, 1963. 327 p.
    Sorokin began as a peasant in Russia, played a role in the Revolution there, was jailed, sentenced to death, but survived to immigrate to the United States, becoming a respected but controversial sociologist.

4256 Southall, James Powell Cocke   **1871-1962**
In the days of my youth: when I was a student at the University of Virginia, 1888-1893. Chapel Hill: University of North Carolina Press, 1947. 197 p.
    Written with a sense of educational idealism and some nostalgia in looking backward, the book confirms his belief in the university as an intellectual aristocracy.

4257 Soyer, Raphael   **1899-**
Diary of an artist. Paintings by the author. Washington, D.C.: New Republic Books, 1977. 316 p. Index.
    A collection of his diaries from the last two decades includes his three

previously published volumes plus his recent writing and portrays a man of gentle wisdom, still a realist in the modern world.

4258 Soyer, Raphael   **1899-**
Painter's pilgrimage: an account of a journey. With drawings by the author. New York: Crown Publishers, Inc., 1962. 127 p.
    His pilgrimage is to the artists and museums of Europe. His journal records conversations, thoughtful impressions, a feeling of beauty.

4259 Soyer, Raphael   **1899-**
Self-Revealment: a memoir. Paintings by the author. New York: Malcenas Press, Random House, 1969. 117 p.
    His diary of 1966-68 includes a sea voyage to Europe, museum visits, and extensive contemplation of the autobiographical nature of his work.

4260 Spalding, Albert   **1888-1953**
Rise to follow: an autobiography. St. Clair Shores, Michigan: Scholarly Press, 1972. (New York: Holt, 1943) 328 p. Index.
    A concert violinist recalls his early years, music lessons, family, study, concerts throughout Europe and the United States, and his musical and intellectual friends.

4261 Spalding, William Andrew   **1852-1941**
William Allen Spalding: Los Angeles newspaperman: an autobiographical account. Edited with introduction by Robert V. Hine. San Marino, California: The Huntington Library, 1961. 156 p. Index.
    Covers the period 1874-1900 during his Los Angeles newspaper career as reporter, business manager, and editor.

4262 *Sparkman, Iva Hall
Journeys with the Senator. Illustrated. Huntsville, Alabama: Strode Publications, 1977. 216 p.
    A devoted wife describes her world travels as her husband, Senator John Sparkman, conducts his work for the Inter-Parliamentary Union. Text includes many of her personal color snapshots.

4263 Sparks, Jacob B.   **b.1886**
Jacob's well of life: new sparks from old time religion; the autobiography of Jacob B. Sparks. Royal Oak, Michigan: Jacob B. Sparks, 1948. 302 p.
    Story of a man who immigrated from Canada to Royal Oak, Michigan, where he became a successful businessman and well-known radio evangelist.

4264 Spellman, Cecil Lloyd   **1906-**
Rough steps on my stairway: the life history of a Negro educator. New York: Exposition Press, 1953. 273 p.
    The difficult and varied experience of a man who became a college professor of education, including interesting details of his boyhood in the Carolinas, college years, and graduate study at Oregon State University.

4265 *Spencer, Carita   **b.1884**
War scenes I shall never forget. New York: C. Spencer 1917. 72 p.
    Originally sold for fifty cents a copy, the expressed purpose of this book was to raise funds for war relief. She traveled through France and Belgium prior to America's entry into the war.

4266 Spencer, Charles Floyd   **1898-**
Wyoming homestead heritage: Memoirs by Charles Floyd Spencer. Hicksville, New York: Exposition Press, 1975. 199 p.
    Since his family settled in Wyoming in 1910 and he spent most of his life there, Spencer's autobiography tells what homesteading was like in the early 1900's. Homebuilding, survival through the harsh winters and dry summers, and learning all about ranching and growing crops presented problems for the neophyte farmers but the country living provided rewards as well.

4267 Spencer, Chauncey E.   **1906-**
Who is Chauncey Spencer? Detroit: Broadside Press, 1975. 150 p.
    This Black pioneer aviator fought for the inclusion of Blacks in the Army Air Corps, was a civil service official, then a police commissioner and city administrator. Throughout his career he has struggled for Black progress and human dignity.

4268 *Spencer, Louise Reid
Guerrilla wife. Chicago: People's Book Club, Inc., 1945. 243 p.
    After Pearl Harbor was bombed, few Americans remained in the Philippines. The author and her husband did, and for two years lived in the jungles of Panay, he fighting with the guerrillas, she fighting for their daily survival, until rescued by submarine in 1944.

4269 Spivak, John Louis   **1897-**
A man in his time. New York: Horizon Press, 1967. 479 p. Index.
    Much admired by Lincoln Steffens, Spivak was an outstanding journalist who wrote about some of the most significant social issues of his time—the labor wars in West Virginia, Sacco and Vanzetti, the Scottsboro case, Georgia chain gangs, Nazism in the United States, and many others.

4270 Spoerl, Howard Davis   **1903-1957**
There was a man; the letters, papers and poems of Howard Davis Spoerl. Edited by Paul B. Zacharias. North Quincy, Massachusetts: Christopher Publishing House, 1972. 193 p.
    Dr. Spoerl was head of the philosophy department of American International College, served on the board of directors of the Swedenborgian Publishing Association, edited *New Christianity* magazine, and wrote articles, poems, and studies on Swedenborgian psychology for various journals. His letters here have been given titles such as "On first causes" and "The relevancy of revelation" to indicate their subject matter.

4271 Sproston, John Glendy   **1828-1862**
Private journal of John Glendy Sproston, U.S.N. Edited by Shio Sakanishi. Foreword by George Alexander Lensen. Second revised edition. Rutland, Vermont: Tuttle, 1968. (Tokyo: Sophia University, 1940) 128 p. Index.
    Sproston was a member of Commodore Perry's expedition to the China Seas and Japan in 1852-54. Sproston's ship, the U.S.S. *Macedonian,* joined the squadron in Edo Bay, Japan, in February 1854; his journal closes in Hong Kong eight months later when he sent it to his family in Baltimore. His discrete personal observations and comments are enhanced by his own pen and pencil sketches.

4272 Spurrier, Steven Orr   **1945-**
It's always too soon to quit: the Steve Spurrier story. As told to Mel Larson. Illustrated. Grand Rapids, Michigan: Zondervan Publishing House, 1968. 157 p.
    Spurrier, 1966 winner of the Heisman Football Trophy, relates the strong familial and Christian influences that with his physical skill contributed to his outstanding performances in high school baseball, basketball, and football and to his outstanding achievements as a football quarterback at the University of Florida-Gainesville. His autobiography conveys a pleasant personality and an unusual sense of team spirit.

4273 Stafford, John Ivy   **b.1870**
Eventful living: the intimate chronicle of a successful life in the happy pursuit of the virtues of the American way. New York: The William-Frederick Press, 1950. 309 p.
    A Midwestern lawyer recalls his boyhood on the family homestead in Indiana, with colorful descriptions of sugar camps, orchards, peddlers, and country life.

4274 Stahl, Frank M.   **1841-1937**
One-way ticket to Kansas: the autobiography of Frank M. Stahl. Margaret Whitemore, oral historian and illustrator. Lawrence: University of Kansas Press, 1959. 146 p. Index.
    An articulate, engaging narrative of Stahl's life as a pioneer and militiaman, Union soldier during the Civil War, proponent of Kansas statehood, advocate of temperance, farmer, and Kansas state legislator. The autobiography provides a humanized history of nearly a century (1841-1937) of Midwestern and Western political and social development.

4275 Stal, Johan
see Steel, John

4276 *Stalvey, Lois Mark
Education of a WASP. New York: William Morrow and Co., Inc., 1970. 327 p.
    An account of one white woman and her family who became cognizant of the inequality and injustice in existing attitudes and prejudices as well as the real and potential dangers in everyday American life. Her step-by-step education began by accident, but led inexorably to her rude awakening to the realities of racism in America and her work in civil rights.

4277 *Stan, Anisoaia   **1900-1954**
They crossed mountains and oceans. New York: The William-Frederick Press, 1947. 386 p.
    Interesting description of her early years in Rumania, of her development as a folk artist and her immigration to New York, where she organized many folk art exhibitions and a plan for a United Nations Ethnographic Museum of Peasant Art.

4278 Standing Bear, Luther   **1863?-1939**
My people the Sioux. Edited by E.A. Brininstool. Introduction by Richard N. Ellis. Lincoln: University of Nebraska Press, 1975. (Boston: Houghton Mifflin, 1928) 288 p.
    In describing the customs of his people, he writes of his own traditional Indian education, including shooting a buffalo. He later traveled with Buffalo Bill's Wild West Show and worked in the pan-Indian movement.

4279 Standish, Burt L., pseud.
see Patten, Gilbert

4280 Standley, William Harrison   **1872-1963**
Admiral Ambassador to Russia. And Arthur Ainsley Ageton. Chicago: Henry Regnery Co., 1955. 533 p. Index.

Based on Standley's notes and diaries, this is a record of his eighteen-month assignment as Ambassador to Russia (1942-43), with chapters on his early life and career.

4281 Stands in Timber, John   1884-1967
Cheyenne memories. And Margot Liberty, with the assistance of Robert M. Utley. Lincoln: University of Nebraska Press, 1972. (New Haven: Yale University Press, 1967) 330 p.

An important contributor to Cheyenne history, Stands in Timber provides insights into the history and culture of his people as they recall and interpret it. He collected reminiscences and lore of his tribe to add to his personal memories for this collective memoir of the Cheyenne.

4282 Stans, Maurice H.   1908-
The terrors of justice: the untold tale of Watergate. New York: Everest House Publishers, 1978. 487 p. Index.

Although Stans briefly mentions his childhood and youth, his book focuses at length on the Watergate scandal and on what he calls the "innocent victims," specifically Stans himself.

4283 Stanton, Edwin F.   1901-1968
Brief authority: excursions of a common man in an uncommon world. New York: Harper and Brothers, 1956. 290 p. Index.

A personal story of his thirty years in the Foreign Service, chiefly in China and Thailand, where he served as U.S. Ambassador.

4284 *Stanton, Elizabeth (Cady)   1815-1902
Eighty years and more (1815-1897); reminiscences of Elizabeth Cady Stanton. New York: Source Book Press, 1970. (London: T. Fisher Unwin, 1898) 474 p. Index.

The author has written the story of her private life as wife, mother, and housekeeper using diary extracts, sketches of her travels, and her opinions on many social questions. Her public career as a leader in the movement for the emancipation of women is described in her *The History of Woman Suffrage.*

4285 Stanton, William Arthur   1867-1955
Awakening of India: forty years among the Telugus. Portland, Maine: Falmouth Publishing House, 1950. 213 p.

An account of the years he and his wife spent as Baptist missionaries in South India, set in a context of the religious and political struggles of the times.

4286 *Stanwell-Fletcher, Theodora C.   1906-
Driftwood valley. Boston: Little, Brown and Co., 1946. 383 p.

During 1937-1941 the author and a friend lived in the north-central British Columbia woods. Based on her diary, this book is a story of the wilderness and their relation to it.

4287 Stapp, Andy   1945?-
Up against the brass. New York: Simon & Schuster, 1970. 192 p.

Stapp objected to what he saw as openly antidemocratic procedures in the U.S. Army, so he joined the Army and formed the American Servicemen's Union. It provides legal aid, information, and moral support for G.I.'s who are at odds with the military establishment.

4288 Stargell, Wilver Dornel   1940-
Out of left field: Willie Stargell and the Pittsburgh Pirates. Edited with interviews by Susan Hall. Photographs by Bob Adelman. New York: Two Continents Publishing Group/A Prairie House Book, 1976. 223 p.

This is an illustrated collection of interviews with Willie Stargell, his wife Dee, and other Pittsburgh Pirates during the 1973 season—Nelson Briles, Steve Blass, Richie Zisk, and Dock Ellis. Stargell discusses his career, racial bigotry in the Texas Leagues, life on the road—easy for him because of admiration and women, but hard on his wife. He emphasizes money and contract negotiations.

4289 Starin, Arthur N.   1889-1971
Growing up, and I find a frontier. Royal Oak, Maryland: Mary Elizabeth Starin, 1973. 154 p.

These reminiscences evoke an atmosphere of the early twentieth century through incidents from his family life, his pleasant recollections of frontier escapades, and amusing incidents in his youth and early manhood as he became a draughtsman and an architect in Duluth.

4290 Starling, Edmund William   1875-1944
Starling of the White House: the story of the man whose Secret Service detail guarded five presidents from Woodrow Wilson to Franklin D. Roosevelt. As told to Thomas Sugrue. Chicago: Peoples Book Club, 1946. 334 p. Index.

After a brief description of his early years in Kentucky, Starling gives a warm and personal view of the presidents he guarded and the inner life of the White House.

4291 *Starr, Blaze   1935?-
Blaze Starr: my life as told to Huey Perry. Afterword by Lora Fleming. New York: Praeger Publishers, 1974. 210 p.

Born during the Depression of the 1930's in backwoods West Virginia, she overcame her poverty-stricken mountain childhood by making use of her body. She became a sensation as a stripper who defied the moral codes of heartland America.

4292 Starrett, Vincent   b.1886
Born in a bookshop; chapters from the Chicago renascence. Norman: University of Oklahoma Press, 1965. 325 p. Index.

A detective novelist and short-story writer, historian and critic, poet and anthologist, essayist and columnist, bibliographer and book collector, Starrett learned early a fascination for books and bookmen. Here is the story of his own adventures with glimpses of the literary life and its participants, particularly the Chicago literary renascence of the early Twenties.

4293 Steamboat Bill
see Heckman, William L.

4294 Stearns, Alfred Ernest   1871-1949
An Amherst boyhood. Foreword by Chief Justice Harlan F. Stone. Amherst, Massachusetts: Amherst College, 1946. 212 p.

Written for the 125th anniversary of the college, the book describes his boyhood in Amherst, where his grandfather was president of the college, and his own college days.

4295 Stearns, Austin C.   1835-1924
Three years with Company K. Edited by Arthur A. Kent. Rutherford, New Jersey: Farleigh Dickinson University Press, 1976. 346 p. Index.

An unpretentious narrative of an infantry soldier's daily life during three years of the Civil War, describing with simple good humor his thoughts and adventures in the Grand Old Army.

4296 Stedman, Ebenezer Hiram   1808-1885
Bluegrass craftsman: being the reminiscences of Ebenezer Hiram Stedman, papermaker, 1808-1885. Edited by Francis L.S. Dugan and Jacqueline P. Bull. Lexington: University of Kentucky Press, 1959. 226 p. Index.

A Kentucky paper manufacturer in the early 1800's describes his life and work, providing an interesting record of the paper industry and of middle- and working-class Bluegrass society.

4297 Steel, John   1848-1928
Johan Stal (John Steel) from Smaland: farm lad to Idaho prune king (completed) by Lilly Ann Steel Loveland. Francestown, New Hampshire: Marshall Jones Co., 1947. 103 p.

After describing his Swedish childhood, he writes of his immigration to America in the 1870's, his homestead in Nebraska, brief years in Leadville, Colorado, and finally settling in Boise, Idaho, to develop fruit orchards.

4298 *Steele, Jennie Koons   1870-1955
I remember . . . with letters to and from Richard St. Clair Steele 1888-1907. Edited by Marion Davault Steele. Illustrated. New York: Vantage, 1977. 357 p.

Chatty, detailed letters between Jennie Koons and her husband-to-be tell of her experiences as a New England conservatory student and music teacher and his as Indian Agent in the Midwest territories at the turn of the century. Photographs and other memorabilia enhance the text.

4299 Stefansson, Vilhjalmur   1879-1962
Discovery: the autobiography of Vilhjalmur Stefansson. New York: McGraw-Hill Book Co., 1964. 411 p. Index.

An adventurous, exciting life full of great achievements that made him a top authority on the Arctic and its people is recorded by the polar explorer, an original thinker who led a vital, active life.

4300 Steffanides, George F.   1908-
America the land of my dreams: the odyssey of a Greek immigrant. Fitchburg, Massachusetts: the author, 1974. 216 p.

When he arrived in the United States from Greece at twelve years of age, he was plunged into the melting pot of Boston. Like many immigrants he struggled to work his way up in the world and found that education supplied the key to success, his own as a professor of biology. He also writes a critique of the problems of modern Greece, American education, and other current educational questions.

4301 Steffens, Joseph Lincoln   1866-1936
The autobiography of Lincoln Steffens. Illustrated. New York: Harcourt Brace Jovanovich, 1968. (New York: Literary Guild, 1931) 2v. Index.

Steffens narrates the story of his life as a muckraking journalist. He focuses on various aspects of organized crime and political chicanery in high and low places, from New York to Philadelphia to Chicago to San Francisco, from the 1890's through the 1920's. This autobiography, an American classic, is a vigorous self-portrait of America's foremost investigative reporter.

4302 Steffens, Joseph Lincoln   **1866-1936**
Letters. Edited with introductory notes by Ella Winter and Granville Hicks. With a memorandum by Carl Sandburg. Westport, Connecticut: Greenwood Press, 1974. (New York: Harcourt Brace, 1938) 2v. Index.

Forty-six years of personal letters to friends, many of them giving warm family anecdotes, others discussing his thoughts and beliefs on current events and social problems. The appendix includes documents showing Steffens' part in certain historical events and his ways of exercising his personal influence. Vol. 1, 1889-1919; Vol. 2, 1920-1936.

4303 Stegner, Wallace Earle   **1909-**
Wolf Willow: a history, a story, and a memory of the last Plains frontier. Lincoln, Nebraska: University of Nebraska Press, 1980. 306 p.

Stegner analyzes his family's four years of summer homesteading in Whitemud, Saskatchewan, 1915-18, as typical pioneer experiences in a quintessential pioneer settlement. He provides a history of the area, which includes French, Indian, English, American, and Canadian explorers and settlers, as a microcosm of prairie history, emphasizing that the possibility for Western pioneering still remains.

4304 Stehling, Kurt R.
Bags up! Great balloon adventures. Chicago: Playboy Press, 1976. 253 p.

A balloonist's exciting adventures from his first solo to record 1000-mile flights, along with dangerous or amusing feats of other daring men and women.

4305 Steichen, Edward   **1879-1973**
A life in photography. Garden City, New York: Published in collaboration with Museum of Modern Art, Doubleday & Co., Inc., 1963. n.p.

An outstanding photographer, Steichen here tells of his first tentative attempts at picture making and his lifetime developing his art. Striking photographs illustrate phases of his art and subjects—scenes, buildings, nature, advertising, fashion, fabric design, theater personalities, and portraits of ordinary and famous people.

4306 Stein, Benjamin   **1944-**
Dreemz. New York: Harper & Row, 1978. 212 p.

This book consists of a year's worth of diary fragments by a former Nixon speechwriter who goes west to Los Angeles to write film scripts and novels. He loves the weather and the people he encounters with their quest for fame, fortune, sex, and drugs. Everyone else hustles, he says, but the author claims to remain true to his ideals—a Spanish-type home in Los Angeles, a Mercedes-Benz with a self-selected license plate "DREEMZ," and a bevy of lovers to admire his success.

4307 *Stein, Gertrude   **1874-1946**
Dear Sammy: letters from Gertrude Stein and Alice B. Toklas. Edited by Samuel M. Steward. Boston: Houghton Mifflin, 1977. 260 p.

During his military service in France in World War II, Steward was befriended by Stein and Toklas, with whom he corresponded thereafter. He visited them after the war in Paris and continued his friendship with Toklas after Stein's death.

4308 *Stein, Gertrude   **1874-1946**
Two: Gertrude Stein and her brother, and other early portraits, 1908-12. Edited by Carl Van Vechten. Foreword by Janet Flanner. Yale edition of the unpublished writings of Gertrude Stein, Vol.1. New Haven, Connecticut: Yale University Press, 1951. 355 p.

In this early period, Stein wrote portraits of herself, her brother, and people she thought were not very important; portraits of characters, not of names. An early experiment writing in the continuous present.

4309 *Stein, Gertrude
see also **Anderson, Sherwood**

4310 *Stein, Judith Beck   **1925-**
The journal of Judith Beck Stein. Washington, D.C.: The Columbia Journal, Inc., 1973. 170 p.

Claiming that there has been a consistent long-term conspiracy of sabotage dedicated to the destruction of her life and values by neofascist groups also involved in the murders of the Kennedys, Martin Luther King, and the deaths at Kent State and Jackson University, Stein asserts that she has been forceably and wrongfully kept in Chestnut Lodge Mental Sanitarium. She believes the sanitarium personnel and others have woven around her "a steel cover of lies, deceit, distortions, manipulations, and deliberately contrived and planted smears within all the communities where I lived or was involved in any way."

4311 Stein, Leo   **1872-1947**
Journey into the self: being the letters, papers, and journals of Leo Stein. Edited by Edmund Fuller. Introduction by Van Wyck Brooks. New York: Crown Publishers, 1950. 331 p. Index.

The papers, primarily letters written between 1900 and 1947, present a chronicle of an intellectual with diverse interests. Stein lived in Paris and outside of Florence during this period except for several short visits to the United States.

4312 Steinbeck, John   **1902-1968**
Journal of a novel; the *East of Eden* letters. New York: The Viking Press, 1969. 182 p.

As a sort of warming-up exercise before each day's stint of writing *East of Eden,* Steinbeck wrote a "letter" to his friend and editor, Pascal Covici. The letters form a part of the notebooks which contain the first draft of the novel and, although they comment on events and random thoughts, they also reflect his serious thinking about the novel and writing in general.

4313 Steinbeck, John   **1902-1968**
Letters to Elizabeth: a selection of letters from John Steinbeck to Elizabeth Otis. Edited by Florian J. Shasky and Susan F. Riggs. Introduction by Carlton A. Sheffield. Illustrated. Limited edition. San Francisco: Book Club of California, 1978. 119 p.

These 44 letters from over 600 that Steinbeck wrote to Elizabeth Otis, his literary agent between 1938 and 1965, do not duplicate those in *Steinbeck: A Life in Letters* (1975). They provide insight into his work habits and creative process. Steinbeck also discusses matters of translations, sales, readers' reactions to his writings, and his efforts to write.

4314 Steinbeck, John   **1902-1968**
Steinbeck: a life in letters. Edited by Elaine Steinbeck and Robert Wallsten. New York: Penguin Books, 1976. 908 p.

Hundreds of letters covering 45 years reveal Steinbeck's early struggles to get published, his lifelong association with agents McIntosh and Otis, his three marriages and two divorces, family deaths, literary successes, war service, and the Nobel Prize for literature. The easy humor in his letters helps shape the portrait of a determined, occasionally unsure, and always loving man.

4315 Steinbeck, John IV   **1946-**
In touch. New York: Alfred A. Knopf, 1969. 202 p.

A straightforward account of his twenty-first year which he spent partly in Vietnam and partly in the United States. He discusses the war, the Vietnamese, the soldiers, the violence, and the prevalence of marijuana usage. Later in the United States he was arrested for marijuana possession, acquitted, and testified before a Senate subcommittee. He questions, enjoys, and tries to get in touch with the issues that are urgent for his generation.

4316 Steiner, Edward Alfred   **1866-1956**
From alien to citizen. Modern Jewish Experience. New York: Arno Press, 1975. (New York: Revell, 1914) 332 p.

An Austro-Hungarian Jewish immigrant, the author converted to Christianity and became a Congregational clergyman and professor of theology at Grinnell College.

4317 Stemmer, Charles C.   **b.1883**
A brand from the burning: from the depths of despair to the gates of heaven. Boston: Christopher Publishing House, 1959. 132 p.

Stemmer gives an account of his unpleasant life and explains why he rejected traditional religion in favor of spiritualism. He describes some of his psychic experiences and mentions several noted people with whose spirits he has spoken, including Ella Wheeler Wilcox and Bernadette of Lourdes.

4318 Stengel, Charles Dillon (Casey)   **1891-1975**
Casey at the bat: the story of my life in baseball as told to Harry T. Paxton. New York: Random House, 1962. 254 p.

A colorful baseball personality since 1912, Stengel here tells of his ups and downs in the game, stunts he pulled, his opinions and ideas. He also picks his all-time ideal American and National League teams.

4319 *Stenhouse, Fanny ("Mrs. T.B.H. Stenhouse")   **b.1829**
"Tell it all": The story of a life's experience in Mormonism: an autobiography. Introduction by Harriet Beecher Stowe. Hartford, Connecticut: A.D. Worthington and Co., 1874. 633 p.

The author writes to tell her own story and to expose the wrongs of Mormon women of Utah, their mistreatment and sufferings under polygamy. Eventually she and her husband, who had published a newspaper, left the Mormon church and she lectured in Washington, Boston and other cities about the evils of Mormonism.

4320 Stephens, Alexander Hamilton   **1812-1883**
Recollections; his diary kept when prisoner at Fort Warren, Boston Harbour, 1865. Edited with introduction by Myrta Lockett Avary. New York: Da Capo Press, 1971. (New York: Doubleday, Page & Co., 1910) 572 p.

Since he was Vice-President of the Confederate States, Stephens was imprisoned for six months after the defeat of the South. His prison diary includes extracts from the Bible and the classics as well as comments on his daily routine, conversations, and thoughts.

4321 Stern, Bill   **1907-1971**
The taste of ashes: an autobiography. With Oscar Fraley. New York: Henry Holt and Co., 1959. 218 p.

In 1941 he became NBC's first sports director. As a result of his drug addiction for over ten years, on New Year's Day, 1956, he collapsed while he was broadcasting the Super Bowl. His book tells of the strain he suffered from the pace of his rapid rise to fame, the continuous pain from a leg amputation in the late Thirties, his struggle against addiction, and his remarkable professional comeback in 1958.

4322 *Stern, Elizabeth (Leah Morton, pseud.)   1890-1954
I am a woman—and a Jew. New York: Arno Press, 1969. (New York: J.H. Sears & Co., 1926) 362 p.
She describes her struggle to free herself from the conventions of her religion and womanhood, and then to find herself. She worked as a social worker, saleswoman, lecturer, and writer. Her books include *My Mother and I* (1917) and *When Love Comes to a Woman* (1929).

4323 Stern, Julius David   b.1886
Memoirs of a maverick publisher. New York: Simon and Schuster, 1962. 320 p. Index.
After his early years as a journalist he became an editor, publisher, successful owner of seven daily papers, and a powerful political figure in New York, New Jersey, and Philadelphia. He often fought for unpopular causes and took positions independent of politics. His book is an interesting history of journalism, a dynamic writer and businessman, and the times.

4324 *Stern, Susan (Harris)   1943-1976
With the Weathermen: the personal journal of a revolutionary woman. New York: Doubleday and Co., Inc., 1975. 374 p.
The story, beginning in 1966, of her transformation from a shy, conventional student to a militant feminist, SDS organizer, and Weatherman committed to violence.

4325 *Sternberg, Cecilia   1928-
The journey. New York: The Dial Press/James Wade, 1977. 576 p. Index.
Countess Cecilia Sternberg tells of her risky departure by train with her husband and daughter from newly Communist Czechoslovakia. She describes their emigration to the United States with much attention to family ties and to the milieu of the very rich in seemingly desperate situations.

4326 Sterne, Maurice   1878-1957
Shadow and light: the life, friends and opinions of Maurice Sterne. Edited by Charlotte Leon Mayerson. Introduction by George Biddle. New York: Harcourt, Brace & World, Inc., 1965. 266 p. Index.
Using Sterne's autobiographical notebooks plus letters, art criticism, and recollections of his wife and friends, the editor has constructed a chronology of Sterne, a painter and sculptor greatly admired by his generation during the years that saw American art coming of age.

4327 Stettinius, Edward Reilly, Jr.   1900-1949
The diaries of Edward R. Stettinius, Jr., 1943-1946. Edited by Thomas M. Campbell and George C. Herring. New York: New Viewpoints, 1975. 544 p. Index.
The record of an industrialist with scant background in international relations thrust into the central positions of foreign policy-making during a crucial period of history.

4328 Stevens, David Harrison   b.1884
Time of humanities: an oral history: recollections of David H. Stevens as director in the Division of the Humanities, Rockefeller Foundation, 1930-50. As narrated to Robert E. Gard. Edited by Robert E. Yahnke. Illustrated. Madison: Wisconsin Academy of Sciences, Arts and Letters, 1976. 151 p. Index.
Stevens describes, in interview format, his direction of the Rockefeller Foundation's Division of the Humanities from 1930-50 and his interaction with many of the pre-eminent scholars of the time. As "a life-long humanist," Stevens was particularly concerned with funding for university presses and for research projects in Far Eastern studies, American studies, and drama. This volume includes his excellent essay, "What are the Humanities?"

4329 Stevens, Wallace   1879-1955
Letters. Selected and edited by Holly Stevens. New York: Alfred A. Knopf, 1966. (Salem, New Hampshire: Faber, 1955) 890 p. Index.
This selection by the poet's daughter from 3300 extant letters covers a span of sixty years. She notes that she has included letters that refer to his own poetry and poetry in general, letters of a high quality in style, and letters containing biographical and other pertinent information. All have been selected on the principle of giving pleasure to the reader.

4330 Stevens, Walter James   b.1877
Chip on my shoulder: autobiography of Walter J. Stevens. Boston: Meador Publishing Co., 1946. 315 p.
The varied life of a Black Bostonian who worked in service at Harvard where he also was informally educated, was home secretary to Edward A. Filene, served in World War I, became a labor investigator and finally a photographer.

4331 Stevenson, Adlai Ewing   1900-1965
Adlai Stevenson's public years: with text from his speeches and writings. Edited by Jill Kneerin. Photos by Cornell Capa and others. Preface by Walter Lippmann. New York: Grossman Publishers, 1966. 160 p.
Stevenson writes, "I discovered that in a political job there are usually two ways to do things: the politically expedient way or the right way; . . . in the long run, the right way is the best politics." His speeches reveal a man serious about America's future and at the same time irrepressibly humorous. This book contains many photographs, some taken by Stevenson's son, John Fell Stevenson.

4332 Stevenson, Adlai Ewing   1900-1965
The papers of Adlai E. Stevenson Boston: Little, Brown and Co., 1972-1979. 8v. Index.
Volume I: The beginnings of education, 1900-1941. Volume II: Washington to Springfield, 1941-1948. Volume III: Governor of Illinois, 1949-1953. Volume IV: "Let's talk sense to the American people," 1952-1955. Volume V: Visit to Asia, the Middle East, and Europe, March-August 1953. Volume VI: Toward a new America, 1955-1957. Volume VII: Continuing education and the unfinished business of American society, 1957-1961. Volume VIII: Ambassador to the United Nations, 1961-1965.

4333 Stevenson, Robert Louis
see **James, Henry**

4334 *Stevenson, Sarah (Coles)   1789-1848
Victoria, Albert, and Mrs. Stevenson. Edited by Edward Boykin. New York: Rinehart & Co., Inc., 1957. 309 p.
Her husband Andrew, a Richmond lawyer, served as Minister to the Court of St. James from 1836 to 1841. Sarah was a favorite in the court and an indefatigable letter writer, the collection being a frank and witty account of the early Victorian court.

4335 Stewart, Donald Ogden   1894-1980
By a stroke of luck! An autobiography. New York: Paddington Press Ltd., 1975. 302 p.
A playboy in his younger days, Stewart seems to have had a constant stream of lucky breaks, good contacts through Exeter and Yale acquaintances, and an inborn knowledge of how to get ahead. Eventually his anti-fascist activities led him to be suspected of communism and to be blacklisted in 1950, after which he moved permanently to England.

4336 *Stewart, Elinore (Pruitt)   1876-1933
Letters of a woman homesteader. Introduction by Jessamyn West. Lincoln: University of Nebraska Press, 1961. (Boston: Houghton Mifflin Co., 1914) 281 p.
The author, who wanted to homestead a place for herself, went to work for a Wyoming rancher who could advise her about land and water rights. She married him and wrote these letters to Juliet Coney, her former employer, about her life, her neighbors, and the beautiful new country she loved. The movie *Heartland* is based on her letters.

4337 *Stewart, Elinore (Pruitt)   1876-1933
Letters on an elk hunt: by a woman homesteader. Foreword by Elizabeth Fuller Ferris. Lincoln, Nebraska: University of Nebraska Press, 1979. 1621 p.
A delightful narrative full of cowboys, mail-order brides, orphans, bull elks, and stampedes fills the letters of Stewart to Mrs. Coney "back east." Of the rough-and-rugged West, she writes in conclusion, "I have experienced about all human emotions. I had not expected to encounter so many people or to get the little inside glimpses that I've had, but wherever there are human beings there are the little histories."

4338 *Stickney, Dorothy   1900-
Openings and closings. Garden City, New York: Doubleday & Co., 1979. 201 p. Index.
An unusually well-written account spanning the actress's childhood in North Dakota through her achievements as an actress. She married an actor-playwright Howard Lindsay. Together they starred in a five-year run of *Life With Father* and in many other plays. Stickney enjoyed a blissful marriage and a triumphant theatrical career.

4339 Still, Clyfford   1904-1980
Clyfford Still. Edited by John P. O'Neill. Illustrated. Bibliography. New York: Harry N. Abrams, 1979. 222 p. Index.
In an introduction to a color catalogue of his paintings exhibited at the Metropolitan Museum of Art, an abstract painter of massive canvases writes of his experiences in galleries and exhibitions on both the East and West coasts. His words reveal an artist deeply concerned with individuality, loath to be associated with any particular "school" of painting.

4340 Still, James   1812-1885
Early recollections and life of Dr. James Still. Freeport, New York: Books for Libraries Press, 1971. (Philadelphia: J.B. Lippincott & Co., 1877) 274 p.
The story of a self-taught Black man who became a doctor, overcoming

his lack of early education through serious application and experience. He recalls some unusual cases and events which impressed him, particularly the Centennial Exhibition in 1876.

4341 Stilwell, Joseph Warren   **1883-1946**
The Stilwell papers. Edited by Theodore H. White. Foreword by Winifred A. Stilwell. New York: Schocken Books, 1972. (New York: William Sloane Associates, Inc., 1948) 357 p. Index.
  The war journals of General Stilwell (December 1941-October 1944), during his command of the China-Burma-India war theater. Blunt and critical, his personal record explains many events which led to his removal from command.

4342 Stimson, Henry Lewis   **1867-1950**
On active service in peace and war. And McGeorge Bundy. New York: Harper & Brothers, 1948. 698 p. Index.
  The introduction states: "This book contains an account of the years of my public service—my actions, motives, and estimates of results—from my point of view." Though Bundy wrote it ("the style and composition are his"), they worked together to make a record which is "an accurate and balanced account" of Stimson's experience in public life.

4343 Stock, Joseph Whiting   **1815-1855**
The paintings and the journal of Joseph Whiting Stock. Edited by Juliette Tomlinson. Compiled by Kate Steinway. Plates. Middletown, Connecticut: Wesleyan University Press, 1976. 180 p. Index.
  Stock's journal (1836-1846) consists primarily of a list of the paintings he did during this time, including the dimensions and price of each painting. It is prefaced by a brief account of his partial paralysis, the result of an accident when he was eleven, and followed by his only extant letter, his will, and reproductions of many of his well-executed folk paintings, mostly portraits notable for their handsome subjects and attention to small, symbolic details.

4344 Stockton, Marcellus Lowry   **1893-**
A general's story. New York: Vantage Press, 1965. 248 p.
  A well-written account of a general's life between the World Wars that consists of anecdotes of military bureaucratic duties mixed with a lively set of experiences in hunting, fishing, and sports in Kansas, Texas, Nevada, Arizona, and California.

4345 Stoddard, Henry Luther   **1861-1947**
As I knew them; presidents and politics from Grant to Coolidge. New York: Kennikat, 1971. (New York: Harper & Brothers, 1927) 2v.
  A review of the period from 1868 through 1926 based on the writer's impressions as he moved along with the years. As a political correspondent he met or knew on close terms the Presidents included here as well as most of the national leaders of both parties, especially those in the East.

4346 Stoddard, Richard Henry   **1825-1903**
Recollections, personal and literary. Edited by Ripley Hitchcock. Introduction by Edmund Clarence Stedman. New York: AMS Press, 1971. (New York: A.S. Barnes & Co., 1903) 333 p. Index.
  Stoddard was a reputable poet in New York who was acquainted with many outstanding contemporary literary figures. He and his wife, Elizabeth Barstow Stoddard, a novelist, were especially close to James Russell Lowell, who encouraged them both in their literary efforts. His book is a quiet recollection of their life among nineteenth-century literati.

4347 Stoddard, William Osborn   **1835-1925**
Lincoln's third secretary: the memoirs of William O. Stoddard. Introduction by William Osborn Stoddard, Jr. Foreword by Edgar DeWitt Jones. New York: Exposition, 1955. 219 p. Index.
  A native of Illinois, Stoddard traces his career in that state as a newspaper editor which led him into an association with Abraham Lincoln, and as a secretary to sign land patents, a post awarded by President Lincoln. The memoirs provide a friend and employee's view of Lincoln and a bureaucrat's experience of the Civil War.

4348 Stoessinger, John George   **1927-**
Night journey: a story of survival and deliverance. New York: Playboy Press/Simon & Schuster, 1978. 216 p.
  A political scientist, winner of the 1962 Bancroft Prize for a book on world politics, and director of the United Nations Secretariat, explores what it means to be fully human. A Jew, he escaped the Nazis by fleeing from Austria to China to the United States. Bored with his successful career, he was lured into a fraud scheme that eventually resulted in a conviction for conspiratorial cover-up. Nearly suicidal, Stoessinger found redemption through fatherhood and teaching in a prison.

4349 Stokes, Carl Burton   **1927-**
Promises of power: a political autobiography. New York: Simon & Schuster, 1973. 288 p. Index.
  The first Black mayor of predominantly white Cleveland, Stokes tried to build Black and white coalitions, politicize the poor, struggle with the power structure, the media, the police, the business community.

4350 Stone, Edward Durell   **1902-1978**
Evolution of an architect. New York: Horizon Press, 1962. 288 p.
  Profusely illustrated with photographs and drawings of buildings he designed, this book tells the story of one of the most outstanding American architects of the twentieth century.

4351 Stone, Kate
  see **Holmes, Sarah Katherine (Stone)**

4352 Stone, Melville Elijah   **1848-1929**
Fifty years a journalist. Freeport, New York: Books for Libraries Press, 1970. (Garden City, New York: Doubleday, Page & Co., 1920) 371 p.
  He grew up in Illinois, worked as a reporter there and in Washington, and returned to found the Chicago *Daily News.* His book describes his active life in journalism, the Associated Press, and national and international politics.

4353 Stone, Willie
I was a Black Panther. As told to Chuck Moore. Illustrated. New York: Doubleday-Signal Books, 1970. 144 p.
  The experiences of a young boy who joined the controversial militant Black Panthers help to explain the attraction American Blacks feel for the movement. An earnest search for identity and for a dignified place in American society are goals the Panthers strive to reach through violent means.

4354 Storey, Del
Collision course. With Laura Watson. Foreword by Gerald Derstine. Epilogue by Laura Watson. Plainfield, New Jersey: Logos International, 1977. 123 p.
  Although written in first person, Storey's experiences as bulldozer-driver-turned-Pentecostal evangelist were apparently set down after his death in a plane crash. His struggles with divorce, the construction business, and church hierarchy—speaking in tongues was contrary to his denomination's dogma—are engagingly presented.

4355 Storke, Thomas More   **1876-1971**
California editor. With Walter A. Tompkins. Foreword by Earl Warren. Preface by Walter A. Tompkins. Santa Barbara: Pacific Coast Publishing Co., 1966. (Los Angeles: Westernlore Press, 1958) 489 p. Index.
  Storke interweaves the account of his long, vigorous career as editor-publisher of the Santa Barbara *News-Press* with a history of the city as it grew from frontier Gold Rush days to the space age and gained a new post office and airport through his efforts. He describes the history of the state of California and of the United States through three wars. In 1938 he was appointed U.S. Senator to fill William G. McAdoo's unexpired term.

4356 Storke, Thomas More   **b.1876**
I write for freedom. Foreword by Adlai Stevenson. Fresno, California: McNally and Loftin, Publishers, 1962. 168 p.
  A seventh-generation Californian, he won the Pulitzer Prize for editorial writing in 1962 after challenging in his articles the activities of the John Birch Society. His book gives the background for his political philosophy, recalling the old days of Spanish and Mexican California.

4357 Story, Joseph   **1779-1845**
Joseph Story: A collection of writings by and about an eminent American jurist. Edited by Mortimer D. Schwartz and John C. Hogan. New York: Oceana Publications, 1959. 228 p. Index.
  Letters, poetry, court decisions, legal commentaries, and autobiographical essays present a mosaic description of Joseph Story, a Boston born-and-bred Justice of the U.S. Supreme Court, 1811-1845. They provide an overview of his accomplishments as a judge, law teacher, and legal writer, including nine great commentaries on the law which established him as "one of the ten outstanding men in American judicial history."

4358 *Stout, Ruth   **b.1884**
As we remembered Mother: memoirs. Hicksville, New York: Exposition Press, 1975. 159 p.
  Though ostensibly about her remarkable mother, this book reveals something of Ruth Stout's own life as well, especially her feelings for her mother and incidents which illuminate both their personalities.

4359 *Stout, Ruth   **b.1884**
I've always done it my way. Hicksville, New York: Exposition Press, 1975. 176 p.
  In an appealing mixture of personal recollection and the politics, manners, and morals of the country since the turn of the century, the author writes of doing famine-relief work, writing for the *New Masses,* and exposing bureaucratic lunacy. She approaches life with humorous, clear-thinking, and intelligent common sense.

4360 *Stowe, Harriet Elizabeth (Beecher)   **1811-1896**
Life and letters of Harriet Beecher Stowe. Edited by Annie (Adams) Fields. Detroit: Gale Research Co., 1970. (Boston: Houghton Mifflin and Co., 1898) 406 p. Index.

The editor has used Reverend C.E. Stowe's biography of his mother to provide connecting links to her letters, constructing a full story of the famous author whose concern for the suffering of slaves influenced the course of history.

4361 *Stowe, Harriet Elizabeth (Beecher)   **1811-1896**
Life of Harriet Beecher Stowe: compiled from her letters and journals. Compiled by Charles Edward Stowe. Illustrated. Detroit: Gale Research Co., 1967. (Boston: Houghton Mifflin, 1889) 530 p.
    This compilation focuses on Stowe's Hartford school days, her youthful conversion to Christianity, her marriage and gradual involvement in abolitionism. The crux of her life was the publication of *Uncle Tom's Cabin*, which made her an instant celebrity and offered travel throughout the United States and Europe. After the Civil War she corresponded extensively with George Eliot and became embroiled in a defense of Lady Byron.

4362 *Strainchamps, Ethel   **1912-**
Don't never say cain't. Garden City, New York: Doubleday & Co., Inc., 1965. 168 p.
    Strainchamps writes humorously on the origins and effects of her Ozark Missouri dialect ("you'uns," "cain't"), how she shed it for standard English and eventually became a successful professional writer, ever aware of the subtleties of language and the discrepancies between spoken and written versions of the same words. She came up the hard way, working her way through high school as a domestic and is sensitive to the nuances of social class and status as manifested particularly in speech.

4363 Strand, Paul   **1890-1976**
Paul Strand: sixty years of photographs: excerpts from correspondence, interviews, and other documents. Profile by Calvin Tomkins. Millertown, New York: Aperture, 1976. 183 p.
    A handsome selection of a photographer's lifetime work, including scenes from around the world and some striking closeups of plants. It is prefaced by Calvin Tomkins's biographical portrait and followed by 31 pages of Strand's autobiographical observations on his life, art, and worldwide travel derived from personal letters, diaries, and interviews.

4364 Strang, James Jesse   **1813-1856**
The diary of James J. Strang: deciphered, transcribed, introduced and annotated by Mark A. Strang. Foreword by Russel B. Nye. East Lansing: Michigan State University Press, 1961. 78 p.
    The diary, laden with commentary on theology and contemporary politics, covers a period (1831-36) in James J. Strang's life when he was teaching in a rural school (Chautauqua County, New York), reading law in preparation for the bar, and courting young women. It gives little evidence of Strang's unconventional future, 1843-1845, as Mormon prophet, colonizer (Beaver Island, Michigan, with 2600 inhabitants), and martyr, which the long introduction explains.

4365 *Strasberg, Susan Elizabeth   **1938-**
Bittersweet. Illustrated. New York: G.P. Putnam's Sons, 1980. 285 p.
    When the daughter of Actors' Studio Director Lee Strasberg and method-acting coach Paula Miller dazzled Broadway at seventeen in *The Diary of Anne Frank*, no one was surprised. But *Bittersweet* details Strasberg's problems with drugs, a failed marriage, her mother's death, her daughter's congenital birth defect, and her ultimate triumph over these crises.

4366 *Straus, Dorothea   **1917-**
Palaces and prisons. Boston: Houghton Mifflin Co., 1976. 209 p.
    In this well-written memoir, Straus combines reflections on her travels to Paris, Venice, New York and elsewhere with vivid recollections of Philip Rahv, Peggy Guggenheim, Edmund Wilson, her brother Philip Rheingold, and his beautiful but bizarre actress wives, Norma Terry and Linda Darnell. Straus meticulously describes houses as well as personalities, placing people in their settings of "palaces and prisons."

4367 *Straus, Dorothea   **1917-**
Showcases. London: Bodley Head, 1975. 200 p.
    In a series of memories and dreamlike vignettes of people and places recalled in mystical fashion, she searches for "a fragment of the divine in the human scene."

4368 *Straus, Dorothea   **1917-**
Thresholds. Boston: Houghton Mifflin, 1971. 183 p.
    A warm and loving memoir of the author's childhood growing up in a German-Jewish family in New York interwoven with a history of her parents and grandparents.

4369 Strauser, Sol
see Bart, Jan

4370 *Strauss, Helen M.
A talent for luck: an autobiography. New York: Random House, 1979. 309 p. Index.
    Strauss's star-studded memoir scorns women's lib and emphasizes that she has always been liberated: as an agent for publishing, television, Broadway, and Hollywood; as a highly paid New York executive; as a woman who never mixed sex and business but enjoyed both. In 1944 Strauss started the literary department of the William Morris Agency.

4371 Strauss, Lewis Lichtenstein   **1896-1974**
Men and decisions. Garden City, New York: Doubleday & Co., 1962. 468 p. Index.
    Having served in high-level positions under four presidents, Strauss writes with knowledge and conviction of momentous decisions and events.

4372 Strausz-Hupe, Robert   **1903-**
In my time. New York: W.W. Norton & Co., Inc., 1965. 284 p. Index.
    Still searching for life's meaning, he writes about his varied experiences, purposes, and interests, particularly in the politics of Europe and the Far East.

4373 Stravinsky, Igor Fedorovich   **1882-1971**
Conversations with Igor Stravinsky. And Robert Craft. Illustrated. Berkeley: University of California Press, 1980. (Garden City, New York: Doubleday & Co., 1959) 140 p.
    These interviews encompass Stravinsky's views on his own compositions and those of others, his anecdotal impressions of a host of contemporary musicians and writers (Schoenberg, Bern, Webern, Proust, Ortega y Gasset), and his views on contemporary music.

4374 Stricklin, Alton Meeks   **1908-**
My years with Bob Wills. With Jon McConal. San Antonio, Texas: The Naylor Co., 1976. 153 p.
    As pianist for Bob Wills and his Texas Playboys off and on for over 25 years, Stricklin traveled with the singer-composer-musician; he writes of the fatigue and loneliness of the road and the spirit of the professional performer.

4375 Stringfellow, William   **1928-**
A second birthday. Garden City, New York: Doubleday & Co., 1970. 203 p.
    When the author moved from New York City to Block Island in 1967, he was ill and following a prescribed course of therapy. When the therapy failed and his condition became grave, a dangerous surgical procedure was the only remaining course. Complications were successfully treated and he survived. His narration analyzes his illness relating it to theological concepts and confirming his Christian understanding of faith, prayer, healing, death, and love.

4376 Strode, Hudson   **1892-**
The eleventh house: memoirs. New York: Harcourt Brace Jovanovich, 1975. 312 p. Index.
    In a busy book crammed with anecdotes and memories, Strode describes a life brimming with nervous energy. He traveled, pursued careers in teaching and writing, met many famous literary and public persons, and seems never to have wasted a minute.

4377 Strom, Erling   **1897-**
Pioneers on skis. Introduction by Lowell Thomas. Central Valley, New York: Smith Clove Press, 1977. 239 p.
    Strom writes engagingly of his life as a cross-country skier in Norway, at Lake Placid (including an account of the 1932 Winter Olympics), in Banff and Mount Assiniboine, and at Stowe, Vermont. He was the first to climb Mt. McKinley on skis and has exciting tales to recount of his cold-weather experiences.

4378 Strong, George Templeton   **1820-1875**
The diary of George Templeton Strong. Edited by Allan Nevins and Milton Halsey Thomas. New York: The Macmillan Company, 1952. 4v. Index.
    A diary of forty years, remarkable for its clarity, precision, and regularity of entries, written always on the same day as events recorded. Volume I, Young Man in New York, 1835-1849; Volume II, The Turbulent Fifties, 1850-1859; Volume III, The Civil War, 1860-1865; Volume IV, Post War Years, 1865-1875.

4379 Strudwick, Peter   **1930-**
Come run with me. With James Rutz. Foreword by Kenneth H. Cooper. Hicksville, New York: Exposition Press, 1979. 146 p.
    A determinedly up-beat diary focusing on Strudwick's attempts to run the Pike's Peak Marathon in 1972 and other long distance races. Born without feet or hands, he runs on padded foot stumps, analogous to "doing 500 miles at Indy on four flat tires."

4380 Stuart, Granville   **1834-1918**
Diary & sketchbook of a journey to "America" in 1866 & return trip up the Missouri River to Fort Benton, Montana. With an introduction by Carl Schaefer Dentzel. Reprinted from the Virginia City *Montana Post* of Jan. 1867. Los Angeles: Dawson's Book Shop, 1963. 50 p.
    A description, illustrated by original sketches, of a five-month journey

in 1866 through the Northern Plains by a keen observer of nature and men.

4381 Stuart, Granville   **1834-1918**
Pioneering in Montana: the making of a state. Edited by Paul C. Phillips. Lincoln, Nebraska: University of Nebraska, 1977. (Cleveland: Arthur H. Clark Co., 1925) 265 p. Index.

Stuart provides a panoramic twenty-year perspective of the settlement of Montana. As a rancher, he offers a poignant testament to the end of the open range, accelerated in 1887 by a severe winter that killed thousands of cattle. As an amateur historian, he details the Indian Wars of the Northwest, 1864-1891, in which the Indians and buffalo gradually became as decimated as the cattle on the open range. As a pioneer, he offers glimpses of prospecting for gold and the development of mining towns.

4382 Stuart, Granville   **1834-1918**
Prospecting for gold: from Dogtown to Virginia City, 1852-1864: Rpt. of original title: Forty years on the Frontier, in the Journals and Reminiscences of Granville Stuart, gold-miner, trader, merchant rancher and politican, VI. Edited by Paul C. Phillips. Illustrated. Lincoln, Nebraska: University of Nebraska Press, 1977. (Cleveland: Arthur H. Clark Co., 1925) 272 p. Index.

A condensation of the author's journals and sketches of his richly varied pioneer experience, particularly in gold mining. With an eye for detail and a sense of humor, Stuart reports on the life and environment of the pioneer. Combats with Indians are described, as are various Indian customs.

4383 Stuart, Jesse   **1907-**
The kingdom within: a spiritual autobiography. New York: McGraw-Hill Book Co., 1979. 168 p.

In novelistic form, this work presents an allegory of Stuart's mental state after a massive heart attack. As Stan Powderjay, he dreams that fully recovered he walked out of the hospital to the railroad station where hundreds of people, all characters from his fiction about his eastern Kentucky homeland, board the train to attend his funeral. He eavesdrops on their conversations and on his funeral service and meditates on his lifetime values—including love for his parents and wife, fairness to others, and bearing personal witness to what he has written.

4384 Stuart, Jesse   **1907-**
My world. Lexington: University Press of Kentucky, 1975. 96 p.

Stuart's book interprets different areas of Kentucky, opens with a 21-page autobiography, and relates his three loves—his native Kentucky hills, his career as a writer, and his wife.

4385 Stuart, Jesse   **1907-**
Seasons of Jesse Stuart; an autobiography in poetry, 1907-1976. Selected with an introduction by Wanda Hicks. Danbury, Connecticut: Archer Editions Press, 1976. 229 p.

Autobiographical poems are grouped under the headings: Youth, Summer, Success, Rebirth, Travel, and Autumn, and follow, in general, the course of his life. Most of them have previously been published elsewhere.

4386 Stuart, Jesse   **1907-**
To teach, to love. New York: The World Publishing Co., 1970. 317 p.

In addition to writing over thirty books, he was a teacher for nearly fifty years. He writes here of teachers and teaching, including many stories of his experiences in Kentucky one-room schoolhouses, in country-school administration, and university teaching.

4387 Stuart, Jesse   **1907-**
Year of my rebirth. Illustrated by Barry Martin. New York: McGraw-Hill Book Co., Inc., 1956. 342 p.

Based on the journal he kept during 1955, the year he struggled to recover from a serious heart attack, his book is a celebration of life.

4388 Stuart, John Leighton   **1876-1962**
Fifty years in China: the memoirs of John Leighton Stuart, missionary and ambassador. Introduction by Hu Shih. New York: Random House, 1954. 313 p. Index.

A Presbyterian missionary recalls his boyhood in China, his missionary training in the United States, and the years he spent first as a missionary, then as an ambassador to China. The author was closely affiliated with Yenching University and was its first president.

4389 *Stuart, Mary
Both of me. Garden City, New York: Doubleday & Co., Inc., 1980. 462 p.

Soap-opera star Stuart relates the parallel and divergent progress of her life and that of the character she has played for 25 years on *Search for Tomorrow*. Her struggle to be a perfect wife and mother as well as a full-time actress is interspersed with flashbacks to a childhood of near-poverty in Oklahoma, a first marriage, and an ultimately disillusioning stint as a Hollywood starlet.

4390 Stuart, Robert   **1785-1848**
On the Oregon Trail: Robert Stuart's journey of discovery. Edited by

Kenneth A. Spaulding. American Exploration and Travel. Norman: University of Oklahoma Press, 1953. 192 p. Index.

The daily account of a harrowing journey from Fort Astoria, Oregon, to St. Louis (1812-1813), which led to the discovery of the Oregon Trail, the first wagon trail to the Pacific which opened the West.

4391 Sturdevant, Carl Alva
Open wider, please. Philadelphia: Dorrance & Co., 1974. 329 p.

Using fictitious names for persons and organizations, Sturdevant has endeavored to present incidents and problems likely to occur in the training and career of a dentist. All of the events actually happened either to the author or to his father.

4392 *Sture-Vasa, Mary Alsop
see ***O'Hara, Mary, pseud.**

4393 *Sturgis, Margie (Marguerite F.)
Let the record show: memoirs of a parole board member. Hicksville, New York: Exposition Press, 1978. 109 p.

The lone female member of the Illinois Parole and Pardon Board for four years (presumably in the early 1970's) writes her interpretation of notable cases and Board activities during this time to set the record straight. In a mixture of penal jargon, formal English, and slang, Sturgis expresses sympathy for prisoners and for the minority (Black and Hispanic) members of the Parole Board, who were often, she says, held to a double standard by white conservative Board members.

4394 Sugrue, Thomas Joseph   **1907-1953**
Stranger in the earth: the story of a search. New York: Henry Holt and Co., 1948. 371 p.

Centered on the author's struggle to overcome a crippling disease which struck him in 1938, the book is the story of his quest for intellectual and spiritual meaning in modern life. In the next ten years he became a prominent author and journalist.

4395 Sullivan, James L.   **1910-**
God is my record. Nashville: Broadman, 1974. 145 p.

Born on a Bible-Belt Mississippi farm, Sullivan became a minister and served in churches in several Southern states before becoming secretary-treasurer and then president of the Baptist Sunday School Board, where he continued spreading the gospel and his sense of biblical ideals and truth.

4396 Sullivan, John Florence
see **Allen, Fred**

4397 *Sullivan, Judy   **1936-**
Mama doesn't live here anymore. New York: Arthur Fields Books, Inc., 1974. 243 p.

After fifteen years of marriage, Sullivan left her husband and daughter in Kansas to go to New York and start a new life of her own, leaving behind the typical American dream of middle-class conventional "success." Her story tells how she arrived at and carried out her decision to make a new life.

4398 Sullivan, Louis Henry   **1856-1924**
Autobiography of an idea. Foreword by Claude Bragdon. New introduction and photographs by Ralph Marlowe Line. New York: Dover Publications, Inc., 1956. (New York: New York American Institute of Architects, 1924) 329 p. Index.

A third person narrative of his life to 1900, his boyhood in Boston, training in Philadelphia and Paris, and his career in Chicago, by a prominent architect.

4399 Sullivan, Mark   **1874-1952**
The education of an American. Illustrated. New York: Johnson Reprint Corp., 1970. (New York: Doubleday, Doran & Co., 1938) 320 p. Index.

A journalist and syndicated columnist with an intense curiosity records a vivid picture of an American life and experience with humor and intelligence.

4400 Sullivan, Tom   **1947-**
If you could see what I hear. And Derek Gill. New York: Harper & Row, Publishers, 1975. 184 p.

The limitations of blindness failed to deter this talented young man who overcame loneliness and self-pity to find joy, love, and a full life.

4401 Sullivan, W. John L.   **b.1851**
Twelve years in the saddle for law and order on the frontiers of Texas. Illustrated. New York: Buffalo-Head Press, 1966. (Austin, Texas: The author, 1909) 284 p.

A series of anecdotes about the author's escapades as a member of the Texas Rangers, trying to bring law and order to a wild West in the post-Civil War era. Sullivan's language belies his sharpshooting, hard riding, and fearlessness: "I told [the prisoner] that while it was my duty to pursue him, it was natural for him to try to escape . . . I told him that

I felt sorry for him because he was in jail and hoped he would lead a better life when he got free again."

4402 Sullivan, William C.   **1912-1977**
The bureau: my thirty years in Hoover's FBI. With Bill Brown. Illustrated. New York: W.W. Norton, 1979. 286 p. Index.
Sullivan writes about working as an FBI agent under Hoover, focusing on Hoover's relationships with the U.S. Presidents from Eisenhower to Nixon. He also describes Hoover's various pecadillos (he was a gambler, an egomaniac, and social butterfly) and the FBI scandals and mistakes Hoover concealed.

4403 Sullivan, William Laurence   **1872-1935**
Under orders: the autobiography of William Laurence Sullivan. Preface by Max F. Daskam. Boston: Beacon Press, 1966. 200 p.
In complex but compelling, occasionally poetic, prose, Sullivan discusses the history and tenets of Roman Catholicism and of liberal Protestantism, using his own life only as a backdrop for the issues. Sullivan moved from the priesthood to an intellectual Unitarian ministry in what Daskam calls "the spiritual pilgrimage of a great soul."

4404 Sulzberger, Cyrus Leo   **1912-**
An age of mediocrity: memoirs and diaries: 1963-1972. New York: Macmillan Publishing Co., Inc., 1973. 828 p. Index.
The third volume of the memoirs and diaries of a journalist who for nearly four decades interviewed history-making individuals and reported on crucial events throughout the world.

4405 Sulzberger, Cyrus Leo   **1912-**
Last of the giants. Illustrated. New York: The Macmillan Co., 1970. 1063 p.
This volume, one of a series of books correspondent Sulzberger has written, contains interviews and assessments of Charles de Gaulle, Khrushchev and Churchill, and entries from the author's diaries from 1954 through 1963.

4406 Sulzberger, Cyrus Leo   **1912-**
A long row of candles; memoirs and diaries, 1934-1954. Illustrated. New York: The Macmillan Co., 1969. 1061 p. Index.
This book is composed of a reporter's notebooks, jottings of remembered conversations or events which were unusual or pleasant or represented important people in his life.

4407 Sulzberger, Cyrus Leo   **1912-**
Postscript with a Chinese accent: memoirs and diaries: 1972-1973. New York: Macmillan Publishing Co., Inc., 1974. 401 p. Index.
This last volume in his series of memoirs and diaries culminates in his 1973 visit to China after seventeen years attempting to gain admittance.

4408 Sulzberger, Cyrus Leo   **1912-**
Seven continents and forty years: a concentration of memoirs. Foreword by André Malraux. New York: Quadrangle/New York Times Book Co., 1977. (Condensed from: New York, Macmillan: *A Long Row of Candles*, 1969; *The Last of the Giants*, 1970; *An Age of Mediocrity*, 1973; *Postscript with a Chinese Accent*, 1974) 688 p. Index.
New York *Times* foreign correspondent Sulzberger presents fascinating excerpts from his journals (1938-1973), emphasizing politics, heads of states, social and military policies of the countries in Europe and Asia he traveled in. His observations are trenchant and concise; "he is offstage in a corner, half visible, half hidden, like the donors of old Flemish paintings," said Malraux.

4409 *Sulzberger, Marina   **1919-1976**
Marina: letters and diaries of Marina Sulzberger. Edited by C.L. Sulzberger. New York: Crown Publishers, 1978. 530 p.
Marina, wife of New York *Times* foreign correspondent C.L. Sulzberger, wrote happy, delightful letters to her Greek mother, children, husband, and hosts of friends, describing her world travels with her husband and commenting sensitively on the people they met and the joys of family life.

4410 Sumner, John Daniel
J.D. Sumner; gospel music is my life. Edited by Bob Terrell. Nashville, Tennessee: Impact Books, 1971. 208 p.
One of the most productive writers of gospel music, he sang with the Sunshine Boys, the Blackwood Brothers, and the Stamps Quartet. He devoted a great deal of time to the Gospel Music Association and was the moving force behind the first National Quartet Convention.

4411 Sumrall, Lester Frank   **1913-**
Run with the vision. With Stephen Conn. Illustrated. Plainfield, New Jersey: Logos International, 1977. 161 p.
As president of the Lester Sumrall Evangelistic Association (LeSea), the author ministers by magazine, radio, and TV to millions of people around the world and has founded and supports a Bible College, orphan homes, and other religious causes.

4412 Sutton, Ernest Venable   **b.1862**
A life worth living. Illustrated by Clarence Ellsworth. Pasadena: Trail's End Publishing Co., 1948. 350 p. Index.
A rambling narrative of pioneer life in Minnesota, North Dakota, and California, with details of town life and the development of the railroads by an ordinary but interesting man.

4413 Sutton, William Francis   **1901-**
I, Willie Sutton. As told to Quentin Reynolds. New York: Farrar, Straus, and Young, 1953. 273 p.
A New York bank robber and jail breaker describes his life as a criminal, fugitive, and prisoner. He explains how he succeeded in crime but how his life was ruined as a result of it.

4414 Sutton, William Francis   **1901-**
Where the money was. With Edward Linn. New York: The Viking Press, 1976. 339 p.
Sutton's account of his career as a gentleman bank robber at the top of his profession is exceptional in its candor, excellent style, and analysis of a robber's motives and methods. For Sutton robbery was an exhilarating art, its success related as much to stylistic finesse as to the amount of money stolen. He eventually won parole to have an operation on a gangrenous leg, having mobilized public sentiment in his favor.

4415 *Svendsen, Gro (Nilsdatter)   **1840?-1878**
Frontier mother: the letters of Gro Svendsen. Translated by Pauline Farseth and Theodore C. Blegen with introduction by Theodore C. Blegen. Northfield, Minnesota: The Norwegian-American Historical Association, 1950. 153 p. Index.
In affectionate letters to her family in Norway, written between 1861 when she immigrated with her new husband and her death in 1878, Svendsen describes her life and feelings in the New World. The letters are detailed and articulate and show her lively curiosity.

4416 Swan, Carroll Judson
My company. Boston: Houghton Mifflin Company, 1918. 263 p.
As Captain of Company D. 101st Engineers, he describes the work of his troops in France laying out roads and building machine-gun emplacements, dugouts, trenches, and barbed-wire systems.

4417 Swanner, Charles Douglas   **1894-**
Fifty years a barrister in Orange County. Claremont, California: Fraser Press, 1965. 165 p.
While describing his own legal practice in southern California, he includes comments on the early history of Spanish and Mexican culture, notable changes in the practice of law, and the phenomenal development of Santa Ana.

4418 Sweeney, William J., III   **1922-**
Woman's doctor: a year in the life of an obstetrician-gynecologist. With Barbara Lang Stern. New York: William Morrow & Co., Inc., 1973. 318 p. Index.
A physician's story of what happens in the delivery and operating rooms, of a surgeon's busy life, of problems encountered, like infertility, venereal disease, and premature delivery. He loves his work and speaks candidly and with understanding of his patients and his profession.

4419 Sweeny, Thomas W.   **1820-1892**
Journal of Lt. Thomas W. Sweeny, 1849-1953. Edited with introduction and notes by Arthur Woodward. Los Angeles: Westernlore Press, 1956. 278 p. Index.
A colorful, gritty account of life in Southwestern military outposts, 1849-53, notably Camp Yuma (Arizona) and San Isabel (California), "where the thermometer averages 108 degrees in the shade and 130 degrees in the sun." This book is full of information about the ways of Indian tribes, Mexican-American relations, and inept U.S. Army administration of frontier and hardship outposts.

4420 *Sweet, Margaret Massling
There must be a better place. As told to Carol Boyle LaPorte. Illustrated by Barbara Sally. New York: Vantage Press, 1976. 120 p.
Sweet describes her childhood in Recklinghausen, Westphalia, Germany, during Hitler's rise to power in the 1930's. She was an ambivalent participant in Hitler's youth-work program, studied nursing, and liked serving as a nurse despite heavy bombing and fighting throughout war-torn Germany. She describes the hardships of war, especially difficult for the very young, the infirm, and aged. After the war's end she married an American sergeant and immigrated to the United States.

4421 Sweezy, Carl   **1881-1953**
The Arapaho way: a memoir of an Indian boyhood, by Althea Bass. Recorded, with little editing, by A. Bass. New York: C.N. Potter, Inc., 1966. 80 p.
The memoir of one of the last full-blooded Arapaho Indians living on an Oklahoma reservation is remarkable for its detail and nobility, as well as the beautiful reproductions of Sweezy's paintings.

4422 Swenson, Birger   **1895-**
My story: immigrant/executive/traveler. Illustrated. Rock Island, Illinois: Augustana Historical Society, 1979. 250 p.

Immigrant Swenson became a Lutheran clergyman in Illinois but eventually found his major contribution as director of a Lutheran publishing concern. His work involved travel for business and religious purposes and, upon retirement, for pleasure. He provides many details about the business aspects of religious publishing.

4423 Swieson, Eddy Ie   **1932-**
When the angels laughed: Eddy Swieson tells his story. With Howard Norton. Foreword and afterword by Howard Norton. Illustrated. Introduction by Mark O. Hatfield. Plainfield, New Jersey: Logos International, 1977. 126 p.

An inspirational account of how Swieson, a Chinese born Ie Swie Sing in Indonesia, was reared from malnourished infancy to physical and spiritual adulthood by his foster mother, Rini Tan. Swieson had a religious experience as a teenager that triggered his conversion from Buddhism to evangelical Christianity. Educated at the Adelaide (Australia) Bible Institute, Swieson and his wife, Debbie, spread the gospel in Indonesia before coming to the Fourth Presbyterian Church in Washington, D.C., around 1970.

4424 Swing, Raymond Gram   **1887-1968**
"Good evening!": a professional memoir. New York: Harcourt, Brace & World, 1964. 311 p. Index.

As newspaperman, foreign correspondent, and radio commentator, his experiences and contacts comprise a roster of noted events and people from World War I through post-World War II.

4425 *Symington, Maude Fay   **1878-1964**
Living in awe. Edited with preface and epilogue by Marshall Dill, Jr. San Francisco: Marshall Dill, 1968. 177 p.

This chatty reminiscence of the author's 25-year career as an opera singer in Munich, Berlin, Budapest, London, and New York has been arranged by the editor by geographic location, opera house (Covent Garden, the Metropolitan Opera), and opera, especially works by Wagner, Strauss, and Verdi.

4426 Symmes, John Cleves   **1742-1814**
Intimate letters of John Cleves Symmes and his family: including those of his daughter Mrs. William Henry Harrison, wife of the ninth President of the United States. Edited by Beverly W. Bond. Cincinnati: Historical and Philosophical Society of Ohio, 1956. 174 p. Index.

A selection of his personal letters and those of his family and intimate friends, intended to portray the everyday family life of the founder of the Miami Purchase.

4427 Symons, R.D.   **1898-1973**
Where the wagon led: one man's memories of the cowboy's life in the Old West. Garden City, New York: Doubleday and Co., Inc., 1973. 343 p.

A cowboy's life on the open range in the days before homesteaders moved in with plows and fences. Symons regrets the passing of a way of life and shares his memories of everyday life on the range, his battles with nature, livestock, rustlers, and progress. Includes glossary.

4428 Szebenyei, Joseph   **1879-1953**
Reporters, kings, and other vagabonds: an autobiography. Caldwell, Idaho: The Caxton Printers, Ltd., 1951. 343 p.

A journalist writes of his boyhood and education in Hungary, his early experience as a Hungarian reporter, his immigration to the United States, and his long career as a reporter, emphasizing his personal experience rather than the events he wrote about.

4429 Szilard, Leo   **1898-1964**
Leo Szilard: his version of the facts: selected recollections and correspondence. Edited by Spencer R. Weart and Gertrud Weiss Szilard. Cambridge, Massachusetts: MIT Press, 1978. 244 p. Index.

An informative account of the developments leading up to and beyond the first atomic bomb, as transcribed from tape recordings, letters, and memos. Many major scientists, politicians, and military people are involved in these exchanges, but always Szilard's perspective appears, a sensitive scientific and humanistic view.

4430 *Taber, Gladys Bagg   **1899-1980**
The best of Stillmeadow: a treasury of country living. Philadelphia: J.B. Lippincott Co., 1976. 348 p.

Selections from seven previous volumes describing the author's life in a country home in Connecticut, bought in the late Thirties to escape the chaos of urban and international affairs.

4431 *Taber, Gladys Bagg   **1899-1980**
Book of Stillmeadow. Philadelphia: Macrae-Smith Co., 1948. 273 p.

To escape from urban living and the threats of war, the author and her friend bought an old farm in Connecticut in the late Thirties. Their new life became the basis for Taber's regular column, "Diary of Domesticity," in the *Ladies Home Journal.*

4432 *Taber, Gladys Bagg   **1899-1980**
Harvest of yesterdays. Drawings by Pamela Johnson. Philadelphia: J.B. Lippincott Co., 1976. 224 p.

A pleasant reminiscence of a writer's early and later years, with charming and amusing anecdotes of people, places and pets.

4433 *Taber, Gladys Bagg   **1899-1980**
Stillmeadow sampler. Illustrated by Edward Shenton. Philadelphia: J.B. Lippincott Co., 1959. 282 p.

Divided by the four seasons and beginning in the spring, this book samples everyday living in the New England country and shares the tranquil contemplation of that life's meaning.

4434 Talbert, William Franklin   **1918-**
Playing for life: Billy Talbert's story. With John Sharnik. Boston: Little, Brown and Co., 1959. 310 p.

In spite of the diabetes he fought from age ten, he became an international tennis star holding several titles for singles and doubles. His book tells of the lifelong struggle between success and disease.

4435 *Talbot, Toby
A book about my mother. New York: Farrar, Straus, & Giroux, 1980. 180 p.

Talbot's book of memories and mourning moves sporadically from one event to another as she recounts incidents in her mother's life, death, and funeral. Jewishness and family life shape this exploration of grief.

4436 Tallmadge, Benjamin   **1754-1835**
Memoir of Colonel Benjamin Tallmadge. Eyewitness Accounts of the American Revolution. New York: The New York Times & Arno Press, 1968. (New York: Thomas Holman, 1858) 70 p.

An account of incidents during the Revolutionary War with which he was primarily connected as head of the Second Regiment of Light Dragoons. He came through the war unscathed and later served in Congress for sixteen years.

4437 Tanous, Alex   **1926-**
Beyond coincidence: one man's experiences with psychic phenomena. With Harvey Ardman. Garden City, New York: Doubleday & Co., Inc., 1976. 195 p.

Citing documentary evidence and scientific verification, Tanous has written about his psychic powers, clairvoyance, healing, telepathic communication, and the uses he has made of these abilities.

4438 Tarkenton, Francis Asbury   **1940-**
Better scramble than lose. As told to Jack Olsen. Illustrated. New York: Four Winds Press, 1969. 126 p.

In a breezy, conversational ramble over his career as quarterback first with the New York Giants and then with the Minnesota Vikings, the author explains successful and controversial plays, shares his feelings when the "scramble" works and when everything he tries falls through, and attempts to make sense of his less-than-cordial relationship with the coach of the Vikings.

4439 Tarkington, Booth   **1869-1946**
Your amiable uncle: letters to his nephews. Indianapolis: Bobbs-Merrill Co., Inc., 1949. 192 p.

Written during his first trip abroad with his wife and parents (1903-1904), Tarkington's imaginative, humorous letters were sent to his three nephews in Indiana. These children furnished material for their grateful uncle's later book, *Penrod.*

4440 Tarleton, Frank L.
Some strike it rich: memoirs and tales of a native son of California. Illustrated. Hicksville, New York: Exposition Press, 1979. 244 p.

This series of anecdotes covers the author's adventures as a prospector, miner, and fisherman during the Depression to his extraterrestrial experiences in recent years. Intermingled are accolades to his dog, his wife, and his ranching experiences.

4441 Tarrants, Thomas A. III   **1947-**
The conversion of a Klansman: the story of a former Ku Klux Klan terrorist. Foreword by Leighton Ford. Epilogue by Harold E. Hughes. Garden City, New York: A Doubleday-Galilee Original/Doubleday & Co., 1979. 130 p.

Tarrants focuses on his activities as a Ku Klux Klan terrorist in Mississippi in the 1960's, which culminated in his attempt to bomb the home of a Jewish businessman in 1968. Captured by the FBI, he was sent to Parchman State Penitentiary, escaped, and was recaptured. His newfound born-again Christianity won him an early release in December 1976.

4442 *Tarry, Ellen   **1906-**
The third door: the autobiography of an American Negro woman. New York: Negro Universities Press, 1971. (New York: David McKay Co., Inc., 1955) 304 p.

Raised in Birmingham, Alabama, she graduated from college, converted to Catholicism, and started a career in journalism which led her to

New York. Later she began working for the interracial Friendship House in Harlem and became well-known for her work in race relations.

4443 *Tartiere, Dorothy (Blackman)   **1903-**
House near Paris: an American woman's story of traffic in patriots. With Morris Robert Werner. New York: Simon and Schuster, 1946. 318 p.
Remembered as the blond heroine in many Charlie Chan movies, she married a Frenchman just before World War II and remained in France throughout Nazi occupation as an important member of the Underground resistance.

4444 Tate, Allen   **1899-**
Memoirs and opinions, 1926-1974. Chicago: Swallow Press, 1975. 225 p. Index.
A collection of essays, some personal memories written for this book, others previously published, and some critical essays meant to intensify the reader's awareness of literature and art—by a distinguished poet and critic.

4445 Tate, Allen
see also **Davidson, Donald**

4446 Tatum, Jack David   **1948-**
They call me Assassin. With Bill Kushner. New York: Everest House, 1979. 251 p.
Tatum, tackle for the Oakland Raiders, discusses his hyper-aggressive style of football, attempting to mitigate his reputation as "the meanest, dirtiest, hardest-hitting, rottenest bastard who ever played the game of football." Yet every illustration supports this contention and belies Tatum's claim that "at heart I'm a friendly assassin who honestly cares about people and the world." He admires his coach at Ohio State for his "hard work, fair play, and honesty"—while acknowledging Hayes' own violent coaching style.

4447 Taub, William L.
Forces of power. Illustrated. New York: Grosset & Dunlap, 1979. 255 p. Index.
Taub's rationale for his book is that he has known powerful people in high places and has been involved in important actions including big favors and big money. These people are now mostly dead or otherwise powerless, so he wants to have his say.

4448 Tawes, Leonard S.   **1853-1932**
Coasting captain: journals of Captain Leonard S. Tawes relating his career in Atlantic coastwise sailing craft from 1868-1922. Illustrated. Newport News, Virginia: Mariners Museum, 1967. 461 p. Index.
Tawes' seagoing career pictures the operation of an American coasting schooner plying the East Coast and Chesapeake Bay before steamships took over. The hazards of fog, shoals, storms, and aggravating pilots and tugboatmen contributed to the excitement of sailing in those early days and add spice to the captain's journals, which he wrote for his grand-daughter.

4449 Taylor, Edward   **1642-1729**
The diary of Edward Taylor. Edited with introduction by Francis Murphy. Springfield, Massachusetts: Conn. Valley Historical Museum, 1964. (Proceedings of the Massachusetts Historical Society, 1880) 40 p.
This diary is a record of his journey from England to Boston, his three years' stay at Harvard, and his overland trip to Westfield where he remained for nearly sixty years as a minister.

4450 *Taylor, Elizabeth Rosemund   **1932-**
Elizabeth Taylor: an informal memoir by Elizabeth Taylor; With photographs by Roddy McDowell plus a collection from Elizabeth Taylor's family album. As told to Richard Meryman. Photographed by Roddy McDowell. New York: Harper & Row, 1965. 177 p.
A superficial, public-relations account of Elizabeth Taylor's fairy-tale life: childhood on a four-hundred-acre English estate: emigration to Hollywood to escape World War II; instant child stardom in *National Velvet*, followed by an unbroken series of star roles, including *Butterfield 8* and *Cleopatra*. Of her five husbands (as of 1965) she remains friendly with actor Michael Wilding. She loved producer Mike Todd dearly until long after his death in a plane crash. She was devoted to actor Richard Burton, her fifth husband, and her children.

4451 *Taylor, Elizabeth Rosemund   **1932-**
Nibbles and me. Illustrated by the author. New York: Duell, Sloan and Pearce, 1946. 77 p.
A diary of the author-actress at 13, describing her affection for her pet chipmunk.

4452 Taylor, Glen Hearst   **1904-**
Way it was with me. Secaucus, New Jersey: Lyle Stuart, 1979. 420 p. Index.
This often hilarious account describes Taylor's career as a singer beginning at fifteen as a vaudeville performer. He later married Dora, another performer, and they toured Idaho and other Western states throughout the Depression. In 1938 Taylor decided to enter politics; he lost several Senatorial campaigns. He won in 1944, but resigned in 1948 to be Henry Wallace's running mate in the Progressive Party.

4453 Taylor, Maxwell Davenport   **1901-**
Swords and plowshares. Illustrated. New York: W.W. Norton & Co., 1972. 434 p. Index.
After serving in World War II, Taylor became Superintendent of West Point, Commander in Berlin, Commander of the Eighth Army in Korea, then Army Chief of Staff, a post he also held under President Kennedy. For Johnson he was a key advisor and Ambassador to Vietnam. Here he discusses lessons learned during his career, offering advice for future national policy.

4454 Taylor, Rinaldo Rinaldini   **1823-1873**
Seeing the elephant: letters of R.R. Taylor, Forty-Niner. Edited by John Walton Caughey. Pasadena: The Ward Ritchie Press, 1951. 107 p.
"Seeing the elephant" meant graduating from the status of greenhorn, which Taylor did on his Panama voyage to San Francisco and in the gold fields, during the year of his California adventure (May 1849-April 1850).

4455 Taylor, Robert H.   **1925-**
Diary of a disbarred lawyer: an autobiography. New York: Vantage Press, 1962. 228 p.
Most of the book is composed of trial transcripts, with narrative interspersed, written by a lawyer convicted of grand larceny in an insurance fraud.

4456 *Taylor, Rosemary (Drachman)   **1899-**
Harem scare'm. New York: Thomas Y. Crowell Co., 1951. 246 p.
Young graduate on vacation tour of Europe and Africa reports on her travels in Morocco with humor.

4457 *Taylor, Susie King   **1848-1912**
Reminiscences of my life in camp. Illustrated. New York: Arno Press, 1968. (Boston: the author, 1902) 82 p.
A view of military life in the Civil War by an educated Black woman whose husband was in the First South Carolina Volunteers, the earliest Negro regiment organized by the Union Army. Mrs. King taught the soldiers to read and write, helped with cleaning equipment, and nursed the wounded. Later she taught school and helped organize an auxiliary of the G.A.R. in Boston.

4458 Taylor, William   **1821-1902**
Story of my life. Edited by John Clarke Ridpath. Illustrated by Frank Beard. The Black Heritage Library Collection. New York: Books for Libraries Press, 1972. (New York: Eaton & Mains, 1895) 2v.
Taylor's life is interwoven with the religious history of his age. He began riding circuit in Virginia, became a missionary in California in 1849, preaching to the sinners, miners, outcasts, and gold seekers. Then his missionary work led him all over the world—Australia, India, Ceylon, South America. Finally he was elected Bishop of the Methodist Episcopal Church for Africa. For over 53 years he devoted himself to his various posts; preaching, founding schools, establishing missions, supplying them with working forces, and spreading the Gospel.

4459 Teale, Edwin Way   **1899-1980**
Dune boy: the early years of a naturalist. Lone Oak Edition. Illustrated by Edward Shenton. New York: Dodd, Mead & Co., 1957. (1943) 275 p.
A naturalist writes with warm affection and nostalgia of his grandparents, their farm in the Indiana Dunes, his excursions and discoveries during his regular visits with them, and the influence of this experience on the development of his values and his career.

4460 *Tempski, Armine von   **1899-1943**
Aloha, my love to you: the story of one who was born in paradise. New York: Duell, Sloan and Pearce, 1946. (New York: Literary Guild of America, 1940) 235 p.
A remarkable, well-written story of her life on a ranch in Hawaii, the early death of her mother, and strong influence of her father's love and values thereafter.

4461 Terkel, Studs   **1912-**
Talking to myself: a memoir of my times. New York: Kangaroo Book/Pocket Books, 1978. (New York: Pantheon Books, 1977) 323 p.
Terkel's stream-of-association roams backward and forward over the high and low spots of life in his beloved Chicago, from childhood escapades in his mother's hotel, to encounters with mobsters in the 1920's, to memorable election campaigns and political conventions. He focuses particularly on quintessential interviews he has conducted with notables over the years, including Mahalia Jackson, A.S. Neill, and Ivy Compton-Burnett.

4462 Tettemer, John Moynihan (Father Ildefonso)   **1876-1949**
I was a monk: the autobiography of John Tettemer. Edited by Janet Mabie. Foreword by Jean Burden. Introduction by John Burton. Wheaton, Illinois: The Theosophical Publishing House, 1974. (New York: Alfred A. Knopf, 1951) 255 p.

After spending 25 years as a Roman Catholic monk, Tettemer made the painful decision to leave the order because he had lost his belief in creed and dogma. As Father Ildefonso he rose to become Consulator General of the Passionist Order at the age of 38, but found the life of a monk no longer tenable and rebuilt his life outside the monastery walls.

4463 Teurlings, William J.   1872-1957
One mile an hour: the priestly memories of Rt. Rev. Msgr. William J. Teurlings. Adapted by Rosalind Foley. New York: Exposition Press, 1959. 99 p.

Father Teurlings spent 62 years in Louisiana parishes, traveling by horse, bicycle, and car, speaking in Creole when necessary. He was an effective religious educator for white and black parishioners and preached with particular eloquence when soliciting money for new church buildings in his rural parishes.

4464 Thach, Harrell G.
God gets in the way of a sailor. Foreword by O. Hobart Mowrer. New York: Exposition Press, 1964. 266 p.

This provocative book raises a profound philosophical and psychological question: Who—according to what system of values or beliefs—has the right to determine another person's sanity? The author, a ne'er-do-well alcoholic sailor, had a religious experience in 1944 that convinced him that "some Great Force was acting on his life in a stern but redemptive manner." As a consequence, he was confined to a naval mental hospital for five months. With extreme difficulty he was released and eventually became a Methodist clergyman.

4465 *Thane, Elswyth   1900-
The strength of the hills. Illustrated. Chappaqua, New York: Christian Herald House, 1976. (*Reluctant Farmer* [original title]. New York: Duell, Sloane and Pearce, 1950) 219 p.

A charming book about Thane's return-to-the-land (she calls it "Driven-Back-to-Eden") from London and New York to a 180-acre farm in Wilmington, Vermont. The book has a Robinson Crusoe flavor, as Thane tells about the installation of heat, electricity, and other creature comforts and the antics of Chee-Wee, her pet finch. She gradually metamorphoses from a New York writer to a Vermont writer-and-farmer, a romantic devotee of rural living.

4466 Theberge, Remy   1929?-
Reluctant rebel in Air Force blues: a unique military autobiography. Illustrated. Attleboro, Massachusetts: Golden Gambit Books, 1977. 220 p.

Theberge writes to explain two court-martial trials involving his alleged robbery of another airman at Travis Air Force Base in 1954. As a consequence of judgments which he claims were vindictive and unjust, Theberge was demoted from staff sergeant to airman basic and given a general (rather than honorable) discharge.

4467 *Theroux, Phyllis   1939-
California and other states of grace: a memoir. New York: William Morrow & Co., 1980. 300 p.

Theroux engagingly writes the story of her life as a child, adolescent, college student at Manhattanville, young wife, and of the memorable relationships that sustained her. Her mother, paternal grandmother, father, and the convent schools in which she was educated were particularly significant in her life.

4468 *Therriault, Selma Crow   1904?-
Southwest ramblins. Illustrated. Philadelphia: Dorrance & Co., 1978. 124 p.

Therriault kept a diary of the winter trips she and her husband, a retired plumber, took to California, Arizona, and New Mexico (1972-77). They enjoyed visiting national parks and monuments, Indian reservations, turquoise shops, friends, and relatives, many of whom lived in trailer parks in Arizona.

4469 Thomas, Alexander   1909-
Many a night's journey. New York: Comet Press Books, 1957. 143 p.

Thomas tried to communicate with and warn relevant people, from friends to presidents, because of visions he had concerning future events. Thomas's particular interest is with events between World Wars I and II in Europe.

4470 Thomas, Ebenezer Smith   1775-1845
Reminiscences of the last sixty-five years. New York: Arno Press, 1970. (Hartford: The Author, 1840) 300 p.

Thomas writes of the life and times in nineteenth-century America. As a journalist he traveled frequently, writing regularly for papers in Charleston and Cincinnati.

4471 *Thomas, Helen
Dateline: White House. New York: Macmillan Publishing Co., Inc., 1975. 298 p. Index.

A White House correspondent under four presidents from Kennedy through Ford seems personally affronted when the president does not arrange news breaks for the convenience of the press or when the First Family tries to snatch a little privacy away from the public eye. As Chief of the UPI White House Bureau, she was in a position to see and tell everything in her zealous pursuit in the name of "the people's right to know."

4472 *Thomas, Jeannette (Bell)   b.1881
The traipsin woman. New York: E.P. Dutton & Co., Inc., 1933. 277 p.

Raised in a poor Kentucky family, she became a county legal secretary which sent her traveling to remote sections of the hill country. Her book recalls this experience with nostalgia for the calico age.

4473 Thomas, Jesse O.   b.1885
My story in black and white: the autobiography of Jesse O. Thomas. Foreword by Whitney M. Young, Jr. New York: An Exposition-Banner Book/Exposition Press, 1967. 300 p. Index.

Thomas has written a compelling narrative of his life, which was largely devoted to the betterment of Blacks and to the promotion of interracial harmony. He was reared on a Mississippi sharecropper's farm, graduated from Tuskeegee Institute, and was befriended by the revered Booker T. Washington. He became chief administrator of Voorhees Institute, a comparable institution in South Carolina; worked six years as the first Black administrator in the American Red Cross (which included pressing for integrated blood banks); was a successful fund raiser for the U.S. Treasury Department (selling war bonds); and founded the Atlanta University School of Social Work.

4474 Thomas, Lowell Jackson   1892-1981
Good evening everybody: from Cripple Creek to Samartana. New York: William Morrow, 1976. 349 p.

Thomas's enjoyment of life and world-wide adventure that he communicated so forcefully in his 45 years of news broadcasts, books, and lectures inspires this tale of his life from boyhood in Cripple Creek, Colorado, until the eve of World War II. Highlights include reporting the Palestine campaign in World War I, in which Allenby took Jerusalem from the Turks; his adventures in Arabia with T.E. Lawrence; journeys to Malaya, Burma, India, and Afghanistan; and the first flight around the world.

4475 Thomas, Lowell Jackson   1892-1981
So long until tomorrow: from Quaker Hill to Kathmandu. Illustrated. New York: William Morrow, 1977. 317 p.

A story of the 1940-1976 adventures of the well-known newscaster who was known by cannibals in New Guinea, presidents, popes, and prime ministers around the world. Filled with wit, wise observations, and lots of stories about skiing, golf, and travel, this second part of Thomas's autobiography is highly entertaining.

4476 *Thomas, Martha Carey   1857-1935
The making of a feminist: early journals and letters of M. Carey Thomas. Edited by Marjorie Housepian Dobkin. Foreword by Millicent Carey McIntosh. Illustrated. Kent, Ohio: Kent State University Press, 1979. 314 p.

From journal entries, letters, and editorial additions, Thomas emerges as a remarkably well-educated young woman intensely aware of her sex and determined to give other women a better chance to be educated. This volume follows her from childhood to a Quaker boarding school, to Cornell University, to Johns Hopkins, through five years of study in Europe where she earned a Ph.D. summa cum laude from the University of Zurich, and deanship at Bryn Mawr College.

4477 Thomas, Matt   b.1888
Hopping on the border: the life story of a bellboy. San Antonio: The Naylor Co., 1951. 170 p.

In 1927 he settled down to hopping bell for hotels in several Southern states, but before that this Black man worked in an incredible number and variety of service jobs, owned a grocery store for a time, later a pool hall, was a fight promoter, bookie, and barber, and most of the time kept a diary, dubbing himself a "successful failure."

4478 *Thomas, Mona Burns
By Emily possessed. Foreword by Allen Potter. Hicksville, New York: Exposition Press, 1973. 165 p.

A busy actress in theater, movies, and television, including eight years on the TV soap opera *The Brighter Day* as Aunt Emily, tells the story of her activities along with those of her actor husband and son, Frank and Frankie Thomas.

4479 Thomas, Piri   1928-
Down these mean streets. New York: Vintage Books, 1974. (New York: Alfred A. Knopf, 1967) 333 p.

An organizer and worker for the rehabilitation of drug addicts, Thomas writes vividly of his childhood and youth growing up in Spanish Harlem, of the sprawling, violent *barrio* life there, the fights, the junkies, the crime, and his own armed robbery attempt and resulting prison sentence.

4480 Thomas, Theodore   **1835-1935**
A musical autobiography. Biography by George P. Upton. Introduction by Leon Stein. Record of works performed. Illustrated. New York: Da Capo Press, 1964. (Chicago: A.C. McClurg, 1905) 378 p.

Thomas's autobiography occupies only 92 pages of this volume; much of the rest is filled with a biographical "Reminiscence and Appreciation" by George Upton. Thomas describes his career as a violin soloist (begun at age 10) and conductor of various orchestras, notably the Chicago Symphony 1891-1905.

4481 *Thompson, Ariadne   **1910-**
Octagonal heart. Illustrated by Arthur Marokvia. Indianapolis: The Bobbs-Merrill Co., Inc., 1956. 221 p.

Recollections of a writer's pleasant childhood among her wealthy Greek relatives in St. Louis, Missouri.

4482 *Thompson, Bertha (Box Car Bertha)   **1903?-**
Sister of the road: the autobiography of Box Car Bertha. As told to Ben Reitman. New York: Harper Colophon, 1975. (New York: Macaulay, 1937) 314 p.

Before she began hoboing at the age of sixteen, she lived in a variety of homes, from railroad camps to experimental communes, associating with the I.W.W.'s, anarchists, and others involved in radical life styles. Her life as a hobo was a natural extension of her childhood.

4483 Thompson, Danny   **1947-1976**
E-6: the diary of a major league shortstop. With Bob Fowler. Minneapolis: Dillon Press, Inc., 1975. 248 p.

The fast-paced story of shortstop Thompson's 1975 season with the Minnesota Twins and his adjustment to the discovery that he had leukemia. He received experimental treatment at the Mayo Clinic and continued playing through the season in top form.

4484 Thompson, Ellery Franklin   **1899-**
Draggerman's haul: the personal history of a Connecticut fishing captain. New York: The Viking Press, 1950. 277 p.

Captain Ellery, well-known and respected draggerman, tells his story like a fisherman examining the haul from his net. He recalls his experiences learning fishing from his father, designing draggers, and trying his hand at music and painting, with natural simplicity and love for his work.

4485 *Thompson, Era Bell   **1905-**
American daughter. Chicago: University of Chicago Press, 1946. 301 p.

The struggle of a young Black girl who grew up in a rural Midwestern farm town, went to college, and then to Chicago in the Thirties to try to find work.

4486 Thompson, Hunter S.   **1938-**
Fear and loathing in Las Vegas; a savage journey to the heart of the American Dream. Illustrated by Ralph Steadman. New York: Random House, 1971. 206 p.

This work first appeared in *Rolling Stone Magazine,* no. 95, November 11, 1971, and no. 96, November 25, 1971. It is ostensibly the story of a wild trip from Los Angeles to Las Vegas taken by the author and his attorney. Drugs and alcohol precipitate much of the action.

4487 Thompson, Mickey   **1928-**
Challenger: Mickey Thompson's own story of his life of speed. With Griffith Borgeson. Englewood Cliffs, New Jersey: Prentice-Hall, Inc., 1964. 273 p.

He won his first racing records with a car named "Challenger" (1959) and during the next three years he set many speed records. His book describes his early experience with cars, the development of his winning cars, and the life of a racer.

4488 Thompson, Wilson   **1788-1866**
Autobiography of Elder Wilson Thompson: embracing a sketch of his life, travels, and ministerial labors, in which is included a concise history of the old order of regular Baptist Churches. Edited with preface by his children. Elizabethtown, Illinois: Ronald L. Nelson, 1979. (Cincinnati: Wilstach, Baldwin & Co., 1873) 502 p. Index.

Thompson describes his spiritual nurturing and growth, the religious experience that convinced him to become a Baptist clergyman, and his career thereafter as a preacher in rural Kentucky, Indiana, Missouri, and Ohio. He discusses various issues of Baptist doctrine and church trials to determine whether some members of the church had violated these doctrines.

4489 Thomson, Alfred Ray   **1889-1943**
Historical letters: a collection of letters of historical interest written by a career officer in the American Foreign Service. Compiled by Mrs. A.R. Thomson. New York: The Hobson Book Press, 1946. 180 p.

Official and personal letters (mostly to his mother) during his career in the diplomatic service, which ended abruptly at the beginning of World War II.

4490 Thomson, Virgil   **1896-**
Virgil Thomson. New York: Alfred A. Knopf, 1966. 424 p. Index.

A composer of opera, symphonic works, and film music as well as critic and witty writer on musical subjects, Thomson comments on his own life and writes portraits of leading musicians, artists, and writers he has known, especially during the decades between the two World Wars.

4491 Thorburn, Grant (Laurie Todd, pseud.)   **1773-1863**
Forty years' residence in America; or, the doctrine of a particular providence exemplified in the life of Grant Thorburn. Freeport, New York: Books for Libraries Press, 1969. (Boston: Russell, Odiorne, 1834) 264 p.

An account of forty years of his life in America, his grocery business, his seed and plant business, his purchases, his marriage, his friendships, followed by a long appendix containing brief unconnected scenes from his life including visits to Boston and Providence, letters, newspaper items, and other miscellany.

4492 Thoreau, Henry David   **1817-1862**
The best of Thoreau's journals. Edited with introduction by Carl Bode. Carbondale: Southern Illinois University Press, 1971. (1967) 327 p.

Selections from the fourteen-volume edition published in 1906 offer a taste of his life and observations from 1837 through 1861. Thoreau drew from his journal for his published works during his lifetime. These selections avoid duplicating those he himself selected.

4493 Thoreau, Henry David   **1817-1862**
Consciousness in Concord: the text of Thoreau's hitherto "Lost Journal" (1840-1841). Notes and commentary by Perry Miller. Boston: Houghton Mifflin Co., 1958. 243 p. Index.

This segment of his journal (July 30, 1840-January 22, 1841) had a curious history as a "lost" volume, described fully by Miller, whose comments are longer than these by Thoreau.

4494 Thoreau, Henry David   **1817-1862**
The correspondence of Henry David Thoreau. Edited by Walter Harding and Carl Bode. Westport, Connecticut: Greenwood Press, 1974. (New York: New York University Press, 1958) 665 p. Index.

A reprint of the first edition which attempts to include every available surviving letter written by and to the famous man of letters and provides a remarkable portrait of his intellectual development.

4495 Thoreau, Henry David   **1817-1862**
The journal of Henry D. Thoreau. New York: Dover Publications, Inc., 1962. (Boston: Houghton Mifflin, 1906) 14v. in 2. Index.

Although extracts from Thoreau's journals were published earlier in various formats, the complete edition did not appear until 1906. It and the reprints offer a complete record of the inner life of an individual, his interests and observations, the conception and evolution of his ideas on a wide variety of subjects—in short, the operation of a thinking man's mind.

4496 Thoreau, Henry David   **1817-1862**
Letters to various persons. Folcroft, Pennsylvania: Folcroft Library Editions, 1975. (Boston: Ticknor and Fields, 1865) 229 p.

Written between 1840 and 1862, these letters were addressed to various persons, many identified only by initials.

4497 Thoreau, Henry David   **1817-1862**
Thoreau's world; miniatures from his journal. Illustrated edition by Charles R. Anderson. Englewood Cliffs, New Jersey: Prentice-Hall, Inc., 1971. 370 p. Index.

Excerpts from the *Journal* provide a sampling of the variety of Thoreau's subject matter. In brief essays, imbedded in the whole journal but intended to stand alone, the author reached a high degree of literary excellence and distinction demonstrated in these 250 examples.

4498 Thoreau, Henry David   **1817-1862**
A week on the Concord and Merrimack Rivers. Edited by Carl F. Hovde, William L. Howarth, and Elizabeth Hall Witherell. Introduction by Linck C. Johnson. Princeton, New Jersey: Princeton University Press, 1980. (Published by the author, 1849) 610 p.

This journal recounts a week's trip that Thoreau and his brother, John, took in 1839 and includes considerable poetry and literary criticism. In emphasizing the river's idyllic aspects, Thoreau presents a posthumous elegiac tribute to his brother and demonstrates his spiritual and artistic growth.

4499 Thoreau, Henry David   **1817-1862**
A writer's journal. Selected and edited with introduction by Laurence Stapleton. New York: Dover Publications, Inc., 1960. 234 p. Index.

Selections from the fourteen-volume edition are here intended to portray Thoreau's work as a writer and reveal the central principles of his philosophy.

4500 *Thoresen, Louise   **1936-**
It gave everybody something to do. And E.M. Nathanson. New York: M. Evans and Co., Inc., 1974. 346 p.

The incredible, bizarre story of a deeply disturbed man who led his wife through a terrifying ten years of stealing, bombing, drug experimentation, gun collecting, violence, and murder before she finally became aware of the danger to herself and shot him.

4501 Thorpe, Elliott R.   **1897-**
East wind, rain—the intimate account of an intelligence officer in the Pacific, 1939-49. Boston: Gambit, Inc., 1969. 307 p. Index.
An intelligence officer in the Pacific before, during, and after World War II tells of blunders in the direction of the war, problems in censorship, and the double dealings of presidents and premiers. He examines the background of the Japanese War Crimes trials and gives a personal appraisal of General MacArthur.

4502 *Thumb, Mrs. Tom
see *Magri, M. Lavinia

4503 Thurber, James   **1894-1961**
Credos and curios. New York: Harper & Row, 1962. 180 p.
A collection of oddments—profiles, stories, reminiscences—of real and imagined events and people.

4504 Thurber, James   **1894-1961**
My life and hard times. Introduction by John K. Hutchens. New York: Harper & Brothers, 1973. (1933) 114 p.
A vintage Thurber collection with hilarious stories of his life in Columbus, including "The night the bed fell," "University days," and "The day the dam broke."

4505 Thurber, James   **1894-1961**
Thurber album: a new collection of pieces about people. New York: Simon and Schuster, 1952. 346 p.
With warm, lively wit, Thurber tells stories about himself, his numerous relatives, and a few friends and colleagues. Most chapters are revisions of articles published in The New Yorker.

4506 Thurman, Howard   **1899-**
With head and heart: the autobiography of Howard Thurman. Illustrated. New York: Harcourt Brace Jovanovich, 1979. 274 p. Index.
Thurman recounts his life as a Black minister and missionary, active in churches and universities in the U.S. and abroad. He notes the advances made in desegregation and the lessening of racial prejudice, as well as his own progress from one who declared he wanted nothing to do with the church to a man devoted to Christ.

4507 *Tierney, Gene   **1920-**
Self-portrait. With Mickey Herskowitz. New York: Wyden Books, 1979. 264 p.
A product of Hollywood's "golden age," she had an apparently ideal life, but was driven to institutionalization and near suicide when she could no longer separate illusion and reality. Tierney describes her own life as her most demanding role.

4508 Tilden, Samuel Jones   **1814-1886**
Letters and literary memorials of Samuel J. Tilden. Edited by John Bigelow. Port Washington, New York: Kennikat Press, 1971. 2v. Index.
Of Tilden's many activities as a public servant, two are most often remembered: his overthrow of the corrupt New York municipal group known as the Tweed Ring and his election by a plurality of the popular vote to the U.S. Presidency. Since no one received a majority vote, the House of Representatives under the Constitution decided the election in favor of Hayes. His letters shed light on many other aspects of his career and personal life as well.

4509 Tilden, William Tatem   **1893-1953**
My story: a champion's memoirs. New York: Hillman, Williams and Co., 1948. 335 p.
One of the early tennis greats who became a part of the Hollywood scene describes his training and development in tennis and his experience among contemporary stars.

4510 Tilghman, Tench   **1744-1786**
Memoir of Lieut. Co. Tench Tilghman, secretary and aide to Washington. Eyewitness Accounts of the American Revolution. New York: Arno Press, 1971. (Albany: J. Munsell, 1876) 176 p.
The Memoir (pp. 1-75), copywritten by a descendent, Oswald Tilghman, in 1876, describes Tench Tilghman's career as Washington's aide. His journal (pp. 79-105) was kept while he served as Secretary of the Indian Commissioners (1775); diary entries and letters document varied experience through 1783.

4511 Tillich, Paul Johannes   **1886-1965**
My travel diary: 1936, between two worlds. Edited with an introduction by Jerald C. Brauer. Translated by Maria Pelikan. Drawings by Alfonso Ossorio. New York: Harper and Row, Publisher, 1970. 192 p.
In preparation for a life-and-work ecumenical conference at Oxford in 1937 examining the interrelationships between church, community, and

state, Tillich took part in a study group in 1936. In his diary he recounted his daily experience and personal reactions; his views on the world situation and on the pressing political problems of the mid-1930's.

4512 Timberlake, Henry   **1730-1765**
The memoirs of Lt. Henry Timberlake: 1756-1765. Notes, introduction and index by Samuel Cole Williams. Marietta, Georgia: Continental Book Co., 1948. (London: The author, 1765) 197 p. Index.
A journal of the French and Indian Wars, depicting the role of the Cherokee Indians in the southern colonies.

4513 Tiomkin, Dimitri   **1894-1979**
Please don't hate me. And Prosper Buranelli. Garden City, New York: Doubleday & Co., Inc., 1959. 261 p.
His book recalls his boyhood in Czarist Russia, his early career as a concert pianist in Europe and the United States, and his success as a leading musician in Hollywood, with interesting descriptions of many famous contemporaries and his difficulty in becoming Americanized.

4514 Tittle, Yelberton Abraham   **1926-**
I pass: my story. As told to Don Smith. New York: Franklin Watts, Inc., 1964. 290 p. Index.
Tittle writes of his long and brilliant career as a football quarterback who attained fame as Player of the Year in 1957, 1962, and 1963. He held many passing records and is considered one of the greatest all-around quarterbacks in history.

4515 Tobin, Richard Lardner   **1910-**
Golden opinions. New York: E.P. Dutton & Co., Inc., 1948. 254 p.
A reporter for the New York Herald-Tribune writes of life in New York, his Irish neighborhood, and his boyhood in the city, the stories colorful and somewhat nostalgic.

4516 Tobin, Richard Lardner   **1910-**
Invasion journal. New York: E.P. Dutton & Co., Inc., 1944. 223 p.
A war correspondent for the New York Herald Tribune, he kept a detailed daily record of his departure from New York on a troop transport, the preparation for D-Day in London, the invasion and after (April-August, 1944), conveying the conditions and stress of wartime.

4517 *Todd, Laurie, pseud.
see Thorburn, Grant

4518 *Toklas, Alice Babette   **1877-1967**
Staying on alone: letters of Alice B. Toklas. Edited by Edward Burns. Introduction by Gilbert A. Harrison. New York: Random House/Vintage Books, 1974. (New York: Liveright, 1973) 448 p. Index.
Chatty, interesting letters written during the twenty years after Gertrude Stein's death, conveying descriptions of Toklas' daily life in Paris, her observations on artists, musicians, and writers, and gossip about many friends and acquaintances.

4519 *Toklas, Alice Babette   **1877-1967**
What is remembered. New York: Holt, Rinehart and Winston, 1963. 186 p. Index.
Her childhood, her friendship with Gertrude Stein, and their years together form the basis of this volume which ends with Stein's death.

4520 Toma, David   **1934-**
Toma: the compassionate cop. With Michael Brett. New York: G.P. Putnam's Sons, 1973. 238 p.
In Newark he became a maverick cop, often working on his own in a variety of disguises for the Bureau of Investigation. His story became the basis of the TV series.

4521 Tome, Philip   **1782-1855**
Pioneer life; or, thirty years a hunter. New York: Arno Press, 1971. (Buffalo, New York: The author, 1854) 238 p.
An outstanding early narrative of the Pennsylvania big-game fields, this book includes exciting scenes of the chase, fights with elk, wolf, and mountain lion, and descriptions of the life of a hunter in the wilderness forests.

4522 *Tomkinson, Constance   **1915-**
What a performance! London: Michael Joseph, 1962. 200 p.
A chorus girl at the Folies Bergère recalls her early years of theatrical training in New York during the Thirties.

4523 Tomlinson, Ambrose Jessup   **1865-1943**
Diary of A.J. Tomlinson, founder of the Church of God, general overseer, 1903-1943—outstanding leader of the Pentecostal and Holiness movement. Edited with notes by Homer A. Tomlinson. New York: The Church of God, World Headquarters, 1949-1953. 2v.
The diary of a minister and faith healer who had a strong and stormy life in the politics of the Pentecostal Church. After describing the division over the administration and government of the Church of God,

Tomlinson gives an account of the revival of the movement with himself as a leader and of the 29-year court trial over the use of the church's name and funds. Volume I, 1901-1923; Volume II, 1923-1943.

4524 Toomay, Patrick Jay   1945-
The crunch. New York: W.W. Norton & Co., 1975. 203 p.
   Toomay earned a starting role as a defensive end on the world-champion Dallas Cowboys in 1970. Here he describes the frustrations, colorful personalities, red tape, player-management relationships, the funny and the controversial aspects of professional football.

4525 Toponce, Alexander   1839-1923
Reminiscences of Alexander Toponce. Illustrated. Introduction by Robert A. Griffen. Norman: University of Oklahoma Press, 1971. (Ogden, Utah: privately printed, 1923) 221 p. Index.
   A picture of frontier life by one who participated to the fullest. He drove a stage coach, rode pony express, was a wagon boss, mined gold, operated a freighting line, drove cattle, chased renegades, raced horses, owned a slaughterhouse, and was full of all kinds of schemes for turning a dollar. He was a strong rough-and-ready pioneer who helped win the West.

4526 *Topp, Mildred (Spurrier)   1897-
In the pink. Boston: Houghton Mifflin Co., 1950. 242 p.
   More nostalgic memories of happy childhood in the South, recorded with a good sense of humor and the times.

4527 *Topp, Mildred (Spurrier)   1897-
Smile please. Boston: Houghton Mifflin Co., 1948. 280 p.
   Pleasant, somewhat nostalgic recollections of her childhood in Alabama, where her mother became a professional photographer to support her family.

4528 Torok, Lou   1927-
Straight talk from prison: a convict reflects on youth, crime and society. New York: Human Sciences Press, 1974. 142 p.
   Compassionate advice from an ex-convict whose three prison experiences provide the background for analysis of prison life and his sincere attempts to dissuade others from criminal behavior.

4529 *Torre, Marie   1924-
Don't quote me. Garden City, New York: Doubleday & Co., Inc., 1965. 254 p.
   In a first-hand report on the television industry, Torre tells of her meetings with entertainment stars, the quiz-show scandals, sponsor interference, her "feud" with David Susskind, and other facts behind stories, including the Judy Garland-CBS dispute because of which Torre went to jail for not revealing her sources.

4530 *Torres, Tereska
The converts. New York: Alfred A. Knopf, 1970. 308 p.
   Novelist Torres' father was a sculptor and her mother, a writer; they were Polish, though they lived in Paris. The revelation of their secret conversion to Catholicism alienated them from their orthodox Jewish relatives and henceforth she lived the life of a traditional French-Catholic convent school student. Later they fled the German invasion, settling in England, but returning to Paris after the war. Eventually Tereska gave way under the strain and loneliness of her life and attempted suicide, survived, and married writer Meyer Levin.

4531 Tors, Ivan   1916-
My life in the wild. Boston: Houghton Mifflin Co., 1979. 209 p.
   Tors's fascinating account of his career as an animal trainer, zoologist, movie writer, and director focuses on the animals he and his three sons have worked with around the world: elephants, lions, leopards, boa constrictors, bears, sharks, dolphins, and gorillas, among others.

4532 *Towne, Laura Matilda   1825-1901
Letters and diary of Laura M. Towne: written from the Sea Islands of South Carolina, 1862-1884. Edited with introduction by Rupert Sargent Holland. Foreword by Alice N. Lincoln. New York: Negro Universities Press/Div. of Greenwood Press, 1969. (Cambridge, Massachusetts: Riverside Press, 1912) 310 p.
   A collection of letters and diary entries that recount Towne's experiences as a social worker and educator on St. Helena Island, one of South Carolina's Sea Islands. Sent in 1862 as an agent of the federal government to take charge of the Blacks whose lives were disrupted by the Civil War, Towne used her medical training to treat smallpox and prevent malaria. For the rest of her life, she founded and administered Penn School, where large numbers of the island's population were educated. She bought Frogmore plantation on St. Helena where she lived until her death in 1901.

4533 Townsend, William Henry   1890-1964
Hundred proof: Salt River sketches & memoirs of the blue-grass. Introduction by Holman Hamilton. Lexington: University of Kentucky Press, 1964. 155 p.

The sketches are of colorful people and incidents during his boyhood in rural Kentucky, written by a man who became a prominent lawyer in Lexington, author of several books on Abraham Lincoln, and long-time friend of Carl Sandburg.

4534 *Tracy, Lena (Harvey)   1860-1941
How my heart sang: the story of pioneer industrial welfare work. New York: Richard R. Smith, 1950. 192 p.
   Raised in rural Pennsylvania, she graduated from college in the 1880's, was ordained a Christian Deaconess, and devoted her life to welfare work. She was the first Welfare Director of National Cash Register Co. in Dayton (1897-1901).

4535 Train, George Francis   1829-1904
A Yankee merchant in Goldrush Australia: the letters of George Francis Train, 1853-55. Introduction and notes by E. Daniel and Annette Potts. London: Heinemann, 1970. 204 p. Index.
   American commercial and other interests expanded greatly during the Australian gold rushes of 1852-55. In order to supply reliable information regarding the Victoria Colony's market requirements, Train sent from Melbourne periodic accounts of the social, economic, and political conditions of the colony, which portray an American's view of the excitement and commercial growth of the period.

4536 *Traubel, Helen   1903-1972
St. Louis woman. In collaboration with Richard G. Hubler. Introduction by Vincent Sheean. New York: Duell, Sloan and Pearce, 1959. 296 p.
   A woman of strong and independent character, she flouted precedent by refusing to confine herself to the world of opera only. Instead, she brought her talents to audiences on all levels: nightclubs, radio, television, and theater, as well as the concert stage.

4537 *Travell, Janet (Graeme)   1901-
Office hours: day and night: the autobiography of Janet Travell, M.D. New York: The World Publishing Co., 1968. 496 p. Index.
   The first woman to become physician to the President describes her early life, the development of her long medical career at Cornell University, and her service to John F. Kennedy and Lyndon Johnson.

4538 Travis, Dempsey
Don't stop me now. With Lester Brownlee and Leonard Grossman. Illustrated. Open Door Books. Chicago, Illinois: Children's Press, 1970. 64 p.
   One in the series of career guidance books for young people, this autobiography tells of Travis' youth, army service, and later success in the real estate business.

4539 Trent, William   1715-1778
Journal of Captain William Trent from Logstown to Pickawillany, A.D. 1752. Edited by Alfred T. Goodman. First American Frontier. New York: Arno Press, 1971. (Cincinnati: Robert Clarke & Co., 1871) 117 p. Index.
   In 1659 King Charles the Second appointed a "Board of Trade and Plantations" to govern related matters in the colonies; it existed until 1782. Trent traveled for the Board to Pickawillany in 1752, the year it was destroyed by the French. At the time it was an important trade center in the Ohio Valley.

4540 Tressler, Donald Kitely   1894-
Memoirs. Illustrated. Westport, Connecticut: Avi Publishing Co., 1976. 88 p.
   A pioneer food scientist recounts his precocious youth (he was a college graduate at 18) and many successes in research, teaching, and publishing. His accomplishments ranged from improvements in food-freezing techniques to a process for making sherry in five days.

4541 Trohan, Walter   1903-
Political animals: memoirs of a sentimental cynic. Garden City, New York: Doubleday & Co., Inc., 1975. 411 p.
   A Washington reporter and columnist for the conservative Chicago *Tribune*, Trohan looks back somewhat cynically on politics and politicians and tells the story of his "life among the leaders."

4542 Troupa, Albert Burton   1881-1959
Grass-roots doctor: memories of a mischievous boyhood and forty fruitful years as an M.D. New York: Exposition Press, 1959. 156 p.
   Troupa devotes half the book to reminiscences of his rural childhood, eating, "bugging" potatoes, husking corn, celebrating holidays, told in homespun language. In the second half, he offers folksy vignettes of his medical education and general practice in a small town.

4543 Trouppe, Quincy   1912-
Twenty years too soon. Illustrated. Los Angeles: S & S Enterprises, 1977. 285 p.
   Trouppe recounts his 22 years in professional baseball with teams in the United States, Mexico, and Puerto Rico, beginning with the Negro National League. Personal anecdotes and notes on baseball celebrities, plus

numerous photographs and team rosters, fill in two decades of Black professional baseball history.

4544 *Truax, Sarah   **b.1877**
A woman of parts: memories of a life on stage. Foreword by Guthrie McClintic. New York: Longmans, Green and Co., 1949. 247 p. Index.
Recollections of stock theater companies and tours during the early twentieth century by a well-known actress; includes vignettes of theater people and parts she played.

4545 Trueblood, David Elton   **1900-**
While it is day: an autobiography. New York: Harper & Row, Publishers, 1974. 170 p. Index.
Telling "what he has tried to do, and how he has tried to think," and of the many people who have helped him along the way, the author shows us a journey through a life built on Quaker principles.

4546 Truman, Harry S.   **1884-1972**
Autobiography. Edited by Robert H. Ferrell. Illustrated. Boulder: Colorado Associated University Press, 1980. 153 p. Index.
An autobiography compiled from various fragmentary manuscript accounts that Truman kept at intervals during his lifetime—1934, 1944, 1945, 1951-2. He discusses his childhood in Independence, Missouri, and on a farm at Grandview; his military service during World War I in France as a member of "Battery D" of the Missouri National Guard; his entrance into politics and election to county judgeship and ultimately to the U.S. Senate and Presidency. Truman's honest, down-to-earth, no-nonsense philosophy is apparent throughout.

4547 Truman, Harry S.   **1884-1972**
Memoirs. Garden City, New York: Doubleday & Co., Inc., 1955-56. 2v. Index.
In a well-written personal account, Truman tells of the seven-and-a-half years of his presidency. He seeks to recapture and record accurately the significant events and decisions of his administration based as nearly as possible upon circumstances, facts, and his thinking at the time, rather than relying on hindsight. The overwhelming purpose which dominated all his thoughts and actions was the prevention of a third world war.

4548 Truman, Harry S.   **1884-1972**
Mr. Citizen. New York: Bernard Geis Associates, 1960. 315 p.
A well-written account of his return to private citizenship in Independence, Missouri, the adjustments to a new life, the building of the Truman Library, and his role as a senior statesman during the Eisenhower administration.

4549 Truman, Harry S.   **1884-1972**
Mr. President: the first publication from the personal diaries, private letters, papers, and revealing interviews of Harry S. Truman by William Hillman. New York: Farrar, Straus and Young, 1952. 253 p.
Selected and compiled by Hillman, a journalist who knew Truman throughout his presidency. Entries have not been edited, though they were not originally intended for publication, and thus provide a remarkable portrait of the man and his views.

4550 Truman, Harry S.   **1884-1972**
Off the record: the private papers of Harry S. Truman. Edited by Robert H. Ferrell. New York: Harper & Row, 1980. 448 p. Index.
Truman's candid private memos and drafts of letters, written to let off steam but seldom mailed, provide a fascinating insight into the President's decision-making processes. Truman was ever-solicitous of his wife, daughter, mother, and aunts, exhibiting in numerous letters to them none of the salty or scathing language he reserves for formidable antagonists. His patriotism, honor, and honesty shine through.

4551 Truman, Harry S.   **1884-1972**
The Truman years: The words and times of Harry S. Truman. Edited by Robert L. Pollen. Editing direction by Michael P. Dineen. Art direction by Buford Nixon. By the editors of Country Beautiful. Waukesha, Wisconsin: Country Beautiful, 1976. 111 p.
This is a heavily illustrated narrative focusing on Truman's years as U.S. President, 1945-52, set in the matrix of the cultural, political, and military events of the time, abundantly illustrated with excerpts from Truman's speeches and with photographs. He deals with the Hot War, the Cold War, the issues of the McCarthy era, the Point Four Program, NATO, and meets them with aplomb, wit, and common sense.

4552 *Truman, Margaret   **1924-**
Souvenir: Margaret Truman's own story. With Margaret Cousins. New York: McGraw-Hill Book Co., Inc., 1956. 365 p.
A warm, personal narrative of her childhood, her teen-age years in wartime Washington, the difficulty of adjusting to life in the White House, and her determination in developing her musical career.

4553 Trumbull, John   **1756-1843**
The autobiography of Colonel John Trumbull, patriot-artist, 1756-1843.

Edited by Theodore Sizer. New York: Kennedy Graphics, 1970. (New Haven: B.L. Hamlen, 1841) 404 p. Index.
For a limited period he was aide-de-camp to George Washington. He did many paintings of Washington's career, though he spent most of his artistic career as a portrait painter. He was commissioned to do several historical paintings for the National Capitol and later for what would become the Trumbull Gallery at Yale.

4554 Tuggle, William Orrie   **1841-1885**
Shem, Ham & Japheth: the papers of W.O. Tuggle comprising his Indian diary, sketches and observations, myths and Washington journal in the Territory, and at the capital, 1879-1882. Edited by Eugene Current-Garcia and D.B. Hatfield. Athens: University of Georgia Press, 1973. 361 p. Index.
Tuggle spent three years (1879-1881) in the Indian Territory (now Oklahoma), observing Indian customs, writing articles, collecting fables and tales. Later in Washington while participating in government duties, he organized his cultural findings about the Creek and other Indians.

4555 Tugwell, Rexford Guy   **1891-**
The light of other days. Garden City, New York: Doubleday & Co., 1962. 404 p.
An account of a turn-of-the-century youth in rural western New York state written with affection and respect for the values of that era.

4556 Tunis, John Roberts   **1889-1975**
A measure of independence. New York: Atheneum, 1964. 307 p. Index.
A free-lance writer whose life bridged the nineteenth and twentieth centuries and who loved sports, words, politics, and freedom has written a modest self-portrait about his adventures, acquaintances, and his achievement of independence.

4557 Tunnell, Emlen   **1926-1975**
Footsteps of a Giant. With William Gleason. Garden City, New York: Doubleday & Co., Inc., 1966. 238 p.
A great New York Giant defensive halfback for fourteen years, 1948-1961, Tunnell writes of the people and the games that have helped him to enjoy his life. Appended are lists of the records he has held and his choices for an All-Pro Team.

4558 Tunner, William H.   **1906-**
Over the Hump. New York: Duell, Sloan and Pearce, 1964. 340 p. Index.
In this dramatic, forceful account Tunner describes his career as commander of the Military Air Transport System (after 1958) and director of other air-transportation groups since the mid-1930's. With unusual sensitivity to military strategy, personnel competency and morale, relations with allies and antagonists, and a strong sense of efficiency and economy, Tunner makes vivid and human the India-China "Hump" operations during World War II, the Berlin airlift in the early 1950's, and transportation of supplies and wounded troops in the Korean War.

4559 *Turk, Midge   **1930-**
The buried life; a nun's journey. New York: The World Publishing Co., 1971. 196 p.
For eighteen years as Sister Agnes Marie she attempted to live the silent, regimented life of a nun within the tradition of the Catholic Church. She finally made the painful decision to leave formal religious life because of conflicts with the hierarchy, the intransigent structure of the Church, and its irrelevance to the problems of contemporary society.

4560 *Turnbull, Agnes Sligh   **1888-**
Out of my heart. Boston: Houghton Mifflin Co., 1958. 158 p.
A spiritual autobiography that explores the important lessons life has presented her, written with idealistic simplicity and humility by the author of *The Bishop's Mantle*.

4561 *Turnbull, Grace   **1880-1976**
Chips from my chisel: an autobiography. Illustrated. Rindge, New Hampshire: Richard R. Smith, 1953. 256 p.
The abundant photographs in this handsome volume attest to Turnbull's skill and acclaim as a sculptor of animals and religious and symbolic figures, and to her expertise as a painter in the manner of Georgia O'Keeffe. Unfortunately, her narrative, though full of accounts of her worldwide travels, art studies in Europe, and service in France with the Red Cross during World War I, does not tell much about her method of work, her choice of media, or her stature in the art world.

4562 *Turner, Clair Elsmere   **1890-1974**
I remember. New York: Vantage, 1974. 179 p.
A recounting of experiences over eighty years with emphasis on unusual events and discoveries in health and education by an emeritus professor at M.I.T.

4563 Turner, Frederick Jackson   **1861-1932**
Dear Lady: the letters of Frederick Jackson Turner and Alice Forbes Perkins Hooper, 1910-1932. With the collaboration of Walter Muir Whitehill. Illustrated edition by Ray Allen Bellington. San Marino, California: The Huntington Library, 1970. 487 p. Index.

A remarkable correspondence attesting to the friendship and mutual esteem between Turner, America's pre-eminent historian of the West, and Mrs. Hooper, the granddaughter of James H. Perkins, author of *Annals of the West*, and daughter of Charles E. Perkins, builder of the Burlington Railroad. Her gifts to the Harvard Library and association with the Harvard Commission on Western History led to the collection of valuable materials for historical research.

4564 Turner, Henry Smith 1811-1881
The original journals of Henry Smith Turner: with Stephen Watts Kearny to New Mexico and California, 1846-1847. Edited with introduction by Dwight L. Clarke. Norman: University of Oklahoma Press, 1966. 173 p. Index.
As adjutant of the Army of the West, Turner actively participated in the conquest of New Mexico and California. His graphic journals and forthright letters present his personal reaction to the men and scenes around him as well as objective comments on practical matters such as problems of water and forage and encounters with the Indians.

4565 Turner, Richard E.
Big friend; little friend; memoirs of a World War II fighter pilot. Garden City, New York: Doubleday & Co., Inc., 1969. 176 p. Index.
He left college to begin his aviation career in 1941, eventually flying nearly 100 missions in Europe and 17 in the Korean War. His book reflects the patriotic values and motivation characteristic of those times.

4566 Turner, Robert E. b.1875
Memories of a retired Pullman porter. New York: Exposition Press, 1954. 191 p.
Turner, who believes "youth is a blunder, manhood a struggle," recounts the characteristics of numerous jobs—a spectrum of those available to Blacks in his time: waiter, bellhop, barbershop porter, shoeshine stand proprietor, janitor, night watchman, culminating in 25 years as a Pullman porter. He enjoyed the travel but devotes considerable space to complaining about racial discrimination and difficult, overly demanding passengers, including those who cheated and stole from the porters and a suspicious Pullman management that tricked the porters and then fired them for violating company rules.

4567 Turpin, James Wesley 1928?-
Vietnam doctor; the story of Project Concern. With Al Hirshberg. New York: McGraw-Hill Book Co., 1966. 210 p.
Turpin combined his two callings as minister and doctor and began Project Concern, a medical mission which opened clinics in Hong Kong, Kowloon, and Vietnam. He heals the sick, fights disease, and struggles to promote health and happiness for people in need.

4568 Turra, Mario 1931-
Mario. Acworth, Georgia: Names of Distinction, Inc., 1975. 174 p.
As a boy, Mario with his family of thirteen lived through the tragic years of World War II, moving from Naples to the village of Pietravairano in an effort to escape the air raids and fighting. After the Italian armistice, German soldiers took Italians into custody, persecuted and exterminated Italian Jews. The family befriended an American pilot, Joe, whose plane had been shot down. Together they hid in a cave when the town was destroyed, but they have not been able to trace Joe since the war.

4569 Twain, Mark, pseud.
see **Clemens, Samuel Langhorne**

4570 Twitchell, Hanford M. 1898-
Brownstone saga: happenings of a New Yorker. New York: Exposition Press, 1973. 146 p.
Short chapters, each describing a remembered event—boyhood pranks, teenage escapades, career stepping-stones, and salutes to New York City—written by a real estate broker who loves New York.

4571 Udall, Morris King 1922-
Education of a congressman; the newsletters of Morris K. Udall. Edited by Robert L. Peabody with the assistance of Tim Wyngaard and Michael Alonge. Indianapolis: The Bobbs-Merrill Co., Inc., 1972. 384 p. Index.
When his older brother Stewart resigned from Congress in 1961 to become Secretary of the Interior, Morris Udall was elected to fill his vacancy. Subsequently he became a leader among House Democrats, placing second in the election for Majority Leader in 1971. These newsletters from the 1960's, arranged chronologically by subject matter, show his thoughts and ideas during that period as he explained his positions to his constituents.

4572 Uhlan, Edward 1912-
The rogue of Publisher's Row: confessions of a publisher. New York: Exposition Press, 1956. 247 p.
The president of Exposition Press writes of his career as an entrepreneur of subsidy publishing, arguing the importance of his contribution to research materials as well as the vanity of many of his authors.

4573 *Underwood, Agness May (Wilson) 1902-
Newspaper woman. New York: Harper & Brothers Publishers, 1949. 297 p.
She started working for the Los Angeles *Record* as a part-time switchboard operator to augment her limited family income. Her book describes her early training in journalism, her years as a Hollywood reporter and then as city editor for the *Herald-Express*.

4574 Unitas, Johnny 1933-
Pro quarterback: my own story. And Ed Fitzgerald. New York: Simon and Schuster, 1965. 188 p.
A famous quarterback tells his personal story, analyzes football strategy and execution, and gossips about training camps, locker rooms, and the players he has known. His wife Dorothy contributed the final chapter to highlight the mind and spirit of her modest, legendary husband.

4575 Unonius, Gustaf Elias Marius 1810-1902
A pioneer in Northwest America, 1841-1858: the memoirs of Gustaf Unonius. Translated by Jonas Oscar Backlund. Edited by Nils William Olsson. Introduction by George M. Stephenson. Minneapolis: The University of Minnesota Press, 1950-1960. 2v. Index.
Originally published in Uppsala in 1861-1862, these volumes reveal the experience and philosophy of one of the earliest and most influential Swedish immigrants in America, describing his experience as a pioneer farmer in Wisconsin and his later work in the ministry of the Protestant Episcopal Church.

4576 *Untermeyer, Jean (Starr) 1886-1970
Private collection. New York: Alfred A. Knopf, 1965. 295 p. Index.
Gathering together portraits of the intelligentsia, customs, and culture of her intense years, Mrs. Untermeyer shows a gallery of portraits of the poets, writers, artists, and musicians whom she counted as friends through the early years of the twentieth century.

4577 Untermeyer, Louis 1885-1977
Bygones: the recollections of Louis Untermeyer. New York: Harcourt, Brace & World, Inc., 1965. 260 p. Index.
A candid account of the life of the poet-anthologist-editor, who met almost everyone in the world of letters, whose life was complicated by four marriages, and who through it all steadfastly advanced the cause of modern poetry in America.

4578 Uphaus, Willard Edwin 1890-
Commitment. New York: McGraw-Hill Book Co., Inc., 1963. 266 p.
An unfortunate victim of the McCarthy era, Uphaus spent a year in jail for contempt of court because he refused to supply lists of names and correspondence of those who attended a camp he established in New Hampshire called World Fellowship, Inc., which state authorities suspected of communist activities.

4579 *Utley, Freda 1898-1978
Lost illusion. Philadelphia: Fireside Press, 1948. (New York: John Day, 1940) 288 p.
The revised edition of *The Dream We Lost: Soviet Russia Then and Now* concerns her disillusionment with communism and "Stalinist tyranny" after six years in Russia.

4580 *Utley, Freda 1898-1978
Odyssey of a liberal: memoirs. Washington: Washington National Press, Inc., 1970. 319 p. Index.
Memoirs of her life before and after her disillusionment in Russia written to record her "far ranging experience as a participant observer of the history of our times." She believes liberals need to free themselves from illusions and recognize the grim struggle for survival experienced by most people before a better world can be a reality.

4581 *Utley, Minnie L. 1925-
Yesterday and tomorrow. New York: A Geneva Book/Carlton Press, 1968. 112 p.
Utley tells of her childhood as one of thirteen children of a Black sharecropper on a plantation in North Carolina—always poor, often hungry, sometimes befriended by charitable whites. She learned self-pride and middle-class values from "the dear old lady" whom she attended as a child, while intermittently working in the fields. A religious spirit underlies her repeated plea for racial harmony.

4582 Valentine, Alan 1901-
Trial balance: the education of an American. New York: Pantheon Books, Inc., 1956. 283 p.
A philosophical, introspective narrative written in third person and modeled in part on that of Henry Adams, by a man who devoted forty years to American education, was President of the University of Rochester (1935-1950), and then became involved in public service.

4583 Valentine, Jimmy
see **Hyatt, Henry**

4584 Valentine, Lewis Joseph   1882-1946
Night stick: the autobiography of Lewis J. Valentine. With an introduction by Fiorello H. La Guardia. New York: The Dial Press, 1947. 320 p. Index.
  Police Commissioner of New York while La Guardia was Mayor, he joined the force in 1903. His book reflects his long commitment to police work and an interesting view of the life of the city, its characters, thugs, and politicians.

4585 Vallee, Rudy   1901-
Let the chips fall. Harrisburg, Pennsylvania: Stackpole Books, 1975. 320 p.
  Vallee's reminiscences of his career as a bandleader emphasize his lust for beautiful women (four of whom he married), his callous disregard for people's sensitivities, his ostentatious spending of money, and love of being seen in the "right" places (mostly nightclubs) with the "right" people.

4586 Vallee, Rudy   1901-
My time is your time: the story of Rudy Vallee. With Gil McKean. New York: Ivan Obolensky, 1962. 244 p.
  Saxaphone, raccoon coat and all, Vallee has played, crooned, acted, and band-directed his way through a long career on stage, screen, radio, TV and night clubs.

4587 Vance, Zebulon Baird   1830-1894
My beloved Zebulon; the correspondence of Zebulon Baird Vance and Harriett Newell Espy. Edited by Elizabeth Roberts Cannon. Introduction by Frances Gray Patton. Chapel Hill: The University of North Carolina Press, 1971. 278 p.
  These 121 letters between Vance and his future wife are primarily love letters, but reveal their hopes, ideals, and salient traits, offering glimpses into antebellum North Carolina society as well. Vance became governor of the state during the Civil War and later was an eloquent spokesman for his state in the U.S. Senate.

4588 Van Cortlandt, Philip   1749-1831
The Revolutionary War memoir and selected correspondence of Philip Van Cortlandt. And others. Compiled and edited by Jacob Judd. Bibliography. Illustrated. Tarrytown, New York: Sleepy Hollow Restorations, 1976. 181 p. Index.
  A collection of his memoirs and selected correspondence provides a comprehensive account of his actions during the American Revolution. Text also contains maps and illustrations, biographical sketch, and full genealogy of the Philip Van Cortlandt family.

4589 Van Cortlandt, Philip   1749-1831
  see also **Van Cortlandt, Pierre**

4590 Van Cortlandt, Pierre   1721-1814
Correspondence of the Van Cortlandt Family of Cortlandt Manor. And others. Compiled and edited by Jacob Judd. Illustrated. Tarrytown, New York: Sleepy Hollow Restorations, 1978. 2v. Index.
  The Van Cortlandt family of Croton, New York, became patriots during the Revolutionary War. Pierre (1721-1814) was lieutenant governor for eighteen years, for a time under George Clinton. The family remained part of an influential political dynasty in New York state throughout the span of this book, as their correspondence with nationally and regionally prominent politicans attests. This compilation also reveals a breadth of commercial, domestic, and religious activities of an energetic, enterprising family.

4591 Van Dellen, Idzerd   b.1871
In God's crucible: an autobiography. Grand Rapids, Michigan: Baker Book House, 1950. 134 p.
  A Dutch immigrant and minister of the Christian Reformed Church describes the history of his life in the church, serving several parishes in the Mid- and South-West.

4592 Vanderbilt, Cornelius, Jr.   1898-1974
Man of the world: my life on five continents. New York: Crown Publishers, 1959. 342 p. Index.
  An engaging, articulate account of Vanderbilt's exciting career as a foreign correspondent ("the billion dollar baby"), information gatherer and press liaison for President Franklin Roosevelt, army intelligence officer, and Nevada rancher. Vanderbilt's world travels (150 transatlantic crossings, 40 transpacific), juxtaposed against his wealthy background and liberal foreground, provide a fascinating perspective of the times.

4593 *Vanderbilt, Gloria (Morgan)   1924-
Double exposure: a twin autobiography. And Thelma (Morgan) Furness, Viscountess. New York: David McKay Co., 1958. 369 p.
  Identical twin daughters of Diplomat Harry Hays Morgan tell of their lives marked by empathy and almost telepathic understanding of each other. Here they tell stories, alternating the anecdotes between them, of their marriages, their families, the peripatetic existence among the society of the day, and the changes in their lives over the decades.

4594 Vandergrift, Archer A.   1887-1973
Once a Marine; the memoirs of General A.A. Vandergrift, United States Marine Corps. As told to Robert B. Asprey. New York: W.W. Norton & Co., Inc., 1964. 338 p. Index.
  During a brilliant military career, he became known as the hero of Guadalcanal, one of the most difficult battles of the Pacific during World War II. Later he was appointed Commandant of the Marine Corps.

4595 *Van Doren, Dorothy (Graffe)   1896-
The professor and I. New York: Appleton-Century-Crofts, Inc., 1959. 246 p.
  A novelist's light, anecdotal narrative of life with her husband, Mark, a well-known author and critic, spending summers on a small Connecticut farm and winters in New York.

4596 Van Doren, Mark   1894-1972
The autobiography of Mark Van Doren. New York: Harcourt, Brace and Co., 1958. 371 p.
  Revered as a professor of literature at Columbia University and an author of poetry, fiction, and non-fiction, Van Doren writes of his boyhood in Illinois, his education, and, affectionately, of his writing over the years.

4597 Van Druten, John   1901-1957
Playwright at work. New York: Harper and Brothers, 1953. 210 p. Index.
  After more than 25 years as a playwright, he writes of his life, his struggle to become successful, and the hard work of being a writer.

4598 Van Druten, John   1901-1957
The widening circle. New York: Charles Scribner's Sons, 1957. 229 p.
  A philosophical quest for the meaning of his life, by a well-established playwright who grew up in England and spent most of his professional life in California.

4599 *Van Hoosen, Bertha   1863-1952
Petticoat surgeon. Foreword by Dr. A.E. Hertzler. Chicago: Pellegrini and Cudahy, 1947. 324 p.
  After growing up in rural Michigan, she finished medical school, started practice in Chicago, and eventually became Head of Obstetrics in the Loyola University School of Medicine.

4600 Van Loon, Hendrik Willem   1882-1944
Report to Saint Peter: upon the kind of world in which Hendrik Willem van Loon spent the first years of his life. Illustrated by the author. New York: Simon and Schuster, 1947. 220 p.
  A fragment left incomplete at his death, the book is limited to his boyhood in Rotterdam. A writer of international reputation for over 25 years.

4601 Van Orman, Ward Tunte   1894-1978
Wizard of the winds. As told to Robert Hull. Foreword by Robert Hull. Illustrated. Saint Cloud, Minnesota: North Star Press, 1978. 278 p.
  This exciting book focuses on Van Orman's balloon races, 1919-1933, when he was a research engineer and inventor for Goodyear. He won many races, national and international, experienced hair-raising trips through storms and hazardous air currents. His good friend was killed when lightning struck their balloon. A lengthy and interesting appendix discusses many of the author's inventions and experiments with lighter-than-air craft.

4602 Van Paassen, Pierre   1875-1968
To number our days. New York: Charles Scribner's Sons, 1964. 404 p.
  This sequel to *Days of our years* continues Van Paassen's eyewitness account of important world events in addition to his personal story. He served in pulpits in Ontario, as a soldier during World War I, explored international affairs through interviews with world political and religious leaders, and championed the Jewish people's national cause.

4603 VanVogt, Alfred Elton   1912-
Reflections: the autobiography of a science-fiction giant. Lakemont, Georgia: Fictioneer Books, 1975. 136 p.
  A prolific writer of science fiction stories, novels, and other books tells about his life and writing career; adapted from recorded interviews in an oral history project.

4604 Vanzetti, Bartolomeo   1888-1927
  see **Sacco, Nicola**

4605 Vasquez, Joseph C.   1918?
My tribe. With Conrad Stein. Illustrated. Chicago, Illinois: Children's Press, 1970. 64 p.
  Written for occupational and career guidance for young people, this book describes Vasquez's youth, his days as a hobo, his various jobs. He eventually worked for Hughes Aircraft Company as a purchasing agent and is active with the Los Angeles Indian Center.

4606 Vauclain, Samuel Matthews   **1856-1940**
Steaming up. With Earl Chapin May. San Marino, California: Golden
West Books, 1973. (New York: Brewer & Warren, 1930) 320 p.
     This reprint of the 1930 edition describes Vauclain's career with the
Pennsylvania Railroad and the Baldwin Locomotive Works.

4607 Vaughan, Stuart   **1925?-**
**A possible theatre; the experiences of a pioneer director in America's
resident theatre.** New York: McGraw-Hill Book Co., 1969. 255 p. Index.
     Written to present "a case history of a creative person working at an
important transitional time in one of the performing arts," this book tells
of the author's involvement with three pioneering resident theater companies, The New York Shakespeare Festival, the Phoenix Theatre, and the
Seattle Repertory Theatre.

4608 Vaught, John Howard   **1909-**
Rebel coach: my football family. Illustrated. Memphis: Memphis State
University Press, 1971. 203 p. Index.
     College football coach Vaught turned the losing University of Missis-
sippi team into a winning football fiefdom. From 1949 until 1971 when he
was forced out by ill health, he built a team with an impressive record
including six Southeastern Championships and eighteen Bowl games.

4609 Vaus, James Arthur   **1918?-**
Devil loves a shining mark: the story of my life. With Julie Maxey. Waco,
Texas: Word Books, 1974. 157 p.
     Reformed criminal and ex-con Vaus quit the syndicate to work with
Hell Gate area street gangs. He established Youth Development, Inc., and
helped troubled kids through youth camps, schools, a ranch for runaways,
a mountaineering program, and his own understanding of and compassion
for their problems.

4610 Veeck, William   **1914-**
Veeck—as in wreck. With Ed Linn. New York: G.P. Putnam's Sons,
1962. 380 p.
     Although his leg was amputated as a result of a World War II injury,
he led an intensely active life as a baseball executive. His book is full of
anecdotes about his executive enterprise and famous baseball characters.

4611 *Veevers-Carter, Wendy (Day)
Island home. Illustrated. New York: Random House, 1970. 345 p.
     Living on a 62-acre island, Remire, in the Seychelles in the Western
Indian Ocean was both adventuresome and hard work for the author and
her family. They depended on fishing, copra production, and other agricultural activities for their livelihood, learning by necessity to become
self-sufficient.

4612 *Velazquez, Loreta Janeta (Lieut. Harry T. Buford, pseud.) b.1842
**Woman in battle; a narrative of the exploits, adventures, and travels of
Madame Loreta Janeta Velazquez otherwise known as Lt. Harry T.
Buford, Confederate States Army.** Illustrated. Edited by C.J.
Worthington. New York: Arno Press, 1972. (Hartford: T. Belknap, 1876)
606 p.
     During the Civil War she served the Confederacy as an officer and spy,
disguised as a man. Afterwards she kept adventure in her life by traveling
widely, working as a secret agent, broker, and a Western miner, among
other things.

4613 Ventresca, Francesco   **b.1872**
**Personal reminiscences: celebrating sixty years in America (1891-1951),
fifty-five years a teacher of foreign languages.** Introduction by Martin J.
Teigan. Preface by Vera Talmage. Illustrated. Chicago, Illinois: the author, 1951. 340 p.
     Ventresca, a teacher of Italian, Latin, and other foreign languages in
Chicago area high schools, 1896-1960, writes of his childhood in Abruzzi,
Italy, and of his immigration to Chicago, his education at Northern Indiana Normal School and the University of Chicago, and his teaching
career. He had a reputation as a brilliant, excellent teacher and translator
of documents during World War I.

4614 Venturi, Kenneth   **1931-**
Comeback: the Ken Venturi story. With Oscar Fraley. New York: Duell,
Sloan and Pearce, 1966. 184 p.
     The story of a golf champion who after winning the National Open in
1964 contracted a rare disease of the hands which nearly ended his career.
An operation at the Mayo Clinic corrected the condition and enabled
Venturi to make a spectacular comeback.

4615 *Vester, Bertha Hedges (Spafford)   **1878-1968**
Our Jerusalem: an American family in the Holy City, 1881-1949. Garden
City, New York: Doubleday and Co., Inc., 1950. 332 p.
     Life in a community center in Jerusalem open to Moslems, Jews, and
Christians for seven decades, under Turkish, British, and independent
rule.

4616 Vickrey, Robert   **1926-**
Robert Vickrey: artist at work. Illustrated. New York: Watson-Guptill,
1979. 143 p. Index.

A painter whose style is reminiscent of Jamie Wyeth tells briefly about
his life, more about how he paints, including some demonstrations step by
step. Vickrey worked as *Time* Magazine artist for a number of years as
well as for other major magazines. As realistic art went out of fashion, he
moved from New York to Connecticut and continued to paint realistically, using his children as handsome models.

4617 Vidal, Gore   **1925-**
Views from a window: conversations with Gore Vidal. Edited by Robert
J. Stanton and Gore Vidal. New York: Lyle Stuart, 1980. 319 p. Index.
     A collection of interviews in which the author discusses his life, inter-
ests, and work as well as America's values and politics.

4618 Vidor, King Wallis   **1895-**
A tree is a tree. Illustrated. New York: Garland Publishing, Inc., 1977.
(New York: Harcourt Brace, 1952) 315 p. Index.
     Vidor's good-humored, fast-paced account of his career as a film direc-
tor spans the first six decades of the twentieth century, in the medium he
wisely labels "the Grand Illusion." He began with primitive films made in
open air and switched to silent films made on sets, including some of his
masterpieces, *The Big Parade, La Boheme,* and *The Crowd.* Thereafter he
made sound and color films (*Hallelujah* and *Our Daily Bread*) and eventually films for Cinerama and television.

4619 *Vining, Elizabeth Janet (Gray)   **1902-**
Being seventy: the measure of a year. New York: The Viking Press, 1978.
194 p.
     In this journal of her seventieth year, Vining exhibits little nostalgia for
the past, commenting instead on contemporary progress. A novelist and
recognized authority on Japan, she observes the modern world with keen
intelligence, humor, patience, and pleasure at aging with vigor.

4620 *Vining, Elizabeth Janet (Gray)   **1902-**
Windows for the crown prince. Philadelphia: J.B. Lippincott Co., 1952.
320 p.
     A chronicle of four years in Japan (1946-1950) where she was ap-
pointed English tutor for Crown Prince Akihito.

4621 Vinton, Bobby   **1941-**
Polish prince. With Robert E. Burger. Illustrated. New York: M. Evans,
1978. 189 p.
     Ethnic pride prevails in Vinton's story of his rise from small-town
musician and band leader to Las Vegas headliner and gold-record-selling
singer. He considers a song he wrote with lyrics in Polish as the apex of
his career and as a rallying point for people of Polish heritage.

4622 Viscardi, Henry, Jr.   **1912-**
Man's stature. Introduction by Bernard M. Baruch. New York: John Day
Co., 1952. 240 p.
     A New York man born with a birth defect, and later in life further
handicapped by surgery, relates the personal and social difficulties he
faced because of his physical disabilities. He also explains his job of helping other handicapped people through the J.O.B. (Just One Break) organization.

4623 Viscott, David S.   **1938-**
The making of a psychiatrist. New York: Arbor House, 1972. 410 p.
     In order to give his readers a sense of what it takes to become a
psychiatrist, Dr. Viscott tells of his training, appraises traditional
attitudes and techniques, and presents the human principles guiding his
own practice and philosophy of psychiatry. He confronts his challenges,
failures, and successes with patients, assessing honestly the changes and
feelings within himself.

4624 *Visono, Maria Assunta Isabella
*see *Dodd, Bella*

4625 Vitkauskas, Arejas
An immigrant's story. New York: Philosophical Library, 1956. 192 p.
     In 1933 he immigrated to the United States from Lithuania. His book
tells of his youth in Lithuania, then of his experience as an American
factory worker. The latter is based on his diary, which makes sharp
contrasts between Lithuanian and American life styles and between the
American dream and the realities of working life.

4626 Vivas, Eliseo   **1901-**
Two roads to ignorance: a quasi biography. Carbondale: Southern Illinois
University Press, 1979. 304 p. Index.
     Philosopher Vivas wrote this autobiography in the third person, claim-
ing that it is an "intellectual quasi biography of an intimate friend . . .
Alonzo Quijang . . . born in the same town in the same year as I," with
whom Vivas has lived intimately ever since. From this perspective he
concentrates on the "mind's adventures," and so discusses such topics as
religion, naturalism, the nature of man, morality and liberalism, and
various philosophers' views on these topics.

4627 Vogel, John   **1909-**
This happened in the hills of Kentucky. Grand Rapids, Michigan:
Zondervan Publishing House, 1952. 382 p.

Vogel tells how he and his wife settled in a tiny log cabin in the
Kentucky hills (near Corbin) so he could practice his ministry. He gradually discovered that his most effective mode of Christian service would
be to run an orphanage, which they founded. The Galilean Children's
Home gradually expanded to include 82 children and many buildings.
Although Vogel intends to dispel the "hillbilly" stereotype, much of the
book consists of Appalachian mountain dialect that reinforces the stereotype.

4628 Vogeler, Robert Alexander   **1911-**
I was Stalin's prisoner. With Leigh White. New York: Harcourt, Brace
and Co., 1951. 314 p. Index.

Vogeler tells his story about work assignments in Russian-controlled
cities, imprisonment, and subsequent ransomed release. Parts of the book
previously appeared as articles in the *Saturday Evening Post.*

4629 Von Mises, Ludwig   **1881-1973**
Ludwig Von Mises: notes and recollections. Foreword by Margit Von
Mises. Translated with postscript by Hans F. Sennholz. Illustrated. South
Holland, Illinois: Libertarian Press, 1978. 181 p. Index.

This collection of miscellaneous papers by economist Von Mises, an
immigrant from Austria in 1940, focuses on Austrian economics, money,
credit, inflation, and social cooperation. Interwoven is information about
his career as an economist with the Austrian Chamber of Commerce, his
teaching in Vienna and Geneva, and devastating observations on world
economic conditions and the personalities of those who exacerbated the
problems before World War II.

4630 *Von Mises, Margit
My years with Ludwig Von Mises. Illustrated. New Rochelle, New York:
Arlington House, 1976. 191 p.

Margit von Mises' loving tribute to her economist-husband Ludwig is
also an appealing story of their fourteen-year courtship in Austria and
their 39-year marriage (1934-73), spent mostly in New York. Margit, a
professional actress and translator, writes with vivid eloquence.

4631 Voorhis, Horace Jeremiah   **1901-**
Confessions of a Congressman. Garden City, New York: Doubleday and
Co., Inc., 1947. 365 p.

After ten years as a U.S. Representative from California, he describes
the life, work, success, and frustration of a liberal Democrat in national
politics.

4632 Waddell, William H. IV
People are the funniest animals. Philadelphia: Dorrance, 1978. 329 p.

Waddell, a veterinarian who practiced medicine in the U.S. Army
Veterinary Corps and as a civilian in Morgantown, West Virginia, and
Fargo, North Dakota, tells rambling tales about his Virginia childhood,
education at Pennsylvania State University, and people and animals he
has known. He believes that "the animal is rich in love, great in fidelity,
wonderful in compassion and, in some respects, able to communicate
better" than people—who "are still the funniest animals."

4633 *Waddington, Mary Alsop (King)
Letters of a diplomat's wife 1883-1900. New York: Charles Scribner's
Sons, 1905. 417 p. Index.

Mme. Waddington, daughter of a president of Columbia College, mar-
ried a French diplomat who served in several posts including Minister of
Foreign Affairs, Ambassador-Extraordinary to the coronation of Czar
Alexander III in Moscow, and Ambassador at the Court of St. James.
Mme. Waddington wrote to her sisters to describe the personages and
incidents of her official life in Russia and England.

4634 *Wadelton, Maggie Jeanne (Melody) (Maggie Owen, pseud.) 1896-
Gay, wild and free: from captain's wife to colonel's lady. Indianapolis:
The Bobbs-Merrill Co., Inc., 1949. 312 p.

Her life as an army wife described with coy and flippant humor, using
silly and fictitious names for people and places, mostly in Georgia and
Oklahoma.

4635 Wadsworth, James Jeremiah   **1905-**
Silver spoon: an autobiography. Illustrated. Geneva, New York: W.F.
Humphrey Press, 1980. 306 p.

Wadsworth recalls a life of enjoyable endeavors, from his education at
Yale to early married years as a farmer and fledgling politician in upstate
New York, to United Nations Ambassador. He focuses on his work with
the State Department during the years of nuclear testing and the founding
and strengthening of the United Nations.

4636 Wadsworth, Peleg   **1748-1829**
**Letters of General Peleg Wadsworth to his son John, student at Harvard
College, 1796-1798.** Biographical chapter and notes by George and
Margaret Rose. Portland: Maine Historical Society, 1961. 44 p.

Letters conveying fatherly advice from a prominent member of a prominent New England family.

4637 *Waerenskjold, Elise Amalie (Trede)   **1815-1895**
Lady with the pen; Elise Waerenskjold in Texas. Edited by C.A. Clavsen.
Foreword by Theodore C. Blegen. Northfield, Minnesota:
Norwegian-American Historical Association, 1961. 183 p. Index.

A portrait of the immigrant colonies of Texas and of her own life seen
through the letters (1851-1895) of a courageous and forceful Norwegian
immigrant woman.

4638 Wagner, Henry R.   **1862-1957**
Sixty years of book collecting. Los Angeles: The Zamorano Club, 1952.
51 p.

A list of important rare-book collections by a noted collector, detailing
the author's intimate knowledge of each and purchase of some. Includes
advice to collectors: "Nothing is easier than to buy at an auction, whether
in person or through an agent, books that you do not really want." Among
Wagner's collections are books on metallurgy, economics, Mexico, the Spanish Southwest, and many others.

4639 Wainwright, Jonathan Mayhew   **1883-1953**
**General Wainwright's story: the account of four years of humiliating
defeat, surrender, and captivity.** Edited by Robert Considine. Garden
City, New York: Doubleday and Co., Inc., 1946. 314 p. Index.

A story of the horror of war and survival, with grisly details of his
experience in Japanese prisoner-of-war camps after the loss of Bataan and
Corregidor.

4640 Waldorf, John Taylor   **1870-1932**
A kid on the Comstock: reminiscences of a Virginia City childhood.
Edited with introduction and commentary by Dolores Bryant Waldorf.
Illustrated. Palo Alto, California: American West Publishing Co., 1970.
198 p. Index.

A memoir of over a decade of childhood (1873-1886) growing up in
Virginia City, Nevada, during its heyday as a silver-mining town exploiting the Comstock lode. Waldorf, a "Peck's Bad Boy," clambered over
waste dumps from the mines, gathered scarce lumber there, stoned innocent Chinese immigrants and ate their funeral food, skirmished with Piute
Indians, and was initiated into gambling, stock speculating, and drinking.
This volume is greatly enhanced by lively interchapters by the author's
daughter on the political and social history of Virginia City.

4641 *Walgreen, Myrtle R. (Norton)   **1879-1971**
Never a dull day: an autobiography. As told to Margueritte Harmon Bro.
Chicago: Henry Regnery Co., 1963. 334 p.

After childhood in a loving but poor family in rural Illinois, she went
to Chicago to become a factory worker, married Charles R. Walgreen and
helped him found his drugstore empire. Simply told, her homely story
nearly disguises her success in horticulture and photography and her
many philanthropic activities.

4642 Walker, John   **1906-**
Self-portrait with donors; confessions of an art collector. Illustrated.
Boston: Little, Brown and Co., 1974. 320 p. Index.

As a museum curator and director, he spent the greater part of his life
collecting collectors who would become donors. Those most important to
him were Bernard Berenson, with whom he lived and studied for three
years, Francis Watson, John Pope-Hennessy, and Kenneth Clark. He
grew up in Pittsburgh, where Mellon and Frick made the fortunes that
produced great collections, and later became director of the National
Gallery of Art, which was developed from Mellon collections.

4643 *Walker, Margaret   **1915-**
How I wrote *Jubilee*. Chicago, Illinois: Third World Press, 1972. 36 p.

Although she began to write her novel *Jubilee* when she was nineteen,
she spent many years in research on Black history and in reflection before
transforming the raw materials into a literary masterpiece finally published in 1966. Here she describes the genesis, growth, and accomplishment of the task which fascinated her through those years.

4644 *Walker, Margaret
see also **Giovanni, Nikki**

4645 Walker, Mickey   **1901-**
Mickey Walker: the toy bulldog and his time. With Joe Reichler. New
York: Random House, 1961. 305 p.

Raised in a middle-class New Jersey neighborhood, he was a fighting
Irishman before and after his success as a boxer. He also tried acting,
singing, radio announcing, and was a sportswriter for the *Police Gazette*
(1948-1955), always with bravado.

4646 Walker, Mickey   **1901-**
The will to conquer. Hollywood: House-Warven, Publishers, 1953. 112 p.

A prize fighter reminisces about his Irish family, his friends, and his
boxing career.

4647 Walker, Stanley   **1898-1962**
Home to Texas. New York: Harper and Brothers, 1956. 307 p.
    After 26 years as a journalist in New York, he returned to the Texas ranch where he grew up. Here he writes of his youth in Texas, his career, and, philosophically, about his return to the land.

4648 *Wallace, Cornelia Folsom (Ellis)   **1939-**
C'nelia. Philadelphia: A.J. Holman Co., 1976. 240 p.
    Cornelia Wallace's memories of childhood and growing up, her occupations—pianist, country singer, composer, actress, and her life as second wife of Governor George Wallace of Georgia including his near-assassination, paralysis, and adjustment.

4649 *Wallace, Elizabeth   **1866-1960**
The unending journey. Minneapolis: The University of Minnesota Press, 1952. 286 p.
    A remarkable narrative of her childhood, her education at Wellesley, her career as a professor of French at the University of Chicago, her friendship with Mark Twain, and her reactions to two World Wars during her own old age.

4650 Wallace, George Corley   **1919-**
Stand up for America. Garden City, New York: Doubleday & Co., Inc., 1976. 183 p. Index.
    A lawyer, Alabama governor, and conservative candidate for U.S. President tells his life story (up from rural poverty to the governor's mansion) and articulates his social and political philosophy. He speaks candidly but without rancor about the assassination attempt that left him paralyzed from the waist down.

4651 Wallace, George Corley, Jr.   **1951-**
The Wallaces of Alabama: my family. As told to James Gregory. Introduction by George C. Wallace. Chicago: Follett Publishing Co., 1975. 256 p. Index.
    The son of Governor George Wallace and Governor Lurleen Wallace tells about his family, his parents' political activities, and the well-publicized events that affected their lives.

4652 Wallace, George J.   **1907?-**
My world of birds: memoirs of an ornithologist. Illustrated. Philadelphia: Dorrance, 1979. 345 p.
    Wallace's fascination with birds is evident from annual lists he made as a teenager in Vermont to his round-the-world explorations in search of exotic species. He describes his studies and years as a professor at Michigan State, intervening stints as warden of a wildlife sanctuary in Massachusetts, and caretaker of a mountain lodge in Vermont while undertaking a study of Bicknell's gray-cheeked thrush. The real stars of the show, however, are the birds themselves. Bird lists are appended to almost every chapter, and his descriptions of bird expeditions are scientifically detailed.

4653 Wallace, Henry Agard   **1888-1965**
Price of vision: the diary of Henry A. Wallace, 1942-1946. Edited with introduction by John Morton Blum. Boston: Houghton Mifflin Co., 1973. 707 p. Index.
    A diary revealing the struggle for authority during his chairmanship of the Board of Economic Welfare, its essential wartime services to the country, as well as his efforts in constructing a thriving and equitable postwar international economy. His goals were "economic democracy, democracy among the races, and political democracy" for all people everywhere.

4654 Wallace, Irving   **1916-**
The writing of one novel. New York: Simon and Schuster, 1968. 250 p.
    A highly detailed account of the "conception," "gestation," and "birth" of Irving Wallace's novel, *The Prize,* involving a complex but fast-moving plot about two Nobel Prize winners and the intrigues, crises, and other human involvements that attend their selection. In the unusual anatomization of this 582-day process, Wallace recounts in detail his 260 days of research, his writing of five drafts, and follow-up activities, including reviewers' observations, fan mail, and his own reactions throughout the process.

4655 Wallack, John Lester   **1820-1888**
Memories of fifty years. Preface and biographical sketch by Laurence Hutton, Illustrated. List of characters played by Mr. Wallack. New York: Benjamin Blom, 1969. (New York: Scribners, 1889) 232 p. Index.
    Wallack, a member of one of the three leading nineteenth-century theatrical families, was born in America, educated and trained for the stage in England, and alternated between the two countries as an actor and producer. He played such roles as Edgar in *King Lear,* Mercutio in *Romeo and Juliet,* and acted in a host of eighteenth-century comedies.

4656 *Waln, Nora   **1895-**
Reaching for the stars. Boston: Little, Brown & Co., 1939. 380 p.
    From 1934 to 1939 the author and her husband lived in Nazi Germany while he studied music. They had many friends among the cultured, music-loving intelligentsia and traveled in Germany, Austria, and Czech-

oslovakia. She describes with clarity the growing Nazi menace and near-destruction of a civilization.

4657 Walsh, James Edward   **1891-**
Zeal for your house. Edited by Robert E. Sheridan. Illustrated. Huntington, Indiana: Our Sunday Visitor, Inc., 1976. 233 p.
    This book is a collection of sermons and speeches by Bishop Walsh over a quarter of a century. He served in the Catholic Foreign Mission Society of America and was imprisoned by the communists for 22 years (1948-1970) in China.

4658 Walsh, Raoul   **1892-**
Each man in his time: the life story of a director. New York: Farrar, Straus, and Giroux, 1974. 385 p. Index.
    Starting as a cowboy-turned-actor in New York, Walsh went to California with D.W. Griffith, became a director, and took part in the birth of Hollywood, its golden era, and its declining years. His book overflows with anecdotes involving himself and the "greats" of the movie world.

4659 Walter, Danton MacIntyre   **1899-**
Danton's Inferno: the story of a columnist and how he grew. Illustrated. New York: Hastings House, 1955. 512 p.
    Broadway columnist, sometime actor, and bon vivant Walker fills this humorous account of his life with anecdotes about hundreds of persons famous (soprano Lily Pons), infamous (madam Polly Adler), and occasionally innocuous. Some of these people he knew well, through cafe society dining and dancing; others he merely observed to write about. He loved to travel and particularly enjoyed Paris while there on military service in World Wars I and II.

4660 Walther, Carl Ferdinand Wilhelm   **1811-1887**
Letters of C.F.W. Walther: a selection. Translated, edited, with introduction by Carl S. Meyer. Seminar Editions. Philadelphia: Fortress Press, 1969. 155 p. Index.
    In a style reminiscent of Pauline epistolary rhetoric, a Missouri Lutheran minister discusses theology and doctrine with his fellow Lutherans, warning against the evils of Catholicism and pietism in particular.

4661 Warbasse, James Peter   **1866-1957**
North star: a contribution to autobiography. Falmouth, Massachusetts: The Kendall Press, 1958. 123 p.
    In *Three Voyages* he described his medical education and practice. This volume, written at 87, relates his family history, his experience in Cuba during the Spanish-American War, and more about his practice of several cooperative philosophies, such as his membership in IWW.

4662 Warburg, James Paul   **1896-**
The long road home: the autobiography of a maverick. Garden City, New York: Doubleday & Co., Inc., 1964. 314 p.
    A banker descended from a family of bankers, he became a public servant and commentator often, as he says in the Preface, "out of step with public policy and majority opinion." A combination of personal memories and historical analysis.

4663 Ward, Andrew   **1946-**
Fits and starts: the premature memoirs of Andrew Ward. Boston: Little, Brown and Co., 1978. 177 p.
    With wit and an eye for minute, revealing details Ward captures the cadence of his childhood, growing up in Chicago and India, and youth in Greenwich, Connecticut. He was receptive to languages and music, maladroit at social relationships and science. He presents a credible and appealing character, who flunked out of Oberlin and has not fully learned to cope by the book's end.

4664 *Ward, Harriet Sherrill   **1803-1865**
Prairie schooner lady: the journal of Harriet Sherrill Ward, 1853. Edited by Ward G. De Witt and Florence Stork De Witt. Los Angeles: Westernlore Press, 1959. 180 p.
    A straightforward account of the author's pioneering trek by covered wagon from Iowa to the California gold fields. She rejoices in attractive scenery, enjoys the Mormon territory, marvels at the altitude when crossing the Continental Divide, and provides a picture of three-generation family life on the wagon trail.

4665 Ward, Samuel   **1725-1776**
Correspondence of Governor Samuel Ward, May 1775-1776: with a biographical introduction based chiefly on the Ward Papers covering the period 1725-1776; and genealogy of the Ward family: Thomas Ward, son of John, of Newport and some of his descendants. Edited by Bernard Knollenberg. Compiler of genealogy, Clifford P. Monahon. Providence: Rhode Island Historical Society, 1952. 205 p. Index.
    The book reprints the letters to and from the man who was Governor of Rhode Island. Some of the correspondence was directed to Nicholas Cooke, another governor, and to the Continental Congress. Ward covered a wide range of topics including the Revolutionary War and the Declaration of Independence.

4666 Ward, Samuel 1814-1884
Sam Ward in the Gold Rush. Edited by Carvel Collins. Stanford: Stanford University Press, 1949. 189 p. Index.
Originally published under a pseudonym (Mides, Jr.) in Porter's *Spirit of the Times* (January-April, 1861), these chapters sketch life in the mining country, by one who promoted and developed gold interests.

4667 Ward, Samuel Ringgold 1817-1866?
Autobiography of a fugitive Negro: his anti-slavery labours in the United States, Canada, & England. New York: Arno Press, 1968. (London: John Snow, 1855) 412 p.
Born to slave parents in Maryland, he and his family escaped to the North where he obtained a liberal education and became a licensed preacher. He lectured for the antislavery cause and aided fugitive slaves in the United States and Canada. In 1853 he went to Great Britain to solicit aid for his cause, becoming known as a great persuasive orator.

4668 Ware, Wallace L. 1892-
The unforgettables. Foreword by Harry S. Young. Illustrated. San Francisco: Hesperian Press, 1964. 160 p.
Ware's reminiscences of his life in California cover his childhood in a large, happy family in Santa Rosa, memorable lectures by Luther Burbank, Tong Wars, the earthquake of 1906, and a pleasant association with Al G. Barnes, circus owner. Ware also includes various speeches he made before civic and educational groups from 1936-1960 and some decisions he made as a trial judge.

4669 *Warfield, Frances 1901-1964
Cotton in my ears. New York: The Viking Press, 1948. 152 p.
Orphaned at four, she disguised her progressive deafness for twenty years, fearing she would be abandoned or socially ostracized. Meanwhile she became a successful young journalist and finally bought a hearing aid.

4670 *Warfield, Frances 1901-1964
Keep listening. New York: The Viking Press, 1957. 158 p.
While growing up she suffered from progressive deafness, but not until her early thirties did she admit it and confront her problem by learning to lip-read, and then getting a hearing aid. Her book reveals the psychological suffering common to those hard of hearing and the practical and prejudicial problems they face daily.

4671 *Warfield, Sandra
see **McCracken, James**

4672 Warhol, Andy 1928-
The philosophy of Andy Warhol: (from A to B and back again). New York: Harcourt Brace Jovanovich, 1975. 241 p.
Painter and motion-picture director Warhol has written a "sex-and-nostalgia book." Sex is too much work, he writes; he obviously prefers offbeat nostalgia of the 1960's.

4673 Warhol, Andy 1928-
POPism: the Warhol '60's. And Pat Hackett. Illustrated. New York: Harcourt Brace Jovanovich, 1980. 310 p. Index.
Warhol namedrops his way through the Pop 1960's—the art exhibits and hip parties, drugs and casual decadence are interspersed with exact recall of contemporary fashions and music. Warhol's Campbell's Soup Can and Marilyn Monroe paintings put him in the artistic vanguard, and his underground films and the "happenings" at the factory (his studio) helped set trends for the 60's counter culture. The fast and loose times changed abruptly when Warhol was senselessly shot by a hanger-on. Warhol recovered, more cautious and more mellow, but the carefree days of smug spontaneity were over.

4674 *Warner, Esther Sietmann 1910-
New song in a strange land. Boston: Houghton Mifflin Co., 1948. 302 p.
The story of two years in Liberia, where her husband was assigned as a botanist for Firestone. A wood carver, she records her experience in exploring African art and customs.

4675 Warner, Jack L. 1892-1978
My first hundred years in Hollywood. With Dean Jennings. New York: Random House, 1965. 331 p.
From early days in Ohio through the first movies, the nickelodeon, talking and sound pictures, Warner tells of his personal struggles, observations and reflections on the Hollywood scene.

4676 Warner, Langdon 1881-1955
Langdon Warner through his letters. Illustrated. Edited by Theodore Bowie. Bloomington: Indiana University Press, 1966. 225 p. Index.
An Orientalist who helped establish the value of the art of Japan, Korea, and China, Warner denied that he was, as others insisted, "the American scholar who had saved Kyoto and Nara from bombing in World War II." The editor has connected selected letters with narrative to reveal Warner's character.

4677 Warren, Earl 1891-1974
The memoirs of Earl Warren. Illustrated. Garden City, New York: Doubleday & Company, Inc., 1977. 394 p. Index.
A former district attorney, attorney general, three-term Governor of California, Vice-Presidential candidate, and Supreme Court Justice offers insights into the workings of government and the personalities of noted government figures, discusses the ground-breaking controversies of the "Warren court," and describes his involvement in the "Warren Commission," investigating the assassination of John F. Kennedy.

4678 Warren, John Collins 1842-1927
To work in the vineyard of surgery: the reminiscences of J. Collins Warren. Edited with appendices, notes, and comments by Edward D. Churchill. Cambridge: Harvard University Press, 1958. 288 p. Index.
Many members of the Warren family have made important contributions to medicine and surgery; since 1782 they have taught at Harvard Medical School; and since 1821, at Massachusetts General Hospital. His book tells of life in nineteenth-century Boston, the history of modern surgery and medicine, as well as his life and recollections of a remarkable family.

4679 Warren, Jonathan Mason 1811-1867
Parisian education of an American surgeon: letters of Jonathan Mason Warren (1832-1835). Notes and introduction by Russell M. Jones. Illustrated. Philadelphia: American Philosophical Society, 1978. 266 p. Index.
The letters of this precisely annotated edition depict the Parisian medical world at its height, focusing on highly detailed accounts of early French surgeons and surgical procedures. They provide an outstanding history of the state of the medical arts in the early nineteenth century.

4680 *Warren, Mercy
see **Adams, John**

4681 Warren, Robert Penn 1905-
A conversation with Robert Penn Warren. Edited by Frank Gado. Schenectady, New York: The Idol, 1972. 23 p.
This tape-recorded interview with Warren was published as a special issue of the Union College journal, *The Idol.* His avowed distaste for the self-consciously avant garde sets him apart from other novelists of the 1920's and 30's, revealed here in his discussion of writing and philosophy.

4682 Washburn, Benjamin Earle b.1885
A country doctor in the south mountains. Illustrated by John Pike. Spindale, North Carolina: The Spindale Press, 1955. 96 p.
An account of health and living conditions in North Carolina hill country at the beginning of this century.

4683 Washington, Adolphus 1923-
Hey taxi! With R. Conrad Stein. Illustrated. Open Door Books. Chicago: Children's Press, 1970. 64 p.
In a career guidance series aimed at young people, the author tells how he became a taxi driver and what qualifications and training are necessary.

4684 Washington, Booker Taliaferro 1856-1915
The Booker T. Washington Papers. Illustrated. Edited by Louis R. Harlan. Urbana: University of Illinois Press, 1972- . v. Index.
Volume 1: Autobiographical writings containing extracts from *The Story of The Negro* and *My Larger Education.* Volume 2-9: Papers written from 1860-1908. With the exception of Volume 1, all material is presented chronologically. Most documents appear in complete rather than excerpted form. Annotation of correspondents and explanatory notes appear but are not intended as exhaustive explications.

4685 Washington, Booker Taliaferro 1856-1915
Story of my life and work. Introduction by J.L.M. Curry. Illustrated by Frank Beard. New York: Negro Universities Press, 1969. (Toronto, Ontario: J.L. Nichols & Co., 1900) 423 p.
Washington founded Tuskegee Institute which pioneered industrial training, agriculture and mechanics, self-respect and self-support for Blacks. He crusaded for better opportunities and better living standards for Blacks through useful education.

4686 Washington, Booker Taliaferro 1856-1915
Up from slavery: an autobiography. New ed. Garden City, New York: Doubleday and Co., Inc., 1963. (New York: A.L. Burt Co., 1901) 243 p.
A later version of his *Story of My Life*, this book describes his youth, education, teaching, and continuing efforts through public speaking and fund-raising to aid his people in various ways, particularly in the establishment and strengthening of Tuskegee Institute.

4687 Washington, George 1732-1799
The diaries of George Washington. Edited by Donald Jackson. Associate editor, Dorothy Twohig. Charlottesville: University Press of Virginia, 1976- . v. Index.
Volume I, 1748-65, includes diary accounts of surveying expeditions, voyages, and plantation concerns. Volume II, 1766-70, concerns his life as

a country squire. Volume, III, 1771-75, 1780-81, begins with domestic occupations, continues through the outbreak of the Revolution, and ends with the Yorktown account of military strategy. Volume IV, 1784-1786, focuses on Washington as a prudent property owner and businessman. More are forthcoming.

4688 Washington, George   **1732-1799**
The George Washington Papers. Edited by Frank Donovan. Illustrated. New York: Dodd, Mead & Co., 1964. 310 p. Index.

An eloquent, abridged selection (with modernized spelling) from Washington's diaries, letters, addresses, and other papers arranged to represent various aspects of his life: surveyor, soldier, commander-in-chief, "peaceful squire." President Washington's writing is forceful, articulate, and to the point: "System in all things should be aimed at; for in execution, it renders everything more easy." Other selected editions have been published.

4689 Wasson, David Atwood   **1823-1887**
Beyond Concord: selected writings of David Atwood Wasson. Edited with introduction by Charles H. Foster. Bloomington: Indiana University Press, 1965. 334 p. Index.

A provocative thinker, Wasson was both like and unlike his contemporaries in New England intellectual history. Some of his writings reflect standard transcendental teachings; others insist on open relations with opposites, the recognition of evil, and the half truth of individualism—avant-garde attitudes for his time. Many of these essays originally appeared in the *Atlantic Monthly, Christian Examiner,* and other periodicals.

4690 Watchorn, Robert   **1859-1944**
The autobiography of Robert Watchorn. Edited by Herbert Faulkner West. Oklahoma City: The Robert Watchorn Charities, Ltd., 1958. 218 p. Index.

As a boy he worked in an English coal mine. He came to America, continued work as a miner, then as a union organizer, an immigration officer on Ellis Island, and finally an oil company executive and philanthropist.

4691 Waters, Donald
see **Kriyananda, Swami**

4692 *Waters, Ethel   **1896-1977**
His eye is on the sparrow: an autobiography. With Charles Samuels. Westport, Connecticut: Greenwood Press, 1978. (Garden City, New York: Doubleday and Co., Inc., 1951) 278 p.

Reminiscences of her long, difficult life from poverty to success as an actress and singer, always sustained by her faith in God.

4693 *Waters, Ethel   **1896-1977**
To me it's wonderful. Introduction by Eugenia Price and Joyce Blackburn. Illustrated. New York: Harper & Row, 1972. 162 p.

A top-ranking actress as well as a blues singer and crusader with Billy Graham, the author is especially famous for her singing of "Dinah," "Stormy Weather," and "St. Louis Blues," and her performance in *Cabin in the Sky* and *The Member of the Wedding.*

4694 Watkins, Paul   **1950-**
My life with Charles Manson. With Guillermo Soledad. New York: Bantam Books, 1979. 278 p.

Watkins explains his wish to tell the truth and express his horror about Charles Manson, his drug-and-sex-oriented hippie "family," and the Tate-La Bianca murders. Watkins' ambivalence permeates the book, for the life free of social constraints and moral responsibility continues to exercise its lurid fascination.

4695 Watson, Charles   **1945-**
Will you die for me? As told to Chaplain Ray Hoekstra. Epilogue by Chaplain Ray Hoekstra. Illustrated. Old Tappan, New Jersey: Fleming H. Revell, 1978. 223 p. Index.

In graphic detail Watson describes his transformation from a clean-cut youth in Copeville, Texas, to a drug-taking member of Charles Manson's satanic "family." Under Manson's evil charisma, Watson killed seven people, including actress Sharon Tate, in 1969. Imprisoned in California Men's Colony, Watson converted to Christianity.

4696 Watson, Deek
The story of the "Ink Spots." With Lee Stephenson. New York: Vantage Press, 1967. 72 p.

A pleasant reminiscence about Watson's career as a singer in a quartet with various members and various names, emerging ultimately and triumphantly in 1932 as "The Ink Spots." The group was composed of Watson, Charlie Fuqua, "Hoppy" Jones, and Jerry Daniels, later replaced by Bill Kenny. Singing in clubs and theaters in Indianapolis (his home town), New York, London, and Australia was exhilarating. Touring throughout the segregated South in the 1930's and 40's produced mortification and anger.

4697 Watson, James Dewey   **1928-**
The double helix; a personal account of the discovery of the structure of DNA. Illustrated. New York: Atheneum, 1968. 226 p.

A scientific adventure story of the events leading to the discovery of the double-helix structure of DNA, work which merited the Nobel Prize in 1962.

4698 Watson, James Eli   **b.1864**
As I knew them; memoirs of James E. Watson. Indianapolis: The Bobbs-Merrill Co., 1936. 330 p. Index.

Elected to Congress in 1894 when he was thirty years old, Watson served in the House and Senate for 38 years. His memoirs are devoted largely to his personal experiences in politics over this long period.

4699 Watson, James Monroe   **1834-1914**
Confederate from East Texas: the Civil War letters of James Monroe Watson. Edited by Judy Watson McClure. Preface. Bibliography. Illustrated. Quanah, Texas: Nortex Press, 1976. 66 p.

The editor's briefly narrated history of Civil War battles provides the matrix for this handful of letters to his family from an uneducated farmer-turned-soldier, reflecting a limited personal view of some minor battles in Arkansas, Mississippi, and Alabama. He talks about his friends, his health, and the economy.

4700 Watson, Jimmy
see **Keating, Michael**

4701 Watt, George William   **b.1878**
Is the liar in?: experience of a Philadelphia lawyer. Clearwater, Florida: George W. Watt, 1948. 327 p.

In spite of the title, a serious analysis of his life and of the law, with emphasis on Pennsylvania.

4702 Watt, Homer Andrew   **1884-1948**
see **Wolfe, Thomas**

4703 Watters, Pat   **1927-**
The angry middle-aged man. New York: Grossman Publishers, 1976. 190 p.

A journalist unemployed at 48 after a thirty-year career examines the impact of this on his mental state (angry) and his life style (more resourceful and more relaxed). He then interviews a dozen other unemployed middle-aged men and finds each "struggling to maintain the integrity and importance of his work." Each holds to "standards and ethics" and adapts to "broken-down situations" to make them work.

4704 Watterson, Henry   **1840-1921**
Marse Henry: an autobiography. American Newspapermen, 1790-1933. New York: Beekman Publishers, 1974. (New York: George H. Doran, 1919) 2v.

As a journalist during the mid- and late nineteenth century in Washington, he was perfectly placed to view and comment on the personalities and events of his day.

4705 Watts, Alan Wilson   **1915-1973**
In my own way; an autobiography, 1915-1965. Illustrated. New York: Pantheon Books, 1972. 400 p. Index.

A philosopher of religion, Watts studied Buddhism, Taoism and Zen, was for a time an Anglican priest and dean of the American Academy of Asian Studies. In writing about theology and philosophies he was particularly interested in showing the West the spiritual significance of Eastern thought.

4706 Watts, George C.   **b.1879**
The long trail. Oakdale, California: The author, 1949. 180 p.

The rugged, difficult life on the Western frontier during the early 1900's, written by a hunter and sheep rancher who settled with his family in Utah and later Wyoming.

4707 Waugh, Alfred S.   **d.1856**
Travels in search of the elephant: the wanderings of Alfred S. Waugh, artist, in Louisiana, Missouri, and Santa Fe, in 1845-1846. Edited by John Francis McDermott. St. Louis: Missouri Historical Society, 1951. 153 p. Index.

An Irish painter and sculptor, he had hoped to join Frémont's third expedition and, when refused, he settled temporarily in the frontier towns of Lexington and Independence, Missouri, and finally traveled to the Southwest, leaving this brief record of his life and the times.

4708 *Wayman, Dorothy (Theodate Geoffrey, pseud.)   **1893-1975**
Bite the bullet. Milwaukee: The Bruce Publishing Co., 1948. 229 p.

Widowed at 27, she returned to Boston and became a reporter for the *Globe,* the first job in her long career as a journalist.

4709 Wayman, John Hudson   **1820-1867**
A doctor on the California trail: the diary of Dr. John Hudson Wayman

from Cambridge City, Indiana, to the gold fields in 1852. Edited by Edgeley Woodman Todd. Denver: Old West Publishing Co., 1971. 136 p. Index.

When Dr. Wayman left his home in Indiana in 1852 to travel to California by the overland route, he expected to reap financial benefits in the Mother Lode country. Eventually he decided that he would practice medicine and invest his income in mines. He is representative of the class of professional people who joined the great migration to California.

4710 Wayne, Anthony   1745-1796
Anthony Wayne, a name in arms: soldier, diplomat, defender of expansion westward of a nation; the Wayne-Knox-Pickering-McHenry correspondence. Transcribed and edited by Richard C. Knopf. Westport, Connecticut: Greenwood Press, 1975. (Pittsburgh: University of Pittsburgh Press, 1960) 566 p. Index.

Commander of the U.S. Army during the Indian Wars (1790-1795), Wayne corresponded with President Washington's three Secretaries of War providing a remarkable record of these often overlooked battles, the Indian tribes and leaders, and his own highly disciplined intellect.

4711 Weaver, Samuel Pool   1882-1963
Autobiography of a Pennsylvania Dutchman. Illustrated. New York: Vantage Press, 1952. 228 p.

In formal language Weaver emphasizes his Pennsylvania Dutch ancestors and their German background, going back to the twelfth century; his career in Spokane, Washington, as a lawyer and professor of constitutional law at Gonzaga University; and presidency of the Great Northwestern Life Insurance Company (begun concurrently with the Depression). Half the book tells of his travels to Europe, the Orient, and the Middle East.

4712 Webb, Samuel Blotchley   1753-1807
Correspondence and journals. Edited by Worthington C. Ford. Preface by William Seward Webb. Illustrated. Eyewitness Accounts of the American Revolution. New York: New York Times and Arno Press, 1969. 3v. Index.

Webb's role in the American Revolution was varied: secretary to the Committee of Correspondence in Connecticut; aide to Major General Putnam and Washington after the Battle of Bunker Hill; and three years of captivity by the British. Released in 1781, he was eventually promoted to Brigadier General. Documents from and to Webb, 1772-1806, reveal his vigorous participation and shed light on military, commercial, and political concerns of the times and of the emerging republic.

4713 Weber, Clarence Adam   1903-
Double trouble: an autobiography of a maverick professor. Bend, Oregon: C.A. Weber, 1980. 421 p.

A self-styled radical, he recounts his checkered career in academia. Text contains a list of his publications.

4714 *Weber, Nancy   1942-
Lily, where's your daddy? New York: Richard Marek Pubs., 1980. 237 p.

New Yorker Weber writes a slick, self-indulgent account of how at 35 and long-established as mistress of Cam (no last name supplied) she seduced the much younger Phillip, a Britisher. Although unsuited temperamentally and in every other way, she forced him to marry her and to father Lily, her much-wanted child. He hated marriage and children and abandoned both within a year.

4715 *Webster, Caroline LeRoy   1797-1882
"Mr. W and I": being the authentic diary of Caroline LeRoy Webster during a famous journey with the Hon. Daniel Webster to Great Britain and the continent in the year 1839. London: Nicholson and Watson, 1949. (Binghamton, New York: Ives Washburn, Inc., 1942) 264 p.

Journals of a European trip with her husband, his daughter, and a companion, by the second wife of Daniel Webster. Includes interesting social and historical material about the life and customs of the 1830's.

4716 Webster, Daniel   1782-1852
The letters of Daniel Webster: from documents owned principally by the New Hampshire Historical Society. Edited by C.H. Van Tyne. New York: Haskell House, 1969. (New York: McClure, Phillips, 1902) 769 p.

Van Tyne has arranged Webster's letters in groups to portray him as local politician, national statesman, family man, friend, farmer, sportsman, businessman, and man of high intellect and moral fiber. From politics to plantings, Webster appears serious, kind, and occasionally charming.

4717 Webster, Daniel   1782-1852
The papers of Daniel Webster: correspondence. Edited by Charles M. Wiltse and others. Hanover, New Hampshire: Published for Dartmouth College (by) University Press of New England, 1974- . v.

Active in public life for forty years, Webster, a strong-willed and strong-minded advocate, legislator, and diplomat, influenced and helped to mold the fledgling United States. He played a leading part in the controversies of his day, supporting the rising nationalism, helping to define the legal framework of the expanding economy, becoming an au-

thority on central banking and currency reform, and taking an early stand against slavery.

4718 *Webster, Margaret   1905-1972
Don't put your daughter on the stage. Illustrated. New York: Alfred A. Knopf, 1972. 379 p. Index.

Picking up where her previous autobiographical effort, *The Same Only Different*, left off in 1937, Webster writes of her theatrical efforts in America: the bus-and-ɪ.unk Shakespeare Company, directing opera at the Met, lecture and recital tours, directing professional, university, and community theater throughout the United States.

4719 *Webster, Margaret   1905-1972
The same only different; five generations of a great theatre family. Illustrated. New York: Alfred A. Knopf, 1969. 390 p. Index.

The first two parts of this book concern Webster's ancestors and her parents. Only in the third part (pp. 259-391) does she take her part in the action which concludes with her second trip to New York in 1938.

4720 Webster, Noah   1758-1843
Letters of Noah Webster. Edited with an introduction by Harry R. Warfel. New York: Library Publishers, 1953. 562 p.

A selection of letters (1783-1843) representing his theory of language, principles of lexicography, his economic and political ideas, and his character traits, by the man most responsible for standardizing the American language.

4721 Wechsberg, Joseph   1907-
Homecoming. New York: Alfred A. Knopf, 1946. 118 p.

A Czechoslovakian Jew who had immigrated to the United States in 1928 and joined the American army, he returned to his hometown in Moravia a few days after it was liberated by the Russians. The story of his attempt to find family and friends is stark and moving.

4722 Wechsberg, Joseph   1907-
Looking for a bluebird. Illustrated by F. Strobel. Westport, Connecticut: Greenwood Press, Publishers, 1974. (Boston: Houghton Mifflin, 1945) 210 p.

After emigrating from Czechoslovakia in 1928, he soon established himself as a night-club musician, often on luxury liners. Many of these pieces describing shipboard life were previously published in *The New Yorker* or *Esquire*.

4723 Wechsberg, Joseph   1907-
Sweet and sour. Boston: Houghton Mifflin Co., 1948. 268 p.

Recollections of his boyhood and adolescence in Czechoslovakia and later in Paris by a journalist who immigrated to the United States. Several chapters appeared previously in *The New Yorker*.

4724 Wechsler, James Arthur   1915-
The age of suspicion. Westport, Connecticut: Greenwood Press, 1971. (New York: Random House, 1953) 333 p.

As editor of the New York *Post*, he had steadily opposed Joseph McCarthy's methods of investigation on the House Un-American Activities Committee. His book reveals the quiet horror of his experience when called to testify before the HUAC, set in the context of the early years of communist influence in the United States and the hysteria which McCarthy generated.

4725 Weed, Steven   1947?-
My search for Patty Hearst. With Scott Swanton. New York: Crown Publishers, Inc., 1976. 343 p.

After his fiancée, heiress Patty Hearst, was kidnapped, Weed searched for her among the radicals, the misfits, the splinter groups of Bay Area subcultures, and later struggled to understand the events and her apparent conversion to the ways of her captors.

4726 Weed, Thurlow   1797-1882
The life of Thurlow Weed. Illustrated. New York: Da Capo Press, 1970. (Boston & New York: Houghton, 1883) 2v.

Volume I comprises Weed's autobiography written at various intervals and arranged to create a narrative of the events and experiences of his life as a politician and newspaper editor. Volume II is a memoir written by his grandson.

4727 Weedon, George   1730-1790
Valley Forge orderly book of General George Weedon of the Continental Army under command of General George Washington, in the campaign of 1777-8. Illustrated. New York: Arno Press, 1971. (New York: Dodd, Mead and Co., 1902) 323 p. Index.

An innkeeper in Fredericksburg, Virginia, before the Revolutionary War, he was commissioned early and became a Brigadier General in 1777. His orderly book details the movements, supplies, and battle plans of the army from Bucks County, Pennsylvania, in August 1777 through the battles of Brandywine and Valley Forge, May 1778.

4728 Weeks, Edward   **1898-**
In friendly candor. Boston: Little, Brown and Co., 1959. 301 p. Index.
    He joined the *Atlantic Monthly* staff in 1924 and in 1938 became its
Editor-in-Chief. Here he writes of his education, many of the friends and
authors he worked with, the cultural importance of reading and education, and some thoughts on editing and the changing times.

4729 Weeks, Edward   **1898-**
My green age. Boston: Little, Brown and Co., 1973. 342 p. Index.
    Editor of the *Atlantic Monthly* from 1938 to 1966, Weeks, as his preface
states, has tried "in this book to recapture the wonder and bewilderment
of one who was struggling to find where he belonged during the first forty
years of this fantastically changing century."

4730 Weeks, Edward   **1898-**
The open heart. Boston: Little, Brown and Co., 1955. 236 p. Index.
    During his long years as editor of the *Atlantic Monthly,* he traveled
widely in search of authors. This book tells of his travels, offering a rich
narrative of his favorite people and places.

4731 Weeks, Lewis George   **1893-1977**
Life-long love affair: the memoirs of Lewis George Weeks. Illustrated.
Foreword by James Daniel. Eulogy by Dana Forrest Kennedy. Postscript
by James Daniel. Westport, Connecticut: Anne Sutton Weeks, 1978.
138 p.
    A happy, articulate account of Week's Wisconsin boyhood, education
at the University of Wisconsin (to which he later donated a building), and
his career. As a field geologist he traveled throughout South America
locating oil sites. He had two exceptionally happy marriages and enjoyed
a retirement filled with good works.

4732 *Weidenfeld, Sheila Rabb   **1895-**
First lady's lady: with the Fords at the White House. Illustrated. New
York: G.P. Putnam's Sons, 1979. 419 p. Index.
    As Betty's Ford's press secretary, November 1974-January 1977,
Weidenfeld recalls events of family life at the White House during the
two-year recuperation from Watergate. Weidenfeld's chatty anecdotes are
often concerned with media and with style—the "decent, compassionate,"
folksy style of the Fords; the personalities and temperaments of the members of the first family; and the styles of the White House decor and the
Fords' clothing.

4733 Weil, Joseph R.   **1876-1976**
The con game and "Yellow Kid" Weil: the autobiography of the famous
con artist. New York: Dover Publications, Inc., 1974. (Chicago:
Ziff-Davis Publishing Co., 1948) 297 p.
    A man of many careers and con games, Weil is said to have been
America's most successful swindler. Here he describes his early years
learning the games and the skills which brought him over $8,000,000.

4734 Weinland, Henry A.   **b.1888**
Now the harvest: memories of a county agricultural agent. New York:
Exposition Press, 1957. 96 p.
    A thoughtful, at times philosophical, account of the author's first 32
years, describing his genesis and maturation as a county agricultural agent
in southern California at a time when the agents' functions were themselves maturing. His observations about politicking among agent
appointments and 4-H prizes are wry and insightful.

4735 Weinstein, Gregory   **1864-1953**
Ardent eighties and after: reminiscences of an interesting decade. New
York: Arno Press, 1975. (New York: International Press, 1928) 242 p.
Index.
    Good description of his hard life after immigration from Russia, his
early work in a print shop, a Jewish newspaper, and general adaption to
American life; with interesting sketches of several important social
reformers of the time.

4736 Weir, John Ferguson   **1841-1926**
The recollections of John Ferguson Weir, Director of the Yale School of
the Fine Arts, 1869-1913. Edited by Theodore Sizer. New York and New
Haven: N.Y. Historical Society; Associates in Fine Arts at Yale University, 1957. 93 p. Index.
    Director of Yale School of Fine Arts for 44 years, Weir was responsible
for considerable improvement in the school: he added sculpture, architecture, and art history to the curriculum, acquired the Jarves Collection of
early Italian pictures for the gallery, and encouraged professional art
education.

4737 *Weisbord, Vera Buch   **1895-**
Radical life. Appendices by Paul Buhle and Mary Jo Buhle. Illustrated.
Bloomington, Indiana: Indiana University Press, 1977. 330 p. Index.
    Weisbord writes with a novelist's consummate skill about the 1920's,
when she and her common-law husband, Albert Weisbord, were communist labor organizers in New Jersey, Pennsylvania, and North Carolina. Though educated at Hunter College and a tuberculosis victim, she
lived the life of the mill workers whose miseries she sought to remedy. She

was jailed for two months as a consequence of a bloody strike in Gastonia,
North Carolina, went north after a rigged trial and, with Albert, left the
local party over a doctrinal dispute. She remained a loyal Marxist despite
FBI harassment throughout the 1950's.

4738 Weissberger, L. Arnold   **1907-**
Famous faces: a photograph album of personal reminiscences. New York:
Harry N. Abrams, Inc., 1974. 443 p.
    Primarily a photograph album of show business and other famous
people, this volume also includes some brief anecdotes and comments by
the author about the occasions when the pictures were taken.

4739 Welch, Herbert   **1862-1969**
As I recall my past century. New York: Abingdon Press, 1962. 144 p.
    Written on that remote level of abstraction common to churchmen, the
book includes recollections of his early life and education and varied
assignments of his ministry, including the presidency of Ohio Wesleyan
University and several missionary posts in the Orient.

4740 Welch, Lew   **1926-1971**
I remain: the letters of Lew Welch and the correspondence of his friends:
Vol. 1: 1949-1960; Vol. 2: 1960-1972. Edited by Donald Allen. Illustrated.
Bolinas, California: Grey Fox Press, 1980. 2v.
    A fascinating but disturbing collection of letters from Welch, an aspir-
ing poet, to his mother and various friends, mostly poets, to whom he sent
texts of poems—Gary Snyder, his Reed College roommate; Jack Kerouac,
whose *On the Road* travels Welch at times imitated; and William Carlos
Williams, his mentor. He published one book in 1960 and two in 1965.
Welch's alcoholism contributed to his intermittent breakdowns, physical
and psychological; in 1971 he committed suicide.

4741 Welch, William Joseph   **1911-**
What happened in between: a doctor's story. New York: George Braziller,
Inc., 1972. 208 p.
    A specialist in internal medicine and cardiology, Dr. Welch believes in
the treatment of people rather than diseases and the importance of human
encounter between patient and doctor. He writes of his innocent childhood, the deprivations of the Great Depression, his successful advertising
agency, his decision to abandon it and study medicine, his encounter with
the extraordinary Gurdjieff, and his philosophy and career as a physician.

4742 Weld, Stephen Minot, Jr.   **1842-1920**
War diary and letters of Stephen Minot Weld, 1861-1865. Illustrated.
Foreword by David Donald. Afterword by Philip S. Weld. Boston:
Massachusetts Historical Society, 1979. (1912) 433 p. Index.
    Weld, a gifted writer, kept a diary throughout most of his
service—ultimately as a lt. colonel—in the 56th Massachusetts Division,
5th Regiment of the Union Army. He enlisted as a twenty-year-old Harvard graduate; the romance of the Union cause was soon overshadowed
by the difficulties of encampment in Tidewater, Virginia (lice, ticks, continual downpours). He dealt forcefully with insubordination and drunkenness among his troops, was imprisoned in Charleston, S.C., for months,
was released, and fought again against the South.

4743 Welk, Lawrence   **1904-**
Ah-one! ah-two! Life with my musical family. With Bernice McGeehan.
Englewood Cliffs, New Jersey: Prentice-Hall, Inc., 1974. 215 p.
    When ABC cancelled Welk's Saturday evening TV show, thousands of
loyal viewers protested. This book tells of his road tour from Hawaii to
New Jersey, of his relationship with his musical family, of his own
convictions, and of his triumphant return to TV and his millions of
viewers.

4744 Welk, Lawrence   **1904-**
My America, your America. With Bernice McGeehan. Englewood Cliffs,
New Jersey: Prentice-Hall, 1976. 182 p.
    Band leader Welk describes what life is like with his "Musical Family,"
all those who work as entertainers or behind the scenes during his band
shows. He enthusiastically explains his "System," the primary purpose of
which is to "develop people—to build humanity" by fulfilling their inborn
talents, and training all employees personally with concern for their "financial, emotional, educational, moral, and social" growth. Welk stresses
wholesomeness, piety, and happiness, and sees his system as "the Golden
Rule in action."

4745 Welk, Lawrence   **1904-**
This I believe. And Bernice McGeehan. Englewood Cliffs, New Jersey:
Prentice-Hall, 1979. 197 p.
    Band leader Welk wrote this book to express his belief in free enterprise
and to show people how hard work, fairness, and profit-sharing make
good sense and good business. He explains how he and his "family" (all
his employees and their families) work together to produce the shows, to
record music, and to run Welk's allied businesses—including a shopping
plaza, office building, apartment house, and restaurant.

4746 Welles, Gideon   **1802-1878**
The diary of Gideon Welles: Secretary of the Navy under Lincoln and

Johnson. Edited with introduction by Howard K. Beale. Asst., Alan W. Brownsword. New York: W.W. Norton & Co., Inc., 1960. (Boston: Houghton, Mifflin, 1911) 3v. Index.

Welles's candid diaries, kept assiduously while he was Secretary of the U.S. Navy under Lincoln and Johnson, shed considerable light on the Civil War and the beginning of the Reconstruction Era. He was concerned with naval military strategy and personnel and provides an insider's partisan perspective on the political scene. This new scholarly edition supplements the bowdlerized 1911 edition.

4747 *Welles, Winifred   1893-1939
The lost landscape: some memories of a family and a town in Connecticut, 1659-1906. New York: Henry Holt and Co., 1946. 299 p.

The story of her New England childhood (pp. 1-79), supplemented by tales of her family, events, and customs in Norwich which are a mixture of fact and fancy.

4748 Wellman, William Augustus   1896-1975
A short time for insanity: an autobiography. New York: Hawthorn Books, Inc., 1974. 276 p. Index.

A highly individual and outspoken movie director remembers events of his life through a haze of pain and opiates in a hospital.

4749 Wells, Charles Knox Polk   b.1851
Life and adventures of Polk Wells (Charles Knox Polk Wells) the notorious outlaw . . . Illustrated. Freeport, New York: Books for Libraries Press, 1971. (Halls, Missouri: G.A. Warnica, 1907?) 259 p.

An exciting career of lawlessness and daring deeds is presented by Wells, a man of warm and kindly heart despite his crimes. Written while he was an inmate of the penitentiary, the book is full of the frontier life of the West.

4750 Wells, Herbert George   1866-1946
see **James, Henry**

4751 *Werfel, Alma Maria Mahler   1879-1964
And the bridge is love. In collaboration with E.B. Ashton. New York: Harcourt, Brace and Co., 1958. 312 p. Index.

Raised among artists and intellectuals in Austria, she was married to Gustav Mahler and later to Franz Werfel. Her book recalls her rich and varied life in Europe and in the United States after she immigrated.

4752 West, Don   1907-1954
Broadside to the sun. New York: W.W. Norton and Co., Inc., 1946. 230 p.

Story of country life in the Arkansas Ozark mountains; typical of the postwar books on old-fashioned values, but realistic in practical details of daily life.

4753 West, Ellsworth Luce   1864-1920
Captain's papers: a log of whaling and other sea experiences. As told to Eleanor Ransom Mayhew. Foreword by Henry Beetle Hough. Illustrated. Barre, Massachusetts: Barre Publishers, 1965. 172 p.

West was a whaler and captain of several whaling ships, 1882-1899, engaging in a highly dangerous but lucrative trade; each whale was worth around $10,000 and was captured with all the excitement of Moby Dick. When he ran the *Horatio* aground on a coral reef in 1899 and it sank ignominiously, West turned to transporting mail, passengers, and supplies to Nome, Alaska, during the Gold Rush—duller but safer.

4754 West, J. Bernard   1912?-
Upstairs at the White House: my life with the First Ladies. With Mary Lynn Kotz. New York: Coward, McCann & Geoghegan, Inc., 1973. 381 p. Index.

As assistant and chief usher of the White House, West was involved in all domestic decisions and all social functions for six presidents and first ladies. Here he recalls those hectic years with humor and understanding.

4755 West, Jerry   1938-
Mr. Clutch; the Jerry West story. With Bill Libby. Illustrated. Englewood Cliffs, New Jersey: Prentice-Hall, 1969. 242 p.

At time of publication, West was considered one of the greatest basketball players in the history of the game, especially famous for his clutch shot and his extraordinary ability in defensive as well as offensive play. His book is of his life in the game.

4756 *West, Jessamyn   1902-
Double discovery: a journey. New York: Harcourt Brace Jovanovich, 1980. 233 p.

West combines letters, a travel diary, and her retrospective interpretations to present a charming montage of a four-month trip from California to New York by train, and then to England, Ireland, and Paris in 1929. Already an accomplished writer, she made observations that are pointed, picturesque, and personal. Her motto: "Never regret travel. Better see the world and cry, than stay home dry-eyed."

4757 *West, Jessamyn   1902-
Hide and seek. New York: Harcourt, Brace, Jovanovich, Inc., 1973. 310 p.

Written during a three-month vacation period alone on the banks of the Colorado River, this work discusses her need for solitude, her special love of nature, the difficulty women writers have in finding solitude, and the guilt they feel having found it.

4758 *West, Jessamyn   1902-
To see the dream. New York: Harcourt, Brace and Co., 1957. 314 p.

Based on a journal she kept while living at her home in Napa, California, and while working in Hollywood with William Wyler, who was converting her novel, *The Friendly Persuasion,* into a movie, her book is a spirited celebration of life.

4759 *West, Jessamyn   1902-
The woman said yes: encounters with life and death: memoirs. New York: Harcourt Brace Jovanovich, 1976. 180 p.

The lives of two sisters and their illnesses: one fights to live and the other embraces death on her own terms. Somehow both courageously affirm the value of life in this moving book, written by a respected novelist.

4760 *West, Mae   1892-1980
Goodness had nothing to do with it. Englewood Cliffs, New Jersey: Prentice-Hall, 1959. 271 p.

A self-proclaimed sex symbol and legend describes her successes in vaudeville, on Broadway, in touring plays, movies, radio, and dinner theaters.

4761 *West, Mae   1892-1980
Mae West on sex, health, and ESP. London: W.H. Allen, 1975. 237 p.

In a fast-talking, sassy book, Mae West gives her advice on the three topics in the title, telling something about her experiences in the process. She's all for good nutrition, no alcohol, and sex.

4762 *West, Mae   1892-1980
The wit and wisdom of Mae West. Illustrated. Berkeley Windhover Books. New York: Berkeley Publishing Corp., 1977. (New York: G.P. Putnam's Sons, 1967) 92 p.

Actress West's wit and wisdom consists of one-liners and double entendres about her voluptuous figure ("Cultivate your curves—they may be dangerous but they won't be avoided."), sex ("Why should I do good when I'm packing them in because I'm bad?"), men ("I like two types of men—domestic and foreign."), and her reputation for seductiveness ("The score never interested me, only the game.")

4763 *Westcott, Cynthia   1898-
Plant doctoring is fun. Princeton: Van Nostrand, 1957. 280 p. Index.

A graduate of Wellesley with a Ph.D. from Cornell, she established a career as The Plant Doctor during the Depression. Since then several of her books on plants have become classics, while she has traveled to lecture at garden clubs, visit and treat gardens all over the United States.

4764 Westmore, Frank   1923-
The Westmores of Hollywood. And Muriel Davidson. Philadelphia: J.B. Lippincott, 1976. 256 p. Index.

With numerous anecdotes about Hollywood stars in relation to their make-up, Frank Westmore discusses the rise and semi-decline of the dynasty of Westmores, Hollywood's supreme make-up artists. His father, George, began the first Hollywood cinema make-up department in 1917, eventually followed by his six sons, Mont (1902-40), Perc (1904-70), Ern (1904-68), Wally (1906-73), Bud (1918-73), and Frank. Despite many personality problems, conflicts, divorces, suicides, and heart attacks, the Westmores continue their artistry.

4765 Westmoreland, William Childs   1914-
A soldier reports. Garden City, New York: Doubleday & Co., 1976. 446 p. Index.

A veteran of forty-years service to his country on and off the battlefield, General Westmoreland writes of the shaping of his life and career, his pride in being a professional soldier, and his part in momentous recent events, especially the Vietnam War.

4766 *Weston, Mary, pseud.
see ***Merritt, Onera Amelia**

4767 Weybright, Victor   1903-1978
The making of a publisher; a life in the 20th century book revolution. New York: Reynal & Co., dist. by William Morrow & Co., Inc., 1967. 360 p. Index.

Growing up in rural Maryland, Weybright dreamed of making great literature easily available to the general public. Ultimately he realized that vision in the establishment of Mentor and Signet paperback books. His story reflects idealistic humanism as well as a realistic assessment of the competitive world of publishing.

4768 Weygandt, Cornelius   **1871-1957**
On the edge of evening: the autobiography of a teacher and writer who holds to the old ways. New York: G.P. Putnam's Sons, 1946. 217 p. Index.

A professor of literature at the University of Pennsylvania and author of seventeen other books writes with warmth and humor of the daily life and background from which those books evolved.

4769 *Wharton, May Cravath   **b.1873**
Doctor woman of the Cumberlands: the autobiography of May Cravath Wharton, M.D. Illustrated. Pleasant Hill, Tennessee: Uplands, 1972. (1953) 214 p.

Wharton's engaging narrative focuses on the forty years of her career as a physician near Crossville, Tennessee. Her services began by treating diseases (often the result of malnutrition and epidemics), expanded to include new baby care, advice on nutrition and sanitation, and eventually resulted in the building of a community hospital and medical center. Wharton loves her work, the people, and the Cumberland region.

4770 Wheeler, Burton Kendall   **1882-1975**
Yankee from the West: the candid, turbulent life story of the Yankee-born U.S. Senator from Montana. With Paul F. Healy. Garden City, New York: Doubleday & Co., Inc., 1962. 436 p. Index.

The controversial Democratic senator from Montana, champion of individualism in politics, did not hesitate to fight for his principles against all comers, from the Anaconda Company to FDR.

4771 Wheeler, John Neville   **1886-1973**
I've got good news for you. New York: E.P. Dutton & Co., Inc., 1961. 320 p. Index.

He started his journalism career as a New York *Herald* correspondent at Columbia University during his undergraduate days. He later became a sportswriter, then a top-notch reporter and syndicate writer. His book includes stories of many famous contemporary writers of news and fiction such as Ring Lardner, Richard Harding Davis, and Ernest Hemingway.

4772 Wheeler, Post   **1869-1956**
Dome of many-coloured glass. And Hallie Ermine Rives (Mrs. Post Wheeler). Garden City, New York: Doubleday, 1955. 878 p.

An unusual collaborative memoir written by a wife and husband, both professional writers who traveled extensively during his long career in the diplomatic service.

4773 *Wheelwright, Valborg Rasmussen   **1875-1957**
Valborg: an autobiography of Valborg Rasmussen Wheelwright. As told to Lorin F. Wheelwright. Introduction. Illustrated. Salt Lake City: Pioneer Music Press, 1978. 224 p. Index.

Wheelwright describes her impoverished childhood in Copenhagen. At twelve she was converted to Mormonism and emigrated to Utah, where she worked as a maid. Ever industrious and enterprising, she served as a missionary, midwife, social worker, community organizer, and was faithful to Mormonism and her family.

4774 Whelen, Townsend   **1877-1961**
Mister rifleman. And Bradford Angier. Epilogue by Bradford Angier. Illustrated. Los Angeles: Petersen Publishing Co., 1965. 377 p.

A thorough, articulate, abundantly illustrated account of Whelen's career as a rifleman in the U.S. Army, 1896-1936, intertwined with a history of the development of the American breech-loading rifle. Whelan was a woodsman extraordinaire and camped and hunted game, big and small, throughout British Columbia, the Canal Zone (where he was stationed while the Panama Canal was being constructed), and the United States—of which he provides fascinating naturalistic lore. Whelen also includes articles he wrote as rifle and shooting editor of *Guns and Ammo Magazine*, 1959-1962.

4775 Whisler, Ezra Leroy   **b.1881**
Shepherd of the Cowlitz: the autobiography of Ezra Leroy Whisler. Exposition by Geraldine Crill Eller. Illustrated. Elgin, Illinois: Brethren Publishing House, 1957. 169 p.

Whisler's own account of his life and ministry as a Church of the Brethren preacher in Richland Valley (Washington) for 36 years is supplemented by a biographical account. The untutored Whisler earned a living as a country storekeeper and particularly enjoyed a happy marriage, a flourishing garden, and woodworking.

4776 White, Elliott P., Jr.   **1903-**
The beautiful Ohio: a pageant of yesterday. Illustrated by George Joseph. New York: Exposition Press, 1950. 196 p.

A business executive from Louisville, Kentucky, muses about life in the good old days before F.D. Roosevelt's New Deal. Described as "a saga of ordinary American life," the book emphasizes a belief in individualism, parental authority, and the freedom to achieve, all of which have been diminished by the increasing power of government.

4777 White, Elwyn Brooks   **1899-**
Letters. Collaborated with Dorothy Lobrano Guth. Edited by Dorothy

Lobrano Guth. Autobiographical commentary by E.B. White. Illustrated. New York: Harper & Row, 1976. 686 p. Index.

This annotated volume is a selection of several hundred letters White wrote throughout sixty years; they cover his high school and college days, his work on *The New Yorker,* his forty-year marriage to Katharine Angell (a superlative *New Yorker* editor), fatherhood, life in New York City and rural Maine, and his meticulous writing of *Charlotte's Web, Stuart Little,* and other classics. Down-to-earth, chatty, witty, and humorous, White's letters are also classics—seemingly simple, but inimitable.

4778 White, Elwyn Brooks   **1899-**
Points of my compass: letters from the East, the West, the South. New York: Harper & Row, 1962. 240 p.

Mostly written for the *New Yorker* between 1954 and 1961, these episodes depict exciting days as well as the quiet New England life he preferred, all described with wit and wisdom.

4779 White, Eugene Elliot   **b.1885**
Experiences of a special Indian agent. Introduction by Edward Everett Dale. Norman: University of Oklahoma Press, 1965. (First published as: *Service on the Indian reservations.* Little Rock: Diploma Press, Arkansas Democrat Co., 1893) 340 p.

Appointed at age 31 as a special Indian agent, he was twenty years younger than any of the other four agents. White set out to learn about his job to investigate Indian problems and be a "trouble shooter." His experiences among the various tribes make delightful and informative reading.

4780 White, Hants A.
How I got published: a Maine author's struggle for recognition. Mars Hill, Maine: Merit Publishing Co., 1977. 348 p.

Farmer White struggled to succeed in business and in writing while holding to his bedrock moral standards and his affection for people, whatever race, color, or creed. Major publishing firms would not publish his books, and vanity presses stole his money, but he persevered and finally got his work published with minimal acclaim—enough to keep him writing. An inspiring book by a stubborn, moralistic, and honest American.

4781 White, Minor   **1908-1976**
Minor White: rites & passages: his photographs accompanied by excerpts from his diaries and letters. Biographical essay by James Baker Hall. Illustrated. Millerton, New York: Aperture Monograph, 1978. 140 p.

A long biographical essay describes Minor White's life, particularly his adult years when he became a famous photograher, teacher, and editor. The excerpts from White's diaries and letters illustrate Hall's point that photographs were White's way of communicating—he would answer letters by sending a copy of *Aperture* magazine to the questioner. The Zen-like quality of his life, his methods of teaching, and his photography—beautifully illustrated in this volume—are visible through words and pictures.

4782 White, Robb   **1909-**
Our Virgin Island. Garden City, New York: Doubleday and Co., Inc., 1953. 284 p.

An author with the dream of settling on a British Virgin Island tells how he and his wife managed to establish a home and career in an exotic and sometimes difficult environment.

4783 White, Theodore Harold   **1915-**
In search of history: a personal adventure. New York: Harper & Row, 1979. 561 p. Index.

Historian and writer White investigates the question "How is history made?", exploring his Boston childhood, revolution and war in Mao Tse-tung's China, World War II in Asia and Europe, and America—tranquil under Eisenhower and dramatic under Kennedy. Finally, he describes how political power often backfires.

4784 White, Walter   **1893-1955**
Man called White: the autobiography of Walter White. New York: Arno Press, 1969. (New York: The Viking Press, 1948) 382 p. Index.

Light-skinned, blond, and blue-eyed, White could have "passed," but chose instead to write fiction and fact about being Negro in America and to work for the N.A.A.C.P. most of his life.

4785 White, William Allen   **1868-1944**
Autobiography of William Allen White. New York: The Macmillan Co., 1946. 669 p. Index.

Newspaper and radio journalist, whose weekly, the Emporia *Gazette,* was distributed and respected nationally. This is a rich narrative of his active life in local and national politics, literature, and journalism.

4786 White, William Allen   **1868-1944**
Letters of William Allen White and a young man. Edited by Gil Wilson. New York: The John Day Co., 1948. 116 p.

The young man is Gil Wilson, whose letters to and from White (1935-1943) depict his years as a struggling young artist and White's support and patronage during that time.

4787 White, William Allen   **1868-1944**
Selected letters of William Allen White: 1899-1943. Edited with introduction by Walter Johnson. New York: Greenwood Press, Publishers, 1968. (New York: Henry Holt and Co., 1947) 460 p. Index.
    Described as a middle-class liberal and spokesman for the greatness of small-town America, White was a nationally known and respected journalist. His letters are a record of the changing American scene during 44 years.

4788 White Bull, Joseph (Pte-san-hunka)   **b.1850**
The warrior who killed Custer: the personal narrative of Chief Joseph White Bull. Edited, translated, with foreword and introduction by James E. Howard. Illustrated by Joseph White Bull. Landmark Edition. Lincoln: University of Nebraska Press, 1976. (1968) 84 p.
    Teton Dakota Chief White Bull's principal claim to fame, though not what he considers his bravest deed, was killing General Custer at the Battle of Little Big Horn. Each line of White Bull's narrative is translated and commented on, as are his interesting drawings.

4789 Whitehouse, Arthur George Joseph   **1895-**
Fledgling. New York: Duell, Sloan and Pearce, 1964. 307 p. Index.
    An aviation writer describes his assignment to the English Royal Flying Corps during World War I. His adventures included surviving defective planes, crash landings, scouting trips hemmed in by fog, and numerous other exciting events.

4790 *Whiteley, Opal Stanley   **1899-**
Opal Whiteley: the unsolved mystery: together with Opal Whiteley's diary, "The Journal of an Understanding Heart." London: Putnam, 1962. (1920) 294 p.
    A record of her early childhood, claimed to have been written in about her sixth year and published in her twentieth, is a remarkable depiction of a child's inner life. She believed she was a descendant of French royalty, secretly given to foster parents who raised her in Oregon. She and her book became literary and social curiosities for more than a decade.

4791 Whitewolf, Jim   **1878-1955?**
Jim Whitewolf: the life of a Kiowa Apache Indian. Edited with introduction and epilogue by Charles S. Brent. New York: Dover Publications, Inc., 1969. 144 p. Index.
    The incursions of the white man's culture which undermined the foundations of the native tribal culture had a profound effect on Whitewolf, an ordinary member of a Kiowa Apache tribe. His story mirrors the reactions to some of these changes—individual property ownership, Christianity, modern education, and alcohol.

4792 Whitfield, Joseph
Treasure of El Dorado: featuring "The Dawn Breakers." Illustrated. Washington: Occidental Press, 1977. 213 p.
    Joseph Whitfield, after a long period of meditation, communicates with El Dorado via mental telepathy. Through five chapters entitled "The Unfolding Plan," Joseph and El Dorado discuss most of the philosophical questions that have ever concerned man, and El Dorado provides answers. There are imaginary journeys to Venus, Saturn, and Orion, and a discussion of the nuclear dynamics of cosmic sex.

4793 Whitlock, Brand   **1869-1934**
Forty years of it. New York: Appleton, 1970. (1914) 374 p.
    The years before World War I were years of hope and faith in human nature when men like Whitlock battled the forces of evil, worked for equitable adjustment of the relations of mankind, and believed in pure ideals of justice. As a four-term reform mayor of Toledo, he maintained his belief in the perfectability of mankind and the great "dream of social harmony always prefigured in human thought as the city."

4794 Whitman, George Washington   **1829-1901**
Civil War letters of George Washington Whitman. Edited by Jerome M. Loving. Foreword by Gay Wilson Allen. Durham, North Carolina: Duke University Press, 1975. 173 p. Index.
    His diary (1861-63) and letters to his mother and brothers comprise an authentic record of a Union soldier's experiences of the Civil War. Walt Whitman's brother survived the bloody fighting at Second Bull Run, First Fredericksburg, Mississippi, Spotsylvania Court House, the siege of Petersburg, and capture and imprisonment by the Confederates. He was a naive observer but his writing makes a strong impact because of its straightforward simplicity.

4795 *Whitman, Sarah Helen (Power)   **1803-1878**
Poe's Helen remembers. Edited by John Carl Miller. Illustrated. Charlottesville: University Press of Virginia, 1979. 528 p. Index.
    Sarah Whitman, a gifted poet and critic, is best remembered as Edgar Allan Poe's fiancée. Her correspondence with John Henry Ingram, Poe's English admirer and biographer, forms a basis of Poe scholarship.

4796 Whitman, Walt   **1819-1892**
Autobiographia; or the story of a life: selected from his prose writings. Folcroft, Pennsylvania: Folcroft Library Editions, 1972. (New York: Charles L. Webster & Co., 1892) 205 p.

A collection of autobiographical prose, including diary entries, edited to give a consecutive account of the poet's life in his characteristic language. Specimen Days furnishes the bulk of the passages but is augmented by the author's hospital diary, nature notes, travel notes, and other selections.

4797 Whitman, Walt   **1819-1892**
Calamus: a series of letters written during the years 1868-1880 to a young friend (Peter Doyle). Edited with introduction by Richard Maurice Bucke. Reprint of the 1898 issue first published in 1897 by Putnam, London. Norwood, Pennsylvania: Norwood Editions, 1974. (Boston: L. Maynard, 1897) 173 p.
    A reprint of the poet's letters to Peter Doyle echoing the emotional turmoil, the reciprocal love relationship, and the sense of community brotherhood contained in his pre-Civil War "Calamus" poems.

4798 Whitman, Walt   **1819-1892**
The correspondence. Edited by Edwin Haviland Miller. New York: New York University Press, 1961-1977. 6v. Index.
    Five main volumes plus the supplement include almost 2900 letters by Whitman, whom the editor names as "America's greatest poet." Some letters indicate the poet's concern with the image he projected; others reveal his warmth and simplicity.

4799 Whitman, Walt   **1819-1892**
Daybooks and notebooks. Edited by William White. New York: New York University Press, 1978. 3v. Index.
    The editor observes that this "should have been called Daybooks, 1876-1891, Diary in Canada, Miscellaneous Journals, Autobiographical Notes, Words, The Primer of Words, Other Notebooks." The Daybooks consist largely of shipping information and sales figures of Whitman's self-published books, tax bills, a record (but not copies of) his correspondence, notes on his comings and goings and important events ("Emerson died, aged 79.") The copious notes provide an interpretive matrix for the cryptic, fragmentary text.

4800 Whitman, Walt   **1819-1892**
Faint clews and indirections: mss. of Walt Whitman and his family. Edited with preface by Clarence Gohdes and Rollo G. Silver. Durham, North Carolina: Duke University Press, 1949. 250 p. Index.
    Previously unpublished manuscripts from the Trent collection at Duke University consist of poems, prose fragments, letters, and postcards by Whitman, and letters to him from his mother and family.

4801 Whitman, Walt   **1819-1892**
Letters written by Walt Whitman to his mother, 1866-1872. Introduction note by Rollo G. Silver. Illustrated. Folcroft, Pennsylvania: Folcroft Library Editions, 1977. (New York: Alfred F. Goldsmith, 1936) 71 p.
    Whitman, a clerk in the Attorney General's office in Washington, D.C., wrote dutiful letters (more-or-less weekly) to his mother in Camden, New Jersey, about his health, his contacts with men he had nursed during the Civil War, the weather, and mutual friends.

4802 Whitman, Walt   **1819-1892**
Walt Whitman's backward glances: a backward glance o'er travel'd roads and two contributary essays hitherto uncollected. Edited with an introduction on the evolution of the text by Sculley Bradley and John A. Stevenson. Philadelphia: University of Pennsylvania Press, 1947. 51 p.
    A study of the evolution of Whitman's essay, "A backward glance o'er travel'd roads," through its early forms and revisions, showing his methods of composition, his reflections on approaching old age, and his purposes and meaning in Leaves of Grass.

4803 Whitman, Walt   **1819-1892**
Whitman and Rolleston: a correspondence. Introduction and notes by Horst Frenz. Indiana University Publications, Humanities Series, No. 26. Bloomington: Indiana University, 1951. 137 p. Index.
    An Irish poet and author, Rolleston founded the Rhymers Club with W.B. Yeats and Ernest Rhys and became an early admirer of Whitman. Their correspondence reflects their friendship, their ideas about poetry, and Rolleston's promotion of Whitman's poetry in Ireland, Russia, and Germany.

4804 Whitmore, Terry
Memphis, Nam, Sweden; the autobiography of a Black American exile. As told to Richard Weber. Garden City, New York: Doubleday & Co., 1971. 189 p.
    The experiences of a Black Marine who fought in Vietnam, was wounded, hospitalized in Japan, then ordered back to Vietnam. Instead he managed to escape and went to Sweden by way of Russia.

4805 Whitney, Cornelius Vanderbilt   **1899-**
High peaks. Foreword by Holman Hamilton. Lexington: The University Press of Kentucky, 1977. 127 p.
    Each of Whitney's short chapters describes a "high peak" of his life, including marriage to Mary Lou; financing Gone with the Wind, Marineland of Florida, and Pan American Airways; experiences in Egypt

and Japan during World War II; establishing the Buffalo Bill Museum in Cody, Wyoming; and entertaining Princess Margaret in Kentucky.

4806 *Whitney, Eleanor (Searle)
Invitation to joy; a personal story. Illustrated. New York: Harper & Row, 1971. 195 p.
As Mrs. Cornelius Vanderbilt Whitney she had all that material wealth could provide. She describes her glamourous, exciting life and some of the famous people she knew. After her divorce she became an "aware Christian" and found a new kind of joy.

4807 Whitney, Frank Peck   **b.1875**
School and I: the autobiography of an Ohio schoolmaster. Introduction and notes by Horst Frenz. Indiana University Publications, Humanities Series, No. 26. Yellow Springs, Ohio: The Antioch Press, 1957. 173 p. Index.
An educator in the Ohio public schools for over fifty years discusses his life and educational theory.

4808 Whittier, John Greenleaf   **1807-1892**
Letters. Edited by John B. Pickard. Cambridge: Belknap Press of Harvard University Press, 1975. 3v. Index.
Volume I: 1828-45 includes all extant letters from this period. Volume II: 1846-1860 includes all extant letters. Volume III is a selection of 527 letters from the 4500 letters he wrote after 1861. From the late 1860's Whittier was a national poet whose popularity rivaled that of Longfellow, hence the increase in the volume of his correspondence.

4809 Whittier, John Greenleaf   **1807-1892**
Whittier and the Cartlands: letters and comments. Edited by Martha Hale Schackford. Wakefield, Massachusetts: The Montrose Press, 1950. 91 p.
Family letters between the cousins were written between 1839 and 1888. These, with recollections of his oldest grandchildren and two short essays, portray Whittier in warm family relationships. Includes genealogy.

4810 Whittier, John Greenleaf   **1807-1892**
Whittier's unknown romance: letters to Elizabeth Lloyd. With an introduction by Marie V. Denervaud. New York: Haskell House, 1973. (Boston: Houghton Mifflin, 1922) 72 p.
Whittier and Elizabeth Lloyd were deeply attracted to each other, and, although they were of differing temperaments, both treasured their rich understanding and friendship. Most of these letters were written during 1859-1860.

4811 *Widdemer, Margaret   **1889-1978**
Golden friends I had: unrevised memories of Margaret Widdemer. Garden City, New York: Doubleday & Co., 1964. 340 p.
As part of the New York literary scene since the Twenties Widdemer knew, and here describes, famous friends. She writes of their personal lives and talents, their feuds and friendships, and her theories about developing literary movements as well as her own life.

4812 Wiener, Norbert   **1894-1964**
Ex-prodigy: my childhood and youth. New York: Simon & Schuster, 1953. 309 p. Index.
A distinguished professor of mathematics at Massachusetts Institute of Technology, Wiener published *Cybernetics* in 1948, dealing with the science of communications in man and machine. This book deals with the period in which he was a prodigy, beginning college before twelve and completing his doctorate before nineteen; he is especially interested in the problems resulting from the acceleration of his youth and how he resolved them.

4813 Wiener, Norbert   **1894-1964**
I am a mathematician: the later life of a prodigy. An autobiographical account of the mature years and career of Norbert Wiener, professor of mathematics at The Massachusetts Institute of Technology and a continuation of the account of his childhood in *Ex-Prodigy.* Garden City, New York: Doubleday & Co., 1956. 380 p. Index.
In technical language, Wiener, who earned a Harvard Ph.D. at 18, discusses his 36-year career as a mathematics professor at MIT, including international teaching and conferences. He describes the work of a number of modern mathematicians and physicists and shows how it relates to his own contributions, including potential theory, prime number theory, and cybernetics.

4814 Wiesel, Elie   **1928-**
A Jew today. Translated by Marion Wiesel. New York: Vintage Books, 1979. (New York: Random House, 1978) 247 p.
Wiesel writes introspectively on what it means to be Jewish in a world that hates Jews. The book is composed of anecdotes and diary entries concerning his thoughts on different meanings of Judaism around the world.

4815 Wilbur, Ray Lyman   **1875-1949**
The memoirs of Ray Lyman Wilbur. Edited by Edgar Eugene Robinson and Paul Carroll Edwards. Stanford: Stanford University Press, 1960. 687 p. Index.

He achieved national recognition as a medical doctor, educator, humanitarian, and public servant. Raised on the Western frontier, he attended Stanford University where he later served as president for 25 years, and became Secretary of the Interior under Herbert Hoover. An outstanding record of his life and times, the book lucidly describes the impact of the modern world on an individual.

4816 *Wildenhain, Marguerite   **1896-**
Invisible core; a potter's life and thoughts. Photos by Fran Ortiz. Palo Alto, California: Pacific Books, 1973. 207 p.
Warm, human stories of her student days at the Bauhaus, the artists who taught her, the hard work in Europe and in establishing her Pond Farm School in California. In addition Wildenhain writes about problems in art, education, pottery and nature, revealing her awareness, personal integrity, and dedication to her art.

4817 Wilder, Alec   **1907-**
Letters I never mailed. Boston: Little, Brown and Co., 1975. 243 p.
An unconventional, self-confessed maverick, composer of orchestral, chamber, and operatic works and popular songs, Wilder's book is made up of purported letters never mailed to friends, enemies, critics, and acquaintances.

4818 *Wilder, Laura (Ingalls)   **1867-1957**
West from home: letters of Laura Ingalls Wilder to Almanzo Wilder: San Francisco 1915. Edited by Roger Lea MacBridge. Historical setting by Margot Patterson Doss. New York: Harper & Row Publishers, 1974. 124 p.
For two months in 1915 during the Panama-Pacific International Exposition in San Francisco, she visited her daughter and wrote letters home to her husband describing the wonders of the trip.

4819 Wiles, Ralph William   **b.1882**
Pipe dreams and memories: an autobiography. Illustrated. New York: The William-Frederick Press, 1953. 312 p.
This narrative reflects a confused and chaotic life. Reared in poverty in Nova Scotia by a sickly stepmother and an aged, indifferent father, Wiles escaped to a logger's life in upstate New York. He was "impressed" into the U.S. Army, served in the Philippines (suppressing the Moro tribesmen of Mindanao), Hawaii, and the Western plains, where he spent much time in whorehouses. He eventually married a good woman and in retirement tried, unsuccessfully, to become a novelist.

4820 Wilk, Max   **1920-**
Every day's a matinee: memoirs scribbled on a dressing room door. New York: W.W. Norton & Co., Inc., 1975. 288 p. Index.
Stage-struck at an early age, Wilk has acted in summer stock, produced shows for the Air Force during World War II, and has written for stage, radio, TV, and movies. His memories are about many show-business greats and their world.

4821 Wilkens, Leonard   **1937-**
Lenny Wilkens story. Introduction by Father Thomas Mannion. New York: Eriksson, 1974. 174 p.
A successful basketball player (eight All-Star games) played with three different professional teams and coached as well. Here he talks about his career, contracts, salaries, integration, team spirit, trades, and other players he has known or played against.

4822 Wilkes, Charles   **1798-1877**
Autobiography of Rear Admiral Charles Wilkes, U.S. Navy, 1798-1877. Edited by William James Morgan (et al.). Introduction by John D.H. Kane, Jr. Illustrated. Washington D.C.: Naval History Division, Department of the Navy, 1978. 944 p. Index.
Rear Admiral Wilkes draws from voluminous diaries and an extensive memory in describing his 65 years of service in the U.S. Navy (1818-1873). He offers a vivid description of early navy life and keen observations on politics, society, and culture. He commanded the U.S. Exploring Expedition, which in four years identified the Antarctic as a continent and explored vast areas of the South Pacific.

4823 Wilkins, James F.   **b.1888**
An artist on the overland trail: the 1849 diary and sketches of James F. Wilkins. Illustrated. Edited by John Francis McDermott. San Marino, California: The Huntington Library, 1968. 143 p.
A portrait painter from St. Louis, Wilkins went on the overland trail to California in 1849 and, "with a view of furnishing a Panorama of the Plains, from Independence to San Francisco," painted the scenery and the people he saw. His diary and watercolor sketches make his journey vivid.

4824 *Wilkinson, Eliza (Yonge)
Letters of Eliza Wilkinson during the invasion and possession of Charlestown, S.C. Arranged by Caroline Gilman. New York: Samuel Colman, 1839. 108 p.
A series of twelve letters written in 1782 by a young widow who lived at Yonge's Island near Charleston, South Carolina. She had to flee from

British troops several times. The final letter celebrates the surrender of Cornwallis.

4825 Wilkinson, Herbert E.   **1892-**
Sun over Cerro Gordo. Ames: The Iowa State College Press, 1952. 289 p.
    The author recalls his boyhood on an Iowa farm in Cerro Gordo County at the turn of the century. He tells of riding behind a team of runaway horses, his first day of school, the advent of the party line, his father's horse trading, and other nostalgic scenes from a bygone era.

4826 Wilkinson, James   **1757-1825**
Memoirs of my own times. New York: AMS Press, 1973. (Philadelphia: A. Small, 1816) 4v.
    Wilkinson's career included service during the Revolution, Indian Wars, and War of 1812. His controversial activities in connection with Aaron Burr and later with an abortive campaign against Montreal led to a general court martial and inquiries into his actions. He attempts to vindicate himself, claiming to have been persecuted by John Randolph and President Madison. Volume IV contains diagrams and plans of battles and campaigns.

4827 *Williams, Alice Cary   **1892-**
Thru the turnstile: tales of my two centuries. Illustrated by Samual H. Bryant. Boston: Houghton Mifflin Co., 1976. 150 p.
    Williams writes of her golden childhood in Boston and on Nantucket Island at the turn of the century. A spirited lass, daughter of Tufts Medical School Dean Harold Williams, she was befriended by her parents' intimates, including Julia Ward Howe and William James. As a young child she was once given a lily by Oscar Wilde.

4828 Williams, Billy Leo   **1938-**
Billy, the classic hitter. And Irv Haag. Chicago: Rand, McNally & Co., 1974. 205 p.
    During fourteen years with the Chicago Cubs, Williams broke many records and was tops in several categories: batting average (1972); runs (1970); hits (1970). Here he tells about some memorable games and seasons.

4829 Williams, Billy Leo   **1938-**
Iron man. With Rick Simon. Illustrated. Open Door Books. Chicago, Illinois: Children's Press, 1970. 64 p.
    The story of a Black professional baseball player and how he worked his way up is presented in this series intended as career guidance for young people.

4830 *Williams, Celia Ann
Diary of a teacher along the journey to Siberia. New York: Exposition, 1972. 156 p.
    In 1967 Williams' contract as a teacher in the Springfield, Missouri, Public Schools was not renewed—"for unethical conduct, insubordination, and inadequacy as a teacher." Here she protests the injustice of this action offering letters, bulletins from administrators, and quotations from the Manual of Operations in support of her assertions of innocence.

4831 Williams, Clyde Elmer   **1893-**
Bridging the gap: my contribution to the growth of industrial research. Arranged and edited by Arthur E. Focke. Cincinnati: Creative Publishers, 1976. 140 p. Index.
    From 1929-1941 and 1945-1958, metallurgist Williams was director of Battelle Memorial Institute (Columbus, Ohio), a nonprofit technological research organization doing $23,000,000 worth of sponsored research annually, as of 1957. He discusses some of Battelle's major projects, including research on bituminous coal and xerography. During World War II, as chairman of the war Metallurgy Committee, he explored sources and uses of tin, aluminum, and titanium.

4832 Williams, Edward Bennett   **1920-**
One man's freedom. Introduction by Eugene V. Rostow. New York: Atheneum, 1962. 344 p. Index.
    A staunch defender of Constitutional rights, he records trials and documents his concern for individual freedoms guaranteed by the Bill of Rights.

4833 Williams, Edward D.   **1921-**
The first Black captain. New York: Vantage, 1974. 110 p.
    One Black man's struggle to rise from a ghetto community to attain dignity and recognition in the police department of Newark. He moved from narcotics detective, to patrol sergeant, to lieutenant, and then captain. He hopes his story will motivate and encourage other disadvantaged youths to seek attainable goals.

4834 Williams, Hank, Jr.   **1949-**
Living proof: an autobiography. With Michael Bane. Illustrated. New York: G.P. Putnam's Sons, 1979. 222 p. Index.
    In a narrative reminiscent of the country music he sings, the son of the idolized Hank Williams tells how he followed in his father's footsteps, stumbling along the road to fame as an entertainer accompanied by drugs,

liquor, and women. After his face was badly injured in a fall down a mountain in 1975, Williams learned love, fortitude, and restraint. He abandoned drugs and liquor, married, and exorcised his father's ghost by making his own music.

4835 Williams, James   **b.1805**
Narrative of James Williams, an American slave, who was for several years a driver on a cotton plantation in Alabama. Philadelphia: Rhistoric Pubs., 1969. (New York: American Anti-Slavery Society, 1838) 108 p.
    Williams' narrative describes his youth as a domestic servant and later experience as plantation driver of his fellow slaves, forced to whip his peers. He escaped in 1837 and was dispatched to England for safety when slave-catchers nearly caught up with him in New York. When it was first published, this book aroused controversy as to its veracity, but it is accepted as an authentic description of slave life whether or not it is true in every detail of time and place.

4836 Williams, John   **1664-1729**
The redeemed captive returning to Zion: or, a faithful history of remarkable occurrences in the captivity and deliverance. Preface to 1853 edition by Stephen W. Williams. Illustrated. Garland Library of Narratives of North American Indian Captives, v. 5. New York: Garland Pub., 1978. (Boston: Samuel Phillips, 1707) 192 p.
    A Protestant clergyman recounts with horror and indignation the events of the capture of himself and his family in King Philip's War 1706-7. He was held captive in Montreal and Quebec and found greatest humiliation in being associated with "Popish" Jesuits, who inhibited his practice of Protestantism.

4837 Williams, John Alfred   **1925-**
Flashbacks; a twenty-year diary of article writing. Garden City, New York: Doubleday (Anchor Press), 1973. 440 p.
    A collection of 24 articles about being a Black writer in the United States covering the period from the early 1950's to 1971, some topical, some about personalities, some personal. He encountered many obstacles as a Black free-lance writer for white publications and prefaces each article with an explanation of how it came to be written.

4838 Williams, Oscar Waldo   **1853-1946**
Pioneer surveyor/frontier lawyer: the personal narrative of O.W. Williams, 1877-1902. Edited by S.D. Myres. Illustrated. Introduction by C.L. Sonnichsen. 2nd. ed. El Paso: Texas Western Press/University of Texas, at El Paso, 1968. (1966) 350 p. Index.
    An interesting, expertly edited compilation of narrative pamphlets about Williams's activities on the Southwestern American frontier during the last quarter of the nineteenth century, focusing on the terrain (which Williams surveyed), vegetation, animals, Indian tribes (Apache, Comanche), economic areas of Texas and New Mexico. The text is accompanied by a biographical preface, abundant explanatory notes, and many illustrations.

4839 Williams, Tennessee   **1911-**
Memoirs. Garden City, New York: Doubleday & Co., Inc., 1975. 264 p. Index.
    The shaping of the life of a successful playwright, the effect of events on his life and art, his struggle to achieve recognition, his family, friends, and battles with alcohol and mental illness.

4840 Williams, Tennessee   **1911-**
Tennessee Williams' letters to Donald Windham 1940-1965. Edited by Donald Windham. New York: Holt, Rinehart and Winston, 1977. 333 p. Index.
    Williams and Windham met through a mutual friend in 1940 when Windham was nineteen. Thereafter they corresponded, Williams's letters reproduced here being running accounts of his activities and thinking.

4841 Williams, Theodore Samuel   **1918-**
My turn at bat; the story of my life. With John Underwood. Illustrated. New York: Simon & Schuster, 1969. 288 p. Index.
    One of the greatest hitters in baseball writes of his boyhood in San Diego, his early days in the minor leagues, and his outstanding career with the Boston Red Sox.

4842 Williams, William Carlos   **1883-1963**
The autobiography of William Carlos Williams. New York: Random House, 1948. 402 p. Index.
    At 68, Williams wrote of his experience as a poet and small-town physician in New Jersey. A close friend of Ezra Pound and many other great artists of his time, he writes with affectionate precision of them as well as his patients and his personal values.

4843 Williams, William Carlos   **1883-1963**
I wanted to write a poem: the autobiography of the works of a poet. Edited and reported by Edith Heal. London: Jonathan Cape, 1967. (Boston: Beacon Press, 1958) 111 p.
    This is an autobiographical annotated bibliography of Williams' works, some fifty volumes of poetry, plays, stories, and translations written

1909-1957. Williams recalled for the recorder salient facts of the intention, composition, publication, and reception of each work.

4844 Williams, William Carlos   **1883-1963**
Interviews with William Carlos Williams: "speaking straight ahead." Edited with introduction by Linda Welshimer Wagner. New York: New Directions, 1976. 108 p. Index.

Williams, a major poet and also a physician in Rutherford, New Jersey, speaks candidly, mostly about American poetry, poetics, and his poetry, to several interviewers (John W. Gerber, Dorothy Tooker, Walter Sutton). The American idiom is "a language dogs and cats could understand." E.E. Cummings "speaks in the American idiom" but writes "conventional" sonnets. "The poet is the happiest of men [who writes from] a passion to make something better in the world than what he sees about him."

4845 Williams, William Carlos   **1883-1963**
The selected letters of William Carlos Williams. Edited with introduction by John C. Thirlwall. New York: McDowell, Obolensky, 1957. 347 p. Index.

Includes letters from 1902, when he was a medical student at the University of Pennsylvania, to 1956, when he retired in New Jersey, a famous poet and physician.

4846 *Williamson, Anne A.   **1868-1955**
Fifty years in starch. Culver City, California: Murray and Gee, Inc., 1948. 245 p.

Although written in third person and set in a narrative frame, the story is apparently the author's own, describing her long and successful career as a nurse in New York and California.

4847 Williamson, John G.A.   **1793-1840**
Caracas diary, 1835-1840: the journal of John G.A. Williamson, first diplomatic representative of the United States to Venezuela. Baton Rouge, Louisiana: Camellia Publishing Co., 1954. 444 p. Index.

Williamson, American consul and chargé d'affaires to Venezuela during its formative years, 1826-1840, kept this perceptive though formal diary during his last five years in office. He records political events (implications of various treaties and diplomatic actions), portraits of people (ranging from liberator Simon Bolivar and Andrew Jackson to pirates), customs (especially of religion), and descriptions of the country itself. His narrative changes from enjoyment to sadness as he finds the diplomatic life increasingly isolating, his beloved wife of four years returns to the United States, and he becomes mortally ill.

4848 Williamson, William   **1875-1972**
An autobiography: William Williamson: student, homesteader, teacher, lawyer, judge, congressman and trusted friend. Foreword by C. Merle Rowe. Illustrated. Rapid City, South Dakota: William Williamson, 1964. 297 p. Index.

Williamson's long life was intertwined with the law, politics, and the state of South Dakota, whose interests he represented in Congress, 1921-1933, until he lost in the Republican debate that accompanied the Depression. Williamson was instrumental in the establishment of Mt. Rushmore National Monument, the Badlands National Park, dams, waterways, and land-use projects.

4849 Willis, Bailey   **1857-1949**
Yanqui in Patagonia. Stanford: Stanford University Press, 1947. 152 p.

Formerly of the U.S. Geological Survey, he went to Argentina in 1910 to explore Patagonia, planning highways, railways, cities, and colonization until 1914.

4850 Willis, William   **1893-1968?**
The hundred lives of an ancient mariner: an autobiography. Illustrated. London: Hutchinson & Co., 1967. 190 p.

Willis describes his life, beginning with childhood memories of Germany. At fifteen he went to sea but after several voyages he settled in Texas, where he tried farming and several other trades. Eventually, he turned to writing and resumed a life of adventures, including the rescue of a prisoner from Devil's Island and several solo sailing voyages at an advanced age. At 73 he made an unsuccessful attempt to cross the Atlantic in an 11 1/2-foot open boat, following a successful Kon Tiki-type voyage on a square-sailed balsa log raft from Ecuador to Australia, 11,000 miles in 204 days.

4851 *Willison, Marilyn Murray   **1948?-**
Diary of a divorced mother. New York: Wyden Books, 1980. 230 p.

The author writes about the problems of being a single parent, the holiday loneliness, dating, and many other difficulties of living alone in a community accustomed to nuclear families.

4852 *Willoughby, Amea   **1909-**
I was on Corregidor; experiences of an American official's wife in the war-torn Philippines. New York: Harper & Brothers Publishers, 1943. 249 p.

From November 1939, when her husband took over as executive as-

sistant to the High Commissioner of the Philippines, Mrs. Willoughby was witness to the events heralding World War II, the coming of war to Manila, the escape to Corregidor, and the final hazardous trip back to the United States.

4853 Wills, Garry   **1934-**
Confessions of a conservative. Garden City, New York: Doubleday and Co., Inc., 1979. 231 p.

A thoughtful and articulate narration of the development and manifestations of his personal and political philosophy, exploring many facets of what "conservative" means to him in respect to the Roman Catholic Church (Wills was once a seminarian), civil rights, Richard Nixon's presidency, economics, journalism, and other topics of public and private concern.

4854 Wills, Morris R.   **1933-**
Turncoat; an American's 12 years in Communist China; the story of Morris R. Wills. As told to J. Robert Moskin. Englewood Cliffs, New Jersey: Prentice-Hall, Inc., 1968. 186 p. Index.

Wills was captured during the Korean War, survived imprisonment by the Chinese for over two years in North Korea, and then chose to go to China instead of returning to the United States. Twelve years later he returned. His book depicts his complicated survival in spite of war, imprisonment, brainwashing, and the guilt of defection.

4855 Willson, Meredith   **1902-**
And there I stood with my piccolo. Westport, Connecticut: Greenwood Press, 1975. (Garden City, New York: Doubleday and Co., 1948) 255 p.

Recollections of the sounds of Iowa, growing up in rural America, then working his way into the music worlds of New York and Hollywood, by the composer of *The Music Man.*

4856 Willson, Meredith   **1902-**
But he doesn't know the territory. New York: G.P. Putnam's Sons, 1957. 190 p.

The third of his autobiographical books, this one as much the story of *The Music Man* as the author, showing a dynamic image of the man in his work.

4857 Willson, Meredith   **1902-**
Eggs I have laid. New York: Henry Holt and Co., 1955. 185 p.

The second of three autobiographical books by the composer of *The Music Man,* this one including many anecdotes about show business and its personalities.

4858 Wilson, Arthur   **b.1888**
Thy will be done: the autobiography of an Episcopal minister. New York: Dial Press, 1960. 213 p.

A moving story of Wilson's intense desire to minister to the poor, which found fulfillment in a Negro parish in Cincinnati in the 1930's while he was separated from his first wife. In order to marry his second wife, he had to relinquish his extremely satisfying career, which he resumed in California thirteen years later, after being reinstated into the clergy upon the death of his first wife.

4859 Wilson, Bertrand   **1908-**
Quest for justice: my confinement in two institutions. Hicksville, New York: Exposition Press, 1974. 112 p.

Wilson tells how he was seized, apparently without cause, and held in mental institutions, denied recourse to a lawyer for a long period of time, and finally was successful in being released. He writes of the violence and mistreatment of inmates and his efforts to receive justice.

4860 Wilson, Edmund   **1895-1972**
Letters on literature and politics, 1912-1972. Edited by Elena Wilson. Introduction by Daniel Aaron. Foreword by Leon Edel. Illustrated. New York: Farrar, Straus and Giroux, 1977. 767 p. Index.

The letters of distinguished critic and author Wilson to a myriad of other eminent writers are witty, precise, and often admonitory, as they comment candidly of the content and style of the correspondents' manuscripts and publications. This collection provides a broad overview of American letters for five decades and the country's political climate, particularly in relation to Russia.

4861 Wilson, Edmund   **1895-1972**
Prelude: landscapes, characters and conversations from the earlier years of my life. New York: Farrar, Straus and Giroux, 1967. 278 p.

Composed of journals and diaries from the years 1908 through 1919 connected with reminiscences added later, this book comprises the story of Wilson's youth including his trips abroad, his years at Princeton, and his army service during World War I.

4862 Wilson, Edmund   **1895-1972**
The Twenties: from notebooks and diaries of the period. Edited with an introduction by Leon Edel. New York: Farrar, Straus and Giroux, 1975. 557 p. Index.

Derived from Wilson's memories and notebook passages, the book views the decade from his position as a central figure in the literary and intellectual circles of the American Twenties.

4863 Wilson, Edmund   **1895-1972**
Upstate; records and recollections of northern New York. Illustrated. New York: Farrar, Straus and Giroux, 1971. 386 p.

Diary selections from 1950 to 1970 and accounts of people who lived in upstate New York, mainly in Lewis and Oneida counties. Wilson's family home in tiny Talcottville and his family and friends have been affected by developments which have changed a once-thriving rural community into a different, but perhaps more democratic, place.

4864 Wilson, Edward Raymond   **1896-**
Thus far on my journey. Richmond, Indiana: Friends United Press, 1976. 308 p.

Wilson carried out his lifetime advocacy of world peace and international understanding through the American Friends Service Committee. As field secretary for its peace section, he traveled extensively in the Far East and Europe, promoting pacifism through political process in the United States and abroad. With his wife and two sons he helped found a cooperative community in Pennsylvania which expressed in its cultural and religious diversity his vision of a "social utopia."

4865 Wilson, Ellen Axson
see **Wilson, Woodrow**

4866 Wilson, Ernest Henry   **1876-1930**
The flowering world of "Chinese" Wilson. Illustrated. With introduction and brief biography by Daniel J. Foley. New York: The Macmillan Co., 1969. 334 p. Index.

Trained as a horticulturist in England, Wilson spent many years exploring and hunting for specific plants in China and other Eastern countries. He became affiliated with Arnold Arboretum (Harvard) in his early years. He introduced many varieties of spirea, azalea, cotoneaster, rhododendron, and numerous ornamental trees to American gardens.

4867 Wilson, Frank John   **1888-1970**
Special agent: a quarter century with the Treasury Department and the Secret Service. And Beth Day. New York: Holt, Rinehart and Winston, 1965. 250 p.

In 1902 after the assassination of President McKinley, the Secret Service was made responsible for the protection of the president's life on a full-time basis. That assignment and the responsibility to protect the currency are the two main duties of the Secret Service of which Wilson was chief from 1936 to 1946.

4868 Wilson, Gil
see **White, William Allen**

4869 Wilson, Gill Robb   **1893-1966**
I walked with giants. Epilogue by Mary Wilson. Illustrated. New York: Vantage Press, 1968. 291 p.

Wilson describes his childhood in western Pennsylvania, his education at Washington and Jefferson College, and emphasizes his lifelong involvement with aircraft, during and after World War I as a member of the Air Services of the U.S. Second Army. This volume provides a detailed, personalized history of the development of aircraft, military and civilian, and accounts of notable facts by memorable pilots, from Wilbur Wright to Amelia Earhart to General H.H. "Hap" Arnold. His poetry about flying is included here.

4870 Wilson, Hugh Robert   **1885-1946**
A career diplomat, the third chapter: the Third Reich. Edited by Hugh R. Wilson, Jr. Westport, Connecticut: Greenwood Press, 1973. (New York: Vantage, 1961) 112 p.

From March 1938, to October 1940, Wilson was Ambassador to Germany and then vice chairman of the Advisory Committee on Problems of Foreign Affairs in the State Department. This volume includes correspondence, diary entries, confidential memoranda, and notes with connecting narrative written by his son.

4871 Wilson, John (Jock) Minnich   **1804-1875 -**
The dark and the damp: an autobiography of Jock Wilson. New York: E.P. Dutton and Co., Inc., 1951. 256 p.

The story of coal-mining life in Indiana begins when the author was thirteen and ends when he leaves for art school almost ten years later. Conditions in the mines, his close relationship with his father and family, his love of outdoor life, and his struggle to complete his high school education are described with realistic detail.

4872 Wilson, Minter Lowther   **1893-**
The light of other days. Boston: Christopher Publishing House, 1959. 283 p.

Wilson's speeches, delivered over a lifetime as a judge in Morgantown, West Virginia, reveal his loyalty to Christian ideals, the U.S. Constitution and the country it represents, the Democratic Party, Theodore and Franklin Roosevelt, home, and motherhood.

4873 Wilson, Sloan   **1920-**
What shall we wear to this party?: The Man in the Gray Flannel Suit, twenty years before and after. Illustrated. New York: Arbor House, 1976. 442 p.

Wilson, author of the best-selling *The Man in the Gray Flannel Suit*, uses this metaphor to characterize himself and his generation of Ivy League, old-boy-network, business-oriented family men. Descended from sailors, he loves the sea, enjoyed his Navy service in Greenland during World War II, and has owned and intermittently lived on boats ever since. Written like a good novel, this book characterizes both of Wilson's spouses, their children, family relationships, and dwellings (mostly in Connecticut and New York) in great detail. Wilson is unsentimental about his alcoholism, now under control, which interfered for years with his writing.

4874 Wilson, Upton Gwlynn   **1889-1945**
My thirty-three years of life in bed. Durham, North Carolina: published privately by the author's family, 1946. 213 p.

At twenty-three, the author was paralyzed from the neck down by a bullet. Thereafter he became an avid student, writer, and journalist whose column appeared regularly in the Winston-Salem *Journal.*

4875 Wilson, William E.   **1906-**
On the sunny side of a one way street. New York: W.W. Norton, 1958. 223 p.

An engaging, often humorous reminiscence of Wilson's childhood and adolescence in small-town Indiana, 1906-1924. He discusses friends, school, illnesses (including his typhoid and scoliosis and his sister's increasing blindness), and the pleasures and pains of growing up—making friends, fighting, earning spending money.

4876 Wilson, William Lyne   **1843-1900**
Borderland Confederate. Edited by Festus P. Summers. Westport, Connecticut: Greenwood Press, 1973. (Pittsburgh: University of Pittsburgh Press, 1962) 138 p.

Raised in the borderland between Virginia and what became West Virginia, Wilson served in the Confederate Army. The editor has linked his diary entries and letters with comments tracing his life during the Civil War, his position as a Latin professor at Columbian College (George Washington University), and later as U.S. Postmaster General.

4877 Wilson, Woodrow   **1856-1924**
A day of dedication: the essential writings & speeches of Woodrow Wilson. Edited with introduction by Albert Fried. New York: The Macmillan Co., 1965. 478 p.

A selection from Wilson's speeches, letters, and state papers arranged chronologically to correspond to political events, which reveals his career and philosophy but not his personal life.

4878 Wilson, Woodrow   **1856-1924**
The papers of Woodrow Wilson. Edited by Arthur S. Link [and others]. Illustrated. Princeton, New Jersey: Princeton University Press, 1966- . v.

Wilson, an outstanding educator and President of the United States during World War I, contributed many ideas to political science and historical literature, educational theories and practice, the formation of modern domestic policies, and the building of a peaceful international community. This comprehensive edition aims to include all important letters, articles, speeches, interviews, and public papers.

4879 Wilson, Woodrow   **1856-1924**
Priceless gift: the love letters of Woodrow Wilson and Ellen Axson Wilson. Edited by Eleanor Wilson McAdoo. Foreword by Raymond B. Fosdick. New York: McGraw-Hill Book Co., 1962. 324 p. Index.

A selection of letters from the 1,400 letters exchanged over thirty years (1883-1913) of courtship and marriage between Ellen and Woodrow Wilson disclosing their deepest thoughts and feelings.

4880 Wilson, Woodrow
see also **Hoover, Herbert Clark**

4881 Winant, John Gilbert   **1889-1947**
Letter from Grosvenor Square: an account of a stewardship. Boston: Houghton Mifflin Co., 1947. 279 p.

U.S. Ambassador to Great Britain during World War II, he writes a story of the war as he saw it from the Embassy.

4882 *Winchell, Florence Sylvester   **b.1876**
Three "incarnations." Illustrated. Boston: Christopher Publishing House, 1954. 268 p.

Winchell spends three-fifths of the book on her first "incarnation" as the only child of her divorced, American dentist father in Berlin, where she was raised and sent to boarding school. Her second "incarnation" as a physician took place in California, where she attended the University of California at Berkeley and established a medical practice in San Francisco, mostly as a women's doctor. Her third "incarnation," coyly identified on the last page, was marriage in her older age to a "velvet-eyed" friend from college days.

4883 *Winchell, Mary Edna   **b.1878**
Home by the Bering Sea. Caldwell, Idaho: The Caxton Printers, Ltd., 1951. 226 p.
An interesting account of her experience as teacher and matron of a mission orphanage in Unalaska, a small fishing village in the Aleutian Islands.

4884 *Winchell, Mary Edna   **b.1878**
Where the wind blows free. Illustrated. Caldwell, Idaho: Caxton Printers, Ltd,. 1954. 176 p.
Winchell was for some fifteen years (c. 1912-1927) the matron of girls at a Methodist mission home for orphans in Unalaska, Aleutian Islands. In this book intended for children, she tells unusual tales of the people, customs, and her experiences in these strikingly beautiful but isolated islands populated by Eskimos, Indians, and whites who live intimately with the sea and cold, fish and whales.

4885 Winchell, Walter   **1897-1972**
Winchell exclusive: "things that happened to me—and me to them". Introduction by Ernest Cuneo. Englewood Cliffs, New Jersey: Prentice-Hall, Inc., 1975. 332 p. Index.
Reporter and columnist on radio and in newspapers, theater critic, and political gadfly, Winchell here reveals in anecdote and gossip some of his scoops and the stories behind them.

4886 Windolph, Charles A.   **1851-1950**
I fought with Custer: the story of Sergeant Windolph, last survivor of the Battle of the Little Big Horn. As told to Frazier and Robert Hunt. With explanatory material and contemporary sidelights on the Custer fight. New York: Charles Scribner's Sons, 1947. 236 p. Index.
A member of Colonel Benteen's troop, he claims to have helped with the burial detail after the battle and gives his own view of events before, during, and after it.

4887 *Windsor, Wallis (Warfield), Duchess of   **1896-**
The heart has its reasons: the memoirs of the Duchess of Windsor. New York: David McKay Co., Inc., 1956. 372 p. Index.
The story of her early life, the events leading to her courtship by the King of England, his abdication, and their later years together.

4888 Winfrey, Carey
Starts and finishes: coming of age in the Fifties. New York: Saturday Review Press/E.P. Dutton, 1975. 183 p.
Winfrey tells a terse and unpleasant tale of the 1940's when his father trained horses in New York, Florida, and California. In the 50's he graduated from Columbia and joined the Marines.

4889 Winkler, Henry   **1945-**
The other side of Henry Winkler: my story. New York: Warner Books, 1976. 151 p.
Winkler, a good Jewish boy from New York, pleasantly discusses his rise to television stardom and makes it sound easy. After graduating from Emerson College (Boston) and the Yale Drama School, Winkler embarked on a Broadway theatrical career until he went to Hollywood to star as "The Fonz." Although the character and the actor are very different, Winkler enjoys the challenge.

4890 Winkler, Max   **b.1888**
From A to X: reminiscences of Max Winkler. New York: Crown Publishers, Inc., 1957. 178 p.
Anecdotes about his life in America, after immigrating from Austria-Hungary in 1907 and becoming a music publisher.

4891 *Winnie, Lucille (Jerry)   **1904-**
SAH-GAN-DE-OH: the chief's daughter. New York: Vantage Press, Inc., 1969. 190 p.
Born of Seneca-Cayuga parents, she describes her life as "completely integrated in the American way" and similar to many other modern Indians. Her story is a plea for understanding which analyzes the difficulties of progress and integration, as well as her own interesting and varied life.

4892 Winslow, Walker (Harold Maine, pseud.)
If man be mad. Garden City, New York: Doubleday & Co., 1947. 435 p.
His fight against alcoholism, his experiences as a patient in various mental hospitals and institutions, as well as his later work as an attendant in those institutions led to his knowledge of the material, medical, and psychological conditions that prevail in the treatment of mental illness.

4893 *Winter, Ella   **1898-**
And not to yield: an autobiography. New York: Harcourt, Brace & World, 1963. 308 p. Index.
An outspoken woman's account of her full life, her protests against injustice, prejudice and exploitation, and her friendships and passions.

4894 Winter, George   **1809-1876**
The journals and Indian paintings of George Winter, 1837-1839. Edited by Gayle Thornbrough. Indianapolis: Indiana Historical Society, 1948. 208 p. Index.
The book includes his unfinished autobiography (1809-1830), color and black-and-white plates of many of his paintings, as well as the journals recording his extensive experience with the Miami and Potawatomi Indians around Logansport, Indiana.

4895 Winter, William   **1836-1917**
Vagrant memories, being further recollections of other days. Illustrated. Essay Index Reprint Series. Freeport, New York: Books for Libraries Press, 1970. (New York: George H. Doran Co., 1915) 525 p. Index.
Winter reminisces about important and interesting actors whom he has known and observed including Edwin Booth, Henry Irving, and Julia Marlowe.

4896 Winter, William   **1836-1917**
The wallet of time: containing personal, biographical, and critical reminiscence of the American theater. Illustrated. Essay Index Reprint Series. Freeport, New York: Books for Libraries Press, 1969. (New York: Moffet, Yard, & Co., 1913) 2v. Index.
A noted drama critic for the New York *Tribune* and other papers, from the fullness of his lifelong experience, wrote these essays spanning sixty years in the nineteenth-century theater in which he "sought to estimate the motives, achievements, and rank of dominant actors, managers, and dramatists . . . and to designate those methods of theatrical administration which are best calculated to promote the welfare of the Theater by making it entirely and nightly serviceable to Society."

4897 Winter, William
see also **Booth, Edwin Thomas**

4898 Winterich, John Tracy   **1891-1970**
Another day, another dollar. Philadelphia: J.B. Lippincott Co., 1947. 204 p.
In recalling his life in Providence, Rhode Island, 1903-1912, he describes his economic education in an atmosphere of small business in a small town with humor and some nostalgia. Later he was editor of the *Saturday Review of Literature.*

4899 Wirt, Loyal Lincoln   **1866-1961**
The world is my parish: an autobiographical odyssey. Introduction by Albert Wentworth Palmer. Los Angeles, California: Warren F. Lewis, 1951. 272 p.
A clergyman's son, Wirt was reared in North Dakota and Wisconsin, educated at Pacific Theological Seminary (Oakland, California), and ordained as a Congregational minister. As a clergyman, he served in Alaska shortly after the Gold Rush began; in Australia, where he was sent to recuperate from overwork in Alaska; and in Mexico. Wirt led a life of adventure and public service all over the world, including field service with the American Red Cross in France, and Western directorship of the educational program of the National Council for the Prevention of War in California and Hawaii after World War I.

4900 Wirt, Sherwood Eliot
Afterglow: the excitement of being filled with the spirit. Foreword by Kenneth Chafin. Grand Rapids, Michigan: Zondervan Publishing House, 1975. 132 p.
A journalist who has served with the Billy Graham evangelistic team around the world describes the entrance of God's spirit into his own inner life.

4901 Wise, Isaac Mayer   **1819-1900**
Reminiscences. Translated and edited by David Philipson. New York: Arno Press, 1973. (Cincinnati: Leo Wise and Co., 1901) 367 p.
Originally published in German, this autobiography begins with his arrival in America in 1846 and covers his early years here, recalling the conditions prevalent in American Jewry and the impact of his powerful personality on the institutional religious development of Judaism in America.

4902 Wise, Stephen Samuel   **1874-1949**
Challenging years: the autobiography of Stephen Wise. New York: G.P. Putnam's Sons, 1949. 323 p.
Describing his autobiography as "heterocentric . . . himself in relation to the world," a Hungarian immigrant and rabbi writes of his participation in liberal affairs, both political and philosophical, and his working concern for Jewish survival. His book includes correspondence, speeches, conversations, and anecdotes about prominent labor, political, and Jewish leaders during the twentieth century.

4903 Wise, Stephen Samuel   **1874-1949**
Personal letters. Edited by Justine Wise Polier and James Waterman Wise. Introduction by John Haynes Holmes. Boston: The Beacon Press, 1956. 289 p. Index.
Letters written to his wife, his children, and his close friend Holmes

reveal the profound humanitarianism that made him a respected leader in the liberal Jewish tradition. A remarkable self-portrait with notes on his friendships with many of his outstanding contemporaries.

4904 Wise, Stephen Samuel   **1874-1949**
Stephen S. Wise: servant of the people—selected letters. Edited by Carl Hermann Voss. Foreword by Justine Wise Polier and James Waterman Wise. Philadelphia: The Jewish Publication Society of America, 1969. 332 p. Index.
   Selected from the thousands of letters he wrote, these best represent to the editor the work and development of the prominent Zionist and leader in the liberal Jewish tradition. A remarkable document of Jewish and American history.

4905 Wislizenus, Frederick Adolphus   **1810-1889**
A journey to the Rocky Mountains in the year 1839. Translated by Frederick A. Wislizenus, Esq. Glorieta, New Mexico: The Rio Grande Press, 1969. 168 p. Index.
   A German doctor who settled in Illinois writes about his trek through Western America in search of physical recreation. He describes the various Indian tribes he and his trapping party encountered, as well as animal life, although he is basically concerned with river formations.

4906 Wislizenus, Frederick Adolphus   **1810-1889**
Memoir of a tour to Northern Mexico: connected with Col. Doniphan's expedition in 1846 and 1847. Robert B. McCoy and John T. Strachan, Publisher's Preface. Armand W. Reeder, "A Tour of Northern New Mexico with Colonel Doniphan." Meterological tables and map by A. Wislizenus. Botanical Appendix by George Englemann. Glorieta, New Mexico: Rio Grande Press, Inc., 1969. (Washington, D.C.: Gov. Printing Office for the United States Senate, 1848) 141 p. Index.
   Wislizenus, a German-born physician who immigrated to St. Louis, was also a noted geologist and naturalist. This vivid and precise account describes the flora, fauna, and terrain of his scientific expedition of 1846-47 along the old Santa Fe Trail from Missouri across Kansas, through New Mexico, and into Mexico.

4907 Wister, Owen   **1860-1938**
Owen Wister out West: his journals and letters. Edited by Fanny Kemble Wister. Chicago: University of Chicago Press, 1958. 269 p. Index.
   The records of his travels on the Western frontier, chiefly in Wyoming, during the years (1885-1895) when he collected materials for his Western fiction, by the author of *The Virginian.*

4908 *Wister, Sally (Sarah)   **1761-1804**
Sally Wister's journal: a true narrative/being a Quaker maiden's account of her experiences with officers of the Continental Army, 1777-1778. Edited with introduction by Albert Cook Myers. Illustrated. Eyewitness Accounts of the American Revolution. New York: New York Times and Arno Press, 1969. (Philadelphia: Ferris & Leach, 1902) 224 p. Index.
   This diary, kept for nine months, 1777-1778, consists of a sixteen-year-old Quaker girl's account of the Revolutionary War, as determined primarily by her association with the American officers quartered in her family's house in Germantown, Pennsylvania. The house was used as General William Smallwood's quarters and, although Sally had a crush on Major William Stoddert, she was not privy to any military information. The introduction and illustrations greatly enhance this volume.

4909 *Wolf, Hannie (Baer)   **1925-**
Child of two worlds. Illustrated. Broken Bow, Nebraska: Purcells, 1979. 151 p.
   "European by birth, American by choice," Wolf recounts her childhood in Germany, her family's trek across Russia, Korea, and Japan to escape the Nazi persecution of Jews, and, finally, her new life as a fifteen-year-old war refugee in Boulder, Colorado. Her journey to America (presented in letters written to her grandmother, who died in the Holocaust) is infused with teen-age exuberance. The shadow of Nazi persecution is described straightforwardly.

4910 Wolf, Howard   **1936-**
Forgive the father: a memoir of changing generations. Washington, D.C.: New Republic Books, 1978. 184 p.
   College professor Wolf juxtaposes his attempts to mature throughout the 1960's with various manifestations of the Vietnam War-protesting counter-culture: drug takers, dropouts, practitioners of free living and free love. His own stance with regard to his hippie artist wife, with whom he cannot live, is ambivalent; he also loves their daughter but does not rear her.

4911 *Wolf, Marguerite Hurrey
How to be a doctor's wife without really dying. Illustrated. Sarasota, Florida: Booklore Publications, 1978. (Coral Gables, Florida: Wake-Brook House, 1967) 146 p.
   Rambling, sometimes repetitive anecdotes constitute this collection of essays about the humorous side of life as a doctor's wife.

4912 Wolfe, Bernard   **1915-**
Memoirs of a not altogether shy pornographer. Garden City, New York: Doubleday & Co., 1972. 312 p.
   A breezy memoir of his early days, miscellaneous jobs, including secretary-bodyguard, drill-grinder, and his first job writing pornography for an Oklahoma millionaire. Once he started writing porn, one job led to another and the books almost seemed to write themselves.

4913 Wolfe, Bertram David   **1896-**
Strange communists I have known. New York: Stein and Day, 1965. 222 p.
   Portrayals of ten men and women, five known personally by the author, who were attracted to the communist movement. Also included is an account of attempts to identify the author of *The Litvinov Diary* and the investigation of the double agent, Roman Malinovsky.

4914 Wolfe, Thomas   **1900-1938**
Correspondence of Thomas Wolfe and Homer Andrew Watt. Edited by Oscar Cargill and Thomas Clark Pollock. New York: New York University Press, 1954. 53 p.
   Letters between the not-yet-famous writer and Watt, who chaired the English Department at New York University during Wolfe's tenure there (1924-1930).

4915 Wolfe, Thomas   **1900-1938**
The letters of Thomas Wolfe. Edited by Elizabeth Nowell. New York: Charles Scribner's Sons, 1956. 797 p. Index.
   A selection of his letters, many of them never sent, revealing his growth and development as a writer during his brief and turbulent life.

4916 Wolfe, Thomas   **1900-1938**
The letters of Thomas Wolfe to his mother. Edited by C. Hugh Holman & Sue Fields Ross. Chapel Hill: University of North Carolina Press, 1968. (New York: Charles Scribner's Sons, 1943) 320 p.
   Held tightly in possessive affection by his mother, Wolfe wrote to her in revealing and intimate letters which provide a basis for understanding the tormented, ambitious, committed, and talented artist he was.

4917 Wolfe, Thomas   **1900-1938**
The notebooks of Thomas Wolfe. Edited by Richard S. Kennedy and Paschal Reeves. Chapel Hill: The University of North Carolina Press, 1970. 2v. Index.
   These two volumes present the bulk of Wolfe's 35 pocket notebooks which he kept from 1926 until 1938. They include random ideas and observations, drafts of material, "jottings of a man talking to himself," opinions, lists, and other recordings of a literary career and of daily living.

4918 Wolfe, Thomas   **1900-1938**
Selected letters. Introduction and explanatory text by Elizabeth Nowell. Selected by Daniel George. London: Heinemann, 1958. 326 p. Index.
   This collection is selected from the American edition (1956), omitting mainly details relating to his lawsuit with Scribner's, his change of publishers, and small family matters.

4919 *Wolff, Mary Madeleva   **1887-1964**
My first seventy years. New York: The Macmillan Co., 1959. 172 p.
   She founded the first theological college and graduate school for women at St. Mary's College, Notre Dame, Indiana. Her book describes her Midwestern childhood and highlights of her career as an educator. She was President of St. Mary's from 1934 until her death.

4920 Wolff, Rick (Richard H.)   **1951-**
What's a nice Harvard boy like you doing in the bushes? Edited by Phil Pepe. Englewood Cliffs, New Jersey: Prentice-Hall, 1975. 216 p.
   In the form of a diary Wolff recorded his first two years in professional minor-league baseball at Anderson, South Carolina, and Clinton, Iowa, teams of the Detroit Tiger organization. After the freedom of Harvard, the baseball towns were a drastic change, but he views his experience with humor and spirit.

4921 Wolfkill, Grant F.
Reported to be alive: an American news photographer is held in brutal captivity for fifteen months by Communist Pathet Lao—and for his courage is awarded the Medal of Freedom by President John F. Kennedy. With Jerry A. Rose. Foreword by Robert F. Kennedy. New York: Simon and Schuster, 1965. 377 p.
   Imprisoned by the Pathet Lao after his helicopter crashed in May 1961, Wolfkill remained a prisoner under enormous physical and psychological pressure for the following fifteen months. His survival under the most savage abuse is a testament to his enduring strength and courageous spirit.

4922 Wolsky, Boris   **1898-**
My life in three worlds. Miami Beach, Florida: Boris Wolsky, 1979. 338 p.
   Wolsky writes to interpret his family for other family members. His "three worlds" are "the world that disappeared"—turn of the century Lithuania, with an enoromous Jewish community victimized by Russian

pogroms; Western Europe, where he lived in Paris from World War I until World War II; and the United States after 1941, where he operated a travel agency in New York and traveled extensively.

4923 *Wong, Jade Snow   **1922-**
Fifth Chinese daughter. Illustrated by Kathryn Uhl. New York: Harper and Brothers, 1950. 246 p.
    The story of a young woman's successful struggle for individuality while growing up in a traditional, disciplined Christian-Chinese family in San Francisco. Her growth is helped by her father's understanding and her own intelligence.

4924 *Wong, Jade Snow   **1922-**
No Chinese stranger. Illustrated. New York: Harper & Row, Publishers, 1975. 366 p.
    The author of *Fifth Chinese Daughter* (1950) writes of her life during the last 25 years in San Francisco's Chinatown. A potter of considerable reputation, she has worked hard to establish a life independent of but relating to the traditions of her family and culture. The last section of this volume describes her trip to China in 1972, among the first after travel became possible.

4925 Wood, Irby F.
Born a gemini; memoirs of a sailor. New York: Vantage Press, 1973. 224 p.
    Vignettes meant to "memorialize a vanishing way of life before it passes from the minds of men" describe this sea captain's life from his first voyage as an ordinary seaman. He touches on many topics—Hurricane Carol (1954), the Shellback ceremony for crossing the equator, the torpedoing of his ship during World War II, and the practice of tattooing.

4926 *Wood, Joan E.   **1945-**
Casting couch and me: the uninhibited memoirs of a young actress. New York: Walker and Co., 1974. 216 p.
    The breezy memoirs of an aspiring actress she had the funny, discouraging, wild, and sometimes frightening experiences she had trying to land modeling or acting roles.

4927 Wood, Leonard   **1860-1927**
Chasing Geronimo: the journal of Leonard Wood, May-September, 1886. Illustrated. Edited with introduction and epilogue by Jack C. Lane. Albuquerque: University of New Mexico Press, 1970. 152 p. Index.
    After 1865 Indian fighting became the principal occupation of the U.S. Army. This diary describes the campaign against the Apache Indians led by the notorious Geronimo, culminating in his capture. The description shows both the brutal character of the undertaking and the courage and endurance required of the soldiers.

4928 *Wood, Peggy   **1894-1978**
Arts and flowers. New York: William Morrow and Co., 1963. 189 p.
    She starred in the popular television series, *I Remember Mama,* for eight years; she was well-known for her roles in *Naughty Marietta, Blithe Spirit,* many other musical and dramatic roles, and for her presidency of the American National Theater and Academy.

4929 Woodberry, George Edward   **1855-1930**
Scholar's testament: two letters from George Edward Woodberry to J.E. Spingarn. Introduction by Lewis Mumford. Norwood, Pennsylvania: Norwood Editions, 1977. (Amenia, New York: Troutbeck Press, 1931) 11 p.
    In the first letter of January 14, 1904, Woodberry announces the resignation of his chaired professorship at Columbia. In the second, he waxes philosophical about the benefits of an independent life of the mind and urges Spingarn to "go on to other things, things of the great world that know nothing of Columbia."

4930 Woodberry, George Edward   **1855-1930**
Selected letters of George Edward Woodberry. Introduction by Walter De la Mare. St. Clair Shores, Michigan: Scholarly Press, 1971. (Boston: Houghton Mifflin Co., 1933) 282 p. Index.
    A representative selection from the lifelong correspondence of this poet-critic portrays his love of humanity and serene urbanity. The letters are written to former students, friends, and literary acquaintances.

4931 Woodford, Jack, pseud.
    see **Woolfolk, Josiah Pitts**

4932 Woodruff, Mathew   **b.1843**
Union soldier in the land of the vanquished: the diary of Sergeant Mathew Woodruff, June-December, 1865. Edited and annotated by F.N. Boney. Southern History Publications, no. 13. University: University of Alabama Press, 1969. 103 p. Index.
    His informal diary reveals a view of the peacetime army of occupation after the Civil War from an unsophisticated soldier's viewpoint. Having served honorably during the war, he had no patience or understanding for the dreary regimentation of the army of occupation after the War's end.

4933 Woodson, Marion Marle (Inmate, Ward 8)   **1882-1933**
Beyond the door of delusion, by Inmate, Ward 8. New York: The Macmillan Co., 1932. 325 p.
    Having committed himself to a state hospital because of his alcoholism, he describes his treatment there—the physicians, the attendants, visitors, and particularly the hopes and fears of the other patients.

4934 Woodward, William E.   **1874-1950**
Gift of life: an autobiography. New York: E.P. Dutton and Co., Inc., 1947. 436 p. Index.
    A pleasant, well-written review of his first 72 years—poor childhood in South Carolina, education at The Citadel, varied work experiences, and his career as a writer of history, biography, and fiction.

4935 Woolf, Robert G.   **1928-**
Behind closed doors. Editing assistance by Mickey Herskowitz. Introduction by Roger Kahn. Illustrated. New York: Atheneum, 1976. 300 p.
    Woolf, a lawyer whose clients are athletes on major sports teams, recounts anecdotes about some of his most lucrative and colorful legal affairs—including successful efforts to have Derek Sanderson's bit part excised from a porno movie. Woolf demands high fees from his clients but works hard to keep them honest, free from drugs, and out of the clutches of shady and speculative investors.

4936 Woolfolk, Josiah Pitts (Jack Woodford, pseud.)   **1894-1971**
Autobiography of Jack Woodford. Garden City, New York: Doubleday and Co., Inc., 1962. 349 p.
    Using Woodford as his pseudonym, he wrote cheap sex fiction—thousands of stories, a shelf full of novels—with amazing commercial success. In a narrative packed with stories about many of the major social and literary figures of his time, he portrays a sense of his cynical distance from the Woodford persona and the constant demands made on it by his public as well as his friends, resulting in a curious comment on American culture and sexual mores.

4937 Woolman, John   **1720-1772**
The journal and major essays of John Woolman. Edited by Phillips B. Moulton. New York: Oxford University Press, 1971. (Boston: Osgood, 1871) 336 p. Index.
    A new edition of the works of a prominent Quaker minister and abolitionist which attempts to produce "a text representing the final intent of the author."

4938 Wootten, Morgan   **1932-**
From orphans to champions: the story of DeMatha's Morgan Wootten. And Bill Gilbert. Foreword by Red Auerbach. New York: Atheneum, 1979. 172 p.
    A basketball coach for 22 years at DeMatha High School in Hyattsville, Maryland, has led the team to nineteen state championships and four national championships; every team member has received a four-year college scholarship. Wooten discusses winning strategies, ways to organize and motivate the team, maintaining morale and morality, and highlights of winning seasons.

4939 Wootton, Richens Lacy   **1816-1893**
Uncle Dick Wootton: the pioneer frontiersman of the Rocky Mountain Region. Edited by Milo Milton Quaife. Oral historian, Howard Louis Conard. Chicago: The Lakeside Press: R.R. Donnelly and Sons Co., 1957. (Chicago: W.E. Dibble and Co., 1890) 465 p.
    A fascinating account of a beaver trapper, buffalo hunter, guide, express carrier on the Santa Fe Trail, rancher, and farmer. The book is also a history of the exploration and economy of the Western territories, Indian culture, and animal life (1836-1889).

4940 Worth, C. Brooke
Of mosquitoes, moths and mice. Illustrated. New York: W.W. Norton & Co., Inc., 1972. 258 p. Index.
    Dr. Worth includes a wealth of fascinating information about natural history in his investigations of the insects, turtles, birds, and mammals around his Cape May County, New Jersey, farm. The index presents scientific names of organisms rather than other topics of discussion.

4941 Woy, William (Bucky Woy)   **1938-**
Sign 'em up, Bucky: the adventures of a sports agent. With Jack Patterson. Foreword by Julius Boros. New York: Hawthorn Books, Inc., 1975. 229 p. Index.
    In the big-business professional sports world the sports agent represents the star, negotiating contracts and promoting business deals, product endorsements, and other lucrative arrangements. Woy tells the frenzied and humorous story of how he became an agent for stars and superstars.

4942 Woytinsky, Wladimir S.   **1885-1960**
Stormy passage: a personal history through two Russian revolutions to democracy and freedom: 1905-1960. Introduction by Adolph A. Berle. New York: The Vanguard Press, 1961. 550 p. Index.
    Part of the Russian social movement since 1905, the author recounts

his participation in the upheavals, his imprisonments and exiles, his progress to Germany and finally to the United States.

4943 Wright, Arthur 1927?-
Color me white: the autobiography of a black dancer who turned white. Foreword by Robert Stolar. Smithtown, New York: Exposition Press, 1980. 372 p.
A victim of vitiligo, a disfiguring disease involving skin pigmentation, this singer and dancer describes how he endured long medical treatments, remained devoted to his art, and learned a great deal about humanity.

4944 *Wright, Catharine Morris 1899-
The color of life. Boston: Houghton Mifflin, 1957. 203 p.
A moving, visual autobiography focusing on the author's philosophy and technique as a painter, interspersed with partial portraits of her husband, four children, and a family of English refugee children they harbored on their farm near Philadelphia during World War II.

4945 Wright, Chauncey 1830-1875
Letters of Chauncey Wright; with some account of his life, by James Bradley Thayer. New York: Burt Franklin, 1971. (New York: Lenox Hill, 1878) 392 p. Index.
Wright, who lived his entire adult life in Cambridge, Massachusetts, worked in the office of the Nautical Almanac to support himself, taught private pupils, was an occasional lecturer and reviewer for newspapers. His letters reveal the philosophical and scientific strengths of his intellect, the real centers of his existence.

4946 *Wright, Cobina d.1970
I never grew up. New York: Prentice-Hall, Inc., 1952. 316 p.
A well-written account of her early ambition to become an opera singer, the conflicts she experienced between her career and family life, the total ruin she and her wealthy second husband suffered in the Great Crash, and her later life as a journalist who wrote "Society as I find it."

4947 Wright, Frank Lloyd 1869-1959
An autobiography. New York: Horizon Press, 1977. (London: Longman's Green and Co., 1932) 620 p.
Architect Wright tells of his early life, running away to Chicago in the "gay 90's," his apprenticeship to Louis Sullivan, his early adversity and success, and the low-cost houses, churches, skyscrapers, and celebrated private homes he designed, all of which revolutionized architecture.

4948 Wright, Frank Lloyd 1869-1959
Genius and the mobocracy. Illustrated. New York: Horizon Press, 1971. (New York: Duell, 1949) 247 p.
Wright's concern is with architectural concepts and what he learned from master-architect Louis H. Sullivan. This book, enlarged from an earlier edition with photographs and additional drawings by both Sullivan and Wright, is a tribute to Sullivan as well as a record of their relationship, which began in 1888 when the Auditorium Building in Chicago was being built.

4949 Wright, Frank Lloyd 1869-1959
A testament. New York: Horizon Press, 1957. 256 p.
A profound discussion of his growth and development in modern architecture.

4950 *Wright, Olgivanna Lloyd
Our house. New York: Horizon Press, 1959. 308 p.
An interesting personal record of her life with Frank Lloyd Wright, the Taliesin fellowship in Arizona, Wisconsin and New York, and their richly productive, disciplined daily life.

4951 Wright, Orville 1871-1948
Miracle at Kitty Hawk: the letters of Wilbur and Orville Wright. Edited by Fred C. Kelly. New York: Arno Press, 1972. (New York: Farrar, Straus and Young, 1951) 482 p. Index.
Selection of about 600 letters from the thousands which have been preserved, which show the differing personalities and ideas of both Wrights. Letters among their close family and to colleagues are arranged chronologically with notes by the editor, who also has written the authorized biography of the Wright brothers.

4952 Wright, Orville 1871-1948
see also **Wright, Wilbur**

4953 Wright, Richard 1908-1960
American hunger. Afterword by Michael Fabre. Illustrated. New York: Harper and Row, 1977. 147 p.
This book was written as the second part of *Black Boy* but was separated before the publication of the former in 1945 and not published until 1977. It delineates Wright's experiences in the North, 1927-1940, especially in Chicago, where he learned to distrust nearly all whites. It also depicts Wright's experiences in the communist movement during the 1930's and includes more bitter political polemic than *Black Boy*.

4954 Wright, Wilbur 1867-1912
see also **Wright, Orville**

4955 Wright, Wilbur and Orville Wright 1867-1912
Papers: including the Chanute-Wright letters and other papers of Octave Chanute; Vol. I, 1899-1905; Vol. II, 1906-1948. Edited by Marvin W. McFarland. New York: McGraw-Hill Co., Inc., 1953. 2v. Index.
Includes the correspondence between Wilbur Wright and Octave Chanute (1900-1910), excerpts from 33 Wright diaries and notebooks and from Wright family correspondence, revealing their contributions to the science of aeronautics as well as their warmth, affection, and wit.

4956 *Wurmbrand, Sabina
The pastor's wife. Edited by Charles Foley. London: Hodder and Stoughton, 1970. 218 p.
The story of her own imprisonment and survival during her husband's fourteen-year imprisonment in communist prisons in Rumania. Her real work during those years was building up the Underground Church and keeping Christianity alive in spite of communist persecution.

4957 Wyeth, Nathaniel Jarvis 1802-1856
Correspondence and journals of Captain Nathaniel J. Wyeth, 1831-6. Edited by Frederick G. Young. Sources of the History of Oregon, V. 1. New York: Arno Press, 1973. (Eugene, Oregon: University Press, 1899) 262 p. Index.
These letters and journals from two expeditions to the Oregon country document Wyeth's efforts to occupy and bring economic enterprise to the territory and match British activity in the area. Although he began the salmon industry and tried to develop business interests, he underestimated the strength of the Hudson's Bay Company and its determination to allow no competition.

4958 Wyeth, Newell Convers 1882-1945
The Wyeths; the letters of N.C. Wyeth, 1901-1945. Illustrated edition by Betsy James Wyeth. Boston: Gambit, 1971. 858 p.
A wealth of letters tracing the writer's evolution from an enthusiastic but naive student of drawing to an expressive artist with a mature perception of his own nature and the world around him. He is especially famous as the illustrator of children's classics *Robin Hood, Treasure Island,* and many others.

4959 Wylder, Meldrum K. b.1877
Rio Grande medicine man. Prefaced by Dennis Chavez, U.S. Senator. Santa Fe: The Rydal Press, 1958. 187 p.
An Albuquerque physician, 1908-58, discusses typical cases, including shotgun marriages and adoptions he helped to arrange. He also discusses night calls (let the wife answer them and ascertain whether they are serious), ethics (every mother has the right to bear a healthy child under healthful circumstances) and doctors' wives (necessary and subordinate).

4960 Wyman, Jeffries 1814-1874
Dear Jeffie: being the letters from Jeffries Wyman, first director of the Peabody Museum, to his son, Jeffries Wyman, Jr. Edited, with preface and notes by George E. Clifford, Jr. Illustrated. Cambridge, Massachusetts: Peabody Museum Press, Harvard University, 1978. 82 p.
Wyman, Harvard anthropologist and anatomy professor, wrote these 59 letters to his young son, Jeffie (b. 1864), between 1866 and 1874. Wyman had to spend winters in Florida and summers in Maine to gain relief from pulmonary tuberculosis; he wrote and illustrated these charming letters to introduce his son to the flora and fauna of the regions he stayed in, focusing on "the rich variety of sights, sounds, forms, smells, and colors that enhance life." (ed.)

4961 Wynn, Keenan 1916-
Ed Wynn's son. As told to James Brough. Garden City, New York: Doubleday & Co., Inc., 1959. 236 p.
Principally a quest narrative by the son of an entertainer in search of his identity which had been initially overshadowed by his famous father. There is a strong element of self justification for the years of struggle, conflict, and perceived failure in his life.

4962 Yamasaki, Minoru 1912-
A life in architecture. Illustrated. New York: Weatherhill, 1979. 195 p.
The beautiful photographs of Yamasaki's major work, notably New York's World Trade Center, are accompanied by an eloquent explanatory text. They are prefaced by "A Life in Architecture," Yamasaki's account of his development as an architect which subtly makes the reader aware of the tremendous racial discrimination he had to overcome in order to succeed. His credo is expressed in "The Aesthetics and Practice of Architecture," another prefatory statement.

4963 *Yancey, Becky
My life with Elvis. With Cliff Lindecker. New York: St. Martin's Press, 1977. 360 p.
Yancey, secretary to rock singer Elvis Presley and his father, Vernon (1952-1975), recounts her view of "The King, the super performer, the super human being." Presley, forever surrounded by his "Memphis ma-

fia" of good ole boys, received tons of fan mail which Yancey coped with, from love letters to underwear to rhinestone guitars.

4964 Yankovic, Frankie 1915-
The polka king: the life of Frankie Yankovic. As told to Robert Dolgan. Illustrated. Cleveland: Dillon-Liederbach, Inc., 1977. 226 p.

Accordionist and polka bandleader Yankovic's childhood was spent in a Slovenian neighborhood of Cleveland, where he first formed bands which entertained at weddings, night spots, and parties in the evenings while he held factory jobs by day. After a stint in the army during World War II, he went into band work full-time, traveling extensively. As the "Polka King," he loves his work though it cost him his first marriage.

4965 Yastrzemski, Carl Michael 1939-
Yaz. With Al Hirshberg. Illustrated. New York: The Viking Press, 1968. 183 p.

His father dreamed of his son's becoming a big-league baseball player and began his training as a young boy. The book describes Yaz's Polish family background on Long Island, but focuses mainly on his years with the Boston Red Sox, being groomed to replace Ted Williams, and winning baseball's triple crown in 1967, the year the Red Sox won the World Series.

4966 *Yates, Elizabeth 1905-
The lighted heart. Pen drawings by Nora S. Unwin. New York: E.P. Dutton & Co., Inc., 1960. 251 p.

In the midst of their active, productive life, her husband lost his sight. Together they established a new life in quieter and simpler surroundings, a farm in Massachusetts. Her book describes their sense of renewal resulting from the joy and freedom they found in country living.

4967 *Yates, Emma Hayden (Eames) 1897?-1950
Seventy miles from a lemon. Illustrated by John O'Hara Cosgrove. Boston: Houghton Mifflin Co., 1947. 234 p.

In 1927 she quit her job as a writer for the *New Yorker* and with her husband built a small stock ranch in Montana. Her book is an interesting depiction of the spirit and reality of modern pioneering.

4968 Yates, Richard 1815-1873
Richard Yates: Civil War governor. And Catherine Yates Pickering. Edited by John H. Krenkel. Danville, Illinois: Interstate Printers and Publishers, 1966. 300 p. Index.

This is a compilation of letters and speeches by and about Richard Yates, Sr., between 1834, when he was a student at Illinois College, and his death in 1873. Inserted in a biographical matrix by Yates's children, most documents concern Yates's political activities in the Illinois state legislature (1842-50), in the U.S. Congress (1850-60), as Governor of Illinois (1860-64), and U.S. Senator (1865-71). A staunch foe of slavery, he cooperated wholeheartedly with Lincoln and U.S. Grant to aid the promulgation of the Civil War.

4969 Yates, Richard 1860-1936
Serving the republic—Richard Yates: Illinois Governor and Congressman/son of Richard Yates, Civil War Governor/an autobiography. Edited by John H. Krenkel. Illustrated. Danville, Illinois: Interstate Printers & Publishers, Inc., 1968. 268 p. Index.

An earnest book marks this account of Yates's duty-bound life following in his father's footsteps as Governor of Illinois (1900-1905) and U.S. Congressman (1918-1932). Yates also served as judge and Illinois Utilities Commissioner. He embodied the cardinal American virtues: hard work, patriotism, party loyalty, love of family, home, and the American heartland.

4970 *Yezierska, Anzia 1885-1970
Red ribbon on a white horse. New York: Charles Scribner's Sons, 1950. 220 p.

Reflections on her struggles with poverty and Jewishness in a Polish village, as an immigrant in New York, and later, after a brief period of wealth in Hollywood, during the Depression in New York, by an author who finally understands her father's spirituality and accepts her own.

4971 Yoder, Sanford Calvin b.1879
The days of my years. Scottdale, Pennsylvania: Herald Press, 1959. 247 p.

Yoder, an Amish Mennonite steeped in the faith, offers a straightforward, thoughtful examination of the Mennonite creed and practices, interwoven with a mixture of church history, the history of the Mennonite Goshen (Indiana) College of which he was president, 1923-1940, and a rich account of his missionary services in Paraguay.

4972 York, Thomas Lee 1940-
And sleep in the woods: the story of one man's spiritual quest. Garden City, New York: Doubleday & Co., Inc., 1978. 221 p.

York, a United Church minister, recalls the events which led to his conversion. In 1962, York fled to Canada with his wife to avoid being sent to Vietnam. Living in solitude, meditation, and prayer led York and his wife to a new understanding of themselves and their relationship with

God. After his conversion, York stood trial for draft evasion and was acquitted.

4973 Yoseloff, Thomas 1913-
The time of my life. Drawings by Al Ostervich. South Brunswick: A.S. Barnes & Co., 1979. 188 p.

Delightful stories of his life in Iowa up to 1935 when he went to New York to establish his career: the Jewish community in Sioux City; the emergence of the Ku Klux Klan, which was then after the Irish, Jews, and Italians; and the exciting years at the University of Iowa where he became critic-at-large for the student paper and met many contemporary writers and intellectuals.

4974 Yoshida, Jim 1921-
The two worlds of Jim Yoshida. With Bill Hosokawa. New York: William Morrow & Co, Inc., 1972. 256 p.

A remarkable story of a Japanese-American youth who, because of legal technicalities, was impressed into the Japanese Army during World War II. His struggle to regain his American heritage after the war led him to volunteer to serve with the allied forces during the Korean War. Eventually he won his suit to reclaim his American citizenship.

4975 Young, Arthur Henry 1866-1943
Art Young: his life and times. Edited by John Nicholas Beffel. Illustrated by Art Young. Hyperion Reprint Series, The Radical Tradition in America. Westport, Connecticut: Hyperion Press, 1975. (New York: Sheridan House, 1939) 467 p. Index.

Young writes vividly of his life as a cartoonist whose illustrations regularly appeared in national magazines such as *Life* and *Judge*, and in socialist and other left-wing publications— *The Liberator* and *New Masses*. This entertaining book, illustrated with Young's cartoons, offers a vigorous view of twentieth-century American socialism, its advocates, and a host of other political groups.

4976 Young, Bennett Harrison 1843-1919
Confederate wizards of the saddle: being reminiscences and observations of one who rode with Morgan. Illustrated. Introduction by E.B. Long. Dayton, Ohio: Press of Morningside Bookshop, 1979. (Boston: Chapple Pub. Co., 1914) 633 p. Index.

Young, a successful attorney and Commander-in-Chief of the United Confederate Veterans Association, recollects and reinterprets events of 55 years relating to his participation in the Eighth Kentucky Cavalry Regiment, Morgan's Raiders, including Morgan's raid into Kentucky (1862), Forrest's raid into West Tennessee (1862), Shelby's Missouri raid (1863) and J.E.B. Stuart's Chambersburg raid (1862).

4977 Young, Brigham 1801-1877
Letters of Brigham Young to his sons. Edited with introduction by Dean C. Jessee. With a foreword by J.H. Adamson. Salt Lake City: Deseret Book Co., 1974. 375 p. Index.

Of Brigham Young's 46 children (by sixteen wives) who reached maturity, seventeen were sons. The Mormon leader enjoyed a warm relationship with his sons, giving fatherly counsel to them when they were away on proselytizing missions for the Church, studying at Eastern universities, traveling for business reasons, or in the military service.

4978 Young, Brigham 1801-1877
Manuscript history of Brigham Young, 1846-1847. Edited by Elden J. Watson. Illustrated. Salt Lake City: E.J. Watson, 1971. 627 p. Index.

Diary entries and letters 1846-1847 contain the history of Young and the Mormons from the last days at Nauvoo through the entrance of the pioneer company into the Salt Lake Valley.

4979 Young, Charles D., pseud.
see **King, Alexander**

4980 Young, Jacob 1776-1859
Autobiography of a pioneer: or, the nativity, experience, travels, and ministerial labors of Rev. Jacob Young. Cincinnati: L. Swarmstedt & A. Poe, 1859. 528 p.

A faithful record of the incidents of the life of an itinerant preacher who was an early supporter of Methodism. He traveled through various circuits in Ohio preaching the gospel and working for the people.

4981 Young, John Orr 1886-1976
Adventures in advertising. New York: Harper and Brothers, Publishers, 1949. 207 p. Index.

Beginning with his early days as an Iowa huckster, he writes of his business and pleasure in building a successful career in advertising.

4982 *Young, Loretta 1913-
The things I had to learn. With Helen Ferguson. Indianapolis: Bobbs-Merrill Co., 1961. 256 p.

Actress Young projects an aura of wholesome glamour and optimism. She includes brief information about her film and television performances between generalizations about manners and mores.

4983 *Young, Rosa   **1890-**
Light in the dark belt; the story of Rosa Young as told by herself. Revised edition. St. Louis: Concordia Publ. House, 1950. (1929) 200 p.
 A simple narrative of the religious life and work of a Black woman who started a school and became a day missionary in rural Alabama.

4984 Young, Stark   **1881-1963**
The pavilion: of people and times remembered, of stories and places. New York: Charles Scribner's Sons, 1948. 194 p.
 Author and drama critic recalls growing up in Mississippi aristocracy, with extensive detail about his family and friends, life in the South, and the art world.

4985 Young, Stark   **1881-1963**
Stark Young: a life in the arts: letters, 1900-1962. Edited with introduction by John Pilkington. Baton Rouge: Louisiana State University Press, 1975. 2v. Index.
 This selection of 939 letters provides, says the editor, "a full . . . spontaneous account of [Young's] life, his writings, his [personal] relationships." Young decried materialism and advocated humanism and the respect for culture and tradition as part of the good life.

4986 Young, Stephen Marvin   **b.1889**
Tales out of Congress. Philadelphia: J.B. Lippincott Co., 1964. 254 p.
 A play-by-play account of the life of a tough old Democrat, Young's narrative gives the details of several state and congressional elections, his diplomatic trips abroad, and his two marriages, as well as a fair sprinkling of Washington gossip. He makes a few stabs at humility but generally writes as if he were campaigning again.

4987 Youngblood, Rufus W.   **1924?-**
Twenty years in the Secret-Service: my life with five presidents. New York: Simon and Schuster, 1973. 256 p. Index.
 Guarding the president from risks, threats, and hazards is a job whose tensions and dangers are sometimes compounded by the chief executives themselves. Here the story is told by a secret service agent who worked for five presidents, from Truman to Nixon.

4988 Younker, Lucas
Animal doctor. And John J. Fried. New York: E.P. Dutton & Co., Inc., 1976. 247 p.
 The story of a veterinarian whose practice for small animals and horses is in southern California.

4989 *Yurka, Blanche   **1893-**
Bohemian girl: Blanche Yurka's theatrical life. Illustrated. Athens: Ohio University Press, 1970. 306 p. Index.
 Yurka describes her career as an actress in plays by Ibsen, Shakespeare, and Aristophanes as well as lesser playwrights. Some great moments of fulfillment in her life have come during great roles on Broadway, but others have been before small-town audiences in out-of-the-way places.

4990 *Zaharias, Babe (Didrikson)   **1913-1956**
This life I've led: my autobiography. As told to Harry Paxton. New York: A.S. Barnes and Co., 1955. 242 p. Index.
 A champion golfer and remarkable woman in many ways writes of her childhood, her sports career, some of her friends—intimate and celebrity—and her struggle with cancer, which took her life soon after her book was published.

4991 Zahorsky, John   **1871-1963**
From the hills: an autobiography of a pediatrician. St. Louis, Missouri: The C.V. Mosby Co., 1949. 388 p.
 Using several classic American autobiographies as models, a St. Louis physician writes of his medical career in the context of major historical events, e.g., the 1904 World's Fair and both World Wars.

4992 *Zakrzewska, Marie E.   **1829-1902**
A woman's quest. Edited by Agnes C. Vietor. New York: Arno Press, 1972. (New York: D. Appleton and Co., 1924) 514 p. Index.
 After emigrating from Berlin in 1852, she became well-known for her medical work among poor women and children of New York and Boston, was founder of an outstanding hospital for women and children in each city, and was dedicated to the training of women doctors.

4993 Zamperini, Louis   **1917-**
Devil at my heels: the story of Louis Zamperini. With Helen Itria. Foreword by Billy Graham. New York: E.P. Dutton, 1956. 251 p.
 A dramatic story of a dramatic life. Zamperini's deliquent childhood was transformed by the recognition he received as a high school track runner, setting the world's interscholastic mile record in 1934. After finishing eighth in the Berlin Olympics of 1936, Zamperini attended U.S.C., but dropped out to enlist in the Air Force. Shot down in the Pacific, he remained afloat on a raft for 47 days until captured by the Japanese, who beat and tortured him. After the war he drifted, but was saved by his born-again wife and conversion by Billy Graham to become a successful evangelist.

4994 *Zassenhaus, Hiltgunt Margret   **1916-**
Walls: resisting the Third Reich—one woman's story. Boston: Beacon Press, 1974. 248 p.
 Now living in the United States, Zassenhaus tells the fascinating tale of her work as an interpreter for political prisoners in Germany during the rise of the Third Reich and World War II. An opponent of Nazism, she used her position to smuggle food, vitamins, books and Bibles into the prisons, and made notations of "send food" on letters given her to censor.

4995 *Zemach, Margot   **1931-**
Self-portrait: Margot Zemach. Illustrated by the author. Reading, Massachusetts: Addison-Wesley, 1978. 31 p.
 Zemach wrote and illustrated this autobiography for children, emphasizing her travels throughout Europe and America and her career. Her illustrations are often peopled with characters from children's books her husband wrote and she illustrated.

4996 Zenger, John Peter   **1697-1746**
Trial of Peter Zenger. Edited with introduction by Vincent Buranelli. Foreword by H.V. Kaltenborn. Westport, Connecticut: Greenwood Press, 1975. (New York: New York University Press, 1957) 152 p. Index.
 The trial in 1735 of printer and journalist Zenger for seditious libel focused on his printing of the political New York *Weekly Journal,* which criticized New York Governor William Cosley's financial malfeasance in office. Although the case itself did not establish either political liberty or freedom of the press, it paved the way for later political and legal reforms promulgated by Andrew Hamilton. Zenger's narrative explains the case and defends free speech and a free press.

4997 *Ziegfeld, Patricia   **1916-**
The Ziegfelds' girl; confessions of an abnormally happy childhood. Boston: Little, Brown and Co., 1964. 210 p.
 Surrounded by luxury and raised by two famous theatrical parents, both somewhat eccentric, her youth was like a fairy tale spiced by show-business personalities and extravagant events.

4998 Zigrosser, Carl   **1891-1975**
My own shall come to me; a personal memoir and picture chronicle. Philadelphia, Pennsylvania: Distributed by Sessler's Bookstore, 1971. 369 p.
 Verbal reminiscences and pictures, a family narrative, essays in art and literary criticism, psychological appraisals, social commentary are included in this volume. Zigrosser, who founded the Weyhe Gallery, was curator of prints at the Philadelphia Museum of Art and later vice-director and acting director.

4999 *Zimmer, Norma Beatrice Larsen
Norma. Foreword by Lawrence Welk. Illustrated. Wheaton, Illinois: Tyndale House Publishers, 1976. 368 p.
 A singer tells of a childhood nearly wrecked by her parents' alcoholism and her father's job problems, her attempt to escape family difficulties through music and the church, her spiritual rebirth, her marriage, her own family, and her rise to success on *The Lawrence Welk Show.*

5000 Zimmerman, Isidore   **1917?-**
Punishment without crime: a lifetime in prison for a crime he did not commit. With Frances Boyd. Introduction by Drew Pearson. New York: Manor Book, 1972. (New York: Clarkson N. Potter, 1964) 320 p.
 Convicted in 1938 of conspiracy to murder a detective, Zimmerman spent the next "twenty-four years and eight months" in various New York state prisons until he was finally released because of evidence that the prosecutor used perjured testimony and deliberately suppressed evidence of Zimmerman's innocence.

5001 Zinn, Houston Jackson (Jack)   **1917-**
Doctor Zinn: autobiography, poems, philosophy, tales, etc. New York: Vantage, 1978. 131 p.
 Although Zinn wrote this book "to encourage young people to buck the odds and do their damndest to achieve their ambition," he spends so much time discussing his hell-raising as a youth, student, soldier, and divorced man that his career as a surgeon appears subordinate.

5002 Zinsser, Hans (R.S., pseud.)   **1878-1940**
As I remember him. Boston: Little, Brown and Co., 1964. (1940) 443 p.
 The reminiscences of a doctor who became a bacteriologist. His success carried him to far countries in search of causes of diseases such as typhus, syphilis, cholera, and infantile paralysis. He hunted for bedbugs, lice, ticks and fleas for scientific purposes and found human nature to analyze as well; he was concerned with philosophy and humanity and tried to understand the contradictions of his age of human achievement on the one hand and the destruction of war on the other.

5003 Zuber, William Physick   **1820-1913**
My eighty years in Texas. Edited by Janis Boyle Mayfield. Notes and introduction by Llerena Friend. Personal narratives of the West. Austin: University of Texas Press, 1971. 285 p. Index.
 Writing in his old age, Zuber describes his part in the fight for Texas

independence, his service protecting the borders, the annexation of Texas, his part in the Confederate Army during what he calls the "Confederate War," and in Reconstruction events. In later life he was active in the Texas Veterans Association, wrote articles, corresponded with other veterans, and participated in Masonic affairs.

5004 *Zuker-Bujanowska, Liliana   1928-
Liliana's journal: Warsaw 1939-1945. New York: Dial Press, 1980. 162 p.
    This is a terrifying account of Liliana's life in occupied Poland and the Warsaw ghetto, 1939-1945. She was eleven at the war's outbreak and matured beyond her years when her mother and grandparents were sent to the concentration camps; she worked in an ink factory and helped to support her family with food the job provided. At sixteen she married a guerrilla who was killed in the Warsaw ghetto uprising. She found the postwar Russian regime too oppressive and escaped to Berlin in 1946 before going to El Salvador to live with relatives and immigrating to the United States in 1953.

5005 Zukor, Adolph   1873-1976
The public is never wrong: the autobiography of Adolph Zukor. With Dale Kramer. New York: G.P. Putnam, 1953. 298 p. Index.
    A movie producer in New York and Hollywood recalls the history of the film industry and the role Mary Pickford played in its development.

5006 Zumwalt, Elmo Russell   1920-
On watch: a memoir. Illustrated. Maps, Charts, and Graphs. New York: Quadrangle/New York Times Book Co., 1976. 568 p. Index.

Zumwalt details his naval career from the Academy to his position as Chief of Naval Operations, giving special attention to his efforts to upgrade U.S. defense readiness, personnel morale, dress codes, and official positions regarding minority personnel in the Navy. Critical of President Nixon, Kissinger, and Admiral Rickover, Zumwalt decries the decrease of U.S. forces in the face of increasing Soviet military strength.

5007 *Zunser, Miriam Shomer   1882-1951
Yesterday: a memoir of a Russian Jewish family. Edited with postscript by Emily Wortis Leider (granddaughter). Illustrated. New York: Harper & Row, 1978. (1939) 274 p.
    This evocative memoir traces the generations of Zunser's extended family, Russian Jews who immigrated to New York at the turn of the century. Zunser, a noted playwright for the Yiddish theater in New York, is sensitive to the dramatic nuances of joy and pathos as she characterizes aunts and uncles, grandparents and children (including herself) with an intense commitment to Judaism, their family, and the arts.

5008 Zweig, Paul   1936-
Three journeys: an automythology. New York: Basic Books, 1976. 182 p.
    A "chance exile from America," the poet sees himself as a "wandering Jew" and describes three journeys: his trip to the Sahara Desert, a "luminous personal space"; a decade in Paris, including a six-year marriage to Michèle; and, in New York, a climactic series of "intense private experiences" triggered by the influence of Swami Muktananda.

Subject Index

clairvoyance,
1622

clairvoyant,
1613, 3760

Clancy, Pat,
0816

Clapp, Frederick M.,
2333

clarinetist,
1522

Clark, Champ,
2397

Clark, D. Worth,
4452

Clark, Dick,
0486

Clark, Edward A., wife of,
0824

Clark, Jonas Gilman,
1894

Clark, Kenneth,
4642

Clark, Mark,
0833, 3340

Clark, Mark, wife of,
0833

Clark, Mark Wayne,
1340

Clark, Monte,
1402

Clark, Mrs. F.C.,
2836

Clark, Tom C.,
3549

Clark, Victor,
3059

Clark, William,
0165, 2734, 3142, 3619

Clark University,
1698, 1894, 3702

Clarke, Anne,
4091

Clarke, Dumont,
0840

Clarke, Helen I.,
3483

Clarke, James Freeman,
2197

classicist,
1871

Clay, Cassius—see Ali, Muhammad

Clay, Henry,
0028, 0043, 0440, 0650, 0845, 1117, 1230,
1502, 1796, 2005, 2364, 2636, 2761, 2762,
2937, 4717, 4726, 4808

Clay, Lucius B.,
2148, 3054, 3340

Cleaver, Eldridge,
2092, 2666, 3247, 3375, 4063

Clemenceau, Georges,
1810, 2177, 4139

Clemens, Olivia Langdon,
0860

Clemens, Samuel Langhorne (Mark Twain,
pseud.),
0047, 0392, 0517, 0591, 0894, 1214, 1253,
1282, 1618, 1784, 2081, 2195, 2199, 2200,
2392, 2460, 2857, 3135, 3787, 4649, 4704

Clemente, Roberto,
1743, 4828

clergy,
0097, 0108, 0148, 0163, 0198, 0202, 0212,
0230, 0297, 0311, 0342, 0366, 0408, 0433,
0459, 0461, 0466, 0474, 0490, 0495, 0502,
0535, 0576, 0640, 0693, 0694, 0718, 0721,
0722, 0765, 0819, 0820, 0830, 0842, 0909,
0973, 0979, 0985, 1001, 1044, 1066, 1088,
1097, 1115, 1133, 1161, 1195, 1247, 1295,
1296, 1302, 1315, 1325, 1337, 1360, 1372,
1391, 1398, 1412, 1456, 1515, 1558, 1629,
1761, 1777, 1844, 1883, 1900, 1903, 1938,
1945, 1948, 1957, 2041, 2044, 2064, 2067,
2080, 2081, 2097, 2109, 2130, 2251, 2258,
2327, 2379, 2386, 2414, 2451, 2470, 2526,
2570, 2634, 2649, 2667, 2675, 2682, 2699,
2727, 2732, 2776, 2839, 2848, 2870, 2875,
2900, 2916, 2956, 2997, 2998, 3052, 3053,
3070, 3207, 3244, 3246, 3251, 3285, 3295,
3314, 3315, 3334, 3376, 3377, 3389, 3410,
3465, 3511, 3557, 3569, 3592, 3640, 3648,
3658, 3664, 3673, 3674, 3696, 3723, 3749,
3802, 3820, 3822, 3910, 3963, 4028, 4051,
4059, 4122, 4129, 4201, 4219, 4221, 4227,
4239, 4395, 4403, 4411, 4422, 4423, 4449,
4458, 4464, 4488, 4506, 4523, 4545, 4567,
4575, 4591, 4602, 4627, 4739, 4775, 4836,
4858, 4896, 4899, 4972, 4980

clergy, Baptist Evangelical,
0484

clergy, daughter of,
2000

clergy, Quaker,
4937

clergy, wife of,
0303, 1114, 1632, 3207, 4114

clergy—see also priest; monk; rabbi; etc.

clerk,
2665, 3679

Cleveland, Frances F.,
1665

Cleveland, Grover,
0264, 0862, 1046, 1157, 1279, 1555, 1665,
1699, 1723, 2181, 3042, 3308, 3622, 3874,
3879, 3884, 4345, 4704, 4827

Cleveland Browns,
0547, 1980, 4514

Cleveland Cavaliers,
4821

Cleveland Clinic,
1018

Cleveland Indians,
0441, 1087, 3490, 3491, 3818

Cleveland Museum of Art,
4676

Cleveland *News*,
3491

Cleveland *Plain Dealer*,
4349

Cleveland *Press*,
4055, 4078, 4349

Cleveland Symphony Orchestra,
2214, 3834

cliff dwellings,
0445

Clifford, Clark,
1328, 2378, 2619, 2751

Clifford, John M.,
1036

Clift, Montgomery,
1375, 4450

Clifton, William,
4687

Cline, Patsy,
2863

Clinton, De Witt,
0846, 2042, 4590, 4726

Clinton, George,
2009, 4588, 4590

Clinton, Henry,
1406, 2009

Clinton, James,
4588

Clinton, Maria,
4590

closed shop,
3855

Clother, Robert C.,
3172

clown,
2467

clubwoman,
2607

Clurman, Harold,
1011

coach,
0105, 0921, 2250, 4557

coach, baseball,
0510

coach, basketball,
0184, 0278, 3082, 3304, 3600, 3938, 4821,
4938

coach, college athletics,
2454

coach, football,
0402, 0403, 0547, 0558, 1089, 1880, 2661,
3087, 3832, 4132, 4140, 4191, 4608

coach, hockey,
4128

coal,
2644

Coale, George Buchanan,
3915

Coan, Titus M.,
3816

Coast Guard, U.S.,
1887, 4557, 4586

Coats, John,
2321

Cobb, Frank Irving,
2588, 2624

Cobb, Irvin Shrewsbury,
0211, 1208, 4355

Cobb, Ty,
2748, 3071, 3344, 3762, 4841

Cobra (sports car),
4115

Coburn, Charles,
0772, 0773

Coca, Imogene,
4146

Cochise,
2192

Cochran, Charles,
1774

Cochran, Jacqueline,
4869

Cocoanuts, The,
2981

Cocteau, Jean,
0680, 1527, 3885, 4490

Cody, William Frederick (Buffalo Bill),
0664, 1533, 2703, 2920, 3059, 3417, 3656,
3734, 4086, 4123

Coe College,
2678, 4137

Coffee, John,
3914

Coffin, Henry Sloane,
0461

Coffin, Mrs. William Sloan (Eva Rubenstein),
3920

Coghlan, Charles F.,
4896

Cohan, George Michael,
0674, 3168

Cohen, Benjamin,
3175

Cohen, Elliot,
1905

Cohen, Mickey,
0326, 3475, 4609

Cohen, Morris,
1173

1459, 1519, 1521, 1534, 1539, 1605, 1711,
1712, 1713, 1721, 1808, 1905, 2012, 2040,
2073, 2102, 2148, 2180, 2253, 2408, 2438,
2475, 2476, 2483, 2561, 2593, 2625, 2630,
2657, 2724, 2922, 2955, 2971, 3005, 3037,
3066, 3117, 3136, 3150, 3215, 3286, 3289,
3291, 3307, 3326, 3409, 3416, 3621, 3775,
3796, 3821, 3859, 3895, 3933, 3957, 4039,
4074, 4137, 4179, 4237, 4302, 4331, 4332,
4402, 4579, 4580, 4629, 4724, 4783, 4832,
4913, 4942, 4953

communism (Chinese),
1210, 1809, 2032, 2032

communism (Manchurian),
0253

communist,
2051

Communist International,
2001

communist leader,
0532, 1153, 1519, 3775

communist movement,
2434

Communist Party,
0789, 0992, 1154, 1191, 1821, 2051, 2475,
3106, 3775, 3808, 3911, 3911, 4737

Communist Party, American,
0341, 0532, 0589, 0751, 0751, 1153, 1193,
1521, 2001, 2922

Communist Party leader,
2001

communists,
2011, 2305, 4332, 4372

Community Development Program (India),
4020

Como, Perry,
3566, 3580

comparative anatomist,
4960

composer,
0099, 0135, 0913, 1033, 1070, 1267, 1375,
1501, 1566, 1572, 1925, 1983, 2115, 2230,
2285, 2579, 2714, 2715, 2988, 3350, 3517,
3654, 3747, 3885, 3978, 4023, 4044, 4233,
4373, 4490, 4513, 4817, 4855, 4856, 4857

Compton, Arthur Holly,
0789, 4429

Compton, Betty (Madam X),
4056

Compton, Carl T.,
4813

Compton-Burnett, Ivy,
4461

computer programmer,
1274

Comstock Lode,
1253, 4640

con games,
2739

con man,
0091

Conant, James Bryant,
0937

concentration camps,
1131, 1442, 2415, 3759, 4814

concentration camps, Japanese,
1913, 4639

concentration camps, Philippines,
0203

concert artist,
3092

Concord River,
4498

Concord School of Philosophy,
0061

Concorde SST,
1879

Concordia College,
1581

Condon, Eddie,
3163

conductor,
0099, 1070, 1375, 2214, 2655, 2947, 4480

Cone, Claribel,
4561

Cone, Etta,
4561

Conerly, Chuck,
4557, 4608

Confederate States of America,
0575, 1106, 2846, 3740

conferences, Lutheran,
4422

Congdon, Charles T.,
1587

Congo,
2207

Congregation of the Propagation of the Faith,
0705

Congregational,
0108, 0408, 0482, 0774, 0775, 1109, 1195,
1259, 1296, 1322, 1329, 1844, 1883, 2386,
2916, 3694, 4316, 4899

Congress, Confederate States,
1106

Congress, U.S.,
0028, 0218, 0264, 0650, 0736, 1224, 1226,
1508, 1912, 1998, 2011, 2288, 2364, 2542,
2624, 2860, 2895, 3037, 3591, 3872, 4079,
4166, 4184, 4571, 4590, 4698, 4878

Congress, U.S. Investigating Committees,
4832

Congress of Panama,
0846

Congress of Venezuela,
4847

Congressional Cup Race,
0949

Congressional Medal of Honor,
2270, 3779

congressman, U.S.,
0113, 0165, 0415, 0487, 0671, 0736, 1019,
1117, 1224, 1998, 2011, 2039, 2382, 2445,
2775, 2850, 2860, 2861, 3093, 3150, 3162,
3591, 3664, 3707, 3784, 3872, 4019, 4079,
4216, 4320, 4436, 4571, 4631, 4848, 4969

congressman, U.S., wife of,
4184

congresswoman, U.S.,
0013, 0798, 0799, 2404

Conkling, Roscoe,
1157

Conn, Billy,
2830

Connally, John,
3396

Connally, Thomas,
2404

Connecticut,
0123, 0257, 0311, 0522, 0584, 0606, 1044,
1296, 1377, 1466, 1607, 1614, 1659, 1755,
1999, 2337, 2534, 2591, 2615, 2704, 2706,
2972, 2998, 3599, 3780, 3937, 4245, 4394,
4430, 4431, 4432, 4436, 4484, 4595, 4596,
4616, 4663, 4712, 4780, 4860, 4873

Connecticut, Bridgeport,
2190

Connecticut, Danbury,
2747

Connecticut, Danvers,
1977

Connecticut, Easton,
1440

Connecticut, Fairfield,
4507

Connecticut, Farmington,
2737

Connecticut, Greenwich,
2787

Connecticut, Hartford,
0283, 0858, 0860, 0861, 4208, 4361

Connecticut, Litchfield,
4360

Connecticut, Middletown,
0015

Connecticut, New Haven,
1527, 1815, 1871, 2128, 2285, 2558, 4553

Connecticut, Norwich,
4747

Connecticut, Preston,
3587

Connecticut, Redding,
4305

Connecticut, Redding Ridge,
4359

Connecticut, Ridgefield,
0996

Connecticut, Rowayton,
4556

Connecticut, Stanford,
1716, 3761

Connecticut, Stratford,
4083

Connecticut, Westport,
0519

Connecticut College School of Dance,
2229

Connecticut Wits,
4208

Connelly, Marc,
1505

Conner, Fox,
1338

Connolly, Bobby,
1760

Connolly, Maureen,
0326

Connors, Jimmy,
2574

Conover, Harry,
2695

Conover, Willis,
2834

Conrad, Joseph,
1005

Conrad, Max,
4869

conscientious objection,
2040, 3160, 3608, 4287, 4971

consciousness raising,
0791

conservation, forest,
0956

conservation and reclamation,
0247, 1177, 2596, 3874

conservationist,
0003, 0247, 0639, 2596

Considine, Alec,
3185

conspiracy,
5000

conspirator,
3131

constable,
0237

Constantine II,
4408

Constitution, Confederate States,
1106

Constitutional Convention,
4688

construction industry,
3715

construction worker,
2696, 4354

consul, U.S.,
1649, 2635, 2636

consul-general to India,
3008

consultant,
1285

Consumers' League of New York,
3356

Continental Congress,
0038, 0041, 0273, 1437, 1551, 1807, 1912,
2648, 2790, 2904, 2990, 3283, 4590, 4665,
4688, 4712

contractor,
3102, 4974

Contrell, Edward,
0023

convenanters,
1852

conventions, medical,
4911

conventions, political,
4041

convents, Catholic,
3446

convert, Catholic,
0214, 0589, 0618, 1130, 1778, 3151, 3152,
3907, 4102, 4156

convert, Christian,
0484, 4156

convert, Jewish,
1121

convict,
0483, 0484, 1496, 3081, 4207

convict, ex-,
3335, 4441, 4528

Conway, Moncure,
2700

Conway, Sally,
4216

Cook, Bill,
4401

Cook, Captain James,
2671

Cook, Edward,
3137

Cook, James,
0454

Cook County Jail (Chicago),
1391

Cook Islands,
1570

Cooke, George Frederick,
1278

Cooke, Nicholas,
4665

cooking,
2856

Cooley, Charles,
2171

Coolidge, Archibald Cary,
2627, 4563

Coolidge, Calvin,
0166, 0276, 0485, 1920, 2152, 2215, 3094,
3099, 3280, 3457, 3519, 3782, 3847, 3884,
3961, 4137, 4226, 4290, 4345, 4698, 4770,
4848

Coolidge, Elizabeth Sprague,
2988

Cooper, Diana,
3013

Cooper, Gary,
2256, 4618, 4758

Cooper, James Fenimore,
0571, 1813, 4152

Cooper, L. Gordon, Jr.,
0695

Cooper, Lady Diana,
0088

Cooper Union,
3230

Cope, Thomas Pym,
1213

Copeland, Charles Townsend,
2663

Copland, Aaron,
0884, 1267, 3747, 4490

Copley, John Singleton,
4553

copper, prospecting for,
2466

copper mining—see mining, copper

Copperhead Party,
3023

Coppolino, Carl,
2031

Corbett, Henry W.,
1134

Corbett, James J.,
1477

Corcoran, Francis,
2438

Corcoran, Fred,
4841

Corcoran, Thomas Gardiner,
3870

Corcoran Gallery,
0121, 1812

CORE (Congress of Racial Equality),
0012, 2515, 3232, 3827

Corman, Cid,
3459

Cornell, Joseph,
2723

Cornell, Katharine,
0056, 0318, 1735, 1737, 2929, 3045, 4989

Cornell University,
0306, 0814, 1285, 1753, 1901, 2271, 2506,
2596, 3432, 3660, 3799, 3851, 4476, 4777

Cornell University Medical College,
4537

Cornfield, Bernie,
3872

Cornish,
3565

Cornish School,
0977

Cornwallis, Charles,
1406, 2009, 2648

coroner,
2668

Corot, Jean B.,
2847

corporation publicist,
4640

corporations,
0189

Corregidor, Battle of,
2873, 3124, 3237, 4852

correspondent,
0739, 1006, 3705, 4109

Corso, Gregory,
1679

Cortiz, Michael,
3956

Cortot, Alfred,
0909, 4185

Corum, Bill,
3935

Corvette (sports car),
4115

Cosby, William,
4996

Cosell, Howard,
3086, 4446

cosmetic industry,
3924

cosmetician,
0897, 3924

Cosmo, Tony,
1196

Cosmopolitan Magazine,
2806

Cossacks,
2784

Costa Rica,
1376, 4181

Costain, Thomas,
1468

Costelloe, Mary Smith,
4798

costume designer,
2004

costumes,
2832

costumes, operatic,
2464

Cotten, Joseph,
2180

Cotton Club, Harlem,
0655

cotton industry,
0849, 1106, 3914

Couch, Charley,
2321

Coughlin, Charles E.,
4269

Coulouris, George,
2180

Council of the Twelve, Mormon Church,
0229

Council of Trent,
0705

Council on African Affairs,
1257, 3808

counsel to President Nixon,
1135

counselor,
3081

counter-culture,
0174, 4673

counterespionage,
0556, 1638

counterespionage—see also CIA; espionage; etc.

counterfeiter,
2622

counterfeiting,
1639, 4867

country life,
0671, 1017, 1248, 1446, 1648, 2633, 2818,
3799, 4193, 4542

country life, Alaska,
1491, 4883

country life, Appalachia,
0404, 4291, 4627

country life, Canada,
1220, 4286

country life, Canadian Wilderness,
2693

country life, East,
0960, 2094, 2456, 2514, 3632, 4224, 4555

country life, England,
1878

country life, Java,
1413

country life, Middle Atlantic,
0054, 4944

country life, Midwest,
0108, 0509, 0513, 1057, 1315, 1460, 1804,
1882, 2056, 2060, 2127, 2149, 2150, 2426,

2544, 2891, 2892, 2976, 3487, 3547, 3951, 4105, 4124, 4943

dancer, ballet,
3469, 4083

Daniel, E. Clifton,
0731, 2367

Daniel, Margaret Truman,
2367

Daniels, Jerry,
4696

Daniels, Josephus,
0264, 2151, 2181, 3869

Danilova, Alexandra,
3469

Danish,
0802, 3178, 3200, 3852, 3856, 4773

Danish West Indies,
0802

Danks, Samuel,
3172

Dantley, Adrian,
4938

Darcy, John Stevens,
1785

Dardanelles,
3966

Darlington, William,
0227

Darnell, Linda,
3180, 4366

Darrow, Clarence,
0023, 1658, 2094, 3952, 4230, 4301, 4302

Dartmouth College,
0402, 0403, 1110, 1308, 2471, 2958, 3531, 4196, 4299, 4717

Dartmouth College Medical School,
3637

Darwin, Charles,
0646, 3561, 4158, 4626, 4945

Daugherty, Harry M.,
3094, 4969

daughter, of clergy,
2000, 2556, 2870

daughter, of evangelist,
4213

daughter, of Frost, Robert,
1575

daughter, of Hazlitt, William,
2003

daughter, of James, Henry, Sr.,
2307, 2308

daughter, of missionary,
0744

daughter, of Pound, Ezra,
3713

daughter, of Stanton, Elizabeth Cady,
0409

daughter, of Sullavan, Margaret and Hayward, Leland,
1999

daughter, of trader,
1570

daughter, of Truman, Harry S.,
4552

daughter, of Ziegfeld, Florenz,
4997

daughterhood,
0147, 1563, 4001, 4325

Daumier, Henri,
2847

David, Jacques,
2877

Davidoff, Sid,
1744

Davidson, James Wood,
4795

Davidson, Jo,
0522, 4302, 4893

Davidson, Thomas,
0915

Davidson College,
2776, 4878

Davies, Henry L.,
1614

Davies, Joseph E.,
0812

Davies, Marion,
0376, 1495, 2822, 3252, 3955, 4593, 4618

Davilova,
1647

Davis, Angela,
1429, 2292

Davis, Benjamin,
2001

Davis, Benjamin J.,
1257, 3808

Davis, Bette,
1495, 2800, 4047, 4180, 4764

Davis, Charles H.,
1284

Davis, Ed,
0368

Davis, Glenn Woodward,
0402, 0403

Davis, Henry Winter,
1284

Davis, J. Richard,
1175

Davis, Jefferson,
0281, 0465, 1117, 1502, 1796, 2061, 2191, 2364, 2447, 2680, 2681, 2846, 2932, 3740, 4320, 4746, 4876

Davis, Joan W.,
0199

Davis, John William,
1112, 1573

Davis, Kathy,
3602

Davis, Meyer,
1103

Davis, Miles,
3570

Davis, Norman H.,
3867

Davis, Rennie,
1989, 4041

Davis, Richard Harding,
4771

Davis, Robert Gorham,
2073

Davis, Roosevelt,
4543

Davis, Sammy, Jr.,
0034, 0208

Davis, Steve,
0412

Davis, Varina,
1108

Davis Cup,
0590, 2574, 3323, 4556

Davison, F. Trubee,
2496

Dawes, Charles G.,
1321, 4345

Daws, William,
3753

Dawson, Horace,
1429

Day, Dorothy,
0912, 2040, 3085

Day, Jeremiah,
1871

Day, Laraine,
1291

Day at the Races, A,
2981

Dayton Daily News,
2794

Daytona 500,
3595

Dead Sea Scrolls,
2502

Dean, Barney,
2154

dean, college,
3603, 4194, 4476

dean, Cornell University,
3799

Dean, Dizzy,
1292, 1571

dean, Graduate School, U.C.L.A.,
2239

Dean, James,
0199, 1440, 2256, 2544, 2993

Dean, John W., III,
1136, 1390, 2237, 2331, 2747, 2913, 2914, 3262, 3396, 3398, 3688, 4029, 4166, 4282

Dean, John W., III, wife of,
1136

dean, Pomona College,
3419

dean, Robert College Engineering School (Istanbul),
4046

Deane, Silas,
0038, 1437, 2685, 4712

Dearborn, Henry,
3619

death,
0074, 1352, 3942

death, by cancer,
0605, 1417

death, by suicide,
0419, 3618, 4010

death, of brother,
3019, 4358

death, of child,
1038, 1860, 3525, 3651, 3820, 4084, 4089

death, of daughter,
0865, 3143, 3154, 3839

death, of daughter, by cancer,
2868

death, of father,
0068, 0791, 2232, 2233, 2500, 2541, 2634, 3074, 3235, 3547, 4120, 4134, 4326, 4924, 4974, 4994

death, of father, by cancer,
0141

death, of father, by suicide,
0419

death, of friend,
0109, 1293, 3301, 4010

death, of husband,
0581, 0643, 1000, 1540, 1972, 2725, 3614, 3652, 4084, 4153, 4708

death, of mother,
0118, 0174, 0313, 0977, 1000, 1293, 1656, 1946, 2105, 2127, 2185, 2541, 2725, 4044, 4358, 4365, 4460

death, of mother, by suicide,
4120

death, of parents,
1884, 3039

death, of sister,
4759

death, of son,
1606, 3094, 3419, 3517, 3618, 3824

death, of son, by suicide,
4577

England,
0007, 0041, 0062, 0082, 0083, 0161, 0169,
0189, 0317, 0409, 0485, 0487, 0520, 0522,
0649, 0889, 0907, 0917, 0917, 0966, 0967,
0990, 1138, 1212, 1234, 1259, 1288, 1313,
1340, 1420, 1422, 1450, 1478, 1520, 1559,
1593, 1614, 1618, 1625, 1640, 1666, 1674,
1699, 1708, 1876, 1878, 1879, 1896, 1984,
2034, 2141, 2176, 2232, 2263, 2275, 2281,
2307, 2308, 2315, 2337, 2338, 2402, 2496,
2501, 2544, 2587, 2625, 2648, 2650, 2659,
2691, 2700, 2732, 2769, 2770, 2771, 2832,
2887, 2961, 3036, 3058, 3215, 3249, 3273,
3300, 3326, 3340, 3466, 3546, 3732, 3790,
3875, 3879, 3966, 3977, 4054, 4074, 4087,
4135, 4137, 4150, 4292, 4329, 4360, 4429,
4458, 4580, 4596, 4613, 4633, 4756, 4764,
4903, 4916, 4994

England, Brighton,
1774

England, Bristol,
0400

England, Cambridge,
1605, 1716, 2075, 2132, 2265, 3351, 4556,
4697, 4729

England, Coventry,
2679

England, Lancashire,
0527

England, Liverpool,
2951

England, London,
0020, 0030, 0038, 0057, 0107, 0140, 0204,
0231, 0235, 0283, 0297, 0560, 0616, 0719,
0745, 0934, 1001, 1051, 1075, 1097, 1112,
1116, 1118, 1160, 1251, 1278, 1304, 1319,
1342, 1368, 1369, 1380, 1544, 1550, 1551,
1617, 1737, 1746, 1769, 1774, 1813, 1852,
1987, 2044, 2084, 2132, 2190, 2304, 2316,
2335, 2437, 2464, 2559, 2618, 2621, 2679,
2709, 2763, 2765, 2788, 2814, 2906, 2907,
2912, 2970, 2993, 3128, 3140, 3166, 3255,
3281, 3325, 3416, 3433, 3469, 3623, 3657,
3690, 3821, 3906, 3980, 3981, 3982, 3995,
3996, 4001, 4109, 4111, 4158, 4177, 4178,
4228, 4332, 4334, 4335, 4425, 4511, 4516,
4577, 4696, 4704, 4711, 4714, 4756, 4789,
4881, 4917, 4995

England, Manchester,
2115, 3965

England, Nottingham,
1097

England, Oxford,
1859, 4225, 4511, 4756

England, St. Margaret's,
4109

England, Wimbledon,
0590, 2574

Engle, Clair,
3957

English,
0030, 0041, 0056, 0155, 0161, 0204, 0229,
0273, 0283, 0362, 0369, 0377, 0387, 0390,
0400, 0509, 0511, 0591, 0648, 0657, 0698,
0719, 0811, 0814, 0818, 0848, 0889, 0900,
0918, 0921, 0926, 1022, 1038, 1039, 1152,
1160, 1164, 1285, 1296, 1300, 1329, 1365,
1404, 1412, 1415, 1450, 1457, 1463, 1498,
1550, 1568, 1569, 1585, 1603, 1694, 1697,
1745, 1769, 1774, 1784, 1785, 1839, 1931,
1933, 2114, 2124, 2154, 2180, 2197, 2210,
2216, 2258, 2279, 2281, 2287, 2290, 2306,
2327, 2337, 2380, 2394, 2418, 2481, 2517,
2534, 2603, 2635, 2644, 2663, 2685, 2695,
2788, 2857, 2859, 2869, 2937, 2954, 2970,
2991, 3009, 3014, 3215, 3242, 3260,
3273, 3292, 3298, 3356, 3374, 3386, 3395,
3400, 3421, 3426, 3466, 3497, 3507, 3565,
3626, 3690, 3727, 3814, 3913, 3915, 3929,
3968, 3996, 4001, 4059, 4066, 4089, 4096,
4122, 4150, 4158, 4162, 4221, 4229, 4240,
4357, 4389, 4450, 4474, 4488, 4580, 4597,
4598, 4616, 4640, 4687, 4688, 4690, 4705,

4711, 4719, 4726, 4731, 4742, 4764, 4819,
4823, 4827, 4843, 4858, 4866, 4908

engraver,
1217, 3996

Enoch, Kurt,
4767

Enright, Dan,
4529

enrolling clerk, U.S. Senate,
4640

entertainer,
0035, 0076, 0215, 0272, 0429, 0560, 0664,
0676, 0729, 1033, 1121, 1486, 1820, 2155,
2156, 2354, 2792, 3170, 3484, 3774, 3907,
3950, 4291, 4696, 4761

entertainer, comedian,
0610

entertainer, radio,
1535, 3899, 4066

entertainer, strip-tease,
2673

entertainer, television,
1190, 1535, 3485, 4066

entertainer, vaudeville,
1982

entomologist,
2933, 4940

environmental protection,
4652

Ephron, Nora,
1381

Ephron, Phoebe,
1381

epidemic, cholera (New Orleans),
0819

epidemic, influenza (1918),
0181, 0247, 1730, 1939, 2046, 2603, 2678,
3137, 3395, 4065, 4065, 4303, 4769

epidemic, typhus (1917-1918),
3137

epidemic, yellow fever (1905),
0315

epidemic, yellow fever (New Orleans),
0819

epidemic, yellow fever (Philadelphia, 1793),
0080

epidemics,
2264, 2867

epidemology,
2264

episcopacy,
0705

Episcopalian,
0053, 0068, 0082, 0086, 0221, 0241, 0310,
0400, 0461, 0466, 0547, 0638, 0655, 0765,
0912, 0939, 1056, 1071, 1134, 1164, 1175,
1304, 1365, 1481, 1508, 1595, 1687, 1821,
1841, 2070, 2125, 2141, 2210, 2418, 2663,
2737, 2938, 3035, 3144, 3262, 3264, 3376,
3461, 3546, 3591, 3618, 3749, 3881, 4059,
4114, 4129, 4375, 4540, 4575, 4635, 4705,
4731, 4858

epistemology,
1173

Eppes, Mary Jefferson,
2346

Equal Employment Opportunity, Committee on,
0524

Equal Rights Amendment,
1725, 4732

Ernst, Max,
1580, 1855, 2723

Ernst, Morris L.,
2724, 4767

Eros Magazine,
1681

Erskine, Albert,
1427

Erskine, John,
1097, 4930

Ervin, Sam,
2217, 3396, 4282

Ervine, St. John,
2630

Esalen Institute,
1864, 4119

Esbjorn, Lars Paul,
3410

Eskew, Jim,
0816

Eskimo, Alaskan,
1800

Eskimo, Nootka tribe,
2359

Eskimo, Wickinnish tribe,
2359

Eskimos,
0072, 0689, 1264, 1637, 1849, 1890, 2027,
2028, 2769, 3555, 3655, 4241, 4299, 4753,
4884

ESP (extrasensory perception),
0893, 0897, 1622, 3522, 4229, 4437

espionage,
0341, 0465, 0544, 0556, 0579, 1265, 1281,
1580, 1638, 2645, 3286, 3443, 3671, 3895,
4165, 4402, 4443, 4628

espionage—see also CIA; secret agent; spy; etc.

Esquire,
1468, 1469, 4853

essayist,
4720

est,
3922

etcher,
3256, 4038

etching,
3027

Ethical Culture School,
2659

Ethiopia,
1021, 2001, 2416, 2611, 3665

Ethiopia, Addis Ababa,
1429

ethnologist,
1052, 2844, 3265, 4027

ethnology,
2222, 2603

Ethridge, Mark,
1397

Eton Preparatory School,
1450

Europe,
0235, 0273, 0409, 0473, 0498, 0507, 0693,
0730, 0780, 0860, 1003, 1148, 1216, 1241,
1270, 1339, 1422, 1469, 1614, 1618, 1745,
1824, 1930, 2008, 2077, 2116, 2152, 2197,
2222, 2337, 2659, 2720, 2770, 2796, 2874,
3082, 3206, 3467, 3851, 3875, 3911, 3956,
4038, 4074, 4137, 4329, 4409, 4424, 4453,
4475, 4476, 4577, 4715, 4783

Europe, Western,
1916

European Defense Community,
4406

evangelical,
0405, 0481, 2226, 3798, 3802, 4106, 4905

Evangelical Christian,
1358

evangelism,
0495, 0633, 1766, 2189, 2839, 3251

evangelist,
0073, 0220, 0604, 0608, 1000, 1146, 1200,
1318, 1957, 1981, 2189, 2203, 2226, 2389,
2839, 3104, 3322, 3501, 3802, 3803, 3948,
3978, 4107, 4238, 4239, 4263, 4354, 4411,
4423, 4609, 4900

Moore, R. Walton,
3867

Moore, Virginia,
4577

Moorer, Thomas,
5006

Moral Rearmament,
1591, 1876, 4467

Morales, Juan Ventura,
2791

Moran, George (Bugs),
2858

Morang, Alfred,
0196

Moravian,
2014, 4734

More, Thomas,
2392

Moreau, Jeanne,
2657

Moreau-Vauthier, Augustin-Jean,
2847

Morehead State College,
2232

Morehouse, Henry Lyman,
1629

Morehouse, Ward,
1068

Morehouse College,
2526, 3020, 4506

Morgan, Arthur,
0023

Morgan, Aubrey,
2769

Morgan, Frederick,
4091

Morgan, Harry Hays,
4593

Morgan, John Hunt,
4976

Morgan, John Pierpont,
0276, 2616, 4592

Morgan, John Pierpont, Jr.,
2616

Morgan, Lewis H.,
0233

Morgan Guaranty Trust,
2615

Morgan's Raiders,
4976

Morgenthau, Elinor (Mrs. Henry, Jr.),
1590, 3860

Morgenthau, Hans,
4348

Morgenthau, Henry, Jr.,
2261, 3308, 3867, 3872, 4547

Morgenthau, Henry, Sr.,
4904

Morgenthau Pogrom Investigation Commission
(1919),
3964

Morison, Ellen Smith,
3271

Morison, Samuel Eliot,
0520

Morley, Christopher,
4292

Morley, Felix,
3741

Mormon,
0106, 0229, 0463, 1152, 1255, 1316, 1461,
2071, 2093, 2242, 2283, 2352, 2676, 3169,
3298, 3308, 3675, 4073, 4319, 4364, 4773,
4977, 4978

Mormon leader,
2676, 4217, 4364, 4977, 4978

Mormon persecution,
3675, 4217

Mormons and Mormonism,
0206, 0718, 1039, 1795, 1935, 2040, 2071,
2093, 2242, 2301, 2920, 3220, 3675, 4217,
4525, 4773

Moro Tribe (Philippine),
4819

Morocco,
2125, 2207, 2751, 3712, 3859, 4456, 4456

Morocco, Fez,
1380

Morra, Umberto,
0347

Morre, Lenny,
4574

Morressey, Paul,
4673

Morrill, Charles N.,
4133

Morris, B. Wistar,
1134

Morris, Bethuel F.,
1479

Morris, Charles,
1173

Morris, Clara,
4896

Morris, Gouverneur,
1912, 2332, 2337, 2685

Morris, Jim,
4401

Morris, Lewis,
4996

Morris, Robert,
0273, 1912, 2895

Morris, William,
0900

Morrison, deLesseps S.,
2011

Morrison, James,
0846

Morro Castle,
1616

Morrow, Dwight, wife of,
3287

Morrow, James W.,
3065

Morse, Charles F.,
2078

Morse, Samuel Finley Breese,
0966, 0967, 1278, 1813, 4553

Morse, Wayne L.,
1223, 1849, 3035, 3549, 3782

Mortimer, Grandma,
4337

Morton, Ellis H.,
1214

Morton, Jelly Roll,
0472, 0927, 1194, 4233

Morton, Oliver P.,
1962, 4968

Morton, Walter,
4601

Moses, Robert,
2016, 2549, 4077

Moslem,
0840

Moss, Stirling,
4115

Most, Johann,
1710, 1711

Most Valuable Player Award,
1980, 3819, 3823

mother, of Carter, Jimmy,
0712

mother, of Graham, Billy,
1766

mother, of Jastrow, Robert,
2329

mother, of Kennedy, John Fitzgerald,
2478

mother, of McCall, Tom Lawson,
3032

mother-daughter relationship,
0157, 0358, 0608, 0687, 0701, 1563, 1725,
1979, 1999, 2706, 3590, 3763, 4358, 4365,
4435, 4467, 4478, 4593, 4756

Mother Earth,
1711

Mother of the Year Award,
4195

mother-son relationship,
0141, 0356, 0358, 0411, 0952, 1017, 1061,
1434, 1656, 2120, 2445, 2567, 2771, 3027,
3172, 4506, 4663, 4916

Mother West Wind books,
0599

motherhood,
0090, 0131, 0146, 0147, 0164, 0195, 0249,
0282, 0287, 0290, 0291, 0324, 0354, 0582,
0664, 0723, 0741, 0802, 0880, 0889, 1028,
1075, 1128, 1154, 1185, 1270, 1322, 1444,
1483, 1491, 1498, 1506, 1513, 1563, 1675,
1766, 1812, 1873, 1926, 1931, 2083, 2176,
2208, 2298, 2427, 2606, 2608, 2618, 2639,
2695, 2770, 2788, 2829, 2863, 2905, 2976,
3036, 3079, 3143, 3144, 3199, 3322, 3332,
3361, 3370, 3411, 3450, 3453, 3507, 3682,
3766, 3831, 3839, 3942, 4084, 4116, 4147,
4325, 4361, 4365, 4389, 4397, 4415, 4450,
4467, 4507, 4630, 4714, 4773, 4911, 4944,
4995, 4999

motherhood, foster,
0203

motorcycles,
2486

motors, automobile,
1042

Mott, James,
3303

Mott, Lucretia,
3663

Mouch, Gene,
0684

Mount Adams,
3930

Mount Assiniboine,
4377

Mount Baker,
3930

Mount Erebus,
3359

Mount Everest,
4022

Mount Hood,
3930

Mount McKinley,
3655, 4377

Mount Palomar, Observatory,
2966

Mount Rainier,
3930

Mount Rushmore,
4848

Mount Rushmore National Monument,
4848

Mount Shasta,
3930

Mount Sinai Hospital, New York,
3432

Mount Washington,
2587

mountain climbing,
0167, 0639, 2107, 3930

mountaineer,
0999, 3930, 4022

Nugent, Elliott,
4503

Nugent, Patrick,
2367

numbers racket,
1266

numerology,
2824

nun,
1857, 2902, 2985, 3361, 4157, 4919

nun, ex-,
0187, 1411, 2463, 4559

nun, Franciscan,
1411

Nunn-Bush Shoe Co.,
3425

Nuremberg trials,
0126, 1660, 2330, 4136

Nureyev, Rudolf,
3487

nurse,
0507, 0614, 1000, 1130, 1818, 2221, 2293,
2845, 3258, 3361, 3505, 3768, 3852, 4420,
4457, 4846

nurse, Civil War,
1922

nursery school teacher,
0143

nursing,
0062, 2898

nursing education,
0507

nursing homes,
2541, 2604

nutrition,
3051

Nutt, George Washington Morrison,
2912

Nye, Edgar Wilson,
3787

Oakes, John B.,
3005

Oakland City College,
3375

Oakland Raiders,
4446

Oakland Seven trial,
1626

O'Banion, Dion,
2858

Ober, Anne Reid,
1468

Ober, Harold,
1427, 1468, 1471

Oberammergau Passion Play,
4178

Oberlin College,
0936, 1649, 2124, 2916, 3156, 4424, 4663

obesity,
1444

O'Brien, Lawrence,
3957

obstetrician,
0574, 2368, 3589, 4599, 4959

Occidental College,
2043, 3592

occultism,
1560, 2414

occultist,
0204

Ochs, Adolph S.,
2588

O'Connor, Ellen,
4798

O'Connor, Frank D.,
2549

O'Connor, William D.,
4798

O'Conor, Charles,
4508

O'Dell, Jacks,
1429

Odets, Clifford,
0992, 1011, 2023, 2438, 2714

O'Donnell, Kenneth,
3435, 3957

O'Dwyer, William,
4141

Of Mice and Men,
4313

off-Broadway,
0743, 4075

Office of National Estimates,
2627

Office of Overseas Schools,
1376

Office of Scientific Research and Development,
0621

Office of Strategic Services (OSS),
2148, 2737, 2884, 3521

Office of War Information,
0668, 2006, 3249, 3516

office worker,
0538

Ogden, James De Peyster,
0967

Oglethorpe University,
1195

O'Hara, Frank,
1848

O'Hara, John,
0737

Ohio,
0118, 0297, 0387, 0547, 0548, 0718, 0769,
0846, 0893, 0995, 1003, 1085, 1199, 1221,
1242, 1247, 1337, 1486, 1614, 1749, 1761,
1784, 1841, 1865, 1975, 1980, 2014, 2051,
2091, 2124, 2469, 2613, 2687, 2794, 2855,
3290, 3384, 3535, 3723, 3755, 4028, 4193,
4214, 4274, 4316, 4488, 4505, 4698, 4710,
4807, 4969, 4980

Ohio, Akron,
1011, 2226, 2783, 3585

Ohio, Berea,
2258

Ohio, Cincinnati,
0104, 0291, 0331, 0486, 0842, 0907, 1190,
1221, 1434, 1865, 1990, 2160, 2279, 2868,
2937, 3022, 3294, 3646, 3846, 3883, 3890,
3891, 4055, 4360, 4361, 4858

Ohio, Cleveland,
0075, 0441, 0544, 0574, 1018, 1139, 1460,
1702, 1717, 1880, 2020, 2154, 2196, 2214,
2382, 2433, 3133, 3138, 3270, 3482, 3585,
3822, 3827, 4042, 4078, 4145, 4169, 4349,
4964, 4986

Ohio, Columbus,
0811, 1057, 2199, 2200, 2201, 3388, 4335,
4504

Ohio, Cuyahoga Falls,
2226

Ohio, Darrowtown,
0089

Ohio, Dayton,
1569, 2773, 3062, 4188, 4534, 4951, 4955

Ohio, Delphos,
3562

Ohio, Dover,
3422

Ohio, Eaton,
1933

Ohio, Erie County,
1460

Ohio, Geauga County,
1460

Ohio, Ironton,
2112

Ohio, Johnson's Island,
0277

Ohio, Lorain,
2517

Ohio, Marietta,
0549, 3575

Ohio, Marion,
1120

Ohio, Martin's Ferry,
2201

Ohio, Massillon,
1687

Ohio, Mt. Vernon,
2531

Ohio, Newtown,
2376

Ohio, Pickawillany,
4539

Ohio, Plymouth,
4806

Ohio, Springfield,
1221

Ohio, Steubenville,
2360

Ohio, Stow,
1031

Ohio, Toledo,
2100, 2609, 3755, 4793

Ohio, Urbana,
1479, 4793

Ohio, Wilmington,
4358

Ohio, Xenia,
4014

Ohio, Yellow Springs,
3384

Ohio, Youngstown,
0323, 1073

Ohio, Zanesville,
2410, 4576

Ohio Company,
2990

Ohio River,
0392, 1357, 2209, 2990, 3512

Ohio State University,
0547, 0825, 1057, 1827, 2577, 3422, 3481,
4014, 4446, 4504

Ohio Valley,
0387, 4539

Ohio Wesleyan University,
4048, 4739

oil,
0627, 3202, 4731

oil boom, California (1909),
0565

oil boom (1901),
4298

oil consultant,
1749

oil drilling,
0370

oil industry,
0948, 1646

Oistrakh, David,
3140

O'Keefe, Specs,
1639

O'Keeffe, Georgia,
4363

Okeh Records,
0472

Okinawa,
0604, 1373, 2449, 2517, 2931, 3582, 3705,
3792

2446, 2462, 2544, 2606, 2641, 2714, 2715,
2716, 2868, 2892, 2913, 2979, 2980, 3068,
3343, 3360, 3390, 3422, 3484, 3485, 3496,
3501, 3596, 3688, 3738, 3815, 3840, 3886,
3891, 3950, 4029, 4066, 4106, 4148, 4149,
4218, 4411, 4478, 4529, 4743, 4889, 4928,
4982

television, soap opera,
1589, 4389

television—*see also* entertainer; sportscaster; etc.

television broadcaster,
1066

television broadcasting,
1843

television commentator,
1584, 2245, 4529

television entertainer,
3485

television interviewer,
2905

television journalism,
2043

television journalist,
1199, 2446

television newscaster,
4349

television performer,
0008, 0486, 1222, 1553, 2185, 2868, 3484,
4743

television producer,
1732, 4732

television reporter,
3850

television soap opera,
4389

television sportscaster,
1758

television talk show host,
1199

television talk shows,
1222

Teller, Edward,
1300, 1605, 2543, 4429

Tellico, First Treaty of,
2288

temperance,
0230, 0369, 0794, 0840, 1479, 1746, 2258,
2443, 2443, 3295, 4274, 4969

temperance lecturer,
1746

Temple, John,
2254

Ten American Painters (art show, 1898),
4150

Ten Commandments,
2059

Tender Is the Night,
1469

Tenerife,
0505

Tennessee,
0152, 0202, 0556, 0708, 0718, 0721, 0834,
0878, 1016, 1019, 1020, 1044, 1106, 1529,
1741, 1832, 1839, 1924, 2138, 2184, 2186,
2224, 2350, 2364, 2488, 2560, 2674, 2781,
2833, 2855, 2862, 2901, 3260, 3512, 3637,
3642, 3716, 3740, 3914, 3935, 4769

Tennessee, Centerville,
3547

Tennessee, Chattanooga,
4794

Tennessee, Cumberland Region,
2288

Tennessee, Franklin,
3547

Tennessee, Henning,
1887

Tennessee, Johnson City,
4272

Tennessee, Johnsonville,
1511

Tennessee, Knoxville,
0173, 2146, 3822

Tennessee, Memphis,
1130, 1893, 1925, 3423, 3682, 3846, 3899,
4608

Tennessee, Nashville,
0723, 1328, 2035, 2146, 2863, 3547, 4238

Tennessee, Natchez,
1474

Tennessee, Oak Ridge,
0789

Tennessee, Pineville,
1919

Tennessee, Rugby,
2216

Tennessee Agricultural and Industrial State University,
0173

Tennessee Conference Female Institute (now Athens College),
2106

Tennessee State University,
2295

Tennessee Valley Authority (TVA),
0378, 2751, 4209, 4371

tennis,
0046, 0162, 0982, 1650, 1651, 1724, 2513,
2574, 3323, 3785, 3786, 4509, 4556

tennis—*see also* player, tennis

Ter-Arutunian, Reuben,
2540

Territorial historian, Arizona,
1902

Terry, Bill,
4318

Terry, Ellen,
0269, 2464, 4719

Terry, Norma,
4366

Teschemacher, Frank,
3163

test pilot,
1403, 2719

test pilot—*see also* aviator

Texas,
0003, 0101, 0175, 0176, 0183, 0196, 0212,
0277, 0288, 0289, 0308, 0663, 0673, 0696,
0723, 0816, 0823, 0918, 0945, 0957, 0972,
1007, 1016, 1019, 1020, 1026, 1069, 1304,
1314, 1415, 1671, 1749, 1782, 1787, 1829,
1840, 1857, 1868, 1900, 1932, 1938, 2054,
2103, 2119, 2123, 2147, 2163, 2178, 2184,
2186, 2206, 2210, 2233, 2319, 2378, 2384,
2392, 2466, 2519, 2524, 2525, 2628, 2664,
2667, 2750, 2781, 2802, 2832, 2846, 2855,
3009, 3102, 3202, 3220, 3260, 3284, 3318,
3328, 3354, 3381, 3455, 3617, 3619, 3633,
3728, 3740, 3797, 3813, 3814, 3838, 3846,
3910, 4101, 4151, 4168, 4184, 4344, 4374,
4401, 4477, 4637, 4647, 4695, 4699, 4763,
4779, 4838, 4906, 4907, 4939, 5001, 5003

Texas, Alvin,
3943

Texas, Amarillo,
1917, 2397, 2976

Texas, annexation of,
0575

Texas, Austin,
3378, 4985

Texas, Beaumont,
4990

Texas, Big Bend,
2628

Texas, Booker,
1293

Texas, Brazoria,
0920

Texas, Corpus Christi,
1801

Texas, Cuero,
0920

Texas, Dallas,
0627, 1327, 2722, 2942, 4048, 4063, 4524,
4987, 4990

Texas, El Paso,
0144, 2749, 4169

Texas, Fort Duncan,
4123

Texas, Fort Worth,
2781, 3064

Texas, Galveston,
0878, 2846, 3378, 4850

Texas, Henderson,
0154

Texas, hill country,
1475

Texas, Hood County,
0661

Texas, Houston,
0082, 1743, 1791, 1851, 1852, 2123, 2330,
2404, 3451, 3501

Texas, King Ranch,
1731

Texas, Lubbock,
0502, 2120

Texas, Mansfield,
1826

Texas, Odessa,
3299

Texas, Rusk County,
0154

Texas, San Antonio,
0301, 0536, 2046, 3792, 3933

Texas, Tilmon,
3805

Texas, Tyler,
3044

Texas A and M,
2119

Texas Land and Copper Association,
2466

Texas Observer,
3284

Texas Playboys,
4374

Texas prison system,
4151

Texas ranger,
1671, 3617, 3617, 4401

Texas Southern University,
2404

Texas State College for Women,
2210

Texas State Women's University,
2210

Texas Technical University,
4191

Texas Technological College,
2120

Thacher, Sherman Day,
2737

Thackeray, William Makepeace,
3300

Thailand,
2153, 2891, 4283, 4501, 4562, 4711

Thailand, Bangkok,
0433, 0734, 0879

Thailand—*see also* Siam

Thalberg, Irving,
2710, 2832, 2979, 3464, 4618

Thaw, Harry K.,
1573

Veterans Administration,
2910

veterans' leader,
5003

veterinarian,
0662, 1446, 1709, 2826, 4632, 4988

veterinary nurse,
1491

vibraphonist,
3477

Vice-President, Confederate,
4320

Vice-President, U.S.,
0055, 0251, 0611, 0612, 0650, 1067, 1508, 1643, 2231, 4546, 4653

Vicksburg, Battle of,
3008

Victor Records,
0472

Victoria, Queen,
4633

Vidal, Gore,
4370

Vidal, Paule,
4329

Vienna State Opera,
2691

Vietcong,
0879

Vietnam,
0917

Vietnam, Saigon,
2479

Vietnam Veterans Against the War,
0879

Vietnam War,
0055, 0201, 0286, 0289, 0290, 0367, 0412, 0423, 0438, 0466, 0501, 0508, 0508, 0539, 0560, 0604, 0654, 0657, 0693, 0734, 0781, 0798, 0799, 0831, 0879, 0879, 0905, 0917, 0926, 0958, 1021, 1021, 1178, 1204, 1205, 1207, 1223, 1239, 1252, 1356, 1373, 1483, 1508, 1626, 1683, 1713, 1721, 1721, 1741, 1744, 1849, 1862, 1926, 1939, 1949, 2052, 2057, 2059, 2092, 2111, 2153, 2153, 2217, 2377, 2393, 2479, 2542, 2542, 2544, 2570, 2571, 2588, 2712, 2747, 2787, 2854, 2913, 2931, 2931, 2953, 2953, 2968, 3005, 3037, 3074, 3077, 3106, 3162, 3167, 3309, 3319, 3325, 3366, 3382, 3396, 3435, 3451, 3494, 3496, 3648, 3728, 3792, 3792, 3931, 3939, 3947, 3947, 4142, 4182, 4212, 4212, 4221, 4237, 4287, 4314, 4315, 4315, 4332, 4402, 4408, 4408, 4453, 4471, 4550, 4567, 4571, 4619, 4694, 4765, 4765, 4783, 4804, 4804, 4853, 4910, 4972, 5006

vigilantes,
1183, 3854

Villa, Pancho,
3471, 3510

Villa Verde Trail,
1669

Village Voice,
1541

Vines, H. Ellsworth,
0590, 2574

Vineyard Gazette,
2173

Vining, Elizabeth Gray,
1138

Vinson, Fred,
1225

violinist,
0950, 3140, 4072, 4169, 4260, 4480

Virden, William H.,
1214

Virginia,
0007, 0036, 0038, 0079, 0114, 0121, 0190, 0261, 0273, 0277, 0320, 0387, 0399, 0503, 0556, 0634, 0638, 0669, 0711, 0713, 0723, 0830, 0841, 0852, 0986, 1038, 1106, 1238, 1272, 1406, 1502, 1523, 1780, 1782, 1912, 1990, 2061, 2106, 2124, 2279, 2327, 2337, 2339, 2341, 2342, 2346, 2391, 2396, 2398, 2406, 2447, 2469, 2482, 2669, 2680, 2759, 2788, 2860, 2903, 2904, 2964, 2990, 3023, 3054, 3062, 3065, 3196, 3226, 3227, 3269, 3283, 3296, 3297, 3314, 3533, 3545, 3546, 3564, 3699, 3720, 3770, 3829, 4028, 4382, 4512, 4685, 4742, 4822

Virginia, Albemarle County,
2340

Virginia, Alexandria,
1481, 4216

Virginia, Appomattox,
2681

Virginia, Arlington,
2681

Virginia, Big Stone Gap,
1531

Virginia, Black Rock Springs,
3196

Virginia, Blue Ridge Mountains,
1187

Virginia, Cape Henry,
4448

Virginia, Charlottesville,
0179, 1059, 2340, 2341, 2345, 3183, 4216, 4256

Virginia, Chickahominy,
3740

Virginia, City Point,
1779

Virginia, Edgehill,
2346

Virginia, Fredericksburg,
1115, 1791, 1966, 3530, 4114

Virginia, Halifax County,
2037

Virginia, Hampton,
3682

Virginia, Harpers Ferry,
3968

Virginia, Lynchburg,
1481, 4267

Virginia, Marion,
0115, 3943

Virginia, Monticello,
2346

Virginia, Mount Vernon,
4687, 4688

Virginia, Newport Hill,
1740

Virginia, Newport News,
1631

Virginia, Norfolk,
1278, 2644

Virginia, Port Royal,
4687

Virginia, Portsmouth,
0220

Virginia, Richmond,
0162, 0461, 0711, 1059, 1108, 1688, 1689, 2061, 2340, 2644, 2681, 2846, 2964, 3183, 3530, 3740, 4114, 4876

Virginia, Roanoke,
4506

Virginia, Sabine Hall,
0711

Virginia, Salem,
3722

Virginia, Shenandoah Valley,
4876

Virginia, Suffolk,
3563, 4619

Virginia, Westmoreland County,
4687

Virginia, Westover Plantation,
0631

Virginia, Williamsburg,
0301, 0630, 0711, 1966, 2341, 2904, 2990, 4619, 4687

Virginia, Yorktown,
0741, 2972

Virginia and Truckee Railroad,
4640

Virginia Declaration of Rights,
2990

visions,
1613

VISTA (Volunteers in Service to America),
2175

viticulturist,
1930

Viva,
4673

Voge, Richard G.,
2140

Vogue Magazine,
0768, 4235

Voice of America,
2180, 4424

Voice of Prophecy,
2583

von Arnim, Gisela,
1367

von Braun, Wernher,
1597

von Keyserling, Hermann,
3330

von Mises, Ludwig,
4630

von Mises, Ludwig, wife of,
4630

Vonnegut, Kurt, Jr.,
3748

von Richthofen, Baron,
2531

von Zedtwitz, Baroness,
4403

Von Zell, Harry,
0610

voodooism,
1275

Voorhees Institute (South Carolina),
4473

Vosper, Robert,
3668

voter registration,
4248

Voting Rights Act,
2404, 4703

Vreeland, Diana,
2695

WAAF (Women's Auxiliary Air Force),
4087

Waddington, C.H.,
4158

Wadsworth, Charles,
1182

Wadsworth, Reverdy,
4635

Wagner, Honus,
2748

Wagner, Richard,
1566, 1717, 2991, 3921, 4480

Wagner, Robert,
0587

Wagner, Robert F.,
2549

wagon trains,
1322

Waite, David H.,
2445